Pius Episcopus Servus Serv[orum Dei]

Universi catholici orbis sollicitudo Summo Pontifici divinitus commissa exigit ut opportune aliquando immutetur. Cum itaque his de causis ecclesiastico[rum]... va exinde Dioecesis... Nos, omnibus mature perpensis, de venera[bilium]... venerabili Fratre Hamleto Joanne Cicognani, Archiepiscopo titulari Laod[iceno]... opus sit, quorum interest, vel eorum qui sua interesse praesumant consensu, Apostolica[e Sedis]... tentem comitatus civiles Ballard, Carlisle, Hickman, Fulton, McCracken, Graves, Livi[ngston], Union, Henderson, Daviess, Hancock, McLean, Ohio, Muhlenberg, Butler, Tod[d]... avulso novam erigimus et constituimus Dioecesim, quam ab Owensburgo urbe Owen[sburgensem]... novae Dioecesis sedem in urbe Owensburgo, a qua Dioecesis ipsa, uti diximus, nomen... in paroeciali ecclesia Deo in honorem S. Stephani dicata, in eadem urbe exstante, figimus, ea[m]... pis omnia tribuimus iura, privilegia, honores, insignia, gratias et favores, quibus ceterae... libus et obligationibus. Quod autem attinet ad huius novae Dioecesis regimen et administra[tionem]... cante, electionem, ad clericorum et fidelium iura et onera aliaque huiusmodi, servanda... vero ad clerum praecipue spectat, decernimus ut simul ac hae Litterae Nostrae ad executionem... Quum autem temporis adiuncta haud permittant ut in cathedrali Ecclesia Owensburgens[i]... tores ad iuris normam eligantur. Mandamus denique ut omnia documenta et acta... ri poterit, Curiae episcopali Dioecesis Owensburgensis tradantur, ut in eius archivo religiose... tersit vel sua interesse praesumant audi[ti] non fuerint, vel praemissis non consenserint, sive... nullitatis vitio seu intentionis Nostrae vel quolibet alio, licet substantiali et inexcogitato, defectu,... ne factas et emanatas perpetuo validas existere et fore suosque plenarios et integros effectus sortiri... ris auctoritate, scienter vel ignoranter contigerit attentari, irritum prorsus et inane volumus... salibusque Conciliis editis, generalibus vel specialibus constitutionibus et ordinationibus Apostolicis... bus omnibus per praesentes derogamus. Ad quae omnia ut supra disposita et constituta executioni... cae Septentrionalis Statibus Delegatum Apostolicum, deligimus etiam propterea necessarias... clesiastica dignitate constitutum, facto eidem onere ad S. Congregationem Consistorialem auth[entica]... rarum transumptis, etiam impressis, manu tamen alicuius notarii publici subscriptis et sigillo... bueretur, si ipsaemet exhibitae vel ostensae forent. Nemini autem hanc paginam dismembrationis... Si quis autem ausu temerario hoc attentare praesumpserit, indignationem Omnipotentis Dei e[t]... Domini millesimo nongentesimo trigesimo septimo, die nona mensis Decembris, Pontifica[tus]...

          R. Thomas Pius C.S. Card. Boggiani

Reg. in Canc. Ap. — Vol. LVIII — N.º 59 — Aloisius Crussardi

Dei Ad Perpetuam Rei Memoriam.

...cum fractiones nuncupatur, sed et nimiam territorii amplitudinem, Diocesium circumscriptio Ludovicopolitanae regionis valde producta esse visum est ut ea in duas dividiretur partes et ex sententia Venerabilium S.R.E. Cardinalium rebus fidei propagandae praepositorum consilio, ac suffragantibus Venerabili Fratre Delegato Apostolico in Foederatis Americae Septentrionalis Statibus, suppleto, quatenus opus sit, consensu quorumcumque in re interesse habentium aut habere praesumentium, praesentium tenore, Apostolica Nostra auctoritate, a diocesi Ludovicopolitana territorii partem illam perpetuo separamus comites Marshall, Calloway, Trigg, Lyon, Crittenden, Caldwell, Christian, Hopkins, Webster, Breckinridge, Grayson, Edmonson, Warren, Simpson, Allen, atque e territorio huiusmodi novam diocesim Oinsboreusem nuncupari volumus, cuius civitas propriae Dioecesis Ludovicopolitanae finibus. Hanc autem novam Dioecesim, quam ex nostra a civitate episcopalis fastigium extollimus, Episcopi regimini subjicimus, eique ad cathedralis Ecclesiae gradum et dignitatem evehimus, tribuimus eique pro tempore Episcopo quaecumque cathedralibus Ecclesiarum Antistitibus quacumque de iure et consuetudine competunt, ipsosque iisdem adstringimus oneribus quibus caeteri Antistites praedicti adstringuntur, ac pro Episcopali mensa dotatione, ad V. Capituli vel ad Administratoris Apostolici, sede vacante, providentiam relegata canonica nec non Concilium plenarium Baltimorense totum recipere et accipere. Quod si factum non fuerit, eo ipso clerici Ecclesiae illi eo adhuc adscripti et in eius territorio degentes exeant, et novum Capitulum modo instituendum, ratumque in litteris, non Canonicis, Dioecesano consilio constet ac Dioecesim rebus cunctis, Canonica Dioecesis Ludovicopolitanae, quam primum fieri poterit. Praesentes autem Litteras et in eis contenta quaecumque, etiam ex eo quod cuilibet eorum interesse et traditum mentione digni sint, nullo umquam tempore de subreptionis, vel obreptionis aut nullitatis vitio, seu intentionis nostrae vel alio quovis, licet substantiali defectu notari, impugnari vel in controversiam vocari posse, sed eas, tamquam ex certa scientia et potestatis plenitudine datas, ab omnibus ad quos spectat inviolabiliter servari debere, nec non super his a quocumque, quavis auctoritate scienter vel ignoranter, iudicari vel definiri posse aut debere, irritumque et inane decernimus et declaramus. Non obstantibus quibusvis constitutionibus et ordinationibus Apostolicis in Synodalibus, Provincialibus, Generalibus, Universalibusque Romanorum Pontificium Praedecessorum Nostrorum dispositionibus caeterisque contrariis, quibuscumque de revocatione cum supra diximus Fratrem Nostrum Joannem Cicognani, in Foederatis Americae opportunas tribuimus facultates atque obligationes ad effectum de quo agitur exemplar Litterarum in eo ecclesiastica dignitate vel officio constitutis, munitas, eadem prorsus tribuimus fides quae hisce Litteris tribueretur, concessionis, statuti, derogationis, mandati et voluntatis Nostrae, infringere vel ei contraire liceat. Si quis autem apostolorum Petri et Pauli se noverit incursurum. Datum Romae apud S. Petrum, anno...

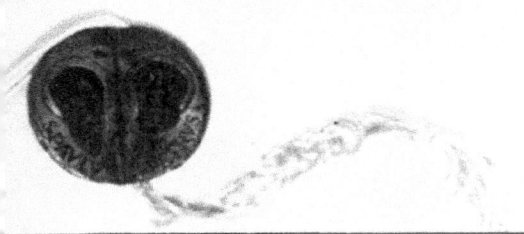

The Roman Catholic Diocese of Owensboro, Kentucky

The Seal of the Diocese of Owensboro

The clasped hands are taken from the great seal of the Commonwealth of Kentucky. Emblazoned upon the cross are the stones and Palm Branch of Victory which represent Saint Stephen, Protomartyr, the Patron of the Diocese and of the Diocesan Cathedral. This Coat of Arms was created for the Diocese by Pierre de Chaignon la Rose.

The Diocese of Owensboro was created by Pope Pius XI, December 9, 1937, separating the 32 counties of Western Kentucky from the Diocese of Louisville which was at that time elevated to an Archdiocese. The Most Reverend Francis R. Cotton, the first bishop of Owensboro, was preconized (appointed) Dec. 16, 1937. The Most Reverend Henry J. Soenneker, appointed March 10, 1961, retired June 30, 1982, was the second Bishop of Owensboro. The Most Reverend John J. McRaith, appointed October 23, 1982, is the third and present Bishop of Owensboro.

TURNER PUBLISHING COMPANY

Copyright © 1995. Roman Catholic Diocese of Owensboro. All rights reserved.

This book or any part thereof may not be reproduced by any means, mechanical or electronic, without the written consent of the Authors and Publisher.

Roman Catholic Diocese of Owensboro was compiled using available information. Neither the Authors nor the Publisher are responsible for errors or omissions.

Turner Publishing Company's Staff:
Publishing Consultant: Douglas W. Sikes
Publisher's Designer: Trevor W. Grantham

Library of Congress Catalog
Card Number: 93-61860

ISBN: 978-1-68162-579-9

Limited Edition. Additional books may be purchased from Turner Publisher Company or the Catholic Pastoral Center, 600 Locust St., Owensboro, KY 42301-2130.

Table of Contents

Letter from Pope John Paul II 3
Letter from Archbishop Thomas C. Kelley 4
Letter from Bishop John J. McRaith 5
Letter from Governor Brereton Jones 6
Letter from Senator Wendell H. Ford 7
Letter from Senator Mitch McConnell 8
Foreword and Acknowledgments 9

Catholicity in Western Kentucky
    Prior to 1938 10
    1938-1987 46
    1987-Present 77
Parish and Institution Histories 96

Family Histories 195
Index 364

Papal Bull Creating Diocese of Owensboro - Dec. 9, 1937

From the Diocese of Louisville we separate that part of its territory comprising the civil counties of Ballard, Carlisle, Hickman, Fulton, McCracken, Graves, Livingston, Marshall, Calloway, Trigg, Lyon, Crittenden, Caldwell, Christian, Hopkins, Webster, Union, Henderson, Daviess, Hancock, McLean, Ohio, Muhlenberg, Butler, Todd, Logan, Breckinridge, Grayson, Edmonson, Warren, Simpson, Allen and from it, we erect a new and distinct diocese, and we will and declare that this diocese be called that of Owensboro from the city of that name, restricting this much the boundaries of the Diocese of Louisville, decreeing further that the seat of the new diocese be fixed in the city of Owensboro, which therefore we elevate to the rank of an episcopal city and to it we grant the rights and privileges which other episcopal cities enjoy; the throne of the Bishop we fix in the parish church of St. Stephen in that same city and we elevate it to the rank and dignity of a Cathedral Church, and to it and its incumbent Bishops, we grant all the rights, privileges, honors, insignia, favors and prerogatives which other Cathedral Churches and their Bishops by common law possess and enjoy, and we bind them to the same duties and obligations.

We constitute this Diocese of Owensboro a suffragan of the Church of Louisville, which Our Most Holy Lord, Pope Pius XI, now gloriously reigning, by his Letters *Quo christifidelium regimen,* written on the tenth day of December last, decreed to be elevated to Metropolitan; therefore we subject the Bishops of Owensboro to the metropolitan jurisdiction of the Archbishops of Louisville.

(This is an English translation of the Latin document shown inside the front cover.)

His Holiness John Paul II

paternally imparts his Apostolic Blessing to

The People of the Diocese of Owensboro

on the occasion of the writing the history of the Diocese.

Letter from the Archbishop

Archdiocese of Louisville

OFFICE of the ARCHBISHOP

Dear Friends:

It is a great joy to celebrate the written history of the Church in Western Kentucky. For many years our dioceses were one family of faith. This history reveals our common heritage as well as how we strengthened each other before and after the establishment of the Diocese of Owensboro. It is a glorious story, with a glorious future.

The Church in Central Kentucky continues to be grateful to God for the many contributions it has received from the Church in Western Kentucky. May the Lord continue to bless and prosper your ways.

With prayerful best wishes,

Devotedly yours in Christ,

+ Thomas C. Kelly, OP
Archbishop of Louisville

Letter from the Bishop

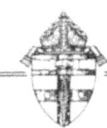

CATHOLIC PASTORAL CENTER
DIOCESE OF OWENSBORO
600 Locust Street • Owensboro, Kentucky 42301-2130   502-683-1545

OFFICE OF THE BISHOP

My Dear Friends,

The contents of this history book is the story of the faith life of western Kentucky -- faith as it is nurtured and lived in the family and in the parish. I am so pleased to have a history book that has the faith of our families as an essential part of the recorded history.

As we read the history of the families and parishes, we realize that we have much for which to be grateful. Those who have gone before us have built a solid road for us to travel. They have created a climate in which faith could grow here in western Kentucky.

This history, I hope, will inspire all of us to realize that we are making history now and that what people will inherit in the future will be what we have prepared for them today.

Thanks to all who worked so hard to make this history a reality. A very special thanks to Sister Joseph Angela, Chancellor of the Diocese of Owensboro, for coordinating the project here in the diocese.

God's blessings on all who have been and who are the Church of Western Kentucky.

Sincerely in Christ,

+ Joe— J. McRaith

Most Reverend John J. McRaith
Bishop of Owensboro

JJM:cih

Letter from the Governor

COMMONWEALTH OF KENTUCKY
OFFICE OF THE GOVERNOR

BRERETON C. JONES
GOVERNOR

THE CAPITOL
700 CAPITAL AVENUE
FRANKFORT 40601
(502) 564-2611

CONGRATULATIONS:

The publishing of the *Western Kentucky Diocese Family History Book*, written during Kentucky's Bicentennial year of 1992, is an appropriate part of the Commonwealth's historical celebration. Roman Catholic settlers were among the heroes who helped build the Commonwealth into the thriving 15th state of the Union.

Catholic pioneers, many of whom were refugees of persecution in other lands, were prominent in the founding of many Kentucky communities, particularly along the Ohio River.

The faith and dedication of your forefathers has been passed on through the generations until it has become a bastion of strength and traditional values that help to anchor family life in Kentucky.

Best wishes as you honor your heritage and an important part of Kentucky's past and future greatness.

With best regards, I am

Sincerely,

Brereton Jones

Brereton Jones

/cmh

AN EQUAL OPPORTUNITY EMPLOYER M/F/H

Letter from the Senator

WENDELL H. FORD
KENTUCKY

COMMITTEES
COMMERCE, SCIENCE
AND TRANSPORTATION
ENERGY AND
NATURAL RESOURCES
RULES AND
ADMINISTRATION

United States Senate
WASHINGTON DC 20510-1701

December 14, 1992

Dear Sister Joseph Angela:

I was pleased to learn of plans to publish the *Western Kentucky Diocese Family History Book*.

A look to the past often provides a glimpse of the future. This celebration of the family is a wonderful way to ensure that the momentous occasions of the Diocese are available for others to learn from and enjoy.

Best wishes for success.

Sincerely,

Wendell Ford

Sister Joseph Angela Boone
Catholic Pastoral Center
600 Locust Street
Owensboro, Kentucky 42301

DISTRICT OFFICES:
- 343 Waller Avenue, Lexington, KY 40504, (606) 233-2484
- 172-C New Federal Building, Louisville, KY 40202, (502) 582-6251
- 19 U.S. Post Office and Courthouse, Covington, KY 41011, (606) 491-7929
- 305 Federal Building, Owensboro, KY 42301, (502) 685-5158

PRINTED ON RECYCLED PAPER

Letter from the Senator

MITCH McCONNELL
KENTUCKY

COMMITTEES
AGRICULTURE
FOREIGN RELATIONS
RULES

United States Senate
WASHINGTON, DC 20510-1702

December 30, 1992

Catholic Pastoral Center
Diocese of Owensboro
600 Locust Street
Owensboro, Kentucky 42301

Dear Friends:

It is my pleasure to write and congratulate the Diocese of Western Kentucky on their effort to publish the histories of families throughout the area.

During the bicentennial of our Commonwealth it is especially important that our heritage and history be recorded. Our children need to know about the men and women of Western Kentucky who have given us a legacy of liberty and opportunity. I commend your efforts to publish the histories of families throughout the 32 counties in Western Kentucky.

Best wishes for the future.

Sincerely,

MITCH McCONNELL
UNITED STATES SENATORS

MM/kah

Foreword and Acknowledgments

(L to R): Bro. Leo Willett, S.M., Sr. Joseph Angela Boone, OSU, Sr. Rose Jean Powers, OSU, Sr. Mary Irene Cecil, OSU and Mel Howard.

We take this opportunity to introduce the History of the Church of Western Kentucky, the Diocese of Owensboro. Through pictures and brief writings, we of the present generation have gathered together the stories of the faith of people who have gone before us.

Any true history of Church holds stories of individuals and families who have been a part of faith communities. These particular stories of faith communities that make up the Diocese of Owensboro are real treasures, the kind of valuable treasures of our past that by knowing about them inspire our own faith life today and will inspire faith life in the future.

We are a vibrant church in Western Kentucky and much of the credit goes to those who have gone before us and who have sown the seeds of faith in the soil of Western Kentucky for the past 150 years or more. By writing their stories in this history book, we can preserve these jewels for future use and enjoyment. I am most grateful to all who took the time to write and submit the beautiful stories and I am in particular grateful to all those who have had any part in making this book a finished product. Please note their names in the Acknowledgment.

Thanks especially to all those whose lives we read about in this history. We pray that you continue to be with this Church today and all the days to come.

God's blessing on all of the people in Western Kentucky.

Sincerely in Christ,

Bishop John J. McRaith

We are grateful to the many parishes, schools, institutions, and families who submitted their histories and family stories. In particular we would like to thank Brother Leo Willett, S.M. of St. Louis, MO (formerly of Fancy Farm) for his tireless efforts in working up the history of the Catholic Church in Kentucky prior to the founding of the Owensboro Diocese. Sister Rose Jean Powers, OSU of Brescia College for writing the first 50 years of our diocese from 1937 to 1987. Sister Mary Irene Cecil, OSU for the history from 1987 to the present date.

We are indebted to the many writers of the history of the parishes and institutions. Their names known only by God. Sister Emma Cecilia Busam, OSU, Mount Saint Joseph, Carmel Wimsatt, and others who spent many hours gathering data, pictures, etc. from the archives of the Diocese and Mount Saint Joseph. Mel Howard for taking and furnishing many photos and for keeping the public aware of the status of the book via the Western Kentucky Catholic. Sister Mary Irene Cecil, OSU for the countless hours of editing and re-editing the written word.

We make a special acknowledgment of Stephen Wall who designed and produced the map showing the 32 counties of the diocese with the Deaneries outlined, the churches, schools, institutions, hospitals inserted into the proper county. We thank Tom Lilly for his part in conning Stephen Wall to do this work. Also for the many other suggestions that Tom has given the writers.

Sister Sharon Sullivan, OSU of Brescia College, for portraying in cartoon the real production of this book as it happened. To all the nameless others for their contributions of time and talent. God bless you. We thank Turner Publishing Company who were the starters of this project and persevered to the end with all of our inexperiences.

We appreciate your patience in waiting for this production. We hope you will find the wait has been well worth your time. May you enjoy reading your own history as well as the many others who were so kind to submit their stories for others to enjoy.

May God Bless All,

Sister Joseph Angela Boone, OSU
Project Coordinator

Catholicity in Western Kentucky Prior to 1938

St. Lawrence Catholic Church near Knottsville, Daviess County. Pictured above is the church as it appears in the 1876 Illustrated Historical Atlas Map of Daviess County.

Introduction

This section, dealing with a brief history of the Catholic Church in Western Kentucky prior to 1938 in the area that became the Diocese of Owensboro in December 1937, has been treated in the following way:
  (1) "Colonial Maryland, 'Cradle of Catholicity', in the United States," by Brother Thomas Spalding, C.F.X. (1985).
  (2) "200 Years of Catholicity—Settlers Laid Foundation for Church in Kentucky," by Joseph E. Duerr (1985).
  (3) Biographies of Rev. Stephen T. Badin (1768-1853) and Rev. Charles Nerinckx (1761-1824), by Rev. John A. Lyons (1976).
  (4) "Reflections of the Bishops of Bardstown and Louisville, KY," by Rev. Clyde F. Crews (1986).
  (5) Biography of Rev. Elisha John Durbin (1800-1887), Patriarch of the Catholic Chruch in Western Kentucky, by Rev. John A. Lyons (1976).
  (6) *Chronology of Events* (1785-1937) related to the area that became the Diocese of Owensboro, with the main source being the extensive files and records of Rev. John A. Lyons (1898-1984), the Louisville Archdiocesan historian and archivist for many years.
     (Note #1: When reading the *Chronology of Events*, it is important to realize that within a particular year, each sentence represents a different, unrelated event.)
     (Note #2: One use of the *Chronology of Events* could be as a source for early and significant history of a particular parish, person or topic.)
  (7) Brief biographies of 56 priests ordained before 1938 (with pictures of most), excerpted mainly from unpublished biographical sketches written by Rev. John A. Lyons. Twenty-three of these biographical sketches appear in the Chronology of Events (1785-1937); the other 33 sketches start on page 35.
     (*Note:* An alphabetical list of these 56 priests (with years of births, deaths, ordinations), for which there are biographical sketches, appears on page 34.
  (8) An alphabetical list of the 40 Diocesan Priests (with dates of birth, death and ordination) who were members of the Diocese of Owensboro when created in December 1937 appears on page 43. (*Note:* the 40 Diocesan Priests have all persevered in their committment to the priesthood.)
  (9) Detailed data by parishes and institutions in the new Diocese of Owensboro, as it appeared in the *1938 Official Catholic Directory* (Also in *The Record*, April 7, 1938).

In compiling this brief history of the Catholic Church in Western Kentucky prior to 1938, I am gratefully indebted to the late Rev. John A. Lyons (1898-1984) whom I first met at Our Mother of Sorrows Rectory, Louisville, in 1979. His extensive files and records, known as the *Lyons Collection*, now located at Bellarmine College, Louisville, was the main source for my research.

Bro. Leo Willett, S.M.

"Colonial Maryland, 'Cradle of Catholicity' in the United States"

by Bro. Thomas W. Spalding, C.F.X.

This shows artist Charles Yardley Turner's mural in the Baltimore courthouse, "Colonist Group," with the ships Ark & Dove *in the background. (Courtesy of the Enoch Pratt Free Library, Baltimore.)*

"On the feast of the Annunciation of the Most Holy Virgin in the year 1634" wrote Father Andrew White, the Jesuit superior who accompanied the Maryland Pilgrims, "we celebrated Mass for the first time on this island (St. Clement's Island). This had never been done before in this part of the world. After we had completed the sacrifice, we took upon our shoulders a huge cross hewn from a tree, and advancing in order to the place appointed, with the help of the governor and his aides and other Catholics, we raised the trophy to Christ our Savior, humbly reciting on bended knees the litany of the Holy Cross with great emotion." Though contrary to the instructions of Cecil Calvert, second Lord Baltimore, the Catholic leaders could not forego this public display of the joy and gratitude they felt for the new era that opened before them.

A few days later, two Jesuit priests and a lay brother converted a bark hut abandoned by the Indians into a chapel on an estuary the colonists called St. Mary's River. The village that grew around it was named St. Mary's City. This "city" was the capital of Maryland for 60 years. There the first legislative grant of religious toleration in the New World was made in 1649.

St. Mary's county is where it all began, "the cradle of Catholicity." There was established the first Catholic parish, the first Catholic school, the first community of religious men in English-speaking America. In St. Mary's County, the initial difficulties of transplanting English Catholicism were met and overcome. In St. Mary's County the vision of George Calvert, first Lord Baltimore, of Catholics and Protestants living in peaceful communion in a small corner of the New World was finally realized. In St. Mary's County the first experiment in separation of church and state in the modern world was attempted.

In terms of numbers, if for no other reason, St. Mary's County remained a vital nucleus in the development of the Catholic Church in English-speaking America. A survey of 1708 revealed that 1,238 of the 2,974 Catholics living in the then twelve counties of Maryland could be found in St. Mary's County. In 1734, the rector of All Faith's Anglican Parish reported: "Papists are supposed now to exceed Protestants at least three to one in this county." In the province as a whole Catholics could claim a ratio of only one in 12. Proportionally the Catholics of St. Mary's County continued to increase, making it perhaps the most Catholic county in the nation. At the time of the establishment of the Patuxent Naval Air Station within its limits in 1947, the county could boast 11,036 Catholics in a total population of 14,626.

The unsung heroes are the plain people. And so it was with the Catholics of St. Mary's County, mostly farmers whose roots in America reached back to almost the beginning of their state. Such immigrant ancestors as John Cissell, Cuthbert Fenwick, Richard Gardiner, John Greenwell, Francis Hayden, Thomas Howard, John Jarboe, Thomas Jenkins, Thomas Mattingly, John Medley, Peter Mills, Thomas Spalding and Robert Thompson, were all there before the "Glorious Revolution" brought an end to the Catholic phase of the colony. Each of them produced a mighty progeny. A sampling of other Catholic names that would constitute St. Mary's County legacy to the country at large would include Aud, Bowles, Brewer, Clark, Knott, Moore, Newton, Morris, Payne, Raley, Shercliffe, Wheatley, Wimsatt and Yates. One might also include those Protestant families who by the time of the American Revolution had sprouted Catholic branches, such as the Abells, Alveys, Lees and Tarltons.

The most important contribution of St. Mary's County to the newly organized church in a nation that had just won its independence from Great Britain was to spearhead the westward expansion of Catholicism. In 1785, the first of several Catholic families from St. Mary's County crossed the mountains to find land in Kentucky, led by the Haydens and the Lancasters, as Archbishop Martin John Spalding, one of the most noted representatives of the Diaspora, tells us. In the 1790's St. Mary's county surrendered 1,538 of its white inhabitants and in the following decade another 520. In the period 1790-1810, in fact, it lost 25 percent of its white population. It was largely a Catholic exodus. Charles and Prince Georges, the two counties with the next greatest number of Catholics, suffered comparable looses but in the decade 1800-1810. The Catholic church in Maryland was deprived of at least a fourth of its membership, mostly farmers, compelled by economic necessity to seek more and cheaper land in Kentucky, Missouri, Georgia, Louisiana and other states. But it was their religion that kept them together in identifiable groupings. So great, in fact, was the number who chose Kentucky as their future home that a diocese was created for those transplanted Marylanders in 1808. *Note: This article by Bro. Thomas W. Spalding, C.F.X., used with kind permission, was an introduction to* Catholic Families of Southern Maryland, *compiled by Timothy J. O'Rourke, published by Genealogical Publishing Co., Inc., Baltimore, MD, 1985.*

Two Hundred Years of Catholicity—Settlers Laid Foundation for Church in Kentucky

by Joseph E. Duerr

Their numbers were small when they crossed the Appalachians two centuries ago to settle in Kentucky and lay the foundation for the Catholic church in this state and in the West.

Like all pioneers, these first Catholic settlers did not know at the time what impact their settlement would have. They shared the hopes of all pioneers—the promise of new land—but their offspring and others who followed would determine the lasting effects of their settlement.

The impact of this settlement is now known—a Catholic faith that not only flourished on the frontier but which grew and expanded in Kentucky and other parts of the country.

"Of all the stories of religious groups that helped tame frontier Kentucky, that of the Catholic settlers and priests is perhaps the most unexpected and certainly the most remarkable," John Boles wrote in his 1976 book, *Religion in Antebellum Kentucky.* "As Baltimore was the mother of the Catholic church in America, so was Bardstown, KY, the mother of the Catholic church west of the Appalachians."

What brought these Catholic families to Kentucky, which at the time was part of Virginia? Boles writes in his history, "General economic conditions combined with the constant threat of religious persecution played a minor role, but the persuasive argument was the promise of bountiful acres across the mountains."

The Catholic pioneers left their imprint. Father Clyde Crews, in a 1973 history of Catholicism in Kentucky noted that the early settlers were "not casual Catholics but were fiercely committed to the faith."

In another article written several years ago, Father Crews, a priest of the Archdiocese of Louisville, who is currently writing a history of Kentucky Catholicism [published in 1987], observed that the pioneer Catholics had a "tradition that combined clerical reverence with a strong streak of lay initiative, religious tolerance and democratic pluralism."

Father Crews added, "The frontier suggested vast open spaces, individualism, adaptability. Catholicism, at least in the popular mind, was more properly represented by urbanity, authoritarianism and disciplined ritual. And yet, by some wonderful chemistry, Catholicism proved to be resilient, even flourishing on the Kentucky frontier."

There were about 300 Catholic families at the time, most in Nelson County and they lived miles apart. Father Badin, who later would help to establish the University of Notre Dame, visited parishioners on horseback.

Father Nerinckx, who came to the state in 1805, established some 10 parishes. He also helped such Kentucky women as Mary Rhodes, Christine Stuart and Ann Hevern found the Sisters of Loretto in 1812 as one of the first native American religious congregations. The Loretto Sisters' Motherhouse still stands at Nerinx, KY.

Other religious communities also have their roots in Kentucky, some of them going back to the wilderness years.

The Sisters of Charity of Nazareth were formed in 1812 by Bishop John Baptiste Marie David and Mother Catherine Spalding, and the Dominican Sisters made their first United States establishment in 1822 near Springfield. The first Dominican foundation in the New World was at St. Rose near Springfield in the early 1800's after the arrival of Father Edward Fenwick.

And there were other firsts. In 1848, the Trappist monks made their first permanent United States foundation not far from Bardstown. Our Lady of Gethsemane Abbey, the first abbey in the New World, was for some years home for the noted monk, Thomas Merton, whose grave is located in the abbey cemetery.

Another landmark event for the church in Kentucky and the West, occurred in 1808 with the establishment of the Bardstown diocese, the forerunner to the Archdiocese of Louisville. The Bardstown diocese was formed the same year that the dioceses were established in New York, Boston and Philadelphia. Until 1808, the Baltimore diocese had jurisdiction over the entire country.

Bishop Benedict Joseph Flaget was the first bishop of the diocese, which then included the states of Kentucky, Tennessee and Ohio and the territories of Indiana, Illinois and Michigan. This diocese played a major role in the expansion of the Catholic Church in the United States and was a stepping stone for Catholicism to spread throughout the Midwest.

One of the highly populated Catholic areas, besides metropolitan Louisville, is the so-called "Holy Land of Kentucky", Nelson, Marion and Washington Counties. It was in this area that the Catholic church took root in Kentucky and that heritage remains today.

"This Holy Land" is unparalleled in the nation for its Catholic history and is certainly unique in the South as one of the few rural areas that are predominantly Catholic," Father Crews observed in one article.

The foundations made by those 25 Catholic pioneer families, 200 years ago, were more than homesteads cut out of the Kentucky wilderness. On these plots, the faith took root, spread throughout the state and developed into the church we know today.

Father Crews wrote several years ago: "Catholicism had become very visibly active throughout Kentucky in the later 20th century in community concerns, peace and justice issues and intensive ecumenical relations. All this was in addition to the traditions of piety, sacrament, virtue and life-shaping creeds and ministries that had crossed the mountains and flowed down the rivers with the earliest pioneers two centuries ago." *This article, used with kind permission, appeared in* The Record, *Sept. 5, 1985, by Joseph E. Duerr, Editor.*

350 year celebration in 1984 – Maryland.

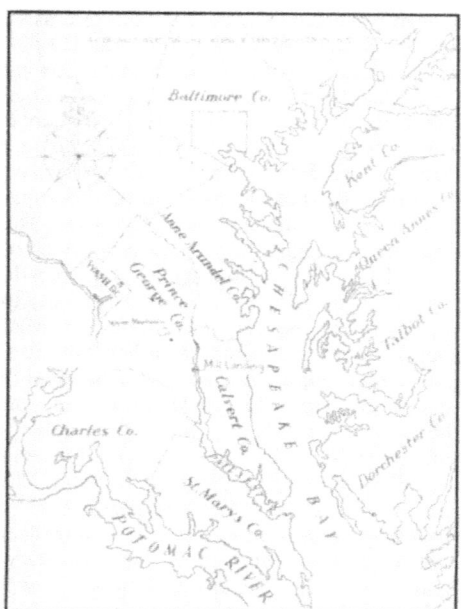
Map of Maryland.

John Carroll, first Bishop of Baltimore (1789–1815)

Reverend Stephen Theodore Badin

Born July 17, 1768 at Orleans, France, he studied for three years at the College of Montaigu in Paris and, in 1789, entered the seminary conducted by the Sulpicians in his native city, where he received tonsure and minor orders. His theological course was well advanced when the terrors of the French revolution forced him to withdraw from the seminary in July 1791. In the following November he sailed for American with Fathers Flaget and David, future bishops of Kentucky, and upon their arrival in Baltimore four months later, he entered the newly opened St. Mary Seminary. Bishop Carroll gave him the subdiaconate Sept. 22, 1791, the diaconate Feb. 23, 1793 and elevated him to the priesthood on the following May 25. He was the first priest to be ordained in what were formerly the English Colonies of America.

In September of that year, 1793, Father Badin in company with Rev. Michael Barriere set out for Kentucky and arrived at Lexington on the last day of November. The older priest moved on to Bardstown, but not finding the missions to his liking, went to Louisiana about four months later and Badin was left alone to attend the scattered settlements. For about 18 months, he made his headquarters at White Sulphur in Scott County and then took up his residence in the Pottinger Creek settlement, near the present Holy Cross in Marion County, for the greater number of Catholics had located in this part of the state. He purchased a tract of land on or adjoining the site of the present motherhouse of the Sisters of Loretto, where he erected a cabin with a small chapel attached, which he called St. Stephen's. Bishop Carroll, was anxious to send assistance to his young priest in the rapidly growing settlements, but it was not until February 1797 that Rev. Michael J.C. Fournier arrived. Father Anthony Salmon came in January 1799 and, in the following month, the convert priest, John Thayer, began his labors in Kentucky. However, Salmon died after nine months of service; Fournier was fatally stricken in February 1803 and Thayer abandoned the mission a few months later. Again, Badin was left alone.

A new era for Catholicity in Kentucky began in July 1805, when Rev. Charles Nerinckx rode up to St. Stephen's. The work of attending the settlements was roughly divided. Father Nerinckx's territory included principally Hardin Creek (St. Charles' in Marion County), Cartwright Creek (St. Ann's near Springfield), Rolling Fork (Holy Mary's, Calvary) and the station in Casey County (St. Bernard's). Father Badin was then able to devote more attention to his congregations at Holy Cross, Bardstown, Cox Creek (Fairfield), Poplar Neck (St. Thomas' in Nelson County), St. John's in Bullitt County, Colesburg, St. Benedicts's in Spencer County and the Scott County missions. His missionary journeys in these early years extended as far west as Breckinridge County. The little town of Louisville was also under his care.

Father Nerinckx frequently assisted Father Badin in his parishes, especially when the latter was on a long missionary tour. Under these

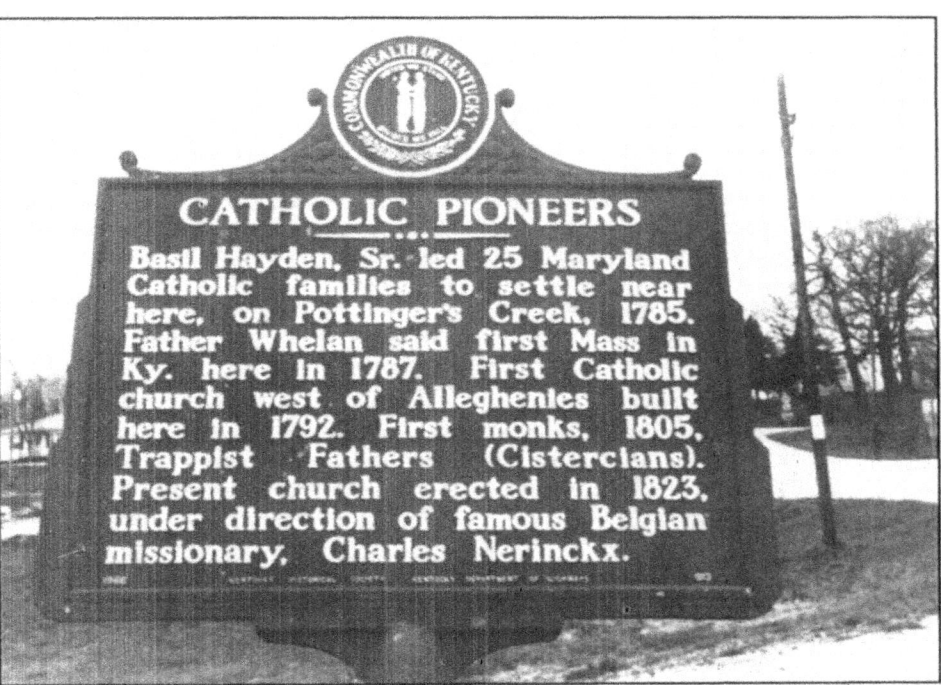

Holy Land of Kentucky. Nelson, Marion, Washington Counties. From Maryland starting 1785.

Holy Cross Church, Marion County, KY. The first catholic church in Kentucky, built in 1790.

conditions, both priests shared in the labor of constructing at least three of the churches during the period between 1805 and 1812. St. Patrick Church in Danville was begun in 1806. It was the first Catholic brick church in Kentucky. St. Michael Church, Fairfield, under construction from 1807, was opened for services on New Year's Day, 1810. St. John the Baptist Church, located close to the southeastern border of Bullitt County, was being erected in 1811, when Bishop Flaget arrived in the diocese. The two missionaries planned to establish a community of Sisters. Father Badin went to Baltimore in August 1807, to receive Bishop Carroll's approval of the project and, on his return in the early part of 1808, began the erection of a convent building on a farm a short distance from St. Stephen's. A few months later, when the work was practically completed, the building took fire by some unaccountable accident and burned to the ground. So ended the first attempt to form a congregation of nuns in Kentucky.

Unfortunately, Father Badin possessed an eccentric and rigorous disposition. His strict and perhaps unreasonable manner of dealing with the laity had left him many enemies. He got into difficulties with Bishop Flaget and it was inevitable that a rift should develop between him and his Bishop. In the spring of 1819, he shook the dust of Kentucky from his feet and returned to his native land. His time was occupied by assisting in parish work at his old home Orleans, and later he devoted his energies in obtaining aid for the American missions. He went to Rome in the fall of 1826, and entered the Dominican novitiate, but when he received a letter from Bishop Richard Fenwick, O.P. of Cincinnati congratulating him and expressing a desire that he become both the provincial of the Dominicans in the United States and his coadjutor, he left the novitiate.

In June 1828, the restless missionary, then approaching his 60th birthday, sailed for America to labor with his younger brother Vincent on the missions in Michigan. Early in 1830, he returned to Kentucky for a visit of several months. He then went to Cincinnati and under the direction of Bishop Fenwick, took charge of the missions among the Potawatomi Indians on the southern shores of Lake Michigan. During the next four years, his field of labor also included the scattered settlers in the northern part of the three states of Indiana, Michigan and Illinois. He spent much time among the tribe of Chief Pokagon along the St. Joseph River and purchased a tract of land near South Bend where the Indians, at his direction, built a small church which was dedicated by him on Nov. 21, 1831. Near the end of 1834, he gave up the missions and went to Cincinnati with the intention of retiring. He traveled much, visiting Baltimore, Washington and St. Louis and he frequently returned to the scenes of his former labors in Kentucky. But his restless spirit would not let him retire and in 1843, when he had passed the golden anniversary of his ordination, he took charge of the missions at Kankakee in Illinois. Five years later he returned to Louisville, this time staying until the end of August 1849.

Father Badin's last years were spent in Cincinnati where he died in the Cathedral rectory on April 19, 1853. He was the last survivor of that group of apostolic priests who laid the groundwork of the Church in Kentucky. After the funeral services in the Cathedral, he was laid to rest in the crypt beside his long time friend, Bishop Fenwick. In May 1906, his mortal remains were removed to Notre Dame and placed in a mortuary chapel erected near the site of the church he had dedicated in 1831. *Rev. John A. Lyons, 1976*

Reverend Charles Nerinckx

Born in Herffelingen in the Province of Brabant, Belgium, Oct. 2, 1761. He studied for the priesthood in his native land and was ordained at Mechlin on Nov. 1, 1785. After laboring as assistant, pastor and chaplain for 19 years, the French Revolutionists invaded Belgium and he was forced to flee to America.

Father Nerinckx landed at Baltimore, MD in November 1804, and proceeded to Georgetown College to learn the English language. A few months later, Bishop Carroll appointed him to Kentucky and he arrived at Father Badin's home (called St. Stephen's) adjoining the present motherhouse of the Sisters of Loretto in Marion County, July 2, 1805. For several years, Father Nerinckx made his headquarters at St. Stephen's.

The work of attending some 25 scattered missions was roughly divided between the two priests, and he took charge of the eastern section which included Hardin's Creek, Cartwright's Creek, Rolling Forks and the settlement in Casey County. He was relieved of the mission at Cartwright's Creek when the Dominican Fathers took it over in October 1806. In addition to his own parishes, he frequently attended those of Father Badin when the latter was visiting the more distant stations throughout the state.

Bishop Carroll sought to appoint Father Nerinckx, Administrator of the troubled diocese of New Orleans in 1808, but the humble missionary declined to accept the promotion.

The first church built by Father Badin's coworker was that of Holy Name of Mary (Holy Mary's), Calvary in Marion County. The cornerstone was blessed Nov. 15, 1805 and the building was erected to replace a hastily and poorly constructed chapel put up a few months previously. That same year, he opened the Chapel of St. Barbara in the home of James Dant, which was located on the present site of the Trappist Abbey at Gethsemane. He rebuilt or enlarged St. Charles Church in Marion County in 1806. St. Clare

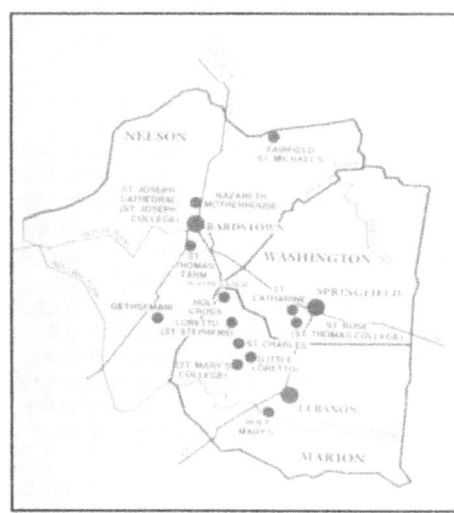

Holy Land of Kentucky. Nelson, Marion & Washington Counties.

Rev. Stephen T. Badin (1768-1853). The first priest ordained in the U.S.; Kentucky Missionary, 1793.

Rev. Charles Nerinckx (1761-1833), an early Kentucky church builder.

Mother Catherine Spalding, S.C.N. (1793-1858).

St. Joseph's Cathedral at Bardstown, Kentucky. It was the first church consecrated in the West in 1819.

Church, Colesburg, begun in 1807 was completed in 1810. In this latter year, he also erected St. Bernard Church in Casey County and began the construction of St. James Church (now called St. Paul's), Big Clifty, Grayson County. In 1812, he built the Church of St. Romuald, Hardinsburg, and the Chapel of the Sacred Hearts in Union County. During this period the Church of St. Anthony, Abbot, Axtel, Breckinridge County was being erected but it was not completed until after 1815. About the year 1812, he built the Church of St. Ignatius (later known as St. John's) in Hardin County. St. Augustine Church, his second church in Grayson County, was constructed in 1815 and that same year saw the completion of the Church of St. Benedict in Spencer County. Besides the above-mentioned buildings, he shared with Father Badin the labors and worry incident to the construction of other churches during the period 1805-1812.

With the arrival of Bishop Flaget at St. Stephen's in June 1811, Father Nerinckx took up his headquarters at St. Charles Church and on April 25 of the following year, he began the foundation of a Community of Sisters of Loretto on a 50 acre farm adjoining the church. The first members were formally received in to the new society June 29, 1812.

In 1823, Father Nerinckx built his last church, the present Holy Cross in Marion County, which replaced the small chapel erected in 1792. The faithful missionary's years in Kentucky were coming to an end. He was discouraged because of the failure of the proposed Brotherhood and grieved that the rules of his Community of Sisters were being mitigated by the authorities. He felt that he could accomplish more good in Missouri where there were many Catholic settlements without a priest, and Indian tribes awaiting conversion. So he set out in June 1824, and arrived at the branch house of the Sisters of Loretto in Bethlehem, Perry County about four weeks later. In August, while on a short missionary tour near St. Louis, he took ill and died at St. Genevieve on the 12th of the month. His mortal remains were buried in the convent cemetery at Bethlehem and in December 1833, were translated to their final resting place in the cemetery of the motherhouse of the Lorettines in Kentucky.
Rev. John A. Lyons, 1976

Bishops of Bardstown and Louisville

by Rev. Clyde F. Crews

Just as Kentucky was the first western star in the American flag, so the Diocese of Bardstown was the first western center of Catholicism in the American Nation. This first inland diocese of the United States, since its establishment in 1808, has been blessed with leadership, both lay and clerical. It could be useful to examine briefly the bishops who led the Kentucky Catholic Church, down to the time of the establishment of the Diocese of Owensboro.

The first bishop to preside over the array of congregations, sisterhoods of educational and healing service and of frontier academies and colleges, was Benedict Joseph Flaget (1763-1850). An émigré from the French Revolution, Flaget was a cultured, affable and pious man. A close friend to countless Catholics and Protestants, the first bishop's life was one of apostolic poverty, zealous preaching and sacramental work. He was a friend to Henry Clay and had visited George Washington on two occasions.

Flaget's original diocese of Bardstown (transferred to Louisville in 1841) was formed by Pope Pius VII in 1808, when the dioceses of Boston, New York and Philadelphia were also carved out of the primal See of Baltimore. Flaget's first administrative responsibilities extended over the area from the Great Lakes to the deep south, from the Appalachians to the Mississippi. Over 30 dioceses in that area today, look to Bardstown-Louisville as their historical matrix.

Bishop Flaget managed to have Rome appoint him three coadjutor bishops: John Marie David (1761-1841), Guy Chabrat (1787-1868) and Martin John Spalding (1810-1872). Kentucky born Spalding, in fact, would become Flaget's successor at Louisville and would serve there from 1850 to 1864; he would then be appointed Archbishop of Baltimore, then considered the most influential place in American Catholicism.

Martin John Spalding was a scholar bishop, a prolific author and a noted lecturer. He lectured from such platforms as the Smithsonian Institution in Washington and the Cooper Union in New York. His orations on Catholic apologetics at the Louisville Cathedral resulted in a book titled, *Evidences of Catholicity*. In Louisville, Bishop Spalding steered a prudent course during the anti-immigrant riots in 1855 known, in the city's history, as Bloody Monday. He was also to bring many foreign-born priests into clerical service in his diocese. During the Civil War, Spalding helped shore up the morale of a badly divided people in border state Kentucky.

The Spalding family, in fact, constituted something of a spiritual dynasty in 19th century

Benedict Joseph Flaget, First Bishop of Bardstown/Louisville (1808-1850).

John Marie David, Coadjutor Bishop of Bardstown/Louisville (1819-1841).

Guy Chabrat, Coadjutor Bishop of Bardstown/Louisville (1834-1868?).

Martin John Spalding, Bishop of Louisville (1850-1864).

Kentucky. Catherine Spalding (1793-1858), was with Bishop David, the foundress of the Sisters of Charity of Nazareth and is considered one of the leading women in American Catholicism in the early 19th century. John Lancaster Spalding (1840-1916), nephew to Bishop Spalding, was another scholar and author who would be called to the episcopacy, becoming the first Bishop of Peoria in 1877. This Louisville priest, would also become one of the founders of the Catholic University of America.

Martin John Spalding was followed in the Louisville bishop's chair by Peter Joseph Lavialle (1820-1867), like Flaget, a native of France. Frail in health, he died after less than two years in office.

Fourth Bishop of Louisville, was William George McCloskey (1823-1909). Authoritarian, strong-willed and stalwart, Brooklyn-born McCloskey would rule the diocese for 40 years. While his tenure saw a steady amount of congregational and institutional growth, it was also to be marked by seemingly endless controversies with his clerics and the religious orders.

When the landmark Vatican Council met in Rome in 1869-70, there was Bishop McCloskey, at first opposing the definition of papal infallibility as untimely; later coming round to its support. A Kentuckian by adoption, he complained once while resident in Rome, that the horses provided him were not satisfactory; not worthy presumably, of a Kentucky gentleman. McCloskey also was present for the vitally important Third Plenary Council of Baltimore in 1884 that would influence Catholic life down far into our own century. (Kentuckian John Lancaster Spalding, incidentally, in addition to his other accomplishments, also had a hand in the composition of the famous Baltimore Catechism at this time.) It was during the episcopacy of Bishop McCloskey that the groundwork would be laid for the eventual establishment of the Ursuline Sisters at Maple Mount as a congregation separate from the Louisville Motherhouse.

Louisville's fifth bishop was to be a gentleman from Indianapolis, Denis O'Donaghue (1848-1925), who presided over his post during the WWI. Being installed as Bishop of Louisville in 1910, he would serve faithfully until Rome pressed for his resignation in 1924. Senility had come upon the worthy old prelate, and a youthful 36 year old monsignor from Nashville, John Alexander Floersh (1886-1968) was named to be his successor.

Bishop Floersh was noted as a linguist, an ascetic in his spirituality and additionally, a genius in the area of real estate. This last talent would serve the bishop particularly well after WWII, when the city of Louisville developed some 30 new suburban parishes in the first post-war generation. Floersh would also place both Catholic charities and education on highly professional bases, and encourage higher education as well, founding Louisville's Bellarmine College, for example, in 1950.

Late in 1937, the same year as disastrous flooding at Louisville, Owensboro, Paducah and other river cities of the commonwealth, Rome established a new diocese at Owensboro, covering the western portion of Kentucky. Named as first bishop, was Francis Cotton (1895-1960), who had been trained for administration in Bishop Floersh's chancery. At the time, Owensboro was constituted a diocese, Louisville was raised to the status of an archdiocese, and thus Floersh was to become Louisville's first archbishop, a post from which he retired in 1967 after 44 years at the helm. His successors would be Thomas McDonough (Archbishop of Louisville from 1967-1982) and Thomas C. Kelly, O.P. (Archbishop of Louisville since 1982).

The Kentucky Bishops "from the Louisville line" had been, without exception, Christian believers who set high moral standards and examples for their people. They brought to an area that began as a wilderness the challenge and the comfort of the ancient faith, translated onto the American scene. Their greatest testaments, one would expect, are the faithful generations of Catholics in this commonwealth, so willing to celebrate, proclaim and serve their common faith in the Christian Gospel. *Note: This article by Rev. Clyde F. Crews, used with kind permission, originally appeared in* A History of St. Jerome, Fancy Farm, KY (1836-1986).

Peter Joseph Lavialle, Bishop of Louisville (1865-1867).

William George McCloskey, Bishop of Louisville (1868-1909).

Denis O'Donaghue, Bishop of Louisville (1910-1924).

John A. Floersh, Archbishop of Louisville (1924-1967).

Reverend Elisha John Durbin (1800-1887)

Patriarch of the Catholic Church in Western Kentucky

REVEREND ELISHA JOHN DURBIN, 1800-1887, was patriarch of the church in Western Kentucky. He was born Feb. 1, 1800 at St. Christopher Mission, near Richmond in Madison Co. Elisha was a son of John and Patience Logsdon Durbin Sr. Most of the Durbins and Logsdons moved from Madison Co. to form the Catholic settlement at Sunfish in Edmonson Co. John Durbin Sr., outlived his wife, Patience, who died at Sunfish on Nov. 8, 1848 on her 77th birthday.

He was ordained Sept. 21, 1822 by Bishop Flaget. In March 1824, he began his long and eventful labors in Western Kentucky. Father Durbin took up his headquarters at Sacred Heart Church, St. Vincent in Union Co. and from there attended the missions throughout the territory that practically embraces the present Diocese of Owensboro. His apostolic journeys frequently took him to the scattered Catholics residing in southern Indiana and Illinois and in April 1832, he began periodic visits to Nashville, TN. For several years he labored alone. Finally, help came with the appointment of assistants and resident pastors in the larger settlements and with their aid, more parishes were established and churches erected.

The veteran missionary was instrumental in the construction of the following churches: St. Mary Church in Perry Co. on the Indiana side of the Ohio River, built in 1825 or 1826; the second Church of St. Theresa in Meade Co., erected in 1826; the first St. Lawrence Church in Daviess Co., opened for services in 1828; the second Church of the Sacred Heart at St. Vincent, Union Co. dedicated Sept. 14, 1828; the first St. Ambrose Church, Henshaw, built about 1833; the first St. Jerome Church, Fancy Farm, erected in 1836; the first St. Francis de Sales Church, Paducah and the first St. John the Evangelist Church in McCracken Co., built in 1849; St. Stephen Church, Smithland in Livingston Co., opened for services in 1860; and the first St. Louis (later Holy Name) Church, Henderson, dedicated in 1861.

In 1867, Rev. William J. Dunn, a former assistant to the veteran missionary, wrote to Archbishop Spalding: "Father Durbin is as vigorous as ever...He may live in his usefulness yet many years. His hope of surmounting all his difficulties before he dies is as unbroken as ever." With the development of the western parishes, nearly all the churches erected during his administration obtained resident pastors and by 1872, his mission territory had been reduced to that section of Kentucky lying roughly between the Tidewater and Tennessee Rivers. The pioneering spirit was still with him and early in 1873, he resigned his pastorate at Sacred Heart Church to devote his full time to his remaining missions. Taking up his headquarters at Princeton, where he purchased property for a church, he attended the Catholics scattered through Caldwell, Livingston, Crittenden, Lyon and Trigg Counties for the next eight years.

Bishop McCloskey removed the zealous old priest, then in his 81st year, from the hardships of the missions and appointed him chaplain at St. Vincent Academy in Union Co. in January 1881. A few months later, he moved to Louisville to become chaplain at Saints Mary and Elizabeth Hospital (12th Street) and in November 1882, he took up his home at St. Joseph College, Bardstown. But retirement did not suit the active Durbin and the last three years of his life were spent as chaplain at the Motherhouse and Academy of the Sisters of the Third Order of St. Francis at Shelbyville, where he died March 22, 1887, in the 65th year of his ordination. Following the funeral services at the Cathedral of the Assumption, the mortal remains of the patriarch of the church in Western Kentucky were laid at rest in St. Louis Cemetery, Louisville. *Bishops and Priests of the Diocese of Bardstown by Rev. John A. Lyons, 1976.*

Chronology of Events (1785-1937)

(Editor's Note: When reading the "Chronology of Events," it is important to realize that within a particular year, each sentence represents a seperate entry.)

1785	25 Catholic families from Maryland settled near Pottinger's Creek, Nelson Co., VA (became Kentucky).
1790	Rev. William deRohan, Irish missionary, arrived in KY; built Holy Cross, first Catholic church in KY (a log cabin). Population of KY: 73,563; population of Louisville, about 200.
1792	Kentucky admitted as 15th State, June 1, 1792.
1793	Rev. Stephen T. Badin (1768-1853), first priest ordained in the United States, arrived in Kentucky with Rev. Michael Barriere (1747-1824),in November; Rev. Badin's "missionary journey in these early years extended as far west as Breckinridge Co."
1801	First Catholic settlers in Breckinridge Co.: Richard and Barton Mattingly and Leonard Wheatley; visited by Rev. Michael Fournier (c. 1755-1803). (Spalding)
1804	Rev. Stephen T. Badin visited "the parish of Rough Creek, which we call St. Anthony," Breckinridge Co.
1805	Rev. Charles Nerinckx (1761-1824), arrived in Kentucky in July; builder of 14 churches; requested permission from Bishop Carroll: *1. To introduce the devotion of the perpetual adoration of the Blessed Sacrament; 2. To establish the confraternities of the Holy Name of Jesus, of the Holy Rosary of the Souls in Purgatory, or any other if deemed advisable, in every congregation of at least 25 Communicants.* Dominican priests established first American foundation, St. Rose, near Springfield, founder Rev. Edward Fenwick (1768-1832).
1807	Rev. Charles Nerinckx wrote regarding Lenten regulations: "Lent is kept very strictly...we have to abstain from meat the first four days of Lent, the entire Holy Week, and on Mondays, Wednesdays, Fridays and Saturdays of every week. This year we were dispensed on Mondays."
1808	Bardstown, KY erected into Episcopal See. Benedict Joseph Flaget (1763-1850), Sulpician, named first Bishop of Bardstown.
1809	Last Rev. Badin's annual trips to St. Anthony, Breckinridge C., and neighboring missions; replaced by Rev. Charles Nerinckx until 1815.
1810	Rev. Benedict Joseph Flaget consecrated Bishop of Bardstown, November 4. Bardstown Diocese: six priests (two seculars, four Dominicans), zero religious women, 16,000 Catholics, ten churches (two brick). Population of Kentucky: 406,511.; Population of Louisville: 1,397.
1811	Bishop Flaget reached Bardstown, June 9. Rev. Guy I. Chabrat (1787-1868), first priest ordained in Kentucky, December 21, by Bishop Flaget. St. James Church (later St. Paul), Grayson Co., erected by Rev. Charles Nerinckx, oldest church in Grayson Co., second church built 1869, burnt 1917.
1812	St. Thomas Seminary, Poplar Neck, Nelson Co., built; Sulpician Rev. John B. David, director. Rev. Charles Nerinckx founded Sisters of Loretto, April 25, first religious community in the West. Rev. John B. M. David (1761-1841) founded Sisters of Charity of Nazareth in December, with co-founder Mother Catherine Spalding. First Synod in Kentucky, February, St. Stephen's, Nelson Co., attended by eight priests. St. Anthony Church, Long Lick (Axtel), Breckinridge Co., started by Rev. Nerinckx; completed 1819 by Rev. Robert Abell. Rev. Charles Nerinckx built St. Romuald Church, Hardinsburg, Breckinridge Co., and Sacred Heart Chapel, Union Co. Sacred Heart Cemetery oldest inscription: Louis A. Fenwick, wife of Richard, born March 11, 1786, died Feb. 19, 1812.
1813	Bardstown Diocese contained about 6,000 souls, 30 congregations, 10 churches.
1814	Bishop Flaget's first visit to Breckinridge Co.
1815	Bishop Flaget's report Diocese of Bardstown to Pius VIII, April 10. St. Augustine Church, Grayson Springs, Grayson Co., built by Rev. Charles Nerinckx.
1816	Rev. William Thomas Willett O.P. (1790-1824), first native priest in Kentucky, ordained; uncle of Samuel Willett, "founder" of Fancy Farm, Graves Co.,1829.
1818	Rev. Robert A. Abell (1792-1873), first native diocesan priest in Kentucky, ordained May 10; succeeded Rev. Charles Nerinckx in care of missions in southern and southwestern Kentucky (1818-1825).

1816 - Rev. William Thomas Willett, O.P. Ordained September 1816. St. Rose Priory, Springfield, KY.

* **REVEREND ROBERT ABNER ABELL,** born Nov. 25, 1792 at Calvary, KY. He was a son of Robert Abell and Margaret Mills, pioneer settlers in the Rolling Fork district in Marion Co. He entered the newly formed diocesan seminary of St. Thomas, near Bardstown, in 1812. He received tonsure from Bishop Benedict Joseph Flaget in April 1814, and the same prelate elevated him to the priesthood at St. Thomas Church, attached to the seminary, May 10, 1818.

Following his ordination, Father Abell succeeded Rev. Charles Nerinckx in the care of the missions in southern and southwestern Kentucky. For the first few months, he made the long missionary circuit on horseback from the seminary and then, to be more centrally located in his Catholic settlements, he took up his headquarters at St. Anthony's, Long Lick (Axtel), in Breckinridge Co. The young missionary erected the Church of St. Paul, near Peonia in Grayson Co. about 1820 and, it was probably in that same year that he began to attend the Catholics in Nashville, TN, where he was instrumental in the building of the first Catholic church in that state. His services in this vast mission field ended in 1825, with his appointment as professor at St. Joseph College, Bardstown. At the end of the scholastic year, he was sent abroad in the interests of the diocese and returned two years later.

In 1859, he took up his residence near his birthplace in the Rolling Fork settlement. He continued to accept light work in the neighboring missions and as he enjoyed a reputation as a brilliant speaker, he was called upon from time to time, to preach at the various church functions. Finally, in his 80th year and after a retirement of 14 years, he moved to Louisville in 1871, to become chaplain of St. Joseph Infirmary (4th Street). His death occurred at the Infirmary, June 28, 1873. The funeral services of the venerable priest took place from the Cathedral and he was interred in St. Louis Cemetery, Louisville. *Rev. John A. Lyons*

Rev. Robert A. Abell (1792-1873).

1819 St. Joseph Cathedral, Bardstown, consecrated August 8; first church consecrated in West; Rev. Robert Abell preached. Rev. John Baptist Mary David (1761-1841), consecrated August 15, Coadjutor Bishop Bardstown. Union Co. church property deeds recorded at Morganfield by Rev. Robert A. Abell. Union Co. Catholics visited earlier by Rev. Stephen Badin and Rev. Charles Nerinckx.

1820 ST. VINCENT ACADEMY, St. Vincent, Union Co., established by Sisters of Charity of Nazareth, December; log cabin church built academy grounds.

1821 Rev. Stephen T. Badin's, *Origins and Progress of the Mission of Kentucky,* published Paris, France. First Catholic service in Daviess Co. by Rev. Robert A. Abell (1792-1873) for Knottsville settlers; became St. Lawrence Parish. Bishop Flaget said Mass Leitchfield, Grayson Co., May 7. Bishop Flaget visited Bowling Green, Warren Co., five Catholic families.

1822 Rev. Elisha John Durbin (1800-1887), ordained September 21, would become Patriarch of the Church in Western Kentucky. Mt. Carmel School established at Long Lick (Axtel) by Loretto Sisters, December; closed 1830 when they opened Bethlehem Academy Hardin Co. Dominican Sisters founded Springfield, Washington Co.; Mother Angela Sansbury first superior.

1823 Second Diocesan Synod Bardstown, August 5; 14 priests attended.

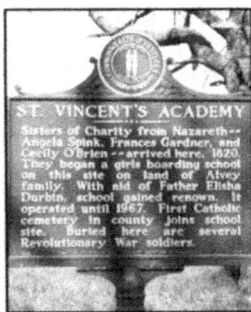

St. Vincent Academy, Union County, KY (Est. 1820).

1824 REV. ELISHA JOHN DURBIN in March began long and eventful labors in western Kentucky, with "headquarters at Sacred Heart Church, St. Vincent, Union Co., and from there attended the missions throughout the territory that practically embraces the present Diocese of Owensboro." Brothers Christopher and John Durbin first Catholic settlers in Edmonson Co.; John and Patience (Logsdon) Durbin, parents Rev. Elisha John Durbin. Rev. Charles Nerinckx died at St. Genevieve, MO on Aug. 12.

1825 Rev. John B. David wrote *The Catechism of the Catholic Religion.*

1826 Rev. Charles J. Cissell (1804-1832), was ordained December 23, born near St. Vincent, Union Co.; assigned missions in Hardin, Breckinridge and Grayson Counties (1827-1832).

* **REV. CHARLES J. CISSELL,** a son of Wilfred and Cecilia Clark Cissell was born near St. Vincent in Union Co. about 1804 and entered St. Thomas Seminary in Nelson Co. in 1818. His theological course was taken at St. Joseph Seminary, Bardstown, where he received the subdiaconate Dec. 18, 1824 and the diaconate Aug. 19, 1826 from Bishop Flaget. Bishop David ordained him, together with Linus Coomes, in St. Joseph Cathedral on Dec. 23, 1826.

Father Cissell was assigned to the missions in Hardin, Breckinridge and Grayson Counties. and from his nominal headquarters at St. Thomas Seminary, he made the month-long circuit to St. Ignatius (later St. John the Baptist) Church "on Rude's Creek" in Hardin Co.; St. Romuald Church, Hardinsburg; St. Anthony Church, "on Long Lick"; Axtel and the Grayson Co. churches of St. Augustine, Grayson Springs, St. James, near Peonia and St. Paul, Big Clifty.

He also attended Mount Carmel School, conducted by the Sisters of Loretto on Long Lick. In 1830, Father Cissell took up his residence at St. Anthony Church and near the end of that year, moved with the Sisters to establish Bethlehem Academy in Hardin Co. His home was a small cabin built on the academy grounds where he died two years later, Nov. 23, 1832. The young priest was buried in the parish cemetery and when the new church, dedicated under the patronage of St. John the Baptist, was erected, his remains were interred beneath the altar. He was the first resident pastor in Hardin Co. *Rev. John A. Lyons*

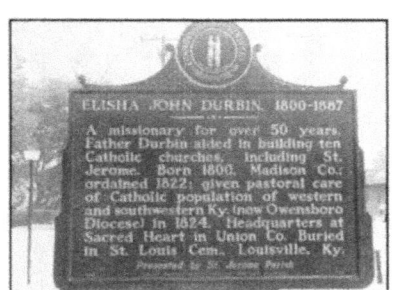

Historical Marker at St. Jerome Church, Fancy Farm, Graves County.

Benedict J. Webb (1814-1897), prominent Catholic layman; established the first Catholic newspaper in Kentucky, the "Catholic Advocate."

1828 St. Lawrence Church, first Catholic church in Daviess Co., built by Rev. Elisha Durbin. Second Sacred Heart Church, St. Vincent, Union Co., built by Rev. Elisha J. Durbin, dedicated by Bishop Flaget on September 14.

1829 St. Ambrose congregation, Henshaw, Union Co., established, St. Ambrose Church built about 1833.

1832 Rev. Elisha Durbin baptized two oldest children of Samuel and Elizabeth (Hobbs) Willett in Graves Co. March 31; his last entry in St. Jerome records Oct. 7, 1884 ("52 years of service").

1833 Rev. John C. Wathen (1801-1841), first resident pastor of St. Lawrence Church, Daviess Co. and missions until 1841; began attending St. Stephen congregation, Owensboro, May.

* **REVEREND JOHN C. WATHEN**, a son of Wilfred and Winifred Coomes Wathen, was born in the Fairfield district of Nelson Co., Oct. 14, 1801 and entered St. Joseph Seminary, Bardstown as early as 1822. He received the diaconate March 6, 1830 and priesthood on the following September 12 at the hands of Bishop Flaget in St. Joseph Cathedral.

After three months at the Cathedral, Father Wathen was appointed assistant to Rev. David Deparcq at St. Charles Church, Marion Co. and given charge of Holy Name of Mary Church at Calvary. It appears from the church records at St Charles, that he moved there from Calvary in November 1831, and was acting pastor during the construction of the second church which was dedicated on Sept. 9, 1832.

Father Wathen's next assignment was on May 5, 1833 when he became the first resident pastor at St. Lawrence Church in Daviess Co. Attached to his parish, were Owensboro where he began attending May 12 and Hardinsburg, August 4. All of the church stations in Daviess and the surrounding counties and the scattered Catholics across the Ohio in Southern Indiana were also under his care. When his cousin, Rev. Charles Ignatius Coomes, resigned his pastorate at St. Theresa Church, Rhodelia in Meade Co., because of ill health in the spring of 1839, this congregation was added to his extensive territory. The energetic priest erected the second church at St. Lawrence in 1839 and about the same time, began the construction of the first Church of St. Stephen in Owensboro.

While making the rounds of his missions, Fr. Wathen was taken sick and died of congestive fever in the home of Stephen Burch at Rhodelia on Oct. 17, 1841. His remains were taken to Owensboro for burial and later transferred to St. Lawrence Cemetery, where they rest in the shadow of the church. *Rev. John A. Lyons*

1834 Bishop Guy Ignatius Chabrat (1787-1868), consecrated Coadjutor Bishop of Bardstown, July 20.

1835 Bishop Flaget departs for Europe; absent about four years.

1836 St. Jerome Church, Fancy Farm, Graves Co., first Catholic Church in Jackson Purchase built by Rev. Elisha Durbin. *Catholic Advocate*, was the first Catholic paper published in Kentucky, established by Ben J. Webb. First St. Benedict Church, Wax, Grayson Co., built by Rev. Augustine Degauquier (1804-1870). Bishop Flaget's report: 36 priests (23 seculars, five Dominicans, eight Jesuits), 260 religious women, 35,000 Catholics, 33 churches (23 brick), three motherhouses, two colleges, 11 schools or orphanages and four Bishoprics formed.

1838 Rev. John B. Hutchins (1803-1879), and Rev. William E. Powell (1803-1840), ordained July 1; two months later they established a school, Mt. Merinio Seminary, near Irvington, Breckinridge Co. Rev. John C. Wathen (1801-1841), preached in Langley, Ohio Co., on "Sacrament of Penance," May 23.

1839 Bardstown Diocese numbered 40 churches, 70 stations, 51 priests, two seminaries, 20 seminarians and nine academies for young ladies. Rev. John C. Wathen "preached on the obligation of hearing Mass at William Hayden's on August 3...the Sacraments on August 31," probably beginning St. Alphonsus congregation, St. Joseph, Daviess Co. Second St. Lawrence Church, Daviess Co., built by Rev. John C. Wathen. Construction began on first St. Stephen Church, Owensboro, by Rev. Wathen.

1841 Bardstown Diocese transferred to Louisville ("immigrants arriving, city beckoned"). "Bardstown years," 75 priests involved ministry Kentucky Catholics: 29 percent Kentucky born, 28 percent French, 22 percent Irish, six percent German. Bishop David died July 12, age 81. Second St. Romuald Church, Hardinsburg, Breckinridge Co., dedicated by Bishop Flaget in October. Rev. Walter S. Coomes (1796-1871) attended Daviess Co. missions until 1855; first church St. Raphael, Daviess Co., built 1842 or 1844 and destroyed by fire in 1857.

* **REVEREND WALTER S. COOMES**, a brother of Rev. Linus O. Coomes and a son of Ignatius Coomes and Sarah Stuart Lewis, was born in Virginia, Feb. 19, 1796 and at the age of 16 years came with his parents to Bardstown. In the following year, the family settled in Breckinridge Co. in the vicinity of Hardinsburg. He entered St. Thomas Seminary in Nelson Co. in 1820 and received his philosophy and theology at St. Joseph College. His elevation to the priesthood, at the hands of Bishop Flaget, took place in St. Joseph Cathedral, Aug. 15, 1831.

Fr. Coomes was sent to Daviess Co. in the fall of 1841 and took up his residence at St. Lawrence Church. He completed the erection of the first church of St. Stephen, in Owensboro, which was dedicated Aug. 21, 1842 and it was probably in the spring of 1844, that he moved to that city and became the first resident pastor. With the rapid growth of Catholicity in Daviess Co. during the next decade, he was aided by assistants and pastors who were his co-workers in visiting the newly formed congregations and in building the first churches in that locality. St. Mary of the Woods, at Whitesville, had its beginning about 1845; St. Raphael, at West Louisville, came into existence shortly afterwards and St. Alphonsus, at St. Joseph, was built in 1854.

In September 1855, Fr. Coomes, with his energies impaired by exhaustive labors on the missions, resigned his pastorate at Owensboro to become chaplain at St. Vincent Orphans Home (Jefferson Street) Louisville, where he remained until his death, Nov. 27, 1871. His funeral services were held from the Cathedral of the Assumption and he was buried in St. Louis Cemetery, Louisville. *Rev. John A. Lyons*

Rev. Walter S. Coomes (1796-1871).

St. Stephen Church, Owensboro, completed by Rev. Walter S. Coomes (1796-1871), dedicated August 21.	1842
Rev. Alfred Hagan (1814-1846), appointed first resident pastor at St. Jerome, Fancy Farm, Graves Co.	1843
Sketches of the Early Catholic Missions of Kentucky, by Martin J. Spalding published.	1844
St. Mary of the Woods Church, Whitesville, Daviess Co., built and rebuilt in 1862 and 1885.	1845
Pope Gregory XVI (1831-1846) died June 1, age 78.	1846
GEORGE THOMAS MONTGOMERY, first Bishop born in area now called the Owensboro Diocese, born December 30 in St. Lawrence, Knottsville, Daviess Co.; ordained Dec. 20, 1879; consecrated Coadjutor Bishop Monterey-Los Angeles April 8, 1894; succeeded to Monterey-Los Angeles, May 6, 1896; Coadjutor San Francisco Sept. 17, 1902; died Jan. 10, 1907.	1847
Rev. Martin John Spalding (1810-1872), consecrated Coadjutor to Bishop Flaget, August 10. Abbey of Our Lady of La Trappe (Trappists), Gethsemani, Marion Co., erected; 44 Trappists from Melleray, France.	1848
Bishop M.J. Spalding, administrator diocese, January 8. Diocese contained 44 churches, 10 chapels, 75 stations, 46 priests, 11 academies for young ladies and population 30,000. First St. John the Evangelist Church, McCracken Co., built by Rev. Elisha Durbin, for farming community Catholic German-speaking families that began settlement in 1832. First St. Francis de Sales Church, Paducah, McCracken Co., built by Rev. Elisha J. Durbin, (property purchased Feb. 15, 1848). First St. John the Evangelist Church, Sunfish, Edmonson Co., built by Rev. Augustine Degauquier (1804-1870). St. Frances Academy, Owensboro, started in former hotel by five Sisters of Charity of Nazareth; named to honor Mother General Frances Gardiner.	1849

* **REVEREND AUGUSTINE DEGAUQUIER**, was born Sept. 6, 1804 in Mourbay, Province of Hainault, Belgium. He began his studies for the priesthood at the College of Ath in his native diocese and was well advanced in his ecclesiastical course when he came to Kentucky in 1832. His theology was completed at St. Joseph Seminary, Bardstown, where he was ordained, probably by Bishop Chabrat in November 1834.

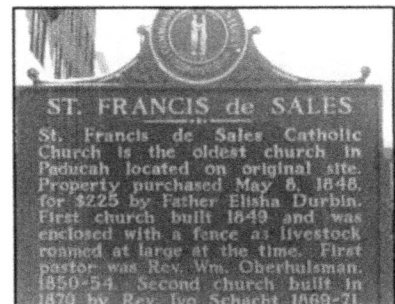

Historical marker, St. Francis DeSales Church, Paducah, KY.

After spending a few months at the Loretto Motherhouse for the purpose of perfecting himself in English pronunciation, Fr. Degauquier went to Louisville to assist the German Catholics during an epidemic in the summer of 1835 and then was given charge of the Grayson Co. missions. From his headquarters at Bethlehem Academy, in Hardin Co., he attended the congregations of St. Paul, near Big Clifty, St. Augustine at Grayson Springs, St. Benedict at Wax and the settlement of Sunfish in Edmonson Co. He built the Church of St. Benedict at Wax in 1836 and the Church of St. John the Evangelist at Sunfish in the winter of 1849. When Rev. Francis Chambige was recalled from Bethlehem to St. Joseph College in Bardstown near the end of 1838, the chaplaincy of the academy and the pastorate of the nearby St. John the Baptist Church were added to his care. He completed the interior of the new Church of St. John the Baptist and at Harcourt, another mission in Hardin Co., he was building St. Ignatius Church late in 1841, when he was transferred to St. Anthony Church, Axtel and from there continued his labors in Grayson and Edmonson Counties which were to last until 1849.

During the Civil War, he administered to the troops stationed along the Louisville and Nashville Railroad in the vicinity of Mumfordsville. A heart attack left him a partial invalid in 1868 and he was forced to retire from missionary work.

In January 1870, he was fatally burned while attempting to light a lamp in his room and died on the 30th day of that month, after about a week of intense suffering. Following the funeral Mass, he was buried in the cemetery of the academy. When the Sisters of Loretto disposed of their property at Bethlehem in 1959, his remains were taken to the motherhouse at Nerinx and re-interred in the convent cemetery. *Rev. John A. Lyons*

Rev. Augustine Degauquier (1804-1870).

1850   Death of Bishop Benedict Joseph Flaget, February 11. Bishop Martin John Spalding succeeded to Louisville Diocese. St. Columba Church, Lewisport, Hancock Co., dedicated April 26.

1851   Bishop M.J. Spalding preached at the courthouse, Hardinsburg, Breckinridge Co., September 25.

1853   Diocese of Louisville divided; Covington Diocese erected July 29. Rev. Stephen Badin died in Cincinnati April 19, age 84, "the last survivor of that group of apostolic priests who laid the groundwork of the Church in Kentucky." Bishop Spalding introduced St. Vincent de Paul Society in Kentucky by establishing conference at Cathedral on November 27.

1854   Holy Guardian Angels Church, Irvington, Breckinridge Co., dedicated February 26 (frame, 50 x 27 ft. with spire). Second St. Augustine Church, Grayson Springs, Grayson Co., dedicated Aug. 28. St. Alphonsus Church, St. Joseph, Daviess Co., built by Rev. Walter S. Coomes (1796-1871). St. Vincent de Paul Society, Louisville, first president Benedict Webb.

1855   St. Stephen Church, Smithland, Livingston Co., established by Rev. Elisha Durbin; torn down circa 1870.

1856   Work begun on the Louisville & Nashville Railroad, many foreign born laborers, majority Catholic. Rev. Joseph deVries (1831-1889), appointed Missionary Rector for Southern Kentucky. Third Sacred Heart Church, St. Vincent, Union Co., built by Rev. Elisha Durbin, dedicated by Bishop Spalding June 1.

1857   Permission granted by Bishop Spalding, June 7, to build church in Hawesville, Hancock Co.; Immaculate Conception Church, Hawesville, built during the Civil War. St. Malachi Church (later St. Rose), Cloverport, Breckinridge Co., built by Rev. Michael Power (1827-1879).

1858   St. Stephen Church, Owensboro, enlargement completed by Rev. Eugene O'Callagan (1821-1897), blessed May 30 by Bishop Spalding; land purchased for cemetery now called Mater Dolorosa. Bishop M.J. Spalding, May 31, 1858, preached in Calhoun, McLean Co. Bishop Spalding blessed St. Alphonsus Church, St. Joseph, Daviess Co., June 1; destroyed by fire, Dec. 3, 1868. Second St. Jerome Church, Fancy Farm, Graves Co., blessed by Bishop Spalding on June 13. Bishop Spalding preached in Clinton, Hickman Co., on June 13, by invitation. Four Sisters of Charity of Nazareth started St. Mary Academy, Paducah, McCracken Co., in August. New St. Vincent Academy, Union Co., in September. *The Catholic Guardian* newspaper established in Louisville by Ben J. Webb, Editor. Ursuline Sisters were established in the Louisville Diocese, October 30. Third Diocesan Synod. Mother Catherine Spalding, first superior Sisters of Charity of Nazareth, died March 20; 145 Sisters in 13 schools, two orphanages, St. Joseph Infirmary, Louisville.

Rev. Eugene O'Callaghan (1821-1897).

* **REVEREND EUGENE O'CALLAGHAN,** was born April 14, 1821 at Carrignavar, County Cork, Ireland. He came to America with his parents in his infancy. He was ordained by Bishop Martin John Spalding in St. Joseph Church, Bardstown on July 28, 1850. Fr. O'Callaghan was first appointed assistant at Sacred Heart Parish in Union Co. and assisted at the missions attached to this church. Around the beginning of February 1852, he became pastor of St. Lawrence Church in Daviess Co. and the missions of Lewisport and Whitesville. Near the end of August 1855, he was transferred to St. Stephen Church, Owensboro, where he completed the enlargement of the church. The edifice was dedicated May 30, 1858. That same year, he purchased land for a Catholic cemetery in Owensboro. About this time, the congregation of St. Sebastian in Calhoun, was organized by him. He also attended St. Alphonsus Church in Daviess Co. for about a year, from 1856-57.

In March 1871, Fr. O'Callaghan was moved from Owensboro to St. Francis Xavier Church, Raywick, but this appointment was only temporary, and in the following month he became pastor of St. Michael Church, Fairfield. The mission of All Saints Church, Taylorsville, was under his care from the summer of that year until the beginning of 1876. At Fairfield, he built the third and present church, which was dedicated Dec. 20, 1883.

Fr. O'Callaghan's pastorate of 20 years at Fairfield, ended in October 1891, when he retired to accept the lighter duties of chaplain at the Motherhouse and Academy of the Sisters of Loretto in Marion Co. His death occurred in the chaplain's residence Feb. 26, 1897. After funeral services in the chapel at the motherhouse, he was laid to rest in the convent cemetery. *Rev. John A. Lyons*

Three Ursuline Sisters, Mother DeSales Reitmier, Sister Pia Schonofer, Sister Maximilian Zwinger, arrived in Louisville from Straubling, Germany on October 31. The Ursulines were founded by St. Angela Mercini in 1535 at Brescia, Italy.

1859   Rev. Joseph De Vries (1831-1889), directed to start parish in Bowling Green, Warren Co., response to Irish Catholics, railroad laborers; St. Joseph small frame church was built.

Rev. Joseph DeVries (1831-1889).

* **REVEREND JOSEPH DE VRIES,** a son of John and Petronella Verhagen DeVries, he was born in Gerwen, Province of North Brabant in the Netherlands on June 30, 1831. His studies were taken at the minor seminary of St. Michael, in Gestel and the major seminary at Haaren. Early in 1853, Bishop Martin John Spalding was at the Haaren Seminary seeking recruits for his Diocese of Louisville and young DeVries, then in subdeacon's orders, offered his services for the Church in Kentucky. He sailed for America with Rev. Lawrence Bax and several other ecclesiastics on the following April 25. Upon their arrival in their new field of labor, he was sent to St. Thomas Seminary in Nelson Co., to complete his theological course. Bishop Spalding conferred on him the priesthood July 16, 1855, at the Cathedral of the Assumption, Louisville.

Fr. DeVries was appointed assistant at St. Catherine Church, New Haven. Also under his care were the missions of Howardstown and Hodgensville. In this latter place, he completed the erection of the church of Our Lady of Mercy in 1856. By the next year, a large number of Catholic laborers were employed in the construction of the Louisville and Nashville Railroad and his missionary territory was extended as far south as Bowling Green, where in April 1859, he was appointed pastor. Upon taking up his residence there, he hurriedly built a small temporary frame building for services and began the erection of a permanent brick church, which was opened for Mass on Easter Sunday, April 8, 1860. When the edifice was finally completed in 1862, it was formally dedicated under the title of St. Joseph. Attached to his pastorate, were mission stations in Warren, Simpson, Logan, Barren and Allen Counties, which he attended for several years. In 1867, he began the construction of St. Mary Church, Franklin.

When the interior of the church of St. Joseph was completed in 1862, the Sisters of Charity of Nazareth came to Bowling Green at the request of Fr. DeVries, to establish St. Columba Academy, which continued in existence until 1912 when the parochial school was opened.

In 1875, Bishop William George McCloskey removed Fr. DeVries from St. Joseph's and sent Rev. Lawrence Bax of St. John the Evangelist Church, Louisville to Bowling Green. Both priests were adverse to making the change and DeVries went to Rome to personally appeal to the Holy See. Two years later, having received a favorable decision, he was reinstated in his parish and Bax returned to St. John's.

With the passing of years, the parish membership increased and the church was rebuilt on a larger scale. The exterior was completed in 1887 and solemnly consecrated May 4, 1889.

But the worry and strain incident to the construction, undermined Fr. DeVries' health and about three months after the ceremonies of the consecration of the new building, he was stricken by apoplexy in his rectory and died suddenly August 10, 1889. His funeral services were held in his church and he was buried beneath the sanctuary. *Rev. John A. Lyons*

1860 Population of Kentucky: 1,115,684; Louisville Diocese: 60,000 Catholics, 76 churches, 100 stations, 74 priests, 20 seminarians and 10 academies. Second St. Benedict Church, Wax, Grayson Co., built by Rev. John B. Vandemergel (1822-1873), attended this church from 1858-1873. Ursuline Academy for girls from poor families was opened.

1861 Rev. Ivo Schacht (1821-1874), first resident pastor of St. Alphonsus Church, Daviess Co.; attended St. Raphael, Daviess Co. until 1864 and probably rebuilt church in 1862. Bishop Spalding "saw for the first time the new church at Uniontown," Union Co. St. Louis Church, Henderson, Henderson Co., used for divine worship "contained 55 pews"; Rev. William J. Dunn (1835-1898), first resident pastor, Nov. 13, 1866. Rev. Michael Power (1827-1879), attended missions in Columbus, Hickman Co. (St. John Evangelist Church built c 1880).

* REVEREND IVO SCHACHT, was born in Bruges, Belgium in 1821. He was well advanced in his studies when he came to Tennessee, heeding the appeal of Bishop Richard P. Miles, who was in Europe in 1840. His theological course was taken in the seminary at Nashville, where he was ordained by Bishop Miles on Dec. 24, 1843.

In September 1861, Fr. Schact affiliated with the Diocese of Louisville and was appointed the first resident pastor of St. Alphonsus parish in Daviess Co. He enlarged the church and erected a school, the forerunner of Mount St. Joseph Academy, which was opened in 1863 by the Sisters of Loretto, who conducted the institution until Dec. 31, 1870, when it was destroyed by fire. His next appointment was as pastor of St. Augustine Church, Lebanon in June 1864. He began the construction of Sts. Peter and Paul Church, Danville, then attended from Lebanon but before its completion, he was given charge of the congregation at Paducah in February 1869. In the following year, he built the second Church of St. Francis de Sales.

The Carmelite Fathers took over all the parishes, with the exception of St. John the Evangelist in McCracken Co., in the Jackson Purchase in January 1871. Fr. Schacht was appointed pastor of St. Stephen Church, Owensboro in the following March. He immediately erected a small church for the German Catholics in his parish. It was dedicated, under the title of St. Joseph, on April 23 of that same year. Grissoms Landing, near Stanley in Daviess Co. and Rome were missions under his care. In the former settlement, he built the first Church of St. Peter of Alcantara in 1872, and in the latter, that of St. Martin in 1873.

Fr. Schacht was stricken on Easter Sunday, April 5, 1874 and lingered for nine days. He passed away in his rectory, on April 14. Following funeral services in his church, he was laid to rest in the Catholic cemetery in Owensboro. He was the first priest to be buried in this graveyard. *Rev. John Lyons*

Rev. Ivo Schacht (1821-1874)

1862 Fourth Diocesan Synod. Rev. Elisha Durbin appointed "Chaplain General" in Western Kentucky by Bishop Spalding.

1863 Second St. Anthony Church, Long Lick (Axtel), Breckinridge Co., built by Rev. John A. Barrett (1838-1893). St. Columba Academy, Bowling Green, Warren Co., established.

* REV. JOHN A. BARRETT, was born near Mallow, County Cork, Ireland, Aug. 15, 1838. He came to Louisville with his parents when he was quite young. His studies for the priesthood were begun at St. Thomas Seminary, Nelson County, about 1853, and upon the completion of his classical course, he entered St. Mary Seminary, Baltimore. On Jan. 1, 1861, he was transferred to Mount St. Mary Seminary, Cincinnati, and he was ordained Aug. 15, 1862, in the Cathedral of the Assumption, Louisville.

Second St. Anthony Church built by Rev. John A. Barrett (1838-1893).

Father Barrett was appointed professor at St. Thomas Seminary and assistant at the adjoining parish church. In November 1863, he was given charge of St. Romuald parish, Hardinsburg, and the mission of St. Anthony, Long Lick (Axtel). He built a new church at Axtel in 1869, when he received the pastorate of St. Jerome Church, Fancy Farm, to which was attached the mission at Hickman. When the Carmelite Fathers took over the territory known as the Jackson Purchase, in Western Kentucky in January 1871, he was transferred to St. Martin of Tours Church, Flaherty. Under his care were St. Patrick Church, Stithton, (now Fort Knox), and Pitts Point, in Bullitt County, where he erected the Church of St. Margaret Cortona, later in 1871.

In March 1872, Fr. Barrett was appointed professor at St. Joseph College, Bardstown, where he remained until 1879, when he was given a leave of absence because of sickness. Upon his recovery, he became chaplain of Saints Mary and Elizabeth Hostpital.

Father Barrett died at the hospital on Nov. 6, 1893. His funeral was held from the Cathedral of Assumption, and he was buried in St. Louis Cemetery, Louisville.

1864   Bishop Martin J. Spalding (1810-1872), transferred to Baltimore Archdiocese, "the Premier See," May 3, 1864.

1865   Rev. Peter Joseph Lavialle (1819-1867), consecrated Bishop Louisville, September 24.

1867   Bishop Peter J. Lavialle (1819-1867), died May 11.

1868   Rt. Rev. William George McCloskey (1823-1909), first rector North American College, Rome, Italy; consecrated Bishop Louisville, Mary 3. Bishop Chabrat (1787-1868), died in France, November 21. St. Mary Church, Franklin, Simpson Co., completed; Rev. James P. Ryan (1842-1919), first resident pastor.

1869   Second St. John the Evangelist Church, Adrian, McCracken Co., built by Rev. Peter Haeseley (1830-1895), pastor. Second St. Paul Church, St. Paul, Grayson Co., built by Rev. John B. Vandemergel, half mile north first church. Six Sisters of Mercy, founded 1831 by Catherine McAuley in Ireland, arrived in Louisville on October 2 from St. Louis. *Catholic Advocate* (1869-1899), first issue June 26, Ben Webb, editor.

Rev. Peter J. Haeseley - (1830-1895).

* REVEREND PETER JOSEPH HAESELEY, an uncle of Rev. Charles A. Haeseley who was ordained in 1878, was born July 1, 1830 at Gipf, near Frick, Switzerland. Having learned the baker's trade, he came to America in May 1856. In the following year, he was employed in his trade at St. Thomas Seminary in Nelson Co., where he expressed his desire to study for the priesthood and was accepted as a student at the seminary. He was transferred to the Provincial Seminary of Mount St. Mary, Cincinnati, in 1856 to complete his theology. His ordination, at the hand of Bishop J.L. Luers of Ft. Wayne, took place in the Cathedral of the Assumption, Louisville, on Dec. 22, 1867.

Fr. Haeseley's first assignment was as pastor of St. John the Evangelist Parish in McCracken Co., where he erected the second St. John's Church in 1869. In his next appointment, in February 1878, he was given charge of St. Joseph Church, Owensboro. Here too, he built a church which was opened for services on March 7, 1880. It replaced the edifice destroyed by fire shortly after his arrival in Owensboro. He resigned his pastorate in September 1886 to take up lighter duties of chaplain at St. Joseph Orphan Home, Louisville. From October 1887 to January 1888, he was chaplain at Sacred Heart Academy on Lexington Road. He then returned to the orphanage, where he remained until late in 1894. In ill health, he resigned from active duty and a few months later, in July 1895, went back to the village of his birth. He died there November 27 of that year. *Rev. John A. Lyons*

1870   Louisville Diocese contained 84 priests, 68 churches, one seminary, 90 seminarians, 15 religious institutes, 15 educational institutes, 25 parochial schools, three orphan asylums and about 100,000 Catholics. St. Joseph Parish, Owensboro, begun by Rev. Paul Joseph Volk (1841-1919), for German speaking Catholics; used building at West 3rd and Cedar for church; first St. Joseph Church built by Rev. Ivo Schacht, 1871, at 9th and Sweeney, dedicated Easter Sunday, April 23. Second St. Alphonsus Church, St. Joseph, Daviess Co., built by Rev. Paul J. Volk. Second St. Francis de Sales Church, Paducah, built by Rev. Ivo Schacht, pastor. St. Mary of the Woods, McQuady, Breckinridge Co., built by Rev. Nicholas Ryan (1837-1918).

1871   All Jackson Purchase, except St. John in McCracken Co., placed in charge of Carmelites; Rev. Peter Thomas Meagher, O.C.C., pastor St. Francis de Sales Church, Paducah (1871-1880); Rev. Meagher (1840-1880), buried at Mt. Carmel Cemetery, Paducah. St. Joseph Church, Leitchfield, Grayson Co., built by Rev. John B. Vandemergel, dedicated August 17. St. Sebastian Church, Calhoun, McLean Co., built by Rev. Paul J. Volk. Preston Park, Louisville, diocesan major seminary (1871-1888), minor seminary (1902-1909).

Rev. Peter Thomas Meagher, O.C.C. (1840-1880) St. Francis DeSales Church, Paducah, KY. (1871-1880).

* REVEREND PETER THOMAS MEAGHER O.C.C., (1840-1880), became pastor of St. Francis de Sales Church, Paducah, in July 1871.

"He was assisted by several Carmelite priests and brothers who conducted a school for boys from 1872 until 1880, in a two-story frame building erected by them on the east side of the church property, fronting on Broadway. In 1874, Fr. Meagher made a visit to Ireland and in the fall of the same year, on returning, conducted what became known as the Irish Pilgrimage to the United States, a notable occurrence. In the party, were four young women, all his relatives, who entered the Nazareth community: Mary Meagher, a cousin who afterwards for 12 years, (1912-1924) served as Mother Rose, was Mother General of the Nazareth community. She died November 2, 1930. Sister Gonzales Meagher, a sister of Mother Rose; Sister Lauretta Meagher, another cousin; and Sister Constance Davis, still another cousin, who was a sister of the late Bishop Davis of Davenport (1917), and of Fr. Richard Davis, at present (1934) chaplain at Nazareth. Fr. Davis was also of this party, as were Fr. Daniel O'Connell, a secular priest who was given a charge at Pittsburgh, PA and Fr. Thomas J. Hayes of Bowling Green, KY, the last named being the only member of the pilgrimage not related to Fr. Meagher. Sister Constance died at Nazareth about four years ago. The others, whose deaths are not recorded here, are still living. Measurably through Fr. Meagher's influence several other relatives embraced the religious life.

About 1876, the health of Fr. Meagher became very poor and he was constantly an invalid until his death at St. Mary's Infirmary at Cairo, IL on August 2, 1880, at the age of 40 years. He is buried in the cemetery which he established, Mt. Carmel at Paducah." *The Catholic Church in Paducah, KY by John T. Donovan, 1934*

Chalice, Paten, Monstrance used by Rev. Elisha Durbin. These sacred vessels are now at St. Mary Church, Shawneetown, IL (across from Sacred Heart Church, Union County, his headquarters until 1873).

1872 Archbishop Martin J. Spalding (1810-1872), died February 7. Third St. Lawrence Church, Daviess Co., first used February 11. SS. Peter and Paul Church, Hopkinsville, Christian Co., erected by Rev. Thomas J. Jenkins (1847-1902). Rev. Engelbert Bachmann (1838-1917), first resident pastor St. Joseph Church, Owensboro.

1873 REV. ELISHA J. DURBIN resigned pastor Sacred Heart, St. Vincent, Union Co., "after 49 years of hard missionary work." Rev. Elisha Durbin given charge of Catholics in Livingston, Crittenden, Caldwell, Trigg and Lyon Counties, with headquarters at Princeton, Caldwell Co. Sacred Heart Church, Russellville, Logan Co., built by Rev. Henry Mertins (1842-1898), pastor Franklin; dedicated April 27 (60 x 30 ft.). First Immaculate Conception Church, Earlington, Hopkins Co., blessed in August; Simon Fegan lay leader of area since 1847.

1874 Five Ursulines to Daviess Co. invitation Rev. Paul Joseph Volk (1841-1919), begin Mount St. Joseph Academy; Mother Pia Schoenhafer, superior; granted state charter 1880. St. Martin of Tours Church, Rome, Daviess Co., built by Rev. Ivo Schacht. Total Abstinence Society formed at St. Mary of the Woods Church in June by Rev. Charles Eggermont, St. Lawrence pastor. Of priests ordained mid-century (1842-1874), serving Louisville Diocese: 38 percent from Ireland, 15 percent from Germany, 11 percent from France, 20 percent from Europe and only nine percent from Kentucky.

* REVEREND PAUL JOSEPH VOLK, a native of Germany, was born May 16, 1841 at Hunfield, near Frankfort, in the Province of Hesse-Nassau. He studied for the priesthood at Fulda, where he was ordained at the Cathedral of the Most Holy Redeemer, March 19, 1865. After laboring in his native diocese for three years, he entered the American College in Louvain, to prepare himself for the missions in the Diocese of Louisville. One year later, in the early summer of 1869, he came to Kentucky.

In January 1870, he became pastor of St. Alphonsus Congregation in Daviess Co., where he built a brick church, which was completed in the following year. In the meantime, the parish school was destroyed by fire, and the Sisters of Loretto, who taught there, returned to their motherhouse. He erected a new building, and upon its completion, in September 1874, Ursuline Sisters from Louisville reopened the school, which today stands as a part of the motherhouse and academy of Mount St. Joseph for in 1912, the Sisters separated from the Louisville Order and became an autonomous community.

Rev. Paul Joseph Volk (1841-1919).

Upon his arrival at St. Alphonsus, Fr. Volk gathered together the German families in Owensboro for services and began what later developed into St. Joseph Parish. At his mission in Calhoun, McLean Co., he erected St. Sebastian Church, which was opened in 1880. At Beech Grove, another mission in the same county, he built a church, St. Benedict's, which was dedicated Oct. 19, 1881. When he was moved to Ottenheim in Lincoln Co., in July 1885, he continued his building operations. His missions extended into the Covington Diocese. St. Boniface Church at Jellico in Whitley Co., was blessed in 1885, St. Francis of Assisi Church, New Austria, was opened on Palm Sunday, April 18, 1886 and St. Sylvester Church, Ottenheim, was dedicated September 12 in the same year. The construction of St. Sylvester Church, East Bernstadt, in Laurel Co., was begun by him in February 1888.

A couple of months later, in the spring of 1888, Fr. Volk sought a new field of labor and sailed for Ecuador in Central America. He built four mission churches for the native Indians in the Provinces of Manabi and Esmeraldes. His next assignment, in September 1891, was to Bocas del Toro in Panama. Bishop William George McCloskey recalled him to Kentucky in June 1893.

Fr. Volk was appointed pastor of Ss. Peter and Paul Church, Danville, with the missions attached. He built St. James Church, Lawrenceburg, which was dedicated July 15, 1894 and also St. Nicholas Church at Rose Hill, Mercer Co., which was blessed December 6 in that year.

A few months later Fr. Volk, having furnished the diocese with a priest, Rev. Joseph Nieborowski, who had been missioned at Ecuador, set out again for Bocas del Toro, arriving there Sept. 29, 1895. He was transferred to the District of Chiriqui, on the Pacific side of the Isthmus of Panama in August 1898, and made his headquarters in a small city called David, where he erected a stone church in 1905. It was dedicated under the patronage of the Holy Family. Then he was sent to Colon. Another stone church, dedicated under the title of the Immaculate Conception, was built by him in 1910.

Fr. Volk returned to Kentucky in May 1915, and in October, became chaplain at Sacred Heart Academy, Louisville, which office he held for several months. But the restless priest needed more activity and although in his 76th year, sought permission to take charge of a poor county parish and was appointed to St. Anthony Church ,Peonia, in Grayson Co. in September 1917. This builder of churches began the erection of St. Joseph Church in the nearby mission of Anneta. However, the infirmities of age forced his retirement from parochial duties in July 1919.

Fr. Volk spent the last few months of his life at Mount St. Joseph, where he died November 2, 1919. After his funeral services, the mortal remains of this faithful missionary were laid at rest in the cemetery of the convent and academy he had established 45 years before. *Rev. John A. Lyons*

1875   Diocese contained 109 priests, 102 churches, 55 seminarians, 27 academies, 53 parochial schools, 400 orphans, 100,000 Catholics, 10 religious institutions and three colleges and seminaries. Rev. Gustave Vantroostenberghe (1847-1919), first resident pastor at St. Raphael, Panther Creek, West Louisville, Daviess Co.; third St. Raphael Church built in 1879, dedicated October; resigned 1890.

1878   Pope Pius IX (1846-1878), died February 7, age 85. St. Ann Church, Morganfield, Union Co., built by Rev. Henry Theophilus Kellenaers (1852-1920), dedicated March; Judge Ignatius A. Spalding Jr. main contributor, church named after mother, Ann Huston Spalding. St. Joseph Church, Owensboro, destroyed by fire, May; rebuilt by Rev. Peter J. Haeseley (1830-1895), with first services March 7, 1880.

Rev. H.J. Theo Kellenaers (1852-1920)

* REVEREND HENRY JACOB THEOPHILUS KELLENAERS, a son of Leonard and Barbara Henckens Kellenaers, was born April 24, 1852 in Meerlo, Diocese of Roermond, in the Netherlands. He was ordained at Villa Frekschueren, near Hasselt, in the Belgium Limburg, by Archbishop Peter M. Francken on Aug. 30, 1874 for the Diocese of Louisville.

Fr. Kellenaers arrived in Kentucky in the following December and was stationed at the Cathedral of the Assumption, Louisville, while attending the Marine Hospital. In February 1875, he was sent as an assistant to St. James Church, Elizabethtown with the care of Our Lady of Mercy Church, Hodgensville. On the following September 1, he was transferred again as an assistant to Sacred Heart Church in Union Co. and attended St. Ambrose Church, Henshaw. In May 1876, he took up his residence at Henshaw, to which was attached the mission of Morganfield, where he built the first Church of St. Ann, which was dedicated in March 1878.

The last assignment of Fr. Kellenaers came in March 1888, when he was appointed pastor of St. Agnes Church, Uniontown and there he built a new church, which was consecrated Oct. 11, 1893. His long pastorate of 32 years at St. Agnes ended with his death from influenza on March 1, 1920. After the Requiem services in his church, he was buried in the parish cemetery. His brother, Charles A.J. Kellenaers, departed this life at Uniontown in 1907. *Rev. John A. Lyons*

1879   *The Record*, established as the official newspaper of the diocese February 15. Sixth Diocesan Synod. St. Thomas Church, Roseville, Hancock Co., built by Rev. Patrick Rock (1850-1924), mission of St. Lawrence, Daviess Co.; area sometimes called Lyonia and/or Pellville; discontinued ca 1911. Bishop McCloskey issued pastoral letter on establishment of parochial schools throughout diocese, November 10.

1880   Louisville Diocese contained 128 priests, 759 religious, 100 churches, 58 stations, 16 monasteries and convents, 16 chapels, four seminaries and colleges, 21 educational institutions, 148 parochial schools, three reformatories, four orphanages, two asylums, three hospitals and about 110,000 Catholics. Rev. Dominic Croghan (1853-1895), named pastor new St. Peter Alcantara Church, Stanley, Daviess Co., July.

1881   Four Carmelite Fathers who served Jackson Purchase missions ten years, withdrawn August 1. Rev. Richard Davis (1854-1941), appointed pastor at St. Bridget (later Sacred Heart), Hickman, Fulton Co., with mission in Columbus, Fulton and Pigeon Mills in Ballard Co. St. Benedict Church, Beech Grove, McLean Co. dedicated October 19.

1883   Mass celebrated for the first time in Sebree, Webster Co., April 19. Third St. Augustine Church, Grayson Springs, Grayson Co., blessed by Rev. E.J. Durbin, December 15; previous church burnt Dec. 9, 1882.

1884   *The Centenary of Catholicity in Kentucky*, by Ben J. Webb (1814-1897), published. *American Catholic Tribune* (1884-1894), *Black Catholic Weekly*, Daniel Rudd (1854-1933), *Black Catholic Layman* reared Bardstown, editor. Second St. Joseph Church, Bowling Green, Warren Co., dedicated April 30. Second St. Mary of the Woods Church, Whitesville, Daviess Co., built by Rev. Kyran King (1853-1899), first resident pastor; dedicated June 8 (40 x 100 ft.).

1885   Rev. Alexander T. McConnell (1842-1919), pastor St. Stephen Church, Owensboro (1885-1919). St. Edward Church, Eddyville, Lyon Co., built by Rev. Richard P. Feehan (1852-1890); members mainly Irish Catholics; blessed by Bishop McCloskey on Nov. 23, 1893; burnt ca 1900.

Mother Mary Paul Carrico, O.S.F. Franciscans, Clinton, IA. Formerly Laura Carrico of Fancy Farm, KY, who joined in 1883 and died in 1954

* REVEREND ALEXANDER THOMAS J. MCCONNELL, born May 5, 1842 in the Diocese of Clogher, Ireland, came to Kentucky in his youth and studied under the Dominicans at St. Rose in Washington Co. His ecclesiastical course was well advanced when he was incardinated into the Louisville Diocese and entered Preston Park Seminary, (site of Bellarmine College), Louisville in September 1871. Bishop William George McCloskey ordained him in the Cathedral of the Assumption on June 15, 1873.

Fr. McConnell was immediately appointed pastor of the Church of Our Lady of the Port, Louisville, where he rebuilt the present church that was opened for services Dec. 14, 1873. His health failed in November 1876, and upon his recovery in September of the following year, he was given charge of St. Francis of Xavier Church, Raywick. At his mission of St. Matthew in the Finley district, he completed the erection of the church. He was recalled to Louisville as pastor of St. Cecilia Parish in November 1883.

The next assignment of Fr. McConnell was to St. Stephen Parish, Owensboro in the summer of 1885. He remodeled and enlarged the church shortly after his arrival. His long pastorate of over 33 years extended to his death. Afflicted with failing eyesight for the last 25 years of his life, he was practically blind when he died at his rectory on Jan. 31, 1919. Following funeral services in his church, he was laid to rest in the Catholic cemetery in Owensboro. *Rev. John A. Lyons*

Rev. A.T. McConnell (1842-1919)

St. Paul Church, Owensboro, established from St. Stephen Church; small church at 4th and Pearl first used for worship March 27, 1887. Holy Name Church in Henderson (replaced St. Louis Church) cornerstone blessed by Bishop McCloskey, October 17; first service held 1891; Rev. Thomas F. Tierney (1853-1901), pastor. St. Martin Church, Central City, Muhlenberg Co., built by Rev. Michael Melody (1846-1926).   1886

* REVEREND MICHAEL FRANCIS MELODY, was born March 25, 1846 at Loughrea, County Galway, Ireland. He was still an infant when his parents brought him to America and settled in the section of Louisville that later became St. John the Evangelist Parish. He was ordained June 21, 1872 by Archbishop Purcell of Cincinnati, in the Cathedral of the Assumption, Louisville.

Fr. Melody had charge of St. Joseph Parish, Bowling Green, during the summer of 1872, while the pastor, Rev. Joseph DeVries, was on a visit to his native land. In the fall of that year, he was appointed pastor of the Church of the Immaculate Conception, Hawesville. He was transferred to St. Joseph Church, Leitchfield, in June 1873 and succeeded the pastor, Rev. J.B. VandeMergel, at the latter's death, July 1. Under his care, were the missions of Central City and Sunfish in Edmonson Co. During his pastorate of 13 years, he completed the interior of St. Joseph Church and in 1886, erected a church at Central City, which was dedicated under the patronage of St. Martin of Tours.

Fr. Melody's next assignment was to Ss. Peter and Paul Church, Hopkinsville in January 1887. His mission territory embraced Central City, Princeton, Golden Pond in Trigg Co. and a small German settlement, near Eddyville. He built a frame church, St. Joseph's, at Golden Pond in 1889, but it was destroyed by a cyclone in the following spring.

Late in 1890, Fr. Melody resigned his pastorate at Hopkinsville to become chaplain of St. Thomas Orphan Home, which was housed at that period in the old St. Joseph College buildings. In November 1892, he was appointed to St. William Church, Knottsville, where he remained for eight months, after which he took up the office of chaplain at St. Vincent Orphan Home, then located at Preston Park. From November 1897 until the following summer, he was at All Saints Church, Taylorsville. The rest of his life was spent in Louisville and with the exception of three months, April, May and June 1890, when he was in temporary charge of St. John the Evangelist Church, he was chaplain at various religious institutions. He observed his sacerdotal golden jubilee at St. Vincent Orphanage, site of Sacred Heart Home, on Payne St. in 1922.

Rev. Michael R. Melody (1846-1926)

Fr. Melody's last appointment, was to St. Helena Commercial College at the north side of St. Joseph Infirmary, 4th St., in November 1924. He died of pneumonia at the infirmary on May 3, 1926. His burial took place from the Cathedral and he was laid at rest in St. Louis Cemetery, Louisville. *Rev. John A. Lyons*

Rev. Elisha John Durbin (1800-1887), Patriarch of the Church in Western Kentucky, died March 22.   1887
Rev. Lawrence Ford (1858-1934), pastor at St. Jerome, Fancy Farm, built first St. Joseph Church, Mayfield, Graves Co., dedicated April 19. New St. Benedict Church, Beech Grove, McLean Co., dedicated May 26. St. Elizabeth Church, Curdsville, Daviess Co., blessed December 11, "the 11th Catholic church in the county."

Second Immaculate Conception Church, Earlington, Hopkins Co., consecrated May 31; Rev.   1888
Alphonsus Coenen (1838-1905), pastor (1872-1905). St. William Church, Knottsville, Daviess Co. built by Rev. James P. Cronin (1862-1922); dedicated Oct. 27, 1889. St. Joseph Church, Sebree, Webster Co., built by Rev. James J. Pike (181851-1920). St. Joseph Church, Laura Furnace, near Golden Pond, Trigg Co., built by Rev. Michael Melody (1846-1926), for German Catholics; destroyed by tornado in 1890; second church built, abandoned c 1914; Rev. Joseph W. Saffer (1906-1971) and Rev. Charles A. Saffer (1914-1989) descended from one of the original German colonists.

Rev. Lawrence B. Ford (1858-1934) built the first St. Joseph Church, Mayfield, KY.

Rev. Alphosus M. Coenen (1838-1905)

* REVEREND ALPHONSUS MARY COENEN, a Belgium by birth and education, was born at Leau, near Brussels on Sept. 2, 1838. His preparatory studies were taken at the College of St. Troud, a short distance from his home and pursued his philosophy at Malines (Mechlin) Seminary. Then deciding to devote his life to the missions in the United States, he entered the American College, Louvain and after three years of theology, he was ordained for the Diocese of Louisville by Cardinal Sterckx at Mechlin on Sept. 21, 1861.

Fr. Coenen arrived in Louisville in June 1862, and was appointed assistant of St. John the Evangelist Church, where he remained until September 1870 when he was transferred as assistant to the Cathedral of the Assumption. His duties also included that of being chaplain of the Sisters of the Good Shepherd on 8th St. He succeeded Rev. John Lancaster Spalding as pastor of St. Augustine Church on Broadway in November 1871.

Early in December of the next year, he was sent to the mission of Earlington and having formally established the parish, he erected a church, which was dedicated under the title of the Immaculate Conception on Aug. 31, 1873. Three months later, he was given charge of St. Louis (later Holy Name) Church, Henderson but resigned his pastorate there in May 1875 to return to Earlington, where he remained until his death 30 years later. His second Church of the Immaculate Conception was consecrated May 31, 1888. He was noted for his great musical ability and published several Masses, which were favorably received. Fr. Coenen departed this life on Feb. 13, 1905. He died in the rectory he built, was buried from the church he had erected and was laid to rest in the cemetery he had established in Earlington. *Rev. John A. Lyons*

1889   St. Rose Church, formerly St. Malachi, Cloverport, Breckinridge Co., dedicated August 27, Rev. Dominic J. Higgins (1852-1951), pastor; destroyed by fire Feb. 28, 1894. Bishop Spalding confirmed: Sacred Heart, Union Co. (69), St. Agnes, Uniontown (23), St. Ann, Morganfield (27), St. Joseph, Mayfield (23), St. Jerome, Fancy Farm (51), St. .Francis de Sales, Paducah (21), St. John, McCracken Co. (23) and Markay's Station, Livingston Co. (8). Second St. Paul Church, Owensboro, dedicated January 13, Rev. Thomas F. Gambon (1837-1901), pastor. Rev. Joseph DeVries (1831-1889), Founder, St. Joseph Church, Bowling Green, Warren Co., pastor (1859-1889), died August 10 (new church consecrated May 4).

1890   Sacred Heart (formerly St. Bridget), Hickman, Fulton Co., dedicated October 5 (brick: 65 x 27 ft); attended by Rev. Thomas A. York (1856-1915), assistant St. Francis de Sales Church, Paducah. New St. Frances Academy, Owensboro, June 17. Sisters of St. Francis (Shelbyville) move to Dubuque, IA.

1891   St. Charles Church, Bardwell, Carlisle Co., built by Rev. Charles A. Haeseley, pastor St. Jerome, Fancy Farm; blessed November 8; dedicated Nov. 29, 1893. Rev. John Riley (1862-1935), first resident pastor at St. Martin of Tours Church, Rome, Daviess Co.; built second church in 1892.

1892   Louisville Diocese: 110,000 Catholics, 130 priests (87 secular, 43 religious orders), 133 churches (28 city of Louisville), 23 academies, three orphanages (261 residents), 10,000 in Catholic schools (70 percent city of Louisville), 1,415 Sisters (600 Charity, 123 Dominican, 13 Littler Sisters Poor, 500 Loretto, 28 Mercy, 151 Ursulines).

1893   Rev. Hugh O'Sullivan (1858-1938), appointed pastor at St. Mary of the Woods Church, Whitesville (1893-1938), Daviess Co.; first Vicar General of Owensboro Diocese. St. John the Baptist Church, Sulphur Springs, Ohio Co., built by Rev. Lawrence Ford (1858-1934), blessed July 23. Second St. Agnes Church, Uniontown, Union Co., dedicated October 11 (130 x 69 ft.); Rev. Henry Kellenaers (1852-1920), pastor (1888-1920). Second St. John the Evangelist Church ,Sunfish, Edmonson Co., built by Rev. Martin O'Connor (1855-1926), dedicated November 19; burnt May 29, 1938. Third St. Jerome Church, Fancy Farm, Graves Co., dedicated November 29; Rev. Charles A. Haeseley (1852-1926), pastor (1888-1920). Rev. Thomas Gambon first Louisville Diocese priest named monsignor.

Rev. Charles A. Haeseley (1855-1926)

* REVEREND CHARLES AUGUSTINE HAESELEY, was born Dec. 14, 1855 at Gits-Oberfrick, Canton of Aargau, Switzerland. He was a nephew of Rev. Peter Joseph Haeseley, who was ordained in 1867.

On coming to Kentucky in November 1868, he entered St. Thomas Seminary, Nelson Co., after which he was sent to St. Joseph College, Bardstown, and in September 1874, was transferred to Preston Park Seminary, site of Bellarmine College, Louisville. He was ordained Sept. 1, 1878 by Bishop William George McCloskey in the convent church of the Sisters of Charity at Nazareth.

He served as pastor of Ss. Peter and Paul Church, Hopkinsville from September 1878 to the summer of 1881. During this time, he erected a log church at his mission at Laura Furnace in Trigg Co. It was probably the last church so constructed in the diocese. He was pastor at St. Mary Church, Franklin and the Russellville Mission from the summer of 1881 to August 1883

He served as pastor of St. John the Evangelist Church in McCracken Co. from August 1883 to September 1888. Also as pastor of St. Jerome Church, Fancy Farm from September 1888 to November 1920. A new church at Fancy Farm was erected by him and dedicated Nov. 29, 1893. Under his supervision, two churches were built on his missions. St. Charles Church near Kirbyton in Carlisle Co. was blessed Nov. 8, 1891 and St. Denis Church near Beulah in Hickman Co. was opened for services Oct. 7, 1914. He was chaplain of St. Joseph Infirmary, 4th St., Louisville from November 1920. It was moved to the new location on the Eastern Parkway in June 1926 and he continued as chaplain until his death four months later.

He died Oct. 19, 1926. His funeral services were held from the Infirmary Chapel and he was buried in the St. Louis Cemetery, Louisville. *Rev. John A. Lyons*

1894 St. Bernard Church, Hampton, Livingston Co., built by Rev. Charles Auer (1867-1942), pastor St. John Church, McCracken Co., dedicated October 16. New St. Rose Church, Cloverport, Breckinridge Co., dedicated October 21, Rev. George Niehaus (1854-1932), pastor.

1895 Salary pastor Louisville Diocese $800, assistant $300 (plus room and board for a priest).

1896 St. Francis Xavier Church, St. Francis, Henderson Co., built by Rev. Henry Kellenaers (1852-1920) as mission to Uniontown, first Mass, May 23. St. Augustine Church, Reed, Henderson Co., dedicated August 21; Rev. James J. Pike (1851-1920), pastor.

1897 Hon. Ben J. Webb (1814-1897), author of *The Centenary of Catholicity in Kentucky* (1884), former editor of the *Catholic Guardian* and *Catholic Advocate*, died February 16. Rev. William Patrick Bourke (1833-1897), died August 8.

1898 Rev. Lucian E. Clements (1872-1942), Knottsville native, first priest ordained in Daviess Co., St. William Church, Knottsville, May 28, by first cousin, Bishop George Montgomery, Bishop of Monterey-Los Angles. St. William Church consecrated by Bishop Montgomery, May 30. Second Holy Guardian Angels Church, Mt. Merino, near Irvington, Breckinridge Co., built by Rev. Celestine Brey (1869-1920).

1900 Third St. Francis de Sales Church, Paducah, McCracken Co., blessed May 13, Rev. Herman Janson (1851-1924), pastor (1882-1909). Third St. Romuald Church, Hardinsburg, Breckinridge Co. dedicated Oct. 17; consecrated Aug. 27, 1903. Of priests ordained late century (1875-1900), serving Louisville Diocese: 25 percent (from Ireland), 29 percent (Kentucky born); 70 percent stayed with the diocese, 25 percent left the diocese but remained priests and three percent left the priesthood.

* REVEREND HERMAN HENRY W. JANSEN, was born in Louisville, Sept. 25, 1851. He was baptized in St. Boniface Church. Bishop William George McCloskey ordained him, May 19, 1875. Fr. Jansen's first appointment was as assistant at the Cathedral of the Assumption. His next assignment, in November 1875, was as assistant at the Church of the Annunciation, Shelbyville, with the care of All Saints Church, Taylorsville. Around the beginning of 1876, he took up his residence at Taylorsville, where he remained until November 1882, when he was transferred as pastor to Paducah. For several years, he had charge of the mission congregations of Maxon Mills in McCracken Co., Golden Pond in Trigg Co. and Eddyville in Lyon Co. The present church of St. Francis de Sales in Paducah, was built by him and dedicated May 13, 1900. He erected St. Thomas Church at Maxon Mills in 1903 and St. Joseph Church, Golden Pond was rebuilt by him about this time. He completed the construction of St. Edward Church near Eddyville, which was blessed Sept. 14, 1905.

In May 1909, after nearly 27 years at Paducah, Fr. Jansen exchanged parishes with Rev. Henry A. Connelly, pastor of St. Brigid Church, Louisville. He built the present Church of St. Brigid. It was solemnly blessed Oct. 5, 1913. The death of Fr. Jansen occurred at his rectory, Aug. 6, 1924, after an illness of two weeks. His funeral was held from St. Brigid's and he was interred in St. Louis Cemetery, Louisville. *Rev. John A. Lyons*

Rev. Herman W. Jansen (1851-1924)

1901 St. Joseph Church, Bowling Green, Warren Co., badly damaged by fire March 29.

1903 Pope Leo IX (1878-1903), died July 5, age 93. Rev. Peter J. McNeil (1876-1946), first resident pastor St. Joseph Church, Mayfield, Graves Co. St. Thomas Church, Maxon Mills (West Paducah), McCracken Co., built by Rev. Henry W. Jansen (1851-1924), pastor St. Francis de Sales Church, Paducah; badly damaged by tornado March 29, 1924, torn down March 15, 1930. St. Anthony Church, Browns Valley, Daviess Co., blessed August 2; Rev. Aloysius Meyering (1871-1940), first pastor (1903-1925). First St. Martin Church building, Rome, moved to Browns Valley in 1902.

1904 Archbishop George Montgomery, Rev. Celestine Brey, Rev. Edwin Drury and Rev. Lucian Clements, November 9 met at St. Lawrence Church, Daviess Co., where they had been baptized, confirmed and received First Communion. St. Paul Church, Princeton, Caldwell Co., renovated within and without, blessed November 13, by Rev. Joseph Welsh (1873-1936), who attended from Hopkinsville.

1905 Third St. Anthony Church, Long Lick (Axtel), Breckinridge Co., built by Rev. John S. Henry (1872-1934); burnt Sept. 15, 1914. Rev. Peter J. McNeil (1876-1946), pastor St. Joseph, Mayfield, in abandoned building in Fulton, Fulton Co., started chapel named Our Lady of Victory, visited every fifth Sunday. St. Leopold Church Eddyville, Lyon Co., blessed September 14; members mainly German Catholics ("Austrian Colony"). New academic building Mount St. Joseph Academy, Maple Mount, Daviess Co., completed April.

Most Rev. George Montgomery D. D. (1847-1907) Coadjutor Archbishop of San Francisco, CA.

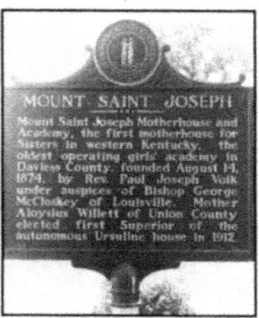

Historical marker, Mt. St. Joseph, Maple Mount, Daviess Co.

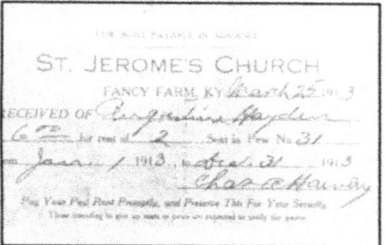

Pew rent receipt.

Rev. Edwin Drury (1845-1913)

1906	Rev. Eugene Spiess, O.S.B., appointed pastor, St. Joseph Church, Owensboro, January 6. St. Elizabeth, Clarkson, Grayson Co., dedicated Christmas, Rev. Anthony Helling (1863-1938), first pastor. Columbian College, Owensboro, with Catholic professors, began September; main building former R. Monarch home; received charter to confer all collegiate degrees 1908; closed c 1912.
1907	Most Rev. George Montgomery, Coadjutor Archbishop of San Francisco, died January 10; born near Knottsville, Daviess Co., Dec. 30, 1847; first bishop born in area now Owensboro Diocese. St. Mary Magdalene, Sorgho, Daviess Co., built by Rev. Joseph Wright (1872-1912), Curdsville pastor. St. Mary Church, La Center, Ballard Co., organized by Rev. Anthony O'Sullivan (1863-1936), of Mayfield; 12 Catholic families; blessed by Bishop McCloskey, November 15.
1908	Centennial year Bardstown/Louisville Diocese. Golden Jubilee Ursulines of Kentucky, November 25. St. Mary Church, Big Clifty, Grayson Co., dedicated August 15; Rev. Anthony Helling (1863-1938), pastor 30 years.
1909	Rt. Rev. William George McCloskey, Bishop of Louisville (1868-1909), died September 17. St. Anthony Church, Peonia, Grayson Co., built by Rev. Anthony Helling (1863-1938), dedicated August 16; Rev. Anselm Kuhn, O.S.B., first resident pastor 1914; church destroyed by fire Oct. 27, 1938. Second St. Mary of the Woods Church, McQuady, Breckinridge Co., built by Rev. John Knue (1878-1945), pastor (1909-1924).
1910	Rt. Rev. Denis O'Donaghue (1848-1925), Rector St. Patrick Church, Indianapolis, named Bishop Louisville, February 7, installed March 29. First St. Peter Church, Waverly, Union Co., blessed October 12; Rev. Peter McNeil (1876-1946), pastor (new parish St. Peter of Antioch began February 1909); church and school destroyed by fire Feb. 8, 1923. Rev. Edward J. Lynch (1854-1920), Holy Name Church, Henderson, pastor (1901-1920), organized Clerical Mutual Aid Association, with 65 provisional members.
1912	Centennial founding Loretto Sisters and Sisters of Charity of Nazareth, celebrated. Decree of Apostolic Delegate making Mount St. Joseph, Maple Mount, Daviess Co., independent Ursuline Motherhouse. St. Joseph Church, Central City, Muhlenberg Co., dedicated Aug. 28 by Bishop O'Donaghue (formerly St. Martin Church). Pew rent main income for many churches. For example, St. Jerome Church, Fancy Farm, KY financial statement 1912: Pew rent $1,551.10; Sunday collections $313.77; Picnic net $496.05; Total receipts $5,093.80; Expenses $4,514.63 plus debt reduction $579.17.
1913	Rev. Edwin Drury (1845-1913), Daviess Co. native, ordained 1872, appointed special missionary to western Kentucky 1899, published *1903 What the Church Teaches,* died February; "leading apologist for Catholicism in diocese."

* REVEREND EDWIN DRURY, a son of Hilary and Teresa Coomes Drury, was born in St. Lawrence Parish in Daviess Co. on June 16, 1845. Archbishop Purcell of Cincinnati, OH, ordained him in the Cathedral of the Assumption, Louisville, on June 21, 1872.

Immediately after ordination, Fr. Drury was appointed pastor of St. Francis Xavier Church, Raywick, where he remained until the late summer of 1874, when he was transferred to St. Francis of Assisi Church, Chicago (now St. Francis), in Marion Co. He attended St. Vincent de Paul Parish, New Hope until July 1883 but continued his pastorate at St. Francis until June 1885, when ill health caused him to resign.

Upon his recovery at the close of 1886, Fr. Drury was given charge of St. Aloysius Church, Rollington (Pewee Valley), and the missions attached. He built a small frame Church of St. John Chrysostom, at Eminence and the Church of the Seven Sorrows at Bedford, which was dedicated July 28, 1889. In the late fall of 1894, his health failed again. Three years later, in November 1897, he was appointed chaplain of St. Thomas Orphan Home, then located at Bardstown.

In August 1899, Fr. Drury became engaged in giving retreats and spiritual missions throughout the diocese, taking up his nominal headquarters at Knottsville. His efforts were especially directed toward the conversion of non-Catholics. Although he was hard of hearing and handicapped by poor health, he was most energetic in his labors and met with unusual success. He compiled a highly praised book, *What the Church Teaches*, in 1903.

Fr. Drury was given the chaplaincy of the Motherhouse and Academy of the Sisters of Loretto in March 1906, an office he was to hold until his death seven years later. In his final sickness, he entered St. Joseph Infirmary, 4th St., Louisville, on Jan. 18, 1913 but failed to respond to medical treatment and died on the following February 2. At his bedside were two of his nephews, Rev. Louis Hilary Spalding, ordained in 1887 and Rev. Celestine Brey, ordained in 1895.

The remains of Fr. Drury were taken to Loretto and following the funeral services in the chapel at the motherhouse, were laid at rest in the Sisters' cemetery. *Rev. John A. Lyons*

1914	Pope Pius X (1903-1914), died August 20, age 79. Benedict XV elected September 3. St. Denis Church, Hickman Co., built by Rev. John Fowler (1886-1957), assistant St. Jerome, Fancy Farm, blessed October 7.

St. Francis Church, Mt. Hebron, Grayson Co., built by Rev. Anthony Helling (1863-1938), dedicated May 6. Holy Ghost Church, Ashbybury, Hopkins Co., dedicated June 15. Todd Family home purchased by St. Joseph Parish, Owensboro, for parish school, became St. Hubertus Academy.

1915

St. Charles Church, Livermore, McLean Co., established June 21; second St. Charles Church dedicated Oct. 20, 1947. Fourth St. Anthony Church, Axtel, Breckinridge Co., dedicated October 15 by Bishop O'Donaghue. St. Joseph Parish, Owensboro, public procession of Blessed Sacrament on Corpus Christi, "first ever in Owensboro."

1917

Rev. Charles Haeseley, Rev. Albert Thompson, St. Charles Church, Carlisle County, 1915.

Rev. Thomas Otho Durbin (1868-1921), born and reared in Sunfish, Edmonson co., great-great-nephew of Rev. Elisha Durbin, ordained June 19 (wife, Melissa Lush, died 1909); two of five children ordained, Rev. Lawrence (1922), and Rev. Paul (1929). Private Elmer Woods of St. Stephen Parish, Owensboro, first Catholic in Daviess Co. killed in WWI, Italy, September 13.

1918

Rev. Alexander Thomas McConnell (1842-1919), died January 31. Rev. Paul Joseph Volk (1841-1919), founder of Ursulines of Mt. St. Joseph, Maple Mount, Daviess Co., died November 2. St. Louis Church, Spring Lick, Grayson Co., dedicated October 1; Rev. Louis Beruatto (1883-1973), pastor; torn down 1938. St. Joseph Church, Anneta, Grayson Co., dedicated November 12. Rev. Samuel Raymond Payne (1888-1919), died April, buried Mt. St. Joseph, Daviess Co.; left written insightful sermons and other notes.

1919

St. Vincent Academy, St. Vincent, Union Co. centennial celebration, June. Rev. James J. Pike (1851-1920, Union Co. native, ordained 1880, author of *History of St. Charles Church, Marion Co. 1907*, died January 14. Other deaths: Rev. Edward J. Lynch (1854-1920, February 25; Rev. Henry Kellenaers (1852-1920), March 1; Rev. Celestine Brey (1869-1920), October 6. Mother Aloysius Willett (1862-1920), elected first superior autonomous Ursuline Sisters, Mount St. Joseph, Maple Mount, Union Co. 1912, died October 1. Rev. Mark Parrette (1893-1968), first pastor St. Denis Parish, Hickman Co. and St. Charles Parish, Carlisle Co., formerly missions of St. Jerome, Fancy Farm, Graves Co. Each state designated when all teachers to be certified; Kentucky postponed certification until 1926, allowing Sisters time to meet state requirements.

1920

Mother Aloysius Willett, co-founder with Rev. Paul J. Volk, of the Ursuline Sisters at Mount St. Joseph, Maple Mount, Daviess County.

* REVEREND JAMES JOSEPH PIKE, was born Aug. 4, 1851 near Waverly, then a Sacred Heart Parish in Union Co. He was a son of Stephen and Beatrix Britannia Vize Pike. He was ordained June 20, 1880 by Bishop William George McCloskey.

He was appointed Professor at St. Joseph College, Bardstown from July 1880 to June 1881. He was also appointed assistant at St. Alphonsus Church, Daviess Co with the care of the McLean Co. missions of St. Benedict, Beech Grove and St. Sebastian, Calhoun from June 1881 to early in 1882. He took up his residence at Beech Grove early in 1882 and from there attended Calhoun and St. Martin of Tours, Rome, in Daviess Co. He began the construction of a larger brick church at Beech Grove in 1884. It was completed in November 1885, but not formally dedicated until the visitation of the Bishop on May 26, 1887. At Sebree, in Webster Co., where Mass was said for the first time in 1883 he began the erection of St. Joseph Church in 1885. The interior of the building was completed by Rev. A.M. Coenen of Earlington, in 1888. Fr. Pike remained at Beech Grove until August 1889.

He was appointed pastor of St. Peter of Alcantara Church, Grissom Landing near Stanley, from November 1893 to July 1899. He built St. Augustine Church, Reed, in Henderson Co., which was dedicated Aug. 21, 1896. Also served as pastor of St. Charles Church, Marion Co., from July 1899 until his death. He erected the present Church of St. Charles, which was dedicated Aug. 15, 1905.

He died Jan. 14, 1920 at his rectory, following a brief illness. His funeral Mass was held from his church and he was buried in the cemetery of the Mount St. Joseph Ursulines, Maple Mount. *Rev. John A. Lyons*

Note: Fr. Pike was the author of a History of St. Charles Church, Marion County, KY, *published in 1907.*

Rev. James J. Pike (1851-1920).

Rev. Francis R. Cotton (1895-1960), appointed assistant pastor at St. Francis de Sales Church, Paducah, in July, until February 1926 [named first Bishop of Owensboro, Dec. 16, 1937]. Rev. Louis Herberth (1866-1922), died December 11; St. Martin of Tours Church, Rome Daviess Co., pastor (1896-1922).

1922

* REVEREND LOUIS HERBERTH, was born Aug. 23, 1866 near Wurtzburg, Bavaria, Germany. He was a son of John and Catherine Rauch Herberth. He was ordained June 29, 1892 at Louvain, for the Diocese of Louisville, by Bishop Augustine Van de Vyver, Bishop of Richmond, who was visiting at the American College at the time.

He was appointed assistant at the Church of the Immaculate Conception, Louisville, from October 1892 to June 1893, when he was taken sick. He served as assistant, pro-tem, at Holy Name Church, Henderson, for a few weeks in the late fall of 1893. He was pastor of St. Mary Magdalen Church, Payneville and the Brandenburg Mission, from November 1893 to late in 1895, possibly December.

Rev. Louis Herberth (1866-1922)

He was appointed assistant at St. Stephen Church, Owensboro, from late in 1895 to July 1896. He served as pastor of St. Martin of Tours Church, Rome, in Daviess Co. from July 1896 until his death, 26 years later. The missions of Calhoun and Ashbyburg were attended by him. He built the Church of the Holy Ghost at Ashbyburg, which was opened for services June 15, 1915. It was destroyed in the 1937 flood.

He died Dec. 11, 1922 at his rectory in Rome. Funeral services were held from his church and he was buried in the cemetery of Mount St. Joseph Motherhouse and Academy, at Maple Mount. *Rev. John A. Lyons*

1923 Rev. William P. Hogarty (1850-1924), celebrated golden jubilee, January 19. Msgr. John A. Floersch (1886-1968), Nashville, appointed coadjutor to Bishop Denis O'Donaghue, April 8.

1924 Bishop O'Donaghue resigned and Bishop Floersch succeeded him, July 28. St. Mary of the Woods Church, McQuady, Breckinridge Co., placed in charge of Precious Blood Fathers, starting with Rev. Leo Landoll, C.PP.S. Second St. Peter Church, Waverly, Union Co., dedicated July 24; Rev. Peter McNeil (1876-1946), first pastor (1909-1924). Rev. Felix N. Pitt (1894-1971), introduced first rural vacation schools in Kentucky.

1925 Bishop Dennis O'Donaghue (1910-1924), died Nov. 7, age 77. Opening of Mount St. Joseph Junior College, Maple Mount, Daviess Co.; relocated to Owensboro in 1950, now Brescia College.

1926 New St. Stephen Church, Owensboro, dedicated September 6. Rev. Charles A. Haeseley (1855-1926), pastor of St. Jerome, Fancy Farm (1888-1920), died October 19.

1927 REV. JOHN A. LYONS (1898-1984), pastor Sacred Heart Church, Russellville, Logan Co., February; transferred August 1932. *(Special Note: Rev. Lyons, Louisville archdiocesan historian and archivist many years; his extensive files and records main source in preparing this chronology.)* Rev. Henry A. Connolly (1846-1936), celebrated golden jubilee, January 9, at St. Francis de Sales, Paducah, pastor (1909-1927). Rev. Edward S. Fitzgerald (1860-1927), pastor St. Paul Parish, Owensboro (1892-1927), died November 22. (Note: April 1948, St. Joseph and St. Paul Parishes merged into SS. Joseph and Paul Parish.) Second SS. Peter and Paul Church, Hopkinsville, Christian Co., built by Rev. James Willett (1894-1965), blessed November 27. Holy Name Church, Henderson, Henderson Co., placed in charge of Order of Holy Cross, Notre Dame, IN; Rev. P.J. Dalton, C.S.C., pastor (1927-1934).

Rev. John A. Lyons (1898-1984)

* **REVEREND EDWARD SHIELDS FITZGERALD,** was born March 24, 1860 in Chelsea, MA. He was a son of Nicholas and Ann Marie Fitzgerald. The family moved to Brookline in suburban Boston when he was four years old. He was ordained on June 14, 1885 by Bishop William George McCloskey.

He was appointed pastor of St. Eugene Church, Bardstown Junction, from Jan. 1, 1886 to early in 1888. He served as secretary to Bishop McCloskey with residence at the Bishop's house located on the southeast corner of Brook and College Streets, from early in 1888 until October 1892. The Catholics in the neighborhood, attended Mass in the Bishop's Chapel, which soon proved to be too small to accommodate their number. Under the direction of the bishop, he erected a church on the adjoining property and became its first pastor. The edifice was dedicated under the title of St. Mary Magdalen. He also was appointed pastor of St. Paul Church, Owensboro, from October 1892 until his death, 35 years later.

He died Nov. 22, 1927 in his rectory, after an illness of several days. Funeral services were held from his church and he was buried in the convent cemetery of the Ursuline Sisters at Maple Mount, over which community he had been spiritual director for 21 years. *Rev. John A. Lyons*

Rev. Edward S. Fitzgerald (1860-1927)

1928 Rev. John M. Higgins (1889-1985), appointed pastor (1928-1953), Sacred Heart Church, St. Vincent, Union Co.

1929 *The Record*, diocesan newspaper for 50 years, February 21. Second St. Peter Alcantara Church, Stanley, Daviess Co., dedicated June 18; Rev. Edward J. Menke (1887-1941), pastor. New chapel and convent at Mt. St. Joseph, Ursuline Motherhouse, Daviess Co., blessed December 18. Bishop Floersh's report: 124,818 Catholics, three deaneries, 153 secular priests and 156 seminarians, (58 major, 98 minor).

1930 Gregory Roberts, member St. Francis de Sales Parish, Paducah, died November 13, age 74; youngest of large family born to slave parents, bequeathed to Rev. Elisha Durbin, freed and placed on tract of land near Fancy Farm, Graves Co.; family moved to Paducah, 1862, members of St. Francis de Sales Parish. Rev. John Fallon (1887-1949), pastor, for first time since he came to Paducah in 1927, gave a brief funeral sermon, "feeling Gregory deserved it."

1931 Roland Pierre DuMaine born August 2, in Paducah, McCracken Co.; ordained in San Francisco, June 15, 1957; consecrated Auxiliary Bishop, San Francisco on June 29, 1978 (second bishop born in area now Owensboro Diocese); first Bishop San Jose, CA, Jan. 27, 1981. Rev. Thomas J. Hayes (1858-1946), pastor St. Joseph, Bowling Green, Warren Co. (1889-1943), celebrated golden jubilee, June 29; Rev. Hayes died March 19, 1946. The original St. Stephen Church, Owensboro, 2nd and Cedar, razed August.

* ROLAND PIERRE DuMAINE, the son of Mary Eulalia Burch and Nolan Amadee DuMaine, was born Aug. 2, 1931 in Paducah, KY. Bishop Pierre Dumaine was named as the first bishop of the Catholic Church for the newly organized Diocese of San Jose, CA on Jan. 27, 1981.

Bishop DuMaine attended the Catholic elementary schools in Paducah, KY until he was about 11 years of age. His family then moved to California, where he attended Catholic schools in Glendale, CA and San Francisco. He received his high school, college and theological studies at seminaries of the Archdioceses of San Francisco: St. Joseph College in Mountain View and St. Patrick's Seminary in Menlo Park. He completed his graduate studies at The Catholic University of America in Washington, DC, receiving his Ph.D. in 1962. In 1978, he attended the Theological Consultation for American Bishops at the North American College, Rome, Italy.

Roland Pierre DuMaine, usually called Pierre, was ordained a Catholic Priest at St. Mary's Cathedral in San Francisco, CA on June 15, 1957. He was named Prelate of Honor (monsignor) on July 28, 1972. On June 29, 1978. he was appointed by Pope Paul VI as Auxiliary Bishop of San Francisco and ordained Bishop at St. Mary's Cathedral on June 29, 1978. Pope Paul II named him to his present position as the first Bishop of the new diocese of San Jose, CA.

Prior assignments of Bishop DuMaine were as follows: assistant pastor at Immaculate Heart Church in Belmont, CA from 1957 to 1958; on the faculty in the Department of Education at the Catholic University of America in Washington, DC from 1961 to 1963; on the faculty of Serra High School in San Mateo, CA from 1963 to 1965; assistant superintendent of Catholic schools for the Archdiocese of San Francisco from 1965 to 1974; superintendent from 1974 to 1978; director of the Archdiocesan Educational Television Center in Menlo Park, CA from 1968 until he became bishop of San Jose.

Most Rev. Roland Pierre DuMaine, Bishop of San Jose, CA. Born 1931 in Paducah, KY, son of Nolan A. DuMaine & Mary Eula Burch, grandson of B. Berkley & Elizabeth Catherine (Willett) Burch.

1933 St. Edward Church, Fulton, Fulton Co., dedicated April 2. Third St. John the Evangelist Church, McCracken Co. built by Rev. Paul C. Barrett (1890-1949), pastor; dedicated June 25 (63 x 105 ft.). Third Holy Guardian Angels Church, Irvington, Breckinridge Co., dedicated October 25.

1934 St. Joseph Church, Mayfield, Graves Co., damaged by fire August 19; replaced by new church in 1938. Second St. Anthony Church, Browns Valley, Daviess Co., dedicated June 1; first church destroyed by fire Oct. 23, 1931.

1935 150th anniversary of Pottinger's Creek Settlement, first Catholics from Maryland at Holy Cross Church, Marion Co., on August 18. St. Mary of the Woods, McQuady, Breckinridge Co., 25th anniversary, November 6. Rev. Albert J. Thompson (1889-1970), appointed pastor at St. Stephen, Owensboro; pastor St. Francis de Sales Parish, Paducah, McCracken Co. (1938-1960). Rev. James L. Whelan (1862-1935), Union Co. native, died May 7 at Maple Mount, Daviess Co.

* REVEREND JAMES LOUIS WHELAN, was born Jan. 26, 1862 near Waverly in Union Co. He was a son of Charles Joseph and Anna Adele Greenwell Whelan. He studied at St. Joseph College, Bardstown and St. Mary Seminary, Baltimore, MD. He was ordained Sept. 24, 1894 by Bishop William George McCloskey.

He was appointed pastor of Our Lady of Perpetual Help Church, Campbellsville and the missions of St. Bernard Church, Clementsville, St. Francis Church, Spurlington and St. Matthew Church, Marion Co. in the Finley district, from October 1894 to August 1896. He was also pastor of St. Patrick Church, Stithton, (now Ft. Knox), from September 1896 to July 1907. He also attended the Brandenburg Mission to 1899. He built a new church at Stithton. It was located in the center of the town, about a mile from the first church. The cornerstone was laid Aug. 4, 1899 and the edifice was opened for services late in 1900. It is still used as a chapel at Ft. Knox, KY. He was chaplain of the Ursuline Mount St. Joseph Motherhouse and Academy, Maple Mount, adjoining St. Alphonsus Church from July 1920 to December 1925. He was pastor of St. Peter of Alcantara Church, Stanley, from December 1925 to January 1927. He returned as chaplain at Maple Mount in January 1927 and remained until his death.

He died May 7, 1935. Following his funeral services in the convent chapel, he was buried in the Ursuline Cemetery at Maple Mount. *Rev. John A. Lyons*

Rev. James Louis Whelan (1862-1935)

1936 Special issue of *The Record*, February 27, celebrating 150 years catholicity in Kentucky; included many historical articles. New St. Paul Church, Princeton, Caldwell Co., dedicated February 23. Holy Ghost Church, Ashbyburg, Hopkins Co., destroyed by flood, discontinued. Three sons of St. Mary of the Woods Church, Whitesville, Daviess Co., offer first Mass: Rev. Joseph E. Payne, July 5; Rev. Anthony Wood, May 23, 1937; Rev. Leonard Boarman, C.S.C., June 27, 1937.

1937 The Diocese of Owensboro, comprising of 32 counties in Western Kentucky was created Dec. 9, 1937 by Pope Pius XI. Most Rev. Francis R. Cotton (1895-1960), named first Bishop on December 16; consecrated Feb. 24, 1938; installed March 8, 1938.

Bibliography

Philip Gleason, editor. *Documentary Reports on Early American Catholicism.* Arno Press, New York, 1978.
Bishop M.J. Spalding. *Sketches of the Early Catholic Missions of Kentucky.* 1844.
Ben J. Webb. *The Centenary of Catholicity in Kentucky.* Charles A. Rogers, 1884.
Mary M. Olson. *A Complete Index to Webb's Centenary of Catholicity in Kentucky.* McDowell Publication, Utica, KY, 1983.
Sister Mary Ramona Mattingly, SCN. *The Catholic Church on the Kentucky Frontier (1785-1812).* Catholic University Press, Washington, DC, 1936.
John A. Lyons. *Bishops and Priests of the Diocese of Bardstown.* 1976.
Clyde F. Crews. *An American Holy Land: A History of the Archdiocese of Louisville.* Michael Glazier, Inc., Wilmington, DE, 1987.
Special Note: Rev. John A. Lyons' (1898-1984) extensive files and records, known as the Lyons Collection, at Bellarmine College, Louisville, was the main source researched in preparing this chronology.

Deceased Priests of the Diocese of Owensboro

Name	Death	Birth	Ordination
Armbruster, Rev. Boniface	04-09-90	03-27-1922	05-18-1948
Barrett, Msgr. Paul	08-12-49	11-10-1890	06-10-1922
Beruatto, Msgr. Louis	07-18-73	11-12-1883	05-13-1906
Borntraeger, Rev. William	12-06-86	08-17-1907	06-10-1933
Bowling, Rev. Charles P.	02-11-80	10-08-1896	06-02-1928
Braun, Msgr. Peter J.	11-13-86	05-30-1901	05-09-1929
Bartolomucci, Rev. John, TOR	10-09-87		
Boarman, Rev. Victor	06-22-93	05-16-1910	06-03-1939
Bomensatt, Rev. Joseph	09-09-94	11-23-1918	12-13-1975
Carrico, Rev. C.R.	02-10-57	08-04-1904	05-30-1931
Clements, Rev. Lucian E.	11-02-42	09-28-1872	05-28-1898
Connor, Rev. Robert	10-31-63	04-20-1912	05-18-1940
Cotton, Most Rev. Francis R.	09-25-60	09-19-1885	06-17-1920
DeChristopher, Rev. Carmen	06-07-87	09-09-1910	06-14-1944
Dienes, Rev. Leo J.	07-24-90	12-19-1919	06-06-1936
Diller, Rev. Otto J., CPPS	11-16-81		
Durbin, Rev. Lawrence	03-05-77	11-26-1897	06-06-1922
Edelen, Rev. Pius	12-30-80	05-05-1907	05-23-1937
Elliott, Rev. Hildebrand	05-17-83	12-09-1899	05-26-1931
Gipperich, Msgr. Robert J.	05-14-79	11-24-1895	05-21-1921
Glahn, Rev. Gerard Jerome	01-18-90	01-14-1933	05-01-1959
Glenn, Rev. John W.	10-20-60	05-25-1901	05-29-1926
Goeff, Rev. Daniel	03-05-94	03-22-1958	05-11-1985
Greenwell, Rev. Paul	11-24-64	10-10-1896	06-02-1928
Haas, Rev. Paul	06-07-79		
Hallahan, Rev. John C.	07-25-79	10-03-1900	05-30-1931
Hayden, Rev. Jolly P.	01-05-41	07-07-1890	06-15-1919
Hayes, Msgr. Thomas Jr.	03-19-46	07-01-1858	06-26-1881
Helling, Rev. Anthony	11-13-38	09-07-1863	06-29-1896
Henninger, Msgr. Gilbert	03-05-90	12-18-1907	05-23-1937
Higdon, Msgr. Anthony	08-19-92	08-19-1911	06-19-1938
Higdon, Rev. James	06-29-54	06-11-1884	06-17-1921
Higgins, Msgr. John M.	01-23-85	10-17-1889	06-09-1918
Hill, Msgr. Raymond G.	05-28-81	02-21-1907	05-28-1932
Huff, Rev. Benedict	08-16-69	05-06-1900	05-26-1931
Hunter, Rev. Donald	04-07-80	07-07-1934	12-20-1959
Jarboe, Msgr. William B.	09-13-84	03-13-1901	06-02-1928
Lauzon, Rev. Peter E.	08-11-95	07-08-1953	01-06-1979
Libs, Rev. Thomas	08-15-57	11-25-1912	06-03-1939
McAleer, Rev. Joseph	06-11-62	02-21-1887	06-10-1911
McAtee, Rev. William M.	08-22-76	07-03-1916	05-30-1942
Mills, Rev. J.W.	07-10-55	10-18-1885	05-25-1929
Murphy, Rev. Thomas A.	01-13-78	08-14-1911	05-04-1943
Nahstoll, Rev. Martin	06-20-78	12-22-1901	06-28-1928
Norman, Rev. James F.	11-07-38	08-02-1875	05-07-1907
O'Sullivan, Msgr. Hugh	07-26-38	11-04-1858	12-12-1892
Pettit, Rev. Clarence	05-10-91	08-09-1913	05-18-1940
Powers, Rev. Ben	09-15-78	01-14-1936	05-10-1975
Russell, Msgr. Edward	03-14-78	09-04-1895	06-06-1922
Saffer, Rev. Charles Allard	09-08-89	05-08-1914	06-07-1914
Saffer, Rev. Joseph W.	01-24-71	05-01-1906	12-08-1931
Smith, Rev. Francis J.	06-27-39	03-15-1895	06-10-1911
Soenneker, Most Rev. Henry J.	09-24-87	05-27-1907	05-26-1934
Spalding, Msgr. Joseph L.	02-08-65	09-17-1901	06-14-1930
Thomas, Rev. Delphin	06-10-85	07-09-1909	06-10-1933
Tompkins, Rev. A.J.	05-11-62	03-06-1896	12-23-1922
Thompson, Msgr. Albert J.	01-05-70	08-03-1889	05-27-1915
Tucker, Rev. Howard L.	05-20-95	03-19-1903	05-20-1971
Ward, Rev. Frank M.	08-09-84	09-11-1911	05-18-1940
Whelan, Rev. Robert A.	01-07-84	07-20-1911	05-23-1937
White, Rev. Carroll L.	12-28-69	02-03-1941	05-04-1967
Willett, Rev. E.E.	12-09-92	04-14-1919	02-24-1945
Wilson, Rev. Robert T.	03-14-82	12-16-1910	06-?-1936
Yunker, Rev. Louis A.	01-09-81		
Zoeller, Msgr. Andrew	03-11-48	04-01-1871	12-27-1894

Biographical Sketches of Some Diocesan Priests Ordained Before 1938

Who Ministered in the Area that Became the Diocese of Owensboro

Name	Birth	Death	Ordination
*Abell, Robert A.	1792	1873	05-10-18
Aud, Athanasius A.	1803	1886	09-04-36
Barrett, Paul C.	1890	1949	06-10-22
*Barrett, John A.	1838	1893	08-15-62
Beruatto, Louis B.	1883	1973	05-13-06
Bourke, William P.	1833	1897	01-06-60
Bowling, Charles P.	1896	1980	06-02-28
Brey, Celestine	1869	1920	07-21-95
*Cissell, Charles J.	1804	1832	12-23-26
Clements, Lucian E.	1872	1942	05-28-98
*Coenen, Alphonsus M.	1838	1905	09-21-61
Connolly, Henry A.	1846	1936	08-26-77
*Coomes, Walter S.	1796	1871	08-15-31
*Degauquier, Augustine	1804	1870	11-00-34
*DeVries, Joseph	1831	1889	07-16-55
*Drury, Edwin	1845	1913	06-21-72
Dunn, William J.	1835	1898	06-10-61
*Fitzgerald, Edward S.	1860	1927	06-14-85
*Haeseley, Charles A.	1855	1926	09-01-78
*Haeseley, Peter J.	1830	1895	12-22-67
Hayes, Thomas J.	1858	1946	06-26-81
Helling, Anthony	1863	1938	06-29-96
Henninger, J. Gilbert	1907	1990	05-23-37
*Herberth, Louis	1866	1922	06-29-92
Higdon, James H.	1884	1954	05-17-21
Higgins, Dominic J.	1852	1951	06-17-83
Higgins, John M.	1889	1985	06-19-18
Hill, Raymond G.	1907	1981	05-21-32
Huff, Benedict F.	1900	1969	05-26-31
*Jansen, Herman H. W.	1851	1924	05-19-75
*Kellenaers, H. J. Theo	1852	1920	08-30-74
Maloney, M. Richard	1882	1965	05-07-07
McAleer, Joseph	1884	1962	06-10-11
*McConnell, Alexander T.	1842	1919	06-15-73
McNeil, Peter J.	1876	1946	01-01-02
*Meagher, O.C.C., Peter T.	1840	1880	
*Melody, Michael F.	1846	1926	06-21-72
Mensa, Guido L.	1889	1936	05-15-13
Meyering, Aloysius G.	1871	1940	06-11-98
Niehaus, George A.	1854	1932	12-18-85
Norman, James F.	1875	1938	05-07-07
*O'Callaghan, Eugene	1821	1897	07-28-50
O'Sullivan, Anthony	1863	1936	05-10-88
O'Sullivan, Hugh	1858	1938	12-18-92
Payne, Samuel R.	1888	1919	08-01-14
*Pike, James J.	1851	1920	06-20-80
Rahm, Charles E.	1885	1942	06-10-11
Russell, Edward	1895	1978	06-06-22
*Schacht, Ivo	1821	1874	06-24-43
Spalding, Louis H.	1861	1920	09-04-87
Thompson, Albert J.	1889	1970	05-27-15
Tierney, Thomas F.	1853	1901	05-14-76
Vantroostenberghe, G. A.	1847	1919	05-19-75
*Volk, Paul J.	1841	1919	03-19-65
*Wathen, John C.	1801	1841	09-12-30
*Whelan, James L.	1862	1935	09-24-94

* appears in the *Chronology of Events (1785-1937)*

REV. ATHANASIUS A. AUD, (1803-1886) was born near Fairfield, KY on February 21, 1803. He was a son of Zachariah Aud and Margaret Coomes.

He entered St. Thomas Seminary in Nelson Co. and later continued his studies at St. Joseph College, Bardstown, but his course was interrupted by sickness in 1823. Then feeling uncertain of his vocation, he left the seminary. We find him in New Orleans in 1825 and he was a student of medicine at Bardstown in 1830-31.

In the following year, he was engaged in teaching at St. Joseph College and a few months later resumed his ecclesiastical studies. On February 27, 1836, Bishop Chabrat conferred on him the subdiaconate in St. Thomas Church in Nelson Co. and a few months later, on September 4, he was elevated to the priesthood by Bishop David.

Immediately following his ordination, Fr. Aud was appointed pastor of St. Thomas Church. Among his missions was the little church at New Haven, In August 1842, he was transferred to St. Joseph College, where he held the office of instructor and disciplinarian until late 1844, when he was given charge of St. Lawrence Church in Daviess Co. He shared the labors of attending the various missions in that county with Rev. Walter S. Coomes, the first resident pastor of Owensboro.

In the summer of 1847, Fr. Aud became pastor of Holy Cross Church in Marion Co. and the church of St. Vincent de Paul, New Hope. Another siege of sickness caused him to resign in April 1850, and he was appointed chaplain of the academy at Calvary and assistant to Rev. D.A. Deparcq in the care of the parish church of Holy Mary. He also had charge of the Lebanon Mission for the next two years. He succeeded Fr. Deparcq as pastor of Holy Mary Church in the summer of 1856. Finally, in September 1874, he relinquished his pastoral duties but continued as chaplain of the academy until his death on March 10, 1886.

His mortal remains were taken to the motherhouse of the Sisters of Loretto and interred in the convent cemetery. The venerable priest had passed his 83rd birthday and had he lived to the next September, he would have observed the 50th anniversary of his ordination. *Rev. John A. Lyons.*

MSGR. PAUL C. BARRETT, (1890-1949) was born November 10, 1890 at Whitesville, Daviess Co., KY. He was a son of Mr. and Mrs. S.D. Barrett. He was ordained June 10, 1922 by Archbishop John Glennon in St. Louis, MO.

He was assistant at the Cathedral of the Assumption, Lousville, from July 1922 to May 1925. He was also administrator of St. Martin Church, Rome, Daviess Co., from May 1925 to October of that year. Also pastor of St. John the Evangelist Church in McCracken Co. from October 1925 to June 1938. He erected a new church of St. John, which was dedicated June 25, 1933.

He was pastor of St. Ann Church, Morganfield, from June 1938 until July 1947. On August 13, 1938, he was appointed to the first body of Diocesan Counsultors in the Owensboro Diocese. Pastor of St. Alphonus Church, Daviess Co., from July 1947 until his death. In July 1949, he was named Domestic Prelate, with the title of Right Reverend.

He died on August 12, 1949 at Our Lady of Mercy Hospital in Owensboro, KY. Following funeral services at St. Alphonsus Church, he was buried in the cemetery of St. Mary of the Woods, Whitesville. *Rev. John A. Lyons*

MGSR. LOUIS BENEDICT BERUATTO, (1833-1973) was born November 11, 1883 in Rivara Canavese, near Turin, Italy. He was ordained May 13, 1906 by Bishop Castranzo Castrale in Turin. He arrived in New York City on December 1, 1906, and then proceeded to Lousville.

He was pastor of St. Joseph Church, Leitchfield, in Grayson Co., from Oct. 9, 1907, with missions of Sunfish in Edmonson Co. and Spring Lick on the Illinois Central Railroad. At this latter mission, he purchased property on the Ellie McGill farm and erected the Church of St. Louis, which was dedicated October 1, 1919. By 1938, most of the families at Spring Lick had moved away and the church was torn down, the lumber being used to build a school at Sunfish.

The Church of St. John the Evangelist, Sunfish, burned to the ground May 29, 1938. He rebuilt the church which was dedicated November 9 of that year. His care of this mission ended in the summer of 1942.

In February 1943, he was elevated to the dignity of Domestic Prelate with the title of Right Reverend, and he was invested with the robes of this office at Leitchfield on the following May 26. He observed his golden sacerdotal jubilee in 1956, and in the following year, after a pastorate of 50 years at Leitchfield, he retired to his native land. He died July 18, 1973 at Turin, in his 90th year of age. *Rev. John A. Lyons*

REV. WILLIAM PATRICK BOURKE, (1833-1897) was born in County Tipperary, Ireland in 1833. He made his ecclesiastical studies at Mt. St. Mary College, Emmitsburg, MD and St. Thomas Seminary in Nelson Co. He was ordained by Bishop Martin John Spalding at the Cathedral of Assumption, Louisville on January 6, 1860.

Fr. Bourke's first assignment was as assistant at Sacred Heart Church in Union Co., with the care of the missions attached to this parish. In August 1861, he became assistant at St. Lawrence Church in Daviess Co. and the missions in Daviess and Hancock Co.'s, where he remained until the spring of 1863, when he was appointed pastor of St. Jerome Church, Fancy Farm and the congregation of St. John the Evangelist in McCracken Co.

Due to conditions brought on by the Civil War, he took up temporary residence at St. Francis de Sales Church in Paducah for several months. During this period, he attended the entire district known as the Jackson Purchase, which included parishes at Paducah, Fancy Farm, St. Johns and Hickman, plus several mission stations.

Fr. Bourke was transferred from Fancy Farm in the fall of 1869, to become a professor at the preparatory seminary then located at Bardstown and assistant at the adjoining St. Joseph Church. Early in 1874, he was made pastor of St. Mary Church, Franklin, and the Mission Church of the Sacred Heart in Russellville, KY. Health forced him to resign in August 1876. He died August 8, 1897 in Louisville and he was buried in St. Louis Cemetery, Louisville. *Rev. John A. Lyons.*

REV. CHARLES PARTICK BOWLING, (1896-1980) was born October 8, 1896 at Athertonville near New Haven, KY. He was a son of Mr. and Mrs. J. Walker Bowling. He was ordained June 2, 1928 by Bishop Floresh in the Louisville Cathedral.

He served as associate pastor at Saint Joseph Church, Bowling Green from November 1928 to June 1929 and associate pastor at the Cathedral of the Assumption, Louisville, from June 1929 to August 1930. He was administrator of Saint Edward Church, Jeffersontown in August 1930 and adminisrator of St. Anthony Church, Browns Valley from September 1930 to January 1932.

He was pastor of Our Lady of the Hills Church, Finley and the Campbellsville Mission from January 1932 to September 1933 and from there served as pastor of St. Peter Alcantara Church, Stanley from September 1933 to April 1939. The Diocese of Owensboro was formed in December 1937 and he became a priest of the newly created See.

He served as pastor of St. Paul Church, Owensboro, from April 1939 to July 1947. With his appointment to Owensboro, he was appointed Vicar General of the diocese. He was pastor of St. Joseph Church, Bowling Green from July 1947 until he retired in 1971. He then moved to St. Augustine Home in Indianapolis, IN.

He died February 11, 1980 at Indianapolis. His funeral services were held from St. Joseph Church, Bowling Green, and he was buried in the family lot in St. Catherine Cemetery, New Haven. Fr. Bowling had four sisters in religion; Sister M. Bernadette, S.L., Sister Mary Regis, S.L., Sister Mary Martin, S.L. and Sister Charlesine, O.S.U. of Mt. St. Joseph. *Rev. John A. Lyons*

REV. CELESTINE BREY, (1869-1920) was born May 6, 1869 in St. Mary of the Woods Parish, Whitesville, Daviess Co. He was a son of Joseph William and Teresa Rose Drury Brey. He was ordained July 21, 1895, by Bishop William G. McCloskey.

He served as assistant at St. Jerome Church, Fancy Farm from August 1895 to February 1897. Also as pastor of St. Mary Church, Fenwick, Washington Co., with the mission of St. Ivo in the Pleasant Run District, Marion Co. from February 1897 to November of that year.

He was pastor of St. Rose Church, Cloverport and the missions of the Guradian Angels, Mt. Merino, near Irvington, Breckinridge Co., Immaculate Conception, Hawesville and St. Columba, Lewisport from November 1897 to the end of July 1912. He built a new church at Mt. Merino, which was dedicated July 16, 1899. He also served as pastor of Holy Cross Church, Louisville from August 1, 1912 until his death. He erected a combination church and school building, which was blessed March 7, 1915.

He died suddenly from a heart attack October 6, 1920, while visiting a sick parishioner. Funeral services were held from his church and he was buried in St. Mary of Woods Cemetery, Whitesville. Fr. Brey was nephew of Rev. Edwin Drury, an uncle of Msgr. Paul Clifton Barrett, who was ordained in 1922. He was also a cousin of Rev. Louis Hillary Spalding. Two of his sisters, Sister Angela and Sister Delphine, were members of the Lorettine Community in Marion Co. *Rev. John A. Lyons.*

REV. LUCIAN EDWARD CLEMENTS, (1872-1942) was born September 28, 1872 at Knottsville, in the parish of St. Lawrence, Daviess Co. He was a son of Charles O. and Appollonia Montgomery Clements. He was ordained May 28, 1898 at St. William Church, Knottsville, by his first cousin, Bishop George Montgomery, then bishop of Monterey-Los Angeles.

He was appointed pastor of St. Joseph Church, Mayfield with the missions of Hickman, Columbus and Fulton from June 1898 to September 1902. He attended Hickman until January 1900. He also served as pastor of St. Lawrence Church, Daviess Co. from September 1902 to September 1914, pastor of St. William Church, Knottsville from September 1914 to May 1915 and pastor of St. Ambrose Church, Henshaw, Union Co. from May 1915 to July 1916, succeeding Rev. Charles E. Rahm, who had attended the parish from Morganfield. He was also pastor of Immaculate Conception Church, Earlington from July 1916 until his retirement late in 1939.

He died November 2, 1942 at St. Joseph Infirmary, Eastern Parkway, Louisville, where he had resided. Funeral services from St. Stephen Cathedral, Owensboro with burial in the cemetery of the Ursuline Sisters at Mt. St. Joseph, Maple Mount. *Rev. John A. Lyons*

REV. HENRY ALOYSIUS CONNOLLY, (1846-1936) was born April 10, 1846 in the parish of Ballahale, County Kilkenny, Ireland. He was a son of James and Brigid Connolly, who came with their family, to the United States and settled in New York City in 1863.

He was ordained August 26, 1877 with Rev. Richard P. Feehan and Rev. Kyran W. King by Bishop William George McCloskey in the chapel of Preston Park. He was appointed assistant at the Cathedral of the Assumption, Louisville, from ordination. In July and August 1878, he was assisting the Yellow Fever victims at Jackson, MS and with the exception of January, February and March 1879, he attended St. Michael Church, 220 So. Brook St., from the Cathedral from 1877 until October 1879.

He served as temporary pastor at St. Anthony Church, Axtel and the McQuady Mission from February 1881 to July of that year and at Annunciation Church, Shelbyville for a few weeks in August 1881. He then returned to the Cathedral until May 1882. He was pastor of St. Romuald Church, Hardinsburg from May 1882 to August 1887.

In May 1909, he exchanged parishes with Rev. Henry W. Jansen, of St. Francis de Sales Church, Paducah, where he remained until February 1929, when failing eyesight and the infirmities of age forced his retirement to St. Joseph Infirmary, Eastern Parkway, Louisville.

He died April 4, 1936 at St. Joseph Infirmary at the age of 87 and the 59th year of his priesthood. Funeral services were held from the chapel of the Infirmary, and his remains were taken to New York for burial. *Rev. John A. Lyons.*

REV. WILLIAM J. DUNN, (1835-1898) was born in Ireland on April 10, 1835. His family emigrated to America when he was very young and settled in Pittsburgh, PA and at the age of 14, he accompanied them to Louisville. Shortly after, he entered St. Thomas Seminary in Nelson Co. His theological studies were made at St. Mary Seminary, Baltimore, MD, where he was elevated to the priesthood by Archbishop Francis P. Kenrick, June 10, 1861. Ordained with him, was the future Cardinal Gibbons.

Father Dunn's first appointment was as assistant at Sacred Heart Church, Union Co., with the care of the mission at Henderson. He moved to Henderson in December 1866, to become the first resident pastor of St. Louis, later Holy Name, Church, and from there attended Earlington and Hopkinsville. He completed the erection of the church at Henderson and purchased a lot in Hopkinsville for a church building. Around the beginning of May 1871, he was transferred to Louisville, as pastor of the Cathedral of the Assumption. The office of Chancellor of the diocese was conferred on him in 1873, and he continued to serve as pastor of the Cathedral until the fall of 1877, when he became president of St. Joseph College, Bardstown. In the following year, he returned to the Cathedral as assistant to Rev. Michael Bouchet.

Fr. Dunn joined the Congregation of the Passion, near the close of 1879, and was known in religion as Fr. Emmanuel. However, in the summer of 1885, he left the Order and was reappointed to the Cathedral and chaplain of St. Joseph Infirmary, 4th St. When St. Helen Church in Glasgow was dedicated October 1, 1893, he preached on the occasion and was so taken up with the little edifice, the gem of the small churches in the diocese, he decided to remain there and became the first resident pastor of the parish. The little congregation could not support a priest and in August 1894, he again went back to the Cathedral.

In 1895, Fr. Dunn took up the duties of chaplain of the Xaverian Brothers and teacher of Latin and Greek in their school on Broadway. He died February 24, 1898 and after funeral rites at the Cathedral, he was buried in St. Louis Cemetery, Louisville, in the family plot of James McCrory, whose wife Jane was a sister of Fr. Dunn. *Rev. John A. Lyons*

MGSR. THOMAS JOSEPH HAYES, (1858-1946) was born August 1, 1858 in Bagnalstown, County Carlow, Ireland. He was ordained June 26, 1881 by Bishop William George McCloskey.

He was appointed as pastor of Saints Peter and Paul Church Hopkinsville from October 1881 to the fall of 1883 and pastor of St. Joseph Church, Bowling Green from September 1889 with co-pastor, Rev. Richard Davis, who had accompanied him from Ireland in 1874. Besides the care of St. Joseph Parish, the two priests attended the missions of Franklin, Russellville, Auburn, Guthrie, Cave City, Glasgow and Glasgow Junction, now Park City. Late in 1890, Hopkinsville was added to their missions. Fr. Davis was transferred to Fairfield in October 1891 and an assistant was sent to Bowling Green. Fr. Hayes continued as pastor until his retirement in September 1943, and remained at St. Joseph Church as pastor emeritus until his death.

Among his many accomplishments at Bowling Green was the erection of a parochial school and a sisters' home in 1912, which replaced St. Columbia Academy, established by the Sisters of Charity of Nazareth in 1862. His investiture in the robes of a Monsignor took place May 19, 1938. Following his long pastorate of 54 years, he resigned in September 1943.

He died March 19, 1946 at St. Joseph Infirmary, Eastern Parkway, Louisville from a broken hip. The funeral of the venerable priest, who was in his 88th year, was held from St. Joseph Church, followed by burial in parish cemetery, Bowling Green. *Rev. John A. Lyons*

REV. ANTHONY HELLING, (1863-1938) was born September 7, 1863 at Rietberg, Westphalia, Germany. His parents died when he was quite young and he came to America in 1885. He was ordained June 29, 1896 by Bishop Van den Branden at Louvain, Belgium.

He was appointed pastor of St. Ambrose Church, Cecilia from the summer of 1896 to July 1898. Among his missions were Harcourt, now White Mills, and Red Mills in Hardin Co. He served as administrator at St. Lawrence Church in Daviess Co. for three months from July to October 1898. He was also assistant at the Church of the Immaculate Conception, Louisville from October 1898 to August 1905.

He was appointed pastor of St. Sylvester Church, Ottenheim for nine months from August 1905 and pastor of St. Elizabeth Church, Clarkson from June 1906 until his death. He was the first resident pastor of Clarkson and erected the first church, which was dedicated at Christmas, December 25, 1906. In practically all his missions, he built or rebuilt churches: St. Mary Church, Big Clifty, dedicated August 15, 1908; St. Anthony Church, Peonia dedicated August 16, 1909; St. Paul Church, Leitchfield dedicated April 30, 1918; St. Agnes Church, in Hart Co. dedicated May 5, 1912; St. Francis Seraph Church, Mt. Hebron dedicated May 6, 1915 and St. James Church, Iberia dedicated about 1914. These latter two churches were built under his direction by Rev. Anselm Kuhn, a Benedictine, who assisted him from October 1913 and five months later moved to Peonia, as resident pastor, relieving him of all his missions with the exception of St. Paul and St. Mary at Big Clifty. About 1935, he received an assistant who attended the missions.

He died November 13, 1938 at his rectory in Clarkson, having suffered a stroke of paralysis about nine months previously. The funeral of the 75 year old priest was held from his church, with burial in the cemetery at Bethlehem Academy in Hardin Co. In the late summer of 1959, the Lorettines removed the remains of their Sisters and those of Fr. Helling, A. Degauquier and J.J. Abell to the cemetery at their Motherhouse in Marion Co., the academy having been closed and the property sold. *Rev. John A. Lyons*

MSGR. J. GILBERT HENNINGER, (1907-1990) was born December 18, 1907 in the parish of St. Peter of Alcantara, Stanley, Daviess Co. He was a son of Mr. and Mrs. Henry Henninger. He was ordained on May 22, 1937 by Bishop Floersh.

He was appointed as associate pastor at St. Benedict Chruch, Louisville from June 1937 to December 1937 and then associate pastor at St. Francis de Sales Church, Paducah from December 2, 1937. A few days after his arrival in Paducah, the Diocese of Owenboro was erected and he became a priest of the new See.

In 1938, he was called to Owensboro to serve as Chancellor and secretary at the Chancery and associate pastor at St. Paul Church. About two years later, he took up his residence at the motherhouse of the Ursuline Sisters at Maple Mount and assisted as chaplain there while maintaining his office at the Chancery. In August 1947, he was appointed Vicar General of the Diocese of Owensboro, and in November 1949 was invested with the robes of Monsignor.

Following the death of Bishop Cotton in September 1961, he was administrator of the diocese until the appointment of Bishop Soenneker in March 1961. In July 1962, he was transferred from the chaplaincy of the Ursuline Motherhouse to the pastorate of St. Martin Church in Rome, Daviess Co. He died on March 5, 1990. *Rev. John A. Lyons*

REV. JAMES HENSON HIGDON, (1884-1954) was born June 11, 1884 in St. Lawrence Parish, Daviess Co., KY. He was a son of Stephen A. and Melissa Ann Carrico Higdon. He was ordained May 17, 1921 by Bishop Joseph Chartrand at St. Meinrad Abbey.

He was appointed pastor of St. Anthony Church, Axtel, Breckinridge Co. from June 1921 to June 1922 and pastor of St. Elizabeth Church, Curdsville, Daviess Co. from June 1922 to October 1933. He served as pastor of St. Ambrose Church, Cecilia, Hardin Co. from October 1933 to January 1937 and pastor of St. Alphonsus Church, Daviess Co. from January 1937 to July 1947. He also served as pastor of St. Peter of Alcantara Church, Stanley, Daviess Co. from July 1947 until his death.

He died June 29, 1954 at Our Lady of Mercy Hospital, Owensboro. Funeral services were held from St. Peter of Alcantara Church. Two of Fr. Higdon's brothers were members of the Xavarian Brothers and two of his sisters were Dominican nuns; Brother Justin, Brother Christian, Sister Maricini and Sister Boniface. *Rev. John A. Lyons*

REV. DOMINIC JOSEPH HIGGINS, (1852-1951) was born in the Diocese of Ardagh, County Leitrim, Ireland. He was baptized October 8, 1852. He was ordained June 17, 1883 by Bishop William George McCloskey.

He served as temporary pastor of Holy Name of Mary Church, Calvary in the summer of 1883. He was appointed pastor of Saints Peter and Paul Church, Hopkinsville with the mission of Elkton and Guthrie from the fall of 1883 to the late summer of 1884. He served as assistant at St. Stephen Church, Owensboro from January 1885 to July of that year and pastor of St. Malachi, later St. Rose of Lima, Church, Cloverport from September 1885 to May 1890. He also attended Hardinsburg from Febuary to August 1888. His new church at Cloverport was dedicated under the title of St. Rose of Lima, August 27, 1889.

Pastor of St. Raphael Church in Daviess Co. from June 1890 until September 1924, 34 years later, when he took an extended visit of two and a half years among relatives in Ireland. He served as chaplain of St. Thomas Orphan Home, then located in the Preston Park Seminary buildings, from late in 1927 to August 1928, when he retired and returned to his native land. He died February 1951, at Drumsna, County Leitrum in his 99th year. *Rev. John A. Lyons*

MSGR. JOHN MARTIN HIGGINS, (1889-1985) was born October 19, 1889 in St. Augustine Parish, Grayson Springs, Grayson Co., KY. He was a son of Thomas H. and Mary Tully Higgins. He was ordained June 19, 1918 by Bishop Denis O'Donaghue at St. Mary Magdalen Church, Louisville.

He was appointed assistant at St. Stephen Church, Owensboro from June 1918 to June 1919 and also pastor of St. Peter of Alcantara Church, Stanley, Daviess Co. from June 1919. He began the erection of a new church at Stanley. The cornerstone was laid in 1922 and the first services were held in the new building in November 1924, but the edifice was far from being completed. Ill health forced his removal from Stanley in December 1925.

He served as assistant at Holy Cross Church, Louisville from the summer of 1926 to November 1928 and pastor of Sacred Heart Church, St. Vincent, Union Co. form November 1928 until he retired about 25 years later. In July 1949, he was elevated to the dignity of Domestic Prelate, with the title of Right Reverend.

For several years after he retired, Msgr. Higgins lived with relatives in Crestwood. In later years, 1979, he resided at Carmel Home in Owensboro. He died January 23, 1985. *Rev. John A. Lyons*

MSGR. RAYMOND GEORGE HILL, (1907-1981) was born February 21, 1907 in Louisville. He was a son of Mr. and Mrs. Michael F. and Lillie Hill. He was ordained May 21, 1932 by Bishop Floersh.

He was appointed associate pastor at St. Joseph Church, Bowling Green from August 1932 to July 1938. The Diocese of Owensboro was erected in December 1937 and he became a priest of the new See. He served as pastor of St. John the Evangelist Church in McCracken Co. from July 1938 to September 1942.

He served as pastor of St. Agnes Chruch, Uniontown from September 1942 to July 1962 and as superintendent of Catholic schools in the Owensboro Diocese from 1953. In March 1959, he became a domestic prelate with the title of Very Reverend Monsignor. He was pastor of St. Alphonsus Church, St. Joseph, Daviess County from July 1962 for a couple of years. He then took up residence at Our Lady of Mercy Hospital, where he was chaplain, while continuing to serve as Superintendent of Catholic Schools.

Failing health caused him to reitre from the school board duties in 1978. He died May 28, 1981 at the hospital. His funeral services were held from St. Stephen Cathedral and he was buried in Resurrection Cemetery, Owensboro. *Rev. John A. Lyons.*

REV. BENEDICT FLOYD HUFF, (1900-1969) was born May 6, 1900 in Perry Co., IN. He was a son of James H. and Nancy Susan Weedman Huff. The family moved to Tell City about 1920.

He was ordained May 26, 1931 for the Diocese of Louisville by Bishop Chartrand at St. Meinrad Seminary Church. He served as associate pastor at St. Martin Church, Louisville and St. Paul Church, Jackson St., Louisville until February 1935. He was pastor of St. Anthony Church, Peonia and the missions of Grayson Springs, Wax and Iberia, in Grayson Co. from February 1935 to October 1939. The Diocese of Owensboro was erected in December 1937 and he became a priest of the new See.

He served as associate pastor at St. Jerome Church, Fancy Farm with the care of St. Denis Church in Hickman Co. and St. Charles Church in Carlisle Co. from October 1939 to August 1951 and as associate pastor at St. Francis de Sales Church, Paducah from August 1951. Before leaving Paducah, he was administrator of St. Thomas More Church around 1960-61. Around 1965-66 he was at St. Mary of the Woods Church, Whitesville.

His last assignment was as pastor of St. Rose Church, Cloverport, where he died on August 16, 1969. *Rev. John A. Lyons*

MSGR. M. RICHARD MALONEY, (1882-1965) was born July 8, 1882 at Aurora, Dearborn Co., IN. He was a son of John and Margaret Tracy Maloney. He was ordained May 7, 1907 in the Cathedral of the Assumption, Louisville by Bishop John Morris of the Diocese of Little Rock.

He was appointed assistant at Saint Alphonsus Church, St. Joseph, Daviess Co. from September 1907 to June 1911 and pastor of St. Augustine Church, Reed, Henderson Co.

from June 1911 to May 1913. He served as pastor of St. Peter of Alcantara Church, Stanley, Daviess Co. from May 1913 to June 1919 and pastor of St. Stephen Church, Owensboro from June 1919 to February 1935. He built the present church, which later became the Cathedral of the Diocese of Owensboro. Cornerstone was laid April 26, 1925 and the church was dedicated September 6, 1926.

He was pastor of St. Brigid Church, Louisville from February 1935 until his death in 1965. Elevated to the dignity of Domestic Prelate with the title of Right Rev., he was invested with the insignia of this office November 22, 1949. He died December 5, 1965 at St. Joseph Infirmary, Eastern Parkway, from pneumonia following an operation. Funeral services from St. Brigid Church with burial in Calvary Cemetery, Louisville. *Rev. John A. Lyons*

REV JOSEPH McALEER, (1884-1962) was born February 21, 1884 in County Tyrone, Ireland. He was ordined June 10, 1911 at St. Meinrad Abbey by Bishop Joseph Chartrand of Indianapolis.

He was appointed assistant at St. Patrick Church, Louisville from June 1911 to January 1918 and pastor of Most Holy Redeemer Church, Chapeze and the Bullitt Co. Missions from January 1918.

Fire destroyed his church and rectory January 28, 1920. He was the last resident pastor of Chapeze.

He also served as pastor of St. John the Baptist Church new Rineyville and chaplain of Bethlehem Academy, Hardin Co. with residence at the academy from July to December 1920. He was pastor of St. Peter of Antioch Church, Waverly, Union Co. from January 1928 to January 1937. He served as pastor of St. Alphonsus Church, St. Joseph, Daviess Co. from January 1937 until his death.

He died June 11, 1962 after a short illness in Our Lady of Mercy Hospital, Owensboro. Funeral services were held from St. Alphonsus Church and he was buried in the parish cemetery. *Rev. John A. Lyons*

REV. PETER JAMES McNEIL, (1876-1946) was born November 11, 1876 in St. Peter Parish, Trenton, Ontario, Canada. He moved with his parents to Olean, NY at an early age. He studied at St. Bonaventure College and Seminary, Allegheny, NY, where he applied for admission into the Diocese of Louisville.

He was ordained January 1, 1902 by Bishop William Geo. McCloskey at the Cathedral of the

Assumption, Louisville. He was appointed as assitant at St. Jerome Church, Fancy Farm, Graves Co. from November 1902. Under his care, was the mission of St. Charles, Carlisle Co. and from May 1903, he began to attend St. Joseph Church, Mayfield, Graves Co.

He was resident pastor at St. Joseph Church, Mayfield from the early fall of 1903. He continued his care of the St. Charles Mission and purchased property for a church at Fulton, Fulton Co. on the Tennessee borderline. He remained at Mayfield until February 1909.

He was transferred to Union Co. in February 1909 to organize a parish at Waverly, where he built a church, school, convent and rectory. The church was dedicated October 12, 1910 under the partronage of St. Peter of Antioch. This church was destroyed by fire February 8, 1923. He rebuilt the edifice, which was blessed August 5, 1924. Three months later he was assigned to Louisville.

He served as pastor of St. Patrick Church, Louisville from November 1924 until his death nearly 22 years later. He died on March 16, 1946 following a lingering illness at St. Joseph Infirmary, Eastern Parkway. Funeral services were held from his Church of St. Patrick, with burial in the cemetery at the motherhouse of the Ursuline Sisters, Mt. St. Joseph, Maple Mount, Daviess Co. *Rev. John A. Lyons*

REV. GUIDO LUIGI MENSA, (1889-1936) was born April 9, 1889 in San Giovanni, suburban Turin, Italy. He was a son of Joseph and Catherine DeMarchi Mensa and a brother of Rev. Secunda J. Mensa. He had prepartatory course in the Turin Archdiocesan Seminary, before following his brother to America for the

purpose of affiliating with the Diocese of Louisville. he continued his studies at St. Bernard Seminary, Rochester, NY and St. Meinrad, IN.

He was ordained May 15, 1913 by Bishop Denis O'Donaghue. He was appointed assistant at St. Paul Church, Owensboro form May 1913 to February 1924 and pastor of St. Raphael church, Daviess Co. from February 1924 to February 1928.

He served as pastor of St. Brigid Church, Vine Grove from February 1928 to February 1932. He erected a new church at Vine Grove and built St. Patrick church at his Grahampton, Meade Co., mission. Both were dedicated May 28, 1929.

He was pastor of St. Martin Church, Rome, Daviess Co. from February 1932 to March 1935 and pastor of St. Alphonsus Church, St. Joseph, Daviess Co. from March 1935. For several years, he was afflicted with a heart condition and died suddenly in the following year. He died on October 2, 1936 at St. Alphonsus. Funeral services were held from his church, with burial in the Ursuline Cemetery at Mt. St. Joseph Motherhouse and Academy, Maple Mount, Daviess Co. *Rev. John A. Lyons*

REV. ALOYSIUS GEORGE MEYERING,

(1871-1940) was born August 28, 1871 in St. Michael Parish, Rochester, NY. He was a son of John and Catherine Mueller Meyering. He studied at St. Andrew Preparatory Seminary and St. Bernard Seminary, both in Rochester.

He was ordained June 11, 1898 with Rev. Denis Murphy, by Bishop Bernard McQuaid in St. Patrick Cathedral, Rochester for the Diocese of Louisville. He spent a year at the University of Innsbruck, Austria and arrived in Kentucky in August 1899.

He was appointed pastor of Guardian Angels Church, Mt. Merino, near Irvington, Breckinridge Co. and the Brandenburg Mission from August 1899 to November 1902. He established St. Anthony Parish, Browns Valley, Daviess Co. in November 1902. He dismantled the former church at Rome in the same county and having rebuilt it at Browns Valley, dedicated it under the invocation of St. Anthony, August 2, 1903. The missions of Livermore and Central City were under his care from 1904 to May 1925, when transferred to Louisville. The present Church of St. Martin of Tours in Central City was dedicated August 28, 1912 and St. Charles Church, a former non-Catholic meeting house, was opened for services June 21, 1917.

He served as pastor of St. Vincent de Paul Church, Louisville from May 1925 to February 1927 and St. Francis of Assisi Church, Louisville from February 1927 until his death. He died December 15, 1940, suddenly from a heart attack. He was concluding Sunday afternoon devotions in his church. Following funeral services in his church, his remains were taken to Maple Mount and buried in the cemetery of the Ursuline Sisters at Mt. St. Joseph Motherhouse and Academy.

Special Note: It was through Fr. Meyering, that the writer of these sketches, Rev. John A. Lyons, became a student for the Louisville Diocese in 1922. *Rev. John A. Lyons*

REV. GEORGE A. NIEHAUS,

(1854-1932) was born Aug 25, 1854 at Vestrup, Oldenburg, Germany. He was a son of John H. and Catherine Spille Neihaus. The family emigrated to Cincinnati, OH in 1861.

He studied in St. Francis Seraphic Seminary at Cincinnati and joined the Francisan Order, September 8, 1879, receiving the name of Boniface in religion.

He was stationed at the Immaculate Conception Church, Higginsville, MO in 1893, when he affiliated with the Dioocese of Louisville. He was ordained on December 18, 1885. He was appointed pastor of St. Rose Church, Cloverport from December 1893 to February 1895. His church, destroyed by fire, was rebuilt and dedicated October 21, 1894.

He served as pastor of St. Martin of Tours Church, Flaherty from February 1895 to September 1914 and St. Lawrence Church in Daviess Co. from September 1914 to March 1931, when he resigned his pastorate because of failing health. He served as assistant at St. Francis de Sales Church, Paducah from March 1931 until his death.

He died February 17, 1932 at the rectory of St. Frances de Sales. Funeral from the church with burial at Mt. Carmel Cemetery, Paducah. *Rev. John A. Lyons.*

REV. JAMES FRANCIS NORMAN,

(1875-1938) was born August 2, 1875 at Manchester, England. He came to America with his parents when he was a child and settled in Providence, RI.

He was ordained May 7, 1907 by Bishop John B. Morris of Little Rock at the Cathedral of the Assumption, Louisville.

He was appointed assistant at St. Cecilia Church, Louisville for five weeks, May-June 1907, then loaned to the Diocese of Little Rock as secretary to Bishop Morris, with residence at the Cathedral of St. Andrew, Little Rock, AK. He returned to Louisville in the fall of 1908.

He served at temporary assitant at St. John the Evangelist Church, Louisville for about a month, Oct-November 1908 and pastor of All Saints Church, Taylorsville and the mission of St. Francis Xavier, Mount Washington from November 1908 to November 1909. He was reassigned as assistant at St. Cecilia Church from November 1909 to October 1910.

He was pastor of St. Romuald Church, Hardinsburg, Breckinridge Co. from October 1910 to November 1928 and pastor of St. Peter of Antioch Church, Waverly, Union Co. from November 1924 to February 1928. He also served as pastor of St. Paul Church, Owensboro from February 1928 and held the pastorate there until his death.

He died November 2, 1938. Funeral services from St. Paul Church, Owensboro with burial in the Norman family lot in the Catholic cemetery at Providence, RI. *Rev. John A. Lyons*

REV ANTHONY O'SULLIVAN,

(1863-1936) was born December 15, 1863 in Pompey, near Syracuse, NY. He was a son of Michael and Ann O'Dwyer O'Sullivan, who moved to Louisville and settled in the Cathedral Parish in 1869. Among his brothers were, Msgr. Hugh O'Sullivan, and Msgr. St. John O'Sullivan who was ordained in 1904.

He studied at St. Joseph College, Bardstown and entered Preston Park Seminary, site of Bellamine College, Louisville in September 1885. He was ordained May 10, 1888 by Bishop Willaim George McCloskey.

He was appointed pastor of St. Augustine Church, Grayson Springs and the missions of Wax, Big Clifty and Peonia from May 1888. When Fr. Egart died in Mary 1890, he moved to Leitchfield and also attended his parish, St. Joseph and the missions of Central City and Sunfish in Edmonson Co. until January 1891. A successor was appointed and he then returned to Grayson Springs, where he remained until March 1894.

He served as pastor of St. Alphonsus Church in Daviess Co. with the mission of Curdsville and Beech Grove from March 1894 until April 1903, when his health broke down and three years passed before he could return to active duty. For the summer of 1906, he resided at St. Francis de Sales Church, Paducah and from there attended the missions of Princeton, La Center, Smithland, Hampton and Calvert City. At La Center, he built the Church of St. Mary, which was dedicated November 15, 1907. His care of these missions ended in the early spring, possibly February 1909.

He was pastor of St. Joseph Church, Mayfield from the early spring of 1909. He attended the missions of St. Charles, Kirbyton, in Carlisle Co. and Our Lady of Victory, Fulton in Fulton Co. He also had charge of Sacred Heart Church, Hickman from January 1913. His health again failed, January 1926, and after spending some time in St. Joseph Infirmary, 4th St., Louisville, he went to California to live with his brother, Msgr. St. John O'Sullivan, who was stationed at the Mission of San Juan Capistrano, where he spent his remaining years.

He died February 4, 1936 at Capistrano. Following services in the mission church, he was buried in Los Angeles. *Rev. John A. Lyons*

MSGR. HUGH O'SULLIVAN,

(1858-1938) was born November 4, 1858 at Pompey, near Syracuse, NY. He was a brother of Rev. Anthony O'Sullivan and Msgr. St. John O'Sullivan, who was ordained in 1904. His parents were Michael and Anne O'Dwyer O'Sullivan. the family moved to Louisville in 1869 and took up their residence in the Cathedral Parish.

He was ordained December 18, 1892 by Bishop William George McCloskey. He was appointed pastor of St. Romuald Church, Hardinsburg and the mission of St. Anthony, Long Lick, Axtel and St. Mary of the Woods, McQuady from January 1, 1893 to September

1893. He also served as pastor of St. Mary of the Woods Church, Whitesville from September 1893 until his death, nearly 45 years later. Under his care, was the mission of St. John the Baptist near Sulphur Springs in Ohio Co.

On February 23, 1938, when the See of Louisville was raised to the dignity of an Archdiocese and the Diocese of Owensboro embracing the western part of Kentucky was created, he was named Domestic Prelate, with the title of Right Rev. The ceremonies of the investiture took place on May 3 of that year at his church in Whitesville, Archbishop Floersh officiating. On that occasion, he was named by the newly consecrated prelate of Owensboro, Bishop Francis R. Cotton, the first Vicar General of the Owensboro Diocese.

He died July 26, 1938 at St. Joseph Infirmary, Eastern Parkway, Louisville. He had been sick about a month after his investiture and a week before his death entered the infirmary. He was in his 80th year and the first priest to die in the Owensboro Diocese. Funeral services were held from his church in Whitesville and he was buried in the family plot in St. Louis Cemetery, Louisville. *Rev. John A. Lyons*

REV. SAMUEL RAYMOND PAYNE, (1888-1919) was born February 7, 1888 in St. Lawrence Parish, Daviess Co., KY. He was a son of Marshall T. and Mary Jane Raley Payne. He was ordained August 1, 1914 by Bishop Denis O'Donaghue. Following ordination, he spent two years in post-graduate studies at the Catholic University, Washington, DC.

He was appointed temporary chaplain at the Ursuline Motherhouse and Academy, Mt. St. Joseph, Maple Mount, Daviess Co. in the late summer of 1916 until his death.

He died April 7, 1919 from pneumonia and the flu, in his rectory at Raywick. Funeral services from St. Francis Xavier Church with burial in the Ursuline Cemetery at Maple Mount. *Rev. John A. Lyons*

REV. CHARLES ERNEST RAHM, (1885-1942) was born May 4, 1885 in St. Patrick Parish, Stithton, now Ft. Knox, KY. He was a son of Henry W. and Emma Brown Rahm. He was ordained June 10, 1911 at St. Meinrad's, by Bishop Joseph Chartrand of Indianapolis.

He was appointed assistant at St. Augustine Church, Lebanon from June 1911 to January 1913 and pastor of St. Ann Church, Morganfield, Union Co. from January 1913 to February 1932. He also attended St. Ambrose Church, Henshaw in the same county from June 1914 to May 1915, from November 1918 to August 1920 and from November 1920.

He also served as pastor of St. John the Evangelist Church, Louisville from February 1932 until his death, ten years later on January 22, 1942. Funeral services were held from his church and he was buried in the cemetery of the Sisters of Charity, Nazareth, KY. *Rev. John A. Lyons*

MSGR. EDWARD RUSSELL, (1895-1978) was born September 4, 1895 in St. Dominic Parish, Springfield, KY. He was a son of Edward McMahon and Sarah Louise Bird Russell. He was ordained June 6, 1922 at Saint Meinrad Abbey by Bishop Joseph Chartrand of Indianapolis.

He was appointed assistant at Holy Cross Church, Louisville, KY from July 1922 to July 1925 and administrator of St. Philip Neri Church, Louisville from July 1925 to December 1926. He served as pastor of St. Anthony Church, Peonia, Grayson Co. and the Grayson Co. Missions of St. Augustine Church, Grayson Springs; St. Benedict Church Wax; St. James Church, Iberia; St. Joseph Church, Annetta; and St. Agnes Church, Dog Creek from January 1, 1927 to February 1935.

He was pastor of St. Jerome Church, Fancy Farm, Graves Co. from February 1935, which office he held for 28 years. Attached to Fancy Farm were the missions of St. Denis, Hickman Co. and St. Charles, Carlisle Co. He built a new church at St. Charles, which was dedicated March 12, 1957. In March 1959, he was elevated to the dignity of Domestic Prelate with the title of Right Rev.

Retiring from parochial duties at Fancy Farm in March 1963, he became chaplain of the Ursuline Motherhouse and Academy, Maple Mount, Daviess Co. From 1968, he resided at Maple Mount, in retirement. He died at Maple Mount, March 14, 1978 and is buried there. *Rev. John A. Lyons*

REV. LOUIS HILARY SPALDING, (1861-1920) was born January 20, 1861 in Holy Name of Mary Parish, Calvary, Marion Co. He was a son of J. Robert and Mary Margaret Drury Spalding. The family moved to St. Lawrence Patish, Daviess Co. He was ordained September 4, 1887 in the Jesuit Church, Louvain, Belgium by Bishop Van den Branden de Rethe. He then went to Rome, Italy and returned to Kentucky in June 1888.

He was appointed pastor of St. Ignatius Church, Harcourt, White Mills, Hardin Co. from July 1888 to May 1889, when his health failed. For the next three and one half years, he was chaplain at Mt. Olivet School, located adjoining Gethsemini, Nelson Co. and conducted by the Sisters of the Third Order of St. Francis.

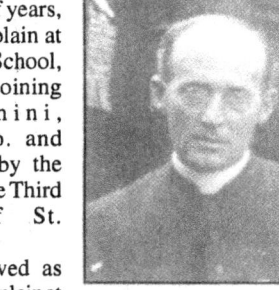

He served as assistant chaplain at the Motherhouse and Academy of the Sisters of Loretto, Marion Co. for 11 months and chaplain at St. Vincent Orphan Home, Jefferson and Wenzel Streets, Louisville for about six months. He was chaplain at Mt. St. Joseph Convent and Academy, Maple Mount, Daviess Co. from May 1892 to July 1893 and pastor of St. William Church, Knottsville, Daviess Co. from July 1893 to September 1914.

He was chaplain at Mt. St. Joseph, Maple Mount from September 1914 until his death on January 22, 1920. He was never in robust health, his condition gradually weakened until he passed away at the chaplain's residence. His funeral was held from the chapel at Mt. St. Joseph and he was buried in the Ursuline Cemetery at Maple Mount. *Rev. John A. Lyons*

MSGR. ALBERT J. THOMPSON, (1889-1970) was born August 21, 1889 in Washington Co., KY. He was a son of Mr. and Mrs. Charles R. Thompson, who moved to Louisville when he was six months old. He was ordained May 27, 1915 by Bishop Denis O'Dohaghue in Saint Mary Magdalen Church, Louisville.

He was appointed assitant at St. Jerome Church,

Fancy Farm, Graves Co. from June 1915 to July 1918. The missions of St. Denis, Hickman Co. and St. Charles, Carlisle Co. were under his care. He was chaplain in the armed forces from July 1918 until he returned from France in August 1919 at the conclusion of WWI.

He was reassigned assistant at St. Jerome Church, Fancy Farm in August 1919 and became pastor in November 1920, retaining that office until February 1935. He served as pastor of St. Stephen Church, Owensboro from February 1935. When the Diocese of Owensboro was created in December 1937, he became a subject of the new See. His church became the Cathedral in which the first bishop, Francis R. Cotton, was installed March 8, 1938 and the priest's house, built by him, became the Cathedral rectory.

He served as pastor of St. Francis de Sales Church, Paducah from May 1, 1938. He was elevated to the dignity of Domestic Prelate, with the title Right Reverend in March 1959 and invested with the insignia of this office on the following April 19. He was pastor of St. Joseph Church, Leitchfield, Grayson Co. from around 1960 until he retired from parochial duties in July 1962. He then served as chaplain of the Ursuline

Motherhouse and Academy of Mt. St. Joseph, Maple Mount, Daviess Co. from July 1962 until his death.

He died Jan. 5, 1970 while on a visit to Madisonville, Hopkins Co. in the 55th year of his priesthood. His funeral services were held from the convent chapel at Maple Mount. *Rev. John A. Lyons*

REV. THOMAS F. TIERNEY, (1853-1901) was born November 29, 1853 at Carbondale, Diocese of Scranton, PA. He was ordained May 14, 1876 by Bishop William George McCloskey.

He was appointed pastor of St. Mary Church, Franklin from May 1876 to the beginning of 1881. Among his many missions and stations was that of Russellville. He served as pastor at Henderson from the beginning of 1881 until his death 21 years later. He erected the present church of the Holy Name of Jesus. The cornerstone was laid October 17, 1886. It replaced the brick St. Louis Church, which stood on the northwest corner of 3rd and Ingram Streets.

He died June 22, 1901. His remains were taken back to Henderson and following funeral services in his church, were interred in a crypt to the right of the altar. *Rev. John A. Lyons*

REV. GUSTAVE ADOLPH VANTROOSTENBERGHE, (1847-1919) a brother of Rev. Edward L. Vantroostenberghe, he was born in Bruges, Belgium February 2, 1847. He entered the American College, Louvain, Belgium in 1872 and 18 months later, came to Kentucky to complete his theology at Preston Park Seminary, site of Bellarmine College, Louisville. He was ordained May 19, 1875 by Bishop William George McCloskey.

Fr. Vantroostenberghe was pastor of St. Raphael Church, West Louisville, Daviess Co. from June 4, 1875 until June 1890. He built the brick Church of St. Raphael, which was dedicated October 12, 1879. The mission of St. Martin, Rome, Daviess Co. was under his care from November 1888, until he left West Louisville for reasons of health, to became chaplain of the Little Sisters of the Poor, 8th St., Louisville. Taken sick again in the following year, he spent some time at St. Joseph Hospital, Lexington.

In summer of 1893, Fr. Vantroostenberghe was given charge of St. Charles Church in Marion Co., where he remained until the late spring of 1899, when he went to Europe to recuperate. He returned in the next November and was assigned chaplain of St. Vincent Academy, St. Vincent, in Union Co. For three years, from October 1900 to October 1903, he

was pastor of Holy Cross Church in Marion Co. With his health in precarious condition, he again journeyed to Belgium and came back in Feb. 1904.

He then served as chaplain at Mt. St. Joseph Motherhouse and Academy, Daviess Co. for about a year. His next appointment, in May 1905, was as pastor of the Church of Our Lady of Mercy, Hodgensville and the mission of St. Ann, Howardstown. This pastorate ended in January 1915, when on a visit to Lexington, the 68 year old priest suffered severe injuries from a fall.

Upon recovery, Fr. Vantroostenberghe was appointed chaplain of the Sisters of the Good Shepherd, Louisville. He died July 15, 1919. His funeral was held from the chapel of the Good Shepherd's. He was laid to rest in the cemetery of the Sisters of Charity of Nazareth. *Rev. John A. Lyons*

Diocesan Priests

When Diocese of Owensboro was Created
December 9, 1937

Name	Birth	Death	Ordination
Barrett, Paul C.	11-10-1890	08-12-1949	06-10-1922
Beruatto, Louis	11-12-1883	07-18-1973	05-13-1906
*Boehmicke, George	04-24-1910		12-08-1935
Borntraeger, William	08-17-1907	12-06-1986	06-10-1933
Bowling, Charles P.	10-08-1896	02-11-1980	06-02-1928
Braun, Peter J.	05-30-1901	11-13-1986	05-09-1929
Carrico, C. Rudolph	08-04-1904	02-10-1957	05-30-1931
Clements, Lucian E.	09-28-1872	11-02-1942	05-28-1898
*DeNardi, Charles	12-25-1909		06-06-1936
Dienes, Leo J.	12-19-1912	07-24-1990	06-06-1936
Edelen, Pius W.	05-05-1907	12-30-1980	05-23-1937
**Egan, Joseph	12-09-1903	06-26-1992	05-30-1931
Gipperich, Robert J.	11-24-1895	05-14-1979	05-21-1921
Glenn, John W.	05-25-1901	10-20-1960	05-29-1926
Greenwell, Paul	10-10-1896	11-24-1964	06-02-1928
Hallahan, John C.	10-03-1900	07-25-1979	05-30-1931
Hayden, Jolly P.	07-07-1890	01-05-1941	06-15-1919
Hayes, Thomas	07-01-1858	03-19-1946	06-26-1881
Helling, Anthony	09-07-1863	11-13-1938	06-29-1896
Henninger, Gilbert	12-18-1907	03-05-1990	05-23-1937
Higdon, James	06-11-1884	06-29-1954	05-17-1921
Higgins, John M.	10-17-1889	01-23-1985	06-09-1918
Hill, Raymond	02-21-1907	05-28-1981	05-21-1932
Huff, Benedict	05-06-1900	08-16-1969	05-26-1931
Jarboe, William	03-13-1901	09-13-1984	06-02-1928
McAleer, Joseph	02-21-1887	06-11-1962	06-10-1911
Mills, J.W.	10-18-1885	07-10-1955	05-25-1929
Nahstoll, Martin	12-22-1901	06-20-1978	06-28-1928
Norman, James F.	08-02-1875	11-07-1938	05-07-1907
O'Sullivan, Hugh	11-04-1858	07-26-1938	12-12-1892
Russell, Edward	09-04-1895	03-14-1978	06-06-1922
Saffer, Joseph	05-01-1906	01-24-1971	12-08-1931
Smith, Francis J.	03-15-1895	06-27-1939	06-10-1919
Spalding, Joseph L.	09-17-1901	02-08-1965	06-14-1930
Thomas, Delphin	07-09-1909	06-10-1985	06-10-1933
Thompson, Albert J.	08-03-1889	01-05-1970	05-27-1915
Tompkins, Anthony J.	03-06-1896	05-11-1962	12-23-1922
Whelan, Robert A.	07-20-1911	01-07-1984	05-23-1937
Wilson, Robert T.	12-16-1910	03-14-1982	06-06-1936
Zoeller, Andrew	04-01-1871	03-11-1948	12-27-1894

*Presently, a retired priest of the Diocese of Owensboro.
**Entered the Congregation of the Passionists in 1941, where he received the name in religion of Father Declan Egan, C.P.

1938 Catholic Directory Diocese of Owensboro

(Dioeccsis Owensburgensis)
Created December 9, 1937
Erected February 23, 1938

Total Square Miles 12,502. Comprises the following thirty-two counties in the Western part of the State of Kentucky: Allen, Ballard, Breckinridge, Butler, Caldwell, Carlisle, Christian, Crittenden, Daviess, Edmonson, Fulton, Calloway, Grayson, Graves, Hancock, Henderson, Hickman, Hopkins, Livingston, Logan, Lyon, McCracken, McLean, Marshall, Muhlenberg, Ohio, Simpson, Todd, Trigg, Union, Warren and Webster.

Most Rev. Francis R. Cotton, D.D.

First Bishop of Owensboro; ordained June 17, 1920; preconized December 16, 1937; Consecrated February 24, 1938; Installed March 8, 1938. Residence, Owensboro, Ky.

Clergy, Churches, Missions and Schools—City of Owensboro

St. Stephen Cathedral, Rev. Albert J. Thompson, Pastor; Rev. Leo Dienes, asst. Residence 614 Locust Street.
Mission-Lewisport, Hancock County, St. Columba's.
Chapel-St. Mary's Home (Ursuline Sisters).

St. Joseph's, Rev. Robert J. Gipperich, Pastor; Rev. Pius Edelen, asst. Res. 508 E. Fourth Street.
School-St. Joseph's. 10 Ursuline Sisters. Res. 507 E. 5th Street. Grade School 330 pupils; High School 80 pupils.

St. Paul's, Rev. James F. Norman, Pastor; Rev. George Boehmicke, asst. Res. 609 E. Fourth Street.

Outside of the City of Owensboro

Axtel, Breckinridge Co., St. Anthony's, Rev. Henry Friedel, C.PP.S., Pastor. P.O. McDaniels, Kentucky.
Mission-Irvington, Breckinridge Co., Guardian Angels.

Bowling Green, Warren Co., St. Joseph's, Rev. Thomas J. Hayes, Dean; Rev. Raymond G. Hill, asst. Res. 434 Church Street.
School-St. Joseph's, 5 Sisters of Charity of Nazareth. Pupils 119.

Brown's Valley, Daviess Co., St Anthony's. Rev. Anthony J. Tompkins, Pastor. P.O. Utica, Kentucky, R.R. No. 2.
School-St. Anthony's, 5 Ursuline Sisters. Pupils 110.

Central City, Muhlenberg Co., St. Joseph's, Rev. Peter Braun, Pastor. School-St. Joseph's, 2 Ursuline Sisters. Res. 115 S. Third St. Pupils 39.

Mission-Livermore, McLean County, St. Charles.

Clarkson, Grayson Co., St. Elizabeth of Hungary, Rev. Anthony Helling; Rev. William Borntraeger, Pastor.
Missions-Big Clifty, Grayson Co., St. Mary's; Mt. Hebron, Grayson Co., St. Paul's.

Cloverport, Breckinridge Co., St. Rose's, Rev. James W. Mills, Pastor.
School - St. Rose's, 2 Ursuline Sisters. Pupils 61.
Mission-Hawesville, Hancock Co., Immaculate Conception.

Curdsville, Daviess Co., St. Elizabeth's, Rev. John J. Glenn, Pastor. School-St. Elizabeth's, 2 Ursuline Sisters. Pupils 57.
Mission-West Louisville, Daviess Co., St. Raphael.
School-St. Raphael, 2 Ursuline Sisters, P.O. Owensboro, Ky. R.R. No. 5. Pupils, 58.

Earlington, Hopkins Co., Immaculate Conception, Rev. L.E. Clements, Pastor, P.O. Box 275.
School-Immaculate Conception, 2 Ursuline Sisters. Pupils 22. *Mission*-Jewel City, Hopkins Co., Church of the Holy Ghost.

Fancy Farm, Graves Co., St. Jerome's, Rev. Edward Russell, Pastor; Rev. Robert T. Wilson, asst.
School-St. Jerome's , 9 Sisters of Charity of Nazareth. Pupils, High School 57, Graded School 272.
Mission-St. Denis, Hickman Co.
School-St. Denis, 2 Ursuline Sisters, P.O. Fancy Farm, Ky., R.R. No. 2. Pupils 37.
Mission-St. Charles, Carlisle Co.
School-St. Charles, 2 Ursuline Sisters, P.O. Bardwell, Ky., R.R. No. 4. Pupils 52.

Hardinsburg, Breckinridge Co., St. Romuald's, Rev. Martin Rosengarten, C.PP.S., Pastor.
School-St. Romuald's, 3 Ursuline Sisters. Pupils 60.

Henderson, Henderson Co., Holy Name of Jesus, Rev. Wm. P. Lennartz, C.S.C., Pastor; Rev. Salatore Fanelli, C.S.C., asst. Res. 511 Second Street.
School-Holy Name, 9 Sisters of Charity of Nazareth. Pupils 253.

Hickman, Fulton Co., Sacred Heart, Rev. C.R. Carrico, Pastor. School-Sacred Heart, 3 Sisters of Mercy, Pupils 44.
Missions-Union City, Tennessee, Obion Co., TN (Nashville Diocese) Immaculate Conception.

Hopkinsville, Christian Co., SS. Peter & Paul's, Rev. Joseph L. Spalding, Pastor. Res. 902 E. Ninth Street.
Missions-Princeton, Caldwell Co., St. Paul's; Outwood, Christian Co., Eddyville, Lyon Co.

Knottsville, Daviess Co., St. William's, Rev. William B. Jarboe, Pastor. P.O. Philpot,
Kentucky, R.R. No. 1.
School-St. William's, 3 Ursuline Sisters, Pupils 104.

Leitchfield, Grayson Co., St. Joseph's Rev. Louis Beruatto, D.D., Pastor.
Mission-Sunfish, Edmonson Co., St. John's.

McQuady, Breckinridge Co., St. Mary of the Woods, Rev. Albin Bauer, C.PP.S., Pastor.
School-St. Mary's, 3 Dominican Sisters. Pupils 50.

Mayfield, Graves Co., St. Joseph's, Rev. Joseph W. Saffer, Pastor. Res. 112 So. 14th St.
School-St. Joseph's, 3 Ursuline Sisters. Pupils 48.
Mission-Fulton, Fulton Co., St. Edward's

Morganfield, Union Co., St. Ann's, Rev. Francis J. Smith, Pastor; Rev. Charles A. DeNardi, asst.
School-St. Ann's, 6 Sisters of Charity of Nazareth. Pupils 153.
Mission-Henshaw, Union Co., St. Ambrose.

Paducah, McCracken Co., St. Francis de Sales, Rev. John C. Hallahan, Adm.; Revs. James B. Stammerman, Gilbert Henninger. Res. 116 S. 6th Street, P.O. Box No.44.
Chapel-St. Mary's Academy (Sisters of Charity of Nazareth).
Missions-LaCenter, Ballard Co., St. Mary's; Eddyville Penitentiary, Eddyville, Lyon Co.; C.C.C. Camps at Paducah, McCracken County and at Murray, Calloway Co.

Peonia, Grayson Co., St. Anthony's, Rev. Benedict F. Huff, Pastor. P.O. Clarkson, Ky, Peonia Star Route.
School-St. Anthony's, 4 Ursuline Sisters. Pupils, High School 60, Graded School 47.
Missions-Grayson Springs, Grayson Co., St. Augustine's; Wax, Grayson Co., St. Benedict's; Iberia, Grayson Co., St. James.

Reed, Henderson Co., St. Augustine's, Rev. Paul J. Greenwell, Pastor.
School-St. Augustine's, 2 Dominican Sisters, Pupils 56.
Mission-Sorgho, Daviess Co., St. Mary Magdalene's.
School-St. Mary Magdalene's, 2 Ursuline Sisters. Pupils 43.

Rome, Daviess Co., St. Martin's, Rev. Martin Nahstoll, Pastor. P.O. Owensboro, R.R. No. 3.
School-St. Martin's, 3 Ursuline Sisters, P.O. Owensboro, R.R. No. 3 Pupils 93.
Mission-Calhoun, McLean Co., St. Sebastian's.

Russellville, Logan Co., Sacred Heart, Rev. Joseph J. Egan, Pastor. Rev. Bernard L. Spoelker, Adm.
Mission-Franklin, Simpson Co., St. Mary's.

St. John, McCracken Co., St. John the Evangelist, Rev. Paul C. Barrett, Pastor. P.O. Paducah, R.R. No. 5, Box 159.
School-St. John's, 3 Sisters of Mercy. Pupils 101.

St. Joseph, Daviess Co., St. Alphonsus, Rev. James H. Higdon, Pastor.
School-St. Alphonsus, 4 Ursuline Sisters. Pupils 136.
Mission-Beech Grove, McLean Co., St. Benedict's.

St. Lawrence, Daviess Co., St. Lawrence, Rev. Willian B. Jarboe, Pastor, P.O. Philpot, Ky., R.R. No.1.
School-St. Lawrence, 3 Ursuline Sisters. Pupils 88.
Mission-Hancock Co., St. Thomas.

St. Vincent, Union Co., Sacred Heart, Rev. John M. Higgins, Pastor. Chapel-St. Vincent Academy, Sisters of Charity of Nazareth.

Stanley, Daviess Co., St. Peter of Alcantara, Rev. Charles P. Bowling, Pastor. P.O. Owensboro, Ky., R.R. No. 4.
School-St. Peter of Alcantara, 4 Ursuline Sisters. Pupils 137.

Uniontown, Union Co., St. Agnes, Rev. J.P. Hayden, Pastor; Rev. Delfin R. Thomas, Admr.
School-St. Agnes, 10 Sisters of Charity of Nazareth. Pupils: High School 80, Grade School 191.

Waverly, Union County, St. Peter's, Rev. Joseph W. McAleer, Pastor.
School-St. Peter's, 5 Ursuline Sisters. Pupils, High School 46, Graded School 112.
Mission-St. Francis, Henderson Co., St. Francis.

Whitesville, Daviess Co., St. Mary's of the Woods, Rev. Hugh O'Sullivan, Pastor.
School-St. Mary's, 6 Sisters of Charity of Nazareth. Pupils, High School 23, Graded School 200.
Mission-Sulphur Springs, Ohio Co., St. John the Baptist.

Institutions in Charge of Religious Communities

Owensboro, St. Frances Academy-Sisters of Charity of Nazareth. Sister Anna Louise Mattingly, Superior. Sisters 21. Pupils 555. Attended from St. Paul's.

St. Mary's Home-Ursuline Sisters. Attended from St. Stephen's.

Maple Mount, Mt. St. Joseph Motherhouse and Convent of the Ursuline Sisters. Mother M. Teresita Thompson, Mother Gerneral. Sisters in the Community 334. Novices 16; Postulants 4. Rev. Andrew C. Zoeller, Chaplain; Rev. Robert A. Whelan; Mt. St. Joseph Junior College and Academy. Sisters 22, Lay teachers 3. Pupils 110. Rev. Andrew C. Zoeller, Chaplain, Rev.

Paducah, St. Mary's Academy, 5th and Monroe Streets. Sisters of Charity of Nazareth, Sister Macrina, Superior. Sisters 18, Pupils 515. Attended from St. Francis de Sales Church.

St. Vincent, St. Vincent's Academy. Sisters of Charity of Nazareth. Sister Mary Leander, Superior. Sisters 20. Pupils 126. Attended from Sacred Heart Church.

Religious Communities of Men in the Diocese

C.S.C.-Fathers of the Holy Cross, Henderson.
C.PP.S.-Fathers of the Most Precious Blood-Axtel, Irvington, Hardinsburg, McQuady.

Recapitulation

Bishop	1
Diocesan Clergy	41
Religious Clergy	5
Total Clergy	46
Churches with Resident Priests	33
Missions with Churches	23
Total Churches	56
Chapels	5
Parochial Schools	29
Pupils	3,081
College	1
Parochial High Schools	7
Academies with Grade and High Schools	4
Pupils in College, Academy and High Schools	1,573
Total young people under Catholic care	4,654
Baptisms	
Infants	856
Adults	99
Total	955
Converts	96
Marriages	371
Deaths	381
Catholic Population	24,059

Well diggers working between St. Paul's Church and the Rectory.

Catholicity in Western Kentucky (1938-1987)

St. Mary of the Woods, McQuady, KY.

St. Lawrence School.

Introduction

The Seal of The Diocese of Owensboro

The clasped hands are taken from the great seal of the Commonwealth of Kentucky. Emblazoned upon the cross are the stones and Palm Branch of Victory which represent Saint Stephen, Protomartyr, the patron of the Diocese and of the Diocesan Cathedral.

St. Stephen was chosen by the Apostles as the first of the seven deacons (Acts 6:1-5). He was stoned to death at the instigation of the Sanhedrin and became the first Christian martyr. His dying prayer obtained the conversion of Saint Paul who was activly engaged in Saint Stephen's martyrdom.

This coat of arms was created for the Diocese by Pierre de Caignon la Rone.

Commenting on the subjective nature of historical writing Carl Lotus Becker, an American historian, once observed that a person could sit all day in the greatest library in the world and nothing in that library would present itself as "wanting to be known". Instead, the researcher, even when just browsing, makes choices about what is brought forth and what is to left for others to uncover. So it was with the writing of the following pages.

The history of the last fifty-six years of the Diocese of Owensboro is extensive, so much so that the file cabinets and shelves at the Diocesan Archives are already filled with materials relative to it, even though the archivist only began officially cataloging records in 1991.

What you will read on the following pages is a distillation of some of the documents found in the Catholic Pastoral Center Archives and in some other resource centers. The approach taken to the materials was to present their content in such a way that a reader could perceive the manner in which the Diocesan Church of Owensboro developed and the direction it charted for itself from the time of its establishment in 1937 to its Fiftieth Anniversary in 1987.

In the telling of this story of the Diocese, this section of the history centers primarily on the guidance given to the Diocese by the three Bishops who have shepherded the Diocese since its creation in 1937: Bishop Francis R. Cotton, Bishop Henry J. Soenneker and Bishop John J. McRaith. It was these people, together with their consultative advisory bodies and administrative staffs, who helped direct the Church of the Diocese of Owensboro in its own formation and in its response to local, regional and world affairs. It is to these people that we, the Church of the Diocese of Owensboro, owe a deep debt of gratitude for the loving stewardship they have shown in their willingness to follow the inspiration of the Holy Spirit in bringing us as Church from the era known in American History as the Depression to the present era, the threshold of the 21st Century.

Structuring the Diocese

As the Catholic laity left the Sunday celebration of Mass in the thirty-three parishes and nineteen missions of Western Kentucky on December 12, 1937, they observed the time honored tradition of gathering in little groups here and there on the church steps, along the street and in the parking lot to exchange news, inquire about relatives, admire new babies, set times for this or that gathering and, in general, take the pulse of the parish community. The economy, in its still depressed state, and the trauma of the great flood in the early months of the year had provided lots throughout 1937 about which to offer opinions and shake heads. But on this day, December 12, 1937, all those topics were put aside. This day was special. This day one topic dominated the conversations. At the Masses they had just attended, their parish priest had announced to them that the news they may have already learned from the newspaper or radio was true. They were all members of a new diocesan church, the Diocese of Owensboro, Kentucky.

The Diocese of Owensboro, according to *Universi Catholici Orbis* (12/9/37), the first of the papal letters issued by Pope Pius XI detailing the information about the new diocese, separated the following counties from the Diocese of Louisville: Ballard, Carlisle, Hickman, Fulton, McCracken, Graves, Livingston, Marshall, Calloway, Trigg, Lyon, Crittenden, Caldwell, Christian, Hopkins, Wester, Union, Henderson, Daviess, Hancock, McLean, Ohio, Muhlenberg, Butler, Todd, Logan, Breckinridge, Edmondson, Grayson, Warren, Simpson and Allen. It took the parishioners just one quick look at a Kentucky map to see that their new diocese, stretching from the Mississippi River to the eastern boundaries of Breckinridge, Edmondson and Grayson counties, included literally all of Western Kentucky.

Universi Catholici Orbis also answered two more questions for the parishioners. Like most other dioceses, the Diocese of Owensboro reflected the name of the city designated as the seat of the Diocese. In this case the designated city was Owensboro, located on the banks of the Ohio River in Daviess County. Owensboro was not only one of the fastest growing cities in Western Ketucky but it was also the home of one of the two largest parishes in that area. The church for this parish, St. Stephen's, became the new Cathedral Church.

Pope Pius XI's second letter dealing with the creation of the Diocese of Owensboro held more immediate interest for the people of Louisville than the people of Western Kentucky. This letter, *Quo Christifidelium Regime*, outlined the relationship that would continue to exist between the diocese of Owensboro and the diocese of Louisville. Pope Pius XI elevated the Diocese of Louisville to the status of an Archdiocese and constituted the newly created Diocese of Owensboro (as well as the dioceses of Covington, Kentucky and Memphis, Tennessee) as "a suffragren" of the Church of Louisville. Basically an administrative decree, this papal announcement made the new and future bishops of Owensboro subject to the metropolitan jurisdiction of the Archbishop of Louisville, who, at this time, turned out to be John A. Floersch, the 51 year old prelate who had already been serving in the capacity as Bishop of Louisville since 1924.

Finally, on December 16, 1937 Pope Pius XI issued the decree entitled *Dilecto Filio*. This was the letter that answered the question that was uppermost among the Catholic populations of the new diocese. It told them the name of their new bishop. The man upon whom Pius XI had bestowed the title of *First* Bishop of Owensboro. This man was the Most Reverend Francis Ridgely Cotton.

In the selection of Francis R. Cotton, Pope Pius XI had chosen a priest whose ministerial experience included the opportunity to become well acquainted with the challenges and possibilities of Western Kentucky as well as the administrative duties that would be required of a bishop. Bishop Cotton had gained first hand experience in Western Kentucky when he served as an assistant pastor for four years (1922-1926) at St. Francis de Sales parish in Paducah, Kentucky. Following that, his work as both assis-

MOST REV. BISHOP FRANCIS R. COTTON

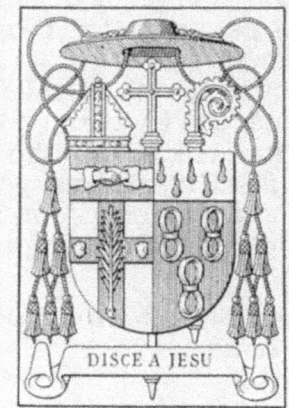

Courtesy of Brother Leo Willett, S.M. Marianist Provincialate

Birth: September 19, 1895, Bardstown, Kentucky
Baptism: October 4, 1895
Family: Only son of three children of Charles and Mary (Moore)
Education: Bethlehem Academy, Bardstown, KY (1903-1908); Valley Field Seminary, Canada (1908-1910); St. Meinrad Preparatory School, Indiana (1910-1915); Sulpician Seminary, Catholic University of America, Washington, D.C. (1917-1920); Applinaris University, Rome, Italy (1932-1934)

Ordination: June 17, 1920

Ministry: St. Joseph's Cathedral, Bardstown (June, 1920); St. Cecilia's Church, Louisville (1920-1922); St. Francis de Sales, Paducah (1922-1926)
(Missions: LaCenter, Hampton, Dyersburg, Mason Mill and St. Marys Academy)
Assistant Chancellor: Diocese of Louisville, (1926-1931)
Chancellor: Diocese of Lousville (1931-1937)
Bishop: Diocese of Owensboro (1937-1960)
Consecration as Bishop: February 24, 1938, Cathedral of the Assuption, Lousville, KY – Archbishop John A. Floresh, Presider
Installaton as Bishop: March 8, 1938, St. Stephen's Cathedral, Owensboro Archbishop John A. Floresh, Presider

Death: September 25, 1960, Owensboro, KY
Burial: Resurrection Cemetery, Owensboro, KY

St. Francis de Sales Parish, 1949. Rev. Francis R. Cotton served as assistant pastor at St. Francis de Sales, 1922-26. (Courtesy of the Mt. St. Joseph Archives)

FORTY MARTYRS
(Diocesan Priests Serving in Western KY at the time of the Creation of the Diocese)

Rev. Paul Barrett	Rev. James Higdon
Rev. Louis Beruatto	Rev. John M. Higgins
Rev. George Boehmicke	Rev. Raymond Hill
Rev. Wm. Borntraeger	Rev. Benedict Huff
Rev. C.P. Bowling	Rev. William B. Jarboe
Rev. Peter Braun	Rev. Joseph McAleer
Rev. Rudolph Carrico	Rev. James W. Mills
Rev. Lucian Clements	Rev. Martin Nahstoll
Rev. Charles DeNardi	Rev. James F. Norman
Rev. Leo Dienes	Rev. Hugh O'Sullivan
Rev. Pius Edelen	Rev. Edward Russell
Rev. Joseph Egan	Rev. Joseph Saffer
Rev. Robert Gipperich	Rev. Francis Smith
Rev. J. Glenn	Rev. Joseph Spalding
Rev. Paul Greenwell	Rev. Delphin Thomas
Rev. John Hallahan	Rev. Albert J. Thompson
Rev. Jolly P. Hayden	Rev. Anthony J. Tompkins
Rt. Rev. Thomas J. Hayes	Rev. Robert A. Whelan
Rev. Anthony Helling	Rev. Robert Wilson
Rev. Gilbert Henninger	Rev. A. C. Zoeller

tant chancellor (1921-31) and chancellor (1931-37) of the Diocese of Louisville kept him updated regarding the growth and the needs of the church in the western third of the state. It came as no surprise to Francis Cotton on March 8, 1938, as he was being installed as Bishop of Owensboro, that despite the tremendous progress since the pioneer days of Fr. Charles Nerinckx and Elisha Durbin, the new Diocese of Owensboro was still, in many respects, "mission territory".

After all, the Owensboro Diocese stretched across 12,502 square miles of mostly rural territory. (Even in 1993 only two cities in the diocese, Owensboro and Bowling Green, had populations exceeding 30,000!). To minister to the 24,000 plus Catholics scattered throughout that vast area in 1938 Bishop Cotton had the grand total of forty-four priests. Forty of these were diocesan priests, three were from the Precious Blood religious community in Atchinson, Kansas and one was from the Holy Cross Fathers religious order at South Bend, Indiana.

The forty diocesan priests, known in later years as the "40 Martyrs" were those who happened to be serving in the parishes of Western Kentucky at the time Pope Pius XI decreed the area separate from Louisville. The creation of the new diocese caught these priests by surprise and called them to serve in a diocese distant from their family members and friends. In spite of this, on the day of Bishop Cotton's installation, the priests through their spokesman, Rev. Charles Patrick Bowling, pledged their "best prayers, loyal support and cheerful cooperation" to their new bishop.

From these priests Bishop Cotton went about choosing the first administrative board for the Owensboro Diocese: the Vicar-General Rt. Rev. Msgr. Hugh O'Sullivan, the Body of Diocesan Consultors, Rev. James Francis Norman, Rev. Francis Joseph Smith, Rev. Paul C. Barrett, Rev. Charles Patrick Bowling and Rev. Andrew C. Zoeller; and the Diocesan Chancellor, Rev. Gilbert Henninger.

In reflection on his early years as bishop, Bishop Cotton probably counted the first two as some of the most challenging years he had ever experienced.

For instance, administratively there were some diocesan concerns that needed immediate attention if diocesan services were to continue without serious interruption in the transition years. It was for this reason that the Diocesan Consultors devoted time during their first meeting (9/30/38) to the issue of the administration and supervision of the Diocesan schools in Western Kentucky. They decided it would be in the best interests of the schools and of the Diocese to let them continue to operate under the supervision of the Louisville Archdiocesan system, which was led by Rev. Felix Pitt. This arrangement turned out to be one of long duration. It would only be in 1953 that the Owensboro Diocese would establish its own school system and name Rev. Raymond Hill, Vicar for Education.

Also in his initial year Bishop Cotton spent much of his time traveling to parishes, making himself personally acquainted with the needs of the individual parishes. A trip early in his episcopacy took him to St. Peter's, Stanley. At this parish, he indicated his interest in the pro-

Father Leo Dienes, Sr. Agnes Francis Osborne and Sr. Elizabeth Marie Sipes join the Stenson boys. Wagon transportation was the only means of transportation (besides walking and horseback or muleback) from the highway to St. James Church, Iberia (Grayson County). (Courtesy of Mt. St. Joseph Archives)

First Communion Day at St. James, Iberia. A mission church of St. Anthony, Peonia Ky. Mass was celebrated once per year. The mission church was started at St. James about 1822. (Courtesy of Mt. St. Joseph Archives)

motion of "good religious practices" and the promotion of Christian values among the youth of the diocese. At St. Peter's, Bishop Cotton announced to the school children that a Diocesan chapter of the Catholic Students Mission Crusade had been established for the Diocese of Owensboro. The C.S.M.C., a national Pontifical missionary society for young people had been founded by an Owensboro native, Rev. Jolly P. Hayden in 1918. Through participation in the organization youths learned concern for people in what in 1995 are called "third world" countries. They participated in leadership activities aimed at providing monies for relief of the underprivileged and for the envangelistic needs of missionaries. Young people in the C.S.M.C. developed public speaking skills through annual oratorical contests on issues relevant to people in mission countries and each year they gathered for a rally demonstrating their solidarity as "youthful evangelizers". Highly drilled in marching precision, they processed (singing hymns and/or reciting the Rosary) throughout the streets of the city hosting the rally. Rev. George Boehmicke, Director of the Society for the Propagation of the Faith, was also Director of the Catholic Students Mission Crusade.

Before Bishop Cotton celebrated the first anniversary of his installation he also experienced lessons in just how quickly crises could arise for the parishioners in the diocese. Tradegy struck in the Eastern part of the diocese when fire destroyed St. Anthony's Church in Peonia on October 27, 1938. Three months later it struck again in Daviess County when the school children at St. Elizabeth's school in Curdsville had to be evacuated at ten o'clock on the morning of January 30, 1939 as flames, starting in the chimney, spread through the two story frame school house. Happily in both instances temporary accomodations were available until the structures could be rebuilt.

For just a little over a year the people of St. Anthony's parish gathered for worship in their school while they built a new church. On November 28, 1940 Bishop Cotton joined these parishioners in dedicating and giving thanks for their new church, a church, remodeled in 1992, which still stands and serves the parish today.

The school children at Curdsville moved "across the street into the old school building" they had used prior to the one that had burned. The teachers for the school, MSJ Ursulines, moved back to the motherhouse convent at Maple Mount, KY (approximately 3 miles away) and commuted daily to their classrooms at Curdsville. This "temporary arrangement" lasted a little longer than initially anticipated. Being a numerically small parish and being located in the close proximity of other parish schools did not bode well for those trying to raise the funds to rebuild St. Elizabeth's. The new school did not become a reality until much later in 1955.

Another tradegy, this one of global proportion, that would directly and significantly impact the lives of every family of the Owensboro Diocese began the same year as the fire at St. Elizabeth's. On September 1, 1939 Germany invaded Poland and World War II began. Letters from Bishop Cotton to the parishes indicated that early in the spring of 1940 the bishops of America began conducting special national collections for aid for refugees and other victims of the war. In May of 1940 this collection became an annual collection. Later that same year a national day of prayer for peace was instituted. The initial national day of prayer, scheduled for September 8, the birthday of the Blessed Mother, was only the first of many such prayer days. In October, 1940 Pope Pius XII issued an encyclical, *Motu Proprio*, in which he asked Catholics throughout the world to offer prayers for the refugees, for prisoners and for a return of peace. Responding to the Pope's plea for public prayer, parishioners throughout the Owensboro Diocese came to their churches on Sunday, November 17, 1940 for holy hours. Convents within the diocese observed the prayer days with exposition of the Blessed Sacrament all day.

After the dreadful events of the Pearl Harbor bombing on December 7 and the consequent formal declaration of war by America on December 8, 1941 the effects of the war were experienced more and more personally in the families across the Diocese. In response to this personal suffering, the annual collection for the victims of war sharply increased. On May 26, 1942 the War Relief and Emergency collection exceeded one million dollars. Bishop Cotton wrote to the parishes explaining that:

"Much of this sum was disbursed through our Holy Father Pope Pius XII and known need was the only criteria for aid to refugees in Russia, Portugal, Italy, the Balkans; and to the starving, the ailing and in many cases the homeless in France, England, Croatia, Greece, Albania, Slovania, Belgium, Luxembourg, Holland, Poland, Lithuania and the Scandanavian Countries. To long suffering China, funds were sent directly through the American Red Cross, and refugees from all countries of the globe were aided by funds allocated to our Catholic Refugee Headquarters in New York City."

As reminders to keep the soldiers and their families in prayer Bishop Cotton urged every parish to display, in the entrance of the parish church, a placque bearing the names of the parishioners who were serving with the armed services during the war.

On September 15, 1942 Bishop Cotton visited the soldiers at Camp Campbell, one of the two military bases in Western Kentucky at the time. While there he gave the invocation at the activation ceremonies. Little did he know then that even three long years later, the war would still be in process and would be impacting even celebrative events in his personal life. Out of deference to the war situation no public ceremonies were held to commemorate Bishop Cotton's silver sacerdotal jubilee in September, 1945.

If the seemingly endless travel throughout the diocese (Remember! Even by car it was much more time consuming than it is today) and a world war were not enough to make the early years of Bishop Cotton's administration demanding, the task of making clergy appointments proved to be so. The difficulty in making the appointments stemmed not from the reluctance of priests to fulfill the offices to which they were appointed but to the untimely deaths of several priests shortly after their assignments to diocesan offices.

One such person was Rt. Rev. Msgr. Hugh O'Sullivan. Rt. Rev. Msgr. Hugh O'Sullivan, at the time of the establishment of the diocese, had the distinction of being the senior priest of diocese. Besides being the second oldest in age (Rt. Rev. Thomas J. Hayes was three months older.) Msgr. O'Sullivan also held the record for years of priestly ministry in Western Kentucky. In fact, his entire ordained ministry had been lived in the geographical area that in 1937 was designated as the Owensboro Diocese and all but eight and a half months of this ministry was spent in one parish, the parish of St. Mary of the Woods at Whitesville, Kentucky. Having begun serving in Western Kentucky immediately after his ordination, December 18, 1892, Msgr. O'Sullivan had not only "seniority status" but also an in-depth knowledge of the church of Western Kentucky. These factors were probably influential in his being chosen as Vicar General by Bishop Cotton. But the added duties, the travel involved in coming to the meetings with the Bishop, and the stress of helping to begin the structuring of the diocese was too much for the 79-year-old prelate. He died on July 26, 1938, just two months and twenty-three days after his appointment.

After the death of Msgr. O'Sullivan the office of Vicar General remained vacant until February 8, 1939 when Bishop Cotton named one of his already appointed Consultors to fill the position. Rev. Charles Patrick Bowling served as Vicar General from that time until 1947 when he moved from St. Paul's parish in Owensboro to St. Joseph's parish in Bowling Green, Kentucky.

A replacement also had to be found for Rev. James Frances Norman. Appointed to the Body of Consultors on August 13, 1938, Fr. Norman brought the experience of having served at five parishes or missions in Western Kentucky as well as four parishes in Louisville. He did not, however, get to share much of this experience with other members of the Body of Consultors. On November 2, 1938, not even three months after his appointment, Fr. Norman suffered a severe heart attack and died enroute by ambulance to St. Joseph Infirmary, Louisville. He was sixty-three years of age.

Though younger than most of the others appointed as Consultors, Fr. Francis Joseph Smith also turned out to be a "short term Consultor". He served at only two parishes in the Owensboro Diocese: St. Ann's parish in Morganfield and Holy Name parish in Henderson. No doubt two of the reasons he had been chosen as a Consultor were because he offered insights concerning the fast growing parishes west of Daviess County and because he

St. Francis Academy and Auditorium, Owensboro. The oldest high school in Western KY, established in 1849. (Courtesy of C.P.C Archives, Diocese of Owensboro)

Rt. Rev. Msgr. Hugh O'Sullivan (1858-1938). First Vicar-General for the Diocese of Owensboro.

Rev. James Francis Norman (1875-1938). Pastor at St. Romuald's, Hardinsburg; St. Peter's, Waverly and St. Paul's, Owensboro.

Rev. Francis Joseph Smith (1895-1939). Pastor at St. Ann's, Morganfield and Holy Name Church, Henderson.

Rev. Jolly P. Hayden (1890-1941). Pastor at St. Agnes, Uniontown and chaplain at St. Mary's Academy, Paducah.

represented the younger clergy. He was on the Body of Consultors long enough to help advise regarding the setting of the first priorities for the diocese, but he was not there to see any of them come to completion. Only forty-four years of age, Fr. Smith died on June 27, 1939 at St. Mary's Hospital, Evansville, Indiana. At the time of his death he had been ordained for twenty years, ministered in Western Kentucky for approximately six and a half years and had served as a Consultor for the Owensboro Diocese only nine and one half months.

Rev. Lucian E. Clements (1872-1942). Pastor at St. William's Knottsville; St. Ambrose, Union County; Immaculate Conception, Earlington.

These deaths meant not only the reappointment of people to the offices that were key offices on which the Bishop depended for advice from his local clergy, but also the naming of new pastors, the switching of parish administrators, etc. And the difficulty of the task was compounded even more by the deaths of three other priests within the first five years after the establishment of the Diocese.

One of these was Rev. Anthony Helling, a native of Westphalia, Germany, who served for thirty-two (1906-38) years as pastor and pastor emeritus for St. Elizabeth's parish in Clarkson, Kentucky and its six missions. Of those 32 years, Fr. Helling did not have the opportunity to complete one full year in the newly created Owensboro Diocese. The seventy-five year old prelate died November 13, 1938.

Rev. Jolly Paschal Hayden was another of the "40 Martyrs" who early on claimed his crown of eternal glory. Born in Daviess County, Kentucky, Fr. Hayden was one of "Owensboro's own" and a classmate of Fr. Joseph Smith's. He began his priestly ministry in Western Kentucky in 1935 as pastor of St. Agnes Church in Uniontown, Kentucky but had to take a sick leave from 1938-1941. While on sick leave he briefly served as chaplain at St. Mary's Academy in Paducah. Then the seriousness of his illness forced him into semi-retirement. He moved to Mount St. Joseph and from there began assisting on weekends at Holy Name in Henderson. It was on one of these weekend visits to Henderson that he died on January 5, 1941.

The *Record*, *The Owensboro-Messenger Inquirer* and *The Lebanon Enterprise* all carried articles and editorials eulogizing Fr. Jolly Hayden. The one theme that dominated the reflections on his life was that of his leadership in not only Church affairs but also in civic and community affairs. While still a seminarian he initiated the first national convention for the organization of the Catholic Students Mission Crusade. As a priest engaged in rural ministry at Holy Cross, Kentucky from 1919-1935 he became a pioneer in the rural cooperative movement. His contributions to this movement were nationally recognized when he was called to be one of the speakers at the first National Rural Life Congress.

Accounts of his civic affairs also indicate that Fr. Jolly Hayden encouraged the building of a community library and gymnasium for the people of Holy Cross and campaigned for hard-surfaced roads and an improved highway system in Marian County, Kentucky. This involvement and interest in petitioning for the betterment of the transportation system was not entirely unrelated to Fr. Hayden's priestly ministry. He pursued this improvement in order that students in the rural areas could more easily have access to education. Toward this same end he consolidated school units in the Holy Cross area and employed busses for the transportation of students.

Fr. Hayden was equally know for his Christian charity as is indicated in the following example supplied by Ramona Bedwell of White Plains, Kentucky at the time of Fr. Hayden's death. "After having a wreck near Henderson on September 8, 1940, Fr. Hayden brought us home (70 miles) and wouldn't accept any pay. We were total strangers. All the way home that painful night I thanked God for putting such a fine man on earth. He was certainly a friend in need."

Another Daviess County native, Father Lucian E. Clements, from Knottsville, KY was the sixth priest to die in the Owensboro diocese. After serving at St. Joseph in Mayfield, Kentucky (with its missions in Fulton, Hickman and Columbus, Kentucky) from 1898-1902, Fr. Clements returned to the parish in which he was baptized, St. Lawrence, Kentucky. He remained there until 1914, after which he became a part of the church history of St. William's in Knottsville, St. Ambrose in Union County and Immaculate Conception in Earlington, Kentucky. Fr. Clements was a recognized "remodeler" of churches—having made improvements at Hickman, Mayfield, St. Lawrence and Earlington. He was also known for being able to raise the funds for remodling and other parish projects and for seeing to it that the parishes were kept out of debt. This feat he accomplished in spite of the fact that some of the parishes in which he worked were recognized as "poor parishes".

Having completed twenty-three years in ministry at his last pastoral assignment, Immaculte Conception, Erlington, Fr. Lucian Clements retired in 1939 at the age of 67. (The Diocese was not yet two years old!) The illness that brought on his retirement would claim his life approximately three years later. Fr. Lucian Clements died November 2, 1942.

Bishop Cotton was able to breathe a sign of relief in that in the same first five years of the diocese, the number of priests ordained to minister in the Owensboro Diocese exceeded by four the number of those who died. Holding the distinction of "the first priest to be ordained" in the Owensboro Diocese was Father Anthony George Higdon. Other "junior clergy" joining him within the next four years were Fathers Victor Boarman and Thomas Libs in 1939; Father Robert Connor, Clarence Pettit and Francis Ward in 1940; Charles Saffer, Henry O'Bryan and Joseph Rhodes in 1941; and William McAtee in 1942.

It would be these priests, along with the remnant of the "40 Martyrs", the religious order priests serving in the Diocese and Bishop Cotton who would gather on February 22, 1943 to establish the Law for the Diocese of Owensboro.

The idea of the Synod first began to take shape at the June 7, 1941 meeting of the Diocesan Consultors. The Consultors unanimously agreed with Bishop Cotton that a synod "would further the good of religion...and serve to better unify us of the Diocese in spirit and practice." In the letters of convocation for the Synod, Bishop Cotton explained that the Synod would enact legislation deemed "necessary or useful for the general welfare of religion in the Diocese."

It is important to note that this Synod was being called at a time in Church history when the Roman Catholic Church was very patriarchal and heirarchical in structure. A popular graphic symbol used for the structure of the composition of the Church was that of the pyramid with the Pope at the pinnacle of the pyramid, the bishops on the next level, the priests on the next level and the laity at the base of the pyramid. This view was still prevalent in the 1940s partially because the priests were the only people within the Catholic Church, with perhaps a few exceptions, formally educated in theology, church law and Scripture studies.

With this being the commonly accepted concept of the Church it is not difficult to understand why at the First Synod in the Diocese of Owensboro, the only people called to participate in any active roles were Bishop Cotton, the Diocesan priests and the priests of religious orders who happened to be serving in the Diocese at the time.

The topics addressed by the laws and regulations that were adopted at this Synod were both diverse and comprehensive. With respect to the clergy, for instance, the laws dealt with specifics ranging from the clerical garb that should be worn by priests to rules forbidding priests to mingle in politics or to hear the confessions of women without a grating between the penitent and the confessor. For purposes of greater communication and consultation the Snyod also divided the diocese into the Eastern, Western and Central Deaneries. (In later years, as population centers shifted and transportation routes changed, the jurisdictional boundaries of the Deaneries would be moved and three more Deaneries—the Bowling Green, Rural and Owensboro Deaneries—would be created.) The duties of the Deans and the Pastors, including duties relative to the administering of the sacraments, the scheduling of the times for Masses and the laws pertaining to mixed marriages, were all spelled out in detail by the Synod.

The Synod also issued statutes and recommendations concerning the observance of sacred places and seasons and divine worship. Under the heading "Divine Worship" were listed numerous devotions. Typical devotions every parish was instructed to offer included: two days of weekly devotions during Lent (a sermon one evening and the Way of the Cross on another evening); the public recitation of the Consecration to the Sacred Heart on the feasts of Christ the King and the Sacred Heart; a novena to the Holy Spirit in preparation for Pentecost; daily devotions to the Blessed Mother during May; and the daily recitation of the Rosary, the Litany of the Blessed Virgin and the prayer "To Thee, O Blessed Joseph" during October. The devotions were promoted so religiously throughout the diocese that people later had difficulty separating devotional prayer from the liturgical and sacramental prayer of the Church.

To promote the knowledge of the Church teachings the Synod called priests to arrange their sermons so that every parish was taught the matter of the Catechism of the Council of Trent at least once every five years. The section on Church teachings in the regulations adopted by the Synod also specified that "Catholics should not attend non-Catholic or undenominational schools nor schools that are mixed, that is open to non-Catholics." Exceptions to this rule could be granted only by the Bishop.

This first Synod in the diocese also set the priests' salary at the sum of $1500.00 annually. In addition to this amount priests were allowed to accept stipends or offerings for Masses but were cautioned that services rendered were not to be dependent upon the payment of a stipend. Rather, services were still to be graciously given to those who were unable or unwilling to make the regular offering. For planning purposes the Appendix to the Synod Book of Regulations also included the dates for the celebration of the Forty Hours in each parish. And, for handy reference, there was included a copy of the Legion of Decency Pledge that was to be recited publicly and "on their knees," by the priests and the faithful on the Sunday following the feast of the Immaculate Conception.

Though just a few of the laws, regulations and recommendations have been mentioned above, the significance of the role of this Synod in the lives of the people of the Diocese of Owensboro should never be minimized. It created a handbook of standards for the religious practice of the people of the Diocese. Once the regulations were set in place, their uniform application and observance across the diocese was expected by the Bishop. It was the strict adherence to these laws that later gained Bishop Cotton the reputation of being "a man who did not know the meaning of compromise. He was personally a kind man, who, no doubt, thought it necessary to carry out the provisions of strictness, perhaps even with severity. In charting a safe course, he ran a tight ship."

"But," Rev. George Boemicke added years later when reflecting on this characterization of Bichop Cotton by *The Record*, "one thing you can say for Bishop Cotton is that he was fair. He never asked anybody to do anything that he did not require of himself."

That he required much of himself is evident in the progress that was made during the years that he adminsitered the diocese as Bishop.

Between 1939 and 1960 (the year Bishop Cotton died) 23 parochical schools throughout the Diocese either opened their doors for the first time or received new classrooms. This tremendous push for a modern, competitive educational system was due to several factors.

To begin with the number of students for enrollment in parochial schools kept pace with the baby boomer age of the late 40s and early 50s. When Bishop Cotton made his five year "Ad limina" visit to Rome in 1959 he noted that enrollment in the parochial schools had increased from 7,182 in 1949 to 8,694 in 1952 and to 10,451 in 1958. He also reported that one half or more of the 598 Catholic children who were of school age but were not enrolled in Catholic schools lived in places were Catholic schools were not accessible.

These 1958 figures plus a 1952 report from Rev. Felix Pitt, the Superintendent of the Archdiocesan School Board, indicated that Catholic education was either a high priority for the people of the Owensboro Diocese or that they took seriously the Synod regulation requiring that they send their children to the Catholic schools. Fr. Pitt wrote that a whopping "93.5% of the students enrolled in Catholic schools were receiving Catholic education from the first through the twelfth grades."

That this was a time of relative prosperity even for a rural diocese such as the Owensboro one is attested to by the fact that in 1959 when the Bishop wrote to the parishes encouraging their first time participation in a Diocesan canvass (capital fund drive) he noted that between 1937 and 1959 the Diocesan office had issued to the parishes one thousand eighty-seven notes ranging in amounts from $500 to $100,000. Despite this tremendous flow of cash the Chancellor of the Diocese during this time had never found it necessary to borrow monies from the bank or from financial agencies. The loans given were also either interest free or, at times, depending on the need, outright gifts to the parishes. This financial prosperity, which incidentally was due to the continous, generous giving of the parishioners to Diocesan collections and to the remembrance of the Diocesan church in the bequests of the people of the Diocese, was a second factor that permitted the tremendous building program that existed in the Diocese particularly in the 1950s, a period that was one of national prosperity as well.

Besides being a beneficiary of grant monies from the Catholic Extension Society (because the Owensboro Diocese was a rural diocese), another financial "break" that allowed for the tremendous expansion of schools at this time was the fact that the parochial schools were staffed by members of religious orders.

All of the following religious communities played a role in the educational system of the Owensboro Diocese: the Sisters of Charity of Nazareth, Ky; the Ursuline Sisters of Mount St. Joseph, Maple Mount, Ky; the Dominican Sisters of St. Catherine, Ky; the Mercy Sisters from the Cincinnati, Ohio province; the Sisters of

RIGHT REVEREND ANTHONY GEORGE HIGDON

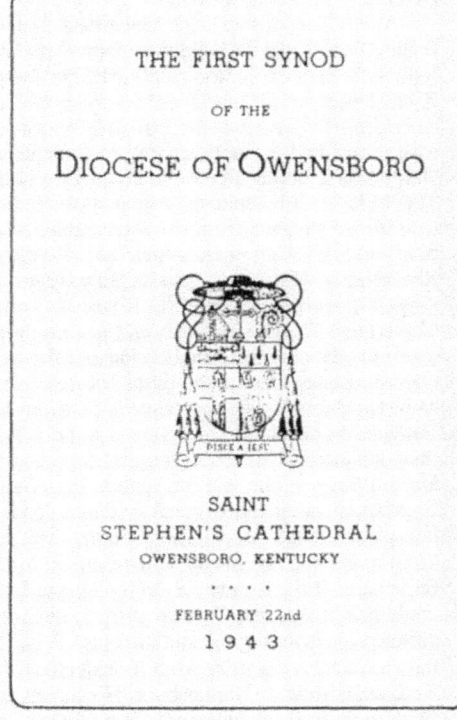

Rt. Rev Anthony George Higdon, the first priest ordained in the Owensboro Diocese, was ordained on June 11, 1938. Born on August 14, 1911 at St. Lawrence, KY, he was the eldest son of Estill and Henrietta Higdon; recieved his educaiton at St. Lawrence School and St. Meinrad Seminary; and served in the paristhes of Holy Name at Henderson, St. Francis deSales at Paducah, St. Paul and St. Stephen at Owensboro, St. Columba at Lewisport, St. Sebastian at Calhoun, Immaculate Conception at Hawesville, Our Lady of Perpetual Help at Patesville, St. John Evangelist at McCracken County, and St. Pius X at Calvert City. His last ministry was as chaplain at Carmel Home in Owensboro where he died August 19, 1992 at the age of 81.

Father Higdon represented the priests of the diocese in numerous capacities. He was Dean of Owensboro and the Western Deaneries. He was also a docesan Consultor. In 1971 he received the honorary title of Monsignor. Msgr. Higdon also served as the state chaplain of the Daughters of Isabella.

The Diocese of Owensboro has had only two Synods: 1943 and 1992.

St. Thomas More School, Paducah (1948). One of the schools from the "building boom" in the late 40s and early 50s.

Loretto, Loretto, Ky; and the Sisters of St. Francis of Milwaukee, Wis. The Glenmary Home Missioners were also working in the diocese at this time offering religious education in the places in which there were no Catholic schools. The Sisters were known for their professionalism in school administration and class-room teaching as well as for their willingness to teach for very little monetary compensation. From 1939 to 1960 the typical salary paid a teacher who was a member of a religious community was $500 per year. In addition to this salary, most parishes provided living quarters for the Sisters.

With the educational system off to such a good start, Bishop Cotton began work on more educational goals for the Owensboro Diocese. On July 27, 1953 the Owensboro Diocese assumed supervision for its own Diocesan Schools. Rev. Raymond G. Hill became the first Superintendent of Education for the Diocese of Owensboro.

Msgr. Hill, as he would later be called by almost everyone in the diocese (He was given the honorary title of Monsignor on April 19, 1959 in recognition of this work for the Church in Western Kentucky), found he had a ready ally and supporter of Catholic education in Sister Christina Echmans, OSU. At the time he was named Superintendent of the Owensboro Diocesan Schools, Sr. Christina was given charge of the newly created teacher education program at Brescia College, the only Catholic co-ed four-year liberal arts college in the tri-state area from St. Louis, Mo. to Louisville, Ky.

The establishment of Catholic higher education in Owensboro had been one of Bishop Cotton's early dreams. He convinced the Ursuline Sisters at Mount St. Joseph to move their junior college from its Maple Mount, Ky location to a "downtown" setting in Owensboro. As it took steps to re-locate, the college had broadened its junior college curriculum to that of a four year baccalaurate degree program and, in 1950, the college received a new name, Brescia College, in honor of the town in which St. Angela Merici, the foundress of the Ursuline religious Community, had lived in Italy. With its education department, Brescia College began awarding degrees and certification not only to many religious Sisters but also to lay people who were beginning to take their place in the Diocesan educational system.

Another major step in the educational system for the Diocese was the building of four secondary schools for the area. St. Romuald's in Hardinsburg, Ky recieved a new high school to replace its out dated one. However, when it opened in 1952 it did so not as a high school just for the students of Hardinsburg, but as a consolidated high school. That is, it offered secondary school opportunities to Catholic students from the surrounding rural parishes: St. Anthony's, Axtel; St. Theresa's, Rhodelia; St. Mary's, McQuady; Holy Guardian Angels', Irvington; and St. Rose of Lima, Cloverport. That the parishes and parents were determined to obtain a Catholic education for their children was evident in the obstacles they overcame to achieve it. For the people of St. Rose, for instance, the obstacle to overcome was the lack of transportation for the students from Cloverport to Hardinsburg. The public school system in Cloverport was an independent system instead of being part of the Breckinridge County system. Their busses did not link up with the busses in the other parts of the county. Even though students could ride busses into Cloverport from the farms surrounding it, the high school students still had to have a system in place that would transfer them the next twelve miles to Hardinsburg. Not having the funds to immediately purchase a bus of their own, the parish contracted with two local taxi drivers to provide transportation for the high school students. When the funds became available, a bus was purchased for this purpose.

Another consolidated high school that was built at this time was Owensboro Catholic High School. In Bishop Cotton's eyes, the building of Owensboro Catholic High School was a tremendous tribute to the people of Owensboro and Daviess County. He started the drive to provide this "modern educational plant" in November of 1949. The school was to serve the parishes of Owensboro, Brown's Valley, Rome, Sorgho and Stanley. Under the leadership of Harry E. Baumgarten and V. J. Steel, Jr. the parishes conducted a fund raising campaign with a goal of $500,000. The dedication and blessing of the new school located at 1524 Parish Avenue was held September 11, 1951.

The opening of Owensboro Catholic was for some a bittersweet achievement. Building and opening it also meant the closing of St. Francis Academy, the oldest high school in Owensboro.

St. Frances Academy had been established in 1849 by the Charity Sisters of Nazareth. The Sisters of Charity would continue to serve at Owensboro Catholic High School, as they would in two other newly built secondary schools, St. Mary in Whitesville (1955) and Holy Name in Henderson (1951). In both Whitesville and Henderson the new buildings replaced older facilities.

Of all the other schools built during this time special note needs to be made of three. Recognizing the need for an outreach to miniorities, but being prevented by the Day Law of 1904 to permit the integration of the Negro students with the students of the Caucasion race, the diocese opened three schools for blacks. The first "Colored School" in the diocese was opened at 5th and Plum Streets in September, 1940 and Blessed Sacrament Chapel was also located near this area in 1946. The second was in Waverly, Ky in 1944 and, lastly, Rosary Chapel and School were established in Paducah on August 2, 1947.

Just three years after the establishment of Rosary Chapel, the Day Law was finally repealed. It had applied to all the educational levels, kindergarten through graduate schools. Its repeal did not mean automatic integration in the public school system. However, the Catholic schools were quick to permit integration. (Mrs. Christina R. Smith enrolled at Brescia College and received her bachelor's degree in 1956.)

The term "modern" as applied to the high schools built in this diocese in the 1950s described the physical plant and the instructional techniques. There was one characteristic in these schools that was not evident in the public school system. It had to do with the "social mix" of the sexes. Coeducational school systems were not approved by the Holy See. The question of co-educational systems was even a matter for the annual clergy conference at St. Maur's monastery in 1957. The school system recommended by the Holy See was a co-institutional system in which there were separate classrooms for the girls and boys and the facilities such as the library and laboratories were used by them at different hours of the day. Since there was only one non-coed secondary school in the Owensboro Diocese, and that was the academy at Mount St. Joseph, the parish priests went away from their conference taking the word back to their parishes that the girls and boys were to be kept separate whenever possible (girls on one side of the room, boys on the other, etc.) Bishop Cotton had to explain in his report to the Holy See the reasons the Diocese could not finance co-institutional systems.

Education was not the only "system" that received attention during this period. Bishop Cotton felt strongly that there was a need for a

Catholic health care system for the diocese. Toward this goal he worked to secure hospitals throughout the Diocese. Construction plans for an 80 bed hospital at the site of Ford Avenue and Robin Road in Owensboro were purposed as early as 1944, but with construction materials still being limited due to the war, there was a delay in the building process. Even though Catholics within Owensboro and Daviess County were encouraged to raise funds for the hospital, the Sisters of Mercy in Cincinnati, who, at the invitation of the Bishop, were to operate the hospital, contributed $388,000 toward the completion of the project. On January 8, 1948, Sr. Mary Leonard Byrne, RSM began the task of ordering the supplies to furnish the new facility which was formally dedicated on Febuary 22, 1948. After just ten years of offering hospital care the capacity of the hospital was all but doubled in 1958 with the addition of a second wing that provided 75 additional beds.

In other parts of the diocese the Catholic health system was provided by the growing number of Catholic doctors practicing in the area; a hospital operated by the Mercy Sisters at Morganfield on the property of the old Vaughn Clinic (This hospital was in operation from 1945 to 1970.); and, another hospital, Lourdes Hospital, located in the western part of the Diocese.

Lourdes Hospital became a possibility when the city of Paducah offered to sell its city hospital at the corner of 4th and Clay Streets. The Roman Catholic Diocese of Owensboro placed a bid of $503,251 for Riverside Hospital. This bid, together with a twenty year agreement to a 41% discount on city charity hospitalization cases to which Riverside Hospital was already committed, was accepted by the Paducah City Council.

It was this hospital to which Bishop Cotton referred when he launched the 1959 five year financial canvass of the diocese. At that time he explained some of the "diocesan" needs that were over and above the local parish needs. Such needs included: "The purchase of a very fine hospital; the erection of a chapel, cafeteria and dorm for Brescia, two absolutely necessary fully new parish plants and a retreat house for ladies."

Renamed Lourdes Hospital when the Sisters of St. Francis of Tiffin, Ohio assumed the administration of the hospital on September 15, 1959, the hospital prospered and was accredited by the Joint Commission on Accreditation of Hospitals.

Another form of health care was provided in the Diocese with the building of Carmel Home, a facility designed to offer care for the retired and the infirmed. Bishop Cotton had persuaded the diocese to purchase 15 acres of land that had become available in 1951. What he bought then was considered fifteen acres of "farm land" in the Southeast section of Owensboro. It did not take the city of Owensboro long to build around the site on Old Hartford Road where, in collaboration with Mother M. Francis of the Carmelite Sisters of the Divine Heart of Jesus, the diocese built a two story brick home for the aged. Placed under the careful direction of Mother Mary Waltrudis, the 47 bed home opened its doors on August 15, 1952. Today it still welcomes people into a Catholic atmosphere in which, assured of both spiritual and physical care, they can live their senior years with dignity.

Finally, another institution that Bishop Cotton encouraged to move to the Owensboro Diocese was a community which would witness to the Diocese through their prayer and solitude. The Passionist nuns, a cloistered community from Scranton, PA sought permission to open a monastery in Owensboro in 1946. When Bishop Cotton assured them that they would be received warmly, they opened St. Joseph Monastery at 1420 Benita Avenue, a then quiet section of the city around which there was a minimum of industrial and residential activity.

Members of the diocese who later entered this Passionist community are Sister Margaret Mary Mattingly, Knottsville; Sisters Rose Mary and Rita Marie Boteler, Knottsville; Sister Marie Michael Aull, Knottsville; Sister Ann Miriam Mills, Owensboro; Sister Mary Elizabeth Sauer, Sorgho; Sister Ruth Marie Carrico, Owensboro; Sister Mary Therese Seitz, Paducah; and Sister Mary Magdalen Wurth, Paducah.

The Passionists were not the only religious community wanting to locate within the diocese. In 1954 South Union became the site at which the Benedictine monks opened St. Maur's Priory and Seminary. Here and at the Passionist Monastery the people of the diocese found opportunities for private and, in the case of St. Maur's Priory, conference led retreats. Many of the Owensboro diocesan priests recieved their theological studies at the St. Maur's (later called St. Mark's) seminary.

Four years later (1958) the Sisters of the Lamb of God also sought permission to open a foundation within Owensboro. Even though their motherhouse was located in France, the Lamb of God Sisters, an order of Sisters devoted to social work and with an unique membership which provided for the inclusion of physically handicapped applicants, had ties to Owensboro prior to establishing a house here. Two Owensboro natives, Sister Mary Thomas Simon and Sister Mary Herbert Woodward became members of the community after having met Sister Mary John as she visited parishes to acquaint the people of the Diocese with the Lamb of God community.

1958-59 was in many ways a pivotal year for the Diocese of Owensboro. On October 9, 1958 the Catholic world was saddened by the death of Pope Pius XII. Bishop Cotton had known Pope Pius XII personally—having made many "Ad limina" visits to him. Bishop Cotton reported "Many of those who have been in a position to observe Pope Pius XII at close range and over a long period of time, have been so impressed, not only by his many virtues and simple holiness of life that they predict that history will probably proclaim him to have been one of the most learned, noble and holy of the Roman Pontiffs."

Shortly thereafter, on October 30, 1958, Bishop Cotton wrote again to the priests of the

The first diocesan-wide fund drive (1959-1962). Canvass Committee Members. Seated-left to right- Randal Carrico, Thomas Meshew, Adam Schmitz, Clarence Elliott, Father Pettit, J. Harold Elliott, Bernard Rule, Harold Cash, and Nicholas De Mareo. Standing-first row- Frank Carrico, Leo Willett, Harry Kempf, C. W. Elliott, Rudy Cash and E. A. Ross. Standing-second row- John Riley, Thomas Hobbs, Frank Rhodes, Houston Carrico, David Stahr, Bobby Rodgers, and Louis Cash.

WE WILL DO IT BY:

FAITH . . . in the ability of every family of St. Joseph Parish to support our canvass.

PRAYER . . . offered every day that our canvass will be successful; that God will give to each of us the strength to know and to do our part.

SACRIFICE . . . Our pledge must be more than convenient, comfortable donations. They must represent SACRIFICE.

. . . Thus it will be done.

HAROLD CASH

"The church is supported by sacrifice"

diocese announcing that John XXIII had been elected and would be crowned Pope on November 4, 1958. Parishes were invited to hold an evening Mass that day (in order to accommodate those who had to work and could not be present at an earlier time.) The evening Mass was not to be before 4:00 p.m. and not later than 6:00 p.m. Bishop Cotton reiterated in his letter a summary of the four main points of Pope John XXIII's first address after his election. This pope, who later would throw open the windows of the church in order to let the Holy Spirit breeze through, let his first address to the world be one of a call for peace. He asked that persecutions cease, that freedom be restored to all peoples, that peace and tranquillity be allowed to exist world-wide and that the leaders of all nations work toward such goals.

1958-59 was also the year for the great Sesquicentennial celebration for Catholicity in Kentucky. In the Owensboro Diocese the celebration, coordinated and directed by Rev. George Boemicke, consisted of what the *Messenger and Inquirer* termed one of the most spectacular productions ever shown here. It was a pageant involving students from every parish in the Diocese. The students were all members of the C.S.M.C. Their pageant took the place of the traditional marching rally. The grand celebration began with a 10:30 a.m. Solemn Pontifical Mass. Then came the pageant - made colorful with elaborate costuming and stage settings - which depicted the history of the Catholic Church in Kentucky. Over 1,500 students took part in the drama that was narrated in prose, poetry, song and pantomine. During the pageant some 5,000 children sang responses. At the conclusion of the pageant models of the churches and schools in the Owensboro Diocese were placed on a large floor map that had been spread out in the Owensboro Sportscenter. Then girls from Owensboro Catholic High and Mount St. Joseph formed a cross which filled the entire Sportscenter area. This pageant was undoubtly one of the greatest highlights of Bishop Cotton's 21 years as Bishop of Owensboro.

A little more than a year after he sat in the audience at the C.S.M.C. pageant and watched the history of the Church in Kentucky, including that of the Diocese that he had personally done so much to structure and nourish, literally march before his eyes, Bishop Francis R. Cotton died. The date was September 20, 1960.

Two words that would be repeated over and over in the eulogies given him were "builder" and "organizer." But perhaps the best characterization was that given by Most Rev. Henry J. Grimmelsman, Bishop of Evansville, as he delivered the sermon at Bishop Cotton's funeral. Bishop Cotton was, Bishop Grimmelsman said, "loyal." Loyalty calls for <u>dedication</u> and it was dedication that Bishop Cotton exemplified for people of the Diocese. Dedication was what he expected from the church of Owensboro - dedication to their God, to their faith, to their church and to their own personal growth. Dedication was the resounding response the Diocese of Owensboro gave between 1937 and 1960.

The planning, financing and building of schools, churches, hospitals, homes for the aged, and new monasteries; the participation in liturgical and devotional worship; and the enrollment in and giving service through parish societies such as the Altar Society, Holy Name Society, Sodality, Legion of Mary, St. Vincent de Paul Society, Knights of Columbus, Holy Childhood Society, or Catholic Students Mission Crusade; all of this required dedication on the part of the people—the laity, the priests and religious working together—the Church of the Diocese of Owensboro.

Architects' sketch for Our Lady of Mercy Hospital, dedicated on Febuary 22, 1948.

Shirley McCauley-Bunch was the first senior to graduate from Rosary Chapel High School... She attended Rosary School from the 1st to the 12th grade!

Sister Marie Bernadette. The Passionists sought to open a monastery in Owensboro in 1946.

Scene from the C.S.M.C pageant held at the Sportscenter in Owensboro in 1959. The pageant was held to mark the Sesquicentennial of Catholicity in Kentucky.

Planting the Seeds of Change

The story is told that when fifty-six year old Rev. Henry J. Soenneker, the spiritual director for St. John's seminary in Collegeville, Minnesota, received a letter marked "Confidential" from the Apostolic Delegate in Washington, D.C., he dropped to his knees fearing that he had done something wrong. After reading the contents of that March 15, 1961 letter he knelt down by his desk again. This second time he was asking for the grace to be a willing servant. The letter told him that he had been chosen by Pope John XXIII to be the second Bishop of the Diocese of Owensboro. Bishop Soenneker, in telling this story on himself, added that he knew then that "I needed to pray as I never had before."

His prayer must have been heard. In 1981, when Bishop Soenneker celebrated his Twentieth Anniversary as the episcopal leader of the Diocese of Owensboro, he would be complimented by Protestants throughout the Owensboro Diocese for his advancement in ecumenical understanding among the various denominational churches and Catholics would describe him as a "people's bishop" who listened to the concerns of his priests and people. His own chief administrator, Rt. Rev. Gilbert Henniger, the Vicar-General for the Owensboro Diocese, would add that he was also a "priest's bishop".

The Church in the Owensboro Diocese needed a listener during the 1960s and 1970s. America became engaged in combat throughout Southeast Asia; many Americans would question the "rightness" [morality] of the war. People would voice their opposition to the war in protests ranging from the burning of draft cards and marching in the streets to fleeing to Canada when they feared their status as "consciencious objectors" would be rejected.

At times these protests became violent. R.O.T.C. buildings were burned. There were clashes between protesters and police. Then in 1970 America was shocked as protesters were fired upon and killed by National Guardsmen at Kent State University in Ohio and at Jackson State University in Mississippi.

The Civil Rights Act and the Voters' Rights Bill were finally passed by the U. S. Congress in 1964. But only four years later, Martin Luther King, Jr., the man who had started the non-violent protests for civil rights for blacks with the bus boycott in Montgomery, Alabama and who had dreamed that he would see the day when his people were "free at last," was assassinated.

The Nation's first Catholic President, John F. Kennedy, was elected. Unfortunately, he and his brother, who also campaigned for that high office, were assassinated.

It was a time when the space age (which had been launched as we tried to stay one step ahead of the Soviet Union—scientifically and militarily—during the Cold War and during the prosperous late 1950s) entered a whole new era with Neil Armstrong's giant step on the moon.

At this same time the poverty levels for single parent families and others in the lower economic strata of America began to drop tremendously and America's homeless took on the new face of "families" for the first time since the depression.

It was a time of young people dropping out of school and church and dropping into LSD and other drugs.

In the early 1960s, one out of four marriages ended in divorce. (The upward trend would continue until statistics would reflect one out of three marriages ending in divorce.)

The Cuban missile crisis reminded everyone that atomic and nuclear weapons, designed to be the deterrents to war, could be used offensively, even against the United States.

Great moral questions were raised concerning the value of life itself. *Roe vs. Wade* ushered in legalized abortions within the United States and the emergence of the Hemlock Society made it almost fashionable to think of suicide as the solution to living with terminal or debilitating illnesses.

The Church of the Owensboro Diocese also needed a listener who would understand as they wondered aloud about all the changes in the Church that were the result of the work of the Catholic bishops of the world assembled together at the Second Vatican Council.

MOST REV. BISHOP HENRY J. SOENNEKER

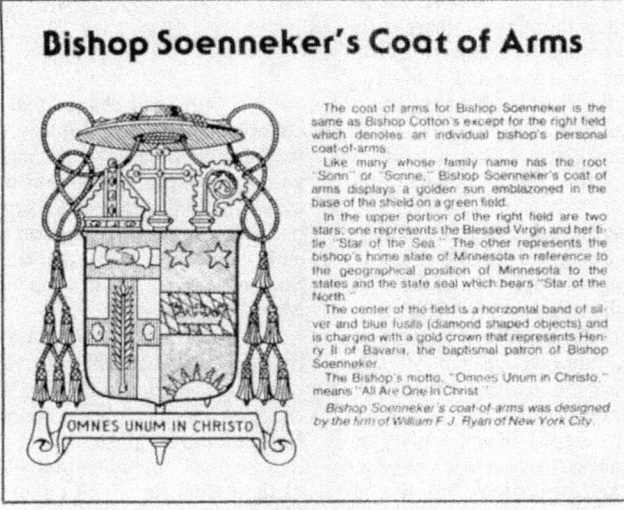

Birth: May 27, 1907, Melrose, Minnesota.
Family: Seventh of nine children of Henry and Mary (Wessel) Soenneker

Education: Small country school, District #164 (Grades 1-7); St. Boniface Elementary School (Grade 8); Pontifical College Josephenium, Preparatory School; Pontifical College Josephenium College; Pontifical College Josephenium; School of Theology; Catholic University of America, Washington, D.C.; Canon Law School, 1948-1950.

Ordination: May 26, 1934

Ministry: St. Anthony's Church, St. Cloud, Minnesota and Chaplain at St. Cloud Veterans Hospital; Chaplain of the Motherhouse of the Franciscans of Immaculate Conception, Little Falls, Minnesota (1940-1948); Spiritual Director at St. John's Seminary, Collegeville, Minnesota (1950-1961); Director of Diocesan Matrimonial Relations Office, 1950; Director of Vocations, Diocese of St. Cloud, Minnesota, 1956; Officialis of the Diocesan Court, dealing with approx. 25 Marriage Cases per year – 1959

Consecration as Bishop: April 2, 1961, St. Mary's Cathedral, St. Cloud, Minnesota, Most Rev. Peter W. Bartholome, Presider
Installaton as Bishop: May 9, 1961, St. Stephen's Cathedral, Owensboro, Archbishop John A. Floresh, Presider
Death: September 24, 1982
Burial: Resurrection Cemetery, Owensboro, KY

Bishop Soenneker was right in thinking that he needed to pray like he never had before.

Installed as Bishop of Owensboro on May 9, 1961, Bishop Soenneker spent the next busy months meeting the priests and people of the Diocese. There were plenty with whom to get acquainted. In 1961 the Owensboro Diocese consisted of 37,845 Catholics who were served by 79 priests in its 67 parishes and missions. Some of these priests he already knew were those on his Diocesan staff and he retained them in their current positions: Rt. Rev. Gilbert, Henninger, the Vicar-General; Rev. Robert Connor, the Diocesan Chancellor; Rev. George Boemiche, Director of the Propagation of the Faith and Rt. Rev. Raymond Hill, Vicar of Education, to name a few.

Besides learning the people of the Diocese, Bishop Soenneker also quickly became acquainted with the variety of concerns with which an administrator of a diocese has to deal. There were celebrative occasions such as the jubilee celebration of St. William's parish in Knottsville, KY. There were listening sessions with pastors and parish trustees of St. Francis de Sales parish as they presented the pros and cons for the purchase of the old Moose Hall that they hoped to convert into a convent for the Sisters and a parish hall. And there were tough decisions like the closing of the mission Church of St. Francis at Smith Mills, Ky. It was reasoned there that the small number of parishioners could be served better by using the good roads and modern means of travel to reach Catholic churches in neighboring towns where parish services were held more frequently than in the little mission church.

But while he was getting acquainted with the Diocese Bishop Soenneker was also making plans to leave to attend the first session of Vatican Council II, called by Pope John XXIII. Bishop Soenneker had been bishop scarcely a year and a half when this first Council session took place.

The Council had been proposed by Pope John XXIII on August 9, 1959. He called it in order to update the church. When Bishop Soenneker spoke to the Owensboro Rotary Club on August 13, 1964, he explained the manner in which the church would be updated: "The Council will not invoke basic doctrines of the Church but will change the methods of presenting these to the priests and to the world...One of the purposes of the Council is to get rid of provincialism... Matters of church law are to be examined... Many such laws were used more than 500 years ago when there was a need for them. These laws were incidental to the basic doctrines of the Church."

Actually Pope John XXIII named "aggiornamento" as the general theme of the Council. Translated, "aggiornamento" meant "getting up to today". The Pope wanted the Church to enter the technological age. Pope John XXIII thought that was the only way the Church was going to be effective in the future. The church needed to secure ways to respond to its present day needs and to refocus its apostolate for the future.

Bishop Soenneker found the first session of the Council to be mostly administrative. It was the session during which the composition of various commissions was studied to try to see that each commission had representatives of both the conservative and the liberal viewpoints present at the Council. When Bishop Soenneker came home from this session he recounted how for the first time members of the Protestant Clergy had been invited as observers at the Council and that work was begun on the first document of the Council. This document, incidentally turned out to be the most significant document of the entire Council. This was the Dogmatic Constitution of the Church.

The Dogmatic Constitution of the Church would be viewed as significant because it was the document that encouraged Catholics to develop a new theological concept, the theology of the marketplace. This was the document that issued the universal call to holiness. What this would mean to the Catholics of the Diocese of Owensboro, as well as those everywhere in the world, was that everyone was encouraged to become evangelizers by living and witnessing their own faith stories. It called for everyone to become minister to each other. It would take some years for the people of the Church to conceptualize how radical the marketplace theology really was.

When the second session of the Council met from September to December, 1963 the familiar joyful, smiling figure of Pope John XXIII was missing. He had died on June 3, 1963. In his place was the former Archbishop of Milan, Cardinal Giovanni Montini or Pope Paul VI, who had been elected Pope on June 21, 1963.

Bishop Soenneker recalled that at this session of the Council the spirit of ecumenism and reconciliation was particularly evident when Pope Paul VI publicly asked the pardon of non-Catholics for any division that Catholics may have caused and asked Catholics to grant forgiveness for any hurt "real or imagined" that they may have suffered in the years since the separation of the churches.

Given his own devotion to the Blessed Mother, Bishop Soenneker must have been particularly happy at this Council session when the Council bishops reaffirmed the importance of the Blessed Mother to the Church. It may have been the study of this woman's role in the history of salvation that made the Council bishops also correct an oversight they had made at the first session of the Council. At the end of this session an invitation was issued to women to come as observers at the future Council sessions.

Due to the death of Father Robert Connor, the chancellor of the Diocese, Bishop Soenneker returned to Owensboro before the closing of the second session of the Council. Father George Hancock was named to replace Father Connor as chancellor.

The work at the second session of the Council that was to have the most immediate impact on the people of the Diocese of Owensboro was the Constitution on the Sacred Liturgy. With the approval of this document the changes in the Church began to be personally experienced back home in the parishes.

On April 2, 1964 the first regularly scheduled afternoon Mass was announced. It was to be held at Our Lady of Lourdes and was "for the convenience of the Catholics who on account of Sunday work schedules [found] it, practically speaking, impossible to attend Mass in the morning."

The 16 Documents of Vatican II

The Constitution on the Sacred Liturgy (December 4, 1963) ■ Decree on the Means of Social Communication (December 4, 1963) ■ Dogmatic Constitution on the Church (November 21, 1964) ■ Decree on the Catholic Eastern Churches (November 21, 1964) ■ Decree on Ecumenism (November 21, 1964) ■ Decree on the Pastoral Office of Bishops in the Church (October 28, 1965) ■ Decree on the Up-to-Date Renewal of Religious Life (October 28, 1965) ■ Decree on the Training of Priests (October 28, 1965) ■ Declaration on Christian Education (October 28, 1965) ■ Declaration on the Relation of the Church to Non-Christian Religions (October 28, 1965) ■ Dogmatic Constitution on Divine Revelation (November 18, 1965) ■ Decree on the Apostolate of Lay People (November 18, 1965) ■ Declaration on Religious Liberty (December 7, 1965) ■ Decree on the Church's Missionary Activity (December 7, 1965) ■ Decree on the Ministry and Life of Priests (December 7, 1965) ■ Pastoral Constitution on the Church in the Modern World (December 7, 1965)

As with each change that was announced concerning the Sacred Liturgy, a note of caution was also announced by Bishop Soenneker. Regarding the afternoon Mass he noted: "Sunday is the Lord's day and it is not proper to spend the preceding night in recreation extending to the early hours of Sunday and then sleep most of Sunday and get up in time for the afternoon Mass."

Also, since people might be crossing parish boundaries to go the afternoon Mass, the instruction was included that "any parish envelopes dropped into the collection during the evening Mass should be given to the proper parish. The loose collection will naturally be for the benefit of the parish [in which the evening Mass was held]."

In April of 1964, the Sacred Congregation of Rites also decreed the change in the form for the distribution of Holy Communion. Now the priest was to hold the host before each Communicant and say the words "Corpus Christi"; to which each person receiving Communion was to audibly profess his/her belief in the presence of Christ by responding, "Amen." Bishop Soenneker called for this practice to be explained to the parishioners and then for it to begin to be used in all the parishes in the entire diocese on May 3, 1964. He cautioned that it was not to be used in any Church prior to that day.

This caution would be typically given each time a new change was introduced into the Sacred Liturgy. Bishop Soenneker was very aware that pastors might get anxious and jump ahead in updating their parishes. But Bishop Soenneker was also very aware that by doing so, pastors might not be sensitive enough to how changes were affecting people throughout the parishes. He thought that symbols could lose their meaning if proper explanation did not precede the introduction of liturgical changes.

In at least one instance, the cautionary approach was also a practical move. In one of the letters to his priests Bishop Soenneker reminded the priests not to buy new Altar Manuals at this time. The changes in the liturgy would be so numerous that it would be difficult for publishers to keep up with them and continual purchasing of updated or revised manuals would run into considerable expense.

Little by little other changes were made in the Liturgy. At first there were changes in the

Prior to Vatican II the altar was far removed from the congregation. The priest did not face the people as he "said Mass." In this photo from St. Josephs Church in Central City, KY the priest is preparing to distribute Communion to those making their First Communion.

wording of some of the prayers. In August and September of 1964, the words "Holy Ghost" were changed to "Holy Spirit" and were to be changed in all the prayers in which Holy Ghost was commonly used. Prayers such as the Sign of the Cross, the Doxology and the Creed and countless other prayers were affected by this change.

Then finally, on November 5, 1964 the change for which many had been waiting was announced. The Liturgy should be prayed in the vernacular. For the people in the United States that meant that the Liturgy would be celebrated in English.

In writing to the priests about the use of the vernacular, the Bishop noted that "Prayers rattled off in English would be a source of disedification to the laity and such an approach to prayer would give the impression of prayer that lacked sincerity, depth and thoughtfulness." It was decided that the use of the vernacular would be introduced into all the parishes on the First Sunday of Advent. In anticipation of the other changes that would be coming in liturgical celebrations and in order to have guidelines by which those changes could be implemented within the diocese, the first Liturgical Commission was established in the Diocese in September, 1964. The following priests made up that first commission: Rev. George Hancock, Chairman; Rt. Rev. Gilbert Henninger; Very Rev. Charles Henry, OSB (Rector of St. Maur's Seminary); Rev. C. P. Bowling; Rev. Eugene E. Ryan; Rev. Bernard Powers; Rev. Joseph Mills; Rev. Joseph Saffer; Rev. Joseph Rhodes and Rev. Lucian Hayden.

The fact that there would be plenty of questions for a liturgical commission to address was illustrated by the example of how the vernacular could be used at funeral Masses. In the fall of 1964 there was no funeral music available in the vernacular. It was decided that at funeral Masses the Latin music could be used until adequate vernacular music began to be published. That sounds like the obvious solution, yet when organists and choirs had previously been schooled to use only approved music in the celebration of liturgies, one can appreciate the quandary in which they found themselves.

The liturgical commission met for much discussion when the next phase of liturgical change took place. This change called for the priests to face the people during the celebration of Mass. The date for this change was March 7, 1965. But the sanctuaries of the churches had to be arranged to accommodate this change. The liturgical commission advised pastors to go the route of placing a temporary altar somewhere between the main altar and the communion rail. This, of course, assumed that later there would have to be renovations within the church buildings to accommodate altars from which the priest would offer Mass facing the people. But major renovations should wait until other liturgical concepts had been assimilated by the congregations.

The liturgical commission was also to prepare ways of teaching the parishioners the reasons for the future changes such as the rituals such as offertory processions, the kiss of peace, and parishioner's placing of a host in a ciborium prior to the beginning of Mass.

Bishop Soenneker wanted to make sure that when these changes were introduced the new symbolism was understood. So he sent a letter in 1964 again instructing parish priests not to begin these practices until the liturgical commission had established clear guidelines as to how the new rituals were to be implemented. The same caution applied to Bible vigils or prayer services. They were not to be introduced without standard procedures that could be followed by all. In fact, demonstration Bible vigils were held in some parts of the diocese in order to teach how they were to be conducted.

In November of 1964 another change was introduced. This one turned out to be a help to parishioners but a great time consumer for the priests of the parishes. Priests were given permission to celebrate more than one Mass daily. They could celebrate two on weekdays and even three on weekends if the size of the congregations indicated a need for that many. The priests were permitted to take liquids between the Masses. (This was before the fasting rules for the receiving of Communion had changed.)

Priests were also given permission to distribute Holy Communion at evening Communion services and to celebrate Mass in social gathering places as long as they had a portable altar stone or Greek antemensis to use in this setting.

Almost all the changes mentioned above and the ones that would come later, particularly those that encouraged the participation of the laity in the role of Eucharistic Minister, Lector and Cantor in the celebration of the Liturgy stemmed from the definition of the Church as it was given by the Second Vatican Council. The Church was the people of God.

For most parishioners these changes, and the teaching that went along with them, made for a wonderful renewal of the liturgical life of the parish with an increased participation on the part of the whole parish. For some individuals, however, the process of coping with the change was either too stressful or offered an already sought for excuse to drop out of participation. Some parishes began to experience a slight decline in membership. That decline, however, was not reflected in the Diocesan-wide membership. Between 1961 and 1971 membership in the Diocese of Owensboro increased from 37,845 to 47,843. It continued to climb throughout the next decade also. In 1982 the Diocese of Owensboro numbered 50,076.

About the same time the number of Catholics in the Diocese was increasing, the Diocese began facing a problem with the continued financing of parochial schools. Some of the smaller schools across the Diocese were closed or grades (such as the 7th and 8th grades) were eliminated. This was a particularly sensitive question for the Diocesan Church because the Church had always looked upon the parochial school as one of its principle means of evangelization of its members.

To begin to address the problem of evangelization of students who were not attending Catholic parochial schools, the Diocesan Office of the Confraternity of Christian Doctrine was established in July, 1967. (The name of this office was changed in 1974 to Diocesan Catechetical Office and in 1980 to the Office of Religious Education.) Bishop Soenneker appointed Rev. Ben Luther as Director of this office.

Originally the office coordinated the training of volunteer teachers in CCD programs across the Diocese. But the goals of the office evolved as more of the laity, most of whom had not had a religious education component included in their teacher training courses, began teaching religion classes in the Catholic schools. Another influencing factor in the changing emphasis in the Catechetical Office was the whole shift in theology that began to be reflected in textbooks after the Second Vatican Council. The CCD Office then became a center for the preparation of and diocesan certification of religion teachers in both the parochial schools and the CCD programs. In addition the CCD Office became a vehicle of adult education and of youth ministry programs.

Through its evolution the CCD Office has had three directors and several staff members. This office was the first diocesan office to have full time lay staff members. The directors, besides Rev. Ben Luther, 1967-79 have been Sister Marie Michael Hayden, OSU, 1979-87, and Sister Kathy Gallo, 1987-93. Program coordinators included Sr. Dolores Gerten, a Victory Noll Sister from Huntingburg, Indiana, Sr. Elaine Burke, OSU, Mr. Bob Lawrence, Mr. Bob Lauer, Mr. Kenneth Heichelbeck and Mr. Phil Spurlock.

The topics for the adult education program over the years have been extensive and diverse. A partial listing includes Church history, the Vision of Vatican II, sacramental preparation, lesson planning, the use of audio-visual materials, Pre-Cana Conferences and Natural Family Planning Seminars.

Since the educational world had entered the age of audio-visuals as teaching tools, a multimedia center was established at the CCD office. The center stocked films, cassette recordings, filmstrips and other audio-visuals resources that could be circulated upon request to parish schools and CCD programs. Ms. LeeAnn McCarty and Ms. Donna Biggs have been the coordinators of this center since it began in 1967.

Other services offered through this office included a newsletter published five times annually, in-service workshops and an annual diocesan-wide conference (beginning in 1974) featuring nationally known keynote speakers.

The CCD staff in the late 1960s was also instrumental in organizing a youth movement, the precursor of the TEC movement within the diocese. Called the "Encounter" movement, this program invited youth from across the diocese to weekend retreats at Knottsville, KY. Frs. Bob Willett, Steve Dunn and Cliff Howard, Sister Elaine Burke and Ms. Joan Perry were just a few of the people who helped to promote and plan these youth gatherings. These retreats reached out to youth who did not have the opportunity for retreats sponsored within the parochial school system. They also helped in a small way to retain for youth that sense of belonging to the larger Church. Retreatants came from different parishes and began to realize that they were members of a diocesan and world Church. This experience had in some measure been fostered with the C.S.M.C. rallies in the Diocese in earlier years. But the C.S.M.C. rallies had ended in 1969.

In 1977 and 1979 attempts were made to revive Youth Rallies, but participation in these rallies did not seem to provide the experience that was needed for the youth of the Diocese. In the fall of 1976, however, a retreat experience was introduced into the Diocese that has been continued with tremendous results even through today. This retreat experience was the Teens Encounter Christ movement. Frs. Steve Dunn and Bob Willett, at the suggestion of some parishioners who had recently moved to Paducah from the Bellville, Illinois Diocese, traveled to Bellville to observe a TEC weekend retreat in progress. They liked what they saw and with a team of dedicated religious and laity they began to plan to offer TEC to the Owensboro Diocesan youth.

The TEC retreat, which continues to be offered several time annually to Diocesan youth, engourages the development of deep faith in Christ, the experience of shared prayer, and the promotion of service and leadership within the Church. The theme of TEC is that of "dying and rising" with Christ. The process includes peer witness talks, conveyed messages of prayerful support from those who made prior TECs and a joyous reunion with prayer partners at the conclusion of the retreat.

Because TEC participants represent a cross section of parishes, particularly at the TEC reunion evenings, an element of diocesan consciousness permeates the retreat experience.

Because there was this obvious need to continue to provide for the needs of the youth of the Diocese, especially since it appeared that the cost of keeping parochial schools competitive in the technological age of education was going to continue to cause the closing of some schools, a Youth minister was named for the Diocese. Fr. Hank Cecil, who was appointed to this position, served primarily as the spiritual director and diocesan coordinator for the TEC movement. This, like most diocesan assignments, was in addition to the job of being a full time pastor.

The youth retreat movement was not the only retreat experience that began to impact the Owensboro Diocese in the 1970s. In 1969 the Cursillo movement was also introduced to the people of Owensboro.

With a goal of deepening the prayer life and promoting Christian leadership among its participants, the Cursillo movement had its beginnings with Bishop Hernas in Spain in the early 1960s when he was looking for a way to help the male population of the Spanish Catholic Church deepen their faith. United States servicemen who happened to be stationed in Spain and to have experienced the Cursillo movement promoted its development throughout the United States.

One place in which the Cursillo movement was introduced was Owensboro's neighboring Archdiocese of Louisville. The interchange of ideas between Louisville and Owensboro soon had people planning a Cursillo for Owensboro.

And, in 1969, in the basement of St. Stephen's Cathedral the first Cursillo was held. Though the first retreats were held for men only, in the 1970s four annual Cursillo retreats began to be sponsored: two for men and two for women. Reflecting the universal call to holiness that was issued by the Second Vatican Council, the planning teams for these retreats were joint ventures including both the laity and clergy. To help people understand that the retreat was fully supported by both the Pope and by the Diocesan Church, a Diocesan spiritual director was appointed for the Cursillo movement. The first spiritual director was Father Charles Fisher.

The Cursillo movement was so effective that over three thousand men and women from the Owensboro have participated in it. There have also been several spin-offs from the Cursillo movement. Ecumenical retreats, known as the Walk to Emmasus, based on the same philosophy and format as the Cursillo, are annual hap-

St. Joseph's Church, Mayfield, KY. A redecorated post-Vatican II sanctuary.

penings within the Protestant/Catholic circles in the Owensboro Diocese. And an ecumenical retreat experience for prison inmates, Residents Encounter Christ (REC), also came to Owensboro after the Knights of Columbus helped sponsor the establishment in Owensboro of a minimum security residence for women. The residence is operated by the Dismas House Charities, Inc.

Finding a place to conduct the Cursillo retreats and the Teen Encounter Retreats emphasized again the large geographic area that was covered by the Owensboro Diocese. Planners wanted the retreats to continue to draw participants from across the Diocese. However finding a location that was central to the diocese and would provide what might be called "equal access" to all the peoples of the Diocese proved to be a challenging quest for the planners. Initially the retreats were held in the basement of St. Stephen's Cathedral. From there they moved to Mount St. Joseph Retreat Center and to St. Francis De Sales Church in Paducah and to St Jerome's parish in Fancy Farm, KY. In recent years the retreats have been held at St. Paul's parish in Princeton, KY.

If the laity saw themselves in a new role as planners of retreats for the Diocese, it was only one of the new ways that they began to see their leadership recognized and requested in involvement in Diocesan matters. It was partly a call for greater collegiality within the Church, partly the simple recognition of talents and skills that people willingly and readily put at the service of the Church and partly the need the Church experienced after the exodus of a number of both priests and religious community members following the changes in the Church after the Second Vatican Council, but in the 1960s and 1970s the laity found themselves with greater representation on parish councils, on local school boards and even on Diocesan Committees and Boards.

One such board was the Diocesan School Board appointed by Bishop Soenneker. When the first school board had been appointed in 1964 all the board members had been priests. Rt. Rev. Raymond G. Hill was the Vicar and Superintendent of Education and was chairman of the Diocesan Board. Other members were Rt. Rev. Gilbert Henninger, Vicar-General; Rev. Robert Wilson, pastor of St. Francis de Sales, Paducah; Rev. Joseph V. Rhodes, pastor of St. Peter's Waverly; Rev. Henry O'Bryan, principal of Owensboro Catholic High School; and Rev. Bernard Powers, a member of the Owensboro Catholic High School faculty and pastor of Sts. Joseph and Paul Church, Owensboro. The Board had as its purpose to administer the affairs of the schools in the diocese.

A decade later the board had evolved to include other representatives. January 1, 1974 the membership included representatives of the laity and of the teaching religious communities that staffed schools within the Diocese. The new representative configuration also included membership from each of the Diocesan Deaneries. This was an attempt to recognize that the school needs of the different areas of the Diocese might differ considerably and that Diocesan policies needed to reflect those differences.

Rt. Rev. Msgr. Hill continued as Vicar and Superintendent of Education. Rev. Henry O'Bryan became the Assistant Superintendent. Rev. Ben Luther joined the Diocesan School Board as representative from the Catechetical Office. At-large representatives from the clergy were Rev. Joseph Mills and Rev. Ezra Willett. Sr. Julia Marie Head, O.S.U. and Sr. Dorothy MacDougall, S.C.N. came on the board to speak for the teaching religious communities. And the first laity serving on the Diocesan School Board were Mrs. Helena Fulkerson, Mr. Paul S. Coomes, Mrs. Mary Rhodes, Mr. Joseph Riney, Ms. Connie Thomas, Mr. Frank Harold and Mr. Leo Marshall. It should be noted that this board had two representatives from the Rural Deanery in Daviess County and two representatives from the Owensboro Deanery. That, at first glance seemed to be highly out of proportion, when only one person represented each of the other deaneries. However, in 1974, sixty-four percent of the parochial school enrollment was in Daviess County. Also, forty-seven percent of the Diocesan Catholic population was located within Daviess County. Based on percentages the composition of the Diocesan School Board reflected additional school board members for the most densely Catholic portion of the Diocese.

As is evident in the example of the diocesan school board, groups of the laity, religious and clergy began to be viewed as consultative channels within the Diocesan Church.

One group whose consultative voice was broadened at this time was that of the clergy. In order to voice their concerns as the changes were taking place in the Church, the priests sought and received permission (even though the permission was hesitantly given) to form a Priest Senate. The difference between this group and the Body of Consultors that was already operative in the Diocese was that members of the Senate were elected by their own peers rather than being appointed by the Bishop.

The Senate established its own study committee to help educate and bring the clergy up-to-date concerning the changes that were called for by Vatican II. Some of these study committees resulted in the revising of Diocesan Committees, such as the Liturgical Commission, and were responsible for initiating clergy workshops that featured speakers such as Father Eugene Walsh and Father Joseph Chaplain, both nationally recognized liturgists at that time.

Brescia College's theology department also also tried to open avenues of continuing education for the clergy, religious and laity in this time of change in the Church. A series of conferences was offered at the College to help open up an interest in Scriptural Studies. The conferences were given by scripture scholars Rev. Barnabas Mary Ahern and Rev. Carroll Stuemueller. Other conferences featured keynote speakers including Fr. Eugene Walsh, Fr. Louis Evely, Mr. Michael Novak, Mr. Alvin Toffler, Mr. Michael Harrington and Dr. Rollo May.

Besides the theological and liturgical changes the clergy had to face there were questions regarding the provisions for priests who were reaching retirement age. Studies indicated that in 1978 there were thirty priests in the Diocese who were over the age of 60 and twenty others were between 50 and 60 years of age. Out of the discussions on such topics came the establishment of the St. Joseph Clerical Aid Society for priests and the plans for a retirement home that would be made available for priests who opted for it at Carmel Home in Owensboro. The first Board of Directors for the St. Joseph Clerical Aid Society included Bishop Soennecker and Fathers Ezra Willett, William McAtee, Richard Danhauer, Joseph Mills, Stephen Dunn and Joseph Miller.

The members of religious communities at this time were also utilizing the opportunity to come together to discuss the changes that were being experienced within their communities and how these changes were impacting on their ministry within the Diocese. In order to better dialogue with each other and with Diocesan personnel, the Sisters formed the Council for Religious. This Council provided them with the opportunity to gather for workshops on topics pertinent to their community lifestyle and how to adapt that lifestyle to the modern age, a charge that was given to them by the Second Vatican Council.

In the process of adapting to the modern age, religious communities studied their community constitutions, studied the charism of their founders and studied the missions for which their communities were founded. They made changes in the lifestyles of their communities based on how they felt these changes would better help them fulfill their particular mission in the world today.

Many of the religious communities also engaged in sociological and actuarial studies of their commuities at this time in order to help project their future needs. From these studies in the late 60s they realized that the "graying of America" would drastically affect their lifestyle. Out of justice to their elder community members they had to begin to think of ways of providing for their care. The studies also confirmed that the costs of providing for the professional preparation for Sisters ministering in the educational and medical areas of ministry would continue to increase in the years to come.

One of the impacts this had on the diocese was that religious had to begin asking for an increase in the compensation they were receiving for their ministry. In the 1970s the Diocese agreed to introduce a salary scale for religious working in the Catholic school system. This, coupled with the salaries for increased numbers of lay teachers, put more strains on the already struggling parochial school system.

Also from the dialogue among themselves and with the priests and bishop a tradition developed in the Diocese for an annual celebration for priests and religious who were observing jubilee anniversaries of the occasion of their respective ordinations and professions of vows.

All of this change, discussion and the need for reassurance that "we are doing the right thing" gave rise to a call from the Priests' Senate for a diocesan-wide means of communication. The diocese took the initial step toward this goal in June 1974 with the first issue of the *Diocese of Owensboro Newsletter*, a monthly publication. Fr. George Boemicke, assisted by Father Henry Willett and Mr. and Mrs. J. R. Clark of St. Pius X Parish in Owensboro, served as editor of the Newsletter which functioned primarily as an informational tool. Items of diocesan interest, notices of workshops, announcements of special events and celebrations found their way to the Newsletter.

Bishop Soenneker also used the Newsletter as a teaching tool. He included a letter of instruction to the Diocesan faithful in each monthly publication. Topics for his letters ranged from Scripture study to explanations of the history of specific Church organizations.

Besides being a means of shared information the *Diocese of Owensboro Newsletter* was itself a product of shared information. Bishop Soenneker gratefully acknowledged that he borrowed the idea for the diocesan newsletter from Bishop Dozier of Memphis. Bishop Dozier shared the idea with him at one of the regional bishops' meetings. The concept of regional meetings for bishops was one more method (after Vatican II) the bishops used for discussion, dialogue and local input before convening at national and international level decision-making meetings.

In discussing the origins of the *Newsletter*, Bishop Soenneker made a statement that revealed a little insight into his own way of dealing with change. He stated that the newsletter format was adopted because "at the present time a diocesan newspaper was considered too ambitious." In this situation as in many others Bishop Soenneker took the cautious approach. If a proposal failed, he did not want the effects of failure to be too severe.

The *Diocese of Owensboro Newsletter* did do its job. By 1977 it had a circulation of 1300. People of the Diocese seemed to like being able to be more aware of the Diocesan happenings. For instance they learned about the following Diocesan developments.

A new Diocesan ministry had opened up as a result of Americans' involvent in the war in Southeast Asia. A Diocesan center was established for service to the Vietnamese refugees who began to come to America to escape persecution after the war and the fall of Hanoi to the North Vietnamese. Bishop Soenneker appointed Fr. Leonard Reisz to head the Diocesan effort to help place Southeast Asian refugees within the Diocese. The parishioners in St. Edward's, Fulton; St. Francis de Sales, Paducah; St. John's, Paducah; St. Mary of the Woods, Whitesville; St. Peter's, Waverly; Sts. Joseph and Paul, Owensboro; and Mount St. Joseph, Maple Mount, KY readily opened their arms to these refugees in the summer of 1975. By December of 1975 over two hundred Vietnamese had relocated throughout the Diocese. And the Diocesan commitment to the refugee ministry became an on going one. Sister Theresa Marie Wilkerson, OSU replaced Father Reisz as Director of the Refugee Ministry and served in that capacity until 1994.

Another Diocesan response to the need of less fortunate people was made when the Diocesan religious and priests answered the call of Vatican II to share their gifts with the Church in developing countries, especially Latin and Central America. The Ursuline Community of Maple Mount, KY commissioned Sisters Louis Marie Bickett (Luisa), Mary Xavier Truijello, Francis Mary Wilhelm and Susan Mary Mudd to parishes in Chile and Venezuela. And the Charity Sisters of Nazareth, KY, while retaining the mission where Diocesan natives, Sisters Mary Jude Hagan, Ann Roberta Powers, and Marie Bernadette (Mary Frances) Sauer were ministering in India, established missions in Belize.

Other Owensboro Diocesan missionaries were Sister Evelyn Stahr in British Honduras, Brother Raban W. Bivins in Peru, Sister Mary Herbert Woodward, A.S. in Cameroon, Africa, Father Clarence A. Clark, C.R. in Bermuda, and the legendary Fr. James S. Tong, S.J. in India.

As the years rolled by the *Newsletter* also acquainted the Diocese faithful with Ursuline missionaries Sisters Mary Elizabeth (Mimi) Ballard, Rosemary Keough, Dianna Ortize and Gia Mudd. It also related that a Diocesan priest had responded positively to the call to serve the U.S. neighbors in Central and Latin America. Father Bill Allard in the 1980s began ministering in Guatemala.

Sharing priests and religious with the people of the Third World was not the only sharing called for in the 1960s and the years following that decade. Another way the Church of Western Kentucky was called upon to sacrifice for the sake of the global Church was by permitting some of its priests to become chaplains in the armed services. Fr. Donald E. Hunter, a pastor at Sts. Joseph and Paul Church in Owensboro, joined the Air Force in August, 1966. He merited the rank of Lieutenant Colonel in 1978. At the time of his death, April 7, 1980 Fr. Hunter was chaplain at Chanute Air Force Bace, Rantoul, IL. Shortly after his death one of the officers' residence buildings at Rantoul was named Hunter Hall as a memorial tribute to him.

Other Diocesan priests who would hear this call to minister within the military were Fathers Richard Powers, Dave Willett and Carroll Wheatley.

The *Newsletter* accounts about the developments in the area of family life ministry within the Diocese faithful drew not only interest from the Diocesan faithful but also the beginnings of much involvement on their part within the Church.

The first diocesan marriage counseling center, directed by Mr. Joseph W. Castlen, Jr., began offering services in 1975. Mr. Castlen, accredited by the American Association of Marriage and Family Counselors, reserved evening and Saturday sessions for the Diocesan Faithful who could either contact him directly or through their pastors. This offer of services by Mr. Castlen was in response to the growing crises among married couples that was accounting for the dramatic increase in divorces among Catholics.

Shortly after the establishment of this service the diocese gained significant help from other diocesan parishioners who had expertise in the area of marriage counseling. Dr. Delbert Hayden, PhD., and his wife, Ellen, M.A.., presented an intense four week course in the fundamentals of marriage counseling to the priests of the Diocese.

Workshops and programs for strengthening and building marriages that could withstand the stress of the 1970s were not limited to the clergy. The Diocese endorsed the Marriage Encounter Retreats as another approach to encouraging healthy marriages. The first Marriage Encounter Weekend was held at the Ramada Inn in Madisonville, KY. Rev. John P. Tachenberry, C.M. of St. Vincent Preparatory Seminary, Cape Girardeau, and three couples from St. Louis, Mo. conducted the first diocesan Marriage Encounter April 30, 1975. Twenty-four couples from the Diocese of Owensboro participated in

Fr. Leonard Reisz was the director of ministry to the refugees from Southeast Asia after the Vietnam War. Over 200 Vietnamese located within the Owensboro Diocese in 1975.

this first retreat. Later retreats were coordinated by Mr. and Mrs. Phil Todd, Dr. and Mrs. Ralph Hines, Mr. and Mrs. Bobby Durbin, Charles and Joan Collins, and Tom and Jane Calhoun. Fathers Gerald J. Glahn, Anthony Zeigler and Henry Willett assisted at the early Marriage Encounter Retreats.

In October, 1978 the Catholic Counseling Service offered the Couple Communication Program to all interested couples in the Diocese. This nationally recognized program helped couples develop their communication skills and strengthen their marriage relationship.

Further help came with the offer of the Natural Family Planning Seminars. These seminars had been part of the adult education classes offered through the Diocesan Catechetical office in the early 70s. The Natural Family Planning method of birth control had been included as a topic for Adult Education because the whole question of birth control had become such a controversial topic for Catholics particularly after Paul Paul VI issued the encyclical *Humanae Vitae*.

Information on the most advanced and Church approved natural family planning method of birth control was also the content of the course taught by the Couple to Couple League that was brought to the Owensboro Diocese through the instrumentality of Mr. Joseph Castlen, Jr. and Mr. Paul Coomes.

The initial meeting arranged for the explanation of this family apostolate, founded by Professor John Kipply in 1971, was attended by over 100 couples. Soon after this meeting, Couple to Couple League groups were organized in Owensboro, Leitchfield, Morganfield, Bowling Green, Hopkinsville and Fancy Farm. By 1981 volunteer teaching couples: Ray and Bobbi Clemons, John and Charlotte Sterett, Richard and Jennifer Corbett and Mike and Suzanne Wurth had taught natural family planning to over 500 couples, had given presentations on Christian sexuality and marriage to high school groups and had helped with Pre-Cana Conferences.

The *Diocese of Owensboro Newsletter*, with the cooperation of people who would send in the information to the editors, also did their part to pay tribute to marriages that survived the test of

Mr. and Mrs. J.P. Keenan on the occasion of their 72nd wedding anniversary in 1976. Couples celebrating special anniversaries were often recognized with a photo in the Diocese of Owensboro Newsletter.

time. The Newsletter printed pictures of couples who were celebrating special anniversaries. One such couple was Mr. and Mrs. J. P. Keenan who in February of 1976 celebrated a record 72 years of married life.

Throughout the Diocese, workshops and programs were scheduled on various topics related to marriage and family life in general. Brescia College offered a workshop in Family Living in 1982. Featuring Fr. Thomas Boland, Director of the Center for Family Ministry in the Archdiocese of Louisville, as the keynote speaker, the day long program celebrated family life and underscored the importance of spiritually healthy families for a healthy Church. And, in St. Charles Parish in Carlisle County, Fr. Bob Willett hosted one of the first diocesan workshops for widows and widowers.

Also, in an effort to help build healthy and loving marriages from the beginning, generous volunteer gave of their gifts to offer conferences and workshops throughout the Diocese. Teaming up to conduct the first preCana Conference in February, 1978 were Fathers Frank Roof, Charles Fisher, and Carroll Wheatley with Dick and Donna Murphy, John and Charlotte Sterett, Jim and Barbara Barr and Greg and Cynthia McCarty.

The next year this effort was further promoted with the initiation of the Engaged Encounter program. The Engaged Encounter was an in-depth weekend in preparation for the Sacrament of Marriage. Conducting this first of the many engaged Encounter programs for the Diocese were Doug and Betty Howard, Rick and Carol Womack and Father Jerry Riney.

In 1980 the priests of the Diocese got a big help in preparing couples for marriage when they were introduced to the Pre-Nuptial Personal Inventory, an instrument that could be used in the marriage preparation sessions. Mr. Joseph Castlen, Jr. held workshops at Stephen's Cathedral and at St. Francis de Sales, Paducah to teach the priests how to administer the inventory.

Also, in 1980, the Diocese tried to draw from experience and offer a set of guidelines that couples planning to marry needed to follow prior to their wedding. These Diocesan Marriage Guidelines were issued with the binding force of Diocesan law. One of these guidelines was a strong indicator of the progress that was being made in ecumenism also. Guideline #10 from the 1980 Diocesan Marriage Guidelines stated: "In an interfaith marriage the Bishop may for serious reason permit the couple to celebrate the ritual of marriage in a non-Catholic Church. Only for the most serious of reasons should a request be made for a dispensation from the Form of Marriage."

This statement was a far cry from the days when "mixed marriages" were held only in the rectory and was much more liberal than the first ecumenical step that permitted the ceremony for mixed marriages to be held within the Catholic church building. That first step in 1965 was worded like this: "Since all marriages are sacred, we should surround them with a religious setting. Permission is hereby given to have all mixed marriages in church (outside the Communion railing)."

The Marriage Guidelines were not the only guidelines that people of the Diocese became acquainted with through the *Newsletter*. There were announcements of the latest liturgical changes, such as the change permitting communicants to receive the host in their hands in 1977. Announcements also informed *Newsletter* readers that there were workshops being held all over the diocese that not only explained the new role of the laity within the liturgical celebrations but also trained all those who wished to be Cantors, Lectors and Eucharistic Ministers.

Invitations, too, were extended through the *Newsletter*. Bishop Soenneker used this means to invite the people of the Diocese to join in the celebration of the Mass of the Holy Chrism at the Cathedral (an event that previously had been reserved primarily for the clergy). He also invited them to come to the Owensboro Sports center to celebrate the Silver Anniversary of the Establishment of the Diocese in 1962 and the Holy Year of Reconciliation, Renewal and Peace in 1975. Other big celebrations that, in a sense, were statements about the continuing progress of the Diocese included: the Ursuline Centennial Celebration in 1974, the Carmelite Sisters' Silver Anniversary of their Ministry within the diocese in 1977; the Passionists' Silver Anniversary of the establishment of St. Joseph Monastery in 1981; and the Mercy Sisters' Foundation Day on December 12, 1981; the 125th anniversary of St. Francis de Sales Parish in Paducah and the 5th anniversary celebration of Christ the King Parish in Madisonville, both in 1974.

The Diocese was also called to rejoice with the Benedictine monks at St. Mark's Priory and Seminary at South Union, KY as they prepared priests to serve not only in the Diocese of Owensboro but also in other dioceses across the United States. St. Mark's Seminary introduced a school of theology especially for the education of older men for the priesthood. Father Clarence Hite, the first alumnus of this program, was ordained for the the Diocese of Owensboro in June, 1973. Other Diocesan priests who received their seminary training in this program were Fr. Joseph Bomensatt, 1976; Fr. Charles Wolford, 1980 and Fr. Arthur Snow, 1980.

Sometimes, too, the announcements were about events that were happening nationally. Catholics were invited to circle September 14, 1975 on their calendars as a special day in the Church history of the United States. On that day the first U.S. born saint, Mother Elizabeth Seton, was canonized. Of national interest also was the death of Pope Paul VI on Aug. 6, 1978 and the election of Pope John Paul II, a Pope who would travel to the United States three times.

Through reading the *Newsletter* the people in one parish could learn who the people were in other parishes who were participating in parish organizations similar to their own. Through networking, parishioners began to share information and to learn from each other. This proved especially helpful when a parish committee or organization was just getting started. One parish organization that was particularly helpful in sharing information with other parishes was the parish council. Parish councils helped to give the laity a voice in establishing and implementing the goals for their parish. They might share information about how the election for the council members was held in their parish; might describe the ceremonies of commissioning of Council members and other ministers within the local Church-ceremonies that recognized the parish members who were assuming new roles of leadership and stewardship within their parish; and they might comment on the fact that now both men and women could be elected to the Council. Also they would share news about what they were doing within their respective parishes.

Networking was not a new thing to the many Christian action organizations that were operative in the Diocese, some of them dating to the time when Bishop Cotton was Bishop and some even before that. Three of these organizations, however, began during the time that Bishop Soenneker was Bishop of Owensboro.

As early as 1974 the Diocese of Owensboro had a dynamic Right to Life Committee. A non-sectarian group, affiliated with the National Right-to-Life Organization, this group had as its purpose to "create and promote reverence and respect for the worth and dignity of all human life." Despite its inclusive goal, the Right to Life organization was usually identified most closely with the anti-abortion movement within the United States. Mrs. Virginia Corley and Mrs. Charlene Baumgarten were the early coordinators of the Owensboro Chapter of the Right to

Life, Inc. and Dr. and Mrs. Steve Maloney headed the Franklin, KY chapter. By 1978 there were Right to Life groups in Madisonville, Marion, Paducah, Hopkinsville, Bowling Green and Hardinsburg. Local units sponsored essays and Christmas card art design contests with pro-life themes, participated in an annual March to Washington to protest the January 22, 1973 *Roe vs. Wade* Supreme Court decision to legalize abortion, and became a very vocal lobby group working for the reversal of that court decision.

Another prolife response to the legalization of abortion was the Birth-right organization. Birthright provides moral support, financial assistance, counseling and housing for any woman who comes to them with an unplanned pregnancy. Their goal is to guarantee that every child have the right to be born. Early promoters of the Birthright movement in the Diocese of Owensboro were Kathy DunLaney, Florence Itschner and Carolyn Sue Cecil.

The third organization that began after Bishop Soenneker came to Owensboro was the Serra Club. Having served as the Director of Vocations in the St. Cloud, Minnesota Diocese, Bishop Soenneker gave his wholehearted support to the formation of the Owensboro Serra Club. It received its charter from Serra International in 1964.

This organization, composed of business and professional Catholic laymen, had as its purpose to foster and promote vocations to the priesthood and religious life and to encourage the spiritual growth of its members. Members of the Serra Club maintained communications with the Diocesan seminarians; sponsored recognition/appreciation events for priests and religious; held retreats and vocation day programs for grade, high school and college students, and encouraged daily prayer for vocations. At the heart of the Serra Club philosophy was the belief that the formation of a prayer based Christian community would naturally promote priestly and religious vocations. This being the case the Serra Club met monthly for the purpose of deepening their own faith and supporting each other in their work of praying for vocations.

Within a few years after the formation of the Owensboro Chapter the Serra Club members began exercising district leadership. In 1975 Ronald Tisch and in 1978 Harry Baumgarten served as District governors with club responsibilities for Owensboro, Jasper, Indianapolis, Terre Haute, Vincennes and Evansville.

Most parishes throughout the Diocese joined in the Serra Club project called "The Thirty-one Club". Large posters were sent to the parish churches. The posters had spaces on them for the thirty-one days of the months so that parishioners could choose one of those days per month to attend Mass for vocations.

Given the descriptions of Bishop Soenneker's devotion to the Blessed Mother, he was probably very happy at the time he came to Owensboro to find numerous active chapters (presidiums) of the Irish initiated organization known as the Legion of Mary. This organization promotes the Rosary prayer and the practice of the corporal works of mercy throughout the parishes in the Diocese. Though the use of terms that are unfamiliar to the general public (presidium, auxiliaries, etc.) and the fairly rigid format for the conducting of meetings may have kept some parishioners from considering the organization, the Legion of Mary functioned as a viable unit of Church leadership.

The goal of the Legion of Mary is to serve and see Christ in one's neighbors through Mary, Christ's Mother. Members meet weekly for the praying of the Rosary and for a reporting of the work they engaged in for the parish that particular week. Also at the meetings they receive assignments for the week to follow. Assign-

St. Mark's Priory. The Benedictines at St. Mark's in South Union, KY offered a special program of study for older seminarians.

The Serra Club, organized in Owensboro in 1964, works to promote vocations to the priesthood and religious life.

St. John's Church at Fordsville is one of the ten churches built in small, rural areas of the Owensboro Diocese in the 1970s and early 1980s.

ments usually consist of visiting the sick and aged and calling associate members who give their moral support of prayer to the active members but do not participate in the meetings or other activities of the Legion. A special mission of the Legion of Mary is to reestablish ties and communication with Catholics who had stopped coming to worship with the local parish community.

When Father Tucker was ordained in 1971, he became the Diocesan Chaplin for the Legion of Mary.

Another women's group that Bishop Soenneker found already functioning within the Diocese when he came in 1962 was that of the Daughters of Isabella. The purpose of this group was to promote unity, friendship and charity throughout the world. The Diocese of Owensboro may have had a small unit of the Daughters, but it was certainly a dynamic one. Mrs. Martine O'Bryan Ward, a native of West Louisville, KY, served as the International Regent for the Daughters of Isabella in 1976. Mrs. Elizabeth Monarch and Mrs. Audrey McKeown of the Owensboro chapter also served as state regents.

There were two long recognized men's Christian leadership groups in the Diocese also. One of these was the St. Vincent de Paul Society. Originally established by Frederick Ozanam in 1833 to help the poor and underprivileged, the St. Vincent de Paul Society spread to the Western Kentucky parishes while they were still a part of the Diocese of Louisville. Prospering under the leadership of people like Sam Monarch and James R. Higdon of St. Paul's parish in Owensboro in 1936, the St. Vincent de Paul conferences within the Diocese of Owensboro grew to 23 units by 1961. In the early years the St. Vincent de Paul Society earned funds to disperse to the needy by selling copies of *Our Sunday Visitor* and *The Register* at the church doors on Sunday mornings. They also placed within each church a poor box in which people could put donations that Society members would distribute for them.

By 1976 the Owensboro St. Vincent dePaul conferences opened a used furniture, appliance and clothing store at 809 East 18th Street. (It later moved to its present location at Sycamore and 7th Streets.) Other conferences opened similar stores in Bowling Green, Morgantown, Whitesville and Paducah.

One St. Vincent de Paul Society conference (Blessed Mother Parish in Owensboro) had a big celebration on the occasion of their 1500th meeting in 1979. At this celebration they gave special recognition to the men who had served as conference presidents during the years 1948-1979. These past presidents included Raphael Lewis, Paul Mischel, Jack Riney, L.B. Fulkerson, Wallace Carrico and Bill Hayden.

The other Diocesan men's group that was still thriving when Bishop Soenneker arrived was the Knights of Columbus. The Knights of Columbus were originally established in 1903 and S. R. Ewing served as the first grand knight. There were chapters of the K of C chartered in Bowling Green, Owensboro, Paducah and Henderson at the time of or shortly after the beginning of the Diocese and by 1950 the parishes in many of the smaller towns such as Uniontown, Waverly, Fancy Farm, and Mayfield also had active Councils. Some of these Councils weathered stern and even adamant discipline from Bishop Cotton concerning the social activities at their meetings, but the Councils prospered with the encouragement of Bishop Soenneker who himself was listed on the K of C membership roster. Diocesan Councils that have received their charters rather recently include Holy Rosary, Paducah; Pope John Paul I Council, Hawesville; St. Romuald's Hardinsburg; Father Connor Council, Sorgho; Fr. Carroll White Council, Grayson County; Fr. Joseph Saffer Council, Murray; Sts. Sebastian and Charles Council, Calhoun; Msgr. Willett Council, Hopkinsville; Sacred Heart Council, Russellville; Holy Trinity Council, Princeton; and the Bishop Henry J. Soenneker Council, Immaculate Parish, Owensboro.

Diocesan priests, Fathers Aloysius Powers and Richard Powers, have both served as the state chaplains for the Knights of Columbus. Also, in 1978, Robert L. Davidson of Henderson was elected to the position of State Deputy. This was the highest office in the Kentucky Knights of Columbus organization. Other Diocesan Knights who have held K of C state offices, include Robert N. Hood who was State Deputy in 1992 and Phillip L. Carr who was State Treasurer in 1993.

The Knights of Columbus, over the years, have been strong supporters of the promotion of religious education of youth, have been active in the pro-life movement, have established a special foundation to help support group and independent living homes for the mentally retarded and have recently established a charitable foundation which helps in the rehabilitation of women in minimum security prisons. Besides keeping the people of the Diocese informed as to the activities of these organizations, the *Newsletter* also regularly introduced them to the names and faces of those who were studying for the priesthood and religious life and to the names and facades of the new buildings for worship in the faith communities throughout the Diocese. These included St. Michael's, Sebree; Sr. John's, Fordsville; the Church of the Sacred Heart, Hickman; Christ the King, Madisonville; St.

Mary of the Woods, Whitesville; Holy Cross, Providence; St. Anthony's, Axtel; St. Stephen, Cadis, St. Denis, St. Denis, KY; and St. Jude, Clinton.

Many of the counties represented by the churches listed above did not have a Catholic church prior to the building of this first one. But that did not mean that they had not had a Catholic presence at work in the county for many years. Being rural mission territory, the Diocese of Owensboro has had the presence of the Glenmary Home Missioners in many of the "unchurched" counties of the Diocese. They have served the people of Ohio, Edmonson, Hickman, Hamilton, Trigg and Lyon counties.

The Diocese also had the presence of Rev. Carl Glahn in some of these counties and Fr. Maurice Teill in others. Fr. Glahn gathered the Catholics together in Webster County and helped them build St. Michael's and Holy Cross at Providence. He did the same for the people of Clinton and they built St. Jude church. Fr. Maurice Teill would be the one to help the people of Lyon and Trigg county work toward that same goal.

Other building projects announced through the diocesan newsletter included the addition of a Science Building (1968) and a Speech and Hearing Clinic (1975) at Brescia College; a new $10.5 million expansion of Mercy Hospital that provided increased bed space as well as new emergency room, dietary, laboratory, radiology and ICU/CCU services; a new personal care home for the elderly (operated by the Lamb of God Sisters) at Knottsville, a new hemodialysis unit and expanded patient care units at Lourdes Hospital in Paducah; a new cafeteria and classroom complex at St. William's school in Knottsville; and new rectories at Christ the King and Precious Blood parishes.

But sometimes the news related through the *Newsletter* was not for rejoicing. Over the years the deaths of many priests and other diocesan leaders were announced to the Diocese. Included among these were Mother Agnes, C.P., foundress of St. Joseph Monastery in Owensboro; Mr. Houston McNutt, husband of Mrs. Dolly McNutt, Mayor of Paducah; Mr. W. O. Kaufman, a parish leader from Hickman; Mrs. Regina O'Bryan, a parish leader from West Louisville; Sr. Joan Marie Lechner, OSU, president of Brescia College; Rev. Carroll L. White; Sr. Mary Joseph Peterson, OSU, former treasurer of the Ursuline community; Mr. Hiram Hancock, Fr. George Hancock's mother; Mrs. Mary Theresa Murphy, parish leader from Owensboro; Fr. Martin J. Frankberger; Fr. Lawrence Durbin; Mr. J. R. Clark, volunteer helper with the Diocese of Owensboro Newsletter; Mrs. Clara Mary Saffer, parish leader from Paducah; Fr. Thomas A. Murphy; Fr. Clarence Clark; Msgr. Edward Russell; Mr. Thomas J. Young, president of the St. Vincent de Paul Society at St. Francis de Sales; Fr. Martin Nahstall; Fr. Ben Powers; Mr. Joseph Hubert Powers, parish leader at Curdsville; Msgr. Robert Gipperich; Msgr. John M. Higgins, Fr: Charles Patrick Bowling; Fr. Donald Hunter; Fr. Pius Edelen; Fr. Louis P. Yunker; and Fr. Robert T. Wilson.

Then in May, 1982 in an almost parenthetical phrase in his monthly letter to the people of the Diocese, Bishop Soenneker also announced his resignation as Bishop of Owensboro. "My resignation as bishop of this diocese will be in the hands of the Holy Father during these days of prayer in preparation for Pentecost." This announcement coincided with Bishop Soenneker's 75th birthday. What were his plans for his retirement? He was going to grow roses.

It should not have been surprising to the people of the Diocese that this Bishop who had grown up on a farm and who, as Bishop, had served on the National Catholic Rural Life Commission would want to go back to gardening upon his retirement.

In one sense of the word "gardening" describes this term of office as Bishop of Owensboro. Bishop Soenneker came in 1961 and found a diocesan church, a garden, all plowed and ready for planting. He got the seed to plant at the Vatican Council, sowed some of the seeds himself and gave some to others but cautioned them to be careful how they planted them. He stayed in close touch with other gardeners to make sure the processes being used in the tending of the plants were good ones. He prayed as the seeds began to take root and to grow. He worried when the young plants were threatened by storms. When he felt confident he had done all he could for the plants, he rested.

Moving into the Future with Faith 1982-1987

On October 26, 1982, just twenty-one years, seven months and eleven days after he had received his own appointment as Bishop of Owensboro, Bishop Henry J. Soenneker announced to the approximately 50,000 Catholics of the diocese that Pope John Paul II had appointed a new bishop for them. Once again a Minnesota farm boy would be coming to Kentucky to become the Bishop of Owensboro. His name was John Jeremiah McRaith. Learning of this appointment to a diocese of seventy-four parishes, Bishop-elect McRaith wrote to Bishop Soenneker:

"I accept this call with the realization that it is the Lord's work and with a trust in Him that He will use me and my limited talents in the way he chooses. My challenge is to be an open, willing instrument in doing His will. It is my prayer that together with the priests, the Sisters and the lay people we will build the kingdom of God in the local diocesan Church of Owensboro."

When he arrived in Owensboro to begin the work of building that kingdom of God, the forty-seven year-old prelate, a native of Hutchinson, Minnesota, brought with him a background of diverse experiences. Besides having been pastor in three rural parishes in the New Ulm, Minnesota diocese, Bishop McRaith had worked with the National Catholic Conference of Bishops as Director of the National Catholic Rural Life Conference and with New Ulm's diocesan offices as the Vicar-General and Personnel Director. He had also served as the principle of St. Mary's School in Sleepy-Eye, Minnesota and had been president of the Minnesota Catholic Education Association. In these offices the newly appointed bishop had worked with priests, religious and lay people from all walks of life.

But probably the most important formative experience that Bishop McRaith brought with him to Owensboro was that of being a priest whose priestly ministry years were almost entirely post-Vatican II. At his episcopal ordination and installation ceremony as Bishop of Owensboro on December 15, 1982, he left no doubt that he was indeed a Bishop influenced by the teachings of this Council. Even the place chose for the ordination and installation cer-

BISHOP JOHN JEREMIAH MCRAITH

Date of birth: December 6, 1934
Place of birth: Hutchinson, Minnesota
Parents: Arthur and Marie McRaith
Education: Elementary School - One room Elementary School, District #46, Hutchinson. Secondary School - St. John's Preparatory School, Collegeville, MN. Higher Education - Loras College, Dubuque, IA. Seminary Education - St. Bernard's Seminary, Dubuque, IA.

Ordination: February 21, 1960 - Most Rev. Alphonse J. Schladweiler, Retired Bishop of the Diocese of New Ulm, MN, presider

Ministry: Assistant Pastor at St. Mary's Parish, Cleepy Eye, MN (1960-1964). Pastor at St. Michael's Parich, Milroy, MN (1964-1967), Pastor at St. Leo's Parish, St. Leo, MN (1967-1968). Pastor at St. Mary's Parich, Sleepy Eye, MN (1968-1971). Director of National Catholic Rural Life Conference, headquarters in Des Moines, IA (1971-1978). Vicar General - Diocese of New Ulm, MN (1978-1982). Personnel Director - Diocese of New Ulm, MN (1979-1982)

Episcopal Appointment: Bishop fo the Diocese of Owensboro - October 26, 1982.
Episcopal Ordination and Installation as the Third Bishop of the Diocese of Owensboro: December 15, 1982.

emony hinted at Vatican II influence. The ceremony was held at the Owensboro Sportscenter.

The spaciousness of this building accommodated all the people of the diocese who could come and participate in the ceremony. It was important to Bishop McRaith that such space be available to the people. Bishop McRaith wanted the people to know from the start that he considered himself a servant of the faithful of the Diocese and, as such, he wanted to give the people the opportunity to be present at this ceremony to acknowledge their acceptance of him. A near capacity crowd, approximately 6,000 strong, chose to do just that. That their new bishop was setting the stage for collaborative ministry throughout the Diocese was evident to the people participating in this ceremony. Bishop McRaith's choice of offical greeters for the installation ceremony demonstrated his strong belief in the teachings on ecumenism and inclusiveness that had been promoted in the Second Vatican Concil. Keith Lawrence, a reporter covering the installation ceremony for the Owensboro Messenger Inquirer made note of this in his December 16, 1982 account of the ceremony.

The list of greeters showed how times had changed since the last bishop was installed in Owensboro 21 years ago. Two of the four members of the clergy from outside the Catholic Church who participated were women. Rabbi Judy Chessin of Temple Adath Israel represented the Jewish community, and the Rev. June Haislip, President of the Owensboro-Daviess County Ministerial Association, represented all of the churches of the County.

The fact that Owensboro area residents who had access to cable television could watch the installation ceremony live from their own homes indicated that Bishop McRaith was also very comfortable using modern technology to help communicate church and faith matters to the public. Bishop McRaith's first letter in the Diocese of Owensboro Newsletter (Jan. 1983) let the people of the diocese know that they could count on continuing to experience decisive leadership from this post-Vatican II bishop trained in team work skills. As he explained in his letter, one of the first steps he took administratively was to move "the chancery" into the Diocesan Service Center located at 4005 Frederica Street. Bishop McRaith made this move so he could work more closely with the Diocesan Staff. Then, in a symbolic gesture, the name of the center was changed to the Diocesan Pastoral Center. This new name indicated the type of ministry Bishop McRaith hoped would be pursueing at the diocesan levels. (Note: In 1988 the center was renamed the Catholic Pastoral Center.)

Six months later Bishop McRaith gave the diocese a further insight into his own vision of the role of the bishop. He wrote in the July, 1983 Diocese of Owensboro Newsletter:

If I were to reduce the role of the Bishop of a Diocese to one sentence it would read as follows: The Bishop, as Pastor and Chief Shepherd of the Diocese, must see the mission of the Church as being carried out in every Faith community (parish and Catholic institution) in his diocese. The mission is carried out through good ministry, and we are all called to ministry in some way in the Church to one another.

To obtain a first hand knowledge of just how the mission of the Church was already being carried out in those Faith communities Bishop McRaith set out "for the parishes, schools, religious education classes and institutions . . . to meet the priests, sisters and all the people." In later years the people throughout the Diocese remarked with amazement that after these initial visits, Bishop McRaith somehow managed to remember their names. In-between visits Bishop McRaith began making appointments to the Diocesan Staff. Msgr. Gilbert Henniger, having served from 1938-47 as the chancellor for the diocese and an additional 36 years in the office of Vicar-General, retired from diocesan administrative work. Bishop McRaith asked Msgr. George H. Hancock to temporarily field both offices. Then, in July 1983, he announced other members of the staff, noting as he did so that others would be added as the ministry needs of the diocese became known. One group he would count on for advice regarding the ministry needs of the diocese was the advisory body known as the Priests Council. He did not appoint this group. They were elected or chosen by their fellow priests. Representing the priests of the diocese were Fathers Victor Boarman, Joseph O'Donnell (Glmy), Joseph Mills, Robert Willett, Bradley Whistle, Gerald Calhoun, Delma Clemons, Jospeh Rhodes, Philip Riney, Thomas Clark and James McCabe (CPPS). This Council consisted of the clergy Consultants (priests elected to represent particular age groups among the clergy) and the Diocesan Deans. Together they functioned in much the same capacity as the former Body of Consultors. With respect to the other staff offices: Fr. Henry O'Bryan continued as Superintendant of Education; Sr. Marie Michael Hayden (OSU) as Director of Religious Education; Fr. Henry A. Cecil as Director of Youth Ministry, Fr. Jodrph O'Donnell (Glmy) as Director of the Office of Ecumenism; Fr. George Boemiche as Director of the Cemeteries; Sr. Theresa Marie Wilkerson (OSU) as Director of Pastoral Ministry for Refugees; and Fr. Edward J. Bradley as Director of Vocations.

As Bishop McRaith promised, new staff offices were created to respond to the needs of the people and the diocese. Sr. Rachel Willett (SCN) became Bishop McRaith's secretary and assumed responsibility for the publishing of the Diocese of Owensboro Newsletter. Fr. Anthony J. Zeigler became the Director of the Pastoral Office of Worship and Spiritual Life; Fr. Gerald Glahn, the Director of the Charismatic Renewal Committee; and Sr. Cheryl Clemons (OSU), the Director of the Pastoral Office for Social Concerns. By 1984 Bishop McRaith was well acquainted with the Diocese and saw the need for other diocesan level appointments. Some of these people did not serve as full time diocesan staff people but did serve on diocesan committees.

From the beginning of the development of these committees, Bishop McRaith encouraged the recognition of the contributions that people from all walks of life could make to church ministry throughout the diocese. When possible, diocesan committee membership included representation from the priests, the religious and the lay people of the diocese. A good example of such a committee was the Committee for Education. Its membership consisted of Mrs. Mary N. (Cissy) Sullivan, Mr. Patrick McNulty, Fr. Joseph Bomensatt, Mr. Thomas Ferreri, Mr. Paul Fritz, Mrs. Carroll Howard, Sr. Annalita Lancaster (OSU), Sr. Teresa Ann Legeay (OSU), Mrs. Donald Mott, Mr. Larry O'Bryan, Mr. Thomas F. Olejnicak, Mrs. Rita O'Reilly, Msgr. Bernard Powers, Sr. Marie Michael Hayden (OSU), and Fr. Henry O'Bryan.

Knowing that the priests of the diocese were much better acquainted with each other and with the immediate needs of the diocese than he was as the newcomer on the scene, the Bishop encouraged the formation of the Priests' Personnel Committee. Functioning in a strictly advisory capacity, this committee was charged with making recommendations regarding the appointments of priests to parish ministry and other ministries within the diocese. The first members of this committee were Frs. Gerald Calhoun, Stephen Dunn, Patrick Reynolds, Joseph V. Rhodes, Jerry Riney and Msgr. George H. Hancock. Another need addressed in the establishment of new Diocesan Staff Offices was that of the continuing education and updating of the priests. Fr. Anthony J. Zeigler, already serving as the Director of Spiritual Life, took on the additional duties as Director for Continuing Education for the Priests. Besides planning for annual retreats for the priests, Fr. Zeigler was responsible for coordinating conferences and workshops that would help keep the priests fully aware of developments in the Church on both the global and national levels.

Probably the one Diocesan Staff Office that, of necessity, reached out to involve the gifts "of all the people" in ministry on committees was that of the Office of Social Concerns. The Office of Social Concerns became an "umbrella" office from which several committees functioned. As time passed and the needs of the diocese became more specifically defined, some of these committees would expand to become separate diocesan offices. In later years, too, some of the committees would be dissolved and new ones would be added. In 1984 five committees operated out of this office. They were: the Office for Family Life, directed by Ms. Marthanne (Marcy) Allman; the Office for Pro-Life Activities, directed by Sr. Kathleen Kaelin (OSU); the Rural Life Committee, directed by Sr. Cheryl Clemons (OSU); and the Mission Office, directed by Fr. George Boemicke. The Office of Pastoral Ministry with Refugees began to function out of the Office of Social Concerns also.

Little did the directors of all the Staff offices know that when Bishop McRaith said he hoped the staff of the Diocesan Pastoral Center would work as a team that they would be involved in a special kind of team effort during the first four years of Bishop McRaith's episcopacy. The reason for this concerted team approach to ministry at this time was rooted in the dream that Bishop McRaith had for the Owensboro diocesan church. Bishop McRaith told the people of the Owensboro Diocese that he envisioned every Catholic in Owensboro coming "forward with their unique gifts and [putting] them at the service of the Believing Community—the parish, instituion, and Diocese." (Newsletter, Jan./Feb., 1984). He first introduced the method through which he hoped to bring this dream to reality in May, 1983 when he established the Office of Lay

RENEW small group sessions were often held in the homes. Gathered here are the parishoners from St. John the Evangelist Church in Sunfish, KY. (L to R): Bill Canty, John Davis, Tom Mattingly, Verena Mattingly, Fr. Gerald Calhoun, Marie Davis, Terry Logan and Cathy Canty.

Sr. Sharon Grant (SCN), Director of the Office of Lay Ministry and RENEW, and her secretary, Kathy Hagan.

Ministry and Renew, directed by Sr. Sharon Grant (SCN). The specific function of this office was to lead the Diocese of Owensboro through a three year program of renewal. Fittingly, the first announcement of the RENEW program for the Owensboro Diocese in May, 1983 coincided with Pope John Paul's designation of the Holy Year of Redemption (March, 1983-April, 1984), the 1950th anniversary of the Death and Resurrection of Jesus. As Director of the new diocesan Office for Lay Ministry and Renew, Sr. Sharon (SCN) assumed the role of coordinator and director of the RENEW process. During the first year, beginning August 1, 1983, Sr. Sharon traveled to each and every parish in the Diocese explaining that RENEW was a three year prayer/study/action process based on five themes: God's call to each of person on the diocese; each person's response to God's call; service to one another; evangelization; and discipleship. Sr. Sharon also explained that even though participation in the RENEW program could be on many levels, the participation that was central to the program was that of small prayer/faith-sharing groups.

Through RENEW the Catholics of the Diocese of Owensboro were encouraged to develop their own leadership roles on many levels in the parish setting. To help them in this process the RENEW program provided training and resource materials for each person who assumed a leadership role.

After the announcement of the year of preparation for RENEW, the Diocese of Owensboro Newsletter regularly carried updates ("On the Road with RENEW") on the steps being taken to prepare the Diocese for the implementation of the program. One step on the road was the formation of a Diocesan Publicity Committee for RENEW. This committee had representatives from various areas of the Diocese. Bishop McRaith must have thought that he was already seeing part of his dream come true as the people gifted with skills in photography and journalism stepped forward and volunteered to put these gifts at the disposal of the Diocese for the RENEW program. These early "volunteers" were: Marcy Allman, Owensboro; Mel Howard, Whitesville; Rose Wyatt, Henderson, Sr. Mary Ruth Gehres (OSU), Owensboro; and Cindy Ozar, Hopkinsville. Also assisting them from time to time were Doug Berry, Madisonville, and Sr. Grace Saia (SCN), a resource person from Nazareth, KY. From the cameras and pens of these people there would come picture after picture and story after story of parish involvement in RENEW. These pictures and stories found their way into the Newsletter of 1984 and the Western Kentucky Catholic in 1985-86. There were stories from St. Henry's parish in Aurora, St. Joseph's Leitchfield, St. Anthony's in Peonia, St. Ambrose's in Henshaw, St. Paul's in Princeton, St. Jerome's in Fancy Farm, St. Denis in Hickman County, St. Joseph's in Central City, Holy Name of Jesus in Henderson, Blessed Mother in Owensboro and numerous other parishes from one end of the Diocese to the other. These pictures and articles revealed the comprehensiveness of the RENEW process.

All levels of parish membership, from school children to senior citizens, were pictured and written about. RENEW was an opportunity for everyone. Besides being a program of spiritual renewal, participation and evangelization for the people of the Diocese of Owensboro, the RENEW process set a precedent for programs promoting diocesan-wide involvement by the people of the diocese. The following description of the RENEW process demonstrates the different levels of participation addessed in the process.

The Priests' Council was the Diocesan body which initally endorsed the Renew Program for the diocese. On May 9, 1983 they met with Rev. Philip J. Murnian, Director of the Committee on the Parishes of the National Conference of Catholic Bishops. He assured them that RENEW would touch on all the issues that were crucial to the life of the parish: personal faith, family, liturgy and social justice.

Sr. Sharon Grant, in the meantime, met with parish staffs and visited Deanery meetings. She also took the RENEW message to the Diocesan parochial and religious education teachers in a presentation she made to them at the Diocesan Religious Education Institute at Owensboro Catholic High School on October 8, 1983.

Bishop McRaith made a special appeal to the religious communities located within the Diocese, urging their members to not only fully participate in the program but also to become the backbone of prayerful support for RENEW. Noting that the RENEW process could be successful only if it were blessed by God, he celebrated special liturgies asking God's blessings for that purpose. These liturgies, to which the public were invited, were held at St. Mark's Priory, the Passionist Monastary, Mount St. Joseph Ursuline Motherhouse and the Sisters of Charity of Nazareth Motherhouse.

Then in January, 1984, the National RENEW service team members, Msgr. Bill O'Bryan and Sr. Donna Ciagnio (OP), arrived from Newark, New Jersey to conduct the first training of parish teams. This training took place at overnight retreats in three locations in the diocese: Paducah, Bowling Green and Owensboro. While the training sessions happened at the overnight retreat sites, parishioners back home in the parishes held prayer vigils for those who were being instructed as leaders. People participating in the prayer vigils were also encouraged, as part of the RENEW process, to further affirm those volunteering as group RENEW leaders by personally communcating their prayer support for them.

That this support and affirmation were needed was evident at the weekend training sessions. It was soon discovered in the sessions that for many involved in the RENEW process, it was the first time they had participated in intensive sharing and interaction in open dialogue groups. They voiced both their thrill at being invited to participate on this level and their nervousness at being requested to share on such topics as Sunday liturgies, homilies, parish planning and social justice issues.

After the parish representatives had been introduced to RENEW through the overnight retreats Sr. Sharon and the total Diocesan Staff once again visited the parishes. This time they outlined the duties of each RENEW committee. There were committees to organize the small sharing groups; to arrange for some total parish gatherings; to plan for special prayer and liturgical celebrations; and to encourage people to participate in the diocesan opening ceremonies for each of the six seasons of RENEW.

The goal of helping all people of the Diocese share their gifts with the total church was particularly evident in the establishment of two important RENEW committees. These committees were created to coordinate and implement adapted versions of the RENEW programs for person with various handicapping conditions and for the youth of the parishes. Once again members of these committees were drawn from across the Diocese. The members on the RENEW Committee Serving the Handicapped included Srs. Marty Blandford (OSU), Whitesville; Kathy Gallo (OSU), Hawesville, Michelle Intravia (OSU), Paducah; Sharon Sullivan (OSU), Maple Mount; Lorena Fleischman (SCN), Paducah and Audry Mary Gold (AD), Owensboro.

The RENEW process for the youth was modeled on that for the adults in that each parish was encouraged to set up its own parish youth committee. Fr. Hank Cecil served as the diocesan resource person for the parish based high school RENEW committees. Fr. Henry O'Bryan and Sr. Marie Michael Hayden (OSU) prepared RENEW materials for elementary school youths. With the training of 870 RENEW parish leaders finished in the Fall of 1984, the Owensboro Diocese then invited all its parishioners to Sign-up Sunday on September 16; the RENEW Kick-off Celebration on September 23 (the official launching of the three year prayer and study process) and Personal Prayer Committment Sunday, September 30.

The Kick-off Celebration gave every indication of a successful beginning for the RENEW process. Approximately 4,000 people gathered for the Liturgy at the Owensboro Sportscenter. Following the Eucharistic celebration a thousand plus worshippers marched, carrying the Blessed Sacrament in procession from the Sportscenter to St. Stephen's Cathedral, to initiate a year of perpetual adoration of the Blessed Sacrament. The perpetual adoration was another means by which the people of the Diocese were encouraged to pray for each other during the RENEW process.

Some of the highlights of the RENEW process centered around the large group gatherings and the Kick-off Celebrations at the beginning of each season of RENEW. These events were visited by speakers such as Fr. Edward Farrell, a nationally known spiritual writer, who spoke at a large group gathering of the Owensboro and Rural Deaneries; Fr. Bryan Hehir, Secretary of the U.S. Catholic Conference Dept. of Social De- velopment and World Peace, who helped prepare leaders for Season III, Empowerment by the Spirit; and Joseph Cardinal Bernardin of Chicago, who was the keynote speaker for the Kick-off Celebration for Season III.

Finally, there was the closing of RENEW in November, 1986. The special flavor of this RENEW season was captured in the celebration of Hospitality Week in every parish church throughout the entire diocese. Some parishes, like St. Mary, LaCenter, used this week to bring the whole parish together in mini-retreats or missions. In other instances parishes used the week as an opportunity to reach out to members of other religious denominations, to the unchurched and to inactive Catholics. They held tours, receptions and information sessions at their parish church. Though there would be little documented evidence* to support their assumption it was not uncommon to later hear parishioners offer the observation that the hospitality extended during this RENEW session partially accounted for the increase in the numbers of people participating in the RCIA (Rite of Christian Initiation of Adults) classes in the late 1980s and early 1990s. (*According to The Book of the Elect used in ceremonies in Paducah, Bowling Green and Owensboro in March, 1986 one hundred thirty four people prepared for entry into the Catholic Church that year. It might be argued that the spirit of renewal brought about in the diocesan Church throughout the first four seasons of RENEW might have helped encourage this large number of catechumens to begin the RCIA process, but this increase was experienced prior to the parish Hospitality Week celebrations.)

Evaluations of the RENEW sessions indicated parishioners were making an effort to make prayer an integral part of parish gatherings; seeking ways to call forth new leadership (though they listed this on evaluations as "a difficulty"); participating more actively in Sunday liturgies; and gaining greater awareness of social justice issues. The evaluations also listed the problems of time commitments and conflicts in scheduling as being the obstacles to greater participation in the RENEW programs. Parishioners from large parishes indicated on evaluations that they were finding a sense of community and belonging in their parishes that they had not experienced before the RENEW process started. They were fearful, however, that this increased participation by parish laity might not be on-going. In response to this fear RENEW leadership was quick to advise that one way to keep the increased participation in parish ministries alive was to establish standing parish committees such as a a Social Concerns Committee, a Hospitality Committee and a Liturgy Committee. These committees, together with existing parish organizations like the Knights of Columbus, the St. Vincent de Paul Society and the Legion of Mary, could help give direction to future programs for the parish.

Another way the spirit of RENEW could be maintained in the parishes was for staff members on the Diocesan Pastoral Center to be utilized as resource persons for the parishes. Actually, the Diocesan Pastoral Center staff had always been available as resource persons but they had not always been perceived as such by the parisioners. A more positive perception emerged as staff members traveled across the Diocese helping people get the RENEW process launched in their parishes and as the laity began to get better acquainted with them. The staff began to be viewed as a group from whom the parishioners could get advice and support as they needed it in their efforts to accomplish some particular goal for their parish. Just as the parishioners became better acquainted with the Diocesan Pastoral Center staff, the staff members, as they trained RENEW leaders and spent time listening in dialogue and shared prayer sessions with the parishioners, began to be keenly aware of some of the needs of the parishioners and their parish faith communities.

The people in the parishes repeatedly expressed two spiritual development needs to the diocesan staff personnel. They hoped for a greater understanding of the theology of Vatican II and for a deeper personal spiritual formation.

In response to the need for deeper spiritual

Fr. Jack Kramer, S.J., the first Director of the Brescia College Ministry Formation Program.

The first graduates of Brescia Ministry Formation Program (1988) meet with Bishop John J. McRaith. (L to R): Rosanna Schadler, Norman Howard, Marianna Schadler, Donna Murphy and Bishop McRaith.

formation and for a more professional preparation for those who wished direct participation in the catecatical and other professional ministries of the Church the Diocese formed a task force to study the question of formation training for the laity of the diocese. The question was studied on two levels.

Initially, a task force was established to make recommendations concerning the type of formation training that might be most beneficial for those of the laity who wished to work in parish ministry. Sisters Kathleen Kaelin (OSU), Marie Goretti Browning (OSU), Margaret Ann Aull (OSU) and Fathers Bernard Powers, Kevin Karl, Tony Shonis and Ed Bradley, meeting in the fall of 1984, proposed that the formation program for lay ministry in the Church include both spiritual development and academic components.

In order to address the question of the academic component of the formation of the laity who wished to engage in diocesan and parish ministries, Brescia College designed a program through which candidates could earn an academic certificate, associate's degree or bachelor's degree. Rev. Jack Kramer, S.J., the first director of the program, welcomed 22 candidates to the first classes in the program in August, 1985. Developed and approved by an advisory council consisting of college faculty, diocesan representatives, and active lay ministers, the Ministry Formation Program at Brescia was unique in the eastern United States in that it incorporated a triple emphasis on theology, ministry and spiritual formation.

Father John Vaughn, who succeeded Sr. Sharon Grant as the Director of the Office of Lay Ministry in August, 1985, chaired three "think tank" session in August, 1986 for the purpose of designing a program that would provide lay volunteers in church ministry with the competencies and the confidence they needed to better serve in their volunteer roles. Priests, religious and lay people attended idea generating sessions. The resulting program was announced in December, 1986 and began February, 1987. It consisted of classes taught one night per week for six weeks in seven locations throughout the diocese (Owensboro, Mayfield Axtel, Madisonville, Sacred Heart in Union County, Bowling Green and Paducah). The courses offered in the program included prayer experiences, spiritual formation studies, and theological and skill building studies related to specific ministries. Initially these courses were taught by priests, religious and lay people who were members of the diocesan staff at the Catholic Pastoral Center in Owensboro. In later years staff members from the Ministry Formation Program and from the Center for Ministry Support (established at Brescia in August, 1989) joined personnel from the Catholic Pastoral Center in offering "out-reach" courses at various parish sites.

At the same time degree programs and outreach classes were being planned to aid those wishing to participate in church ministeries, the Diocesan Religious Education Office began to examine ways it could further help catechists with their professional preparation. One way they decided they could help was by making the diocesan media center much more accessible to the catechists.

A grant from the Catholic Extension Society, provided the Religious Education Office with the means to accomplish that goal. A van, equipped with audio-visual and teacher training materials and religious text books, became a mobile classroom which the Director of the Office of Religious Education could take to the parishes for on-site demonstration lessons with the catechists.

In addition, the catechetical religious educators, directors of religious education, and pastoral ministers from across the Diocese began to participate in the Mid-South Catholic Educational Conferences. Attendance at these professional meetings not only gave the participants opportunities for continuing education but also provided time for dialogue and exchange of ideas with peers from the Dioceses of Birmingham, Memphis and Nashville.

The acquistion of the mobile classroom and participative membership in the Mid-South Catholic Educational Conferences were only two of the accomplished goals of the Office of Religious Education in the 1980s. Under the directorship of Sr. Marie Michael Hayden (1979-1987) and Donna Biggs, the director of the Media Center (1976-present), the Office of Religious Education served those in the catechetical ministry by: making parish visitations to assist catechists in their teaching methods; maintaining a library of curriculum materials and periodicals as resource materials for teachers; supplying teachers with audio-visual aids from the Media Center library; publishing a bi-monthly newsletter to generate new ideas among the catechists and to give recognition to the accomplishments of parish programs; conducting workshops on curriculum for Summer Bible Schools and for parish programs; assisting with the sacramental preparation of children in catechetical programs; offering correspondance courses; promoting and assisting with the establishment of the SPRED program for the handicapped; and conducting bi-monthly in-service days for the Directors of Religious Education (DREs) in the parishes.

To keep aware of the methods and curricula being used by others in the catechetical field, the Office of Religious Education materials for teachers; supplying teachers with audio-visual aids from the Media Center library; publishing a bi-monthly newsletter (UPDATE) to generate new ideas among the catechists and to give recognition not only to individual teachers but also to parish programs; assisting with the sacramental preparation of children in catechetical programs; offering correspondence courses; and conducting bi-monthly inservice days for the Directors of Religious Education (DREs) in the parishes.

In order to keep aware of the methods and curricula being used by others in the catechetical field, the staff of the Office of Religious Education met periodically with other colleagues who were members of the National Conference of Catholic Leadership and the National Conference of Diocesan Directors. On a more local level the Directors of Religious Education who were members of the Catholic Conference of Kentucky also routinely gathered for sharing and planning sessions.

The information shared at these meetings bore fruit in the Diocese in many different ways.

The Directors of the Religious Education Office frequently would meet people at the conferences whom they would invite be to be featured speakers at workshops for the teachers of the Owensboro Diocese. At these conferences, too, people would share information about programs that had proved successful within their dioceses.

One such program was SPRED. SPRED, Special Religious Education, was initiated in the Diocese of Owensboro in 1986. Designed especially for children with disabilities, SPRED was spearheaded in the Diocese by Judy Colby who was trained by the National SPRED office in Chicago. Through the efforts of Ms. Colby and Lorena Fleischmann (SCN) the program was quickly organized at Holy Name of Jesus parish in Henderson and at Lourdes, Blessed Mother and Sts. Joseph and Paul parishes in Owensboro. The difference in this program and other religious education programs that had been previously offered for special education was that it was parish based. It also had a special format calling for one adult volunteer for each child in the class and for a master catechist who conducted the class portion of each group session. The goal of the program was for the development of a faith community for the special education children. The Religious Education Office hoped to help establish a SPRED program in every parish in which there was a need.

Just as the Office of Religious Education tried to find ways to provide the best religious education for the children of the diocese who for one reason or the other did not have the privilege of education at one of the Catholic schools in the diocese, the Catholic Schools Office looked for ways to constantly upgrade the education received by those in the diocesan Catholic schools.

Bishop McRaith, in his letter to the people of the Diocese in August, 1983, left no doubt that he supported the diocesan Catholic school system. Citing the Code of Canon Law (#773-#776) he noted that it was the duty of parents, pastors and the diocesan bishop to provide for the catechesis of children. He also reminded pastors that the diocese and the parishes needed to offer opportunities for adults to continue to educate themselves in the Faith.

In order to have help in determining the future development of the Diocesan Catholic schools and the CCD and adult education programs, Bishop McRaith appointed a Committee for Total Catholic Education. Comprised of priests, religious and lay persons, this committee was charged with assisting the bishop in the development of policy and directional goals for the Catholic education efforts throughout the Diocese.

In 1985 Fr. Henry O'Bryan retired as Superintendent of the Diocesan Catholic schools. Amelia Stenger (OSU), who had served as Fr. O'Bryan's Associate Superintendent in 1984 became the Superintendent. Sr. Amelia outlined two directional setting goals for the diocesan Catholic school system. Both goals received approval by the Total Education Committee and the Bishop.

These goals proposed that the diocesan Catholic schools strive to fulfill two functions: that of providing an excellent academic preparation for the students and that of assisting parents in their efforts to teach the Gospel message to their children.

The staff in the Catholic Schools office could easily document the fact that the teachers in the Catholic schools were succeeding in providing excellent academic preparation of the diocesan students. They could point to high scores on CTBS achievement exams, to student academic teams placing in regional and state academic tournaments, and to scholarships awarded to graduates of the Catholic schools.

Regarding the ways they were assisting parents in teaching the Gospel message, the staff could demonstrate how the Catholic school children were participating in the RENEW program, in sacramental preparation programs and in other developmentally based religious education studies. They could also take pride in special events celebrated by the students in the Catholic schools. One such event, the RAINBOW MASS, began to be celebrated on an annual basis. Like the CSMC rallies of earlier days this event helped students to develop a sense of community with their peers throughout the diocese.

In spite of evident successes, the Catholic schools entered a critical period in the 1980s. Operational costs, particularly with respect to books, educational technology, and teacher/staff salaries, began increasing at a rate whick parishes found harder and harder to fund. At the same time they were being asked to meet these higher expenses, parishes were also trying to give a fair share to the other educational needs of the people of the parish. These needs included funding teachers for CCD classes and for programs in adult education. It became increasingly clear that parishes were faced with the task of weighing, even more carefully than they did in the past, every program into with they invested their parish funds.

With an eye toward accountability, efficiency and affectiveness, the Catholic Schools office and the Total Education Committee began a study of the Catholic schools in 1985-86. This study concentrated especially on the areas of long range planning, finances and academics. To determine how crucial this study was the committee members needed only consider the number of students who would be affected by their decisions and the finances involved in the education of those students. In 1985 a total of 6,647 students were enrolled in secondary and elementary schools throughout the diocese. Budgets for the diocesan schools that year totalled approximately $8 million dollars or $1,100 per student.

Knowing that the Catholic schools could be kept open only if they received total parish support, the question of the future of the Catholic schools was taken directly to the parishioners. Through town hall discussions, self-studies and surveys parishioners helped explore the options that were open for Catholic education in their area of the Diocese. Some parishes, like Sacred Heart in Russellville which had only sixteen students taught by two full time teachers and a part time aide in 1985, had to make make the difficult decision to close their school. Other parishes engaged in fund raising efforts like bingo, magazine drives and candy sales to supplement tuition and tithing contributions which formed the basis of financial support for the school.

Good stewardship in the form of making use of what was available helped some parishes find ways to renovate existing parish structures rather than build new buildings to expand school facilities. For instance, St. Mary's Elementary in Paducah converted the former St. Thomas More Ursuline convent into regular classrooms, a library and rooms to accomodate music and learning disabilities programs.

Other parishes used the opportunities afforded by the town hall to recommit themselves to providing a Catholic school education for the children of their parish, even though the organizational structure that that Catholic education took on differed drastically from what they were used to in the past. The schools thus affected were located in the city of Owensboro and in Western Daviess County. Schools located in parishes that were already experiencing significant decreases in enrollment due to the aging of their parish population or that were facing extraordinary increases in operational expenses were closed and the students from these schools were incorporated in a newly organized consolidated school system.

Schools that were closed in this 1988 consolidation process were St. Stephen's Cathedral School, Sts. Joseph and Paul School, St. Alphonsus School (St. Joseph, KY), and St. Martin of Tours School (Rome, KY).

The remaining schools (St. Pius X, Precious Blood, Immaculate, Lourdes, Blessed Mother and St. Mary Magdalene [Sorgho]) were reorganized on the middle school concept and were renamed. The new names for the schools were a symbolic gesture to help people realize that these schools crossed parish boundaries and that funding assessments of parishes went to support the total school system instead of a particular school. The names selected for the schools housing kindergarten through sixth grades in this process were as follows: Francis R. Cotton School (St.Pius X); Henry J. Soenneker School (Precious Blood); Catherine Spalding School (Lourdes); Angela Merici School (Blessed Mother); and Holy Angels School (St. Mary Magadelene).

Immaculate School became the Owensboro Catholic Middle School offering education for the Catholic students who were in the seventh and eighth grades in the Owensboro Consolidated Catholic School system.

Four schools in the Owensboro and Daviess County area were not included in the consolidated system: Owensboro Catholic High, which continued to offer Catholic education on the secondary level to students from the city of Owensboro and western Daviess County; and, Trinity High School, St. Mary and St. Mary of the Woods Elementary School and St. William Elementary School, which served students in the eastern part of Daviess County. Trinity High School was already a consolidated school. It had merged with Knottsville's St. William High School in 1969.

Because of the complexities of a consolidated system involving so many schools, the organizational structure of the Owensboro Consolidated Catholic School system also called for the appointment of a Director of those schools. Larry Bishop was the first person named to this office.

Another topic addressed by the Total Education Committee was the question of adjustment of salaries and benefits for the teachers in the Diocesan Catholic school system. As more lay teachers became involved in the school system, various personnel policies had to be studied and either rejected or incorporated into the diocesan policies. Diocesan officials knew they had one group from whom they could solicit input concerning these matters. DOCE (the Diocese of Owensboro Catholic Educators, INC.) had, with Bishop McRaith's blessing, formed an organization in November, 1983. They did not consider themselves a union in the labor organization sense of the word, but envisioned a two fold purpose for their organization.

First, they wished to work to improve Catholic education by a continuous upgrading of the teaching methods and standards in its system. Second, they committed themselves to helping to maintain a stable work force of dedicated teachers in the Catholic school system by working to assure the teachers the personnel benefits that would be typical of those received in other comparable educational systems. In November, 1985 their members met and contributed their perspective on topics such as contracts; leave of absence (maternity and educational); provisions for sick days and personal days; tuition discounts for members of teacher's families; and the curriculum offered in the diocesan schools. Their voice represented approximately 170 of the 290 lay faculty involved in the diocesan Catholic schools in 1985-86.

DOCE, Bishop McRaith and Amelia Stenger (OSU), the superintendent, all realized the importance of encouraging increased membership in DOCE. Unity among the lay faculty of the Catholic schools was and would continue to be a key factor in maintaining good education in the Catholic school system. To assure the teachers in DOCE that they would have a direct link to the diocean committees on education, DOCE representatives were appointed to the Diocesan Committee for Total Education and to the Principal's Association of Catholic Elementary and Secondary Schools (PACESS). The DOCE organization itself began a vigorous communications campaign through the *Western Kentucky Catholic* helping acquaint the people across the diocese with not only the situation facing the schools in the diocese but also the activities and members of the organization. "DOCE Happenings" and "Teacher of the Month" began to be regular features in the diocesan newspaper.

In 1985-86 DOCE members were gratified to learn that a benefits package was established for all full time diocesan employees. The retirement part of the plan became effective on July 1, 1985 and the insurance part of the plan began in September 1985. Bishop McRaith, in his letter explaining this benefits package to pastors, cited Canon Law which stated that diocesan employees have a right to not only a living wage but also pension, social security and health benefits.

Along with securing the financial support for regular school sessions, one school found itself facing a crisis situation in December, 1985. Trinity High School, Whitesville, KY suffered a fire on December 1, 1985. Caused by an aronist, the fire itself was contained mostly to the biology and chemistry laboratories but smoke and soot damage was throughout the building. Though the shock and the damage of the fire was extensive, the teachers and students from the school and the people from the St. Mary and St. William parishes, plus organizations from outside the Whitesville community, bonded together to re-open the school in one week's time.

To help address the financial questions faced by parishes as they tried to provide funds for not only the Catholic schools throughout the diocese but also all the other needs of the Church, a new staff position was created at the diocesan level of administration. The Office of Development opened on September 1, 1984 with Clark Shackelford as Director.

Under his guidance each parish installed a computer system for budgeting and cost control for the parish accounts, thus establishing a consistent system of accounting throughout the entire diocese. Based on the information received from the parishes, the Office of Development was then able to assist on both the parish and diocesan level in the planning of financial funding and the establishing of long-range goals.

In an attempt to help in the funding of the long-range goals of the diocese Bishop McRaith worked through the Development Office to establish The Catholic Foundation of Western Kentucky. This foundation was set up as a charitable, non-profit corporation for the expressed purpose of accepting tax deductible contributions that could in turn be used to help meet the Church needs in Western Kentucky.

The Catholic Foundation of Western Kentucky had as its scriptural basis the letter of the Apostle Paul to Timothy (I Tim. 6-7). Explaining that in this reference Paul is encouraging all Christians to be good stewards of the gifts they have received from God and to use those gifts for the building of the Kingdom of God on earth, Bishop McRaith later changed the name of the Office of Development to that of the Office of Stewardship. Through this office the faithful of the diocese were encouraged to contribute from their time, talents and resources for the building up of God's Kingdom. In later years, Tom Lilly became the Director of this Office.

The Office of Development was not the only diocesan office that had a direct impact on the parishes throughout the diocese. As the diocesan staff members worked with the parishioners in the training sessions during the RE-NEW process, the parishioners began to get better acquainted with them and they began to feel much freer to request assistance from them.

The office the parishioners turned to when they needed a deeper understanding of the liturgical renewal of the Church was that of the Office of Worship and Spiritual Life. Directed by Fr. Anthony Zeigler, who was later assisted by Sr. Kathleen Kaelin (OSU) as co-director, this office provided training for parish liturgical ministers. It offered workshops for cantors, educated liturgical committees regarding the planning of the environment for liturgical celebrations, and helped parishes assess and meet the spiritual needs of the parish.

As they worked with the people on the parish liturgy committees, the staff of the Office of Worship frequently heard the request for a reference tool to guide them in their planning. In response to this need the Office of Worship joined with the Diocesan Liturgy Committee and published a set of diocesan guidelines for use in all the parishes. Using these guidelines the parishioners could feel more confident in the selecting, training and commissioning of the Eucharistic ministers for the parish; in the planning of wedding liturgies; and in the preparing of the art and environment in the places in which liturgical celebrations were held.

Providing ongoing education with respect to changes in the celebration of Roman Catholic liturgies was another concern of the Office of Worship and Spiritual Life. In response to this need they published a Liturgy Newsletter and made opportunities available for parishioners to meet and discuss with nationally known speakers.

The Office of Worship also helped secure the services of Jim Hansen as Coordinator of Liturgical Music for the Diocese of Owensboro. Based at Brescia College from the fall of 1986 to the fall of 1990, Mr. Hansen conducted workshops for parish musicians and offered a series of minicourses for people involved in the ministries of Church music and liturgy.

This nationally renowed coordinator of the National Pastoral Musicians School of Cantors introduced parish coordinators of music to national periodicals, workshops and organizations that would encourage both the young and old musicians and liturgy planners to keep current.

In their efforts to assist parishioners with the development of their prayer life, the Office of Worship and Spiritual Life was readily assisted by the Mount St. Joseph Retreat Center, opened by the Ursuline Sisters in 1983 as a retreat facility which could accomodate directed, private, and/or preached retreats for all age groups. With the opening of the center the people of the Owensboro diocese not only had a place where they could make a retreat, but they had available to them spiritual directors who could guide them in the development of their prayer life.

Another help to the Office of Worship and Spiritual Life was the continued development of the Charismatic Renewal within the diocese. Under the leadership of Fr. Jerry Glahn, the diocesan liason for the Charismatic movement, the diocese hosted annual Charismatic Conventions. Sometimes held at parishes, like the one hosted at St. Piux X parish on Novermber 18, 1985, the Charismatic Conventions were opportunities for the people of the diocese to come together to share faith stories and to pray, sing and celebrate the Eucharist together. Often the speakers at the conventions were from the diocese itself. (For instance, the featured speakers at the Pius X Convention included Dick and Donna Murphy, Doug and Pat Howard, Cathy Hagan, John Henderson and Wayne Henderson.) At other times the Conferences or Conventions addressed special topics and guest speakers were invited to lead the conference.

Father Robert DeGrandis led such a conference on the topic "The Healing Ministry" in September, 1985 at St. Stephen's Cathedral.

Another movement that continued to positively influence the prayer life of the people of the Diocese was the Cursillo movement. Held four times annually since the early 70s, the Cursillo retreats predated Bishop McRaith in the diocese by approximately ten years. The people who had made these retreats were quick to respond to the call to offer their leadership for the RENEW process in the diocese. In fact, in order to fully dedicate themselves to the promotion of the renewal of the diocese, Cursillo retreats were temporarily suspended during the RENEW seasons.

When they began to be held again in 1988, the board in charge of the retreats worked hard to find a place that could be perceived as centrally located for those traveling to the area for the retreat and at which the Cursillo teams could leave supplies, etc. for their retreats. The place eventually settled upon for this purpose was St. Paul's in Princeton, KY.

The parish at St. Paul's permitted the Cursillo retreatants and the TEC retreatants to use part of what was formally used as the elementary school and convent. In so doing, however, the parish still maintained sufficient space to continue to offer Catecatical classes and other parish sponsored events.

The dilemma the Cursillo retreatants were trying to solve by looking for a place that was fairly centrally located in the Diocese was the same dilemma faced by most groups that tried to hold meetings with representatives from across the Diocese. As people began to be more represented on Diocesan committees the complaints began to be voiced about always being the ones who had to travel "long distances" and that ways should be found to equalize the time and travel demands that were made on people who were willing to serve on diocesan committees and in other service roles for the Diocese. In response to this either real or perceived need, the Bishop made his office more accessible to the people of the Western most section of the Diocese by holding office hours in Paducah at least one day per month. Likewise many diocesan committees began scheduling their meetings in places other than the Catholic Pastoral Center.

Many of these committees found Christ the King Parish Center in Madisonville, KY a good alternate meeting place. Its location seemed to be fairly equidistant for representatives from the Eastern most and Western most parishes and also seemed to be fairly equidistant for people from Owensboro and Bowling Green.

One diocesan office that could not easily shift locations for meetings was the Marriage Tribunal. However, the office did become much more accessible to the people of the diocese after Bishop McRaith began directing the Diocese. Bishop McRaith increased the number of people working on the Marriage Tribunal staff from one in 1982 to four full time staff and eight part-time volunteers by 1986. Fr. Joseph Mills became the Judicial Vicar in April, 1983. He replaced Msgr. George Hancock who had served as both Judicial Vicar and Chancellor of the Diocese at the same time. Five people working part-time initially assisted Fr. Mills in determining the sacramental validity of the marriage cases submitted to the Tribunal. These people were Frs. Leonard Alvey, John Vaughn, Kevin Karl and Patrick Reynolds, and Sr. Vivian Marie Bowles (OSU).

The increased staffing meant that people could now have their annulment cases heard and decided within a reasonable length of time. The staff studying the annulment cases, cases in which they determined whether or not there was any possiblitiy of the marriage being deficient in some essential quality which prevented the apparent marriage from being a true marriage in the eyes of the Church, consisted of highly trained people.

They had studied: the interpretation of the New Code of Canon Law, as it applied to marriages; procedures and jurisprudence applicable to all types of marriage cases in church courts; formal procedures used in nullity cases; the psychological basis and other grounds for nullity; and the tests required to determine with moral certitude whether nullity had been proven in a given case.

It did not take the 1983 Marriage Tribunal staff long to realize they needed even more assistance with the lengthy procedures of collecting testimony and studying cases for decision. Mrs. Kay Rhodes and Mrs. Mary Ann Kurz became the secretaries for the Marriage Tribunal and Mary Russell (OP) joined the staff full time for the year 1983-84. Fr. Pete Lauzon completed studies in Canonical Law at Catholic University and began work with the Marriage Tribunal in 1983. Two others, Annalita Lancaster (OSU) and Fr. Severin Messick, (OSB) also assisted on the Tribunal in its early years.

Besides working on the cases presented to them, the Marriage Tribunal staff conducted workshops in Paducah and Owensboro in October, 1984 for the purpose of bringing people up-to-date regarding the New Code of Canon Law as it related to marriages. (The New Code of Canon Law was promulgated in November, 1984.) They also used these workshops to answer questions people might have regarding the processing of annulments.

Believing strongly in the indissolubility and holiness of the sacramental marriage, the Marriage Tribunal became one of the greatest promoters of the new Marriage Policy that became effective throughout the diocese on January 1, 1986. But the Marriage Tribunal members were not the only ones who were strong backers of the new policy. Initially it was the Priests' Council which requested the appointment of a Marriage Policy Commission to study and write a marriage policy for the diocese. The members for this commission represented people of all walks of life in the diocesan Church: Tim and Marcy Allman, Vivian Marie Bowles (OSU), Tom and Jane Calhoun, Joe Castlen, Cathy Clark, Ray Clark, Joe and Marilyn Hayden, Wayne and Carol Johner, Fred and Helen Meister, Rev. Joseph O'Donnell, Rev. Phil Riney, Paul and Alice Roof, Darla Wethington, Mike and Suzanne Worth and Rev. Tony Zeigler. Ms. Carolyn Sue Cecil provided secretarial services for the commission.

The new marriage policy they proposed outlined the importance of home taught marriage values. It also emphasized the role that each Christian has in encouraging and supporting the development of good marriages.

Although the guidelines set forth in the new policy addressed the various circumstances that might be associated with proposed marriages in today's society (such as mixed marriages, pregnancy at the time of marriage, remarriage and validation of marriages) the main emphasis was on the engaged couple' preparation for marriage. Due to the serious nature of this preparation the engaged couples were required to contact their pastor at least six months prior to their anticipated wedding date. Accordingly, the members of the Marriage Tribunal hoped that the assessments, marriage instructions and even the possible recommendation of a delay in marriage might help prevent many cases from later being referred to them for determination of a decree of nullity.

Bishop McRaith took this Marriage Policy so seriously that he requested the parish priests to take three Sundays and talk to their parishioners about the theology of marriage, the nature and context of the Marriage Policy and the highlights of the Policy. Ater this initial introduction to the Marriage Policy, each parish household received a copy of the policy.

Bishop McRaith went even further to try to encourage the development of marriages and families that would be wholesome and sound. Toward this end in September of 1983 he hired Marcy Allman as the first Director of the Office of Family Life.

Ms. Allman was not a newcomer to the Pastoral Center staff. She had been volunteering her services to the Diocese as part of the Office for Social Concerns. In her new position as Director of the Office of Family Life she determined that her job was to "help families see holiness in the messiness of everyday life." To do this she offered family-centered programs to the students at Brescia College and in local high schools as well as to families throughout the diocese. She also became the "family advocate" in diocesan planning sessions. In these sessions she repeatedly emphasized the role of the home as the primary teacher of faith, love, care, service, and moral and social values.

The Family Life Office sought to contribute to the many different groups represented in family life. For those preparing for marriage, the Family Life Office encourage the adoption of the Sponsor Couple approach to marriage preparation.

In response to the 1984 request for married couples who would "walk with" the couples preparing for marriage, over fifty couples from across the Diocese offered to help.

And for those whose marriages, despite efforts to the contrary, ended in separation and/or divorce, the Family Life Office offered seminars and programs to help in the healing process. The Family Life Office considered this family-centered healing process especially important if there were children involved in the separated family. As a result of this family healing ministry, a Diocesan Day of Prayer with Separated and Divorced Catholics was scheduled on October 29, 1983. Following this day of prayer support groups for separated and divorced Catholics were established in Henderson and Owensboro. These groups were coordinated by Bruce Farley and Marcy and Tim Allman. In 1984 a third group, headed by J. R. Bone, was organized in Madisonville, KY.

The Family Life Office officially welcomed Mrs. Ellen Hayden as an Associate for Family Life Ministry in 1985. This was an "official" welcome because Ms. Hayden had actually been associated with and contributing to the Diocesan family ministry programs since she and her husband began offering workshops for the Diocesan Catholic Counseling Service.

A certified marriage and family therapist, Mrs. Hayden, in conjuction with the Family Life Center she and her husband, Del, had established at the Western Kentucky University Newman Center, presented programs for widowed persons as well as programs for effective parenting.

The Family Life Office also continued to encourage the already established Diocesan marriage programs such as the Marriage Encounter, the Couple-to-Couple League, the Engaged Encounter and the Pre-Cana Conferences. In addition, to these the Family Life Office introduced a new Diocesan tradition, the celebration of World Marriage Day.

St. Anthony's Parish in Brown's Valley hosted the first diocesan observance of World Marriage Day on February 10, 1985. The celebration included a Mass and special blessings for the married couples. The "longest married couple" in the Diocese was also given special recognition at this celebration. Sherman and Ethel Howard received the first such Diocesan recognition. They had been married 70 years. Also recognized at the celebration were Claude and Rose Catherine Payne who had been married for 67 years.

The Family Life Office encouraged the Diocesan faithful to think of the home as the basic unit of the parish community. From this basic unit of the home and from the larger Church community another Diocesan Office, that of Social Concerns, invited parishioners to reach out to address the justice and charity issues that could be found on local, state, national, and global levels. Initially established in August, 1983 with two half-time staff members, Sr. Kathleen Kaelin (OSU) and Sr. Cheryl Clemons (OSU), the work of this office was so extensive that it was evident it needed at least one person who could give it undivided attention. Sr. Cheryl Clemons became that person in August, 1985 and Carolyn Sue Cecil joined her in the office as her secretary.

Responding to the justice and charity issues of the 1980s called for the creation of seven commissions operating in conjuction with the Office of Social Concerns: the Commission for Persons with Disabilities, the Women's Commission, the AIDS Task Force, the Rural Life Commission, the Respect for Life Commission, the Black Catholics' Commission, and the Peace and Justice Commission.

In addition to organizing these commissions and coordinating their activities, the Office of Social Concerns also began the process of encouraging each parish to initiate its own parish social concerns committee so that the diocesan office could better network with the parish groups for communications purposes and, at times, for the coordination of a total Diocesan response to a justice or charity issue.

There were some issues in the 1980s that immediately called for the attention of the Social Concerns Office. As was true of so many of the other Diocesan Offices, the Office of Social Concerns learned that the diocesan faithful desired updated education regarding the Church's position on issues of justice and charity. For this updating, the Office of Social Concerns turned to the National Conference of Catholic Bishops which issued several pastoral letters in the 1970s and 80s that addressed justice issues. The Office of Social Concerns was able to use some of the pastorals as teaching tools and in other instances was instrumental in bringing people together from across the diocese to supply data for the Bishops' consideration as they wrote the pastorals. The three pastoral letters available for teaching purposes were *Brothers and Sisters to Us, A Pastoral Letter on Racism in our Day*, issued November 14, 1979; *The Challenge of Peace: God's Promise and Our Response*, issued on May 3, 1983; and *Economic Justice for All*, issued on November 18, 1986.

In 1984 the Commission on Women started the process of gathering local input for consideration by the National Conference of Bishops as it prepared a national pastoral letter on women and women's role in the Church. These women not only supplied ideas and research, they also critiqued and made suggestions for the first two drafts of the pastoral letter. When the pastoral letter, *Women in the Church*, was issued in 1989, the women of the Owensboro Diocese may not have agreed with all that it contained, but they had had the opportunity to thoroughly discuss it and were well informed of its message.

The Office of Social Concerns also kept the people of the diocese well informed concerning the U.S. involvment in the civil war raging in El Salvador and in the murders of Archbishop Romero and the four American women martyrs: Sisters Ita Ford (MM), Dorothy Kazel (OSU), Maura Clark (MM) and Ms. Jean Donovan. In March of each year the Office of Social Concerns encouraged the celebration of Central American Week. These celebrations helped the parishioners become aware of the inequity of the distribution of wealth and resources in the Central American countries. They also became aware of the many ways they could become active promoters of the Gospel as it related to these matters. Through the Office of Social Concerns parishioners learned of organizations in which they could participate and methods they could use to voice their concerns to elected officials and others who might directly influence the outcome of a particular issue.

Another 80s issue that claimed the attention of the Office of Social Concerns was the outbreak of the AIDS epidemic. In September of 1987 in an effort to find ways to minister locally to people with AIDS and to their families and to find ways to educate the public about the disease, Bishop McRaith appointed a twelve member task force of people from across the diocese. Prominent among the members of this task force were health care representatives from Mercy and Lourdes hospitals, educators and counselors. The task force saw their goal as one of taking a pro-life stand with respect to the people with AIDS and and sought ways the diocesan Church could make a difference in the quality of life for people with AIDS and their families. As a result of their work, in November of 1987, Bishop McRaith issued a document, "'Go and Do Likewise': Responding to the AIDS Crisis". The document called for a Christian response of prayer, solidarity and compassion with people with AIDS and their families. It also urged justice in employment and health care for people with AIDS and advocated adequate funding for research aimed at treatment and cure of the disease.

After 50 years the tree of fruit in the Diocese of Owensboro continues to bear the fruits of a community committed to charity and justice.

In order to continue in solidarity with people with AIDS the AIDS Task Force became a standing committee working with the Office of Social Concerns. Its efforts to educate the public included sponsoring talks at the Education Institutes in the diocese, distributing literature, about AIDS, and planning annual memorial services for people with AIDS. One of the most positive steps of solidarity with the families and friends of people with AIDS was the step taken at Sts. Joseph and Paul parish in Owensboro, KY. In this parish the people started a support group (STAFF) that met regularly once a month for these friends and families. The AIDS Task Force was also charged with establishing employment policies for all Church employees with life-threatening illnesses, including AIDS.

People with AIDS were not the only people in the diocese who still faced discrimination. The Social Concerns Office urged an end to racism within the Church. Toward this end and to increase the awareness of the gifts, talents, and rich culture of Black Catholics in the Owensboro Diocese Bishop McRaith established the Black Catholic Commission.

Through the efforts of the Office of Social Concerns and the Black Catholic Commission area Catholics especially from Paducah and Owensboro, cities in which there had been Black Catholic communities for many years, gathered to celebrate special days like Martin Luther King, Jr.'s birthday (observed as a national holiday for the first time January 20, 1986) and to study the history of Black Catholicism. Terri and Clarence Hanley and Cathy Meadows represented the diocese at the National Black Congress, a meeting of U.S. Bishops and Black Catholic leaders, who together worked to discover ways the Catholic Church in the United States could work to end racism and promote more opportunities for Black leadership in society and in the Church.

Rosary Chapel in Paducah, under the leadership of Rose Lowery, would find one way to bring Black leadership to the diocese and that would be the ministry of song and dance. She developed a choir at Rosary Chapel that was frequently asked to give guest concerts in other churches throughout the diocese.

In 1987 Rose Lowery and the Hanleys would also represent the Owensboro diocesan Black Catholics in an audience with Pope John Paul II as he met with Black Catholics in New Orleans,

Mel Howard, Director of the Office of Communications, proudly displays the first copy of the Diocese of Owensboro Newsletter *printed in Newspaper format, November 1984.*

LA when on his visit to the United States in September of 1987.

Another group of people for whom the Office of Social Concerns sought equality was people with disabilities. One of the greatest injustices the people with diabilities had to endure was that of simply being forgotten or ignored by the Church, especially when it came to the planning of liturgical celebrations and/or the drawing up of building or renovation plans for parish buildings. The Diocesan Commission for the Handicapped (later called the Diocesan Disabilities Commission) chose as one of their first goals an education of the diocese with respect to barriers faced by parishioners with disabilities when they wished to participate fully in liturgical celebrations in their parish churches. Largely through the efforts of this commission the diocese began to include interpreters for the deaf at large group gatherings in the diocese, like the Chrism Mass at the Sportscenter, and they made attempts to organize support groups for the deaf. Priests in the diocese who were fluent in sign language (Fr. Marty Hayes and Fr. Louis Piskula, for instance) celebrated the Liturgy in sign language on special occasions for the these support groups. Church planners were encouraged to think of building ranps to entrances instead of steps or having entrances on ground level for people in wheelchairs. Social Concern Committees in parishes were also encouraged to form transportation committees for people who might be physically able to come to parish liturgies and functions, but might be lacking transportation to the same.

One leader on the Diocesan Disabilities Commission who was able to demonstrate very graphically the barriers faced by people with disabilities was Tommy Malone of Owensboro. Though crippled with cerebral palsy, Tommy worked tirelessly at sensitizing people to other peoples needs.

The pro-life approach the Office of Concerns took in trying to provide quality life for the marginalized in society was also evident in its promotion of observance of Respect Life Sunday, advocacy for the rights of the unborn and efforts to make alternatives to abortion available to any woman in the diocese who might find herself facing an unwanted pregnancy.

Two very positive steps taken to reach out to women and their unborn children were the establishment of the Birthright Center in Owensboro, KY and the Opportunities for Life, Inc. hot-line.

The Birthright Center was directed by Carolyn Sue Cecil and Florence Itschner of Owensboro. It opened on January 22, 1985, offering a place residence, supplies, and counseling to women in need.

The Opportunities for Life, Inc. was the name for the state-wide alternative to abortion program sponsored by the Catholic dioceses of Kentucky. Its purpose was to recruit and train volunteers for crisis counseling and for coordinating parish based help for women in need. Barbara Koonce of Mayfield, KY served as the program director of Opportunities for Life, Inc.

The Office of Social Concerns had another opportunity to witness to the consistent pro-life ethic that is the teaching of the Catholic Church when the state of Kentucky began deliberating the reinstatement of the death penalty as the punishment for particular crimes. Cheryl Clemons (OSU), director of the Office of Social Concerns put together a source book on Capital Punishment. This source book provided input for the Bishops' pastoral Choose Life: Reflections on the Death Penalty". To educate the public regarding the Church's stand on the death penalty the Office of Social Concerns used opportunities like the Respect Life Day at Brescia College to speak to large gatherings of people and they participated in protests against the reinstatement of the death penalty in Kentucky. They chose Eddyville state prison as the site for the demonstrations.

Other groups reached out to specifically by the Social Concerns Office included the unemployed and widows/widowers. For both of these groups the Office of Social Concerns planned prayer days and sought to establish parish based support groups.

Another group needed more than that and because their needs were so great a part-time diocesan worker was assigned specifically to work with them. This group consisted of the refugees from Southeast Asia and from Poland who were coming to the United States to escape the persecution they feared in their own countries. Theresa Marie Wilkerson (OSU) succeeded Fr. Leonard Reisz in the special ministry to the refugees. She helped to find them adequate housing, get them enrolled in classes so they could learn to speak English (if that was needed), obtain the proper papers from the immigration office in Louisville and, in general, get established within the area. Between 1975 and 1982 approximately 500 refugees from Southeast Asia and Poland had been sponsored by the people of the Owensboro Diocese.

After 1982, it was not uncommon for the refugees to move out of the Diocese to other areas. Reasons for leaving usually were job or family related. In many instances they would learn of relatives who had also immigrated to the U.S., but had located in another area due to sponsorship by some group in that area.

The efforts that Sr. Theresa Marie made to help the refugees, that the Office of Social Concerns made to educate concerning the "seamless garment" approach taken by the Church regarding pro-life issues and the many different ways the laity of the diocese were participating in small and large group gatherings during RENEW were shared with the rest of the diocese through the work of the people in the diocesan Office of Communications. Bishop McRaith appointed Mr. Mel Howard to direct this office in August, 1984. In 1985-86 he was assisted one day a week by Fr. Maury Riney. Besides publishing *The Diocese of Owensboro Newsletter,* which assumed a newpaper format and the name *Western Kentucky Catholic* in November, 1984, the Office of Communications helped launch the diocesan offices into the technological world. With the help of a grant from the Catholic Communications Campaign in December, 1985, the Office of Communications was able to purchase equipment needed to link up with the Catholic Telecommunications Network of America, a network owned by the National Conference of Catholic Bishops. Programming from this network could be made available through cable TV stations throughout the diocese. The educational value of this television media was demonstrated to many of the diocesan faithful as they participated in teleconference classes at the Catholic Pastoral Center.

During the RENEW years in the Diocese, the Office of Communications helped spread the news of the RENEW celebrations, small and large group activities in parishes, schedules and, in general, the spirit that was being experienced throughout the diocese. *The Western Kentucky Catholic* became a tool of evangelism as well as information sharing. Like Bishop Soenneker, Bishop McRaith used the diocesan newspaper as a means of teaching. Each month he wrote a letter to the people through the newspaper.

And in February and March, 1986, the newspaper also explained how each of the pastoral staff offices served the people.

Of particular note to the laity was the Office of Lay Ministry, Rev. John Vaughn replaced Sharon Grant (SCN) in this office in August, 1985. (He also became Vicar General of the Diocese, replacing Rev. George Hancock who had been doing that ministry along with being Chancellor

With the completion of this church in December 1986, only one county in the Diocese, Todd County, was left without a church.

for the Diocese.) This office coordinated the formal work of establishing the Lay Ministry program for the diocese. The goal of the ministry program was to help all the laity become more aware of their mission to "make Christ and His Church present in the marketplace."

Other diocesan offices that could help the laity fulfill this mission were the Office of Vocations, directed by Rev. Ed Bradley; the Office of Ecumenism, directed by Rev. Joseph O'Donnell; and the Office of Youth Ministry, directed by Rev. Henry Cecil. The staff of these offices were very involved in the promotion of RENEW, in representing the diocese at functions related to their office and as consultants for the bishop and others throughout the diocese when they needed input on matters related to these offices.

AS RENEW kept helping questions surface through small and large group gatherings, there was much consulting with all the diocesan offices and there was much to study and to celebrate throughout the diocese.

That there were still poverty issues to be confronted, especially among the women, children and farmers in Kentucky, was acknowledged and studied in a series of documents written in 1986 by the Catholic Conference of Kentucky and published in the diocesan newspapers. (The series was called the "Faces of Poverty".)

That there was still a need for vocations to the priesthood and religious life was made real with studies that indicated that there were approximately 240,000 unchurched people in the 32 counties of the Owensboro Diocese in 1983. And that many were giving serious consideration to those vocations was celebrated by the fact that seven seminarians would be ordained for the Diocese in 1989.

As the Diocese planned to keep addressing these questions and working to promote the Kingdom of God in Western Kentucky, two events would make Bishop McRaith's fifth year in leading this diocese very memorable. Both of these events occurred in the fall of the year.

On September 25, 1987 Most Rev. Henry J. Soenneker died as a result of a stroke. He was 80 years old. Archbishop Kelley from the Archdiocese of Louisville presided at his funeral liturgy on Monday, September 29. Eight other bishops co-celebrated this Mass of Resurrection and more than 700 people in the congregation joined their prayers with those of the clergy. Bishop McRaith would eugulogize Bishop Soenneker as a "gentle person, who, though frugal with himself, had always been generous with others." Perhaps it was the best of both of those characteristics that had helped Bishop Soenneker leave the Diocese of Owensboro financially sound when he retired in 1982.

Bishop Soenneker was also remembered as an effective leader, one who had to deal with the changes of both the Church and American society of the 60s.

That the Church had been guided carefully through those turbulent years was one of the reasons the second event in the fall of 1987 was such a celebrative one. This event was the celebration of the 50th Anniversary of the Diocese.

The Diocesan Jubilee committee consisted of Clark Shakelford, Bettye Bowlds, Paul Coomes, Fr. Ray Goetz, Fr. John Vaughan, Bishop McRaith, Barbara and John Becker, Max and Sarah Feller, Sr. Joseph Angela Boone, Marianna Robinson, Mary Ann Thrasher and Mel Howard. *The Western Kentucky Catholic* published a series of historical essays and stories about various places and events in the "first fifty years" of the diocese and Judy Hayden compiled a commemorative history of the diocese entitled "Thus Far By Faith". The stories told in the historical essays and in the commemorative book reminded people of lots of other stories that could have been related.

And there was a time for the Church of the Diocese of Owensboro to share those stories. That time was on October 10, 1987 at 4 o'clock in the afternoon at the Owensboro Sportscenter. With flags, color and great pagentry and with songs that gave thanksgiving for each of the 32 counties in the Diocese, Most Rev. Archbishop Pio Laghi, the Aposolic Delegate presided at the Jubilee Liturgy. Afterwards the congregation of over 7,000 spilled out of the Sportscenter to a barbecue picnic in Moreland Park where they stood in little groups, sat at benches, or strolled the park telling their stories of blessings of the fifty years of the Diocese.

May 1990, Diocesan Staff at 600 Locust St., Catholic Pastoral Center.

Kevin Osborn, a Seminarian student visiting Grayson County, led the children in a song during final day activities at a county-wide Vacation Bible School held at St. Joseph in Leitchfield June 8-12. (Photo by Edna Duggins)

Catholicity in Western Kentucky 1987-Present

Chronology of Events

1987   Office of Lay Ministry established; First move toward training laity in parishes; Core Course designed and presented for training of laity; Diocesan Pastoral Council established; 50th anniversary celebration, October 4, 1987; First History of Diocese written; Bishop Soenneker's death, September 24, 1987; Bishop Cotton Apartments for Retired Priests built

1988   Closing of St. Mark's Seminary; Bishop McRaith's first Ad Limina Visit; First graduates in Ministry Formation

1989   Office of Planning created; Introduction of synod; Consolidation of Catholic schools in Owensboro-Daviess Co.; Full-time director in Office of Youth Ministry, July 1989; Adult Formation combined with Office of Lay Ministry; St. Mark's, Eddyville completed, fulfilling the goal of a Catholic Church in every county; Monsignor George Hancock retired from Office of Administration and Sister Joseph Angela Boone appointed; Marian Shrine established in Bowling Green; Full-time Director in Office of Youth Ministry, July 1989; Addition to Bishop Cotton Apartments for Retired Priests

1990   Lay Deanery Councils formed in all six deaneries; Second Diocesan Synod promulgated at Chrism Mass, April 9; Formation of Deanery Councils
Catholic Pastoral Center moved from 4005 Frederica Street to 600 Locust Street; College classes taught in rural areas for first time

1991   Two college classes for certification in rural areas ; Second Synod of the Diocese held October 18-20; Synod Speak-ups, March 1-April 18; Office of Stewardship created in July 1991; Part-time Archivist hired; Glenmary Sisters move to Owensboro; Lourdes Hospital transferred to sponsorship of Mercy Health Systems; Passionists Nuns decision to relocate

1992   Scripture Classes in four rural sites; Office for Outreach part-time; Office for Black Catholics; Bishop John McRaith's Pastoral Letter, Respect and Justice-Rooted in the First Church"; TEC #100 held at Mount Saint Joseph; Western Kentucky Catholic mailed to households, October; Bishop McRaith's 10th anniversary as bishop; Father John Vaughan to Rome; First non-ordained Chancellor named; Father Joe Mills appointed Vicar General; Mount St. Joseph Ursulines renovate their chapel

Overview of the Years 1987-Present

The Catholics of Western Kentucky trace their heritage to the Catholics of Maryland who came to this country seeking religious freedom. Standing on the shoulders of strong and determined people of faith, the Church of Western Kentucky carries forward into the next century, the legacy of strength that has been handed down to it from the 1700's into the 21st century, the "faith—and the spread of it—is a way of life, a reason for life."(1)

Through the years of Bishop Cotton (1937-1960), religious leader and executive builder, the diocese was firmly rooted in faith and growth. During the span of Bishop Soenneker (1961-1982), zealous and faithful guardian and educator, the faith deepened and Catholics held on to commitments while striving to adapt amid changing cultures and transforming challenges of the Second Vatican Council. The following account is an attempt to record the happenings of the period beginning in 1987 to the end of 1992 under the shepherding of Bishop John Jeremiah McRaith (1982-), third bishop of the diocese. It addresses the movements that thrust Catholics into the deeper realization of what it means to be a church of people with "faith become living, conscious, and active..."(2) in the world.

The first section, Toward a Church of the Laity, describes events that helped to shape the response of lay people to their baptismal call. The section, Toward a Church with a Mission, illustrates the development that happened with the knowledge that the Church of Western Kentucky must carry the message of Jesus into the world. The last segment, Toward a Church in Gratitude and Celebration, marks the blessings that God has bestowed upon the diocese during these years.

Toward a Church of the Laity

Equipping the Laity

Bishop John J. McRaith, a rural bishop for a rural diocese, proved himself to be pastoral in the real sense of the word. He made himself known as a listener and as a bishop with the needs and concerns of the people at heart. One of his great loves was to visit parishes and meet the people. Out of the need to be in touch with parishes at a distance from Owensboro, the Diocesan See, he opened an office in Paducah, where he spent one day each month. Early in his episcopate, it became evident that he desired to draw the laity into their rightful role of shared responsibility in the Church. An Office of Lay Ministry was created, Renew, was begun and a Lay Ministry Think Tank was instituted. The Think Tank captured Bishop McRaith's vision of training the laity for ministry and designed the Ministry Formation program at Brescia College which officially began in 1985. Renew proved to be the major contributor toward igniting the flame of lay involvement. In 1987, following

Father John Vaughan and Sister Cheryl Clemons present a session of the Core Course at the Catholic Pastoral Center.

The Parish Hall at St. Joseph and Paul Parish is filled to standing room only for the Core Course.

Participants in Old Testament Class at St. Romuald, Hardinsburg, Fall 1992, Sr. Marian Powers, Mila Whittler, Kin Brumfield, Carol Bair, Marie Rose, Connie Critchelow, Debbie Oelze, Dorothy Payne, Rosemary Dowell, Wilma Hayse.

Renew in an effort to meet the laity's call for greater growth, the diocesan staff planned and presented across the diocese a six-weeks course of training for ministry. This "Core Course" included theological foundations for ministry and spiritual formation. Approximately 2,000 people participated in these learning sessions.

For the first time in the history of the diocese, volunteer ministers along with Catholic school teachers were able to become trained and certified for their roles as religious educators. Most importantly, a desire for spiritual growth was awakened as never before. From this, grew the need for training in specific ministries. Brescia College, the diocesan staff, and Mount St. Joseph Center began to present workshops for various ministries, committees and councils across the diocese. All of these, as well as Brescia's Ministry Formation Program became part of the certification of religious educators and ministers. The diocese made strides in ministry training and the laity was at a point of no turning back in church involvement. The Spirit had truly been at work in the hearts of the people in the Church of Western Kentucky.

A further development within the diocese was the effort to train catechetical leaders for parishes in rural areas. In 1990, through the collaboration of the diocese and Brescia, the Ministry Formation Program was inserted into the Weekend College. At first glance, this may not seem significant but, indeed, it was. It allowed women and men in full-time work to take classes on weekends in the Ministry Formation Program. Thus volunteer ministers in parishes could receive professional certificates or degrees for ministry. In addition, in 1991 two college classes were taught in four rural sites of the diocese as an effort to help volunteers in small parishes. By 1992, this number increased to four classes in four places off-campus making it possible for more ministers to become professionally certified through Brescia College and also further their own faith development. Bishop McRaith's enthusiasm and foresight for the need to equip the laity to fulfill their rightful role in the Church caught on and continues to grow. The interest and participation in the opportunities made available is a sure sign that it is of the Spirit.

Involving the Laity
Diocesan Pastoral Council

An important step toward lay involvement was the formation of the Diocesan Pastoral Council. It came into being on August 17, 1987 after a year of study and work by an appointed task force to formulate guidelines for such a council. The original members of the task force were: Sidney Ebelhar and Mike Thompson, Owensboro Deanery; Ted Nally and Gloria Adams, Eastern Deanery: Charles Shade and Joyce Greenwell, Central Deanery; Pat Eubank and Philip Hayden, Rural Deanery; Curtis Hixon and Joyce Tidwell, Western Deanery; Jean Fulkerson, Stella Flaherty and Mary Watson, Bowling Green Deanery; Rev. Robert Drury, Rev. Louis Piskula and Rev. Carl Wise, CPPS, priests' representatives; Sister Patricia Froning, OSF, and Sister Suzanne Sims, OSU, sisters' representatives; Dave Pennaman, Committee for Total Catholic Education; Susan Silva, Social Concerns Committee; Rose Warren, Administration Committee; and Carolyn Basehart, Worship Committee. All but five of these original members committed themselves to serve on the newly formed Diocesan Patoral Council beginning in August 1987. Ted Nally was replaced by Jim Lynch for the Eastern Deanery, Steve Schuhmann and Kenny Buckman became the Bowling Green representatives and Rev. Carl Wise, CPPS, withdrew leaving two priests as the by-laws specified. In 1992, the membership included two new committees formed since the diocesan Synod: Family Life, represented by Ron Segebarth and Spiritual Life whose representative was Father John Meredith. Members of the Diocesan Pastoral Council in 1992: Drury Howard, Joanne Stevens, Philip Hayden, Ann Mulligan, Pat McGruder, Thomas Buerhle, Curtis Hixon, Jim Tidwell, Gloria Adams, Jim Lynch, Kenny Buchman, Steve Papciak, Fay Higdon, Sister Mary Margaret Cooper, SCN, Father Gary Payne, Mike Thompson, Ron Segebarth, Father John Meredith, Sister Clarita Browning, OSU, Sister Eula Johnson, SCN and Father Larry Hostetter.

The original Diocesan Pastoral Council gathered in meeting.

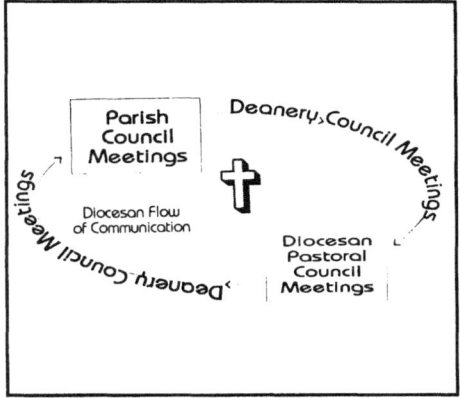
Symbol portraying the flow of communication made possible by Deanery Councils.

April 9, 1990 Chrism Mass – Bishop McRaith officially announces the Second Synod of the Diocese.

Members of the Faithful participate in a Speak-Up held at St. Joseph and Paul Parish Hall prior to the Synod, March 1, 1991.

The Diocesan Pastoral Council is the chief consultative body for the bishop. Its responsibilities are to review, plan and evaluate pastoral activities of the diocese and set forth conclusions that contribute to fulfillment of the mission for the Church of the diocese.(3) The creation of this council allows the consultative process to become a reality in the diocese.

Deanery Councils

One of the first major steps taken by the diocesan Pastoral Council was the formation of Deanery councils, groups of lay people from each deanery to serve as liaisons between the Diocesan Pastoral Council and Parish councils. By 1990, these six Deanery Councils were formed with representatives from each parish and two Diocesan Pastoral Council representatives from their respective deaneries. With the formation of these councils, the chain of communication between the Diocesan Pastoral Council and Parish Pastoral Councils was completed and a new link existed between and among the parishes of the deaneries. Also, more people assumed an active role of shared responsibility in decision making in the Church. Deanery Council representatives bring to the diocesan level issues from the parish that are of concern to the whole Church as well as take back to the parish information that needs to be shared by all. It is a circle of communication—from parish level to diocesan level and back to diocesan level. Such exchange of ideas and resources pertaining to

Participants of a Speak-up at St. Anthony, Peonia, April 9, 1991.

Synod Delegates at Work, October 19, 1991.

the pastoral life of the Church promote greater understanding and unity in carrying out the mission of the people of God in Western Kentucky.

Diocesan Synod

Another way of involving the laity began with the creation of an Office of Planning in July 1989, with Father John Vaughan as director. This office would, over the course of time, call forth many lay persons to assist in planning for the church's mission. An initial endeavor of this office was to introduce the idea of a diocesan synod. After extensive consultation with the priests and the faithful of the diocese and upon the recommendation of the Diocesan Pastoral Council, the synod became official. At the Chrism Mass on April 9, 1990, Bishop McRaith read the decree announcing the Second Synod of the Diocese of Owensboro, naming Father John Vaughn Director of the Synod. This was a memorable event. It had been over 40 years since the first and only synod of the diocese (1943) and at that time none of the laity were involved. In a letter from the Vatican Secretariat of State, Pope John Paul II gave his commendations and prayerful support of this endeavor and invited "the members of the Synod to find the inspiration and motivation for all their efforts in the teaching of the Second Vatican Council on the nature and mission of the Church."(4) Bishop McRaith stated four goals for this synod: First, a long range plan for the diocese; second, a greater sense of diocesan church; third, the spiritual renewal of all; and fourth, a reminder that all are to be evangelists. In the months that followed the announcement, a year and half-long preparatory process began under the guidance of Sister Kathy Warren, OSF, of Rochester, Minnesota. A central committee and eight preparatory commissions were formed and the process was in motion. The focus was on the current status of diocesan programs in administration, education, communications, family life, personnel, social concerns, spiritual life and worship in light of the demographic make-up of the diocese. Data of the past five years was compared with the current situation and forecast statements of trends for five years ahead were written. This information was considered in Speak-up Sessions around the diocese. Every Catholic was invited to attend the Speak-ups and voice an opinion about future needs. From March 1-April 1991, the Catholics of Western Kentucky from Owensboro to Scottsville, from Irvington to Fulton, shared a unique moment in their history. Approximately 1,500 persons took this opportunity to express to the bishop their concerns about the local church of the future. Every idea for change was recorded and clustered. Then during October 18-20, 1991, delegates from every parish, institution and committee along with invited observers gathered at the Executive Inn in Owensboro for the three-day synod facilitated by Sister Donna Kenny, SCN. After months of preparation, it was now the responsibility of the delegates to deal with the information gleaned at the speak-up sessions. To the surprise of many, Bishop McRaith did not speak but he listened to his people in order to allow the Spirit to work as the delegates prayed, shared and made decisions. Through this process, ten goals were determined for the Church of Western Kentucky for the next five years. On October 20, the Synod officially concluded at the Sportscenter with approximately 2,500 Catholics participating in a beautiful liturgical celebration. The Synod was over, but the experience of the three days was fresh in the hearts of those present. Their lives had been touched and they knew it was a sacred moment for the Church of the diocese as well as the whole Church. They were indeed privileged to have been chosen to represent their parishes at this joyful event. The Spirit was and is active in and through them as they celebrated a new vision of the Church of the diocese and the accomplishment of the goals for the synod. Comments of the delegates attest to this: "We are a diocesan Church not a county with surrounding neighbors." "I was afraid when I started this process that we were just to be a 'rubber stamp' group, but... despite our varied backgrounds, we were being drawn together in the Spirit to create something new, not to rubber stamp the status quo."(5)

Diocesan Staff

Another way of involving the laity was effected through changes in the diocesan staff and the inclusion of lay staff members. Each addition had an impact on the movement toward becoming a Church of the Laity. As early as 1983, an Office for Family Life was directed by a lay person as was the Office for Social Concerns by 1987. In July 1989, a lay person was hired as the first full-time director of the Office for Youth Ministry.

In the Office for Youth Ministry, Tony Cooper, replaced Sister Martha Keller, OSU, who was interim director during 1988-89. Father Henry Cecil served as the diocese's youth leader from 1983-88. He empowered many lay person to take initiative in working with young people who would become active leaders for tomorrow's Church.

One office which had the particular duty of leading the laity in their role of taking responsibility in the Church was that of Lay Ministry. When the office was formed, Father John Vaughan, its leader, had the charge of coordinating the training of lay people for ministry and for pastoral councils. In July 1989, an Office of Adult Formation was coupled with the Office of Lay Ministry and Sister Mary Irene Cecil, OSU, became its director. One of her first tasks was that madated by the Diocesan Pastoral Council to design and implement the formation of the Deanery Councils. These councils proved to be a most effective means by which more of the laity took an active role of shared responsibility in the Church as it lived out its mission.

Still another office change that had an impact on the laity, was the appointment of Sister Joseph Angela Boone, OSU, to the Office of Administration, when Monsignor George Hancock retired after some 40 years of service. In this office, Sister Joseph Angela had the

Closing Liturgy of the Synod at the Sportscenter, October 20, 1991.

The Church of Western Kentucky at Worship – Closing of the Synod, October 20, 1991.

special ministry of all areas of business and finance and it positioned her to empower people at the parish level, who were responsible for those areas. The growth and development of the diocesan staff continued to come about as needs arose and each change was made in light of the responsibility of the laity to their Baptismal call to mission and ministry.

Toward a Church in Mission

The Call to Mission

The Renew process deepened the realization that Catholics are a church with a mission, the mission of Jesus: namely, to share the good news of God's love. Bishop McRaith, in his role as teacher continually challenged all the faithful that the message of Jesus must be acted out in their lives, in their families and in the world. In order to model this directive, he set about developing the essential ministries to enable the people of the local Church to become effective evangelists.

Stewardship for Mission

The diocesan paper, *The Western Kentucky Catholic*, carried as a regular feature a letter from the bishop to the people of the diocese. It is one way he can speak to all the faithful and fulfill his role of teacher. In it, he also challenges and encourages Catholics to be what they profess by their baptism. There are constant messages of the call to be mission-minded, to share the faith and to reach out to the needy. More frequently, he has written in terms of the responsibility to share God's gifts of time, talent and treasure because all are gifts received from God and not any person's private possession. Such sharing is for the disciple the measure of salvation. (6) So strong was the bishop's conviction that in 1991, an Office for Stewardship led by Tom Lilly was added to the diocesan staff as a beginning effort to make this challenge a reality throughout the diocese. For Bishop John, stewardship is a sign of true discipleship which touches all areas of life, all of God's creation. Personally he has taken this challenge seriously, responding responsibly and accountably. He believes that God exacts an accounting of the gifts he has received both personally and as shepherd of the diocese. Each year he has published in the diocesan newspaper a financial report of how moneys have been spent in the care of the diocese. The Synod goal for the Office for Administration supported his desire to develop a comprehensive program of stewardship education in the parishes to meet the needs of the mission. This program was Tom Lilly's first major task and he jumped into it with whole heart from the beginning of his employment in July 1991.

Mission to Others

No one could listen to this bishop for very long, without hearing him voice his concern for hurting Catholics and the unchurched around us. The need to reach out to them as a part of the mission of the Church of Western Kentucky seemed to have a greater urgency because of its proximity to the Bible belt and because of the small percentage (6.5) of Catholics in the 32 county area. Bishop McRaith believed that all Catholics are engaged in evangelization no matter the ministry, no matter the workplace. One goal of his was fulfilled by the opening of houses of Catholic presence where there was none in the diocese. To accomplish this, Bishop McRaith established houses of ministry for sisters in places such as Benton in Marshall County; Caneyville in Grayson County; Horse Branch and Fordsville in Ohio County; Greenville in Muhlenburg County; Marion in Crittenden County and Smithland in Livingston County. He promoted the Christian Initiation of Adults as one of the best ways of welcoming new members into the faith community. In 1992, he implemented the Synod goal of outreach by appointing Sister Patricia Froning, OSF, as part-time for outreach in the Office for Lay Ministry.

The Church of the diocese was not amiss in Vatican II's exhortation to be ecumenical. As director of the Office for Ecumenism, Father Joseph O'Donnell (Glenmary) was involved in various interfaith dialogues, the Catholic Conference of Kentucky and the Kentucky Council of Churches. Inter-church relationships through prayer and faith sharing services are held in individual parishes. Priests and pastoral associates participate in local ministerial associations.

Close to Bishop McRaith's heart was the rich heritage of the Church's social teaching and the Gospel call to live those teachings. His response to them was the creation of an Office for Social Concerns only a few months after having been made bishop. This office, directed by Sister Cheryl Clemons, OSU, at its outset, came under the leadership of Dan and Laura Robinson from 1987-91. These directors led the development of a Diocesan Social Concerns Committee and seven working commissions: Black Catholic Commission, Commission for the Handicapped, Peace and Justice Commission, Respect Life Commission, Rural Life Commission, Aids Task Force and Women's Commission. The Office of Social Concerns and these groups dedicated themselves to educating others in an awareness of social needs. Much time and effort was given to training parish committees for direct services and social action. In 1992, Sister Judy Morris, OP, became the director of this office continuing to focus on the Church's role in promoting the dignity of all persons. Besides offering training for Social Concerns Committees, she networks with other churches and agencies who minister to human needs.

Of particular concern to Bishop McRaith from the start, were the black Catholics in the diocese. He continually sought to support them and question how the church can draw them into active participation. Each year he participated in a Day of Reflection conducted by the Black Catholic Commission. In July 1992, he attended the Seventh Black Catholic Congress held in New Orleans, LA. On return, he wrote in the *Western Kentucky Catholic*: "I came home with a renewed conviction and commitment to make our African American sisters and brothers more a priority—both in how they can enrich the Church in Western Kentucky and what the faith community (diocese) can do to assist in solving some of the serious social issues."(7) It was not long before he proved his commitment by creating an African American Catholic Ministries Office and naming Father William S. Odom-Green as its director, effective January 1993.

Mercy Hospital in Owensboro.

Lourdes Hosptial in Paducah.

Bishop McRaith's Pastoral Letter on the Role of the Family.

Catholic Inmates on Death Row in Eddyville State Prison with Bishop McRaith and Father Peter Hughes – April, 1991.

An added concern in 1992 was the influx of Hispanics, most of whom were migrants, but nevertheless of Catholic background and very needy in every aspect of life but more particularly in the area of worship and religious education. According to Glenmary Researchers, there are 10,000 Hispanics in the diocese at this time. If they are not a part of the ministry of the diocese, they will become lost for lack of care. There is a Refugee Services Center for the diocese directed by Sister Theresa Marie Wilkerson, OSU, which works with the resettlement of immigrants, helping them find homes and work and apply for permanent residence in this country. These are people displaced by war or political and economic situations. For migrants, the story is different yet much the same. They are strangers in a strange land, yet they cannot be strangers in the Church. The Church of Western Kentucky must find ways to minister to them, so speaks the bishop.

Bishop McRaith is no stranger to the Catholic inmates on death row at the Kentucky State Penitentiary in Eddyville. He makes regular visits there, offering Mass, administering the sacrament of Confirmation and visiting the inmates. Bishop McRaith took a stand with the other bishops of Kentucky in a pastoral letter published on June 14, 1984 entitled "Choose Life-Reflections on the Death Penalty," condemning the death penalty and he has remained adamant in this position.

The church of the diocese makes an impact by its care of the sick. The two Catholic hospitals, Mercy in Owensboro and Lourdes in Paducah, are leaders in health care, especially for the poor and those without the benefit of insurance. Both hospitals are members of the Mercy Health Care System. Originally Lourdes was Riverside Hospital for the city of Paducah. In 1959, it was purchased by the diocese and became a Catholic hospital. The Sisters of St. Francis of Tiffen, Ohio managed and/or sponsored Lourdes from 1959-82. The diocese was its sponsor from 1983-90. On Jan. 1, 1991, the diocese transferred sponsorship to the Mercy Health Care System.

Mission to Ourselves

Becoming a Church for others, necessitates strenghtening the faith within ourselves. To look back through the last decade is to find a strong commitment to deepen faith and enhance growth. The diocese through the Family Life Office,

Bishop Cotton Apartments – Home for Retired Priests.

QUEST #4, St. John's Paducah, March, 1990.

TEC #100, Mount St. Joseph, September, 1992.

directed by Marthanne F. Allman, strives to promote a family perspective in all ministries. This is effected in a number of ways. Programs, training and resources are made available for all aspects of family: singles, pre-marriage couples and marriage enrichment. These include training in parenting and on sexuality. Special support sessions are provided for developing and hurting families, for divorced families and for those in bereavement. The Family Life Committee is responsible for implementing the Synod goal of assisting all parishes to address every aspect of family ministry, particularly by promoting inter-family support. Following Pope John Paul II's initiative, emphasis is placed on the family as the Church of the home, the smallest community of faith where people encounter God in the joys and struggles of their closest relationships. Bishop McRaith highlighted this essential role of the family in the mission of the Church in his pastoral letter, "Respect and Justice—Rooted in the First Church" in November 1992.

The Diocesan Tribunal continues to be active in judicial matters pertaining to church law in regard to the validity or non-validity of marriages. Rev. Joseph Mills has served as the Judicial Vicar since Feb. 1, 1983. In April 18, 1989, Father Peter Lauzon was named Adjutant Judicial Vicar. Others were called to assist them in this ministry. Among them are: Sister Annalita Lancaster, OSU, Sister Vivian Marie Bowles, OSU, Rev. Kevin Karl, Rev. J. Patrick Reynolds who began studies in Canon Law in 1992 and Father John Vaughan.

Faith life is expressed especially as a worshipping community and in worship faith is renewed. The diocesan Office for Worship, focuses its ministry toward improving communal liturgical celebrations. At its creation it was combined with the Office for Spiritual Life. Father Tony Ziegler and Sister Kathleen Kaelin, OSU as co-directors led the diocese in both spiritual growth and liturgical renewal with the help of diocesan Liturgy Committee. They provide workshops and training for lectors, cantors, musicians, RCIA teams and homilists. Parish Liturgy Committees are encouraged to evaluate their experience of liturgy and public prayer. Since "...liturgy is the summit toward which the activity of the Church is directed...the fount from which all her power flows" (8) every effort is being made to promote the Sunday Eucharistic liturgy as the center of the spiritual life of the parish. The Synod goal for worship calls not only for formation but also for evaluation of presiders, homilists and liturgical ministers to enable Spirit-filled liturgical celebrations in each parish community. The Diocesan Liturgical Committee began immediately its work of implementing this goal. In 1992, Father Larry McBride was appointed Director of the Office for Worship, Kevin Kinnaird accepted the position of Diocesan Music Director and assistant director of the Office of Worship. As diocesan Music Director, his role is to assist parishes to assess their liturgies and to offer workshops to help them enhance their worship through music. In addition to those duties, he directs the diocesan choir for such liturgies as the Chrism Mass, the Rite of Election and other diocesan events.

The Office for Worship and the Office for Spiritual Life were combined until 1987. At this time, the Office for Spiritual Life was assumed as a role of the Mount St. Joseph Retreat Center with Sister Mary Matthias Ward, OSU as the director until 1988 when Sister Marie Goretti Browning, OSU became director. While many people throughout the diocese benefit from the services and programs offered by Mount St. Joseph Center, the spiritual life needs of the diocese cannot be fully met by one retreat center. Following the Synod a Spiritual Life Committee was formed to assist in planning for the spiritual life needs of the people of the diocese. Father John Meredith was appointed as chairperson. The goal of the Synod which called for trained spiritual directors who could provide opportunities regionally for people in the parishes indicates both growth and hunger, thanks to Bishop McRaith's urge toward renewal and involvement in mission.

Two other movements were effective in reawakening the faith in people of the diocese—the Cursillo Movement and the Charismatic Renewal. Both continue to lead men and women to a turning point in their lives and inspire them to become active disciples in their families, in the marketplace and in the parish. Cursillo was under the direction of Sister Mary Matthias Ward, OSU until 1989, when Father Gerald Calhoun became the director. Father Gerard Glahn was the leader of the Charismatic Renewal until his death in 1990. At that time Father John Meredith took the leadership.

The Catholic life of the diocese moved with the times and responded as needs arose. Like the nation, this local Church was not exempt from aging. Concern for its priests, who were elderly and infirm led to an agreement in June 1987, with the Carmelite Sisters of Carmel Home in Owensboro, to build four rooms for infirm priests as an extension to their nursing home. In 1989, the diocese completed four additional apartments to the existing Cotton Apartments for retired priests which are located behind Carmel Home. The Cotton Apartments contain eight individual apartments, a chapel, a community

50th Anniversary Mass, October 4, 1987.

Procession with Banners at the Anniversary Mass.

Catching up on the News in The West Kentucky Catholic.

The First History of the Diocese.

Diocesan Heritage Cookbook

Judy Hayden, Editor of This Far by Faith.

room and an exercise room. Priests who live there can take meals and participate in activities at Carmel Home as well as receive the personal care they need.

Educating For Mission

Another way of building a church with a mission is through education. Bishop McRaith views communication as one means of education and he supports an Office for Communications for this purpose. As a member of Catholic Telecommunications Network, this office makes national teleconferences available for use to the diocese. The diocesan paper, *Western Kentucky Catholic*, is also an educational tool. Under Bishop McRaith's direction it became a means of building a sense of unity in the local church, an instrument of faith sharing and a way to publish parish happenings. It began as a simple four-page newsletter. In 1984, under the leadership of editor Mel Howard, the newsletter was expanded and given the name, *Western Kentucky Catholic*. Its purpose is to publish news events and happenings of parishes around the diocese. From its beginning, it was distributed at the Church door with the parish bulletin. Only later came the decision to mail the newspaper to every household in order to reach all parish families particularly the homebound. This decision was implemented for the first time with the October 1992 issue.

Passing on the faith to children in each parish was and is a priority for the diocese. From their beginning, Catholic schools have been communities of faith in which the Christian message, the experiences of community, worship and social concerns are integrated in the total experience of students, parents and members of the faculty. This perspective is not new to Bishop McRaith who had been a Catholic school administrator and educator. He gives his wholehearted support to Catholic education and presents the challenge that schools truly be what they professed to be. During this decade, however, schooling in the nation became both complex and costly. Catholic schools are not exempt from this adverse situation. Due to many reasons—changing values, economics, birth rate, fewer sisters and brothers as teachers and many others— parochial schools decreased in number and more children attend parish religious education classes. To make the best use of reorganization in the Owensboro-Daviess County area resulted in the second largest Catholic Consolidated System in the nation (1989). In 1992, there remained in the diocese, 17 parochial and inter-parochial grade schools, two middle schools and three high schools. Sister Amelia Stenger, OSU served the diocese as Superintendent of Schools from 1984-1991. H. Joseph O'Bryan took the position in 1991. Under his leadership, the Catholic school system continues to be a strong influence in both the Catholic and civic communities.

With a re-awakened understanding that the role of the parish is to offer opportunities for all its member to have access to religious education and the reality that Catholic schools are not available to everyone, came renewed emphasis in the area of religious education. The development of catechetical leaders for parishes is considered of primary importance. Through special collaborative efforts with Brescia College, the diocese intensified what it was already doing toward catechetical leadership training. For both parishes and schools the development of parish programs involves enhancing the role of the parents in the religious formation of their children along with greater participation on the part of the entire parish. Bishop McRaith gave full support toward the improvement of such programs and toward encouraging those who serve as catechetical leaders and catechists. The Office for Religious Education under the direction of Sister Kathy Gallo, OSU offers assistance and resources to parishes and schools for their programs. With the major goal of the calling forth and enablement of catechetical leaders, she directs much time and effort toward its accomplishment. Because of this emphasis, more parishes have directors and coordinators for their religious education and many volunteers are becoming certified for ministry.

One of Bishop McRaith's first moves for Catholic education was to re-activate the Diocesan Board of Education altering its focus and expanding it to serve as a diocesan Committee for Total Catholic Education. This committee's membership is inclusive of lay representation from each deanery as well as representation of the priests and sisters. Its chief function is to consider the religious education needs of people of all ages and to make policy recommendations to the Diocesan Pastoral Council and to the bishop. It strives to foster a vision of lifelong religious education and to help parishes realize their role in passing on the faith. Five diocesan directors are staff to this committee: Directors of the Offices for Religious Education, Adult Formation, Youth Minisry, Catholic Schools and Communications. Together they strive to offer a united effort toward the faith development of all people of the diocese. In 1992, in response to the Synod goal, a Religious Education Task Force was formed to plan a diocesan Religious Education Convocation which will call each institution and faith community to evaluate its experience of religious education and develop a plan for lifelong religious formation.

Renewal surfaced other areas of need, one of which was the young people of the diocese. In response to an expressed concern, in July 1989, Bishop McRaith employed the diocese's first full-time Director for Youth Ministry. Tony Cooper. As director, he is responsible for providing training, resources and consultant services for parish youth ministry. These include experiences and opportunities that build a wider sense of Church and world through ministry, education and retreats. Important among the goals of this office is training youth and adults for Christian ministry. One effective way used to accomplish this goal, is the Christian Leadership Institute held each summer. More than 200 young people and 60 adults, have participated in this training since it began in 1988. Many youth and adults have attended national regional youth ministry conferences. Workshops on building a youth ministry in the parish are provided for adults and key youth leaders across the diocese. Some well received firsts are: an overnight Diocesan Youth Rally in March 1992, and special liturgies for youth celebrated in each of the deaneries. Bishop McRaith gives time to young people at their conferences and rallies because he sees them as the young Church of today, who will be the adult Church of tomorrow.

One retreat experience that continues to influence the lives of young people, is the Teens Encounter Christ Weekend (TEC). TEC provides an opportunity for high school seniors to look at the place Christ holds in their lives and to choose to make other decisions in life in light of this first commitment. Since 1976, when this weekend experience was first introduced into the diocese, over 2,000 young people and adults of Western Kentucky have been enriched by this sharing event. In September 1992, TEC #100 was celebrated at Mount St. Joseph Center.

In order to offer an experience similar to TEC to younger teens, QUEST is held in some deaneries. QUEST is a 24 hour coming together for those in the first and second years of high school. Based on the three circles of love—love of self, love of God and love of others—this experiences draws young people together to share about their basic call to lead Christian lives.

People with special needs are important in the diocese and efforts are made to show this. The SPRED program (Special Religious Education and Development) for the handicapped is coordinated by Judy Colby and Sister Kathy Gallo, OSU. The Knights of Columbus have been and continue to be active in their generous support of this program.

Toward a Church in Gratitude & Celebration

As people of faith, Catholics have reason to celebrate. To look back and recall stories of the past, to ponder the many blessings is to be drawn to be grateful. Anniversaries are such times.

Procession at Bishop McRaith's 10th Anniversary Celebration.

People raise hands in blessing over Bishop McRaith. Bishop McRaith's Mother is in the wheelchair.

Bishop McRaith and Father Joe Mills at the 10th Anniversary Mass of Thanksgiving, December 13, 1992.

Friends enjoy chatting with Bishop McRaith at the reception after the Liturgy.

Celebrating 50 Years

A highlight in 1987, was the celebration of the 50th anniversary of the diocese. It was the occasion of much rejoicing in the gifts that God had showered on the Church of Western Kentucky. In this first 50 years, the number of Catholics doubled; parishes were established in all counties except one. The diocese could boast for many reason: 77 parishes, two Newman Centers, the largest Catholic school system in the nation percentage wise, a Catholic college, two Catholic hospitals, two Catholic homes for the aged and a Church of involved people who make an impact in the civic community. In a letter in the diocesan newspaper in September 1987, Bishop McRaith wrote: "...the real miracle and real growth is the growth of the faith that lies deep in the hearts of all... ".(10) He recalled the thousands of faithful, the many religious and priests who were pioneers of the diocese and he lauded in particular his two predecessors, Bishop Francis R. Cotton and Bishop Henry J. Soenneker, faithful successors of the apostles, who laid the foundation on which this church stands.

The celebration was held on Oct. 4, 1987 at the Sportscenter in Owensboro. It was glorious event for the Church of Western Kentucky. Nearly 6,000 Catholics from 32 counties assembled to glorify God for the gift of faith and to celebrate the many blessings they shared. Archbishop Pio Laghi, the Pope's personal representative and Apostolic Nuncio to the United States, was the main celebrant at the liturgy. Celebrating also were: the six bishops of the province: Archbishop Thomas C. Kelly and Bishop Charles G. Maloney, Louisville; Bishop William Hughes and Bishop J. Kendrick Williams, Covington; Bishop James Niedergeses, Nashville; Bishop Daniel Buechlin, Memphis; Abbot Timothy Sweeney, OSB, St. Meinrad Archabbey, Bishop John McRaith and 80 priests.

From every corner of the diocese, people came in cars and buses. It was a day to remember, a liturgy that shouted the praise of God, a crowd that filled the Sportscenter. Chosen representatives formed the entrance possession carrying banners bearing the names of every parish and institution of the diocese. A diocesan choir, directed by James Hansen, led the singing of a striking, new litany of praise. It invoked the names of the deceased of the diocese and the saints of the parishes to which the whole assembly responded "Pray for us." There was no doubt that those who had gone before were present at this joyful celebration.

After the final hymn and procession, the celebration ended with a dinner unique to Western Kentucky—a picnic of barbecued chicken and burgoo. Also unique was what happened in the park across the street from the Sportscenter. Rather than being the scene of a ballgame for the little league, Moreland Park was transformed into the picnic grounds for the Catholics of Western Kentucky. The meal, prepared and served by the Knights of Columbus, was enjoyed as people visited with friends, made new acquaintances, and talked with bishops of other dioceses. Archbishop Pio Laghi commented on how much better it was to picnic together than to be rushed off for a meal at some hotel where they could not meet people.

A history entitled, *This Far By Faith: the Story of Catholicity in Western Kentucky*, was written by various people and edited by Judy Hayden, to chronicle the diocese's beginning. The first to be written about this local Church, it portrays a partial history of the development of the church in the western part of the state and of the first Catholics to come to Kentucky. It speaks of the heritage that belongs to the Church of this state and of this diocese. Miss Hayden, who contributed several of its stories, wrote: "If Maryland is the proverbial 'door' to Catholicity in America, then Kentucky is, if you will, the foyer. For it was our state, the 'dark and bloody ground' that provided, once again, a much needed avenue of escape so our ancestors could practice freely the faith of their ancestors." (11)

A diocesan cookbook of favorite recipes was published as a commemorative souvenir. Many people across the diocese sent their best-loved recipes to be printed for all to enjoy.

A note of sadness was in the hearts of all at this anniversary, over the fact that the former bishop, Bishop Henry J. Soenneker, who had served the diocese for almost half of its existence, was not here to be a part of the celebration. He had died on Sept. 24, 1987, just ten days prior. Bishop Soenneker retired in 1982, but continued to reside in Owensboro. It had become home to him and the people were at home with him. They had been struck by his deep faith and touched by

Father John Vaughan, Vicar General, July 1985–December 1991.

Chrism Mass at the Sportcenter – May, 1991.

Rite of Election at the Cathedral – Febuary 12, 1989.

his simple lifestyle. Bishop Soenneker was one of the reasons the diocese could boast of its first 50 years and give praise to God.

Celebrating Ten Years with Bishop McRaith

In 1992, the diocese celebrated another anniversary. This is the year that marked Bishop McRaith's 10th anniversary as Bishop of Owensboro. St. Stephen Cathedral was filled to overflowing on December 13 for Mass of Thanksgiving. The liturgy began with a procession of representatives from every diocesan committee and institution bearing symbols to represent the development and growth in ministry during the past 10 years. Among them were: the RENEW banner, the book of Synod goals and objectives, a framed copy of the first *Western Kentucky Catholic*, a Bible representing the word taught by Bishop McRaith as first teacher of the diocese and a plaque with the image of Jesus washing the feet of a disciple, the emblem of Ministry Formation at Brescia College and the inscription: Bishop John J. McRaith, "Thanks for the Dream," 1982-91. The Diocesan Pastoral Council members marched at the end of the procession.

Music for the liturgy was led by the diocesan choir, directed by Kevin Kinnaird. Bishop John's chosen favorite at his ordination as bishop, "Here I Am, Lord" was sung as the Communion hymn.

In his homily, Bishop John presented John the Baptizer's question about Jesus in Matthew's Gospel as a challenge to all, saying: "Now, as the people of Western Kentucky go about their journey to the Lord–they might well look at us and say: Are you the one with the mission of Jesus? Are you truly disciples of Jesus? Or should we look for another?" (12)

After communion, Father Joe Mills, Vicar General, presented Bishop John with a vial of Western Kentucky soil sprinkled with water blessed at the Synod to be inserted in the center of his pectoral cross which bears soil from his other places of ministry. Then children brought forward a child's red wagon filled with personal congratulation cards made by the girls and boys in Catholic schools and parish religious education programs throughout the diocese.

After the liturgy all were invited to a reception in the newly renovated undercroft of the Cathedral. Tables were spread with delicious food prepared by the people from the various parishes. Members of the staff served as people enjoyed the food, shared stories and expressed their appreciation to Bishop John. It was truly a day of gratitude and praise to God.

Blessings to Celebrate

There are other reasons to celebrate: people of faith continually responding to the Spirit's call to holiness and to share the light of Christ, the gift of seminarians and ordinations of priests for the diocese, many generous people volunteering time, talent and treasure in ministry in the Church, new members coming to join the communities of faith, the services of women religious and on and on.

Growth

The people's response to the call to renewal and involvement in the mission of the Church is truly a gift and it has its own effects. Not only do the Catholics assume their rightful roles in ministry, many others are attracted to join the faith community. The process of Christian Initiation of Adults, better known as RCIA, had been introduced and Bishop McRaith gave full support to it as one of the best ways of welcoming new members. As it flourishes in the parishes, not only do many join the parish community each year on Holy Saturday, but many catholics experience anew their own renewal as they participate with the catechumens and candidates. In the process, lay people serve as directors, team members and sponsors–a new kind of ministry for many of them but one which is their role in the mission of Jesus. They experience the Church happening as they work to make it happen.

Bishop McRaith endeavors to make avail-

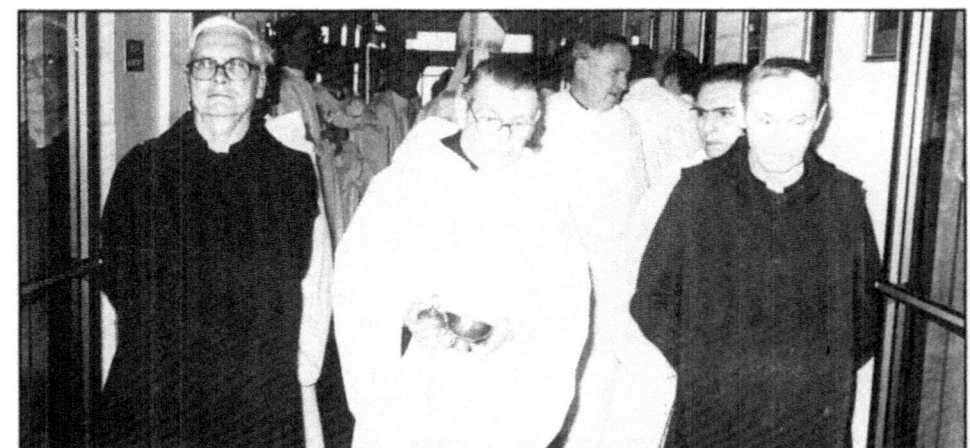
Processional of Closing Liturgy at St. Mark's Priory – Febuary 16, 1988.

Bishop McRaith Celebrates the Closing Liturgy at St. Mark's.

Glenmary Sisters, 405 Parrish Avenue, Owensboro.

able for all the experience of the larger diocesan Church worshipping together. Each year the Chrism Mass is celebrated at the Sportscenter in Owensboro and all the people of the diocese are invited to be a part of that celebration. In the spring Masses for the Rite of Election are held at the Cathedral or at two sites in the diocese to allow larger numbers to participate in welcoming new members into the faith community. He also promotes the concept that the Sacraments of Initiation are total parish celebrations. Yearly anniversary liturgies celebrating the priesthood, religious life and marriage are held for the entire diocese. The married couple who has been married the greatest number of years receives special honor on the diocesan marriage day.

To name the laity as blessing is not to discount the leadership of the Church in West ern Kentucky. It is because of the chief shepherd and the priests that those who are led can respond so fully. The diocese is truly blessed with its bishop and priests. Faithful and committed disciples, they stand tall in their commitment and their service to the Church. Unlike many dioceses, there are no priestless parishes here at this time, though some priests do serve two parishes and many have other part-time ministries. Most of the parishes that have no resident pastor, have a pastoral minister. Being so blessed, the diocese graciously shares of its bounty with other places of greater need. Three diocesan priests serve in the armed forces; three are involved in higher education; two in hospital ministry, two are spiritual directors in seminaries and one is serving in the Third World. In the decade of Bishop McRaith, 24 men have been ordained and the number of those studying is better than that of other dioceses of comparable size. Such a blessing of the Spirit can only happen where faith is strong.

The diocese continues to receive the services of priests as pastors from religious communities of men–the Society of the Precious Blood, the Benedictines and the Glenmary Home Missionaries. Through them many blessings come upon the Church of Western Kentucky.

Responding to the Spirit continually calls for changes and adjustments some of which do not carry visible reasons for gratitude. One which left its effect was the call of the Vicar General, Father John Vaughan to serve as Spiritual Director at the North American College in Rome in January 1992. His going was a loss to the diocese though it was gain for the North American seminarians in Rome. While the diocese rejoiced in having one of its priests chosen for ministry in Rome, he would be missed at home. Nor was filling his place here as simple as finding a replacement. Since he served as Vicar General, Chancellor, Coordinator of Staff and directed the Office of Planning, four persons were appointed to take these roles. Father Joseph Mills became Vicar General; Sister Joseph Angela Boone, OSU, Chancellor; Sister Mary Irene Cecil, OSU, Coordinator of Staff and Cathy Hagan was named Director of the Office of Planning. No seminarians are in attendance at the North American College in Rome at this time, though there have been in the past, Father John among them. Presently the diocesan seminarians study at seminaries in this country: Mundelein in Chicago, IL; Josephinum in Columbus, OH and St. Meinrad, in Indiana and others.

Since 1948, a seminary where some priests of the diocese studied, St. Mark's Priory, was located at South Union, Kentucky. Serving late vocations to the priesthood, this seminary and retreat house, was operated by the Beneditines. In February 1988, St. Mark's was forced to close its doors due to too few seminarians to study there. With a note of sadness, the diocese said good-by to the monks at a Mass celebrated by Bishop McRaith on Feb. 16, 1988. The monks who had prayed, worked and helped out across the diocese have been missed. They left a legacy in the hearts and lives of thousands of people of Western Kentucky. The 47 acre property has been purchased by the Father of Mercy who use it to train candidates for their order.

Women Religious

A reason for gratitude that does not often receive mention is the presence of women religious who have enriched the Church of Western Kentucky by their ministry for many years and continue to do so. At this writing, there are 17 different religious communities of women serving the people of this local church. They are: Adorer of the Blood of Christ, Wichita, KS and Ruma, IL;

St. Joseph Passionist Monastery, 1420 Benita Ave., Owensboro.

Interior of St. Mark Church, Eddyville, Kentucky.

Mount St. Joseph Chapel, 1992.

Benedictine Sisters, Ferdinand, IN and St. Mary's, PA; Sisters of Charity, Nazareth, KY; Carmelite Sisters of the Divine Heart of Jesus, St. Louis, MO; Sisters of St. Dominic, Adrian, MI and St. Catherine, KY; Sisters of St. Francis, Rochester, MN; Tiffon, OH and Clinton, IA; Sisters of Mercy, Cincinnati, OH and Detroit, MI; School Sisters of St. Francis, Milwaukee, WI; Sisters of Providence, Terre Haute, IN; Passionist Nuns, Sisters of the Lamb of God, Home Mission Sisters of America, Owensboro, KY and Ursuline Sisters, Maple Mount, KY. They are ministering in schools, in hospitals, in parishes, in the diocesan offices, in higher education, in counseling and in mission areas among the poor. The contribution they have made and are now making to the diocese, is invaluable and cannot be measured in human ways and God blesses this Church through them.

Two motherhouses located in the diocese from their foundation are the Ursulines of Maple Mount and the Passionist Nuns. Another community of sisters moved its home offices to the diocese in the summer of 1991. The Home Mission Sisters of American better known as the Glenmary Sisters are now based at 405 West Parish Avenue in Owensboro. In addition, they established a Mission Training Center in Livermore, KY. This group of sisters was founded in Cincinnati, OH, where they remained until this move. With fewer numbers and far distance from mission fields, the Spirit prompted them to settle closer to mission territory. Thus they came to this diocese in Western Kentucky. Their sisters serve in mission houses in Guthrie, Elkton and Smithland in this local Church as well as in other dioceses in the south.

The Cloistered community of Passionist Nuns has been a part of the diocese since 1947. This group of 18 nuns minister to the Church in Western Kentucky by prayer, solitude and the making of altar breads for the churches of the diocese. Little was known about them except that they went quietly about their daily schedule in the monastery at 1420 Benita Avenue in Owensboro. In the summer of 1990, things began to stir in this community. On the occasion of a formal visitation, Bishop McRaith challenged them to the renewal of their lives and to become more effective for the life of the Church in the essentials of their contemplative vocation. His words were "...The better the Passionist Nuns are, the better off the Church in Western Kentucky will be." The acceptance of this challenge meant that the Passionist Sisters needed to look at their mission and its meaning for the church in this century. After prayerful discernment together and in consultation with church officials, they have made the decision to relocate the monastery to an area outside the city which will be more conducive to solitude and contemplative prayer. In addition, they hope to provide a space where others can come for solitude. Implementation of the decision was begun immediately and in the spring of 1992 land was purchased for the new monastery near Whitesville, Kenutcky. With God's blessing, at a future date the Passionist Nuns of Benita Avenue in Owensboro will be praying and serving God and the Church of the diocese in the open space surrounded by woods. Much good cannot help but come upon this Church through their prayer.

The new Catholic Pastoral Center, 600 Locust Street, Owensboro.

Another group of religious not new to the diocese, are the Sisters of the Lamb of God, a French community who have been located here since 1958. Their uniqueness is that they welcome into their community women who are physically handicapped. Their ministry is to serve in the areas of need to which they are called by the gifts God has given to them. Presently they are administrators and caregivers at Bishop Soenneker Home at Knottsville in Daviess County.

The Ursuline Sisters whose motherhouse is at Maple Mount continue to serve the diocese. Their ministries in this century range from classroom teacher to pastoral associate, from parish minister to sister visitor, from diocesan office staff member to serving the poor. Two of their ministries that are very significant for the diocese are Brescia College and Mount St. Joseph Center. Through their influence, many people receive spiritual and educational formation and growth. In 1991-1992, the Ursulines took a noteworthy step in faith in the renovation of the Chapel. It was an effort to enhance their liturgical prayer and worship, to express hospitality and provide accessibility to community members and visitors alike. As Ursulines called to serve the Church, they continue the vision of their foundress, Angela Merici, and follow the example of their pioneer sisters who moved forward with courage and high hope. On Nov. 21, 1992, they celebrated the 80th anniversary of their autonomy as a religious community.

Sisters of two other communities who have a long history of service in the diocese and who are presently still in ministry here are the Sister of Charity of Nazareth and the Sisters of Mercy of Cincinnati. Their dedication and commitment remain constant in various ministries: higher education, parish and hospital ministry, schools, social services and with the elderly. Their long years of service have made them a part of the diocese.

Church Building and Renovation

The growth the diocese experienced brought the erection of new churches and renovation of existing structures. It was with gratitude to God that in September 1987, a new parish, St. Anthony of Padua, was established at Grand Rivers in Livingston County. This moved the diocese further toward the goal of having a Catholic

Bishop John McRaith with Pope John Paul II – First Ad Limina Visit, May, 1988.

church in every county. That goal was fulfilled two years later with the institution of St. Mark Parish at Eddyville in Lyon County on July 13, 1989. St. Mark Church was completed and blessed by Bishop McRaith on Sept. 17, 1989.

Along with the erection of new churches, attention is given to the renovation of older ones for the purpose of enhancing liturgical worship and making them accessible to all. An Art and Architecture Committee formed in 1989 developed Directives for Building, Renovation or Redecorating Places of Worship in the diocese. Use of these directives contributed to the quality and appropriateness of the art and architecture of a number of new and newly renovated churches, among them are: St. Elizabeth, Clarkson; St. Columbia, Lewisport; St. Anthony, Peonia; Mount St. Joseph Chapel, Maple Mount; St. Mark, Eddyville and Immaculate Conception, Earlington. A number of parishes took the necessary measures to make their buildings accessible for the handicapped.

New emphasis in parish life and developments in the diocesan church necessitate other changes that contribute to lay involvement and the enhancement of parish life. A church and a school building no longer provide enough space for all the groups who meet weekly and monthly in a parish. This trend has its impact not only on parishes but also on the diocesan offices. In the spring of 1990, the diocesan office building known as the Catholic Pastoral Center, located at 4005 Frederica was sold to Our Lady of Lourdes Parish and St. Stephen Cathedral School at 600 Locust Street was renovated to become the new

Catholic Pastoral Center for the diocese. Moving day, June 30, 1990 was phenomenal experience. Trucks of all sizes made trips from one end of the city to the other and many people volunteered time, energy and expertise to put offices in shape for work to go on. Sept. 16, 1990 was the day of blessing and dedication. Before the blessing, a dinner was served to all who had contributed to the renovation. After the blessing, guided tours led people through the renovated building and to the first floor for cookies and punch. This move was beneficial to both Lourdes and St. Stephen Parishes and the diocese. Lourdes gained a much needed parish hall, St. Stephen found a use for their building, and the diocesan offices were located near the Cathedral and in a less affluent area of the city.

With the move into new space, a room was designated as Archives and a part-time Archivist, Sister Emma Cecilia Busam, OSU was employed in 1991. The diocesan which celebrated 50 years has a history that needs to be recorded and documented. It is proud of its past and wishes to preserve its story.

Ad Limina Visit

Bishop McRaith made his first Ad Limina visit to Rome in May 1988. The Ad Limna visit, which takes place every five years, is the regular visit of the bishop with the Pope to keep him informed about the diocese. A written report is sent some weeks ahead of the visit. All of the bishops of the province meet together with the Pope and then each bishop has a private audience. 1993 is the year for the next visit. At this time, Bishop McRaith will speak personally to the Pope about the people and the growth of the diocese. It is an occasion of gratitude for the Church, the church that traces its origin from Jesus and the apostles and is directed to the Kingdom of God.

Traditions

The people of the diocese remain grateful for the traditions passed down by their forebears. Devotion to Mary is one of these traditions that is important. The year 1987-88, named the Marian Year by Pope John Paul II, gave special impetus to this tradition. As part of the observance of this Marian Year, Bishop McRaith declared 12 churches of the diocese as pilgrimage churches with certain privileges for those who visited them and he encouraged all parishes to have significant celebrations in honor of Mary. Special Marian Days were held in Owensboro and Paducah in April 1988. A Marian Pilgrimage Shrine was established at St. Joseph Parish in Bowling Green on May 7, 1989. Father Ben Luther, Director of the Marian Shrine, with a committee of interested people, continue to plan pilgrimages and celebrations to be held at the shrine and around the diocese.

Epilogue

The aim of this history is to bring together events of this local Church from its beginning in 1937 through the first 55 years of its life and growth. It is a story of the faith of the Catholics of Western Kentucky as it is nurtured and lived in the home and in parish family. No story of development stands alone; neither does this one. It builds on its past and carries forward the legacy it received. The first Catholics who came to this region brought a deep and lasting faith and planted its roots firmly in soil of these 32 counties. According to Father C.P. Bowling in a talk given at the time of the establishment of the diocese in 1937, "Owensboro Diocese is large in territory, small in wealth but rich in zeal and elevation. (13) This story depicts that rich heritage and illustrates how that foundation was the basis for its growth up to the present and into the future. Just as no history can portray a complete picture, so this one can offer only glimpses of its recent past and its present. For a clearer perspective of this period, one must walk among the people, listen to their stories, observe their lives. What is written in these pages speculates a narrative that remains unfinished and whose deeper meaning will only be known in the next century. This book, then, intends to bring light on the past and convey a broader view of the maturing of the Catholic faith in this part of the state of Kentucky. Even that is done inadequately because it has named only a few of those from its midst who have joined the Communion of Saints. It ventures, however ineptly, to give credit and praise to the abiding presence of the Spirit of God in the hearts of both the leaders and those being lead.

May the generous showering of blessings and the gracious response of the people remain constant as the faith of the people grows to full flowering.

Notes

1. Hayden, Judy, editor, *This Far by Faith: The Story of Catholicity in Western Kentucky*. 1987, pg. 11.
2. *Sharing the Light of Faith*, National Conference of Catholic Bishops, 1973, pg. 4.
3. Diocesan Pastoral Council, Diocese of Owensboro, By-laws, 1989, pg. 1.
4. Second Synod of the Church in Western Kentucky Diocese of Owensboro, Oct. 19-20, 1991, pgs.4.
5. *Western Kentucky Catholic*, December 1991.
6. Ibid., January 1987, September 1990, April 1991.
7. Ibid., August 1992.
8. Sacrosanctum Concilium, 10.
9. Second Synod of the Church in Western Kentucky Diocese of Owensboro, Oct. 18-20, 1991, pg. 20.
10. *Western Kentucky Catholic*, September 1987.
11. *This Far by Faith*, pg. 3.
12. Homily given by Bishop John J. McRaith at his 10th anniversary as Bishop of Owensboro, Dec. 13, 1992.
13. *This Far by Faith*, pg. 38.

The Official Catholic Directory

Anno Domini

1993

Diocese of Owensboro

logo

Catholic Pastoral Center-600 Locust St., Owensboro, KY 42301. Tel: 502-683-1545; Fax: 502-683-6883. Refer all official business to this address.

Most Reverend John J. McRaith, D.D.

Bishop of Owensboro; ordained February 21, 1960; appointed October 23, 1982; consecrated December 15, 1982. Res., 501 W. Fifth St., Owensboro, KY 42301.

Address correspondence to: 600 Locust St., Owensboro, KY 42301 Fax: 502-683-6883;

Created December 9, 1937.
Erected February 23, 1938.
Square Miles 12,502.

Comprises the following thirty-two Counties in the Western part of the State of Kentucky: Allen, Ballard, Breckinridge, Butler, Caldwell, Calloway, Carlisle, Christian, Crittenden, Daviess, Edmonson, Fulton, Graves, Grayson, Hancock, Henderson, Hickman, Hopkins, Livingston, Logan, Lyon, McCracken, McLean, Marshall, Muhlenberg, Ohio, Simpson, Todd, Trigg, Union, Warren and Webster.

For legal titles of parishes and diocesan institutions, consult the Catholic Pastoral Center.

Statistical Overview

Bishop	1
Priests: Active inside diocese	64
Priests: Active outside diocese	6
Priests: Diocesan, Foreign Missions	1
Priests: Retired, sick /absent	12
Diocesan Priests	83
Regligious Priests in Diocese	13
Total Priests in Diocese	*96*

Ordinations:

Religious Priests	1
Total Brothers	1
Total Sisters	264
Parishes	78

With Resident Pastor:

Resident Diocesan Priests	45
Resident Religious Priests	8

Without Resident Pastor:

Administered by Priests	25
Pastoral Centers	2
Catholic Hospitals	2
Total Assisted	115,356

Health Care Centers	1
Total Assisted	100
Homes for the Aged	2
Total Assisted	177
Day Care Centers	4
Total Assisted	267
Special Centers for Social Services	2
Total Assisted	15,977
Colleges and Universities	1
Total Assisted	800
High Schools, Diocesan/Parochial	3
Total Students	914
Elementary, Diocesan /Parochial	19
Total Students	4,225

Confraternity of Christian Doctrine:

High School Students	1,199
Elementary Students	3,337
Total Students under Catholic Instruction	10,498

Teachers in the Diocese:

Priests	2
Sisters	20
Lay Teachers	288

Baptisms:

Infant	913
Adult	223
Received into Full Communion	269
Total Baptisms	1,405
First Communions	1,112
Confirmations	1,190

Marriages:

Catholic	220
Interfaith	262
Total Marriages	482
Deaths	554
Total Catholic Population	50,134
Total Population	776,314

Former Bishops-Most Rev. Francis R. Cotton, D.D.,First Bishop of Owensboro; ord. June 17, 1920; appt. Dec. 16, 1937; cons. Feb. 24, 1938; died Sept. 25, 1960.-Most Rev. Henry J. Soenneker, D.D., Second Bishop of Owensboro; ord. May 26, 1934; appt. March 10, 1961; cons. April 26, 1971; installed May 9, 1961; retired June 7, 1982; died September 24, 1987.

Vicar General-Rev. Joseph M. Mills, J.C.L., Res., 5856 Ky. 81, Owensboro, 42301.

Chancellor-St. Joseph Angela Boone, O.S.U.

Archivist-Sr. Emma Cecilia Busam, O.S.U.

Diocesan Tribunal-
  Judicial Vicar-Rev. Joseph M. Mills, J.C.L.
  Adjutant Judicial Vicar-Rev. Peter E. Lauzon, J.C.L.
  Defenders of the Bond-Revs. Kevin Karl; J. Patrick Reynolds.
  Judges-Revs. Leonard Alvey; Peter Lauzon, J.C.L.; John Vaughan, J.C.L.
  Adovcates-Priests and pastoral ministers of the diocese.

Case Promoters-Sr. Vivian Marie Bowles, O.S.U.
Administrative Assistants-Mrs. Mary Ann Kurz; Mrs. Kay M. Rhodes.

Diocesan Boards and Councils

Diocesan Pastoral Council-Mr. Mike Thompson, Chm.; Ms. Gloria Adams; Ms. Ann Mulligan; Ms. Fay Higdon; Sr. Maggie Cooper, S.C.N.; Mr. Jim Tidwell; Ms. Pat McGruder; Mr. Steve Papciak; Mr. Phillip Hayden; Mr. Curtis Hixon; Sr. Clarita Browning, O.S.U.; Mr. Tom Buehrle; Mr. Jim Lynch; Mr. Ron Segebarth; Mr. Kenny Buckman; Sr. Eula Johnson, C.S.N.; Mr. Drury Howard; Revs. John Little; Larry Hostetter; John Meredith; Gary Payne; Ms. Joanne Stephens.

Consultors-Revs. Joseph M. Mills; Pike Powell; Jerry Calhoun; W. Jerry Riney; Larry Hostetter; Mr. Martin Mattingly.

Deans-Western Deaners: Rev. Ben Luther; Bowling Green Deaners: Rev. Lucian Hayden; Central: Rev. John Meredith; Owensboro: Rev. J. Edward Bradley; Rural: Rev. Joseph O'Donnell; Eastern: Rev. Greg Trawick.

Priests' Council-Revs. Joseph M. MIlls; John Meredith; Joseph O'Donnell; Ben Luther; Lucian Hayden; Martin Mattingly; Pike Powell; Jerry Calhoun; W. Jerry Riney; Larry Hostetter; J. Edward Bradley; Greg Trawick.Schoenborn, G.H.M.S., Pres.

Council of Religious-Sr. Elaine Burke O.S.U.; Sr. Eula Johnson S.C.N.; Sr. Marian Powers, O.S.U.; Sr. Mary Anne Yanz, O.P.; Sr. Alicia Coomes, O.S.U.; Sr. Jeannette Haas, R.S.M.; Sr. Mary Leon Riney, O.S.U; Sr. Catherine Schoenborn, G.H.M.S., Pres.

Pastoral Office for Administration-Sr. Joseph Angela Boone, O.S.U., Dir.

Pastoral Office for Stewardship-Mr. Tom Lilly, Dir.

Committee for Administration-Mr. Homer Barton; Ms. Janet Berry; Ms. Becky Luckett; Sr. JoAnn Mark, A.S.C.; Mr. Charles Kamuf; Mr. Joseph Hancock; Mr. Pete Buser; Mr. Louis Haas; Revs. E.E. Willett; Phil Riney;

Joe Mills; Mr. Mike Thompson.

Pastoral Office for Planning-Cathy Hagan.

Pastoral Office for Education-
- *Director of Education*-Sr. Mary Irene Cecil, O.S.U.
- *Superintendant of Schools*-Mr. Joseph O'Bryan
- *Director of Religious Education*-Sr. Kathy Gallo, O.S.U.

Committee for Education-Mr. Del Hayden, Chm.; Ms. Elaine Grant; Rev. J. Edward Bradley; Sr. Teresa Riley, O.S.U.; Rev. Richard Powers; Ms. Judy Simpson; Mr. Al Mattingly; Ms. Dee Black; Ms. Mildred Stribling; Ms. Barbara Hertel; Ms. Fay Higdon; Ms. Mary Lou Joseph; Sr. Margaret Turk, R.S.M.

Director of Ecumenism-Rev. Joseph O'Donnell, Glmy., Box 106, Beaver Dam, 42320. Tel: 502-274-3414.

Director of Youth Ministry-Mr. Tony Cooper

Director of Communications-Mr. Mel Howard

Pastoral Office for Worship-Rev. Larry McBride, Dir.

Diocesan Liturgical Committee-Revs. Thomas Clark; Sr. Loraine Lauter, O.S.U., Chm.; Darrell Venters; Gary Payne; Ms. Barbara Woodward; Mr. Mike Conley; Ms. Sue Eckmans; Mr. Norman Howard; Sr. Annalita Lancaster, O.S.U.

Pastoral Office for Spiritual Life-Sr. Marie Goretti Browning, O.S.U., Mount St. Joseph, Maple Mount, 42356. Tel: 502-229-4103.

Cursillo-Rev. Gerald Calhoun, Dir., 2232 Smallhouse Rd., Bowling Green, 42104-4141. Tel: 502-842-7777.

Pastoral Office for Adult Formation-Sr. Mary Irene Cecil, O.S.U. Dir.

Pastoral Office for Outreach and Lay Ministry-Sr. Patricia Froning, O.S.F., Dir.

Pastoral Office for Social Concerns-Sr. Judy Morris O.P.

Diocesan Social Concerns Committee-Janet Barkley; Margaret Ann Huston; Lisa Kemper Johnson; Jim Settles; Robbert Hagan; Sr. Mary Margaret Cooper, S.C.N.

Catholic Relief Service Director-Sr. Judy Morris O.P.

Campaign for Human Development-Sr. Judy Morris O.P.

Respect Life Office-Sr. Judy Morris O.P.

Rural Life Office-Sr. Judy Morris O.P.

Mission Office-Rev. Joseph M. Mills.

Pastoral Ministry with Refugees-Sr. Theresa Marie Wilkerson, O.S.U.

Pastoral Office for Family Life-Marthanne F. Allman.

Diocesan Family Life Committee-Rev. Gary Hayes, Margaret Swanberg; Camilla and Jim Schumakers; Ron and Marsha Segebarth; Judy Kapelsohn; Martha Crabtree; Kathy and Jim Gardner; Bernadette and Hank Hayden; Yvonne Hatcher; Joyce and Tom Hayden.

Couple to Couple League-Marthanne F. Allman.

Pastoral Office for Personnel-
Priest Personnel Committee-Revs. Aloysius Powers; Joe Mills; J. Ed Bradley; Danny Goff; Richard Meredith; Larry Hostetter.

Vocation Office-Rev. Kevin Karl, Sts. Joseph and Paul, 609 E. Fourth St., Owensboro, 42301. Tel: 502-683-5641.

Continuing Education for Priests-Rev. Anthony J. Ziegler.

Roman Catholic Diocese of Owensboro Charitable Trust Fund, Inc.-Most Rev. John J. McRaith; Revs. Joe mills; Kevin Karl.

Organizations

St. Vincent de Paul Society-Edward Hayden, Pres., 771 Covington St., Bowling Green, 42101. Tel: 502-843-3562.

Scouting Activities-Mr. Tony Cooper, 600 Locust St., Owensboro, 42301. Tel: 502-683-1545.

Holy Childhood Association-Rev. Joseph M. Mills.

Teens Encounter Christ-Mr. Tony Cooper, 600 Locust St., Owensboro, 42301. Tel: 502-683-1545.

Legion of Mary-

Clergy, Parishes, Missions and Parochial Schools
City of Owensboro

(Daviess County)

1-St. Stephen Cathedral, Revs. J. Edward Bradley; Mark Anthony Jones; Richard Meredith; J. Edward Bradley; Mark Anthony Jones; Richard Meridith. Pastoral Assocs.: Mr. Larry Lyon; Sr. Margaret Ann Aull.
    Res., 614 Locust St., 42301. Tel: 502-683-6525 [JC]

Blessed Sacrament Chapel-602 Sycamore St., 42301.

2-Blessed Mother, Revs. C. Phil Riney; Dave Johnson; Jan Storm, Admin. Asst.; Julie Whitten, Music Coord.
    Office: 515 E. 22nd St. 42303.
    Res: 601E. 23rd St. 42303. Tel: 502-683-8444.

3-The Immaculate, Revs. Richard Powers; Sr. Clarita Browning, O.S.U., Pastoral Assoc.
    Parish Office: 2516 Christie Pl., 42301. Tel: 502-683-0689.
    Res. 2601 Christie Pl., 42301. Tel: 502-683-0689.

4-Our Lady of Lourdes, Revs. Delma Clemons; Ray Clark; Sr. Mary Oliver Reising, O.S.B., Pastoral Assoc.
    Res., 4029 Frederica St., 42301. Tel: 502-684-5369.

Catechesis/Religious Programs-Sr. Rosanne Spalding, O.S.U., D.R.E.
    Students 113

5-Precious Blood, Rev. Darrell Venters; Sr. Lorraine Lauter, O.S.U., Pastoral Assoc.
    Res., 3306 Fenmore St., 42301. Tel: 502-684-6888.

6- St. Pius Tenth, Revs. Larry McBride; Steve Ulrich. In res., Rev. Anthony J. Ziegler.
    Res., 3512 E. Sixth St., 42303. Tel: 502-684-5517.

7-SS. Joseph and Paul, Revs. Kevin Karl; William S. Odom-Green.
    Res., 609 E. 4th St., 42301. Tel: 502-683-5641. (JC)

Outside the City of Owensboro

Aurora, Marshall Co., St. Henry, Rev. Msgr. George H. Hancock.
    Res., R.R. No. 1, Box 471, Hardin, 42048. Tel: 502-474-8058.

Axtel, Breckinridge Co., St. Anthony, Rev. Bruce Fogle.
    Res., R.R. 3, Hardinsburg, 40143, Tel" 502-257-2132. (CEM)

Bardwell, Carlisle Co., St. Charles, Rev. Terry Devine.
    Res., R.R. 2, Box 317, 42023. Tel: 502-642-2586. (CEM)

Beaver Dam, Ohio Co., Holy Redeemer, Rev. Joseph O'Donnell, Glmy.; Sr. Luisa Bickett, O.S.U., Pastoral Assoc.
    Res., P.O. Box 106, 42320. Tel: 502-274-3414.

Big Clifty, KY, Grayson Co., St. Mary, Recors kept at St. Joseph's church, Leitchfield.

Bowling Green, Warren Co., St. Joseph's, Rev. Alan McIntosh, O.S.B.
    Res., 434 Church St., 42101. Tel: 502-842-2525. (JC)

Holy Spirit, Revs. Gerald Calhoun; Henry Wieder; Ms. Rosanna Schadler, Youth Coord.
    Res., 2232 Smallhouse Rd., 42104-4141. Tel: 502-842-7777.

Catecheses/Religious Programs-Ms. Anita Willoughby, D.R.E.
    Students 320.

Brown's Valley, Daviess Co., St. Anthony, Rev. Peter Lauzon.
    Church, 261 St. Anthony Rd., Utica, 42376. Tel 502-733-4341. (CEM)

Cadiz, Trigg Co., Stephen, Rev. Richard T. Danhauer.
    Res., Box 1043, 42211. Tel: 502-522-3801.

Calhoun, McLean Co., St. Sebastian, Rev. Maury Riney.
    Res., 180 Ky 136, 42327. Tel: 502-273-3185. (CEM)

Calvert city, Marshall Co., St. Pius Tenth, Rev. Aloysius Powers, Admin.
    Res., P.O. Box 495, 42029. Tel: 502-395-4727.

Clarkson, Grayson Co., St. Elizabeth of Hungary, Rev. Charles G. Fischer.
    Res., 1821 St. Paul Rd., Leitchfield, 42754. Tel: 502-242-7436.

Clinton, Hickman Co., St. Jude, Rev. Martin E. Hayes; Sr. Annalita Lancaster, O.S.U., Pastoral Assoc.
    Res., 42031. Tel: 502-653-6869.

Cloverport, Breckinridge Co., St. Rose, Rev. Walter Hancock.
    Tes., 118 Chestnut St., 40111. Tel:- 502-788-6422. (CEM)

Curdsville, Daviess Co., St. Elizabeth, Rev. James C. Hite.
    Mailing Address: P.O. Box 9-A, 42334. Tel: 502-229-4134.
    Res., 6143 First St., 42334.

Dawson Springs, Hoplins Co., Resurrection, Rev. Martin Mattingly.
Res., 530 Industrial Park Rd., 42408. Tel: 502-383-4743.
Church, Tel: 502-797-8665.

Earlington, Hopkins Co., Immaculate Conception, Rev. Martin Mattingly.
Res., 125 S. Day St., 42410. Tel: 502-383-4743.

Eddyville, Lyon Co., St. Mark Church, Rev. Maurice J. Tiell. Pastoral Assocs.: Sr. Frances Spalding, O.S.U.; Sr. Rose Theresa Johnson, O.S.U.
Res., 302 Peachtree Ln., P.O. Box 1205, 42038-1205. Tel: 502-388-2133.

Elkton, Todd Co., St. Susan, Rev. John T. Brown, Glmy. Res., P.O. Box 788, 42220. Tel: 502-265-5263

Fancy Farm, Hickman Co., St. Denis, Rev. Terry Devine.
Res., St. Charles Church, R. 2, Box 317, Bardwell, 42023. Tel: 502-642-2586. (CEM)

Fancy Farm, Graves Co., St. Jerome, Revs. J. Raymond Goetz.
Res., P.O. Box 38, 42039. Tel: 502-623-8181. (CEM)
Catechesis/Religious Programs-Mary Lou Joseph, D.R.E.
Students 315.

Fordsville, Ohio Co., St. John the Baptist, Rev. Joseph O'Donnell, Blmy.; St. Diane Marie Payne, O.S.U., Pastoral Assoc.
Res., 42343. Tel: 502-276-3619.

Franklin, Simpson Co., St. Mary of the Woods, Rev. James L. Wood, Glmy.
Res., 504 Eddings St., 42041. Tel: 502-472-2742.

Grand Rivers, Livingston Co., St. Anthony of Padua, (Grand Rivers Catholic Church) Rev. Msgr. George H. Hancock.
Res., P.O. Bos 55, 42045. Tel: 502-362-8636.

Grayson Springs, Grayson Co., St. Augustine, Rev. Gary Payne.
Mailing Address: c/o St. Anthony Church, 1256 St. Anthony Church Rd., Clarkson, 42726. Tel: 502-242-4791.
Res., 1256 St. Anthony Church Rd., Clarkson, 42726.

Guthrie, Todd Co., Sts. Mary & James, Rev. John T. Brown, Glmy.
Res., P.O. Box 325, 42234. Tel: 502-483-2571.

Hardinsburg, Brechinridge Co., St. Romuald, Rev. J. Brad Whistle. Pastoral Assocs.: Rosemary Dowell; Sr. Clarence Marie Luckett.
Res., 40143. Tel: 502-756-2356. (CEM)

Hawesvill, Hancock Co., Immaculate Conception, Rev. William Allard.
Res., 42348. Tel: 502-927-8419. (CEM)

Henderson, Henderson Co., Holy Name of Jesus, Revs. Thomas H. Clark; Gary Hayes; Richard Lynn Cash. Pastoral Assocs.: Sr. Sharon Bittner, O.S.B.; Bro. Dominic O'Brien.
Res., 511 Second St., 42420. Tel: 502-826-2096. (CEM)
School-618 Second St., 42420.
Sisters of Charity of Nazareth 1; Lay teachers 29; Students 465.

Henshaw, Union Co., St. Ambrose, Rev. Albert A. Reed, C.PP.S.
Res., c/o St. Francis Borgia, 1302 Adms St., Sturgis, 42459. Tel: 502-333-4645. (CEM)

Hickman, Fulton Co., Sacred Heart, Rev. Martin E. Hayes; Sr. Rose Marita O'Bryan, O.S.U., Pastoral Assoc. Tel: 502-236-2071.
Res., 504 Eddings St., Rulton, 42041. Tel: 502-472-2742.

Hopkinsville, Christian Co., SS. Peter and Paul, Rev. Gerald H. Baker.
Res., 902 E. Ninth St., 42240. Tel: 502-885-8522.
School-Lay teachers 8; Students 162.

Irvington, Breckinridge Co., Holy Guardian Angels, Rev. Walter Hancock.
Res., 40146. Tel: 502-257-2132. (CEM)

Knottsville, Daviess Co., St. William, Rev. Leonard Arcilesi.
Res., 9515 Ky, 144, Philpot, 42366. Tel: 502-281-4802. (CEM)
School-Mary Carrico Memorial School. Ursuline Sisters 3; Lay teachers; Students 158.

LaCenter, Ballard Co., St. Mary, Revs. Robert T. Drury, Canonical Pastor; Robert Willett; Sr. Elaine Byrne, O.S.U., Pastoral Assoc.
Res., P.O. Box 514, 42056. Tel: 502-665-5654.

Leitchfield, Grayson Co., St. Joseph's Rev. Gregory G. Trawick.
Res., 109 W. Walnut St., 42754. Tel: 502-259-3028. (CEM)

Lewisport, Hancock Co., St. Columba, Rev. William Allard.
Res., P.O. Box 219, Hawesville, 42348. Tel: 502-927-8419.

Livermore, McLean Co., St. Charles, Rev. Maury Riney.
Res., St. Sebastian Church, 180 Ky. 136, Calhoun, 42327. Tel: 502-685-2559.
Church, 506 Hill Ave., 42352.

McQuady, Breckinridge Co., St. Mary of the Woods, Rev. Bruce Fogle.
Res., R.R. 3, Hardinsburg, 40143. Tel: 502-756-2093. (CEM)

Madisonville, Hopkins Co., Christ the King, Rev. John Meredith; Sr. Mary Leon Riney, O.S.U., Pastoral Assoc.
Res., Rt. 6, 1600 Kingsway Dr., 42431. Tel: 502-821-5494.
School-Sisters 3; Lay teachers 8; Students 160.

Marion, Crittenden Co., St. William, Rev. Maurice J. Tiell. Tel: 502-388-2133. Pastoral Ministers: St. Rose Theresa Johnson, O.S.U.; Sr. Frances M. Spalding, O.S.U.
Res., 860 S. Main St., 42064. Tel: 502-965-2477.

Mayfield, Graves Co., ßt. Joseph, Rev. Patrick Bittel.
Res., 702 W. Broadway St., 42066. Tel: 502-389-2287. (CEM)
School-Lay teachers 8; Students 132.

Morganfield, Union Co., St. Ann's Rev. Severin Messick, O.S.B.; Sr. Beatrice Koerper, O.S.F., Pastoral Assoc.
Res., 304 Church St., 42437. Tel: 502-389-2287. (CEM)

Morgantown, Butler Co., Holy Trinity, Rev. Joseph A. O'Donnell, Glmy.; Sr. Marcan Freking, O.S.F.; Patoral Assoc.
Res., 766 Logansport Rd., P.O. Box 222, 42261. Tel: 502-526-3723.

Murray, Calloway Co., St. Leo, Rev. Peter Hughes.
Res., 401 N. 12th St., 42071. Tel: 502-753-3876; 759-1621 (office).

Paducah, McCracken Co.,

1-St. Francis de Sales, Revs. Robert Willett; Kevin Osborne; Sr. Barbara Woodward, Pastoral Assoc.
Res., 116 S. Sixth St., 42001. Tel: 502-442-1923. (CEM)

2-Rosary Chapel, Revs. Robert Willett; Kevin Osborne; Ms. Marianna Romero, Pastoral Assoc.
Res., 711 Ohio St., 42001. Tel: 502-444-6383.

3-St. John the Evangelist, Rev. Benjamin F. Luther.
Res., 6705 Old U.S. Hwy. 45, 42003. Tel: 502-544-3810.
School-7450 St. John Church Dr., 42003.
Lay teachers 7; Students 87.

4-St. Thomas More, Revs. Jerry Riney; Anthony Bickett; Sr. Marjorie Wisor, O.S.F., Pastoral Assoc.
Res., 3211 Buckner Ln., 42001. Tel: 502-444-7404. (JC)

Peonia, Grayson Co., St. Anthony's, Rev. Gary Payne.
Res., 1256 St. Anthony Church Rd., Clarkson, 42726. Tel: 502-242-4791. (CEM)

Philpot, Daviess Co., St. Lawrence, Rev. Leonard Arcilesi.
Res., 9515 Ky 144, 42366. Tel: 502-281-4802. (CEM)

Princeton, Caldwell Co., St. Paul, Rev. Anthony Stevenson.
Res., 813 S. Jefferson, 42445. Tel: 502-365-6786. (JC)
Stations-Kentucky State Penitentiary; Western Kentucky Correctional Complex.

Providence, Webster Co., Holy Cross, Rev. Carl J. Glahn.
Mailing Address: c/o St. Michael Church, P.O. Box 705, Sebree, 42455. Tel: 502-835-2584.

Reed, Henderson Co., St. Augustine, Revs. Larry Hostetter.
Res., 16777 Hwy 60 E., 42451. Tel: 502-764-5570. (CEM)

Rome, Daviess Co., St. Martin, Rev. Joseph M. Mills; Rose Ann Payne, Pastoral Assoc.
Res., 5856 Ky 81, Ownsboro, 42301. tel: 502-685-0339.

Russellville, Logan Co., Sacred Heart, Rev. Lucian P. Hayden.
Res., 296 W. 6th St., 42276. Tel: 502-726-6963.

Scottsville, Allen Co., Christ the King, Rev. James L. Wood, Glmy.; Sr. Mary Lou Ruck, S.P., Parish Min.
Res., P.O. Box 463, 42164. Tel: 502-586-4515; 237-4404.
Summer Station-St. Peter the Fisherman, Barren River.

Sebree, Webster Co., St. Michael, Rev. Carl J. Glahn.
Res., P.O. Box 705, Church St., 42455. Tel: 502-835-2584.

St. Joseph, Daviess Co., St. Alphonsus, Rev. Msgr. Bernard A. Powers.
Res., 7950 Cummings Rd., Owensboro, 42301. Tel: 502-229-4566. (CEM)

St. Paul, Grayson Co., St. Paul, Rev. Charles G.

Fischer.
Res., 1821 St. Paul Rd., Leitchfield, 42754. Tel: 502-242-7436. (CEM)
School-1812 St. Paul Rd., Leitchfield, 42754. Ursuline Sisters 2; Lay teachers 4; Students 81.
Sorgho, Daviess Co., St. Mary Magdalene, Rev. Daniel Goff.
Res., 7232 Ky 56, Owensboro, 42301. Tel: 502-771-4436.
Stanley, Daviess Co., St. Peter of Alcantara, Rev. Paul P. Powell.
Res., 81 Church St., Owensboro, 42301. tel: 502-764-1983. (CEM)
Sturgis, Union Co., St. Francis Borgia, Rev. Albert A. Reed, C.PP.S.
Res., 1302 Adams St., 42459. Tel: 502-333-4645.
Sunfish, Edmondson Co., St. John the Evangelist, Rev. Gregory G. Trawick.
Res., 42284. Tel: 502-286-4366. (CEM)
Uniontown, Union Co., St. Agnes, Rev. Henry L. Frantz, C.PP.S.; Sr. Theresa Kinkel, O.S.F., Pastoral Assoc.
Res., P.O. Box 607, 42461. Tel: 502-822-4416. (CEM)
Waverly, Union Co., Sacred Heart, Rev. E.E. Willett.
Res., Rte 1, Box 132, 42462. Tel: 502-389-4224. (CEM)
St. Peter, Rev. E. E. Willett.
Res., Route 1, Box 132, 42462. Tel: 502-389-4224. (CEM)
Wax, Grayson Co., St. Benedict, Rev. Gary Payne.
Res., St. Anthony Church, 1256 St. Anthony Church Rd., Clarkson, 42726. Tel: 502-242-4791. (CEM)
Whitesville, Daviess Co., St. Mary of the Woods, Revs. Louis Piskula; William J. Hagman; Bruce McCarty; Sr. Sheila Higdon, O.S.U. Pastoral Assoc.
Res., 10534 Main Cross, P.O. Box 1, 42378. Tel: 502-233-4196. (CEM)
School-St. Mary's Grade School. Lay teachers 14; Students 274.
High School-Trinity High School. Lay teachers 11; Students 144.

Non-Parochial Assignments:

Reverend Fathers:
Alvey, Leonard J., Brescia College, 717 Frederica St., Owensboro, KY 42301
Reisz, Leonard, 617 E. 23rd St., Owensboro, KY 42301
Shonis, Anthony, Chap., Mount St. Joseph, Maple Mount, KY 42356
Speaks, John, Chap., Mercy Hospital, 1006 Ford Ave., Owensboro, Ky 42301
Ziegler, Anthony J., Catholic Pastoral Center, 600 Locust St., Owensboro, KY 42301

On Duty Outside the Diocese:

Reverend Fathers:
Byrd, Freddie, St. Meinrad, IN St. Meinrad Seminary
Reynolds, J. Patrick, Divine Word College, 1025 Michigan Ave., N.E., Washington, DC 20017
Vaughan, John R., North American College, 00120 Vatican City, Italy

Absent on Leave:

Reverend Fathers:
Dunn, Stephen

Military Chaplains:
Reverend Fathers-
Roof, Francis M., Chap., PSC 1501 Box 1111, APO, AE 09704.
Wheatley, Carroll, Office of the Chaplain, Naval Training Station, NTS 30, Orlando, FL 32813-5010
Willett, William D., Fort Campbell, P.O. Box 146, Fort Campbell, KY 42223

Retired:
Reverend Fathers:
Boarman, Victor, Bishop Cotton Apartments, 2501 Old Hartford Rd., Owensboro, KY 42303
Boehmicke, George, 2501 1/2 Old Hartford Rd., Apt. 6, Owensboro, KY 42303
Bomensatt, Joseph, Bishop Cotton Apartments, 2501 Old Hartford Rd., Owensboro, KY 42303
Clements, Richard, Bishop Cotton Apartments, 2501 Old Hartford Rd., Owensboro, KY 42303
DeNardi, Charles A., 1705 St. Paul Rd., Ambassador Shores, Leitchfield, KY 42754
Miller, Joseph C., Box 319, Nevis, MN 56467
O'Bryan, Henry, P.O. Box 114, Owensboro, Ky 42302-0114
Rhodes, Joseph, Joseph, Bishop Cotton Apartments, 2501 Old Hartfor Rd., Owensboro, KY 42303
Tucker, Howard, Sts. Joseph & Paul Church, 609 E. Fourth St., Owensboro, KY 42303
Willett, Henry L., 423 Bolivar St., Owensboro, KY 42303. Tel: 502-686-7666
Wolford, Charles, Nazareth Village, I Apt. 318, P.O. Box 210, Nazareth, KY 40048

Institutions Located in the Diocese

(A) Colleges and Universities
Owensboro. *Brescia College*, 717 Frederica st., 42301.
Tel: 502-685-3131.
For a complete listing, refer to the Colleges and Universities section.

(B) High Schools, Inter-Parochial
Owensboro, *Owensboro Catholic High School*, 1524 Parish W. Ave., 42301. Tel: 502-684-3215. Mr. Harold Staples, Prin.; Rev. Larry Hostetter, Chm. Religion Dept.; Mrs. Marian Bennett, Devel. Dir. Priests 1; Sisters 1; Lay teachers 39; Students 596.
Paducah. *St. Mary High School*, 1243 Elmdale Rd., 42003. Tel: 502-442-1681. Mr. Michael J. Collens, Prin. Sisters 1; Lay teachers 17; Students 175.
Whitesville. *Trinity High School*, 42378. Tel: 502-233-5533. Mr. John R. Calhouns, Prin. Priests 1; Lay teachers 11; Students 143.

(C) Elementary Schools, Inter-Parochial
Owensboro. *St. Angela Merici School*, 525 E. 23rd st., 42303. Tel: 502-683-6989. (Grades K-6). P.J. Hayden, Prin. Ursuline Sisters 3; Lay teachers 20; Students 400.
Catherine Spalding School, 4017 Frederica St., 42301. Tel: 502-684-7583. (Grades K-6). Mrs. Doris Waldeck, Prin. Lay teachers 17; students 344.
Francis R. Cottom School, 3418 Hardinsburg Rd., 42303. Tel: 502-683-2268. (Grades K-6). Mrs. Joyce Hoffman, Prin. Ursuline Sisters 1; Lay teachers 12; Students 215.
Henry J. Soenneker School, 3400 Fenmore St., 42301. Tel: 502-684-6487. (Grades K-6). Mr. Phil Spurlock, Prin. Ursuline Sisters 1; Lay teachers 7; Students 128.
Holy Family (Middle) School (Owensboro Catholic Middle School), 2540 Christie Pl., 42301. Tel: 502-683-0480. Mr. James T. Duffy, Prin. Lay teachers 20; Students 314.
Bowling Green. *St. Joseph School*, 416 Church St., 42101. Tel: 502-842-1235. Ms. Joanne Powell, Prin. Lay teachers 11; students 264.
Hardinsburg. *St. Romuald School*, N. Main St., 40143. Tel: 502-756-5504. Sr. Jolinda Naas, O.S.B., Prin. Sisters 2; Lay teachers 10; Students 188.
Morganfield. *St. Ann Interparochial School*, 320 Church St., 42437. Tel: 502-389-1898. Mr. Daryl Hagan, Prin. Ursuline Sisters 2; Lay teachers 14; Students 215.
Paducah. *St. Mary Elementary*, 377 Highland Blvd., 42003. Mrs. Nancy S. Collins, Prin. Lay teachers 19; Students 333.
St. Mary Middle School, 1243 Elmdale Rd., 42003. Ms. Rosann M. Whiting, prin. sisters 1; Lay teachers 7; Students 148.
Sorgho, *Holy Angels Elementary*, P.O. Box 7244, Ky. Hwy. 56, Owensboro, 42301. Tel: 502-771-4773. Ms. Mary Kennedy, Prin. Lay teachers 8, Students 160.

(D) General Hospitals
Owensboro. *Mercy Hospital*, P.O. Box 2839, 1006 Ford Ave., 42301. Tel: 502-686-6100.
For a complete listing, refer to the Hospitals section.
Paducah, *Lourdes Hospital*, P.O. Box 7100, 1530 Lone Oak Rd., 42002-7100. Tel: 502-444-2444.
For a complete listing, refer to the Hospitals section.

(E) Home For Aged
Owensboro. *Carmel Home*, 2501 Old Hartford Rd., 42303. Tel: 502-683-0227.
For a complete listing, refer to the Special Care Facilities section.
Knottsville. *Bishop Soenneker Home*, 9545 Ky. 144, Philpot, 42366. Tel: 502-281-4881.
For a complete listing, refer to the Special Care Facilities section.

(F) Monasteries and Residences of Priests and Brothers
Hartford. *Glenmary House*, 300 Peach Alley, 42347. Tel: 502-298-9886. The Home Missioners of America. Bro. Jack Henn, Dir. Brothers 1; Brother Candidates 1; Priest Candidates 3.
South Union. *Fathers of Mercy*, 42283. Tel: 502-542-4146. Very Rev. John O'Brien, C.P.M., Supr. Gen.; Revs. Joseph Burgdorf, C.P.M.,

Novice Master; John Molloy, C.P.M., Mission Dir.; Kenneth Frye, C.P.M., Novice Master; William Casey, C.P.M.; Frank Sherry, C.P.M.

(G) Convents and Residences for Sisters
Owensboro. *The Glenmary Center*, P.O. Box 2264, 42302. Tel: 502-686-8401. Glenmary Home Mission Sisters of America. Sr. Christine Beckett, Pres. Professed Sisters in Community 14.
Siena Guild of the Glenmary Sisters, Mrs. Rose McCabe, Pres.
St. Joseph's Monastery, 1420 Benita Ave., 42303. Tel: 502-683-5483. Religious of the Passion of Jesus Christ, (Passionist Nuns, Cloistered Comtemplative). Sr. Mary Agnes Higgs, C.P., Supr.; Rev. George Boehmicke, Chap.
Livermore. *The Glenmary Center for Mission Training*, 220 E. 7th St., 42352. Tel: 502-278-5239. Formation Program Sr. Mae Koenig, Dir.; Sr. Martha Schuler; appointed Assoc. Dir.
Maple Mount. *Mount St. Joseph*, 42356. Tel: 502-229-4103. *Motherhuose and Convent of the Ursuline Nuns of the Congregation of Paris*. Sr. Mary Mathias Ward, Supr.; Rev. Anthony J. Shonis, Chap. Professed Sisters in the Community 270.

(H) Retreat Centers
Maple Mount. *Mt. St. Joseph Retreat Center*, 42356. Tel: 502-229-4103. Sr. Marie Goretti Browning, O.S.U., Dir. Assoc. Directors: Rev. Msgr. Bernard Powers; Sr. Elaine Burke, O.S.U.

(I) Newman Centers
Bowling Green. *Western Kentucky University Newman Center*, St. Thomas Aquinas Chapel, 1403 College St., P.O. Box 10170, 42102-4770. Tel: 502-843-3638. Rev. John Little, Dir. Students served 1,100.
Murray. *Murray State University*, 220 N. 13th St., 42071. Tel: 502-753-1391. Joan C. Frisz, Newman Chap.; Rev. Peter Hughes. Students served 750.

(J) Miscellaneous Listings
Owensboro. *The Catholic Foundation of Western Kentucky*, 600 Locust St., 42301.
Paducah. *St. Mary High School Benefit Fund*, 1243 Elmdale Rd., 42003.
Our Lady of the Pines Prayer House, Inc., 717 S. 6th St., 42001. Tel: 502-443-3650.

Religious Institutes of Men

Represented in the Diocese
For further details refer to the corresponding bracketed number in the Religious Institutes of Men or Women section.
(0200)-*Benedictine Monks.*-O.S.B.
(0560)-*Third Order Regular of Saint Francis.*-T.O.R.
(0570)-*Glenmary Home Missioners.* (Glendale OH).
(1060)-*Society of the Precious Blood.* (Cincinnati Prov.).-C.PP.S.

Religious Institutes of Women

Represented in the Diocese
(0100)-*Adorers of the Blood of Christ.*-A.S.C.
(0230)-*Benedictine Sisters of the Pontifical Jurisdiction.* (Ferdinand, IN).-O.S.B.
(0360)-*Carmelite Sisters of the Divine Heart of Jesus.*-Carmel D.C.J.
(0500)-*Sisters of Charity of Nazareth.*-S.C.N.
(1070-13)-*Dominican Sisters.*-O.P.
(1540)-*Sisters of Saint Francis, Clinton, Iowa.*-O.S.F.
(1680)-*School Sisters of St. Francis.*-O.S.F.
(1720)-*Sisters of the Third Order Regular of St. Francis of the Congregation of Our Lady of Lourdes.*-O.S.F.
(1760)-*Sisters of the Third Order of St. Francis of Penance and Charity.*-O.S.F.
(2080)-*Home Mission Sisters of America.*
(2260)-*Sisters of the Lamb of God.*-A.D.
(2575)-*Institute of the Sisters of Mercy of the Americas.* (Cincinnati, OH; Detroit, MI).-R.S.M.
(3170)-*Religious of the Passion of Jesus Christ.*-C.P.
(3360)-*Sisters of Providence of Saint Mary-Of-The-Woods, Indiana.*-S.P.
(4120)-*Ursuline Nuns, of the Congregation of Paris.*-O.S.U.

Interparochial cemeteries
Owensboro. *Mater Dolorosa Cemetery*, 1860 W. 9th St. *Resurrection Cemetery*, 5404 Leitchfield Rd., 42303. Mr. Art Hodde, Dir.

Necrology
Higdon, Anthony, Owensboro, KY Carmel Home.-Died Aug. 19, 1992.

Current Parish and Institution Histories
The following Histories were submitted by parishes and institutions of the Diocese of Owensboro.

Past Parishes, Missions, Schools and Institutions

Parishes/Missions	City	Opening	Closing
Holy Spirit	Ashbyburg	1915	1937
Our Lady of Perpetual Help	Patesville	1848	1983
Our Lady of Victory	Fulton	1906	?
St. Benedict	Beech Grove	1881	1925
St. Bernard	Hampton	1894	1923
St. Edward	Eddyville	1885	1900
St. Francis Xavier	Smith Mills	1818	1900
St. James	Iberia	1915	1950
St. John the Baptist	Sulphur Springs	1892	?
St. John the Evangelist	Columbus	1880	?
St. Joseph (later St. Stephen)	Cadiz	1846	1926
St. Joseph	Golden Pond	1878	1925
St. Joseph	Owensboro	1864	1948
St. Joseph	Sebree	1885	1902
St. Joseph	Smithland	1915	1937
St. Mary	Big Clifty		
St. Raphael	W. Louisville	1832	1982
St. Stephen	Smithland	1855	1870
St. Thomas	Hawesville	1879	1964
St. Thomas	Maxon Mills	1880	1924

Institutions	City	Opened	Closed
Our Lady of Mercy Hospital	Morganfield	1945	1970
St. Maur's Priory	South Union	1948	1988
St. Columba Academy	Bowling Green	1889	?
Columbian College	Owensboro	1906	1913
Mount Carmel	Axtel	1823	1830
Mount Merino Seminary	Irvington	1838	1838
Outwood Hospital	Earlington	1930	?

School	City	Opened	Closed
Blessed Martin	Waverly	1943	1962
Blessed Sacrament	Owensboro	1948	1960
Holy Name H.S.	Henderson	1899	1970
Immaculate Conception	Hawesville	1949	1969
Mount St. Joseph Academy	Maple Mount	1874	1983
Sacred Heart	Russellville	1947	1972
St. Agnes	Uniontown	1922	1963
St. Alphonsus	St. Joseph	1901	1964
St. Anthony	Peonia	1927	1979
St. Charles	Bardwell	1921	1966
St. Frances Academy	Owensboro	1849	1950
St. Jerome H.S.	Fancy Farm	1892	1985
St. John Evangelist	Sunfish	1941	1965
St. Joseph	Bowling Green	1912	1965
St. Columbus Academy	Bowling Green	1863	1912
St. Joseph H.S.	Mayfield	1945	1964
St. Joseph	Owensboro	1924	1948
St. Mary	Whitesville	1882	1967
St. Mary's Academy	Paducah	1858	1965
St. Paul H.S.	Leitchfield	1917	1967
St. Romuald H.S.	Hardinsburg	1876	1992
St. Vincent Academy	St. Vincent	1820	1967
St. William H.S.	Knottsville	1937	1967
Immaculate Conception	Hawesville	1948	1992
Immaculate Conception	Earlington	1890	1978
Rosary School	Paducah	1947	1967
Sacred Heart	Uniontown	1885	1887
Sacred Heart	Russelville	1947	1972
St. Alphonsus	St. Joseph	1901	1989
St. Anthony	Browns Valley	1912	1966
St. Anthony	Axtel	1939	1970
St. Augustine	Reed	1922	1964
St. Benedict	Wax	1941	1962
St. Charles	Bardwell	1921	1966
St. Denis	Fancy Farm	1921	1963
St. Edward	Fulton	1947	1961
St. Elizabeth	Curdsville	1911	1973
St. John Evangelist	Sunfish	1941	1943
St. Joseph	Central City	1923	1975
St. Joseph	Leitchfield	1951	1970
St. Lawrence	Philpot	1920	1961
St. Martin	Rome	1916	1989
St. Mary Magdalene	Sorgho	1923	1989
St. Mary of the Woods	McQuady	1922	1967
St. Paul	Princeton	1948	1973
St. Peter	Waverly	1910	1973
St. Peter Alcantra	Stanley	1911	1982
St. Raphael	St. Raphael	1900	1963
St. Rose	Cloverport	1916	1967
St. Sebastian	Calhoun	1952	1967
St. Stephen	Owensboro	1939	1989
Sts. Joseph and Paul	Owensboro	1948	1978
St. Hubertus	Owensboro	1879	1915
St. Joseph	Owensboro	1915	1948

Parish Membership
1994-1995

Parish	City	Families	Members	Opened
Blessed Mother	Owensboro	891	2466	1948
Blessed Sacrament	Owensboro	60	103	1933
Christ the King	Madisonville	317	909	1968
Christ the King	Scottsville	27	52	1964
Holy Cross	Providence	28	59	1978
Holy G. Angels	Irvington	78	240	1877
Holy Name	Henderson	1354	3289	1824
Holy Redeemer	Beaver Dam	87	216	1958
Holy Spirit	B. Green[1]	846	2500	1968
Holy Trinity	Morgantown	27	60	1940
Immaculate	Owensboro	763	1981	1954
Im. Conception[2]	Earlington	74	173	1873
Im. Conception[2]	Hawesville	150	350	1858
Newman Center	Murray			1986
Our Lady of Lourdes	Owensboro	792	2198	1959
Precious Blood	Owensboro	382	1088	1960
Resurrection	D. Springs[3]	42	106	1900
Rosary Chapel	Paducah	119	250	1947
Sacred Heart	Hickman	45	87	1858
Sacred Heart	Russellville	250	538	1858
Sacred Heart	Waverly	50	129	1819
St. Agnes	Uniontown	298	901	1859
St. Alphonsus	St. Joseph	209	550	1839
St. Ambrose	Henshaw	46	121	1832
St. Ann	Morganfield	600	1790	1812
St. Anthony	Axtel	230	540	1801
St. Anthony	B. Valley[4]	116	316	1902
St. Anthony	Peonia	107	205	1822
St. Anthony of Padua	Grand Rivers	24	36	1987
St. Augustine	Gray. Springs[5]	30	60	1815
St. Augustine	Reed	60	130	1896
St. Benedict	Wax	66	124	1835
St. Charles	Bardwell	99	337	1891
St. Charles	Livermore	34	80	1917
St. Columba	Lewisport	123	280	1850
St. Denis	Fancy Farm	90	296	1914
St. Edward	Fulton	60	162	1932
St. Elizabeth	Clarkson	52	143	1906
St. Elizabeth	Curdsville	60	185	1887
St. Francis Borgia	Sturgis	102	274	1952
St. Francis de Sales	Paducah	700	1465	1848
St. Henry	Aurora	100	192	1983
St. Jerome	Fancy Farm	650	1950	1836
Sts. Joseph and Paul	Owensboro	557	1142	1948
St. John Baptist	Fordsville	28	62	1898
St. John Evangelist	Paducah	325	823	1843
St. John Evangelist	Sunfish	60	130	1830
St. Joseph	B. Green[1]	223	519	1859
St. Joseph	Central City	103	255	1886
St. Joseph	Leitchfield	249	684	1872
St. Joseph	Mayfield	545	1310	1887
St. Jude	Clinton	48	101	1982
St. Lawrence	St. Lawrence	115	294	1821
St. Leo	Murray	265	693	1949
St. Mark	Eddyville	70	140	1989
St. Martin	Rome	184	494	1873
St. Mary of Fields	LaCenter	112	208	1906
St. Mary Magdalene	Sorgho	178	562	1902
St. Mary of Woods	Franklin	113	233	1867
St. Mary of Woods	McQuady	70	182	1870
St. Mary of Woods	Whitesville	678	2200	1830
St. Mary and St. James	Guthrie	20	50	1949
St. Michael	Sebree	48	125	1977
St. Paul	Leitchfield	200	575	1811
St. Paul	Princeton	88	192	1899
St. Peter	Stanley	104	283	1873
St. Peter	Waverly	213	605	1909
Sts. Peter and Paul	Hopkinsville	551	1372	1872
St. Pius X	Calvert City	168	361	1954
St. Pius X	Owensboro	625	1800	1957
St. Romuald	Hardinsburg	390	1050	1812
St. Rose of Lima	Cloverport	130	400	1887
St. Sebastian	Calhoun	62	180	1880
St. Stephen	Cadiz	124	248	1966
St. Stephen	Owensboro	1051	2526	1839
St. Susan	Elkton	54	125	1963
St. Thomas Aquinas[6]	Bowling Green			1962
St. Thomas More	Paducah	759	1999	1943
St. William	Knottsville	331	792	1887
St. William	Marion	69	144	1966
Total		19148	49790	

(1-Bowling Green; 2-Immaculate Conception; 3-Dawson Springs; 4-Brown's Valley; 5-Grayson Springs; 6-Newman Center)

Blessed Mother Parish
Owensboro

Blessed Mother Parish is a vibrant faith community that lives and flourishes in the heart of the Owensboro Diocese. Established under the leadership of the Most Reverend Francis R. Cotton in 1948, this parish was dedicated to the Mother of God. The parish began in 1991 to celebrate the Feast Day of the parish on August 15th, the Assumption of Mary into Heaven.

Boundaries for the parish were defined on April 3, 1948. Father William B. Jarboe was installed as the first pastor and on July 25 the Dedication Sunday Mass was celebrated. The church building itself was intended to be temporary. The original plan had the church building becoming a gym and a new church building being built later. Blessed Mother School opened its doors on December 6, 1948. 299 students were enrolled in classes taught by five Ursuline Sisters that first year. Sister Callista Langan was the first principal of the school. There were five classrooms in the school building. Three rooms served as living quarters for the Sisters. The north half of the present church building was used as a cafeteria for the children. By the summer of 1951 there was already an addition of four class rooms to the school building, thus providing for its rapid growth.

In 1957 an addition was made to the rectory in anticipation of a full time assistant pastor.

The summer of 1962 showed further growth and the addition of more facilities. Then, by 1963, the Ursuline Sisters moved from their apartments in the school building into a new convent on 22nd Street.

In 1965 the parish's first religious vocation was realized. Sister Rose Marita O'Bryan, daughter of M/M Marion Albin O'Bryan, made final Profession as an Ursuline Nun at Mount St. Joseph Motherhouse, Maple Mount, Kentucky.

Sister Mary Damien Abell became the principal of Blessed Mother School in 1966 and continued to serve the parents and students for nineteen years. Her impact on Blessed Mother Parish continues today. During her years, Blessed Mother School grew and prospered, and built quite a reputation. She will always be remembered as "A legend in her own time."

By 1968 the school facilities were again outgrown. Four new classrooms, a new cafeteria, a new and larger library were added to the school. The church building was completely renovated at this time and the former cafeteria was incorporated into the present church, thus began the longest aisle in the city.

The silver jubilee of the parish was celebrated on July 22, 1973. The Most Reverend Henry J. Soenneker presided at the Mass with Msgr. William B. Jarboe, Father Richard Clements, Father Robert Whelan, and Father Francis Roof as con-celebrants.

In March 1977 Bishop Soenneker came for a special commissioning ceremony for twelve men who were to serve as Blessed Mother's first Eucharistic Ministers.

In 1981 the parish was again bursting at the seams. In August a new parish building was raised which included a gym, kindergarten and first grade classrooms, and two meeting rooms which also served as classrooms.

In August 1984 the parish pulled together to host their first parish picnic in twenty years. The spirit of the parish was at a high when Renew started in the fall of 1984. During the next three years more and more people got involved in parish ministries and parish organizations.

On May 28, 1988, Kevin Osborne, son of Bob and Francis Osborne, was ordained a priest, the first from Blessed Mother Parish. The first Parish Pastoral Council was elected June 25 and 26, 1988.

After 2 years of planning and struggle the Owensboro Catholic Consolidated School System was formed on July 1, 1989. Blessed Mother School closed and the school buildings were leased to the Owensboro Catholic Consolidated School System. The former Blessed Mother Elementary School became St. Angela Merici School.

In July 1990 the parish offices were moved out of the priests' home into the new Parish Center which had been the Sisters' convent. Minor renovation was done to the building to provide not only offices but also a Parish Center. Meeting rooms and The Greatroom provided much needed space for Parish Activities.

The year of 1991 brought about the ordination of Fr. Ray Clark. Ray, the son of Harold and Ann Clark, attended school at Blessed Mother.

In order to conform with the Vatican II Constitution on the Sacred Liturgy (1963) and the American Bishops' Statements on Environment (1974 & 1978) the Parish Council expressed a Dream of Renovation of the Church Building to the Parishioners of Blessed Mother in June of 1991. A fund was established as a savings for future Church Renovation. The dream consist of a new floor plan for a worship space where the altar is centrally located, where all can see, hear and participate. An enlarged Cry/Bridal Dressing Room, inside restrooms, Place of Reservation for the Blessed Sacrament, Reconciliation Chapel, and Gathering Space are envisioned in the dream.

Blessed Mother Parish has come a long way over the years and we continue to grow and to share the Spirit. Many have said they find us to be a warm and welcoming parish. We will strive to continue to spread that warmth, to be the sunshine of a faith-filled community, and to love one another!

Blessed Mother Catholic Church.

Pastors

Msgn. William B. Jarboe	1948-1965
Fr. Richard Clements	1965-1983
Fr. Charles G. Fischer	1983-1989
Fr. C. Phil Riney	1989-

Associate Pastors

Fr. John C. Hallahan	1957-1967
Fr. Richard Hallenkamp	1967-1968
Fr. Leonard Alvey	1968
Fr. Gerald Calhoun	1968-1970
Fr. Philip Field	1970-1972
Fr. Francis Roof	1972-1973
Fr. Robert Whelan	1973-1974
Fr. John Speaks	1974-1977
Fr. Louis Piskula	1977-1982
Fr. Robert Drury	1982-1984
Fr. Martin E. Hayes	1984-1987
Fr. Gregory Trawick	1987-1989
Fr. Larry Hostetter	1989-1990
Fr. Freddie Byrd	1990-1992
Fr. Dave Johnson	1992-

BLESSED SACRAMENT CHAPEL
OWENSBORO

According to Mrs. Fannie Myles (85) one of the oldest members of Blessed Sacrament Congregation, evangelization took place as early as 1933 in a house located at Fifth and Plum Streets, in Owensboro. Father Robert W. Connor, ordained May 18, 1940, was assigned chaplain of Blessed Sacrament Chapel by Bishop Francis R. Cotton and remained chaplain from 1940 until 1959. In 1940 two Sisters of Charity of Nazareth under Father Conner's direction, opened the CATHOLIC COLORED HIGH SCHOOL. This school was located at the corner of Fifth and Plum Streets. This school remained in operation at this location till 1947 when it had to be moved. The CARTER COUNTY SCHOOL, located at Seventh and Sycamore was purchased and used as a school house and church services. In 1959, due to low enrollment paired with lack of funding the school was closed. Black students were then bussed to St. Stephen Cathedral School. As Father Connor was already involved in evangelistic work in the black neighborhood, he felt the need to give the members of the Community something to call their own. Therefore, thru community involvement, many picnics held over the years, plus help from the EXTENSION SOCIETY, the dream of a church for the black Catholics began to materialize. Blessed Sacrament Chapel was built and dedicated in 1948. This church was built directly behind the Carter School. In 1966 Blessed Sacrament Chapel was rented to the Owensboro School System for the Owensboro Area Museum. The Museum closed in 1970 and Bishop Soenneker requested the building from the Museum and Father John Bartolomucci, an Italian Franciscan priest re-opened it as a chapel. He also utilized the building for many other purposes: church services, day care, community services and a food and clothing bank for needy persons. During the 1970s, these services were coordinated by the Sisters of the Lamb of God. Since Father Connor's death in 1963, numerous other priests have played a significant role in the history of Blessed Sacrament Chapel. The name and location remain the same, BLESSED SACRAMENT CHAPEL, 602 Sycamore Street, Owensboro, KY, a memorial to many.

Blessed Sacrament Chapel. (Courtesy of Fannie Myles)

CHRIST THE KING PARISH
MADISONVILLE

Christ the King Church, Madisonville, KY.

On Saturday, January 20, 1968, an announcement was made by Bishop Henry J. Soenneker that a new Catholic Church would be erected on a 22-acre plot of land just north of Madisonville, a city long known as "the smallest town in the nation with a Shrine Temple and the largest second class city without a Catholic Church. The acreage was made possible through the generosity of Mr. and Mrs. Albert Whittington. Rev. Gerard J. Glahn, previously served parishes in Hickman and Fulton counties, was named the first pastor of the community of less than 125 families.

The parish hall, the first building to be erected on the site, included a meeting/social hall and temporary living quarters for the pastor and housekeeper. The people continued to participate in weekend liturgies in their old parish, Immaculate Conception, Earlington, but held meetings and parish activities in the new hall. The church building, with a seating capacity of 400, was dedicated on June 15, 1969, by Bishop Soenneker and is constructed in a contemporary design (in the round) with pews facing the altar on three sides.

In 1975, plans began to take shape to build a parish school to accommodate the children from grades K-8 for both parishes. The children from the new parish continued to attend school in Earlington but the building had grown too small and was in need of extensive repairs. These problems led to the decision to build a new structure. The new school was to be located in Madisonville and it became a reality much through the generosity of Eleanor and Bob Tapp. After the construction of the rectory, the former living quarters of the pastor became housing for the Ursuline Sisters who moved from Earlington to staff the new school that was to have the capacity for 200 students.

In 1971, the Diocese, with the help of Albert and Mildred Whittington, purchased the Old Branch Street Elementary School for use in the service of youth. It was destined to become the first home of the St. Vincent de Paul Store established by Eve Markham and Eileen Ainsworth. The store has moved twice in the past years; the building now being used is the property of the organization, and the store is still managed by Eve Markham.

Christ the King Parish family has grown from the original 125 families to its present 300 families. During the early years of the parish, there was an annual parish outing on the grounds in the woods on the hill, highlighted with an outdoor Mass on the stone altar that still graces the top of the hill. The parish picnic, that is held every year on the third Saturday of September, is the largest of many parish activities that keeps the life and spirit of community thriving and growing. The parish remains a transient one basically due to the fact that Madisonville is a transient community with many of the town's industries keeping their company headquarters located elsewhere. And so new faces appear and old faces disappear on a regular basis.

The parish hall was converted to a preschool and day-care center in 1987 called the Learning and Growth Center. It offers an invaluable service to about ninety families in the community. Since the parish had long outgrown the original social hall, on Sunday, March 22, 1992, the community of Madisonville saw the groundbreaking of Christ the King's new 10,000 square foot parish center.

The priests who have served the parish since its establishment are: Rev. Gerard Glahn, 1968-1981; Rev. Delma Clemons, 1981-1985; Rev. Alan McIntosh, 1985-1988; and Rev. John Meredith, 1988-Present. *by Charles G. Melton*

CHRIST THE KING PARISH
SCOTTSVILLE

Christ the King Church, Scottsville, KY.

Christ the King Church, Scottsville, a Glenmary parish is located in the southeast corner of the Owensboro diocese and is the only Catholic Church in Allen County. Its history began in 1964 with Father Raymond Berthiaume, a Glenmarian and pastor of St. Mary of the Woods, Franklin (Simpson County), serving eight Catholic families in Allen County. (Three of the original families are still in the parish: Hall, Taylor, and Wheat). Mass was first celebrated in a trailer across from White Plains School. In these early years, religious education classes were held in the Hall's home, and there was one young convert as a result of the classes. Clarine Taylor tells of a young visitor who was so impressed with the smallness of the parish that upon returning to her school, inspired the class to sell encyclopedias, sending the money to Scottsville!

In 1965, four and one-half acres in Colonial Manor were purchased and the trailer moved there. Two years later an all-purpose building costing $40,000 was erected. While Father Del Holmes was pastor, in 1981, a Mass station was built near Barren River Dam on land donated by Marcus and Frances Cook. Mass is celebrated there on the summer holiday weekends.

True to the spirit of Glenmary, despite opposition from some parishioners and other Scottsvillians, an early pastor, Father Gus Guppenberger, reached out to non-Catholics in the county, especially Blacks and the unemployed. However, early records also show support of Catholics from members of one Baptist congregation who refused to heed their preacher's opposition. Dell Hall tells of a group of Methodist women helping her make a canopy for the trailer. Pastors and the present Parish Minister have been active in the county's Ministerial Association.

Shortly after the building was finished, Christ the King Church opened its doors to a special education program serving handicapped children from poor families. This program has been moved to the school system. Many parishioners serve the community in their careers and in volunteer work.

Joining the eight original families were two from Tennessee. The Catholic population in both areas grew and eventually Lafayette, Tennessee's Catholics built a church and Christ the King's population declined.

In 1988, the first non-Glenmary pastor, Father James Wood from the Rockville Centre, New York diocese, began service in Simpson and Allen counties. Two years later, in consultation with the parish, Sister Mary Lou Ruck, a Sister of Providence from St. Mary-of-the-Woods, Indiana, was hired. Sister resides in Scottsville and has taken over most of the daily running of the parish. With a full time staff person in Allen County, parish membership grew. In 1991-2, there were an unusual number of deaths and there were also several families transferred from the area. Though numbers declined, parish spirit remained high.

From a small seed planted in 1964, through numerical growth and decline, members of Christ the King continue to worship together and bring the message of Jesus Christ to their world.

HOLY GUARDIAN ANGEL PARISH
IRVINGTON

In 1930 it was decided that Holy Guardian Angel Church, completed at Mount Merino and dedicated in 1898, was in need of too many major improvements and too far removed from the major population area. Even though it was during the Great Depression, the decision was made to build a brick Gothic Church on High Street in Irvington.

Mr. Aloysius King, the only member of our congregation who worked on the construction 50 years ago recalls the following:

In spite of the fact that many of the parishioners were very much attached to the Church at Mount Merino and were very much upset with the decision to tear it down practically all the able-bodied men pitched in to help with the new construction. Practically the entire congregation were farmers. Together with their farm equipment - wagon, horses, etc. - the men contributed their labor. They dug the basement with teams of horses and slip scrapers. With picks and shovels, they straightened up the basement walls and leveled off the floor. For mixing the concrete they hauled water in barrels from the railroad roundhouse.

In wagons they hauled everything that they could salvage from the church at Mount Merino to the new site. They used the 2x6 inch timber for the subfloor in the new church, the stained glass windows, the pews and many other items.

Paul Whalen, the head carpenter, directed the parishioners in construction work. Fr. Jerry Hoepf also was considered a competent carpenter. Nick Malls, a skilled finishing carpenter, rebuilt the pews by hand. All of the construction work was done without precision and power tools.

The parishioners feared they would not have sufficient funds with which to finish the Church. Whereupon, during a Sunday Mass Fr. Jerry announced that he felt if each parishioner, besides paying the pew rent (salary) would give a dime a Sunday they would manage somehow. Astonishingly, when the Church was dedicated, the parish was free of debt.

The solemn ceremony of the dedication of the new Gothic structure took place on the morning of October 30, 1933. The dedication was presided over by the Most Rev. John A. Floersh, Archbishop of Louisville. During the course of the homily, Archbishop John A. Florsh observed: "More than 75 years ago the first Church was erected in this locality. The old church building was torn down. But the spirit of saintly pioneers of those days will be brought here because their spirit has descended upon their children's children as an heirloom...I wish to extend to the Rev. Pastor, Father Jerome Hoepf, C.PP.S. and the faithful parishioners, my congratulations on having erected so beautiful an edifice, small but beautiful in its smallness."

Holy Guardian Angel Church, Irvington. (Courtesy of Lilly Lucas)

In December of 1937 Irvington became part of the new Diocese of Owensboro.

Between 1933 and 1983, the basement with kitchen facilities was completed, and air conditioning installed throughout the structure. On May 3, 1981 during a covered dish supper the parishioners approved each detail of the building committee's final plans for the restoration of the church in compliance with the updated Liturgy. Bishop Soenneker on October 4, 1981 solemnly blessed the renewed structure.

Priests serving Holy Guardian Angel Church 1933-1983: 1933—Rev. J. Hoepf, C.PP.S.; 1938—Rev. J. Froede, C.PP.S.; 1946—Rev. A. Zumberger, C.PP.S.; 1951—Rev. E. Murphy, C.PP.S.; 1952—Rev. M. Storms, C.PP.S.; 1958—Rev. A. Meiring, C.PP.S.; 1968—Rev. J. Minch, C.PP.S.; 1979—Rev. W. Donohoe, C.PP.S. 1986 Father Tony Stevenson became pastor of Holy Guardian Angel Parish. There were only 16 families then and when he left on June 16, 1992, there were 65 families. Father Tony got the people to have fish fries and picnics and put on a Saturday evening Mass at 5 P.M. and he had Mass on Sunday morning at 8 A.M. Father Walter Hancock became Pastor of Holy Guardian Angel Parish on June 16, 1992 and continued the programs of Fr. Tony Stevenson. In July 1992 more walks were made on side of the Church and the front of the Church.

A rough Historical sketch of Holy Guardian Angel Church, 1832-1933 follows:

In 1832 a tract of land called Mount Merino was sold to Dr. Benedict Wathen and Dr. Richard M. Wathen. The Wathen brothers established the Mount Merino seminary there in 1838 under the direction of W.E. Powell and Rev. J.B. Hutchens. The school closed in 1843 when its director, Rev. B.J. Spalding was transferred to other duties. In 1854 the Mount Merino farm became the home for Holy Guardian Angel Church, then a mission of St. Theresa parish in Rhodelia.

On the 26th of December 1888 the Merino Post Office in Peter P. Roberts' store was renamed Irvington. The name was chosen by the developers in honor of an official of the Texas railroad.

The year 1898 saw major growth in Irvington, in that same year, after several near disasters and bad weather. J.K. Bramlette completed the new Holy Angel Church at Mount Merino.

Priests serving Holy Guardian Angel Parish 1838-1898: Rev. Spalding, Rev. Wasterman, Rev. Craney, Rev. O'Cornor, Rev. Hennesy, Rev. Niehaus, Rev. Carol and Rev. Pike.

Priests serving Holy Guardian Church 1899-1932: Rev. Brey, 1897; Rev. A.G. Meyering, 1899; Rev. Augustine Zoeller, 1903; Rev. Stephen Holieran, 1905; Rev. M. Rosengarten, C.PP.S., 1925.

September 4, 1992, Father Walter A. Hancock is Pastor and Holy Guardian Angel Parish is mission of St. Rose Church, Cloverport, KY. There are 70 families in Holy Guardian Angel Parish in Irvington, KY, Sept. 4, 1992.

Holy Name of Jesus Parish
Henderson

In 1810, the Reverend Charles Nerinx reported in a letter to Archbishop Carroll of Baltimore that there were 10 Catholic families living in Henderson.

In 1992, there are some 1400 families registered as members of Holy Name of Jesus parish, making it the largest parish in the Diocese of Owensboro.

The celebration place of Mass has grown as much symbolically, as well; from a room in a Third Street home to a small 55-pew church on the corner of Third and Ingram, to the impressive Gothic structure on the corner of Second and Ingram, which can seat about 600 people. Many believe that the reason for constructing such a massive structure in 1886 for a small parish was that Father Tierney believed—and hoped—that some day, Henderson would be the seat for the diocese that he was sure would be established.

The first parish in Henderson was named after St. Louis, but when the cornerstone was laid for the "new" church on the feast of the Holy Name, Father Tierney named the church after the feast day. (The cemetery, however, retains the name of St. Louis).

There have been many milestones in the growth and life of Catholicity in Henderson, centered around the church and the school. The "heyday," perhaps was in the early sixties, when there reached a peak of 15 Sisters of Charity teaching at the grade and high schools. The convent was so full that bedrooms for the sisters were set up in the attic to accommodate them. The peak year for students was in 1965-66 with 730 enrolled in both levels of education. These accomplishments, however, were also at the beginning of a very painful time in the life of the parish.

Coinciding with other factors, such as Vatican II and the leaving of thousands of clergy and religious, state regulations regarding schools, the financial strain of operating an educational institution from grades one through 12 caused some heart-wrenching decisions to be made.

Eventually, the parish decided to discontinue the high school, and channel faith, monies and energy toward running a grade school. 1970 saw the last class graduate from Holy Name High School.

In 1992 Holy Name Elementary School, which now includes kindergarten, is the heartbeat of the parish. Normal enrollment for the past several years has been about 500 students a year, but again, the financial strain and other factors are making it an effort to keep the school open. For the first time in its history, a lay principal is at the helm and there is only one Sister of Charity in the parish.

But as is the power of God, He can make positive come from negative. With the *decrease* in religious numbers, there has been an *increase* in active lay people, and that is always good. No longer do we Catholics depend on "Father" or "Sister" to "do it." More often, we are ministering to others ourselves...visiting the sick...feeding the poor...comforting the lonely and heartbroken...and Holy Name people are doing it with almost 1000 active in church ministries.

We boast a St. Vincent dePaul Society which ministers to the financially needy, a Good Samaritan League which helps people from all walks of life who fall through the cracks of health care. We have a bereavement league which caters to families and friends after a funeral. The list goes on, but the sentiment is the same...Holy Name people are living their faith. *by Judy Hayden*

Holy Name of Jesus, Henderson.

Holy Redeemer Parish
Beaver Dam

For almost 100 years the few Catholics in the northeastern part of Ohio County were served by St. John the Baptist Church, originally near Dundee and later, in 1960s, moved to Fordsville. Because of the large geographic area comprising Ohio County, this parish had practically no influence in the southwestern area of the county.

In 1950 Father Walter Hancock began visiting a few scattered Catholics in the southwestern half of Ohio County. He soon started to offer Mass once a month at the home of Edwin Sharp in Hartford. Then in 1954 he offered an occasional Mass at the southern edge of Beaver Dam in the home of William Pierce. (William was a former Methodist minister who joined the Catholic church in his later years.) On the first Sunday of Lent in 1958 Father Hancock started offering Mass every Sunday at Bill Pierce's home. In the Fall of that same year a house on Main Street in Beaver Dam was purchased by the diocese for the purpose of establishing some permanent Church residence. At this time Father Bill Hageman, newly stationed at St. Mary's Church in Whitesville, came to offer weekly Mass. In 1961 Bishop Soenneker asked the Glenmary Home Missioners if they would assume pastoral responsibility for the southern half of Ohio County as a mission of Holy Trinity Church in Morgantown.

At this time there were about ten practicing Catholics. Due to the booming coal industry in Ohio County during the 1960s, the number of Catholics began to increase. Father Carl Boehler was the first Glenmary Priest to serve here. The number of Catholics migrating from other areas (particularly from Daviess County) brought quite an increase in membership.

In 1963 Bishop Soenneker arranged for the purchase of property at the northern end of Beaver Dam to serve as a permanent location of Holy Redeemer Church. The construction of the present church on this property began in 1964. In 1965 Father Boehler was elected the treasurer of the Glenmary Missioners and moved to their headquarters in Cincinnati. In October of that year Father Joe O'Donnell arrived to be pastor. On September 11, 1966 Holy Redeemer Church was formally dedicated by Bishop Soenneker.

In the Spring of 1967 Brother Jerry Dorn arrived to begin a five-year assignment working with Father O'Donnell. He influenced greatly the youth, both Catholic and Protestant, of the whole area raising a positive Catholic image countywide.

September 22, 1967 the first Ecumenical Prayer Service was held at Holy Redeemer. The pastor of the Beaver Dam Baptist Church, Rev. Glenn Armstrong, preached the sermon. In 1970 Tony Shonis, later Father Shonis, was ordained a deacon at Holy Redeemer Church. (He had

Holy Redeemer Church, Beaver Dam.

spent a year doing mission work in Ohio County from 1966-67.)

Until 1973 Glenmarians and other church volunteers lived in the church basement. A rectory was constructed by the Glenmary Building Crew in 1973. During the course of this parish's short existence there were many Glenmary priests, brothers, and sisters who came to do great mission work in this area. Also effective witness has been given in Ohio County by several diocesan priests and many Ursuline sisters.

In 1976 Father O'Donnell left the parish to do ecumenical work with the Southern Baptist Convention. Father Ed Gorny then became the pastor. In 1981 Father O'Donnell returned as pastor. He is, at present, still pastor and finds the experience both rewarding and stimulating.

In 1984 Sister Luisa Bickett, O.S.U. came to Holy Redeemer to do mission work, after spending many years in the missions of South America. With the cooperation of the people of Holy Redeemer parish she began to live in the Horse Branch area of the county and is still there giving a missionary witness where few Catholics live.

Over the years Holy Redeemer parish continues to grow slowly but surely. When Father O'Donnell began offering Mass in 1965 there were an average of about 30 people attending Sunday Mass. Now the Sunday worship usually has over 150 people present.

This parish has never had the experience of a Catholic school. However, it has been blessed over the years with many parishioners who have moved in with a fine background of Catholic education both on the grade, high school, and college level. The parish family has been very cooperative in parish life and has done much to make the Catholic Church acceptable to the other people of the county. One example of fine Catholic leadership was the establishment of the Parish Council in the Fall of 1967. For 25 years now this council has met regularly on a monthly basis.

With the members living in an area extended over so many square miles, one of the great challenges is religious education. Because of the cooperation of the parishioners there has been a strong effort and concern for handing on the faith. One of the special highlights of the Church Year is the annual two-week Summer School of Religious Education. Besides lay teachers this Summer School has been blessed over the years with the teaching of many religious sisters. Each year children receive their First Communion at the end of the Summer School. Every other year the Bishop comes for Confirmation around the same time.

The parish always has had a deep appreciation for the concern and enthusiastic support of the bishops of Owensboro. The people of this parish have had Glenmary provide the priestly ministry. As a matter of fact, Glenmary for the past five years has had the first year of its training program for candidates to priesthood and brotherhood at a center established in Hartford.

There are a few members still in the parish who lived here when it was first established. They alone with many others are a testimony to the vital faith of Catholics who moved into an area where the Church is very much in a mission situation. The future for Holy Redeemer parish continues to look promising.

Holy Spirit Parish
Bowling Green

In a letter dated August 4, 1967, the Most Rev. Henry J. Soenneker, D.D., Bishop of the Diocese of Owensboro, decreed the erection of the new parish of Holy Spirit in Bowling Green. He named Fr. Henry Willett as the first pastor of Holy Spirit which was originally part of the historic St. Joseph Parish on Church Street. There were 225 families in the newly formed parish. However, the construction of the facility was delayed. It was not until December 6, 1970 that the new facility consisting of church, hall, and rectory were dedicated and Mass was celebrated in the church on Thanksgiving Day, 1970.

The parish began to grow and continues growing today. Rev. Joseph Mills was the second pastor of the parish. Due to the rapid growth of the area and the parish Rev. Ben Powers was appointed Associate Pastor in 1975. Rev. Powers served in that office until his fatal car accident in 1978.

From the time of Rev. Powers to the present a number of associate pastors have received their training at Holy Spirit. Between the years of 1978 and 1992 those serving the parish as associate pastors were Rev. Peter Lauzon, Rev. Bradley Whistle, Rev. Greg Trawick, Rev. Gary Payne, Rev. Anthony Jones and Rev. Henry Wieder. From 1975 to 1984 these associate pastors also cared for the spiritual needs of St. John the Evangelist Church in Sunfish, Kentucky. This church in Edmonson County was a mission church of Holy Spirit.

Under the leadership of Rev. Joseph Mills, Holy Spirit Parish put special emphasis upon the values of family life. During Rev. Mills pastorate many parishioners were involved in the Catholic Family Movement, the Marriage Encounter, and the Cursillo Movement.

Rev. Thomas Clark, the third pastor, pastored Holy Spirit until 1989. Being an accomplished liturgist, the various liturgical ministries began to flourish. The parish liturgical worship was enhanced by the formation of a permanent Choir and Guitar Musical Group. Eucharistic Ministers were appointed as well as training workshops for Lectors, Ushers and Greeters. The sanctuary was arranged to be liturgically correct in appearance.

In 1989 Rev. Gerald Calhoun became the fourth pastor of Holy Spirit. By this time the parish had outgrown its ability to effectively carry out its programs in its original facilities. A massive building campaign was organized in 1992 with ground breaking ceremonies planned for October of that year. The plans call for a new rectory and parish hall. The existing rectory will be converted into office space and the parish hall into class rooms and meeting rooms space.

In 1988 Holy Spirit hired its first Youth Director, Rosanna Schadler. The Religious Education office expanded its services to include a number of adult programs under the direction of Anita Willoughby who was hired in 1990.

As Bowling Green continues growing, so does the Holy Spirit Parish community continue to grow in its ministry to the local church.

Holy Trinity Parish
Morgantown

Holy Trinity Catholic Church. (Courtesy of Shirley Hamilton)

The summer of 1942 witnessed an unusual event in Butler County, Kentucky, when two Glenmary Home Missioners, Father Raphael Sourd and Father Clement Borchers, visited Morgantown, the county seat, and set up their mission tent. During the following week they preached on the front lawn of the County Courthouse, visited the people, and acquainted them all with the teachings of the Catholic Church, a little-known entity in the area. No immediate conversions surfaced, but the experience provided groundwork for future development.

In 1944, Father Francis Massarella began to work in Butler County, and two acres of land bordering Logansport Road were purchased in the name of the Church. A small house on the property provided a room for Mass and religious services, as well as living space for a priest who could remain for any length of time.

Father Richard Boland and Father Francis Wuest took care of the Church in the county from 1946 to 1949, followed by Father Joseph O'Donnell, who was stationed at Sunfish. Father O'Donnell was made pastor in 1950, but when the known Catholics moved away, religious services were discontinued, except for occasional visits from priests in neighboring counties. The construction of a bridge across the Green River in the early 1950s provided a transient congregation of bridge-builders which vanished with the completion of the bridge.

Father Joseph O'Brien came to Morgantown in 1958, at which time there were only a few known Catholics in Butler County. The parish grew remarkably under his leadership, and in 1960 Father Carl Boehler was appointed pastor. Plans were begun for building a church, and Father Patrick O'Donnell was engaged as architect. On September 8, 1963, ground was broken for the church, designed in the shape of a cross, with a unique roof structure, beginning two feet from ground level and rising to a copper steeple crowned with a fourteen foot cross. Over the mosaic doorways and copper-covered doors, large antique-glass windows were set in redwood frames. A double course of hand-chiseled sandstone formed both interior and exterior walls.

Included in the building project was the erection of a rectory joined with a fellowship hall, all built by the Glenmary Brothers Building Crew under the direction of Brother Robert Hoffman, assisted by Brother Peter McQuade and Brother Gregory Woods, and with the help of local parishioners and others.

The first Mass in the new church was celebrated on Christmas Eve of 1964. Bishop Henry Soenneker officiated at the dedication held on June 13, 1965. In October of that year, Father Joseph O'Donnell was named pastor of Butler and Ohio Counties. When diocesan boundaries shifted, Beaver Dam became the parish center, with Morgantown and Fordsville as mission parishes.

Father Louis Yunker served in Butler County from 1969 to 1971, when Father Brian Kennedy began his ministry here. He was followed by Father Michael Caroline, and the next year by Father Thomas Charters. Father Terrence Jackson also assisted in the area, as did several young seminarians, among whom were Chester Artysiewicz, Dennis McAuliffe, and Wayne Swatlowski. Glenmary Brothers who have served here are Brother James Dorn and Brother Marion Placzek.

In 1976, Father Edward Gorny became pastor, followed by Father Robert Valenza. Father John Zeitler from Des Moines, Iowa, offered his services as pastor from April of 1979 to May, 1981. Father Joseph O'Donnell returned as pastor in November of 1981, and remains pastor at present.

Many Sisters from different areas have worked in Butler County over the years. 1971 marked the beginning of the Glenmary Sisters' service here, with Sister Mary Frances Simon and Sister Catherine Schoenborn, followed by Sister Nora Mulchrone and Sister Christine Beckett. Sister Grace Nash, a Franciscan Sister from Iowa, also served here for a year. In the fall of 1979, Sister Ann Kelley, a Sister of Notre Dame from Massachusetts, began working in the parish, and remained until December of 1983. Sister Marcan Freking, a Sister of St. Francis of Rochester, Minnesota, is presently Pastoral Associate in Butler County.

Immaculate Conception Parish
Earlington

Immaculate Conception Church, Earlington

The history of Immaculate Conception Church dates back to 1847, when an Irishman named Simon Fagan settled in Hopkins County. He and his family were the only Catholics in the county. Father E.J. Durbin, the pioneer priest of Western Kentucky, whose mission extended from Vincennes, Indiana to Nashville, Tennessee, celebrated the first Mass in the Fagan home and offered Mass there once a year for the next 25 years.

The settlement which is now Earlington was formerly called "Hall's Post Office." In the late 1860s, when the railroad was being laid, Father Durbin's assistant, Father Dunn, offered Mass for the workers in a farmhouse near the site, where later the L&N depot was built. The town received the name "Earlington" in 1870. By that time coal mining was becoming an important industry in Hopkins County. In 1871 Father Jenkins, then pastor of Holy Name Parish in Henderson, KY offered Mass for the few miners who had just started to work in the first mine of the St. Bernard Coal Company in Earlington.

On Dec. 11, 1872, Immaculate Conception Parish was formally established by Bishop Wm. George McClosky, Bishop of Louisville, KY. Father Alphonsus Marie Coenen was appointed pastor, with approximately 15 Catholics to begin the new congregation. The first church was dedicated in August, 1873. Simon Fagan built the foundation, and the lots were donated by the St. Bernard Coal Company.

The cornerstone for the present church was laid on October 16, 1886. By 1901, 300 Catholics were living in Earlington, 30 in Madisonville, 10 in Barnsley, 15 in Morton's Gap, and 28 scattered throughout Hopkins County.

The Ward-Miller Hall, which stands behind the church and rectory, was completed in the summer of 1985. It is named in honor of Father Frank Ward, pastor from 1968 to 1984; and Father Joseph Miller, pastor from 1984 until 1986. The hall was dedicated on December 8, 1985, by the Most Reverend John J. McRaith, Bishop of the Diocese of Owensboro, KY.

Immaculate Conception School—In September, 1875, four Sisters of Loretto opened a parochial school in the church; the sanctuary was closed off by folding doors. A two-story brick school was built, with Father Coenen as principal. In 1890 four Sisters of Charity of Nazareth took over the school, and added a commercial department. In 1914 the Ursuline Sisters from Mount Saint Joseph Motherhouse took over the school. By

Immaculate Conception Church, Earlington

1921 the brick school was in disrepair, and was torn down. It was replaced by a temporary frame structure. A new brick two-story school was built in 1925 with an auditorium that doubled as a gymnasium.

The Immaculate Conception School was mainly an elementary school, but was expanded to a secondary school from 1955 until 1962. The school continued until 1978, when the school facilities were transferred to the newly built Christ the King School in Madisonville, KY. The Sisters' house and school were both torn down in August, 1978.

Priests who have served Immaculate Conception Church of Earlington are the following: Fathers Alphonsus Marie Coenen (1872-1905); Martin O'Connor (1905-1906); John Patrick McParland (1906-1916); Lucian Edward Clements (1916-1939); George Boehmicke (1939-1943); Clarence Pettit (1943-1949); Wm. Borntraeger (1949-1961); Henry Willett (1961-1968); Frank M. Ward (1968-1984); Joseph C. Miller (1984-1986); Gerald Baker (1987-1989); and Martin Mattingly (1989-present).

The parish has 84 families and 192 parishioners.

Immaculate Conception Parish
Hawesville

Immaculate Conception, Hawesville, 1958.

This history of the Catholic Church in Hawesville dates back to the earliest days of the county. The immigrants came by boat and ox-drawn wagons to the little village of Hawesville. In those early days a priest stationed many miles away traveled great distances to visit the community several times a year. For services, the Catholic families would gather at the homes of members before the church was built.

In 1854, at the request of Bishop Spalding of Louisville, Father Bede O'Connor who resided at Cannelton, Indiana, began preparations for the construction of a church at Hawesville. On August 17, 1858, Bishop Spalding purchased a lot from Mr. & Mrs. Stephen Powers and Mr. & Mrs. James E. Stone for $400.00. On this lot was constructed the first church. The building was constructed of hand-hewn stone, a product of this area, by Mr. Bill Snowden. It was completed in 1871.

During most of these earlier years there was no resident pastor at Hawesville. For many years the pastor resided at Cloverport and, due to the large congregation there which required two Masses on Sunday, it was necessary for services to be held at Hawesville on Saturday.

When Fr. Rives became pastor, he was stationed at Reed, Kentucky and commuted by the L&N Railroad, coming to Hawesville on Saturday afternoon, offering Mass at 6:00 AM on Sunday, and returning to Reed on the 7:00 AM train, which enabled him to have Mass there later in the morning.

In 1937 flood did extensive damage to the altar and interior of the church, which necessitated much repair work. During Father Gerst's pastorate, the church was redecorated throughout.

In 1947 Bishop Francis Cotton of the Owensboro Diocese purchased a house and some land from John and Catherine Robbins. The house was repaired and used for a rectory. He appointed Father Anthony Higdon, pastor of Browns Valley, to come to Hawesville to oversee the building of a Catholic elementary school. Through the generosity of the parishioners, the money was obtained and the first Catholic school in Hancock County was dedicated on November 1, 1947, staffed by the Sisters of Loretto whose residence was built over the school. Hawesville received its first assistant priest at this time.

In 1949, under the pastorate of Fr. Anthony Thompkins, a high school was constructed which also included a cafeteria. The parish grew until it became necessary to make plans for the con-

Original Immaculate Conception Church, Hawesville.

struction of a larger church.

A house and lot were purchased on the east end of Main Street from Mrs. Ella Givens Heavrin in November, 1957. The cornerstone for the new church was laid in September, 1958 and the church was dedicated on February 19, 1959. The stained glass windows from the original church were put into the church.

The Immaculate Parish
Owensboro

"The good of religion and the care of souls will be much affected by the erection of a new parish."

With this decree, Bishop Francis R. Cotton created the Church of The Immaculate on April 19, 1954. The new parish was part of the diocesan observance of the Marian Year, and in celebration of the 100th anniversary of the dogma of the Immaculate Conception. Fr. Charles Carrico of St. Jerome Fancy Farm was named its first pastor. The Ursuline Sisters staffed its new school.

The 10 acre grounds were cut from a cornfield. All around were new houses in subdivisions pushing Owensboro south and west. The parish had 200 families when the large building housing church, school, rectory and sisters' residence was opened. The first Mass was celebrated on Aug. 22, 1954, the feast of the Immaculate Heart of Mary.

History was made by these parishioners that first year: Robert Eugene Mehlbauer and Robert Anthony Steele were the first infants baptized on Aug. 22, 1954. George Negley Barnett and Martine Durbin were the first couple married on Oct. 9, 1954. John Edward Gatton was the first parishioner to be buried on Jan. 31, 1955.

The four-room school opened in August, 1954. Sr. Callista OSU was the first principal and taught grades 6, 7, and 8. There were 166 pupils the first year. More rooms were added the next year.

The St. Vincent dePaul Society was organized May 2, 1955. Paul Mischel was the first president. The Altar Society was formed May 17, 1955. Mrs. Horace Temple was the first president. Mrs. James I. Payne was vice-president.

Fr. Carrico became ill in the summer of 1956. Fr. Clarence Pettit became interim pastor. On Sept. 15, of that year Fr. Leo J. Dienes was appointed pastor. He built Immaculate to the needs of its people. During his 19 years as pastor the parish grew to 600 families. A new wing was added to the school, a new rectory was built, and the former church became the school gymnasium. The Christian Family Movement (CFM) was begun; Cana Conferences were held; a Youth Club was started; Boy Scouts, Cub Scouts, Girl Scouts and Brownie Troops were organized.

Fr. Dienes appointed the first Lay Eucharistic Ministers in 1973. They were Joseph Wedding, David Gasser, Al Clark, James Jackson, Joseph Lauzon and his son Peter, a seminarian. They distributed Communion on Sunday and at holyday Masses.

The school doubled its enrollment in 5 years. Mrs. Marita Englert was the first lay teacher in 1958. (In 22 years there would be no nuns at the school and Immaculate would hire its first lay principal.)

Msgr. Bernard Powers became the third pastor of Immaculate in 1976. Fr. Maury Riney became assistant pastor in 1978.

Fr. William Allard served as pastor from 1984 to 1987. Immaculate parish had grown to 865 families. Fr. John Meredith was associate pastor followed by Fr. Vincent Boyle. The first parish council was organized in 1985 with Mrs. Sue Hill as president. Two Ursuline nuns joined the staff. Sr. Marie Goretti Browning was named parish coordinator; Sr. Julia Marie Head was director of religious education.

From 1987 to 1989 Fr. Frank Roof was pastor of Immaculate. Fr. Peter Lauzon was associate pastor. He was followed by Fr. Richard Cash. Linda Shipp was hired as youth director. The positions of parish coordinator and director of religious education were combined and Sr. Angela Wethington SCN became pastoral associate.

When Fr. Roof joined the Air Force as chaplain, Fr. Richard Powers, then serving as a Navy chaplain, became pastor of Immaculate, assuming his duties in January, 1990. Fr. Stephen Montgomery, a Franciscan, was associate pastor. Fr. Thomas Joyce became associate pastor in March, 1991. The parish bought a residence for the priests in 1991, located across the street from the church. The former rectory became the administrative offices.

Sr. Clarita Browning, OSU, became pastoral associate in June, 1990. Dennis Morris served as youth minister during 1991-1992.

Immaculate merged with other parochial schools in the fall of 1989 and the Owensboro Catholic Consolidated School System was formed. The former Immaculate School became the Owensboro Catholic Middle School.

Three vocations came from Immaculate parish. Fr. Peter E. Lauzon son of Mr. and Mrs. Joseph L. Lauzon was ordained in 1979. Fr. Ray Goetz, ordained in 1981 is the son of Mr. and Mrs. Bernard Goetz. Fr. Tony Jones, son of Mrs. Wanda Jones, was ordained in 1989.

The Immaculate Church, Owensboro.

Our Lady of Lourdes Parish
Owensboro

Our Lady of Lourdes Catholic Church.

It was the day before Labor Day, Sept. 6, 1959. The headlines in Owensboro's *Messenger and Inquirer* reported that French President Charles DeGaulle would visit the United States and the U.S. Senate voted to raise the federal gas tax from 3 to 4 cents.

There were few candidates for Owensboro City Commissioner, Penney's advertised wool skirts for $4.98 and Dragnet was on television at 6:30 p.m.

But the big news to 218 Owensboro families that day was happening on the south end of Frederica Street. It was the day Our Lady of Lourdes Catholic Church celebrated its first Mass and began a tradition of close-knit worship.

"The parishioners were very close," said Ettie Murphy, who along with her husband Joe Bob are original members. "We had a bond in physically building a church. We all started on kind of an even plane."

Lourdes drew its parishioners from Blessed Mother and Immaculate parishes. Organizations were formed by the future members and they held meetings anywhere they could find.

The first building included the church and four classrooms. The rectory was built next, and in following years the school got a new wing and a convent for the Sisters of Charity. A social hall was built behind the school in 1964 and was used for classrooms for several years.

Lourdes' first pastor was Father Victor Boarman, who stayed in that role for 23 years molding the parish. "He was the one who got it off to a good start," said Bob Strehl, a 74-year-old original member. "The church shaped us individually because of Father Boarman."

The next major step for Lourdes was in 1966, when the current church was built and the old one was converted to classrooms. Mrs. Murphy, who converted to Catholicism shortly after Lourdes opened, said the school was always the catalyst for the church.

"Everyone was real happy with the new church," she said. She remembered making choir robes for the girl's choir that sang at the new church's opening. "They were white with red bows, and the girls had red bows in their hair."

Father Anthony Ziegler was appointed the second pastor in 1982 and served three years until the current pastor, Father Delma Clemons, was appointed in 1985. Father Clemons has helped tutor several new priests at Lourdes namely Father Terry Devine, Father Larry Hostetter, Father Henry Wieder and, currently, Father Ray Clark.

In 1990, the Catholic Pastoral Center moved its offices to the former St. Stephen School. Our Lady of Lourdes Building Committee worked for several months negotiating with Bishop McRaith for the purchase and renovation of the building that currently houses the parish offices, day care and parish hall.

Lourdes Parish has now grown to 745 families. The Parish Council, Altar Society, St. Vincent dePaul Society, Men's Club, Administration Committee, Liturgy Committee, Lay Ministry and many others are very active organizations working within Our Lady of Lourdes Parish.

The success of Lourdes is the result of a family atmosphere, members said. "It feels like home," Mrs. Murphy said. "I think a lot of people feel that way. As far as my husband's concerned, Sunday's not Sunday if he doesn't go to Lourdes."

Strehl, one of about 30 or 40 people who attend Mass every day at Lourdes, enjoys the friends he's made at the church. "Ten or 15 of us go to breakfast after church each day, and we'll get 25 on Sunday," he said. "It's a regular fellowship."

Precious Blood Parish
Owensboro

Precious Blood Parish.

Precious Blood Parish is located on the west side of Owensboro facing north on Fenmore Street between Dalton and Greenbriar Streets. It encompasses many city blocks of northwest Owensboro and some bordering rural communities. Bishop Francis R. Cotton dedicated the new church on September 5, 1960 and Father George Boehmicke was installed as the first pastor.

School opened on September 6, 1960 with an enrollment of 244 students and Sr. Callista Langan, OSU was the first principal.

Mrs. Edward Garvin was the first organist. The first infant baptized was Thomas W. Mills, and Elizabeth Mae Devins was the first adult to be received as a new Catholic into Precious Blood Church. The first funeral Mass was celebrated for Miss Marie Delphine Osborne, and the first couple to exchange Marriage Vows was John Raymond Thomas and Sara Beverly Grant.

On March 27, 1963, Father Clarence Pettit became the second pastor of Precious Blood Church. During this time Bishop Henry J. Soenneker extended the parish to its present boundaries.

On August 2, 1966, Father Maurice J. Tiell became the third pastor of Precious Blood. Although it was during this period of nine years that the Second Vatican Council began visible and significant changes in the way we worshipped, parishioners of the time remember this as our pre-vatican II period.

In July of 1975, Father Richard Powers began serving as pastor of Precious Blood Parish and parishioners experienced lots of changes. Community building was the trademark of this spiritual leader. "Parish Renewal," Sunday Liturgy celebration of Baptisms, outdoor Masses and large group social gatherings were characteristic of this period in our parish history.

Father Robert Drury was appointed as administrator on March 17, 1982. Father Joe Mills was appointed as pastor in August of 1982. Father Robert Willett came to Precious Blood in February of 1983 and served as pastor for 6 years. During this time, Sr. Barbara Peterson was hired as the first of several women religious to serve in the role of Pastoral Associate. It was also during this time that the cost of Catholic schools became an overwhelming factor in parish operations. With the support of many lay parish leaders, Father Willett introduced a system of accountability to parishioners. This highly-akin forerunner to the Diocesan Stewardship program required parishioners to respond in very tangible ways of time, talent, and treasure to God's call to us as his people. The renovation of our church building will long stand as evidence of parishioners' response to that call. The Renew program served as the major spiritual growth impact upon the people of Precious Blood.

Father Robert Drury came to Precious Blood in June of 1989. The Catholic schools underwent reformation into the Consolidated School System. The Precious Blood School became Bishop Henry J. Soenneker Elementary School.

Father Darrell Venters became the ninth pastor of Precious Blood in June of 1992. Though only a little time has passed at this writing, parish leaders look forward and hopefully expect a period of renewed spirituality and growth.

Thirty-two years have brought many changes to this small Owensboro parish, but through the wisdom and efforts of its spiritual leadership, the mission given to us by God is always in view and only a dawning away from fulfillment.

RESSURECTION PARISH
DAWSON SPRINGS

The first permanent Catholic known to have settled in Dawson Springs was Mrs. Lee Dempf Holeman. She came as a young bride in February, 1896, when the small town had a population of less than 1,000.

The nearest Catholic church to Dawson Springs was in Earlington, Kentucky. At that time there were no highways connecting the two towns, so the only practical means of covering the 14 miles was by railroad. Train schedules seldom coincided with the time of Mass. In 1916 the Holemans bought a touring car. In good weather, the journey could be made in 45 minutes to 1-1/2 hours. In the winter time the trip was not possible, and even in the summer months a rain could make the trip impossible.

Sometimes priests on vacation in the health resort near the town offered Mass. In 1922 the U.S. Veterans Hospital, called "Outwood," was dedicated, three miles from Dawson Springs. A priest named Father John O'Hara came, as Irish as his name, and very much looked the part. The Catholics in Dawson Springs were then able to attend Mass at Outwood, offered by the priests who ministered to the patients and staff. A priest who came later, Father John W. Vance from Sts. Peter and Paul Parish in Hopkinsville, gave spiritual care at Outwood from 1932 to 1936.

After the diocese of Owensboro was established, the following diocesan priests have served the Catholics in Dawson Springs: Fathers George Boehmicke (1939-1943), Clarence Pettit (1943-1948), Richard Clements (1948-1955), Carl Glahn (1955-1960), Jerome Glahn (1961-1963), Thomas Clark (1963-1971), Delma Clemons (1971-1981), Francis Roof (1981-1987), Gerald Baker (1987-1989), and Martin Mattingly (1989-present).

The construction of Resurrection Church— Late in the summer of 1968, while Father Thomas Clark was pastor at St. Paul Parish in Princeton, and served as pastor to the Dawson Springs Catholics, Bishop Henry J. Soenneker selected a site for building a Catholic Church. The property measured 300 feet by 265 feet in depth.

Bishop Soenneker said the building would start as soon as possible. The total cost of lots and church was about $43,000.00. The Diocese lent the parish enough, at 2-1/2% interest, to cover the cost of the building. The Extension Society contributed $10,000.00; and the Diocese matched, dollar for dollar, most of the payments.

At the time the church was being built, the number of Catholics who attended Mass at Outwood were about six adults, namely: Virginia L. Holeman, D. Fletcher Holeman, John P. Rhody, Noel V. Wise, George Iott, and Millie Iott. Linda Randolph sometimes came to Outwood, but at other times she and her two children went to Princeton. Oswald and Bonnie Pike and their children attended Mass in Earlington. Soon after Resurrection Church was built, Dr. James Freeman and Elizabeth Freeman became members of the congregation.

In 1982 the interior of the building was redecorated, rearranged, and some stained glass was added for a total cost of $27,000.00. All of the above costs have been paid, and at the present time the parish has saved more than $27,000.00 for a community center.

The church currently has 42 families, with 103 parishioners.

Resurrection Church

Rosary Chapel
Paducah

Rosary Chapel, Paducah.

Rosary Chapel was established in 1947 by Rev. Albert Thompson, pastor of St. Francis de Sales Church—the only Catholic Church in Paducah at that time. Because of the custom of segregation prevailing, Fr. Thompson felt that Black Catholics had no sense of identity at St. Francis and needed a church of their own. The members of Rosary Chapel cooperated in building Rosary by contributing time and labor to help renovate the first buildings. Initially, the property consisted of three small houses, one of which was converted to a small chapel, and the other two houses were used for classrooms for Rosary Chapel School. Mass was first offered in the spring of 1947 and school opened in September of that year. Fr. Richard Wersing, C.S.S.P. was the first pastor. Two Ursuline sisters from Maple Mount, KY took charge of the school. Many members living today remember walking miles carrying bricks, cement, mortar, and other materials to reconstruct the existing buildings.

The community at large helped Rosary Chapel and School grow spiritually and materially. The number of children attending Rosary Chapel School grew from 23 students to 150. This necessitated building a larger school. A three story brick building with classrooms for twelve grades was constructed in 1952 under the supervision of Fr. Joseph Rhodes.

The amazing growth of the congregation, mostly through converts— some 87 in the first ten years of the church, led to the construction of a church. The modern, A-frame structure was built under the direction of Fr. Phillip Riney. The church was dedicated by Bishop Francis R. Cotton in 1958 as Rosary Chapel. The construction of the new church and the support of the pastor led the community to continue to invite and receive new members. The church grew fast during the 1960s. After the close of the school in 1967 due to declining enrollment, Rosary went through several pastor changes in a short time, but the faith of the people continued the growth of the church.

In the summer of 1976, Fr. Harold Diller, C.P.P.S. came to Rosary Chapel. He found a community that was strong and self directed. Recognizing the gift of the people, Fr. Diller started the first Pastoral Council in 1976. This council began the work of setting a direction for the community. In the late 70s, again at the encouragement of Fr. Diller, members of Rosary began to become involved in the National Black Catholic Congress. Under the direction of Rose Lowery, the Rosary Chapel Choir was formed. This choir helped to introduce black hymns into the worship at Rosary as well as throughout the diocese. Later, again Liturgical reform at Rosary would also help the larger church to experience Liturgical Dance. Meanwhile, under the care of such watchful stewards as Curtis Hixon, Buford Wilson, Leo Hunter, Shirley Bunch, Charles Davis, Edna Davis, William and Sarah Payne, the church continued to grow.

During the early 1980s, several women religious, and priest ministered with the people of Rosary to continue the mission that had become very much a part of the life of Rosary—to minister with and evangelize in the African American community. Always seeking better ways to carry out its mission, in June of 1988, Rosary Chapel hired Marianna Schadler (Romero) as its first full time lay minister.

Rosary is a multicultural Parish, with a particular mission to the African Americans. The Parish is currently in the process of developing a five year plan. Today, as in the past, it is the faith, the work, and the commitment of the people that keeps the mission of Christ and Rosary Chapel alive. Strong lay leadership, dedicated folks who give generously of their time, and folks who have endured the struggle, lead Rosary into the next chapter of our history.

Sacred Heart Parish
Hickman, KY

The people of Hickman first began receiving Catholic religious services in 1850, when priests of the Carmelite Order, stationed in Paducah, included Hickman in their western Kentucky missions of Columbus, Mayfield, Fancy Farm and Fulton. Services were held in the Sherron House on West Main Street (later the corner of Buchanan-Moulton Streets).

Catholics in Hickman took their first step toward a real church in 1853, when Bishop Martin J. Spalding of the Louisville Diocese bought a lot from C. F. Young on Magnolia Street for $30.50 in cash and a note for $90.50. The bishop planned to build a church there, but for reasons unrecorded, the plans were never carried out.

Five years later, in June, 1858, the bishop paid $200.00 for two lots on Brooklyn Street in West Hickman owned by J. C. Catlett. Members of the church at that time carried the names of Dillon, Sherron, Hartwick, Barry, McDermott, Glaser, Steele, Effinger, Knoerr, Cusick and Cravens. The predominantly Irish congregation, led by Father Patrick Bambury, decided that the church would be called St. Bridget.

In the latter part of the 19th century, Hickman's Irish Catholics became outnumbered by an influx of Germans with names of Lattus, Mangold, Stahr, Hellner, Werner and Witting. St. Bridget became too small and a new church was needed. In July 1890, John and Catherine Witting sold two lots on Moulton Street to Bishop William George McCloskey for $200.00. The name "St. Bridget" was abandoned and Sacred Heart was chosen as the new church name.

Dedication ceremonies took place on Oct. 5, 1890. Bishop McCloskey and Father William Dunn came from Louisville to conduct services with the pastor, Father Thomas York. Both Catholics and protestants alike attended, for Protestants had helped to raise the $2300.00 cost of the church.

Building a school was the next goal of Sacred Heart parishioners. Until one was built, catechism was taught in the Sherron House. Miss Annie Sherron, who lived to be nearly 100 years old, taught generations of Hickman children in Hickman Public School and conducted the catechism lessons in her home.

Father Fred J. Gettelfinger was pastor when the school opened in 1928. Four Sisters of Mercy from Louisville staffed the school, a single building which the church members had built by remodeling and combining two houses behind the church. Ruth Johnson was the first pupil to graduate from the eighth grade.

In 1949, a new school building was opened and a high school added to the grade school. The brick building was built with funds left by the Augustus McCary Family, Mrs. Catherine Costello Bradley and parishioners and citizens from Hickman.

Sacred Heart School served both Catholic and non-Catholic children in Hickman, but in the last decade, it became victim to those causes which have closed many schools. The high school was closed in 1961 and the grade school in 1968. Religious Education continued with members of the parish alternating as instructors. Summer classes were conducted by Sisters of Mercy from St. John in Paducah.

In 1977, the church building was torn down and a new church and rectory were completed under the supervision of Father Emmett Zachman. The new church was built on the original site and formally dedicated on June 17, 1977, with the Most Reverend Henry J. Soenneker, D. D., Bishop of Owensboro, presiding. Father Zachman, a members of the Crosier Order, was responsible for the red Italian Marble altar in the new church. The altar was a gift from the Crosier Monastery in Anamia, Minnesota. The stained glass windows, Stations of the Cross, statues, pedestals and some furniture from the old church were restored and incorporated into the new Sacred Heart Catholic Church.

October 7, 1990, Sacred Heart Parish celebrated its 100th anniversary as a faith community in Hickman with Liturgy of the Eucharist, dedication of the original Sacred Heart Parish Bell and a reception. Together, the Most Rev. John J. McRaith, Bishop of Owensboro; Rev. Martin E. Hayes, Pastor; Sacred Heart Catholic Church parishoners and friends gave thanks to God for a century of faith and prayed for blessings on the future.

From this parish have come the following religious:

Sister Michaella Dillon, SCN
Born: August 1, 1843
Vows: January 6, 1864
Died: May 4, 1888

Sister Imelda Sherron, SCN
Born: January 10, 1855
Vows: March 25, 1878
Died: August 7, 1933

Sister Marie Frances Burgess, RSM
Born: October 1, 1926
Vows: August 16, 1949
Died: 1978

Father Patrick Bradley
Born: December 6, 1905
Ordained: September 22, 1945
Died: July 22, 1974

Father Vincent Kaufman
Born: February 23, 1936
Ordained: May 28, 1960
Died: September 25, 1979

Sister Elizabeth Ann Lattus, SCN
Born: July 10, 1928
Vows: December 8, 1948
Died: December 26, 1988

List of former pastors

1859	Rev. Patrick Bambury
1860-1863	Rev. John Martin Beyhurst
1861	Rev. J. Jarboe
1864	Rev. Michael Power
1864-1869	Rev. William Bourke
1868	Rev. Edmund O'Driscoll
1869-1871	Rev. John Aloysius Barrett
1871-1881	Carmelite Fathers: Rev. Peter Meagher, Rev. Brocard Murphy (died yellow fever, age 27), Rev. Anselm Duhl, Rev. John Feehan, Rev. P.J. Haeseley, Rev. Gregory Forrestal, Rev. Anastasurs Kreidt, Rev. Joseph Walsh, Rev. Theodore McDonald
1881-1887	Rev. Richard Davis
1884-1887	Rev. Daniel J. McShane
1886	Rev. Kyran W. King (January - July)
1886-1887	Rev. H. Jansen
1887-1888	Rev. Lawrence B. Ford
1888-1891	Rev. Thomas Amos York
1891-1893	Rev. George A. Weiss
1893-1897	Rev. Kyran W. King
1898-1900	Rev. S.E. Clements
1900-1907	Rev. Joseph A. Minch
1907-1908 and	Rev. Anthony O'Sullivan
	Rev. William P. Hogarty
1908-1911	Rev. Paul M. Guerin
1911-1913	Rev. Secundo Joseph Mensa
1913-1925	Rev. Anthony O'Sullivan
1926-1927	Rev. E.F. Callahan
1927-1933	Rev. Fred J. Gettelfinger
1933-1937	Rev. Joseph L. Spalding
1937-1943	Rev. C.R. Carrico
1943-1950	Rev. Thomas Libbs
1950-1956	Rev. Clarence Pettit
1956-1960	Fathers of Mercy: Rev. William P. Carroll and Rev. Edward L. Tarrant
1960-1965	Rev. Carl J. Glahn
1965-1966	Rev. Leonard Alvey
1966-1967	Rev. Gerald Glahn
1967-1969	Rev. William Field
1969-1973	Rev. William Hagman
1974-1975	Rev. Leonard Reisz
1975-1980	Rev. Emmitt Zachman, OSC
1980-1985	Rev. Carl J. Glahn
1985-1988	Rev. John Meredith
1988	Rev. Thomas O'Connor
1988	Rev. Martin E. Hayes

Assistants

Date	Name
Aug. 20, 1950	Rev. Martin Mattingly
June 12, 1952	Rev. Leonard Reisz
Oct. 7, 1954	Rev. Thomas Murphy

Pastoral Associates

1985-1989	Sister Ann Legeay, SCN
1989-1990	Sister Janice Rospert, OSF
1991-	Sister Rose Marita O'Bryan OSU

Sacred Heart Parish
Russellville

Around 1830 Father Elisha Durbin was assigned to care for the Catholics in the area now comprising the Diocese of Owensboro.

The Parish of Sacred Heart, Russellville, Kentucky, includes the whole area of Logan County, Kentucky.

Many Irish families came to this area with the railroad construction in the late 1850s, including the Lennons, Waldrons, O'Briens, O'Connells, Burkes, Johnsons, McTiques, Phillips, Ryans and Shehees. Father Patrick Bambury was sent to Bowling Green and stayed until 1859 when Father Joseph DeVries was put in charge of the southern Kentucky missions.

As the Catholic population grew, Father DeVries oversaw building of a church in Franklin in 1867. Father James Ryan was appointed as resident pastor there and also served the mission at Russellville.

Father Henry Mertins was assigned to Franklin and Russellville in 1869. In 1872 a church was built for the growing Russellville flock at the corner of Fifth and Winter Streets and was dedicated under the title of Sacred Heart of Jesus on April 27, 1873.

In late 1873 Father William Bourke succeeded Father Mertins at Franklin and Russellville. About this time a shift in the Catholic population occurred probably due to the opening of the L & N shops in Russellville and junction points both there and in Guthrie.

The Catholic directory for 1882 lists sixteen stations besides Russellville as being attended from Franklin, including Adairville, Auburn, Cave Spring, McLeod, and Red River; the last five being in Logan County.

Father William Dunn Pike became the first resident pastor of Russellville in 1894. He also served the missions at Franklin and Hopkinsville as well as the stations at Auburn, Guthrie, Howell, Kelly, and Rockfield. Father Pike was succeeded in 1897 by Father Benedict Joseph Wight and was pastor until August 1899.

When Father Jules Dreville assumed charge of Sacred Heart Parish November 1, 1907, he embarked upon the longest pastorate in the history of the parish, a period of 20 years. He attended to the missions and stations which by 1911 were reduced to Franklin and Glasgow. (Father Dreville was a native of France.) Father Dreville was more than a spiritual servant. He advised his parish on real estate and legal matters. During World War I, he traveled Logan County giving speeches; earning the name of the "Three Minute Man".

Father John Lyons succeeded Father Dreville as pastor of Sacred Heart in 1927 and remained until August 1932 when Father Leo Dreckmann took charge of Russellville and its missions. He was succeeded in February 1935 by Father Joseph Egan. Father Egan's term as pastor abruptly ended when he was seriously injured in an automobile accident in April 1937. Sacred Heart Church in Russellville was Father Egan's first parish, and as this is being written, Father Egan died at age 89 on June 26, 1992, Feast of the Sacred Heart and buried at Sacred Heart Monastery in Louisville, Kentucky.

Sacred Heart, Russellville, KY. First church, 1873.

Sacred Heart Church, 1992.

Russellville and its missions were then put under the care of Father Bernard Spoelker. It was during his short period that the church in Franklin burned to the ground on January 1, 1938; the old school building was then used for church services.

On December 9, 1937, the Diocese of Owensboro was created which embraced the western 32 counties of Kentucky.

The first pastor of Russellville under Bishop Francis Cotton was Father John Hallahan who was appointed on May 1, 1938.

In 1942, Bishop Cotton turned to the Home Missioners of America (also known as Glenmary Missioners) for help in supplying priests for the various parishes of the Diocese. Father Benedict Wolf became the first Glenmary Missioner to serve as pastor at Russellville.

Father Wolf arranged for the Glenmary Sisters to open a parochial school at Sacred Heart. Sacred Heart School opened with one pupil, but the numbers grew to 92 in a short time. His assistant, Father Robert Healy, helped take care of the missions at Guthrie and Franklin. Father Healy succeeded Father Wolf as pastor of Russellville in 1950. Perhaps the most beloved

Glenmary nun was Sister Mary Francis Simon.

Father Healy, with his assistant, Father Patrick O'Donnell, oversaw the rebuilding of the church at Franklin in 1953.

Father Venantius Preske came to Russellville to be Father Healy's assistant in January, 1954 and became pastor in June 1955. He organized the St. Vincent De Paul Society in 1956; and had both a Senior and Junior Praesidium of the Legion of Mary working successfully.

Father Preske inaugurated the building program for a new church and school in Russellville but was transferred in June 1961 before the main work was begun.

New pastor, Father Eugene Ryan, oversaw the building of the new church and school at Sixth and Winter Streets, and the purchase of the rectory at 296 West Sixth Street. The buildings were dedicated on September 1, 1963.

On July 29, 1965, Father Ryan was succeeded by Father Paul Pike Powell. At the same time, the teaching Glenmary Sisters were succeeded by the Ursuline Sisters of Mount St. Joseph. Father Powell carried stones from Joe Rohrer's farm and built the Blessed Mother Grotto himself. On March 17, 1971, Father Powell was transferred to St. Pius Tenth in Owensboro, Kentucky.

Father William McAtee became pastor on March 17, 1971. During his pastorate the Ursuline Sisters were recalled and the school was left without teaching sisters. A school board, CCD board, and Parent-Teacher Society were all formed. Father McAtee also took the parish through the Centenary Celebration; a truly inspirational event.

Father Louis Telegdy was sent to Sacred Heart Church in 1973, where he was active with the Boy Scouts of America. Father is living in retirement in Cathogeno, Ohio.

After the transfer of Father Telegdy, the Bishop of Owensboro, the Most Reverend Bishop Henry J. Soenneker, D.D., entrusted the care of Sacred Heart Parish, church and school, to the Benedictine Fathers of St. Mark's Priory, South Union, Kentucky, in Logan County.

Prior Joseph Alexander, O.S.B., sent Father Thomas O'Connor, O.S.B., to care for Sacred Heart Parish; an associate came from St. Mark's in 1976 to help. The associate was Father Alexander Korte, O.S.B., founder of St. Maur's which became St. Mark's.

Father O'Connor's accomplishments were many including organizing the Knights of Columbus under the patronage of the Sacred Heart of Jesus. The K.C.'s are a strong, active council now, giving monies earned from Bingo and Tootsie Roll Drives to St. Vincent de Paul Society and Jesus Community Center, and the Logan County Association of Retarded Citizens. Father O'Connor helped sponsor many refugee Laotians coming here from Owensboro Refugee Services. He also tried to keep alive a floundering school and continued the Legion of Mary.

Father O'Connor relates that teaching moral theology at St. Maur's - St. Mark's, and being pastor of Sacred Heart Church, were his most interesting experiences.

After seven years, Father O'Connor was succeeded by another Benedictine, Father Francis dos Remedios, O.S.B., who called himself an interim pastor until the Bishop procured a diocesan priest for Sacred Heart. In Father Francis's brief year, he endeared himself to the little children by teaching them religion. Father was so unassuming no one knew that he had several higher degrees including an L.L.B., and Master of Divinity (Theology). He was ordained in 1982. Father was sought by many in this area as a kind confessor and spiritual director until he left St. Mark's in 1988 for Assumption Abbey, North Dakota.

In 1984, Father Robert Drury came to Sacred Heart. He saw the closing of Sacred Heart School in 1986 (a sad time for many). Father Drury guided the Parish through the Renewal process, and our Parish debt was retired. Because of his rapport with people of all persuasions, he was chosen Chairman of Russellville Ministerial Association and was a frequent, interesting guest on Don Neagle's Feed Back Program on WRUS.

June, 1989, saw the arrival of Father Walter Hancock. No one had ever seen the likes of Father Hancock with his ready smile, flying paint brush, and his familiar red sweater. The Cougar and Panther Football Teams presented Father with their official sweaters for his outstanding support and cheer. Father kept the lawn mower humming and the grounds immaculate. He remodeled the Parish Center, had stained glass windows installed, along with Carillon bells, and new Church doors. All of this made the Church more meaningful and attractive. Father Hancock was in charge of making the 131st Year Pictorial History of Sacred Heart. June 16, 1992, Father Hancock was assigned to St. Rose Church at Cloverport. He jokingly called this transfer "going North up the river".

On June 16, 1992, Father Lucian Hayden came to Sacred Heart with his many years of priestly experience, bringing with him a remarkable nun as his Associate Pastoral Assistant. She was Sister Mary Aloysius Conlon of the International Order of the Daughters of Jesus (France). Sister had been with Father Hayden for eleven years in four parishes. Sister remained at Sacred Heart only seven weeks visiting homes, counseling, beginning and teaching RCIA, taking the good news of Jesus to residents in the nursing homes and the jail, dispensing words of encouragement, comfort, hope and love. Sister led a life of self sacrifice. She had vast experience in hospital and nursing, and teaching in Honduras and West Indies, Canada and the United States. In Honduras, Sister administered several parishes where priests came only once a month. Wherever she was, she served God and His people generously without wanting favor for herself. Sister was called to her Provincial House near London for a rest and to visit her native Ireland.

Every parish needs a Sister like Sister Mary Aloysius Conlon. God be with her!

With Father Lucian Hayden, our expectations for spiritual growth in Sacred Heart Church are high. He is truly a "man of prayer". He is also a man of action, already setting the Council on a spiritual and pastoral path of action. He has the view of evangelization to bring back our members who have left us for some reason, while at the same time reaching out to others. Father Hayden is teaching the RCIA Class that Sister Aloysius began; and his teaching is being well received. All are called to be saints; on our pilgrimage to holiness we would do well to observe Father Hayden's prayer life and seek his guidance. Father serves the Fathers of Mercy as a confessor and pastoral guide.

For forty years (1948-1988), the Benedictines were at Saint Maur's (St. Mark's). They had touched so many lives, only God knows how many. It was sad to see them leave in 1988. Yet, this was God's Providence for them. The Fathers of Mercy, who bought the Benedictine property, made it their national headquarters, renaming it St. Joseph's Novitiate. In a short time, we have found ourselves blessed with the coming of the Mercy Fathers. At this writing, their numbers are growing dramatically with outstanding young men joining their congregation. We can trust that they will have a great and wide spiritual influence, especially because of their devotion to the Holy Eucharist and Our Blessed Mother in their prayer life.

There has been a Catholic presence in Logan County for 133 years. We dedicate this history of Sacred Heart Parish to those faith-filled early Catholic families who in 1872 built our first church with their own hands, working at night. We thank those early members for naming their church (and ours) for the Sacred Heart.

The early period of Sacred Heart Parish history relied heavily on the notes of Brother Thomas Whitaker, O.S.B., of St. Mark's Priory, South Union, Kentucky and the research of Ron Switzer.

Thanks to Father Lucian Hayden for his quiet encouragement, and to our typist, Mary Pat Helton, for her hard work. Our thanks to Linda Patterson for her review and helpful advice.

We are grateful to Father Egan, Father Lyons, Father Preske, Father O'Connor, and other former pastors, as well as parishioners, who shared their happy memories. *Compiled by Clara (Mrs. Ed) O'Brien and Laura (Mrs. Kevin) Lennon.*

SACRED HEART PARISH
WAVERLY

Sacred Heart Parish of Union County, Kentucky, is the oldest Catholic Parish west of Breckinridge County. Bishop Benedict Joseph Flaget of the Diocese of Bardstown, Kentucky, the first diocese west of the Allegheny Mountains, and Father Charles Nerinckx visited the area of Union County in 1811. There is some evidence that perhaps Fr. Stephen Badin also visited the few Catholic families in the territory during those early years of the nineteenth century. Father Badin along with Fr. Nerinckx and Bishop Flaget were the missionaries, who established the Church in Kentucky. At any rate, Fr. Nerinckx built a small log chapel on what was to become the site of St. Vincent Academy. This first chapel was built in 1812. Since there were only five or six priests for the whole territory west of the Alleghenies, the Catholics of this area were able to have the services of a priest only at very irregular intervals.

In 1818 Fr. Robert Abell, who was stationed at Elizabethtown and Axtel was given charge of the Mission of Sacred Heart, Union County, KY. The first sermon was preached at the courthouse in Morganfield. About 360 acres of land was acquired in northeast Union County in 1819 and with the recording of the deeds the church was permanently established.

In 1820 the Sisters of Charity of Nazareth arrived in Union County to establish a school beside the Sacred Heart log chapel. In 1821 the Rev. Charles Coomes became the first permanent pastor. His tenure was to last only three years. The successor to Fr. Coomes was to become a legend in the annals of the history of the Church in Kentucky: The Reverend Elisha Durbin - the Patriarch of Western Kentucky. He was to be on the scene for forty-nine years: 1824-1873.

Fr. Elisha Durbin ministered to catholics in an area from Breckinridge County to the east to the Mississippi River in the west; from Vincennes, Indiana to the north to an occasional visit to Nashville, Tennessee in the south. He made all of his travels by horseback, traveling 7000 miles a year.

Fr. Durbin replaced the little log chapel built by Fr. Nerinckx in 1812 with a larger one in 1828. The October 4, 1828 edition of the U.S. Catholic Miscellany notes that the new building was solemnly blessed by Bishop Flaget on September 14, 1828.

As St. Vincent Academy for girls became firmly established a large portion of the original land purchase was turned over to the Sisters of Charity in order that the academy might be more self sustaining. A few acres, however, were set aside for a cemetery for the burial of the Catholic people of the area. In fact the catholic dead were brought here from as far away as Henderson, Kentucky, Mt. Vernon, Indiana, and Shawneetown, Illinois for burial. It is interesting to roam around the cemetery and read the dates and inscriptions on the tombstones.

Fr. Durbin constructed the two story brick portion of the parish house in 1836. Aware that

Sacred Heart Parish, Waverly

the Academy was well established and would need the space where the Church was located for expansion, it seems that plans began to be formulated for the erection of a new house of worship for the growing congregation in the area of the parish house. However, this would not materialize until 1856. The tower of the Academy building stood on the spot of the original log chapel.

The beautiful new, big Church was begun in 1854. The dimensions being 100 x 54 ft. At that time there was slave labor and no doubt much of such labor was used on the building. The bricks were burnt here on the grounds and after the clay had mixed and been made ready the mud was packed and placed in the wooden forms the size they wanted the brick. Then the forms were set aside in the sun to dry; and along came the little pigs and chickens to leave their "little tracks on the mud of time". All this was much in evidence when the building burned on the 24th of March 1950 and the process of clearing away the sad remains of what had been a grand spiritually fruitful past. The new church was dedicated by Bishop Martin John Spalding, June 1, 1856.

Fr. Durbin continued to minister to the catholic population in the vast territory of Western Kentucky, threading his way through much of the roadless expanse to offer spiritual strength to the isolated Christians. Although he would have preferred to remain in Union County to continue serving the needs of the people, he was persuaded by his bishop to end his labors here and take up residence in Princeton, Ky., in 1873, after forty-nine years of tireless service to Union County and points west and south. In Princeton he continued for about ten years to serve the Catholic population of the Elizabethtown to Paducah Railroad headquartered at Princeton, Caldwell County, Ky. Finally, after sixty-five years of Herculean endeavors he retired to Bardstown, KY, where his earthly life ended on March 22, 1887. A spiritual giant had fallen; an era had ended.

For several years after the departure of Fr. Durbin there were a number of temporary pastors at Sacred Heart Parish. Frs. T.J. Jenkins, James Crawley, and James Cronin. In July of 1881 Rev. William P. Hogarty began a pastorate that would last until 1897. During his tenure a boys' school was erected in the area of what is now the parking lot of the Church. This was a two story building which would stand until it was torn down during the early years of the pastorate of Monsignor John M. Higgins. No enrollment number of this boys school is available, but since St. Vincent Academy is solely for girls, The Catholic newspaper, in its February 18, 1882 edition, notes that the school was well attended. In later years the Academy allowed boys to attend, as day students.

After the completion of Fr. Hogarty's term as pastor, Fr. Cyrinus Thomas was pastor for eight years. A rather long pastorate was held by Fr. Bernard Cunningham - 1905 to 1926. He steered the congregation of Sacred Heart with a competent hand which saw it increase both in numbers and fervent faith. Two brief pastorates followed, held by Frs. Walter Heally and Henry Keil. In December of 1928 a new pastor was installed to preside over the parish of Sacred Heart for 45 years - Father John Martin Higgins.

Fr. Higgins was born Oct. 17, 1889 in Grayson County, KY, in the little community of Grayson Springs. He was ordained to the priesthood June 9, 1918. For the first ten years of his ministry Fr. Higgins served in parishes in Louisville and Owensboro. At his arrival in Union County he took the reins of the parish of Sacred

Heart, St. Vincent, Ky., and under his guidance the congregation continued to prosper in both spiritual and material ways. Besides the usual duties of pastoring a parish, Fr. Higgins spent much of his time as an instructor at St. Vincent Academy, located across the road from the parish house. Due to his contact with the hundreds of young people who attended the Academy during his residency, Fr. Higgins was instrumental in gaining the confidence of these future leaders of church and state and instilling in them Christian values that would enable them to be a credit to the community and the country.

The community of St. Vincent and Morganfield benefited from the sense of loyalty which Fr. Higgins had for the civic sector. With the advent of World War II the United States Government acquired fifty thousand acres of Union County Land adjacent to St. Vincent and Morganfield for the establishment of Camp Breckinridge Army Center. Fr. Higgins spearheaded the efforts in organizing the USO for the benefit of the thousands of service men at the Camp. In the late forties and early fifties Fr. Higgins lent his close relationship with the community of Morganfield in assisting the Sisters of Mercy to acquire the Vaughn Clinic and convert it into a hospital. The work for both church and state prompted Bishop Francis R. Cotton of the Diocese of Owensboro to petition Pope Pius XII to bestow on Fr. Higgins the honor of Domestic Prelate with the title of Right Reverend Monsignor.

In the history of any pastor and parish there are moments of trial. No doubt one of the greatest moments of sadness for both pastor and people occurred on March 24, 1950. About 3:00 P.M., as the children from St. Vincent Academy were waiting for the school buses, they noticed smoke coming from the church tower. Miss Jo Ann Greenwell, a former student of St. Vincent Academy, was leaving the Academy after a visit, and noticing the smoke turned in the fire alarm. Although fire fighting equipment from Morganfield and Camp Breckinridge answered the alarm, soon the tall tower of Sacred Heart Church, which had stood as a Union County Landmark for 96 years, was gone. Msgr. Higgins had gone to Uniontown after having conducted religious services at 2:00 P.M. He rushed back to see the beautiful, historic church in ruins. A $15,000.00 renovation and beautification project had been completed a few months previously.

One hero of the conflagration was a young sophomore at St. Vincent by name of Jerry Manning, son of Mr. & Mrs. Paul Manning. He had been altar boy during services and knew where the tabernacle key was located. Jerry and Sr. George Mary, third grade teacher, went into the smoke-filled church, and although they could not see the altar, they were familiar enough with the church to find their way. They became separated inside and were unable to find each other for a few minutes. Jerry went first to the right sacristy for the key, then to the altar to unlock the tabernacle and remove the vessels containing the Blessed Sacrament.

At a meeting of the congregation on Sunday following the fire, various committees were appointed and one group, the grounds committee, was on the job Monday morning tearing down the remaining walls and removing debris. Plans were formulated to start rebuilding with the permission from Bishop Cotton already given. "What our forefathers can do, we can also accomplish." Msgr. Higgins said, "There will always be a Sacred Heart Church, and we will attempt to build a new one more beautiful, perhaps, than the one which burned." During the rebuilding process religious services were conducted in the auditorium of St. Vincent Academy.

The old church had been dedicated on June 1, 1856 by Bishop Martin John Spalding. The rebuilding of the new church progressed expeditiously so that on November 24, 1951, Bishop Francis R. Cotton dedicated the new debt-free church.

For one hundred and fifteen years St. Vincent Academy had been a beacon of learning for thousands of young people from Union County and surrounding states. However, in the early 1960s with the decline of available Sisters of Charity to staff the institution, indications that the Academy might have to close began to be sensed. At the close of the 1967 school year the Academy High School held its final graduation, and the Academy property was sold.

For a time the Sacred Heart grade school continued in a building which had been constructed apart from the Academy. After a couple of years it merged with St. Peter's School from Waverly and was conducted by the Ursuline Sisters of Mount St. Joseph, Maple Mount, KY. Due to declining enrollment this arrangement was dissolved in 1973 at which time Sacred Parish purchased the school building for use as a parish-hall. On Aug. 18, 1976 this building was sold at public auction for $58,100.00. Many of the pupils of the parishes of Sacred Heart and St. Peter's are now transported by bus to St. Ann School in Morganfield.

Having been pastor of Sacred Heart for forty-five years and now being 83 years old, Msgr. Higgins was granted permission to retire from active parish duty by Bishop Henry J. Soenneker on February 13, 1973. Until his death January 23, 1985, Fr. Higgins remained active and healthy in his retirement at Carmel Home in Owensboro. Due to the friendly interest he took in civic affairs during his lengthy stay in Union County and his natural ability to show concern for all people, the community expressed its appreciation and affection for Msgr. Higgins by giving a number of appreciation affairs in his honor in the weeks immediately preceding his departure. The sincere Christian conduct of Msgr. Higgins with people of all faiths made it easier for all denominations to work together. He, like one of his predecessors - Elisha Durbin - was a 'pillar of faith' for more than just members of his congregation.

With the retirement of Msgr. John M. Higgins, Sacred Heart parish was without a resident pastor for the first time in one hundred and twenty-two years. Bishop Soenneker designated Sacred Heart a mission of St. Ann, Morganfield, where Fr. Thomas Clark was pastor. In August of 1975 Fr. Stephan Pirtle was assigned co-pastor of the two churches.

Fr. Kevin Karl came to St. Ann's in 1980 and helped carry on the labor of love at Sacred Heart until his transfer in 1983. That change brought Fr. Aloysius Powers to St. Ann's, as pastor, with Fr. Ray Goetz as assistant. Fr. Goetz was here only one year. When Fr. Ray Goetz was transferred, once again Sacred Heart was transferred. It was October 1984 and Fr. E.E. Willett was assigned the responsibility of caring for our oldest and dearest establishment - Sacred Heart parish. Fr. E.E. Willett is the pastor of St. Peter's parish, Waverly, Kentucky and thus Sacred Heart is "his Mission Church".

Presently there are approximately 58 families in the parish. The majority of them are direct descendants of the first catholic families who settled here in the early eighteen hundreds. The cooperation, willingness to support the church, and firm faith still remains. May it always be so.

Research for this article was done by Fr. Tom Clark, originally used in the 1977 Church Directory; & updated for this article by two "Faithful Secretaries".

St. Agnes Parish
Uniontown

Fr. Elisha J. Durbin organized St. Agnes Parish in 1859. According to the History of Union County, Kentucky, "Catholicity in Union County, and in all Southwestern Kentucky is intimately connected with the name and personal labors of Rev. Elisha J. Durbin." Fr. Durbin's mission was from the Ohio River to Tennessee, and from the line of Jefferson County to the Mississippi. He served this alone for many years and was headquartered near Morganfield in Union County.

St. Agnes Church was built in 1860 on a lot donated by William David, a non-Catholic. In 1870, Fr. G.A. VanFroostenberghe became pastor of our growing congregation. In 1878, Fr. VanFroostenberghe was succeeded by Fr. B.E. Daly who in turn was replaced by Fr. M. Dillon in 1880. During their residency, two tracts of land were purchased south of the city for the parish cemetery.

Rev. Theophilus Kellenaers became pastor in 1888. It was during his 33 years as pastor that we acquired our present beautiful church. It is of Romanesque style and contains irreplaceable stained glass windows. The foundation was laid in the fall of 1891. The entire church was built for $38,000 and was completely free of debt before consecration ceremonies on October 11, 1893.

August, 1920, brought us Fr. R.C. Ruff. Fr. P.C. Barrett served as pastor pro-tem from February to May, 1924. He was followed by Rev. J.T. Pieters. Soon after his arrival in Uniontown, he had the church redecorated. The most beautiful addition to the church was the frescoes painted on the ceiling and around the doors and windows (later removed). Improvements also included the purchase of a $10,000 Kilgen pipe organ which is still in use today. It is the largest and most beautiful organ in the area.

Much of the rich history of St. Agnes parish is recorded in the annuals kept by the Sisters of Charity of Nazareth who were closely connected to the school here until the closing in 1989.

Some highlights from the sisters' accounts are: 255 students enrolled (May 1933), terrible windstorm, rumors of rising water (Jan. 1937). Water up to first floor of convent. People coming and going by boat. Water reached four feet in convent, six feet in church (Feb. 1937). Modern brick convent built (Oct. 1941). Another flood. River crested at 54.6 feet compared to 64.6 feet in 1937 (March 1945). Knights of Columbus furnished suits and equipment for newly organized high school basketball team (Oct. 1950). Parish-wide fund raiser netted $66,726. A new grade school will be built (Sept. 1959). Open house held at new grade school. It was announced by the Bishop that the high school would be closed on May 4 (March 1963). Grade school closes (May 1989).

Fr. Pieters' successors were Frs. J.P. Hayden (1935-36), Delphin R. Thomas (1937-38), Robert Whelan (1938), and A.J. Thompkins (1938). The summer of 1942 brought the arrival of Fr. Raymond G. Hill. During his 20 years at St. Agnes many improvements were made to the church.

Fr. Pius Edelen was assigned to St. Agnes parish from 1962 to 1976. The church was repaired and completely redecorated in 1975. On July 20, 1976, Fr. Charles G. Fischer was appointed pastor of St. Agnes. In January, 1981, a major renovation program was begun and completed in the spring. The renovation included painting throughout, new pews, two restrooms added, installation of carpet and tiling of vestibules. Parishioners did 99% of the work. Fr. Jim Miller, C.PP.S., became pastor in June, 1983. During this period extensive exterior improvements were made: tuckpointing of the brick, new concrete for the entrance steps, terrace around the church and sidewalks. Ramps for the handicapped were also installed. Central air conditioners were installed.

The 125th Anniversary of St. Agnes Church was celebrated in 1984. During this celebration, many former pastors and teachers came to visit and reminisce. Fr. Henry Frantz, C.PP.S., has been pastor since January 15, 1985.

Sr. Theresa Murphy, SCN, came to St. Agnes parish in 1984. She taught at the school, served as principal, and later served as pastoral associate. She accepted another assignment in the summer of 1991.

Sr. Teresa Kunkel, OSF, has been serving as pastoral associate since August, 1991.

Many people are engaged in all forms of ministry. At the present time, plans are being considered to rebuild our Kilgen organ and to build a new rectory.

St. Agnes Catholic Church, Uniontown.

St. Anthony of Padua Parish
Grand Rivers

July 12, 1966 six acres purchased from Mrs. Dorothy Thompson located at 1518 J.A. O'Bryan Ave. in Grand Rivers.

Summer of 1967 Mass was offered in the open air. Early spring 1968, a pavillion was built to accommodate Catholics who lived or vacationed in the area. Mass was celebrated from Memorial Day weekend until Labor Day weekend. It was called the "open air" Mass.

In the fall of 1985, the pavillion was enclosed and the following year finishing touches were made. Mass has been offered every Sunday since Christmas 1986.

The parish, which includes all of Livingston County, was officially established September 4, 1987 with the name of St. Anthony of Padua. Bishop John J. McRaith blessed the Church on October 18, 1987. Msgr. George Hancock was named the first pastor.

The name, St. Anthony of Padua, was suggested by Mr. and Mrs. Roy S. Rohter of Santa Barbara, California, who, through the Catholic Extension Society contributed toward the construction of the church.

St. Anthony of Padua Church.

The parish presently has 38 active resident members. Two Glenmary Sisters, Sister Mary Joseph and Sister Rosemary, live in Smithland and do missionary work in the parish. A parish council has aided in the development of the parish.

St. Alphonsus Parish
St. Joseph

In the early days the people of St. Alphonsus community were served by missionary priests. The first known of these was Fr. E.J. Durbin who served from 1825-1831.

Fr. John Wathen followed until 1837. Fr. Walter Coombs came to St. Alphonsus and built the first log church on five acres of land donated by John Rodman in 1854. After the church was completed there was Mass once a month.

The first resident priest was Fr. Ivo Schacht who enlarged the church and built the first log cabin school which opened in September 1861. The Sisters of Loretto came to teach in the school in 1863 and it became known as St. Joseph Academy. The school was destroyed by fire on Dec. 30, 1870 and the sisters returned to their Motherhouse. Fr. Schacht was succeeded by Fr. Charles Eggermont in 1864 and was pastor when the log church burned in 1868. In 1870, Fr. Paul Joseph Volk came as pastor and his first task was to rebuild the church. He attended to the burning of the brick and helped to erect the building personally. It was 84 by 45 feet in size.

Next Fr. Volk set to work rebuilding St. Joseph Academy. He called five Ursulines sisters from Louisville to teach in the academy. Fr. Martin Oberlinkels, who succeeded Fr. Volk as pastor in 1885, built the rectory. The first grade school known as St. Alphonsus was built by Fr. Anthony O'Sullivan in 1901. After three years, it closed because of financial reasons only to be reopened in 1913 by Fr. James Whelan. During this time, the church was remodeled and the sanctuary added. In 1941, a new brick school was erected by the pastor, Fr. James Higdon. This building served as a school until the consolidation of the Catholic Schools in the county. The building then became the parish hall and space for Religious Education classes.

St. Alphonsus Pastors

Years	Pastor	Years	Pastor
1861-1864	Fr. Ivo Schacht	1937-1947	Fr. James Higdon
1864-1869	Fr. Charles Eggermont	1947-1949	Fr. Paul Barrett
1870-1885	Fr. Paul Joseph Volk	1949-1962	Fr. Joseph McAleer
1885-1888	Fr. Martin Oberlinkels	pro tem	Fr. Leonard Reisz
1888-1894	Fr. Wm. McCarthy	30 days	Msgr. R.G. Hill
1894-1903	Fr. Anthony O'Sullivan	1962-1965	Fr. Frank Ward
1901-1906	Fr. D.J. Gallagher	1965-1972	Fr. Walter Hancock
1906-1907	Fr. J.M. Dreville	1972-1979	Fr. Joseph Miller
1907-1920	Fr. James Whelan	1979-1983	Fr. Bob Willett
1920-1927	Fr. John Abell	1983-1985	Fr. Richard Clements
1927-1935	Fr. Joseph J. Diermert	1985-1989	Fr. Carl Glahn
1935-1936	Fr. Guido Mensa	1989-1994	Fr. Bernard Powers
Pro tem	Fr. Joseph McPherson	1994-	Fr. Bob Drury

St. Ambrose Parish
Henshaw

St. Ambrose Church, Henshaw, KY. (Courtesy of Mary E. Dayberry)

Union County's second oldest Catholic Church stands nine miles west of Morganfield on Highway 270 near the Henshaw community. This tiny rural church owes its existence to the dearly loved, Rev. Elisha J. Durbin, pioneer priest of Western Kentucky.

History shows that Father Durbin was born in Boonville in 1800 and at age 16 entered St. Thomas Seminary at Bardstown. In 1824, two years after ordination, he moved to Union County. As a resident pastor at Sacred Heart, he ventured to establish a new congregation and four years later in 1832 built what then was known as the "lower chapel". The construction took place on a 186 acre tract donated by Martin Thomas Cropper of Virginia. Local farm families at that time included, the O'Learys, Heavrins, Lindles, Binghams, Collins, Henshaws, and the Huckebys.

Father Durbin and his assistant, Edward A. Clark served the congregation until 1860 when St. Agnes Church in Uniontown took over responsibilities. In 1875, the church received a resident pastor, Rev. Theodore Kellenaers, who retained this position for thirteen years. He was replaced on September 16, 1888 by Rev. J.F.A. Donahue who remained until October 7. He was followed by Rev. Patrick Walsh, who served until Nov. 2, 1889 after which Rev. Robert Craney cared for the parish almost 10 years.

On Sept. 13, 1899, Rev. Joseph Odendahl arrived. He remained until May 10, 1910. Rev. Francis X. Havelburg, a Jewish priest, tended the congregation until June 15, 1913. At that time, the church returned to mission status under the rule of Rev. Charles E. Rahm of St. Ann's. About May 2, 1915, Rev. Lucian E. Clements took over as pastor and remained until April 1916. Pastors next were Rev. Joseph Newman; Rev. Joseph Fitzgibbon, a former parish member, and Rev. Joseph Gettlefinger.

For the next 25 years, St. Ambrose again found itself a mission of St. Anne. It was served by Rev. Rahm, Rev. Francis Smith, Rev. Paul C. Barret, and their assistants, Rev. Delphin Thomas, Rev. Thomas A. Murphy, Rev. Henry Willett and Rev. Pius Edelen.

St. Ambrose once more regained status as a separate parish when in Feb. 1946 Rev. Francis Ward was named pastor. He was succeeded on June 15, 1949 by Rev. Edelen.

In Sept. 1952 the Most Rev. Francis R. Cotton, Bishop of Owensboro, divided the parish to form the present parish and St. Francis Borgia of Sturgis.

In July of 1962, Rev. Leonard Reisz came to St. Ambrose. The following year he constructed a new rectory at St. Francis Borgia, hence the pastor's residence moved to Sturgis. In Jan. 1965, Rev. Wm. Hagman was assigned as pastor. Fr. Hagman introduced many Vatican II Council changes and initiated the parish council. Rev. Joseph Pilger who arrived in Jan. 1969, continued that work and involved more parishioners by implementing the lay apostolate. Rev. Alan Pierson followed Fr. Pilger for a brief period. Rev. Louis Telegdy C.PP.S. was then assigned to shepherd the parish. Fr. Telegdy is best remembered for the time and energy he invested in support of the Boy Scout Council.

A native Union County priest, Rev. James C. Hite, became pastor in Aug. 1974. Father Hite was a "natural" for this parish, having been a local family farmer prior to joining the priesthood. Rev. Henry A. Cecil then was assigned. Fr. Cecil added new energy to the parish by his emphasis on youth involvement. Fr. Cecil played an active leadership role in the Teens Encounter Christ movement. Since that time the present pastor, Rev. Albert A. Reed, C.PP.S., has served the small parish.

The small wilderness church, a vague memory to most, is a reality at Henshaw. St. Ambrose continues to be a dynamic farm parish. The church community prides itself on annual social events including trail rides, and parish homecomings; and on its warm welcoming attitude. After worship services are over, most see fit to linger to share tales of the week's occurrences.

But the primary emphasis at St. Ambrose remains on the spiritual growth of its parishioners.

A small pastoral worship, an American legend.

At St. Ambrose the legend is eternal!

St. Ann Church
Morganfield

St. Ann Church in Morganfield was erected in 1876-77 on land donated by prominent attorney and State Senator Ignatius A. Spalding, Jr.

Senator Spalding's house, as that of his father, had been used as the church station of Morganfield prior to the church's construction.

The church was built under the direction of a committee made up of Senator Spalding, Dr. T.J. Shoemaker, Ben Thomas, Charles Alvey, and Louis Wathen. The original construction cost was $9,000. St. Ann was dedicated in March 1878 and was named St. Ann after the mother of the Virgin Mary. The name Ann was also in honor of Senator Spalding's wife.

There are at least two accounts of the naming of the church. One has it that Mrs. Spalding's name was Ann, while another account notes that Mrs. Spalding was known as "Aunt Nancy". The later account tells us that Louisville Archdiocese Bishop McCloskey was in Union County for confirmation at St. Agnes in Uniontown and at St. Ambrose near the Henshaw/Grove Center communities.

He visited the construction site, accompanied by Fr. Elisha Durbin. Later, while riding back with Fr. Durbin, the bishop asked Fr. Durbin what Mrs. Spalding's name was. Fr. Durbin replied—"Why, Aunt Nancy". The Bishop took this to mean Ann.

Still another account tells us that Mrs. Spalding's name was Susan A. Johnson of Daviess County. Ann, Nancy, or Susan, was not Catholic, but she had a great affection for the Catholics of the Morganfield area. She hoped that the congregation would flourish and it did. Mrs. Spalding converted to the Catholic faith shortly before her death.

St. Ann Church was blessed on November 25, 1878 and St. Ann remained a mission of St. Ambrose until 1889 when Fr. Robert Craney became the first resident pastor. A few years later St. Ambrose became a mission of St. Ann. St. Ann was the fourth Catholic Church to be built in Union County.

By the early 1900s, the Catholic population had so increased in the Morganfield area that the decision was made to build a school. St. Ann School was built in 1912 under the supervision of Fr. Robert Craney. The school opened with 50 students and was staffed by four Sisters of Charity from Nazareth. Enrollment increased steadily and a fourth room was added in 1923. By 1925 the school had 150 students. Enrollment continued to grow and a new section was added in 1949 when enrollment had grown to 260. The enrollment increased to 286, the next school year and in 1958 the school had its largest enrollment at 379.

Another addition was added to the school in 1962 under the guidance of pastor Fr. Joseph Spalding. A renovation of the front part of the school took place in 1975, under the supervision

St. Ann Church, Morganfield. (Courtesy of Mary Dayberry)

of Fr. Thomas Clark. As in many rural Catholic schools, enrollment declined steadily and by 1976-77, St. Ann had 255 students. Enrollment hovered around the 300 mark for a few years in the mid 1980s and then began to dwindle slightly.

A kindergarten was added in 1988-89. At the end of school in 1989 St. Agnes school was closed and the students were enrolled at St. Ann school for the beginning of school that fall. The 1991-92 enrollment was some 250 students. The school had 15 teachers and two aides in the 1991-92 school year. The staff included two Ursuline Sisters, Sr. Clara Johnson and Sr. Margaret Marie.

The school year of 1985-86 would be the last year the Sisters of Charity would run St. Ann School. Sr. Molly Thompson was the last Sister of Charity principal, which would interrupt a continuous history since the opening of St. Ann School. Sr. Molly and Sr. Martha Clan, who had taught the first grade, had shared their love and knowledge with the children at St. Ann's for twelve years. The children that began the first grade the first year they were here, graduated out of high school the May that they moved away.

A home for the nuns stationed at St. Ann was built in 1912 and it was torn down in the late 1980s, when talk of the need for a new parish hall surfaced. The rectory was built sometime before 1912 and was originally situated close to the front of the church, near Church Street. The rectory was later moved to the rear of the church, where it remained until it was torn down in 1985, after a new rectory was built.

When the old rectory was moved, (estimated to have taken place in the mid to latter 1920s) it was no easy task. The rectory was originally built in the shape of an "L" and it had to be cut in half before it could be moved. It was reassembled in the shape of a square.

When the church was built in 1876-77, a 500 pound bell was donated by Robert Spalding and his wife of Atlanta, Georgia. It was said to be the largest and finest toned bell in the county and cost $150. The church was lengthened to its present dimensions in 1913 under the direction of pastor, Fr. Charles Rahm. The extension now makes up the sanctuary and sacristies.

Fr. Rahm oversaw a complete renovation of the church's interior, including the installation of 14 stained glass windows from Innsbruck, Austria. The Tyrolese Tradition windows were donated by various church groups and individuals, in 1925. The church was renovated in 1969-70 under pastor Fr. Joseph Saffer.

When the land for the church was donated by Senator Spalding, he also donated land for a cemetery. The cemetery was originally six acres, with three and a half acres making up the burial plots and the remainder being used as a playground for the school children. In 1973, some six acres were added through donations and purchase. It contains 5,500 burial plots in five sections.

During the 115 year history of the church, there have been a large number of young ladies who have become nuns. They include Mother Aloysius Willett, Mother Mercedes Wathen, Sister Mary Charlesetta Bowen, Sister Mary Antonia Wathen, Sister Jean Marie Wathen, Sister Mary Caroline Wathen, Sister Mary Aloysius Wathen, Sister Thelma Cambron, Sister Jean Louise Thomas, Sister Martha Ann Cargile, and Sister Elizabeth Jean Mills.

At least three men of the parish have become priests—Fr. Harold Luckett, Fr. Donald Hunter and Fr. Tony Bickett.

Thirteen priests have served as pastor of St. Ann Parish: Fathers Theophilus Kellenaers 1876 to 1888; Patrick Walsh 1888 to 1889; Robert Craney 12/22/1889 to 1/9/1913; Charles E. Rahm 1/10/1913 to 1/31/1932; Francis J. Smith 2/1/1932 to 7/2/1938; Paul C. Barrett 7/3/1938 to 7/19/1947; Joseph L. Spalding 7/20/1947 to 2/8/1965; Joseph W. Saffer 6/1/1965 to 1/24/1971; Thomas Clark 3/17/1971 to 8/20/1982; Aloysius F. Powers 8/20/1982 to 6/13/1989; J. Bradley Whistle 6/13/1989 to 6/26/1991; J. Patrick Reynolds 6/26/1991 to 6/15/1992, and Severin Messick is currently assigned to caring for St. Ann Parish.

There was no record kept of the many faithful assistants, who have spent many long and tiring hours here at St. Ann's, but they will be remembered and held in highest esteem. Many of them were sent here shortly after ordination, and brought with them many new ideas and much young energy.

St. Anthony Parish
Axtel

St. Anthony Parish was founded even before the first church was built. In 1791 three Catholic families moved into the Southern area of Breckinridge County. These early settlers were Leonard Wheatley, Richard Mattingly, and Veticel Hinton. It was in the Mattingly home that services were held prior to the building of the first church.

The first priest to visit the area was Michael Fournier, followed by Stephen T. Badin before the construction of the first church was begun by Charles Nerinckx in 1812. This first church, built of logs, was not completed until 1819, after Father Nerinckx had left and Robert Abner Abell had come to Long Lick in 1818 (now known as Axtel, Rough River Area).

Father Abell was newly ordained and only 26 years old upon coming here and was the first resident priest. He not only saw the completion of this first church, St. Anthony the Abbott, but also built a priest house near the church. It was he, also, that started the first school here which was held in the Mattingly home. Three Sisters from the Sisters of Charity of Nazareth came and resided in the Mattingly home as well. The school did not survive long and in 1823 Father Nerinckx sent six sisters from the Community of Sisters of Loretto to reopen the school, called Monastery of Mt. Carmel.

Father Abell left in July 1824 and until Thomas Butler came to Long Lick in 1825, St. Anthony's was attended occasionally by Elisha J. Durbin as he passed through the area. Father Butler's duration was short and he left in 1826, thereby leaving St. Anthony parishioners with only an occasional visit by a passing priest, one of these being Charles J. Cecil. He later took up residence at St. Anthony in 1830, then left with the sisters before the end of that year.

After Christmas of 1830 Joseph Rodgers came to Axtel and he who opened a school for boys in the convent and school that had been used by the Sisters of Loretto. In 1836 he closed the school and resigned as pastor due to his health. The Long Lick congregation was once again periodically attended by Father Durbin.

Augustine Degauzuier resided part of the time at St. Anthony up until October 1846. From this date to 1851 Father William Fennelly, of St. Romuald parish, and Father Patrick McNicholas served the St. Anthony congregation. At last, in 1851, Thomas Joyce took up residence. He was followed by Patrick Bambury in March 1854, another newly ordained priest, having St. Anthony as one of his missions. Father Bambury, 27 years old at the time, was transferred in 1857, three years before his death at 34 years of age.

Fathers Michael Power, Patrick Cassidy, and John A. Barrett served St. Anthony as a mission parish until 1864, when the second church was built. Father Barrett knew the church at Long Lick mission was too small and he saw to it that a larger frame church was built before he left the area in 1869.

St. Anthony, still just a mission church, was attended by several priests: Fathers Nicholas Ryan, James J. Crowley, and Thomas J. Jenkins. They all attended at various times until June 1876 when Mathias Oberlinkels was appointed resident priest. He was responsible for a new rectory built at St. Anthony. Henry A. Connolly took temporary control in 1881, when Father Oberlinkels left, and remained for only three months. In Sept. 1881 Lawerence B. Ford became the pastor and reigned until June 1884, followed by Charles P. Raffo in June-Sept. 1888. From this date to 1899 Long Lick was attended as a mission from St. Romuald's at Hardinsburg.

During this time, Fathers Dominic J. Hygins (Higgins), John A. Creary, James J. Pike, Michael Dillon, Hugh O'Sullivan, Lawerence B. Ford (again) and William C.L. Gabe were all priest's who attended St. Anthony as a mission. It was not until Dec. 1899 that St. Anthony again had a resident priest, John Stafford Henry.

Father John Stafford Henry built the third church at Axtel because the second church was becoming too small. In June of 1905 the new church was open for services. Before leaving Axtel in July 1907, Father Henry also saw to it that a new rectory was built.

Rudolph C. Ruff continued Father Henry's work until April 1908. At that time John Francis Knue became the resident pastor at McQuady and St. Anthony became his mission parish. He was attending St. Anthony's when the 100th anniversary was observed. He continued to serve until May 1913.

In May 1913, Joseph R. Odendahl was appointed resident pastor. He quickly paid off a $400.00 debt from the building of the new church and rectory Father Henry had built. He tore down the old church in 1914 (the second church). Only a few weeks later disaster struck and the new church burned to the ground. The rectory, standing nearby, was saved through strenuous effort. During the winter, Mass was said in the dining room of the rectory and on the front porch, weather permitting. It wasn't until spring of 1916 that the new church was opened for services. Father Odendahl stayed at St. Anthony until July 1921, looking after the congregation and overseeing the spiritual growth of the fourth church at St. Anthony.

James Henson Higdon came to St. Anthony in 1921, but spent only one year here, being followed by Robert J. Jenne whose stay was also brief due to illness. As a result of Father Jenne's illness Father Knue again took charge from McQuady. St. Anthony returned to being a mission church until Oct. 1924.

Jerome Louis Hoepf came to St. Anthony in Oct. 1924. He was the first Precious Blood priest at Axtel. He began a Vacation Religion School, classes being held in the church and the rectory, and taught by Ursuline Sisters. Before he left in 1938, he had already started plans and raised funds for a school and a Sisters residence. While under his leadership, St. Anthony became part of the Diocese of Owensboro. The Diocese of Louisville was divided in 1937. Until this division, St. Anthony had been under the jurisdiction of the Diocese of Louisville.

Henry J. Friedal was at St. Anthony from 1938-1946. It was during his tenure that a school and a sisters house were erected. Both buildings were erected from old Army barracks, hauled from Ft. Knox by truck.

In Nov. 1946, August H. Zumberge came to St. Anthony. He saw to it that a basement was dug out under the rectory. He used his carpentry skills in the remodeling of the rectory. On Sept. 10, 1951 Father Zumberge was killed in a collision between the school bus he was driving and a milk truck.

Edwin J. Murphy was sent to St. Anthony temporarily following Father Zumberge's death. In 1952 Michael A. Storm took charge, during his stay a new school was built. Father Storm was at St. Anthony until 1958 when Arnold Meiring came onto the scene. It was during his time that the highest attendance at the school was obtained, 84 students. Father Meiring remained at St. Anthony until 1968.

Upon Father Meiring's transfer, James Minch was welcomed at Axtel. The school was closed in 1971 due to failing enrollment and a decline in Sisters available to teach. He left St. Anthony in 1979, but not before he had overseen the building of the fifth church at St. Anthony's.

It was in May 1973 that the new and present church was built. At this time the parish had grown to about 140 families. William Donohoe came to St. Anthony in 1979. He is of the Precious Blood Order. He saw to the renovation of the rectory and remodeling of the closed school, turning it into a Catholic Community Center. Father Donohoe left in 1987.

After Father Donohoe left the congregation, they welcomed into their midst Roy Anthony Stevenson. Under his guidance a pavilion and storage building for picnic supplies were built. Even more remodeling and updating of existing structures were accomplished, as well as having a new steeple erected with electric chimes. Father Stevenson was great at raising funds for the church. Picnic and raffle tickets were constantly changing hands. Father Tony, as he was known, left in June 1992. Father Bruce Fogle came to St. Anthony upon Father Tony's departure. He is the present pastor.

St. Anthony Parish
Browns Valley

St. Anthony Church, Browns Valley. (Courtesy of Theresa McCarty)

In 1902, Father Fitzgerald came from Owensboro to celebrate the Eucharist in the homes of Sam Bumpus and John Murphy. Thus was the beginning of the parish of St. Anthony in Browns Valley, KY. A frame church building was erected in 1903. The pastor, Father A.G. Meyering, lived in the sacristy of the church until the parish rectory was built in 1904.

In September, 1912, a new school was opened for the education of the parish children. It was staffed by the Ursuline Sisters of Maple Mount, KY.

On October 31, 1931 disaster struck the little church. Fire completely destroyed the building. The altar, statues and pews were saved. Sunday services were held in the school hall until a new church was dedicated on May 31, 1934.

St. Anthony's began to hold picnics to raise needed funds. In 1914, six acres of ground were donated to the parish for its use.

Over the years, much needed remodeling was done. In 1941, the school had new siding put on and storm windows installed along with new indoor restrooms. In 1951, it was the church's turn. The grounds were landscaped and the exterior of the church was covered with St. Meinrad Stone. New pews and floors were installed and a new baptistry was added.

Because of dwindling attendance, the parish school was closed in 1966 and the students were bussed to Our Lady of Lourdes in Owensboro. The old building was demolished and a new hall was built to be used for parish functions, such as Wedding Receptions, Pancake and Sausage Breakfasts, Wednesday night Bingo. Proceeds from Bingo were used to air-condition the church and blacktop the parking lots.

In 1990, the old rectory was demolished to make way for a new rectory. Father Peter Lauzon moved into the beautiful new rectory in September, 1991.

In its 90 year history, St. Anthony's has been served by 22 pastors. Its history is built on a solid spiritual foundation of many hundreds of people, working together to keep the parish alive for these 90 years.

St. Anthony of Padua Parish
Peonia

According to all information presently available the fourth Catholic church established in Grayson County was that of one under the patronage of St. Paul at Peonia. The first church built was erected in 1822 and was located at the site of the cross in the cemetery on top of the hill. The spot is now marked by an outdoor altar. The church is said to have been erected under the direction of Rev. Robert A. Abell, who is known to have served the Grayson County area from 1818 to 1824. One conflicting report has it that an earlier church was built near the site by Fr. Nerinckx around 1812 also under the name of St. Paul. However this probably is not accurate, and the source may have this mixed up with the St. Paul Church in the present St. Paul community.

The fate of the church built in 1822 is unknown, however it is known that another church was built on the same site in 1869 by Rev. John Baptist Vandermergal.

The 1869 church, on top of cemetery hill burned around 1890. The congregation was left without a church for about 20 years. The spiritual needs of the people were served by St. Augustine at Grayson Springs or St. Benedict at Wax. St. Augustine had a resident pastor for most of the period from 1851 to 1906. Rev. Anthony Helling was the last resident pastor assigned to St. Augustine. Shortly he left there to move to Clarkson where they were completing a new church. Under the direction of Fr. Helling a new church was built at Peonia. The new church was dedicated on Aug. 16, 1910 under the patronage of St. Anthony of Padua. This was also the patron saint of Fr. Helling. With additions to the front and rear, the building measured 25 feet by 104 feet.

Father Anselm Kuhn, O.S.B. was assigned as assistant to Fr. Helling in October, 1913 and was placed in charge of the Peonia Missions and became our first resident pastor in late 1913. The first residence was a small box house across the road from the church along with a plot of land purchased from Zack Higdon. Fr. Jacob Rahm succeeded Fr. Kuhn in February 1916 and served until his health failed in 1917. He was succeeded by the venerable missionary and founder of Mount St. Joseph Ursuline Convent, Rev. Paul Joseph Volk.

Next came the noted Rev. John Nicholas Dudine with his assignment July 2, 1919, 10 days after his ordination. Fr. Dudine achieved many accomplishments during his tenure. Due to his influence new roads were built into the area, on March 29, 1921 a new rectory was blessed, the church property across the road from the church was deeded to the county and a public school was built. The county allowed the Ursuline sisters to teach in the school and this provided a Catholic education for the local children. Fr. Dudine left

St. Anthony, Peonia.

on Jan. 17, 1927 and was replaced by Rev. Edward Russell, however Fr. Dudine returned July 22, 1944 to celebrate his 25th jubilee of Ordination with Mass at St. Anthony.

During Fr. Russell's stay in 1930 a new modern convent was erected just west of and near the church. This was later destroyed by fire.

Father Russell was replaced by Rev. Benedict Huff on February 24, 1935 who remained until October 27, 1939.

Disaster struck the Peonia community on the morning of October 27, 1938. The church which had stood for 28 years and 2 months, along with the nearby convent for the nuns, was totally destroyed by fire. Fr. Huff's first order of business was to build a new convent for the nuns. The new house was built about 150 feet to the west of the church site to remove the danger of future fires. Fr. Huff laid the groundwork but asked to be relieved of the strain of building a new church, and was replaced on Oct. 27, 1939 by a younger priest, Rev. Robert T. Wilson.

The new church was dedicated on Nov. 28, 1940 by Bishop Francis R. Cotton. An unsigned narrative of the event is on file in the Confirmation Register book for St. Anthony. The sermon was delivered by a former pastor, Rev. Edward Russell. A copy of this is also on file at the rectory from this we find this excerpt to be very fitting today: "IN THANKFULNESS FOR ALL THESE UNUSUAL BLESSINGS RESOLVE THIS DAY THAT YOU WILL KEEP IN THE BEST REPAIR THIS TEMPLE OF GOD, AND TO FAITHFULLY SUPPORT YOUR PRIEST WITHOUT WHOSE ADMINISTRATIONS, BUILDINGS OR NO BUILDINGS THERE WOULD BE NO RELIGIOUS SERVICES. THE FEAST OF THE DEDICATION OF THIS CHURCH SHOULD BE TO EACH OF YOU THE ANNIVERSARY OF YOUR OWN PARTICULAR FEAST."

Fr. Wilson was called to duty as a Navy Chaplain at the end of Dec., 1942. On Jan. 9, 1943 Rev. Leo J. Dienes was assigned as his replacement. In Dec., 1948 Fr. Dienes was replaced by Rev. Victor C. Boarman. While Fr. Boarman was here the land on which the county school stood was deeded back to the parish, additional land was purchased, and a new modern school was built by the church. An arrangement was made with the county to lease the building and allow the nuns to continue to teach.

In 1959 Fr. Boarman was replaced by Rev. Walter Hancock. Due to the impending closing of St. Benedict School at Wax for the building of Nolin River Reservoir, Fr. Hancock soon began preparations for the additional children from Wax. During his tenure additional rooms were built to the existing school and the convent was enlarged to provide living space and a chapel for the nuns. A later project by Fr. Hancock was the erection of a gym and lunchroom addition to the school.

Succeeding pastors were Rev. David H. Warren, Rev. Clark G. Fields, and Rev. Joseph Miller. Near the end of his first term, Fr. Miller sold the old rectory, and had a new brick rectory built in 1972.

Due to the consolidation of the Grayson County School System, the Peonia School was forced to close at the end of the school year 1973-74. The building was used very little the next few years and began to deteriorate. The Knights of Columbus, Father Carroll White Council 6743 made arrangements with the parish to lease the building. Extensive repair and renovation projects were undertaken and the hall was dedicated on May 2, 1981 under Grand Knight Bernard Lush.

Succeeding pastors included: Revs. William Borntraegar, Steven Dunn, Carmen DeChristopher, Joseph Miller, Ray Goetz, George Curran, Brad Whistle, and presently Gary Payne.

In 1990 some discussion arose within the parish council about the need to do something to celebrate the upcoming 50th anniversary of the church's dedication. Something that began as only a small sprucing up project turned into a full scale renovation project. With the blessing of the bishop, and very much physical labor and financial support from both the members of the parish and others, a project of complete renovation of the interior and exterior of the church was accomplished which has been estimated would have cost three times the $115,000.00 to have done this by contract. The newly remodeled church was blessed and dedicated by Bishop McRaith on June 30, 1991.

St. Augustine Parish
Grayson Springs

As early as 1810 Rev. Charles Nerinckx visited the missions of Grayson County. The first documented Catholic family living in the Bear Creek - Grayson Springs area was that of James Higdon, showing up in the tax record in 1808. Shortly more families with Catholic names began popping up including Alvey, Boone, Clark, Clements, Coomes, Durbin, Higgins, Hill, Jarboe, Kelly, Mattingly, Mollihorne, Mudd, Powell, Roby, Sims, Thompson, and Webb. Reportedly, in 1815 the second Catholic Church erected in Grayson County, St. Augustine, located on Bear Creek in the Grayson Springs community, was erected under the direction of Fr. Nerinckx. No resident pastor was assigned to St. Augustine in the early years. The other early priests who served the area included: the Revs. Peter Schaeffer, Robert A. Abell, Charles J. Cissell, and perhaps an occasional visit by Elisha J. Durbin. In 1831 entries begin showing up for "Bear Creek" in the record book of St. John the Baptist Church near Rineyville in Hardin County. The entries were made by Rev. Augustine Dequaquier. The 1839 issue of the National Catholic Directory lists the churches in Grayson County and the pastor by whom they were served: "St. Paul (on Big Clifty), St. Benedict (on Nolynn River), and St. Augustine (Grayson Springs) attended by Rev. Francis Chambige". Fr. Chambige resided at Bethlehem in Hardin County. Two other priests known to have served the area were Rev. Francis Lawler and Rev. John F. McSweeney.

The first resident pastor at St. Augustine was Rev. Charles Ignatius Coomes. He began a baptismal record Dec. 12, 1851. His last entry was Dec. 12, 1853. Other priests assigned to the area included: the Revs. John Joyce, Thomas Joyce, Patrick Bamburry, John Baptist Vandermergal, Michael Francis Melody, Joseph Henry Carmens, Edward W. Fahrenbach, Henry L. Egart, Anthony M. O'Sullivan, William L. Gabe, Andrew C. Zoeller, Laurence Bernard Ford, Francis X. Havelburg, and the last to be assigned to St. Augustine, Anthony Helling.

In 1854 the brick St. Augustine Church was built as it presently stands. George Smith (1891-1980), a long time resident owning the farm adjoining the church grounds has often pointed out the site on his farm where the clay was dug and the pit where the bricks were fired for the church. Reportedly the church was built at the sole expense of a Catholic lady, Mrs. J.D. Bellchase, whose husband, John died in 1852. The church was built over the grave of Mr. Bellchase. A marble tablet on the wall to the left of the front entrance has this inscription: "D.O.M....John D. Bellchase, born in New Orleans, August 24, 1810...Died at Grayson Springs, August 17, 1852". Mr. Bellchase had been visit-

St. Augustine Church, Grayson Springs

ing the local mineral springs spa at Grayson Springs, the waters of which supposedly had medicinal healing values.

On Dec. 7, 1882 the roof and the interior were destroyed by fire, leaving the walls and probably the floors intact. Signs of charred timbers are still evident in the cellar under the north end of the church. The church records that had been kept there for the years ca. 1870 to 1882 were also destroyed. These would have included the records for St. Anthony and St. Benedict. Rev. Edward Fahrenbach restored the church to its original condition. The restored church was dedicated Dec. 5, 1883.

Around the end of 1913 Rev. Anselm Kuhn was assigned as the first pastor of St. Anthony at Peonia. Since that time St. Augustine has been a mission of St. Anthony. A list of the priests ministering to the area up to the present time are included in the St. Anthony history.

In the fall of 1954 the church was remodeled. Central heat was installed, the interior was replastered and freshly painted, new roof and gutters were installed, the badly leaning wooden bell tower was removed and replaced with a tower on top of the roof, also the stained glass windows were restored. The only major change in the original appearance was in the bell tower. In Dec. 1954 Rev. Victor C. Boarman celebrated a High Mass with an all day exposition of the Blessed Sacrament to celebrate the closing of the Marian Year, then in progress, to commemorate the new renovation project just completed, and to celebrate the centennial of the erection of the church.

Today, St. Augustine is the smallest parish in Grayson County and probably the Diocese, but it has the distinction of being the second oldest parish and the oldest one still located on the same site and using the same building.

A priest having close ties with St. Augustine was the late Rev. Carrol Lewis White. Fr. White was born just across the field from the church. His parents Hugh and Trecy White and his brother and sisters were all members of the parish. Fr. White was killed in an automobile accident on the Western Kentucky in December of 1969. He was buried in St. Joseph cemetery in Leitchfield.

Presently St. Augustine church is in need of repair. The parish council is presently making plans to do this in order to preserve a piece of history.

ST. AUGUSTINE PARISH
REED

According to available records, in point of time, the first institution in the little settlement of Reed was the St. Augustine Church, founded in 1896. This church served the Catholics of the area until 1916, when it was destroyed by fire. The faith of the people led to the erection of the second church in 1917.

St. Augustine School was built in 1922 and staffed by the Dominican Nuns of St. Catharine, KY. In 1964 the school closed and most of the students were enrolled in St. Peter's School at Stanley.

The second church burned on March 11, 1944 and 4 years to the day a new, more beautiful church was dedicated. During those 4 years the congregation worshipped in the school basement.

During the 1937 flood, the school was used as a refuge for a number of people until the rising waters caused them to have to leave by boat. The present church is of Spanish Mission design, built of St. Meinrad sandstone. The cost was approximately $51,000. Father Robert Wilson, who had been a chaplain in the Navy during World War II, received much help from his former friends in the service. At that time there were some 45 families and 270 parishioners. Enrollment in the school stood at 50 students in 8 grades—40 Catholics and 10 Protestants.

The first child baptized in the original St. Augustine Church was Louis Sylvester Patry— on Aug. 28, 1896—by Father J.J. Pike. Among the Priests serving the church later were Frs. J.J. Muyssen, Eugene Spiess, O.S.B., Thos. A. McGuire, J. Odengahl, Richard Maloney, S.J. Mensa, Richard W. Mattingly, O.S.B., J.J. Rives. Apparently the first resident pastor was, Fr. J.J. Rives (1920-28); following him were Frs. S.W. Luley (1928-32); (Fr. J.P. McGee filled in in 1929); C. Hooiveld (1932-35); Paul Greenwell (1935-43); Frank Ward (1943-1945); Robt. T. Wilson (1945-57); Fr. Henrly L. Willett filled in (in 1949 & 1950); Aloysius Powers (1957-63); Wm. J. Hagman (1963-64); Wm. McAtee (1965); again Fr. Robt. Wilson (1981); Carmen deChristopher (1982-87); Larry Hostetter (1992-) The last 3 resident pastors lived in a mobile home after the rectory was torn down.

During the intervening years when there was no resident pastor, it was served from Sorgho or Stanley. Fr. Paul P. Powell cared for St. Augustine from Stanley from June 1987 to June 1992.

At present the parish has some 45 families and 140 parishioners. For a number of years Arnold Mills and family have lived upstairs in the school and he has acted as custodian. CCD classes are held in the classrooms; and the basement, recently renovated, serves as a meeting place for community groups, for picnics and showers. In 1988 a large shelter was erected for serving barbecue dinners. It was built in memory of Father Carmen De Christopher and appropriately, but unofficially, named "Dee's Diner." The 4th of July Picnic has been a tradition for many years. People from all over the tri-state come to partake of the barbecued mutton and chicken and the burgoo.

St. Benedict Parish
Wax

According to an article written by Rev. Louis Beruatto in 1942, the fifth Catholic Church built in Grayson County was that of St. Benedict at Wax. The exact date of the establishment is unknown, however it can be assumed to be prior to 1835. The oldest tombstone still standing in the cemetery is that of Benedict T. Carrico, born Jan. 27, 1780, died Aug. 15, 1835. The first church was a log structure on the north bank of Nolin River on a site reportedly donated by Absolum H. Johnston. Mr. Johnston was the ancestor of the present day Johnston families living in the area. St. Benedict served the Catholic settlers, and continues to serve the Catholic families on both sides of Nolin River in Grayson, Hart, and just down the river, eastern Edmonson County. The church has never had a resident pastor. In the early years it was served by priest from St. John the Evangelist at Rineyville, then from the Bethlehem Academy both in Hardin County along with the other missions in Grayson County.

In 1851 Rev. Charles Ignatius Coomes was assigned as the first pastor of St. Augustine at Grayson Springs with the missions of St. Benedict and St. Anthony. This was a distance of about 10 miles away and due to nothing more than crooked wagon roads at the time it is doubtful that Mass was held more often than once a month at St. Benedict. In late 1913 Rev. Anselm Kuhn was assigned as the first pastor of a new church built at St. Anthony at Peonia. With this assignment came the missions of St. Benedict, St. Augustine, St. James of Iberia, St. Agnes of Dog Creek in Hart County, and later St. Joseph of Annetta. No doubt the early priests assigned to St. Anthony still were limited to the time they could spend at each church. St. Agnes served several families south of Nolin River in Hart and Edmonson Counties for several years. With the building of a bridge at Wax around 1930 there was little need for the church, being located only about a mile from St. Benedict, however it remained open with occasional services until

St. Benedict Catholic Church

around 1960 when the building was finally torn down leaving only the cemetery.

The second church was probably the one that stood in the cemetery for so many years. Old pictures show it being a frame church in a very poor dilapidated condition. On November 20, 1940 a new frame church was dedicated by Bishop Francis R. Cotton. This church standing further up the hill was erected under the direction of Rev. Robert Wilson, and was the one that stood until the early 1960s.

Around 1940 a Catholic school was started at St. Benedict. Classes were held in a frame building with additional classrooms in the church basement. Ursuline nuns were assigned as teachers. In the early 1950s a new modern concrete block school was built, also providing living quarters for the nuns. The school year of 1948-49 recorded an attendance at St. Benedict of 97 pupils. Also the same report showed 352 total parishioners.

The area of "old" Wax, including St. Benedict Church, school, and cemetery was in the flood plain of the Nolin River Reservoir. The property was purchased by the U.S. Government Corps of Engineers in the early 1960s. The school was torn down by members of the parish and the material was used to build additional classrooms to the school at Peonia where the children were transferred. Under the direction of Rev. Walter Hancock property was purchased about one mile east on Highway 479 where a new church was built and the cemetery was relocated. In 364 days after the new church was dedicated it was completely destroyed by fire from unknown reasons. The present identical church was built the following year on the same foundation.

With several of the local families being forced from their farms with the coming of Nolin Lake, St. Benedict Parish consists today of some of the original families and several newer members who have retired to nearby subdivisions surrounding the lake.

St. Charles Parish
Bardwell

The first Catholic settlers in eastern Ballard County (Carlisle) arrived in 1834. For the first few years, they received the Sacraments and attended to their religious duties at St. Jerome Church, Fancy Farm.

It was not until 1891 that hopes for a church of their own began to be realized. The new church was christened "St. Charles."

For the next few years, the priest at Fancy Farm traveled over the poor roads and through all kinds of weather once a month to celebrate Mass and care for the spiritual needs of his parishioners.

By 1917, these visits had increased to two per month. Then in 1920, preparations were under way to provide a school for the children. For forty-six years and through many a crisis, this school lasted. And then because of lack of teachers, it had to be closed in 1966.

A new church was built in 1956 and dedicated March 12, 1957 by Most Rev. Frances R. Cotton, D.D. During the building of the church, members of St. Charles Parish, with Father Pike Powell as pastor, furnished more than 500 days of volunteer labor. It was built without the aid of an overall contractor. Only the masonry work and heating were contracted.

After the school was closed, a need arose for a new plane of religious education. In 1968, the present C.C.D. program was started. It is kept going by the constant and untiring effort of volunteer members of the parish. It is supplemented in the summer by the Ursuline Sisters who come for a one-week Summer Religion Program.

August 1970, the old school was sold. In the spring of 1972, after all traces of the school had been removed, blacktopping for an improved parking lot was started and more added the following year.

The following year, St. Charles ceased being a mission of St. Jerome's. Fr. Bob Willett was named pastor of St. Charles, St. Dennis, and St. Mary's. The rectory to the church was purchased in 1975. Restrooms were added in 1981, and a ramp was constructed in 1948. Remodeling of the inside of the church took place in 1990.

ST. CHARLES PARISH
LIVERMORE

In the late eighteen hundreds, Catholicism was well established in Western Kentucky, but only a few Catholics resided in Livermore and the surrounding area. There was no church at first so that Masses were said at various locations by a visiting priest who traveled by train to reach Livermore. After 1902, Mass was celebrated in the home of Nellie Corrigan Quigg. In 1905, Karl J. Meyer arrived from Troy, IN to start a chair manufacturing business in Livermore. He was also interested very much in establishing a permanent Catholic parish in Livermore. With the permission of the Bishop of Louisville, Mr. Meyer was permitted to set aside a room in his home for the celebration of holy sacrifice of the Mass. This arrangement continued until larger quarters were needed for the congregation. In 1915, a frame church edifice at Fifth and Hill Streets that had been previously owned by the Presbyterian Church was purchased and remodeled for Catholic services. It was named in honor of St. Charles Borromeo, noted archbishop of Milan.

And so St. Charles was established and became a mission of Brown's Valley under Rev. Aloysius G. Meyering. Since there was no resident pastor in the early years Mass was said only on alternate Sundays. From the time of its dedication in 1917 until 1935 St. Charles remained a mission of St. Anthony Church in Brown's Valley.

Around 1916, a school, located across the street from the Church on Hill Street between Fifth and Sixth Streets, became available. Mr. Karl J. Meyer purchased the building and donated it to the church. In 1919, it opened as the St. Charles Parochial School with twenty students. The school continued in existence for five years

until 1925, at which time it was closed due to falling enrollment. One year later the building burned.

In 1917, the St. Charles Cemetery was established.

By 1941, the parishioners of St. Charles, with the permission of Bishop Francis R. Cotton of Owensboro, were planning a new church. The plans were drawn by Nolan and Nolan architects of Louisville, Kentucky, and all the preparations were made at that time but they could not be carried out because of building restrictions necessitated by World War II. The foundation was laid in 1943 and took all summer to complete since the work was done by parishioners. In 1945, after the war was

over it was decided to resume construction of the new church. Fr. Victor Boarman, the pastor of St. Charles at the time, asked Clarence Charlet and K.J. Meyer, Jr. to oversee the work on the new church and even though the war was over construction was still plagued by lack of building materials. At this point, Karl J. Meyer was able to provide the necessary lumber as owner of the Green River Chair Company; he was able to purchase the lumber, cut it and dry it. The sheeting was processed at the Logsdon Saw Mill and Hartz and Clark of Owensboro served as building contractors. Construction was finally completed in 1947 and the new church was dedicated on October 20, 1947. Due to the dedication and generosity of many people the construction of the new church was completed at a cost of less than twenty thousand dollars and has provided a beautiful worship space since that time for the people of St. Charles parish.

In 1946, Fr. Victor Boarman, pastor of St. Joseph Church in Central City and of St. Charles, decided to send the children to St. Joseph's Catholic school. The children gradually graduated from riding in a station wagon to their own school bus to get to school. Children from St. Charles attended school at Central City until 1972.

From 1935 until 1972, St. Charles was a mission of St. Joseph Church in Central City and in 1972 St. Charles became a mission of St. Sebastian Church in Calhoun, KY. It has been a mission of St. Sebastian since that time. St. Charles has continued to prosper since its beginning and we look forward to a much longer history here in McLean County.

ST. EDWARD PARISH
FULTON

The beginnings of the Catholic Faith in Fulton, Kentucky can be traced to 1891 to 1892. During that period Mass was offered once every three months in the home of John Weis. Fr. George Weiss came from Paducah for these times.

An interesting event in 1905, when trains were the predominant means of travel, brought the Church to this town. One day while Fr. P.J. McNeil was assigned at Mayfield he visited Fr. Joseph Minch, Pastor of Sacred Heart in Hickman. On his return he had to change trains at Fulton and was approached by a stranger. This man, who identified himself as not being Catholic, suggested that Catholic Church was badly needed at Fulton. Fr. McNeil returned to Fulton the next week and offered Mass in the home of John J. Gavin, a railroad official. Another non-Catholic offered the use of vacant rooms in an office building where Mass was celebrated for the next several months.

Later an abandoned school building was

purchased on the present site of Saint Edward. They broke ground in November of 1931 and laid the cornerstone December 4, 1932. Catholics as well as non-Catholics contributed $1100 to make the opening of the Church possible. Apparently someone in the town had an old discarded Blessed Virgin Altar in his shop and donated it to the Church. The new Church was dedicated by Bishop Floersh on April 2, 1933,

which happened to be Passion Sunday of that year. Fr. Harold Luckett, Pastor of St. Joseph in Mayfield, was appointed Pastor of the new Parish.

In 1947 the Dominican Sisters from Springfield, Kentucky opened a school at Saint Edward. The school lasted until 1961 when the students were taken through Union City, TN to Hickman.

Through the course of years Fulton was no longer dependent solely on the railroad. Other industry came to and near the town. The companies brought several Catholics from other areas of the country to Fulton. As we begin our 60th year as a parish there are very few Catholics who were raised in Fulton. The Church has gone through many changes over the years. Most of our parishioners are grateful to the preceding generations for the facilities we have now. The history of the faith in Fulton is being formed from the diversity of the people who have moved into our area.

St. Columba Parish
Lewisport

The first St. Columba Church was built in 1850, on an acre of land donated by Miley Johnson. The land is across from property known as the Claude Roberts Farm. On this site a small log frame church was built. A part of the acre was used as a final resting place for the faithful and is known as the "Old Catholic Cemetery".

The stones in the cemetery reveal that the first person to be buried there was Michael (Miley) Johnson, born October 21, 1820 died March 26, 1864. Other stones of interest are: William Gibbony, native of Ireland, County of Downs; born December 20, died August 5, 1867. Benedict Long, St. Mary's County, Maryland; born July 25, 1816, died August 25, 1877.

The log church served as a place of worship for the Catholics of the whole neighborhood. Because many of the parish were of Scotch-Irish descent and had migrated from St. Mary's County, Maryland and Ireland, may explain the selection of St. Columba, and Irish Saint, as the patron of their small church.

The first church, which at the time was in the Diocese of Louisville, Kentucky was served by Father Rock, who traveled from the St. Lawrence Parish.

August 30, 1867, Bishop Spalding of Louisville, purchased a lot on Pell Street in Lewisport on which the second and third St. Columba Churches would be built. The first church built on Pell Street was a small framed building. This church was served by priests from the St. Rose Church in Cloverport, Kentucky.

Fr. Anthony J. Tompkins was appointed pastor of Immaculate Conception and St. Columba in 1949. Father Tompkins would build the fourth church on a track of land purchased from the Earl Simmons family in 1958. Father Tompkins died May, 1962 while serving as pastor of both churches.

Permission to build the church was granted by the Most Reverend Francis Cotton, Bishop of Owensboro in the spring of 1959. Construction began in April and the cornerstone laid June 29, 1959. The Parish Hall was added, adjacent to the church, by Father Philip Riney in 1968. This large colonial design church would serve the Catholic community of Lewisport until the morning of August 9, 1989 when it was destroyed by fire which started in the electrical wiring.

The parish is now in the process of rebuilding. In the summer of 1990 the Most Reverend John J. McRaith, Bishop of Owensboro, directed that planning for the new building should begin. July of 1990 the Parish Council appointed Denny Long and Doris Marsch to chair a core committee with Father Emil Schuwey, C.PP.S., Pastor for the planning of the new St. Columba Church which is to be constructed on the site where the fourth St. Columba Church stood.

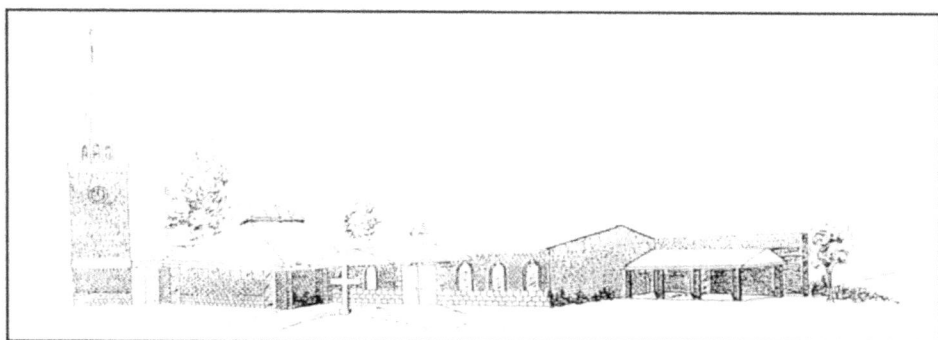
St. Columba Catholic Church, Lewisport, 1992

St. Columba Catholic Church, 1868-1937

St. Columba Catholic Church, 1937-1959

St. Columba Catholic Church, 1959-1989

St. Denis
Fancy Farm

At the request of Father Charles A. Haeseley, Bishop Denis O'Donohue sent a priest to establish a parish in Hickman County to meet the needs of the people.

Father John Fowler was sent to Fancy Farm and under his supervision the church was built. The church was named St. Denis in honor of the bishop and dedicated on October 7, 1914. Father Albert Thompson came in 1915 and a few years later he volunteered for chaplain during World War I. During his absence Father Haeseley traveled twice a month to St. Denis. Upon Father Thompson's return, he found a need for the school in 1920. Before the school was finished Father Mark Parrette replaced Father Thompson. It was under his care that the school was finished. The Ursuline Sisters from Mount St. Joseph, Maple Mount, Kentucky came to teach school in 1921. A small rectory was built for the priest to live in part time.

Other priests that followed were: Fathers Durbin, Harold Luckett, William Jarboe, James Mills.

During the Great Flood of 1937, Father Robert Wilson came, and Father Benedict Huff in 1939. The church and school were wired and a water system was installed. In 1948 the rectory was sold and the priest lived at Fancy Farm.

In 1948 Benedictine Fathers wishing to open a religious house in Kentucky came to St. Denis. They were Father Alexander Korte, Harvey Sheperd and two brothers.

In 1951 they moved near Bowling Green,

Kentucky, Father Huff became pastor. Others that followed were: Fathers Rudolph Carrico, Pike Powell, Richard Danhauer, William Allard, William Hagman and Clark Field.

In 1963, Father Charles DeNardi assumed responsibilities of St. Jerome and the missions of St. Denis, Hickman County and St. Charles, Carlisle County. During his stay a gas heating system was installed, and the church was carpeted. Because of a lack of teachers the school was closed in June 1964. The school was turned into a community hall.

Father DeNardi was assisted by Fathers Clark Field, William McAtee, Raymond Waldruff, David Linderman, Hubert Wolf, and Donald Howard.

In 1972 Father Walter Hancock became pastor. He provided a new organ, black topped around the church and community hall and planted new trees. St. Denis, at this time, ceased being a mission of St. Jerome in Fancy Farm and became a parish of its own.

In 1973 Father Bob Willett became pastor. Looking at the needs of the people he formed a Parish Council, commissioned Eucharistic Ministers to help at Mass and the needs of the sick in the parish.

There was a need for a new church. Before the new church got underway, Father Willett left.

In 1979 Father Joe Bomensatt came. He continued with the plans of the new church. On May 30, 1982, the new church was dedicated by Bishop Soenneker. Father Joe was replaced by Father Allen McIntosh who stayed a year.

In 1985 Father Bruce Fogle came to St. Denis, St. Jude, and St. Jerome as an assistant pastor to Father Jerry Riney, pastor. Once again there arose the need for a new parish hall. A committee was formed under the leadership of Father Bruce and Father Jerry.

In 1987 Father Terry Devine came, assistant to Father Riney. They continued with the building plans and on November 29, 1987 Bishop John McRaith dedicated the new parish hall.

Father Riney left on June 10, 1989, and Father Terry Devine became pastor of St. Denis and St. Charles.

Let us remember the religious from our parish: Sisters Paul Joseph Durbin, Albert Mary Durbin, Rose Kathleen Durbin, Teresa Ann Ellegood, Joseph Mark Hayden, and Bro. Ferdinand Hayden.

St. Henry Parish
Aurora

February 21, 1967 - 32 acres of land purchased from Dale and Mildred Leneave for a future church.

Summer of 1967 - Mass was offered for tourists in the open air, under the trees, near Highway 68 and 80.

Early spring of 1968 - an outdoor pavilion, consisting of a metal roof and concrete slab floor, was constructed and completed in time for Mass for the Memorial Day weekend.

From Memorial Day weekend 1968 until Labor Day weekend 1982, Msgr. Hancock offered Mass during the summer months for tourists and Catholics living in the area.

Fall of 1982, plans were formulated for the construction of a new Church, with construction beginning in January.

St. Henry Church was blessed on September 18, 1983 by Bishop John J. McRaith, with Bishop Henry Soenneker giving the homily.

The church was named in honor of Bishop Soenneker, the last of many churches approved for construction during the 21 years of his episcopate in the diocese. Msgr. George Hancock was named the first pastor of St. Henry's.

The beginning parish census was 45 persons. Today 178 practicing Catholics. Since its beginning some 40 persons have either been baptized or received into the Church by Profession of Faith.

The parish has a parish council, a CCD program, a choir, a monthly pot luck during the Fall and Winter and other activities.

St. Elizabeth of Hungary Parish
Clarkson

St. Elizabeth of Hungary was constructed in 1906 and was dedicated on Christmas Day of that same year. It was the first of seven churches to be built by Father Anthony Helling.

Prior to 1906, Father Andrew Zoeller had said Mass in a building owned by Miss Ellen Kellehur, located where the Bank of Clarkson now stands. Father Helling came to St. Augustine, Grayson Springs, May 6, 1906. He also served the missions at St. Paul and St. Benedict. He immediately realized the need for a Catholic Church in Clarkson and began soliciting donations. Miss Bettye Baker donated ground for the Church, a school and rectory. The people held socials and picnics to help finance the project. The first infant baptized in the new Church was Lawrence Earl Pearl; the first couple to be married was Robin Taylor and Ophelia Higdon.

A parochial school consisting of one room was built in 1910; another room was added later. Grades one through eight were taught, with an enrollment of sixty to seventy students, before the school closed in 1913. Father Helling served as pastor for over thirty years until his death at the rectory on November 13, 1938.

Since 1906 St. Elizabeth has been served by the following priests: Fr. Anthony Helling, Fr. Huff, Fr. Charles DeNardi, Fr. William Borntraeger, Fr. Pike Powell, Fr. James Wathen, Fr. Richard Danhauer, Fr. Griffith, Fr. Ben Luther, Fr. Arthur Snow, Fr. Tony Stevenson, Fr. Maury Riney, Fr. Charles Fischer, with Frs. DeNardi and Borntraeger serving on two separate occasions.

Father Tony Stevenson and Father Maury Riney began plans for a new church. The annual picnic was revived to help raise funds. Father Charles Fischer, who came in June 1989, continued, completed and finalized the plans. Construction was started in August 1991. The first Mass was celebrated in the new church on the Fourth Sunday of Advent, December 22, 1991.

Bishop John McRaith presided at the Mass of Dedication on January 19, 1992. Several former pastors and diocesan priests were present for the Mass and reception.

The new church consists of a parish office, kitchen, large meeting room, rest rooms, sacristy, Blessed Sacrament Chapel, and a large worship area. Several of the stained glass windows which were imported from France, and the main altar, which was sent from Germany, were removed from the old church and incorporated into the new building. The large cast iron bell and the smaller brass bell from the old church will be utilized in a new bell tower to be constructed beside the new church.

St. Elizabeth is located on Clifty Avenue in Clarkson four miles east of Leitchfield on Ky. Highway 62. Going east, turn left at the caution light, right across the railroad track, and left on Clifty Avenue.

St. Elizabeth of Hungary, present facility.

St. Elizabeth of Hungary, 1906.

St. Elizabeth Parish
Curdsville

As early as 1797, the first pioneer men and women settled in the forests and clearings on the corners of Daviess and McClean Counties in the area later called Curdsville. Its location on the Green River and Panther Creek enhanced its growth as a trade port and by 1890, it had a population of 341. The first Catholics in the area went to St. Raphael Church (established in 1854). With the increase of Catholics, the need for a church at Curdsville became apparent and Father Oberlinkels responded by building St. Elizabeth Church in 1887. It was dedicated on Dec. 11 of that year. A large crowd, many of them Protestants, gathered for the dedication. The Mass was offered by Father Oberlinkels with a sermon by Father McCarthy.

The first Baptism recorded is that of Raymond Borgia Clayton on Nov. 6, 1881 by Father James Pike. The marriage of Matthew Mason and Anna Johnson on Feb. 7, 1915, is the first on the register for the parish. In November 1903, Father Edwin Drury gave a mission for non-Catholics. Many converts resulted from this mission.

In the first years, there were no resident pastors. Among the priests who served during these years were Fathers James J. Pike, John H. Riley, W. P. McCarthy, Joseph Neesen, Engelbert Schmitt, A. D. Sullivan and D. J. Gallagher. In all probability, these priests were missionaries for the various outlying districts and included St. Elizabeth on their rounds. A note in the register on Feb. 11, 1902, indicates that St. Elizabeth would be a mission of St. Alphonsus. The first appointed pastor was Father Joseph Wright who came in 1910. He resided at St. Alphonsus until a rectory could be built at Curdsville.

Father Wright opened a school in 1911 seeking the Ursuline Sisters of Mount St. Joseph as teachers. The first school was the Sweikart residence, located a block or so from the Church. It was used as a school until 1938. High school classes were offered from 1918 to 1934. In the summer of 1938, when the area public schools were consolidated and that school building vacated, the parish purchased it. Everyone was happy because it was conveniently located across from the church. St. Elizabeth School was opened in this newly acquired building by October 1938. Then, on Jan. 30, 1939, sad news spread through Curdsville, when this school was destroyed by fire. Once again, the old school building was put into service and continued to be used until a new school was erected on the lot across from the church in 1955. Due to decrease in enrollment, the school closed in May 1973.

In 1925, the Church was enlarged and transformed by Father James H. Higdon. The original structure was preserved but veneered by Rugby Brick. The sanctuary, two sacristies and a tower were added and the gallery was enlarged. This improvement doubled the capacity of the Church. Over the years, the church was redecorated several times as needed and particularly for the celebration of the first hundred years in 1987. A beautiful new rectory was erected during the time that Father Robert Whalen was pastor.

The parishioners of St. Elizabeth Parish continue to display a deep faith and generous family spirit. Over the years, they were seen as people who not only worked together to preserve their church and school, but who also reached out beyond the parish working to help neighboring parishes in times of need. even though the parish roll remained small in number, its members were large in enthusiasm and service to the church. Records show four native diocesan priests and ten women religious.

Rev. Joseph Wright	1910-1912
Rev. Bernard A. Gillenbeck	1912-1913
Rev. Christian Weigand	1913-1914
Rev. Robert Joseph Jenne	1915-1922
Rev. James H. Higdon	1922-1933
Rev. John J. Glenn	1933-1950
Rev. Henry Willett	1950-1961
Rev. Robert Whalen	1961-1962
Rev. Thomas Murphy	1962-1965
Rev. Robert Whalen	1965-1969
Msgr. Peter Braun (4 months)	1969-1969
Rev. Clifton Howard (Jan.-Aug.)	1970-1970
Rev. Francis Howard	1970-1972
Rev. Hubert Wolf	1972-1973
Rev. William McAtee	1974-1976
Rev. Joseph Mort, OSB	1976-1982
Rev. Carmen DeChristopher	1979-1982
Rev. J. Edward Bradley	1982-1983
Rev. Boniface Armbruster	1983-1990
Rev. Clarence Hite	1991-

St. Francis Borgia Parish
Sturgis

The dedication of St. Francis Borgia Church on September 30, 1952 met a need for a Catholic church in southern Union County. The impetus for building a church in Sturgis came from a letter written to Bishop Francis Cotton by Regina Long. She and her husband, James L. Long Sr., a non-Catholic, donated a series of lots on the east side of Adams Street between Thirteenth and Fourteenth Street in Sturgis.

The name of the church, St. Francis Borgia, stems from the first name of Mr. and Mrs. F.L. Lewis of Chicago, IL who gave a sizeable donation through the Catholic Extension Society. A local contractor, Fred Alloway, was chosen to build the 45' x 80' building which has a seating capacity of approximately 200 persons. The cost of the construction was $35,000.00. The first Sunday Mass after the official dedication was celebrated on October 5, 1992. When the parish was founded there were only 21 adults as registered members.

Initially St. Francis Borgia was a mission parish of St. Ann Church, Morganfield, KY. Rev. Joseph Spalding was pastor of St. Ann's and Fr. Philip Riney was associate pastor. Fr. William Allard and Fr. Richard Danhauer succeeded Fr. Riney as associates and took care of St. Francis Borgia until 1962 when Fr. Leonard Reisz was assigned as the first resident pastor of St. Francis Borgia. He lived at St. Ambrose, Henshaw, KY while the rectory was being constructed in Sturgis. The rectory was completed in 1963. St. Ambrose parish, Henshaw, KY then became a mission parish taken care of from St. Francis Borgia.

A new parish of St. William, Marion, KY was established in August, 1962 and also became a mission of St. Francis Borgia Parish. Fr. Reisz then had the pastoral responsibility for St. Francis Borgia, St. Ambrose, Henshaw and St. William, Marion, about 20 miles southeast of Sturgis. Fr. William Hagman became pastor of these three parishes in 1965. During the early days of St. Francis Borgia Parish, any students who wished to attend parochial school had to be bussed to St. Ann School, Morganfield and for a few years to St. Peter School, Waverly.

After the II Vatican Council a strong CCD program was developed in the parish to meet the need for the religious education of the students who did not attend parochial schools elsewhere in Union Co. Fr. Ben Luther provided formal training for the CCD teachers, and was helpful in developing the religious education program. With the formation of the CCD program, more space was needed for classroom facilities. In order to meet this need and to provide space for a social center in the parish, a new building was contracted for on October 26, 1968 and completed under the new pastor, Fr. Joseph Pilger in 1969. This building is located on the corner of Fourteenth and Adams Streets.

St. Francis Borgia, Sturgis, KY.

Fr. Pilger also undertook the job of renovating the interior of St. Francis Borgia Church. Marble was added to the interior walls, the Communion rail was removed. Gordon Braddock and C.E. Johnson were appointed as Pastoral Ministers while Fr. Pilger was here. Fr. Pilger served all three parishes until December of 1971.

Fr. Alan Pierson and Fr. Ben Luther served the parishes briefly until Fr. Louis Telegdy, C.PP.S. was assigned pastor in 1972. He served until 1974 when Fr. James C. Hite came to St. Francis Borgia Parish as pastor. Fr. Hite guided the growth of the three parishes until December of 1982 when Fr. Henry Cecil was given the assignment of the pastoral care of these parishes.

St. Francis Borgia continued to grow, and by 1984 additional space was needed for religious education classes and for the increasing number of social and community functions on the calendar. For some years, now, St. Ambrose Parish had shared our facilities and responsibilities for the CCD program. It was evident that any additional building project would have to be large enough to meet the needs of the combined parishes. Accordingly the new parish hall project was a joint project for St. Francis Borgia and St. Ambrose parishes. In May of 1986 in a joint meeting of the Pastoral Councils of St. Ambrose and St. Francis Borgia, a unanimous vote was recommended to Fr. Cecil that bids be taken for an addition to the education building.

Ground breaking for this new addition took place on June 21, 1986. Because of the cooperative effort and volunteered service of these two parishes, the 3760 sq. ft. building was completed at a cost of $18.00 per sq. ft. The first function in the new building was on November 1, 1986. On this occasion a "Time-Capsule" was sealed in the cornerstone of the building to allow future generations the opportunity of having a detailed history of the planning and construction process. The new addition was formally blessed by Bishop John H. McRaith on December 14, 1986. With the completion of this new building, which contains a large community room, kitchen and restroom facilities, the present need for space has been met.

However, the Pastoral Council for St. Francis Borgia, anticipating the future growth needs, advised the pastor, Fr. Henry Cecil, to purchase additional property in the block fronting Main Street. The purchase was made possible by a loan from the Diocese of Owensboro. This 1988 acquisition included an office building, which is currently being rented to the Union County School District, and houses the Head Start program in Sturgis.

In September of 1988, Fr. Albert A. Reed, C.PP.S. was appointed pastor of St. Francis Borgia and St. Ambrose parishes. During the summer of 1988 St. William Parish in Marion was assigned to Fr. Maurice Tiell, who also began the new parish of St. Mark, Eddyville, KY. At present, St. Francis Borgia is a strong and vital community, looking forward to spiritual growth in the coming years, but ever conscious of the love, perseverance and dedication given by earlier members. Its members are working hard to pass on this heritage of their faith community to future generations.

St. Francis De Sales Parish
Paducah

Begun by Fr. Elisha Durbin, St. Francis De Sales Church is a historical landmark in downtown Paducah, having served the Catholic community since 1850. Three brick church buildings have provided a worship space: the first was completed in 1850; the second, larger and closer to Broadway, was built in 1870; the third, the present Church with twin bell towers topped with copper domes and now a famous part of the Paducah skyline, was built in 1899-1900.

As the Catholic population in the area increased, three parishes branched out from St. Francis De Sales. Established were St. Mary's Parish in LaCenter (1907), St. Thomas More (1943) and Rosary Chapel (1947).

Through the years, many improvements and renovations have enhanced the beauty of the present Church building. In 1933, renovations included a terrazza floor, new doors containing art glass, and a vestibule finished in polished red gum wood at the front entrance. In 1936, the mural of the Ascension was placed above the altar. In 1949, this painting was restored, portraits of saints were added along two upper walls, and the portrait of St. Cecilia in the choir loft was restored. During an early 1970s renovation, the baptismal area was converted into a new side entrance which includes a restroom and a ramp leading to the parking area. Air conditioning and bells were also installed at this time, and one of the confessionals was changed into a shrine area to include statues of saints and votive candles. A sacristy near the sanctuary was changed into a Blessed Sacrament Chapel, a place for small group Masses and for private prayer in the Lord's Eucharistic presence within the Tabernacle. An extensive interior and exterior restoration occurred between 1979 and 1984. This included cleaning of outside bricks, improvements to the bell towers, new sanctuary furnishings, building of a small porch at the front entrance, restoration of paintings and statues, and redoing of confessionals to meet liturgical requirements. Just as the Church building has changed over the years, so have there been many changes and different efforts at ministry on the part of the Church, that is, the people. To help meet the needs of the needy, a St. Vincent De Paul Society Conference was organized in 1922 and has continued numerous and generous works of charity to the present day. In 1989, the St. Vincent De Paul groups from St. Francis De Sales and from St. Thomas More united to form one conference to represent the Paducah Catholic Community in outreach to those in need.

Other societies organized include: The Altar Society (1869), The Sodality of the Blessed Virgin Mary (1872), The Holy Name Society (1912), The Knights of Columbus (1905), The Daughters of Isabella (1923), Knights of Columbus Ladies Auxiliary (1906) and Catholic Boy Scouts (1917).

From 1858 until its closing in 1965, St. Mary Academy (under direction of the Sisters of Charity of Nazareth) provided Catholic School education for students in Grades 1-12. In 1965, St. Mary High School, an interparochial Catholic school, was established while St. Francis De Sales Grade School began in the former St. Mary Academy building at 4th and Monroe. In 1974, this grade school was moved to the former Rosary Chapel School building and, in 1982, St. Francis De Sales Grade School and St. Thomas More Grade School were consolidated into St. Mary Elementary School. St. Mary Middle School was established in 1991 and a new building for St. Mary Elementary School was completed in 1992. The St. Mary School System continues the tradition of providing Catholic School education for the families of St. Francis De Sales Parish.

"Catechism" lessons have been offered through the years for students in public schools. In the late 1960s, a CCD program was organized and, with the help of many generous people, continues to provide religious instruction and formation. In 1989, the CCD programs of St. Francis De Sales and St. Thomas More were united to form the Paducah CCD Program.

With the Vatican II Council's urging of more involvement of lay persons, the first Parish Council was initiated in 1970. The first Eucharistic Ministers were appointed in 1973. In 1975, the people of the parish began welcoming and relocating of 25 Vietnamese families. As more members became actively involved, more trained leadership was needed in addition to the priests. In 1974, two Sisters of Charity of Nazareth began as Pastoral Ministers in the parish, becoming some of the first in this ministry in the Diocese. In 1983-86, the RENEW process involved even more people in faith-sharing groups and apostolic action. The Parish continues to thrive and the number and variety of ministries increase as more and more members share their time, talent and treasure.

St. Francis de Sales, Paducah, KY.

St. Jerome Parish
Fancy Farm

WE REMEMBER, WE CELEBRATE, WE BELIEVE
WITH GRATITUDE AND HOPE!

June 10, 1992: 100th Anniversary of the death of Samuel Willett (1808-1892), the "founder" in 1829 of "the Catholic Settlement" with his wife, Elizabeth d/o Jesse & Mary (Elder) Hobbs.

In the 1830s "the Catholic settlement" included at least the following families: Stephen Ballard; Charles Bright; Cornelius & Henry Carrico; James & John Cash; Thomas Curtsinger; James Elliott; George, Henry, John, Samuel, Thomas Jr., Thomas Sr., & William Hayden; Alfred, Horatio, Jerome, John, Joseph, Mary, & Samuel W. Hobbs; John B. Pierceall; Solomon Riley; Benjamin & John S. Roberts; Samuel & William Thomas; Hilary, Stanish Lloyd, & William Toon; and Samuel Willett. Most of the pioneers were from St. Rose Priory Parish (Dominicans), Springfield, Washington Co.

Fall 1992: 100th Anniversary of the arrival of the Sisters of Charity of Nazareth.

Franciscan Sisters of Shelbyville (now Clinton, IA) at St. Jerome School from 1882-1890; Sisters of Charity of Nazareth from 1892-1975, and as pastoral ministers from 1983-1989 and since 1992. Vocations: Priests (13); Religious Sisters (88: SCN - 48, OSU - 15, OSF - 10, Others - 15) Brothers (6); Bishop R. Pierre DuMaine of San Jose CA, whose mother, Mary Eula Burch, was from Fancy Farm.

March 15, 1993: 150th Anniversary of the establishment of a Post Office.

The post office at Fancy Farm was established on March 15, 1843, with John Peebles as the first postmaster. Thus, the first use of the name Fancy Farm to designate a particular area in northwest Graves Co. was in 1843. On the first Saturday of August each year, a blend of politics, community spirit and home cooking puts the Fancy Farm Picnic in KY Headlines.

April 16, 1993: 150th Anniversary of the first resident pastor.

Resident pastors at St. Jerome: Revs. A. Hagan (1843), P. McNichols (1847), W. Oberhulsman (1850), P. Bambury (1857), J. Beyhurst (1859), W.P. Bourke (1863), J. Barrett (1869), Carmelite Fathers (1871), R. Feehan (1881), L. Ford (1884), J. Taylor (1888), C. Haeseley (1888), A. Thompson (1920), E. Russell (1935), C. DeNardi (1962), W. Hancock (1972), W.J. Riney (1983), L. Hayden (1989), R. Goetz (1992). St. Jerome Community was served by Rev. Elisha J. Durbin, the Patriarch of the Catholic Church in Western KY, with his first baptisms recorded in 1832, and the last in 1882.

November 29, 1993: 100th Anniversary of the dedication of the present church.

The first church at St. Jerome, which was the first Catholic church in the Jackson Purchase, was a small log building, built in 1836 by Rev. Elisha J. Durbin. The second church, erected in 1854, was of brick. The third, and present St. Jerome, was completed in the fall of 1892, and was solemnly blessed by Bishop W. George McCloskey on November 29, 1893. In the 1986 Sesquicentennial Celebration of the first church, there was included the publication of "A History of St. Jerome, Fancy Farm, KY" (266 pgs, 827 pictures).

St. John The Baptist Parish
Fordsville

In August of 1893 Father Lawrence Ford offered Mass for the first time in the newly completed mission church of St. John the Baptist in Ohio County. Father Ford will long be remembered for his generous work in Ohio County. Before him other priests had visited this area of Ohio County from St. Mary's in Whitesville, but no parish had been established as of yet. In 1896, Bishop McClosky visited the mission and administered the Sacrament of Confirmation to nine people. This parish is still in existence today although it is now moved to Fordsville.

In the 1940s a more consistent effort at evangelization began in this area. Visiting beyond the immediate area of St. John Church, Father Henry O'Bryan contacted some Catholics as far away as Rosine and Adaburg. Then Father Walter Hancock and after him Father William Hagman began to offer Sunday Mass at St. John's. The Catholic congregation began to grow a little. But then the migration towards town slowly depleted the parish numbers once again.

In early 1965 Bishop Soenneker asked the Glenmary Home Missioners to accept St. John's as part of their mission territory, which would now cover the whole of Ohio County. The loyal Catholic families still present in the area began attending Mass on Sunday evenings at 6:00 pm.

In October of that year Father Joe O'Donnell was appointed pastor of the mission (while also taking care of Holy Redeemer in Beaver Dam and Holy Trinity in Morgantown.) It became evident to him and the parishioners that the future growth of St. John Parish would depend on the willingness of all to move this base parish to Fordsville. A mission team of Glenmary seminarians and other volunteers was sent to the Fordsville area where they discovered a few more Catholic families. (Among them was the future Father Tony Shonis, now a priest of the Diocese of Owensboro.)

The first Mass offered in Fordsville was in the lunchroom at the public school on the Feast of the Assumption 1966. Soon after that, a Protestant couple let the Catholics move a chapel trailer onto their property. This became the present site of St. John Church. Sunday Mass was offered weekly. Soon the mobile chapel was filled to overflowing each Sunday. The adjacent house and property were purchased by the diocese. The first floor was gutted out for a temporary church. (That house was later converted to a social hall, now known as Father Yunker Hall.) The congregation continued to grow in number and spirit.

In 1971 Father Louis P. Yunker, a retired priest of the Diocese of Pittsburgh, Pennsylvania, took up residence at St. John's in Fordsville. As he became more known in town he soon became a loved figure among all the Protestant community. Also among those who did significant church work in the area was Brother Jim Dorn (later a Glenmary priest). He was especially appreciated for his effective leadership with young people.

In 1976 the Glenmary Building Crew came to Fordsville and constructed the present church building. The church was dedicated by Bishop Soenneker on July 11, 1976. The congregation continued to grow. The appreciation for the Catholic Church as an accepted part of the community was more and more taken for granted. Father Yunker continued his priestly presence until serious disability forced him into complete retirement.

During this time a young woman, Beatrice Meany, who had done several years of lay mission work in Africa came to Fordsville as a missionary. She did a wonderful job of bringing this small community of Catholics together to make a vibrant witness-group throughout the area. Tony Shonis spent a year doing mission work at St. John's and gave instructions to the people who were interested in joining the Church. Among others who helped the parish of St. John's with sacramental ministry were Father Ed Gorny of Glenmary and Father Joe Mills a diocesan priest of Owensboro. Many others also helped.

When Father O'Donnell returned as pastor in 1981 he found it most difficult to give a meaningful witness in three parishes. There was a real need again for genuine Catholic leadership by someone who could live in town. On August 13, 1983 Sister Diane Marie Payne, an Ursuline sister, came to reside in the apartment attached to the church building. (She was the first sister of her community to go into pastoral ministry.) Due to the effective ministry of Sister Diane the congregation continued to grow. Converts came into the Church. On many Sundays the new church building was full. Sister Diane is now in her ninth year at St. John's and continues to be well-appreciated by the whole community of Fordsville.

With the shortage of priests, Father O'Donnell found it necessary to have Mass on Sunday evening at 6:00 pm at St. John's. Even though this difficult change has forced some people to go to other churches for Liturgy, the parish core remains firm in its loyalty to St. John's. There is great hope for the future. Thanks be to God.

St. John The Evangelist Parish
Paducah

*"If we work upon marble, it will perish.
If we work upon brass, time will efface it.
If we rear temples, they will crumble to dust.
But if we work upon men's immortal minds,
if we imbue them with high principles,
with the just fear of God, and love of their
fellow men, we engrave on those tablets
something which no time can efface and
which will brighten and brighten to all
eternity."* —Daniel Webster

From its beginning at gatherings in neighbors homes during the first half of the nineteenth century, and continuing through the construction of three church buildings, the tenures of countless religious, and generations of parishioners, the faith of the congregation of St. John the Evangelist Catholic Church has continued to grow and flourish. St. John school has given hundreds of children instruction in their religion as well as basic subjects through the years. Through the selfless efforts of diocesan priests, religious sisters, and devoted parents, our parish has fostered many religious vocations, successful farmers, business professionals, and even professional baseball players. The following history traces the development of the small settlement of German immigrants and the accomplishments which have shaped the parish into its present form.

The first Catholics to settle in southern McCracken County began to arrive in the area now known as St. John around 1834. The lives of these German immigrants were very hard, having suffered many hardships and, for some, the loss of family members on their journeys to this country. Unfortunately, little written testimony of these travels is available. It is known, however, that those staunch pioneers brought the faith with them, and it has been the heart and soul of the St. John Community ever since.

Founding

The Centenary Of Catholicity In Kentucky by Ben J. Webb notes "about the year 1834 Father Elisha J. Durbin began visiting a number of German Catholic immigrants who had settled a distance of twelve miles from Paducah."

These early parishioners were visited by Father Durbin who had been assigned the missions throughout the territory that today make up the Diocese of Owensboro. His apostolic journeys frequently took him to scattered Catholics in southern Indiana, Illinois, and Tennessee. His headquarters was at Sacred Heart Church, St. Vincent in Union County, Kentucky.

The story of Father Durbin's arrival at the small community known then as Adrian, Kentucky, has been told in this way. Several men were standing in a field talking when a stranger approached and inquired if any were Catholic. One man, Adrian Grief, answered that he was. Father Durbin asked him if he might say Mass in his home the next morning. Mr. Grief looked into the weather-beaten face of the priest with much doubt, for the weary priest looked like anything but a priest. Seeing his doubt, Father Durbin dismounted his horse, removed his saddle bags and displayed the chalice, altar stone and vestments. With great joy Father was welcomed into the Grief home and the first Mass ever offered at St. John was said there the next morning. For many years thereafter, whenever a missionary priest visited, Mass was offered in the Grief home.

The privilege of Mass and the Sacraments was not accorded the people of the St. John community very often in these early days since Father Durbin's missionary journeys covered such a large area with the Catholic population being widely scattered. Horseback journeying an average of 200 miles a week was not uncommon for Father Durbin. In later years, it was estimated that he had traveled over 500,000 miles on horseback.

Church at St. John

On October 8, 1849, as recorded in McCracken County Deed book E, page 484, John W. and Rosena Roof donated to Benedict Joseph Flaget, Roman Catholic Bishop of Louisville, Ky and to his successors in the office of Bishop as aforesaid, a certain tract or parcel of land containing 20 acres in form of a square, lying on the South Eastern corner of the North West quarter of section twenty-nine township six range one East bought by me of William Enders and being the part of said quarter section on which the Roman Catholic Chapel of Saint John is now built to have and to hold the same forever in trust for the use and benefit of the Roman Catholic Congregation attending the said Church.

This first church, a log building, was raised by the parishioners under the direction of Father Elisha Durbin. The log church burned and was replaced by a larger frame structure in 1869, during the pastorate of Father Peter Haeseley. Nothing else is known of the log church, but the frame church was used for sixty-three years. At the construction of the present church building, the frame structure was moved across the road. Even though the moving process took several days, each morning Mass was held inside the building before the day's activity began. Mass continued to be offered in the old church until the new church was completed. From 1938-1956, it was used for the high school. Later it was sold, dismantled, and used in the construction of the current home of parishioner Albert Gill.

It is known that the people of St. John donated generously to the building of the new church. Many borrowed money to do so during the midst of the Great Depression. One family, Louis Wurtz, unable to make the requested cash contribution, donated twenty acres of land which was located at the corner of Old Highway 45 and Lebanon Church Road. A lake was developed on the property to use in addition to Jeffrey Springs at Leeder Bottom, as a source of water for livestock during periods of dry weather. It was also used by the community for fishing and swimming. The lake was later closed and in May 1974 was sold to Howard Cash.

In addition to the monetary contributions, parishioners donated manual labor and the use of horse and mule teams for hauling, pulling, and leveling.

Unfortunately, little information remains concerning the building of the brick church. Blueprints, supply lists, and other pertinent information no longer exists. With construction estimates of $35,000,00, a Paducah native William B. Roetteis was hired as the contractor. Thomas J. Nolan, Sr. of Louisville was the architect.

Ground was broken for the new church on July 28, 1932, and the cornerstone was laid September 4th of that year. Sealed within a steel box in the cornerstone are various documents, listing pastor, sisters, parishioners, and members and officers of the various church sodalities and societies. Included also were copies of the local newspaper and the Catholic paper the *The Record*. The interior walls of the church were constructed of used brick which was hauled from Paducah by parishioners before the start of construction. Many trips were needed to transport the brick due to the weight and the inability of the teams to pull heavy loads over the hilly roads.

The church structure is described in *Architecture of Paducah and McCracken County* by Camille Wells as "a brick nave-plan structure with a polygonal apse, corner bell tower, and advanced front vestibule. Salient buttresses, corner pinacles, and lancet, or pointed openings give the church a weighty, English Gothic quality." The carved sandstone details are similar to those of the Broadway Methodist Church and the Westminister Presbyterian Church in Paducah and have been attributed to the same skillful artisans.

On Sunday morning, June 25, 1933, the new church was dedicated by the Most Rev. Bishop John A. Floresh. The interior and exterior walls were blessed after which the doors were opened the first time for divine service. Solemn Mass was celebrated by pastor Rev. Paul Barrett, assisted by nine priests. Bishop Floersh preached the dedicatory sermon entitled, "Why We Have Churches," in which he complimented the zealous and sacrificing labor of the pastor and parishioners.

It is unclear where the first resident priests lived while serving in our parish. Reportedly, it was not uncommon for priests to live in the church buildings during that period.

Father Francis Felton who served as pastor from 1895-1898 is credited with the building of the two-story wood frame rectory. It was used until the present rectory was completed in August of 1964 during the pastorate of Rev. Richard Clements. The new one story structure was designed in the same style, using the same color of brick with stone trim, as used in the other buildings on the church grounds.

St. John The Evangelist Parish
Sunfish

The history of St. John the Evangelist Parish, Sunfish, Kentucky, the only Catholic church in Edmonson County, began as most Kentucky parishes with the missionary activities of many great priests such as: Father Whelan, the first priest sent to Kentucky by Bishop Carroll in 1787; Father Stephen Baden in 1793; Father Nerinckx in 1797; and Father M. Salmon in 1799. Father Baden visited the Durbin and Logsdon families in Madison County from which several families migrated to the Sunfish area, probably around 1796.

Father Nerinckx was probably the most active and efficient of all the priests sent to Kentucky. By 1805, he had erected at least ten churches helping with the manual labor. He spent much of his time traveling around the state on his horse, Printer.

The family of John J. Durbin and Patience Logsdon was living in Scott County in 1816 (Edmonson County was not formed until 1825) when their son, Elisha, age 16, entered the seminary at Bardstown. In 1822, when Father Elisha was ordained, almost all his family lived in Sunfish.

The first church in Sunfish was built in 1830 on the land given to Father Elisha by his father. The present church still stands on this ground. This pioneer priest outranked even the fabulous Father DeSmet in the extent of his frontier journeys. His travels earned for Father Elisha the epithet of "Apostle of Western Kentucky" and "Patriarch-Priest of Kentucky." Father Elisha Durbin was given the care of western and southwestern Kentucky, about one-third of the state. He then began a missionary career of over 60 years, hardly paralleled in the U.S. He rode a total of 500,000 miles on horseback, stopping at log cabin churches and eating at farmers' houses after hearing Confessions the whole morning. Often his only fare was cornbread, salt pork, and water. He died in 1887.

In 1835, Father Degauquier was given the mission of Central Kentucky which included the church at Sunfish.

St. John is a mission of St. Joseph in Leitchfield. It is eighteen miles to the south of St. Joseph. According to records, Rev. Louis Beruatto, pastor of St. Joseph, spent many years ministering to the Sunfish people. He performed marriages and baptisms from 1908 to 1949.

The first resident priests were the Glenmary priests from Ohio. Father Clemens Borchers came in 1942. There was a small school where the Sisters of St. Francis from St. Francis, Wisconsin taught about eighty students, grades 1-12, from 1941 to 1971. They lived on the second floor of the school, while a small two-room shack had been built to accommodate the occasional overnight stay of Father Beruatto. Father Howard Bishop, the Glenmary founder, referred to it as a "frame shack of about the type used as camp shacks and hunting lodges." It was a Spartan rectory, heated by a wood-burning stove; a hundred yards away was the water cistern and the outdoor toilet facility about that same distance from the house. Father Borchers did not complain about the primitive rectory, he said: "Hardships? Where are they? I left all of that in the city. What a sweet, peaceful serenity always."

In 1944, a new three-room house was built which was used as a rectory until August 1990 when the Mount Saint Joseph Ursulines began their ministry working with the people in this beautiful setting. This Holy Saturday of 1992, ten people were received into the Church, the following Sunday three more were baptized.

The Glenmary priests were here from 1942-1971. Others were: Rev. Richard Bolands, Rev. Joseph O'Donnell, and Rev. Joseph Nagele.

The Diocesan priests were: Rev. William and Phillip Field; Rev. Benjamin Powers, who was killed in an accident between Sunfish and Bowling Green while performing his priestly duties at Sunfish; Rev. Brad Whistle; Rev. Gerald Calhoun; and Rev. Gregory G. Trawick, who is the present pastor. The parish consists of 67 families.

St. John, Sunfish, KY.

The New Sunfish Rectory, St. John Fr. Clem Borchers, ca. 1940. This building is now the convent.

St. John (L to R): Fr. Charles DeNardi, Fr. John Dudine, Fr. Louis Beruatto and Fr. Clem Borchers.

St. Joseph Parish
Bowling Green

One of the historic landmarks of Bowling Green, KY is St. Joseph Catholic Church, at 434 Church St., situated in the oldest part of the city- "between the river and the railroad". In 1975 the church was listed on the National Register of Historic Places as possessing exceptional interest and worthy of preservation because of its history and artistically significant architecture. Its history is an integral part of the story of Catholic Christianity in Kentucky and the c.1859 parish provides its own thread of beauty and diversity to the colorful tapestry that is Bowling Green-Warren County history.

Kentucky was the first western star in the American flag when it entered the Union in 1792. Catholic settlers came first to Kentucky in 1775 emigrating chiefly from Maryland. By 1808, the number of frontier Catholics had grown so steadily that a Bishop, Benedict Joseph Flaget, had been consecrated for this people. Thus the oldest inland American Diocese of Bardstown was underway. Bishop Flaget and his priests rode horseback over 800 miles to minister to his flock. In 1841, the headquarters of the Bardstown Diocese was moved to Louisville, a much larger and growing riverport. A little later Louisville became also the railhead of one of the major railroad lines of the nation - the L. & N.

It was this same Louisville and Nashville Railroad which in 1856 began the construction of a bridge over the Barren River. Bowling Green became a scene of great activity as many German and Irish Catholic laborers were drawn to the area. They urgently requested a priest from then Bishop of Louisville, Martin John Spalding. He appointed as missionary pastor of the southern Kentucky counties, Rev. Joseph DeVries, who had come to Kentucky in 1853 from the seminary in his native Holland and was ordained a priest by Bishop Spalding in 1855. In 1859 Fr. DeVries was asked to organize a parish and build a church at Bowling Green.

During that summer a crude frame building was hurriedly built on a lot donated by a non-Catholic friend, Euclid Covington, a member of a prominent Warren County family. This small temporary mission sat north of the present Rectory on the corner of what is now Church and Barry Sts. It served as a school during the week and was converted to a church for Mass on Sundays. Immediately, work was begun on a brick church dedicated to St. Joseph. Mass was celebrated there for the first time on Easter Sunday 1860, but due to the outbreak of the Civil War, it was not completed and dedicated until 1862.

St. Joseph Church as it is today rose in stages from this small 1860 brick building through an 1870 addition at the east end of higher and wider

walls containing the semi-circular apse with the sanctuary and three altars. This served until 1884 when further enlargement became imperative. The higher walls were extended to the street completely surrounding the original church which was then torn down. This final addition and enlargement of the magnificent cathedral-like structure that is St. Joseph Church today took five years for completion. It was consecrated May 4, 1889. Fr. DeVries had spent the years 1875-77 in Europe on leave from his parish. He no doubt visited the Cathedral at Cologne, as it was being completed in the 1870s after having been started in the 14th century. When he came back, the young pastor envisioned the enlarged church as a modified replica of Cologne. The interior is classic Gothic architecture with its tall ribbed vault ceilings, massive pillars with Corinthian capitals, and the apse which contains the sanctuary and three hand carved altars, separated from the nave of the church by a handsome curving communion rail of native cherry.

The wall-hung Stations of the Cross, the ornate Baptismal Font, and many of the sculptured images in the church, finished in soft polychrome and outstanding in their beauty, were in the church in 1889.

Fr. DeVries died three months after the consecration of his "miniature Cologne" erected to the honor and glory of God in Kentucky. In deference to his wishes, he was buried in a vault under the main altar. A marble slab on the sanctuary wall marks his resting place. His beloved church became thus his monument and his tomb.

The second pastor, Rev. Thomas J. Hayes served the parish 54 years. An Irishman and a fine musician, his first legacy was the installation in 1898 of the Grand Organ. This magnificent instrument has thirteen ranks of pipes, a case of white quarter-oak with wood carved angel trumpeters on pedestals high above the console. The choir, formed and nurtured by Fr. Hayes, was renowned in the Diocese of Louisville for its excellence for many years.

The original (1903) fresco artwork was an exuberant interpretation of the Gothic style of decorating all interior members to the utmost; the dome filled with choirs of angels in clouds of glory and the ribs entwined with garlands of roses. Louisville artists Charles and Guido Leber executed the original artwork. Their descendants were involved each time the frescoes were renovated and simplified until the complete redecoration in 1986, painted by L. Sylvester of Bloomington, Illinois.

In 1911 St. Joseph Parochial School and convent home for the Sisters of Charity of Nazareth, who taught there some 60 years, were built. Fr. Hayes was the oldest priest in the Diocese of Owensboro when it was created in 1937. He died March 19, 1946. His successor was Rev. Joseph Spalding, who had been his associate for three years.

Rev. Charles P. Bowling, 1947-1971, was only the fourth pastor of the church in its one hundred year history. He presided at the Centennial celebration in 1959. In preparation for this, the interior was redecorated and some additions were made to the frescoes. An exquisite grill-work pattern of gold leaf chalice and grapes was added to the sanctuary walls at this time. The 1898 organ was electrified then. The original Gothic canopied hand carved pulpit that had been attached high on the front right column, was removed for safety reasons. Fr. Bowling guided St. Joseph's through the first liturgical changes made by Vatican II and also the transition period when the parish was divided and Holy Spirit Parish was formed. St. Joseph became the "mother church" in Bowling Green. It is still held dear in the hearts of its former parishioners and pastors. Structural repair, and renovation continue, but the changes dictated by liturgical reform and modern life-style have all been done with an eye to retaining the integrity of the original.

The history of a church is best told in its people. The priests, nuns, and loyal laity of St. Joseph Parish, will all be remembered as the "people of God" who worked in the construction and preservation of this historic church, as one of God's best gifts in the beauty of his Creation.

St. Joseph Parish
Central City

The first Mass celebrated in Central City was in the home of Tom & Ellen May shortly after the Civil War. At that time, the Diocese was located in Bardstown, and priests had to travel on horseback throughout the state. With such an area to cover, a priest would come to Muhlenberg County only once or twice a year. The first recorded Baptism in the County was that of Martin Richardson in 1892.

In November of 1885, Mr. DuPont Edwards, President of Central Coal & Iron Company donated property located on West Second and Walnut Streets for the building of a Catholic Church. Local railroad men built the original church on this land in 1886. The Church was named St. Martin Catholic Church. Father M.F. Medley came from Leitchfield to offer Mass and helped in building the church. After a short time at that location, the Church was moved up the street to West Second and Main due to construction of the Illinois Central Railroad. Not long after the relocation, the Church burned to the ground.

In 1909, Edward and Mary Miller donated to the Diocese of Louisville a parcel of land located on the corner of South Third and Broad Streets. The present Church was built on this property in 1912, at which time the name was changed to St. Joseph Catholic Church. Dedication services were conducted on August 12, 1912 by the Most Rev. D.D. O'Donaghue, Bishop of Louisville. Father P.H. Monaghan was celebrant of the Mass. The beautiful stained glass windows which adorn the church were crafted by a German firm in St. Louis, Missouri and were donated by the parishioners.

Property was acquired in 1919 for a Catholic School. In 1923, St. Joseph School opened its doors under the tutelage of the Ursuline Sisters of Mt. St. Joseph. During the pastorate of Father Lucian Hayden, funds were obtained for the building of a new school to replace the inadequate two story frame building which housed grades one through ten plus the Sisters. Under the direction of Father James Wathen, the new school was constructed behind the Church in 1969. In 1975, the Ursulines returned to Mt. St. Joseph and the school was maintained by a lay faculty until its closing at the end of the 1984-85 school year.

In February of 1928, St. Charles Church in Livermore became a mission of St. Joseph. It remained a mission of St. Joseph until 1970.

Records indicate that Father Rudolph Ruff was the first resident pastor, assigned to Central City in 1899. He was transferred to Leitchfield and St. Joseph Church became a mission until Father Charles Marshall was assigned as resident pastor in February 1928. At that time, there were 230 parishioners on record.

Prior to 1940, the priests who ministered in Central City lived in the Gish Apartments of Broad Street. In the mid 1940s, a house on Third and Reynolds Streets was donated to the Church to be used as a Rectory. The present rectory on South Third Street was purchased in 1956.

The parish is presently administered by Franciscan Father Francis Mastrovito, T.O.R.

St. Joseph Church
Leitchfield

As far back as 1840 there were Catholics in and around Leitchfield. The spiritual needs of these Catholics were attended to by zealous missionaries from Hardin County and from St. Augustine Church in Grayson County. Among these pioneer priests were Father Thomas Joyce, Father Patrick Bambury and Father Augustine Degauquier. According to past recollections, Mass was said at the home of Joe Edelen which used to stand about one block south of the Court House. In the same house, the visiting priests heard confessions and instructed the children in their Catechism.

Church services were also conducted in the house of John Owens, a prominent merchant of Leitchfield. Among the prominent members of the congregation at the time were: Joe C. Edelen, John Owens, W.L. Conklin, Justin Higdon, Mrs. M. Goldsbury, Henry Horrell, James Burtle, Andrew Burtle, James Mattingly, Gustie Higdon, and A. Mudd.

In 1869 the local congregation bought the Valentine Yates property where the church parsonage is still located. Father Vandermergel moved to Leitchfield from Grayson Springs where he was pastor of St. Augustine Church, the oldest Catholic church in Grayson County. He took up residence in the year 1870.

At first a lot on Market Street had been bought from J.J. Rogers as a church site, but the congregation became dissatisfied with the idea and a committee composed of J.C. Edelen, Dan O'Riley, James Burtle, G. Higdon, and W.L. Conklin was named to solicit funds to erect the structure on its present location. At that time the railroad connecting Elizabethtown and Paducah was being built through Grayson County, this brought a number of Catholic families into the area. Several of the Irish Catholics cooperated with the pastor to the best of their ability in building a new church. Father Vandermergel remained in Leitchfield until his death July 1, 1873. He was succeeded by Father Melody.

Father Melody came from Lewisport. The interior of the church was finished and the inside of the rectory was improved under his direction.

During Father Melody's stay of about six years, the church had a parochial school on the corner of North Main and West Chestnut. The school was taught by two graduates of Nazareth College, Misses Nora Leary and Fanny Wilkerson. The pupils numbered sixty including non-catholics.

The school which began under encouraging auspices closed five years later in 1880 due to low enrollment.

Father Melody, determined to have a school, purchased a two story residence from Hoza Bishop for two thousand dollars. This building was sold in 1890 because many prominent catholics had moved away from Leitchfield and Bishop McClosky ordered the sale.

Father Melody remained as pastor in Leitchfield until 1886. He was then sent to Hopkinsville.

Immediately after ordination on December 21, 1887, Reverend Henry L. Egart was sent to St. Joseph's where he remained as pastor until his death on March 29, 1890.

Father Anthony O'Sullivan took over as pastor until February 1891. He was followed by: Rev. Englebert Schmitt, who remained until January 1892; Rev. Martin O'Conner, who had charge until July 1903; Rev. R.C. Ruff, who stayed until 1907; Rev. Joseph Minch, who was here until October 1907; Rev. H.J. Muyssen, who was the pastor here until July, 1908.

On October 9, 1908, Father Louis Beruatto became pastor of St. Joseph Church. In the three quarters of a century of its existence, St. Joseph had eleven pastors, Father Beruatto staying longer than his ten predecessors, namely 48 years. Father Beruatto was ordained on May 13, 1906 in Turin, Italy and in November of that year came to the United States. In October of 1908 he arrived here to serve as pastor of St. Joseph Church. In February of 1943 Father Beruatto was elevated to the rank of Domestic Prelate of the Pope with the title of Right Reverend Monsignor by Bishop Francis R. Cotton.

While at St. Joseph's his greatest achievement was the opening of the parochial school in 1948 with the Sisters of St. Francis from Minnesota in charge. Later the Ursuline Sisters of Mount Saint Joseph had charge of the school.

Msgr. Beruatto was here until 1956 at which time he returned to his native Italy.

Rev. Charles Hughes followed Msgr. Beruatto and was here until 1957. Father Richard Danhauer was here during the summer of 1957. Some years later he returned to Grayson County as pastor of St. Paul.

Rev. Albert Thompson came in 1957 and was here for about four years. Father Thompson purchased new pews and made new steps during his stay.

He was followed by Rev. George Hancock who was here until the fall of 1963. He then became Chancellor of the Diocese.

He was followed by Father Raymond Berthianume who remained here until the spring of 1964.

Father Bernard Powers assumed his duties as pastor until 1967. Then he was made Chaplin at Mount Saint Joseph.

On Thursday, May 4, 1967 a most solemn and impressive ceremony was held at St. Joseph Church, when Rev. Carroll Lewis White, son of Mr. and Mrs. Hugh White was ordained as a priest by the Most Rev. Henry Soenneker, Bishop of Owensboro.

To our great sorrow Father White was killed in a car accident in December, 1969. His body lies in St. Joseph Cemetery, Leitchfield.

Rev. William Borntrager was pastor from 1967 until 1969.

Rev. Robert Wilson, who had been pastor at Peonia returned to Grayson County and pastor of the Leitchfield church arriving to assume his duties in 1969. He was active in civic events and President of the local Ministerial Association. In the fall of 1970, Rev. William Fields came to assist in the work of the parish. He became pastor at St. John's, Sunfish in 1971.

In 1970 the school was closed by Father Wilson.

In 1972 a new rectory was made possible under the direction of Father Wilson with the combined funds of Delma Mauzey, Mrs. Richie Cannon and St. Joseph Parish.

Father Wilson was known as the "Builder Priest." He was transferred in 1977 when Father Leo J. Dienes was appointed to St. Joseph. Father Dienes was here until 1985.

During the time that Father Dienes was pastor, three young men from St. Joseph parish were ordained to the priesthood. Richard Meredith, ordained on June 3, 1978, and John Meredith, ordained on January 12, 1980, are the sons of William Percy and Margie Mae Simpson Meredith. Anthony Stevenson, son of Floyd and Mary Clark Stevenson, was ordained on January 10, 1981.

Father Anthony Stevenson was appointed here for a few months until Father Gerald Calhoun could assume his duties later in 1985. Father Calhoun was pastor until 1990 when he was appointed to Holy Spirit in Bowling Green.

Presently, Father Gregory G. Trawick is pastor of St. Joseph.

On January 2, 1991 the old school building next to St. Joseph church was demolished to make room for a new Parish Center. Plans for the new center were formulated under the leadership of Father Calhoun, but actual work on the new building did not begin until Father Trawick became pastor. The building was dedicated on September 29, 1991 with Bishop John McRaith presiding.

St. Joseph Parish
Mayfield

The history of St. Joseph Parish began over one hundred and eighteen years ago with the purchase of a plot of ground, where the present Church now stands for $125. The building of the Church began in 1887 by Father Lawrence Ford. It was dedicated on April 19, 1887. Prior to this time all of the spiritual needs of the parish were taken care of by the pastor at Fancy Farm. A plot of ground was donated by J.R. Blanford, to be used as a cemetery.

Among the names of members about this time were Jack Willett, Victor Lebre, James Touhey, Jack Conroy, Hugh Murphy, Martin Erwin, John Lenihan, James Hyland, John Kinney, Martin Leonard, John Sweeney and the Tom Carman family.

During the following years there was a succession of devoted pastors: Father Thomas A. York, 1889-1892; Father George Weiss, 1892-1893; Father W. King, 1893-1897. These priests also had charge of missions at Columbus, Kentucky, and Union City, Tennessee. Mass at St. Joseph's was now being said once a month on Sunday. Father King established a school here.

January 1898 found Father L.E. Clements in charge. He continued the school, with twenty-five students, both Catholic and non-Catholic. It was taught by Mrs. Ella Curtsinger. Father Clements also added a tower and choir loft to the Church and donated the bell which was rung for the first time on Easter Sunday of 1900.

In 1902 Father Clements was succeeded by Father George Cone who was succeeded by Father P.J. McNeil in May 1903. Father McNeil established a mission at Fulton and built a rectory at St. Joseph's. He purchased new pews for the Church, as well as having concrete walks built around the property.

Father Anthony O'Sullivan came to St. Joseph's in 1909 and remained here until 1926. He took a great interest in the youth, Catholic and non-Catholic alike, and was a Boy Scout leader. He was given a leave-of-absence in 1926 because of ill health, and left to help his brother, also a priest, restore a Mission in California, where, ten years later, he died. He was buried next to his brother at San Juan Capistrano, California.

Father Louis Millard came here in March, 1926 and remained until 1932. During his time at St. Joseph's, he started having daily Masses.

Father Millard's successor was Father J.H. Luckett, who served us from 1932-1937. In 1934 the property east of the Church was purchased, and the first Sisters' School began, with the Ursuline Order of Sisters in charge.

Father Joseph Saffer came to St. Joseph's in 1937 and bent his entire efforts toward the building of a new Church. This was accomplished, and dedicated on May 4, 1938, by Bishop Francis R. Cotton.

In 1949 Father Saffer was succeeded by Father Leo J. Dienes under whose supervision the new school was completed in 1951 with living quarters for the Sisters on the third floor. The High School was discontinued in May, 1965.

From 1957 to 1963 Father Clarence Pettit was pastor. During his stay, he organized the St. Vincent de Paul Society.

From 1963 to 1969 Father Aloysius F. Powers was pastor. It was under his direction that the present rectory was built in 1964.

In August of 1969 Father Francis Mastrovito of the Franciscan Order was assigned to St. Joseph's. Father Francis made many physical changes to the inside of the Church. He extended the playground for the children. He dismantled the old Church, and in its place he built the St. Joseph Parish Center. In 1974 a local chapter of the Knights of Columbus was formed.

In 1983 Father Francis was succeeded by Father John Speaks. He was responsible for introducing the Renew Program into the parish, and did much of the preparatory work for our Centennial Celebration in 1987.

Father Peter Chiodo of the Precious Blood Order was assigned to St. Joseph's in July 1987 and remained until July, 1988. During this time he purchased the lot to the south of the school to add to the property.

Father Henry Cecil arrived here in July, 1988. He has been instrumental in enlarging the children's playground and putting a new roof on the school which is still flourishing.

Father Patrick Bittel was appointed Pastor in June, 1990. Under his direction the Church grounds have been landscaped including the children's playground. A cry room was added to the Church which was badly needed for years. Also a new reconciliation room with a very warm atmosphere was put together by Father and the Knights of Columbus. We have purchased more property in order that we have sufficient parking for the future. Our Church Roster now stands at 500 family units. Our school continues to grow and operate a balanced budget yearly as does our Parish. Father Bittel continues to urge all to get involved in parish and community activities. Our Youth are responding beautifully under Father's leadership.

We look forward to the coming years and what they will bring as we strive to build the kingdom.

St. Joseph Parish
Owensboro

St. Joseph Church in Owensboro was born out of the unrest that swept Germany about 1830. A young missionary priest by the name of Joseph Kundek, ordained in 1833, heard of the need for missionaries in America. In the fall of 1838 he arrived as rector of the mission of Jasper, Indiana. He created a "little Germany" in the hills of Southern Indiana. By 1850 more than 150,000 Germans had come to the United States and some of these settlers drifted south of the Ohio River to live in Owensboro. Because of the diversity of the cultures in the area, clashes resulted. Since St. Stephen was the only Catholic Church, the German Catholics had to attend it in order to celebrate Mass. However, they were allowed to worship only from the back pews of the church. Prejudice against the Germans continued for years.

In 1870 Father Paul Joseph Volk came to St. Alphonsus Parish in Daviess County. Being from Germany himself, he was called upon to minister the German Catholics in Owensboro. Under his guidance they established their own school at the corner of West Third and Cedar Streets. Intent on "preserving the faith and their German customs," the founders of the school insisted that only German children be allowed to attend. Ursuline Sisters from the Sacred Heart Community in Louisville were the teachers. In 1871 they built their first church on Triplett Street at McFarland. This was the first site for St. Joseph Church which was dedicated by Father Ivo Schacht, Pastor of St. Stephen Church who also held the first services at St. Joseph. The German people began the St. Hubertus Society when a man, Mr. Rose, was bitten by a rabid dog. Sure to die, he promised St. Hubertus, who was once a German king, that he would start a society in the saint's honor if he were spared. The St. Hubertus Society was comparable to the present day Knights of Columbus, bringing material and spiritual aid to widows and orphans in need.

Father E.M. Bachmann became the first resident pastor of St. Joseph Parish, Owensboro, in June 1872. A position he held until 1878 when Father P.J. Haeseley assumed the pastoral duties.

On May 12, 1878, St. Joseph Church was struck by lightning and destroyed by fire. Bishop McCloskey ordered that a temporary church be built on the site. The parishioners erected a twenty feet by thirty feet building. However, the resulting strife within the parish was caused by more than the lightning. The trustees of the church wanted to move the church nearer the city. After much turmoil it finally came to be built at Fourth and Clay Streets. Since the parish was not allotted money from the diocese of Louisville to build the church, the people paid for it themselves. They borrowed on their own personal notes and donated money to the parish for the construction of the church. A Mr. Kamuf traveled to several states soliciting funds for the church from other German Catholics. Still not having enough money to hire an architect to design the new church, a priest whose name is unknown, gave them building plans used by another church. The approximate cost of the building and the lot was $10,000. On

March 7, 1880 the church was blessed and the first services were held by Father Haeseley although work on the church was not completed. Bishop McCloskey having wanted the church to be built at Seventh and Frederica Streets, ordered the church to be closed. However the parish continued to hold services in the new church which was not officially dedicated until 1883.

With the resignation in 1886 of Father Haeseley, Father Louis Conrad Ohle was appointed pastor. A requisite for a pastor in these early years was that he be able to speak the German language. Although the Mass was in Latin, prayers, sermons and confessions were spoken in German. During World War I, the German language was discontinued because its use was forbidden by the government. Father Ohle remained pastor until 1891. During his pastorship Father Ohle built the rectory, which in the early 1980's became the home for Birthright. In 1891 Father Henry Joseph Carmens became pastor until his health failed and he returned to his native land.

Father Edward Fehrenback was pastor from November 1901 until late 1904. Then the parish was temporarily placed in the charge of Father Edward Fitzgerald, pastor of St. Paul Church. Father Thomas McGuire who had been ordained for the Cleveland Diocese, but who made frequent trips to Kentucky was asked to go to St. Paul Church and care for St. Joseph Church as well. After two years, Father McGuire's health failed and he left Owensboro.

On January 6, 1906 Father Eugene Spiess arrived at St. Joseph's. He found things in disrepair with even the widows falling out in the church. Some of the men and women helped him fix up his rectory and to make much needed improvements in the church. They also constructed streets to make the church and rectory accessible. In 1921 Father Spiess was sent to the Diocese of Corpus Christi, Texas. When he left St. Joseph's, the parish debt was paid off with $5,000 over for Father Philip Bauer, his successor. Father Bauer was pastor from 1921 to 1926. It was during his pastorship that St. Joseph Academy was built.

There were six spacious classrooms, four for grade school and two for the high school along with a large auditorium. This school was dedicated by Bishop John A. Floresh in September 1924. Enrollment grew and remained large until 1948 when the high school students were sent to St. Francis Academy.

Father Martin Frankenburger was pastor of St. Joseph parish from 1926 to 1935. During his tenure the school debt was reduced from $65,000 to $28,000. Father Robert J. Gipperich succeeded Father Frankenburger as pastor from 1935 to 1939. He was given the job of paying off the school debt before he could return to Holy Family Church in Louisville which he had recently organized. However in 1937 the Owensboro Diocese was formed and Father Gipperich was never able to return to Holy Family. When the debt was paid at the end of 1937, Father Pius Edelen was assigned as St. Joseph's first assistant pastor. Father Peter Braun came to St. Joseph as pastor from July 1939 to 1948.

On April 3, 1948 the announcement was made that St. Paul Church and St. Joseph Church would merge to become Sts. Joseph and Paul Parish. St. Joseph High School was to be disbanded and the students transferred to St. Frances Academy which would be the Central Catholic High School for Owensboro and surrounding parishes. Father Braun sought to achieve a smooth transition. He maintained one parish with two churches until the winter of 1977. At that time, in order to cut fuel costs for the two buildings, St. Joseph Church was closed. Much effort was made subsequently to save St. Joseph Church building. Due to the deteriorated condition and cost of structural repairs however, the decision was made in the summer of 1989 to demolish the church. The beautiful stained glass windows were removed and given to Owensboro Museum of Fine Arts to be placed in its new addition. A monument, made from some of the brick and the cross from the church, was constructed on the site of the old Church at the corner of Fourth and Clay Streets as a reminder of "Times gone but not to be forgotten."

Sts. Joseph & Paul Parish
Owensboro

St. Joseph Church was organized through the efforts of the German Catholics who had migrated into Daviess County from small towns in Southern Indiana. Prior to the establishment of the church, a school was begun for the children of German origin. They were permitted to attend the Masses held at St. Stephen Church, but the Germans were only allowed to sit in the back of church away from the rest of the congregation.

The Germans met with Father Paul Volk of West Louisville as early as 1868 for religious instruction. Officially, in 1870, St. Joseph Church was organized by the German members of St. Stephen.

In 1871, the German Catholics built their first church, an eighty by thirty foot frame building, in the old precinct of Triplett and Sweeney Streets. The church was dedicated by Father Ivo Schaacht, pastor of St. Stephen, who also held the first services in the new church.

On May 12, 1878, St. Joseph Church was destroyed by a fire caused by lightning. A temporary church was erected on the sight by order of Bishop McCloskey of Louisville.

In October, 1878, the people of the German church purchased a lot at the southeast corner of Fourth and Clay Streets. Bishop McCloskey did not wish for a church to be built at this location, for he had planned that a church be built at Seventh and Frederica Streets.

The German parish was not allotted money from the diocese to build the church. Instead, the people paid for the new building themselves. Work was begun on the eighty-six by forty-three foot brick church building in late 1878. On March 7, 1880, the church was blessed and services were held.

When Bishop McCloskey received news that the church had been built, he ordered that it be closed. Services continued to be held in the church despite the Bishop's wishes. It was not until 1883 that the church was officially dedicated.

In 1868, before the church had been built, a Catholic school was opened and located at Third and Center Streets. After the church was built at Fourth and Clay Streets, an effort was made to move the school closer. The second site was located in a two room frame building behind St. Joseph Church and was known as St. Hubertus Academy. In 1904, a more commodious school was built at Ninth and Sweeney Streets to accommodate the increasing number of students, grade school and high school alike.

Around 1912, property at Fifth and Clay Streets was purchased and remodeled into a school.

As enrollment grew, St. Joseph Parish made a drive to secure money for a new school. The new $65,000. school was dedicated in 1924 by Bishop John A. Floersh and was changed to St. Joseph Academy. The Academy consisted of high school and grade school students.

When St. Stephen Church could no longer accommodate the growing numbers of their congregation, St. Paul's Church was formed. The first official announcement of the division of St. Stephen was recorded as of December 5, 1886. All those Catholics who lived east of St. Ann Street would belong to the new parish.

Most of the founders of St. Paul Church were associated with the distilleries of Owensboro; they were the Irish "whiskey people." This affluent group of people did not like to associate with the German people. The "whiskey people" did not understand the German language and thought of the Germans as "dirty."

Under the direction of Father Thomas Gambon, the appointed pastor of the new congregation, a small temporary church was built on a lot at the corner of Fourth and Pearl Streets. The first members worshipped there on Passion Sunday, March 27, 1887. Shortly thereafter, the lot on which the present church stands was purchased for $4000, and ground was broken on July 6, 1887, for the new church.

St. Paul Church was dedicated on Sunday, January 13, 1889, by Rev. William George McCloskey, bishop of Louisville.

On April 3, 1948, an announcement was made by Bishop Francis R. Cotton concerning the parishes in Owensboro. In the announcement, one of the many proposals made called for a merger of the two parishes of St. Joseph and St. Paul with Father Peter Braun as pastor. In addition to the proposal, the high school of St. Joseph's Academy was to be moved to St. Francis Academy, the new central high school for the Owensboro parishes. St. Joseph school was to be known as Sts. Joseph and Paul Grade School with all grade school students of the newly combined parishes to attend classes there. Because of the continued increase in enrollment at the grade school, an addition to the school was built in 1953 consisting of four classrooms and an office.

The announcement brought considerable consternation to both parishes. Both had been entities within themselves. In order to minimize the friction between the two parishes, St. Joseph Church would remain open for two Masses on Sunday and one during the week, while the rest of the Masses were to be held at St. Paul's Church.

Due to the rapid rise of fuel costs in 1977, the parish could no longer afford the operation of two churches. In addition, enrollment had been declining for several years in both St. Stephen and Sts. Joseph and Paul Schools. Also, Sts. Joseph and Paul Grade School was in disrepair and had been condemned by the fire marshall. In the Spring of 1977, the diocese decreed the merger of Sts. Joseph and Paul School and St. Stephen School. It would be called The Cathedral School.

In June of 1978, St. Joseph Church was closed to the public.

In 1985, Sts. Joseph and Paul Grade School

Pastors of Sts. Joseph & Paul Church

1948-1969	Msgr. Peter Braun
1969-1976	Rev. Alousius Powers
1976-1982	Rev. Maurice J. Tiell
1982-1990	Rev. Henry L. Willett
1990-	Rev. Kevin Karl

was demolished with the exception of four classrooms that remain standing on Clay Street.

On October 29, 1978, the parish was presented certificates by the Kentucky Heritage Commission declaring St. Joseph Church and St. Paul Church as Kentucky landmarks. The certificates have no legal connotations for the preservation of these historical sites.

On December 25, 1984, the interior of St. Paul Church was ruined by a fire that had started in the cellar of the church. Until October of 1985, all Masses were said at St. Joseph Church.

St. Paul Church was ready for occupancy in October, 1985 and the rededication ceremonies were held in January of 1986 with Bishop John McRaith in attendance.

The parish celebrated the centenary of St. Paul Church in 1987.

In 1986, the Preservation Alliance and the Daviess County Historical Society were continuing to search for a use for St. Joseph Church. In order to preserve the church, a very large sum of money was needed to repair it.

For four years, time passed with no funds available to anyone for repairs to the church. On March 19, 1990, demolition procedures took place on the property. The sixteen priceless stained-glass windows were raised from the church and donated to the Owensboro Museum of Fine Arts where they remain on display today. Other possessions of St. Joseph Church such as the Stations of the Cross, The Corpus, and presider chair are presently being used as decor in the interior of St. Paul Church.

Today, in 1992, the existing part of the old Sts. Joseph and Paul Grade School now houses the Help Office which serves as a non-denominational outreach program for the poor and needy in the city of Owensboro. The old St. Joseph rectory and later the Ursuline Convent for the grade school now houses Birthright, Inc. which provides a place of residence for battered women who are pregnant. Sts. Joseph and Paul Parish continues to be a thriving faith community of five-hundred and twenty families. The laity are involved in various ministry programs offered by the parish. Under the new Owensboro Catholic Consolidated School System, the parish shares a school building with St. Pius X Church known as Bishop Francis R. Cotton Grade School and supports the Owensboro Catholic Middle School and High School. The parish also directs its own Religious Education program for those children who do not attend a Catholic School.

St. Lawrence Parish
Philpot

Amid the hills of the extreme eastern part of Daviess County stands the Church of St. Lawrence, the pioneer church of this section of the state.

The first record of Daviess County's Catholic history began when Father Charles Nerinckx, from Bardstown, visited a few Catholics and held a service as far back as 1821. As early as 1822, Rev. A.A. Able conducted services which resulted in the organization of the St. Lawrence Parish. The first house of worship was a log structure erected by Father E.J. Durbin, of Uniontown, Kentucky, who made this structure his home and Mission. Records show his activity here for we find the first grave opened in the parish cemetery in the year 1823.

Enterprising land owners donated a tract of land for church purposes. With the erection of a log church in 1831, many families settled near the church located near the Hardinsburg Road two miles east of Knottsville. In 1833, Fr. John Wathen became the first resident Pastor and was also a part-time school teacher of the youth of his parish. It appears that Fr. Wathen's school may have been the first parochial-educational effort in Daviess County. In 1839, a brick church was built, but because of defective work, it was replaced by the present church in 1870. The whole of Daviess and adjoining counties as far as St. Theresa, Meade County, were attended from here. There were as many as thirteen stations attended to by Father Wathen traveling through the wilderness living out of his saddlebags, which contained the requisites for church services and a little sack of cornmeal for his food. Father Wathen died in 1841 at St. Theresa, but his remains rest in St. Lawrence Cemetery opposite the church.

Today, St. Lawrence Parish is a mission to St. Williams Parish of Knottsville. Its inside appearance has changed due to remodeling, and even though it has not grown much in its number of families, it is the proud mother to countless citizens of Daviess County. Though advanced in years of interesting history, St. Lawrence still remains an active Mother Church as can be seen from the spirit and active works of the parishioners in recent times.

St. Lawrence Parish

Saint Lawrence claims the distinction of being the Mother church of the Catholic community of Daviess County in Kentucky. It was in 1821, in the home of Mr. and Mrs. Ezekiel Henning, on what is now the Aull Road, east of Knottsville, that Father Charles Nerinckx, of Bardstown, Ky, offered the first Mass in Daviess County, for the small group of Catholic settlers in what is now the Knottsville community. Later Father A.A. Abell and Father Elisha Durbin attended to the spiritual needs of this community of Catholics. Father Durbin built a log structure which served as his residence and as a church. His missionary activities extended from Vincennes to Nashville and from Daviess County to the furthest parts of Western Kentucky.

The erection of a log church in 1831 gave impetus to the settling of Catholics in the area. Two years later, 1833, Father John Wathen became the first resident pastor, who built a new structure which later became the Sisters' residence which to this day is still in use as the home of the custodian of the church and church property, including the cemetery, which dates back to 1823. The remains of Father Wathen, the first resident pastor who died in 1841, are in the cemetery.

In 1839, a brick church was built to replace the log structure. Because of defective workmanship, that church structure had to be replaced by the present structure in 1870, under the pastorate of Father M.M. Coghlan. This church was dedicated on February 11, 1872.

St. Lawrence was truly a mother church, having as many as 13 mission stations throughout Daviess and surrounding counties, the farthest being St. Theresa's in Meade County. Among daughter churches in Daviess County are St. Stephen Cathedral; St. Raphael, West Louisville; St. Joseph, Owensboro; St. Mary's, Whitesville; and St. William, Knottsville. After on hundred and fifty-five years, St. Lawrence remains a very active and thriving parish, with nearly one hundred families as members. However, St. Lawrence is now a mission parish attended from St. William's. The children from the St. Lawrence community attend school at the Mary Carrico Memorial School in Knottsville and Trinity High School in Whitesville. Rev. George Niehaus was the last resident pastor, serving from 1914 until his retirement in 1931. After this time, the old rectory was demolished.

In 1984, under the direction of Father Clarence Hite, an up to date parish hall that can easily accommodate 250 people was completed and paid for. The church was extensively remodeled in 1965, during Father Tiell's pastorate. Currently, the church is being restored to the extent possible by the current pastor, Father Len Arcilesi.

Pastors of St. Lawrence Church

Rev. Charles Nerinckx	Missionary
Rev. Robert A. Abell	Missionary
Rev. Elisha J. Durbin	Missionary
Rev. John C. Wathen	1833-1841
Rev. Linus O. Coomes	1841-1845
Rev. Athanasius A. Aud	1845-1848
Rev. Michael Coghlan	1845-1872
Rev. Charles Eggermont	1872-1879
Rev. Peter J. Rock	1879-1885
Rev. Thomas F. Cambon	1885-1887
Rev. Thomas J. Jenkins	1887-1895
Rev. Oscar P. Ackerman	1895-1898
Rev. Anthony Helling	1898-1898
Rev. James B. Monaghan	1898-1902
Rev. Lucian E. Clements	1902-1914
Rev. George Niehaus	1914-1931

St. Leo Parish
Murray

St. Leo Church has its roots in the services supplied to the Catholic members of the Civilian Conservation Corps Camp established at Murray in 1933. The chaplain provided came from St. Francis De Sales Parish, Paducah, KY. During 1938 and 1939, the priests serving the CCC Camp were Frs. Albert Thompson, Stammermen, Thomas Libs, and Joseph Saffer.

The Camp was closed in 1939, and Mass was continued for the local Catholics in the private home of Mr. and Mrs. Harry J. Fenton. Fr. Joseph Saffer, pastor of St. Joseph, Mayfield, served the Camp prior to its being disbanded, and the Mission of St. Leo until 1948.

Mass was offered at the Fenton home for a little over two and a half years until Bishop Francis Cotton felt that a church should be erected in Murray. Two lots were chosen, and purchased for a cost of $450.00 in October of 1942. The site was the corner of North 12th and Payne Street (at that time this area was outside the city limits of Murray). Construction of the church was financed through the Extension Society from a grant of $9,000.00 left in the will of Fr. Leo Gleason. Fr. Saffer also had a hand in the construction work by building the pews that would serve the Catholics in this area for the next 20 years that the church would be in use.

In January of 1943, a program for the training of the Naval Air Corps, the "V-5 Program" was initiated at Murray State College. Mass was still being offered in the Fenton home while construction was being done. Because of the numbers of Catholics that were in the program, and who came to Murray State College, the Fenton home became too small to hold them. Mass was then offered on the campus of MSC in the "Little Chapel", then the gym, and later in Wilson Hall.

Upon completion of the church, attendance had risen to 175, and although the church was adequate for local Catholics, with the V-5 Program, college students, and visitors Catholics often found themselves standing outside the front doors, and peering in through the windows.

Over the years St. Leo's had been a mission to various parishes. 1930s—St. Francis De Sales, 1940s—St. Joseph, Mayfield, 1950s—Sacred Heart, Hickman, St. Jerome, Fancy Farm. In August of 1961, St. Leo's was raised to the status of an independent parish with Fr. Martin Mattingly as the first full time pastor.

Over the years, the religious education needs of the youth were not only taken care of by the priests, but by various religious congregations: Ursuline Sisters from Mayfield, Dominican Sisters from Fulton, and Sisters of Charity from Fancy Farm.

It was during Fr. Mattingly's pastorate that the present church was built, Seton Hall (our religious education center), and more land for parish expansion secured. It was during the 80s that Rand McNally published a list of the best places to live, and Murray received favorable mention. What occurred was an Exodus from the north to Murray and St. Leo's began to experience a "population explosion".

With this, St. Leo's became blessed with a broad spectrum of ages and backgrounds. With Murray State University we have the energy of our college students, and with Rand McNally we have the wisdom of many retirees. Industry and the university have blessed us with many families from all over who bring their talents and beliefs into this community.

Priests who have served St. Leo's are: Frs. Albert Thompson, Stammerman, Thomas Libs, Joseph Saffer, Leo Dienes, Clarence Pettit, Leonard Reisz, Thomas Murphy, Msgr. Edward Russell, Richard Danhauer, Pike Powell, Martin Mattingly, Ben Luther, Louis Piskula, Msgr. Bernard Powers, Stan Tillman, Pete Sharkey, Gerald Glahn, Larry McBride, and Pete Hughes.

As St. Leo grows, developments to the property have also been undertaken. November 8, 1992 marked the dedication of an addition to Seton Hall. The old Parish Assembly area was divided into four new classrooms, a larger Parish Hall was added as well as expanded kitchen, an additional classroom. The total cost of renovation and construction was $215,000.00. The building stands as a tribute to St. Leo's looking to the future, building community.

The Diocese of Owensboro has responded to the needs of the Catholic students of Murray State University since the inception of the Newman Club in September of 1961. Faculty advisors were Dr. Peter Panzera, and Dr. John Mikulcik. Gleason Hall, the original church St. Leo's, was the Newman Center. Personnel that worked with Newman Campus Ministry are as follows: Sr. Mary Julian Baird 1967-68, Extension Society volunteers - Jane Duggan, Ellen Wilkinson 1968-69, Ann Henkel, Colleen Lane 1969-70, Eva Admas, Trish Novicke 1970-1972, Mary Catherine Kletzel, Arlene Meyerhofer. The Extension Program was phased out in the summer of 1971, but Miss Kletzel, and Miss Meyerhofer stayed an extra year. Fr. Bill Field came to Murray in May 1972, and on September 10th Fr. Martin Mattingly took over. The various pastors who followed also became the Newman chaplain as well as pastor. As the duties of St. Leo Parish increased, the need for extra personnel for Campus Ministry did as well. In September of 1985, Fr. Jack Coakley arrived along with Fr. Stan Tillman to Murray, Fr. Stan as pastor, and Fr. Jack as Director of Newman House. Due to an illness, Fr. Jack had to leave his post, and Fr. Pete Sharkey was sent to replace him in July of 1987. To make the ministries more distinct, Bishop John McRaith purchased the land that the present Newman House sits on. The present campus minister was hired as Ms. Joan Frisz.

The present St. Leo's with Gleason Hall in the background.

Bishop Francis Cotton leaving St. Leo's upon dedication of the church in October 1943.

St. Jude Parish
Clinton

St. Jude Parish began with a Mass, celebrated on June 28, 1982, at 11:30 a.m. in the Hickman County Recreational Center on Cresap Street in Clinton, Kentucky. The Reverend Carl Glahn, pastor of St. Edward in Fulton, Kentucky officiated, with approximately 50 people in attendance. This marked the first Catholic Mass ever held in this city.

On August 24, 1982, the Most Reverend Henry J. Soenneker, Bishop of Owensboro officially named the congregation The Church of St. Jude.

On October 18, 1982, ground was broken for the construction of the church building. The project was abundantly blessed from the very beginning. With Father Glahn's unrelenting pace, with contributions coming from both Catholics and non-Catholics alike throughout the area, monetary and furnishings, and with many of the parishioners donating time, energies and talents, the building was completed in nine and a half weeks.

On December 24, 1982, Christmas Eve Mass was held in the new Church.

On May 1, 1983, dedication of the new church was celebrated by the Most Reverend John Jeremiah McRaith, our newly appointed Bishop of Owensboro.

On December 27, 1984, the last payment was made on the debt and on February 17, 1985, the Hickman County Recreational Center was rented once again—this time to celebrate as a parish family the burning of the mortgage. The theme of this celebration was "believe in miracles."

Pastors and Ministers

Rev. Carl Glahn	1982-1985
Rev. Jerry Riney	1985-1990
Rev. Bruce Fogle (assc)	
Rev. Terry Devine (assc)	
Rev. Martin Hayes	1990-
Sr. Annalita Lanceste (Pas. Min.)	1990-

St. Mark Parish
Eddyville

The formation of the Lyon County Catholic Community with headquarters in Eddyville, KY began when Fr. Maurice J. Tiell took up residence at 210 Kenoak Drive in Eddyville on June 10, 1987. On June 14, 1987 54 gathered for the first Liturgy of the Eucharist at 9:00 A.M. at the Lee Jones Park building. On August 2, 1987 the building in the park was not available, so the Hilltop Nursing Home became another temporary place of worship. On August 9, 1987 they began to share the temporary "Church Home" of the Eddyville Assembly of God Church in an old Five & Dime store building in Eddyville. On September 27, 1987 the Kuttawa United Methodist Church became their last temporary place of worship. On July 13, 1989 the Lyon County Catholic Community was given name, Saint Mark. Then by a decree of Bishop John J. McRaith dated September 4, 1989 the Saint Mark Community became a full-fledged parish. The members of the building committee were: Paul Bachi, Marilyn Cash, Andy Cimprich, Ed Priester, and Leo Voytek. On the furnishings committee were: Celia Bachi, Casey Migacz, Mary Parker, and Carolyn Sims. Architect was James Bob Gresham of Gresham Associates of Paducah. Construction of the 7,300 square feet church-hall facility

was entrusted to the Hayden Construction Company of Owensboro. Sixteen participated in the first Liturgy of the Eucharist in the new St. Mark Church on November 14, 1989 and there were seventy six at the first Sunday Liturgy on November 19, 1989 at 8:30 A.M. An "Open House" was held for the community January 7, 1990. More than 300 attended the Dedication of Saint Mark Church at 3:00 P.M. on April 1, 1990. Joining the Pastor in anointing the walls of the church building were Msgr. Anthony G. Higdon, Fr. Paul Pike Powell, and Fr. Thomas O'Connor, OSB (donor of a statue of St. Mark that was once enshrined at St. Mark Monastery at South Union, KY). As of April 1992 St. Mark Parish had grown to 70 families or 138 parishioners.

St. Martin Parish
Rome

St. Martin Parish dates back to the year 1873. Rev. Ivo Schacht, a pastor at St. Stephen Parish in Owensboro, organized the rural Catholic people into a new parish. The first church was built in 1873. The record of the first deed of land to St. Martin is recorded in the Chancery Office April 20, 1872.

During the early formative years of the parish, Holy Mass was offered on Tuesday since there were not enough priests to take care of the spiritual needs of the people. St. Martin was served by St. Stephen Parish, St. Peter Parish, Stanley, KY and St. Raphael Parish. In November, 1891, Rev. John Riley was appointed the first pastor of St. Martin Parish.

On July 25, 1896, Father Louis Herberth was assigned to the pastorate at St. Martin and remained there until his death in December 1922. The beautiful stained glass windows that are in the church today, were donated (1908-1910) to the old church by the parishioners. In a deed dated August 30, 1912 a tract of land containing an acre was donated and Father Herberth started to build the first parochial school at St. Martin. This was a long frame building with sliding doors dividing it in the center and thus making two classrooms. At this time he also built a two story frame house for the Ursuline Sisters of Louisville, KY. Four Sisters came to St. Martin.

In 1919, the school enrollment was increased to such an extent that Fr. Herberth saw the need for a larger school. Again land was donated for the building of a new school. The school consisting of four classrooms on the first floor and an auditorium on the second was completed during the year 1920 and the Ursuline Sisters of Mount St. Joseph took charge of the teaching with a faculty of three sisters.

In 1954, the parishioners recognized the need for a new school building. Led by the Rev. Joseph W. Saffer, the parish began a three year fund drive which would not only include the new school, but a new church, rectory and sisters quarters.

In May, 1957, the cornerstone of the new church was laid. Fr. Saffer acted as his own contractor and worked many hours as a laborer on the construction. Many parishioners donated labor and materials.

On December 17, 1957, the Church was dedicated by Bishop Francis Cotton and Fr. Saffer offered the first Mass. Msgr. Gilbert Henninger came to St. Martin in 1962. He built the new rectory in 1964 and in 1966, he completed the school. Rev. Victor C. Boarman was appointed as pastor at St. Martin in 1982. He was instrumental in organizing the Parish Council. Under his guidance, both lectors and Eucharistic Ministers began serving our parish, thus enhancing the liturgy. After fifty years of dedicated service to the Church, Fr. Boarman retired in June of 1989.

The parishioners at St. Martin are proud to have Rev. Joseph M. Mills as pastor (1989-). During the three years that Fr. Mills has been in the St. Martin community, the involvement of the parishioners has grown...Religious Education Classes & Adult Religious Education have started. A parttime Pastoral Minister, Rose Ann Payne, has been employed by the parish. Many renovations and needed repairs have been made.

The parishioners look forward to the years that Fr. Mills will spend at St. Martin and know that they will continue to grow as a faith filled Church community under his spiritual direction.

St. Mary Magdalene Parish
Sorgho

The Catholic Church in the community of Sorgho became a reality on June 27, 1908. Profits from St. Elizabeth's picnic in 1906 got the construction started in the summer of 1907. Father Joseph Wright was the first pastor of the new church which was a mission of St. Elizabeth. It was a wood frame church with a white cement interior and a natural wood finish. The furnishings of the church were mostly of wood. It had carved wooden statues. Some 36 families made up the first church. Seven of these families still have their family members attending.

Reverend Robert Jenne arrived in 1915 and opened the first Catholic school at St. Mary Magdalene in 1918. The first five years of the school it was staffed by lay teachers. In 1922 Fr. James Higdon became pastor and secured two sisters from Maple Mount.

In 1928, St. Mary Magdalene was removed from St. Elizabeth and put under the direction of St. Augustine, Reed. Rev. S.W. Tuley took over the parish. By 1929 the membership of the parish had increased to 83 families. Rev. Hooiveld came in 1932 and stayed a short while. In 1935 Rev. Paul Greenwell arrived. He entertained the idea of a new church around 1939 when some fund raisers were held. The old church was getting too small and was getting in bad need of repairs. Fr. Greenwell left in 1943 when Father Frank Ward became pastor for the next three years.

In 1946 Fr. Robert Wilson arrived in Sorgho. He got the construction of the new church started in 1948. The new church was built of St. Meinrad sandstone. The dedication took place on January 27, 1949 with Bishop Cotton celebrating a high Mass. Shortly after the completion of the new church, Fr. Wilson opened a new school. It was opened in 1951 and was also built from St. Meinrad sandstone.

Fr. Aloysious Powers followed Fr. Wilson in 1957. The school reached its peak enrollment of 134 students in 1962. In September 1964, Rev. William Hagman thought the time had come for a resident pastor. He helped to supervise the construction of the rectory which was built out of sandstone. The rectory was finished in February, 1965 and Fr. William McAtee was the first resident pastor. After 57 years, St. Mary Magdalene was not a mission parish. Three months later the parish purchased two additional acres. At this time the parish had around 119 families.

In 1966 Rev. George Boehmicke arrived. The following year the parish bought a house across the highway for the sisters who taught at the school. In the summer of 1975 a new parish hall was built for the parish functions. It was dedicated by Bishop Soenneker on November 9, 1975.

Father Boehmicke retired after 17 years at St. Mary Magdalene. He was the longest residing priest. He was replaced by Rev. Henry O'Bryan. With Father O'Bryan several fund raising projects took place for the remodeling of the church. New paint, lights, carpeting and speaker system were installed in the church as well as the stone altar being turned around to replace the wooden portable altar.

In 1989 Rev. Kevin Karl along with Rev. Danny Goff came to St. Mary Magdalene. The parish had just finished renovations on the rectory. Fr. Kevin stayed only one year. For Fr. Danny it was like a homecoming. He made his First Communion at St. Mary Magdalene where he attended school his first six years. In January 1991, the parish replaced the worn out boiler in the church and school with a new heating and air conditioning units.

St. Mary Magdalene has an active Youth Group with several spirited high school members. They are also blessed to have an active Senior Citizens group in the parish as well as an active Christian Mother's Society.

The parish is also blessed with an active Men's Club.

The annual picnic is probably the biggest event of the year for the parish participation. It is always held on the last Saturday before the 4th of July. It is a day of hard work but is enjoyed by all.

St. Mary Magdalene also participates in the annual Barbeque Festival held in Owensboro each year. They won the very first year in 1979 and by 1989 had won the fourth time.

After St. Raphael's church burned, St. Mary Magdalene received the bell from that parish. It first rang in its new home on Easter Sunday in 1984.

St. Mary of the Woods Parish
Franklin

The early foundations of what would become the parish of St. Mary of the Woods, Franklin, can be traced back especially to Father Elisha Durbin, a priest who cared for all the far-flung Catholic families of south central Kentucky, and Lawrence and John Finn of Franklin who took the responsibility to host the Catholic worship for the area. Their commitment to their faith in the early 19th century allowed others to build on a firm foundation.

Throughout the 1850s, large numbers of railroad laborers came to this part of the state, and many were Roman Catholic Irish. Father Joseph DeVries, a priest assigned to Bowling Green in 1859, was very aware of the changing situation, particularly that the Finn House was no longer adequate for Franklin's Catholics. In 1867, he organized the people to build a church and named it St. Mary of the Woods. Built on the site of the present church, the woodframe church was completed and dedicated in 1868. Father Henry Mertins, who succeeded Father James P. Ryan (the first resident pastor), opened the parish school in 1869. The school served the parishioners up until the turn of the century. Due to economic changes, St. Mary's congregation shrank and in 1887 the resident pastor was removed and priests began coming from Bowling Green and Russellville. The biggest physical tragedy for the parish happened on January 1, 1938 when the 70 year old church burned to the ground. Part of the old school building (the site of the present rectory) was used for church services until the new church was built.

Two important events color the history of St. Mary after World War II. One was the great growth of industry in the Simpson County area which attracted many Catholics from other parts of the country. The other was the involvement of Glenmary Home Missioners with the Parish, at first from Russellville and after 1966 as resident pastors. (Glenmary Home Missioners is a Catholic religious order of Priests and Brothers dedicated to work in areas of our country that have small numbers of Catholics). Glenmary was able to raise the needed money in order to build the current church by 1953. Acquisition of more property next to the church allowed the parish to meet the spiritual and physical needs of an ever-growing congregation.

St. Mary of the Woods
McQuady

In 1840 the Diocese of Louisville listed the home of James and Priscilla Mattingly, a station where a priest would come once a month (weather permitting) to serve the needs of the Catholic families in the neighborhood. James Mattingly and Priscilla Wayne had been married at St. Charles Church at St. Mary's, Kentucky (now Marion County), August 12, 1812, and came to Breckinridge County c1814. They had eight children, 63 grandchildren and 331 known great-grandchildren.

Two letters dated March 18, 1861, and April 26, 1861, from Bishop Martin J. Spalding to James Mattingly have been preserved by the descendants. They are replies to letters written by James, evidently discussing building a church and having a pastor assigned. Bishop Spalding was not encouraging about assigning a priest on any basis other than what then currently existed. However, plans to erect a building continued, no doubt to relieve the crowded conditions of congregating in a private home, as well as the determination of these people to have a church.

In 1870, a simple frame building was completed and called Saint Mary's. Father Nicholas Ryan began holding monthly services there. On December 14, 1870, James Mattingly died. The deed for the three acres of land for the church and cemetery is dated December 15, 1870, the next day after James' death. Grantors were John Askins Sr. and John Askins Jr., at the time, both sons-in-law of James. Was this act in response to a dying wish expressed by James, or a sort of memorial of his long years of struggle to have a church?

In 1876, Leo Mattingly (eldest of James' children) gave an acre of his property for the purpose of building a school for the Catholic children in the area. This site was located about a mile North of the church property. There is no record of this school, except for the property deed, but a few people still living today recall that their parents families attended school there. From the records of families living in the area at that time, there could have been about 25 or 30 children who attended this school. The parents paid a sort of tuition in order to pay a teacher. A Mr. J.J. Friel was thought to be the last teacher of this school.

During the 1890s a new sanctuary was built on the end of the church to enlarge the body of the church in order to relieve the crowded conditions that existed by then.

In April of 1908, Father John Francis Knue, was appointed pastor of St. Anthony's at Axtel, with St. Mary's as a mission. He was assigned the task of building a new church. Father Knue was then 30 years of age and perhaps best described as a gentle giant.

Many of the events and feelings of the people at this time were described by a lady who wrote her memoirs several years ago. She was

an eye-witness, though young, her remembrances give a feeling of the times. "Becoming a parish on our own turned out to be far more of an upheaval in our religious lives than anyone had ever dreamed it would be. We knew we must have a new church building, but people in our neighborhood expected it to be built on the site of the old church. Learning it would be at McQuady was a terrible shock - how would we ever manage to get to church every Sunday if we had to go so far! It was even worse for the people in the Bailtown community - we lived at least two miles nearer McQuady than they did."

When the new pastor, Father Knue arrived to take over, he won everyone's hearts with his pleasing and genial ways, but he lost no time in really waking up the sleepy heads among us. He was a real go-getter.

First, of course, came the planning stage, just persuading the people they could build a church took some doing on his part. They had expected to get by with a simple frame building similar to the old one, but he had other ideas and when he explained to them, everybody knew it couldn't be done. We didn't have that kind of money - ten thousand dollars sounded like a million to us.

The work began, and little by little, the new St. Mary Church was built by the hands of Father Knue and his parishioners, he worked right along with the men every day. The stone for the church building was quarried nearby and hauled to the site with wagons and teams, Every able-bodied man was supposed to help. Each Sunday, Father Knue read a list of names of those who were to work through the coming week. Any man who could not come on his appointed day was expected to see that another came in his place. Slowly, but steadily the stone walls rose. The cornerstone was laid in October 1909.

While the building was in progress, Father Knue lived in a small tenant house on the Tom Sheeran farm nearby. He drove a horse and buggy to the old church for Mass every Sunday.

St. Mary of the Woods was an appropriate name for the new church. The old church was in the woods and the new one also. Most of the new church property was in woods. There were no buildings near it, except on a farm across the road. The rectory was built at the same time as the church, so Father Knue moved into his home at the same time the church was finished. His housekeeper was a Miss Catherine Lucid. In his later years here, Miss Elizabeth Sherron of the parish became his housekeeper and remained with him for the rest of his life.

The church of rough sandstone, about 45 x 80 feet in dimension, was built in American style architecture. The stained glass windows, the Stations of the Cross and three altars were all special donations to the church. The only paid labor for the church building was a stone mason and two carpenters. The stone mason was George Seitz. Both carpenters were men of the parish, David Crews and John Ruppert. All the woodwork in the church and rectory was done by these two men.

The church was dedicated on November 6, 1910. There was an over-flowing crowd and many people never got inside the church. The old church was stark, no decorations except for a large picture of the Assumption above the altar, a very subdued picture. Only two candlesticks, severe and plain. A neighbor put flowers on the altar in summer and that was the only bit of color, save for the priest's vestments. Mrs. Beavin wrote that when she stepped inside the new church the first time, she thought she was in Heaven. Beautiful colors everywhere, the ceiling a soft ivory, the walls were two shades of green, with dark green carpet in the sanctuary. The new pews were beautiful and three altars - all white and gold - the shining tabernacles, candelabra and candlesticks. She had never seen a large statue before, nor ever been to a High Mass. There was a new organ, a good choir and beautiful music. The first organist was Miss Lillian Sheeran of Kirk.

In 1920, construction of a school was begun. The parish still had a debt from the church building and Father Knue's dream was a parish school built of stone like the church. The Bishop said the school should be built at once, so once again Father Knue and the men of the parish were in the construction business.

Because of the debt, they could not afford the expense of the stone, so a large frame building was erected over a full basement made of concrete block. There were three large classrooms on the first floor, the second floor was the Sisters' convent and chapel. One large room in the convent area was used as a high school classroom. The school opened in the fall of 1922, staffed by four Dominican Sisters from St. Catherine's at Springfield, Kentucky. Father Knue helped teach the high school students. The first nuns were Sister Thecla, Sister Jamesetta, Sister Raphael and Sister Scholastica. The high school was discontinued in 1932. The cost of building and operating the school had increased the parish indebtedness and during the depression years it was many times impossible to do more than pay the interest. Finally, in 1938 when Father Albin Bauer was pastor, the debt was $2,200. Father Knue told Father Bauer that if the parish would raise money to pay half the amount, he himself would pay the other half. The parish somehow raised the money and Father Knue came to the "note-burning" celebration.

Following Father Knue's 16 years as pastor, in October 1924, he was sent to pastor St. Columba in Louisville. His successor was Father Leo Landall, a member of the Precious Blood Society of Carthegena, Ohio, and priests from this order served the parish until 1983. Father Landall was transferred in 1926, and the following priests of the Precious Blood Society were pastors: Father Remigus Monnin, 1926-1931; Father Louis Pottkoetter, 1931-1936; Father Albin Bauer, 1936-1938; Father Frederick A. Stock, 1938-1943; Father Albert Kaiser, 1943-1951; Father Henry W. Wibbles, 1951-1958; Father Herbert R. Renner, six months; Father Gabriel Brenkus, one year; Father Henry Balster, 1959-1969; Father Fred L. Koch, 1969-1972; Father Cornelius Fenton, 1972-1982; Father James McCabe, 1982-1983.

Father Leonard Reisy of the Owensboro Diocese was assigned our pastor in 1983, but due to illness, he was unable to come for several months. Father Maury Riney, pastor of St. Rose at Cloverport served as interim pastor until Father Reisy was able to come. He served as pastor until his retirement in February 1986. Father Pete Hughes was our pastor from 1986-1990 and was succeeded by Father John Little. In June 1992, Father Little was sent to serve the college students at the Newman Center in Bowling Green, Kentucky and Father Bruce Fogle was named as pastor of St. Anthony at Axtel and St. Mary of the Woods.

Our church has been blessed with several young people who embraced the religious life through the years. They include one priest and 17 sisters. The priest is the Rev. James William Hinton, a member of the Society of the Precious Blood. He was ordained in 1943

The young women of the parish to enter the Ursuline Order of nuns at Mount St. Joseph were Sister Fidelis Weise in 1911, Sisters Rosine and Miriam Hinton and Sister Mary Frances Weise in 1913. Others to join the same order were Sister Mary Gesine Sherron in 1924, Sister Mary Concepta and Sister Mary Anslem Beavin in 1930 and Sister Mary Carl Sherron in 1945.

In 1923, two young women entered the Dominican Order at St. Catherine. They were Sister Rosella Mattingly and Sister Mary Benvan Hinton. Others later entering the same order were Sister Kathleen Mattingly, Sister Vallina Sheeran and Sister James Vincent Mattingly in 1932. Sister Frieda Payne in 1943 and Sister Rose Marie Mattingly in 1938.

Two of St. Mary of the Woods young women entered the order of the Sisters of Charity at Nazareth, Kentucky. The were Sister Helen Frances Sheeran in 1934 and Sister Louise Catherine Kennedy in 1932.

In 1959, Bishop Soenneker commissioned our pastor, Father Henry Balster, and the parish to build a new school. A fund raising drive began, and again, with volunteers from the men of the parish, a new building was erected. At the time, the Army Post at Fort Knox was in the process of dismantling several buildings that had been erected during World War II and Father Balster and the men of the parish made several trips there and salvaged structural lumber that could be used in the basic construction of the new building. The exterior of the building is faced with stone, so it is similar to the church. The building was completed with two classrooms and living quarters for the two teachers. School began in the new building in the fall of 1962. Our pride in our accomplishments seemed short-lived however, as on a hot Sunday morning in the summer of 1967, Father Balster, with tears on his face, read a letter from the Bishop saying that our school would not open in the fall.

During the years after World War II, more county roads were improved and new ones built and as passable roads were available, the county school bus system also grew. The students of the parish now had transportation available to attend St. Romuald's at Hardinsburg, which became an inter-parochial school.

After the school had closed, Father Balster continued to live in the rectory but when Father Koch came to pastor, he established his residence in the living area of the school building. The rectory was removed in 1987. Our school building now serves as a parish hall and other rooms are used for small group meetings and CCD classes. In August of 1987, Father Pete Hughes arranged for Sister Marian Powers, OSU, to live in the former convent rooms and assist in various parish duties, both at St. Rose in Cloverport and at St. Mary of the Woods. She was with us until July 1991 and now serves in the same capacity at St. Anthony, Axtel, Kentucky.

Our parish is largely made up of the descendants and relatives of the original builders, and we are proud of the legacy they left us. In the 1960s when the decision was made to have the altar facing the people, the original communion railing was removed and two sections of it were used as a base for the new altar. When renovations has been needed, we have strived to keep the style and appearance much the same. Our altar linens are still trimmed with hand-made lace.

Father Knue remained a loyal friend to the parish he built and at his request at his death in 1945, his remains were interred in our cemetery.

St. Mary of the Woods Parish
Whitesville

The important details surrounding the beginnings of St. Mary of the Woods parish have been lost with the sands of time. However, there are some references to the fact that Fr. Elias Durbin and Fr. Charles Nerinckx visited the area for sacramental ministry in the early 1820s. Fr. Durbin baptized William Lanham July 3, 1825, probably at the Lanham home in the Desserter Creek settlement to the South of present-day Whitesville. Mass was offered in the home of Thomas Clark Hagan during this early period. This area later became known as Hagan's Station.

In 1833 Fr. John C. Wathen was appointed first pastor of St. Lawrence and tended the faith community at Hagan's Station as his mission. Fr. Walter Coomes became pastor in 1842 and served until 1848 with the assistance of Fr. Linus Coomes and A.A. Aud. In 1845 Richard W. Barrett donated an acre and five poles of land upon which was built a 30 X 46 ft. log Church, with a 14 X 20 ft. addition on the back to serve as a sacristy. The name St. Mary of the Woods was given to this new church.

Bishop Martin John Spalding administered the Sacrament of Confirmation in 1849 at St. Mary's where Fr. Michael Coghlan was now the pastor, showing 163 parishioners. The names of this early community include some which are still common to the area. Fr. Coughlan directed the parish in building a frame structure to serve as Church building in 1862. This building was later moved from the hilltop in the current cemetery to Whitesville where it was used as a school building from 1886-1918.

Fr. Charles Eggermont served as pastor 1872-1878 when St. Mary's became an independent parish. Fr. Kyran W. King became the first resident pastor and soon began work on the "new" brick church which was dedicated on June 8, 1884. Fr. John Sheridan led the community in worship in the church between 1885-1888, even though the interior was not finished until Fr. Lawrence Ford (1888-93) arranged for its completion. Fr. Ford established the mission of St. John the Baptist in Ohio County, which grew slowly for 70 years until a parish was erected in Fordsville.

The Fr. Hugh O'Sullivan era (1893-1938) saw many improvements in the parish plant: a brick kiln was built on the property which was used to fire bricks to build the present rectory (1898), the stables (presently being used as parish office), and a new school building, completed in 1918. This building, O'Sullivan Hall, continued to grow over the next 11 years as the school enrollment increased and more classroom space was required. Bricks from the brick yard were sold to help pay for improvements at the parish; many buildings in Daviess and Ohio counties can boast of having Whitesville bricks in them.

O'Sullivan Hall also served as the convent for the Sisters of Charity of Nazareth who worked in the parish from 1901 until 1990. Other Religious Orders serving the community were the Franciscan Sisters during the 1880s, the Mount St. Joseph Ursuline Sisters from 1967-1989, and the Benedictine Sisters from Ferdinand, Indiana during the late 1980s.

St. Mary of the Woods Church frame structure, built in 1862.

St. Mary of the Woods present building.

The parish rejoiced as the Diocese was established because their pastor was named Vicar General and given the dignity of Monsignor. These honors were short lived, however, as Msgr. O'Sullivan died July 26, 1938. Fr. Joseph Egan replaced him temporarily until Fr. William B. Jarboe was named pastor, serving until 1947. Frs. Frank Ward, Henry O'Bryan and Pius Edelen worked as assistant pastors during this time. Frs. O'Bryan and Edelen continued as assistants for Fr. Martin Nahstoll along with Frs. Martin Mattingly, Walter Hancock and William J. Hagman. Fr. Nahstoll led the parish in erecting a new High School building in 1954-55. Fr. Benedict Huff became pastor in 1961, assisted by Frs. Hagman, David Warren, and William Field. It was under Fr. Huff's administration that the current grade school building was completed (1965). Fr. Charles Fischer succeeded Fr. Huff and ushered in the establishment of Trinity High School which serves the parishes in Eastern Daviess County. Fr. Fischer was helped by Frs. Lewis White, Phillip Field, Phillip Thomas, Jerry Riney, and Carroll Wheatley, who later taught at Trinity.

A newly formed Booster club raised funds to build a gym in which the first ball game was played on Nov. 19, 1971. It was also during this year that school boards were established for both schools and a parish pastoral council was formed to assist in the task of leading the parish community. A dining room was added to the rectory in 1976.

Fr. Charles Philip Riney assumed the duties

of pastor in 1976, assisted by Frs. John Meredith and Ray Goetz. On October 6, 1978 the fourth church building was blessed and dedicated. Fr. Stephen Dunn succeeded him with the help of Frs. Gerry Baker, William Hagman, Anthony Bickett, Severin Messick, O.S.B. and Larry McBride. In 1986 the O'Sullivan building was dismantled, much to the dismay of many in the community.

Sr. Ann Legeay, S.C.N. came to work as a parish minister in 1980 and was influential in getting a Senior Citizen Center program started in the community. Sr. Terri O'Sullivan, S.C.N. worked as parish minister (1986-88) and was succeeded by Sr. Brenda Engelman, O.S.B. who worked as pastoral associate from 1988-90. She was followed by Sr. Mary Sheila Higdon, O.S.U. who also served as Director of Religious Education.

Sharon Cinnamon worked as director of parish business affairs for 11 years until Sue Batman assumed those duties in 1991. 1989 saw still more new faces of leadership arrive at St. Mary's: Fr. Joseph Mills came as interim pastor during the Spring. In June Fr. Louis F. Piskula was named pastor and Fr. Len Arcilesi came as his associate. Fr. William Hagman continued to be in residence with special duties as needed around the Diocese.

In 1990 the Longtrail stable was extensively renovated to accommodate the parish office, and the rectory first floor was remodeled into living space for the clergy. The church roof was replaced with a copper roof in 1991 and repairs were made to the rectory roof in Spring 1992. Fr. Richard L. Cash served as 1/2 time associate and 1/2 time with Trinity High School (1990-92). Fr. Bruce McCarty was appointed associate pastor in 1992 with special duties and ties to Trinity High School.

Over the years there have been various programs and organizations as well as countless unnamed persons which have contributed to the life and growth of this parish: The Total Abstinence Society, Knights of Columbus, Legion of Mary, St. Vincent de Paul, Catholic Family Movement, Altar Society, Cursillo, Army of Mary, Parish Renewal Weekends, Marriage Encounters, Teens Encounter Christ, Engaged Encounters, Block Rosaries, Renew, to name but a few which have offered approaches and tools for growth to segments of the parish. In February 1992 the entire parish embarked upon a Stewardship process, allowing the Word of God to confront the way in which we live and share all aspects of our life.

The faith community continues to grow through the efforts and generosity of many dedicated persons, and by the grace of God. The vision of our ancestors has sparked a flame of faith, whose torch has been handed on to us who run the course of history. Our challenge is to run the race well with the flame of faith alive in our hearts and to pass along that burning desire to attain an everlasting place in God's Kingdom. Our prayer is that our efforts, however small and meager, may in some way bring others closer to our loving God.

ST. MARY OF THE FIELDS PARISH
LACENTER

"On November 24, 1907 at LaCenter, Ballard County, Right Reverend William George McCloskey, Bishop of Louisville, dedicated the church of St. Mary of the Fields." These official words from the church register testify to the eighty-five years Saint Mary has served the Roman Catholics of this far-western county of the Diocese.

Originally, Mass was celebrated in homes in Wickliffe, and for a number of years, only on Monday morning. Earliest members of the church include M.K. Church, Mrs. Tom Tharpe, Lon Bullock, Mrs. Ben Curtis, N.L. Cannon, Willie Poole, and E. Weidenbenner. The Goughs, Ballards, Haydens, Mattinglys, Aubreys, and Harrisons were also numbered among the first families.

Plans for a brick structure were begun under Father Rhodes, pastor from 1944-1955, and construction began during the pastorate of Father Phil Riney. The new Saint Mary was blessed by Bishop F.R. Cotton (who had earlier served as pastor) on November 5, 1956, with its patronal feast designated as the Assumption.

The only Catholic Church in the County, Saint Mary is one of fifty-one churches of various denominations within Ballard's one hundred ninety-eight square miles. The less-than-two-percent Catholic population is spread not only across the fields, but also in the settlements of Kevil, West Paducah, Gage, New York, Blandville, Barlow, Wickliffe, Oscar, Bandana, Ingleside, Lovelaceville, and Monkey's Eyebrow.

The church is centrally located at LaCenter, the heart of the County.

Saint Mary has been aligned at various times with St. Francis de Sales, Rosary Chapel, Sts. Charles and Denis, and most recently, Lourdes Hospital. The gifts and talents of the two hundred plus members of the parish are coordinated by the five commissions of the Pastoral Council (established in 1971 by Father Bob Willett) and by the recently formed Ladies' Sodality.

The only salaried positions in the parish are the non-resident sacramental minister and the resident administrator, both part-time. Parish volunteers chair Adult Education, CCD, RCIA, RCIC, Records, Altar Care, Ministry to the Homebound, and Music Ministry. Father Bob Drury presently serves the parish as canonical pastor, in addition to chaplaincy duties at Lourdes Hospital. Sister Elaine Byrne, OSU is in her fifth year as pastoral administrator of Saint Mary, and serves on the Vocation Ministry Team for her Ursuline Community.

SAINTS MARY AND JAMES PARISH
GUTHRIE

In the mid 1940s Mass was offered in the homes of Joseph Sanders, Sr. and Clarence Covington by the Pastor or assistant priest from Russellville, KY. In 1948 Father Robert Healy bought two barrack buildings from near-by Fort Campbell. With the help of parishioners from Russellville, a Guthrie carpenter, Wallace Craggs and the volunteer assistance of a railroad work crew who were replacing signals on the L & N Railroad, Father Healy converted the barracks into Sts. Mary and James Mission Church. With Bishop Francis Cotton presiding and the Founder of the Glenmary Home Missioners, Father William Howard Bishop, celebrant, the church was dedicated on March 9, 1950.

The missions of Franklin and Guthrie continued to be served by the assistant priest and two of the Glenmary Sisters out of Russellville. The Sisters conducted religion classes throughout the school year and, along with volunteers held Bible schools in the summer and engaged in social service work in the Guthrie, Elkton area as well as in Simpson County. In 1957 the property next to the church was purchased. In 1965 the parish of Russellville was turned back to the Diocese of Owensboro and staffed by a diocesan priest. Father Frank Wuest was assigned as Pastor in Elkton and served the Guthrie mission from there. The Glenmary sisters subsequently left the Russellville parish and were succeeded by two Ursuline Sisters from Maple Mount, KY. The Glenmary Sisters again came back with volunteers for summers from 1968 to 1973. The Ursuline Sisters taught Bible schools in the summers of 1981 and 1983 in Guthrie. In 1975 the Glenmary sisters took up residence to serve full time in Todd County. The house next to the parish house was purchased in 1990. The Sisters continue to reside in this house. At the time of this writing the pastor, who resides in Elkton, and two Glenmary Sisters serve as a team in Todd County, ministering to and with the people of the area.

ST. MICHAEL PARISH, SEBREE
HOLY CROSS PARISH, PROVIDENCE

In 1976, Webster County was the only county in the Diocese without some kind of Catholic Presence. This was a worry to Bishop Henry J. Soenneker and especially since he had been approached by some business people and residents requesting a church in the area of Providence, a city of 6000 people. On July 15, 1976 the Bishop sent Father Carl Glahn to investigate the possibility of a church. Catholics showed up out of nowhere. The Providence State Bank invited the Catholic Community to use the Social room in the basement for Sunday Mass. Someone quipped "Jesus Saves" about the same time the members of the Aluminum Workers of America offered their Union Hall for Mass at Sebree. This meeting room was on the third floor of the Sebree Deposit Bank, approached only by a fire escape. It was said that Webster County had the Highest and Lowest Masses in the diocese. The congregation seemed to grow each Sunday and soon there was talk of a permanent church at both Sebree and Providence. There was some difficulty in getting church sites. In time, three acres were purchased on Highway 41 North at Providence and a downtown lot across from the post office was procured at Sebree.

The Catholic Church had been present in the county many years before, when priests came from neighboring counties to offer Mass at the coal mining camps near Providence and this dates back as far as 1893. The Church of St. Joseph was founded in Sebree in 1885 and existed until 1901. The building was later used as a public school and was destroyed by fire in 1922. The Church was on Dixon Street.

With the response from the people, building began immediately at Sebree. The Bishop assigned the name of St. Michael's to the new church. It was dedicated November 20, 1977. Holy Cross was the name of the new church at Providence. The harsh winter of 1977 held up construction and the church was not dedicated until May 14, 1978. By 1981 some 300 people were attending the two churches. Father Herman Moman was pastor in 1981. Father Maury Riney was pastor in 1983. Father Maurice Tiell came in 1983 to 1987. Father Tiell added a real ecumenical look to the churches and integrated them into the religious picture of Webster County. In 1987 the two parishes were divided. St. Michael's was taken care of by Monsignor Bernard Powers who was pastor at St. Alphonsus, St. Joseph, KY. Holy Cross became a mission of Immaculate Conception Parish at Earlington, KY. Father Gerald Baker was pastor. Father Baker engineered an extensive renovation to the interior of Holy Cross Church and it became one of the most beautiful little churches in the diocese. In 1989, Father Glahn was reassigned to the Webster County churches with residence at St. Michael's in Sebree and the two parishes were linked together again. A Parish Hall was added in 1989, a Rectory in 1991 and the church was remodeled and enlarged in 1992.

These churches were built on the sacrifices, prayers and the faith of the people. It was not always easy, so many in the area misunderstood the church. One man said "There are two kinds we don't want in our town, Mormans and Catholics." In time the churches were very well received by the good people of the county. God blessed the churches through it all and they stand today re-echoing the voice of Christ to Webster County—1992.

Saint Paul Parish: 1810-1992
Saint Paul School: 1917-1992
Leitchfield

In the year 1810, Fr. Charles Nerincx, the pioneer of Catholicism in Grayson County, formed the first congregation of Catholics in the county. The following year, 1811, with the help of the people, he erected the first Catholic Church in the county. Built of logs, the first church stood on the site of our present cemetery.

In 1860, because of the increasing number of parishioners, Fr. J. B. Vandermergel, under the guidance of Billy Burkhead, built a new church where the present church now stands. The frame church was constructed on land donated by Mr. Wilford Clark.

In June, 1906, Fr. Anthony Helling was assigned to the care of St. Paul Parish. On June 10, 1917, lightning struck and burned the church built by Fr. Vandermerel. Fr. Helling built a new church shortly afterward in June 1917 with donated materials and labor. Also around this time, the people of St. Paul, along with Fr. Helling, built a new school and convent for the Sisters. Ninety-three students attended the first school. After serving the Catholics communities of Grayson County for 32 and one-half years, Ft. Helling died at Clarkson on Nov. 13, 1938.

On April 20, 1939, Fr. Charles DeNardi began his duties as pastor of St. Paul and its missions of St. Elizabeth at Clarkson, KY and St. Mary at Big Clifty, KY. His first project was to start a parochial school at St. Paul. After renovating the old two room school, the parochial school was opened in September 1940. In 1941, a high school was opened at St. Paul. The first high school graduates were Mary A. Milliner, Margie Pearl, Dolores Harris and Thomas Clark.

In 1944, Fr. Charles DeNardi moved the rectory from St. Elizabeth in Clarkson to St. Paul. On August 1, 1945, under the leadership of Mr. Willie Casey and help from the men of the parish, construction began on a new school building. The school was completed and dedicated on May 6, 1946. With the opening of the new school, the old two room school building was torn down and the lumber was used to build a dwelling across the road from the church which was used as the caretakers home. It was later remodeled and served as a convent for the Sisters.

Pupils from all the parishers of Grayson County were accepted at the new school, increasing its enrollment to 210. In 1953, a seperate building was constructed across the road from the church and was used as a high school. The new school was finished and dedicated in 1956.

On September 20, 1957, Fr. DeNardi was transferred to St. Francis DeSales in Paducah, KY. He was succeeded as pastor of St. Paul, St. Elizabeth and St. Mary by Fr. Pike Powell. Fr. Powell added two classtooms to the high school in 1963 and it became known as the "Grayson County Catholic High School." Fr. Powell renovated the church of St. Elizabeth in Clarkson and was in the process of renovating the church of St. Paul when he was transferred to Sacred Heart Church in Russellville, KY.

Fr. Richard Danhauer succeeded Fr. Pike Powell as pastor of St. Paul and its missions. After enlarging the caretakers home, it became the new convent for the Ursuline Sisters who were teaching at St. Paul School. The old convent was then demolished. At the end of the school year in 1966, the Grayson County Catholic High School closed and the building was then used for the St. Paul Grade School. The old frame building then served as the school cafeteria and parish hall. In the summer of 1987 two rooms were remodeled and are presently being used for classrooms.

On July 21, 1968, the church was struck by lightening and destroyed by fire, along with the contents. Fr. Danhauer immediately began plans for a new church. The foundation was laid in March, 1969, but Fr. Danhauer was transferred before the church was completed.

Fr. William Borntraeger became pastor of St. Paul and its mission of St. Elizabeth and St. Mary on July 12, 1969. Under his supervision, the new church was completed. It was dedicated by the Most Rev. Henry J. Soenneker on Dec. 21, 1969. Fr. Borntraeger continued to serve the people of St. Paul and its missions until he was transferred on Aug. 10, 1972.

Fr. Charles DeNardi, who served St. Paul and its missions from 1939 to 1957, was reassigned to St. Paul in August, 1972 for his second term as pastor. He served until his retirement in March 1984. He left St. Paul on March 9, 1984.

Fr. Art Snow replaced Fr. DeNardi in March 1984 at St. Paul. Later in the same year, June 14, 1984, Fr. Gerald Calhoun moved to Leitchfield to become pastor of St. Joseph as well as pastor of Grayson and Edmonson Counties. Fr. Art Snow moved to St. Joseph, Leitchfield and Fr. Tony Stevenson moved to St. Paul's in June 1984. Thus began the Grayson County Team Ministry.

Fr. Tony Stevenson lived and served in the St. Paul Community for three years until he was assigned to St. Anthony's in Axtel, KY and Holy Guardian Angel in Irvington, KY in June 1987. During Fr. Tony Stevenson's time at St. Paul, he worked with the youth of the parish, RENEW and was involved in major improvements to the church.

Bingo was started in January 1986. The proceeds from Bingo helped pay part of St. Paul's tuition and other church expenses.

In April 1986, St. Mary Church in Big Clifty, one of the mission parishes of St. Paul, was closed and the ground and Community Building were turned over to the East Grayson County Volunteer Fire Department.

On June 7, 1987, Fr. Maury Riney arrived at St. Paul to begin his new assignment.

On June 13, 1989, Fr. Charles G. Fischer came to be pastor of St. Paul and St. Elizabeth Parishes. In September 1989, Fr. Fischer started RCIA Classes for the first time in our parish. On June 24, Fr. Fischer celebrated his 40th Anniversary in the priesthood with a Mass in Thanksgiving and a reception with many friends.

Fr. Fischer continues to be devoted to his work as our pastor and leader. He has the love and cooperation of the people of the parish.

The following priests served the parish during its long history: Fr. Charles Nerinckx (1810-unknown), Thomas Joyce (September 1853-1855), Bambury (February 1854-58), J. B. Vandermergel (1858-1875), Joseph Carmanns (February 1875-May 1876), Jacob Farenback (May 1876-January 1888), H. S. Egart (January 1888-May 1888), Anthony Sullivan (May 1888-March 1894), Andrew Zoeller (March 1894-January 1896), Gabe (January 1896-April 1896), L. B. Ford (April 1896-July 1896), Frank X. Havelburg (July 1896-June 1906), Anthony Helling (June 1906-November 1938), Charles A. DeNardi (April 1939-September 1957), Pike Powell (September 1957-July 1965), Richard Danhauer (July 1965-July 1969), William Borntraeger (July 1969-August 1972), Charles A. DeNardi (August 1972-March 1984), Arthur Snow (March 1984-June 1984), Anthony Stevenson (June 1984-June 7, 1987), Maury Riney (June 7, 1987-June 13, 1989), Charles G. Fischer (June 13, 1989-present)

St. Paul Parish
Owensboro

St. Paul Parish is an offspring of St. Stephen Parish, the first Catholic Parish in Owensboro. When St. Stephen Church became too small for the growning numbers of their congregation, St. Paul Parish was formed. In the early years, it was a mission of St. Lawrence in eastern Daviess County. The first official announcement of the division of St. Stephen Parish is recorded on December 5, 1886. Under the direction of Fr. Thomas Gambron, the first pastor, a small temporary church was built on a lot at Fourth and Pearl Streets. The parishioners worshipped there for the first time on Passion Sunday, March 27, 1887. Shortly after, a lot was purchased on the corner of Fourth and Bolivar Streets for $4000. Ground was broken for the church building on July 6, 1887.

St. Paul Church was dedicated on Sunday, Jan. 13, 1889 by Bishop William George McCloskey of Louisville. He was assisted by Rev. James Cronin of Knottsville and Rev. P. M. J. Rock of Louisville. The first wedding took place on Jan. 15, 1889. Richard H. Rudd and Mary Belle Field were married with Bishop McCloskey performing the ceremony. On May 12, 1889, a class of 20 boys and 26 girls received their first Holy Communion. Records show that the first mission was given in October 1890 by Jesuit Fathers Mueller and Finegan.

Most of the founders of St. Paul Church were associated with the distilleries of Owensboro; they were the Irish. Among the parishioners were also businessman, politicians and realtors. They were noted for their religious fervor and their commitment to God and their faith.

In 1892, Fr. Gambron received a new assignment. He was called to serve as secretary to the bishop in Louisville. Fr. Edward S. Fitzgerald was appointed pastor of St. Paul. Fr. Fitzgerald came to Owensboro as a young priest in 1892 and remained at St. Paul to become a legend in the community. He was affectionately regarded by not only the Catholic people, but also by ministers of other faiths and by the civic community. The entire populace of Owensboro was shocked at the news of his sudden death on Nov. 22, 1927. He is buried in the Mount St. Joseph Cemetery at Maple Mount, KY.

In 1911, a new rectory was built at St. Paul. Then, in 1917, the church was improved by the addition to the sacristy and by the frescoing of the church. Needed repairs and modernization to both the church and the rectory were made between 1939 and 1946. On October 29, 1978, the parish was presented with a certificate by the Kentucky Heritage Commission declaring St. Paul Church as a Kentucky landmark.

On April 3, 1948, Bishop Francis R. Cotton announced the merger of St. Paul and St. Joseph Parishes. They would henceforth be known as Sts. Joseph and Paul Parish. Fr. Peter Braun was pastor at the time of the merger.

On December 25, 1984, the interior of St. Paul was ruined by fire that had started in the cellar of the church. After restoration St. Paul Church was rededicated by Bishop John McRaith in January 1986.

Left, Rev. W. P. McCarthy, Pastor at St. Alphonsus, 1888-1894. Rift, Rev. Thomas Gambon, Pastor at St. Paul, Owensboro.

Rev. Thomas Gambon, Pastor and builder of St. Paul's Church, Owensboro, 1887-1892.

Pastors

Rev. Thomas Gambron	1886-1892
Rev. Edward S. Fitzgerald	1882-1927
Rev. James F. Norman	1927-1938
Rev. George Bowhmicke	1938-1939
Rev. Charles P. Bowling	1939-1946
Rev. Willaim B. Jarboe	1946-1948
Msgr. Peter Braun	1948-1969

St. Paul Parish
Princeton

St. Paul Church, built in 1917. Beside the church is the rectory.

St. Paul Church

Sister's Convent at St. Paul Parish

The early Masses offered in the Princeton area were in private homes of the members by circuit-riding priests coming from Fancy Farm, Hopkinsville, Paducah, and Henshaw. Father E.J. Durbin, who rode mule-back over a wide area, was the first priest to serve this territory. Other priests who conducted services and administered to the Catholics of this area were Fathers Patrick O'Sullivan, Havelburg, Welch, Vance, Spalding, Boehmicke, Clements, Carl Blahn, Gerald Glahn and Thomas Clark, the first resident pastor. Father Delma Clemons was assigned to St. Paul in March 1971 and continued to serve as pastor during the major expansion of parish facilities. More recent pastors were Fathers Frank Roof, Patrick Bittel, Peter Hughes, and Anthony Stevenson.

Some of the family names appearing in the early history of Princeton who were members of the Church are Bohanon, Downs, Kelley, Moss, Sweeney, McGovern, McNamara, Adams, Linton, McKinney, Orange, Skees, Loftus and Walker. Many descendants of these families still live in the area and continue to make up the membership of the present congregation.

Property was first acquired in Princeton in 1871 and 1873 on the corner of Washington and Harison Streets, the present site of the United States Post Office building. The first building used as an assembly place for the Catholic families appears to have been built in 1874. A second structure or renovation of the old building seems to have taken place around the corner lot was sold to the Post Office Department for ten thousand dollars and the church was erected for that amount. The building previously used as a Rectory was purchased in 1948 and housed a parochial school until 1963. The twelve acre tract of land on the Old Eddyville Road was purchased in 1961 for the location of a new education building as well as for a future church structure. The school was built in 1963 and the first classes were held there on November 7, 1963. The enrollment continued high for a number of years, particularly under the capable leadership of Mrs. Carmen Richardsville as principal.

The old St. Paul Church and Rectory properties in downtown Princeton were sold to the General Services Administration in March 1971 to make possible further expansion of the Post Office. The money received paid off the mortgage on the school building and let funds for the porch of a mobile home as the temporary rectory as well as a nest egg for a new church. In the meantime, Mass was offered in the Chapel located on the lower floor of the school building.

A successful building fund drive was conducted in August 1972 and approval was received from Bishop Henry J. Soenneker for the construction of a new church. The new church building was blessed and dedicated on Saturday, April 20, 1974. Capital improvements continued in St. Paul Parish with the blacktopping of the parking lot in the summer of 1974 and the building of a new rectory adjacent to the church. The rectory and its furnishings were a gift of Mr. and Mrs. Howard Day in memory of their son John Moser. The Rectory was blessed on Sunday, February 23, 1975, with many of the parish members present.

In 1986 following a feasibility study conducted throughout the Diocese, the decision was made to close St. Paul School. This took place at the end of the school term in May 1986. The former school facilities presently serve the parish at St. Paul Catholic Center. Among other groups who regularly use the Catholic facilities are: the local chapter of A.A., Catholic and Ecumenical Cursillos and retreats for small high school groups.

St. Peter of Alcantara Parish
Stanley

Two gentlemen by the names of John Gaw and N.M. Lancaster first proposed the idea of building a church in the area of Oakford in western Daviess County. After 2 meetings, sufficient funds were raised to build the church and the location at Bernard Hill was decided upon. The first priest involved was Father Eugene Callahan of Owensboro, who attended the planning meetings. The building committee consisted of Thos. J. Monarch, John Gaw, N.M. Lancaster, J.C. Grant and T.C. Hill. At a cost of $4000.00, the church was constructed in 1873 and was dedicated by Bishop McClosky. The first pastor, Father T.P. Faunt, was there from Nov. of that year until the spring of 1880, when Father Croghn took charge. In 1883 the congregation numbered about 60 families. (This church was located on what is called the Oakford Road, north of the present Clement Mitchell residence. The old frame rectory still stands.) In the teens a temporary church and school were erected on the present church site. In 1922, under Father John M. Higgins, the present church was erected. The basement was divided into classrooms, which were used until a 4-room school and Sisters' quarters were built in 1952. In the early 1960s 4 more rooms were added to the school. For many years St. Peter's had both grade and high school.

Ursuline Sisters taught in the school until 1982 when the school was staffed by all lay people.

Declining enrollment dictated the closing of the school in 1984, at which time St. Peter's students went to the Cathedral School. When all the Catholic schools of western Daviess Co. and Owensboro consolidated in 1988, Holy Angels School at Sorgho became the "home" of St. Peter's students.

In 1972 the church was completely renovated by Father Carl Asplund. A beautiful wooden raredos was installed and the side altars were removed. The old St. Peter Cemetery on Overstreet Road (known as Lancaster Cemetery) has long since been out of use and a larger, well-kept cemetery is located about 3/4 mile from the church on Highway 1554. Among the priests from the parish were Father James Smith, O.M.I. (dec.) Father Pat Thompson, O.M.I., who is in Mexico; Msgr. Gilbert Henninger, (b. 1907-d. 1990) who was Chancellor and Vicar General of the diocese for many years; and Fr. Bruce Fogle, presently pastor of St. Anthony's Axtel.

The original St. Peter of Alcantara Church and Rectory on Oakford Rd., Stanley, KY.

St. Peter's Church, Stanley, KY 1992.

The following pastors followed Fr. F.J. Groghan; Fr. J.J. Abell (1889-91); Fr. Joseph Niesen (1889-92?); J.J. Pike (1892-99); J.G. McKearney (1899-1910); Thomas F. McGuire (1910); J. Odendall (1910-1915); R. Maloney (1913-1919); John M. Higgins (1919-1925); Jas. S. Whelan (1925-26); E.T. Menke (1927-33); Chas. P. Bowling (1933-39); Martin Nahstoll (1939-47); James Higdon (1947-54); Geo. Hancock (1954-60); again M. Nahstoll (1960-69); Carl Asplund (1969-74); Richard Powers (1974-76); Wm. J. Hagman (1976-82); Paul Pike Powell (1982-).

There are at present about 110 families in St. Peter Parish with a total parish population of about 275.

St. Peter of Antioch Parish
Waverly

St. Peter of Antioch, Waverly, KY was the fifth Catholic parish established in Union County, KY. The town of Waverly having a railroad station made it a logical place for a church.

The choice site containing four acres was purchased from Mr. and Mrs. John S. Payne for $400.00. Bishop O'Donaghue, of Louisville, appointed Father Peter J. O'Neil as first pastor. He arrived from Mayfield, KY on February 8, 1909 to take on the duties of establishing the parish.

He visited all parishioners to make their acquaintance and secure a pledge of financial support in constructing the parish buildings.

The Church, a two-story structure was ground level with the school on the second floor. On either side was a rectory for the Pastor and a Convent for the Sisters.

Construction costs was $20,000.00 and $10,000.00 for furnishings. Each family constructed their own pew. Easter Sunday March 27, 1910 was the first Mass in the new church.

Dedication and Blessing was October 12, 1910.

In 1918 the original debt was paid off and school enrollment was 174.

A grade school staffed by the Ursuline Sisters of Mount St. Joseph was opened in 1910 and continued until 1973.

Fire was discovered in the church February 8, 1923. All contents were destroyed but by the efforts of parishioners the Rectory and Convent were saved. It was rebuilt and dedicated August 5, 1924. The school was in the basement and the church above ground.

The fiftieth Anniversary was celebrated August 4, 1974 with Bishop Soenneker, of Owensboro, present. In 1988, with Father E.E. Willett as pastor, the Church was renovated.

St. Rose Parish
Cloverport

The first Catholic Mass in the Cloverport area was celebrated in the home of Richard P. Carter, about three miles up the river at Carter's Landing in about 1853. In 1857, Father M. Power built the first church in Cloverport. It was a small brick church which stood across the railroad from the present Church. It was called St. Malachi. St. Malachi was served by priests from Hardinsburg before receiving its first resident pastor. In 1884 Father Sheridan became pastor. He was followed by Father D.J. Higgins. Father Higgins soon began construction of a new church on the lot which had been purchased across the railroad by Father Connolly a priest from Hardinsburg. The church a large frame church was built about where the present rectory now stands. It was dedicated in 1887 to St. Rose of Lima. A new frame rectory was built where the present church now stands. Father Higgins was succeeded by Father P.F. Hennessy, Father James Cronin and Father George Niehaus. On February 28, 1894, St. Rose Church and rectory burned to the ground. Construction was begun almost immediately on a new church and rectory. On February 21, 1894, the new St. Rose Church was dedicated by Bishop McCloskey. The original pews are still being used. Father M. Carroll came as pastor in 1895. He was followed by Father Celestine Brey. Father Brey started the first parochial school in Cloverport in 1900. It was taught by a Mrs. Durry in her home but lasted only a few months. Father J.S. Henry came as pastor in 1912. He built the St. Rose parochial school in 1916. It was at that time both a grade school and a high school. It was staffed by the Ursuline Sisters of Mount Saint Joseph. A few years later the sisters house was built. In 1925 Father J.T. Neeson took Father Henry's place as pastor. He remodeled the sanctuary and installed large Gothic altars. He remained pastor until 1928 when he was succeeded by Father Joseph Rives. In 1935, Father C. Leo Smith became pastor. He remained until 1937 when he was succeeded by Father James W. Mills. During the last year of his pastorate Father Mills made extensive repairs on the church. In 1948 Father C. Hallahan became pastor. He was followed in 1949 by Father Thomas L. Carter who was pastor for about a year. On August 20, 1950 Father Frank Ward became pastor of St. Rose, a position which he held until 1962. It was during his pastorate that our high school students began going to St. Romuald in Hardinsburg. In 1962 Father Aloysius Fisher, O.S.B. assumed the duties of pastor. The most outstanding of his contributions was the building of the parish hall, called "Aloysius Hall" in his honor. In 1965 Father Charles Fischer became pastor. Under his guidance the church was extensively renovated and remodeled in conformity with the requirements of the new liturgy. Father Fischer remained pastor until 1967 when he was followed by Father Benedict Huff. Father Huff remained only about three years when he became gravely ill and died in 1969. In 1969 Msgr. William Jarboe was appointed pastor. He devoted much effort toward organic gardening projects. He built a greenhouse and spent much time and energy improving the landscape of the lawn. In 1973 Msgr. Jarboe was succeeded by Father William Borntraeger who served as pastor until September 1976 when Father Frank Roof became pastor. Under Father Roof's direction the old St. Rose School was extensively renovated and was named "St. Rose Parish Center." He was succeeded by Father John Vaughn. While he was here Father Vaughn started the Parish Renewal which brought the parish closer together spiritually. He also made some renovations in the church. He tore the white ceiling down and restored the rafters to the original finish. He also built a closed in walkway joining the bathrooms and parish hall together. He served as pastor for 4 years when Father Maury Riney came in 1983. Serving as pastor for two years, he was succeeded by Father Peter Hughes in 1985. It was during his pastorate that our annual Homecomings began. He formed the finance committee. On May 17, 1987 at 6:30 a.m. Father was awakened by a phone call saying the church was on fire. The front of the church was extensively damaged while the rest of the church suffered considerable smoke damage. The extreme heat disfigured the windows and walls. With the help of the parishioners and Father Pete the church was cleaned and renovated without sacrificing the original pews and statues. In 1991 Father John Little became our pastor. He was only to stay a year but he touched many people in different ways. Now on June 16, 1992 St. Rose Parish has to open their arms and hearts to yet another priest, Father Walter Hancock. We wish all the ones before him the best of luck and God's blessings, and to those who are to come in the future. We the parishioners of St. Rose today can be very proud of our heritage and now give thanks to God for the faith and zeal of our ancestors. The life and vitality of St. Rose Parish today is a credit to those pastors and faithful who have gone before us.

STS. PETER AND PAUL PARISH
HOPKINSVILLE

Organized Catholicism in Hopkinsville/Christian County dates from 1866. Prior to that time, there were a limited number of Catholic families in Hopkinsville and Mass was celebrated in the private homes of various residents. This missionary church was tended by Rev. Elisha Durbin, then pastor of Sacred Heart Church, St. Vincent, Kentucky.

In November, 1866 Rev. William J. Dunn, who had been assistant to Fr. Durbin since his ordination in 1861, was appointed as the first resident pastor of Holy Name Church in Henderson and given the care of the Hopkinsville station. In this capacity he purchased a lot on Nashville Street (later to be called East 9th) with the expectation of building a church on the site at some future date.

Hopkinsville was originally part of the Diocese of Bardstown (founded in 1808). In 1841, the rapid growth of Louisville caused the diocese to be transferred from Bardstown to Louisville and Hopkinsville remained as part of the Louisville Diocese for the next 70 years.

In 1871 Fr. Dunn was transferred to the Cathedral in Louisville, and succeeded by Rev. Thomas J. Jenkins. It was under Fr. Jenkins' auspices that the first church was constructed. It is presumed that the construction began in the spring, 1872. The all frame structure was built on the Nashville Street lot originally purchased by Fr. William Dunn in 1866. The church measured 20' x 40' in size and sat on a site between the present church and rectory. It stood on a red brick foundation and was accessible by a small wooden stairwell. The divided front doors were panelled and very narrow. A simple foyer was overshadowed by an attractive belfry, which waited for a bell for a number of years. Three floor length windows graced each side of the church, and the building contained 25 pews - 13 on one side and 12 on the other. The space of the 13th pew was occupied by a pot-bellied coal-heating stove. Music was provided by a walnut cased Victorian pump organ. The church was named Saints Peter and Paul. The dedication date of this first church is not recorded in the archives of the Archdiocese of Louisville, and it is supposed that it was never canonically erected.

In 1873 Fr. Jenkins was transferred to Saint Vincent's Church in New Hope and succeeded by Rev. Elisha Durbin who served as missionary pastor from 1873-78 on a fulltime basis, and 1878-80 on a parttime basis. The first entry in the parish records, which begin in 1873, is the baptism of Margaret Kearney on March 15, 1873.

In the fall, 1878 Saints Peter and Paul became an independent parish with a fulltime resident pastor - Rev. Charles A. Haeseby. While pastor, Fr. Haeseby built the first rectory in the spring, 1879 - a white frame dwelling that stood at the approximate site of the present rectory.

After two and one-half years, Fr. Haeseby was transferred and succeeded by Rev. Thomas J. Hayes in November, 1881. Under his leadership the parish made great progress both spiritually and materially. During 1882 the Catholics of Hopkinsville demonstrated their high esteem for their zealous and untiring pastor by their numerous gifts to the parish: a handsome wrought iron fence was erected around the church lot; a cross was set up at the church; stations of the cross were presented and installed; a bronze bell for the belfry was donated; and a trio of fine handmade altars were obtained.

In 1883 Fr. Hayes was transferred to the Cathedral in Louisville and succeeded by Rev. Dominic J. Higgins for one year, and then by Rev. Richard Feehan.

Rev. Michael F. Melody succeeded Fr. Feehan in January, 1887 and remained three years. When he left in 1890, the parish reverted to a mission and was attended from Saint Joseph's in Bowling Green. In 1895 Rev. William Pike, assistant at Bowling Green, was named pastor of Sacred Heart Parish in Russellville and attended Hopkinsville until his transfer in 1897. Saints Peter and Paul continued to be attended by Sacred Heart's pastor until 1901.

In September, 1901 Rev. John Thomas Hill became resident pastor of Saint Peter and Paul and remained until April, 1903. During his pastorate a limestone foundation was laid for a proposed new church, but the church was never completed.

Pastors continued to change frequently until the appointment of Reverend Joseph P. Welsh in July, 1904. Rev. Welsh continued as pastor until 1925. He was known as a great advocate of the parochial school system and was interested in building a new church, though he never had the chance to do so.

Fr. Welsh was succeeded by Rev. James H. Willett in 1925 who began an active drive to replace the church. In 1927 the frame structure was razed and replaced by the current structure. Fr. Willett's campaign to build a new church was far-reaching. His former parish, St. Brigid, held a social to raise money for the mission church in Hopkinsville. The ladies of Saints Peter and Paul hosted many fund-raising projects, including several suppers held in the business district.

In late 1926 Neal Curtin, a Louisville architect, was contracted to design a new church. The building contract was awarded to S. Lee Oldham Contracting firm of Hopkinsville and personally supervised by Mr. Oldham himself. The cornerstone was blessed on June 28, 1927 by Rev. E. Erle Willett, brother of Fr. James H. Willett, who officiated for Bishop John A. Floersh. The building was completed in mid November, 1927 and formally dedicated by Bishop Floersh on November 27, 1927.

It was reported that the new church would hold 250 people. The two stained glass windows of St. Peter and St. Paul were gifts of former parishioners and imported from Europe. When the church was completed, the old bell which was removed from the old belfry was installed in the new one, and the main altar was also transferred from the old building to the new one. It was trimmed in gilt by Mr. Hugo Hisgen of Hopkinsville. The new church was supported by some 25 local families and was completely paid for when erected.

Fr. Willett was transferred in January, 1928 and succeeded by Rev. John W. Vance who, in addition to Saints Peter and Paul, had the care of Princeton, Outwood Veterans Hospital, and the mission at Eddyville. He built the present rectory in the era of 1928-1930, as well as a new church in Princeton.

In 1937, a little over a century after Fr. E.J. Durbin began his missionary labors in western Kentucky, the centenary was observed by the establishment of the Diocese of Owensboro.

That same year Fr. Vance was succeeded by Rev. Joseph L. Spalding. During his pastorate the summer school was initiated, the mission near Eddyville was blessed with a new church, and the basement of Saints Peter and Paul was refurbished to help entertain the soldiers of nearby Camp Campbell before the USO was founded. Additionally, Fr. Spalding greatly intensified the duties of chaplain at Western State Hospital.

Fr. Spalding was succeeded in 1943 by Rev. George Boehmicke whose greatest contribution was the parish school. He opened the first school and built the present school building. Fr. Boehmicke had charge of Princeton until it was detached from the parish in the fall of 1948. He resigned due to impaired health in 1954.

The parish school was started in 1947 with an enrollment of 15 students and was conducted by three members of the St. Catharine of Siena Congregation, St. Catharine, Kentucky. It was located in a frame dwelling on 9th Street that served as a combined school and convent.

In 1951 the lot next to the rectory was secured for a new school building and construction began in 1952. The school contained grades Kindergarten through 8th Grade until the parish voted to phase out 7th and 8th Grades at the end of the 1967 school year due to inadequate classroom facilities.

Fr. Boehmicke was replaced by Rev. Leonard Reisz who served as pastor pro-tem from 1954-1955. He was replaced by Rev. Thomas Libs in 1955, who died prematurely in 1957 at the age of 44.

Fr. Libs' vacancy was filled by Rev. Ezra E. Willett in 1957 who continued as pastor until 1965. His contribution to the parish included the expansion of school facilities, redecoration of the interior of the church, and an added expanse to the rectory.

In 1961 an assistant, Rev. Gerald Calhoun, was assigned to Saints Peter and Paul. This position was later filled by Rev. Gerald Griffith.

In 1963-64 there was a move to build a new church in Hopkinsville. A proposed structure was designed and would have been located at the site of the then-existing church parking lot on East 7th Street. The final decision, however, was to renovate the existing building.

In June, 1965 Fr. Willett was succeeded by Rev. Carl J. Glahn. In 1966 it was decided to renovate the church to provide more space. The architecture of the church remained unchanged, but only extended to accommodate 21 additional pews. The plastered walls were panelled, restrooms added, and improved lighting installed. The two side altars were removed, but the main altar left in place. With the renovation came the construction of off-street parking facilities. In addition to the duties of Saints Peter and Paul, Fr. Glahn was responsible for Saint Stephen Church at Cadiz and the chaplain responsibilities at Western State Hospital.

The school reached its peak enrollment in 1966-67 when 180 students registered. The school closed at the end of the 1969-70 school year because it was no longer possible to obtain the continued services of the Dominican Sisters, and Fr. Glahn's attempts to acquire the teaching aid of other religious orders were regrettably futile.

In July, 1976 Fr. Glahn was succeeded by Rev. Steve Dunn. In addition to implementing the changes directed by Vatican II, Fr. Dunn was successful in reopening the school (grades Kindergarten through Sixth Grade) with a full staff of lay teachers and built the Parish Hall.

In July, 1981 Fr. Dunn was transferred to Whitesville and succeeded by Rev. Martin Mattingly. Under Fr. Mattingly's guidance, much-needed repairs were begun on the church properties. The roofs of the rectory and the church were replaced, the church was tuckpointed and the stained glass windows repaired and covered with Lexan, and the church was recarpeted.

In July, 1983 Fr. Mattingly was succeeded by Rev. Frances Mastrovito who continued the extensive repair program started by Fr. Mattingly. Fr. Frances proceeded with repairs on the rectory, installed central heat and air conditioning in the church, changed the lighting in the church, refinished the main altar (which in previous years had been covered with white enamel) returning it to its original wood and gilt finish, and installed the backdrop and canopy over the altar. Additionally, Fr. Frances began repairing the school by installing a new roof, painting the classrooms, replacing carpeting and desks where needed, and installing new light fixtures. A lot adjacent to the school was purchased and converted to a teachers' parking lot.

In July, 1989 Fr. Frances was succeeded by Rev. Gerald H. Baker. Under Fr. Baker's direction the parish has made significant strides in expanding and improving church properties. Since his installment as pastor the parish has purchased the lot adjacent to the parking lot and landscaped it, purchased two houses facing 7th Street adjacent to the church property and instituted extensive renovations allowing the buildings to be used for parish and school purposes, purchased the lot at the corner of Belmont and 9th Streets and developed it into a parking lot, and acquired the lot across 9th Street formerly occupied by Young's Tobacco Warehouse and reclaimed it as a grassy area. One of the units on 7th Street was named St. Vincent de Paul and houses the St. Vincent de Paul Store previously located on Walnut Street. Additionally, a large conference area was created on the second floor to allow for additional meeting space. The building also houses St. Joseph's Workshop, the maintenance shop for the groundskeeper. The second unit has been named St. Michael's and is being readied to house the Pre-School, Kindergarten, and extended care programs for the school.

Fr. Baker has continued the school refurbishment started under Fr. Frances. He has converted the Kindergarten room to a new school library, and the former library has been converted to office space for the now fulltime principal. New heating and air conditioning wall units have been installed in the library and principal's office. A computer lab has been installed with state-of-the-art computers, and the teachers' workroom and lounge areas have been restructured.

The church offices and the rectory have been refurbished, all landscaping of the church properties has been replaced, lighting on the church properties has been improved, the church parking lot has been extended and resurfaced. A marble statue of the Blessed Mother was purchased through the generous donations of parishioners and installed outside. Fr. Baker has expanded the size and operation of the parish committees and staff to aid in the accomplishment of long-term goals.

Since the late 1940s Saints Peter and Paul's growth has been largely influenced by active and retiring military families making their homes in Hopkinsville and new industry moving into the area.

St. Pius X Parish
Calvert City

Some forty-five years ago the chemical complex was established on the Tennessee River some 20 miles east of Paducah, KY, in Marshall County. With the coming of the plants to Calvert City, there came a number of workers to the plants...up to that point in history, Catholics in Marshall County were very few. The Catholics who came with the plants had to drive some 50 miles round trip for Sunday Mass. Because of shift work, many found it almost impossible to attend Mass.

St. Pius Tenth Parish began as a Mission of St. Francis De Sales, Paducah. In February, 1953 Mass was offered each Sunday in the American Legion Building. Religious instructions for the children were conducted in the home of Mr. and Mrs. James Gootee.

In the spring of 1954, land was acquired for a Parish Church and School. Immediately plans were implemented and the Church-School Building was completed and blessed by Bishop Francis R. Cotton on the Sunday before Labor Day, 1954. School opened the same September with two Sisters of Charity of Nazareth. At first the Sisters lived in a mobile home and moved into a new convent in 1956. Because of the drop in Religious vocations, the school closed in 1968 with a number of children being bussed into Paducah Parish Schools.

All these building projects were done by the enthusiastic efforts and work of the parishioners. There was a completed parish plant with the erection of the rectory in 1962 with Rev. Wm. Marvin McAtee becoming the first resident Pastor. In the same year, 1962, St. Pius Tenth was elevated to the status of a Parish, the first Catholic Church in Marshall County.

For many years, St. Pius Tenth Parish has served the Catholic Community and also to care for the many campers and vacationers that come to the Kentucky Lake Area.

In 1978-79, Fr. Ben Luther, headed up an extensive renovation program for the Parish Church. In the early Pastoral leadership of Msgr. Anthony Higdon the new entrance was finished.

St. William Parish, Marion

Early in 1960 Jim Fred Mills sent a letter to the Most Reverend Francis R. Cotton, Bishop of the Diocese of Owensboro, to ask the Bishop to consider a Catholic Church in Marion, KY. In a letter dated April 6, 1960 Fr. Joseph L. Spalding, Pastor of St. Ann Parish in Morganfield, KY, Jim Fred Mills was informed that the feasibility of a Catholic Church in Marion was being considered. In August of 1960 Fr. William Allard, Fr. Spalding's Assistant Pastor, and Jim Fred Mills began the task of searching for Catholic families in Crittenden County. About fifteen families showed an interest in having a Catholic Church located in Marion, KY. The first Mass was celebrated in the basement of the home of Jim Fred Mills on August 5, 1962 at 4:00 P.M. with 33 in attendance. The new parish was designated as a mission from St. Ambrose of Henshaw, KY with Fr. Leonard Reisz as the first pastor. The Parish was given the name, Christ the King. In June of 1963 the congregation moved to a house on the present property. With the removal of several walls, three rooms were turned into Christ the King Chapel. It was during that time that Mass was celebrated at 11:00 A.M. The present church was erected by The Hayden Construction Company of Owensboro. Upon the request of Mr. William O'Bryan, a major benefactor through the Catholic Extension Society of America, the name of the church was changed to St. William of Vercelli. The Patronal Feast of the Parish became June 25. On the Feast of Christ the King in 1966 St. William Church was dedicated by Bishop Henry J. Soenneker. Fr. William Hagman was pastor at that most memorable day in the history of St. William Parish. An addition to the back of the church later provided four classrooms. To provide living quarters for two Ursuline Sisters as Pastoral Ministers a mobile home was located behind the education building. St. William had been a mission from St. Francis Borgia in Sturgis until July 6, 1988 when it became a mission from the new parish of St. Mark in Eddyville, KY. As of April 1992 Saint William Parish had 77 families or 175 parishioners.

St. Pius X Parish
Owensboro

It was in 1957 that the first word got around of plans being made for the building of a new church in the Owensboro area. Knowing how rumors are not many people took this information seriously and then one day a tree stump was pointed out as the sight for a new Catholic church. Soon after this revelation Father George Boehmicke began visiting families and organizing a "Christian Family Movement" group for the new parish.

As construction on the Church started families began visiting the site to watch the progress of their new parish home. There was great enthusiasm among the people and they were dedicated to making this dream become a reality. The Choir was one of the first organizations formed followed by an Altar Society and St. Vincent de Paul organizations.

The church building was dedicated on December 27, 1957. The dedication was presided over by Bishop Cotton and the first pastor Rev. Robert T. Wilson. Many of the furnishings for the church were supplied by the people and the celebration was truly a community celebration with the choir singing and the men of the parish filling in as altar servers. The generosity and dedication of the people brought this parish into reality and have sustained it through the years. Rev. Robert T. Wilson served as pastor until 1963, followed by Rev. George Boehmicke who served as pastor from 1963-1966. Rev. Clarence Petitt served as pastor from 1966-1971, and then Rev. Paul Powell from 1971-1976. In 1976 Rev. Robert T. Wilson returned to St. Pius to again serve as the pastor. In 1981 Rev. Jerry Glahn was assigned as the pastor and served until 1989. Rev. Bruce Fogle served as pastor from 1989-1992. Rev. Larry McBride currently serves the parish as pastor. The parish has been blessed with many other priests who have served as associates and have lived in residence plus many religious and lay ministers who have ministered in the parish.

Our School opened September 2, 1958. Five Ursulines from Mount St. Joseph, under the direction of Sr. Cecelia Jean, made up the faculty during this first year. Since that first year, hundreds of students have had the opportunity for a quality education in a Catholic school. In 1989 the Catholic Schools in Daviess County consolidated and the school site at St. Pius became the Bishop Cotton School. Students were welcomed from Sts. Joe and Paul Parish and the emphasis has remained on offering all children a quality Catholic education.

In 1971 Sr. Mary Mercy started the kindergarten and daycare which has continued as a tremendous asset to the parish and community. The daycare program is currently directed by Jaunita Fogle and continues to offer excellent care for children.

Other parish structures were added as years went on with the opening of the school in 1958, the Rectory in 1962, the addition of the west wing to the school in 1964. Remodeling of the church occurred in 1967, 1973, and 1986. The renovation of 1986 was performed almost entirely by parishioners and culminated a two year process of study, planning, and prayer. The convent was remodeled in 1976. In 1981 our school/gym parish hall was completed.

In 1974, Sister Mary Lois and Father Powell worked to form a Parish Council. Twelve members were chosen to serve on this first council in January 11, 1976. The council has continued to serve as a valuable asset to the parish.

Since 1957 the parish has continued to grow in number and in growing sense of community. Many changes and challenges have faced this community but always at the center of this community has been a deep faith and commitment to sharing that faith with others.

St. Raphael Parish
Panther Creek

She was a Catholic Church in every sense of the word for her 135 years of service. And, additionally was the hub for a community hewn from the wilderness and provided the spiritual light as well as the communal gathering crossroads for each of the rural Catholic families. She weathered the storms through life with the greatest of dignity until her demise. Her spirituality was equally strong at the end as it was at the beginning. The second effort burning by the arsonist(s) possessed by a warped delusion for old churches standing with dignity in a sparsely populated farming area decreased in numbers through mechanization and consolidation of what we knew as 'the family farm' when Mom and Pop fed the family primarily from the garden and what was produced thereon. Those who attended the last Mass Sept. 25, 1977, constituted the same cohesive parish as did those gathered early for the first in the Hayden log home. Sheer numbers, availability of priests, and fire damage costs were factors necessitating that St. Raphael's parishioners, residing nearby three neighboring churches, to join with their respective congregations; Sts. Alphonsus, Mary Magdelene, Martin.

Her birth was christened as the Panther Creek Station, pastored by Rev. John C. Wathen of St. Lawrence. If one reflects back in time, duties and ministrations of the Holy Word, this priest may well have the most enviable record for the Diocese in that he served missions at Yellow Banks, Hardinsburg, and thirteen outlying stations, one to become St. Raphael's. Our parish family originated with "Little Willie" Hayden from the collection of Catholic families migrating from Holy Cross parish near Loretto in Marion County, KY. The Hayden family name permeated our community throughout the life of this church and the extended community. The nearest of the one room public schools when their numbers were legion, was the Haydentown School. There were numerous other family names who extended Catholic worship westward from the centered diocese headquarters in Bardstown and the counties of Nelson and Marion.

Our St. Raphael's was birthed and born as a creek station for a few farming families, and was soon to be granted a dowry for those who had settled and for those Catholics yet to come. Land Barons and Brokers in the mid-eighteen hundreds held title to vast tracts of land emanating from colonial grants plus those to be acquired through the tax defaulting processes. Two hundred acres were bequeathed to Bishop Flaget at Bardstown, 'for the purpose of establishing a respectable Catholic community for those now living there and for those to benefit who are yet to come'. The first small log church was erected in the center of the farm along a trail meandering from east to west. This structure burned and was replaced, and later was to be replaced by a brick 'permanent' church located on the hill at the farms corner and near the crossroads intersecting to spread throughout the community in all four directions of the compass. Confirmed genealogists can find many references to St. Raphael in early writings and in the history stored in the Ky. Room of the Public Library at Owensboro.

Her storms of life were most likely typical in an average parish. However, when a loss of the temple by burning is experienced, all find the grit of family in rebuilding. When the first 33 years are administered in a mission status, true faith to the church is essential. And then when a community has 53 years of 'pastor on board', guided by two who must have been clones of Moses' abundances of faith had to have been stored for the last 49 years functioning again as a mission church. The good times and Christian brotherhood far exceeded the rocky times.

Our first pastor to be assigned in 1875, - the builder of the foundation - truly the doer, erected the brick church, parsonage and school with quarters for sisters. He came with a great name for all Irish farming Catholics to remember, Rev. Gustav A. Vantroostenberge, and in the building process quickly became Fr. Van. His fifteen years were without question unmatchable. He was to be followed by an Irishman to the core, Rev. Dominic Higgins, who was to remain for 33 years. He was a liturgist, and had little patience for the discussion of alternatives. The schools functioning under his management fell on hard financial straights as well as methodology and was soon closed for the duration of his parsonage. Rev. Guido Mensa was to follow and soon opened the school as a priority which was to succeed for almost forty wonderful years, thanks to the Ursulines from the Mount, who endured many adversities; inadequately heated facilities to include their quarters, mud roads to a depth that tried the patience of the most hardy, and transportation which at best kept all parties guessing as to time and quality.

School operation was the most consummate function reaching enrollment of one hundred plus at the end of Fr. Van's tenure and was a massive number to be reckoned with by the public school system, upon its closing soon thereafter. Its twenty year period of non-operation must have had a profound effect. Without question upon its reinstitution there began the frequent discussion of its merits whenever two or more gathered together. Those who had the good fortune to be in attendance for those eight elementary formative years will always be heard to express remembrances with gratitude. Even having to drink the water from the cisterns, with or without the wiggletails, was sufficient to leave an indelible mark. The summer picnics were always the focal point in determining how successful the finances of the school would fare.

Cemeteries are a fulfilling part of our Catholic faith, where we terminate this short journey on earth, and await Gabriel's call. St. Raphael's truly experienced this importance. The first small one at the old log church was to record 37 graves plus or minus. In frank honesty and candor it was abandoned and when a concerted effort was made at restoration, efforts to identify individual graves was difficult. Identity of names is as near accurate as possible. Many not so comforting remarks have been heard as to how abandonment was possible. When the permanent church was decreed to be suppressed, the well being and maintenance of the cemetery became a primary item as to how it was to be cared for in its hallowed spot. At this writing there are funerals being held for young and old, children, parents, spouses, relatives, and recall fondly the times that they attended school on the hill at St. Raphael's and chose to be interred in her soil.

St. Raphael's may possibly be the one spot in the diocese where a church will one day be erected in reverse order to the usual. First the church, then the cemetery; possibly my children's children will see a church erected to join a cemetery.

St. Romuald Parish
Hardinsburg

The heritage of St. Romuald Church begins with the settlement of Fort Hardin in 1780. Religion at the fort was given attention at an early date when Fr. Charles Whalen erected a log chapel in the fort to serve the needs of the early Catholics who had emigrated to the area from Maryland. Fathers Wm. DeRohan, Stephen Theodore Badin, Michael Barrieres, Michael Fouriner, Anthony Salmon, and John Thayer were among early missionaries.

By the year 1810, the number of Catholics in the county had grown so that a church building was deemed necessary. Under the guidance of the legendary Fr Charles Nerinckx, the first Catholic Church in Breckinridge Co. was built. It was a simple log cabin structure and was located near the center of the present cemetery. For several years the church remained without a roof, and so became known as the "Fair Weather Church," since Mass could only be offered when the weather permitted. It was named Saint Rumoldus for the Cathedral in Mechelen, Belgium, but was later changed to St. Romuald. Fr. Nerinckx was from Belgium. In 1814, Bishop Benedict Joseph Flaget made his first visit.

In 1818, Father Robert A. Abell was given charge of the area and when he visited Hardinsburg, Father Abell said Mass in the "Fair Weather Church," and Father Nerinckx assisted as his altar server. In 1820, when Father Abell became seriously ill, Bishop Flaget came to Hardinsburg to attend Father Abell and for six weeks took care of the missions of Western Kentucky.

From 1824, when Father Abell was moved to Louisville until 1829, St. Romuald had no pastor. The church was visited occasionally by priests from Louisville and Union County. After 1829, Father J. Cissell and Father Joseph Rogers served Saint Romuald.

In the year 1841, under the direction of Father John C. Wathen, a new and much larger church was erected and dedicated the same year by Bishop Flaget. Since this church was built with red brick, it was affectionately called "The Little Red Brick Church." It was located in the front part of the present cemetery and about two hundred feet south of the present church building. Father Wm. E. Powell, who had taught at the Mount Merino Academy near Irvington, was buried under the high altar of this church. Unfortunately, his grave was not marked when the church was torn down.

The next priest to take care of St. Romuald was Father Adams, then from 1848 to 1850, the missions of Breckinridge County were under the direction of Father William Fennelly whose pastoral residence was Hardinsburg. From 1850 to 1856, the mission was attended by Father Patrick McNicholas from Flint Island.

By the year 1897, the congregation needed a larger church, and with Father William Gabe as pastor, the foundation for the third and present church was laid. It was two years later before the superstructure was completed. This church too was constructed of red brick, and with its two towers and extensive paneling, its architecture would be classified as modified Gothic. This church

Pastors of Our Parish

Father Charles Nerinckx	1805	Father James J. Pike	1889-92
Father Robert A. Abell	1818	Father Michael Dillon	1892-92
Father J. Cissell	1829	Father Hugh O'Sullivan	1892-93
Father Joseph Rogers		Father S.B. Ford	1893-94
Father John C. Wathen	1837	Father William Gabe	1894-07
Father Adams		Father Cyrinus Thomas	1907-10
Father Wm. Fennelly	1848-50	Father James Norman	1910-24
Father Patrick McNicholas	1850-56	Father Martin Rosengarten	1924-48
Father William Powers	1856-60	Father Wm. Roth	1948-48
Father Patrick Cassidy	1860-63	Father Leo Hoying	1948-56
Father John A. Barrett	1863-69	Father Cletus G. Bihn	1956-64
Father Nicholas Ryan	1869-72	Father Lawrence F. Mertes	1964-68
Father J.J. Crowley	1872-74	Father Arnold J. Meiring	1968-79
Father Thomas Jenkins	1874-82	Father James Miller	1979-83
Father Henry Connoly	1882-87	Father Peter Edward Lauzon	1983-85
Father D. Higgins	1887-88	Father J. Patrick Reynolds	1985-91
Father John Creary	1888-89	Father Brad Whistle	1991-

Early home of the Wheatleys, six room plantation house, erected circa 1800, destroyed by fire, 1955.

was blessed by Father Michael Bouchet, Vicar General of the Diocese of Louisville, on October 17, 1900. Bishop Denis O'Donoghue consecrated the new church on August 27, 1903. In 1911, Saint Romuald celebrated its centennial.

In 1962, under the guidance of Father Cletus Bihn, the church was completely remodeled with its seating capacity nearly doubled. It was consecrated on February 17, 1963, by Bishop Henry J. Soenneker of the Diocese of Owensboro. (Saint Romuald became a part of the Diocese of Owensboro in 1937.)

In 1985, under the guidance of Father J. Patrick Reynolds, members of the parish remodeled the church sanctuary and renovated the church. The Pieta and an Altar from the old church were located and brought back to Saint Romuald.

Saint Romuald's 175th anniversary was celebrated on October 5, 1986, and Bishop John J. McRaith blessed the monument erected in memory of Father William Powell who died and was buried in the cemetery, but whose grave had never been marked. A new and much larger pipe organ was dedicated and blessed by Bishop McRaith on Nov. 8, 1987. A stained glass window depicting the life of Saint Romuald was given to the church in 1990.

Father Brad Whistle hired our first Pastoral Assistant in 1991. A new addition to the cemetery was opened in 1992.

The first school on the parish grounds was built near the church in 1876, and was staffed by the Sister of Charity until 1887, and from that

St. Romuald Church, Rectory and School, early 1900s.

date, until 1903, by the Ursuline Sisters of Louisville. In 1903, a new school was built and staffed by the Ursuline Sisters of Mount Saint Joseph, Maple Mount, Kentucky. The third and present grade school building was constructed in 1952, while Father Leo Hoying was pastor. In 1966, a separate building for the high school was built. In 1990, the Benedictine Sisters of Ferdinand, Indiana joined the staff at our school. The High School closed in 1991.

Saint Romuald has given two priests to the church and eleven young ladies from the parish have become nuns in various religious orders.

Saint Romuald is a rural parish of approximately 375 families striving to carry on the faith, determination, and the commitment to Catholic education of those who came before us. Our annual picnic held the third Saturday in June draws many back to their church and school roots.

St. Sebastian Parish
Calhoun

The Catholic faith has been alive and well for 121 years here in McLean County. The first reported services were held by Father Eugene O'Callagran, the pastor of St. Stephen Church in Owensboro, nearly 122 years ago when he began having Mass in the home of Mrs. Thomas Quirk. Mass was celebrated whenever possible and sometimes more than a month would elapse between celebrations of the Mass. Occasionally, Father Charles Eggermont from St. Lawrence Church in Daviess County would also come and help with the celebration of the Mass.

It wasn't until 1871 when Father Paul Volk, pastor of St. Alphonsus Church in Maple Mount, KY, began the undertaking of organizing the ragtag band of Catholics who had been meeting in homes into an official parish. In the Fall of 1871, Fr. Volk constructed the first mission church in Calhoun, KY. Fathers James Pike and G. Schmitt from St. Benedict Church in Beech Grove, KY also helped with the mission at Calhoun as well as Fr. McCarty from Mount Saint Joseph Academy.

In 1891 the mission of St. Sebastian became attached to Saint Martin Church at Rome, KY, which was then under Fr. John H. Riley. It was in 1891 that the first recorded Confirmation was celebrated on October 29, 1891 by the Right Reverend William G. McCloskey, Bishop of Louisville. He confirmed seven people on that occasion. St. Sebastian remained a mission of Saint Martin Church for a number of years.

Rev. Louis Herberth, pastor of St. Martin Church took charge of the mission of St. Sebastian in 1896. Due to the very poor conditions of the roads at the time it took Fr. Herberth two days to get from Rome to Calhoun. He would take the road to Owensboro on horseback and then take a train from Owensboro to Livermore where he would proceed by boat to Calhoun. With the death of Father Herberth, the pastors at St. Martin's in Rome, KY, continued to minister to the mission of St. Sebastian.

In 1937 and 1938, during the time of Father Martin Nahstoll and Father William "Barney" Borntraeger there were some 15 families in St. Sebastian, all of whom must be admired for their loyalty to the church and their faith in spite of the hardships they had been forced to endure. Some of the families at this time were - Mr. and Mrs. Thomas Quirk, Mr. and Mrs. Lewis Moore, Mr. and Mrs. August Moore, Mr. and Mrs. John Rearidon, Mr. and Mrs. James Boyle, Mr. and Mrs. Charles Straney, the McLaughlin family, Mr. and Mrs. John Downey, the Towerys, the Durbins, and Mr. and Mrs. John Trunk.

During the fall of 1947, while Father Anthony Higdon was pastor of St. Anthony Church in Brown's Valley, KY, St. Sebastian became a mission of Brown's Valley. Assisting Fr. Higdon with the mission of St. Sebastian were Fathers Henry O'Bryan and Walter A. Hancock. Heretofore, there had not been a regular schedule for the celebration of Sunday Liturgies. Now the families of St. Sebastian would have the privilege of attending Mass regularly.

St. Sebastian continued as a mission of Brown's Valley for a while longer. In 1952, Father Thomas Libs began a drive to move from the old church to its present location, and to open a Catholic school in McLean County. With a lot of hard work and struggle to raise funds by Fathers Thomas Libs and Charles Fischer and the families of St. Sebastian, Fr. Libs was able to purchase a roller skating rink and renovate it into a church, a school with a Convent and a recreation hall. In actuality, it was a Mrs. Ollie Belle Leachman who bought the roller skating rink from Chester Stratton and then she sold it to Fr. Libs. Fr. Charles G. Fischer renovated a garage into an apartment and continued to serve the people of the community until around 1962. He would spend some of his time in the parish and some at Brown's Valley where he was officially stationed.

The school opened in the Fall of 1953 and St. Sebastian had its first Communion in the new church on November 25, 1953 and its first Confirmation class on March 14, 1954. The school continued in existence until 1967 when it was closed due to the lack of teachers.

In 1962, Fr. James Wathen became the first resident pastor of St. Sebastian Church as the parish finally became independent of Brown's Valley. St. Charles Church in Livermore, KY became a mission of St. Sebastian in 1972 and has continued as a mission since then.

In 1981, the Knights of Columbus, Council 7831, was formed in McLean County and began doing some good things among the people in the County. They continue to this day to do good work in the County and the parish.

St. Sebastian bought the Vandiver property in 1984 and it was used as a pre-school until the summer of 1990 when it became the rectory for the new pastor. During these past 121 years St. Sebastian has made much progress and hopes to make even greater progress in the future. We ask God's blessings upon our future work.

St. Stephen Parish
Cadiz

On August 14, 1966 Bishop Henry J. Soenneker blessed the new church and offered the first Mass in the new parish of St. Stephen's, Cadiz. It embraces the entire Trigg County of Kentucky.

Back at the turn of the century there had been a Catholic church in Trigg County, at Golden Pond. A state historical marker stands today on highway 68 West at Golden Pond, bringing attention to the former existence of St. Joseph Church. The church cemetery still exists today, back in the woods about two miles from the historical marker.

For 15 years St. Stephen's was a mission parish of Sts. Joseph and Paul parish of Hopkinsville, being served by the various pastors there. During his pastorate Rev. Steve Dunn enlarged St. Stephen's church building, and Rev. Carl Glahn built a small rectory next to the church.

In 1981 Rev. Joseph Nagele, a retired Glenmary Home Missioner, became the first resident pastor at St. Stephen's, serving for three years. In 1984 Rev. Richard Danhauer became pastor and serves to this day. Presently plans are being worked on for the construction of a parish hall, much needed to serve the needs of the parish's present 125 families.

Nancy Lee Rutherford was the first infant baptized in the new church, on February 19, 1967. William Amberg and Margaret Gray were the first couple to marry in St. Stephen's, on June 3, 1967.

St. Stephen Parish
Owensboro

The Beginning
In this year of Kentucky's Bicentennial, it seems appropriate to look at the special history of Catholicism in Western Kentucky. Missionary priests celebrated Mass at Yellow Banks, as Owensboro was once called, as early as 1822. Eleven years later, the first church was established at Knottsville with St. Stephen's as its mission. In 1939, Reverend John C. Wathen, then pastor of St. Lawrence at Knottsville, was also appointed pastor of St. Stephen Church in Owensboro, thus establishing it as the first parish in Owensboro and the second in Daviess County. A church building for the fledgling parish was erected at Second and Cedar Streets in that same year. It was described in archives of the church as being "40 x 40 with Gothic windows." This first building was completed in 1842 and dedicated by Reverend J. McGill of Louisville. By 1848, the population of the young parish had doubled and so did the size of the church building. Upon completion, the building addition was dedicated in 1858 by the Most Reverend Martin J. Spaulding.

The first resident pastor of the new church in Owensboro was the Reverend Walter S. Coomes. Successive pastors were the Reverends Eugene O'Callahan, Ivo Schacht, Hugh Brady, Dominic Crane, Thomas Gambon, and Reverend Alexander McConnell, who brought the church into the twentieth century.

Education
Catholic education in a formal setting also began early in Daviess County. In 1849, the Sisters of Charity of Nazareth established Saint Frances Academy, the first Catholic school in the county. In fact, it preceded by twenty two years the establishment of the first public school in the county! Both boys and girls attended the Academy until the public school system was founded in 1871. After that time, the boys attended for grades one through three, then moving on to the public school. Girls of that day attended St. Frances for all grades.

In 1879, St. Stephen Boy's School began operation and continued until 1914. St. Frances Academy continued as the girl's school during this time. When St. Stephen Boy's School closed, the Academy became the "church school" and remained so until 1939.

At that time, the old Knights of Columbus hall at Seventh and Frederica Streets was converted into classrooms for grades one through five and named "Our Blessed Mother." Grades six through eight continued to attend Saint Frances Academy. In 1948, the school at Seventh and Frederica was renamed Saint Stephen School. In that year also, Blessed Sacrament Chapel was established by Father Robert Conner as a mission of St. Stephen Cathedral. By 1951, the girl's and boy's schools were merged to form Owensboro Catholic High School located, as now, on Parrish Avenue. In 1962, construction for an elementary school to serve grades one through eight was begun. The school was an

integral part of the parish until 1989 when it was closed as a part of the school consolidation program. The building now serves as the Diocesan Pastoral Center and houses the parish preschool.

Organizations
The earliest parish group to organize was the Altar Society which began in 1848. It was not until 1880 that the St. Vincent de Paul Society established itself in the church community and not until 1936 that the Society was chartered at Saint Stephen Church. Immediately after the turn of the century, in 1902, the Blessed Virgin Sodality was begun. The following year, the Knights of Columbus was chartered in Owensboro. In 1927, the Holy Name Society was established. The League of the Sacred Heart was begun at St. Stephen in 1941.

The Second Vatican Council, responding to the call of Pope John XXIII for a spiritual renewal and *aggiornamento*, or "updating" began an era of involvement by the laity which continues and expands even to this time. A parish council to assist the pastor was established in 1971. Ministries to involve parishioners as choir members, lectors and ministers of Communion were also begun. In addition, ministries to the homebound and to those in the two community hospitals were also created. Recognizing the importance of serving the youth of the church community and keeping their involvement at a high level has resulted in the establishment of a Youth Ministry which has both a Middle School and High School group. In 1985, in response to community-wide needs, a soup kitchen was established in the undercroft of the church building. Although the parish school was closed in 1989, a preschool and kindergarten were established to meet the needs of the youngest members of our faith community.

The Building
In 1924, the third Saint Stephen Church was begun at the site of the present church, 614 Locust Street. Completed and dedicated in 1926, the Church is of Italian Lombardian architecture, a cruciform design of 150 x 83 feet with a campanile of 83 feet. The Stations of the Cross and Holy Water fonts were brought from the original church. In 1972, in order to conform with the changes made by the Second Vatican Council, the church was completely renovated. The walls were lined with marble and contemporary mosaics adorn many areas of the church, most notably behind the main altar, the Tabernacle and the Baptismal font. Equally notable are the stained glass windows, rich in symbolism, which remain from the original construction.

Leadership
It was in December of 1937 that the Church of Western Kentucky came of age when Pope Pius XI created the Diocese of Owensboro with the Most Reverend Francis R. Cotton, D.D. as its first Bishop. Saint Stephen Church was designated as his Cathedral in 1938. Bishop Cotton was succeeded in May, 1961 by the Most Reverend Henry J. Soennecker, D.D. who served as Bishop from that year until 1984. On December 15, 1984, Most Reverend John J. McRaith, D.D. was installed as the third Bishop of Owensboro at a Pontifical Mass celebrated at the Owensboro Sportcenter.

The aforementioned Reverend Alexander McConnell was pastor of St. Stephen Church for thirty-four years, until 1919. Reverend Richard Maloney became pastor at that time, serving until 1935, overseeing the completion and dedication of the new building as well as continued growth and change in the church. Serving as pastor in successive years were Reverend Albert J. Thompson, Reverend Joseph Egan, Reverend Leo J. Dienes and Reverend William M. McAtee. In 1949, Reverend Anthony G. Higdon was named rector of Saint Stephen Cathedral. He had been the first to be ordained in the new church, in June 1938. Monsignor Higdon continued to serve as rector of the Cathedral until 1969 when Reverend Joseph V. Rhodes was appointed pastor. Fr. Rhodes ministered to the Cathedral until 1985 when the present pastor, Rev. J. Edward Bradley was appointed.

In addition, the parish has been ministered to, and the Catholic Faith lived and taught by many assistant pastors.

St. Stephen Cathedral Church, along with the Universal Church, has sustained through controversy and change and surmounted it all, as Christ promised we would. The same pioneer spirit which brought the Catholic Church to Western Kentucky remains in those who persevere through struggles both personal and public. It is not the building, as beautiful as it is, nor those who have led us, as much as we owe to them for their leadership. It is the love of the greatest gifts of all, the gift of the Eucharist and the gift of Faith, which sustain us and will continue to sustain as they are passed on to succeeding generations of the Cathedral faith community.

St. Susan Parish
Elkton

Through the cooperative efforts of Bishop Henry Soenneker and the Glenmary Home Missioners, a Catholic church was established in Elkton. The Glenmary Missioners already had one Todd County mission at Guthrie, twelve miles south of Elkton. J. Stanley Howard, an active Todd County farmer who was also the Todd County Agricultural Extension Agent, also played an important role in bringing the Catholic Church at Elkton.

On September 9, 1963, Father Robert Dalton, a Glenmary Missioner, became associate pastor at Sacred Heart Church in Russellville. As associate pastor, Father Dalton was in charge of the Todd County mission. Father Dalton celebrated the first Mass in Elkton on January 12, 1964 in a 3-1/3 room duplex apartment rented from Mrs. Frances Lynn. Among those braving the ice and snow to attend the first Mass were J. Stanley Howard and his son, Sheril; Mrs. Talmadge Moseley and her son, Andrew; Clarence Covington and three of his children, Robert Paul, Tamara Dawn, and Mary Charles; Mrs. Geri Reding and two of her children, Charlotte Marie and Charles Maurice. The Covingtons and Redings were visitors from the mission of Saint Mary and Saint James at Guthrie.

Father Dalton asked Mr. Howard to locate a site for a Catholic Church in Elkton. In March 1964, 4-1/2 acres of land and a three bedroom brick house were purchased from Loyce Simon for $18,000. The Simon house served as a meeting place for Catholics and later became the rectory. The first Mass was celebrated in the Simon house on March 30, 1964.

In September 1964, the Glenmary Brothers converted a large mobile home into a beautiful church chapel where Mass was offered until a church was built in 1965.

Michele Arms was the first person baptized in the parish on February 6, 1966 by Father Wuest in the trailer. Bob and Rube Henning were married there November 6, 1966.

When plans to build a church began the building site showed Goebel Avenue going through the property to the Elk Fork Creek and Sunset Drive running from Highway 68 to Goebel Avenue. Building committee members J. Stanley Howard, Talmadge Moseley, and Michael Schwab worked with the city council through a form of court to close Sunset Drive and a portion of Goebel Avenue crossing the church property.

In June of 1965, a tract of land south of the driveway became available. The purchase of this land completed the land area now owned by Saint Susan Parish.

On July 25, 1965, the Glenmary Missioners left Russellville and Elkton became a separate parish with Saints Mary and James at Guthrie as a mission. Also in July of 1965, Father Francis Wuest was assigned to Elkton and became the

first resident priest ever to live in Todd County. He was well received because of the enormous good will effected by Father Dalton. Father Dalton left Elkton August 1, 1965.

Work on a church building began soon after Father Wuest arrived in Elkton. The total cost of the building was $31,050.00. $15,000 of the funding was a bequest of the Leslie O'Bryan family of Chicago in memory of Ronald and Susan O'Bryan and $10,000 came from the estate of Mr. and Mrs. August Bauman. Both came through the Catholic Church Extension Society. Bishop Soenneker dedicated St. Susan Church on June 2, 1967.

Three Glenmary Brothers served in Elkton during the time Father Wuest was the pastor. The brothers were Brother Jerome Herbert, July 28, 1965-January, 1967; Brother Kenneth Woods, February 3, 1967- September 1, 1968; Brother Marion Placzek, December 29-March, 1970.

Glenmary and Ursuline Sisters from Russellville and later Guthrie did much visiting and good in the area over many years.

Wayne, Janet, Terry and Lisa Gibbs were the first baptized in the new church, May 13, 1967 by Fr. Wuest, while the old hall was still under construction. Virginia Shanklin and Sheril Howard were the first couple to get married in the new church, February 8, 1968 by Father Nobert Howard.

When Father Wuest suffered a heart attack in February 1969, Father Francis Schenk filled the post as administrator while Father Wuest was convalescing. Father Schenk arrived March 1, 1969 and stayed until Father Wuest returned in September 1969. Father Wuest remained as pastor an additional year until August 1971. During the time Father Wuest was pastor, several converts were received into the church. Among the early converts were the Wayne Gibbs family, Virginia Hightower and some of her family members, and Ann Sebree and her children.

On August 8, 1971, Father Joseph Nagele arrived in Elkton. He was to be the pastor for the following ten years. During the time he served in Todd County he won the respect of the community by his dedication and hard work. For example, he unearthed many outcroppings of limestone and personally broke them into smaller stones so they could be removed. He was able also, with the help of the sanitation department, to install field tile to reroute the sewage away from the front of the church property. He was perhaps best known for the abundant gardens he grew each year to share with the needy.

On August 27, 1981 Father Patrick O'Donnell replaced Father Nagele as pastor of Saint Susan.

Through a loan from the Saint Vincent De Paul Society, a building on Streets Avenue was bought in October 1982. The building was bought to house a thrift store to provide low cost clothing and household items for those in need. Known as "The Something Else Shop" it opened for business on November 12, 1982 and remains open to the present time. Ladies of the parish are assisted by volunteers from the Ladies Missionary Circle of Petrie Memorial Methodist Church.

In late summer of 1983, ground was broken for an addition to the church. The Christ Center includes a parish hall, offices, classrooms, and quarters for volunteers on the second floor. The parish hall features a large, natural stone fireplace, a spiral staircase fashioned entirely from cherry wood, and a modern kitchen. At the same time, the interior of the church was redesigned and new sanctuary furnishings were made. The round altar symbolizes the eternity of God while the three supporting stipes represent the Trinity. Except for $1,100 donated by two parishioners, funding for the building and renovation project was provided by Father O'Donnell's many friends and supporters outside of Todd County. Father O'Donnell left Elkton in August 1987.

Father John Brown came to Elkton as the new pastor in August 1987. He replaced the pews in the church with oak pews which were a gift from Saint Peter Church in Waverly, Kentucky. Parishioners rebuilt, stripped, refinished and installed the pews. Father Brown also organized Saint Susan's first administrative council. The first members were Bryan Blount, Sheril Howard and Judy Prince. The councils have paved the parking lot and driveway, put up a basketball goal and worked to finish the hall and surroundings. The county wide CCD program and the Cub, Boy and Girl Scouts began using the hall, along with parish families for personal celebrations. Bible schools and joint Christmas plays and parties with Guthrie are held there. Father Brown continues as pastor of Saint Susan, as a team with Sisters Bernadette and Catherine from Guthrie.

St. Thomas More Parish
Paducah

As St. Thomas More Catholic Church approaches the 21st century it does so with a deep sense of pride in-the-past and a profound sense of anticipation for the future.

Dedicated on May 2, 1948, the church is currently being served by its tenth pastor, the Rev. W. Gerald "Jerry" Riney. St. Thomas More Catholic Church was dedicated by the Most Rev. Francis R. Cotton, who, coincidentally, was the first bishop of the newly-formed Diocese of Western Kentucky.

The first pastor of the church was the Rev. Charles Carrico, who actually began his work five years before the fledgling church had a home (1943). That was the year the Catholic community decided a second church was necessary, due to severe overcrowding of the mother church, St. Francis de Sales, whose membership had reached 3,000. However, World War II prevented construction of the church building until 1948. Since its inception, the church has held Mass in the facility that was designed originally for a school gymnasium.

Father Carrico served as pastor until 1950 when the Rev. John J. Glenn became pastor, leading the church for the next 10 years. Subsequent pastors have been the Rev. Benedict Huff, 1960-1961; the Rev. Martin Nahstoll, 1961-1962; the Rev. Joseph Saffer, 1962-1965; the Rev. E.E. Willett, 1965-1969; the Rev. Richard Danhauer, 1969-1976; the Rev. Aloysius Powers 1976-1982; the Rev. Lucian Hayden, 1982-1989; and at present, Father Jerry Riney.

In 1970 the parish community accepted the guidance of its first Pastoral Council. The present council uses a shared wisdom model and is collaborative in nature. Five major Commissions or Committees form the "working arms" of the Pastoral Council. These chairpersons serve as liaisons to the parishioners. Every parish organization flows from one of these committees or five major commissions: Administration, Worship and Spiritual Life, Education, Social Concerns and Community Building.

Throughout the years, St. Thomas More Catholic Church has strived to meet the varied needs of its congregation. Most recently this has been seen in the construction of a new elementary school, the revamping of its middle school and the renovation of the "brothers' quarters" into a new Catholic Community Center.

With the elementary school vacating its present site on Buckner Lane to become adjacent to the middle school and high school facility on Highland Boulevard in Paducah, St. Thomas More parishioners are left with the unique situation of deciding "where do we go from here?"

In January 1993, Fr. Jerry Riney and the parish community began a series of meetings with the help of Fr. Richard Vosko, a nationally recognized liturgical design consultant from the Albany Diocese of New York, to determine the better option—renovate the present church of erect a new church on another site. The end result was the purchase of a tract of land on Highway 62 near the I-24 Intersection for a new Church. The Groundbreaking Ceremony was held on July 31 and a new church will be the place of worship for the St. Thomas More parishioners for many years to come.

As the St. Thomas More parish community looks to the future, growth is inevitable—not only in terms of its physical facilities, but in an ever-widening circle of service, not only to its members, but to the Catholic Community and Paducah at large.

St. William Parish
Knottsville

St. William's

Chronology of St. William

May 1, 1887	St. Williams Parish is established.
May 1887	Altar Society established
May 27, 1888	Laying of Cornerstone of St. William's Church.
Sept. 1897	St. John Berchman's Sanctuary Society organized.
May 28, 1898	First Priest from parish ordained.
Sept. 1899	Young Ladies Sodality of the B.V.M. organized.
Nov. 23, 1908	Holy Name Charter granted.
Sept. 1912	St. William's school opened.
Sept. 1937	St. William's High School established.
Dec. 11, 1949	St. Vincent De Paul Society organized.
1950	Four-Room block addition to school made.
Oct. 8, 1958	Sisters moved into their new convent.
May 20, 1962	Diamond Jubilee of St. William's Parish celebrated.
May 5, 1963	Mary Carrico School opened.
Sept. 1967	St. William's High School Consolidated.
Dec. ?, 1968	St. William's Church remodeled.
Oct. 27, 1968	Knottsville Home opened.
March 1974	Allen Organ and air-conditioning added to church.
Oct. 14, 1979	Dedication of Parish Hall & School Addition.

St. Lawrence

Down the winding Hardinsburg Road thirteen miles East of Owensboro, Kentucky, one will see a small town once known as "Heart's Delight." One fall day in the year of 1827, Leonard Knott built the first house, followed by a blacksmith shop. Twenty years later the Hon. William R. Griffith, Representative to the Legislature, named our prospering settlement "Knottsville." To meet the educational needs of this growing community, a log school was erected about 1854. By 1883, Knottsville had grown to such an extent that it was able to point with pride to a drug store, a shoe shop, two general stores, a saw and grist mill, a blacksmith and wagon shop, a flouring mill, two undertaking establishments and three tobacco factories.

Catholics of the village of Knottsville attended church at nearby St. Lawrence, Kentucky. The St. Lawrence parish is the oldest Catholic parish in Daviess County, the services being held as early as 1822 by Father Robert Abel in the home of William Jarboe. The first church was built in 1828 by Father Elisha John Durbin. Father John C. Wathen was the first resident pastor in 1833. By the year 1883, two hundred families attended St. Lawrence Church. Such remarkable growth necessitated the establishment of another parish.

The people of Knottsville will never forget that great historic day on May 1, of 1887 when Father Thomas Jefferson Jenkins, pastor of St. Lawrence Parish was having company. One by one they arrived—Rt. Rev. Msgr. Thomas F. Gambon, Rev. John Sheridan, Dr. Drury, Misters J.B. and H.T. Aud and W.S. Hazel. At this memorable meeting of the clergy and laity a division of the old St. Lawrence congregation was made. In this manner St. William Parish of Knottsville, Kentucky came into existence.

Pastors of St. William Parish: Rev. James P. Cronin, 1887-1892; Rev. Michael F. Melody, 1892-1893; Rev. Louis H. Spalding, 1893-1914; Rev. Lucien E. Clements, 1914-1915; Rev. Francis J. Timoney, 1915-1920; Rev. Joseph McAleer, 1921-1928; Rev. Francis X. Laemmle 1928-1933; Rev. William Byrne Jarboe, 1933-1938; Rev. Joseph J. Egan, 1938-1942; Rev. Robert A. Whelan, 1942-1959; Rev. Maurice Jerome Tiell, 1959-1966; Rev. Lucian Hayden, 1966-1973; Rev. Henry L. Willett, 1973-1982; Rev. James C. Hite, 1982-1989; Rev. Anthony Bickett, 1989-1992; Rev. Leonard Arcilesi, 1992- .

Brescia College
Owensboro

Brescia College, established in Owensboro in 1950 by the Ursuline Sisters of Mount St. Joseph, is a direct outgrowth of the Company of St. Ursula, founded in 1535 by St. Angela Merici in Brescia, Italy.

The pioneer Ursulines who came from Louisville to St. Joseph, Kentucky (1874), established an elementary school and academy. A postsecondary program began in the early 1900s; in 1925 Mount St. Joseph Junior College for women was established. Brescia College represents the expansion and transformation of Mount St. Joseph Junior College.

Church bulletins in the late 1920s indicated that Ursuline Sisters were even then offering college courses in Owensboro. In 1946, three Ursulines taught evening "commercial" classes at the old St. Joseph High School. Classes were welcomed by returning servicemen (World War II had just ended) and teachers motivated by increasing state requirements.

By 1947 the extension offered a full day/evening schedule in Mary Hall — a brick house on Seventh Street owned by the Ursulines since 1919 — and next door in a recently purchased white frame residence. The Sisters worked and lived in these two buildings. One Sister volunteered to sleep in the attic so her room could be used as a chapel.

By 1948 Owensboro enrollment surpassed that at Maple Mount. In 1950, at the request of the Owensboro community, the junior college relocated in Owensboro at Brescia College. There were 111 students and a staff of 15 Ursulines and one priest. Two residences were purchased to house women students and Sisters; a former church at Seventh and Frederica provided the first auditorium, library, and music department. Advertisements for the new college emphasized Christian values, liberal arts, serious scholarship, and family spirit. Older students were welcomed; students paid $7.50 per semester hour.

During the first decade the Maple Mount administration governed the college, with the Ursuline Superior as president. The academic dean served as day-to-day administrator. The earliest faculty and administration were dedicated pioneers whose energy and sacrifice assured a firm foundation for this new endeavor.

Plans to establish a 4-year program began immediately. Under affiliation with The Catholic University of America, Brescia awarded its first baccalaureate degrees in 1953. Since 1957 the college has been continuously accredited by the Southern Association of Colleges and Schools.

By 1960 enrollment had surpassed 500. Twelve structures comprised the physical plant, including a new administration building, library, and Merici Hall (chapel, cafeteria, convent, and women's residence facility). During these building years the Ursuline Community, assisted by loans from the Owensboro diocese, financed the college.

Brescia's second decade opened with the appointment of Sister Joan Marie Lechner as college president. Her administration brought new growth in every area. In fall 1961 over 170 community leaders met to lay out a 10-year plan. Brescia's first appeal for public support came at this time. In the mid-1960s the college began its first fundraising drive—the Science Building Campaign, bringing contributions of $600,000. In 1969 this 5-story facility was dedicated. The college continued to acquire and renovate neighboring properties. By 1968 enrollment surpassed 1000.

The 1960s brought major governance changes. As early as 1955 there was an Advisory Council with predominantly lay membership. Beginning in 1963 a Board of Community Trustees advised the president on policy and development. In 1964 the college was incorporated independently from Mount St. Joseph; four years later the Board of Directors (the Ursuline Superior and Council) merged with the lay board to form the Brescia College Board of Trustees.

The late 1960s and early 1970s saw major academic expansion. Brescia established the first Kentucky program for teachers of the educable mentally retarded. The Speech and Hearing Clinic provided (and continues to provide) comprehensive service to the region while preparing students for careers in speech therapy and audiology. The Christian Femininity (now Contemporary Woman) program attracted nationwide attention. The college established preprofessional programs in medicine, dentistry, and other science-centered areas. By this time Brescia offered a crowded schedule of day, evening, and summer courses, together with continuing education for adults.

In 1974 Sister Joan Marie Lechner retired from the Brescia presidency. In April 1974 the Trustees named Brescia's second president: Sister George Ann Cecil, a Daviess County native. A quiet person by nature, Sister George Ann invested tremendous energy and singleminded dedication in this work.

Brescia's second 25 years began with another period of energetic growth: the opening the college Counseling Center, the first Greater Owensboro Music Camp and Festival at Maple Mount, establishment of the federally funded Student Support Services program which continues —with noteworthy success— to provide intensive assistance for handicapped, low-income, and first-generation college students. At this time gift and scholarship income began to increase substantially. Physical plant expansion continued with both land and facility acquisitions. A new Speech and Hearing Clinic, funded entirely through federal and private grants, was dedicated in 1975.

In 1983 the college undertook its second major fund drive: a Capital Endowment Fund Campaign, providing more than its $2 million goal for academic programs, plant maintenance, scholarship and general endowment funds.

The early 1980s saw the establishment of an immediately successful Weekend College program and in intercollegiate athletic program. In fall 1985, in collaboration with the Diocese of Owensboro, Brescia inaugurated a degree program in Ministry Formation designed to provide academic, professional and spiritual preparation for lay persons seeking careers in church ministry. This and related religious education programs continue to serve Western Kentucky and surrounding dioceses. By fall 1992, 21 persons had completed degrees in ministry formation; the majority of these graduates now minister in the Owensboro Diocese.

On December 12, 1985, Sister George Ann Cecil died after an illness of over a year. In February 1986 Sister Ruth Gehres was named third president of Brescia College. This administration faced the new challenge of a state-supported community college in Owensboro. Part-time enrollment decreased dramatically during this period. Intensive recruiting of resident students helped Brescia maintain its full-time base.

In 1987 the Board of Trustees launched a $3 million campaign for a student services building on Frederica Street between Seventh and Eighth Streets. Over 800 donors contributed $3.5 million. The Brescia College Campus Center, dedicated in May 1989, was completely free of debt by February 1992. This facility provides a functional center for the Brescia campus and a handsome landmark for the college in downtown Owensboro.

In fall 1992 Brescia college counted over 800 students and nearly 4,000 graduates. Among these alumni are over 200 clergy and members of religious community serving in the Owensboro Diocese and elsewhere. Brescia College provides employment for over one hundred persons, including forty-full time faculty. The college itself provides over $500,000 annually in scholarship and other student assistance; a large majority of students receive financial aid. New degree programs include Graphic Design, Art Therapy, and a Bachelor of Social work degree beginning fall 1993.

In the year 2000 Brescia College will celebrate its 50th anniversary in Owensboro. Founded in two modest houses by a small but dedicated group of Ursuline Sisters, Brescia is moving into the future with confidence, faith in God, gratitude toward all whose support makes fulfillment of its mission possible, and a pledge of continuing service to the Diocese of Owensboro and all the people of this region.

BLESSED SACRAMENT SCHOOL
Owensboro

At Right: Sisters Michael Ellen Regan and Martha Louise Walsh at Blessed Sacrament School, Owensboro.

Sisters

Ann Elizabeth Maloney	Aug. 1947-Aug. 1955
Antonia Schiebert	Aug. 1944-Aug. 1947
Frances Benita Clark	Aug. 1955-Aug. 1960
Helen Joseph Wise	Aug. 1940-Aug. 1942
Joseph Rita (Rita Englert)	Aug. 1943-Aug. 1944
Marcella Cameron	Aug. 1947-Aug. 1954
Margaret Patrick Gallagher	Aug. 1940-Aug. 1941
Mary Carmelite Molohon	Aug. 1946-Jan. 1947
Mary Felix Taylor	Aug. 1941-Jan. 1943
Michael Ellen Regan	Aug. 1956-Aug. 1960
Patrick Maria Bowling	Aug. 1942-Aug. 1946
Robert Vincent (Mary Ross)	Aug. 1954-Aug. 1956
Rose Veronica (Rose Fitzmorris)	Jan. 1943-Aug. 1943

Enrollment Figures

1940-1942	38
1942-1944	36
1944-1946	32
1946-1948	50
1948-1949	54
1949-1950	58

Catholic Newman Center—WKU
Bowling Green

In 1962, Fr. Bill Allard (with the encouragement of Bishop Henry Soenneker), moved from Morganfield to begin establishment of a Catholic Church at Western Kentucky University. He moved into a large clapboard house and began the Newman Center at Western.

Fr. Allard made signs and distributed fliers advertising his first service which attracted a small gathering of worshipers at his house. However, as Western's enrollment grew, so did Fr. Allard's congregation. The old house was torn down in 1967 and a modern Newman Center was built in its place in 1968.

There were many who supported the new construction, including some of the university's faculty and its president at the time - Mr. Kelly Thompson (who remains a member today).

The new 15,000 square foot, two-story structure, has undergone several changes since its construction. Fr. Allard previously lived in the downstairs apartment with Mass being held on the second floor. Eventually, partitions were put into place, and rooms were constructed, so that the former worship space could be turned into the rectory. The current worship space was constructed adjacent to the rectory.

The facility has continued to expand and today continues to serve the university students well. The facility contains several study rooms, a large meeting room and lounge, kitchen, priest's office, library and prayer chapel. There are two complete apartments - one for the priest and one which is rented out to a university students(s). The center also has a non-alcoholic night club (the Catacombs) which is open one evening a week during the school year. The Catacombs once served as a free speech area during the turbulent '60s.

Under the direction and inspiration of Fr. Ray Goetz (who served at the Newman Center for five years), and Fr. John Little (current director), a major renovation of the chapel has been undertaken. The project, which continues at this writing, includes changes in accordance with current Church guidelines. The altar has been placed in the center of the chapel with pews surrounding it in a semi-circle fashion. A new altar and ambo have been constructed, a new lighting system put into place, and new carpet laid. At this time, a Eucharistic chapel, confessional and cry room are being constructed and a new baptismal font will be built in the new future.

There are many activities for students to be involved with, including the Newman Club which is a spiritual, social and social justice group open to all students. The center currently served about 400 Catholic students and approximately 150 families from the Bowling Green area. It is financially supported by the Diocese of Owensboro, the students and local members.

Fathers of Mercy
South Union

Both photos: In 1854, the building was erected by the Shakers, making their own bricks. It was used as a men's and women's dormitory (note two stairways). The structure is now owned by The Mercy Fathers, South Union, KY. It is used as a religious retreat home by the Fathers of Mecry.

On March 1, 1988 the Fathers of Mercy returned to Western Kentucky. From 1956 to 1960 the Community staffed parishes in Hickman and Fulton. It now occupies the former Benedictine Priory in South Union.

Founded in France in 1808 to preach parish missions, the Congregation is continuing this work in the United States. The Community also staffs rural parishes in Glasgow, KY, and Iota, IA. It is ready to serve wherever a Bishop will invite it.

The original constitutions of the Fathers of Mercy were approved by Pope Gregory XVI in 1834. Since that time it has been a pontifical Community. The Congregation undertook missionary work in this country in 1839. In 1960 the Congregation was reorganized and revised its constitutions in accordance with present canonical demands.

Today, the Fathers of Mercy is a small, entirely American, foundation under the protection of Mary in her Immaculate Conception and the title of Our Lady of Mercy. The priests, clerics and seminarians are all dedicated to Our Holy Father and the Magisterium.

Mercy Hospital
Owensboro

Founded on the legacy of hope and care left by Mother Catherine McAuley, Mercy Hospital Owensboro first opened on March 1, 1948. Originally named Our Lady of Mercy Hospital, it was built after the Sisters of Mercy of Cincinnati along with the people of the Owensboro diocese raised $510,000 for the building fund.

Archbishop John Floerish of Louisville, Bishop Francis Cotton of Owensboro and Bishop Henry Grimmelsman of Evansville celebrated a Pontifical High Mass to open the new hospital. Bishop Grimmelsman used this passage from Luke's Gospel as his homily's theme: "And He sent them forth to preach the kingdom of God, and to heal the sick."

Within 10 short years the eighty bed hospital needed more room and added space for forty-five additional beds in what is now called the west wing. Between 1981 and 1987 the surgery suite was expanded. Laser surgery was added in 1987.

In 1988 the School Nurse Program started delivering free health care to students in schools located in Owensboro's poorer neighborhoods. The next year, the Mercy Medical Plaza was built adjoining the west side of the hospital. This building is occupied by 24 physicians representing family medicine, general surgery, plastic surgery, orthopedic surgery, anesthesia, internal medicine, cardiology, psychiatry, oncology, nuclear oncology, pediatrics, and urology.

In 1990, a twenty bed Regional Rehabilitation Unit, the only one in Western Kentucky, opened its doors for service. A year later, this Rehab Unit was certified by Kentucky as an official Qualified Rehabilitation Facility which will allow Mercy to assess workers injured on the job and refer them to the proper rehabilitation program.

In 1991, the McAuley Center was certified as a special health clinic by the State of Kentucky. This Center now delivers free health care to residents of a west end public housing project in Owensboro.

In mid-1992, two more operating rooms were added to the surgery suite, bring the total to five in the hospital. Every type of surgery is now done at Mercy, except open heart.

Mercy Hospital continues to diversify its services to meet the changing health needs of the community and to secure health care for the poor. The hospital seeks to provide holistic health care for everyone in need of its service within the limits of its resources and without regard for race, creed, status of ability to pay. Mercy is still firmly rooted in Mother McAuley's belief in connecting "the rich to the poor, the healthy to the sick, the educated and skilled to the uninstructed, the influential to those of no earthly consequence, and the powerful to the weak, all in order to do the work of God on earth."

Glenmary Home Mission Sisters of America

The Home Mission Sisters of America, more familiarly known as the Glenmary Sisters, were founded in 1941 by Father William Howard Bishop. Their purpose is to serve the needs of people in small towns and rural areas of America where the church is not present in its fullness. Their apostolate has a four pronged thrust; to build up the Catholic community, to reach out to the unchurched, to promote ecumenism, and to free the needy from the shackles of poverty.

RUSSELLVILLE

Three years after their founding, the women made their way to their first mission assignment in Russellville, Kentucky. At that time the women were called Miss, rather than Sister, as it would be nine more years before they would receive canonical recognition entitling them to be called a Sister.

For the first three years the mission only operated in the summers, but became a permanent, full-time mission in 1947. In the Fall of that year two of the Sisters opened an elementary school which Glenmary Sisters operated for nineteen years. In 1966, the Ursuline Sisters from Owensboro took over operation so the Glenmary Sisters could return to Father Bishop's original idea that, as missionaries, they would not own or manage institutions like schools, hospitals or clinics.

Glenmary Sisters have continued to be present in the Diocese of Owensboro ever since.

MORGANTOWN

In 1948, three Glenmary Sisters were missioned in Morgantown to teach Bible school and do outreach with the poor and unchurched. However, the permanent mission in Morgantown did not exist until Sister Mary Frances Simon and Sister Catherine Schoenborn opened it in 1971.

The mission served Butler and Ohio counties and the three parishes in Morgantown, Beaver Dam and Fordsville. The Sisters worked with Glenmary Priests Joseph O'Donnell and Edward Gorny. In 1979, the mission had to be closed due to the illness of one of the Sisters. In all, seven Glenmary Sisters served the Morgantown mission the eight years it was open. With them were a number of women in training, two volunteer Sisters of other congregations, and more than 200 lay volunteers.

GUTHRIE

During the years of the Russellville mission, the Sisters also had outreach services to the Guthrie area. A summer mission was opened in Guthrie from 1968-1973. Sister Mary Joseph Wade opened the permanent mission in Guthrie in 1975. Through her efforts the town organized a much needed Senior Citizen's Center, housing for the elderly and poor, and the establishment of a clinic. Today, the Sisters are working as pastoral associates, social workers, and religious educators. Presently Sister Bernadette Hengstebeck and Sister Catherine Schoenborn are missioned in Guthrie.

OWENSBORO

For the first 50 years of their existence, the Sisters' central residence was located in Cincinnati, Ohio. But, in July of 1991, the Sisters moved into their central residence and administrative offices located at 405 West Parrish Avenue, in Owensboro. Sister Christine Beckett, elected to her second term as the Community's President, resides at this central residence.

Although there were several considerations involved in the decision to move, the Sisters believe the move was a "positive step towards the growth and renewal of their community."

In May of 1991, they opened the new mission training house and mission in Livermore, Kentucky, and in August of that year, a new full-time mission was opened in Smithland, Kentucky. Currently, Sisters Mae Koenig and Martha Schuler, and Glenmary candidate Suzanne Jelinski are living in the Livermore mission, while Sisters Rosemary Esterkamp and Mary Joseph Wade are missioned in Smithland.

Together with the mission in Guthrie, Kentucky, the Sisters have three full-time missions, and the central offices, in the Owensboro Diocese. They also serve missions in eastern Kentucky, South Georgia and Tennessee.

At right: Sisters Bernadette Hengstebeck, Mary Frances Simon and Mary Joseph Wade with Fr. Benedict Wolf and the first group of students at the Russellville School. Above: The Glenmary Center in Owensboro—central residence and administrative offices for the Sisters.

Glenmary Home Missioners

The Glenmary Home Missioners invites men who have reached that point in their discernment when they desire to explore the possibility of missionary life in the rural South, to participate in the Candidacy Program. This exploration calls for an openness to listen and to learn, to give and to grow. The Candidacy Program is a hands-on experience of mission life, "trying Glenmary on for size" to see if it fits ones gifts and ones call from God to serve. It involves sharing the journey and discovery with others who are seeking a deeper relationship with God and a way to spread God's Good News.

The program is located in Hartford, Kentucky. Glenmary has been working in this area for more than 25 years. The candidates live close to the center of town in a former rooming house that has been converted into a homey residence.

Candidacy House (Glenmary), Hartford, KY.

The local people have given the candidates a warm welcome to their community.

The Candidacy Program is a nine-month experience which begins in late August and concludes at the end of May. Each year a new group of men form a class and begin their year of exploration. The first group started in August, 1986. The August 1992-May 1993 program marks the seventh group of men to begin the journey. The number of candidates who have participated in the program totals 33.

The Candidacy Program blends elements of action, information and prayer/reflection.

The dimension of action entails local outreach in Ohio and Butler Counties. Candidates spend a portion of each work working on projects such as religious education, youth ministry, and outreach to the elderly and handicapped.

The information segment consists of courses in Scripture, Spirituality and Catholic Belief at Brescia College and various workshops conducted at the house. The program is bound by prayer and reflection. With the rich experiences of daily personal and communal prayer, retreats and spiritual guidance, one is nourished for this year of discovery.

Carmel Home

In 1951 Bishop Francis R. Cotton purchased 15 acres farmland from Mr. and Mrs. Fleming Bowlds. The Haycraft homestead stood near the rear of the property. Bishop Cotton desired to have a home for the elderly built on this property. He requested Father Robert T. Wilson to find some Sisters who would be interested in operating a Home for the elderly in Owensboro. In December Father Wilson visited Mother M. Francis, the Carmelite's major superior in America. She agreed to travel to Kentucky in the spring to study the possibility of establishing a foundation in Ky. In June the Community agreed to start a Home for the elderly in the Owensboro Diocese. Seven and one-half acres of the original fifteen acres was sold to the Carmelite for a small sum. A.J. Schneider was contracted to build a home large enough for forty seven residents.

On August 16, 1952 Mother M. Francis arrived in Owensboro with Mother M. Waltrudis, the first superior of Carmel Home. She was accompanied by Sr. M. Gottfrieda and S. M. Bernadette. They cleaned and prepared the home which was blessed by Bishop Cotton on September 28th, 1952. Miss Taylor was the first resident, Father Henry O'Bryan served as Chaplain till 1964 at which time Fr. Joseph Mills became Chaplain.

In 1962 Mother Marianna had the convent's refectory, office, and community room added. The Home's dining room and kitchen were enlarged, a wooden gable roof was added giving the Home a more attractive appearance. In 1964 an elevator was installed. In 1964 the final check for payment of the home was sent to Bishop Henry J. Soenneker.

In 1967 the first of many major additions were made. This involved a wing which housed

a new chapel, a large main lobby area, forty private rooms, a laundry and a sun porch.

In 1968 Mother M. Teresa-Irmina obtained a licensure from the State for Intermediate Care. Twenty of the new rooms was set aside as an infirmary. This allowed the residents to remain in the Home when requiring special care.

From 1970 - 1979 Sr. Imelda served Carmel Home as Local Superior and Administrator, Fr. Gerald Calhoun served as Chaplain. Sr. Andrea was named Administrator and Local Superior in 1982. She directed the construction of a new activity wing, kitchenette, storage areas, arts and crafts room, beauty parlor shop, maintenance shop and a nice lounge for the employees. Bishop John McRaith blessed and dedicated this new wing on March 19, 1983.

In 1984 more construction was underway, a new Solarium, and an addition to the main kitchen and dining areas. This was made possible by a sizeable donation from Mrs. Mae Diener, a resident who died at Carmel Home in 1982.

In 1984 the Hycraft homestead was torn down and the diocese built a four apartment complex on part of the property. These apartments were to be made available for the use of the retired priests of the diocese. Msgr. Gilbert Henninger was the first priest to move in.

In 1985, Carmel Home made a park. About two acres of land was developed. A beautiful shrine to the Virgin of the Poor was built. At the same time a new infirmary wing was begun as a result of the generosity of Mrs. V. J. Steele through the Steele Foundation $500,000 was donated to make this infirmary wing possible. It was dedicated on June 22, 1986 by Bishop John J. McRaith to the Infant Jesus of Prague.

In 1987 major renovation of the chapel occurred. To insure that the Infirm priests of the diocese would have a place when they became ill, the diocese had four large rooms added to the Infant of Prague Infirmary wing. Father Clarence Pettit was the first resident priest to use the room.

In 1989 more major construction and renovation occurred. The small rooms in the original building were enlarged to accommodate the needs of our Residents. A new convent was built and the present convent was renovated to make more rooms for residents. Sister M. Bernadette was appointed local superior with Sr. Mary Catherine serving as Administrator. On March 19, 1991, Bishop J. McRaith blessed and dedicated these areas. In November Sr. M. Josephine was appointed local Superior with Sr. M. Francis Teresa serving as Administrator. In January 1992 Father Joseph V. Rhodes was appointed Chaplain.

In June 1995 Bishop McRaith granted Carmel Home the privilege of hosting Perpetual Eucharistic Adoration. In the past forty years of Carmel Home history the building and property have undergone many major and minor "facelifts", but our mission has always remained the same —to provide a real "home away from home" for our elderly Residents. God has blessed Carmel with many good and dedicated staff members and volunteers for which we are eternally grateful . . . .

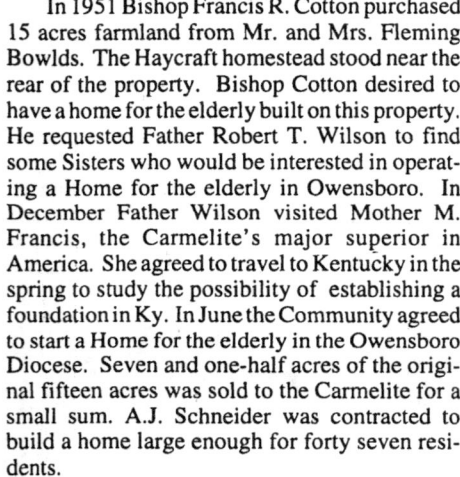

Lourdes Hospital
Paducah

In 1905, Riverside Hospital, the predecessor of the present Lourdes Hospital, was built on the Civil War site of Fort Anderson, now the northeast corner of Fourth and Clay Streets, in Paducah. Because of innumerable problems, the city offered Riverside Hospital for sale to a private group.

On July 15, 1959, the Roman Catholic Diocese of Owensboro purchased the hospital for $503,251 and an agreement to discount city charity medical cases for twenty years. The Diocese asked the Sisters of St. Francis of Tiffin, Ohio to assume operation of the hospital and on September 19, 1959 they did so. The hospital was renamed Lourdes in honor of Our Lady of Lourdes, who, in appearing to the French peasant girl, Bernadette Soubirous, left in history one of the most remarkable healing impressions of all time.

Lourdes Hospital continued to develop under the direction of The Most Rev. Francis R. Cotton, the first Bishop of the Diocese of Owensboro, and his advisors until his death in 1960. At the request of the newly installed bishop, The Most Rev. Henry J. Soenneker, the Sisters from Tiffin took over the sponsorship of the 124-bed facility in 1963 and continued a history of health care which would span more than a quarter century and encompass millions of dollars worth of growth.

The relocation of Lourdes to its present facility on Lone Oak Road occurred in 1973. This was made possible by the generosity of the citizens, employees, business and industry of the area and the determined efforts of many.

In September, 1982, the sponsorship of the hospital was reassumed by the Diocese of Owensboro just prior to the installation of the Most Rev. John J. McRaith as the third bishop of the Diocese.

Changes in Medicare reimbursement and a general change in philosophy in the health care system in the 1980s made it important for Lourdes to seek affiliation with a national system.

In 1989 Lourdes entered into a management contract with the Mercy Health System of Cincinnati, Ohio. In January 1991 sponsorship of the hospital was transferred to the Sisters of Mercy from the Diocese of Owensboro and Lourdes became a full member of the Mercy Health System.

The story of Lourdes Hospital is more than a story of expansion, growth, new buildings, ground breakings, blessings, and the start-up of new services. It is a story of dedication — the dedication of many: the employees, the Sisters of St. Francis, Mercy Health System and the Sisters of Mercy, the Board of Directors, the medical staff and the volunteers. All who have served the hospital over the years have made it what it is today.

Top photo: Riverside Hospital, 1908.

Bottom photo: Lourdes Hospital

OWENSBORO CATHOLIC HIGH SCHOOL
OWENSBORO

The first Catholic High School in Owensboro was Saint Frances, 1849, located in a two-story frame building on Third and Saint Ann Streets where the Y.M.C.A. building later stood. It was moved into a newly erected brick structure on Fifth and Allen Streets in 1889.

Saint Hubertus Academy was a small frame building located on Ninth and Sweeney Streets, 1879. In 1915 it was moved into a large, remodeled home on Fifth and Clay Streets. The name was changed to Saint Joseph School. In 1924 a new brick structure was completed just across the street and Saint Joseph School first graduating class was in June of 1925.

As a result of a thorough survey and study of the Catholic School System in Owensboro it was decided in the spring of 1948 to have one central high school. In the fall of that year the necessary transition was made using Saint Frances Academy as the Catholic High for all Catholic students in Owensboro and the surrounding area with the intention of building as soon as possible. In 1951 the school was moved to the new Diocesan High School building at 1524 Parrish Avenue. The legal title Assumption High School, is better known as Owensboro Catholic High School.

The first faculty at OCHS consisted of nineteen Sisters and four Priests. Bishop Francis R. Cotton celebrated a Pontifical Mass on September 12 to bless the school. There were priests, faculty, about 585 students and others in attendance.

The first School Evaluation Program was conducted in 1952. The team was very pleased with the permanent record system, guidance program, library services and lunchroom program. In the first graduating class, June 5, 1952, one hundred three seniors received diplomas in the exercises held at Memorial Recreation Center. The guest speaker was the Right Reverend Mosignor Felix Pitt, executive secretary of the Louisville Archdiocese Schools.

The enrollment grew steadily from 651 students in 1952 to 1122 in 1964. Because of financial and other reasons enrollment declined for a few years. In 1984 the enrollment was 1040 and presently is 605.

In January, 1955, new classroom space was planned. One classroom of the new wing was used in the fall of 1956. At one time the eighth graders from Blessed Mother School were in attendance at OCHS.

In 1958, Mr. Philip Hayden became the first lay faculty member. The next year five priests, twenty-three Sisters and two more laymen joined the faculty.

In 1964, another wing was added to the school. This included space on the second floor for school offices, a student chapel, small gym, cafeteria and classrooms. The first floor of the new building was used for labs, the second for the Religion Department and cafeteria. This section extends across the back of the previous school, enclosing a courtyard which beautified the campus. Soenneker Hall was created in 1982 from the former location of the early cafeteria and locker room.

In 1988 Mr. Tom Lilly became the first development director. In 1989 Premium Allied Tool Corporation installed a computer lab, ($110,000), in honor of Father Henry O'Bryan, the first Diocesan supervisor of Parochial Schools.

Principals of OCHS have been: Sister Mary Auxilium, S.C.N.; Sister Joseph Mary, S.C.N.; Sister Helen Constance, S.C.N.; Rev. Henry O'Bryan; Rev. Gerald Calhoun; Rev. Edward Bradley; H. Joseph O'Bryan and Harold Staples.

OCHS is noted for: Class plays; Catholic Students Mission Crusade; participation in the annual Christmas Parade float competition; success of the Art Department in local, state, and national competition; success of the Science and Math Departments in competitive undertakings; sports activities. The Pep Club has always been a great asset in promoting school spirit. The Acettes drill team was formed in 1970. In 1971 the marching band was organized and later a flag and rifle corps was added. Religious, social and cultural achievement has always held priority at OCHS.

OWENSBORO CATHOLIC PAROCHIAL SCHOOL SYSTEMS

For some time the Owensboro and Daviess County Catholic Parishes conducted their own parochial schools:

Saint Hubertus/St. Joseph	1879-1978
Blessed Mother	1948-1989
The Immaculate	1954-1989
Saint Pius X	1958-1989
Precious Blood	1960-1989
Saint Stephen	1948-1989
O.L. of Lourdes	1959-1989
Saint Raphael	1900-1963
Saint Alphonsus	1902-1989
Saint Peter	1910-1973
Saint Elizabeth	1911-1973
Saint Anthony	1912-1989
St. William/Mary Carrico	1912 to date
Saint Martin	1916-1981
Saint Lawrence	1920-1961
St. Mary Magdalene	1923-1989
Sr. Mary, Whitesville	1918 to date

A search for a director to consolidated the parochial school system of Owensboro and Daviess County began in 1988. Mr. Larry Bishop was named director in May of that year.

During the summer of 1989 all Owensboro Catholic Elementary Schools were closed and reopened in August under a new system. Four schools were designated as city parochial schools, one county school and a middle school as a regional parochial school.

Saint Angela Merici (former Blessed Mother School) welcomed students, kindergarten age through sixth grade from Blessed Mother and St. Stephen (Cathedral) parishes. Sister Rita Scott, O.S.U. was named principal.

Bishop Henry J. Soenneker (former Precious Blood School) met students kindergarten age through sixth grade from Precious Blood Parish and those in the northwestern part of Owensboro. Mr. Philip Spurlock, principal.

Bishop Francis R. Cotton (former St. Pius X) greeted students from Saints Joseph and Paul and St. Pius X parishes with Ms. Joyce Hoffman as principal.

Catherine Spalding (former Lourdes) welcomed students from kindergarten age through sixth grade from Saint Anthony, Our Lady of Lourdes and Immaculate parishes. Mr. P.J. Hayden was the first principal.

Holy Angels (former Saint Mary Magdalene) became the center for: Saint Mary Magdalene, Saint Alphonsus, Saint Elizabeth, Saint Martin, Saint Peter and Saint Augustine parishes. All students from kindergarten age through the sixth grade met with Ms. Mary Kennedy as principal.

Owensboro Catholic Middle School (former Immaculate location) opened its doors to all students in seventh and eighth grades. Sister Michael Marie Friedman, O.S.U. was principal.

Enrollment for the above schools totaled: 1823 students in 1989-1990; 1872 in 1990-1991 and 1816 in 1991-1992.

Schools in the eastern part of the county were not affected by this change. (Mary Carrico Memorial; Saint Mary of the Woods and Trinity High).

In May of 1991 the Priests Deanery voted to include Owensboro Catholic High School in the Consolidated School System. Owensboro Catholic High School Development Office was extended to include kindergarten through grade 12. Marian K. Bennett became the director in July 1991.

The Passionist Nuns
Owensboro

The Passionist Nuns were founded in the 18th Century Italy by St. Paul of the Cross. He had previously founded the Passionist priest and brothers. Over his long life of preaching missions and retreats, and giving spiritual direction to men and women in all walks of life, Paul of the Cross became more and more convinced that when we forget the Passion and Death of Jesus, we no longer realize how precious we are to God and how loved by Him.

The Passionist Nuns of Owensboro, Kentucky is a community of Cloistered nuns dedicated to the Passion of Christ through a contemplative ministry of prayer in solitude. They witness to timeless values and to the primacy of God amid the breathtaking pace and noise of the changing world. They fulfill their Passionist vow through a monastic life of prayer, work, penance and community, as well as by sharing with others the fruits of their contemplative prayer.

The foundation of St. Joseph Monastery on October 7, 1946, was initiated by the community of the Passionist Nuns at St. Gabriel's founded in 1926 in Scranton, PA. The first five Passionist Nuns came to Owensboro in 1946, where they have continued the contemplative aspect of the mission of the church for 46 years.

The following are the five Sisters that were chosen to make this foundation:

Mother Mary Agnes Roche, C.P., Superior; Mother Mary Bernadette Rohling, C.P., Assistant Superior; Mother Mary Cecilia Taylor, C.P., 1st Counselor and Novice Directress; Mother Jeanne Marie Wehmhoefer, C.P., 2nd Counselor; Mother Francis Marie Livoti, C.P., Assistant Novice Directress.

Those who have served as Superior of St. Joseph's Monastery from 1946-1992 are the following:

Mother Mary Agnes Roche, C.P., October 1946-October 1955; Mother Jeanne Marie Wehmhoefer, C.P., October 1955-October 1958; Mother Mary Agnes Roche, C.P. October 1958-December 1967; Mother Jeanne Marie Wehmhoefer, C.P., December 1967-January 1974; Mother Margaret Mary Mattingly, C.P., January 1974-January 1986; Mother Catherine Marie Schuhmann, C.P., January 1986-June 1992; Sister Mary Agnes Higgs, C.P., June 1992-

Mother Mary Agnes Roche died in 1974, and Sister Jeanne Marie died in 1988. Sister Mary Dunnigan, who was the community's first postulant, came from the Scranton community in 1946 shortly after the Nuns arrived, died in 1966 at the age of 64.

The Nuns were welcomed to the Diocese of Owensboro most graciously by all. The Priests and Religious of the Owensboro Diocese, since 1946 until the present day, have supported the Nuns by their prayer, appreciation and their spiritual and material assistance. The Passionist Fathers supported the Nuns in every way, mainly by giving yearly retreats, and their spiritual assistance and encouragement. The Laity have been equally helpful and supportive throughout these many years by showing appreciation for the contemplative life and offering the Nuns their material assistance. Many have offered their personal services to the community over the years. The Nuns could not have done without these services.

During those very early years up to 1960, the community continued to grow in numbers and develop with the support of Bishop Cotton. From the long period between 1969-1982, the community continued to experience the same interest and support from Bishop Soenneker. Bishop Soenneker constantly encouraged the Nuns in their community decisions throughout the difficult years after Vatican II when the church called all religious back to the original inspiration of their Founders and Foundresses. One major decision was that, in order to regain a solid identity as cloistered nuns, they needed either to build a separate retreat house or discontinue retreats altogether. Because the limited space on the monastery grounds made building a separate retreat house impossible, the retreats were discontinued in 1968. It was after this decision that the Nuns experienced a noticeable decline in vocations.

The Nuns have experienced Bishop McRaith's continued support over the past 10 years and he frequently expresses his appreciation for their contemplative vocation and their presence in the Diocese.

In 1978, the Church issued a document from the Holy See, in which all religious, especially contemplatives, were urged to share the richness of their prayer life with the people of God. In May, 1991, after conferring with Bishop McRaith, the community unanimously adopted a plan of relocation which would allow them to share their prayer, resume the retreats and that would assure the continuation of their ministry into the 21st century and beyond. Bishop McRaith supports the Nuns 100% in their relocation project. Doors began to open for the Nuns sending a steady stream of helpers to donate time and talents to this project.

After a 4 1/2 month search for a new property, a 150-acre plot of woodland two miles southwest of Whitesville, Kentucky was discovered. The new St. Joseph Monastery will be built on this property of great natural beauty - where heaven and earth seem to merge, and one can easily discern the close presence of God. The vistas are ideal for a monastery and retreat house for they inspire peace and prayer. And the 150-acre site will assure solitude for decades to come.

The new monastery will afford **men and women of all faiths** the opportunity to enter into a deeper relationship with God — the opportunity and facility for sharing in the Passionists' liturgical celebrations, while renewing and strengthening themselves spiritually and physically. And, it will preserve the rich tradition of the Passionist charism for new generations of women whom God will call to this form of religious life.

The Nuns continue to build their lives on the faith and trust in Providence that was handed down to them from their Founder, St. Paul of the Cross and their Mother Foundresses. Today they number 18 professed religious in the community and their median age is fifty. There are no postulants or novices at this time. However, there are young people expressing interest in the life and this gives the Nuns added hope for the future.

The new leadership since June of this year, 1992 are as follows:

Sister Mary Agnes Higgs, C.P., Superior; Sister Joseph Marie Snyder, C.P., Assistant Superior; Sister Rita Marie Boteler, C.P., Counselor; Sister Mary Therese Seitz, C.P., Formation Director.

The Nuns continue to educate their religious in all areas of life that is in accord with the teaching church and which they see as so beneficial in our day and time.

Serra Club
Owensboro

Serra is a Catholic organization for lay men and women devoted to fostering vocations to the priesthood and religious life. The club's name is taken from Father Junipero Serra, the noted Spanish Franciscan missionary who played a leading part in early missionary efforts in the West. Serrans belong to different parishes, but are all interested in the future of ministry in the Church.

The local club's beginnings were in mid 1962, when Bishop Henry J. Soenneker encouraged a group of local businessmen to work toward the formation of a Serra Club in Owensboro. Included in the initial group were:

Dr. James A. Baumgarten; Leo T. Bowles; William T. Carroll; Paul S. Coomes; James W. Danhauer; J. Richard Flaherty; Norbert J. Greenwell; Richard D. Kennedy; J. Ray Topper; Jack R. Wilson

After eighteen months assistance from the Serra Club of Evansville, the Serra Club of Owensboro was granted Charter No. 254 on January 21, 1964. The Very Rev. Msgr. Raymond G. Hill was the first chaplain, and served in that capacity until 1980. Reverend Louis F. Piskula served as chaplain until 1982, when the current Chaplain, Reverend Joseph M. Mills assumed the office. Of the thirty-seven charter members, Joseph W. Castlen, Jr., George S. Hagan, Jr., and Joseph L. Hagan are still on the roster. The Serra Club of Owensboro currently has 46 members, and Fay Higdon serves as president. Past presidents of the Serra Club of Owensboro include:

Homer L. Barton, Dr. James A. Baumgarten, Harry E. Baumgarten, Jr., Raymond Eugene Boone, William H. Booth, Richard D. Booth, Leo T. Bowles, Joseph W. Caslen, Jr., Paul S. Coomes, James W. Danhauer, J. Richard Greenwell*, George S. Hagan, Jr.*, Donald E. Hayden, Eugene B. Hayden, Fay Higdon, Donald J. Johnson, Louis Johnson, Robert L. Osborne, Robert W. Slack, Ronald M. Sullivan, Dr. Shelby Thompson, Ronald R. Tisch*, J. Ray Topper, Abram B. Walker, Jack R. Wilson.

*Past District Governors of Serra International

Past and present activities of the local Serra Club include grade school and high school essay and poster contests concerning vocations, the altar boy and vocation cross programs in parishes, and days of recollection, picnics and luncheons for seminarians and religious candidates in formation. Serrans adopt seminarians and religious candidates and pray that they will persevere in their vocation. There is at least one Serran at Mass every day of the year praying for vocations.

St. Joseph Interparochial School
Bowling Green

The history of Catholic schooling in Bowling Green dates back to the influx of Catholics in 1858 who came mostly from Ireland, and found work building the L and N Railroad and bridges. Fr. Joseph DeVries was directed to establish a parish for this community. In the summer of 1859 a small wooden building was built as a temporary church and used for a school during the week and for Mass on Sundays.

In 1863 four sisters from the Sisters of Charity of Nazareth came to Bowling Green to teach, and in 1869 opened St. Columba Academy. In 1912 the sisters occupied their new convent and taught in the new St. Joseph School, both buildings being adjacent to the St. Joseph Church with Fr. T.J. Hayes as pastor. High school classes were taught from 1955-1965. In 1960 an additional classroom building with a gymnasium was added.

In 1969 the school became St. Joseph Interparochial School upon the establishment of Holy Spirit Parish in Bowling Green. The following year the Sisters of Charity gave up the staffing of the school and the first school board was instituted with Julian Durbin as chairman. Ursuline Sisters taught at St. Joseph from 1974 through 1988.

St. Joseph Interparochial School today has kept pace with developments in technology, good educational practices, and community needs while striving to enrich the religious lives of the students. The school presently houses preschool classes through the eighth grade. Child care during the day is provided for the four and five year olds when they are not in class as well as after school care for all grades that need it.

Fr. Jerry Calhoun serves as the priest-pastor of the school and is the pastor of Holy Spirit Parish. Fr. Henry Wieder is the associate pastor of Holy Spirit Parish and Fr. Alan McIntosh, O.S.B. is the pastor of St. Joseph Parish. The school board consists of Al Arbogast-chairman, Laura Caswell, Mike Caudill, Buzz Colburn, Leslie Gillock, Warren Irons, Janile Martin, Joan Martter, Mike Murphy, Patrick Petty, and Jane Wilson. Joanne Powell has served as principal since 1984. Certified teaching faculty includes Mary Anne Davenport, Siggy Gorman, Winkie Huddleston, Donna Kanaly, Jan Lange, Rita Larimore, Alicia McFarland, Turtle Moore, Angela Nunn, Lynn O'Keefe, Ann Pollard, Bruce Simmons, Connie Simpson, Susan Webb, and Mary Ann Wolfram. Additional staff includes teachers' aides, clerical, transportation, maintenance, food service and development.

St. Joseph School
Bowling Green

St. Joseph Interparochial School, which serves Bowling Green and surrounding communities, joins with Catholic Schools throughout the United States in celebrating Catholic Schools Week, January 31 through February 6, 1993. Catholic Schools Weeks is a good time to reflect on who we are, what we are about, and who are our partners in this enterprise in the name of the Lord Jesus.

Documents form the Second Vatican Council declare that parents are the first and foremost educators of their children. These same documents further state that parents need help in the education of their children. This is the mission of St. Joseph Interparochial School.

One of the greatest strengths of Catholic Schools in this country is the Catholic educators' practical recognition of the fact that though we educators stand in the place of parents, it is the parents who have entrusted us with their children thus maintaining their obligation to educate their children. The Catholic School serves as a special place where the Catholic faith and values of the parents is passed on to the children while they receive an excellent academic education.

Our bishop, Most Reverend John J. McRaith, has been quoted saying, "Every bit of research shows that the Catholic School does the best job in training and forming people in their faith - a faith that will evangelize the community by education, celebration, and service."

The faculty and staff of St. Joseph School thank you for your support in our endeavors and pray that God blesses you in all you do. We hope you enjoy seeing some of our students pictured on these pages as they go about their school activities.

Dedication of the new St. Joseph School (on the right) and convent (on the left) Bowling Green, KY, Sept. 1912.

St. Joseph School. Frame building is original church, 1859. On the left is the back porch of the convent. Behind these buildings is the present church, built in 1890.

St. Joseph School, Facult/Staff, 1992-1993. Front row (L to R): Ann Pollard, Turtle Moore, Lynn O'Keefe, Rita Larimore, Bruce Simmons, Connie Simpson, Joanne Powell. Back (L to R): Angela Nunn, Donna Kanaly, Jan Lange, Siggy Gorman, Mary Ann Wolfram, Charlene Fortier.

Fourth grade students entering the front entrance of the school building.

Sisters Of Charity Of Nazareth

The Congregation of the Sisters of Charity of Nazareth was founded December 1, 1812 near Bardstown, Kentucky, by Reverend Jean-Baptiste Marie David, later Bishop David, Co-adjutor Bishop of Bardstown.

Catherine Spalding, who joined the first two members, Teresa Carrico and Betsy Wells, a few months later, and who was elected first superior, is considered co-founder because of her vibrant leadership and because of the influence of her spirit and personality upon the young community.

The motto of the community has been from the earliest days "caritas Christi urget nos": "The Charity of Christ urges us on" (11 Cor. 5:14).

When the Owensboro Dioces was created in 1937, the SCNs had been serving the region for 117 years. In 1963, the number of Sisters of Charity serving our diocese peaked at 111. In 1987 there were 19 sisters serving the diocese.

St. Vincent Academy, Union County. In 1820, a band of three sisters was sent to Union County, riding the 150 miles on horseback. They opened St. Vincent Academy.

An interesting description of Sister Angela Spink, one of those first three sisters, can be found in the history of the congregation by Anna Blanch McGill.

She toiled in the fields and woods; she readied her own harvests thus helping to provide a livelihood for the other Sisters and the means for building a school . . .

That the school was a success can be attested by an article in the Louisville Post in 1919. "One of the oldest and most successful institutions in the South is St. Vincent Academy in Union County, conducted by the Sisters of Charity of Nazareth, KY, and order famed for the ability and experience of its members."

In 1967, after 147 years, the Sisters of Charity closed St. Vincent.

St. Frances Academy, Daviess County. A second band of five sisters came to Owensboro in 1849 on a flatboat from Louisville. They opened St. Frances Academy, named for Mother Frances Gardiner (one of the first three sisters at St. Vincent Academy) who was Mother at the time. As she bade good-bye to the five sisters, Mother Frances said, "My daughters, review, study. Never think you have reached a point beyond which you need not aim. Onward, ever."

In 1923, St. Frances Academy was affiliated with the Department of Education, Frankfort; with Catholic University, Washington, D.C.; and with the Southern Association.

The excitement caused by the creation of the Owensboro Diocese can be glimpsed from

St. Vincent's Academy, near Uniontown, Union Co., KY.

the following excerpt in the St. Frances Annals, March 7, 1938:

"The academy was decorated in the papal colors and U.S. flag honoring Bishop Cotton who entered the Episcopal City. A very splendid reception was given him at the Knights of Columbus auditorium."

In 1949, the centennial of St. Frances, there were 35 SCNs living at the academy, including three full-time music teachers and two teachers who taught at Blessed Sacrament School.

In 1951, St. Frances, having become a diocesan high school, moved to 1524 Parrish Avenue where it was known as Owensboro Catholic High School. Enrollment there peaked at about 1350. The last SCN left OCHS in 1983.

St. Jerome, Graves County. The sisters staffed St. Jerome School in Fancy Farm in 1892. Almost immediately it was noted throughout the area for its academic achievements. Anna Blanch McGill called the school "the Parnassus of Graves County." In 1933, St. Jerome became a state school; however, it continued to be staffed by the sisters.

An interesting entry in the 1949 annals of the SCNs at St. Jerome convent attests to the continuance of excellence in education maintained at the school:

Mrs. Deweese, wife of the County Superintendent of Schools, conducted achievement tests in the senior and freshman classes . . . St. Jerome rated first in the county."

St. Mary of the Woods, Daviess County. At the request of Father O'Sullivan, three SCNs arrived to teach at St. Mary of the Woods, Whitesville, in September 1901. From the beginning, music was an important part of the children's education. Singing classes were held after school and on Saturday. For the second Christmas after the SCNs arrived, the children sang the Christmas Mass in Gregorian Chant.

Later, the school developed into a secondary school with its first graduating class in 1914. The Sisters of Charity withdrew from the high school in 1967 and were replaced by the Ursuline Sisters.

St. Mary Academy, McCracken County. In 1858, the Sisters of Charity opened St. Mary Academy, Paducah. Prejudice and primitive living conditions marked the early years. A sister writes, "the whoop of an Indian and the cry of a panther were the only sounds that disturbed the solitude." Their poverty was so great that at one time there were only two pairs of good shoes for the three sisters so only two could go out at a time — never three together.

During the Civil War the sisters closed the school to nurse both the Blue and the Gray. Sister Lucy Dosh, the youngest, died of a fever contracted while nursing the soldiers. Her patients insisted she be given a military funeral with an equal number of Confederate and Union soldiers as a military honor guard.

In 1937, when Western Kentucky became a diocese, there were 18 SCNs at St. Mary Academy. Today there are none — the last SCN having left in 1983.

Holy Name, Henderson County. Four Sisters of Charity arrived at Holy Name, Henderson in 1872 for the purpose of teaching Catholic children.

In 1946 the Holy Name High School opened with 99 students. In 1965 the number of students peaked at 730 — 554 in grade school and 176 in high school.

In 1970, a simple note in the SCN's annals states: Holy Name High School held its final graduation under the able direction of Sister Mary Catherine Clarkson. It was with deep regret that we closed our doors to our high school classes, but it was a parish decision.

Bowling Green. In 1862, the Sisters opened a school in Bowling Green on State Street. Seven years later they opened St. Columba

Academy. In 1920, St. Joseph Parochial School opened. The sisters withdrew from St. Joseph School in 1971.

Other Missions of Sisters of Charity:

1872 - Three SCNs arrived in Uniontown and opened St. Rose Academy. The graduation exercise of 1807 was described by a local newspaper as a "brilliant affair." In 1922 the name of the school was changed to St. Agnes. At that time, fourteen sisters were serving at the school.

1876-Three Sisters staffed St. Romuald School in Breckinridge County. They withdrew in 1887.

1886-St. Lawrence School opened in Ohio County. The three Sisters remained 18 months.

1886-A Boys Parochial School opened in Owensboro and served until 1920.

1940-Two Sisters opened Blessed Sacrament School in Owensboro.

1944-Blessed Martin School in Waverly.

1954-St. Pius X School in Calvert City.

1956-St. Edward School in Fulton.

1959-Our Lady of Lourdes School in Owensboro.

1960-Sacred Heart School in Hickman.

1965-St. Frances de Sales School in Paducah.

The Sisters of Charity had to withdraw from most of these schools due to the death of Sisters, for the Nazareth Community was not immune to the upheaval following the Second Vatican Council.

Educators - The primary thrust of the work of the SCNs in the Owensboro Diocese has been in the field of education. From the early days of the congregation, excellence in education has been an important goal. In 1814, Ellen O'Connell from Baltimore entered the new community. Already a qualified teacher, she assisted Father David, who was highly educated, in the training of the young sisters. Early records describe Sister Ellen O'Connell as "the giver of lectures on Christian doctrine comparable to a priest, an artist, a mathematician, musician, and writer of considerable charm."

Several decades later, another educator with an interesting background joined the Kentucky community. Marie Menard, born in France, was the first graduate of St. Mary Academy, Paducah. Returning to Paris to complete her education, Marie had to follow the lecture at the Sorbonne from behind a screen and received her degree from Louis Napolean.

After having joined the SCN community during the Civil War, Sister Marie developed a correspondence course for the sisters in the branch houses ensuring better informed teachers and a higher calibre of teaching throughout the community.

The Sisters of Charity of Nazareth are keenly aware that their lives are a constant struggle to serve as Jesus served and their best efforts will never attain this. With their diminishing numbers and with the enormous changes in society and the Church, the Sisters do not know what the future holds for their community. However, imbued with the frontier spirit of Catherine Spalding, they are preparing for it the best they can because the charity of Christ urges them onward.

SISTERS OF THE LAMB OF GOD
OWENSBORO

In 1958 at the invitation of Bishop Cotton of the Owensboro Diocese, a group of Sisters of the Lamb of God came to America from France and settled in the Owensboro Diocese. They were offered a wonderful civil war house for their convent located next to Catholic High on Parrish Avenue. The house offered the French nuns a lesson in American History as they learned how and where slaves were believed to have been hidden in the great attic and where moonshine was supposedly made up there.

By taking census for various parishes in the diocese, going door to door, the sisters came to know many people. They also cared for the sick and those with other needs in their homes. In 1964 the sisters opened the first kindergarten in the area. A year later it was moved from their house to a room in Catholic High.

The sisters have served in the parishes of St. Stephen's Blessed Sacrament, St. Augustine, Blessed Mother, Immaculate, and St. Williams. They have also given many years to the Robert Connor Center day care, Bishop Soenneker Home in Knottsville, and ministered at the Wendell Foster Center.

While the sisters over the years have included many French sisters, the Americans include two from the Owensboro Diocese, Sr. Mary Herbert Woodward, and Sr. Mary Thomas Simon. The other American sisters are mostly from the northern states. It is a wonderful experience to belong to this group of people from four different countries, (France, Switzerland, America and India), backgrounds and a mixture of people with good health and with physical disabilities. It is what the church family is all about—richness in diversities, many different parts, but all one body.

Sisters of the Lamb of God. (L to R): Front, Sr. M. Katherine, Mary, Sr. M. Agnes and SR. M. Raymonde. Back: Sr. M. Bernadetta, Sr. M. Madeleine and Sr. Monica

Sisters of Loretto
Daviess County

In 1861 the Reverend Ivo Schacht was sent by the Most Reverend Martin John Spalding, Bishop of Louisville, to care for the Catholics settled in the Green River hills of Daviess County.

The new pastor soon saw the need for a school and persuaded his parishioners to build a 20 x 50 foot log schoolhouse. He then employed two lay teachers to conduct the classes. Unfortunately they remained for only one year.

Father's next recourse was to Mother Berlindes Downes, Superior of the Sisters of Loretto in Marion County who agreed to send four Sisters to conduct a boarding and day school. This foundation experienced some of St. Paul's perils—perils of water at the beginning and perils of fire on ending. While on their way, a terrible storm arose that threatened to carry boat and passengers to the bottom of the river. Seven years later fire was to put an end to the mission.

Having survived the ordeal of the journey, the four Sisters, Sister M. Agnes Carrigan, Superior, Sisters Agnes Tucker, Harriet Moore and Francisca Pike, experienced another shock when they beheld the little log cabin in the woods. Their first night in this new home was to produce further surprises. There was no such thing as a fence to protect the house from animals in the woods. The hogs that foraged under the trees for acorns seemed to think that they owned the shelter of the convent floor, little more than two feet above the ground, for their nightly shelter. Whether or not they were the cause of the plague of fleas that infested the house, the Sisters spent the next day clearing away debris and undergrowth around the convent school and endeavoring to discourage any further nightly visits from the unwanted "guests".

The fleas, as well as the pigs, were soon dislodged and school was opened on October 1, 1863. In December, Mother Agnes made a trip to Loretto to see if she could get another Sister to help in the growing school. Sister Athanasius Wathen was chosen for the mission, and it is from memoirs that we receive our information about the St. Joseph foundation.

The two westward bound Sisters left Loretto on the afternoon of December 31. Once again the hazards caused by the weather threatened to make this their final journey. Because of ice in the river, the Sisters spent two days and two nights aboard the *Gray Eagle* before they were able to begin their perilous journey to Owensboro. Sister Athanasius writes:

On arriving at Owensboro some time before noon we took dinner with the good Sisters of Charity. Mr. Billy Clark was waiting with his two horse wagon to take us out to St. Joseph. Sister Isabella wrapped us up in two large double blankets and put hot bricks to our feet, but not long did they remain there for the ground was so rough we could scarcely keep on our chairs. After fifteen miles jolting, we arrived at our cold home in the woods. Father Schacht was just ringing the Angelus bell which he was faithful to do three times a day."

For the next six years the efforts of the Sisters were blessed and St. Joseph Academy in Daviess County enjoyed a period of success as both school and community increased. Mother Agnes Corrigan was replaced as Superior by Sister Agnes Tucker and Mother Matilda Drury later took her place. Five more Sisters were added to the community.

When the school was more flourishing and affairs were assuming the permanency that time alone can give, fire destroyed the buildings on December 30, 1870. St. Joseph Academy was a complete loss and the Sisters were stranded. Grateful that their pupils were at home for the holidays, and therefore not endangered by the fire, the Sisters might have returned by boat to Loretto, but the Ohio was frozen over and no boat could run.

The nine homeless ones: Mother Matilda Drury, Sister Francisca Pike, Sister Januarius Quigley, Sister Anselm Handley, Sister Concordia Henning, Sister Rosine Green, Sister Mary Clement Hamilton, Sister M. Joseph Dennis and Sister Athanasius Wathen were given shelter in the homes of Mr. Rodman and several other good friends in the vicinity for the next three weeks while they awaited instructions from Loretto. They would gladly have continued their arduous work at St. Joseph, but the Superiors recalled them to the Motherhouse. Thus ended the Loretto mission at Daviess County.

The next Loretto foundation in the Owensboro diocese was neither as primitive nor as fraught with hardship and adventure as the St. Joseph mission.

Shortly after the Reverend Anthony Higdon was named the first resident pastor at Immaculate Conception Church in Hawesville in 1947, the Sisters of Loretto were asked to take charge of the Parish School.

The Sisters assigned to Hawesville were: Sister Bernadette Bowling, sister of Reverend Charles P. Bowling, former Vicar General of the diocese, Sister M. Blanche Elder, who had spent her childhood in Hawesville and Sister Theresa Louise Wiseman.

The Sisters got their first view of their new home on August 27. The unfinished condition of the school raised some concern about where they would teach on the following Monday for Father Higdon had assured the people that the school would open on schedule.

On September 1, Labor Day; fifty-nine happy youngsters arrived eager to begin their journey on the path of learning. Since the school building was still not finished, the first lap of the journey was begun in the unfinished rectory. Sixth, seventh and eight grades met in the kitchen; fourth and fifth in a bedroom; third, second and first in the priest's office. Crowded quarters did not daunt these youngsters, but the teachers were not sorry when the school building was ready for occupancy on October 29.

Until the convent was completed, the Sisters had to rely on the kindness and hospitality of the Ursuline Sisters at St. Rose convent in Cloverport. The move to the completed convent took place on October 18.

The following year saw the ninth grade added to the school and a fourth Sister, Sister Coaina Mudd, added to the community.

In the ensuing years, the increase in enrollment as grades were added to the high school necessitated the addition of a new building and the shifting of grades in the elementary school. The first high school graduation was held on May 11, 1952. Members of this class were: Dan Hagman, Lois Johnson, Mildred Gray, Charles and Clay McBride.

The tenure of the Sisters of Loretto at Hawesville terminated very unexpectedly in 1961. The shortage of teachers made it prohibitive to have two Sisters for so few high school pupils. It was felt necessary to close the high school or at least to withdraw the two high school Sisters.

It was suggested that perhaps another religious community of Sisters might exchange grade schools and furnish the high school teachers for Hawesville. The Ursuline Sisters of Maple Mount were contacted and they were willing to exchange their Hillsboro, Missouri School for the Hawesville grade and high school. This change was approved by His Eminence, Cardinal Ritter of St. Louis by Bishop Henry Soenecker of Owensboro, Mother Wilfrid, Superior General at Maple Mount and Mother M. Luke of Loretto. The change became effective at once so that the Sisters could make the transfer and be ready for the opening of school in both places.

THE SISTERS OF THE THIRD ORDER OF ST. FRANCIS OF PENANCE AND CHARITY TIFFIN, OHIO

Upon invitation from the Most Rev. Francis R. Cotton, first Bishop of the Diocese of Owensboro, Kentucky, the Sisters of St. Francis came to Paducah, Kentucky with the mandate to manage and staff the recently purchased Riverside Hospital on behalf of the diocese. On September 19, 1959, seven Sisters of St. Francis began the work of Catholic health care ministry in the Jackson Purchase in the 124 bed facility now renamed Lourdes Hospital.

Bishop Cotton and his clergy advisor formed the Board of Trustees. Sister Mary Eleanor Rahrig served as the first administrator.

The Diocese of Owensboro sponsored the hospital under Bishop Cotton until his death in 1960. In 1962, the Most Rev. Henry J. Soenneker, newly installed as Bishop, requested that the Sisters of St. Francis assume sponsorship and the debt of the hospital.

The early years were years of great struggle, challenge and blessing. The census was low and expenses out-distanced income. Breaking the traditions of institutionalized racial discrimination was met with anger and resistance. The need for repair and replacement of equipment, furnishings and building was evident everywhere. The mission of serving God's people in the name of Christ ("in so far as you did this to one of the least of these... you do it to me." [Mt. 25:40]) was the motivating force for the Sisters who found themselves working seven days a week and often sixteen hours a day and foregoing any financial remuneration for several years. The support and encouragement of the chaplains, the local parish priests, and the sisters of the area; the dedication of the Sisters of St. Francis; and the tremendous support of the people of the Paducah Catholic parishes combined to form an enduring thrust in the healing mission of Christ and a simple and rooted presence of the Church in Western Kentucky and Southern Illinois.

The hospital grew in care, reputation and service in the state and the region. In 1973 a new facility, relocated to Lone Oak Road, opened its doors to patients. Lourdes Hospital has continued to develop services and has grown to a 385-bed capacity.

Early in 1982 Bishop Soenneker reassumed the sponsorship of Lourdes Hospital on behalf of the diocese. The Sisters of St. Francis continued to work there and serve on the Board of Directors. With the escalation of the technology, regulation and complexity of the health care industry and the accompanying demands of sponsorship the Most Reverend John J. McRaith, third Bishop of the Owensboro Diocese, together with the Board of Directors, reached the decision in 1990 to transfer the sponsorship of Lourdes Hospital from the Diocese to the Mercy Health System (Health Ministry of the Sisters of Mercy of Cincinnati, OH).

A recent survey shows that forty-three (43) Sisters of St. Francis have ministered at Lourdes Hospital in some capacity. Over the years, the Sisters have taught at the Paducah Community College and have taken an active role in diocesan, parish, state and local concerns. Twelve (12) Sisters have taught at St. Mary High School, Paducah; three (3) have managed and worked at Toddlers' Inn; three (3) have served as Pastoral Associates in various parishes; and four (4) have done volunteer summer work in the diocese.

The Sisters of St. Francis continue work in the Diocese in health care, child care, parish ministry, and diocesan ministry.

(L to R): Sister Mary Eleanor Rahrig, Sister Mary Luke Schill (now Sister Helen Schill), Sister Marilyn Keller, Sister Mary Gerard Linder (now Sister Gerard Linder), Sister Mary Leo Siebenaler (now Sister Elizabeth Jean Siebenaler), Sister Mary Aquinas Makin (now deceased). Early 1960. The photo was taken in the park along the Ohio River, just across the street from the hospital at Fourth and Clay Streets, where the Executive Inn now stands.

St. John Elementary School
Paducah

The first Catholics to settle in southern McCracken County began to arrive in the area now known as Saint John around 1834. The early settlers were visited by Father Elisha Durbin who had been assigned the territory that today is the Diocese of Owensboro. Father Durbin had a pattern of making sure the congregation attended to the educational needs of their children. Therefore he established Saint John School soon after beginning his ministry in the community.

School was conducted at first in a small log cabin which had been used as a Post Office for the community which was still called Adrian. It was termed "spring school" because it lasted about six weeks during good weather. Its main purpose was to prepare the children for the sacraments of Penance and Holy Communion. Later it was conducted for six months of the year, the children being taught by priests and laymen. Mrs. Ada Reber Wurtz was for many years as instructor in the school at St. John.

The little log school, covered with sheet metal, was used for many years as a classroom even after the building of the larger frame schoolhouse. It was referred to as the "University." Today the little log school is still in existence, though in very bad repair. The school house was purchased by the Folsomdale Feed Mill in 1956 when the brick school was constructed. The large frame school house was built around the same time as the frame church and is used by the community as a gym.

The Sisters of Charity of Nazareth, Kentucky were the first nuns to teach at St. John. They came to the parish in September of 1900 at the request of Rev. Charles Auer. Under Father Auer's direction a frame convent was built which, with several additions, was used by both the Sisters of Charity and later by the Sisters of Mercy who lived there until the brick convent was constructed in 1957. The Sisters of Charity taught elementary education classes here until June of 1912, when they gave up the school. The Sisters of Mercy reopened the elementary school in September of 1913.

To better educate and prepare our young people for their adult life, a two-year high school program was introduced in 1938. A number of St. John students continued their high school education and graduated from St. Mary Academy in Paducah. In 1946, the curriculum was extended to four years with the first class graduating in 1950. In 1956, during the pastorate of Rev. Richard Clements, the brick school was built. The high school was not to remain on the church grounds, however, as the last and largest class to graduate from St. John was in 1965. At this time a centrally located St. Mary High School was built to consolidate the area Catholic high schools of St. John, St. Mary Academy in Paducah, and St. Joseph of Mayfield, Kentucky.

Since the consolidation of the high schools in 1965, a number of other significant changes have been made to the school. After construction of the gymnasium/cafeteria building, a kindergarten program was introduced at St. John in 1975. Since 1987, the seventh and eighth grades have been taught at St. Mary High School with seventh and eighth grade classes from St. Mary Elementary. Beginning in the fall of 1989, a preschool program was offered at St. John.

The first school building at St. John.

Large frame schoolhouse used for many years.

St. John School, built in 1956.

St. Mary Academy
Paducah

The history of Catholic education in Paducah began with the opening of St. Mary Academy on October 12, 1858. There were no public schools at the time, and the few private schools were conducted by individuals in their homes. The academy opened under the direction of the Sisters of Charity of Nazareth, Kentucky, with Sister Martha Drury serving as principal. The school opened with a faculty of four Sisters and an enrollment of sixty students.

The Sisters arranged for the purchase of the Judge George H. Morrow property on the southeast corner of Fifth and Monroe, which initially served as the convent and school. As enrollment continued to increase, and faculty increased two-stories were added to the small convent, and a new school building was erected in 1860. After the addition was made to the convent, boarding students were accepted.

In 1907, forty-nine years after St. Mary Academy was established, the school had outgrown the original building erected in 1860 and a new one was begun to served as both grade and high school (this building was eventually sold to Draughon Business College). At the time, the new St. Mary Academy, was considered one of the largest and most imposing buildings in Paducah. The Sisters of Charity continued to administer the K-12 Academy until 1965.

The Sisters, after 106 years, elected to close the Academy at the conclusion of the 1964-65 school term. Bishop Henry J. Soenneker, Bishop of Owensboro, upon being informed of this decision, sought the services of the Christian Brothers of the St. Louis Province to continue the tradition of educational excellence so well established by the Sisters.

A fund campaign was launched to build a new high school. Five parishes cooperated in the financing of the new building. The Paducah parishes of St. Francis De Sales, St. Thomas More, St. John, Rosary Chapel, and St. Pius X in Calvert City. Over $1 million was raised through public subscription by a committee headed by Bob Claussner. The site for the new school was purchased off Lone Oak Road from the J.R. Smith estate.

Plans were completed and the ground-breaking ceremony was held August 22, 1964 for the present St. Mary High School located at 1243 Elmdale Road. One year later, the school was dedicated and blessed by Bishop Soenneker.

Great interest and support was shown for the new St. Mary High School. The first faculty included three Christian Brothers, eight Sisters of Charity, two Ursuline Sisters, two Sisters of Mercy, and two Franciscans. The founding principal was Bro. Ignatius Brown, FSC. Enrollment at the new high school was 312 on opening day, and increased to an all time high of 396 students during the 1968 fall semester. In addition to those belonging to the Paducah area parishes, the student population included students from St. Joseph in Mayfield and as far away as Cairo, Illinois.

With the opening of the new St. Mary High School, Catholic education in Paducah now consisted of one high school, and two grade schools: St. Francis De Sales Grade School located at 5th and Monroe, and St. Thomas More Elementary School located at 3230 Buckner Lane. In 1974, St. Francis De Sales moved from the original St. Mary Academy School building to the former Rosary Chapel School at 7th and Ohio.

Enrollment in the Catholic schools fluctuated over the years. As the nation's Catholic schools decreased in enrollment, so did enrollment in our Paducah Catholic Schools. In 1981, in an effort to best utilize facilities, the 7th and 8th grades of St. Thomas More and St. Francis De Sales grade schools moved to St. Mary High School. In 1982, St. Francis De Sales and St. Thomas More Grade Schools consolidated to form St. Mary Elementary School at 3230 Buckner Lane in the former St. Thomas More Elementary School. In the mid-1980s, the school boards of the elementary and high schools voted to consolidate and St. Mary High School and St. Mary Elementary School comprised the newly formed St. Mary School System. At this time, the school boards merged and the St. Mary School System Education Committee became the governing board of the school system.

Toward the end of the 1980's, interest once again turned to the educational opportunities of our Catholic schools. Enrollment began to grow and the need for a new elementary schools to replace the outdated building on Buckner Lane became a primary concern. In addition, research showed the need for creating a middle school to house grades six through eight. In the spring of 1990, a $2.8 million capital campaign, designated "Forward 2000", was launched with Louis A. Haas named as chairman. In a whirlwind community-wide campaign, the money was raised within 18 weeks and plans were made to begin construction. Ray Black & Son was hired as contractor.

In April of 1991, renovation of St. Mary High School was begun to include the new middle school. The two academic corridors were extended north toward Lone Oak Road. The east wing (100 corridor) was renovated to house St. Mary Middle School. New administration offices and restrooms were added on the north end and a sidewalk extending off of the bus loop allowed a separate entrance for middle school students. The west wing (200 corridor) was extended with additional classrooms to accommodate the move of all high school students to the west side of the building. St. Mary Middle School opened in September 1991 with Mrs. Rosann Whiting serving as its first principal. Serving as an administrative team with Mrs. Whiting, Mr. Michael Collins was hired as principal of St. Mary High School and Mrs. Nancy Collins was hired as principal of St. Mary Elementary School.

The first phase of "Forward 2000" was completed with the opening of St. Mary Middle School and construction of the new elementary school was begun. Property at 377 Highland Boulevard, adjacent to the St. Mary High School baseball field, was purchased from the city of Paducah for its new site. St. Mary Elementary School opened its new facility in the fall of 1992 with Mrs. Collins as principal.

The St. Mary School System has enjoyed a rich heritage and its indebted to the many religious orders and diocesan priests who have served our Paducah Catholic schools ince 1858. The lasting success of our Catholic school system is a beautiful tribute to the dedication and commitment of the founding Sisters of Charity, the Christian Brothers, the Urusline Sisters, the Sisters of Mercy, and the Franciscan Sisters.

St. Vincent De Paul Society
Owensboro

Our pioneer heritage in this region began circa 1865 in St. Louis. There, Christian lay persons felt the need to "bear witness" to their Christian faith by actions rather than words. They modeled their actions from the life of Frederick Ozanam. In the mid 1830's, this twenty year old student, along with some other young friends, felt inspired to unite themselves in service to the poor. In a humble and discreet manner, they proceeded to help others in simple ways; their time, presence, conversation, and giving from their modest means. They patterned their life after St. Vincent de Paul, a priest in the 1600's, who actively cared for the poor, the lonely, and those who had no one to help them.

Around 1880, this spirit of love found roots in Louisville, which spawned and nourished other groups in that region. The first conference in the newly-formed Diocese of Owensboro was St. Stephen's in 1935. From this hub of Western Kentucky Catholicism sprang many other parishes, and with them, groups of Christian-minded men and women who called themselves Vincentians. They honored and accepted Jesus' command to "love one another" By unpretentious means, they answered the "cry of the poor"; giving of themselves in time, talent, and treasures.

From being blessed by their good works, active Vincentians continually sought for new and better methods of reaching the needy. Again, the Holy Spirit gave Vincentians a means to achieve their goal. This concept was to have a store, whereby clothing, furniture, appliances, and other household items could be obtained for free, if the person was truly in need, or at a very reduced price. This gave people the opportunity to provide for themselves or their families, based upon their means, and for them to maintain some dignity as human beings. By being associated with a conference, the store provided some funds for the conference to help those who need food, medicine, shelter, etc.

The first Owensboro St. Vincent de Paul Store began operations in 1961 at the site of the present store. By providing a needed community service and with efficient operation, it showed other parish communities how to begin and develop their stores. Stores were started in Bowling Green, Paducah, Henderson, Russellville, Madisonville, Elkton, Morganfield, and Whitesville. In each location, civic and religious leaders attest to the positive Christian influence which these stores have on their community.

The number of parish Saint Vincent de Paul Conferences started increasing in the 1950's. The parish conferences' association, named the Owensboro Central Council, began with eleven affiliated conferences. The records show a gradual increase for the next thirty years. In 1984, a total of twenty Saint Vincent de Paul Conferences were affiliated with the Owensboro Central Council.

Today, the eighteen parish conferences, with its 400 members, have provided over $200,000 of goods and services; have devoted over 25,000 hours of services; and have helped 22,000 persons in the Owensboro Diocese by 1991. The St. Vincent de Paul Society is a major charity arm of the Catholic Church. Its goal is to make each encounter spiritually enriching for both parties as well as easing our clients' temporal burdens. The Society's conferences have a major role in evangelization; not so much by mere words, but by their good works and prayers.

The Society continues to have dedicated Christian leadership so necessary for its primary role in the church. Beginning with the Bishops, to the parish clergy, spiritual advisors, to the conferences' board members, and extending to the ever-faithful members, so many men and women have given of themselves in this ministry of charity. May it be sufficient to say that God knows how you have "tended to His lambs and have fed His sheep." We strive to bring God's love, His "Good News," to those who need it and to see it in action.

Trinity High School
Whitesville

Trinity High School opened its doors in August, 1968 in the buildings of the former St. Mary High School in Whitesville which closed when the Sisters of Charity of Nazareth found it necessary to withdraw their sisters from St. Mary High School due to a lack of personnel. The Mary Carrico Memorial School at Knottsville, grades 1-12, was also experiencing the national trend of dropping enrollment in Catholic Schools, so Diocesan Schools superintendent, Msgr. Raymond G. Hill, and the pastors of three eastern Daviess County parishes, Fr. Lucian Hayden, pastor of St. William, Knottsville, and St. Lawrence Parishes, and Fr. Charles Fischer, pastor of St. Mary of the Woods Parish in Whitesville, met with small groups of parish leaders from the three parishes to form an interparochial Catholic high school to be supported by the three parishes in order to ensure Catholic secondary education for students in eastern Daviess County.

Fr. Fischer wrote in the 1967 St. Mary of the Woods Parish Directory: "An entirely new high school has been established at Whitesville. It is Trinity High School, an interparochial school for the Knottsville and Whitesville children. It is under the supervision of a schoolboard composed of the Principal of Trinity High School, the Pastor of St. Mary's, the Pastor of St. William's and five laymen from each parish. It is administered by the Ursuline Sisters of Mount St. Joseph ably assisted by four Lay Extension Volunteers, two other lay teachers, and a lay secretary. The buildings occupied by Trinity are those formerly used by St. Mary High School. The east wing of the old St. Mary School (named the Msgr. Hugh O'Sullivan Building) has been remodeled into a convent for the eight Ursuline Sisters who are on the faculty of Trinity High School. Present enrollment of the school is 297, 84 from Knottsville and 213 from Whitesville." Fr. Lew White was Trinity's first assistant counselor.

The first school board members of Trinity High School were Fr. Lucian Hayden, Sister Regina, principal, Fr. Charles Fischer, Robert Howard, John Boarman, Jr., Clarence Logsdon, Vincent Johnson, Charles Roby, J. Andrew Hardesty, Gene Lanham, James Hagan, Jerome Hamilton, and Carl Logsdon. The first Ursuline Sisters on the faculty were Sr. Mary Daniel, Sr. Nazaria, Sr. Joseph Mark, Sr. Regina, principal, Sr. Jane Francis, Sr. Charles Mary, Sr. Justina, and Sr. Lennora. The Lay Extension Volunteers were Sue Fitzgerald, Bob Laur, Carolyn Burns, and Bob Lawrence. The two lay teachers were Bryce Roberts, the school's first basketball coach, and Mrs. Ann Daugherty. The first Trinity Booster Club officers were Joseph Montgomery, Thomas Conder, James Aud and Charles Varble, Jr.

The principals of Trinity High School were: Sr. Regina Boone, OSU, 1967-1969; Sr. Lennora Carrico, OSU, 1969-1971; Virgil Sublett, 1971-1973; James Hurm, 1973-1977; Joseph Delehunt, 1977-1981; Donald Freeman, June, 1981 - October 1981; Katie Williams, Interim principal, October 1981-June, 1982; Christopher Cameron, 1982-1985; Sr. Stephanie Warren, OSU, 1985-1989; Daniel Fuller, 1989-1991; Katie Williams, Interim principal - 1991-1992; John Calhoun, 1992-.

Trinity High School is located in the extreme eastern end of Daviess County, and students are transported to school by county buses and parents; some students drive to school. Tuition was initially set at $100 per year, with tithing families exempt from tuition. Tuition in 1993 was $2,600 per student with families paying $200 per student plus working at the school fundraiser. The parishes paid the remaining $600 per student. School enrollment in 1993 was 147.

Trinity High School has survived in many conflicts and cultural stresses through the years because as Bishop Henry Soenneker said, "The Catholic Communities of Eastern Daviess County need and can support a good Catholic High School. Trinity is the answer."

Ursuline Sisters, Mount St. Joseph
Maple Mount

Mount Saint Joseph is a community of Ursuline Sisters who trace their founding and spirit to a sixteenth century woman, Angela Merici. Angela was born in Italy in 1474 and, following an inspiration she received while very young, established in 1535 at Brescia, Italy, the Ursuline Order. It was the first community of women promoting apostolic ministry, that is, women who worked with the people rather than in a cloister. Ursulines carried Angela's educational idea of rechristianizing family life from Italy to France, then Belgium, Holland, Germany, Switzerland, Ireland, England, Poland, Greece, Canada, the United States and South America.

Of the fourteen original foundations in the United States, Immaculate Conception Ursuline Convent in Louisville, Kentucky was the ninth. Martin John Spalding, Bishop of Louisville, went to Straubing, Germany to solicit teachers for his Episcopal city. In 1858 under the guidance of Father Leander Sterber three Ursulines brought their educational methods to Kentucky. Their schools spread throughout Louisville and into other areas of Kentucky, seven other states and countries.

Mount Saint Joseph Academy was founded as a mission from Louisville in 1874 when five Sisters came to open an academy in Daviess County, Kentucky. In 1880 Father Paul Joseph Volk, pastor of Saint Alphonsus Parish, obtained a charter from the State Assembly under the title: Mount Saint Joseph Female Academy.

With the increase in enrollment of students at Mount St. Joseph, the community in Louisville sent additional teachers as needed. The school flourished and other mission schools were opened. Often the Ursulines pioneered in isolated areas, teaching in one-or-two room schoolhouses. In 1895, under the direction of Bishop McCloskey, an English speaking Novitiate was established at Mount Saint Joseph and five candidates were received into the Novitate. It should be noted that Ursuline Sisters profess the vows of poverty, chastity, obedience and a fourth vow of instruction.

By 1912 there were close to one hundred young women who had asked to be admitted to the Ursuline way of life. It was in that year that autonomy was granted by the Holy See and the Mount Saint Joseph Motherhouse was established.

Mount Saint Joseph Junior College was opened in the fall of 1925. In 1950 it was relocated in Owensboro, Kentucky, sixteen miles northeast of the Mount and named Brescia College. In 1934 a government post office began operating on the campus. Mount Saint Joseph, Maple Mount, Kentucky was officially added to the state maps in 1975. In 1979 the older buildings on the campus were added to the register of National Historic Buildings.

To date 873 young women have entered the Order and have served in approximately 275 parishes or schools in: Kentucky, Indiana, Illinois, Missouri, Nebraska, New Mexico, Tennessee, California, Oklahoma, New York, and South and Central America. Often the women of this Community blazed the trail to take education into isolated areas. At present there are 263 living members teaching in schools for kindergarten, primary, intermediate, junior and senior high, and college. Some tutor, teach English as second language, some work in administrative positions, pastoral, health and personal care; others in food service, youth ministries, hospitals, with refugees, parishioners and parishes. Ursulines are open to new ministries that will serve the needs of the church, especially among the poor and underprivileged.

Mount Saint Joseph Academy was discontinued in May, 1983. In the fall of that year Mount Saint Joseph Center began. The center offers various educational, religious, social and cultural programs in keeping with the needs of the times and of the people served. Programs are designed for interested persons or groups of any race, color or creed.

Since its foundation the Congregation of Ursulines has preserved the teaching concepts promoted by Saint Angela, not merely by mechanically giving out facts and rules and demanding obedience, but by an education worthy of imitation today. The congregation strives to bring forth the good in each person and teaches only what is first practiced with great insight, faith and courage.

Top: Ursuline Sisters Motherhouse, Mount St. Joseph.

Bottom: Mount St. Joseph Chapel.

Ursuline Sisters
Benton and Calvert City

Mother's Day 1994. (L to R): Lisa Walter, Sister Aloise Boone, Virgie Strobel, Sister Therese M. Mattingly

In 1984, Sister Therese Martin Mattingly and Sister Aloise Boone responded to their Superior's and Bishop John J. McRaith's request to go to Benton, KY. They started their ministry by first teaching Summer Religion Classes at St. Pius X in Calvert City. They were informed that there were "no Catholics, no blacks and no alcohol in Benton." With this information, they took up their residence in the Brown Gable Apartments. This was an ideal spot for their ministry of "reaching out" to the people. It was near Marshall County Hospital, Long Term Nursing Home, the bank, post office, grocery stores, jail, court house and the public library. Judge Miller gave permission for Bishop John J. McRaith to celebrate the first Mass in Benton in the Court House. After the Eucharistic Celebration, there were refreshments and time for people to meet Bishop McRaith, and to socialize with one another.

The Ministry of these two Sisters consists of many things, but mostly visiting the hospitals in Benton, Paducah and Murray, visiting the Nursing Homes, taking people to the doctor, to treatment centers, to get groceries, attending meetings like" Red Cross, Cancer Support, Coalition for Health Concerns, Home Makers (SWEEP), Marshall County Need Live, etc. At a HABITAT Meeting one individual admitted his efforts to keep Catholics out of the area, but now he is glad that he was not successful.

They have a Communion Service each Sunday at Brithaven even if only one Catholic is in residence. While there, they visit many of the other residents.

Much listening takes place over a cup of soup, coffee or tea. Many poblems, hurts, sorrows are sorted, discussed and even solved and resolved. Bishop McRaith, seeing the apparent good being done in this area, has started similar ministries in other locations in the Diocese.

In 1988 Msgr. Anthony Higdon asked Mt. St. Joseph for two Sisters to help with parish work. Sister Mary Mercy Hayden and Sister Mary Ethel Sims were asked to come. They came August 13, 1988. They lived in the house where the Sisters of Charity lived when they had a school here. Since it had been used as classrooms for CCD students, it was in need of some repair. The people worked hard to dress it up for the Sisters.

At the beginning Sister Mary Mercy taught the 4th grade. Msgr. Higdon and Sister Mary Ethel were the team members for the RCIA class. There were four people interested and their sponsors in the class.

In October 1988 Msgr. Higdon had a heart attack and had to leave the parish. Another pastor was not appointed until two weeks before Christmas. During the time in between the parish had a Rent-a-Priest week-end. Father Alan Mcintosh was appointed and stayed until June 1989. Then Rev. Aloysius Powers was appointed as pastor and remains so today.

The two Sisters are still at the parish but their duties have increased. Sister Mary Mercy is now teaching the second grade which also means preparing the children for the reception of the Sacraments of Reconciliation and Holy Eucharist. Sister Mary Ethel now teaches the 6th and 7th grades and has the responsibility of preparing the 7th and 8th grades for the Sacrament of Confirmation. She is the only organist in the parish and plays for the 5:00 p.m. Mass on Saturday and the 10:00 Mass on Sunday. Besides visiting and helping at the convalescent home, when it is St. Pius Tenths' time to do so, they take Holy Communion to the shut-ins in the parish. Visiting other people in the parish is also important and they help with the many duties that go on in a parish. *The Sisters at St. Pius Tenth Parish, Calvert City, Ky 42029*

James Everett Schwartz and Lona Belle Schwartz

Roman Catholic Diocese of Owensboro Family Histories

This building was oginally St. Leo's. It is presently Gleason Hall.

ALLEN, ERIC CLARK, son of Eric T. Allen and Veronica L. Reil, of Paducah, KY. He is the paternal grandson of Samuel C. and Mildred Allen. Samuel is the son of William T. and Johnnie Allen while Mildred is the daughter of Joe Kimble, the son of June and Marguerite Kimble and LaVerne Kimble, the daughter of Virgil and Nellie J. Muscovalley Clark.

Eric is the maternal grandson of Thomas E. and Essie B. Burgess. Thomas is the son of Francis and Joanna Burgess and Essie is the daughter of Chester A. and Maultie Clapp.

ALLEN, WILLIAM AND RITA, live in the St. Paul Parish in Grayson County. They have five children: Ann, Jimmy, Karen, Brenda and Marsha.

The Allen Family

Bill is originally from Breckinridge County and joined the Catholic Church on their wedding day. Bill works at Phillip Morris Company in Louisville, KY, and commutes to work each day. Rita works at home caring for their children, garden and helping on their farm.

ALVEY, BERNARD A., Bernard Aloysius, (Feb. 5, 1907-July 10, 1971) son of Mr. and Mrs. Andrew Claude Alvey, married Eugenia Busam, (April 11, 1908-), daughter of Mr. and Mrs. John William Busam, on May 6, 1930. They lived in Owensboro all their lives and were members of the Roman Catholic Churches in Owensboro.

Bernard, owned and operated service stations, coal mines and later became a contractor and builder. He was an active businessman, and a devoted husband and father.

Mr. and Mrs. Bernard A. Alvey. Picture taken in the 1960s.

Eugenia was an accomplished violinist who played in the first Owensboro Symphony Orchestra in 1919, a member of the Women's Clubs of Owensboro and was active in religious, civic and local concerns.

Their sons: Bernard Eugene Alvey married JoAnn Tamborn, of Chicago, IL, in 1953 and John Andrew married Sharon McKaey of St. Louis, MO, in 1957, later Donna Brazil in 1983.

Their grandchildren are: Miriam B. Alvey-Burich, Berdette A. Alvey-Anderson, Bernard T. (Chip) Alvey, children of Bernard E. and JoAnn, and John Andrew II, William Gerard; Mark W., children of John Andrew and Sharon.

ALVEY, BERNARD EUGENE, son of Mr. and Mrs. Bernard A. Alvey, born March 24, 1931. Bernie married JoAnn Tamborn, whom he met in Saint Louis while attending St. Louis University. Married on Nov. 26, 1953. JoAnn is the daughter of John J. Tamborn and Anne Zarnowiecki of Chicago, IL.

They moved to Owensboro in 1965 when he became a partner with his father in business. Their children are: Miriam B. who married John Burich in 1977, now residing in Louisville, KY; Berdette A. who married Richard Anderson in 1980, and lives in Memphis, TN; Bernard T. (Chip) who is a financial advisor in Nashville, TN.

The Bernard E. Alvey Family (1977)

After graduation from Saint Louis University Engineering School, Bernard has been an active business man. He served as major in the United States Air Force. Was stationed at Boeing in Seattle, WA and later Arnolt Corporation in Los Angeles, CA, residing in the Pacific Palisades. He was plant manager in charge of research and development. After moving to Owensboro he became a realtor and joined his father in lumber and construction enterprises. He built two churches in the Owensboro Diocese: St. Henry's Aurora and Saint Anthony of Padua, Grand Rivers. At present he is beginning a manufacturing company. The Alvey's reside in Spring Bank, a subdivision designed by the family in Owensboro.

JoAnn is active in civic events and volunteer work. She served on the first mayor's committee of the Fine Arts Commission in the city of Owensboro; she served two terms as president of the Owensboro Symphony Auxiliary. Served on the Family Board, and has been on the board of directors for the Owensboro Area Museum for 10 years.

Bernard and JoAnn are members of Saint Stephen Cathedral Parish. They have five grandchildren: Kristen Ann, Whitney C. and Hilary A. Burich all of Louisville, KY and Rachel Marie and Richard N. (Tripp) Anderson of Memphis, TN.

ALVEY, CARRIE LUSH, born Feb. 15, 1912, and the late Clarence Alvey, born Nov. 9, 1908, were born and reared in the Louisville Diocese. They received the sacraments, including marriage in St. Benedict Church, Wax. Their early married life began in 1937, the same year Western Kentucky became Owensboro Diocese and The Most Rev. Francis R. Cotton was appointed first bishop, Dec. 16, 1937.

The couple made their first home on a farm in Hart County, a beautiful setting overlooking the Nolin River. They were blessed with seven children: Wendell, Walter, Leon and George Thomas Alvey, Mary Frances Swenson, Rita Ferrell and Leoma Grant.

Carrie Alvey

The children received elementary education in St. Benedict School. The school was taught by the Ursuline Sisters from Maple Mount, KY. They commuted from St. Anthony Convent, Peonia. Sharing meat, eggs and vegetables from the farm was a valuable lesson in social concerns for the Alvey children.

During this time the Alvey family was active in parish and school activities: Holy Name, Altar Society and P.T.O. There were no pastoral councils or school boards. The parishioners cooperated to meet challenges of parish life. The Alvey family, along with other parishioners, cut saw logs from their wooded area to build the second church at St. Benedict.

The family moved from their Hart County farm in 1963. They built a home on the Leo and Ida Johnston Lush estate in Grayson County. Clarence was called to his eternal reward, Dec. 19, 1975.

Due to circumstances, the Alveys are presently members of St. Anthony Parish, Peonia. Carrie says her later ministries have been feeding tired, hungry pastors en route to and from the parishes. During their lifetime in the diocese, the Alveys have experienced many changes over the last half-century. The growth and spiritual enrichment of their parishes and the diocese as a whole, have been enhanced by their dedicated priests and three zealous bishops.

ALVEY, JAMES MARLIN, was born on Nov. 27, 1948 to Arnold Alvey and Anna Mary Clemons Alvey. He was baptized at St. Anthony Parish. Marlin is a Vietnam veteran. He served in the Army from 1969 to 1972. Then he went to work on construction until he became disabled in 1975. His father, a construction worker and his mother a housewife, both are now deceased. Veronica Lynn Higdon was born on July 4, 1955 to Wilbert Higdon and Geneva Hill Higdon. Wilbert worked in a Louisville Cooperage Factory and Geneva was a housewife, both now deceased. Lynn was baptized at St. Anthony Parish. Marlin and Lynn married Nov. 18, 1972. Lynn works at Vermont American in Leitchfield. They have two children, Kimberly Lynn Alvey and James Matthew Alvey. Kimberly was born on June 4, 1974 and baptized on July 21, 1974. Matthew was born on Feb. 20, 1978 and baptized on March 22, 1978. Lynn is a Parish Council member, lector and Children's Catechists. Kimberly is a Eucharistic Minister. They reside in Clarkson, KY.

ALVEY, FATHER LEONARD, was born in Walter Reed Hospital, Washington, DC on March 21, 1933. His father was Sgt. Leslie Alvey in the Army Medical Corps, and his mother Martine Weaver was a registered nurse. His maternal grandparents were Leonard and Pauline Weaver, members of St. Stephen's Cathedral, Owensboro, KY.

Father Alvey went to nine different schools in the first eight grades since his father was a military person. Two of these schools were St. Paul's School, Tell City, IN, and St. Stephen's School, Owensboro. He was confirmed and made his First Communion in St. Stephen's Cathedral, Owensboro. While he was visiting his grandparents in Owensboro, he decided to enter the seminary for the Diocese of Owensboro. He was accepted by Bishop Cotton and entered St. Meinrad Seminary where he studied from 1946-1952. From 1952-1954, he went to St. Mary's Seminary, Baltimore, MD. From 1954-1958, he went to St. Maur's Seminary, South Union, KY.

Father Leonard Alvey

Bishop Cotton ordained Father Alvey on May 3, 1958. His first assignment was assistant pastor at St. Stephen's Cathedral. In 1960 he was assigned to St. Thomas More Parish, Paducah, KY and Lourdes Hospital, Paducah, KY. In 1965, he was appointed pastor of Sacred Heart Parish, Hickman, KY and St. Edward's Parish, Fulton, KY. In 1966, he transferred to Owensboro Catholic High School where he served as teacher of Latin and Religion and director of Pupil Personnel for two years. He then went to Catholic University of America where he earned an MA in philosophy and began teaching at Brescia College, his present assignment. While at Brescia, he has earned an Ed.S. in counseling. At present, Father Alvey teaches philosophy at Brescia College and is in its counseling center. His residence is at St. Martin's Parish, Rome, KY.

ALVEY, MARY PAULETTE, was born and raised in Union County, Morganfield, KY, and now lives at Carmel Home, Old Hartford Road in Owensboro. She is the daughter of Robert Douglas and Heniette Newcom Alvey. She attended and graduated from nursing school at St. Mary's in Evansville, IN. She worked as a registered nurse for 50 years.

ALVEY, ROBERT LEE (BOBBY), was born to Curtis Edward and Teresa Evelyn Alvey on Dec. 15, 1951 in Daviess County. A month earlier, Mary Ann Keller was born to Lucian Dennis and Regina Keller (Bud and Gean) on Nov. 4, 1951 in Daviess County also. They met in high school where they attended Owensboro High School. They were married on Oct. 16, 1970 at St. Martin's Church in Rome. They built a small house in Stanley but later moved across the road. Bobby became a self-employed farmer, and Mary Ann became a self-employed caterer, later a school cafeteria worker. They attended St. Peter's Parish in Stanley.

Bobby and Mary Ann started a family and now have three children. The oldest son, Robert Lee Alvey Jr., (Robby) is 21, and attends Owensboro Community College. The middle child, Benjamin Ryan Alvey (Ben) is 16 and attends Owensboro Catholic High School. The youngest child, Sara Beth Alvey, is 13 and attends Owensboro Catholic Middle School. Robby and Ben both assist their father on their farm. When the Alvey family goes to church, Mary Ann is in the choir, Ben sometimes serves, and Robby and Sara are lectors.

THE ALVEY FAMILY, the Ruth Marjilee Hayden Alvey family was raised in the St. Alphonsus Parish at St. Joseph. Marjilee attended Beech Grove Grade School, Mount St. Joseph Academy and has a degree in medical technology from Brescia College. She worked many years at Our Lady of Mercy Hospital and was chief technologist for eight years. She married Joseph Damian Alvey on Sept. 27, 1958 at St. Alphonsus, Fr. Joseph McAleer officiating. Three children were born to this couple, Gracia Elaine, Daniel Joseph and Jack Linus. They were legally separated in February 1962 and divorced in June 1975.

Alvey Family. Adults (L to R): Gracia, Dan, Terrie, Marjilee, Jack and Susie Children (L to R): John, Rachael, Ben, Rebekah and (not pictured) Beau.

Marjilee is the daughter of the late Joseph Henry and Verna Marie Ball Hayden. She gives much credit and thanks to her parents for helping raise her children. She is a member of the Altar Society/Christian Mothers, the Army of Mary and sings in the Army of Mary Choir. The Catholic faith was brought to them through grandparents of the late J. Sid and Victoria Blandford Hayden. The Hayden line extends back to the early Maryland Catholic settlers.

Gracia is an organist at St. Alphonsus, holds a degree in biology from Brescia College and is presently office manager and bookkeeper at Our Tennis House. She and her mother live on a farm near Beech Grove.

Dan married Terri Jean Cremer on June 23, 1984 at St. Alphonsus, Rev. Jose Ramon, O.S.B. officiating. Terri is a convert and was received into the church in 1985 by Fr. Carl Glahn. They have five children: Rebekah Brooks, Johnathan Daniel, Rachael Ruth, Benjamin Joseph and Beau Edwin. Dan farms, raising mostly soybeans, corn, tobacco and hogs. Terri is a graduate of Murray State University and works at the Thrifty Nickel. Rebekah and John attend Holy Angels School.

Jack married Carol Sue Haight on July 9, 1988 at Holy Family Church in Ashland. Jack has a master's degree from the University of Kentucky. He is a farmer. Susie is a convert, U.K. graduate and is presently working on her master's degree. She teaches fifth grade at St. Angela Merici School. Jack and Susie attend St. Stephen's Cathedral.

ANTHONY, LAVERNE, was born in Providence, KY. The seventh child of Will and Ida Cox on March 25, 1909. They were members of Pleasant Hill Baptist Church. She was a 1928 graduate of Rosenbald High School. She served as pianist of the same church. Married John T. Anthony in 1934 in New York City. She was a 1936 graduate of Orchids School of Beauty Culture. Attended business school and later was blessed with owning and operating a successful business, LaVerne's Beauty Salon, in New York City.

LaVerne Anthony

They returned to Kentucky in 1969 for retirement. Attended Christ the King Catholic Parish in Madisonville, KY. They were confirmed Easter Sunday 1975 and helped establish the Holy Cross Catholic Parish in Providence, KY. God called John before the building was finished on Feb. 7, 1978. He was eulogized at Christ the King Parish. LaVerne had the honor of being a charter member of the same, a long happy life, and the Catholic faith.

ARCILESI, REVEREND LEONARD JOSEPH, born on July 12, 1928, in Louisville, Kentucky, and baptized at the Old St. Michaels Church, on Aug. 16, 1928. He was born of Italian and Anglo-Saxon ancestry, his father Frank Arcilesi, was born in Alcomo, Italy and came to the U.S. at the age of 18. His mother, Hazel Mary was born in New Albany, IN. Both parents are deceased. His mother died when he was 12. His father died when he was 38. His father's second wife Nettie, died four years ago. He has one sister Vita Miller, no brothers. Rev. Arcilesi's extended family lives in Chicago, Detroit and other urban centers. His home was in the downtown area of Louisville, where he attended St. Boniface Church and School. Later went to St. Xavier High School, graduated and went to Xavier University in Cincinnati, and then transferred to Bellarmine College in Louisville, gaining a BA degree in history and English, with minors in economics and biology.

From his earliest years in St. Boniface School, Rev. Arcilesi served Mass and began to form his desire for the priesthood or religious life. In 1953, he studied for the Louisville Diocese for one year, then departed the seminary and went to the service for two years. Then he began a 31 year career as a professional educator in the high schools of Cincinnati, OH, 14 years in the classroom, teaching history, sociology and economics. For the next 17 years he was either assistant-principal or principal of junior and senior high schools. Rev. Arcilesi retired in 1985, after being principal of a 1,600 student high school in Central Cincinnati, with nine specific programs.

During his educational career, Rev. Arcilese also served in the teachers' unions, as an officer and during his four years as president, he led the first teacher's strike in Ohio and they negotiated the first teachers' negotiated contract in Ohio. Later he served on the Ohio Educational Association Board of Directors and was president of the OEA for two years, with offices in Columbus, OH. During his term, they had 14 strikes and won everyone of them, resulting in salary increases and better teaching conditions. Retirement benefits were greatly improved.

Reverend Leonard Joseph Arcilesi

Another extra personal interest was to develop real estate, supervising building crews and directing plans. This along with renovating old homes and selling them was a interesting avocation. However, he never dropped the idea of becoming a priest; most of his life plans were often directed by this vocational call.

Rev. Arcilesi dated many wonderful girls and was engaged to be married several times, but could never make the commitment because of a desire to become a priest. He spent 10 years in discernment for the priesthood before he dropped all the wonderful and profitable pursuits to enter the seminary. Along the way he earned an M.A. in history-economics; an M. ED. in education, an Ed. specialist degree, completed all doctoral works for D.ED degree and earned the M. Div. at Mount St. Mary of the West Seminary, in Cincinnati, OH.

In preparation for entrance to the seminary, he studied graduate philosophy at Xavier University in Cincinnati and took many courses at the seminary, so that he was advanced one year when he officially entered as a seminarian. Rev. Arcilesi was ordained on May 27, 1989, by Bishop McRaith at the sportscenter in Owensboro. A real support in his vocation, has been Bishop McRaith's fraternal concern and encouragement. His most important interests in the church are the study of scripture, liturgy and preaching. Working with youth and young people have always been a major interest and satisfaction.

AUD, The Aud family has been in Daviess County since its formation. As part of the Catholic migration from Maryland to Central Kentucky in the late 18th century, it has been prominent and distinguished in each generation. Today's many Aud families contribute much to the church and community.

In *The Centenary of Catholicity in Kentucky*, by Ben Webb, the family of Zachariah Aud and Margaret Coomes Wathen is recorded. One of their most prominent sons, Father Athanatius A. Aud, was one of the first Catholic priests in Daviess County and served as pastor of St. Lawrence Church and the administrator of many baptisms and other sacraments.

Michael Aud, another of their 12 children, was born in 1812 in Nelson County, and married Angela Speak. They came to Daviess County in the late 1830s. His 15 children's descendants include all the Auds in Daviess County, and family ties to Payne, Sanders, Head, Higdon, Mattingly, Nugent, Bowlds, etc. of Knottsville, Whitesville, Owensboro and throughout the U.S.

Their fifth child, Richard Henry Aud and his wife, Mary Ann Poole, built a house south of Knottsville. Their children included William Thomas Aud who married Mary Matilda Payne. Their children included Sylvester Leo and his sisters, Margaret (married Victor Franzen of Waucoma, IA), Mary Agnes (Sister Monica, OSU, who died at Maple Mount in 1988) and Rose Ann, who died as a teenager in 1920.

Leo married Lattie Martina Fulkerson, of Beech Grove, in 1937. They had six children: William J., F. Leon, Raymond L., Charles E., Thomas LaVerne and Mary A. Leo who died in January 1965. Lattie married Wilfred Lanham Payne in 1974, who died in 1982. Lattie still lives in Owensboro.

Throughout the history of Daviess County, the descendants of Michael Aud have served as strong Catholics, priests, nuns, farmers, real estate agents, lawyers, librarians and many other positions. The strong ties of God, family and home continue as prominent values maintained by the Aud families everywhere.

AUD, BARRY DEAN AND KAREN MARIE (EDGE),
were both born and raised in Whitesville, Daviess County, KY. Barry is the son of Jay and Hazel Aud. Karen is the daughter of Fabian (Dude), deceased, and Loretta Edge. Barry works as a mail carrier. They are members of the St. Mary's Parish. They have three children, Emily Marie, born Sept. 19, 1978; Kyle Dean born Aug. 26, 1980; and Lyndsay Diane born Nov. 2, 1982.

AUD, FRANCIS LEON,
was born on Dec. 7, 1940 in Daviess County, KY. He is the son of Leo Aud and Lattie Fulkerson Aud Payne. Leon in presently a maintenance man at Mount St. Joseph. While growing up he liked to help his dad with the farm. He attended St. William School for 12 years. Leon went to Owensboro Junior Business College for two years before going into the Navy for six years. He married Cecilia Marie Higdon, born Aug. 21, 1943 in Daviess County. She is the daughter of Norbert Ignatius Higdon and Bertha Orene Knott Higdon. Cecilia is a homemaker for her family at St. Joseph, and also works at Catherine Spalding School on the after school program. She went to St. Mary of the Woods School and Parish while growing up. Cecilia and Leon met through a blind date and were married on Jan. 5, 1963 at St. Mary of the Woods Church in Whitesville.

They have eight children: David James (29), Stephen Joseph (28), Michael Dominic (25), Catherine Marie (22), Mary Elizabeth (19), Loretta Anne (17), Jonathan Patrick (15) and Paul Gabriel (13). Catherine attends University of Louisville, Mary attends Brescia College, Loretta and Jonathan attend Catholic High, and Paul attends OCMS. David, Stephen and Catherine have moved away. David and Stephen are married.

AUD, DR. WILLIAM JOSEPH (B.J.),
was born May 26, 1954 in Owensboro, KY. Karen F. Warren was born March 16, 1954 in Owensboro. B.J. and Karen married in 1976 at Lourdes Church. They later moved on to Louisville after Karen received her bachelor's degree in science. B.J. went to the University of Louisville to become a dentist after receiving his bachelors. B.J. and Karen had two children in Louisville and moved around for awhile until they decided that Owensboro was their home. B.J. started two dental practices with his brother, Gary Aud, one in Owensboro and the other in Henderson, KY. B.J.'s parents are Bobbie Ray and William Ernest. Karen is the daughter of Odie B. Warren and Martine Crow.

B.J. and Karen had four children: Aaron (13), Casey (11), Stephen (6) and Kara (2). The Auds now belong to Lourdes Parish and take part in parish activities.

BACON, JOHN SHAW,
the son of Andrew Clark Bacon and Clara Shaw Bacon, daughter of George Lyle Shaw and Mary Ann Curlin. Other children of Andrew and Clara include Andrew and Mary Lyle, both deceased, and Dorothy.

Margaret Mary Johnson is the daughter of Ernest Duval Johnson and Loula Ramage Johnson.

John Shaw Bacon married Margaret Mary Johnson on July 27, 1940. They are the parents of four children: Mary Cecilia, Margaret Elizabeth (Betty), Agnes Teresa and John Shaw. Mary Cecilia married Gerald Love Harris. They have three children: Laura, Cindy and Mary Carol. They are members of Sacred Heart Parish in Hickman, KY. Margaret Elizabeth married Lt. Col. Richard Ciccolella (Ret.). They have two children Richard (Dickie) and Heather. The family resides in Virginia. Agnes Teresa married James Toler from Owensboro and gave birth to a daughter, Melissa. Agnes, divorced from James, married Robert Barron from Owensboro. John Shaw Bacon married Nancy Jo James of Union City, TN. They have twins, Kelly and Kim and one son James Andrew. John remarried Kathy Keightley from Union City, TN. She has a son Brad and a daughter Kim.

John Shaw Bacon and Mary Margaret Johnson Bacon

John and Margaret live on the family farm in Hickman, KY, and are members of Sacred Heart Parish.

BAKER, ROBERT CARSON,
born in Earlington, KY, the son of Godfrey and Virginia Baker. He is a graduate of Murray State University and Marquette University Dental School in Milwaukee, WI. He is a convert to the Catholic faith and was baptized June 10, 1958 in St. Paul's, Owensboro.

Rose Mary Bowlds was born in Owensboro, the daughter of Wilbur and Anna Doreen Drury Bowlds, members of St. Paul in Owensboro. She is a graduate of St. Francis Academy in Owensboro and St. Bernard College, Cullman, AL. She was a teacher in the Owensboro Public School System. They married Aug. 23, 1958 in St. Joseph's, Owensboro (because St. Paul's was being redecorated), and moved to North Chicago, IL, where Bob was in the Navy at Great Lakes Naval Base. Next they moved to Milwaukee, WI, where their three children were born while Bob attended Marquette Dental School.

The Robert C. Baker Family

The family returned to Owensboro in 1966. They attended Our Lady of Lourdes Church. In 1968 they moved to Marion, KY where Bob opened a dental practice. They were members of St. William Church. Bob and Rose Mary taught CCD classes and were active in parish life. They currently attend Holy Cross in Providence.

Jeffrey was born June 24, 1964, lives in Chicago, IL, and was married May 2, 1992, to Terri Perlman of Chicago. Twins Gregory and Jennifer were born Sept. 8, 1965. Greg lives in Lexington, KY. Jennifer married Mark Pieper April 27, 1991 in Evansville, IN. She died suddenly of a heart attack on June 17, 1992. The Baker children all graduated from the University of Kentucky in Lexington.

Bob has practiced dentistry for over 25 years with Rose Mary as his office manager for the past 10 years.

BAKER, ROBERT JOHN AND ALETA (GREAYER),
John was born in Cleves, OH, in the same house where his two brothers and sisters were born. The doctor came to their house and delivered them for $65. He married Aleta Greayer who was born in St. Peter Hospital in New Brunswick, NJ. He is a member of several organizations including the United Way and Kiwanis, which sometimes takes him overseas.

Robert and Aleta have three children: Tara, born April 11, 1980 in Lexington, KY; Gretchen Ann, born April 28, 1981 in Paducah, KY; Erin Allyse born Jan. 25, 1988 also in Paducah. All attend St. Joseph School in Mayfield, KY.

BALL, JOSEPH BERTEL AND KATHERINE CRUNE MCMICHAEL,
were married on Feb. 3, 1934 at St. Michael's Catholic Church at Fairfield, KY (Nelson County). J.B. was the oldest of the eight children. J.B.'s mother and father were William Francis Ball and Sophie Hall Ball. They lived in Nelson County, KY. They formed and owned a grocery store. Katherine was the youngest of the eight children. Katherine's mother and father were Miles McMichael and Kate Crune McMichael. They farmed and lived in Nelson County, KY. J. B. and Katherine had nine children. One child Charles Phillip passed away one day after his birth. The children are: Elizabeth Juanita Fogle, Helen Jean Fogle, Joyce Ann Henning, Katherine Marie Weber, Joseph Wayne Ball, William Lee Ball, Agnes Pauline Trent and Mary Sheila Frank. There are 20 grandchildren and three great-grandchildren.

J.B. is a farmer and does construction work, Katherine a housewife. J.B. and Katherine moved from Nelson County in 1948 to Meade County. They lived in Meade County four years and then moved to Breckinridge County in 1952. Katherine passed away Jan. 19, 1991. J. B. will be 80 years of age on Nov. 27, 1992.

BALLARD, EDMUND E.,
was born in Owensboro, KY. Went to school at St. Francis Academy. He was baptized, made his First Communion and Confirmation at St. Paul Church. Worked as a cabinet maker and in the furniture industry for 20 years. He was self-employed, servicing wood working and aluminum industries cutting tools. His father, Evaristus Ballard, was born in West Louisville, KY and worked as a machinist in the furniture industry. His mother, Birdie Wayne Leigh, was born in Henderson County, KY, and was a housewife. They had eight children.

Edmund E. Ballard and Mary Martin Howard Ballard

Mary Martine Ballard, born at Dermott, KY, outside of Owensboro. Made all her sacraments at St. Paul Church.

Her mother, Nora Ellen Clark, was born in Grayson County, at Big Clifty, she was a housewife. Her father, was born in Ohio County, and was a farmer. They had eight children.

Edmund and Martine were married May 11, 1935 at St. Paul Catholic Church in Owensboro, they have nine living children, 32 grandchildren and seven great-grandchildren. Two of their children were born in Owensboro, two in Louisville, KY, five at Stanley, KY, where they have lived since 1944. All of the children have made their sacraments there, went to grade school there, graduated from Catholic High School and some went to Brescia. Three of the sons were in the military, one serving 20 years in the Air Force. Martine and Edmund still live on the farm they bought in 1944 when they moved back to Daviess County from Louisville. After they retired, they bought a 22 foot travel trailer and Blazer self-contained and travelled over the U.S. spending several winters in Florida.

Martine and Edmund celebrated their 50th Wedding Anniversary May 11, 1985 at St. Stephen Cathedral with Fr. Joe Rhoades and Fr. Baker officiating. All nine children and families were present.

BALLMANN, JOSEPH AND ANNA WHEATLEY, *A Brush with History*, Joseph, (1871-1949) born of immigrant refugees from German Revolution 1848 at Dukes, Hancock County, KY. Farmer.

Anna, born also at Dukes (1879-1950) was assistant school teacher until marriage in 1898 at first nuptial Mass, St. Rose Church, Cloverport. Wheatleys came from Bristol, England to Jamestown Colony, VA in 1639 and could not practice their faith in public until American Revolution. In 1740 George Wheatley of Virginia married Mary Darnall of St. Mary's City, MD, the cousin of Fr. John Carroll of Upper Marlboro who founded America's first Catholic College (Georgetown, now a university) and became America's first bishop and archbishop of Baltimore. His brother, Daniel Carroll furnished the land for building the U.S. Capitol. Mary was also a cousin of Charles Carroll of Carrolton, a signer of the Declaration of Independence.

Mary and George's grandson, Leonard served in the Continental Army. When marching to Yorktown they met Washington's Army with news of the British surrender. Leonard and family migrated to Breckinridge County, KY in 1791, its first Catholic family. Thomas and Elijah Wheatley were in Sherman's March to the Sea.

Joseph and Anna had 13 children:

Joseph (1898-1928). Member of Student's Army Training Corps, (SATC) during World War I. School teacher.

Lawrence (1900-1964). Married Ruth Southard. Pennsylvania Railroad employee and farmer.

Christine (1902-1991). First graduate of St. Rose High School, Cloverport, school teacher, nurse, superintendent of nurses St. Joseph Infirmary, Louisville, U.S. Indian Service, Army nurse (captain), Pacific Theatre, Graduate Brescia College, Spalding College, and master's degree University of St. Louis. Teacher Spalding College.

Carolyn (1903-1990), school teacher, technical writer and engineering consultant for Navy Department, Washington, DC. Attended American University. Officer Catholic Daughters of America.

Charles (1905-1980). Married Helen Riedl, builder-developer, Columbus, OH. Six children: Rose Marie, Mary Rita, Charles, Robert and Doris. Paul was lost in an automobile accident.

Celestine (1908-1984). Actor, travelling shows, and had minor parts in five movies. Los Angeles. Married twice. First wife lost in automobile accident within one year. Married Marcella Lombardi who lived for 22 years. No children. Absent from family for 53 years. Found by brother Francis six months before his death.

Bernard (1910-1988). Married Clara Barton, great niece of founder of American Red Cross. Maintenance engineer, Ohio State Hospital. Columbus, OH. Three step-children.

Leo (1912-1991). Married Evelyn Simmons, Jadwin, MO. Foreman of Master Mechanics, North American-Rockwell, Columbus, OH. Eight children: Carolyn, Michael, David, Stephen, Loretta, Teresa, Douglas and Margaret.

Agnes (1914-). Graduate Louisville Academy of Cosmetology. Owner Powder Puff beauty Shop, Owensboro. Later computer systems analyst Sears Roebuck. Married Forest Riggs (deceased). No children. St. Petersburg, FL.

Cecilia (1915). Died in infancy.

Regina (1916) Statistical analyst. Department of Interior, Washington. Married John F. Sheehan. One son, Clyde. Philadelphia.

Eugene (1919-1992). General Electric 35 years. Usher at St. Stephen Cathedral 53 years.

Francis X. (1920-) Pacific World War II. Later 1st Lt. Air Force Reserve. Graduated from Georgetown University, School of Foreign Service, George Washington University, Law School, Senior statistician, Department of the Navy on staff of assistant secretary of the Navy for Financial Management, Architectural Archivist Georgetown University, Member Family Life Board 10 years, Archdiocese of Washington, representing the hurting families, Three years Maryland State Chairman of PTA Committee for Exceptional Children. Secured legislative enactment of program for Gifted Children. Initiated movement for law raising drinking age one year at a time from 18 to 21. Movement resulted in a federal law in 1986. Married Marion Muller. Four children: Susan, Francis X. Jr., Joseph and Richard. Rockville, MD.

This family history has charter members in the Diocese of Baltimore (1790), Bardstown (1808), Louisville (1841) and Owensboro (1938).

BARROW, SISTER MICHAEL, was born June 23, 1880 at Winchester, KY. She was the daughter of David and Elizabeth (Curry) Barrow.

She entered Mount Saint Joseph Novitiate on Jan. 27, 1907, received the Habit on May 31, 1907 and took her first vows on July 14, 1909.

Sister attended school in Washington, DC from 1922 to 1925. She received an MA in History from the Catholic University of America in 1925. She authored "The Foundations of the Ursulines in the United States" in 1925. From 1926 to 1954, she was involved with work at various missions including: Calvary, KY; Mt. St. Joseph; Waverly, KY; Waterflow, NM; and Brescia College at Owensboro, KY.

In 1946, she released her second book, "Candles of the Lord (Missionary life in New Mexico)."

Sister Michael was a delightful person to know, a lover of history and vitally interested in promoting education. In 1949 she was constantly reminding Bishop Francis R. Cotton that the Ursulines had spent 25 years at MSJ Junior College campus with little growth. It was time, she thought, to move to Owensboro to better serve those interested in going to college.

Her almost weekly calls to the Chancery Office produced results. The move to 7th Street took place August 1950 and on Oct. 4, 1950 concrete evidence that Sister's labors and prayers were productive with the laying of a cornerstone on the property at 120 West 7th Street, Owensboro, indicating that the Mount St. Joseph College had been transplanted and renamed Brescia College.

At this time she envisioned the Campus as occupying the entire block, east-west, Allen to Frederica and north-south, 7th to 8th Street, with a library on the corner of 7th and Allen - where it is now located. She frequently repeated this statement ending with "I will not live to see it, but you will."

A student remarked when Sister left Brescia in April 1953, "she paved the way for many apprehensive students entering collegiate life." Her *European Civilization* course was described as "one of the most cultural courses we ever took; it was an hour of rich delight, in which just to be present was a joy."

Sister Michael passed away on May 21, 1956.

BARTLEY, HEZEKIAH KENDRICK, was born Feb. 22, 1793 in Maryland, the son of John and Sarah Bartley. In 1824, Hezekiah married Elenor Madden in Washington County, KY, and about 1838 the Bartley's moved to Union County, KY. They became one of the early families of Sacred Heart Church. As Hezekiah tilled the soil of his Union County farm, his family prospered, eventually numbering 16 children: Reuben L., Milton, Walter, Mary, Solomon, Matthew, Henry Harrison, Louisa Ann, Nancy, Margaret Catherine, Sarah Elizabeth, Eliza Magdalin, Martha, Hezekiah Jr., Susanna and Elisha Alexander.

Elenor Madden Bartley died in Union County, Jan. 19, 1881, and Hezekiah Bartley died there Oct. 18, 1884 at the old age of 91. Both are buried in St. Ann Cemetery, as are many of their descendants. Also, the Bartley name can be found on several markers in Sacred Heart Cemetery in Union County, KY.

Although the Bartley name has died out in Union County, descendants of Hezekiah and Elenor Bartley continue to live there with names such as Veatch, Tucker, Stewart and Collins.

BATSON, ANNA LORENE HOWARD, (husband, William H. Batson deceased), was born in Bowling Green, KY on May 28, 1920. She was baptized at St. Joseph Church by Rev. Thomas J. Hayes. She is the daughter of Wilhelmina Bittner Howard and Webb A. Howard.

Golden Wedding Anniversary Picture of Bernard and Clara Ballmann February 22, 1948. Left to right: Bernard and wife Clara, Agnes, Christine, Joseph (father), Charles, Lawrence, Joe, Anna (mother), Francis, Carolyn, Celestine, Eugene, Leo and Regina. Pictures inserted are Joe (deceased), Charles and Celestine.

William H. and Anna Howard Batson

Member of the Holy Spirit Parish in Bowling Green, past member of St. Joseph Parish also in Bowling Green. Lorene is also a member of Legion of Mary, Our Lady of Sorrows Praesidium.

She has nine children: Mary Annette Bostick, Bernadette Franklin, Michael Howard Batson, Rita Clare Carroll, Wilhelminz Shelton, Paula Shannon Boddie, Hatton Nicholas Batson, Ann Loretta Micale, Agnes Lorene Chittenden. Lorene and her son Michael live in Bowling Green, KY.

Lorene's great-grandfather Francis was an architect and Kister built St. Joseph Church.

BAYER, MARY E., was born and raised a Catholic christian in St. Brendan Parish, New Haven, Connecticut Dec. 23, 1946. She was baptized and confirmed in the usual manner of ways. One particular incident involved her "transplantation" to Daviess County, Owensboro, KY-a vocation to the religious life. However, after having incurred a medically traumatic accident, (cerebral anoxia), earlier in her youth, she found her handicaps not to be compatible with community. Having been involved with the Legion of Mary back East, and concerned with the involvement of handicapped people in society, she sought her own involvement in a more religious environment, according to her own gifts and abilities. Not being able to fraternize in community because of physical and stressful circumstances, she lives independently as a Secular Sister, who will be consecrated to a life of Virginity, May 9, 1992, by her spiritual director, Fr. J. Edward Bradley, current pastor of St. Stephen Cathedral, Owensboro, KY.

Mary E. Bayer, Sec.

Having a deep understanding of blind people in a sighted society, Mary records textbooks and various literature for the blind and visually impaired students who attend regular classrooms; and for those professionals who have made their contribution to society in spite of their visual impairments. She also, does what she can for St. Stephen Cathedral Parish.

Keeping her own diary of sorts, there are particular thoughts she thinks are wise for all to remember: If commitment is not understood, it will probably be short-lived or shallow. Faith is the substance of things hoped for, the evidence of things not seen.

BEATTY, JOHN LYNN AND DONNA JEAN HIGDON, are members of St. Mary's Parish. John is the son of John W. and Mary Beatty. Donna is the daughter of Henry and Mary Jo Higdon. They currently live in Daviess County, KY. They have two children Mandy, born June 1, 1979 and Matthew born Jan. 5, 1983.

BEAVEN, RICHARD JOSEPH, was born June 15, 1957, son of Donald and Carolyn Beaven of Route 1, Sturgis, KY. Richard is a graduate of Union County High School and employed at Pyro Mining Company in Sturgis, KY.

He married Mary Diana Payne on Nov. 29, 1991 at Holy Name of Jesus Catholic Church in Henderson, KY. She was born Sept. 22, 1960 and is the daughter of Herman J. and Edith C. Payne of Whitesville, KY. Diana is a graduate of Trinity High School and is employed at Hagerman Plumbing and Heating Company in Owensboro. They currently live in Corydon, KY, and are members Holy Name of Jesus Catholic Church. Past member of St. Francis Borgia, Sturgis, KY and Diana is past member of St. Mary of the Woods, Whitesville, KY. Richard is a Eucharistic Minister, lector, parish council and CCD teacher. Diane serves as guitarist and cantor, lector.

Richard and Diana Beaven

Richard's grandparents, George B. and Teresa Beaven (still living) belonged to St. Agnes Parish in Uniontown. They were farmers. Now members of St. Ann, Morganfield, KY. His grandparents, Charles and Mary Mattingly (still living) lived in Morganfield, KY, until early 1960s, then moved to Evansville, IN.

Diana's grandparents, Kyran and Delpha Clark (both deceased) of Whitesville, KY. Her grandparents, Lawrence and Anna Payne (both deceased) originally from Knottsville, KY moved to Owensboro, KY.

BEAVEN, WILLIAM R. AND MARY HILDA WURTH, were both raised in Union County, KY. William was born there and Hilda was born in McCracken County. They now live in Morganfield, KY and are members of St. Ann Parish.

They have two sons and two daughters, Tammy Kay Beaven Blue, born April 21, 1961 married to Joe Blue with one son Joey who is 3; William R. Beaven II born Sept. 15, 1962; Robin M. Beaven Oliver born Sept. 30, 1963, two girls Wendy M. (9) and Melissa D. (7); Bryan Keith Beaven born Feb. 6, 1968.

BECKNER, MARY MARGARET (BUSH), was born on June 12, 1940. She was baptized, made her First Communion and Confirmation at St. John Church, Sunfish. She graduated from St. John in May 1958, then moved to Lake Charles, LA where she married in the Immaculate Conception Church Oct. 1, 1960. Mary has three sons, James of Pedal, MS who is married to Emma Outland and had one son, James F. III. Timothy D. married Dede L. McMannis in 1985, they have two girls. Timothy is a captain in the U.S. Army stationed at Ft. Knox, KY. Thomas is managing a store for Pick Way in Aroura, IL.

Mary currently lives in Brownsville, KY, and is a member of St. John Evangelist Church in Sunfish, KY. Past member of parishes in Lake Charles, Kokomo, IN, Omaha, NE, Agana Guam, Michigan, New York, Alaska and Kentucky. She taught CCD for about 12 years until her sons graduated from school. She now takes care of the cemetery fund for St. John's and finds it very rewarding.

She is one of four children, Pleas M. Bush, Frances C. Davis, Abe C. Bush. Her mother was Jessie Agnes Hayes and her father was Edward Monroe Bush. Her grandparents were Rall Dean Mary Farris and Joseph Benedict Hayes, James William Bush and Martha Maria Robinson. They were all from Sunfish and are buried in St. John Cemetery.

She remembers as a little girl always wanting to be a saint, and being read a story by the nuns about St. Agnes. So she took her name at Confirmation (it was also her mother's name). She took her sons to Mass every Sunday, took part in their religious training and prayed to live until they were grown. (This stems from the fact that her mother passed away when she was only 6 years old, and knowing how difficult it was to grow up without a mother.) Her sons all now have families of their own. Both daughters-in-law are converts, and three grandchildren are Catholic. She states that now she is alone again and still struggling to be a saint.

BETHEL, SISTER ADELINE, was born in West Louisville, KY on Nov. 7, 1874 to Benjamin and Nannie Burns Bethel. She was baptized on Feb. 27, 1875 and given the name Leona. The facts of her early life are few although it is known that she had a sister, Florence. Leona herself went to school at Mount St. Joseph Academy from 1892-1895. She entered the convent there on April 21, 1907 and made vows on July 14, 1909.

Sister Adeline's missions were St. James, Louisville; Immaculate Conception, Earlington; St. Martin, Rome; St. Raphael, West Louisville; Mount St. Joseph Academy; and St. Mary Home, Owensboro.

Sister Adeline died on Dec. 7, 1948 and is buried at Mount St. Joseph.

BEYKE, DWIGHT ALAN, was born on a farm five miles from Whitesville, KY on Jan. 20, 1950. His parents were John H. and Anna Marie Barrett Beyke. He was the third of seven children, six boys and one girl. His family were farmers and helped manage a tobacco warehouse in Owensboro. He married Rebecca Jane Johnson, daughter of Paul and Anastasia Coomes Johnson of St. Lawrence on Aug. 13, 1976 at St. Lawrence Church.

Dwight and Becky both attended Catholic schools for 12 years; Dwight graduated from St. Mary of the Woods in 1967 and Becky from Trinity High School in 1968. They both graduated from Brescia College; Dwight in 1972 and Becky in 1977.

Dwight and Becky were full-time farmers until the winter of 1988. At that time they sold their farming equipment and Dwight began work with Kentucky Central Life Insurance Company in 1989. He is currently sales manager of the Owensboro area. They have two daughters, Kathy age 15 and Christina age 12. They have been foster parents for over 40 different children. Dwight has been active in the Whitesville Lions Club since 1972, the Owensboro Serra Club since 1989. He was chairman of the St. Mary's Picnic Committee for three years and chairman of the finance committee of the church for two years.

Dwight and Becky both enjoy gardening and travel. They attend St. Mary-of-the-Woods Church.

BICKETT, SISTER AGNES IRENE, was born Oct. 16, 1916 in Union County, Morganfield, KY. Her father James Henry Bickett, born April 30, 1874 and passed away Feb. 27, 1937, her mother Mary Alma Stewart was born Dec. 31, 1881, passed away April 29, 1953.

She had 12 brothers and sisters: Emma Ruth Bickett (Whitfield) (July 28, 1898-Oct. 6, 1972); Mary Josephine Bickett (Oct. 31, 1900-Jan. 2, 1902); James Lewis Bickett (Oct. 23, 1902-Jan. 8, 1966); Mary Ellen Bickett (Sister James Alma Bickett) (Feb. 6, 1904-Dec. 16, 1985); Robert Paul Bickett (May 11, 1905-March 31, 1965); Alice Cecilia Bickett (Dayberry) (Sept. 12, 1906-April 2, 1965); Margaret Catherine Bickett (Girten) (Nov. 1, 1907-); Lucian Nathaniel Bickett (Nov. 28, 1908-Dec. 3, 1984); Benjamin Franklin Bickett (Nov. 5, 1910-Oct. 21, 1984); Mary Blanche Bickett (Sister Blanche Rita Bickett (March 20, 1912-); Alma Elizabeth Bickett (Russelburg) (June 12, 1915-); and Agnes Lucille Bickett (Sister Agnes Irene Bickett) (Oct. 16, 1916-).

Sister attended school as a child in Hitesville and Hancock in a little one room school. Then she went to the Mount for high school, to Brescia College and Murray State University.

Her missions were: Knottsville, St. Lawrence, Waverly, New Mexico, Nebraska, St. Louis, Affton, Owensboro, Vine Grove and Hardinsburg.

BICKETT, ANN, was born in Whitesville, KY on Feb. 8, 1926 and baptized by Fr. Hugh O'Sullivan. She is a member of St. Mary of the Woods Church; a Eucharistic Minister, member of the Legion of Mary, the Altar Society and works at the picnics. Her father is Gilbert Hagan, a farmer. He died in 1987 at the age of 91. Her mother, Oretta Russelburghe, a housewife and homemaker, died in 1991 at the age of 89. Both were members of St. Mary Church in Whitesville.

Ann Bickett

Ann married William Bickett, from Knottsville, KY, on July 9, 1949. They have two children and six grandchildren. Her husband died Oct. 29, 1976 at the age of 49. After graduating from St. Mary High School, Ann worked at the Ken Rad for 12 years, they owned and operated Bickett's Grocery for 10 years. She worked at St. Mary's lunchroom for 18 years and is now employed part-time at St. Mary's rectory.

BICKETT, INA BELLE, lives on the farm which has been home to her and her family for more than 50 years-located between West Louisville and St. Raphael's. She is the widow of Henry Bickett, she was born Sept. 8, 1903. Her parents were Helen (Cain) and David Crowe. Her early religious formation came from her pious Baptist family and Church Community. She married Henry Bickett, son of John P. and Mary Elizabeth (Payne) Bickett in 1923 and joined the Catholic church at that time. They attended St. Thomas Mission Church near Roseville when a priest came usually every other Saturday, if the weather wasn't too bad.

They earned their living by farming, at first in Hancock/Ohio Counties where six of their ten children were born: Lucille (O'Neill), Alvin, Geraldine (Owdziej), Marcellus (Sister Louis Marie (Luisa)), Edmund and Dennis.

Henry and Ina Belle Bickett Family. (Family reunion, 1953, at St. Raphael's.)

In 1935 they moved to a farm in Daviess County near St. Raphael Church and school. The four children, Jim, Jeannie (Calhoun), Kenneth and Carol were born there. Many of their 51 grandchildren and their families live in the Owensboro Diocese.

Ina Belle and Henry were always active in their parish. Helping with church cleaning and laundry, or the parish picnic was no problem. She never forgot her first experience of the children's First Communion - "white clothes" for three children at once was a major affair.

Life has not been the same for her since Henry, her husband of 61 years, died in 1984. Aging has taken its toll, but she still finds reason for her healthy laugh that was so common in the days when the families at St. Raphael visited for an hour or two in front of church after Sunday Mass. Now she is ministered to by St. Alphnosus Parish which they attended after St. Raphael's closed.

BICKETT, JOSEPH ALVIN, was born Feb. 8, 1926 in Hancock County. He is the second of 10 children of Henry Louis and Ina Belle (Crowe) Bickett. The family moved to Daviess County in 1935 and attended St. Raphael Church. Alvin attended St. Raphael Elementary School and West Louisville High School.

He married Betty Joy C. Rumage on June 9, 1951. Betty is the oldest of eight children of Bob and Martine (Wink) Rumage of Owensboro, KY. Betty attended St. Mary Magdalene Elementary and Mount St. Joseph High School.

Alvin and Betty moved to Rumsey, KY, McLean County, after they married where Alvin is engaged in farming. They attend St. Sebastian Church in Calhoun, KY. They have eight living children and 12 grandchildren.

The children are Joseph A. Jr., married to Jan Lamb, has one daughter, one son, lives in Owensboro, KY; Mary Beth married to Wes Andrews has two daughters, lives in Frankfort, KY. Stephen Wayne married Holly Ward and has two daughters and one son. They live in Slaughters, KY. Vicky Ann married Donnie Gibson, has one daughter, lives in Bowling Green, KY. Lisa Marie married Steve Young, has one daughter and lives in Calhoun, KY. Paula is married to Jeff McGuire with two sons and lives in Rumsey, KY. Gary William married Karen M. Wiggins, lives in Lexington, KY. Amy has one son, and lives in Bowling Green, KY.

Alvin is on the Parish Council, picnic committee and other church activities. Betty is on picnic committee and other church activities.

BICKETT, SISTER LOUIS MARIE (LUISA), an Ursuline of Mount St. Joseph, Maple Mount, KY, is the fourth of 10 children born to Henry and Ina Belle (Crowe) Bickett. She and five brothers and sisters were born on a farm that was mostly in Hancock County, but partly in Ohio County. Her family attended the old St. Thomas Mission Church near Roseville.

The four youngest were born in Daviess County on a farm near West Louisville in the St. Raphael area. One of her early memories is the move when she was 5. She remembers how important it was to her Dad to buy a farm near a "Sister's School," because Father Jarboe had told him he needed to take his family to a more Catholic area with Catholic schools if he wished to better assure that faith in his family. Sister attended St. Raphael's Grade School and Mount St. Joseph Academy. Life growing up was pretty much farm, school and church.

Sister Louis Marie (Luisa) Bickett

On finishing high school in 1947, she entered the convent. With the exception of one year in Jeffersontown, KY, she taught in parochial schools in New Mexico until 1965 when she was missioned to a Jesuit Boys School in Santiago, Chile. In the more than 17 years in Chile, she worked nine years in pastoral work in a slum area of Chillan. During those years, she began to be called by the Spanish form of her name, Luisa, which is the name by which she is known by most outside her family and community.

She returned to the United States in 1983 and has worked in Ohio County, sponsored by Holy Redeemer Parish in Beaver Dam since 1984. In 1987, she moved to Horse Branch, 13 miles away, where she represents the Catholic church in an almost total non-Catholic area.

BICKETT, RONALD DEAN, was born in Sterling, IL, and is one of 12 children of Anselm James (A.J.) and Elizabeth (Sis) Bickett. Several years after Ronald's birth, his family moved back to Whitesville, KY, where his parents grew up.

His father retired from Fields Packing Company in Owensboro. His mother is a homemaker and teacher's aide at St. Mary Grade School at Whitesville, KY.

Ronald attended St. Mary Grade School and Trinity High School. He served three years in the U.S. Army. He presently works at Owensboro Grain Company.

Ronald and Susan Bickett family

Susan Johnson was born at Our Lady of Mercy Hospital in Owensboro, KY, and is one of 10 children. Her father, Lawrence Johnson, is a carpenter and her mother, Dortha Lanham, is a homemaker who graduated from St. Williams School in 1951 with 12 years of perfect attendance. Susan attended Mary Carrico Memorial Grade School at Knottsville, KY and Owensboro Catholic High School. She presently works as a registered nurse at Owensboro Daviess County Hospital.

Ronald and Susan were married on Sept. 1, 1979 at St. William Church by Rev. Henry Willett and Monsignor John Higgins. They have three children: Sarah born Jan. 29, 1984, Rebecca born April 10, 1985 and Nicholas born Nov. 10, 1987. They have lived at Pellville, KY since 1983 and are members of St. Lawrence Parish.

BITTELL, THOMAS AND JULIE CHAPPEL, were married on Dec. 7, 1968. Thomas was the youngest of 13 children by Robert and Mary Bittel. Julie is the middle child of seven children by Charles and Mary Chappel.

Julia is a deputy jailer at the Daviess County Detention Center and Thomas is deceased. He was employed at Groves Construction Company until his death.

Julia is a believer in Catholic schools. She has worked two jobs since 1978 to be able to afford for the children to attend Catholic schools. All three children have had Catholic educations.

Julia has three children, one daughter and two sons. Her daughter, Tammy, is 20 years old and is a teacher's aide. Her son, Tommy is 20 years old and is employed at Billy Gaddis and Sons Excavating Company. Her youngest son, Timmy, is attending Catholic High and has a part-time job at Wyndall's Foodland. He graduated in 1993.

BICKWERMERT, CHRIS AND RUTH (WARD), were both born and raised in Daviess County. Chris in Eastern part of Owensboro, and Ruth in Philpot. Chris was born Aug. 1, 1957 and Ruth was born May 17, 1959. They are members of St. Mary of the Woods Parish, Chris was formerly a member of St. Pius. He works as MPD operator; Ruth is a homemaker.

They have five children, C. Matthew (seventh grade), Kevin (fifth grade), Bradley (fourth grade), Teresa N. (kindergarten), Andrea M.(2 years), and Ruth is expecting their sixth child in November.

BLACK, MARVIN RAY, was born in Cool Springs, KY. Family moved to Detroit, MI when he was a child. He spent every summer with grandparents on the farm in Cool Springs. Attended school both in Michigan and Kentucky. Worked as truck driver. Served four years in U.S. Air Force.

Marvin married Dolores (Dee) Maier of Detroit, MI at St Francis De Sales Church in June 1957. She attended St. Francis De Sales School for 12 years. Oldest child of 10. Worked as secretary after graduation. They currently live in Beaver Dam, Ohio County, KY, and are members of Holy Redeemer Parish. Past members of St. Benedict Church in Highland Park, MI. Marvin serves as Pastoral Council secretary, Dee is Religious Education Committee member and teacher, also Liturgy Committee member.

Marvin and Dee Black

Marvin serves as Audubon Area District Commissioner for Boy Scouts of America, Assistant Scoutmaster-Troop 173, a member of Lions Club and American Legion. He is a retired coal miner. Dee is a member of Courthouse Players Community Theatre group, treasurer; and actor. She serves as parish secretary.

They have six children: Barbara, May 1958; Robert, March 1959; William, April 1961; Elizabeth, May 1962; Bridget, August 1965; Brian, December 1970. Nine grandchildren to date.

Marvin was received into the Catholic Church after taking instructions from the Scout Chaplain for the Archdiocese of Detroit, who was also associate pastor at St. Benedict Church. Marvin, his son William, and 7 year old brother-in-law, Marty, all received their First Communion at a home Mass in 1969. Dee and Marvin have taught several religious groups (grade school to adult) at Holy Redeemer including several confirmation preparation groups during the past 15 years. In 1978, Marvin and Dee each made a Cursillo and a Marriage Encounter weekend.

BLACKWELL, MARY CATHERINE CRONIN,
was born Sept. 3, 1932 in St. Louis, MO to Francis and Irene Cronin. She received baptism at Immaculate Conception Church, Holy Communion and confirmation at St. Theresa Church in St. Louis. She attended St. Theresa and Sacred Heart Catholic Schools until moving to Symsonia, KY in 1946. In Kentucky she became a member of St. Francis De Sales in Paducah. She has since moved her membership to Rosary Chapel in 1981. She wed Victor L. Blackwell at St. Francis De Sales on June 11, 1949; witnessed by Father Albert Thompson.

Mary and Victor Blackwell, Brian and Victoria

Mary has two children Victoria L. Auchenbach of St. Louis, MO and Brian D. Blackwell of Fort Worth, TX. Two grandchildren, Lauren Michelle Auchenbach of St. Louis, MO and Sean M. Auchenbach of Atlanta, GA. Both Victoria and Brian attended St. Mary Academy, St. Francis De Sales Grade schools and graduated from St. Mary High School. They both attended Paducah Community College and graduated from the University of Kentucky. They received the sacraments of Baptism, Communion and Confirmation at St. Francis De Sales Parish in Paducah, KY. Mary has been a member of Daughters of Isabella and has served on the Finance Committee at Rosary Chapel.

She credits the strong Catholic beliefs to her mother Irene C. Thweatt who is also a member of Rosary Chapel.

BLAIR, BEN AND STANETTE EMBREY,
were married on Aug. 24, 1968. Ben has been a member of St. Augustine Parish all of his life. Stanette was a member of Precious Blood Parish until she was married to Ben. Ben and Stanette both attended Catholic schools all their lives and graduated from Owensboro Catholic High School in 1966.

The Blairs have 10 children, three boys and seven girls. Phillip, 22, is in the Army, stationed at San Antonio, TX and is married to Jennifer McNulty. They have a 2 year old daughter named Mary Beth. Bethany, 21, is engaged to Cary Greenwell and works in Accounts Receivable at Clark's Restaurant Service. She graduated from Owensboro Junior Business College. Gretchen, 20, lives in Hubert, NC, with her husband, Michael Young, who is in the Marine Corps. She is currently working at a crab and oyster restaurant. Jared, 18, works at Big Dipper and attends the Owensboro Community College. Liane, 17, is a senior at Owensboro Catholic High School and is a member of the Acette Drill Team, Student Council, St. Augustine Youth Group and church choir. Josh, 14, is a freshman at Owensboro Catholic High School, serves at St. Augustine Parish and is a Youth Group member. Rebecca, 12, is in the seventh grade at Owensboro Catholic Middle School, is in the Youth Group, the church choir, and plays the flute in the Middle School band. Ellany, 9, is in the fourth grade at Holy Angels, where she is a cheerleader and sings in the church choir. Marietta, 6, is in the first grade at Holy Angels. Margaret, 3, is home with mom.

Ben is a member of the Parish Council and works at Devon Oil Company. Stanette plays the organ during Sunday Mass, types the bulletin for the church, is in the church choir, and, of course, is an extremely busy mother.

BLAIR, DANIEL (FUZZ),
was born in Newman, KY to Jay and Mary Emma, farmers, and baptized at St. Augustine, Reed by Father Robert Wilson. He attended school at St. Peter's in Stanley, four years at St. Augustine, and graduated from Catholic High in 1965. Lucy Edge was born to John and Gladys, farmers, in Whitesville, KY, and baptized by Father Martin Nahstoll in St. Mary of the Woods Parish and graduated from high school there in 1963.

Fuzz and Lucy married May 6, 1967 at St. Mary of the Woods with Father Charles Fischer officiating. They live in St. Pius X Parish, where they celebrated their silver anniversary this year with Father Bruce Fogle officiating.

Daniel E. Blair Family

Fuzz and Lucy are very proud of their children. They were all baptized at St. Pius X, attended school there for eight years and graduated from Catholic High. Jude, 24, works at Tom Watson's Prosthetics and attends Community College. Ralph, 21, attends Kentucky Wesleyan and starts on their football team. Tasha, 18, attends the nursing program at Kentucky Wesleyan. They have one handsome grandson, Jordon, 1, baptized at Blessed Mother Parish by Father Freddie Bird.

The Blairs have all run the Bottle Ring stand at the picnic for 15 years, along with Lucy making many items for other booths, and Fuzz, helping to cook the night before. While Fuzz worked at NSA for 22 years, Lucy did a little baby sitting in their home for extra money and helped the children through school and sports. She was head of the concession stand at St. Pius for 10 years and served as secretary of the Booster Club for one term.

Fuzz was a KC member and has donated his time mowing grass at the 10th Street location for the past three summers.

BLAIR, JOHN P. (JAY),
born in Daviess County, KY, was a convert to the Catholic faith and baptized by Fr. Paul Greenwell on Dec. 23, 1938. Mary Emma Murphy, born in Evansville, IN, was baptized at Sacred Heart Church in Evansville. At the age of 3, Mary Emma moved to St. Augustine Parish at Reed, KY, where she married Jay on Dec. 26, 1938. The couple lived in St. Augustine Parish for three years then moved to St. Martin, Rome, KY, for three years. They returned to St. Augustine's and have lived there ever since.

John P. (Jay) and Mary Emma Blair with friends and family.

Jay and Mary Emma had eight sons and two daughters. Their two oldest sons were baptized at St. Augustine, Reed, KY. The second son lived only one month and was buried at the church cemetery. Their next two sons were baptized at St. Martin, Rome, KY. The remaining children were all baptized at St. Augustine's. The family now includes 34 grandchildren and 14 great-grandchildren.

Jay was a farmer all his life. He also worked at Murphy Miller for 11 years. Mary Emma worked in the home caring for their 10 children. Mary Emma has been active in the Altar Society for 54 years, where she served as President for five years.

Jay and Mary Emma celebrated their 50th Wedding Anniversary in 1988. Jay died on Oct. 11, 1991. Mary Emma still lives on the farm and attends St. Augustine Church.

BLAIR, MICHAEL JOSEPH, SR. AND ELSIE MAE BICKETT,
were married on Aug. 7, 1965 in Shawneetown, IL. They were remarried in the Catholic church a year later. Mike's parents were John Phillip Blair and Mary Emma Blair. They belong to St. Augustine Parish. Grandparents were: Joseph Thomas Murphy and Mary Augusta Murphy, John Francis Blair and Birdie Blair.

Elsie's parents were James Monica Bickett and Beulah Mae Bickett. Grandparents were: Archie Rogg Barnett and Cliffie Lee Likens Barnett and Martha Raye Barnett, James Monty Bickett and Zula Mae Bickett. She was a member of St. Joseph and Paul Church and Precious Blood Church.

Mike and Elsie have five children: Charlene Michelle McGehee, Daphne Gayle Blair-Robeson, Michael J. Blair Jr., Shannon Nicole Blair, Matthew Damion Blair.

Charlene is married to Rex Anthony McGehee and they live in Owensboro, KY. They have four children: Jason Nakia, Jamie Noah, Jenny Nicole and Jeremiah Nolan McGehee.

Daphne is in the U.S. Navy stationed in San Diego, CA. She has one child, Brianna Evangline Robeson.

Michael Jr. is married to Angelina King. They are stationed in San Diego, CA, where he serves in the U.S. Navy. They have two children: Lisa Renee and Jazzilynne Rose Blair.

Shannon in a senior at Henderson County High School in Henderson, KY. She works part-time at Henderson Dairy Queen.

Matthew is a junior at Apollo High School in Owensboro, KY.

Mike and Elsie have been married for 27 years. They are members of St. Augustine Church in Reed, KY, they lived in Newman, KY, for 17 years before moving to Reed, where they have lived for seven and one-half years.

Elsie belongs to the St. Augustine Choir. Mike participates in church functions.

BLAIR, ROBERT A. AND LAURA GAIL (SIMON),
were married Sept. 24, 1977. Robert was born Nov. 10, 1957; a high school graduate and truck driver. He is the son of John Phillip Blair (deceased) and Mary Emma Murphy Blair. Gail was born Jan. 23, 1957, the daughter of Silas Edward Simon and Catherine Loraine Feldpausch Simon of St. Augustine; high school graduate and housewife. They are members of St. Augustine Parish in Reed, KY, and now live in Owensboro, KY, Daviess County. Past members of St. Alphonsus, St. Joseph, KY. Gail is a member of the Parish Council, president of Altar Society, cantor and lector.

They have four children: Katie Lee Blair, born Nov. 15, 1979, lector; Kimberly Gail Blair, also born Nov. 15, 1979, lector; Robert Aloysius Blair, born Jan. 25, 1982, altar boy and cantor; and Dustin Jeremiah Blair who was born May 14, 1989.

BLAND, J.W. AND LORENA FLOOD,
the J.W. and Lorena Flood Bland family have lived in Breckinridge County all their lives. They married Aug. 5, 1946 in the rectory of St. Romuald Church in Hardinsburg. J.W. is the son of Walter and Delilah Jackson Bland of McQuady. Lorena is the daughter of Peter and Rachel Alexander Flood of Hardinsburg. J.W. and Lorena have been farming since they married. They have seven children, three sons and four daughters, and nine grandchildren.

J.W. and Lorena Bland

David is married to Shirley Robbins. They have two sons, Jamie and Bobby. David served two years in the Vietnam War. He is employed at the Murray Tile Plant in Lewisport. Lois is married to Don Hill and has one son. Lois is a registered dietitian. Harold is single. He is employed at Airco in Meade County. He served three years in the U.S. Navy. Nancy is married to August Henning and has one daughter, Christy and two sons, Nathan and Aaron. They have their own business as building contractors. Janet is single and is employed at the Galante Studio. Joe is married to Carol Mays. She has two daughters, Carla and Lisa Lane. He is employed as a carpenter. Angie, their seventh child, is married to Walter Pate and has one son, Jordon. She is employed at the local Jr. Food Store.

Lorena has belonged to St. Romuald Parish all her life. She attended St. Romuald Grade School. They sent all seven children to St. Romuald Grade and High School and very proud of it.

In 1986, Lorena and Janie Jackson spent many hours collaborating on the "History of St. Romuald." She is currently serving on the St. Romuald cemetery committee.

BLANDFORD, GEORGE AND NETTIE,
George was born on Dec. 24, 1873 and died on May 10, 1959. Nettie Bland was born on Feb. 13, 1879 and died Nov. 29, 1961. George and Nettie were married on Oct. 12, 1898. They were from Marion County, where they were probably married, as the St. Charles Church records show.

Front row (L to R): Walter, Lucille, Ella Mae, Ed and Charlie; Second row (L to R): Alice, George, Nettie and Tillie; Back Row (L to R): Al J. Cash, Father Russell and Tommy Cash 60th Wedding Anniversary.

They came to Carlisle County in the early 1900s by wagon. Four families came together looking for a better place to live. They attended St. Charles Catholic Church. George was a farmer and according to Nettie "a jack-leg" carpenter. Nettie was a housewife. They had 11 children: Jack, lived in Chicago and married Alice; Tillie married Hervie Toon and lived in Carlisle County; Tommy (deceased); Alice married Alton Thomas and lived in Carlisle County; Charlie lived in Chicago and married Leslie; Walter lived in Chicago and married June Kapusha; Edward lived in Chicago and married Geneviene Wajiuckecwicz; Lucille lived in Chicago for several years and married Aubery Thomas. He died and she married Florian Cereny. They now lives in Chicago. Joe was killed in World War II at Normandy; Ella Mae live in Graves County and married Albert Cash. Mary Praxedes died at birth.

BLANFORD, SISTER MARIE BERNADETTE,
daughter of Francis Palmer Blanford and Mary Daisy Head was born March 30, 1912 at Holy Cross, KY. She was baptized on April 8, 1912. Her baptismal name was Elsie. She was confirmed in September 1919.

Her father was a farmer in Marion County, KY, near Holy Cross, KY. Her mother was housekeeper and homemaker. She has several brothers and sisters: Beulah Blanford Ballard, now living in Louisville; Viola Blanford Lyvers, now living in Holy Cross, KY; Earl Blanford, also of Holy Cross; Roberta Blanford Ball, employed with Louisville Public Schools; one brother, Thomas Alfred Blanford deceased. Other family members: Earl Blanford died as a child, Mary Blanford died at birth; Gladys Blanford died at age 17; Mary David died at birth and Carl died at about 6 months of age.

She studied at Mount Saint Joseph Academy and college from 1930 to 1935. She entered the convent Sept. 8, 1933, received the habit March 18, 1934 and was professed March 19, 1936. She taught schools in Indiana, Kentucky and Missouri.

After teaching for about 50 years, she returned to the motherhouse at Mount. St. Joseph. She worked in the museum, and outreach programs.

BOARMAN, CARL JOSEPH,
was born March 24, 1965 in Owensboro, KY, son of Kenneth Raymond Boarman and Catherine Glahn Boarman of Utica, KY. Kenny is a farmer with Boarman Brothers Farms. Johanna is owner of Glahn's Tax Service. Carl is a farmer working with his father and brothers.

Linda Catherine Thomas Boarman was born Feb. 2, 1968, daughter of William Thomas and Catherine Marie Roby Thomas of Philpot, KY. William is a retired farmer and cabinet maker. Catherine is a homemaker. Linda is a registered nurse in the recovery room at Mercy Hospital.

Carl and Linda married Nov. 18, 1988 and have two daughters. Catherine Johanna "Katie" Boarman was born May 11, 1989 in Owensboro and named after her maternal and paternal grandmothers. Jessica Gabriell "Jesse" Boarman was born in Owensboro on May 6, 1990.

BOARMAN, JOHN O. JR.,
better known as "Bud" around Whitesville, married Mildred Eileen Edge on Dec. 27, 1944 at St. Mary of the Woods Catholic Church in Whitesville. She is known as Minnie by a lot of folks.

First Row (L to R): Jackie, Bud, Mildred, Amanda. Second Row (L to R): Bill, Joetta, Deliloh, Sandra, Jamie and Jeff. Third Row (L to R): Mickey, Greg, Johnny and David.

Snow was on the ground and ice was so thick that they were three hours late for the wedding. Fr. Wm. B. Jarboe called and asked if they wanted to postpone, Bud said no way because he had been drafted and was to leave for the Navy in 10 days. The only people at Mass were Bud and Mildred, his brother Dick and sister Camilla, two altar boys, Sister Eileen Howard played the organ. They both agree there has never been a day more beautiful since.

Bud is the son of John O. Boarman Sr. and Mary Agnes Henning Boarman. Mildred is the daughter of Wm. Ross Edge and Mary Ethel Clark Edge.

They were both baptized and received the sacraments at St. Mary's where they are lifetime members.

Bud was postmaster of the Whitesville Post Office for 28 years and Mildred is a homemaker. They have six sons Johnny, Billy, Mickey, David, Jeff and Greg. Greg, the youngest of 12, was born on his mothers 36th birthday. Their six daughters are Sondra, Jamie, Delilah, Jackie, Joetta and Amanda. They have 32 grandchildren and three great-grandchildren.

Bud is president of the Pastoral Council. They are both Eucharist ministers. They are also a Sponsor Couple in marriage and have worked with the R.C.I.A. since it began at St. Mary's.

BOARMAN, LUCIAN PAUL,
was born on Aug. 29, 1915, the seventh child of James Caleb and Ann Catherine Curtsinger Boarman who were married on April 17, 1904 at St. Joseph Church in Central City, KY. Paul has remained single through his life and is an avid student of American history, Catholic Church history and a genealogist. One of the loves of his life has been tracing the Boarman and Curtsinger families. He can provide

James Caleb and Anna Catherine Curtsinger Boarman

information about many other families in Daviess County, as well, thanks to his many hours researching courthouse records and other genealogical sources.

James and Anna Catherine Boarman had nine children: Martin Hollie, James Noble, William Hugh, Joseph Celestine, Charles Robert, Xavier Ignatius, Lucian Paul, Teresa Marie and Raymond Aloysius. Most of the Boarman family was born near Oakley, KY. Martin, James, Joseph and Charles are dead. Raymond was a Passionist Brother from 1939-1944. Father Victor Boarman, a priest of the Diocese of Owensboro, is his first cousin, once removed.

Paul is a member of Sts. Joseph and Paul Parish in Owensboro. He continues to be faithful to his daily prayers and devotions though he is unable to get out much to attend Mass and parish activities. Paul shares in the work of the church through prayer for the pope, bishops, priests and all the people of the church. Paul has been and continues to be one of the people who support the many works of the church through personal sacrifices and prayer. He lives in Owensboro, KY.

BOARMAN, MARTIN HOLLIE, was born May 9, 1905. He was the first child of James Caleb and Anna Catherine "Katie" (Curtsinger) Boarman. He and six of his brothers and their one sister, were born near Whitesville, KY. They were baptized at St. Mary Church by Monsignor Hugh O'Sullivan. Another brother, Raymond, was born after the family moved to Owensboro, and was baptized by Monsignor Richard Maloney at St. Stephen Church.

Professionally, Hollie was an accountant; but beyond that his interests and activities were numerous. Being very dedicated to his faith, he attended daily Mass and received Holy Communion. His works of charity extended to the education of seminarians, helping finance Indian Missions in the Dakotas, and many acts of local charity toward his fellow man. He was a close friend and confidant of the late Bishop Cotton. After years as a parishioner of St. Stephen Cathedral, his last parish was Sts. Joseph and Paul.

Martin H. Boarman, son of James Caleb Boarman and Anna Catherine Curtsinger; Raymond Boarman, brother of Martin H. Boarman.

Martin's hobby was genealogy. He traced the Boarman lineage back to 1645 in Colonial Maryland where our Pioneer Major William Boarman (1630-1709) was one of the nine first manor Lords of the Colony. In the late 1600s William added a chapel to his manor house during the suppression of the Catholics; this chapel became St. Mary Church at Bryantown, still one of the oldest parishes in Maryland.

Of interest to the Diocese of Owensboro is this: one of William Boarman's great-grandsons, The Reverend Leonard Neale, S.J. (1747-1817), became the second archbishop of Baltimore; and, it is known that the Diocese of Owensboro was once in the Baltimore Diocese. Archbishop Neale had four brothers who were also members of the Jesuit Society.

Following Hollie's death on Feb. 6, 1962, he continued his brother's research. When the renowned genealogist Mary Louise Donnelly was preparing to publish the Boarman Family genealogy-*Major William Boarman . . . His Descendants* (Privately published, Ennis, TX, 1990) he sent to her their vast collection of Boarmans in Kentucky data.

Regarding myself: After service in the U.S. Navy during World War II, I migrated to California. Attended the U.C.L.A. School of Dental Technology and for many years have owned my Holly-Dent Laboratory in Hollywood. My parish is the Incarnation, where I reside in Glendale.

He considers it a great blessing to have been raised in Owensboro, and to have been a student of the dear Ursulines in old St. Joseph School.

BOARMAN, TERRY AND YVONNE (BONNIE), the Terry and Yvonne Boarman family started on Nov. 10, 1973 when Terry, the son of Wm. Hugh Boarman and Grace Rapier, and Yvonne, the daughter of Owen Payne and Virginia Roberts, married at Blessed Mother Church with Fr. Robert Whelan presiding.

Terry and Yvonne Boarman family

Terry was raised at Sorgho, KY, and attended St. Mary Magdelene Grade School and graduated from OCHS. Terry also attended Brescia College. Bonnie was born and raised in Knottsville where she went to school at St. Williams Grade School and graduated from Daviess County High School.

Terry has been a self-employed farmer for 20 years and belongs to the Knights of Columbus. Bonnie is a homemaker and works part-time in catering.

They have five children, Lee (14), Lori (13), Billy (11), Stefonie (7) and Robby (5). Lee and Lori attend OCMS and Billy and Stefonie attend Catherine Spalding School. Robby will start kindergarten in the fall of 1992.

BOARMAN, WILLIAM HUGH AND GRACE, William Hugh was born near Whitesville, KY, baptized by Fr. Hugh O'Sullivan who was his namesake. His father James Caleb was a school teacher, and his mother Anna Catherine Curtsinger was a teacher from Graves County, KY before she married. Grace Rapier was born in Owensboro, her father William Frederick Rapier was the owner of Rapier Grain Mill. Her mother was Chrissa Hart, the daughter of a blacksmith.

Hugh and Grace Boarman

Hugh and Grace were married on June 2, 1936 at St. Stephen Church in Owensboro, and moved to Ninth Street where they ran Boarman Brothers Grocery with his brother, Noble. Their oldest children were born in Owensboro, and the three youngest were born at Sorgho after they sold the store. While they ran the grocery in Owensboro, Hugh also farmed. They shipped clothes to Indian missions. After they retired they traveled and also enjoyed square dancing. They have 10 living children, 33 grandchildren and 12 great-grandchildren. Hugh and Grace celebrated their 50th Wedding Anniversary. Grace passed away on May 19, 1989. Hugh still lives at their home on the Lyddane Bridge Road and attends Mass at St. Mary Magdalene at Sorgho.

BOBBETT, CHARLES AND JENNIFER ELAINE WOOLDRIDGE, were both born and raised in Graves County, Mayfield, KY. Jennifer is the daughter of Mary Donna Wooldridge born Feb. 9, 1943 and Joseph Wooldridge who was born Nov. 9, 1940. They are members of St. Joseph Parish in Mayfield. Charles works as an over the counter clerk/dispatcher. They have one daughter, Jessica Leigh Bobbett who is in the second grade at St. Joseph School.

BOEHMANN, GENE, was born in Owensboro, KY. He works at the Daviess County Hospital. Margaret Boehmann was born in Evansville, IN. She is a teacher at Bishop Soennecker School, and she's been teaching for 22 years. Gene and Margaret were married in Newburgh, IN. They belong to St. Pius the Tenth Parish. Margaret Boehmann's parents are Mary and Lawrence Raibley. Mary is living in Evansville and Lawrence is deceased. Gene Boehmanns parents are Bernice and Aloysius Boehmann. Bernice is living in Owensboro, and Aloysius is deceased.

Jon Boehmann, the oldest child, was born in Tell City, IN on Jan. 2, 1977. He attends O.C.H.S. Joe Boehmann was born on June 23, 1979. He attends O.C.M.S. Mayme Boehmann was born on April 30, 1984. Seth Boehmann was born on Feb. 22, 1988. The three youngest were born in Owensboro. Jon and Joe serve and go to the youth group.

BOEHMICKE, FATHER GEORGE, was born April 24, 1910 in Louisville, KY. He was the son of Karl and Eileen Boehmicke, both of Louisville, KY. He was of Irish and German descent.

Fr. Boehmicke received his Holy Orders on Dec. 8, 1935. He served as auxiliary chaplain, U.S. Army. He worked with the St. Vincent Assembly. He was a member of the Knights of Columbus, 4th Degree; Director of Propagation of the Faith; Director of Diocese Cemeteries; Chaplain to the Daughters of Isabella.

He has one brother, Richard Boehmicke, born Nov. 18, 1912, a priest in the Archdiocese of Louisville.

BOGGESS, CATHERINE R., daughter of Wm. F. Rapier and Chrissa Hart Rapier, is the last surviving member of six children. She was born March 4, 1909. Her father settled in Owensboro in the early 1900s having moved from Curdsville, KY.

The Rapier ancestry can be traced back to the 1700s to Richard James Rapier who brought a group of Catholic families from St. Mary County in Maryland to Bardstown, KY. He helped found St. Thomas Church near Bardstown.

His direct descendant, Charles Rapier's son, Frederick Gwynn Rapier, married and settled in Curdsville, KY. There his son, Wm. F. Rapier, was born on March 24, 1886. As a young man, William, excelled in the organization and running of the Ellendale Fair.

Catherine R. Boggess

Later he married Chrissa Hart and settled in Owensboro, KY. He was the owner of the Rapier Sugar Feed Mill. Catherine R. Boggess, his third oldest child, married Wallace R. Boggess in 1928 and had five children. Called to work in order to support her children, Catherine excelled in the business world. She joined the Prudential Insurance Company in 1945 and retired in 1973.

In 1965 she was elected president of the Owensboro Estate Planning Council. She currently holds a lifetime membership in the Kentucky Underwriter's Association and was a eight year National Quality Award Winner. In 1973 she was awarded the coveted C.L.U. designation by the American College of Life Underwriters.

During this time Catherine saw to the religious education of her daughters. She attended Mass frequently during the week and was a member of St. Stephen's choir. When Blessed Mother was built, she and her family joined it and sang in its choir.

Today she spends her time quietly enjoying her golden years. Two of her daughters, Joan Boggess and Joyce Moodey, care for her. She has 11 grandchildren and nine great-grandchildren.

BOONE, SISTER ALOISE, the first girl of the William Joseph Boone and Mary Josephine Greenwell Boone family was born on Aug. 6, 1914. She was given the name Mary Joan. Being the oldest girl after two older brothers was not an easy job with many new family members soon to follow. It is no wonder that she decided early in her young life to give her life to God by becoming an Ursuline educator. Her teaching years took her to: St. James School, Louisville, 1936-1937; St. Columba School, Louisville, 1937-1949; St. Joseph School, Raywick, 1949-1951; St. Mary Magdalene, Sorgho, Principal 1951-1953; Sts. Joseph and Paul, Owensboro, Principal 1953-1959; St Alphonsus School, St. Joseph, Principal 1959-1960; Director of the Mount St. Joseph Novitiate, 1960-1970; St. Teresa, Glennonville, MO Principal, 1970-1971; St. Margaret Mary, Louisville, Principal, 1971-1979; St. Francis School, Loretto, Principal, 1979-1984; Benton, KY 1984-present time.

Sister Aloise Boone

BOONE, SISTER JOSEPH ANGELA, the 12th child of William Joseph Boone and Mary Josephine Greenwell Boone was born in New Haven, KY on Sept. 20, 1928. She was given the name of Mary Bernice. Early formation took place at the knees of her parents with the help of older brothers and sisters. Formal education was received at the St. Catherine Grade and High School in New Haven under the direction of the Mount St. Joseph Ursulines. This formal instruction and the inspiration of her parents and two older sisters, Sister Aloise and Sister Regina, influenced her decision to become a member of the St. Joseph Ursulines. This vocation as an Ursuline educator has been fulfilled in various ways: Sts. Joseph and Paul School, Owensboro, 1949-51 and 1959-61. St. Denis School, Louisville, 1951-59.

She spent 1961-63 as a graduate student at Catholic University of America studying mathematics and physics. Brescia College became her home for the next seven years. She was head of the mathematics department, Dean of Women and helped design and plan the science building which was completed in March 1969. In January 1970 she was assigned to be the general treasurer of the Ursuline Community-a job which she held until July 1989 when she became director of administration for the Diocese of Owensboro. In January 1992 she was officially appointed as chancellor for the diocese. The first time a non-cleric had held that position in the history of the diocese.

BOONE, SISTER MARY REGINA, the fifth child of William Joseph Boone and Mary Josephine Greenwell was born on Jan. 31, 1919. She was given the name Mary Elizabeth-Becky for short. Early education outside of the home was at St. Catherine Grade and High School in New Haven, KY. In 1936 she decided to follow her older sister-Joan and to become a member of the Mount St. Joseph Ursulines. Her first 12 teaching years were at St. Columba School in Louisville. There she taught grades four through seven. Several of these years were with her older sister, Sister Aloise who also taught grades four through seven. This often caused a little confusion to the parents of the children who really didn't know one from the other.

From 1954-1965 she taught at St. Romuald High in Hardinsburg. Returned as principal, 1969-74. Principal of Mary Carrico Memorial High School, 1965-1967 and Trinity High School 1967-69. Lourdes High School in Nebraska, 1974-79. Mount St. Joseph Academy, 1979-83. She taught a math class at Brescia College, 1983-88 along with being director of hospitality at Mount St. Joseph.

BOONE, RAYMOND O'CONNELL, was born in Nelson County, Bardstown, KY. He was the son of James Raymond Boone D.D.S., born in Hodgeville, KY and Gertrude Stroker of Bardstown. Raymond was baptized at St. Joseph Cathedral in Bardstown by Fr. O'Connell for whom he was named.

He married Mary R. Hayden at St. Joseph Church in Owensboro on Dec. 27, 1933. She was the daughter of Joshua Burch Hayden, a real estate broker and Mary Byrne Hagan who was baptized at St. Stephen Church and was the daughter of Prof. Robert Abell Hagan and Julia Blincoe. Joshua Burch was a brother of Father Jolly P. Hayden the founder of C.S.M.C.

After spending the first year of their married life in Louisville, KY where their first son was born they returned to Daviess County where their next eight children were born. There are four sons and five daughters. Six of their children reside in Owensboro. They have two daughters who are in Memphis, TN and one daughter in Indianapolis, IN.

Today they have 24 grandchildren and 11 great-grandchildren.

Raymond was one of the first students at Brescia College after it opened in Owensboro and was a self-employed accountant for over 40 years. Mary Robert was a member of St. Stephens Altar Society and served as president for one term. Raymond was a lector/Eucharistic minister in the parish before his death on March 11, 1981.

Before becoming members of St. Stephen Parish in 1954, they were members of St. Joseph and Paul Parish.

BOONE, WILLIAM JOSEPH, born April 12, 1885-March 21, 1969 and Mary Josephine Greenwell Boone, July 8, 1891-Feb. 26, 1965. Had 15 children. Two girls died as infants and the oldest boys, Joseph Aloysius and Joseph Frederica are buried in St. Catherine Cemetery in New Haven, KY.

The other Boone family members are: Sister Aloise, (Joan), Mrs. Hugh Johnson, (Margie), Sister M. Regina, (Becky), Mrs. Earrol Johnson, (Cecilia), Mrs. Edward Hagan, (Mary Jean), Mrs. Joseph Dworzan, (Josephine), Mrs. John L. Newcomb, (Edna Marie), Sister Joseph Angela, (Bernice), Mrs. Frank Keene, (Catherine), Mrs. Patrick Thompson, (Teresa Marie) and one son, Joseph William Boone. Three of the girls became members of the Mount St. Joseph Ursuline Community. Josephine graduated from Mount St. Joseph Junior College in 1942, Catherine was in the last class to attend Mount St. Joseph before it moved to Owensboro and became Brescia College in 1949. Teresa Marie and her youngest daughter both graduated from Brescia College and are now teachers. Another daughter, Regina is married to Denis Jacobs, Residential Life Director at Brescia College and has attended classes at Brescia.

BOSWELL, DAVID E. AND SANDI L., were married at St. Alphonsus Church in St. Joseph, KY. David was born in Henderson County, KY and later moved to Daviess County, KY. David's parents are the late Otis Allen Boswell and Francis Mulligan Boswell O'Bryan. Otis owned his own car lot in Sorgho, KY, until he passed away in 1983. Sandi's mother, Audra Sparks Bell, died when Sandi was 2 years old, and her father, Harry Lee Bell died when she was 23 years old. Sandi was raised by the Mount St. Joseph Ursuline Sisters. David is employed as a State Senator for District Eight and also is a land agent for Addwest Mining. Sandi is employed at Owensboro Daviess County Hospital. David and Sandi attend St. Mary Magdalene Church in Sorgho, KY.

David and Sandi have two sons, Todd C. Boswell and David E. Boswell Jr. Todd is 13 years old and in the eighth grade at OCMS. David Jr. attends University of Kentucky as a senior, he also has a summer job working for Parkway Construction. Todd will be confirmed this year at St. Mary Magdalene Church and will be a freshman at Apollo High School next year. David Jr. will graduate from University of Kentucky in 1993 and will work for Parkway Construction until he is accepted into law school.

BOURGOIS, LOUIS G. JR., was born in Cairo, IL, April 22, 1927, to Louis G. Bourgois Sr. and Margaret Geneva Courtney Bourgois. He is a descendant of Solomon Courtney, one of the pioneer settlers of this area, and August Bourgois, who arrived in this country from the area of Paris, France in the late 1840s. He was baptized at St. Joseph Catholic Church in Cairo. He spent many of his early years living in Fancy Farm, KY with his grandmother, Mary Imelda Toon Courtney and went to St. Jerome Catholic School. In the fall of 1936 he moved to St. Louis, MO with his mother and sister Dorothy Rose Bourgois. His mother died in October 1939 and is buried at Fancy Farm. Later he moved to Henderson, KY to live with his sister who was now married to Paul E. Youngblood of Cairo, IL. They moved to Paducah in May of 1944. He went to work for the Illinois Central Railroad at that time and finished school at Dorian Private School. He was drafted into the U.S. Army in 1945 and discharged in 1947 and then went to Central Technical Institute in Kansas City, MO where he graduated

The Boone Family

as a broadcast engineer. He went to work for Union Carbide at the Paducah Gaseous Diffusion Plant in Paducah in April of 1952 and later met and married Emma Jane Smith on Nov. 20, 1954 at St. Thomas More.

Louis G. and Robyn Lesley Fisher Bourgois III; Louis G. and Emma Smith Bourgois Sr.

He is a member of the Knights of Columbus and Emma is a longtime member of the choir and Altar Society. They have one son Dr. Louis G. Bourgois III who was born Jan. 27, 1956. He was baptized at St. Thomas More Church. He is now married to Robyn Lesley Fisher of Lexington, KY where they reside. He is a professor of music at Kentucky State University, and a member of the Knights of Columbus and she is a music teacher in the Fayette County School System.

BOWLDS, HARVEY AND CATHY MARIE CLARK, were married on Sept. 28, 1985. They have three children, Christopher, Mary Anne and Michael. They are members of Our Lady of Lourdes Church, Owensboro, KY.

Harvey is the son of the late Ora Dozier Bowlds and Catherine Marie Lott Bowlds of St. William Parish, Knottsville, KY.

Cathy is the daughter of Harold Raphael and Anne Clark of Blessed Mother Parish. The Catholic Church has always been an important part of Cathy's life. She recalls, "I lived across the street from Blessed Mother Church. As a child, I loved to go to church and sing. I sang so loud people would turn around and smile at me. As I grew older, I sang in the choir and played the organ from the time I was 9 years old until I was 26 years old."

Harvey and Cathy Bowlds Family-September 1992

Fond memories Cathy has are about Fr. Jarboe and Fr. Hallahan, two of the early priests of Blessed Mother. "Fr. Hallahan always had a stick of gum in his pocket for me and Fr. Jarboe would say, "My Cathy, my Cathy. What would I do without my Cathy?" "I think the greatest gift I can give my children is the gift of a Catholic education. That is one reason my husband and I chose to live close to a Catholic school, so our children can walk to school."

Harvey was a small-group leader for Renew and a Eucharistic Minister. Cathy was involved in TEC, Renew and Catholic Singles (where Cathy and Harvey met). Cathy plays the organ at Lourdes.

BOWLDS, ORA DOZIER AND CATHERINE MARIE MOTT, were married on July 30, 1938. They were members of St. William Parish, Knottsville, KY.

Ora D. Bowlds parents were Dozier Francis Bowlds and Vina Bickett. Catherine's parents were Harvey Ernest Lott and Ethel Boarman.

Ora D. and Catherine Bowlds Family

Ora D. and Catherine Bowlds have six children, Dan, Bonnie, Oran, Loretta, Harvey, Barry and 26 grandchildren.

Daniel Patrick Bowlds married Elaine Richardson, daughter of Sherman Richardson and Alice Bivins. They live in St. Lawrence Parish and have six children, Kelly, Andy, Danny Joe, Noah, Joshua and Rebecca Bowlds.

Bonnie Bowlds married Gary Roberts, son of J.L. Roberts and Dorothy Roberts of Knottsville. They now live in Nashville, TN with their nine children: Neil, Raymond, Brian, Damien, Jason, Angela, Katresa, Maria and Laura Roberts. Bonnie is active in Pro-life ministry.

Oran Bowlds married Nancy Roberts, daughter of J.L. and Dorothy Roberts, of Knottsville. They have three children, Kevin, Adam and Miranda Bowlds. They are members of St. Lawrence Parish.

Loretta married Ronnie Carr and lives in Florida with their five children Kristen, Ronnie, Matthew, Corey and Naomi. Loretta is active in the music ministry, playing the guitar and singing.

Harvey Bowlds married Cathy Clark, daughter of Harold and Anne Clark of Blessed Mother Parish, Owensboro, KY. Harvey and Cathy have three children, Christopher, Mary Anne and Michael and are members of Our Lady of Lourdes Parish, Owensboro. Harvey was a small-group leader of Renew.

Barry Bowlds is engaged to marry Helen Shank, of Owensboro, on Oct. 3, 1992 at St. Williams Church, Knottsville, KY. Helen is the daughter of Betty King of Owensboro.

BOWLES, SISTER VIVIAN MARIE, is the daughter of James L. Bowles and Willa K. Francis (Bowles) Stein. James L. was born Aug. 30, 1909 in Louisville, KY. Willa was born Feb. 26, 1919. James has served as an accountant and as mayor of Jeffersontown, KY. Willa served as a government clerk. She had one sister, Mary Catherine Bowles (March 13, 1942-March 15, 1942).

She attended St. Edward School, Jeffersontown, KY; Mount Mercy at Pewee Valley and Mt. St. Joseph at Maple Mount.

She entered the Mt. St. Joseph Ursulines on Sept. 8, 1957. Final profession was Aug. 15, 1963. Sister Vivian ministered all 35 years in the Diocese of Owensboro: St. Pius X, St. Joseph, St. Thomas More, Immaculate and Brescia College.

She graduated from Brescia with an AB in English and History; Murray with a MA in counseling and psychology; Western with an Ed.S. in counseling and from the University of Arkansas with an Ed. D. in counseling, education, marriage and family therapy.

Sister Vivian is presently serving as Professor of Psychology at Brescia, Director of Counseling at Brescia and serves as a Perita on the Diocesan Marriage Tribunal. She is a member of the Mt. St. Joseph Ursuline Leadership Team.

She enjoys traveling to such destinations as Asia, Europe, Australia, New England. She has also visited the Holy Land, Russia and Ireland.

BOWLING, REV. CHARLES PATRICK, was born Oct. 8, 1896, the son of Joseph Walker Bowling, C. and Mary Alexine McGee, C. his wife, at Athertonville, KY, and was baptized Charles Patrick Anthony Bowling at St. Catherines Church, New Haven, KY by the Rev. George A. Weiss, and confirmed there by the Rt. Rev. Denis O'Donahue, D.D., Bishop of Louisville, KY on Oct. 16, 1910. He made his first Communion on May 1908 at the same church under the pastorate of Father Buckman.

Rev. C.P. Bowling

At the age of six he started to school at Athertonville, where, probably, Abe Lincoln went a "few years previously". From the second to the eighth grade he attended St. Catherine School, New Haven. (A number of them walked a distance of about three miles each day each way.) Went to Gethsemani College for a month, until it burned down. The next fall he went to Jasper College for two years. (As a matter of record only, during this time, he received several prizes for high grades in various subjects. One year he got a gold medal, representing the highest average in school for Christine Doctrine). These were the years 1911-12, 13. Between then and 1917 he was out of school working part of the time on the home farm, in a general merchandise store, and for the Illinois Central Railroad Co. in Chicago. Later he was accepted by Bishop O'Donahue as a student for the Louisville Diocese. He went to St. Meinrad College on Oct. 8, 1917. He finished fifth class there in 1922; was transferred to Kenrick Seminary, St. Louis, MO along with a number of other seminarians, September 1922. There he spent six happy years. At Kenrick he received all of his orders, except priesthood from his Grace, the Rt. Rev. John J. Glennon, D.D. He was ordained to the Priesthood at the Cathedral of the Assumption on June 2, 1928 by His Lordship, the Rt. Rev. John A. Floersh, D.D.

For the first four years after ordination he had about 18 assignments as "locum tenens", assistant, vicar, administrator, principally at Bowling Green; Cathedral in Louisville, Jeffersontown, and Brown's Valley and Calvary. Then in 1932 he was made pastor of Finley; from there to Stanley in September 1933; to St. Paul's in April 1939; to Bowling Green in July 1947.

His "talents" or hobbies have run along the lines of oratory, music, sports, raising monies for paying Church debts, improving Church property, and convert making.

BRADEN, EMILY LANE, and family have been in Immaculate Parish since 1977. The Braden family's Catholic roots began in New Brunswick, Canada. Emily's mother, Mary Simone Theriault, married B.K. Lane of Sturgis, KY on Jan. 26, 1946 and they settled in Western Kentucky. Emily grew up a member of Immaculate Conception Parish, Earlington, a 40 mile round trip from their home in Providence. Early memories of church include holding Father Borntraeger in great awe and later Father Henry Willett.

While at Immaculate, Emily has served as a lector, school board member and parish council member. Jonathan performed as a tympanist with the Diocesan Choir on several occasions, including the dedication of the Brescia College Campus Center in 1989. He is pursuing an economics degree at Western Kentucky University. Ellan has been an active participant in youth groups in Precious Blood Parish, St. Stephen Parish and Immaculate Parish as well as serving as a Eucharist Minister, lector and youth

Emily, Jonathan, Ellen, Jim and Nathan Braden

formation committee member at Immaculate. She was a member of the youth team led by Father Richard Cash that went to Western Kentucky to street preach in 1990. She feels this was a particularily faith strengthening experience for her. She is on staff at Camp Ondessonk, a Catholic youth camp in the Ozarks. Ellen is pursuing psychology and sociology majors at Brescia College. Jim and Nathan have attended Immaculate and Catherine Spalding Grade Schools and OC Middle School, participating in football and baseball programs and band. Both boys also participate in the Owensboro Area Youth Hockey Program.

BRADLEY, CHARLES C. (CHUCK), was born at Dog Creek, Hart County, KY, on Aug. 25, 1938. The son of Maudie L. Bradley (deceased). He attended school at Poplar Corner at Dog Creek, KY, St. Benedict Grade School at Wax, KY, and graduated from St. Paul High School. He also attended Western Kentucky University and Elizabethtown Community College and received a BS degree in business administration. He is currently employed by the Hartford Steam Boiler Inspection and Insurance Company as a boiler and pressure vessel inspector in the states of Kentucky, Ohio and Indiana.

He was married to Wanda (Netherton) Bradley on June 6, 1970. Wanda was born in Waterview, Cumberland County, KY, on Dec. 7, 1943. The daughter of Estus and Zella (Wright) Netherton (both deceased). She attended grade school at Brandenburg Elementary and graduated from Meade County High School. She also attended and graduated from Bryant and Stratton Business College in Louisville, KY. She is currently employed by Baillie Lumber Company in Leitchfield, KY.

They have one son, Charles Stephen Bradley, who was born on March 10, 1971. Steve attended St. Paul Elementary School, Grayson County Middle School and graduated from Grayson County High School. He is currently employed by Campbell-Hausfield, in Leitchfield, KY.

All three are active members of St. Benedict Catholic Church, Wax, KY, (Wanda is a convert from the Methodist faith). They reside in Clarkson, KY.

BRADLEY, REVEREND JOSEPH EDWARD, was born, April 24, 1943, in Hart County, KY is one of 10 children of Martin Ward Bradley and Anna Lee Sims Bradley. A farm in Grayson County was home until his parents death. All of the children helped with the farm work. Social life revolved around Saint Anthony Parish and School. Baptized by Father Leo Dienes. His life was greatly influenced by Father Victor Boarman who understood that the needs of young people must be affirmed and complimented. His kind and gentle way was greatly admired and respected by all. A fond memory was the Friday afternoon ball games. The students from St. Benedict Wax were brought to Peonia to play baseball. Fr. Boarman was both coach and umpire.

Joseph Edward graduated from St. Paul High School in 1960. Fr. Walter Hancock had a big influence on the youth of Grayson County. He began a TEEN CLUB at St. Anthony Parish. The big events were the dances with the students from Whitesville. There they met new faces and broadened their social life.

It was the Mount Saint Joseph Ursulines who inspired Joseph Edward to be a teacher and thus to enter the congregation of the Brothers of the Poor of St. Francis in Cincinnati, OH. He taught in schools in Ohio, New York and New Jersey and attended universities. After 10 years of teaching and studying, he decided to enter the Josephinum Seminary and was ordained a priest for the Owensboro Diocese on Aug. 9, 1975. His next 10 years were spent at Owensboro Catholic High School as dean of students and principal. He was diocesan vocation director until May 1987.

Reverend Joseph Edward Bradley

He was appointed pastor of the St. Stephen Cathedral in May 1985. He has worked on many church and civic organizations and committees. These 18 years as a priest have been fulfilling and challenging. He enjoys the ministerial priesthood and finds great satisfaction working with the people of God in the Diocese of Owensboro.

BRADLEY, MILLIE WILSON, was born on July 3, 1885, and married John Thomas ("J.T." or "Dick") Bradley, who had been born on Nov. 12, 1871. The couple lived on a farm and J.T. (Dick) ran a general store at Dog Creek, KY (Hart County). They belonged to the old St. James Parish at Dog Creek. When that parish closed, they became members of St. Benedict Parish, Wax.*

Millie and Dick raised three children of their own: Vera (Johnston), George and Alvey Bradley. In addition, Millie helped raise the large family of her daughter, Vera, who had married Ewell Johnston. The Johnston family first lived with Millie and Dick, and later moved a short distance up the road, before eventually settling across the river in Grayson County. Finally, Millie helped raise the eight children of her son, George, who had married Catherine Stinson. George and Catherine lived with his parents until the Nolin Flood Control project took the farm in 1959-1960.

From bottom left, clockwise: Millie Wilson Bradley (85), Vera Bradley Johnston (59), Bernita Johnston Sims (43), Janet Sims Lashley (24) and Kenneth Lashley.

After a brief time spent with George and Catherine who had moved to Flaherty, Millie returned to Grayson County to live with her daughter, Vera Johnston.

Dick died of heart failure on Sept. 28, 1950. Millie remained with her daughter, Vera, who was able to care for her at home until shortly before her death on Nov. 24, 1976.

*(After the establishment of the Owensboro Diocese, the Nolin River separated it from the Louisville Archdiocese. However, most Catholics in Hart County continued to attend St. Benedict in Wax; it was closer than the nearest church in the Archdiocese.)

BRADY, SISTER MARY PIERRE, was born March 11, 1901. She was baptized Mary Genevieve. Her parents were Charles B. Brady who was born Feb. 15, 1863 and Mary Ellen French who was born Dec. 31, 1871. They were both born in Union County and died young in the flu epidemic of 1909, only four days apart. Charles belonged to the W.O.W. Club. Her brothers and sisters included: John Oscar, Charles Bowlds, William Edward, Anna Christine, Thomas Cyrene, Clara Josephine, all single, deceased.

Mary attended grade and high school of Mount St. Joseph Academy. Interested in needlework and crocheting especially. She entered the convent May 5, 1918. Missioned in New Mexico, Missouri and public schools of Kentucky.

BRANDLE, MARGRET MARIE RHODES, is a member of St. Lawrerance Catholic Church. Marie was born in Owensboro, KY on Aug. 13, 1939. She was baptized on Aug. 20, 1939 by Father Bolling at St. Paul Church.

Marie had her First Communion on May 1945 and was also confirmed in 1948 at St. Mary of the Woods Church. She went to St. William Catholic School in Knottsville, KY. She graduated in June 1958.

She married James Franklin Brandle on Dec. 2, 1967 by Rev. Carroll White. This was Rev. White's first and only celebration of marriage. He was killed going to his parents' house for the Christmas holiday.

James was born on Feb. 26, 1942 in Hancock County. He was baptized at the Hawesville Baptist Church by Brother Ezra D. Meadors. He went to the Hawesville Beachmont School, which is now the Hawesville Grade School. He graduated in May 1960. James entered the Army in 1964 and he was discharged in 1966. When he was discharged he made the rank of SP4.

James and Marie decided to start a family and on September 3, 1968 they had their first child, it was a son, named James Wade; on September 27, 1969 they had a daughter, Anita Carol; on March 1, 1972 they had a 3rd child, a daughter, Elizabeth Marie; on May 26, 1976 they had another daughter, Regina Lynn.

They were all baptized at the St. Lawerance Catholic Church by Father Lucian Hayden. All of their children graduated from the Hancock County School, except for the youngest who is still in high school.

Four years after Wade graduated he married Sonya Carol Snyder on Oct. 12, 1990 and one year after they were married they had a son, Christopher Wade, born on Aug. 6, 1992.

Two years after Anita graduated she married Bobby Lewis Renfrow on March 12, 1989. They had a daughter on May 3, 1989, Brandy Natasha. Then on June 10, 1990 they had a second daughter, Ashley Victoria.

Libby and Regina are still single and living at home.

BRANDON, MARY EILEEN, daughter of Mr and Mrs. Edgar Leonard Hayden, Paducah, KY, was born Nov. 25, 1916, baptized by Rev. Henry Conley, pastor of St. Francis De Sales Church. Her mother, Myrtle Helen Raley Hayden is daughter of Robert Andrew Raley and Sarah Elizabeth Garrison Raley of Paragould, AR. Family were members of St. Mary Catholic Church, Rev. Joseph Hoflinger, pastor. Mr. Edgar Leonard Hayden, father of Mary Eileen, is son of William Hilary Hayden and Ida Elliott Hayden, Fancy Farm, KY.

Clifford Greyson, son of Roy Young Brandon and Grace Myers Brandon, was born on Jan. 19, 1917. Family lived in rural Hazel, KY and were members of South Pleasant Grove Methodist Church. Clifford was baptized in the Methodist Church at the age of 5.

Clifford Greyson Brandon and Eileen Hayden were married on Dec. 27, 1939 in the rectory of St. Francis De Sales Church, Rev. Albert Thompson, pastor. The Brandons were blessed with six children as follows: Clifford Greyson Jr., Margaret Ann, Tommy, Betty, Bobby and Marilyn Jane. Clifford and Margaret Ann were baptized by Rev. Albert Thompson, St. Francis De Sales. Tommy, Betty and Bobby were baptized by Rev. John Hallahan, Pastor of St. John The Evangelist. Marilyn Jane was baptized by Rev. John Glenn, pastor of St. Thomas More Church.

Mr. and Mrs. Clifford Greyson Brandon

All children were married. Clifford and Judy Rueff Brandon have five children. Kelly Marie, Carrie Lynn, Clifford G. III, Kasey Leigh and Karen Machelle. They live in Owensboro, KY and belong to Immaculate Church. Margaret Ann is married to Dr. John Merjavy. They have two sons, Stephen Andrew and Matthew Paul. They reside in St. Louis, MO and are members of Christ, Prince of Peace Catholic Church. Tommy is married to Violet Greathouse and they live in Owensboro, KY. Betty is married to August Legeay Jr. They have a son, Christopher Michael and a daughter, Jennifer Marie. They are members of St. Gabriel's Church, Indianapolis, IN. Bobby is married to Kelly Hinchey and they have two children, Robert Keith and Kelly Dean. They live in Paducah and are members of St. Thomas More Church. Marilyn Jane was married to Walter Thomas Christopher. They have three children, Tara Ann, Bradley Thomas and Mark Brandon. Mrs. Christopher and children are members of St. Ann Church of Decatur, AL.

Mr. Brandon, employed by R.J. Reynolds Tobacco Company for 38 years, retired in 1974 due to health problems. Clifford was received into the Catholic church on March 5, 1988, Fr. Lucian Hayden, pastor of St. Thomas More, officiating. Mr. Brandon is deceased as of March 9, 1988. The Brandons made their home in Paducah for 48 years and three months of marriage. Eileen Brandon remains in Paducah and attends St.Thomas More Parish, Fr. Jerry Riney, pastor.

BRAUN, FATHER PETER J., was born May 30, 1901 in Wilkes Barre, PA. He was the son of Peter Sr. and Anna Powers. Ordination took place on May 9, 1929 under the direction of Rt. Rev. James J. Hartley at St. Joseph Cathedral in Columbus, OH. He served as assistant pastor at St. Martin and St. Therese, both in Louisville; He served as pastor at St. Joseph, Central City; Cursdville, KY; St. Joseph, Owensboro, KY; Saints Joseph and Paul at Owensboro, KY and as chaplain at the St. Joseph Monastery. He was appointed to the office of monsignor in November 1949. He entered Carmel Home in October 1983. Died Nov. 13, 1986.

Father Peter J. Braun

BROWN, BERNARD C., son of John and Georgia Clark Brown, married Jane Hancock, daughter of Virgie and Clem Hancock, on June 8, 1948. Ironically, these two were introduced by Fr. Henry Willett at a St. Ambrose social because he felt they were suited for each other. His intuition must have been pretty good because 44 years later, they are still together.

Bernard and Jane have five daughters, Mary, Janet, Charlotte, Martha and Bernadette and one son, John. All six children attended St. Ann School in Morganfield, KY and the oldest daughter was in the last graduating class from St. Vincent Academy.

Bernard and Jane Brown with six children and first and second grandchildren, Todd Harper (2 1/2) and Jenny Reitz (6 months).

Traditions in the church were established early. Christmas season revolved around encouraging the children to do good deeds to earn straws for the baby Jesus' manger. The children were divided into teams to see which team could do the most good deeds and that team received the honor of placing the baby Jesus in his manger on Christmas Eve night.

The children's First Communions were highlights of the church year. After the children were older, the honor of being an angel and being able to lead the first communicants into the church was bestowed on several daughters. The crowning of the Blessed Mother during the May processions was also an anticipated event.

Bernard has always been active with the Knights of Columbus and has had the distinction of being a Grand Knight. Since retirement and an empty nest has been accomplished, Bernard and Jane are able to attend daily Mass and volunteer with the St. Vincent DePaul Society and the Knights of Columbus.

The Browns have 13 grandchildren who are not the beneficiaries of the religious traditions. They are making their journeys of faith with the guidance of their parents.

Bernard, age 74, has been an active member of St. Ann Parish most of his life. He began serving as an altar boy at age 9 and on occasion, still serves the priest.

BROWN, CORA THERESA, was born June 30, 1914 to John Young Brown and Mary Viola Osborne. John was born Aug. 6, 1879 in Hardin County, KY near Vine Grove, was a farmer and Mary was born April 23, 1887. Cora grew up on a farm; attended grade school and three years of high school at St. Martin of Tours Parochial School. She entered the Ursuline Convent, Mount St. Joseph, Maple Mount, KY Sept. 8, 1931, received habit and veil March 19, 1932; received the name, Sr. Mary Denise; professed vows for three years March 20, 1934, final profession for life came on March 20, 1937. Taught grade school and high school from 1937-1977 all in Kentucky except for one year that was spent in Nebraska City, NE. The last 16 years from about 1960-1977 she taught math. She served in the business office at Mount St. Joseph as medical clerk. She retired from active duty January 1990.

She had five brothers and two sisters: William Denis born Oct. 12, 1912 married Alice Teresa Byerly who was born Feb. 3, 1914, they had eight children. Cora Teresa was second born. Thomas Albert Brown born Sept. 18, 1915 married Oct. 27, 1942 to Teresa Catherine Hager born Jan. 16, 1915, they had eight children. Frances Rebecca Brown born June 25, 1917 and entered Sisters of Loretto, in Kentucky September 1939, became Sr. Domitilla. Mary Rita Brown born 1919 married Charles Benjamin Jerkins on Jan. 17, 1920, they had six children. John Leslie Brown born Feb. 26, 1924 married Mary Ellen Padgett who was born March 14, 1924 on Sept. 4, 1946, they had eight children. Charles Patrick Brown born May 31, 1927 married Anna Maxine Lancaster born July 31, 1933, had four children. He married Marianne Koenig-Adair from Germany Jan. 16, 1928 and had one child. James Aloysius Brown born Feb. 22, 1932 married Frances Janette Whelan who was born Dec. 10, 1938 on Jan. 12, 1957. They had three children.

BROWN, JAMES ROY SR., and Agnes Alverda (Greenwell) Brown moved to Irvington in 1942 from Payneville, KY. They moved their membership from St. Mary Magdalene Church to Holy Guardian Angel. They had two sons: James Roy Brown Jr. and Theodore Charles Brown.

James Roy Brown Jr. married Betty (Raymer) Brown and they have one son, James Richard Brown who also has one son, James Ryan Brown. They live in Brandenburg and attend Ekron Baptist Church, Ekron, KY.

Theodore Charles Brown married Barbara (Allen) Brown and they have one daughter and one son, Karen Y. Brown and Kevin Charles Brown.

Karen Y. Brown married Hal Basham and they have two sons, Michael Christopher Basham and Brandon Dawson Basham. They are all members of Holy Guardian Angels Church.

Kevin Charles Brown married Rebecca (Lawson) Brown and they have two daughters, Whitney Leigh Brown and Chelsey Myranda Brown. In 1988 they had stillborn twin daughters, Emily Chastity Brown and Elisabeth Celeste Brown. They are buried at Mount Merino. They are members of Holy Guardian Angels Church.

First Row: Alverda Brown, Whitney Brown, Theodore Brown. Second Row: Brandon Basham, Karen Basham, Hal Basham. Third Row: Kevin Brown, Rebecca Brown. Fourth Row: Barbara Brown, Michael Basham.

James Roy Brown Sr. died on March 26, 1966. He is buried at St. Mary Magdalene in Payneville, KY. Alverda Brown is 83 years old and a member of Holy Guardian Angels Church.

BROWNING, SISTER CLARITA, born March 19, 1929, the fifth child of J. Lee Browning and Agnes Abell Browning in Calvary, KY. She attended Holy Name of Mary Elementary School, Calvary, Mount Saint Joseph Academy for grades nine-12, and after graduation she entered the Ursuline Novitiate at Maple Mount. Her elementary teaching career began at Sts. Joseph and Paul, Owensboro, followed by St. Thomas More, Paducah, St. Margaret Mary, Louisville, St. Christopher, Radcliff and Immaculate in Owensboro. She graduated from Indiana University in Bloomington.

Sister Clarita Browning

IN, with a master's in education, later attaining a master's in religious education from Saint Meinrad School of Theology at Saint Meinrad, IN. The following 22 years found her teaching at Brescia College in Owensboro. She has since served at Mount Saint Joseph Retreat Center and as a pastoral associate at The Immaculate Parish in Owensboro.

The four older members of her family are: Fr. Lawrence Browning, CP, serving in Chicago, Fr. William Browning, CP, serving at the Passionist Monastery in Louisville, Emma Rita Neudecker, deceased, and Josephine Browning, Lebanon, KY. The two younger members are Sister Marie Goretti Browning, director of the Mount Saint Joseph Retreat Center, at Maple Mount, KY and Agnes Marie Watts, Louisville. Sister Clarita also had three aunts who were members of the Ursuline Order. They are Sister Mary Otho Abell residing at Mount Saint Joseph Motherhouse, Sister Ann Vincentia Abell and Sister Mary Lawrence Abell both deceased.

BRUMLOW, JAMES L., was born at Fancy Farm, KY on March 20, 1913. Married to Julie Norsworthy at St. John Church. Graduated from Saint Jerome High School in 1932. Served in the U.S. Army for five years with service in the South Pacific for two and one-half years. Moved to St. John Parish in 1957. He is currently the last living descendant in the original Brumlow family. He resides in Paducah, KY and is a member of St. John's the Evangelist Parish and is a member of the church choir. Also he was a past member of St. Francis De Sales Parish.

BRYAN, JAMES H. GRIFFIN, (Sept. 24, 1856- Jan. 11, 1927), native of Atlanta, GA, married Rachel Heim, (Feb. 25, 1856-July 18, 1943) of Louisville, KY.

Griffin moved to Cannelton, IN, with his parents as a child. He became a foreman of the Indiana Cotton Mills where he worked most of his life.

Mrs. Bryan, daughter of Martin and Mary Heim came with her parents to Cannelton when she was 3 years of age. Her father, a stone mason, came to help build St. Michael Catholic Church. The family were devout Catholics and Christian in every sense of the word. They remained in Cannelton and Mr. Bryan opened a monument business.

Griffin and Rachel moved to Ardmore, OK after his retirement in the 1930s. One of their sons provided a home for them. Mr. Bryan died from a stroke and was brought back to Cannelton for burial. After her husband's death, Rachel made her home with two of her daughters, Fanny in Cannelton and Cecelia in Owensboro, KY. She was greatly loved by all who knew her and was affectionately known as "Mamma Bryan" by her family, friends and neighbors. She was a member of St. Ann Sodality. She is buried in St. Michael Cemetery.

Their children and place of residence at the time of their death: J. Augustus (June 24, 1877-) Henderson, KY; Charles Griffin (Feb. 12, 1880-) Chicago, IL; Mary Cecilia (June 9, 1883-July 4, 1967), Mrs. John W. Busam Sr., Owensboro, KY; Martin Harry, (Oct. 15, 1886-) Memphis, TN; Frances Anna (March 2, 1889-) Mrs. Joseph Thiry, Cannelton, IN; Emma Drucella (Nov. 11, 1891-1981) Sister Mary Angela, Poor Clare, Memphis, TN; Agnes Ella (May 8, 1897-) Mrs. Martin L. Frink.

BUCKMAN, DANIEL BROOKE AND SHERRY LYNN LEAR, are members of St. Peter Parish and past members of St. Ann Parish. Daniel was born June 28, 1962 in Union County at Our Lady of Mercy Hospital, the son of James Elbert Buckman and Dorothy Ann Bickett Buckman. James a retired coal miner and Dorothy, a Hospice volunteer. Sherry Lynn was born April 19, 1961 in Mulenburg County, Greenville, KY, the daughter of Roy Lear and Ima Nell Brown Lear. Roy, a factory worker and farmer and Ima, a factory worker. Sherry lived in Mulenburg County until 1972 then moved to Union County.

Daniel and Sherry have two sons and one daughter: David Daniel born June 18, 1982 in Crittenden County, KY, a student at Uniontown Elementary; Thomas Anthony born Aug. 5, 1983 in Crittenden County, also a student at Uniontown; and Laura Lynn born April 11, 1988 in Henderson County, a headstart student at Morgan Elementary.

The family helps with church picnics, festivals, and Sherry is a Bible School "helper."

BUCKMAN, DONALD AND ELLEN, were married Oct. 28, 1954 and have been members of Sacred Heart Church, near Waverly, KY for 35 years. Ellen was originally a member of St. Ambrose and Donald had always been at Sacred Heart, except for three years when they were first married and lived in Henshaw. They have always attended a country church and they remember long, cold journeys that were a real effort to get to Mass, when warmed bricks, quilts and pot-bellied coal stoves at church kept them from freezing.

Donald is one of 12 children and Ellen one of 10. Their parents are Robert and Mary Leo Buckman and George and Jane Dayberry. They have seven children of their own ranging from ages 20 to 37. They are Jennifer, Theresa, Kathy, Steve, Ken, Greg and Julie. They have 13 grandchildren and at the time of this writing one on the way. They all live close enough to visit and share many special days together which, they say, they are really grateful for.

They have witnessed a lot of the transitions of the church including Latin to English and the altar placement. They agree that most of these have been for the good and that it has given the church more warmth. Ellen says, " I used to be scared to death of the priests and sisters, but now some of them are very good friends. I have worked with them in different movements of the church." In this regard Donald and Ellen are most grateful for the movements within the church and can't understand why all of the people wouldn't want to take advantage of them. They say where you can really encounter Christ is in "God's people". They have made Cursillo, Marriage Encounter, Teens Encounter Christ and Life in the Spirit Seminar. They have also attended workshops in religious education. Both credit the Cursillo weekend as that time in their lives when they examined their faith and felt a rebirth of the Holy Spirit and that is why they have dedicated a lot of their time and evangelizing by working in the movements. They credit T.E.C. as being the lifesaver that God threw at them when they had five teenagers at one time and prayed for help. God answered their prayers and they became one of the first total T.E.C. families in the diocese. They believe T.E.C. to be a powerful witness that young adults can't get by just attending Mass and Catholic schools.

Donald Buckman Family

Donald has been a vocational instructor at E.C.C. Job Corp for 26 years where he has had many opportunities to minister and instill good values in these minorities. He completed his B.S. in V.T.I. from Murray State while teaching there. Ellen says she has always been in the choir someplace, not so much by talent but because music really moves her. She is presently a cantor at Sacred Heart and is taking ministry classes at Brescia College. Both are members of the Parish Council and Donald serves as Eucharistic Minister.

They believe the church has much to offer today for a person's spiritual enrichment but with many either leaving the church or attending irregularly there is much work to be done. They believe that this is the result of not forming a correct conscience that creates the trend of "I don't feel that certain things the church teaches that are wrong are wrong for me." Don says that the answer is to study God's word.

BUCKMAN, JAMES ANDREW, son of Dorothy Ann Bickett and James E. Buckman was born on April 25, 1960 in Union County, KY. Was baptized at St. Ann's Church in Morganfield. Married Mary Lee Berry on Dec. 11, 1978. Daughter of J.W. Berry and Wanda Lee Ritch, born on Jan. 4, 1963 in Union County. She was baptized at St. Peter Church in Waverly. Their children are: James Lucian Buckman born March 22, 1979 in Union County, attends Union County Middle School; Bridget Renea Buckman born Oct. 7, 1983 in Henderson County, attends Uniontown Elementary; Salena Kaye Buckman born Aug. 6, 1987 in Henderson County; Joseph Andrew Buckman born Feb. 20, 1990 in Henderson County.

Mary helps with C.C.D. class. She is a homemaker. Andy is a truckdriver for Home Oil and Gas Company.

BUCKMAN, JAMES ELBERT, married Dorothy Ann Bickett on Aug. 10, 1957 at St. Ann Parish in Morganfield, KY with Rev. Joseph L. Spaulding officiating. He is the son of William Robert Buckman and Mary Leo Willett. Dorothy is the daughter of James Louis Bickett and Eva Christine Sheffer. They were both born and raised in Union County, KY.

Their children are: Anna Marie Buckman born July 15, 1958, married to Anthony Earl Heriges with two children, Laurel Elizabeth Heriges and Adam Elijah Earl Heriges; James Andrew Buckman born April 25, 1960, married to Mary Lee Berry, they have four children, James Lucian Buckman, Bridget Renea Buckman, Salena Kaye Buckman and Joseph Andrew Buckman; Daniel Brook Buckman born June 28, 1962, married to Sherry Lynn Lear with children David Daniel Buckman, Thomas Anthony Buckman and Laura Lynn Buckman; Christopher Lynn Buckman born Dec. 30, 1963; Thomas Edward Buckman born June 8, 1966; Judith Carol Buckman born July 14, 1968, married to Joseph Lloyd French with one child, Malorey Ruthanne French.

Jim is a retired coal miner where he worked as a welder and mechanic; member of the Knights of Columbus; born in Sacred Heart Parish. He has been a member of St. Ann Parish in Morganfield since 1957.

Dorothy was born in St. Ann Parish. She is a homemaker. They have both been C.C.D. teachers and are Eucharist Ministers for the nursing home and sick of the parish; active in RCIA Programs.

BUCKMAN, JOHN SIMMS was born Aug. 21, 1791 in Maryland. He moved to Kentucky with his parents about 1797. He lived in the Rolling Fork settlement around Calvary, KY, where he married Elizabeth Roberts (born Feb. 8, 1795) on Jan. 14, 1812. They were united in marriage at Holy Mary Church, Calvary, KY, by Father Charles Nerinckx.

In 1821, they moved to Union County, KY. They then moved to Monroe County, MO, arriving there in 1836. All of their children were born in Kentucky, except Robert P., who was born in Missouri. Their children were: Joseph P., Nov. 5, 1813-Nov. 23, 1880; William A., March 5, 1815-Feb. 10, 1894; Benedict J.F., April 19, 1817-Jan. 22, 1837; Mary Jane, Feb. 15, 1819-Aug. 10, 1838; John R., Jan. 12, 1821-Aug. 15, 1834; Margaret Ann, Aug. 24, 1822-ca. 1865; Susann, Feb. 29, 1822-March 1849; George William, Jan. 14, 1862-Jan. 24, 1902; James Matthew, Sept. 22, 1827-April 8, 1889; Aloysius (Doc) Simms, March 3, 1830-Sept. 20, 1904; Thomas M., Sept. 2, 1831-Jan. 17, 1906; James Ignatius, 1832-1832; (Gov) Pius, Sept. 12, 1833-Sept. 23, 1897; John Robert, Feb. 18, 1835-Sept. 25, 1913; Robert F., Jan. 26, 1837-Jan. 31, 1917.

John Simms died May 5, 1865; Elizabeth died March 3, 1868.

THOMAS EDWARD BUCKMAN, was born and raised in Union County. He served in the Marine Corps. He married Denise Anne Monica on April 17, 1993. She was born and raised in Lebanon, NH and attended Keene State College.

Eddie and Denise now reside in Lebanon, Grafton County, NH. He works as a herdsman for Tadmor Farm and Denise teaches school in Grahtham, less than 20 minutes from her home. They attend Sacred Heart Parish of Lebanon.

BURCH, CHARLES M. AND ROSAMOND (BLINCOE)

On Nov. 28, 1871 Charles Montague Burch married Clarissa Rosamond Blincoe. Both were of English descent. Their ancestors came to America during the 17th century and fought in the Revolutionary War. By 1800 both their great-grandfathers had migrated to Nelson County, KY: Walter Burch from Charles County, MD; Benjamin Blincoe from Loudoun County, VA. Grandchildren of Walter and Benjamin moved westward in Kentucky: the Burches to Henderson County and the Blincoes to Daviess County. The wedding of Charles and Rosamond took place in the home of her father, Dr. Benjamin Berkeley Blincoe, in St. Joseph, KY. The Blincoes belonged to St. Alphonsus Parish.

After their marriage Charles worked as farm manager in Daviess, Union and Henderson Counties. In 1886 the Burch farm equipment and farm animals were put on a river boat. Charles and Rosamond and their seven children traveled down the Ohio River to Paducah. Upon landing, horses were hitched to the farm wagon, and the family rode to their new farm in St. Jerome Parish, Fancy Farm, Graves County. Six more children were born. All grew to adulthood except Caroline, who died at the age of 2, and Will at age 12. Berkeley, the eldest son, married Elizabeth Willett; Samuel married Katie Elliott; Charlie married Effie Carrico; Watt married Ida Ryan; Robert married Rosalie Goatley. Francis Merriman, the youngest son, was ordained a priest in 1929 and served the church in Kentucky until his death in 1968.

Mary Rosamond married Malcolm Willett; Julia married Solomon T. Ross; Margaret married Dr. Ernest Merritt; Susan married James M. Cash. Hampton married Edgar Elliott; their son Burch Elliott was ordained a Benedictine priest at St. Meinrad, IN in 1931, bearing the name Fr. Hildebrand. He labored for two years among the Sioux Indians of South Dakota and 38 years among the Chippewa of North Dakota. After his retirement he returned to Kentucky and ministered in rural parishes of the Owensboro Diocese until his death in 1983.

Charles M. and Rosamond (Blincoe) Burch

The Burch family members remained in St. Jerome Parish, Fancy Farm, and raised their children there. Altogether there were 70 grandchildren. Three granddaughters became Sisters of Charity of Nazareth: Sister Agnes Clarissa Burch, daughter of Samuel; Margaret Ross, daughter of Julia; and Theresa Cash, daughter of Susan. Sister Jacquelyn Doepker, a great-granddaughter, is a Franciscan Sister at Tiffin, OH. Her mother is Margaret Merritt's daughter, Elizabeth Doepker.

A grandson, William Burch, son of Charlie, was ordained a priest in 1934 and served the church in Kentucky until his death in 1980. A great-grandson, Richard Cash, was ordained a priest in 1989; he is the son of Susan's son Charles. He is now associate pastor at Holy Name Parish, Henderson. Another great-grandson, Pierre DuMaine, son of Berkeley's daughter Eula DuMaine, was ordained a priest of the Archdiocese of San Francisco in 1957. In 1978 he was appointed auxiliary bishop of San Fancisco, and in 1981 was transferred as bishop of the newly created Diocese of San Jose, CA.

These and other grandchildren and great-grandchildren of Rosamond and Charles Burch are now extending the roots of St. Jerome Parish from Alaska to Hawaii.

BURCH, JAMES OSCAR

was a descendant of Teresa Hagan Burch and Walter Burch, two of the early Catholic immigrants coming from Maryland to Kentucky in the 1790s. James Oscar, son of Romanus Washington Burch and Mary Ellen Spink Burch, was born in 1856 in Oolite, Meade County. As a young man he worked as a cook on steamboats along the Ohio and Mississippi Rivers. In 1883 he married Frances Ann McGill of St. Romuald Parish in Hardinsburg, Breckinridge County. Frances was the daughter of Joseph and Margaret McGill. The couple settled on a farm just outside Hardinsburg: Mary Marcella Burch-Sheeran, Mary Margaret Burch-Haley, Robert Romanus, John Allen, Joseph Carroll, William Everett and James Vernon. Frances died in 1901.

James Oscar Burch

In 1904 James Oscar married again to Martha Gallagher at St. Romuald. The family lived in Hardinsburg until about 1905, then moved to Kewanee, IL and eventually to Flint, MI. Seven children were born to James Oscar and Martha: Alberta, Helen Bernadine, Catherine Laverne Burch-Driskill, Mary Josephine, John Donald, Paul James and Frances Rita. James Oscar and Martha both died in Flint, MI in 1924. The children, grandchildren and great-grandchildren of James Oscar Burch now live throughout the United States. In June of 1993, they and the many descendants of Teresa Hagan Burch and Walter Burch gathered for a Burch family reunion at Otter Creek Park near Louisville to honor the ancestors who passed on the faith to them, and to learn more about their family heritage.

BURD FAMILY.

The Burd's were early settlers in the Jackson Purchase of West Kentucky. They moved into Marshall County in the early 1820s from Caldwell County (later Trigg County) where they had immigrated to from the Spartinburg district of South Carolina about 1807.

John Henry Burd ran away from home in Marshall County in 1853 when he was 14 years old and came to the Dublin community in Graves County. His father, Isaac had died around 1848-49 and his mother, Martha was getting married again.

(L to R): Margaret Irene Burd, Linda Marie, Johnnie Burd, Mary Ellen and Rudy Dale Burd

He entered Confederate service when the War Between the States commenced, and fought the duration of the war. Most of the time he served in regiments of General Nathan Bedford Forrest's Calvary Corps.

After the war he married Ann Keeling of the Dublin community and moved to Pulaski County, IL near Ullin where he died Jan. 3, 1883. His wife, Ann had preceded him in death about 1876-77. Their two surviving sons, Edward born 1869 and Edmound born 1871 were brought back to Graves County by their Keeling relatives.

In 1903 Edmound married Kattie Charlottie Kirby who was born 1880 in Graves County. They had three sons Eddie Jr., (1903-1926), John Henry (December 1905-June 2, 1980), Flavious (1907-1978). John Henry met and married the beautiful Margaret "Maggie" Irene Pierceall, eldest daughter of Carl and Ellen Pierceall of St. Jerome Parish in 1934. Johnnie, his mother Kate and younger brother, Flavious were all converts to the one true church.

Children of John Henry Burd and Margaret Irene Pierceall Burd: Carl Edmound Burd born May 21, 1937 Graves County, died June 6, 1944 in Detroit, MI; Rudy Dale Burd born Sept. 27, 1939 in Graves County married Juanita P. McKenzie in November 1964 Lincoln, NE; Linda Marie Burd born Aug. 8, 1945 married first to Jason Nall and second Robert Foy; and Mary Ellen Burd born Jan. 11, 1950 married David Sullivan.

BURKE, AUDREY

was born on April 26, 1924 in Edmondson County, KY, to John R. Durbin and Sarah Elizabeth Durbin. Audrey has one daughter, Rita Fowler and two grandsons, Joey and Daren Fowler. Audrey is the eldest of seven children, has one sister and five brothers. She has lived half her life in the St. John Parish in Sunfish KY. Audrey lived about 18 years in Louisville, KY, until the death of her husband, Bill Burke, she has recently built a house in the Sunfish Community.

Audrey's parents, grandparents and great-grandparents on both sides of the family lived in the St. John Parish and Sunfish community.

Audrey Burke

According to family history handed down, the first Durbins came from Virginia in the late 1700s or early 1800s. Audrey is a full stock Durbin. Audrey's mother Sarah Elizabeth, was born a Durbin, and married a Durbin as was Sarah Elizabeth's mother and one of her aunts.

Through her childhood days and teenage years Audrey and her sisters and brothers walked four miles a day or rode a wagon to and from church and school over dirt roads. At times in bad weather the roads were so muddy wagons and vehicles would mire down and the only mode of transportation was your feet.

The Durbin family enjoyed life, worked hard and were never bored. Audrey can remember stripping sugar cane by moonlight to make molasses.

Audrey loved the St. John Parish and the people. She expects to live the rest of her life there.

BURNS, JIM AND DONNA,

the Jim and Donna Burns family attend St. Martin Church in Rome, KY Donna has been a member since 1965 and her husband Jim since 1985 when they were married. They have two sons Aaron and Nathan. Donna's mother attended St. Charles Church in Livermore as a child. Her grandparents were the first Catholic couple to be married in the mission church there. Later, Donna's mother and father would be the first Catholic couple to be married in the new church built by

Fr. Victor Boarman and the parishioners. Her mother recalls the days of street preaching when Fr. Boarman and the parishioners would set up chairs in the street late in the evening in the summer. They got to see modern day apostles in their work.

Donna is part-time housekeeper for Fr. Joe Mills at St. Martin, secretary of the Altar Society and a member of the Army of Mary.

BUSAM, SISTER EMMA CECILIA, O.S.U.,

daughter of Mr. and Mrs. John William Busam Sr., born July 27, 1921 in Owensboro, KY. Her childhood was spent among a loving family and friends. She attended St. Joseph Grade and High School in Owensboro.

After graduation in 1939, Emma Cecilia was employed at the Ken Rad Tube and Lamp Corporation and played the trumpet with the Ken Rad Tubeadores for three years. She enjoyed sports, parties and travel.

In 1942, Emma entered the Ursuline Community of Mount St. Joseph. She became Sister Emma Cecilia on Aug. 14, 1945.

Her teaching career began in September of 1945, and has taught all grades from first through twelfth. Her experiences as teacher included college classes, training of student teachers, Adult Education classes as well as C.C.D. and other summer programs. Her teaching assignments were in: Central City, Knottsville, Louisville, Holy Cross, Bardwell, Axtel, Owensboro and Mount St. Joseph.

During her novitiate she attended Mount St. Joseph Junior College, later St. Francis College in Jolliet, IL where she received her first degree. Her master's is from the University of Notre Dame in Indiana. She has received many grants and fellowships which took her to Hawaii, North Carolina, Pennsylvania, Colorado, Oklahoma, Ohio, New York and Virginia.

Sister Emma Cecilia Busam, O.S.U., Mount Saint Joseph, Maple Mount, KY

In the fall of 1983 she became archivist for the Mount St. Joseph Ursulines and director of the Museum. In this position she has studied in Washington, Canada, Illinois and Kentucky. She has received grants for the development of archives and historic places. Her knowledge and experiences have been shared with hundreds of workshop participants and those seeking consultation from many archives. She is presently serving on several committees and/or boards related to the community and archives.

BUSAM, FRANCIS XAVIER ALOYSIUS, (June

16, 1845-Nov. 9, 1919), son of Michael Busam and Mary Kern, both of Badan, Baveria, were married on May 6, 1828. They became naturalized citizens of the United States on April 9, 1884.

F.X., as he was called, had four brothers and sisters: William (March 28, 1829), born in Alsace, France; Mary Elizabeth (no date); Louisa (no date); and Christian A. (April 6, 1839) all born in New York. Christian served with Co. H., Ninth Regt. and was killed during the battle of Antietam, Sept. 17, 1862.

Mr. Busam married Mary Hummel (Aug. 3, 1849, Bavaria, Germany-Sept. 19, 1900) in Cannelton, IN in 1870. They returned to New York City for several years where he followed his profession, a lithograph printer. He was also known as an expert painter.

Mrs. Busam came to the United States at the age of 3 years and lived in New York until 1870, the year she was married. She was a kind, loving mother and a dutiful wife, beloved by all who knew her. She was a member of the Catholic Church and a member of the Ladies' Society. Mary died of flux contracted by errands of charity. Two of their children were unable to attend the funeral of their mother because of the disease.

Their children were: Francis Joseph (May 20, 1871-March 3, 1858); Charles Jacob (Jan. 23, 1874-April 3, 1947); John William (July 16, 1876-Oct. 26, 1960), born in New York; and William J. (June 18, 1879-Aug. 17, 1960); Mary Ann (July 31, 1882-Nov. 17, 1965); Chlotilda Elizabeth (June 26, 1885-May 11, 1952); Michael Lawrence Nicholas (March 12, 1888-Sept. 11, 1960), born in Cannelton, IN.

BUSAM, JOHN WILLIAM, and Mary Cecilia Bryan

were married July 26, 1904 at St. Michael's Catholic Church in Cannelton, IN.

In Cannelton, John and his brother, Frank operated Busam's Wallpaper Store. In 1906 John was commissioned to decorate the interior of McAtee's Department Store in Owensboro, KY. The Busam's became life long members of St. Joseph Catholic Church. John, a woodcarver and cabinet maker opened a Decorator's Store in the 300 block of Frederica Street from 1907 to 1917, reserving a section for religious articles. John was employed as head cabinet maker for Forbes Manufacturing Company, makers of church goods until the company moved out of Kentucky in 1930. He continued his art until death in 1960. His work could be seen in most of the Catholic churches and many Protestant ones in Owensboro as well as many states in the nation and foreign countries. John was a dedicated husband and father.

Mary Cecilia, a devoted homemaker and mother, collected slippers as a hobby. Several hundreds are in the Mount Saint Joseph Museum, the others divided among their children.

Their children: Rachel Agnes Eugenia, (1908-), Mrs. Bernard Aloysius Alvey, (1930); John William Jr., (1919-1979), married Margaret Hayes, 1944 in England during World War II, later Alice Morgan; Emma Cecilia, (1921-) an Ursuline Sister at Mount St. Joseph; Mary Agnes (1927-) Mrs. Antonia M. Caruso and after her husband's death, she married Otis Vance.

Mr. and Mrs. John William Busam Sr. 50th Wedding Anniversary, July 26, 1954.

At the time of Mrs. Busam's death in 1967 they had eight grandchildren and six great-grandchildren.

Grandchildren: Bernard Eugene Alvey, John Andrew Alvey, John William Busam, III, Henry Siril Busam, Eugenia Lee Busam-Matthews, Mary Cecilia Caruso-Vetterl, Antoinette Maria Caruso-Hanson, Josephine Marie Caruso-Patten.

Cannelton Telephone ran an article on March 15, 1900 as follows: John Busam has at his home on Front Street a very pretty little pleasure boat which is one of the most complete and perfect of any we have ever seen. He made the design and the completed boat is a sample of his handiwork. He is now at work on a motor which is to furnish the motive power. It will be operated by a battery of several cells containing chemicals and, as soon as he determines on what he will use, will set the little vessel into the water. It will carry about five persons.

Cannelton Enquirer, May 21, 1904, ran an article: John Busam, one of our painters, was the central figure of attraction on Tuesday afternoon, not only for the ladies as he always is, but for all the residents of Cannelton. He climbed the scaffolding that has been erected to St. Michael Church tower and mounted the big iron cross to give it a coat of paint. He looked like a minnow on a fish hook as he sat on the cross arms and worked.

BUSAN, MARGARET HAYES, was born in

Cheshire, England in 1921 to Henry Sirl Hayes II (1893-1933) and Sara Agnes Riley Hayes (1893-1978). Sara Hayes remarried in 1935 to Herbert Hallows (1890-1969), a wonderful husband and step-father.

So much is known about the Busan (Busam) side of this family, and included is a little bit about the Hayes family. Her grandparents on her father's side were Henry Sirl Hayes Sr. and Charlotte Holmes Hayes, both of Cheshire, England. Her grandparents on her mother's side were Patrick Riley (born near the Blarney Stone in Ireland) and Ann Jane Riley of Cheshire, England.

Donna Helfrich Busan, John W. Busan III, John W. Busan IV "Jay".

She has two brothers, Henry Sirl Hayes III (born 1917) and Arthur B. Hayes (born 1924). She also has one sister, Marie Hayes (born 1928).

John William Busan Jr. and Margaret Hayes Busan were married in Andover, England in 1944. With John being in the Air Force, Margaret moved to Owensboro, KY in 1946.

John Busan Jr. was a draftsman/architect after he was discharged from the Air Force. The home they lived in on Colonial Court was actually designed by John Busan Jr. They had two children, John William Busan III (born 1947) and Henry Sirl Busan (born 1950).

For 30 years Margaret Busan worked at the General Electric Plant in Owensboro, KY.

Margaret Busan now resides in Newburgh, IN, just across the Ohio River from Owensboro, KY. Also residing in Newburgh are John III and Henry Busan. John William Busan III and Donna Helfrich Busan married in 1984. They have one son, John William Busan IV (born 1989); they call him "Jay." Henry Sirl Busan and Jane Wilhite married in 1969 and had one daughter, Amanda Jane Busan (born 1970). Henry married Nancy Chase in 1992.

BYRD, FRED AND CHARLOTTE MITCH-

ELL, were married in Indianapolis, IN on July 22, 1950. It seems ironic that their first date was at a St. Ambrose Parish picnic. Fred and Charlotte are the parents of three children, Fr. Freddie Lee, Shelia Faye and Linda Darlene. Fr. Freddie was the second priest called to Holy Orders from the long history of St. Ambrose Parish. Fr. Freddie was ordained a deacon at St. Ambrose on Sept. 26, 1987 and ordained a priest at the SportCenter in Owensboro on May 28, 1988. The presider at both celebrations was Bishop John McRaith. Shelia married Don Slusher at St. Ambrose on Aug. 20, 1988. Shelia and Don are the proud parents of two girls, Sara Elizabeth and Lora Dawn. Linda Darlene died shortly after birth on April 26, 1956. Fred passed away suddenly of a massive heart attack Aug. 31, 1992. Charlotte lives in the city of Henshaw where she was born and raised.

BYRNE, JOHN D. AND ANNA MARIE

COOMES, (each from a family of 14) were married in 1939 and parented seven children: Margie, John Jr., J.L., Elaine, Mary Lou, Eddie and Tony. The family owned a

96-acre farm, but supplemented their income by tenanting crops on four other farms, and by raising cattle, pigs and chickens. John D. died of a heart attack in 1963, but Anna Marie and the children continued to make a living from the farm, with the three older children working at public jobs as well.

Margie is married to Jim Rode and has one daughter, Kristen. John married Barbara Loney and has one stepdaughter, Carla and three grandchildren: Scott, Jon and Jeff. J.L. married Joan Fulkerson and has three daughters: Jackie, Karen and Jenny; and three grandsons: Michael, Joshua and Garrett. Mary Lou is married to Darrell Payne and has four children: Charlie, Jill, John Paul and Kaitlyn; and one granddaughter, Brittany. Eddie married Alo Dant and has four children: Bryan, Sean, Heath and Tera (who died as an infant); and one grandson, Cody. Tony is married to Betty Drury and has five children: Lisa, Michael, Michele, Erica and Bradley.

Elaine celebrated her Silver Jubilee as a Mount St. Joseph Ursuline in 1990, and has ministered in various parishes and schools for 24 years.

Presently, Marge and her family are members of Our Lady of Greenwood near Whiteland, IN; Elaine ministers at St. Mary, LaCenter; and the other siblings reside in Daviess County, where Mary Lou is active in Right-to-Life and is a member of St. William, Knottsville; J.L. is involved at St. Mary Magdalene, Sorgho and Eddie and Tony at Lourdes in Owensboro. The brothers share a special interest in barbeque functions.

Anna Marie, who died in 1990, was the daughter of J. Watt and Hattie Coomes of West Louisville. John D.'s parents were D. L. and Ettie Byrne of Curdsville.

BYRNE, SISTER MARY IGNATIUS, was born April 23, 1930 about half a mile west of Newman in Daviess County to Sylvester Ignatius and Mary Ethel Murphy Byrne. She was baptized Agnes Pauline in St. Augustine Church in Reed on May 18, 1930. She was the fourth child of 12 children born of her parents. There were four boys and eight girls of which one boy and one girl older than she are dead.

It was a family custom to say Grace before meals and kneel around the parents bed for 20 minutes of night prayers.

She attended four years of schooling at St. Augustine taught by the Dominican Sisters, six and one-half years at St. Peter Alcantara in Stanley taught by the Ursuline Sisters and two years at St. Frances Academy taught by the Sisters of Charity from Nazareth. She graduated from high school June 9, 1949.

Sister Mary Ignatius Byrne

After high school she worked a few months at Our Lady of Mercy Hospital as a nurse-aide.

She entered the Carmelite Sisters of the Divine Heart of Jesus in Wauwatosa, WI Sept. 15, 1950. She made her First Profession of the Holy Vows July 2, 1952 and Final Profession July 2, 1957.

Her vocation to the religious life was influenced by a Franciscan Father who gave a Mission in St. Augustine Church when she was 16 years old. She thinks the call to the Carmelite Community was through the intercession of St. Theresa, the Little Flower of Jesus. The family made a novena to the Little Flower for a cure of a severe illness when she was 12 years old. The late Rev. Robert T. Wilson was pastor of St. Augustine Church in Reed and was instrumental in her vocation to the Carmelite Sisters, D.C.J. because he has asked the Sisters to come to the Owensboro Diocese to open a home for the elderly.

She has been stationed in St. Joseph Home Kenosha, WI, St. Joseph Home Jefferson City, MO, St. Joseph Home St. Charles, MO, St. Agnes Home Kirkwood, MO and Carmel Home in Owensboro.

CALHOUN, EDWIN PATRICK, was born on March 27, 1950 and is 42 years old. He is a manager at Diebold Inc. Linda Kay Barnett was born on May 3, 1954 and is 38 years old. She works full time in admissions at Owensboro Community College, part-time in jewelry and cosmetics in Bacons, and is a Riverpark Center volunteer. Edwin's parents are Robert P. and Catherine Calhoun. Linda is the daughter of Charles and Bernadean Barnett. Ed and Linda were married on July 7, 1978 at St. Pius X Parish, where they still attend church. Ed is on the Parish Council and school board. Linda is a lector and Eucharistic Minister.

Jennifer Kay Calhoun was born on March 31, 1979 and is 13 years old. She attends Owensboro Catholic Middle School. Edwin Patrick Calhoun Jr., was born on July 27, 1982 and is 10 years old. He attends Bishop Francis R. Cotton School.

CALHOUN, FATHER GERALD, was one of eight children born of Everett and Pauline Calhoun. His birth on Dec. 23, 1935 was a shock to his parents as his mother gave birth to twin boys. Besides his twin brother, Sherrell, other members of the family are Mary Lucy Strehl, Martha Warren, Juanita Riney (dec.), Julian, James Henry (dec.) and Robert Calhoun.

Fr. Calhoun received his education at St. Joseph Grade School, Owensboro; St. Francis and Owensboro Catholic High School. His seminar training was from St. Mary's, Marion County and St. Maur's, Logan County. After his ordination on May 20, 1961, he received his BA from Brescia College and his MA degree from Western Kentucky University.

Fr. Gerald Calhoun

Fr. Calhoun served as associate pastor at Sts. Peter and Paul Church, Hopkinsville and St. Stephen Cathedral, Owensboro. He was teacher, dean of students and principal in Owensboro Catholic High and served as chaplain at the Carmel Home until 1980. Calhoun was principal at St. Mary High School, Paducah, for four years. Named pastor of St. Joseph Church, Leitchfield in 1984 until present assignment as pastor of Holy Spirit, Bowling Green in 1989.

Fr. Calhoun has served the diocese as vocation director, on the Board of Consultors under both Bishop Soenneker and Bishop McRaith, Dean of the Western Deanery, on the Personnel Board and Diocesan Total Education Committee.

Fr. Calhoun says he has been happy in his priesthood, although he has seen many changes and expectations in the priesthood. He found his years in education as the most challenging years as well as years of personal growth. However, he says it was a great joy when he received his assignment as a pastor. Fr. Calhoun says, "It was the opportunity to fulfill the mission to which I felt called from the day of my ordination." "Thank God for His Goodness."

CALHOUN, SHERRELL AND JEANNIE, live in Madisonville and are a part of Christ the King Parish. Sherrell was born in Owensboro, KY, son of Everett and Pauline (Payne) Calhoun and baptized in St. Stephen Cathedral along with his twin brother, Father Gerald Calhoun. He is from a family of nine children. He attended St Joseph Grade School in the West Louisville, KY, area. Jeannie is the daughter of Henry L. Bickett and Ina Belle (Crowe) Bickett, one of 10 children. She attended St. Raphael Grade School, Mount St. Joseph Academy and Brescia College.

Sherrell and Jeannie were married at St. Raphael Church on Dec. 27, 1958. In 1962 they moved from Blessed Mother Parish in Owensboro to Madisonville and were a part of Immaculate Conception Parish in Earlington until 1973. They are now a part of Christ the King Parish.

Their children are Jerry, Johnny, Cheryl Ann Lutz, David and Michael, who all attended Immaculate Conception School, Earlington, KY, or Christ the King, Madisonville. All four sons received their Eagle Scout Award from Troop 90, sponsored by the church and Cheryl Ann received highest honor in Girl Scouts. Sherrell and Jeannie both have been active on Christ the King Parish Council, school board, Altar Society, St. Vincent De Paul and building committee.

CALHOUN, THOMAS PAUL, was born on Sept. 21, 1947 to Joe and Edwina Calhoun. Tom grew up with 11 brothers and sisters in Curdsville on a 65 acre farm. The Calhoun family went to St. Elizabeth Catholic Church in Curdsville. On June 25, 1951, Margaret Jane Higdon was born to James E. and Eloiwise Higdon. Jane and her family went to St. Pius X Catholic Church in Owensboro. Jane lived on Pleasant Valley Road. Tom was good friends with one of Jane's brothers and that is how Tom and Jane met. They were married on April 8, 1972. Then during August of 1976 they went to Marriage Encounter, and for four years Tom and Jane were involved with Marriage Encounter. After that time they were presenting team couple for Engaged Encounter from late 1980 until early 1992. They are now the finance couple for Engaged Encounter. Tom is working for Pinkerton Tobacco Company. He was in the church choir, a Encharistic Minister, previous Parish Counsel member and a member

Sherrell and Jeannie Calhoun Family

f the picnic committee. Tom and Jane were teachers for the eighth grade youth group and are both lectors at St. Pius X Catholic Church. Jane was also a teacher for Children's Liturgy and she works at home.

Tom and Jane had four children. Their first child, Jill Suzanne Calhoun, was born on Nov. 22, 1973. Jill is now in her second year at Bellarmine College in Louisville. During the summer she has been working at Foodland. Their second child, Denise Marie Calhoun, was born Oct. 3, 1975. Denise attends Owensboro Catholic High School where she is a junior and a member of the Thespian Society. Their third child, Curtis Alan Calhoun, is 14 and he attends Owensboro Catholic Middle School. He was born on Oct. 10, 1978 and he is an alter boy. Curt mows yards during the summer and he is involved with the OCHS marching band. The fourth child, Steven Ray Calhoun, is 10 years old and goes to Bishop Francis R. Cotton Elementary School. Steven was born on Sept. 5, 1982 and will soon be an altar boy. He is in Cub Scouts and he mows his yard for pocket change in the summer.

CAMBRON, THOMAS EDWARD, was born in December 1879 in Union County, KY. His father Ralph was a farmer and his mother Ellen Drury attended Sacred Heart Church at St. Vincent, KY. Fr. Elisha J. Durbin founded the parish and served the people in southwestern Kentucky, along with churches in Tennessee, Indiana and Illinois. Tom married Connie Thomas from Daviess County. They met when 8 and 10 years old, when dad led her to his mother saying "Ain't she pretty, Mom?" When in high school Connie attended St. Vincent Academy and Tom visited her with her cousins. The wedding took place 16 years after their initial meeting.

The Cambrons migrated from Scotland to Maryland then to Kentucky. The historic records give the names of those who fought with George Washington in the American Revolution.

Ralph and Ellen had 13 children. They were 87 and 89 years of age when they died and are buried at St. Ann Cemetery, Morganfield, KY. Tom and Connie had nine children, who are scattered all over the U.S.A. The oldest daughter is deceased. Only one, Mrs. Allen Gordon resides in the Owensboro Diocese and attends St. Stephen Cathedral.

After Tom retired from farming they moved to Morganfield and attended St. Ann Church. He sold seed corn for the Pioneer Seed Company for several years. They celebrated their Golden Jubilee in 1955 and also lived to celebrate their 60th. After retiring they spent time driving their friends around.

Father Rahm was the beloved pastor at St. Ann's when the Cambron children attended St. Ann School. Tom was a faithful member of the Catholic School Board, as well as the County School Board. Father Rahm frequently borrowed Tom's horse so he could go riding, when the Cambron children weren't riding themselves.

Tom and Connie's children grew up in a happy household with much popcorn popping over an open fire place, also fishing, roller skating on the wide concrete porches and even playing tennis. Yes, Tom built them a tennis court to play tennis at St. Vincent Academy, where she attended high school.

CARRICO, FRANCIS MARION AND ELIZA JANE (WILLETT), Francis Marion (1854-1897) son of Henry C. and Nancy (Wethington) Carrico, was born in Casey County, and his family moved to Daviess County before the Civil War. Francis Marion and his brother, William Alexander, moved to Graves County before 1880. William Alexander and Martha (Brewer) Carrico were the parents of Laura, who was taught at St. Jerome School by the Franciscan Sisters of Shelbyville (later Clinton, IA) who were there from 1882-1890. In 1883, Laura joined the Franciscans, whom she would later serve as Mother M. Paul for more than 30 years. She died Jan. 12, 1954.

Francis Marion married Eliza Jane (1844-1922) Willett (see Samuel Willett biography), eight children.

Alphonsus Kramer (1871-1943) son of Francis Marion and Eliza Jane married Dora Francis Marshall (1879-1938), who was born in Scott County, MO, at St. Jerome on Jan. 29, 1900, nine children (see Memorial Record of Western Kentucky, 1904).

Joseph Otto (1912) son of Kammer and Dora married Mary Ella (1917) daughter of Henry Tyler and Nellie Pearl (Stephens) Bugg on Dec. 29, 1935 at St Jerome. They had four children, namely, Donald Anthony (1938); Frances Marilyn (1939), who married first William Robert Driscoll on June 8, 1957 at St. Mary Magdalene in Melvindale, MI (six children), and married second Roy Neill Hughes; Dennis Michael (1941-1942); and Richard Leon (b/d 1948).

Otto and Mary Ella Bugg Carrico, Wedding Day 1935

In 1943 Otto and Mary Ella moved to Detroit, MI. They were active in the *Kentuckians in Michigan Club,* and they started their extensive scrapbook collection of clippings from *The Mayfield Messenger* and *The Paducah Sun,* on items related in any way with the Fancy Farm community. They were away from home and their heritage for over 32 years, but never away in spirit and interest. When Otto retired in 1975 they returned home to Fancy Farm. Their collection of clippings was very helpful to the editor and compiler of "A History of St. Jerome, Fancy Farm," 1988. (Note: As both Otto and Mary Ella are ill, the above family story was written for them, his friends, in admiration and gratitude by Bro. Leo Willett, S.M.)

CARRICO SISTERS, Did you ever hear of a father and mother losing three daughters in one day . . . by having them enter a convent? Well, this is what happened to Charles and Elizabeth Carrico, longtime members of the Saint Lawrence Community. With both joy and sadness in their hearts they experienced the loss of their three daughters. This happening may be the first and only such event in the history of religious orders.

Lucy, the oldest, Ann and Angela being twins, all graduated from high school at Saint Frances Academy, Allen Street, Owensboro in June 1933. Immediately thereafter all three sisters started working at the Ken-Rad plant in order to earn enough money to buy the necessary personal items required for acceptance into the Novitiate of the Sisters of Charity at Nazareth, Kentucky. They, along with another classmate, Mary Jane Cecil, now Sister Teresa, left the Carrico farm near St. Lawrence headed for Nazareth on Sept. 24, 1933. Their pastor, Father William Jarboe, drove them in his 1928 Chevrolet sedan . . . loaded with three young girls, suitcases and other luggage . . . cramped quarters on a very hot day.

The Carrico Sisters

Upon completing their novitiate training they made vows on March 25, 1935. Soon thereafter they each left the Nazareth Motherhouse having been assigned to careers in teaching and nursing. After getting a degree in nursing Sister Angela Maria served as Dr. Irvin Abell's operating nurse at St. Joseph Infirmary, the doctor who was known nationwide for his skilled surgery and charity. Later Sister earned a master's degree in nursing at the Catholic University. She was then assigned to Georgetown University, Washington, D.C. as dean of their School of Nursing. In later years she taught at the University of Kentucky College in Henderson. After more than 50 years of service to the Charity Community of Sisters she died a happy death on March 20, 1988.

Sister Ann Maria, Angela's twin, also had an outstanding career. As a teacher she taught various primary grades in Bellaire, OH, Memphis, TN and other Charity schools before earning her master's degree in mathematics at St. Xavier University. For several years she taught math at the Owensboro Catholic High School. As a teacher and religious instructor she was always highly respected in that community. Sister Ann Maria is now a patient at the Order's Nazareth Care Home in Louisville.

Sister Lucy, the oldest of the three sisters, now teaches at the Order's Montessori Children Center at the Nazareth Motherhouse. She too has had an outstanding career as a Sister of Charity. She earned a degree in nursing at Catherine Spalding University in Louisville. She served her community at several Charity hospitals in a supervisory capacity, mainly St. Joseph Infirmary, Sts. Mary and Elizabeth, as well as Mount Vernon, OH and Little Rock, AR. Sister Lucy is still very active within the community at the age of 78. She is extremely proud of the fact she was instrumental through a contact within the Jesuit Order in establishing the Sisters of Charity with a house in India. The Order is now flourishing and doing extremely well in that country.

All three of the Carrico Nuns celebrated their Golden Anniversary on March 25, 1985 at St. Stephen Cathedral. Father Joseph Rhodes, one of their classmates at St. Frances Academy, officiated.

All three sisters, Lucy, Ann and Angela . . . along with their three brothers, Edwin and Henry of Owensboro and Gerald Emmanuel of Leesburg, FL thank God for the deep faith of their father and mother and for the excellent examples of faith by their many friends, both lay and religious, in the St. Lawrence community as well as the entire Owensboro Diocese.

CARRICO, SISTER CARMENCITA, was born June 2, 1920 in Manton, KY. She is the daughter of J.B. Carrico (Jan. 20, 1880; Nelson County, KY) and Alma (Bell) Carrico (March 29, 1886; Nelson County, KY). J.B. Carrico passed away on July 28, 1948. Alma Carrico passed away on June 24, 1944. Sister Carmencita has seven brothers and four sisters (only three brothers and three sisters are still living). Her brothers and sisters: Perry (deceased), John, Nixon C. Clarkson (deceased), Lester, Eric, Maurice, Tess C. Elder, Booth Carrico, Jr., Maxine (Sister Corda OSU), Norma C. Hagan and James.

Sister Carrico entered the convent on Sept. 7, 1938. She received the Habit on Aug. 14, 1939. During her ministry, she enjoyed being a teacher for Grades 1-4. She has served at Paul, NE; Plattsmouth, NE; Princeton, KY; St. Margaret Mary, Louisville, KY; Affton, MO; SS. Joseph & Paul, Owensboro, KY; St. Ignatius, Louisville, KY; Mother of Good Counsel, Louisville, KY; St. Thomas More, Paducah, KY; Precious Blood, Owensboro, KY; and St. Catherine, New Haven, KY.

Her main hobby was riding horseback.

CARRICO, CHARLES E., was born the eldest son of Charles Raphael and Elizabeth Johnson Carrico in 1911. The family also included two brothers, Henry I. and Gerald E. Carrico, three sisters, the late twins Sister Angela Marie and Sister Ann Maria and Sister Lucy Carrico. They were born in the St. Lawrence community of Daviess County, KY.

Charles E. Carrico married Mary Virginia Boarman on May 1, 1943. From this marriage came the births of 14 children and 23 grandchildren. They were married at St. Mary of the Woods Church, Whitesville, KY.

The children are as follows: Robert Patrick, Charles David, Phillip Anthony, Richard Joseph, Mark Edwin, Karen Ann, Francis I., Samuel Lee (deceased), Christopher Michael Carrico, Mary Jeanette Smith, Lucy Elizabeth Goetz, Carol Jean Hurm, Judith Marie Bielefield and Janice Marie Walker.

Charles was employed for 33 years at Fleishman Distillery before retirement. Virginia is a retired cafeteria worker and housewife. Their favorite pastimes are gardening and entertaining family and friends at their St. Lawrence farm, where they often reside. This farm is the original homeplace for Charles E., as well as a dedicated memorial to the memory of Sam, a son who died in a 1987 automobile accident. With each gathering, they still feel the loss, but celebrate having known him.

CARRICO, CHARLES R. was born on Oct. 15, 1876 to David R. and Susan Head Carrico in Daviess County, KY. Charles married Elizabeth Johnson on April 1, 1910 in St. Lawrence Church, St. Lawrence, KY. Elizabeth Johnson, born on May 19, 1885 in Blackford Creek, Hancock County, was the daughter of Henry P. and Marcelie Hazel Johnson. Charles and Elizabeth were members of St. Lawrence Parish until they moved to Owensboro in 1955. They were then members of Sts. Joseph and Paul Parish and later of St. Stephen Cathedral. They had six children.

Charles Edwin, born Jan. 3, 1911, married Mary Virginia Boarman; Henry Ignatius, born July 17, 1912, married Mary William Boteler; Lucy, born Jan. 27, 1914, professed vows as a Sister of Charity of Nazareth, Nazareth, KY, on March 25, 1935; Angela and Ann Marie, born Feb. 24, 1915, professed vows as Sisters of Charity of Nazareth, Nazareth, KY, on March 25, 1935; Gerald Emmanuel, born Sept. 13, 1916, married Oda Mae Osborne, and after her death, Marcy Walker.

There are 27 grandchildren. Charles R. died on June 12, 1965; Elizabeth died on Jan. 17, 1979; both are buried in St. Lawrence Cemetery, St. Lawrence (Daviess County), KY. Sister Angela Marie died in Owensboro on March 20, 1988; Sister Ann Marie died at Nazareth Home, Nazareth, KY on Sept. 4, 1992; Sister Lucy teaches at Montessori School, Nazareth, KY; Henry and Edwin live in Owensboro; Gerald Emmanuel lives in Leesburg, FL.

CARRICO, CHARLES R. AND ELIZABETH, my parents, recited their marriage vows at St. Lawrence Church in Eastern Daviess County on April 4, 1910, God must have showered down upon them a very special blessing. This undoubtedly provided them with the necessary grace and courage to withstand the hardships of married life in a time when making a living and raising a family on a small farm was indeed difficult. As a result of this special blessing they survived during depression-like times and reared their six children according to God's commands. They instilled in their children the values of living a good Catholic life, teaching them to respect God's laws and the laws of His church. This meant regular attendance at Mass on Sunday's and all Holy Days as well as on special occasions such as First Friday's, morning and night prayers, a special devotion to the rosary, regular confessions, a Catholic study program both at home and at school, a true respect for others and a respect for hard work on the farm.

Mom and Pop reaped very few worldly rewards for their hard work on the farm. Instead, they reaped many spiritual benefits. They became spiritually rich from their good works as good Catholics and from the graces God gave them in raising six children, three daughters who entered the congregation of the Sisters of Charity, Nazareth, KY, all three entering on the same day, and three sons who gave them the many blessings of 26 grandchildren.

Like my parents, many other members of the St. Lawrence Parish were blessed in similar ways by living out their marriage vows. Undoubtedly these self-sacrificing commitments must have been in God's plans during the erection of this esteemed church in the year 1870. Proof of this lies in the reality of faithful performance over the years by its present members and those already enjoying their rewards. In my opinion the St. Lawrence Cemetery is the earthly home of many of God's saints. Undoubtedly this parish has produced as many priests, brothers and nuns, possibly more than any other parish within the Owensboro Diocese. I am indeed proud to be a part of the spiritual history of St. Lawrence, I am also proud to be a son of Charles R. and Elizabeth Carrico and a brother to Charles Edwin, Henry I., Sister Lucy and her deceased twin sisters, Sister Angela Marie and Sister Ann Marie.

May God continue showering His blessings on all the members of the St. Lawrence community.

CARRICO, HENRY I. was born on July 17, 1912, to Charles R. and Elizabeth Johnson Carrico in St. Lawrence (Daviess County), KY. Henry married Mary William Boteler on Aug. 17, 1944 in St. William's Church, Knottsville, KY. Mary William, born on May 7, 1923, was the oldest daughter of Severious Aloysius and Virgie Mae Winkler Boteler of Knottsville (Daviess County), KY. After their marriage, Henry and Mary William became members of Sts. Joseph and Paul Parish.

The Henry Carrico Family: Seated (center) Henry and Mary Williams; between them, James Matthew; on Mother's left: Thomas Andrew and John Gilmary; on Dad's right; Marilyn Elizabeth and Geraldine Mae; standing (left to right) Timothy Aloysius, Kathleen Marie, Stephen Joseph, Michael Henry, Rose Mary, Ruth Ann. Picture taken in their home by George (James C.) Washington a couple months prior to Aug. 15, 1964.

The Henry Carrico Family today

They had 11 children: Ruth Ann, born Jan. 22, 1946; Rose Mary, born Aug. 12, 1947, married James Thomas Wieder Jr.; Michael Henry, born May 18, 1949; Stephen Joseph, born Dec. 1, 1950, married Anna Marie Wieder; Kathleen Marie, born Dec. 18, 1951, married Gary William Campbell; Timothy Aloysius, born Dec. 17, 1952, married Mary Beth O'Bryan; Geraldine Mae, born Dec. 17, 1953, married Joseph Larry Jarboe, Sr.; Marilyn Elizabeth, born Feb. 8, 1955, married Randy Wayne Aldridge; John Gilmary, born Oct. 20, 1956, married Kelly Jo Marvel; Thomas Andrew, born Oct. 28, 1957, married Terri Joan Edge; and James Matthew, born July 21, 1960.

There are 22 grandchildren. Mary William died March 20, 1976, and is buried in St. Lawrence Cemetery, St. Lawrence, KY. Henry, retired manager of Budget Loan Company, Owensboro, lives in Owensboro, KY. He is a member of Sts. Joseph and Paul Parish.

Tim and Mary Beth Carrico live in Scott (Layfayette Parish), LA. John and Kelly Carrico live in Wadesville, Posey County, IN. All the other children live in Owensboro and surrounding areas (Daviess County, KY).

CARRICO, JAMES AMBROSE AND ROSE CARRICO are members of the St. William Parish, Knottsville, KY. They have lived in Knottsville since 1948. They were married July 4, 1947 at St. Joseph Church, Owensboro, KY. Father Joseph McAleer officiated at their wedding. They have six children and nine grandchildren.

James was born in Knottsville, a son of Ligouri and Nora Haynes Carrico. He is a descendant of one of the first Catholic families in Eastern Daviess County.

Rose was born in Daviess County, a daughter of Frank and Rose Simon Gilles, and was a member of St. Joseph Church, Owensboro, KY.

James Ambrose and Rose Carrico

James served three years in the Army during World War II, being stationed in Europe.

He retired from General Electric Company, Owensboro, KY with nearly 42 years of service. After their children were grown Rose worked eight years at the Bishop Soenneker Home.

They live at Knottsville, KY, on the Short Station Road.

CARRICO, SISTER LENNORA was born in Fancy Farm (Graves County), KY, Dec. 8, 1915. She was the oldest of a family of seven; four sisters and two brothers. Her parents Aubrey and Mae Carrico were born and reared in St. Jerome Parish in Fancy Farm, KY.

Sr. Lennora Carrico

Her earliest education was under the Sisters of Charity of Nazareth, KY, who taught both grade and high school. She entered the Ursuline Community at Mount St. Joseph in 1938 after a year of college.

Her assignments as an Ursuline are many and varied. She was a teacher for 38 years in both high school and Brescia College.

Her second career was working among the elderly in Senior Citizen activities and pastoral ministry work.

She has also worked as a volunteer at Mercy Hospital in Owensboro. For many years she worked in the Hospice program. She has been involved with the RCIA program in the parish.

At present she is working part-time in the MSJ Shop and being on call for small jobs that come her way at Mount St. Joseph, Maple Mount, KY.

CARRICO, LEON AND DOROTHY. Leon Carrico son of J. H. Carrico (1893-1987) and Mary Irene

(Thomas) Carrico (1898-1977) and Dorothy M. Riley daughter of Joseph Aubrey Riley, 1910-1986, and Mary Wilma Garnett Riley (1912) were married by Father Rudolph Carrico (Uncle of Leon) at St. Jerome Church in 1952.

Their children and grandchildren are: Rebecca, married Russell Dalton, parents of Kelly, Cliff, Clint, died 1973, Jessica and Kyle; Stephen, married Barbara Lee, parents of Heather and Holly; Margaret (Margie) married Johnny Dossett, parents of Tara, Dereck and Matthew; Donald, married Kelli Parrott, parents of Sam, Whitney and Ty; Timothy Joseph, married Susan Mills, parents of Katie, Jodi, Mitchell and Elyse; Lorrie, married Mike Forgey parents of Jennifer, died 1978, Ashley, Dana, Emily and Waylen; Dr. Jeffrey, married Lisa Elliott, parents of Adam; Mark, married Beth Ivie; Russell, married Ellen Wilson, parents of Lauren, died 1988 and Madison.

They have been members of St. Jerome Parish, except for October 1955 until June 1960 when they were members of St. Vincent De Paul Parish in Newport, KY.

Leon is the grandson of William Constantine and Allie Bridget (Cash) Carrico and Robert and Lucetta (Hayden) Thomas.

Dorothy is the granddaughter of Lucelia Elvis and Elizabeth (Mills) Riley and Edward and Artie (Roach) Garnett.

CARROLL, FRANK AND MARY ANN.
The Frank and Mary Ann Carroll family lived on a farm near Wilson Station and attended Holy Name Church.

Frank was born April 15, 1857 to Eliza Kelly and Redmond Carroll. They were from Mayo County, Ireland. Mary Ann was born Oct. 22, 1872 to Winefred Jourdon and Michael Cunningham. Michael was from Cincinnati, OH and came to Henderson to help build the Ohio River Railroad Bridge.

Frank and Mary had nine children: Elizabeth, Redmond, Francis, Alice, John, Agnes, Katherine, Billy and Maria.

Frank, with his three sons farmed until his death Feb. 20, 1935. He was attending a dance at Holy Name School when he died.

Mary continued to live on the farm and with her sons John and Billy helping to operate the farm. Alice taught school and also lived at home.

Francis died in infancy; Redmond married Mary Konsler; Elizabeth married Hal Cates; Agnes married Gordon Konsler; Katherine married Sam Hamilton and Maria married Adam Werner.

Mary Ann was a very devout and religious person. She often prayed her rosary that she kept in her pocket. She was a member of Holy Name Altar Society.

She loved to see and spend time with her children and 15 grandchildren until her death April 5, 1958.

THE CARROLL FAMILY.
Michael Carroll and Catherine Broffey were born and raised in Cork County, Ireland. They were married in St. Patrick's Cathedral in Cork County in the early 1860's. After their marriage, they started their voyage to America. It is not known if any of their families came to America before them.

Upon arriving in America, they came as far as Breckinridge County, KY, settling at Holt's Bottom, on the Burk family farm. All of their seven children were born there. Around 1885, they bought a small farm in the same vicinity and lived there until they died. They are buried at St. Romuald Catholic Cemetery. They were members of St. Rose Catholic Church in Cloverport, where their five daughters were married. Their son, Lawrence, was married at St. Romuald Catholic Church in Hardinsburg, KY.

All of the children settled around Cloverport, where all of their children were born. Later in life, Lawrence and his family moved to Louisville, KY, where his children are still living. Julia and her family moved to Paynesville, in Meade County, KY. This is where her children are still living. Margaret and her family went to Oklahoma at the turn of the century. They were one of the first to claim territory there, settling close to Enid, OK. This is where all of her family was raised and where some of them still live today. Bridget and her family lived in Cloverport, KY.

Catherine married John Flood. They are buried at St. Romuald Catholic Church Cemetery in Hardinsburg, KY. Their children are: Philip Flood, Elizabeth (Flood) Basham, Kathleen (Flood) Basham, John C. Flood, Mary Agnes Flood, Anna Mildred (Flood) Popham, Bridget Flood, Helen R. (Flood) Scuhmann and Michael Carroll, Flood.

Michael Carroll, born in Cork, Ireland (1830-1893); Catherine Broffey, born in Cork, Ireland (1843-1918)

Nellie Carroll died young. Elizabeth Carroll married James Flood. They are buried at St. Romuald Church Cemetery. Their children are: Bridget Agnes (Flood) Potts, Michael William Flood, Mary Nellie (Flood) Roach, Peter Paul Flood, Katherine Flood, Margaret Cecelia (Flood) Henning, Lawrence Flood, James Vincent Flood, John A. "Doc" Flood, Julia Elizabeth (Flood) Kidder and Catherine Lorena (Flood) Fischer.

Most of the Catherine "Carroll" Flood and the Elizabeth "Carroll" Flood families are still living in Breckinridge and Meade Counties in Kentucky. Their families are double first cousins.

Michael Carroll had a brother, Lawrence Carroll, who married Sarah Hinton, but nothing is known of their life. Michael's sister, Elizabeth "Carroll" Sherran, of McQuady, KY, had three children: Dennis Sherran, Margaret (Sherran) Askin and Bridget (Sherran) Mattingly. Their descendents still live in the Hardinsburg and McQuady, Kentucky areas.

CARROLL, REDMOND
was born in Mayo County, Ireland in 1814. He married Mary Doland in 1843. A daughter, Maria, was born in 1844. Mary died the same year. Redmond later married Eliza Kelly; Henry was born in 1850. Redmond and Eliza with two children came to America in 1851 and settled in Kenton County, KY, where they lived for 20 years.

Six more children were born: Anthony, Redmond, Frank, James, Elizabeth and Catherine, before moving to a farm near Wilson Station in Henderson County in 1871.

Eliza Kelly Carroll died in 1872 and was the first person buried in St. Louis Cemetery in Henderson. Now, 50 or more direct descendents are buried there.

Redmond continued living in the small log dwelling called "The Old Place" until his death in 1889.

The entire family were life long members of Holy Name Church in Henderson. When the church was built the five Carroll sons donated money for one of the stained glass windows which bears the names of their mother and father, Redmond and Eliza Carroll.

It has been 141 years since the Redmond Carroll family left their home in Ireland and came to America. Today the descendents of this courageous Irish couple embrace six generations and reside throughout the United States. They are blessed with a precious heritage of faith, family affection and love of country.

CARROLL.
The Redmond and Mary Carroll family lived in Henderson County and attended Holy Name of Jesus Catholic Church.

Redmond was born Aug. 4, 1895 to Mary Ann Cunningham and Frank Carroll. He grew up and went to school at Wilson Station. Mary was born Oct. 8, 1901 to Julia Adelle Griffin and Anthony Konsler. She grew up and went to school at Posey Chapel, graduated from Barrett High School, attended Western Kentucky University and graduated from the University of Evansville in 1960.

They were married Aug. 9, 1930 at Holy Name Rectory by Rev. P.J. Dalton. Mary was a convert to the Catholic Church in 1942.

Mary and Redmond had four daughters, Mildred (married Lamar Egart), Joyce (married Billy Don Greenwell), Mary Julia (died in infancy) and Ruth Ann. They have 14 grandchildren and 13 great-grandchildren.

Redmond farmed until he retired and moved to Henderson. He then worked at the Audubon State Park Museum and for the city of Henderson. Mary taught school many years and retired in 1970.

After retirement they both enjoyed attending daily Mass at Holy Name Church, visiting their children, grandchildren, brothers and sisters.

They celebrated their 50th Wedding Anniversary in 1980 with Mass at Holy Name Church. Many of their friends and family attended.

Redmond died Oct. 31, 1982. Mary moved to Waverly, KY, to be near her daughter, Joyce. She enjoys her new home and St. Peter Parish by going to daily Mass, belonging to the Altar Society, and has made many new friends. She still enjoys seeing and visiting with all her family.

CASH, CHARLES FREDERICK
was born Dec. 12, 1950 in Fancy Farm, KY. His parents were Robert Edwin Cash and Mary Pauline Willett Cash. He graduated from Fancy Farm High School and Murray State University, BS agriculture. He married Marilyn Susan Felhoelter Cash Aug. 19, 1972, who was born Nov. 13, 1946. She graduated Assumption High School (Lou) and Brescia College in Owensboro; received a BA in French, worked as a teacher; currently living in Eddyville, KY. Members of St. Paul Parish in Eddyville since 1977. Past members of St. Paul, Princeton, Immaculate Conception, Union City, TN and St. Leo, Murray, KY. Fred worked as dairy supervisor for West Kentucky Correctional Complex. He was murdered May 9, 1986.

Fred was a member of Parish Council, usher and Eucharistic minister. Marilyn taught and served as secretary and bookkeeper at St. Paul and a member of Women's Auxiliary, PTA, Band Boosters and 4-H.

They had three children: Christopher Patrick born Feb. 23, 1973, Karen Diane born June 30, 1975 and Kathleen Marie born June 1, 1982.

CASH, JAMES R. AND CYNTHIA (SANDERS),
were both born in Graves County and still live there. James is the son of R. Allard and Lucille (Hayden) Cash and the grandson of Robert and Anna (Boarman) Cash and James P. and Millie Hayden. Cynthia is the daughter of Barney Sanders and Mary Sue Perkins Sellers, and the granddaughter of George Dewey and Hazel (Seaford) Sanders and John and Beulah (Wyatt) Perkins.

They are members of St. Joseph Parish in Mayfield, KY. Cynthia is on Parish finance committee. James and Cindy co-chair St. Joseph annual Christmas auction which in 1991 made over $17,000.00-the largest fund raiser in St. Joseph history. He is the owner of James R. Cash Auction Company.

They have three children, Mary Katheryn Cash born June 5, 1983, attends St. Joseph School in Mayfield; James R. Cash II "Jay" born Oct. 24, 1984 also attends St. Joseph; and Amanda Caroline Cash born Jan. 11, 1989.

CASH, ROBERT LOUIS AND ANNA
lived at Fancy Farm, KY. They were blessed with 12 children: Bennett, Vernon, Otha Gertrude, Roberta, Irvin, Ethel, Alice, Nettie, Joseph, Edwin and Allard. Irvin died at 2 years of age.

They always lived in Fancy Farm in a large house near beautiful St. Jerome Church and school where they received a good education, attended church and were raised as strict Catholics. They were all taught by the Sisters of Charity of Nazareth.

All the boys and their father farmed, as their father owned a farm. The girls attended boarding schools while in high school at Mount St. Clare in Clinton, IA, Mount St. Joseph and Nazareth, KY.

Their parents were blessed with three Nuns, Gertrude (Sister Mary Henrietta) became a Sister of Charity of Nazareth in 1922, where she served as a teacher in elementary school in Kentucky, Massachusetts, Tennessee and Arkansas. After 41 years on missions she lived at Nazareth Motherhouse for 16 years. Her last eight years were spent at Nazareth Home, Louisville, KY. On April 7, 1988 she died peacefully at the age of 88.

At the age of 16, Roberta (Sr. Anne Rita) came to Mount St. Joseph, Maple Mount, KY, where she completed her education. A few months later she entered the convent at the Mount. For 53 years she taught small children in parochial and public schools in Kentucky, Missouri and New Mexico, while receiving all her college degrees. She spent 21 years in public schools in Marion County, and became a certified tutor in the Literacy Program. In 1986 Sister came to the Motherhouse and helped the sick nuns. God gifted her by taking her home Oct. 11, 1991 at the age of 88.

Ethel (Sr. Roberta Ann) completed her high school at St. Jerome. In 1924 she entered the School of Nursing at St. Joseph Infirmary in Louisville. She entered the Convent at Nazareth in 1932. She spent 14 years as supervisor of Surgical Dept. and Instructor in School of Nursing. She was director of Nursing at St. Joseph's Hospital, Lexington and Ss. Mary & Elizabeth Hospital and St. Joseph Infirmary Louisville. In 1975 she completed a course in Pastoral Care Department at Ss. Mary & Elizabeth Hospital and worked in that department until 1984. Since then she has served in the department as a volunteer.

Their mother Anna Cash died December 1934 and their father Robert L. Cash died September 1951 followed by Bennett in August 1961, Vernon Sept. 8, 1976, Otho September 1989 and Alice on Feb. 23, 1984.

Sister Roberta Ann and Nettie are the only girls still living. Nettie (Hicks), wife of the late Harry Hicks is a widow living at Water Valley, KY, a member of St. Edwards (Fulton, KY). Joe and wife Helen, Edwin and Pauline, Allard and Lucille are retired and continue to live in Fancy Farm.

Their parents Robert and Anna have 44 grandchildren and 52 great-grandchildren.

CASTLEN, DAVID,

was born in Owensboro in 1951. His parents are Ann and Ray Castlen. Ray is now deceased. Edie Wightman was born in Lakeland, FL, in 1958. Three years later she was moved to Owensboro. Her parents are Martel and Ann Wightman. They attend First Presbyterian Church. Edie attended Owensboro High School. When they married in 1974 Edie converted to the Catholic Church. Edie now belongs to Immaculate Parish and David attends St. Pius X.

Their children are Stacy, Luke and Wayne, all born in Owensboro. Stacy is 16, Luke is 14 and Wayne is 10. Stacy attends Catholic high school as a junior; Luke is in the eighth grade at Owensboro Catholic Middle School; Wayne is in the fourth grade at Catherine Spalding. Luke is active in the Immaculate Youth Group. Stacy in now working for the Water Works.

David is working at the Ragu Foods, Inc., and Edie works for the Owensboro Postal Service.

CASTLEN, GERALD P. AND BONNIE LEA (MURPHY),

the biography of the Gerald P. Castlen and Bonnie Lea Murphy Castlen family consists of three children: Patrick Lee (1986), Alexander James (1988), Stuart William (1990). The credit of their Catholic faith is due in large to their parents and ancestors.

The parents of Gerald P. Castlen are Mrs. Anna Louise Volk Castlen (1925-), and the late James Roy Castlen (1922-1982). Roy and Anna (Sis) Castlen raised seven children, being: Daniel, Joyce, David, Becky, Larry, Gerald and Mary Jo.

The Castlen line has been traced back to Virginia in the 1800s. Andrew Castlen and Anna Turner from Hanover, VA married in 1783. Their son John Castlen (1800-1835), wife Elizabeth Leet Castlen lived in Madison, IN. Their son Lee P. Castlen (1833-1905), wife Fannie Minnis died. Lee remarried Elmira Gillim and moved to Daviess County in 1862, they settled in Thruston. Their son, John Wilson Castlen (1858-1938), wife, Mary Christina, lived in Thurston on the same farm. John W. Castlen, a Methodist, converted to the Catholic faith before he died. Their son William E. Castlen (1896-1982), wife Mary Ellen Woods (1900-1988) attended St. Pius Tenth Church in Daviess County.

The Volk line is more vague due to being immigrants from Germany on the Volk side. Anna Louise Volk's father was the late Joseph E. Volk (1866-1984), wife, Anna Lorenes. His parents were Juluis Volk (1866-1901), wife Mary Holinde (1869-1911). Anna Lorenes parents were Phillip Fuerst and Anna Kleuk.

Bonnie Lea Murphy Castlen's parents are William Bernard Murphy (1917-) and Mary Helen Kerrick (1918-). They raised 11 children being: Miles, Daniel, Dennis, Dorthy, Alan, Gwendolyn, Shelia, Pamela, Bonnie, Donald and Linus.

Mr. Murphy's parents were Joseph Thomas Murphy (1888-1968), wife Mary Augusta Bickwermert (1893-1975). He was a carpenter and farmer, they moved to Newman when Bernard was a small boy. His mother's parents were William Bickwermert and Elizabeth Krampe. Mr. William (Ben) Bickwermert was a carpenter during the time of Fr. Pike at Maple Mount. He planted two rows of trees from convent to corner.

Mary Helen Kerrick Murphy's parents were James Miles (1880-1964), wife, Mary Lillian Hayden (1894-1963). Her grandparents were George Rose Kerrick (1855-), wife, Elnora Price (1855-). The Kerrick line can be traced back to Bordeaux, France.

CECIL, CLEM,

was born on March 17, 1912 in West Louisville, KY. He was baptized at St. Alphonsus Church. He was the first baby baptized by Father John Abell, thus John was added to his baptismal name and he was baptized John Patrick Clement Cecil. As the waters of baptism flooded over Clem, he joined his ancestors in embracing the Catholic faith. According to Webb's *Centenary of Catholicity in Kentucky*, published in 1880, the Cecils were conspicuous for their sterling worth and strong adherence to Catholic truth. The Cecil ancestors came from England to Maryland and then to Washington County near St. Rose Church in Springfield, KY. Clem's grandfather, Sylvester Clement Cecil, along with Clarence Mackin, came from Springfield by horseback to settle in the St. Raphael area. He farmed the St. Raphael Church farm in the late 1880's. It is said he died from working in the wet tobacco patch. At the age of 40, he left a widow with eight young children. Clem's father, Joseph Oliver was the second child. He married Loretta Murphy. They had nine children. Clem was the oldest child. He married Ann Elizabeth Wink. She died June 28, 1980. They had 11 children. Clem later married Mary Castlen. She has seven children.

Clem Cecil

Clem is a retired farmer. He has been active in the parishes where he lived, St. Martin, Rome; Blessed Mother, Owensboro; St. William, Knottsville; and St. Pius Tenth, Owensboro. He is a burgoo maker at parish picnics. He served as a member of St. Vincent De Paul Society. Clem has a strong devotion to the rosary and the Eucharist. He has attended Mass and received the Eucharistic almost daily for many years. He is currently active as Eucharist minister. He ministers to friends and family in the area rest homes.

CECIL, SISTER GEORGE ANN,

daughter of Charles Leo and Georgia Ann Mattingly Cecil, was born on Dec. 30, 1927 at West Louisville, KY. She was the fourth of ten children, three girls and seven boys. At her baptism on Jan. 12, 1928 in St. Alphonsus Church where the family belonged, she was given the name, Helen Doris. Early education for her was at St. Alphonsus School and Mount St. Joseph Academy. After high school graduation she entered Mount St. Joseph Novitiate and committed her life to God's service. She attended Brescia College for her first degree in Elementary Education and St. Louis University for a master of education degree. Later she earned an education specialist degree from Peabody College.

Sister George Ann taught at Saints Joseph and Paul School, Owensboro, KY and at Seven Holy Founders School in St. Louis, MO prior to joining the faculty at Brescia College in 1967. At Brescia she was assistant professor in special education. In 1974 she began an 11-year term as president of the College and led it successfully through much growth and development. Her tireless dedication to the college and to higher education and her personal interest in the students will long be remembered by all whose lives she touched. This and her leadership in the civic affairs in Owensboro gained her a number of city, state and national awards.

Sister George Ann died on Dec. 12, 1985 after a courageous bout with cancer.

The other members of her family are Marie Simmons, Hugh, Bernard, Robert, Leon, Paul, Frank and Mildred Higdon. Sister George Ann had four aunts who were Ursuline Sisters and an uncle who was a Dominican brother. Sisters Alicia, Celestine, and Mary Clement Cecil, Sister Paul Joseph Mattingly and Brother Martin Mattingly.

CECIL, JAMES AUGUSTINE,

was born near Knottsville, KY in 1922. His father William Ignatus was a farmer. His mother, Mary Martha O'Bryan, taught school until they married at St. William in Knottsville. Rose Ann Payne was born near Whitesville, KY in 1922. Her father William Guy Payne was a farmer, carpenter and blacksmith. Her mother, Mary Bertha Boarman, a daughter of George E. Boarman, a farmer that had moved to Whitesville from Marion County, KY. Rose and James were married Nov. 25, 1943 at Camp Crowder, near Neoshia, MO, while he was serving with the Army Signal Corps. He was shipped to Europe in October 1944 and served there until the end of World War II. Rose lived with her parents and had their first child during that time.

James Augustine and Rose Ann Payne Cecil

They lived in Owensboro for four years. In the fall of 1949 they bought 183 acres near Whitesville and moved there. They lived there three years, when Rose's health, asthma, forced them to move to El Paso, TX, a warmer climate, with their six small children. He worked for Mountain States Telephone Company until they transferred back to Kentucky with South Central Bell. They bought a small farm near Whitesville at this time. They have eight children, five boys and three girls, 31 grandchildren. In 1980 Rose, James and their third son, Michael bought the funeral home in Whitesville and renamed it Cecil Funeral Home. After retiring in 1986, he worked part-time until he retired in the spring of 1992. Rose and James now live in Whitesville. They are members of St. Mary of the Woods Catholic Church.

CECIL, JAMES CLEMIE, son of William Lawson and Clara Mae Cecil and Jaqueline Anne Hood, daughter of Newell Justin and Mary Bernice Hood, have lived in the Diocese of Owensboro since birth. They were married on May 17, 1958 at St. Mary of the Woods Church in Whitesville by Rev. Martin H. Nahstoll and became members of Blessed Mother Parish. They moved to St. William Parish in 1960.

Five children were born into the family, two of which died at birth. Their three daughters live in the Owensboro Diocese and all have productive careers. They are very proud of them and their five grandchildren.

Clemie supported his family by working at Green River Steel until it closed in 1985. Clemie was an active member of Lions Club and a volunteer fireman.

CECIL, JOE AND BARBARA (WEAFER), were married at St. Stephen Cathedral in 1979. Joe is the son of James A. and Rose Cecil. He was one of eight children raised on a farm in Whitesville, KY. He grew up in the St. Mary of the Woods Parish and graduated from Trinity High School. Barbara is the daughter of Lillian P. Weafer and the late Richard E. Weafer. She is one of nine children who grew up in St. Stephen Parish. Her family spent two years in St. Peter Parish in Stanley. During this time, Barbara attended school at St. Mary Magdalene in Sorgho. The change from St. Stephen's school with 500 students to St. Mary Magdalene with only 125 students was quite an adjustment! However, the return to St. Stephen's took an even bigger adjustment. There was a huge difference in the attitudes of "country kids" and "city kids!" Barbara graduated from Owensboro Catholic High School and Brescia College.

Joe and Barbara joined Blessed Mother Parish after their marriage, and are currently active members there. They have five children: Shelly, Brian, Alicia, Kristin and Aaron. Four of the children attend St. Angela Merici School and are active in scouting and sports. It should be no surprise that Joe and Barbara were both scout leaders and coaches for the school's volleyball team and the parish's pee-wee baseball team. Joe was also the first PTO president for the school. Barbara has been the coordinator for Blessed Mother's Children's Liturgy Program since it began in 1989.

Joseph L. and Barbara A. Cecil Family

Their children are learning the importance of parish involvement. Shelly helps in the nursery during Sunday Mass and Brian is anxiously waiting for next year when he can serve as an altar boy during Sunday Liturgies.

CECIL, MARION WILLIAM was born Sept. 6, 1923 near West Louisville, KY. He was baptized September 1923 at St. Alphonsus Church. His parents Thomas Arthur Cecil and Irene Hite Cecil were farmers. They had five children and Marion was the oldest of the five. Marion graduated from St. Alphonsus Elementary School and then went on to West Louisville High School and graduated in 1941. After graduation, Marion completed a course in electricity and was certified to wire homes. This was soon after current was brought to the rural area. He also operated his father's farm and started a dairy.

Elizabeth Maxine Riney was born Jan. 1, 1924 near West Louisville, KY. Her parents were Francis Guerdon Riney and Mabel Catherine Kelly. Maxine was baptized at St. Raphael Church in January 1924. Maxine graduated from St. Alphonsus Elementary School and then graduated from Mount St. Joseph Academy in 1942. After graduation Maxine worked as a secretary for a law firm.

On Feb. 18, 1943 Marion and Maxine were married at St. Alphonsus Church, St. Joseph, KY by Rev. James H. Higdon. They lived on the Cecil farm and had eight children: Mary, Bill, David, Alice, Pat, Mike, Janice and Betty all of whom are now married. They have 17 grandchildren and two great-grandchildren.

Marion and Maxine Cecil

Now that Marion has retired, he has turned the farming over to their son, Mike. Mike, his wife Tracy and two children operate the farm and run the dairy that Marion started many years ago. Mike lives in the home Thomas A. Cecil built in 1917. Marion and Maxine still live on the farm and are members of St. Alphonsus Church. They celebrated their 50th Wedding Anniversary on Feb. 18, 1992.

CECIL, SISTER MARY IRENE, was born near West Louisville, KY. Her father, Thomas Arthur was a farmer in Daviess County and her mother, Irene Hite, was from Union County. Early education and faith formation for her took place at St. Alphonsus Parish and School. After graduation at Mount St. Joseph Academy she entered the Mount St. Joseph Novitiate to become an Ursuline Sister. She taught in the diocese of Owensboro at Immaculate Conception, Earlington and St. Joseph, Leitchfield also in the Archdioceses of Louisville and St. Louis. She served as school supervisor and consultant in the Archdiocese of Louisville during 1969-1975. In 1975 she returned to the Motherhouse to serve the community in the ministry of leadership. In 1987 she began the ministry of service on the staff of the Diocese of Owensboro in the Office of Lay Ministry and Adult Formation and later as Coordinator of Staff, Director of Education and Adult Formation.

Brothers and sisters in her family are Winifred Marie, Marion William, Martin Hite, Thomas Arthur Jr., and two who died at birth, Hubert Joseph and Mary Irene.

Many vivid memories stand out in the life of her childhood. In the days before electricity was available to rural areas, her father went from house to house creating interest and support among farmers. Through his initiative, Green River Rural Electric extended its service to Western Daviess County. He served as a member of that organization until his death in 1969. Her mother is remembered as a person who used her gifts to serve the need of others. As a seamstress, she made many an outfit for friends and neighbors. While she sewed, she listened to their concerns with empathy. Irene died in 1977. In their later years, both her parents enjoyed their grandchildren and spent much time with them.

St. Alphonsus Parish was the center of the sacramental life of the Cecil family. Next to home this was the first awakening to God's working in their lives. They were part of all parish activities from Holy Name and Altar Societies to St. Alphonsus School and parish picnic. Both Arthur and Irene are buried in St. Alphonsus Cemetery.

CECIL, ROLAND EDWARD, was one of three children born to Alexander Cissell and Lucinda Lanham on Nov. 27, 1867. The other two children were: Catherine Rebecca and Annie Victoria. There were also four half brothers and sisters: Mary Frances, Lucinda's daughter by a prior marriage; Hilary David, John Baptist and Barbara Ellen, children of Alexander by a previous marriage. Both had known the sorrow of burying two spouses, before they met and were married.

The Cissell's were English/Irish Catholic. They were descendants of the Catholics, who migrated from Maryland and first settled in the Nelson County, KY area; later moving west and helping to establish Sacred Heart Parish in Union County. Roland was a blacksmith, carpenter and did some farming.

Roland met and married Mary Hulda Dyer, daughter of John William Dyer and Susan Catherine Fowler. Mary Hulda was the third child of eight. (See Dyer story)

Roland E. and Mary Hulda Dyer Cecil

Roland and Mary Hulda had six children: John Dyer, who married Elsie Rathman and had no children; Catherine Henrietta (Hettie), married George Reckinger, no children, but five step-children; William Alexander, married Laura Susan Veatch, adopted one daughter, Rita Marie; Roland Edward Jr., married Mizie Walker had no children; (he had one daughter by a previous, unsuccessful marriage); and Margaret Clara, who married Frederick Owen Collins, brother of Martin. They had two daughters- Clara Roberta and Ada Agnes. After being a widow for 18 years, Margaret married Herman R. Moman and had a son, Herman Roland and a daughter, Margaret Ann.

Besides raising their own children, Roland and Mary Hulda took care of her aging parents until their death.

Sometimes during the life of Roland, the spelling of Cissell was legally changed to Cecil.

CERHAN, ROBERT WILLIAM SR., was born into a Catholic family from North Liberty, IA in 1918. His father came to this country from Czechloslovakia at age 5. In 1941, Robert came to Kentucky by way of Fort Knox where he was stationed during World War II. He later settled in the New Albany and Louisville area. He is the father of two daughters and two sons. He is also the grandfather of several grandchildren and great-grandchildren.

Robert W. Cerhan Sr. and Katherine L. Shain

In 1973, he moved to the Rough River area of Grayson County. He attended St. Anthony Church at Axtel. In 1979 he became acquainted with Katherine Shain, a lifelong resident of Grayson County. They now manage Stinnett Insurance Agency and Bob's Woodcrafting. Katherine resides with her mother near Leitchfield. Bob continues to live near Rough River State Park.

They began attending St. Joseph Catholic Church in Leitchfield and in 1986, Katherine was baptized into the Catholic faith. Robert is longtime member of the Knights of Columbus, both third and fourth degrees. Katherine is active in the Ladies Auxiliary. Both are active members of their parish. At present both are serving on the stewardship committee and Robert is also serving a term on the parish council.

CINNAMOND, ROBERT AND SHARRIE,
have been instrumental in evangelizing the youth of our diocese, and simply bringing people to meet Jesus.

It began in 1972 when they each made Cursillo. Their four children; Debbie, Don, Anne and Sue remember, "After their Cursillo, they were so peaceful, ready to spread the good news."

Sharrie began teaching CCD at Holy Name in Henderson where they were parishioners. Bob began working with the Inner-City Group to tell them about Jesus. Before long, the whole family was involved. The kids went with their parents to Ultreyas every week and they said nightly prayers together also. "Christianity was a way of life in the household. The presence of Jesus was always there."

Bob and Sharrie worked with a team of others to begin their T.E.C. movement. They longed for the day their children could make a T.E.C. They were lay directors for T.E.C. and began working in Youth Ministry.

In 1979, God sent the Cinnamonds to Whitesville.

Debbie finally made the T.E.C. 13, then Don T.E.C. 20; Anne, T.E.C. 13 and Sue, T.E.C. 54.

Bob and Sharrie were working on Cursillo, Y.E.S. and R.E.C. weekends. They were active in RENEW and Youth Ministry.

Bob and Sharrie Cinnamond

In 1983, while Sharrie was Archivist for the National T.E.C. board, the National T.E.C. Convention was held in Owensboro and the whole family was involved. Sharrie worked as administrative assistant for St. Mary of the Woods Parish and also earned a degree in Pastoral Ministry. Today, she works for the Glenmary Sisters in Owensboro. Bob served on the T.E.C. Board, Catholic Cursillo board and also earned his doctorate in mathematics. He is an associate professor and now chairman of the Math Department at Brescia.

The children have followed in their parents' footsteps by working on T.E.C. and Cursillos, helping with Youth Ministry and by instilling a strong faith in their own children.

Debbie and Gary Hagan have two children, Marie and Allen.

Don graduated from Brescia and is teaching high school.

Anne and Danny Howard have three children, Ben, Ashley and Brian.

Sue graduated from Franciscan University of Steubenville and is also teaching.

"Our parents, over the years, gave us the best gift that parents could: Love of God and life. We Cinnamonds will always be active in spreading the good news of Jesus."

CISSELL, ALEXANDER,
was born in Nelson County, KY, on March 1, 1817; the son of Charles C. and Catherine (McPherson) Cissell. The other three children, Helen, John T. and Elizabeth Ann were born after they moved to Union County. They arrived there in 1820 and helped to establish Sacred Heart Parish.

The Cissells were fruit growers and planted trees wherever they went.

Alexander Cissell — Lucinda Lanham Cissell

In 1840 Alexander married Elizabeth Blandford and fathered three children: Hilary David, John Baptist and Barbara Ellen. Elizabeth died when Barbara Ellen was only a few days old. Later in 1863 Alexander married Olivia Riggs. She lived less than one year after their marriage. Then on Nov. 22, 1864, Alexander married Lucinda Lanham, who had also lost two spouses to death. Lucinda was the daughter of William and Catherine (Shehan) Lanham from Washington County, KY. She had one daughter from a prior marriage-Mary Frances. Alexander and Lucinda had three children of their own: Catherine Rebecca, Roland Edward and Annie Victoria. They were both buried in St. Agnes Cemetery within three years of each other.

Alexander was six feet tall in his stocking feet and Lucinda was very small.

CISSELL, JOSEPH BENJAMIN AND HETTIE JANE (HAYDEN).
Margaret Catherine, daughter of George Silas and Martha Jane (Mayes) Cissell, born April 8, 1845 was baptized at Sacred Heart, Union County, on May 18, 1845. The family of Silas and Martha was listed in the 1860 Hickman County Census.

In 1870 Hickman County Census there appears: Silas (49), Martha (43), George (20), Frances E. (18), Martha E. (14), John I. (10), James T. (6), Barney (3) and Joseph B. (1).

Silas and Martha (died 6/1/ 1904) had 13 children, seven died young, and six grew to adulthood: Frances Ellen (died 6/1/1904) married Jim Courtney, Martha Eleanor, John Ignatius married Annie Hayden, James Thomas married Etta (Dotson) Hayden, Barney married Amanda Luella Glisson and Joseph Benjamin born (8/20/1869 died 3/4/1959) married Hettie Jane Hayden born (10/22/ 1871 died 5/30/1940) (a sister of Annie) on Jan. 7, 1892 in Cairo, IL. Hettie is the daughter of Jessie A. Hayden (4/21/1843-1/25/1919) and Jane Carrico (dates unknown).

Joseph Benjamin and Hettie had 13 children: Artie (1893-1928) married Guy Piersall; Joseph Felmyr (1894-1971) married May Pease; Charles Edwin (1896-1984) married Liza Kate Felts; Annie (1897-) married Bernard Elliott; Alice (1899-1978) married Herman Curtsinger; Beatrice (1901-1985) married Joseph Leslie Wilson; Celestine (1902-1969) married Nell Phipps; Joseph Benjamin (1904, died at birth); Martha Jane (1906-1972) married Vernon Bugg; Teresa (1908-1957) married Jack Tibbs; Jesse Bernard (1910-1913); Jane Cecilia (1912-)

Joe Ben Cissell and Hettie Jane Hayden Family Back row: L to R: Alice, Felmyr, Artie, Edwin, Anne Middle Row: Beatrice, Joe Ben, Hettie, Martha, Celestine Front Row: Teresa, Bernard, Cecilia (on Hettie's lap) Note: Eleanor was born at this time.

married Josh Gupton; Eleanor Pauline (1914-) married Eugene Templeton.

Eleanor told Sr. Dorothy Wilson (daughter of Beatrice) that Martha Mays and her sister were orphans and grew up at St. Vincent's, KY. She was a "little bidy" woman, smoked a clay pipe after breakfast and supper each day and served as a mid-wife in the area. Beatrice told Sr. Dorothy that Mass was celebrated at Hettie's parents home before St. Charles Parish was formed. Hettie's youngest sister, Dona (1884-1955) joined the Little Sisters of the Poor in 1904 and was known as Sr. Martine de l'Immaculee.

CLARK, HAROLD RAPHAEL SR. AND ANNE TERESA KELLER,
were married on Jan. 12, 1952 at St. Stephen Cathedral, Owensboro, KY. They have been active members of Blessed Mother Parish for 40 years. They have four children: Joan, Father Ray Clark (Harold Raphael Clark Jr.), Patricia and Cathy Clark Bowlds.

Anne's parents were George Keller and Rose Schrecker Keller. She grew up in Rome, KY and was a member of St. Martin Parish. Rose Keller was a very devout Catholic and she passed that on to her children. The Catholic church always played a very important part in Anne's life. She felt the most important gift she could give her children was the gift of a Catholic education. Anne and Harold are daily communicants.

Harold R. and Anne Clark Family

Harold's parents were Virgil Dyer Clark and Orean Schadler Clark. The Schadler's were members of St. Elizabeth Parish in Curdsville, KY.

Their daughter, Joan, a teacher is married to Jim Toth and lives in South Carolina. Joan is a CCD teacher, Eucharistic minister and a lector. When Joan lived in Owensboro, she was a small-group leader for RENEW, taught CCD at Blessed Mother, and was in the Legion of Mary.

Their son, Harold Raphael Clark Jr., a teacher, was ordained a priest on May 25, 1991. Father Ray was assigned to Our Lady of Lourdes Church in June 1991.

Their daughter, Patricia, a teacher, lives in Colorado with her husband, Dan Schlesinger and their two daughters, Kimberly and Catherine. Patty played the organ at Blessed Mother Church.

Their daughter, Cathy, a teacher, married Harvey Bowlds. They have three children, Christopher, Mary Anne and Michael and attend Our Lady of Lourdes in Owensboro.

Harold and Anne are Eucharistic ministers for the sick and are members of Legion of Mary. Harold is in the St. Vincent De Paul and is very active in the Sierra Club.

CLARK, JESSE A. AND ROSE AGNES (HARRIS),
were married May 25, 1910 by Father Anthony Helling in St. Elizabeth Church in Clarkson. They were descendants of early Catholic settlers who came to Kentucky from Maryland, and originally settled in Washington and Nelson Counties, and later migrated to Grayson and Hardin Counties.

Jesse and Rose spent their married life on his father's farm, situated midway between Clarkson and St. Paul. They had nine children: Edwin, Clarence, Rudolph, Margie, Aloysius, Louis, Mary Camilla (died in infancy), Thomas and Rebecca. The surviving children today are Margie Clark, Thomas Clark and Rebecca Darst.

Two of the sons became priests, Fr. Clarence, a member of the congregation of the Resurrection, who died

Feb. 2, 1978 at St. Theresa Cathedral, Hamilton, Bermuda. Fr. Tom was ordained in 1955 and is presently the pastor of Holy Name of Jesus Church in Henderson, KY.

The Clark Family

The Clark family was steeped in traditional Catholic practices of the time. Living equal distance from St. Elizabeth in Clarkson and St. Paul on Big Clifty-Tar Hill Road in Grayson County, both churches were attended whenever services were held. Travel to these churches was either by walking or by wagon. Frequently Mass would be held only once a month at St. Paul due to road conditions caused by bad weather.

Jesse would be called an early church activist, since he would drive Bishop O'Donoghue, Bishop of Louisville in a horse drawn buggy to the many Catholic Churches in Grayson County when he was in this area for administering the sacrament of Confirmation.

The descendants of Jesse and Rose were quite numerous, 20 grandchildren, 27 great-grandchildren and one great-great-grandchildren.

Presently, Margie and Rebecca are active members of St. Paul Parish, St. Paul, KY.

CLARK, JOSEPH DALE AND ANNA JEAN, were married at St. Paul Parish in Grayson County on Sept. 18, 1971. They had five children: Carl, Nancy, Gary, Joseph Paul and Mary Elizabeth. Carl was killed in an accident on Aug. 14, 1986.

Dale's parents are Joseph Mitchel Clark and Mary Pauline Hazelwood. They have six children. Dale was the oldest, then came Janice, Susie, Tom, Roger and Marsha. Marsha, their youngest died in 1963 from a congenital heart defect.

Anne's parents are Joseph Paul Clark and Rosa Catherine Milliner. They have 10 children, but the oldest two died at birth. Fortunately, the next eight survived, they are: Norbert, Sammy, Martina, Danny, Lowell, Christina, Kathleen and Anna Jean. When Anna was born, her mother, Rosa died. With plenty of help from the parish, her father managed to send Anna along with her four brothers and three sisters to St. Paul Catholic School. Dale's parents did the same with their five remaining children. When Anna was still too young to officially attend school, the good sisters of Mount St. Joseph who taught at the school, allowed her to come and sit with her sister, Kathleen in the double, wooden desk. They gave her plenty of warm love when the weather was too cold for her to accompany her father to the fields. The loving help that Anna has received from them and her surrounding parish has caused her to remark often, "I didn't have "A" mother; I had a whole parish full of them!"

CLARK, JUSTIN AND VIRGINIA, have lived in St. Paul Parish, Grayson County all their lives. They married, Dec. 27, 1941. Rev. Charles A. DeNardi officiated at their wedding. Justin was in the service for about four years (1942-January 1946). Virginia spent that time at her parents home. They lived briefly in Louisville returning to their farm in a few months, where they farmed and Justin commuted daily to Louisville as a carpenter helper. With no children of their own, they had nieces and nephews all summer long every summer, during school vacations. Justin has now retired from carpenter work and farming. They have been and still are very active in church and school work. He has served on the parish council and ushers. He mowed the St. Paul Cemetery for several years, still does some mowing around church and helps with the up-keep of the grounds. She is always helping with the picnic and socials, funeral meals, member of St. Paul Ladies Quilters and active in the R.C.I.A.

Justin and Virginia Clark

They celebrated 50 years of marriage in December 1991. Their anniversary celebration was at the same parish, same priest officiated (Rev. Charles A. DeNardi) and attendants were the same-Michael Darst (brother of Virginia) and Margie Clark (cousin of Justin) were still here to help them in the renewal of their vows.

Virginia is the daughter of Joseph Ernest and Annie Ruby (Tackaberry) Darst. Justin is the son of James I. Clark and Sarah Ellen (Pearl) Clark.

CLARK, THOMAS A., was born Feb. 1, 1920. Mary Marguerite Clark was born Sept. 26, 1918. They were married Feb. 26, 1926. They have lived in Whitesville, Daviess County, KY, since birth. Marguerite is the daughter of William Guy Payne (born Feb. 16, 1888 died April 1983) and Mary Bertha (Boarman) Payne (born April 9,1895 died Feb. 19, 1981) who came from Marion County. Thomas is the son of John Samuel Clark (born Aug. 21, 1875 on a wagon train in Iowa) and Florance Agnes (Mills) Clark (born Aug. 13, 1882 died Feb. 8, 1960) who came from Grayson County. John Samuel died Aug. 9, 1949. Thomas served in World War II for four years.

They are members of the St. Mary of the Woods Parish. Marguerite is a member of the Altar Society and works at the quilt stand at the church picnics. Thomas worked for years carving meat at the picnics.

Thomas Andrew and Mary Marguerite (Payne) Clark

They have nine children and 33 grandchildren: Anna Jean Clark Wathen (Nov. 19, 1940), Edward Andrew Clark (May 24, 1948), Doris Mae Clark Howard (Jan. 26, 1950), Darrell Raymond Clark (Oct. 12, 1951), Margie Loraine Clark (Feb. 21, 1953), Kathy Maxie Turner (Sept. 30, 1954), Jaycee Cecilia Payne (Jan. 14, 1958), William Paul (Dec. 8, 1959) and Thomas Joseph Clark (April 29, 1961).

CLARK, LUCILLE (Sister Tresine), was born May 31, 1909 in Uniontown, KY. She was the daughter of Robert S. Clark (1878-1923) and Rillie Pike (1885-1914), their only child. At the death of her father, she went to live with her grandmother, Cordelia Pike, in Rhodelia, KY. Lucille attended grade school and two years of high school at Raywick, KY where her aunt, Sister Amadeus Pike, OSU, was teaching. The last two years of high school were spent at Mount Saint Joseph Accademy, Maple Mount, KY.

In September of 1932, Lucille entered the convent of the Ursuline Sisters at Mount St. Joseph where she was given the name, Sister Tresine. Sister Tresine began her studies to become a teacher at Mount Saint Joseph Junior College and completed her higher education at Nazareth College in Louisville. She taught in grade schools of Kentucky for fifty-four years. Eighteen of these years of teaching were spent at Saints Joseph and Paul School in Owensboro where she trained Student Teachers from Brescia College.

In August of 1988 Sister Tresine retired from teaching and went to live at the Motherhouse.

CLARK, VIRGINIA B., Thomas Roland Mattingly married Sally Genoa Roberts and attended St. Stephen Church. He was born in Breckenridge County. Sister Mary Sylvester SCN was his sister. Above grandparents of this recorder gave birth to Virginia, Cora and Barney Mattingly. Cora married Fred Burris and produced nine children. Fred was not Catholic but married Cora at St. Martin, Rome, KY, 1919. Virginia Irene, oldest of nine (recorder) was baptized with two younger children at this time. Future children were baptized at St. Stephen Church, after the family moved to Owensboro, and recieved First Communion and Confirmation.

This recorder married Robert C. Clark Sr. in 1931, St. Julian Church, Ashland, KY. Born in 1906, Robert was baptized at St. Paul, in Owensboro, where he received First Communion and Confirmation. The Clark family lived in Eastern Kentucky where two children were born and baptized, Robert C. Clark III and Doris Marie Clark. The family returned to Owensboro in 1939 and attended St. Stephen Cathedral. The children were educated at Blessed Mother School and graduated from St. Francis Academy.

Doris spent two and one-half years at Nazareth Juniorate. After graduation she married Herbert Anthony Hayden, son of Ferdinand and Borgia Hayden in 1950. They produced nine children. Anthony died in 1989. Doris later married Raymond Haragan.

Robert C. Clark III served as altar boy, graduated from St. Bernard Junior College and Brescia, joined the Navy, married Marie Honnold of Chrisman, IL. They produced two children.

Robert S. Clark Sr., was vice-president of the Holy Name Society, member of St. Vincent De Paul Society at St. Stephen, usher, weekly hospital visitor and prayed the rosary daily. Robert died in 1973.

Virginia B. Clark

His wife, Virginia Burris Clark was secretary/treasurer of the Altar Society at St. Stephen, belonged to the Sacred heart League, Legion of Mary and continues faithful to the Catholic tradition.

CLARK, WILLIAM PAUL AND SHARON MARIE (MILLS), were both born and raised in Daviess County, now living in Whitesville. William is the son of Thomas A. Clark and Marguenile Payne Clark. Sharon is the daughter of John William Mills and Elizabeth Eloise Burch Mills. They are members of St. Mary of the Woods Parish. Bill is a supervisor for McDonald's Corporation, Sharon is a registered nurse in the surgery department at St. Mary Hospital. They have two daughters, Jillian Marie Clark born Feb. 26, 1982 and Jennifer Michelle Clark born Nov. 13, 1983. Both attend St. Mary of the Woods Church.

CLEMENTS, LeROY AND JOYCE ANN (HAYDEN),

have lived in Owensboro all their lives. They have been members of the Immaculate Parish since its beginning. They were married at Immaculate by its first pastor, Father C.R. Carrico, on Sept. 17, 1955. They have two daughters-Janet Kathryn, now married to David Harris and living in Owensboro, and Terri Ann, who resides in Evansville, IN.

LeRoy worked for Sears for 19 years; then worked as an account executive for WVJS for seven years, leaving to go into the home exterior business for himself. He is now retired.

Joyce is retired from the city of Owensboro, where she worked for 23 years. She was a senior analyst/computer programmer at city hall.

LeRoy and Joyce Ann (Hayden) Clements

The Clements' have three grandchildren. The oldest, Melissa, attends OCMS, while Michael and Michelle attend St. Angela Merici School.

LeRoy is past president of the Immaculate Men's Club, past president of Brescia Alumni and Downtown Merchants. He is active in the St. Vincent De Paul Society, the Knights of Columbus and is a hospitality minister at Immaculate. Joyce is a past president of the Immaculate Altar Society, and is a Eucharistic Minister.

LeRoy's mother and father, nee Evelyn Shelton and Thomas Earl Clements, attended St. Paul Church. They are both deceased. Joyce's mother and father, nee Virginia Medley and Charles Al Hayden, were in the Immaculate Parish family from its beginning. Mr. Hayden died on Sept. 27, 1992 and Mrs. Hayden is now residing in a nursing home in Paducah, KY, where Joyce's brother, Bernard lives.

CLEMENTS, ZENA CATHERINE WEAVER,

(1907-1991) was an active member of the Western Kentucky Diocese during her 83 years. Zena was one of nine children of Martin and Elizabeth Birchler Weaver. The Weavers originated from Indiana—by way of Switzerland and Germany—and settled in Utica, KY. Zena married Joseph Earl Clements (19?-1954) and they had a daughter, Mary Earlene. Zena was an active member of St. Anthony Parish where she served as a cook for the school and cleaned house for the priests. When she later moved to Owensboro (following the deaths of her husband and parents), Zena remained active in her faith. She was a dedicated parishioner of Sts. Joseph and Paul and a loyal member of the Army of Mary, the Legion of Mary, the Altar Society and the Confraternity of Christian Mothers. Zena was also a dedicated missionary as she helped lead several people to the Catholic faith.

Following some heart problems, Zena moved to Riverside Manor in Calhoun, near her daughter and family. She took up painting and won recognition for some of her work—even being published in the national Collection of Art and Poetry by the Hillhaven Corporation.

Zena's daughter, Earlene, married Jerry Roberts Abney in 1959. They are members of St. Sebastian in Calhoun, where they have been active in the Knights of Columbus Altar Society and the CCD program. The Abneys have five children and three grandchildren: Cathy and Todd Burden and Emily of Hopkinsville; Rob and Katie Abney and Joe and Jenny of Lexington; LeeAnn and Scott Starkey of Richmond; and Greg and Nicholas Abney of Calhoun.

Zena Catherine Weaver Clements

Zena is also survived by her niece, Carole Weaver Peak, whom Zena raised following the death of Carole's mother. Carole and her husband, Tommy, have two children, Steve and Kristen. They reside in Owensboro.

Zena is also survived by two brothers, Leo Weaver and Eugene "Slick" Weaver, of Evansville and Owensboro, respectively.

"Daney" as Zena was a wonderful person and an exemplary model of Catholic living. She is sorely missed by all.

CLEMONS, CARMEL AND ODALINE.

On Tuesday, April 19, 1949, at the 8:00 a.m. school Mass at Wax, Odaline Johnston, born in Dog Creek on April 10, 1930, daughter of Vera and Ewell, married Carmel Clemons, born in Pearman on March 7, 1926, son of Nora and Clarence. Carmel walked one and one-half miles up the creek from Wax to the Johnston homeplace to pick up Odaline for the early wedding.

Carmel had clerked his father's second general store at Wax from 1939-42, and served in the Army from 1945-47, spending the first year in post-war Japan. Odaline had helped her parents on the farm with 10 younger children. Both had eighth grade educations.

The Clemons' lived on (and worked) his father's farm in Pearman until 1960 (they worked it even longer), growing tobacco, corn, hay and livestock. Carmel and Daymon Clemons also ran a three county hay-baling business, producing up to 100,000 bales in busiest years. During these years, the first five of their eight children were born, beginning with the oldest, Dwayne, now living in Frankfort. All eight children were born in St. Joseph Infirmary, Louisville.

In 1957, the couple bought a nearby 160-acre farm and began, along with their oldest children, to clear it of brush and rocks. In 1960 they moved into a new home where Odaline and Carmel continue to live in retirement.

Carmel and Odaline Clemons

In 1962, Carmel began a fertilizer/farm supply business which continued to expand until his retirement in 1989.

Carmels' retirement hobbies are lawn care, dabbling in the stock market, Red's baseball and U.K. basketball games. Odaline likes to read, sew and visit the sick and elderly.

Odaline and Carmel have always been members of St. Benedict Parish. In 1963 when the almost new church burned, they discovered the nighttime fire. Since the Wax area had no telephone service, Carmel drove several miles to phone the fire department and pastor.

Because of living next to the church, Carmel has taken care of various needs/problems with the building; Odaline belongs to a bereavement committee providing meals after funerals.

CLEMONS, CHARLES HUBERT AND MARY EDITH "BILLIE" MERCER,

were married on Aug. 11, 1961. He is the son of the late Dillard Clemons and Maude Sims Clemons. Hubert was born on April 15, 1939 and has been a lifetime member of St. Anthony Church, Peonia, KY. He was baptized by Fr. Benedict Huff on May 13, 1939. He was employed at Brown Williams in Louisville, KY for 20 years while also farming in Peonia and is presently farming as well as running a dairy. Hubert is actively involved in the parish as a parish council member, Eucharistic minister, an RCIA sponsor as well as other commitments to the church.

Billie Mercer was born on June 26, 1945. She is the daughter of the late Hezzie Mercer and Zelphia Scott Mercer of Leitchfield. She is a housewife. She became a full member of the Catholic church on Easter Sunday of 1990 and was baptized by Fr. Gary Payne. Billie is also actively involved in the parish.

Billie and Herbert have five children: Tammy Embry of Leitchfield, Charlie Clemons of Clarkson, Zina Higdon of Clarkson, Chris Clemons and Shannon "Sled" Clemons of Clarkson. They also have five grandchildren.

Billie and Herbert were both involved in the 1991 renovation of St. Anthony Church in Peonia.

CLEMONS, SISTER CHERYL (SUSAN),

born on March 29, 1951, was the second child of Odaline and Carmel. She attended St. Benedict and Peonia Grade Schools, and graduated from Mount St. Joseph Academy in 1969. She enrolled at Brescia College in August 1969 and entered the Mount St. Joseph Ursuline Community the following January (1970).

Cheryl graduated from Brescia College with a BA in French in 1974 and made final vows in the MSJ Community on July 24, 1977. She taught two years (1973-75) at St. Romuald High School, Hardinsburg; four years (1975-79) at MSJ Academy; one year (1979-80) at Lourdes High School, Nebraska City, NE; and three years (1980-83) at Trinity High School, Whitesville. During this time, she completed her MA in theology from the University of Dayton, graduating in 1984.

Cheryl (Susan) Clemons

Cheryl was director of the office of Social Concerns for the Diocese of Owensboro from 1983-1987. In January 1988, she began work on her Ph.D in historical theology from the Catholic University of America in Washington, DC. She is currently writing her doctoral dissertation on the writings of St. Gertrude the Great, a 13th Century Benedictine mystic.

In July 1992, Cheryl was elected to a four year term of leadership on the Mount St. Joseph Community Council.

For relaxation, she enjoys walking, reading, M.A.S.H, Perry Mason and Star Trek re-runs; music and visiting with community, friends and family.

CLEMONS, DARREN (LEE),

eighth and last child of Carmel and Odaline, was born on April 22, 1969. He attended Clarkson and St. Paul Grade School and Grayson County High School. He graduated in 1987. He has taken courses at University of Kentucky and has begun working towards a civil engineering degree through Elizabethtown Community College and U.K.

Darren (Lee) Clemons

Darren worked in the family fertilizer business until his father's retirement, and continues to work part-time in his brother Kendell's surveying business.

His hobbies include golf and sports of every kind, including deer hunting. He lives in Leitchfield and belongs to St. Joseph Parish, Leitchfield.

CLEMONS, DELMA THOMAS, was born in Jan. 9, 1939 in Pearman, KY, Grayson County, the 12 of 14 children of Clarence L. Clemons and Nora Frances Sims. Their dad was a farmer, businessmen and postmaster. Their family was deeply rooted in the Catholic faith. They always prayed together and attended their parish church, St. Benedict, Wax, KY. St. Benedict School was staffed by the Ursuline Sisters of Mount St. Joseph. Fr. Turner Wilson baptized Delma. The first priest that he recalls was Fr. Leo Dienes who scared him to death in confession. Fr. Vic Boarman was their next pastor. He and Sr. Martin Gertrude were instrumental in fostering his vocation to the priesthood, along with the living faith exemplified by his parents and family. He entered St. Thomas Seminary, Louisville, KY, following the eighth grade in 1954. From there he attended St. Mary Seminary, Marion, KY, from 1960-62. He studied theology at St. Maur's Seminary, South Union, KY, 1962-66. He was ordained to the priesthood for the Diocese of Owensboro, KY, on May 1, 1966 in St. Benedict Church, Wax, KY. Fr. Clemons first assignment was to St. Joseph Church, Bowling Green, KY under Fr. Charles Patrick Bowling. After one year he became associate pastor of St. Joseph and St. Paul, Owensboro, KY under Monsignor Peter Braun. He served there from 1966-71 when he was assigned pastor of St. Paul, Princeton, KY, Resurrection, Dawson Springs, KY and chaplain of Kentucky State Penitentiary, Eddyville, KY. This assignment continued for 10 years-1971-81. He was finally paroled and assigned as pastor of Christ the King Church, Madisonville, KY, 1981-85. In 1985 Bishop John McRaith assigned Fr. Clemons pastor of Our Lady of Lourdes Parish, Owensboro, KY, where he continues to serve today.

Delma Thomas Clemons

Priesthood for Fr. Clemons is a wonderful life of joy, excitement, satisfaction and fulfillment. His security and support comes from the wonderful people of faith in his own family and the parishes. God's people are accepting, loving, enthusiastic, generous and courageous. He is overwhelmed by the faith and goodness of God's people.

CLEMONS, (JEFFREY) CRAIG, born on Sept. 12, 1959, was the fifth child of Odaline and Carmel. He attended Peonia Grade School, Clarkson and Grayson County High Schools, graduating from the latter in 1977. In 1985, he graduated from the University of Kentucky with a BS in civil engineering, and obtained his state license in 1991. He presently works for the State Highway Department in Bowling Green.

On Aug. 26, 1989 at St. Anthony Church, Peonia, Craig married Regina Powell, born on Aug. 15, 1961, the daughter of Waymon Powell and Lavada Powell of Leitchfield. Regina received her RN from Elizabethtown Community College in 1988 and is currently employed as a home health care nurse in Grayson County.

Craig and Regina Clemons

In 1989, Regina joined the St. Joseph Parish RCIA Program and was received into the Catholic Church on Holy Saturday 1990.

Craig and Regina are members of St. Joseph Parish. Craig's hobbies include playing golf, watching football, basketball and playing cards. Regina spends her spare time caring for her family, her grandmother and her two nieces. Both Craig and Regina enjoy working outside in their yard.

CLEMONS, (LAWRENCE) KENDELL, was born on Dec. 2, 1953, the third child of Carmel and Odaline. He attended St. Benedict and Peonia Grade Schools. Throughout high school, he played basketball for his home team of Leitchfield High; he graduated in 1972.

Kendell attended the University of Kentucky for two years before returning home to work in the family fertilizer business and help take over the care of the farm. He also began to do land surveying. In 1985 and 1986, he and his father, Carmel, were joint partners in the fertilizer/farm supply business.

On Sept. 28, 1985 he married Deneace Wilson of Caneyville, KY, daughter of D.B. and Helen Wilson. Deneace was born on Nov. 6, 1958. The couple lives in Leitchfield.

In 1986 Kendell went into the land surveying as a full-time business. In 1985 he became county surveyor. Deneace has an associate degree in nursing, a BA degree in dietetics and institution administration and an MS in public health. She works as director of dietary services in the Leitchfield/Grayson County Hospital.

For their hobbies, Kendell enjoys sports; the couple enjoys garden and yard work, entertaining friends and travel.

CLEMONS, NORA (FRANCES) SIMS, daughter of Mr. and Mrs Joseph Sims, was born on Christmas Day, 1899. In January 1918, she married Clarence (Lee) Clemons, son of Mr. and Mrs. A. J. (Andy) Clemons, who had been born on Christmas Day, 1898. Nora had two brothers, Albert and Robert. Clarence had one brother, Arnold; two half-sisters, Lela (Alvey) and Ola (Powell); and two half-brothers, Williard and Leonard. Ola grew up in her brother Clarence's home, where she lived until she married.

In their first year together, Clarence and Nora lived and farmed in Snap, Grayson County. In the early 1920s, they moved to Pearman and took over the farm and general store from his father. Clarence ran the store, which included a U.S. Post Office, until 1967. At one time, he also had another store at Wax.

Clarence and Nora Clemons, 50th Anniversary

The couple had 14 children, three of whom died in infancy. The 11 who lived to adulthood were Leta (who married Courtland Clemons), Kenneth (married Eugenia "Jo" Pierce), Hazel (married Arthur Higdon), Carmel (married Odaline Johnston), Audrey (married Daymon Clemons), Melvie (married Edward Clemons-brother of Damon), Mildred (married Lionel White), Ernestine "Norma" (married Jack Robinette), Daris (married Dorothy Bradley dec., married Sue Metcalf), Delma (Owensboro diocesan priest) and Paul (married Brenda McKinley).

Clarence and Nora belonged to St. Benedict Parish all their married lives. Clarence served as a parish trustee for many years, along with Claude Johnston.

Clarence died in March 1970 of kidney disease. Nora continued to live in the family home connected to the store until her death in 1982 by a stroke.

CLEMONS, TOMMY, was born near Wax, KY, in Grayson County on March 20, 1941. He was baptized by Fr. Robert Wilson at St. Benedict Church in Wax. His father, Arthur Clemons was a carpenter and farmer. He died in 1977. His mother, Elsie Hill Clemons is a homemaker. She lives in Grayson County and is member of St. Anthony Church in Peonia, KY. Tommy has 10 brothers and sisters, most of whom still live in Grayson County.

Tommy works at Ford Motor Company in Louisville, KY, and farms part-time. He is an usher at St. Anthony Church and a member of Knights of Columbus.

Tommy Clemons Family

Judy Johnston was born in Hart County, KY, on Aug. 3, 1944 and was baptized by Fr. Leo J. Dienes at St. Benedict Church in Wax, KY on Sept. 3, 1944. Judy's family moved to a farm near Wax, KY when she was an infant. Her father, Ewell Johnston was a farmer. Judy's mother, Vera Bradley Johnston, was a homemaker. They raised 14 children. She died in 1984. Judy married Wendell Wadell in 1962. They had one son David, born on March 21, 1963. Wendell died when David was 5 years old. In September 1971, Tommy and Judy were married at St. Benedict Church in Wax, KY. They moved to Peonia, KY. They have one daughter, Jill who was born May 16, 1975. She was baptized June 24, 1975 by Fr. Steve Dunn at St. Anthony Church. Jill is a senior at Grayson County High School. Judy is a secretary for the churches of St. Anthony, St. Benedict and St. Augustine. She is a Eucharistic minister, a catechist for Children's Liturgy and is on the

Parish Council and Finance committee. She is also active in the Knights of Columbus Ladies Auxiliary.

Both Tommy and Judy continue to be involved in the various activities of St. Anthony Church.

COCKE, EUGENE H. SR., was born in Pewee Valley, KY. Upon completion of college he moved to Owensboro to take a job. There he met and married Clara Benjamin Hagan. They had five children, Gene Jr., Jule, Bob, John and Tom. When Gene Jr., was 6 years old the family moved to Paducah where he attended St. Mary School. Upon graduation he attended the University of Kentucky. Two years later his father died and he returned to Paducah to help close his father's business. He didn't return to UK but took a job as an accountant in South Carolina.

In 1941 he was drafted into the Army and sent to Ft. Knox. There he had a blind date with Mary Ford, who lived and worked in Louisville. They were married in 1943. Mary was not a Catholic at this time but joined the church two years later. Gene was in the Army Finance Corps and during World War II was sent overseas to Ie Shima, an island in the Pacific.

Mary moved to Paducah, KY to await his return almost four years later. They had five children, Judy, Mike, Kathy, Patrick and Elizabeth Ann. Elizabeth Ann was dead at birth. They were members of St. Francis De Sales until they moved near St. Thomas More and became members there.

Upon graduation from St. Mary High School, the children left home for college and took jobs out of town, except Kathy, who works in Paducah and lives near Smithland, KY.

Eugene H. Cocke Sr. Family (1967 or 1968)

Gene was active in the Knights of Columbus, Boy Scouts, 4-H Club and American Legion. He was diagnosed as having advanced cancer in 1983 and died Jan. 25, 1984.

Mary still lives in Paducah and is active at St. Thomas More and is a member of Lourdes Hospital Auxiliary. She has four grandchildren.

COLE, JOHN LESLIE AND MARGARET ROSE ELDER, John Leslie is the son of Hubert Lee Cole and Thelma Lee Carter Cole and Margaret is the daughter of Charles Anthony Elder and Frances Aline Elder. She is the granddaughter of George Elder and Annie Toon Elder. Margaret was raised in Graves County, and John Leslie was raised in Hickman County. She works as a beautician and John is a construction worker. They are members of St. Jerome Parish in Fancy Farm, KY.

John and Margaret Cole

They have two sons, John Jeffrey Cole who was born Sept. 22, 1966 and Henry Albert Cole who was born Jan. 28, 1969. John Jeffrey married Melinda McGee Cole. They belong to St. Jerome Church.

COLLINS, JOHN WICKLIFFE, son of Phillip and Amanda Francis (Smith) Collins was born Feb. 1, 1871, the 11th child of 12 children. James W. and America Alice were his half brother and sister; their fathers were brothers. The others were: Louis B., Juliett, Jonathan Catlett Taylor, Marian Elizabeth, Mary Catherine, Phillip Otto, John B., George Simpson and Amanda Eleanor. His parents and forefathers were of English/Irish descent and active in the Baptist Church. But Wick, George and an older sister, Mariam Elizabeth met and married Catholics. They chose to become Catholics prior to their marriages.

Wick's bride was Mary Magdalene (Mollie) Veatch, the daughter of Benjamin and Eliza Magdaline (Bartley) Veatch. Mollie's brothers and sisters are listed in the Veatch story.

Not long after Wick and Mollie were married, they bought a farm near Grove Center, KY, in Union County, making them members of St. Ambrose Parish. There they remained and raised five children: Benjamin Gilbert, married Beatrice Virginia Vandiver and had six children, Virginia, Elizabeth, Robert, Margaret, Dorothy Jean and Betty Ann. (After being a widower for years, married Jessie Young Paris.) Virginia Magdaline "Virgie," married Hilary Elias French and had two daughters, Edan and Martha. Frederick Owen married Margaret Clara Cecil and had two daughters, Clara Roberta and Ada Agnes. Martin Andrew (see his story). Harry Ambrose died before he was married. They are buried in St. Ann Cemetery, as are all five of their children and the deceased members of their families.

John Wickliffe Collins Family. (L to R): Martin, Fred, Wick, Virgie, Mary, Ben and Harry (sitting in Nick's lap).

They dated on horseback or in a buggy. The boys used to love to play tricks on each other. The last one in at night would tie the others feet to the bed and when they were called to breakfast, naturally he would be the first one downstairs.

COLLINS, MARTIN, was one of five children born to John Wickliffe and Mary Magdalene (Veatch) Collins in 1898. The other siblings were Benjamin Gilbert, "Virgie" Virginia Magdalene, Frederick Owen and Harry Ambrose. They were born and raised on a farm in the St. Ambrose Parish, where they attended church. The earlier Collins' were part of the settlers, who came from Virginia to settle in Kentucky.

Martin met Annie Mary Cecil at a dance and later made her his wife. She was from Sacred Heart Parish and the daughter of Roland Edward and Mary Hulda (Dyer) Cecil. She was one of six children: John Dyer, "Hettie" Catherine Henrietta, William Alexander, Roland Edward, Annie Mary and Margaret Clara. The earlier Cecil's were with the original Catholics who migrated from Maryland in 1785.

Martin and Annie were married Jan. 2, 1924 at Sacred Heart Church, St. Vincent, KY, and set up housekeeping in the St. Ambrose Parish, where they remained for about 40 years. They farmed, first with his dad and brothers and later bought their own farm.

They eventually had eight children: Mary Elsie, Wick Edward, Hazel Anne, Reburn Martin, Margaret Catherine, "Tom" Thomas Joseph, "Susie" Barbara Susan and Therese Veronica. Martin raised corn, hay, hogs and cattle. Annie always had a huge garden and raised chickens, selling eggs and cream. They sent the children to St. Ann School and St. Vincent Academy. Annie used to read the Bible History to the children when they came home from school and they said the family rosary before going out to play and do chores.

Back Row (L to R): Wick, Martin, Mary Elsie, Annie, Hazel Front Row (L to R): Reburn, Catherine, Tom, Susie and Therese Collins.

Finally after the children grew-up, married, and moved away, they retired in Morganfield, St. Ann Parish. Wick, the oldest son, now owns and runs the family farm.

Martin and Annie had 18 grandchildren and 17 great-grandchildren.

CONDER, JODY AND ETHEL, have lived in Whitesville and belonged to St. Mary of the Woods all their lives. Jody is the only son of Charles and Mary Rose Conder, Ethel is the daughter of Fred and Mary Wright, who also belonged to St. Mary's. Jody and Ethel were married in the old St. Mary of the Woods Church on Aug. 24, 1937. They were farmers until they retired, even during the years Jody worked at Green River Steel.

Ethel belong to the Altar Society for many years. Most of their children, a lot of their grandchildren and even great-grandchildren are lectors, ushers, Eucharistic ministers, altar boys, song leaders, choir members, etc. in the Catholic church. Jody and Ethel have 15 children: Rose Brooks, Charles Conder, Vince Conder, Barb Roberts, Louis Conder, Judy Connor, Doris Hamilton, Margaret Henderson, Ina Mattingly, Connie Coomes, Debbie Connor, David Conder, Jerry Conder, Hope Brey and Terry Conder, 55 grandchildren and 27 great-grandchildren. All their lives the Conders have been affiliated with the activities concerning the Catholic education of their families; parish picnics; chili suppers, bar-b-que, quiltmaking for raffles, bingos and many other things.

The Joe Conder Family

Three of their grandsons, Tony Conder, Elwood Conder and Bruce Roberts, were active in the Persian Gulf War.

Many a Mass, many a prayer has been offered at the Conder home. Special prayers were offered during the war, and Masses have been offered for Ethel and birthdays and other occasions have been celebrated there.

Jody and Ethel have participated in the senior citizens group for several years. He now resides in Whitesville, quite different from home after living on the farm all his life. Jody and Ethel celebrated their 50th Wedding Anniversary with family members and friends in August 1987 prior to Ethel's passing away in April of 1988.

CONN, JOSEPH E. AND HELEN (COLLINS),
were united in matrimony Nov. 24, 1949 at St. Ambrose Rectory with Rev. Pius Edelen officiating. Joe is a convert to the faith. He served in World War II in the U.S. Army; entering in 1941; discharged in 1944. Five children were born into this union; three sons and two daughters: Mike, David, Joseph A., Cynthia and Constance. Mike, David and Joe served as altar boys at St. Francis Borgia. David was the first baptism at St. Francis Borgia in October 1952. Rev. Phillip Riney was the associate pastor. Cindy and Connie contributed to the music at St. Francis Borgia. Cindy was an organist. Connie and Cindy both played the guitar. Joe and Helen reside on the Conn farm with son, Mike who is engaged in farming with his father.

David married Anna Danhauer Feb. 21, 1976 at St. Ann Catholic Church. They have three children, Kelly, Karla and Will Tom. They attend St. Ann School. David is employed at Rayloc. Anna is with the U.S. Postal Service.

Cynthia married George Cole July 3, 1976 at St. Peter Catholic Church. They have three children, Sara, Georgie and Annie. Cynthia has a bachelor of science degree in elementary education. She teaches in Bowling Green, KY. George is associated with Barren River Comprehensive Care.

Joseph E. Conn and Helen (Collins) Conn

Connie married Joe Daniel June 12, 1981 and lives in Bowling Green, KY. She has an associate degree in nursing. Her husband is associated with Professional Builders. They have two daughters, Catherine Ann and Jenna Marie.

Joseph A. married April Lee Holeman Nov. 12, 1988 at St. Francis Borgia. Joe is associated with Buckman's Construction. April is employed at Richman Brothers Clothing Company. They reside in DeKoven, KY.

CONNER, GUY F. AND LINDA (SIMMONS)
were born and raised in Daviess County, KY. Guy was born March 31, 1940 and is the son of Guy and Wenona J. Conner. Linda was born Sept. 14, 1942 to Virgil J. and Lura M. Simmons. They now live just outside of Owensboro on Griffith Station Road. They are members of the Precious Blood Parish. Guy is a farmer and Linda works as a machine operator for Pinkerton Tobacco Company.

Their daughter Michele, was born Dec. 12, 1961. She is married to Michael Scott Young, and they have two children, Michael Stephen and Lindey Michele. Michele works in marketing at Pinkerton Tobacco Co.

Guy and Linda's older son, Guy "Fred" F. Conner Jr. was born Sept. 1, 1963. Fred is married to Rita M. (Ruckdaschel) Conner. They have one child, Christian, and Fred works for United Parcel Service.

Their other daughter, Selina, was born Dec. 30, 1964. She is married to Ricky L. Holder, and they have two children, Terry L. and Travis L. Holder. Selina works as a waitress at Canton Gardens.

The Conner's second son, Brian, was born May 4, 1966 and is married to Tammy Hagan Conners. Brian is employed by Frito-Lay, and Brian and Tammy work with the youth group at Precious Blood Parish.

Guy and Linda have been members of Precious Blood for more than 26 years and have been diligently active in the Men's and Women's Club, Marriage Encounter, Parish Council, St. Vincent De Paul, Eucharistic Ministry, picnics and sports.

COOMES, J. EUGENE
was born March 15, 1918, in St. Augustine, FL, far from his parents home state of Kentucky. Ordained June 1948, he worked in Belize, Central America, 1950-1979; then was assigned to St. Louis University, St. Louis, MO.

His great-grandfather was Richard Coomes, 1768-1856, eldest son of Francis Ignatius, 1718/26-1822, who was born in Maryland, Port Tobacco, Charles County.

Richard grew up in North Carolina. Family tradition has it that in his travels in the early 1790s, he met a Catholic priest, who gave him a book on the Catholic faith. He decided that the family should move to Kentucky, where they could be in a Catholic community.

Richard's son, Richard P. came to Daviess County in 1841, and settled at Knottsville.

Cebert C., Richard's youngest son, was married twice: 1861, Springfield, KY, to Anna Hanson, daughter of Peter Hanson and Mary Worland; and 1879 at St. Mary, to Fidelis Russell, daughter of William Russell and Sarah Mudd. Fidelis "Delia" was previously married to James Raphael Mattingly. A daughter of Cebert and Anna was Mary Mercy, 1862-1909 Sr. M. Ida, S.L.

Cebert C. Coomes (1830-1902) at age 22

Charles Edward, 1880-1978, was the son of Cebert and Fidelis. When Edward was 3 1/2 years old, the family moved from St. Mary to Osage Mission (St. Paul), KS, in Neosha County, west of Walnut, where Cebert's older brother, Pius, had settled in 1867. From 1887 until 1890 they lived in Joplin, southwest Missouri; then in 1894 they were in Knottsville, near Owensboro. For four years Edward attended high school with Anna Crouse, daughter of Jacob Crouse and Rebecca O'Bryan. The two were married, 1905, by Edward's cousin, Fr. Louis Spalding, pastor.

J. Eugene Coomes is the son of Edward and Anna. The other children are: Charles, born 1906; Catharine, 1908-1992; Albert Francis, ordained 1941, 1910-1986; William Egan, 1914, died an infant, Anna, 1915.

COOMES, MARY JOSEPH (Sister Marie Joseph)
was born May 9, 1940 to Joseph Bernard Coomes and Amanda Josetta Knott at Philpot, KY. Her paternal grandparents were Joseph I. Coomes and Clara M. O'Bryan; maternal grandparents were Arnold Knott and Mary Maron. Mary Joseph was baptized May 18, 1940 at St. Lawrence Church by Rev. Joseph J. Egan and given the name Mary Joseph. She received her First Holy Communion and was confirmed in the faith in 1947 at St. Lawrence. She attended St. Lawrence School from 1946 to 1955 and St. William High School from 1955 to 1959.

Mary Joseph had four sisters, Mildred Ann, Lois Marie, Margaret Cecelia, Theresa Rose and four brothers, Thomas Ignatius, Robert Aloysius, William Eugene and David Lawrence.

Mary worked for four years after graduating from high school then she entered the Mount St. Joseph Ursuline Community. She received the name Sister Marie Joseph on Aug. 15, 1965. She made final vows on July 23, 1973. As an Ursuline she was trained to be a teacher, receiving her B.S. from Brescia College in Elementary Education and an M.A. from Western Kentucky University. She spent ten years teaching primary grades in the schools in Kentucky.

In 1978 she was called to serve in the ministry of hospitality at the Ursuline House of Prayer and in the health care needs of the Ursuline Sisters at Mount St. Joseph.

COOMES, STEVE AND DIANE (SIMON).
Steve was born on March 14, 1949 in Daviess County, KY. He works at Owensboro Grain Company as a safety engineer. His parents are Marion Coomes and Mary Howard. Diane Simon was born April 1, 1953 in Daviess County, KY. She works as an Avon sales representative and a homemaker. Her parents are James Simon and Clara Ambo. Steve and Diane were married on May 11, 1973 in Sts. Joseph and Paul Parish and are still members of that parish.

Steve and Diane have five children. There is Shanda, the oldest, who is 17. Next there is Chad who is 13, Stacey is 10; Grant is 8 and Alex is 1 1/2.

Shanda goes to school at Daviess County High School, Chad goes to Owensboro Catholic Middle School, and Stacey and Grant go to Bishop Francis R. Cotton School. Shanda and Chad are involved in the Catholic Youth Organization (CYO) and Stacey is in the youth group. Steve works bingo often and Diane takes turns with others to teach children's liturgy at the 10:00 a.m. Mass.

COSSEY, RAY AND ELIZABETH (SCOTT)
have lived in Kentucky most of their lives. Ray is a convert, and a son of Clifford and Beulah (Snyder) Cossey. He was born in Neosha, MO on Oct. 31, 1921. The Cosseys came to Bowling Green in 1921. Ray graduated from Western Kentucky University's College High in 1939 and entered Western. In January 1941 he was called to active duty with the 149th Regt., Kentucky National Guard. After the war Ray joined the reactivated National Guard. When he retired in 1981 he was a lieutenant colonel and commander of the 3rd Bn. He worked at the Bowling Green Post Office from 1948-79 as city carrier, night supervisor and rural carrier. In 1976 Ray was received into the Catholic Church at Holy Spirit Church by Fr. Joe Mills.

Lib, a cradle Catholic, one of nine children of William Addison and Catherine Leonora (Spalding) Scott, was born Nov. 27, 1918 in Morganfield, KY. The family lived on a farm a mile from Sacred Heart Church and St. Vincent Academy, a girls' boarding school established by the Sisters of Charity, Nazareth, KY in 1820. The Scott children attended the academy as day scholars. In 1935 Lib and her sister Helen, graduated from St. Vincent Academy in a class of 17. That fall six girls from the class entered the Novitiate at Nazareth along with an older sister of one of the girls. Lib graduated from Mount St. Joseph Junior College in 1937. She taught in a two room rural school in Union County until December 1942.

On June 20, 1942 Ray and Lib married in a chapel at Camp Shelby, MS, by Fr. James McMahan, chaplain. Ray and Lib had four children: Gerald Ray (1943-1984), married Susan Jackson; Carolyn Elizabeth (1951-) married Robert Fleming; Mary Anne (1957-) married D. Wayne Powers; and Alisa Jane (1962-).

In the late 1960s Lib enrolled at WKU. She earned a BS and two master's degrees. She was a library faculty member at WKU from 1971-1976.

COTTON, BISHOP FRANCIS R.
was born in Bardstown, KY on Sept. 19, 1885 to Charles and Mary Moore Cotton. He received his A.B. and A.M. degrees from St. Mary Seminary in Baltimore, MD. He attended the Sulpician Seminary at the Catholic University of America in Washington, DC from 1919-1920 and was ordained to the priesthood on June 17, 1920. He served as assistant pastor of St. Joseph's in Bardstown, St. Cecelia's in Louisville, St. Francis De Sales in Paducah. He was assigned assistant chancellor of the Diocese of Louisville in 1926. In 1931 he became chancellor of the diocese, a position he retained until December, 1937 when he was appointed the first bishop of the newly formed Diocese of Owensboro. A position he held until his sudden death from a heart attack on Sept. 25, 1960. Bishop Cotton will always be remembered as an intelligent hardworking priest who used his business and architectural skills much to the benefit of the diocese.

COURTNEY, LEO BYRL AND BERNARDINE (PIERCEALL). Byrl (1885-1939) son of James Sylvester and Sarah Rebecca (Warden) Courtney, and grandson of Solomon and Lucinda (Cash) Courtney, married Sarah Bernardine (1888-1962) daughter of Martin Andrew and Anna Irene (Toon) Pierceall, and granddaughter of Benedict Joseph and Mary Elizabeth (Austin) Pierceall, on Feb. 27, 1911 at St. Jerome, Fancy Farm; 10 children.

Byrl and Bernardine (Pierceall) Courtney

In 1892 the Sisters of Charity of Nazareth began teaching school in Fancy Farm. Sister Samuella, the first principal, was the one who began training students to become teachers for the one-room rural schools, with the encouragement of Fr. Charles Haeseley, the pastor (1888-1920). After completing the 10 grades at St. Jerome, students obtained certification by successfully passing an examination administered by state officials. And some of these teachers taught their students Christian Doctrine after school. Bernardine Pierceall, who attended Mayfield College also, was one of these teachers. It is known that she taught at Pelo, Hickman County, during 1906-1907 and 1907-1908, and at Pirtle, Graves County during 1910-1911.

Anna Rita (1914), third child and second daughter of Byrl and Bernardine, married Thomas Everett (1914) son of Robert Leo and Anna Belle (Hobbs) Wilson (see Jerome Hobbs and James Wilson biographies) on Dec. 26, 1935 at St. Jerome; 15 children.

Anna Rita and Everett's children are: Willene (1937), Carolyn (1938), Mary Gladys (1940-1941), LaVerne (1941), Lawrence (1942), JoAnn (1943), Rose Marie (1/1945), Maurice Edward (12/1945), Glenn (1947), Bernard (1948), Frederick (1949), Judith Ann (1951), David Ray (1953), Albert Eugene (1954) and Steven (1956). Anna Rita and Everett have 39 grandchildren and 13 great-grandchildren.

Monsignor Edward Russell (1895-1978) was pastor at St. Jerome, Fancy Farm, from 1935 to 1962. He officiated at the wedding of Everett and Ann Rita, and he baptized each of their 15 children. This is an accomplishment seldom equaled.

CRABTREE, VIRGINIA (ALLEN), was born March 25, 1920 at St. Landry Parish, LA. Growing up in Cajun country made the Catholic religion a natural part of life, since everyone was of the faith.

Fred Crabtree was born in Gainesboro, TX, on Feb. 23, 1917. His family moved to Bowling Green, KY, when he was 3 years old. After serving in the military in World War II, he and his brother, Frank, bought land in Butler County, KY. Fred passed away on March 3, 1986. Virginia continues to live on the family property, and is a member of Holy Trinity Parish in Morgantown.

Fred and Virginia have one daughter, Teresa Elaine, born Feb. 5, 1947. Teresa now lives in Taylor, MI, and has three children, Anthony, Andre' and Nicole Bell.

Anthony Bell lives in Butler County, and is married to Theresa Belcher. Andre' attends college, while working at a sales position in preparation for a business career. Nicole is presently in sixth grade at Taylor.

With her French background, Virginia is occasionally called upon to translate letters written in that language. She has been the faithful director of the parish Thrift Shop, even though a stroke on March 15, 1992 brought partial paralysis. Recovery is slow but continuing as she resumes an active part in parish and civic activities.

She has belonged to Homemakers for 17 years, and had not missed a meeting prior to March of 1992. At various times she has held membership on the Community Action Board, Mental Health Board and the BRADD Board.

In 1988, Virginia received news that her cousin, Fr. Curtis Guillory, had been named auxiliary bishop of Houston, TX. Bishop Guillory's mother and Virginia's mothers, Camelia (Guillory) Allen, were first cousins. Bishop Guillory is a member of the Divine Word Missionaries of Bay St. Louis, MS.

CRAWFORD, DEBORAH, has lived in the St. Paul Parish all of her life. She is the oldest daughter of Tony Darst and Rebecca Clark Darst. She has three children, Jeremy David, Kyle Edward and Cari Nicole.

Deborah Crawford Family

Debbie is active in parish functions while seeing that her children receive a Catholic education. Kyle and Jeremy served as altar boys. Jeremy is a sophomore at Grayson County High School were he made the basketball and baseball team. Kyle is in the seventh grade at St. Paul Grade School and plays baseball in the summer time. Cari is in the second grade at St. Paul Grade School and plays softball in the summer.

CRAWFORD, NEIL AND LYNDA, are both natives of Grayson County. Neil was born Nov. 10, 1957 to John and Rose May Allen Crawford. Lynda was born July 9, 1959 to Tony and Rebecca Clark Darst. They were married Aug. 25, 1978 at St. Paul's Church by Rev. Thomas Clark, Lynda's uncle.

Neil and Lynda Crawford Family

They have two daughters, Carla Elaine (11) and Cindy Rose (7). They both attend St. Paul Catholic School. Neil was baptized into the Catholic church April 1990. Lynda has been a member of St. Paul Parish all of her life and attended St. Paul School.

Lynda and Neil are active members in the parish and help with parish and school activities. They both coach teams for the summer youth programs.

CRISP, JOHN ALEXANDER, was born March 31, 1842, died July 9, 1920 married Mary Elizabeth Cecil who was born Oct. 7, 1854 and died Feb. 8, 1889. John's parents were Allen Crisp and Laura Willams. One of Allen Crisp's descendents by his first wife (who was a Mudd) was Admiral Ion Purcell of the U.S. Navy. Admiral Purcell returned to Kentucky after his retirement and worked tirelessly to advance literacy in Kentucky. Mary Elizabeth Cecil Crisp's parents were George Cecil and Tabitha Barrett. Her grandparents were Richard Wheeler Barrett and Mary Wedding Barrett.

John Alexander Crisp came to Whitesville at an early age from Raywick in Marion County, Kentucky. He was a Union veteran of the Civil War, a farmer, a Republican and very anti-slavery.

The Cecil family came from Cecilia, KY, and originally had large land holdings along old Highway 54 from Hickory Road to Haynes Station Road and then back to Haynes Station. The Barrett family were natives of Maryland who came to Ohio County in the latter part of the 18th century. Richard Wheeler Barrett though not a Catholic donated in 1845 "one acre and five poles" to St. Mary of the Woods Catholic Church.

The Barrett-Cecil-Crisp families included several nuns among whom, of recent date, are Sister Dorothea Oberst, S.C.N. and Sister Eileen Howard, O.S.U. There was at least one priest, Father Paul Clifton Barrett.

John and Mary Elizabeth had eight children: Annie married Alonzo (Lonnie) Brown; Joseph married Pearl Smith; Marietta married John William (Gid) Fuqua; Agnes married James L. Shively; Lawrence married Emma Howard; Thomas died as a young boy; Zita Theresa married Elmer L. Berry; and Emma Isabelle married John Luke Oberst Sr.

CRITCHELOW, CHARLES ORTON, was born Feb. 7, 1953 to Charlie and Jean O'Donoghue Critchelow, McDaniels, KY in Breckinridge County. They were members of St. Anthony Parish, Axtel. The following year Barbara Marie Greenwood was born Feb. 2, 1954 to George and Dorothea Greenwood, Stephensport, KY in Breckinridge County, who were members of St. Theresa, Rhodelia Parish, Meade County.

Ort attended St. Anthony Grade School and St. Romuald Grade School where he met Barbara who attended St. Romuald Grade and high school. They graduated in May 1972. Married Dec. 29, 1972.

Ort worked for the state park and Barbara was attending WKU. They lived at Axtel, were members of St. Anthony Parish for nine years. During this time, Charles Orton II was born Dec. 15, 1976; Barbara received her BA from Western in education and Ort was hired at Commonwealth Aluminum, then Martin Marietta. Barbara taught one year at St. Romuald then Mark Aaron came along Sept. 28, 1980. The following year, the family moved to Hancock County, Lewisport and joined St. Columba Parish during which time Mary Lynn, born Jan. 26, 1983 and Amanda Gail born Oct. 17, 1985 were added to the Critchelow family. Barbara received her MA from Western and the family built a house near Hawesville where they have resided for five years. Barbara taught one year at Catholic High and on Sept. 20, 1989, Kyle Joseph was born. The family presently are members of Immaculate Conception Parish.

Ort is employed at Commonwealth Aluminum; Barbara is presently a homemaker and substitute teacher. Both are active church and school members. Their oldest child, Charlie is a freshman at Hancock High. Mark, fifth and Lynn, third are at Immaculate Conception, Hawesville where Amanda will be next year as a first grader.

CROWE, WILLIAM (BILL) AND ANGELA, were united as a family on Feb. 12, 1955 by the late Fr. Joseph Saffer at St. Martin Church in Rome, KY. They now have four sons, three daughters, five grandchildren and two step-daughters.

Peter, single, an over-the-road truck driver; Michael, married, two children, lives at Danville, KY; Thomas, single, Hartford, KY; Theresa, single, Opportunity Center; Sharon Garrett, married, a U.S. Marine, Oceanside, CA, one child and two step-children; Mary Jane Wood, married, two children, going to Daviess County Technical School; and Henry, single, Tampa, FL.

Bill is the son of Joseph and Martha Barr Crowe. He was the second of 13, 11 boys and two girls. They were share-crop farmers, living in several communities, including Reed for about 15 years. He was an altar boy and belonged to a youth group. He now belongs to the Men's Club, the Kentucky Wesleyan Panther Express

Basketball Bus Fans, and an usher and meat cooker for the picnic.

Angela is the daughter of Henry and Mary Catherine O'Bryan Wink. She is the oldest of 10. They moved to St. Martin Community in 1940. The whole family were active supporters in the church. She attended St. Martin and Catholic High Schools, class of 1953. She has been manager of A & W Hot Dogs and More, for over 14 years and she loves it. She is a Eucharist Minister and feels it is an honor and humble experience. She has been minister of music for 12 years, full-time at St. Martin, a member of the Diocesan Choir, St. Martin's Christian Mother's, the Diocesan Spred Group, and a member of the Owensboro Council of Retarded Citizens.

Theresa Crowe has started to work at the Opportunity Center this summer. She belongs to the SPRED Group, and some programs through Green River Comp Care. Her hobbies include watching TV, writing and looking at books.

The whole family enjoys all kinds of sports from watching to playing, country music and reading.

CUMMINGS, PAUL AND ANNE,
Hopkinsville, KY. The Cummings family arrived in Hopkinsville in August of 1975. The family moved from Weiherhof, West Germany after Paul received orders to Fort Campbell.

Paul is originally from Houlton, ME, and Anne is from Bayrisch Eisenstein, Germany. They have three children: Larry, Danelia and Sandra. In his career in the Army, Paul and the family have lived in several different areas including Arizona and Oklahoma. After retirement from the military, Paul and Anne decided to make their permanent home in Kentucky.

The Paul and Anne Cummings Family

The children however have since moved on. Larry is now a priest serving the Diocese of Owensboro. He is currently full-time at Owensboro Catholic High School and pastor of St. Augustine Church in Reed, KY. Danielia (Dee) is married and living in Hilliard, OH, with her husband and two sons, Jeffrey who is 9 years old, and Wesley who is 1. Sandra (Sandy) and her husband are both in the Navy, living in California and expecting their first child.

Paul is a member of the Methodist Church and Anne belongs to the parish of Sts. Peter and Paul in Hospkinsville.

CURTSINGER, JAMES E. AND FRANCES PEARLE WILLETT,
were married on Oct. 26, 1946 at St. Joseph Church in Bowling Green, KY. James was born April 15, 1916 and Pearle was born May 11, 1922. They are descendants of Samuel Willett and Thomas Francis Curtsinger, early settlers of Fancy Farm and St. Jerome Parish.

James, son of Mark A. and Verena Ryan Curtsinger, attended school and graduated from St. Jerome School in 1935 and worked four years in California before entering the U.S. Postal Service as a railway mail clerk in Kentucky. He served four years in the U.S. Navy during World War II doing duty in the southwest Pacific area. He is now retired after 40 years in the mail service. A life-long member of St. Jerome Parish, he has served as Trustee and a member of parish councils under Frs. Russell, DeNardi, Hancock, Riney and Hayden for over 45 years, and continues to serve as Sacristan under Fr. Ray Goetz. He served over 35 years on the board of directors of the Fancy Farm Credit Union.

Pearle, the daughter of Lyndal and Lois Carrico Willett, was born in Mayfield, KY, and attended schools there and graduated from Holy Name High School in Henderson, KY, in 1940, and from Mt. St. Joseph Jr. College in 1942. She worked for two years as a secretary for the Dean of Western Kentucky State University, and for two years as secretary in the personnel office of General Electric Company in Bowling Green. Since their marriage, she has been active in Altar Society, Homemakers Club, taught CCD for several years, and worked as co-editor with Brother Leo Willett and Sister Rachel Willett on the *St. Jerome Fancy Farm Sesquicentennial History Book*.

James E. Curtsinger Family, St. Jerome Parish, Fancy Farm, KY, James, Pearle and children-Lois, Del, Don, Richard, Maria, Susan and David.

James and Pearle are the parents of seven children: Lois Ann (born Jan. 6, 1948) married to Cletus Don Bell. Parents of John Robert and Patricia Leigh Bell. Members of St. Joseph Parish, Mayfield, KY.

Delbert Anthony (born Feb. 18, 1949) commander U.S. Navy, married to Jeanette Ann Haddon. Parents of Sheryl Ann and Mark A. Curtsinger. Now stationed at U.S. Embassy, Paris, France.

Donald Eugene (born Aug. 21, 1950) single. He is a member of St. Francis DeSales Parish, Paducah, KY.

Richard Wayne (born Oct. 31, 1951) married to Mary Mac Nowell. Parents of James Richard and Joseph Nowell Curtsinger. Members of St. Edward Parish, Fulton, KY.

Maria Katherine (born Oct. 22, 1953) married first David E. Johnson. Married second Standford Bell. Parents of Jennifer Carol and Michael James Johnson. Members of St. Jerome Parish, Fancy Farm, KY.

Susan Carol (born May 16, 1955) married to Frederick L. Thompson. Parents of Aaron Lloyd, Andrew Willett and Angela Marie Thompson. Members of St. Charles Parish, Carlisle County, KY.

David Ryan (born Oct. 18, 1963) married to Susan Maria Elliott. Members of St. Francis of Assisi Parish, Louisville, KY.

The accompanying picture was made in 1986 on the 40th Wedding Anniversary of James and Pearle.

CURTSINGER, JOSEPH "CARMON" SR.,
was born and reared in St. Jerome Parish, Fancy Farm, KY, the youngest child of Luke Sr. and Mary Ella Burshears Curtsinger. An educator, he was committed to Catholic faith.

The Joseph Curtsinger Family

Post World War II he married Mary Elizabeth Heuser Curtsinger on Aug. 16, 1947 at St. Augustine's Church Jeffersonville, IN. She was the third child (only daughter) of George and Carrie Heuser. "Betty" sacrificed her clerk-stenographer position at the Jeffersonville Quartermaster Depot for a life of Catholic and family values. Together they sacrificed for the Catholic education of their eight children.

Carmon earned a bachelor's degree in business from Murray State University (1949) and a master's from the University of Louisville (1952). He worked 30 years as teacher and senior guidance counselor at Louisville's Shawnee and Manual High schools. He served as principal at Ahrens Trade and Atherton night schools.

As athletic director Carmon was constantly involved with Louisville High School athletics including the Mason Dixon games and the State Track Committee. He was elected chairman of the St. Barnabas Parish Council and Bellarmine College Board of Overseers.

Betty and Carmon's six daughters all graduated from Assumption High School. Their two sons graduated from Trinity. All eight children earned a minimum of a college bachelor's degree. Their children: Mary Beth born Aug. 31, 1948, master's in elementary education. Married Roger Lee Haney, Harrisburg, IL, June 8, 1968, St. Barnabus. Children: Julia Katheryn Haney (CPA), Aug. 2, 1969, Murray, KY; Stephen Lee Haney, Aug. 31, 1970 Murray, KY. Family resides in Fayetteville, AK.

Barbara Jeanne, Dec. 19, 1950, Doctorate Auburn Veterinary School, May 1975. Married to Rockne B. Gibson, Sissionville, WV, June 20, 1980, they have one child, Christopher Benjamin Gibson born April 11, 1983, Danville, KY. Owns and operates Danville Animal Clinic.

Margaret Ann, April 8, 1954. master's in nutrition, Murray State. First Lieutenant U.S Air Force Reserves, works for Food and Drug Administration and resides in Washington, DC.

Joseph Carmon Jr., June 23, 1955. Doctorate University of Louisville Medical School, 1980. Completed surgery residence, 1992, at St Elizabeth's Hospital, Boston, MA. Established residence and private vascular surgery practice in Paducah, KY.

Judith Frances, Oct. 4, 1956. bachelor's in accounting and business administration, Murray State University, 1978. Kentucky Certified Public Accountant, 1986. Resides in Fancy Farm. Member of St. Jerome Parish Council.

Catherine Rose, Oct. 31, 1958. Medical Technologist, Murray State University, 1980. doctorate in pathology, University of Kentucky Medical School, 1990. Married John Soldo, Bethlehem, PA, July 29, 1988, St. Jerome. They reside in Philadelphia, PA. Twins born April 22, 1994 - Jerome Samuel and Christiane Michaela.

Dorothy Louise, Feb. 9, 1960. bachelor's in journalism, Murray State 1982. Married Dr. Robert Zimmerman (Syracuse, NY) 1984. Children: Andrew Zimmerman, Venezuela, Dec. 18, 1986; Thomas Zimmerman, Murray, KY, June 26, 1990. The family resides in Raleigh, NC.

Robert Walter, June 23, 1961. bachelor's in criminology, Murray State University, 1983. Employed for Toyota Manufacturing in Georgetown, KY. Captain U.S. Reserves, 1990. Married Kim Higgins, St. Denis, April 1983. Their children are: Jason Robert, born July 11, 1983 in Murray, KY; Patrick Scott, born April 2, 1986 in Germany; and Nicholas Jordon, born Dec. 17, 1988 in Murray, KY.

In April 1979, Carmon and Betty retired and returned to Fancy Farm, KY. Carmon served as chairman of the Fancy Farm Picnic and St. Jerome Pastoral Council. He served as president of Graves County Retired Teachers and ran a full-time farm operation, Betty worked with Liturgy, Altar Society, Red Cross board.

In 1991, together they received the Graves County Bank Outstanding Achievement Award.

On May 16, 1992, an operation at Lourdes Hospital revealed Carmon to have lung cancer. The children returned home to care for him as he struggled to overcome it. He died Dec. 27, 1992. They are very grateful to the community who were overwhelmingly supportive of the family.

CURTSINGER, THOMAS ALTON,
son of Luke and Mae (Burshears) Curtsinger, was born Sept. 17, 1921 in Fancy Farm. Rose Irene (Lickteig), daughter of William and Anna (Oechsli), was born March 17, 1928 and baptized at St. Denis, Louisville.

They were married May 29, 1954 in St. Denis. Their children are: Pamela (1955) and Mary Jo (1957) who were born in Louisville and baptized at St. Columba while Beverly (1959), Tommy (1960) and Patricia (1962) were born in Lebanon and were baptized at St. Domonic, Springfield. All college graduates.

Alton graduated from St. Jerome in 1940, made 77 trips over the "Hump" in World War II as a radio operator, graduated from University of Kentucky in 1948, worked for Armour 10 years followed by 33 years as County Agent in Springfield and Owensboro where he retired, December 1990. A K.C. member since December 1945, was secretary and president of Kentucky County Agents, president of Springfield Lions, secretary of Daviess County Lions for 20 years and now vice-president.

Rose grew up on a vegetable farm in Jefferson County, graduated from Valley High School in 1946. Worked for South Central Bell until 1955, then a housewife for 18 years followed by 13 years a school bus driver in Daviess County. She has been a member of Daviess County Farm Bureau Womens' Committee, and an advisor to the Young Farm Bureau for 20 years, volunteers as minister of Eucharist at Mercy Hospital since 1984, a member and secretary of the Immaculate Parish Council for three years.

Both have been members of the Immaculate Parrish since moving from Springfield in 1968, where Rose is a member of the Altar Society and a Eucharistic Minister. Tom is a lector, and both are ushers and members of the "Over 50 Club."

D'ANGELO, CARMEN AND ELEANOR (JONES), were married Dec. 17, 1955 in Chicago, IL. Carmen was born March 17, 1921 in Chicago, and Eleanor was born April 5, 1927 in Golden Pond, KY. She is the daughter of Louis Saffer and Lena (Saffer) Jones. Carmen served in the U.S. Marine Corps from 1942 until 1945. They are currently living in Murray, KY, and are members of St. Leo Parish. They are past members of St. Turibius Parish. Eleanor is active in K of C, the Women's Guild, and as a housewife. Carmen is retired from the trucking industry.

They are the parents of three children, Craig, Micheal and Kevin and four grandchildren, Amanda, Laura, Emily and Nicholas.

DARST, ALOYSIUS AND JANICE, are members of St. Paul Parish in Leitchfield, KY. They were married Sept. 6, 1974 by Rev. Thomas Clark, uncle of Aloysius at St. Paul Church. Janice is the daughter of Leslie Milliner and Sarah Whitten Milliner. Aloysius is the son of Tony Darst and Rebecca Clark Darst.

Aloysius and Janice Darst Family

They have two children, Kristie Lynn and Byron Thomas and they both attend St. Paul Grade School. Byron serves as an altar boy as his father did as a boy. Kristie participates in school activities and sports.

DARST, ANTHONY (TONY) AND REBECCA, were both born and raised in Grayson County, Leitchfield, KY. Tony was born Dec. 12, 1927 to Joseph Ernest and Ruby Tackaberry Darst. Becky was born June 6, 1930 to Jesse and Rose Clark.

They both attended grade school and high school at St. Paul Catholic School in Grayson County. They were married Nov. 4, 1950 at St. Paul Catholic Church by Rev. Clarence Clark, Becky's brother. Rev. Charles DeNardi was pastor at St. Paul Church at the time. Tony and Becky have nine children, Wayne, Justin, Al, Debbie, Lynda, Cathy, Aubrey, Teresa and Lisa. They have one deceased daughter Mary Rebecca. All of the children attended St. Paul Catholic Elementary and are still members of St. Paul Parish. Several of them have served on the Parish Council and school board.

Anthony (Tony) and Rebecca Darst Family

Tony and Becky have operated Darst Grocery in St. Paul for over 20 years. Tony worked at Olin Chemical in Brandenburg, KY, for 22 and one-half years until he retired in 1983.

They have 15 grandchildren and so far all of them attend St. Paul Catholic Elementary School.

On Feb. 11, 1992 Tony passed away. We live on with special memories we have of him.

DARST, DALE AND DONNA, live in the St. Paul Parish in Grayson County. Dale has been a member of the parish all his life. They were married July 16, 1983 at the St. Paul Church with Rev. Charles DeNardi officiating of the ceremony.

Dale and Donna Darst

Dale works at Twin Lakes Regional Medical Center and IMS Mfg. in Leitchfield, KY. Donna cares for the home and does babysitting.

DARST, JOSEPH ERNEST, was born in Irvington, KY, Oct. 16, 1898 and baptized Dec. 25, 1898. He is the son of Henry and Anna Darst. He moved to St. Paul Parish along with his parents as a child. At this time, St. Paul Parish was a part of the Louisville Diocese. Later, he met Ruby Tackaberry of Big Clifty, KY. Ruby was born in Big Clifty, KY, Oct. 19, 1900 and baptized Sept. 27, 1903. She is the daughter of John and Mary Ellen Tackaberry. Ernest and Ruby were married in St. Paul Church by the Rev. Anthony Helling, April 18, 1917. They lived on a farm on the St. Paul Cemetery Road where they raised 10 children, four boys and six girls. One girl, Marcella died at the age of 15 months and one boy, Donald Dale died at the age of seven days. Five of their eight living children live in St. Paul Parish; Mike, Virginia, Trudy, Tony (died February 1992) and Deanna. The remaining three live in Louisville, KY, and belong to St. Timothy Parish. Ernest was a farmer and a member of the ASCS in Grayson County. He later worked for the highway department. He built a grocery store at St. Paul May 6, 1946 in which his wife, Ruby, and some of their children worked. Soon after the store was built they moved to an apartment connected to the store. Later in 1957 they built a stone house near the store. Ownership of the store was sold to a son, Tony, in 1973.

Ruby and Ernest were also very dedicated and committed parish members who participated and assisted in parish functions and activities. Ernest was a trustee of the parish and Ruby a member of Altar Society. Because of their excellent example, their children are also active and dedicated members of their church.

The Joseph Ernest Darst Family

Ernest died June 19, 1981. Ruby continued to live in the stone house until 1988. She is now a resident of Leitchfield Health Care in Leitchfield, KY.

They have several grandchildren and great-grand-children living at St. Paul and attending St. Paul School. The tradition continues.

DARST, JUSTIN AND NANCY, are members of St. Paul Parish, Leitchfield, KY. Justin is the son of Tony Darst and Rebecca Clark Darst. Nancy is the daughter of John and Allean Lucas. Justin and Nancy were married Dec. 22, 1973 in St. Paul Church by Rev. Charles DeNardi. Their attendants were Larry and Debbie McGrew.

Justin and Nancy Darst Family

They have four children, Jamie Michael, William Anthony, Sarah Margaret and Hannah Kathryn. All of the children attended St. Paul School. Justin and Nancy are active in school and parish functions. Justin also serves on the Parish Council, school board and picnic committee.

DARST, MICHAEL AND HETTIE, live in the St. Paul Parish near Leitchfield, KY, in Grayson County. They have lived in this area for most of their lives. Michael was raised in the same house and lived on the farm all his life.

Michael and Hettie Darst Family

Michael and Hettie were married on Nov. 6, 1948 with Rev. Charles DeNardi officiating the wedding at St. Paul Church. They are proud of their 10 children: Tom, Rita, Dale, Billy, Charles, Raymond, Richard, Ruth Ann, Pat and Mary. Seven of the 10 children are now married with their own homes; and all except one son who resides in Mount Vernon, KY, belong to St. Paul Parish.

Michael was an active farmer taking care of his livestock and field crops. He has now retired and has passed much of his farming experience on to his three sons who live at home and care for the farm. Michael still has a strong interest and active part in farming.

Hettie worked at home caring for their children and helping on the farm when needed. She occasionally babysits for their 10 grandchildren of whom she is very proud.

Hettie attended St. Paul School when the school opened in 1940 from fifth grade through high school. Their 10 children also attended St. Paul School through eighth grade. Their oldest son was fortunate enough to attend and graduated from Grayson County Catholic High School, formerly St. Paul High School, before it closed in 1967.

Michael and Hettie have been married more than 43 years and are looking forward to celebrating their 50th Wedding Anniversary shortly.

DARST, RICHARD AND LORI, live in the St. Paul community near Leitchfield, KY with their son, Christopher. Richard and Lori were married on April 20, 1985 at St. Paul Church by Fr. Tony Stevenson.

Richard and Lori Darst and their son Christopher

Richard has lived in the St. Paul area all of his life. He graduated from Western Kentucky University in May 1983 and is presently employed at Vermont American Corporation in Leitchfield. Lori is originally from Cincinnati, OH; and it is a big change for her moving from the large city to the small town of Leitchfield.

In 1989, Richard and Lori celebrated a very special Easter when Lori entered the Catholic Church during Easter vigil services.

DARST, WAYNE AND MAUREEN, have lived in St. Paul's Parish, Leitchfield, KY all of their lives. They were married June 15, 1974 at St. Paul Church by Rev. Charles DeNardi.

Maureen is the youngest child of Cletus Whitfill and Clara Milliner Whitfill. Wayne is the oldest child of Tony Darst and Rebecca Clark Darst. They have two children, Amy Maureen and Joshua Matthew. They both attended St. Paul School.

Wayne and Maureen Darst Family

Wayne and Maureen have participated in many parish activities. Maureen has served on the Parish Council and the school board. She has been a leader of the 4-H Club taking the children to district championships and also performing at the Kentucky State Fair.

DAVENPORT, RICHARD ALAN, his wife Gail and sons, Duane, Scott and Kyle are members of St. Joseph Church, Central City. He is the son of Genevieve and Norman Davenport, the maternal grandparents are Mary and Tatum Burden with paternal grandparents, Bess and Ben Davenport. Richard and his sons were baptized and confirmed at St. Joseph Parish. He and his wife Gail Goldwasser of Denver, CO, were married by Fr. Richard Danhauer at St. Joseph Parish on Dec. 16, 1976. Richard and Gail are very involved in parish activities. Richard is RCIA and High School CCD instructor, Gail is on the Welcome Committee, treasurer of the Altar Society and sponsor of parish youth groups.

Richard Davenport Family

Richard was a member of the United States Marine Corps from 1968 to 1970 and the United States Army Special Forces (Green Berets) from 1974 to 1976 and served in Vietnam. He works at the Tennessee Valley Authority at Paradise Fossil Plant as a steam plant operator. He attended Austin Perry University in Clarksville, TN.

Gail after graduating from high school went to work in the banking profession before becoming a wife and mother.

DAVIS, GERALD W., was born March 29, 1954 to James R. Davis and Elizabeth L. Roberts of Reed, Henderson County, KY. He graduated from Henderson County High School in 1972. After high school he joined the Army and was stationed in Korea. Upon his discharge from the service, Jerry attended Owensboro Business College and was employed at Wetzel's Supermarket. There he met his future wife, Debra Ann Merimee, daughter born on April 9, 1956 to Joseph W. Merimee and Marjorie A. Kamuf. Debbie was a member of Sts. Joseph and Paul Parish, Owensboro, and graduated from Owensboro Catholic High School in 1974. She attended Brescia College; taught kindergarten and met her future husband while working as a clerk at Wetzel's. On April 24, 1976, Jerry and Debbie were married by Rev. Aloysius Powers. They made their home on the family farm in Reed, KY, and became active members of St. Augustine Parish. Soon they were blessed with five children. The first, Timothy Scott, was born March 3, 1977; followed by Gordon Michael on July 11, 1979; Nathaniel James on July 19, 1981; Hannah Louise on Jan. 22, 1983; and Patrick Joseph on April 8, 1992. The children attend Holy Name Elementary in Henderson, KY. Jerry is a Eucharistic Minister and instructs his sons and the other altar boys. Debbie restores statues and other church artifacts. They plan to spend the rest of their lives building a family homeplace in Reed and preserving their family oriented parish.

DAVIS, JAMES RICHARD, was born March 12, 1932. His parents were James Clarence Davis and Mary Ellen Drace of McLean County. In April of 1953, James was baptized by Rev. Joseph Saffer. In June of 1952, he met Elizabeth Louise Roberts, daughter of B. Drury Roberts and Elizabeth Agnes Payne (Leona) of Daviess County. She was born at Rome, KY, Sept. 7, 1933. One year later after meeting, they were married at St. Martin Church, Rome by Rev. Joseph Saffer on June 6, 1953. They lived in Owensboro for the first three months of their marriage then moved to Reed in September of 1953. They bought a farm on KY 811 from Will Clary. On March 29, 1954 they were blessed with the first of three children, Gerald Wayne; then their second child was born Linda Gail. But not until 14 years later was their third child born, Jamie Lenore. They currently have six grandchildren.

James R. and Betty Davis

Since moving to Reed, the family has belonged to St. Augustine. James supervises the parking of cars and Betty supervises the Bingo stand at their church's annual picnic on the 4th of July.

In May of 1992, James retired from Whirlpool after 40 years of service. Elizabeth for the past 22 years has been working for Henderson County school system driving a bus.

DAY, JOSEPH PAUL FAMILY. Helen Ann Riney, daughter of William Hugh Riney and Mary Helen Hartz, was born Jan. 20, 1953 in Owensboro, KY. She went to St. Martin School and later to Catholic High. There she met Joseph Paul Day, son of John Philip Day and Mildred Delilah Brashear. Joe was born March 27, 1953, and went to Immaculate School.

Joe and Helen Ann dated in high school. After high school, Helen Ann went to nursing school, and got a job at Daviess County Hospital. Joe went to college for two years. He got a job at W. R. Grace with his brother, Steve. Joe and Helen Ann got married on June 29, 1974 at St. Martin Church. They lived in an apartment on Legion Park Drive for one year and then moved to Carryback Ct. One year later, Joseph Matthew was born Dec. 12, 1976. April Suzanne followed April 18, 1979. After April was born Helen Ann quit her job at the hospital and began working at a doctor's office. Andrew Riney was born April 14, 1983. Abby Marie entered the world on May 12, 1985, and Helen Ann began working only part-time. Paul William was born April 28, 1987. The family moved to a rental house owned by Helen Ann's parents on Highway 81. Joe's father, John died a year later. Finally, the family found a house on Needles Ct. They moved in and a year later, Johnna Marie, the sixth child, was born Feb. 7, 1989.

Matt is going on 16, April is 14, Andy is 9, Abby age 7, Paul age 5 and Johnna is 3. The family attends Immaculate Parish. Joe is in the Men's Club, Helen Ann is in the Confraternity of Christian Mothers. Matt is an altar server. Helen Ann and the children are active members of the Army of Mary.

DEVINE, ROBERT AND SANDY HARDISON, were married by Fr. Willet in 1984. Robert had three children from a previous marriage: Brad, Ryan and Heath. Sandy also has three children from a previous marriage: Scott, Becky and Greg. Robert and Sandy were married in Precious Blood Church, where Heath attended school for six years. He then went to OCMS, and is now at OCHS. Roberts' other children, Brad and Ryan live with their mother and Robert, now, is the father of Sandy's children.

Vicki Devine and Denny Howe were married at Precious Blood Church in 1989. Vicki is the mother of three, Byron, Jennifer and Heath. Denny was a father of two, Bryan and Stacy. Brian and Stacy also attended Precious Blood Church and School.

After Robert and Sandy were married, Robert converted into the Catholic faith, and later, Heath was baptized. Robert decided to become Catholic because the more he read and learned about God, the more convinced he was that God loved him. Roberts' converting into the Catholic faith has made the family stronger both mentally and spiritually. They were able to share their problems together and they can talk with each other better then they ever could before.

DEWEESE, CATHERINE CAROLYN, just getting born that 20th day of February, 1921 in the small southern Illinois town of Cairo was a monumental undertaking for Catherine Carolyn DeWeese. So uncertain was the outcome that both pastor and God-parents were present in the DeWeese house on Fourth Street. Little Catherine Carolyn was baptized at birth. Whatever else transpired, the baby was safely in the grace of God.

Catherine Carolyn was the second child born to Ray Paul and Catherine Mary DeWeese. Ray Paul was a Kentucky-born Methodist, son of a minister and a convert to Catholicism. Catherine Mary was English born, of Irish and Scottish ancestry traced to the time and influence-of St. Patrick. Two brothers, Bernard John and Raymond Paul, completed the family.

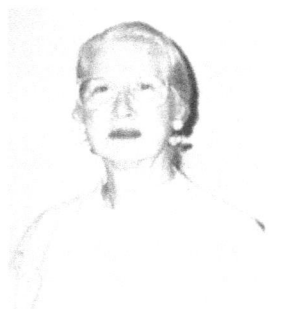

Catherine Carolyn DeWeese

Childhood and young womanhood were spent in Northern Illinois near Chicago. Schooling was parochial, and after the schooling came a business career. In her idle hours, Carolyn fostered a native talent for painting and writing.

After the death of her parents, and her retirement, she and her brother Paul came to Kentucky in search of their father's roots. The search culminated in a miraculous discovery of a colonial ancestry and a family in Butler County she never dreamed existed. A new sense of faith also called them both. They found themselves not only engrossed in their family of cousins but in church as well.

Carolyn and her brother purchased a house in Morgantown just two-tenths of a mile from Holy Trinity Church and moved permanently to Kentucky.

At Holy Trinity, Carolyn partakes fully in the life of her parish. She reads scripture at Mass as her turn arises. Occasionally, she serves as parish reporter to both the *Western Kentucky Catholic* and local newspapers. She is active in community affairs as a member of the Daughters of the American Revolution, the Historical and Genealogical Society, the Big-Bend Rural Development Club, County Bi-Centennial Committee and the Green Rivers Writers Association.

In the summer of 1991, she received the "Best of Show" and the "Memorable" awards for a painting she exhibited in the George Dabbs Memorial Art and Photography Show.

DEWEESE RAYMOND PAUL, was "Sunday's Child," born Aug. 10, 1924, in Kankakee, IL to Ray Paul and Catherine M. DeWeese. Childhood was typical of any medium-size town in Northern Illinois-parochial school, marbles at recess, roller skates, bicycles, swimming, Saturday afternoon movies, children's Mass on Sunday's and Holy days, altar boy, Boys' Choir, Boy Scouting and camping, school dances and outings.

Adulthood brought different diversions, different schooling, and a career in engineering that spanned 43 years. He was holder of several patents in his field of industry. In his parish church he served as usher, Parish Council member and Extraordinary Minister of the Eucharist. He was a member of the Fourth Degree of Knights of Columbus, Bishop McNamara Council.

Raymond Paul DeWeese

Retirement in 1985 ushered in new interests. Among these was the pursuit of history and genealogy and a desire to research his ancestry. That desire led into a new-found life in Butler County, KY where the DeWeese family settled in the 1830s, and where grandfather and father had been born. After several years of intense research, he co-authored a DeWeese Family History, published in the fall of 1988.

In Butler County, Ray Paul discovered not only his family roots but a new dimension to his faith. Bearing a letter of recommendation from his former pastor, he became a full member of Holy Trinity in Morgantown. He serves again as Extraordinary Minister of the Eucharist and member of the Parish Council. He also serves as sacristan, occasional usher, parish representative to the newly formed Bowling Green Deanery Council and its present chairman. He was parish representative to the 1991 Diocesan Synod.

Ray Paul is active in his community as a member of the Sons of the American Revolution, the County Historical and Genealogical Society, being its past secretary/treasurer, the County Bi-Centennial Executive Committee and the Big Bend Rural Development Club. He is presently extracting data from Butler County Court Record to be published as a research tool.

He currently resides in Morgantown, KY. Having never married, he shares a home with his sister, Catherine Carolyn.

DIEROLF, RONALD KENNETH JR. AND GAIL LYNN (DAUBY), have been members of St. Thomas More Church in Paducah, KY, since 1972. Ron was born July 4, 1949 in Oak Park, IL, and Gail was born July 14, 1952 in McLeansboro, IL, raised in White County, IL. They now reside in Paducah, McCracken County, KY. Gail was the daughter of Clarence Dauby and Betty (Mitchell) Dauby, who were farmers; the granddaughter of Henry and Katie (James) Dauby and Frank and Viola (Dutchke) Mitchell of Cannelton, IN. Viola is the daughter of Gus and Anna (Hardesty) Dutchke. Ron the son of Ronald K. Dierolf Sr., a dairy engineer, and Barbara (Harvey) Dierolf, a teacher, who was married July 3, 1948. He is the grandson of Tom and Ethel (Gish) Harvey of Chicago, IL, and Ken and Hope (Anderson) Dierolf of Peoria, IL. Ron works as a chemical engineer for Martin Marietta and Gail is a medical technologist at Lourdes Hospital.

Ron and Gail have three children: Jennifer Rebekah Dierolf born Sept. 24, 1977, attends St. Mary School in Paducah; Jamie Elizabeth Dierolf born June 8, 1981, attends St. Mary School-adopted from Korea in 1987; and Christopher Kenneth Dierolf born Sept. 11, 1985, also attends St. Mary.

DIETRICH, DANIEL A. AND ROWENA A. (SELLERS), are members of St. Francis De Sales in Paducah, KY. Daniel was born May 11, 1952 in Chicago, IL and Rowena was born April 4, 1951 in Chicago, IL. Except for their youngest son Aaron, they were all born in Cook County in Chicago, IL and presently live in Paducah, KY, having moved there in October 1986 to take a job with the Paducah and Louisville Railway.

August 13, 1989, in front of St. Francis De Sales Church after the baptism of Aaron. The baptism was administered by Fr. Dave Johnson.

They have three sons, Daniel who was born Feb. 6, 1974, attends Murray State University; Nicholas J. Dietrich, born Sept. 22, 1977 attends St Mary High School; and Aaron A. Dietrich born June 25, 1989.

DONAHUE, SISTER JANE FRANCES, was born June 14, 1903 at Holy Cross, KY. She is the daughter of John Webb Donahue (April 5, 1873-Dec. 14, 1946) and Frances Beatrice Clark Donahue (March 5, 1879-June 17, 1958) both born in Nelson County, KY. She had four sisters and three brothers: Mary Carolyn (Sr. Rose Catherine); Hubert died May 19, 1929; John died Aug. 4, 1963; Fidelma (Sr. Mary Beatrice); Augustine; Joseph died 1912; Margaret (Sr. M. Camilla, S.C.N.); Catherine (Mrs. Anna Donahue); and Adeline who died in 1949. Served in many missions throughout Kentucky, from 1921 until 1982. Taught primary through high school.

DORAN, THOMAS, NICHOLAS AND FRANCIS, migrated to Kentucky, from Harford County, MD, about 1792. They and seven siblings were born in 1753-1775 to Hugh Doran and wife Margaret McCarty. Hugh died 1778 and Margaret 1791. Their family was active in St. Ignatius, Hickory. Hugh and sons Patrick and John signed the Oath of Allegiance in 1778 in Harford County.

Patrick, who served in the First MD Line Sixth Regt. until 1784, received land warrants in Ohio and Western Maryland. He died unmarried in 1798 before he and his siblings received a MD Land Patent to Monto Santo, Harford County.

Brother, Edward served in the PA Militia at Long Island, NY in 1776. He was given power of attorney and became the emissary between the Kentucky brothers and their Maryland land interests, later buying them. Edward married Mary Allman of Philadelphia and named a son Francis.

The youngest brother, Philip, served in the War of 1812 at the Battle of Baltimore. Philip and sister, Catherine, never married. Hugh's daughters, Margaret married Aubrey Jones and Mary Ann married Edward Kean of Pennsylvania. John had five children: Bennett, single; and four daughters who married Shipleys and Suttons.

Thomas, Nicholas and Francis, all apparently bachelors, served in the Fourth Regt., Washington Co., KY Militia. Thomas built a grist mill on the Rolling Fork at New Market near the Old Holy Mary Cemetery. He died in 1807 returning from Natchez.

Nicholas farmed in the same area attending the Holy Mary Catholic Church. He died in 1809.

Francis worked in Thomas' mill and on Nicholas' farm and acquired their estates. He sold all his possessions before leaving Kentucky in 1812 with the militia in the Illinois-Indiana Campaign. He returned to Calvary, Marion County, and resumed participation in the church. No records after 1817 are found for him. Hugh Doran's surname continues only through his son Edward.

DORE, RANDY AND RHONDA ANN (SMITH), the daughter of Robert W. Smith Jr. and Margaret Mary Thompson comes from a long family line of Catholics. Grandparents of Rhonda, Robert W. Smith

Sr. and Gladys Spink Smith. Other grandparents, Robert and Francis Whelan Thompson came from early pioneer Catholics. The Thompson line came from England to St. Mary's, MD in 1634 with the *Ark* and *Dove*. The Whelan ancestors came to Daviess County in approximately 1827.

Rhonda married Randy Dore and they became the parents of two daughters, Brandi Noel and Tara Margaret Dore. The daughters were baptized at Holy Guardian Angel and St. Anthony Catholic Church in Breckinridge County. Brandi and Tara received their First Communion at Holy Guardian Angel Church at Irvington, KY. Rhonda taught CCD at Holy Guardian Angel Church and was a active Girl Scout leader.

Rhonda's daughters attended St. John Catholic School, Brandenburg, KY where Rhonda was a library volunteer at the Catholic school. *Submitted by Rhonda Smith Dore.*

DOSSETT-DURBIN, THOMAS LEO,

was born Oct. 10, 1914 to Oscar Lee (Pete) Dossett and Mary Bessie Goins Dossett married Mary Levena Durbin, May 22, 1921 daughter of Christopher (Kit) Columbus Durbin and Amy Irene Ballard on June 29, 1937.

They have 13 children: Shirley Dossett Hobbs (Jan. 21, 1939); Dorothy Dossett Hobbs (Aug. 8, 1940); James Dalton Dossett (Sept. 12, 1942); Thomas Wayne Dossett (June 25, 1944); William Earl Dossett (Aug. 30, 1946); Thomas Larry Dossett (May 3, 1948); Brenda Dossett Slaybough (Jan. 11, 1950); Barbara Dossett Doughty (Sept. 10, 1951); Johnny Ray Dossett (Jan. 7, 1953); Marilyn Dossett Bosecker (May 8, 1954); Rose (Angie) Dossett Keeling (Sept. 12, 1955); Mary Donna Dossett Roberts (April 24, 1957); and Kimberly Dossett Bennett (July 10, 1960).

Mary Levena and Thomas Dossett

Members of St. Jerome Catholic Church in Fancy Farm, KY.

Thomas Lee Dossett served in World War II, was a butcher at Brown Thompson Packing House for 40 years. Mary Bessie Dossett was the cook for the Sister of Charity Nuns in Fancy Farm for many years. Oscar (Pete) Dossett was a convert and the janitor for the church. Amy Irene Durbin was a cook at the school cafeteria and Christopher (Kit) Durbin was a sharecropper.

Tom and Levena celebrated their 50th Wedding Anniversary in 1987. They have 13 living children, 28 grandchildren and five great-grandchildren.

DOWDY, DAN,

was born in Madisonville, KY on Feb. 11, 1951, the Feast of Our Lady of Lourdes. The third of four children, he attended grade school in Earlington at Immaculate Conception School. He attended St. Thomas Seminary in Louisville and graduated from Madisonville North Hopkins High School. He attended Madisonville Community College and the Area Vocational School.

He met the former Katharine Ellen Jackson, also of Madisonville, and they wed on Dec. 27, 1982. Shortly after their marriage, they moved to Louisville at the request of Dan's employer. While there, their first child Benjamin Wesley was born. Feeling called to relocate to Owensboro, they did so just before the birth of their second child, Hannah Rose.

He currently attends Our Lady of Lourdes Church in Owensboro and is involved in various parish ministries, as is Kathy. Both are lectors, music ministers, RCIA team members, and are sponsor couples helping others prepare for their marriage commitments. In the past, Dan has served on liturgy committees and had been active in the diocesan choir.

The Dan Dowdy Family

Dan appreciated the opportunity to serve, especially in the music ministry, and selects Holy Week and the Triduum as his favorite liturgical celebrations. His most memorable celebration, other than his wedding, was the Easter Vigil that Kathy joined the church of Western Kentucky. He credits his family and the church community, especially in his younger years, with his continued commitment to the Catholic faith. He has enjoyed his affiliation with Cursillo and Western Kentucky Teens Encounter Christ (TEC).

DOWDY, DEAN,

was born on Dec. 13, 1912 in Mayfield, KY. After graduating from Mayfield High School, he enrolled at Murray State Teacher's College as a pre-medicine student. Becoming involved in a chorus there, he changed his major to music and was among the first graduates to receive a music education certificate.

His first, and only, teaching position was in Madisonville, KY, where he met and married Edna Mae Brown of Owensboro. They had four children, Judy, Cathy, Dan and Herbert Dean Jr. (also known as Bud). Active in music education for the Hopkins County School System, he naturally served the Immaculate Conception Parish in Earlington as a music minister. As the first practicing Catholic in Madisonville, he was on numerous boards and helped with the building of the parish facilities in Madisonville, Christ the King Parish.

He credits his successes in music to a daily prayer, asking God to use him as a means to touch the children he taught, in spite of his inability to know if the road he was travelling was the correct one. His bands, orchestras and choruses were known throughout the Midwest and southeast for their superb performances, and he was able to impart a love for music to those he taught. He directed the Madisonville Community Choirs' annual Christmas presentation of Handel's Messiah for 25 years, helping make it a truly inspirational event, especially for the performers.

After Mrs. Dowdy's death in 1968, he remained single until his recent marriage to Bette Eastwood in December 1990. He continues to reside in Madisonville and to attend Christ the King Parish there.

DRURY, FAMILY,

(Taken from William Rodman's letter to Dr. H.D. Rodman, dated March 12, 1914)
Dear Brother:
Ignatius Drury and Charles Drury were grandmother's brothers. She (grandmother) named her first-born Ignatius.

Zachariah Drury was an older half-brother of grandmother. As to Mary M. Drury and Anna S. Drury-these were probably full sisters of Zachariah or his wife and the wife of Ignatius, Charles and Elizabeth possibly husband and wife.

I am under the impression our great grandmother Drury was a widow when she left Maryland. She had a stepson, Zack, I know and maybe a step-daughter, but I think not. This great-grandmother Drury's name was Alice Anastasia (French) Drury. She had six children, Ignatius, Charles, Dolly or Dorothea Payne, Elizabeth or Betsy Jarboe, Martha or Moccie Warren, Eleanor or Nellie Hogan.

Our grandmother was the youngest child of the family.

Billy.

The following was taken from the records at Bardstown, KY:
Deed to Mary M. Drury from Jonkim Reynerson 1809, Abraham Hite, 1811, Anna S. Drury, Hezekiah Murphy, 1814, Charles Drury, David Cox, 1817, Jas Anderson, 1828, Ignatius, Francis Donohoe, 1832, Charles Drur, Thomas Smith, 1836.

An appraisement of the estate of Zachariah Drury in Order Book G page 334.

Ignatius Drury will probated-inventory and appraisement examined-settlement-sale bill.

Charles Drury will appraisement and sale bill-exams-settlements-Elizabeth Drury will probated.

Mother's grandfather's name was either Ignatius or Zachary Drury. His wife, (mother's grandmother) was Anastasia French. (She was Grandfather Drury's second wife.) The name of his first wife is not known. From the first union came Charles Drury formerly of Beech Grove, Daviess County, KY.

To Ignatius or Zachary Drury and Anastasia French were born the following children, one son, Charles Drury and four daughters, namely, Dorothy called Dolly, Elizabeth called Betsy, Martha or Monica called Moccie, Ellen, or Eleanor, or Helen, called Nellie.

Dorothy or Dolly Drury married John called Jackie Payne. From this union sprung all the Paynes in Knottsville, Daviess County, including Ignatius Payne of West Louisville.

Elizabeth or Betsy Drury married a Mr. Jarboe. From this union came Ignatius Jarboe, formerly of Knottsville, KY, also "Algie" Jarboe of Knottsville. There were probably other descendants but they are not known.

Martha, or Moccie Drury married_____Warren. From the union came the Warrens of Hardin County and Archbishop Montgomery.

Ellen, Helen or Eleanor Drury known as Nellie, married William Hogan of Fredericksburg, Washington County, KY. From this union came William and Ignatius Hogan and several daughters. Hilary Drury of Fredericksburg was a brother to Charles Drury mentioned above.

Bishop Montgomery's grandmother was daughter of Charles and Moccie Warren.

DRURY, FATHER EDWIN,

Father Drury's ancestors were among the Catholic settlers of Maryland in the 17th century. His father, Hilary Drury was born in Maryland in 1799, and came to Kentucky in 1808. [Sister Jamesetta, our present school principal, also traces her ancestry back to Hilary.] Father Drury's mother, Teresa Coomes, was born in Kentucky in Sept. 7, 1797 Teresa's father, Francis Coomes, also came from Maryland to Kentucky, having first tarried several years in Virginia and North Carolina, arriving finally in 1795 with his family.

Father Drury was born on June 16, 1845, in St. Lawrence Parish, Daviess County, KY. At an early age he entered old St. Thomas Seminary, near Bardstown, and completed his course at Preston Park Seminary [now Bellarmine College campus] in Louisville. Ordained a priest on June 21, 1872, at the cathedral in Louisville.

Father Drury assisted at his home parish until the fall of that year (1872), when he became pastor of St. Francis Xavier Church, Raywick. In the spring of 1874, he bought three acres of land about four miles from Finley and built St. Matthew's station in lower Marion County. In 1907, when the church at Finley was built, the station was closed and only small cemetery remains to mark the site of St. Matthew's.

On Nov. 11, 1874, Father Drury was appointed second resident pastor of St. Francis of Assisi Church at Chicago (St. Francis), KY. In 1880 he built the first parochial school.

In June of 1885 ill health forced Father Drury to resign his pastorate. Upon recovery in late 1886 he became pastor of the Pewee Valley missions, which post he held until his health failed again in 1894. In the fall of 1897 he accepted lighter duties as chaplain at St. Thomas Orphanage, then located in Bardstown, and began giving missions in Peoria, IL, from August 1898 to August 1899 when he began his mission preaching throughout the Diocese of Louisville.

On March 23, 1906, Father Drury was appointed chaplain at the Loretto Motherhouse, Loretto, KY, which office he held until his death at St. Joseph Infirmary (Fourth Street location) on Feb. 2, 1913. He was buried in the Motherhouse Cemetery.

An old church ledger, in Father Drury's handwriting, states that the church expenses between Aug. 20, 1874 and Aug. 1, 1875, were $1,092.40. The income for the same period was listed as $915.82.

DRURY, MARY MARGARET, was born on March 19, 1948, the oldest of 12 children born to Maurice and Margaret "Dot" Hodskins Drury of West Louisville, KY; the family had been lifelong members of St. Alphonsus Parish, St. Joseph, KY.

Mary Margaret attended St. Alphonsus Elementary from 1954 to 1962 and Mount St. Joseph Academy from 1962-1966.

Mary Margaret Drury

After high school, Mary Margaret started working for the Diocese of Owensboro in the Catholic Schools' superintendent's office on June 10, 1966. Working for the church has been Mary Margaret's only career. One of the first lay women to work for the Diocese of Owensboro, and serving in two bishops' administrations, Mary Margaret stayed in the Education Office for 19 years until 1985. She has also been a strong supporter of the St. Vincent De Paul Society.

Mary Margaret remembers that all of the principals, teachers, the pastors were such a nice group of people to work with because they were all working for the same purpose, teaching young people about life and God. She enjoyed working with Catholic educators because they all believed in what they were doing and did it well.

In 1984 and 1985, Mary Margaret worked in two diocesan offices, education and administration, to help fill in for another person on maternity leave. In 1985, Bishop John J. McRaith asked her to work in the Administration Office, which she has done up to the present.

Working for the Owensboro Diocese for 26 years, Mary Margaret can say, "They have all been very good years. The people of Western Kentucky are truly like family to me."

DRURY, MAURICE LEO AND MARGARET "DOT" HODSKINS, Drury, born Aug. 26, 1929, son of Pius Earl Drury and Ola Christine Luttrell Drury and Margaret Hodskins, born June 24, 1930, daughter of Clarence E. and Mary Emma Galloway Hodskins were married on Nov. 25, 1947 at St. Alphonsus Church, St. Joseph, KY by Fr. Paul Barrett.

Maurice worked as a coal miner, a mechanic and a farmer; Margaret has worked as a housewife and farmer with Maurice. They have eight girls and four boys: Mary Margaret Drury, Joanne Cecil, Betty Byrne, Barbara Hutchins, Judy Johnson, Kay Revlett, Maurice Jr., Billy Joe, Marie Lindsey, Kris Weise, Timmy and Bobby. All 12 children attended St. Alphonsus School. The girls attended Mount St. Joseph Academy; the boys attended Owensboro Catholic High School. One graduated from Brescia College.

The family prays the rosary every night. Everyone attended Mass on Sunday, and received the Sacraments. Family life centered around the home, children and parents entertaining one another, learning traditional Catholic values and how to make do with what they had. The children made their own toys and, because there were so many living in one home, they had to learn the art of getting along with each other, taking care of babies, cooking, cleaning, doing housework, yardwork and farm work. The boys were trained as mechanics by their father in the garage at home. The girls worked alongside their mother and father; the first six worked at Mount St. Joseph Academy for their high school education.

Maurice and Margaret helped work at parish picnics and clean the parish church, but the greatest contribution they have made to the church in Western Kentucky has been to raise 12 good Catholics and teach them Christian values and the art of community life. They are very proud of each of their children, all of whom are involved, caring citizens in the church and their own communities.

DUFRESNE, ETTA, was born to Mary Jane Lindsey Burden and Clarence Burden on Oct. 28, 1921 on a small farm in Butler County, KY. She was the sixth child in a family of 10 children. They moved to Equality in Ohio County when she was 6 years old and she grew up as a member of the Baptist Church.

In 1938 she married Elmer Geary and they had two daughters, Lois and Mary. They lived in Louisville, KY until they were divorced in 1956. She and her daughters moved to a suburb of Boston, MA.

She was later to be baptized into the Catholic faith at St. Anthony Church in Allston, MA. They then moved to the town of Reading, MA and joined St. Agnes Parish. She met Roland Dufresne, who was also Catholic, and they were married at St. Agnes in 1960.

In 1963 they decided to move to Equality, KY on a farm she owned in Ohio County, KY. They became members of the Catholic church in Beaver Dam, which at that time was having Mass in a house on Main St. It was a proud day for Catholics when the new Holy Redeemer Church was built in their community in 1966.

In 1984 Roland passed away and one year later she moved to Beaver Dam to be closer to her daughter, her church, and her favorite recreation, bowling.

Roland and Etta Dufresne

At the present she still resides in Beaver Dam and attends Holy Redeemer. She is also believed to be the oldest remaining active member who attended when the new church was built.

DUNBAR, ROBERT E. AND MARY ENDA WILLINGHAM, were married Oct. 28, 1914 in St. Augustine Church Reed, KY. In 1935 they moved to Owensboro with their five children-Robert Lee, Elizabeth, James (Jack), Jesse and Ruth Ann, enrolling the three youngest at St. Joseph School where they graduated. Robert Lee joined the Navy and in 1935 married Kathryn Roberts of Reed, KY while stationed in Long Beach, CA. They have one son, Walter Lee. Elizabeth married Bernard Dorth of Henderson, KY in a double ceremony with her brother, Jack and the former Emma Rose Coomes at St. Joseph Church, Owensboro. Elizabeth and Bernard have four children, Sallie Ann, twins, Lou and Lea, and Mark Jack and Emma Rose have three children, Mary Frances, James David and Michael and are members of Blessed Mother Parish, Owensboro.

Jesse moved to Akron, OH after World War II and in 1949 married Mary Thomas, and they have four children, Cheryl, Jesse Jr., Mimi and Don. Ruth Ann married Jessie Mattingly in St. Joseph Church, Owensboro in 1947 and are members of St. Joe and Paul Parish.

Robert E. Dunbar 1888-1960; Mary E. Dunbar 1893-1989; Robert L. Dunbar 1915-1985; James (Jack) Dunbar 1920-1987.

DUNCAN, VIRGIL JR., is the son of Virgil Lee Duncan Sr. and Mary Cleveland. He was born in Henderson County and graduated from Smith Mills High School. Virgil Lee Duncan is a production supervisor at W.R. Grace and Company, Organic Chemical Division in Owensboro.

Mr. and Mrs. Virgil Lee Duncan Jr.

Barbara Reynolds Duncan is the daughter of William Nick Reynolds and Ethel Wimsatt Reynolds. Born in Daviess County and graduated from Owensboro Catholic High. Barbara is a bookkeeper at Tom Blue Furniture, Inc. in Owensboro. In 1948, Barbara's mother, Mrs. Reynolds, was working in the cafeteria at St. Francis and her sons Andy was a senior, James was a junior, her daughters Mary Lee was a freshman and Barbara was in the sixth grade.

Their daughter, Janna Lee graduated from Apollo High School and Wesleyan College and is an auditor at Owensboro National Bank.

Drury Family Wedding, October 1974

DURBIN, ELISHA J., was born in Madison County, KY, on Feb. 1, 1800. His birth took place 16 miles from the historic Fort Boonesboro, founded by frontiersman Daniel Boone.

His parents were John D. Durbin and Patience Logsdon.

As a boy, Elisha attended church at St. Francis in Scott County. His religious fever soon kindled and at the age of 16 he entered St. Thomas Seminary near Bardstown.

Elisha spent six years in the seminary and he soon gained the reputation as a hard and tireless worker, two traits that would later serve him well.

He was ordained a priest by Bishop John B. David on Sept. 21, 1822.

Fr. Durbin spent his first several months as a priest at St. Joseph College High School and St. Joseph Cathedral in Bardstown.

Elisha J. Durbin

Fr. Durbin was not surprised by the fact that he was no great orator and one anecdote of the pioneer priest tells us that a non-Catholic attended one of his early services about six months after his ordination and found the best part of his sermon to be its brevity! But what Fr. Durbin lacked in oratory skills, he more than made up for with his zeal and tireless work to bring the gospel of God to the faithful of Western Kentucky.

In 1824, Fr. Durbin was entrusted with the pastoral care of the entire Catholic population of Western Kentucky, with his headquarters at St. Vincent in Union County.

Fr. Durbin also served the Catholics that lived in the counties of Illinois and Indiana that bordered the Ohio River. And from 1832, he also made at least one visit per year to Nashville, TN.

When Fr. Durbin reached his mission in Union County, he found a small log chapel built by the Sisters of Charity of Nazareth, who came to St. Vincent in 1820 to open a school on land that had been donated.

Fr. Durbin visited several settlements in his vast parish and these included Caseyville in Union County; Flint Island in Meade County, Fancy Farm in Graves County; Knotsville and Panther Creek in Daviess County; Paducah in McCracken County; Henderson; Bell's Mines, Marquettes and Dycusburg in Crittenden County; Eddyville in Lyon County; and Hardinsburg in Breckinridge County.

Several so-called "minor stations" were set up where Fr. Durbin would visit when time and weather permitted.

The first church built by Fr. Durbin was Sacred Heart of Jesus at St. Vincent, near the site of the old log chapel.

The property was deeded to Bishop Flaget from John F. and/or Robert Alvey, in 1818. The land, where the church was built, was released by the heirs for $1.

When the church was completed, it was the only church designed for Catholic worship west of Breckinridge County and east of the Mississippi River. The church was soon outgrown and a new church was built at the cost of $20,000 and dedicated on June 20, 1855.

The second church built was at Flint Island in Meade County and the third was St. Jerome at Fancy Farm.

The second church in Union County was built at St. Ambrose, a few years after 1830 when Fr. Durbin's first assistant was named. He was Fr. Edward Clark, who established the congregation at St. Ambrose.

Fr. Durbin spent 50 years as a missionary priest and spent an average of 200 miles a week on horseback, which based on 62 years as a priest, comes to well over 500,000 miles of travel.

Fr. Durbin endured the discomforts of horseback travel in a sparsely populated landstress from weather, hunger, thirst, from loss of sleep and from the countless accidents.

The book, *The Centenary of Catholicity in Kentucky,* had this to say about Fr. Durbin, " He organizes congregations and builds churches. He takes thought of the rising generation and multiplies its resources for more perfect Christian culture and training. He follows the straying sheep and brings them back to the fold."

Fr. Durbin shunned ill health and was robust in nature. He ate simply and his drink was only "what nature provided." Perhaps his daily routine, which would tire even the most physically fit man of today, and his fondness for fresh air, were the reasons Fr. Durbin had such a healthy life. He was described as being 5'10" in height and weighed about 160 pounds.

Though a quiet person, Fr. Durbin was known to jest and gave signs of "pleased interest in exhibitions of wit and humor."

In 1873, Fr. Durbin was relieved of his pastoral duties in Union County.

But Fr. Durbin did not retire at the age of 73 because his 51 years of service did not quench his fire or zeal to do God's work.

He was placed in charge of the Catholics who lived along the railroad between Elizabethtown and Paducah. His headquarters were at Princeton in Caldwell County.

A few years later, he was prevailed upon by the bishop to spend his remaining years at St. Joseph College in Bardstown. "He is surrounded in his retirement by those who consider it an honor to be permitted to minister to his wants."

Fr. Durbin died in Shelbyville in 1887 at the age of 87. He was serving as chaplain of a convent of Franciscan nuns at the time of his death.

He is buried at the St. Louis Cemetery in Louisville.

DURBIN, JAMES RALPH, son of John Allen and Eva (Tomes) Durbin, was born in Sunfish, KY on Nov. 11, 1913. He graduated from Sunfish High School and attended Western University to obtain a normal teaching certificate. He returned to Sunfish and taught school. The bright lights of the city beckoned, and Ralph found employment with the Naval Ordnance in Jeffersonville, IN. He began dating Lena Marie Hayes, daughter of George Washington and Susan (Durbin) Hayes, born May 11, 1913. Marie left Sunfish at the age of 16 and began work in Louisville.

By 1934 the couple decided to be married. On Christmas Eve Ralph drove his car as far as Bee Springs, where the road became impassible. He called his father and the couple traveled the last nine miles by wagon. On Christmas Day the father took them to Leitchfield in the same wagon to be married by Fr. Louis Beruatto who had baptized them. After a wedding dinner back at Sunfish, the bride and groom returned to their car, and were back in Louisville in time for work on December 26.

Ralph and Marie Durbin-1980

In 1943 the couple returned to Sunfish and bought a dairy farm. Ralph and Marie were never blessed with children, but they encouraged and helped financially to keep 11 children in school.

Except for the 14 years spent in Louisville, St. John the Evangelist has always been Ralph and Marie's parish. Ralph served on the Parish Council. The couple were godparents for 12 children. In 1990 Ralph and Marie were honored by Bishop McRaith with a certificate recognizing their 56 years of faithful love.

In 1991 Ralph died of leukemia. Marie missed him very much but she carries on his wish to see the church grow. She sponsored two young men in the RCIA, and was their godmother at the Easter Vigil, 1992.

DURBIN, JOHN RAYMOND AND SARAH ELIZABETH "LIZZY," were married April 4, 1923 at St. John the Evangelist Church, Sunfish, KY by Fr. Louis Beruatto. Monsignor Beruatto also baptized their seven children. Four of their children: Audrey, Juanita, James E. and Basil, belong to St. John Parish. Louis is dead, Norman lives in Louisville, and Terry Ray in Bowling Green. Three sons served in World War II. At different times Lizzy cared for a younger brother and sister and a niece and nephew.

Both Lizzy and John R. trace their ancestry back to Ireland, through the John J. Durbin line. John J. gave the land for St. John Church. He was the father of Elisha Durbin, the Kentucky Missionary Priest. With the exception of six years when the father worked in Louisville, Lizzy and John R. always belonged to St. John Parish. John suffered a stroke and was unable to speak for two years before he died in 1977.

Basil, James, Louis, John R., Elizabeth, Audrey, Juanita, Norman and Terry Durbin.

The Church was the focal point of the Durbin family's religious and social life. The children were taught by the Franciscan Sisters at St. John School. Lizzy cooked in the school cafeteria for one year. She was a member of the Altar Society, and served meals in her home to many Glenmary and diocesan priests who came from Bowling Green and Leitchfield to minister at St. John. She followed the changes in the church, and was overjoyed at the first Mass celebrated in English. Lizzy's aunt, also from St. John, became a MSJ Ursuline, Sister Loretto Durbin, in 1915 and died in 1973. Lizzy still shows visitors a tiny infant Jesus that sleeps in a toothpick manger, that was given to her by Sister Loretto.

The Durbins stay close together. In October 1991, the children had a surprise birthday party for Lizzy. Most of the 21 grandchildren and 26 great-grandchildren were present.

DURBIN, JOHN AND RUDINA, The John and Rudina Durbin family rejoined the diocese at St. John the Evangelist, Paducah, in September, 1982 after five years away in Columbia and St. Louis, MO. They have three living children, daughters Aubrey (December 1980) and Lindsay (September 1984) and son William (December 1991). Their third daughter, Kristen, was full-term stillborn in January 1990 and is greatly missed.

John's father is Richard Anthony, a life-long member of St. John. His mother, Helen Luigs, passed away as a member of St. John in 1966. John, born 1956, is the eighth of 10 children. John credits his sisters for helping "raise" him after his mother's death at age 45. John attended St. John Elementary School and St. Mary High School in Paducah.

Rudina's full name is Mary Rudina Smith, and is the daughter of C.J. and Blanch Smith, members of the St.

Thomas More Parish in Paducah. Rudina, born 1956 has a brother and a sister. She was named after a nun. Rudina, an RN, attended St. Thomas More Elementary School in Paducah and St. Mary High.

John and Rudina Durbin, Lindsay (standing), Aubrey (sitting) and William (baby).

In recent years, John, a CPA, has served on the Parish Pastoral Council and the Finance Council. Rudina has been active in the PTA, serving as an officer, and with the parish Girl Scout troop. They co-chair the raffle ticket sales for the annual picnic.

A memorable trip in Spring 1990, made by the Durbin's included over 30 members of John's father's immediate family to the final resting place of John's great-grandfather Richard Francis in the Catholic community of Sunfish, KY near Leitchfield. After attending Mass, a visit to the parish cemetery revealed that nearly 20 percent of the departed were Durbins. Visiting was also done with several living women of the Sunfish Durbin family.

DURBIN, LAWRENCE ROBERT AND GERALDINE WURTZ,

were both born on Feb. 20, 1945. In keeping with the custom at St. John in 1945, they were baptized on the weekend following their birth in a joint ceremony. Their wedding vows were exchanged in the same church 20 years later.

Lawrence is the son of Richard A. and Helen Luigs Durbin. Geraldine's parents are William E. and LaVera Kaufman Wurtz. Both families trace their roots to the first members of the St. John community.

The Durbins are parents of three sons, Keith, Randall and Matthew. Randall is married to Shanna Ellis and Andrew Tyler is the newest member of the family.

Lawrence serves as a Eucharist Minister and is a member of the Lourdes Hospital Board of Directors. He has served on the St. John Parish Council, St. John Finance Committee, the St. Mary High School Board, and served as parish chairman during the St. Mary High Forward 2000 Campaign. Geraldine is a member of the choir and has served on the St. John Picnic Committee, St John Education Committee and the Sesquicentennial Committee, where she coordinated and edited the commemorative parish history.

DURBIN, LAWRENCE T.,

was born on June 12, 1922 in McCracken County, KY. His parents were Dora and Riley Durbin. He and his nine siblings lived near St. John Church where Riley had a blacksmith shop. Lawrence worked in Iowa on a farm as a youth where he was inducted into the Army during World War II. He served in Europe. He married Delene Ray who was received into the church upon their marriage. They had one son, Louis. Delene died in 1968. Lawrence worked with his brother Richard at Durbin's Garage for 42 years. He is a farmer now.

Dorothy Marie Fogle and her twin sister, Rosa Lee, were born on Aug. 12, 1935 in Daviess County. Their parents were Uldine and Curt Fogle. Their only brother is Clyde Fogle. Dorothy Marie attended Mount St. Joseph Academy and Brescia College and was organist for St. Raphael choir before marriage.

Dorothy Marie Fogle and Paul J. Willett were married at St. Raphael Church by Paul's uncle, Fr. Henry Willett on Jan. 17, 1959 in Daviess County. They lived in McCracken County. They had four children; Theresa Marie, Stevie, John and Cathy, before Paul died of cancer in 1964. One daughter, Mary Paula, was born later.

Lawrence T. Durbin Family

Lawrence Durbin and Dorothy Marie Willett were married at St. John Church on Sept. 14, 1968. They have four children: Laurie, Randy, Rose and Joseph. They made the Cursillo, TEC and Marriage Encounter. Lawrence is lector at St. John, Red Cross Volunteer and involved with St. Mary athletic programs. Dorothy Marie is song leader at St. John. They have 13 grandchildren.

DURBIN, RICHARD A.,

the first Durbin in this country, "Christopher" came from Ireland and settled in Baltimore. Father Elisha Durbin, (known as the horseback priest) grandson of Christopher, was the founder of Saint John in McCracken County.

Richard Francis Durbin, father of James Riley Durbin lived and died in Sunfish, KY. Riley moved here in 1916, married Dora Poat (daughter of Anthony Poat) and lived in sight of St. John the rest of their lives.

Richard, second of 10 children born to Riley and Dora grew up and attended St. John School and Church. He learned the art of repair in Dad's Blacksmith shop, which stood as a landmark for 50 years. He and Helen Marie (Luigs) were married by Fr. Raymond Hill, June 18, 1940.

Richard Durbin's family from left-Kenneth, John, James, Steven, Elizabeth, Richard A., Ruth Ann, Lawrence, Carolyn, George and Richard E.

Richard and Helen built a house on Florence Station Road, one-half mile from St. John, that was to be home for 10 wonderful children. They are: James, married Elizabeth Marshall, they have five children: Theodore, Philip, Bryce, Joy and Katie. Carolyn, married Henry Beavin, they have four sons: Jeffery, Christopher, Michael and Mark. Lawrence, married Geraldine Wurtz, they have three sons: Keith, Randal and Mathew. Ruth Ann, married Arvil McKendree, they have two daughters: Jennifer and Jessica. Richard Edward, married Susan Cash, they have three children: Emily, Timothy and Rebecca. Elizabeth, married Joe Gorline. Their two sons are Kevin and Thomas. Steven is married to Karen Meredith, their daughter is Meredith Leigh. John is married to Rudina Smith, they have three children: Aubrey, Lindsay and William. George is married to Sharon Rollins. Kenneth, married Lisa Cherry. All live near St. John except James and Carolyn who live in Columbus, OH and Louisville, KY, respectively.

Helen died May 25, 1966 and is buried in St. John Cemetery. Richard enjoys his children, 23 grandchildren and three great-grandchildren, who visit him regularly and lovingly.

DURBIN, RICHARD EDWARD AND SUSAN (CASH),

are members of St. John the Evangelist Parish. Richard was born and raised in McCracken County, KY, and Susan was born in Graves County and raised in McCracken County. They now reside on Old Highway 45 in Paducah. Susan is the daughter of Howard and Stella Willett Cash. Richard is the son of Richard A. Durbin. He is a businessmen and Susan works as a physical therapist. They have three children: Emily, born Dec. 10, 1974 a student at the University of Louisville; Timothy, born May 12, 1977 a student at St. Mary High School and Rebecca born July 11, 1979 a student at St. Mary Middle School. Richard is a member of the Knights of Columbus; media and advertising coordinator for St. John's Annual Picnic and Susan is a raffle ticket salesperson at other parishes for picnic.

DUVALL, (MARY) CARMA CLEMONS,

born on Sept. 20, 1957, was the fourth child of Odaline and Carmel. She attended Peonia Grade School, Clarkson High School, and was among the first graduating class of Grayson County High in 1975. After graduation, she went to work at the Bank of Clarkson.

On Sept. 19, 1976 at St. Benedict Church, Wax, she married (Charles) Stanley Duvall, the second child (of four) of Charles and Agnes Sanders Duvall of Anneta, KY. Stanley, born on July 15, 1957, had also graduated from Grayson County High School in 1975. He worked at Hoover Sing, and is currently employed at ALCATEL in Elizabethtown.

Their daughter, Kelly (Nicole), was born on Oct. 16, 1979. She presently attends Leitchfield Middle School, plays softball in the summer and takes piano lessons.

Stanley, Carma and Kelly Duvall

Carma is presently pursuing an associate degree in banking at Elizabethtown Community College. She has completed the Kentucky School of Banking Program from UK/UL.

Besides their two full-time jobs, the Duvalls annually lease a tobacco crop and raise a garden. Stanley does carpentry, plumbing, electrical and telephone work and a variety of other jobs on the side. For relaxation, he likes to fish and watch "Star Trek." He also coaches girls' softball in the summer. Carma does sewing, home canning, craft work of all kinds, cooking and shopping.

In 1986, Stanley joined the RCIA Program in St. Joseph Parish, Leitchfield, and became a Catholic on Holy Saturday night, 1987. The family belongs to St. Joseph Parish. Carma serves in the Religious Education program for the parish.

DYER, JOHN WILLIAM,

was the son of Nathan Harris Dyer and Mariam Griggs of Union County. His father was shot in the head in front of his blacksmith shop at the beginning of the Civil War. He was a very young man at the time, and witnessed this horrible scene.

Later he met Susan Catherine Fowler at a dance and afterwards married her. The family story says that she was eating a sweet potato, when he asked her to dance. She turned to a friend and said, "Hold my sweet potato while I dance with this man with a store bought suit."

John William, Henrietta (standing) and Susan Catherine Fowler Dyer.

Susan Catherine was the daughter of Richard Fowler and Margaret Jarboe who were married in Nelson County, KY, descendants of the early Catholics from Maryland. Susan and John were married at Sacred Heart Church in St. Vincent, KY. They remained in this parish and raised their family. Their children were: Edward, Margaret Mary, Mary Hulda, Richard Samuel, Henrietta Eleanor, Nancy Catherine, Clara Rosalie and John Thomas. Most of these children, if not all attended St Vincent Academy.

John helped to raise a Catholic family and finally was baptized at Sacred Heart at the age of 79. He and Susan spent the final years of their lives with their daughter, Mary Hulda and Roland Cecil.

(A list of Susan Catherine's brothers and sisters can be found in 'Richard Fowler' story.)

DYER, RICHARD LEON, was born in 1903 at Flourney near Morganfield, KY. His father, Richard Samuel Dyer, was a carpenter and blacksmith. His mother, Mary Lucinda Brown, a housewife. Richard was one of 14 children. They attended Mass at St. Vincent.

Mary Louise Raley, 1902, was born in Union County near Waverly. Her family moved to Henderson County when she was 2. Her father, William George Raley, of Waverly was a farmer. Her mother, Mary Ann Byrne, of Uniontown, a housewife. Louise was one of nine children, their only daughter.

Richard and Louise married Sept. 22, 1922 at Holy Name Church in Henderson. They lived in Morganfield. Richard was a mechanic for Truitt and Richards Motor Company. Their sons, Robert (1923) and William (1927) were born there. The family moved to Marion in 1929 for one year. Richard worked at Crittenden Motor Company. Their family, Frances Gray and Eugene Mackey, were the only Catholics in the county. Going to Mass meant travelling to Princeton or Henderson on dirt roads in a Model T, at first. Their daughter Margaret was born in 1931. In 1936 they moved to Evansville, IN, and enrolled the boys at St. Benedict. Richard worked at Hancock Truck Line. They lost practically everything in the 1937 Flood and returned to Marion. The children attended the schools in Marion and graduated there. Margaret attended Mount St. Joseph one year.

The children grown, Louise worked at Ben Franklin, Gene's Market and was an LPN at the Marion Hospital. More Catholics had moved to Marion. Mass was celebrated each Sunday in the James F. Mills home. St. William Church was built in 1966. Louise died in 1988. Richard still lives at home. That one year has expanded to 62.

EBELHAR, ANTHONY AND JULIE (GILLIM), were married Oct. 25, 1982. Anthony was born July 15, 1959 and Julie was born Oct. 26, 1961. They have lived in Owensboro all of their life and are members of the St. Mary Magdalene Parish, past members of the Immaculate Parish. Anthony served as a Parish Council member of the Immaculate Parish.

They have three sons: Alex, born Aug. 30, 1984; Jeremy born Feb. 10, 1987; and Adam who was born Feb. 2, 1992.

EBELHAR, CLARENCE AND SIDNEY, have lived in Daviess County most of their lives. Clarence, son of Leo and Helen Russell Ebelhar and was born 1930 in Sorgho, KY. He attended school at St. Mary Magdalene and graduated from St. Frances Academy in 1949, and Brescia College in 1964. He began working at Southern Bell Telephone in 1949 and entered the Navy in 1950 for four years.

Sidney was born in 1933, daughter of Lamar and Ozetta Hayden Riney and attended St. Alphonsus, graduating from Mount St. Joseph. They were married in 1952 and lived in California and Henderson, KY, before settling in Owensboro in 1956.

They have five children: Ronald Joseph, Richard Leo, Robert Keith, Mary Beth and David Brian and nine grandchildren.

They have been active members of the Immaculate Parish. Clarence was a Charter Member of the Men's Club, coached Little League, worked with Boy Scouts and served as secretary on the first Pastoral Council. He also was a representative of Immaculate on second Diocese Synod. He is a past-president of the Telephone Pioneers and remains quite active with this organization.

Clarence and Sidney Ebelhar Family

In 1967, Clarence and Sidney helped form a Cursillo Secretariat of Owensboro Diocese under Bishop Soenneker. Clarence served as Lay Director, First Director of Leaders School and on the Regional and National Secretariats and worked throughout the diocese and region on workshop teams.

They were instrumental in forming an Ecumenical Movement and Walk to Emmaus in Methodist Church, also Cursillo in Evansville and St. Louis Diocese.

Clarence retired from Bell South in 1992 after 42 years service.

Sidney served as secretary for the Immaculate Altar Society and had a Renew Group in their home and presently serves as lector. She was rector for First Women's Cursillo in Owensboro and St. Louis, MO and worked on Ecumenical teams. She served on Regional Secretariat and workshop teams, also first Diocese Pastoral Council and Adult Formation Committee. She worked as assistant in Follow Through at Goodloe School for seven years, helped organize food bank at Help Office and served as coordinator and board member. She is presently working as bridal consultant at Abbington's Bridal House.

The Ebelhars are looking forward to retirement and serving the Lord for many years to come.

EDELEN, JAMES CHRISTOPHER III, was born and raised in Daviess County, and Deborah (White) Edelen was born and raised in Henderson County. James was the son of James C. Edelen Jr. and the late Edna Tabor Edelen. Deborah is the daughter of Ewing White and Lorraine Neely White. They currently live in Daviess County. James worked as supervisor for Big Rivers Electric Corporation, Deborah works at a shop at home as a hairdresser. He is a life long member of St. Peter Parish, Stanley, active in Parish Council and Eucharistic Minister. Deborah is a convert since 1976.

They have four children: James C. Edelen IV, born Jan. 16, 1970, a student at Pharmacy College University of Kentucky; Michael A. Edelen, born May 29, 1973, a Western Kentucky University student; Benjamin Beau Edelen, born Sept. 6, 1977, a Owensboro Catholic High School student; and Amy Lynn Edelen Oct. 7, 1981 a student at Holy Angels.

EDGE, ANCEL V., was born near Whitesville, to his father, Lawrence Edge who was a farmer, his mother, Florence Horseman, a housewife. Huberta Rysselberghe was born near Whitesville, daughter of John Rysselberghe and Agnes Howard both baptized at St. Marys of the Woods by Fr. O'Sullivan. They married, Oct. 30, 1951, at St. Mary's by Fr. Nahstoll, and moved to Whiting, IN, where he was employed. Three children where born in Whiting, baptized at Sacred Heart Church. They moved back to Owensboro where three more children were born. One child baptized at St. Joe and Paul and two at Precious Blood. All six graduated from Owensboro Catholic High School.

Richard Wayne married Laura Westerfield has three children, is plant manager at Southwire: Sue Carol is married to Greg Doggett, one child has lived in Alaska for the past 17 years. Works for Alaska Department of Natural Resources; Denise Ann had one daughter and works as a registered nurse at Owensboro Daviess County Hospital; Joseph Torrence married Tina Hancock, three children, owns Edge's Business Machines; Jeffrey Curtis is single, worked at Fields Packing, unemployed at this writing; Byron Keith is single and works for state of Kentucky. Ancel passed away July 26, 1987. Huberta remains at their home in Owensboro, with the two single sons. She belongs to Precious Blood Parish, a member of the Over 50s Club at church, works bingo, picnic, Helps Office once a week and attends Mass at Medco Nursing Home every Wednesday.

EDGE, GLADYS, has lived in Whitesville, KY, one block from St. Mary of the Woods Church since her husband of 61 years died in 1982. She is one of the oldest members of St. Mary's and is sometimes called the "Mother of Whitesville." Gladys celebrated her 90th birthday Nov. 5, 1992 with many family and friends including her new great-great-grandson. All five generations were present. Gladys lives by herself; does her own business; goes to Mass and prays many rosaries devoutly everyday; has been in the Altar Society 72 years, Legion of Mary for 20 years, Army of Mary for 10 years, and helps at the Senior Citizen Center.

Gladys Edge

Gladys was born in 1902 and baptized in St. Anthony, Peonia, by Father Myron. She and her parents moved to Whitesville in 1904. She married John Nov. 16, 1920 at St. Mary's. Father Hugh O'Sullivan officiated. They were farmers and raised 11 of 15 children and 10 still living and one died while in the service. The doctor called Gladys "the neighborhood nurse" since she was always

James C. Edelen III and Family

there to help with the sick and childbirth. Gladys remembers a lot about "the good old days" and loves to tell her 43 grandchildren, 45 great-grandchildren and one great-great-grandchild about them.

Teachers ask her to come to school to tell about her childhood; walking to school barefooted and not being able to go in bad weather; the Depression and how hard it was to get food. She recalls courting John in a horse and buggy and going to barn dances. She still loves music and dances a little. A couple of years ago she had to give up a lifelong hobby crocheting, because of her eyesight. She used to crochet at least 50 items for the picnics country store each year.

EDGE, JAMES L., was born on Feb. 2, 1942. Sarah Steele was born June 28, 1942. They were married on May 27, 1967 at St. Stephen Cathedral. James is self-employed as a salesman. James' parents were Alphonsus Edge and Agnes Pinkston. Sarah's parents were V. J. Steele and Pauline Hagan. James and Sarah belong to Blessed Mother Parish.

Anne (22), Mike (21), James (20), John (16), Robert (13), Nick (11) and Laura (9) are their children. Anne graduated from Belmont Abbey in North Carolina last year. Mike is a senior at St. Louis University; James is a sophomore at O.C.C.; John a junior at O.C.H.S.; Robert is in eighth grade at O.C.M.S.; Nick is in sixth grade and Laura is in the fourth, and they will go to St. Angela Merci School.

EDGE, JOEY, was born on March 12, 1978 in Fort Knox, KY. His brother, Jimmy Jones was born in November 1973 in Germany. His mom, Darlene Edge was born in Curdsville, KY. His mom has five brothers and one sister.

When Joey started school he went to St. Pius the Tenth through kindergarten and first grade. Then they moved to Knottsville, KY. He went to school there is second grade year. Then they moved to Hawesville, KY. He went to school there his third grade year all the way until his eighth grade year. He will graduate from Hancock County High School in 1996.

Joey's dad, Pat Edge was born on March 18, 1938 in Kentucky. He works at NSA, drives a fork truck. His mom stays home, cleans the house and takes care of bills.

EDGE FAMILY, LOUIS AND NORA, have lived in Whitesville in eastern Daviess County all their lives. They were married on May 2, 1938; Monsignor Hugh O'Sullivan, the first Vicar General of the Owensboro Diocese officiated at their wedding. Louis and Nora have been grocers, farmers and shipbuilders. Louis worked in an Owensboro steel mill until he retired; Nora has worked in the home nurturing their 14 children, two of whom died as children.

Nora remembers when Louis was called into the Army in World War II. She stayed on the farm with their four children during his 13 months of service. Nora said, "We had very good neighbors. All of them helped us when crops needed doing or food needed gathering or just whatever. And we haven't forgotten about their generosity."

The Edge Family

Louis and Nora are proud of their children, all of whom have found useful careers. Some have farms, some work professionally. Many have children and grandchildren. Louis and Nora have 12 living children, 47 grandchildren and 21 great grandchildren. They celebrated their 50th Wedding Anniversary in 1988 with over 200 people, most of them family who still live nearby in Daviess County.

Louis and Nora have a special ministry in the "Whitesville Hoedowners," a country music band which they lead. They play at retirement homes and at the Wendell Foster Center in Owensboro and about anywhere people call them.

Louis has been a St. Vincent DePaul Society member for 28 years, has been on the St. Mary Parish Pastoral Council for four terms, and belonged to the Men's Club. Nora has been in the Legion of Mary for 28 years and in the Altar Society for 53 years. She is an active organizer of a parish quilting club at St. Mary's.

EDGE, PATRICK JOSEPH, was born in Whitesville, KY, one of eight children to Phillip Lawrence Edge and Mary Florence Horseman. Pat followed in his father's footsteps as a farmer and eventually married Anna Leah Payne of Knottsville, KY. Leah is the daughter of Franklin Elisha Payne and Margaret Dell Millay. She has one brother, two sisters and eight half-brothers and one half-sister.

Pat and Leah married Oct. 23, 1928 and lived in Whitesville. They moved back and forth from Whitesville to Knottsville over the next few years and were blessed with eight living children: Joseph, Margaret, Anna, Bobby, Joyce, Mary, Patsy and Dorothy. Pat has worked in South Bend, IN for a short time as well as made a living farming. Leah has worked at the Cigar Factory and as a housewife.

Patrick Joseph and Leah Edge

Pat lost his eyesight 53 years ago, never seeing his two youngest children, but continued farming, carpentry work, and providing for his family even after he became blind. Pat and Leah have been active at St. William Parish since moving from Whitesville's St. Mary of the Woods Parish. They have called bingo, worked at parish picnics, and been a part of the senior citizens group at Knottsville.

They presently have 43 grandchildren, 80 great-grandchildren and are celebrating their 64th Wedding Anniversary in 1992. Pat and Leah still attend Mass at St. Williams where it is not uncommon to see them walking arm in arm from their home on Free-Silver Road to the church.

ELDER FAMILY, CHARLES AND ALINE, Three of John M. Thompson's sons migrated to Kentucky to the area serviced by St. Jerome's Church around 1890 at Fancy Farm, KY. John M. Thompson died in Henderson, KY in 1870.

One of his sons, William Horace Thompson, married Eliza Frances Fuqua on Sept. 9, 1865. They were the parents of eight children. Their youngest daughter, Alice, met and married Wm. Don Helm of Whitesville, KY Daviess County. He was a non-Catholic and was instructed and baptized by Fr. Mattingly of Mayfield, KY and married the following day Jan. 18, 1909. They had nine children. One of their daughters, Frances Aline Helm, married Charles Anthony Elder, son of Geo. Wm. Elder and Annie Idella (Toon) Elder.

George Wm. is the grandson of Thomas G. Elder who migrated from Maryland to Fancy Farm, KY. Annie Idella Toon is the daughter of Elisha Toon and Elizabeth Jane Burgess Toon of St. Dennis Parish, Hickman County.

Charles A. Elder and Frances Aline (Helm) Elder have 14 children, 37 grandchildren and 23 great-grandchildren.

Charles Anthony Elder died May 15, 1986 and is buried at St. Jerome's Cemetery, Fancy Farm, KY.

Charles A. Elder was a farmer and raised his family on a farm at Fancy Farm, KY. All of his children were born in Graves County.

ELDER, EDWARD NELSON, was born in Mayfield, KY to Donald and Mary Ruth Elder. Carol Elizabeth (Elliott) Elder was born in Graves County, KY, to Joseph Rudy and Judith Loretta Elliott. They now live in Fancy Farm, KY and are members of St. Jerome Parish in Fancy Farm. They are the parents of Jacob Edward Elder who was born June 13, 1983 and attends St. Joseph School in Mayfield, Cody Joseph Elder born Aug. 5, 1985 also attends St. Joseph and Nathaniel McKinley Elder born Dec. 3, 1991.

ELLIOTT, CHARLES WILLARD SR., is the only living son of James William Elliott and Victoria Cash Elliott. He was born on Dec. 6, 1905 in Fancy Farm, KY, and later baptized by Father Haesley.

Willard married Cecelia Carrico in March 1927. Cecelia is the daughter of Henry Carrico and Augusta Hayden Carrico.

Willard and Cecelia are the parents of five children, Charles Willard Jr., married to Lois McCabe; Rosa Nell married to the late Howard Burch; Joseph Rudolph married to Judith Garland; James Howard married to Jaqueline Gordon; and Joseph Kenneth married to Mary Virginia Hobbs.

At age 86 Willard still attends Mass daily and often assists children and grandchildren in building, roofing and many other carpentry tasks.

Willard and Cecelia have 23 grandchildren and 22 great-grandchildren.

ERWIN, JERRY THOMAS, was born July 17, 1940 to Lewis and Virginia Erwin in Graves County, KY. Norma Marie (Carrico) Erwin was born June 2, 1943 to Harold and Wilmuth Carrico also in Graves County. They

The Charles and Aline Elder Family.

now live in Mayfield, KY, and are members of St. Joseph Parish in Mayfield. Jerry works as a utilityman at General Tire and Rubber Company in Mayfield and Norma is a secretary at St. Joseph School.

They are the parents of four children: Jean Marie Erwin, born Dec. 7, 1968 a student at University of Kentucky; William Thomas Erwin, born Jan. 20, 1970, student at University of Kentucky; Gerri Anne Erwin, born July 21, 1972, student at University of Kentucky; and Carrie Mary Virginia Erwin who was born Nov. 1, 1976, is a student of Mayfield High School.

ESPY, EDWARD CHARLES, the Espy family is of Irish decent having come to the United States in the late 1700s. Dr. James A. Wilson served in the Indiana legislature in the mid-1850s. He lived in Rossville, IN, but later moved to Lafayette, IN, where he practiced medicine. He was the grandfather of Ada Wilson who married George Espy, a farmer whose family had settled near Rossville. Ada Wilson and George Espy were married and moved to Indianapolis, IN.

The Espy family have been members of Sacred Heart Parish since Nov. 17, 1945, when Ruth Helen Roberts married Edward Charles Espy at a chapel at Camp Breckinridge, KY, where he was stationed in the Army. Monsignor John M. Higgins officiated at the wedding.

They have a son, Edward Charles II who is married to Judith Ann Woodruff, whose parents were Amelia Graves and Harry Woodruff. They have a daughter Laura Ann who is a graduate of Union County High School.

Ruth Helen Roberts Espy is the daughter of Francis M. Roberts and Robert E. Roberts who were also members of Sacred Heart Parish, Waverly. Their parents and grandparents helped establish this parish. From these families there have been several members who chose the religious life, Sisters of Charity, Ursuline Sisters, Sisters of Mercy, a Dominican Nun and a Dominican Priest. Most of the women in these families were educated at St. Vincent Academy or Mount St. Joseph. The men were sent to St. Joseph at Bardstown, KY, or to a school in Jasper, IN. There was a grade school for boys at Sacred Heart, St. Vincent and from there they went on to public schools.

They live in one of the oldest houses in Union County. Their life time hobby has been restoring the home. Their house is on a farm that was owned by his parents. They farmed for awhile, then Ed went to work on the river for a barge line and she was a medical secretary at Job Corps Center until retiring.

ESTEP, J.P., was born April 25, 1927 in Celina, TN. J.P. was in the Army; attended Bulova School of Watchmaking in Woodside, NY, where he met Rosemary Prinz Estep who worked as secretary and receptionist. They were married June 22, 1957; purchased jewelry store in Franklin, KY, in March 1959; operated the store until they retired in 1985. Rosemary now works for her son in sporting goods store in Franklin. They joined the St. Mary of the Woods Parish in Franklin, KY in March 1959, and are past members of the St. Mary of Christians in Winfield, NY. Rosemary is active in Ladies Guild, Past Pastoral Council member, Bible School teacher and past CCD teacher.

J.P. and Rosemary Prinz Estep

They have two sons: John H. Estep, born July 16 in Woodside, NY; Joseph J. Estep born June 26 in Franklin, KY. They also have five grandchildren: Jeremy Estep born Jan. 27, 1986; Magen Estep born May 9, 1988; Carey born Feb. 20, 1978; Hilary born Aug. 19, 1984 and Jay Allen born Sept. 14, 1992.

EVANS, MARTHA JEAN SCOTT, was born in Paducah, KY, and baptized at St. Francis De Sales Church. She attended St. Mary Academy and Draughon Business College in Paducah. She married Norman Oscar Evans in 1950 and was widowed in 1978. They have four children. Norma Jean married Gordon Wirt. They live in Lexington, KY, and have two daughters, Melissa and Maria. Mark Wayne married Barbara Wells. They live in Marshall County. Nancy married Rich Harms, and resides in Brunsville, IA. Matthew Lewis married Donna Wring. They live in Louisville, KY and have one daughter, Jessica.

Martha has always lived in Paducah. She was a member of St. Francis De Sales until her marriage. Since that time, she has ben a member of St. Thomas More Church. She sings in the choir, is active in RCIA, is on the Bereavement Committee, a Eucharistic Minister, a former member of the Parish Council and a member of the Altar Society. She is an active member and Past Regent of the Daughters of Isabella.

Great-great-grandparents of Martha J. Evans

Martha is employed by Prudential Insurance Company in Paducah. Her parents are Reba Johnson Scott, originally from Marshall County, KY. She is a convert and is a member of St Francis De Sales. Harry Franklin Scott was Martha's father. He was originally from Livingston County, KY. He was a member of St. Francis De Sales. He died in 1951.

Martha's great-great-grandparents were Barney and Malinda Paydon Markey. Barney was originally from Ireland. They were the leading spirit in establishing the Catholic Church at Hampton, KY in Livingston County in 1894. At Barney's request, the church was named St. Bernard after his patron saint. The church is no longer there. The altar and pews were removed to St. Mary Church at LaCenter, KY. Some of the candlesticks were taken to St. Francis De Sales, Paducah. This information was from a book called *The History of Catholic Church in Paducah, KY,* copyright 1934. At that time there was a Catholic cemetery at Hampton called Markey Cemetery.

EZELL, JANE LEA (ROBERTS), met Leslie Davis Ezell 19 years ago (1993). During this time Davis' parents were in the process of a divorce. His was a Baptist family then he switched to the Catholic faith when he married Jane Lea. Jane Lea's family has been Catholic all of their life. Jane Lea's parents are Johnny and Mary Jane Roberts, which have been married 50 years. Davis and Jane Lea were married on Dec. 27, 1975.

On March 4, 1979 Davis and Jane Lea had their first of two children. They named their baby girl, Courtney Michelle Ezell. At this time Davis and Jane owned a Sonic on Parish Avenue. They soon sold the Sonic and Davis worked for McDonalds, while Jane went to nursing school in Henderson, KY, where she soon became a registered nurse.

On May 26, 1984 they had their second child, this time a son and named him Jacob William Ezell, after Davis' uncle Willie. Four years later Davis graduated from Brescia College and got a job with Fruit of the Loom in Bowling Green, KY, where they lived for two years. After that two years, the family got transferred to Harlingen, TX. The family lived there for two years and Davis remains there while Jane and the kids live in Owensboro, KY.

Courtney is now 13 and attends school at Owensboro Catholic Middle School and Jacob is 8 and goes to Bishop Soenneker School in Owensboro, KY.

Jane and Davis are still married and hope to be together again very soon. When this happens they hope to move back to Bowling Green, KY and stay there for a long while.

FARLEY FAMILY, THE MALCOLM, began in 1947, with the marriage of "Mac" and Betty Ann Cambron, at Holy Name Rectory, Henderson, with Rev. Robt. Gipperich officiating.

Malcolm's mother was Barbara Elizabeth Feix and his father was George Jesse Farley. Betty Ann's mother was Lilla Mae Graves and father was George Leonard Cambron. In 1948 James M. Farley Jr. was born; 1950 Debra Teresa; 1951 Christopher Len; 1954 Bruce Cambron; 1955 Marcia Ann; 1957 David; 1959 Thomas Robert; 1961 Richard Kennedy; 1962 Timothy Ray; 1963 Joseph Patrick; 1967 Dianne Maria; 1968 Elizabeth Mae.

The George Cambrons moved from Union County to the Corydon Community and began attending St. Peter Church in Waverly in 1931. When they bought a farm near Cairo, they started going to Holy Name Church in Henderson. Betty Ann was 8 years old at that time. Malcolm became a Catholic in 1961.

From 1964 to 1973, four of their 12 children died of cystic fibrosis, a lung and pancreas disease. Debra at age 14, David was 9 years, Dianne was 22 months and "Buffy" was 5 years old. Tim and Charyl Hoover, of Bowling Green, KY have daughters, Elizabeth and Jennifer, with cystic fibrosis. Their oldest is David and second child Nicholas, died in his sleep at age 2 1/2. The five children are buried in St. Louis Cemetery in Henderson.

The other grandchildren are Jim's Jamie Leigh. Her mother, Pauline Deel, is from Pilgrim Knob, VA. Bruce married Patti Bradley Gibson and has two stepchildren, Nat and Jessica Gibson; Bruce Jr.; Kristine and Rebecca. Marcia's son Michael Vanover graduated number five in the 1992 class of Henderson County High School (the oldest grandchild), the daughter of Marcia and Mike Vanover is Barbara Marie. Tom married Kim White and their daughters are Lauren and Leslie Ann. Richard married Sabrina Christian and have Betsy Jo; Christian and Issac.

FENTRESS, JOSEPH WILLIS, was born Aug. 19, 1894 at Axtel in Breckenridge County. His father Charles, a nonCatholic, was a farmer and his mother was a housewife. Before her marriage she was Mary Joanna Lewis daughter of William Richard Lewis and Mary Margaret Jarboe. The Lewis and Jarboe families were some of the earliest settlers in our area, and have a rich Catholic heritage.

(L to R) Attendants Iva Mattingly and Oliver Finley with groom (seated) Joseph W. Fentress and bride, Pauline Rose, April 11, 1923.

Joseph Willis was baptized by Father William Gabe and was a life-long member of the St. Anthony Church. He served in the Navy during World War I. He attended the Ky. State Normal School in Bowling Green and taught eight years in the rural county schools. He married Pauline Rose who was born in Ammons, KY. She was the daughter of Robert Lee and Amanda Swink Rose. At the time of their marriage she had moved to Owensboro where she was employed at Murphy Chair Company They were married at St. Stephen Church April 11, 1923, bought a farm adjoining his parents and remained there until the last few years of their lives. They were the parents of five children: Mary, Joseph, Lois, Clinton and Kathryn, 20 grandchildren and 16 great-grandchildren.

Joseph Willis and Pauline celebrated their 50th Wedding Anniversary April 11, 1983, and lived to celebrate their 66th anniversary. Pauline passed away Nov. 9, 1989 at the age of 85. Joseph Willis passed away Sept. 13,1991 at the age of 97. They are interred in the St. Anthony Cemetery.

FENWICK, RICHARD IGNATIUS,

Among Maryland Catholic pioneer arrivals to Nelson County, KY were Richard Ignatius Fenwick Sr., 1750-1816, wife and children, Elizabeth Abell Thomas, 1754, widow, Mark Thomas and Walter Burch, 1757-1822, wife, Theresa Hagan and children.

October 1836 Robert Fenwick, 1805-1862, married Elizabeth Burch, 1829-1856, father, John Hanson Burch, 1788-1852, remarried 1814 to Nancy Greenwell, father, Joshua Leonard Greenwell, 1756-1821 and Elizabeth Newton, father, William. They returned to Chasey Creek farm in Union County and attended Sacred Heart Church at St. Vincent, one mile west of Waverly. Of eight christened children, youngest two, Mary Ellen "Ella" 1854-1933, and Mary Lucinda, 1852-1822, married 1876, respectively, Newton Abner Long, 1849-1883, merchant and Elisha Richard Bondurant, 1847-1909, carpenter from Meade County, KY.

Fenwick/Long House

With Lucinda's burial at St. Vincent alongside two infant sons, parents and grandparents, Elisha Richard returned to Brandenburg with infant son, James Henry, 1877-1956. Elisha remarried 1879 to Laura Ann Garey, 1858-1942, father, Jonathan, 1823-1875, Harrison County, Mauckport, IN. Their daughter, Imogene, 1899-1914, married 1907 to half-cousin, William Burch Long, 1800-1953, engineer/artist/poet, oldest of three children of Newton Abner and Mary Ellen "Ella" Fenwick Long.

They returned to Waverly Pit Coal Mine employment until it closed; next helped erect Ohio River flood control dams. Widower Burch Long's two daughters, Annie Laura, 1910, married 1927 Joseph Thomas Perdue, 1905-1930, father, George Thomas Perdue, while Minnie Elizabeth, 1912, married 1932, Jefferson County, Robert Reed Young Sr. 1909-1956, Meade County farmer.

Burch remarried, 1933, Agnes French, 1893-1967, father, Dan. They resided in Thomas Fenwick Henderson home until burial beside Imogene in Cap Anderson, Brandenburg and Agnes' parents and his mother in Waverly.

FERRIELL, SISTER JEAN PASCHAL,

was born June 4, 1902 at Holy Cross, KY to Thomas Ferriell and Catherine Peake. She was baptized as Edna on June 7, 1902. Edna entered the convent on July 16, 1920 and received her habit on March 19, 1921. She took her vows on Aug. 15, 1923, Aug. 5, 1924 and Aug. 15, 1926. She had the following brothers and sisters: Bernadette, James, Angela (deceased), Clara, Imelda, Stephen George, Carl, Kendrick, Marcella, Joseph and Alton.

She was a music teacher and served at the following missions: St. Angela Home, Louisville; Nebraska City, NE; Affton, MO; Jeffersonville, IN; St. Francis, KY; St. Paul, Louisville; St. Columba, Louisville; Buechel, KY; St. James, Louisville; Affton, MO; Buechel, KY.

FIELD, ROBERT EDWIN AND HELEN BOOTH,

were married June 2, 1923, at St. Stephen Church, Owensboro, KY. They had seven children: Edward Booth Field, born 1926-died 1938; Robert Edwin Field Jr., born 1927-died 1932; Jane Caroline Booth Field, S.C.N. (Sister of Charity of Nazareth) presently at the Motherhouse, Nazareth, KY; William Overstreet Field, presently living in East Orleans, MA; Clark Gabriel Field, presently living in Evansville, IN; Phillip Slack Field, presently living in Evansville, IN; and Elizabeth Overstreet Field, presently living in Evansville, IN.

Robert E. Field was born in Owensboro, May 20, 1901; died Jan. 21, 1973. He attended St. Francis Academy, Owensboro, and graduated from Senior High School, Owensboro. Attended Notre Dame University for one year. Was an accountant and active in Democratic politics; was chairperson of North Precinct in Owensboro for many years. He was baptized and buried from St. Joseph and Paul Parish (was St. Paul's at baptism). Member of St. Stephen Parish most of his married life, though some years in Precious Blood Parish. Robert was the son of John Edwin Field (born 1873-died 1937) and Mary Ella Slack (born 1873-died 1938). He was the grandson of Robert Winfield Slack (born in Bardstown, KY in 1848-d. 1924) and Susan Lavely (born in Bardstown, KY in 1851-died 1926) and John William Morton Field (born 1844-died 1903) and Elizabeth Hanning (born 1844-died 1926). Elizabeth went to daily Mass and was the daughter of John Green Hanning (born 1815-died 1890) and Mary Jane Hagan. John Green Hanning became a Trappist Monk at Gethsemani, Bardstown, KY and is subject of the book, *The Man Who Got Even With God*. John William Morton Field's father was Thomas Field (born 1805-died 1847).

J.W.M. Field helped build St. Paul Church and attended Mass with his family faithfully every Sunday even though he was not a Catholic. He was a large man, so they had the first pew in church made for him. It was built larger than any of the rest of the pews. This was the way the pews were until the recent renovation of the church. They were distillers and owned the Field Distillery in Owensboro until the 1939 Great Depression. The Field family probably attended St. Stephen until St. Paul was built. He was brother to Susan, Morton, William, Phillip, Nanny and Dorothy.

Helen Booth was born June 8, 1903-died May 30, 1992. She was baptized and buried from St. Stephen Cathedral, in Owensboro. Helen was the daughter of Edwin Galt Booth (born April 12, 1869-died January 1951) and Jane Caroline Overstreet (born April 21, 1873-died June 1933), both of Owensboro. She had two brothers, Henry O. and Samuel. Her grandparents were Henry Overstreet (born 1850-died 1915) and Ella Clark (born Nov. 25, 1864-died November 1957). Henry was from Calhoun and Ella from Maple Mount, St. Alphonsus Church. After marriage she moved to Owensboro. Henry was a lawyer and Kentucky state senator. He stopped practicing law and went into farming because, as he said, "You can't practice law and stay an honest man." Helen attended a one-room, Carrico School House, in elementary grades in Barn Harbor Hills near Ben Hawes State Park now. Attended St. Francis Academy in Owensboro in high school, also attended Nazareth High School in Bardstown, KY, and graduated from Owensboro Senior High. She was very active in both church and politics. She was a member of St. Stephen Altar Society and Legion of Mary. She made yearly retreats at the Passionests' Nuns, St. Joseph Monastery, in Owensboro. In politics, she was North Precinct chairperson for many years; worked hard in the Democratic Party driving rural folks to the voting (polls) booths, calling, campaigning door to door, etc.

This story appeared in the Owensboro newspaper. Elizabeth's great-grandfather, Henry Overstreet, had had a stroke. He was in a coma. He had been great friends with Fr. Volk, considered a saint in the diocese at the time. Fr. Volk was called to come and anoint her great-grandfather.

Now, even though these two men were friends, Henry O. greatly disliked priests, was not a church-goer, nor a Catholic either. Her great-grandmother (Ella O.) somewhat tentative called Fr. Volk. When Fr. V. received the message, he was saddened that he could not immediately go. However, he called Jolly Hayden, then a deacon and a cousin of Ella O., saying, "Take the nearest priest, and I will do the rest."

When Jolly Hayden and Fr. Higgins (John Martin Lancaster Spalding Higgins) arrived, he went to her great-grandfather's bedside. The family were all kneeling around the room praying but feeling a little tense with the situation.

This was Fr. Higgins first anointing since he was newly ordained. When he called her great-grandfather's name he opened his eyes and began to respond positively to Fr. H.'s questions about sorrow for sin and desire to be anointed. Elizabeth's great-grandfather's reconciliation with the church caused all in the room to weep and was considered a miraculous event attributed to the holiness of Fr. Volk.

FISCHER, FATHER CHARLES,

was born June 7, 1924, the third child of Henry I. Fischer and Julia Rosalia Reisz. His brothers and sisters are: Henry Jr., Marie (deceased as an infant), Ann (deceased), Frank, Bernard, Ruben and Eugenia. They lived on a farm at Brown's Valley, KY until he was 10 years old. His father ran a store at Stanley in 1935, then they moved to Owensboro. He attended St. Anthony School, Brown's Valley, St. Peter School, Stanley, and graduated from St. Frances Academy in Owensboro.

His first real call to the priesthood came in his junior year of high school at a retreat held at St. Stephen Cathedral. He went to the seminary in September 1942. He attended St. Charles College, Cotonsville, MD, and St. Mary Seminary, Baltimore. His ordination was by Bishop Cotton on May 30, 1950.

Fr. Charles Fischer

His first assignment was assistant at St. Anthony, Brown's Valley and St. Sebastian, Calhoun. He was also teaching at St. Frances Academy and then at Owensboro Catholic High School. In 1962 he left Daviess County and was assigned to Rosary Chapel, Paducah and St. Mary, LaCenter.

In 1965 he was transferred to St. Rose, Cloverport. Two years later he went to Whitesville where he helped organize Trinity High School. In 1967 he made the Cursillo, which was a real turning point in his life. He was transferred to St. Agnes, Uniontown in 1976. Seven years later he went to Blessed Mother, Owensboro. In 1989 he moved to St. Paul and St. Elizabeth, Grayson County.

He has enjoyed all of his assignments and the good people he found in each place. He is grateful to so many people who have loved and accepted him over the years. He is very grateful to Almighty God.

FISCHER, LORENA FLOOD,

was born near Stephensport, KY. Baptized by Father Norman on March 14, 1911 at St. Romuald Church, Hardinsburg. Daughter of James Edward Flood, farmer and carpenter, and Mary Elizabeth Carroll. They were born in Breckenridge County. Their parents immigrated from Ireland in the middle 1800s.

The Carroll family, Michael and Catherine, settled near Cloverport, St. Rose Parish; John and Bridget Flood settled near Stephensport, St. Romuald Parish.

Robert and Lorena Fischer

James Flood and Elizabeth Carroll were married February 1888, St. Romuald Church. Elizabeth died Dec. 13, 1914. James died Jan. 18, 1923. Parents of 11 children. Lorena, the youngest, spent three years in convent school, Hardinsburg; four years at St. Rose School, Cloverport.

In 1929 Lorena entered nurses training school at St. Anthony Hospital in Louisville, KY. Graduated 1932, did post graduate work in New York City. Nursed mostly in Kentucky and surrounding towns.

Married Robert Fischer at St. Philip Neri Church in Louisville Oct. 14, 1941, son of Frank and Margaret Klien Fischer of Dale, IN. Robert was a construction worker and carpenter. He was drafted into the Army in 1942. Spent most of three and a half years in Italy, radio operator on the front line, wounded three times. Received the Purple Heart.

Family moved back to Cloverport in 1950, St. Rose Parish. Children: Robert Sue Thompson, July 1942, teacher; John Robert Fischer, April 1947, metallurgic engineer; and Jane Elizabeth Powers, December 1949, teacher. All three attended St. Rose Grade, St. Romuald High School. Robert died Dec. 16, 1990 at age 76. Buried at St. Romuald Cemetery, Father John Little, clergyman. Lorena moved to an apartment after selling their home. There are seven grandchildren: Lesley, Lara, Mac, Amanda, Jennifer, Michael and Jill.

FISCHER, SYLVESTER ROBERT AND BARBARA,
Sylvester was born in Rome in Daviess County, KY, on July 9, 1944. His father, Robert Fischer, was a lifelong farmer in the Rome community and married Audrey Payne from Curdsville on April 3, 1937. Sylvester has one brother and seven sisters all living in the Owensboro area. Sylvester married Barbara Howard, daughter of George C. Howard and Beulah Mayfield Howard, from Whitesville on July 17, 1965 at St. Mary of the Woods Church, with the late Father Benedict Huff officiating.

Sylvester and Barbara Fischer

Sylvester and Barbara have lived in Rome their entire married life and are members of St. Martin Church. They have four children: Brian, Jerry, Debra and Christa. Jerry is married to the former Michelle Lashbrook and they have one son, Robert. Brian is a student at Brescia working toward a degree in Chemistry and both sons work in the family farming operation. Debra presently lives in Lexington and is a physical therapist at UK Medical Center. Christa is a student at Brescia College working toward a degree in communication sciences and disorders.

In addition to farming, Sylvester is supervisor of sales and secretary-treasurer for the Owensboro Tobacco Board of Trade. He is a member of the Knights of Columbus, a director of Daviess County Farm Bureau, and a member of St. Martin Mens' Club. Barbara is a homemaker and a member of St. Martin Altar Society.

The Fischers enjoy family get-togethers, bar-b-ques, volleyball, and hope to be able to travel in the years to come.

FLAHERTY, MIKE AND ANN,
arrived in Owensboro in April of 1988 from Rutherfordton, NC into the Parish of The Immaculate. Mike took a job as a child/youth psychologist at Green River Comprehensive Care Morehead Center in order to be closer to family (in Louisville, KY where both Mike and Ann are from originally) and to be able to send his children to Catholic schools. Mike brought his wife, Ann, and their two boys, Michael and Aaron. They officially registered with Our Lady of Lourdes Parish in July and enrolled Michael in kindergarten at Our Lady of Lourdes School. Within two weeks, Ann had gotten a call from the principal who asked her to teach fifth and sixth grade math, science, religion and spelling as a team teacher. She accepted and taught there until giving birth to her third child, Hannah, the following April. At this time Ann decided to stay home, work on her masters in school counseling and get involved in Lourdes Parish and Catherine Spalding School where both of her boys now attend. In the past three years she has taught sixth grade CCD, become an Eucharistic minister, was elected to Parish Council and became a sponsor couple with her husband, Mike. Mike ushers for Lourdes and plays on their men's softball team. Ann has also enjoyed being a homeroom mother and helping with prayer days, field trips, carnivals and other activities associated with her sons' school life. Michael, the Flaherty's oldest son, made his First Communion and first Penance last year and now proudly serves for Lourdes Parish.

Ann has just completed her masters through Western Kentucky University and has been hired by Catholic High to become their academic counselor. She looks forward to serving and supporting the wonderful Catholic school system here in Owensboro.

FLEISCHMANN, BROTHER CONRAD,
Monk-Abbey of Gethsemani, Trappist, KY. Marvin Aloysius born April 7, 1929 near Brown's Valley, KY. He attended; St. Mary Magdalene grade school, Sorgho, KY with his twin brother Melvin Joseph. They attended St. Alphonsus High School, graduating in 1947.

Bro. Conrad Fleischmann

Marvin Aloysius worked at Ideal Pure Milk Company, then served in the Air Force for four years.

With encouragement from Fr. Aloysius Powers, who was assistant pastor at St. Paul Church at the time, he entered the Trappist Monastery, on a sunny October day in 1957. Fr. Aloysius accompanied him to Gethsemani.

He took Novice habit April 7, 1958; Temporary Vows, April 18, 1960; Solemn Vows, Jan. 26, 1966; Silver Jubilee, Oct. 7, 1982. He soon learned the sign language, and was quite comfortable with it. Long robes were worn even out in the fields at that time. Some changes have taken place. Sign language has been replaced with the spoken word. The monks now wear denim work clothes.

Though the Trappists are cloistered, his family have yearly visits, his nieces and nephews eagerly look forward to visiting their uncle, Bro. Conrad.

Some rules have been relaxed. Bro. Conrad now has the option, which he takes very seriously, such as attending the funeral for a loved one, brother, sister or parents. He used that option the first time, with the abbot's approval, to attend his brother Leo's funeral in March 1991 in Owensboro, KY.

He has had a few "jobs" at the monastery. He was cellarer, then farm manager for a number of years, which he took rather seriously.

True to his vow of obedience, and saying yes, when asked by his abbot, to take another assignment; he is now in charge of the cheese making at the monastery.

FLEISCHMANN, EMIL HENRY AND ALMA MARY WEAVER,
were married on April 27, 1927 at St. Anthony's Church, Brown's Valley. Emil was born in Fulda, IN, and moved to Daviess County with his parents at an early age, and attended St. Anthony School. Alma was born in Daviess County, baptized at St. Joseph Church in Owensboro, and later became a member of St. Anthony Parish. Emil was a farmer, and Alma was a homemaker. Emil was also grave-digger for St. Anthony and burgoomaker for over 20 years for St. Anthony's annual picnic.

Back row (L to R): Joe, Erma, Gene, Bonnie. On couch (L to R): Martin, Emil holding Vickie, Alma, Ann. Front row (L to R, on floor): Edwina, Lorena and Charlene.

The couple have 10 children: Ann Barr, Martin Fleischmann, Erma Millay, Joe Fleischmann, Gene Fleischmann, Bonnie Miles, Sister Lorena Fleischmann, SCN, Edwina Fleischmann, Charlene Williams and Vickie Head. All the children were baptized, confirmed, received their First Communion and Reconciliation at St. Anthony; the girls were also married in this parish. Sister Lorena made her final profession as a Sister of Charity of Nazareth in this parish also. The children attended St. Anthony Grade School. The older ones attended St. Francis Academy; the younger ones went to Catholic High.

Living on a farm in the country made this family aware of God's many blessings, as shown through the beauties of nature. Much time was spent together as a family in work, play and prayer. The parish community, church as well as school, was the center of life and activity, with picnics, socials, Lenten services, Friday night novenas and people just standing around and talking after Mass. God blessed this family with a special child, Edwina, who had Down's Syndrome. In many ways, she brought love and unity to the family. The family also suffered many heartaches: Alma has died of cancer, Emil with Parkinson's Disease; Martin was killed in Vietnam, Edwina died of pneumonia, and Vickie was recently killed in a car accident. However, the bond of love is as strong in death as it is in life. It's their faith in God that binds them together.

FLEISCHMANN, EUGENE HUBERT SR.,
born Feb. 13, 1937 in Utica, KY; graduate Owensboro Catholic High School; Captain on Owensboro Fire Dept., joined the fire department December 1960. Also lives and farms in western Daviess County since 1972. Married July 5, 1958 to Dorothy Ann Tromly born May 28, 1940 in Owensboro. She is a graduate of Owensboro Catholic High School. They were married at St. Joseph Church in

Owensboro. Eugene is the son of Emil Henry Fleischmann and Alma Mary (Weaver) Fleischmann. He was raised in Brown's Valley, St. Anthony Parish. Dorothy is the daughter of Aubrey Wilhite Tromly and Elizabeth (Clark) Tromly, raised in Owensboro, Sts. Joseph and Paul Parish. They are presently members of St. Alphonsus and past members of St. Joseph and Paul 1958-1962, Blessed Mother 1962-1972. Gene is an Eucharistic Minister and former member of the Parish Council. Dorothy is an Eucharistic Minister; represents St. Alphonsus on the Rural Deanery Council.

Gene and Dorothy Ann Fleischmann

Eugene is a member of Knights of Columbus and likes to hunt and bowl. Dorothy likes to bowl and quilt. They both like to travel and visit the grandchildren.

They have three sons. Eugene Hubert, 1981 graduate Murray State University, was born May 6, 1959. He married Karen Gough of Morganfield on May 30, 1981 and they have two children, Ryan Eugene and Amy Mischelle. They live in Richmond, TX near Houston.

Randall Joseph Fleischmann was born Oct. 23, 1960 and is a graduate of Murray State University. He married Maria Goretti Taylor of Daviess County at St. Joseph in January 1986. They have two children, (twins) Karl Joseph and Erin Elizabeth. They live in Katy, TX.

Kevin Dwayne Fleischmann was born Aug. 27, 1962 and is a 1985 graduate of Murray State University. He married Miller of Beech Grove, KY on June 30, 1984 and they have two children, Kyle David and Sara Hope. They live in Meridianville, AL.

FLEISCHMANN, JOSEPH ALOYSIUS,

was born Sept. 7, 1873, one of nine children. Joseph Aloysius' first marriage was to Julia Wigger. They had two children Emil and Edwin. Emil born June 1902 married Alma Weaver, having 10 children. Emil died 1985. Alma, his wife, died 1975. Edwin born 1905, married Ila Green, had three children, live in Kankakee, IL. Edwin died 1986. Julia Wigger Fleischmann died August 1911 at Brown's Valley, KY.

J.A. Fleischmann and first wife.

Ann Fischer's first marriage was to Robert Fleischmann, at St. Meinrad, IN. They too were blessed with two children, Lorena and Eugenia, born in Poseyville, IN. Eugenia born September 1907, married Sidney Miles, in Louisville, KY June 22, 1946. Sidney Miles died in 1971. Lorena born May 28, 1909, entered the convent October 1929 at Mount St. Joseph taking for her religious name Sister Robert Angela. Having taught school for 60 years, is now retired and resides at Mount St. Joseph, Maple Mount, KY. Robert Fleischmann died June 1906.

Mary Anne (Fischer) Fleischmann married the brother of her first husband, Joseph Aloysius Fleischmann, 1912. Blessed with eight children from this second union. So you see, your children, my children and our children all 12, grew up as brothers and sisters. They farmed near Browns Valley, KY, where all their children were born.

Oscar Aloysius born 1913, married Cecelia Roby in 1947. Cecelia died Feb. 28, 1992. Oscar married Imogene Knott McDaniel Nov. 6, 1992. Paul born Nov. 19, 1917 married Elizabeth (Betty) LeBeau Jan. 25, 1941. They had seven children, one deceased. They live in California. Elizabeth died Sept. 29, 1990. Paul's second marriage was to Jeane Aug. 17, 1991. Hubert born April 11, 1916 married Mary Eunice Donahue, 1947 and had five children, live in Kankakee, IL. Urban born 1919, married Arlene Leiedecker 1947, have three children. Arlene died 1991. They too live in Kankakee, IL. Rita, born April 7, 1922, married Carl Fahrendorf Oct. 13, 1956, four daughters. Carl died 1992. Leo born Aug. 12, 1925, married Margaret Feaster 1950, they had six children. They are all living in Daviess County. Leo died in his 66th year on March 19, 1991. Marvin and Melvin, twins born April 7, 1929 near Brown's Valley, KY baptized at St. Anthony Church. Melvin married Helen Maxine Jones Oct. 1, 1960 at St. Paul Church. They were blessed with five children all living in Daviess County, KY. Marvin Aloysius entered the Trappist Monastary, Our Lady of Gethsemani, Trappist, KY and has persevered for 35 years.

FLEISCHMANN, LEO ALOYSIUS AND MARGARET LAVELLE FEASTER,

were married on July 5, 1950 at St. Paul Church, Owensboro. They met while making a novena to the Blessed Mother at St. Paul Church. They were the parents of six children, David Allen, born April 8, 1951; James Vincent, April 7, 1952; Mary Joanne, April 10, 1953; Amy Carolyn, Feb. 26, 1955; Sue Elaine, Jan. 24, 1956; and Joseph Aloysius, Jan. 26, 1958. The children attended parochial schools, have married and lead productive lives in the community. They have given their parents 16 grandchildren.

Leo was the son of Joseph and Mary Fleischmann and the 10th child in a family of 12. He served his country as a member of the Coast Guard during World War II. He held a variety of jobs during his lifetime and was employed by the Daviess County Board of Education when he retired because of his health in 1988. Leo was an active member of St. Pius Tenth Parish. He and Margaret came into the Charismatic Renewal movement of the Catholic Church in January of 1983 and served the renewal in many ways. Leo died of leukemia on March 19, 1991. This is the Feast of St. Joseph, husband of Mary, who was his lifelong patron saint.

Margaret was born to William Allen Feaster who died in 1930 and China Mary O'Bryan. She returned to the work force after their last child started school. She was cafeteria manager at St. Pius Tenth, then Daviess County Middle School and finally Daviess County High School, retiring in 1990. She served her parish in various ways. Currently she is an Eucharistic Minister, a McAuley Minister at Mercy Hospital and a team member for the annual Charismatic conference held at Mount St. Joseph.

FLEISCHMANN, MELVIN JOSEPH,

the last of 12 children, was born April 7, 1929 near Brown's Valley, KY. He is the son of the late Joseph Aloysius Fleischmann and Mary Ann (Fischer) Fleischmann. Melvin married Helen Maxine (Jones) Fleischmann on Oct. 1, 1960 at St. Paul Church in Owensboro, KY. Fr. Bernard Powers officiated. Helen Maxine is the daughter of the late Bernard Cecil Jones and Edith Francis (Millay) Jones.

Melvin worked for a number of years for Sears, and is presently employed at Mitchell Sales Company. Maxine is employed at Canteen Service in Owensboro, KY. They have five children, two adopted. Mary Edell born May 27, 1960 in Louisville, KY. She has two children, Heather Lynn and Sarah Ellen, who live in Owensboro, KY. Angel born and died Aug. 3, 1991. Anne Elizabeth born Jan. 20, 1960 in Louisville, KY. Anne Elizabeth is married to Dale Edward Payne and they have four children, Amanda Nicole, Laura Elizabeth, Rebecca Lynn and Nolan Daniel. They live in Booneville, IN and attend St. Clement Church. Andrew Joseph, born Oct. 23, 1964, works for the Ohio Valley Marine Service. Helen Marie born Nov. 3, 1965, works for Hunter Douglas, and Jonathan Lee born Jan. 18, 1972, is employed at Jagoes. All born in Owensboro, KY and all live in Owensboro, KY.

Melvin and Maxine Fleischmann

They have been active in church, community work all their married lives. After encouragement from Fr. Richard Powers, Fr. Delma Clemons and Fr. Bernard Powers, they became foster parents. They were foster parents for 21 years, taking into their home 49 children. Some came at 6 days old, to and including teenage boys and girls. A full time job for Maxine. The first person to be placed in their home was a teenage young man. He was an inspiration and blessing to the Fleischmann family. From a broken home and in trouble, is now happily married to a wonderful woman, they have two teenage children and they have a successful business and live in Daviess County.

Melvin and Maxine are members of St. Joseph and Paul Church, in Owensboro, KY. Melvin is a member of the Legion of Mary, The Victorious Missionaries, and is active in church ministry.

FLEISCHMANN, PAUL A.,

was born Nov. 9, 1917 in Farm Tuck, KY. "Tuck" was located on Smith Road, about two and one-half miles from Petit, KY and five miles from St. Anthony Church, Brown's Valley, KY. He is the son of Joseph A. Fleischmann and Mary Anne Fischer Fleischmann. He has two half-brothers, Emil and Edwin, deceased and two half-sisters, Eugenia Miles of Louisville, KY and Lorena (Sister Robert Angela), Mount St. Joseph, Maple Mount, KY. He has one sister, Rita Fahrendorf, Owensboro, KY and six brothers, Oscar, Owensboro, KY; Hubert, Kankakee, IL; Urban, Kankakee, IL; Leo, Owensboro, KY, deceased; Melvin, Owensboro, KY; and Marvin (Brother Mary Conrad) Monk, Gethsemani, KY.

He was baptized at St. Anthony on Nov. 11, 1917. First Holy Communion, St. Anthony Spring 1924 or 1925. Confirmation the same day. He married Elizabeth A. La Beau on Jan. 25, 1941. He later married B. Jean Mistkowski on Aug. 17, 1991. They were both widowed at the time of their second marriages. They were married at St. Patrick Catholic Church, Grass Valley.

His father, Joseph was born in Fulda, IN. He was the son of Henry and Mary Fleischmann, who were from Lachen, Switzerland. Henry was the son of Jacob and Anna (Hammerlin) Fleischmann, also from Lachen, Switzerland. His dad, Joseph, moved from Indiana, around the turn of the century, to the farm at "Tuck," KY. (Tuck was located between Petit and Mosleyville on the Smith Road.) He went to St. Joseph (German) Catholic Church in Owensboro, later to St. Anthony, Brown's Valley, KY. He was possibly instrumental in the establishment of the St. Anthony Parish. Paul went to school there for six years. He was an altar boy at St. Anthony. Then to St. Peter Catholic School in Stanley, where he graduated from the eighth grade. He was in the Civilian Conservation Corps for three and one-half years. He became field leader and barracks sergeant. He had the authority to use a truck to take C.C.C. members to various churches for Sunday morning worship. He went to St. Patrick in Placerville, CA.

His parents were very serious about their religious duties. It was five miles to St. Anthony Parish on a dirt and gravel road. When the road was too muddy for the car they went by buggy, surry or team and wagon. Yes, sometimes they were late. They went to school by buggy or surry. Sometimes his sister Lorena and Oscar went alone to school, on horse or mule.

The work on the farm was long and hard, however, when supper dishes were done, they all knelt down and prayed the rosary, led by his mother. Dad made sure they all stayed awake.

He is thankful for his early spiritual and religious training, which has remained with him all his life.

He has always practiced his faith. When he attended St. Felicitas he was an active member in the Holy Name Society and Men's Club. He taught CCD five years. After retirement he moved to Grass Valley, and became active in St. Patrick Catholic Church. He joined the Knights of Columbus and is active in other church functions.

He believes the "successful road to heaven" like any other success is paved with many prayers and sacrifices.

FLEISCHMANN, SISTER ROBERT ANGELA,
was born on May 28, 1909 at Poseyville, IN to Robert Joseph Fleischmann (born Jan. 10, 1876-died June 29, 1910) of Fulda, IN and Mary Ann Fischer (born Dec. 7, 1882-died Dec. 20, 1964) of St. Meinrad, IN. Her baptismal name is Lorena Philomena. She was baptized in St. Francis Xavier Church in Poseyville, IN on May 31, 1909.

She entered the convent at Mount St. Joseph on Sept. 8, 1929 where she was recommended by Father Fitzgibbon. She received her habit on March 19, 1930 taking her vows on March 19, 1932 and March 19, 1935.

Her missions include: St. Columba, Louisville; Bardwell, KY; Curdsville, KY; Holy Cross, KY; St. James, Louisville; Raywick, KY, St. Joseph; Princeton, KY; St. Alphonsus, St. Joseph, KY; St. Margaret Mary; Fredrickburg, KY; St. Francis X, Raywick, KY; St. Ignatius, Louisville; Hardinsburg, KY; St. Boniface, Louisville; St. Angela Ed Center, Louisville.

Her brothers, sisters and their spouses include: Emil Henry - Alma Weaver; Edwin - Ila Bernice Green; Oscar Albert - Cecelia Roby; Hubert Peter - Mary Eunice Donoghue; Paul Aloysius - Elizabeth Ann Flanagan; Urban Robert - Arlene Liedecker; Leo Aloysius - Margaret (O'Bryan) Feaster; Melvin - Maxine (Millay) Jones; Eugenia - Michael Sidney Miles; Rita - Carl Aloysius Fahrendorf; and Marvin (Brother Conrad) OSCO.

FLOOD FAMILY, JAMES VINCENT,
James V. Flood was born to James and Elizabeth Carroll Flood. His wife, Elizabeth Pearl Jolly, was born to Henry Clay Jr. and Ida Elizabeth Meador Jolly. Children: Bernard Jolly, Harold Vincent, Ruby Catherine, Agnes Elizabeth, Mary Eliza, Shirley Jean, Robert Clay, Julia Nellie, Lawrence Dale.

Bernard J. married Frances Marie Alexander. Their children are Bernard James, Paul Vincent, Linda Ann, John Michael, William Kenneth, Rita Susan, Edward Carroll, Wanda Jane and Catherine Marie.

Harold Vincent married Mary Agnes Kanapple. Their children are Harold Donald, Gerald Patrick, Philip Leon, James Richard, Rosemary, Sharon Ann, Brenda Marie, Vincent Jerome and Joseph Michael.

Ruby Catherine married Francis "Pat" Whealey. Their children are Shelia Ann, Keith Patrick, Stephen Gerard, Thomas Joseph, David Anthony and Lisa Michelle.

Agnes Elizabeth married James Franklin Critchelow. Their children are Monica Gale and Dale Franklin.

Mary Eliza married William Anthony Wallace Jr. Their children are Karen Maria, Bryan Albert, Kimberly Susan and William Anthony.

Shirley Jean married Marvin Bernard Manning. Their children are Rhonda Ann, Pearl Marie, Bernard Wayne, Jerome Keavin, Donna Jean and Jennifer Lynne.

Robert Clay is single.

The James Vincent Flood Family. Front row: Shirley Jean, Julia Nellie, Mary Eliza, Agnes Elizabeth. Back row: Robert Clay, James Vincent, Bernard Jolly, Elizabeth Pearl, Lawrence Dale, Ruby Catherine, Harold Vincent.

Julia Nellie married Charles Wayne Hardesty. Their children are Charles Wayne, Janet Carol, Gregory Eugene, Jennifer Lynne and Timothy Gerard.

Lawrence Dale married Patricia Kaye Moorman. Their children are Scott Dale and Deanna Kay.

Bernard James married Virginia Ann Critchlow. Paul Vincent married Debra Kay White. Linda Ann married Ralph Carwile. John Michael married Charlene Dare Voyles. William Kenneth married Garlana Elain Benham. Rita Susan married William Dewayne Carwile. Edward Carroll married Terry Hale. Wanda Jane married Charles Edward Laslie. Harold Donald married Janet Sue Carman. Gerald Patrick, single. Philip Leon married Susan Jane Roach. James Richard married Vicky Dian White. David Anthony married Katherine Lorraine Sturgeon. Rosemary married John Darrell Neff. Sharon Ann, single. Brenda Marie married Dewight Lee Wheatley. Vincent Jerome married Rebecca Lynn Burchs. Shelia Ann married Daniel Glen Drane. Stephen Gerard married Terri Ann Lewis. Lisa Michille married Richard Armes. Bryan Albert married Mary Elvlyn Akers. Kimberly Susan married Jennarro Fredrick Federico. Monica Gale married Paul Frances Jarboe. Dale Franklin married Connie Moore. Rhonda Ann married Charles Bernard Fitter. Jerome Keavin married Laura Jean Harper. Charles Wayne married Sandra Kay Jonson. Janet Carol married Todd O'Neil Board. Gregory Eugene married Denise Michelle Smith. Jennifer Lynne married Kennith Lanier Eskridge.

James Vincent and Elizabeth Jolly Flood and families are all strong Catholics still around St. Romuald Church. They have nine children, 44 grandchildren, 73 great-grandchildren and five great-great-grandchildren.

FLOOD FAMILY, JAMES,
James Flood was born March 9, 1861 to John Flood and Bridget Douling Flood. They were both born in Ireland. James was married to Elizabeth Carroll Feb. 8, 1833, at St. Romuald Church. She was born Dec. 14, 1867. Her parents were Michael and Catherine Broffey. They were also born in Ireland. James died Jan. 23, 1923. Elizabeth died Dec. 13, 1912. All were buried at St. Romuald Church Cemetery at Hardinsburg, KY. Several of the children of James and Elizabeth Flood were also buried here.

Children are: Bridget Agnes, June 12, 1889-Dec. 23, 1987, married Harvy Potts, Nov. 7, 1907-May 2, 1881 on June 24, 1949. Michael Miliam, Oct. 18, 1891-Oct. 4, 1960 married Feb. 14, 1914 to Lenora Wilson Jan. 3, 1896-Sept. 12, 1951. Mary Helon (Nellie), Aug. 10, 1893-June 23, 1975 married John Lee (Jack), Oct. 29, 1919-Feb. 13, 1990 on Sept. 26, 1881. Peter Paul, March 24, 1895-Aug. 6, 1973 married Feb. 10, 1920 to Mary Rachel Alexander, Nov. 2, 1898-May 16, 1981. Katherine, March 11, 1897-Jan. 2, 1902. Margaret Cecilia, March 27, 1899-Jan. 4, 1984 married on Feb. 8, 1922 to James Edward Henning, Nov. 24, 1896-still living. Lawrence, March 24, 1901-Aug. 26, 1944, single. James Vincent, May 23, 1903-April 2, 1983 married Elizabeth Pearl Jolly, June 10, 1906-still living, on April 24, 1924. John Andrew (Doc), April 18, 1905-Aug. 9, 1970 married Ruby Ellen Brown, Aug. 11, 1915-Feb. 9, 1915 on June 7, 1943. Julia Elizabeth, Aug. 13, 1908-Sept. 13, 1967 married March 19, 1946 to George McKinley Kidder, Feb. 18, 1917-Dec. 24, 1966. Catherine Lorena, March 14, 1911-still living, married Robert Aloysius Fischer, March 18, 1914-Dec. 16, 1990 on Oct. 14, 1941.

These are very strong Irish Catholic families. The Flood families were all born, lived, died, for the Lord. "We Don't Fear No One But God."

FLOOD FAMILY,
John Flood and Bridget Douling Flood were both born in County Cork, Ireland and came to America in 1845 as young people.

John had two brothers that came with him, however, they stayed in the East and we have no knowledge of what happened to them.

John came to Cannelton, Perry County, IN, where he went to work in a small factory.

John Flood (1823-1892) born in Dublin, Ireland and Bridget Douling (1830-1909) born in Dublin, Ireland.

Bridget Douling had two sisters, Martha Douling and Annie Douling Carney. They also came to Cannelton, IN, where Bridget went to work in the cotton gin mills. Soon after meeting, Bridget Douling and John Flood were married at St. Patrick Catholic Church in Cannelton, on Aug. 26, 1855. This church is now known as St. Michael Catholic Church.

After their marriage, John and Bridget moved to Breckenridge County, near Stephensport, KY, to a small farm where all of their children were born. After John died, the home burned and was rebuilt on the same location.

Their son went to Oklahoma. Mary Ann Flood was married at St. Romuald Catholic Church in Hardinsburg, and later went to Henderson, KY. All of her family lives there today. Margaret Flood Mullen was married and also lived in Henderson, KY. James and John Flood married Carrolls (notice Carroll Family). They stayed in Breckenridge County all their lives. Peter Flood died young. Thomas Joseph Flood married Mary Elmora Dutsehke. Their family still lives here in Breckenridge County, KY. William, Philip and Patrick Flood all died young.

There are still generations of Floods living in Breckenridge County today.

FOGLE FAMILY, PAT AND HELEN,
Charles Patrick Fogle and Helen Jean Ball were married on May 12, 1962 at Holy Guardian Angels Catholic Church, Irvington, KY.

Pat is from Stanley, KY (Daviess County). His mother and father are Joseph Frank Fogle and Katherine Krampe Fogle. There were eight children in his family. Helen is from Irvington, KY and her mother and father are J.B. Ball and Katherine C. Ball. There were nine children in her family.

Pat and Helen have three children. The children are Patrick Todd Fogle, Stephanie Ann Fogle and Angela Marie Fogle. Todd is 28 years old and married to Pamela Severs and they live in Lexington, KY. Stephanie is 23 years old and presently in Europe. Angela Marie is 14 years old and a freshman in high school.

Pat is self-employed in the restaurant business. Pat has been Mayor of Irvington, KY for 19 years. Helen is a housewife.

Pat has three aunts who were nuns at Maple Mount, KY, Sister Antionette, Sister Angela Marie and Sister Mary Ann. Sister Mary Ann is still living.

Pat also has a nephew who is a priest, Father Bruce Fogle.

FORD, WILLIAM PRENTICE, single, studied commercial art at Memphis State University. He was born May 7, 1937 in Memphis, TN. He has resided in Columbus, MS, Corinth, MS, Picayune, MS, Bowling Green, KY, Fulton, KY, Union City, TN, Birmingham, AL and Cape Cod, MA. He has always been an artist or designer.

William presently lives in Paducah (McCracken County), KY (since 1990) and attends St. Francis De Sales. He serves in the music ministry with the 9:30 a.m. Sunday Choir and Prayer Line.

He is Acquisition Chairman of Yeiser Art Center, Paducah Board Member, member Market House Museum, Paducah, Graphic Artist, Paducah Main Street and member of PCC Community Choir.

William joined the St. Frances De Sales in March 1991 when he moved from Fulton, KY. He is an interior designer at Rust & Martin in Paducah, KY. He became a Catholic in 1991. His mother, Louise Hill Ford, is Baptist. His father, Henry Wesley Ford, was Catholic. The Catholic side of his family is from Mississippi and Tennessee. He was raised in both religions.

FOWLER, RICHARD FAMILY, Richard Fowler born c. 1809 in the Rolling Fork Settlement, was baptized by Fr. Nerinckx on July 16, 1809 at Holy Name of Mary Church, Calvary, in Washington County, now Marion County, KY. He was the son of John Fowler and Mary Pierceall, daughter of Richard Perceall of Marion County, KY.

Richard married Margaret A. Jarboe on Jan. 22, 1830 in Washington County. Margaret was born Dec. 22, 1807, the daughter of John Reed Jarboe and Mary Hayden. Both families came directly from Maryland to the Nelson County area. And their lineage can easily be traced further back in Maryland.

Margaret died Sept. 28, 1875 and Richard died December 1881, no date recorded, but he was buried Dec. 22, 1881. Most of their family history is unknown to present families, but at least four of their children still have descendants residing in Union County.

Their children were: Mary Elizabeth (died young)*, John James (history unknown), Richard Ignatius*, William Thomas (history unknown), Susan Catherine*, Peter Nathaniel*, Martha Matilda Frances (history unknown), Charles Robert*, Sarah Ellen (history unknown), Julia Victoria*, Margaret Ann (history unknown) and Virginia Jane*. (Asterisk indicates children that are known to be buried at Sacred Heart Cemetery, St. Vincent, KY.) All these children were born in Union County.

FOX, SAMANTHA LYNN HOLLIE AND GORDON, were married at St. Romuald Parish Church in Hardinsburg, Breckinridge County, KY on Dec. 8, 1990 by Fr. J. Patrick Reynolds. Samantha and Gordon were married on the Feast of the Immaculate Conception which is the anniversary of the day they met in 1985.

From left: Sue Ann Hale, Samantha (Hollie) Fox, Gordon Fox, Mary Lillian Potts, Harold Hale.

Samantha was baptized at the request of her parents Sue Ann (Potts) Hollie and Larry D. Hollie in December 1969 at the Church of the Immaculate Conception in Lake Charles, LA. Samantha's sponsors are her maternal grandparents, James Flood Potts and Mary Lillian (Brown) Potts.

Samantha and Gordon announced to her mother Sue and step-father Harold Hale that their first child is to be born in September 1992.

FRANCIS, CYNTHIA LONG, daughter of Mave and Rome (born May 2, 1960 in California), (baptized Queen of All Saints, Concord), service Communion, confirmation, minister of Eucharist was married at St. Frances De Sales May 24, 1987 to Randall Dean Francis of Independence, MO, son of Sharon Francis Bissert (Mrs. Gene Bissert) and Norman Francis. Attended parochial kindergarten, elementary and high schools. Class of '78 St. Mary High School. Member of church and school choirs, Girl Scouts, CCD Instructor, St. Mary High School substitute teacher, Altar Society, attended UK-Paducah Community College, studies are continuing at college in Kansas City, MO. Employed at Gordon Jewelers, Oaks Mall while teaching days at St. Mary High School; assistant manager Gordons, Independence Mall; IRS, Service Merchandise, assistant manager jewelry; Data Proc Adjustor, Kansas City, MO.

Christopher Francis, grandson of Mrs. Marie Long

Christopher Jeremy Francis, son of Randall and Cynthia Long Francis, born May 25, 1990 in Independence, MO.

MASTROVITO, FATHER FRANCIS, T.O.R., pastor of St. Joseph Church, Central City, KY. Born July 1, 1924 in Indiana, PA. Family moved to Detroit in 1934. Entered Franciscan Prep. Seminary on Sept. 3, 1939. Entered Catholic University of America in Washington D.C. in 1942. There until ordination on June 5, 1951. Received M.A. in English Literature. First assignment - assistant pastor of St. Anthony Church in Johnstown, PA. In 1953 pastor of St. Anthony Church in Windber, PA. Came to Kentucky on Feb. 12, 1967. Pastor of St. Joseph Church in Mayfield, KY for 14 years. Then to Sts. Peter and Paul Church in Hopkinsville, KY for six years. Presently serving as pastor of St. Joseph Church, Central City, KY.

FRENCH, DONALD ALEXANDER AND MARY HÉLENE HAGAN, manager French's Supermarket, sales director Mary Kay Cosmetics. Donnie was born and raised in Morganfield, Union County and Hélene was born and raised in Waverly, Union County. Presently living in Morganfield, Union County. They are members of St. Ann.

They have three children: Kathryn Hélene French, 6 1/2 years old, first grade; Alexander Guy French, 4, preschool; and Elizabeth Hagan French, deceased at 9 1/2 weeks.

FRENCH, GEORGE FRANCIS, was born in Uniontown on April 28, 1917. He has spent his life in farming except for time spent in the Air Force in World War II. At the end of the war he married Nancy Pike. They have three children, Frances Ann Boarman of Philpot, Pat and Daniel French of Union County.

George Francis French

The French family has always lived in Uniontown and are members of St. Agnes. Frank is a member of Fourth Degree Knights of Columbus.

Frances is married to Ronald Boarman of Philpot and they have one son, Benjamin French Boarman. Pat married Teresa French formerly of St. Ann Parish and they have two children, George Douglas and Amy Elizabeth. Daniel is married to Vickie Wedding, also formerly of St. Ann Parish, and they have a son Adam Daniel.

Both of them attended St. Agnes grade and high school. Nancy is a graduate of Nazareth College and the University of Evansville and spent 26 years teaching.

FRENCH, JOSEPH LLOYD AND JUDITH CAROL BUCKMAN, are members of St. Ann Parish. Joseph was born on April 4, 1966 and is the son of Robert Lewis French and Pansy Jane Dayberry French. Carol was born on July 14, 1968 and is the daughter of James Elbert Buckman and Dorothy Ann Bickett Buckman. They were both born in Union County, KY at Our Lady of Mercy Hospital. They were raised and currently living in Union County.

Joey is a student (studying electricity) and Carol is a homemaker. They have one daughter, Malorey Ruthanne French, born July 21, 1990. They are members of St. Ann Parish.

FRENCH, LEROY AND ANN RHODES, were married May 4, 1955 at her home parish, Sacred Heart at St. Vincent, KY by Monsignor John Higgins.

Leroy and Ann French

Her parents were Bill and Lena Brady Rhodes. His parents were Rabe and Leona Mills French.

He served in the Air Force for four years. They then moved to Indiana to his former job in the steel mills.

They lived in Merrillville, IN for 30 years and raised five children, Vince, Bill, Brenda, Paul and Danny. They live in that area except Bill who is in Houston, TX and Paul who is in the Navy. They are grandparents to Joey French, Alyssa and Keith Wachter and Kelsey French.

He retired from the steel mill with 37 years of service. They returned to Union County and live at his parents' home place, where they are parishioners at his home parish, St. Ambrose at Henshaw, where he is a council member and Eucharist Minister.

He is custodian at St. Ann School in Morganfield and member of Knights of Columbus Durbin Council 1004. She is a member of the Ladies Guild.

FRENCH, MICHAEL VINCENT (MIKE) SR., of Hitesville, in Union County, where he grew up with two sisters and two brothers was the fourth child born to Clyde F. and Margaret Buckman French on June 10, 1961. He married Cynthia Kay (Cindy) Beck French, the sixth child born to Walter Owen Beck and the late Betty Jo Clark Beck of Henderson, where she grew up with seven brothers and three sisters and was born on Aug. 16, 1960.

They married on July 11, 1980 at Holy Name of Jesus Catholic Church in Henderson and moved to Hitesville, where they lived for 11 1/2 years. They currently reside at the corners of Hite School and Chapman Roads in Union County, where "they" just built a new house. They maintain a "mini-hay field" with their three children, Michael Vincent Jr., 10; Amber Michelle, 8; and Nathan Heath, 3.

Mike works at United Technology Automotive in Morganfield as a Process Technician. Cindy is a mother and housewife. She is a member of St. Ann School Board, and is the PTO Treasurer. Michael is in the fifth grade and Amber is in the third grade at St. Ann Interparochial School in Morganfield. Nathan is momma's sidekick of the day, and daddy's little helper of the evenings.

They belong to Sacred Heart Parish in Waverly. Cindy is a lector and choir member. Michael serves as an altar boy.

FREY, EUGENE EDWARD JR., was born on Feb. 9, 1935. He was the son of Eugene Edward Frey Sr. and Olivia Marie Collignon. He was born just out of Owensboro. Gertrude Marie Sims was born on Sept. 21, 1939. She is the daughter of Joseph Robert Sims and Mary Teresa Long. She was born in Owensboro. Gertrude Sims and Eugene Frey were married on Nov. 26, 1959. They met in a grocery store where they both worked. Today, Gene is a coal handler and Gertie is a domestic engineer. They and their family attend St. Pius Tenth Church. They live in Owensboro and have six children.

Their children's names are Pamela Marie Randolph, 32; Vicki Lynne Frey Thompson, 31; Sharon Renee Tipmore, 29; Mary Suzanne Cain, 25 and Gary Alan Frey, 25 (twins); and Natalie Anne Frey, 13. For school they all attended St. Pius Tenth and O.C.H.S. Pam is a human resource supervisor for Comp Care. Vicki is an independent dentist. Sharon is a pharmacy technician at Daviess County Hospital. Mary works in the bottling department at United Distilleries. Gary is a janitor at O.M.U. Natalie is a student at O.C.M.S. All of the children are a part of all parish picnics. At church, Gertie, Gene and Pam are eucharistic ministers. Pam is also on the scholarship committee.

The three oldest children are married and have children.

FRONING, SISTER PATRICIA, a Sister of St. Francis of Tiffin, OH is a member of St. Stephen Cathedral Parish in Owensboro. Sister Pat was born in Coldwater, OH (Mercer County) and is the daughter of Clem and Marie Froning who reside in St. Sebastian, OH and are the parents of eight children (seven daughters and one son), 30 grandchildren and 15 great-grandchildren. A sister, Sister Joan Froning, also a Sister of St. Francis, worked at Lourdes Hospital, Paducah in a variety of nursing and nursing administrative positions from 1968-1988.

Sister Pat entered the congregation of the Sisters of St. Francis in 1952. She has taught in rural schools in the Toledo Diocese and in 1966 began work in hospital administration at Lourdes Hospital in Paducah, KY. She served in Paducah from 1966-1970 when she was elected to the General Council and later to the Office of Community Minister for the Sisters of St. Francis. During those years, 1970-1982, she served as a member of the board of directors for the hospital. From 1983-1986 she worked as Pastoral Associate in Holy Name Parish, Henderson, KY, then returned to Lourdes Hospital as vice-president of Mission Services from 1986-1990. Sister Pat worked for one year as Pastoral Associate in St. Ann Parish, Morganfield, KY. In July 1992 she began her work as the director of the Office of Lay Ministry for the Diocese of Owensboro.

Patricia Froning, CSF

During her years in the Owensboro Diocese, Sister Pat has served as a member of: the Council of Religious; the Diocesan Pastoral Council; and the Health and Hospital Committee of the Kentucky Catholic Conference.

GARLAND, WILLIAM MCKINLEY SR., was born on Nov. 25, 1898 in Livingston County, KY. He was baptized in the Catholic faith in 1919, when he met and married Mary Magdalene Saffer, daughter of William and Mary Johanna Saffer of Paducah, KY.

William and Mary Magdalene Garland settled in Fancy Farm, KY after being forced to leave Paducah, KY during the 1937 flood.

Since Fancy Farm was a Catholic community with a Catholic school and they had 11 children to raise, William and Mary chose to remain in Fancy Farm.

All 11 children graduated from St. Jerome School in Fancy Farm. Joseph William Garland married to Jeanean Russell Garland and Judith Loretta Garland Elliott married to Joseph Rudolph Elliott now reside in Fancy Farm.

Margaret Ross married to the late Edward Ross; Lucille Carrico married to the late Thomas Francis Carrico and Louise Carrico married to Randal Carrico reside in Mayfield, KY. Dorothy Stafford married to Murray Stafford live on Hilton Head Island, SC. William McKinley Garland Jr., married the late Cecelia Skinner Garland, lives in St. Charles, MO. Theresa De Sai married to Sharod De Sai lives in Indianapolis, IN. Rose Ann Thomas married to James Lyndal Thomas lives in Elsmere, KY. Sister Joan Marie Garland resides in Louisville, KY and Robert Lewis Garland married to Marjorie Curtsinger Garland live in Murray, KY.

William McKinley Sr. died in May 1950 and Mary Magdalene Garland died in December 1940.

In 1943 William married Ann Frances Toon Garland and had two daughters; Frances Ellen Garland now married to Danny Forester and Marilyn June Garland now married to Byron Miller. Frances Ellen and Marilyn and families live in Mayfield, KY.

Ava Frances Garland still resides in Fancy Farm, KY.

GARRETT-FISCHER FAMILY, Hilary E. Garrett and Aline A. Fischer were married at St. Stephen Cathedral in Owensboro, KY on Jan. 8, 1946. They both have at least 100 years of ancestors living in the area that is now the Western Kentucky Diocese.

Hilary's father, John H. Garrett joined the Catholic Church as a young man, after coming to Owensboro. He was from Centertown, KY. No one in his family was Catholic. Hilary's mother, Mary Ann Rodman's family, before moving to Daviess County, came from the Bardstown, KY area. Mary Ann's grandfather, John H. Rodman joined the Catholic Church while helping to build St. Joseph Cathedral in Bardstown. His wife and children were Catholic.

Aline's parents, Martin O. Fischer and Sadie M. Collignon were both born and raised in the Rome, KY area. Their ancestors, in this country came from southern Indiana to Kentucky. According to church records obtained from Germany, both families have been Catholic for centuries.

Hilary and Aline Garrett

Hilary and Aline have two children. Their daughter Linda Marie is married to J. Steven Dixon. They have two daughters: Casey Dianne and Christy Lynne Dixon. Their son is Patrick Joseph and he is married to Debra Ann Koblenz. Linda and family live in Daviess County and are members of St. Pius Tenth Church. Patrick and Debra live in Arlington Heights, IL and they are members of St. James Church in Arlington Heights.

Hilary and Aline are charter members of St. Pius Tenth Church. They have both always been active in church work, such as: choir, lector, Eucharistic Ministers, etc.

Hilary belongs to the Knights of Columbus and is a member of the Veterans of Foreign Wars. He served in the European Theatre of War with the Air Force during World War II. They both are members of the Loyal Order of the Moose.

GILSTRAP, MONICA, Gerald and Monica Gilstrap were married Feb. 27, 1975, at St. Martin Church. Gerald was born in Evansville on July 30, 1955. Monica was originally a Murphy before she married Gerald. She was born in Ohio on Sept. 17, 1955. They now live in Owensboro and have two kids. Gerald works at OMU as a line-man and Monica works at Pam's Hair Care as a beautician.

Their two children are Jamie, who is 13 and attends Owensboro Catholic Middle, and Miranda who is 4 and does not go to school but goes to Our Lady of Lourdes Day Care Center.

The family attends Mass at Our Lady of Lourdes. Monica, Jamie and Miranda have all been baptized but Gerald has not. Even though Gerald hasn't been baptized he still attends Mass with his family.

GIPSON, RICHARD AND MARTHA, On Nov. 23, 1963, the day after President John F. Kennedy was shot, Richard Harold Gipson married Martha Ellen Willett at Saint John Catholic Church in McCracken County Martha's uncle, Father Henry R. Willett performed the ceremony. Richard is the son of the late Harley and Flora Ella Holder Gipson. Martha is the daughter of Bertram Willett and the late Lydia Dunaway Willett.

Richard and Martha Gipson

Richard and Martha built on her parents' farm. They have three children, Dewain Richard, Ella Marie and Darla Jean. Dewain married Sara Ann Burrows, daughter of Iva Hargett Burrows and the late Walter "Buddy" H. Burrows Jr. Dewain and Sara own and live on 32 acres in the Saint John Community that was once part of the original farm Dewain's great-great-grandfather owned. Dewain, with his grandfather, Bertram Willett, is still farming the land today. Ella Marie married Christopher "Chris" Andrew Garland, son of Joseph W. Garland and the late Rose Ella Cash Garland. Chris and Ella own a farm in the Saint John Community. Their 75 acres are also farmed by Dewain and Ella's grandfather. Darla Jean married Dewayne Keith Martin, son of Dewayne L. and Edith "Edie" Black Martin. Darla and Keith live in Millington, TN, where Keith is stationed with the United States Navy. Darla and Keith Martin are the parents of twins born Dec. 16, 1992, Ashley Marie and Brandon Dewayne.

Richard worked 32 years at Modine Manufacturing Company before taking disability. Before the children were born, Martha worked at South Central Bell as a telephone operator. After staying home with the children for 10 years, she went to work at Saint John School where she helped start the school lunch program. She worked there for 11 years. From there she went to work at Western Baptist Hospital, where she is currently a dietary supervisor.

One of Martha's hobbies is sewing. She made Ella and Darla's bridesmaid dresses for Dewain and Sara's wedding. Ella chose to wear her mother's wedding gown and Martha made the bridesmaids' and flower girls' dresses. For Darla's wedding, Martha fulfilled a dream by making Darla's wedding gown and also making the bridesmaids' and flower girl's dresses.

GLAHN, ANNE LOUISE, was born to Virginia Osborne and George Anthony Glahn, Easter Sunday, March 29, 1959. She was baptized by Fr. Wilson at St. Pius X. She attended Sts. Joseph and Paul Grade School and graduated from Owensboro Catholic High School in 1977. Anne received her associate degrees in marketing/accounting and real estate from the Owensboro Junior College of Business in 1979. On May 14, 1983, Anne married Bobby Joe Mulligan (son of John M. and Mary Louise Dant Mulligan). Anne survived a complete brain tumor removal in October of 1986. She has her real estate license, worked as a bookkeeper for 11 years and now owns and operates Balloons Over Owensboro, Inc. Bobby and Anne have three children: Kari Anne, Ryan Joseph and Robert Clay. They are members of Sts. Joseph and Paul Parish in Owensboro, KY, where Anne serves on the finance council. Bobby is employed in the trucking industry.

GLAHN, CARL ANTHONY, was born Nov. 1, 1962 to Virginia (Osborne) and George Anthony Glahn and baptized at St. Paul Church in Owensboro. He attended St. Joseph and Paul and St. Pius X Grade Schools and graduated from Owensboro Catholic High School in 1981. He graduated from University of Evansville with an associate degree in transportation management in 1983. He remained a member of St. Joseph and Paul Parish until he married Linda Roberts at St. Stephen Cathedral Nov. 17, 1990 by Father Ed. Bradley. Linda received instructions and had been baptized, Easter 1989, by Bishop John McRaith. Their son, Matthew Tyler was born May 24, 1992 and was baptized at St. Stephen Cathedral also by Bishop McRaith. They are members of St. Stephen Cathedral Parish.

GLAHN, CARL J., "What can I render to the Lord for all that he has given to me?" This must be Carl's prayer as he looks back on 40 years in the priesthood. His name is Carl J. Glahn, oldest survivor of 10 children, born to George J. Glahn and Catherine Johanna Froehlich. He thinks that God talked to him when he began to serve as an altar boy in the fourth grade. His instruments were three wonderful priests. Father James Norman, pastor of St. Paul's in Owensboro and his two assistants Father Gilbert Henninger and Father George Boehmicke. In 1940 Bishop Cotton sent Carl to St. Meinrad and he was ordained in 1952. His first assignment was St. Francis De Sales in Paducah with a zealous pastor, Father Albert J. Thompson. Besides working in a big parish, he was teaching three courses at St. Mary High School, census work in the many trailer camps brought about by the Atomic Plant Boom in 1952, then census work in Marshall County as Father Thompson planned the new St. Pius the Tenth Parish at Calvert City.

Carl J. Glahn

In 1955, Bishop Cotton thought it would be nice if Carl moved to Earlington as an assistant to Father Wm. Borntraeger to start a high school and transport children from Dawson Springs and Princeton. In 1960, after a three-hour lecture from Bishop Cotton, he sent Carl to Hickman to consolidate the small schools at Fulton, KY and Union City, TN at Sacred Heart in Hickman. Their bond was "Ole Yellar" the faithful school bus, piloted by Carl, for the 112 mile trek each day. Then in 1965, their new Bishop Soenneker, sent Carl to 11 happy years at Hopkinsville and St. Stephen at Cadiz came into being in 1966 and the school was reopened in 1972 with all lay faculty. In 1976, Bishop Soenneker wanted someone to go to Webster County, the last county in the diocese without a Catholic presence. St. Michael Church in Sebree was dedicated in 1977 and Holy Cross in Providence was dedicated in 1978. In 1981, the Bishop asked Carl to go to Hickman for a few weeks and the beautiful parish of St. Jude at Clinton was born in 1982. The few weeks added up to 179 weeks when Bishop McRaith moved Carl to St. Alphonsus Church in Daviess County in 1985. Then when he had a close encounter with the eternal sand man in 1989, he was sent back to Webster County to take care of St. Michael and Holy Cross. He renders thanks to God for his happy and blessed life.

GLAHN, EVA MARIE, was born Dec. 8, 1957 to Virginia (Osborne) and George Anthony Glahn who were members of St. Joseph and Paul Parish, Owensboro, KY where she was baptized. She attended St. Joseph and Paul Grade School and graduated from Owensboro Catholic High School in 1975.

Eva and David Jonathan Atkinson of Rockport, IN were wed at St. Paul Church on June 17, 1978 by her uncle, Father Jerry Glahn. She graduated with Magna Cum Laude honors from Brescia College in 1979 with a B.A. degree in psychology. She completed her Master of Arts degree in counseling from Western Kentucky University in May 1991 and works as a counselor at a chemical dependency treatment center in Evansville, IN. She and her husband also own and operate Andria's Candies in downtown Owensboro. She has been a member of the St. Stephen Cathedral Parish.

GLAHN, GEORGE ANTHONY "TONY," was born in Louisville, KY, Dec. 26, 1930, the third of eight surviving children. His father, George Jacob (Oct. 30, 1899-Dec. 26, 1963) was a self-employed tax accountant, and his mother, Catherine Johanna Froelich (May 28, 1899-April 6, 1965) sang in the choir at St. Stephen Cathedral upon their moving back to Owensboro when Tony was three. Tony graduated from St. Frances Academy in 1949 and attended Brescia College.

Virginia Louise Osborne was born in Owensboro, KY, June 22, 1932, the youngest of seven surviving children. Her father, William Charles (Sept. 29, 1885-June 19, 1956) was a farmer, living his entire life in eastern Daviess County as a member of St. Paul Church in Owensboro, KY. Her mother, Mary Eva Mason (April 20, 1893-Oct. 18, 1981) was the daughter of a lawyer and the then Daviess County Prosecutor: Elliott Brown Mason (who was last heard from while homesteading during the Oklahoma Land Rush in 1919). Mary Eva studied music at the Mount St. Joseph, Maple Mount, KY, and then worked at McAtee Department Store until retiring in 1955. Virginia graduated from St. Frances Academy in 1950, attended Brescia College, and worked at Texas Gas for a few years. Tony Glahn married Virginia Osborne, June 16, 1956, at St. Paul Catholic Church by Fr. Carl Glahn, one of his only two brothers (both who are priests). William Charles Osborne stating that he had no daughters to "give away," Virginia's hand was given in marriage by one of her brothers (Joseph Osborne).

The George Anthony Glahn Family

All six of their children (Eva, Anne, Carl, Jerry, Tony and Eric) were born in Owensboro, KY, attended grade school and high school in the Owensboro Catholic School System. As members of Sts. Joseph and Paul, Saint Pius X then returning to Sts. Joseph and Paul, Tony works in the trucking industry and Virginia is a housewife. They have six grandchildren.

GLAHN, REV. GERARD JEROME, was born in Louisville, KY on Jan. 14, 1933 to George Jacob Glahn and his wife, Catherine Johanna (Froelich). He was the fourth of eight surviving children, his brothers are Tony and Rev. Carl Joseph Glahn; his sisters are Betty, Mary, Martha, Alice and Johanna.

Rev. Jerry Glahn

Father Jerry attended grade school at St. Frances Academy in Owensboro. At the age of 14, he entered the seminary in St. Mary, KY for high school and two years of college. He then went to St. Mary, Paca Street for philosophy study and his last two years of college in Baltimore. He remained in Baltimore at St. Mary, Roland Park for four years of theology, Father Jerry was ordained on May 1, 1959, in Owensboro at St. Stephen Cathedral by Bishop Francis R. Cotton.

St. Joseph and Paul Parish in Owensboro was his first assignment. In 1960, he came to Immaculate Conception Parish, in Earlington, as assistant pastor, also taking care of St. Paul Parish in Princeton, KY, and Outwood Hospital. In 1963, he was assigned as assistant at St. Stephen Cathedral. He was assigned as pastor of Sacred Heart Church in Hickman, KY in 1966. In 1967, he was assigned back to Immaculate Conception to start Christ the King Parish in Madisonville, KY, which until that time, was the largest city in the U.S.A. without a Catholic Church. Father Jerry was moved to St. Pius X Parish in

Owensboro in 1983 and remained until June 1989 when he moved to the parish in Murray, KY. Father Jerry became ill in the fall of 1989 and succumbed to cancer Jan. 18, 1990. Father Jerry was a priest, a poet, a fisherman, a traveller, an orator, a singer and a friend to all.

GLASSCOCK, KENNETH EARL,

was born in Louisville, KY on Sept. 22, 1952, and baptized by Father Neeson at St. Dennis Church in Louisville, KY. His father, John Alonzo, was a truck driver, and his mother, Geneva Irene, was a housewife. On Feb. 2, 1974 he married Anita Faye Mattingly of Payneville, KY. They were married at St. Mary Magdalen of Pazzi Church in Payneville, KY, by Father Phillip Bronk. Her father, Alphonsus, worked at Fort Knox in Ammunition Depot. Her mother, Leola Agnes, also worked in Fort Knox in laundry.

Kenneth and Faye lived in Payneville, KY for six years, and then, in 1980, moved to Union Star, KY where they now are raising nine children. They are presently members of St. Romuald Church in Hardinsburg, KY.

Kenneth has been a self-employed truck driver for 18 years. Faye is a licensed hair dresser and housewife.

GOFF, FATHER DANIEL LEE,

was born March 22, 1958 in Daviess County, KY, the oldest of five children and only son of Leander and Janet Barr Goff. He was baptized at St. Martin Church in Rome, March 30, 1958, by Fr. Joseph Saffer.

Fr. Daniel Lee Goff

From a young boy, he has always wanted to be a priest and would "play" Mass with pencil candles and a piece of light bread fashioned into a host. As a server, he remembers his pastor advising him to pay particular attention to where everything belonged for the day when he would become pastor.

He loved to study, starting school in 1965 at St. Mary Magdalene in Sorgho, KY, transferred to Sorgho Public in 1968, returning to St. Mary Magdalene for the fifth and sixth grades. In 1971, his family bought the homeplace and moved to Rome where he completed his elementary education at St. Martin School. After graduating from Owensboro Catholic High School in 1977, he began pre-medical studies at Western Kentucky University in Bowling Green, KY. Searching for something more, he entered the Seminary of St. Pius X in Erlanger, KY graduating in 1981 with a BA in philosophy. He continued his studies at St. Meinrad School of Theology in St. Meinrad, IN graduating with an M. Div. in 1985.

June 16, 1984, he was ordained a deacon at St. Martin Church in Rome, KY and assigned to Blessed Mother Parish in Owensboro, KY under Fr. Charles Fischer. May 11, 1985, he was ordained a priest at the Sportscenter by Bishop John McRaith with Frs. Terry Devine, Gary Payne and Greg Trawick. His first priesthood assignment was to be associate pastor to Fr. William Allard at Immaculate Church in Owensboro. During his two years there, he taught religion at Owensboro Catholic High School eventually becoming chair of the religion department. During this time, he served as chaplain for the Wendall Foster Center and the Roosevelt House. In 1990, he was named pastor of St. Mary Magdalene Church in Sorgho, his boyhood parish.

In addition to parish duties, he sits on several community service boards and diocesan committees. As Diocesan Coordinator of AIDS Ministry Resources he has held board positions for both state and national AIDS organizations.

Often discouraged in his vocation because of his health, he loves being a priest and considers it to be a real gift from God. He and several family members suffer from hemophilia, a genetically transmitted blood disorder that causes crippling. His family feels that this has made them strong-willed, determined and assured in their faith. "I have the strength to face all conditions by the power that Christ gives me." Phil 4:13. He feels that God has blessed him by allowing him to witness his hand at work in the church and credits his vocation to the support of his loving family, and to the example of the priests of his childhood.

GOFF, LEANDER AND JANET BARR,

have lived in Daviess County, KY for most of their lives. Lee was born Nov. 18, 1937 to Leander Isidore and Mayme Pearl Shaney Goff of Rome, KY. Janet was born Aug. 17, 1938 to William Garrett and Ruth Cecilia Payne Barr of Browns Valley, KY. Lee and Janet were married June 1, 1957 at St. Anthony's in Brown's Valley, KY by the Rev. Martin Mattingly.

The Leander Goff Family

Lee has worked as a milk route salesman for nearly 35 years. In the early years of their marriage, Lee's job forced them to move about a lot - moving from Rome to Leitchfield, Elizabethtown, Philpot, Birk City and then back to Rome. Janet works in the lab of the local hospital. Lee and Janet now reside at Lee's boyhood home in Rome, KY. They belong to St. Martin's Church where Lee grew up and went to school.

The Goffs are very proud of their family and work hard to be a close family. Lee and Janet have five children and eight grandchildren. Their oldest and only son, Fr. Daniel Lee Goff is a priest of Diocese of Owensboro and is pastor of St. Mary Magdalene Church in Sorgho, KY. Sharon Ann, of Rome, is married to Billy Dean Clary and they have three sons, Jeremy, Jason and Jared. Jackie, of St. Charles, MO, is married to Tim Wehr and they have a daughter, Danielle Lee. Elaine, of Magnet, IN, is married to Bruce Miller and they have two children, Kayla and William Garrett. Lisa, of St. Joseph, KY, is married to Pat Mattingly and they have two children, Ryan and Ashley.

The Goffs mostly enjoy being with each other. It is not unusual to have them gather on Sunday at home to laugh and talk over a cup of coffee.

Suffering and illness are no stranger to the Goff family. Several members suffer from hemophilia, a genetically transmitted blood disorder that can cause crippling. Most of the family agrees that this has made them strong-willed, determined and assured in their faith. "I have the strength to face all conditions by the power that Christ gives me." Phil. 4:13.

GRANT, DENNIS,

was born on Dec. 31, 1949. He was born in Owensboro. His father Richard Grant was a farmer that lived out in the country. Dennis worked on the farm all his life and still is a farmer today. Sarona Murphy was born on Jan. 17, 1954. She was born in Owensboro and lived out in the country. She worked at a little country grocery store until she was 18. She then got a job at Owensboro National Bank. She still is working there.

They now have five kids. Their names are Nathan, 16; Ryan, 14; Scott, 11; Ginny, 8; and Jake, 4.

Sarona and Dennis both attended the same parish, Saint Peter of Stanley.

GRANT, ISHMAEL AND CATHERINE,

were members of the Western Kentucky Diocese ever since it was made a diocese. He was a member of Saint Anthony's Parish of Peonia and she was a member of Saint John The Evangelist Church at Sunfish, KY. They were married on May 8, 1948 at Saint John Evangelist and celebrated their 40th Anniversary at Saint Anthony's Church at Peonia, KY with Father Marty Hayes as celebrant with family and lots of friends.

Ishmael and Catherine Grant, 40th Wedding Anniversary, St. Anthony's Church.

Ishmael's father and mother originally were members of Saint Benedict's at Wax and were farmers. Catherine's mother was Hattie Bright of Fancy Farm, KY and father was Emmett Hayes of Saint John Evangelist of Sunfish.

Ishmael was the oldest son of George and Eva Pierce Grant of a family of nine children. Catherine was the oldest of 10 children, two of which died in infancy and eight are living in Kentucky, Indiana, Illinois and Nebraska.

Catherine graduated from Sunfish High School in Edmonson County in 1938. She attended college at Mount Saint Joseph for a semester. She went to work at Grayson Manor Nursing Home for 20 years, retiring in 1988.

Ismael has been a farmer all of his life and they became members of Saint Joseph Parish at Leitchfield in the 60s. They are proud to be members too.

Catherine had been served by Monsignor Louis Beruatto since childhood while he lived in Leitchfield. There were few good roads so he didn't get to Sunfish very often. Their mothers taught them their religion and had prayers in their homes on Sunday.

Father Howard Bishop from the Home Missioners of Glenmary came to visit and sent Father Clement Borchers as the first pastor.

Their pastors have joined the Ministerial Association and it is good to have an association with all religions of their county and their neighbors. They have a regular tent meeting in the fall for a week where all religions come together to pray and listen to the word of God.

GRATZER FAMILY, BERNARD DAVID AND DOROTHY ANN KELLY,

were married at St. Pius in Owensboro in 1966. Previous to the formation of St. Pius in 1957 three generations of his family had been members of St. Paul's in Owensboro.

The Gratzer family arrived in the United States at New York on Sept. 11, 1853, on the ship "Uncas." They had resided at Einsiedeln, Switzerland, where Benedict Gratzer Sr., died while farming about 1842. His widow, Gertrude Gratzer, and children, Catherine, Joseph M., August, Stephen A. and Benedict, were accompanied by her brother, John M. Kaelin, to the U.S. For awhile they lived at Cincinnati, OH. They were among the first purchasers of lots in Tell City, IN in 1859, when it was laid out by the Swiss Colonization Society. Members of the St. Michael's Church at Cannelton, IN, Gertrude Gratzer was buried there in 1889.

Benedict Gratzer, Josephine McCallister Gratzer (on right), their daughter, Gertrude Young and granddaughter, Josephine Young. Taken about 1902.

Benedict Gratzer Jr. (1842-1917) married Josephine McCallister (1848-1934) in Perry County, IN in 1867. A Catholic convert, she was the daughter of Granville McCallister and Nancy Dixon. A year or so later they moved to Owensboro, KY. A successful farmer and produce dealer he became known as "the Potato King of Kentucky". He owned farms on the Hardinsburg Road (just north of the Owensboro Memorial Gardens) and where Chautauqua Park is now. Initially members of St. Stephen in Owensboro, in 1887 upon the building of St. Paul Church they became members there. To them were born: Emma "Gertrude" (married Rinehart Young), "William" Thomas, Albert, "Ernest" Peter, Arthur "Lee," "Joseph" Matthew, "Mary" Josephine and two other children died in infancy.

Ernest Gratzer (1877-1954) married Mable Catherine Paulin (1900-1938), a native of Cannelton, IN and daughter of Cornelius Paulin and Elizabeth Feirstein. To them seven children were born: three died in infancy; Louise and Robert are single; Mabel married Mitchell C. Long, the parents of Mitchell C. Jr. and Jerry Long; and Bernard Gratzer, who by his marriage has three children, David, Christopher and Michael.

GREENWELL, BILLY DON AND JOYCE,
live on a farm near Waverly, KY in Union County and attend St. Peter of Antioch Church.

Billy Don was born July 24, 1929 to mother, nee, Mary Regina Clements and father Sylvester Greenwell. He was baptized at St. Ann in Morganfield and grew up near Uniontown in St. Agnes Parish. Joyce was born Sept. 7, 1934 to mother, nee, Mary Euginia Konsler and father Redmond Carroll. She was baptized and grew up in Holy Name Parish in Henderson, KY.

Billy Don attended Hite School, St. Agnes School and graduated from St. Vincent Academy. He served in the Air Force from 1951-1955. Joyce attended Weaverton School and graduated from Holy Name High School and worked as a dental assistant. They married, March 2, 1957, at Holy Name Church with Rev. Robt. J. Gipperich officiating.

Billy Don farms with his three sons, another son is a coal miner. Joyce has taken care of their eight children. Julie was baptized at St. Agnes and Ralph, Jason (married Sherri Floyd), Paul, Carol (married Jeff Ratley), Amy (married J.D. Kramer), Bryan and Lana at St. Ambrose near Henshaw, KY. Their daughters work professionally as a dental hygienist, speech therapist, beautician and occupational therapist student.

Billy Don is a member of the Knights of Columbus, has served on St. Peter's Parish Council, Union County Water District Commissioner and Union County Industrial Committee.

Joyce is a member of St. Peter's Altar Society, served on the Owensboro Diocesan Pastoral Council, is a lector, and serves on the liturgy committee.

They enjoy their four grandchildren and having all their children living near them. Each Christmas they love to be host for the 75 or more members of the Sylvester and Regina Greenwell family.

GREENWELL, JASON PATRICK AND SHERRI ANN,
of St. Peter Parish in Waverly, KY have three children John Kirk, Sarah Rose and Drew Patrick.

Jason was born Sept. 27, 1960 and baptized at St. Ambrose in Union County, KY by Rev. Pius Edelen. He grew up and served as an altar boy there until 1975 when he moved with his parents, Billy Don and Joyce Carroll Greenwell, to Waverly, KY. He attended grade school at St. Ann and St. Peter's. He graduated from Union County High School in 1979. He is engaged in farming with his father and three brothers. He also has four sisters.

Sherri was born, Sept. 21, 1965, and baptized at St. Agnes Church in Uniontown, KY. She grew up and attended grade school there. She graduated from Union County High School in 1983. Her parents are Charles Hamilton and Rose Buckman Floyd and she has four brothers and two sisters.

They were married, Nov. 18, 1983, in St. Agnes Church with Rev. James Miller officiating.

Jason serves on the St. Peter's Church Pastoral Council and is a member of the K of C Uniontown Council.

Sherri does volunteer work at St. Ann Interparochial School and devotes her time caring for her family.

GREENWELL, SISTER LUCITA,
was born March 5, 1906 at New Haven, KY. She entered the parish on Sept. 7, 1924 and received her habit on March 19, 1925. She took her vows on Aug. 15, 1927 and Aug. 15, 1930. She was baptized as Edna M. on March 9, 1906 and received her confirmation on Oct. 19, 1913.

Sister Lucita is the daughter of Nicholas S. Greenwell (born Dec. 26, 1867-died Nov. 4, 19??) and Mary Veronica Bowling-Greenwell (born May 7, 1876-died Nov. 16, 19??). Her brothers and sisters include: Joseph Raymond Greenwell (born Aug. 14, 1896-died Jan. 14, 1977) married Agnes Bompart; Mary Elizabeth Greenwell (born Dec. 11, 1898-died Sept. 19, 1973) married William J. Logsdon; Mary Ruth Greenwell (born Jan. 13, 1905) single; Mary Louise Greenwell (born Oct. 23, 1903-died Oct. 30, 1982) married E. Leon Ballard; Edna Marie Greenwell (born March 5, 1906) now Sr. Lucita Greenwell; Mary Lucita Greenwell (born Nov. 5, 1908-died June 3, 1984) married Thurmond Smith; Robert Nicholas Greenwell (born Jan. 19, 1915) married Katherine Ducette; and Mary Dolores Greenwell (born Aug. 15, 1920) married Henry Payne.

Sister Lucita's missions include: Jeffersonville, IN; St. Denis, Shively, KY, St. Bernard, Nebraska City, NE, St. Alphonsus, St. Joseph, KY, Glennonville, MO, St. Joseph, Owensboro, Mt. St. Joseph Academy, Mistress of Novices, Leitchfield, KY, St. Paul, St. Romuald, Hardinsburg, KY, New Haven, KY, St. Margaret Mary and Mother of Good Counsel, Louisville, St. Edward, Jeffersontown, Mount St. Joseph, Archives.

GREENWELL, SISTER MARY CLEMENT,
is the daughter of Matthew and Elizabeth (Sauer) Greenwell. Her father was a farmer at Curdsville. He was raised in Whitesville while her mother was raised at Stanley, KY.

Her brothers and sisters are Clement Greenwell, Celestian, Julius, Homer, Emma (Clements) Greenwell, Rose (Ruihe) Greenwell, Miles, Wallace, Leo and Augusta Byrne.

She attended St. Elizabeth Curdsville from grades one-11 and finished high school at Mount St. Joseph. She entered the novitiate Jan. 21, 1927. She received her novitiate training from Sister Leo Johnson. During the second semester of the second year, she was sent to Stanley, New Haven and Chicago, KY to substitute for sick Sisters.

In 1929 she was assigned to teach in St. Joseph in Owensboro. During the depression years she was in Glennonville, MO teaching the primary grades for 10 years. Later she was sent to St. Charles, Holy Cross and St. Joseph in Marion County, Fredericktown, Waterflow and Farmington in New Mexico.

Her last schools included Blessed Mother, Immaculate, St. Margaret Mary in Louisville and St. Louis, MO.

After 50 years of teaching she stayed at their retirement house in Louisville and did various volunteer jobs, such as, Red Cross, hospital and nursing home visiting, teaching refugees English and teaching converts for 11 years.

She is now retired at the Mount since 1989. She loves it and is thankful for it all.

GREENWELL, MARY HELEN,
is one of four children born to Marie and Hogarty Greenwell in Nelson County, KY on Aug. 31, 1938. She was a member of St. Catherine's Catholic Church, New Haven, KY and attended St. Catherine's Grade and High School. She was taught by the Ursuline Sisters who had a great influence on her Catholic faith and religious vocation.

Sr. Margaret Marie Greenwell, OSU

Her parents were blessed having two daughters to enter religious life. Her sister, Sister Paul Marie Greenwell is also a Mount Saint Joseph Ursuline.

She entered the Ursuline Order of Mount Saint Joseph on Sept. 7, 1954 and was given the name Sister Margaret Marie. On Aug. 15, 1957, she professed her temporary vows and three years later, Aug. 15, 1960, she professed her perpetual vows. During this time, she attended Brescia College and received a bachelor degree in elementary education. Later, she attended Western Kentucky University and received a masters degree in elementary education.

She has taught in Vine Grove, KY; St. Columba and St. Denis in Louisville; and St. Mary Elementary in Paducah as a primary teacher, religion teacher and principal.

She is presently working at St. Ann's Morganfield, KY, part time in the school as religion teacher of the students with Non-Catholic teachers and part time in parish ministry.

During these 38 years of religious life, she has been richly blessed by God, her family, her friends and the students she's taught. For this, she is eternally grateful.

GREENWELL FAMILY, SYLVESTER AND REGINA,
live near Uniontown in Union County and are members of St. Agnes Parish.

Sylvester was born May 24, 1898 to mother, nee, Margaret Mills and father Sylvester Greenwell. He grew up near Waverly, KY in St. Peter's Parish with his brothers and sisters: Bernard, Annie, Matilda (Sr. Cleophas), Ida, Helen and Margaret. Regina was born July 23, 1906 to mother, nee, Mary Frances Rapier and father Joseph Robert Clements. She grew up near Uniontown in St. Agnes Parish with her six brothers; Willie Ben, Bernard, Pat, Rapier, Jimmy and Lyle.

Sylvester attended Hancock School, graduated from St. Peter's High School, and attended St. Mary of the Woods College. Regina attended St. Ann School and graduated from Morganfield High School.

Sylvester and Regina married, Nov. 3, 1924, with

Rev. R.C. Duff officiating at St. Agnes Church. Sylvester farmed and Regina devoted her time to their eight children—Charlotte, Helen Dean (married Leonard Thomas), Billy Don (married Joyce Carroll), Joan (died Jan. 12, 1976), Tommy (married Elizabeth Thomas), Gerald (married Marilyn Welge), Patsy (married Roger Whitaker) and Marie (married Mike Guillerman).

They celebrated their 65th Wedding Anniversary with Mass at St. Agnes in 1989 with their family. They have 33 grandchildren and 32 great-grandchildren.

Sylvester belonged to the Knights of Columbus and was honored as a Pioneer Farmer. He passed away April 3, 1991. Regina remains in her home on the farm operated by her sons and grandsons. She enjoys her family and visiting her friends.

GRIEF, RUTH ANN, the daughter of Charles Rowan Ballard and Anna Maude Ballard Ballard (both deceased). Married Richard Thomas Grief Sr. (Tom died 1979) July 3, 1937 at St. Frances De Sales in Paducah. Ruth is a member of St. Frances De Sales parish. She and Tom had five children, all graduated from St. Mary's High School.

Ruth Grief family, left to right; Ruth, Richard, Marilyn, David, Phyllis and Howard. The occasion was Ruth's 75th birthday, Aug. 13, 1992.

Phyllis Kathryn, married William Richard Darnell (Dick) they attend Our Lady of Mount Carmel, in Carmel, IN and have four children: William Richard Jr. (Ricky), married Jean Clarke; Londa Marie, married Richard Dowden (Rick); Jennifer Lynne, married Tim Melone; and Christopher Allan (Chris).

Phyllis has three grandchildren, Amanda (a stillborn) and Taylor Anthony born to Londa and Michelle Lynne, Jennifer's child.

David Michael, St. Frances De Sales had a stillborn child Maria.

Richard Thomas Jr. (Skippy), life time member of St. Francis De Sales, two children, Monica Lynn and David Anthony.

Howard Anthony, life member of the Owensboro Diocese and a member of Rosary Chapel, two children: Robert Anthony (Robbie) and Angela Marie (Angie).

Marilyn Ruth, life time member of St. Francis De Sales, wife of Michael Stephen Mayes (Mike).

Ruth has three sisters and four brothers: Evelyn married Nicholas Roberts (both deceased); James lives in Chicago; Wilbur (deceased) married Lillian McNally; Frances married Earl Watson and lives in La Center, KY, attends St. Mary's; Charles Anthony (deceased) married Neva Resser a member of St. Francis De Sales; Margie lives in Chicago, married Thomas Carey (deceased) and William (Earl) lives in Chicago.

HAAS, ELDRIDGE H. AND CAROLYN THELMA (BENHASE), were both born and raised in Hamilton County which is Cincinnati, OH. They now live in Calloway County, and belong to St. Leo Parish in Murray, KY. They've been here since May 1989, when they moved from Marion, OH. They celebrated 35 years of marriage in August 1992.

Eldridge retired from the General Telephone Company of Ohio in 1988. Carolyn retired from the Marion County Social Service Department in 1980; both jobs were in Marion County, Marion, OH.

Their three grown children, Margaret, Richard and Ronald have given Eldridge and Carolyn six grandchildren. The three children were born and raised in Ohio, except for two years when the family lived in Connecticut. One grandson lives in Florida with his father, Ronald and Margaret is the mother of the other five grandchildren. Margaret lives in Massillon, OH. Richard, a newly-wed who visits Murray frequently, lives in Florida.

Eldridge joined the Knights of Columbus at St. Leo, having been invited to join by Frank Morris of St. Leo. Carolyn attends meetings of the Ladies' Guild of St. Leo and Bible classes held by Sister Mary Anne Yanz there. They belong to St. Joseph Circle at St. Leo and enjoy the activities of the Circle and other Church functions, including the Dedication of the new Parish Center by the bishop on Nov. 8, 1992 at St. Leo. They act as Ministers of Hospitality, greeting Mass-goers, taking up the collection, and making sure everyone has a Bulletin when he or she leaves. This past October when the children of the parish held their Halloween Party, Eldridge and Carolyn decided to attend the party, taking treats and helping the children have fun. Being with youngsters brings back wonderful memories of earlier Halloweens.

Eldridge and Carolyn watch the historic events taking place in Israel with special interest, since they visited the Holy Land in 1979. They also saw Pope John Paul II in Rome, Italy that year.

HAAS FAMILY, George, 1833-1915, and Catherine, 1836-1893, Haases arrived in America from the Alsace-Lorraine area of Germany circa 1856. Economic conditions and political unrest prompted their immigration to this country to settle in Cincinnati, OH. Their children were Allie, George, Adam, Kate Dahm and Lizzie Grief all born in Germany. Adam, grandfather of the present Haas family in St. John Parish, was 13 years old when arriving in this country. He married Clara Weimer of Cincinnati and came by flat boat down the Ohio River to Paducah with their furniture and household possessions and settled in the St. John community as a young married couple. Their metropolitan backgrounds as saloon keeper and dry goods store clerk did not enhance their skill to provide for their six children on a farm. Their determination, frugality and hard work became a way of life. Their home was at the end of a long lane on the Contest Road near Lone Oak. Two log rooms of the original home are still standing on the original property and used for recreational outings. Children of George and Clara were Helena and Henrietta, twins who died in infancy, Charlotte and Leon, who died in early years of tuberculosis, Clara Louise Yopp and George Adam Haas. Newspapers, language and prayer were printed and spoken in German well into the 20th century. The German influence was seen in celebrating and cooking for special occasions in varied ways. Traditional Christmas practices were commemorating the feast of St. Nicholas on December 6 by leaving goodies in the shoes of family members, a tradition still observed by the Haas and Yopp families today, and decorating the Christmas tree with candy and cookies.

George Adam Haas married Margaret Mary Roof. They have six children: Rose Marietta, Charlotte Marie and Sister Mary Jeanette Haas, Barbaranelle Tackett, George Edwin and Louis Alfred Haas. Rose Marietta and Charlotte Marie are unmarried. Mary Jeanette is a Religious Sister of Mercy. George Edwin married Judith Ann McGarry and has three children, Mary Kathleen, Matthew Edwin and Daniel Adam. Barbaranelle married Robert Tackett and has three children: Colleen Ann married to Bruce Edwin Tincher, Cynthia Rose married to Erik Paul Sandefer and Carol Maria. Louis Alfred Haas married Lanera Kaye McKinney. They have four children, Terrance Patrick married to Laura Michelle Shoulta, Timothy Joseph, Michael Andrew and Christopher Mark Haas.

HAAS FAMILY, LOUIS ALFRED AND KAYE MCKINNEY, Louis Alfred Haas was born Nov. 6, 1941, son of George Adam Haas and Margaret Roof Haas.

The Haas family were members of St. John the Evangelist Church near Paducah. Louis attended school at St. John for 12 years. After playing four years of professional baseball, Louis graduated from Western Kentucky University, earning a BS degree in accounting. He married Kaye McKinney on Nov. 26, 1964.

Kaye was born on Aug. 31, 1942, daughter of Emory Dean McKinney and Elizabeth Langston McKinney. The McKinney family were members of St. Francis De Sales Parish in Paducah, KY. Kaye graduated from St. Mary Academy which, at the time, was located downtown at Fifth and Monroe in Paducah.

They have lived in the St. John Parish in Paducah, KY all of their married life. Louis is a business executive and Kaye is a full time homemaker. They are the parents of four sons. Terry Patrick was born Sept. 19, 1965. He attended St. John Elementary and St. Mary High School, graduated from St. Louis University and earned an MBA from Notre Dame University. He is married to Laura Michelle Shoulta. Timothy Joseph was born on June 29, 1967. Tim received his education from Lone Oak School in the Special Education program. Tim is employed at a local car dealer as a file clerk. Michael Andrew was born on Jan. 4, 1971, attended St. John Elementary, graduated from St. Mary High School and is a senior at St. Louis University. Christopher Mark was born Oct. 15, 1976. Chris completed eight years at St. John Elementary and is in his second year at St. Mary High School.

Their family has a very special interest in Catholic education and are involved in activities that support the local Catholic school systems.

HADDAD, JACK AND THERESA, have been members of St. Edward Parish in Fulton, KY for 27 years. Jack, who is a convert, received First Communion on their wedding day in 1965 from the same priest who gave him instructions to enter the church. Theresa was born in Lebanon and came to the United States in 1948. Jack's parents were born in Lebanon. Theresa taught at a Catholic elementary school before coming to St. Edward. At St. Edward she has at one time or another been teacher and CCD coordinator, president of the Altar Society, Renew leader, Eucharistic minister, parish council member and sponsor and leader of the sponsors in RCIA. Jack has been a lector, usher, finance committee member, president of the Men's Club and chairman of the Parish Council.

Christmas 1991

They have three daughters: Lori, who was organist for 10 years at St. Edward and now attends Holy Name in Henderson with husband Michael; Christy, who was a lector at St. Edward for many years; and Jackie, who is presently the organist at St. Edward and has been for four years. They also have two grandsons, Michael and Joshua.

The Haddad family said a nightly rosary for many years and placed family prayer and Mass attendance two-three times weekly as very high priorities.

HAGAN FAMILY, DARYL AND JILL, live in Henderson County and have been members of Holy Name Church since birth. They were married on Jan. 5, 1985 at Holy Name Church in Henderson, KY. They have one son, Maxwell Lincoln, born on Feb. 21, 1992.

Daryl and Jill have been very active in Catholic schools. He taught at Christ The King School in Madisonville, KY, Holy Name School in Henderson, KY and is currently the principal of St. Ann Interparochial School in Morganfield, KY.

Jill has been assistant coach for one of the girls basketball teams at Holy Name when she is not working as a financial analyst for Berry Plastics, Inc.

HAGAN, EVELYN HARDESTY HOWARD,

was born in Lockland, OH near Cincinnati. Her parents, Virgil and Dessi Wimsatt Hardesty, moved there to enroll their deaf sons (twins) Edward and Edgar in a Catholic school, St. Rita School for the Deaf.

The Evelyn Howard Hagan Family

Her mom and dad were born and raised in Daviess and Ohio County, KY. When their twin boys were born in 1921, they soon detected a hearing problem. They knew the boys would have to have special education, hoping for a Catholic education if possible. One day when the boys were around 4 years old, a magazine called *The Silent Advocate,* from St. Rita School for the Deaf in Ohio, appeared in her grand-father Hardesty's mailbox. They never knew how it came to be there. That led her parents to Ohio. They lived there until 1937; they moved back to Whitesville, KY just after the roads were clear from the '37 flood.

Evelyn went to school at Stevens School and St. Mary, Whitesville. She married James Edgar (Pete) Howard in 1950, they had 11 children. They are: Michael, Richard, Becki, Karen, Bobby, Vicki, Jerry, Sandy, Pam, Kenny and James Edgar Jr. (who died at birth). All live in the Owensboro Diocese. Pete was a farmer and steel worker, he died in 1967. She married James W. Hagan in 1990 and still lives in Whitesville, and attends St. Mary of the Woods Church.

HAGAN, SISTER FRANCES THERESE,

was born on Oct. 21, 1911 at Holy Cross, KY. She was baptized as Mary Pauline. She is the daughter of Charles Hagan and Ellen Porter. Her brothers and sisters are: Marie Ballard, Robert Hagan, Guy Hagan (deceased), Theresa Thompson, Emmanuel Hagan, Sister Frances Emmanuel S.L., Guy Hagan, Adolphus Hagan (deceased), Charles Hagan Jr., Rev. Joseph Hagan (Hubert) and Elizabeth Hagan Osborne. She entered the convent on Sept. 8, 1929 and received her habit on March 19, 1930. She took her vows on March 19, 1932 and March 19, 1935.

Her missions include: St. Columba; New Haven, KY; Buechel, KY; Bardwell, KY; Sorgho, KY; Fredericktown, KY; St. Columba, Louisville; Waverly, KY; St. Benedict, Nebraska City, NE; St. Alphonsus, St. Joseph, KY; Calvary, Lebanon, KY; Holy Cross, Loretto, KY; Precious Blood, Owensboro; St. Romuald, Hardinsburg; St. Catherine, New Haven, KY.

HAGAN, GARY M.,

son of W.F. and Lillie Mae Hagan, married Debbie M. Cinnamond, daughter of Bob and Sharrie Cinnamond, May 14, 1982. They have two children Marie Nicole (11) and Allen Michael (8). They are active members of St. Mary Church, Whitesville. Their children attend St. Mary Grade School. Debbie is originally from Henderson having lived there from birth to 17 years of age. In 1979 her family moved to Whitesville, where she met Gary.

They presently reside in Philpot, KY and attend Saint Mary of the Woods, Whitesville. Past parish memberships include Holy Name of Henderson. Debbie has been very active in the Social Concerns Committee from 1986 to 1992. She has withdrawn for a short time to spend more time with the children. Debbie reads at Mass on Sunday, is a member of the Altar Society and teaches the Children's Liturgy of the Word regularly.

Gary M. and Debbie M. Hagan with Allen (6 weeks) and Marie (3 years).

Debbie is currently Den Mother for 10 Wolf Cub Scouts. Gary is member of Knights of Columbus in Whitesville.

"I just want to say that an "outsider" moving in to a new parish is very difficult and St. Mary was not extremely open or welcoming. But as I became active in the church the parishioners opened up. As I learned more names and faces the parish seemed to be more like home. I urge all those who don't feel part of the parish to get involved, volunteer for something, anything. It will do wonders for you."

HAGAN, JAMES W.,

has lived in Whitesville all his life. James married Catherine M. Higdon in 1950. They had five children: Francis E., Lucia Marie, Richard A., Darrell A. and Mark W. They all live in the Owensboro Diocese. James was a farmer, carried mail part-time and sold and serviced chainsaws at his home two miles north of Whitesville. He is a former member of the Parish Council, Trinity High School Board, Knights of Columbus and Whitesville Credit Union.

James W. Hagan Family

The Hagan name has been associated with the Catholic Church for many generations. His great-great-grandfather, Thomas C. Hagan, was among the first Catholic settlers of Daviess County. Mass was celebrated in his home (Hagans Station) before there was a church in Whitesville. Thomas' father was with the first boat loads of Catholics from Maryland to settle in Kentucky in 1785.

His wife Catherine died in 1989. In 1990 he married Evelyn Hardesty Howard. She had 10 children. Now when they get the families together, it is quite a party with 15 children and 23 grandchildren.

HAGAN, JOSEPH BIRCH,

was born May 5, 1893 in St. Lawrence, KY. His father, Robert Abel Hagan was a real estate developer, and his mother Julia (Blincoe), was a daughter of a physician. Stella Mae was born May 29, 1897. Her father Samuel Hamilton was a farmer and married Fronica (Stennett). Joseph's occupation was that of a draftsman, and he and Stella were married at St Stephen Church on Oct. 31, 1917. They were members of St. Stephen Parish and had four children who were raised in Owensboro, Daviess County, KY.

Of their four children, Joseph Richard (March 13, 1918) married Fladge Teresa Birkhead and they have three daughters and one son. Joseph Richard died Oct. 25, 1980. Estelle Marie (March 19, 1920), married Robert A. Oberst and they have six daughters and two sons. Robert A. Sr. died Oct. 23, 1974. Phyllis Elaine (Sept. 21, 1921), married Harold Chapman and have one son. Robert Daniel (March 12, 1923), married Wilma Jean Morphew and they have one son and one daughter.

Joseph Birch passed away on Oct. 19, 1957. Stella lives at the Carmel Home on Old Hartford Road in Owensboro and would love for friends to call on her there.

HAGAN, JOSEPH LAWRENCE AND ANNE (ROLPH),

are members of St. Ann Parish living in Union County, currently in Morganfield. Larry is employed in agriculture sales and Anne is a secretary. He was born and raised in Union County while Anne was born in El Paso, TX. Her father was in the Army, so they moved a lot.

They have four children. Lori Ann, born July 18, 1969 is married to Timothy Buckman and has one daughter, Angela Buckman. Lori is a secretary and Tim is a machinist. Susan Marie, born Jan. 18, 1973 is a sophomore at Western Kentucky University. Elizabeth Lynn, born Dec. 1, 1975 is a Junior at Union County High School. Bradley Lawrence, born June 30, 1979 is an eighth grader at Union County Middle School.

HAGAN FAMILY, RICHARD ALAN,

Richard Alan "Doc" Hagan, wife Shawna Denise Norris Hagan, daughter Rachel Rene Hagan and son Weston James Hagan live in Whitesville, KY. Richard grew up in Whitesville. He entered Western Kentucky University and graduated in mechanical engineering in 1978. He accepted a job in Albany, OR as a paper plant engineer. He is a finance committee member and helps with the St. Mary picnics.

In Albany Richard met Shawna Norris. She was born in Aurora, MO, but grew up in Southern California, Michigan, New York and Oregon.

Richard returned to Whitesville in 1984 to begin farming full-time. He owned the farm next to his parents. About a year later Shawna came to live in Owensboro, KY, working as a travel agent. The two were married at St. Mary of the Woods on Oct. 4, 1986. They live on the farm where they built a home in 1991.

Their first child, Rachel René was born Dec. 24, 1989 and their second child, Weston James was born on May 8, 1991. Their favorite sport is snow-skiing. They also enjoy traveling.

Richard's parents are James William Hagan of Whitesville and Catherine Marcelline Higdon (deceased). Shawna's parents are Bobby Lynn Norris of Salt Lake City, UT and Cle Ella Caroline Mattox Norris of Harbor City, CA.

HAGAN, WILLIAM FRANCIS,

son of William Gibson Hagan, Henderson County and Olivia Kathern Strobel, Daviess County and Lillie Mae Simon, daughter of Silas Francis Simon and Laura Frances Durbin both from Edmonson County were married Nov. 18, 1941 at St. Paul Church Owensboro. Rev. C.P. Bowling officiated.

The Hagans have lived in Daviess County and farmed all their lives except the 37 months William was in service in World War II.

Lillie remembers being left with a 6 week old baby, a cow to milk, hogs to feed and six and one-half acres of tobacco to get to market. Friends and families were life savers.

The Hagans have been members of St. Mary of Woods, Whitesville, for 33 years. They are hospitality ministers, involved in R.C.I.A.; social concerns, parish picnics, volunteer St. Vincent De Paul Store, Whitesville and are very active in the Catholic Cursillo movement in Owensboro diocese. Lillie is member of Altar Society.

Daughters of Isabella and tutors for Kentucky Literacy program.

William and Lillie Mae Hagan Family November 17, 1991, 50th Wedding Anniversary.

The Hagans have nine children, 28 grandchildren and five great-grandchildren. All of their children graduated from St. Mary and Trinity High. Their sons are Leo, Donald, Paul, Gary and Thomas. Their daughters are Linda Milligan, Darlene White, Frances Logdson and Ann Lanham.

William remembers riding the street cars in Owensboro and riding the train to Stanley to visit his maternal grandparents.

Lillie remembers going to school in the St. Raphel Church after the school burned.

William and Lillie celebrated their 50th Wedding Anniversary, November 1991, at St. Mary with Mass and renewal of vows. Rev. Louis Piskula officiated. Mrs. Hagan's brother Silas Simon Jr., Newman, KY and niece Mrs. Mary Cathern Fogle Baush, Semore, IN, their original witnesses were also present.

Reception was at Whitesville Knights of Columbus Hall where more than 300 friends and family members attended.

HAGAN-WINSTEAD FAMILY, Robert Hagan, son of Sam Hagan and Mary Howell Hagan was born near Calhoun, KY Oct. 10, 1926 and baptized by Father Blandford. His father Sam Hagan was a farm hand and laborer, his mother Mary Howell was a housewife from McLean County, KY. Louise Winstead was born to Willie (Buck) Winstead and Minnie Belle Curry on June 20, 1937 in Owensboro, KY. Robert and Louise were married on April 16, 1956 at St. Stephen Cathedral. They presently reside on Maple Street in Owensboro.

Robert Hagan

Robert and Louise had eight children. Five are still living. Robert is a retired employee from the City of Owensboro where he worked for 13 years and from Texas Gas Corporation where he worked for 12 years. Robert is very active in St. Stephen Cathedral and Blessed Sacrament Chapel where he ministers as a lector, Eucharistic Minister, altar server, etc. Robert belongs to many church organizations such as Blessed Sacrament Parish Council, St. Stephen Pastoral Council, African-American Catholic Commission, Owensboro Deanery Council, Social Concerns Committee and the Army of Mary. Robert graduated from Catholic Colored High School in 1945. He pursued a course of study for the priesthood at St. Augustine's Seminary in Bay St. Louis, MS from 1943 to 1944.

HAGMAN, DANIEL JOHN, was born in Skillman Bottoms, near the town of Hawesville, KY, June 24, 1934. He was baptized at St. Rose, Cloverport. He is the son of Harold Victor Hagman, who was a farmer. His mother was Dorothy Rose Johnson of St. Lawrence, KY. He was one of 11 children. Dan graduated from Immaculate Conception School in 1952. He attended St. Bernard College and graduated in 1954. He served in the Naval Airforce for four years.

Shirley Kurz was the daughter of Fred Kurz, a long time foreman of General Electric of Owensboro. She was baptized and raised in St. Stephen Cathedral Parish, graduated from Catholic High in 1952. Her mother was Goldie Whelan and (the mother of) 10 children.

Shirley and Dan were married on Aug. 13, 1960 and live in Hawesville, KY where Dan is a farmer and Shirley is the parish secretary for Immaculate Conception and St. Columba churches. Shirley is also on the RCIA team and teaches in the religious program at Immaculate Conception. Dan is a member of the Third and Fourth Degree of the Knights of Columbus.

They are the proud parents of four children and four grandchildren. Dan loves to play golf and they enjoy traveling on their vacation.

HAGMAN, VICTOR, the son of Harold and Dorothy Johnson Hagman was born in Hawesville, KY. He attended St. Rose School in Cloverport for eight years and four years at St. Bernard in Cullman, AL. After serving four years in the U.S. Navy, he returned to the family farm in 1955 and became a partner with his dad. They were members of Immaculate Conception Parish, Hawesville.

Left to right, back; Matthew, Joseph and Mary Rose. Front row, left to right; James, Vic, Barbara and Paul.

In 1965 Vic married Barbara Frey. She was the daughter of William Charles and Mary Agnes Bryan Frey. They were life long members of St. Joseph and Paul Parish in Owensboro. Barbara attended St. Joseph School for eight years, St. Francis Academy two years and graduated from Catholic High in 1953.

They have five children. Their oldest son Joseph is a partner with his dad on the farm and his Uncle Francis. Matthew is currently in the U.S. Navy. James is also working on the family farm and plans to become a partner. Mary Rose is a student at Brescia College. Their youngest son, Paul, is attending Owensboro Community College.

Their five children attended Immaculate Conception School for eight years and St. Romuald High School in Hardinsburg for four years, except Paul. The school closed his junior year. He graduated from Hancock County High School.

Vic and Barbara have been married for 27 years.

HAIRE, KIMBERLY "ANN" CLEMONS AND PHILIP "RAYMOND," were married on May 14, 1983, at St. Stephen Cathedral in Owensboro, KY.

Kim was born on Sept. 18, 1961, the sixth child of Carmel and Odaline. She attended Peonia Grade School; she spent two years at Grayson County High and two years at Mt. St. Joseph Academy, graduating in 1979. She received her BA in accounting and an associate degree in computer science from Brescia College in 1983. She has worked at EnTrade Corp. and Texas Gas Corp. in Owensboro.

Phil and Kim, Amy and Andrew Haire

Phil was born on April 18, 1960 in Louisville, KY, the eighth child (of nine) of James and Beverly Thompson Haire. He attended St. Polycarp Grade School and Pleasure Ridge High for two years (both in Louisville), and graduated from Owensboro Catholic High School in 1979 after his family moved to Immaculate Parish in Owensboro. He attended Brescia College for two years. He is currently store manager of Midwest Electric Supply in Paducah.

Kim and Phil have three children: Andrew (Philip), born Aug. 28, 1984 in Evansville, IN; Amy (Elizabeth), born Feb. 19, 1987 in Owensboro; and Logan (Bradley), born March 6, 1992 in Paducah. Andrew and Amy attend St. Thomas More School.

Members of Thomas More Parish, Phil serves as chair of the Building and Grounds Committee and as Minister of Hospitality. Kim serves on the Welcoming Committee of the parish.

When she has time apart from the children, Kim enjoys reading, window shopping, playing the piano and visiting with friends; Phil enjoys woodworking; sports, especially golf; and helping coach children's sports.

HALE, HAROLD AND SUE ANN (POTTS) HOLLIE, were married at St. Romuald Parish Church in Hardinsburg, Breckinridge County, KY on Dec. 4, 1983 by Fr. Peter E. Lauzon. To this union Harold brought a son Myron Hale and daughter Cherie D. Hale and Sue Ann brought Laura Ann, Samantha Lynn and Elaine Marie Hollie. Laura (Hollie) Hamlet Miller has presented the family with two grandchildren, Julie and Michael.

From left; Laura Miller, Sue Ann Hale, Samantha Fox, Elaine Hollie. Harold Hale (in back).

Harold has worked at Commonwealth Aluminum for 25 years, May 7, and Sue Ann is currently employed with the Breckinridge County Fiscal Court. Sue Ann has been a member of St. Romuald Parish from birth in 1946. Sue Ann is a member of the choir, an Eucharist minister, works with the youth ministry program, has taught CCD and helps with the annual picnic.

HALE, KRISTI, was born May 12, 1978 in Hardinsburg, KY at Breckinridge Memorial Hospital. Her father, Leroy Hale was born in Brandenburg, KY and her mother, Neita Clark Hale, was born in Waverly, IL.

Kristi's paternal grandparents are Gene and Mary Hazel Hale. Gene was born at Fall of Rough, KY and Hazel was born at Kirk, KY.

Kristi's maternal grandparents are John Preston Clark Jr. and Mary Lucille Clark of Payneville, KY. John was born in Axtel, KY and Mary was born in Cloverport, KY.

Her paternal great-grandparents are the late Harry Hale Sr. and Laura Leigh Wheatley Hale who now lives at McQuady, KY. Her paternal grandmother's parents were Joseph and Lillis Wells Martin. They lived at Axtel, KY.

Kristi's maternal great-grandparents are the late John Preston Clark Sr. and Mary Louise Berry Clark of Louisville, KY and the late Austin and Jessie Mae VanConey DeWitt of Cloverport, KY. Jessie Mae VanConey was born in Cannelton, IN.

Kristi graduated from Immaculate Conception School in Hawesville, KY and she will be attending Hancock County High School in August.

HALL, MEAGAN, was born on Dec. 11, 1979 in Owensboro, KY and was raised in Lewisport, KY. Her parents are Cythia Goodwin and Clinton Hall. She has one brother, Wesley Hall.

There are many interesting stories throughout her family history. One example is when her grandfather on her father's side, Albert Hall, had to change his name.

When Albert was born, his mother had already had several children. So when her doctor came out to ask what she wanted to name him, she replied, "I don't even care if you name him John Henry!"

It was after he was taken home she decided to name him Albert Ray Hall. After Albert was an adult, he decided he would get a birth certificate. So he called the county courthouse. The person there said that there was no Albert Hall listed there, and he needed to give them more information about his family. They called him back to say the only person in his family was named John Henry! He had to have five witnesses saying he had been going by the name Albert Hall.

There is another interesting thing in Meagan's family history. Her great-grandmother was the first telephone operator in Lewisport. Her great-grandfather helped install the first telephone lines in Lewisport.

Meagan goes to Immaculate Conception School in Hawesville, KY. She is 12 years old and is in sixth grade.

HALL, RITA AND DAVID, have been happily married for 17 years. They were married into the church at Our Lady of Lourdes. Rita's mom was born in Ireland and has been Catholic all her life. Nathaniel Lyons, her dad, converted to be a Catholic in 1968.

David and Rita have eight kids; five girls and three boys. Their names are Lori, Erin, Dustin, Mary, Joseph, Anna, Jesse and Christian. Lori, Erin, Dustin and Mary were baptized by Fr. Boarman. Joseph and Anna were baptized by Fr. Ziegler and Jesse and Christian by Fr. Clemons. They were all baptized in Our Lady of Lourdes parish. The whole family has lived in Daviess County all their life. The family attends Mass along with Rita's parents every Sunday at Lourdes. The Hall family now lives on Tennyson Dr.

HAMILTON, CAROL RAY AND PATRICIA LOUISE PAYNE, Carol Ray was born on Sept. 24, 1947 in Daviess County near Whitesville. His parents are James and Anne Hamilton. Patricia Louise Payne was born Dec. 5, 1947 in Daviess County near Knottsville.

Patty moved to Whitesville in 1963, there she met Ray. They both attended St. Mary High School and graduated in 1965.

They were married April 23, 1966. Ray has worked at Green River Steel for over 20 years and he is a part-time farmer. He is also a volunteer fireman for the Whitesville Community. Patty has worked at Valley Institute of Psychiatry for the last five and one-half years. Patty served as secretary/treasurer for St. Mary Altar Society for six years and one year as vice-president. She has also served on the grade school board three years.

Ray and Patty have served their parish by giving of their time, labor and money. They have supported Bishops Relief Fund, the Lion's Club, Good Neighbor Fund, Cystic Fibrosis Foundation, United Way and Foreign Missions over the past 26 years.

Ray and Patty have four children. Patricia Carol, born Dec. 1, 1967, graduated from Trinity High in 1985. She was married Dec. 28, 1991 to Joseph Vincent Ebelhar III. Mary Katherine, born July 31, 1969, graduated from Trinity in 1987. She was married to Brian Michael Boehman on April 22, 1988. James Francis Hamilton, born March 5, 1972, graduated from Trinity in 1990. He has received a Certificate of Appreciation for Outstanding Performance while serving on board Shipping Port ARDM-4 in the United States Navy. He received an honorable discharge in October 1992. Ronald Ray Hamilton, born June 16, 1974, is a senior at DCHS and he is participating in the FFA program.

Ray and Patty have four grandchildren: Kristin, Brandon, Joshua and Whitney. Ray and Patty reside on the old Leitchfield Road at Whitesville. They are members of St. Mary of the Woods Parish.

HAMILTON, CHARLES AND ANDREA, Charles Ray Hamilton, son of Patrick Abraham Hamilton and Anna Mae Adams Hamilton, was born Sept. 27, 1941 at home in Philpot, KY, Daviess County. He has lived in Daviess County all his life. Andrea Joan Downing Hamilton was born Oct. 13, 1948 in Fort Knox, KY in Hardin County. She is the daughter of Robert Gordon Downing and Doris Mae Robinson Downing. Andrea was raised in Kentucky. They were married on March 17, 1965.

Charles and Andrea are farmers and currently living in Utica, KY. They are members of St. Anthony Parish at Browns Valley, KY. Their children are:

Darrel Ray Hamilton, born Oct. 5, 1965, graduated from Apollo High in 1984. Married May 22, 1992 to Mary Beth Wink Taylor, daughter of Maurice Wink and Shirley Blandford Wink. Mary has one son Alexander Blake Taylor, born Aug. 25, 1989.

Robert Patrick Hamilton, born Sept. 2, 1967, graduated from Apollo High in 1986. Married March 6, 1987 to Barbara Sue Galloway, daughter of Donnie Galloway and Patsh Galloway Shock. They are the parents of twins, Cesley Rochelle Hamilton and Wesley Patrick Hamilton, born Sept. 13, 1988.

Twin: Anna Faye Hamilton, born Jan. 24, 1970, graduated from Apollo High in 1988 and Brescia College in 1992. She is teaching Primary at Utica Elementary School.

Twin: Diana Kaye Hamilton Fulkerson, born Jan. 24, 1970, graduated from Apollo in 1988 and Owensboro Tech in 1991. Opened K's Country Kids Daycare in September of 1991. Married June 13, 1992 to Ken Martin Fulkerson, son of Patrick Fulkerson and the late Edna Krampe Fulkerson.

HAMILTON, DAVID ALLEN, of St. Mary of the Woods Parish in Whitesville, KY married Rose Ellen Payne Oct. 7, 1967. They have six children, Christina Jane, (born Sept. 4, 1968) married Jeff Connor and now have a 4 year old boy, Dustin and 23 month old girl, Chrystal; Mary Denise (born Feb. 15, 1970) married James Garrett Lee and has a little girl, 16 months old, Rosalyn Denise; Davida Rose (born Oct. 29, 1973), a cosmetologist working with her mother; JoAnna (born March 4, 1975) is a senior at Trinity High School; Regina Belle (born Jan. 16, 1979), eighth grader at St. Mary's; Merrill Allen (b. Nov. 1, 1980), a sixth grader at St. Mary's. They live on the family farm on Jack Hinton Road. David is the son of James and Anna Hamilton. Rose is the daughter of Francis and Mabeline Pope.

Christina now lives at Webbertown on Hawesville Route and they attend St. William or St. Lawrence Parish.

Gary and Denise live on the farm next to David and Rose and attend St. Mary's Parish.

David was born on Oct. 22, 1948 and Rose was born on Feb. 7, 1949.

HAMILTON, JAMES CAROLL JR., was born on March 29, 1951 in Daviess County. His parents were Theresa Brown and James Caroll Hamilton Sr. James attended Sts. Joe and Paul and then went to Catholic High. He started working at NSA at 21. He married Linda Sue Knight on Oct. 14, 1972 at Sts. Joe and Paul. Linda was born on Oct. 12, 1955 in Daviess County to Arnold Knight and Ann Whittaker. She went to Foust and then to Senior High. After she had four children, she attended OCC and Henderson Community College to fulfill her goal as a RN. She now works at Daviess County Hospital. Their family now attends Blessed Mother Parish.

James and Linda have four children. April Michelle Hamilton was born on March 31, 1973 in Owensboro. She attended St. Pius X and then Daviess County High School. She is currently working at Wetzels and attends classes at OCC. James Daniel Hamilton was born on Jan. 12, 1975 in Owensboro. He went to St. Pius X and then went to Daviess County High. He is now working at a hardware store and is looking for a good college to go to. Tracy Jean Hamilton was born on April 14, 1979 in Owensboro. She went to Blessed Mother and is now at Owensboro Catholic Middle School. Laura Beth Hamilton was born on April 8, 1985 in Owensboro. She is now going to Blessed Mother.

HAMILTON, ROBERT MARSHALL "BROTHERS" AND SHIRLEY MARIAN, after living out west 27 years, and rearing Lawrence Edward, Robert Michael and Shirley Marie, in Riverside, CA, decided in 1984 to move closer to "home" to do genealogy.

Robert and Shirley Hamilton

Reside in Morgantown, Butler County, attend Holy Trinity, Morgantown, where "Bob" was baptized in 1985 by Fr. Joseph O'Donnell. Father Joe also baptized granddaughter, Alicia in 1991. At age 12, she claims "It took all my life."

Born in Lexington, second of three sons of John Raymond Brothers and Ethel Taylor. After World War II, he moved to Cincinnati with his mother, four brothers, a sister and stepfather James David Hamilton, and assumed the name Hamilton. Met Shirley, the daughter of Theodore Elwood Davis and Angela Clara Phillips, and married in 1951.

Illness took the family west in 1957, where he worked and retired from the California Transportation Department.

He served in the Navy during the Korean conflict, aboard the Flagship, *USS Helena*, with his two "Brothers."

She attended St. Vincent De Paul and Seton High Schools in Cincinnati, OH. Grew up with one brother Leroy, who witnessed the blessing of her marriage at St. Michael in 1956. In California, she worked for Denny's Restaurants for 13 years, and enjoyed singing with Sweet Adelines. Now loves grandparenting Shane, Alicia, Nicole, Adrianne and Curtis.

Bob, a descendant of the first Catholics into Kentucky from Maryland, circa 1780s, researches the paternal ancestors surnamed; Brothers, Mattingly, Riggs, Downs, Newton, Cooper, Mills, Cissell, Wimsatt, Hinton, Gilkey, Pottinger, Clark, Smith, Springer and Quigley. All settled in Nelson, Washington and Marion counties, where some built the first Catholic Church, Holy Cross and others built the first cathedral, St. Joseph at Bardstown.

Parish community includes lectoring, Eucharistic Minister, Liturgy Committee, Parish Council, and occasional helping hand at the church Thrift Store.

HAMILTON-CARROLL, Samuel Richard (Sam) Hamilton Jr. was born July 26, 1898 in Waverly, KY. He died April 18, 1973. He married Mary Kathryn (Katie) Carroll Nov. 10, 1924 at Sacred Heart Catholic Church in St. Vincents, KY. Samuel Jr. was the son of Samuel Richard Hamilton Sr. and Emma Augusta Hite Hamilton. Mary Kathryn was born June 23, 1901 in Henderson County, KY and died Dec. 24, 1968. She was the daughter of Francis Joseph (Frank) and Mary Ann Cunningham Carroll. Sam and Katie had six children, Sarah Rebecca, William Frank, Mary Ann, Samuel Richard III, Emma Jane and Nancy Carroll.

Sarah Rebecca was born Sept. 3, 1925 and married Leslie Jennings Jr. They had five children, Sarah Kathryn, Patricia Alice, David Leslie, Paul Hamilton and Helen Jane.

William Frank was born Aug. 27, 1929. He married and divorced Patricia Joanne Hill. They had two children, Richard Lyman and Mary Patricia. He later married Barbara Galloway.

Mary Ann was born May 18, 1932 and married Cecil Thrasher Jr. They had three children, John Cecil, Mary Anne and Margaret Jane.

Samuel Richard III was born June 19, 1935. He married and divorced Ann Sandefur. They had one son, Stuart Leslie.

Emma Jane was born Sept. 11, 1937. She married and divorced Walter Nussbaun Jr. They had one son Frank Hamilton.

Nancy Carroll was born Oct. 16, 1940 and married Dennis Neel Wrinkles. They had five children, Nancy Caroline, Susan Kathryn, Mary Kathryn, Emily Ann and Alexander Neel.

Sam was a farmer and a horseman in retirement years. He and Katie are buried in St. Louis Cemetery, Henderson, KY.

HAMILTON-HITE, Samuel Richard Hamilton Sr. was born Oct. 3, 1862 in Washington County, KY four miles west of Springfield, KY on Bardstown Road. The house is still there and was built by his father in 1854 and is listed in the *National Historical Homes*. Samuel Richard Sr. was the ninth and youngest child of Thomas Goddard Hamilton and Lelitia Smith. He married Emma August Hite, born in 1861 in Waverly, KY and daughter of George Hite and Elizabeth Spalding. Samuel Richard Sr. was a farmer and lived on a farm three miles from Waverly, KY. Their children were all born there and house and farm is now owned by the William Don Greenwell family.

Children of Samuel Richard Hamilton Sr. and Emma Augusta Hite:

Thomas Alexander Hamilton born 1888. He married Mona Mae Pike. Their children are Eloise Hamilton, Francis Lamar Hamilton, Thomas Edward (Jack) Hamilton and Emma Susan, who died at the age of 2 of meningitis. Thomas Alexander Hamilton died in 1970 and is buried in St. Louis Cemetery in Henderson, KY.

Mary Lucile Hamilton born July 31, 1889. She married Hudson Damian Payne. Their children are Margaret Reginia born Jan. 17, 1915, Anna Cecilia Payne, born Nov. 17, 1916, Hudson Damian Payne Jr., born April 14, 1919, Mary Susan Payne, born Aug. 5, 1922. Mary Lucile Hamilton Payne died March 11, 1972 and is buried in St. Peter Cemetery, Waverly, KY.

George Albert Hamilton born Feb. 28, 1891. He married Ellen Brown. Their daughter is Mary Elizabeth Hamilton. George Albert died Feb. 18, 1920 of influenza. He is buried in St. Louis Cemetery in Henderson, KY.

James William Hamilton born Jan. 2, 1894. He married Minnie Pike. His daughters are Aileen Hamilton (deceased) and Alberta Hamilton b. May 2, 1921, died Dec. 31, 1972, buried in St. Louis Cemetery in Henderson, KY. James William Hamilton died Jan. 18, 1961, buried St. Louis Cemetery.

Susan Helen Hamilton born July 9, 1896. She married Louis H. Rogge. Their son Louis Phillip, born Feb. 12, 1930. He joined Carmelite Order and was ordained July 4, 1954 in Rome, Italy. His first Mass was August 1955 in Louisville, KY. Fr. Louis P. Rogge has been engaged in education in Canada, U.S. and Peru; he taught at Loyola University of Chicago before being called to Rome, Italy where he works for the Carmelite Institute. His mother Susan Helen Hamilton died April 10, 1982 and is buried in Calvary Cemetery in Jordon, MN.

Samuel Richard Hamilton Jr. born July 26, 1898. He married Mary Kathryn Carroll. Born to them were six children. Sarah Rebecca Hamilton, Sept. 3, 1925, William Frank Hamilton Aug. 27, 1929, Mary Ann Hamilton May 18, 1932, Samuel Richard (Buddy) Hamilton III, June 19, 1935, Emma Jane Hamilton, Sept. 11, 1937, Nancy Carroll Hamilton, Oct. 16, 1940. Samuel Richard Hamilton Jr. died April 18, 1973. Buried in St. Louis Cemetery in Henderson, KY.

Alice Cecilia Hamilton born Dec. 20, 1899. She joined the Ursuline order in 1916 at Maple Mount, KY as Sister Mary Samuel. She taught music for 44 years. She was elected member of General Council as Assistant Mother of Maple Mount. She died Aug. 21, 1977 and is buried in Mount St. Joseph Cemetery, Maple Mount, KY.

Gertrude Lelitia Hamilton born 1903. Married Charles Sinnott. They had a daughter Dorothy Louise Sinnett. Gertrude died June 1983 and is buried in Hartford, CT.

Emma Lilly Hamilton born July 5, 1905. She married Joseph Henson Clements and he resides in Louisville, KY. Emma Lil died 1980 and is buried in St. Louis Cemetery in Henderson, KY.

In 1916 Samuel Richard Hamilton Sr. and his wife Emma Augusta and family moved to Henderson, KY and were members of Holy Name Parish. Samuel Richard Sr. died May 10, 1927 and his wife died Sept. 26, 1933 and both are buried in St. Louis Cemetery in Henderson, KY.

HAMILTON-JENNINGS, Sarah Rebecca Hamilton was born Sept. 3, 1925 in Henderson County. Daughter of Samuel Richard Hamilton Jr. and Mary Kathryn (Katie) Carroll. She married Leslie Jennings Jr. of Henderson County Oct. 25, 1944 while Leslie was on leave from U.S. Navy during World War II. Leslie is son of Leslie Jennings Sr. and Vivian Jane Williams. Leslie and Sarah had five children.

Sarah Kathryn born July 30, 1947, and married L. Michael Greenfield. They have two children. Sean Michael born April 26, 1976 and Anne Marie Greenfield born July 15, 1977. They reside in Evansville, IN and are members of St. Teresa Parish.

Patricia Alice Jennings born Aug. 20, 1949 married Ralph Steven Tweddell and they have four children. Richard Steven born Jan. 12, 1974, Patrick Vincent born Sept. 26, 1975, Sarah Elizabeth born June 13, 1977 and Joshua Jennings born Feb. 7, 1981. The Tweddells live in Henderson, KY.

David Leslie Jennings born July 27, 1951 and died July 30, 1951. He is buried in St. Louis Cemetery.

Paul Hamilton Jennings born July 15, 1956. Paul married Kelle J. Gentry, born to them Samuel Jackson Jennings born Jan. 17, 1975. Paul and Kelle divorced. Paul later married Alice Clark Gibson. Alice has a daughter Andrea Keri Gibson born Jan. 14, 1978. Paul and Alice have a daughter Alice Kathryn Jennings born Sept. 14, 1984. They reside in Collierville, TN.

Helen Jane Jennings born Aug. 13, 1958. She married Jeffrey Woodcock and are the parents of Rachel Leslie Woodcock born Oct. 18, 1986. Helen and Jeffrey divorced May 1992. Helen and Rachel reside in San Diego, CA.

HAMILTON, WILLIAM DONALD, was born near St. Lawerence, KY. Sylvia Faye Hester was born in Owensboro, KY. After being married on Jan. 31, 1959 at St. Stephen Cathedral in Owensboro; they moved to Reid Road and St. Pius Parish where they have been members for 33 years.

Through the years they have been active in the parish and Don has been a member of the cooking team for several years. They have four children: Vickie Lynn, Terry Donald, Kimberly and Shelly Marie. Vickie Lynn married William Hagan, they have three children: Zachary Elijah, Isaiah Nathaniel and Madalyn Olivia. Terry Donald married Bonnie Roberts, they have two children: Jesse Aaron and Cassie Nicole. Kimberly Faye married Jeffery Johnson. Shelly Marie is living at home. They all attended St. Pius Elementary School and graduated from Owensboro Catholic High School as did Sylvia.

Don has worked at W.R. Grace for 30 years, and Sylvia worked at G.E. in early years, but retired to raise the family.

The Hamilton family has enjoyed being members of the St. Pius Parish and will continue to for many years to come, as Sylvia and Donald celebrate their 34th Wedding Anniversary in January 1992.

HANCOCK, MONSIGNOR GEORGE H., J.C.L., was born in Waverly, KY, Union County on Feb. 2, 1919. He is the son of George Hiram Hancock and Virginia R. Fenwick, both Catholic, united in a good Catholic marriage. They are both deceased. The family was well-known and respected in the community and county. They owned their own family farm. They were hard working and thrifty people.

Monsignor Hancock attended St. Peter Catholic Grade School and High School in Waverly, KY. After high school he attended St. Meinrad Seminary for the first two years of college. His scholastic grades there were excellent which earned him a three year Basselin scholarship in philosophy at the Catholic University. He received a master's degree in Philosophy. He remained at the Catholic University for the four year course in theology. He has superior intellectual talent which he uses in a humble way for the Church. After his ordination, Bishop Cotton sent him to Rome for two years to earn the Licentiate in Canon Law at the Lateran University.

Monsignor George Hiram Hancock

Bishop Francis R. Cotton ordained Fr. George Hancock in the Cathedral of St. Stephen, Owensboro, KY on May 27, 1947. He was born within the Diocese of Owensboro. He belongs to this diocese and has always lived there except when he was in Rome and in other seminaries preparing for priesthood.

Upon his return from Rome he was appointed administrator of the parish in St. Peter of Stanley, KY and also appointed Ecclesiastical Notary and secretary of the Diocesan Tribunal. He continued his parish work at Stanley and was appointed pastor of this parish and Officialis of the diocese in September 1957. On July 23, 1962 he was appointed pastor of St. Joseph of Leitchfield, KY and dean of the deanery. On Nov. 18, 1963 he was appointed chancellor of the diocese. He also took care of the finances of the diocese. Upon retirement in 1989, he became pastor of St. Henry, Aurora and St. Anthony of Padua, Grand Rivers.

HANCOCK, ROBERT IRVIN JR., the oldest son of Robert Irvin Hancock Sr. and Jane Catherine Payne, was born Sept. 23, 1917. He was raised on a farm and graduated from St. Peter High School in 1935. His parents were long time parishioners of St. Peter Parish, Waverly, KY in Union County.

Irvin Jr. and Mary Frances Clements were married Sept. 16, 1941 in the old Sacred Heart Church, which burned in 1950. The church dates back to the beginning of Catholicity in Union County.

Mary Frances was the daughter of William Patrick Clements and Mary Margaret Proctor, who were farmers and life long members of Sacred Heart Church. She attended school at St. Vincent Academy, founded by the Sisters of Charity, Nazareth, KY, and graduated in June of

1938. They were happy years of learning, and all were saddened by the academy closing in 1967.

Irvin and Mary Frances have lived on the same farm since their marriage, and have raised four sons Robert, William, Joseph and Denis and one daughter, Carolyn. They are very proud of their children, who have all chosen professional careers outside of farming, and are happily married. They are also proud grandparents of 13 grandchildren.

Mr. and Mrs. Irvin Hancock and Family - 50th Wedding Anniversary.

The Hancock and Clements families were pioneer settlers of these Catholic communities.

Irvin and Mary Frances celebrated their 50th Wedding Anniversary at St. Stephen Cathedral in Owensboro, KY September 1991.

HANCOCK, FATHER WALTER, and his two sisters Sister Jane Mariam and Sister Jane Irvin, were born in the country in the little town of Waverly, KY. Their parents were Irvin Hancock and Jane Catherine Payne. They were married at St. Peter Church, Waverly, KY on Oct. 25, 1916. They had 14 children, four of which died a few weeks after birth-Teresa, Frank Cruz, Florence and Paul Joseph. The following 10 are still living-Robert Irvin, Mary Catherine, Walter Anthony, John, Rita, Ann, Martha Jane, Ben Hite, Louise and Gertie.

Walter became a priest on May 27, 1947. He studied at St. Meinrad Seminary, St. Meinrad, IN. His first assignment was an assistant at Brown's Valley, KY. He was also assistant at Hawesville, Lewisport, Patesville and Calhoun, KY. He was pastor of Peonia, Wax and Grayson Springs, KY. At Wax, KY, he built a church, St. Benedict; he built a gym, cafeteria and library at Peonia, KY.

In 1965, Fr. Hancock became the pastor of St. Alphonsus, St. Joseph, KY. There he renovated the Church, the school and the rectory.

Father Walter Hancock

In 1972, he became the pastor of St. Jerome, Fancy Farm, KY. There he put on the Fancy Farm Picnic for 11 years. The first years the picnic grossed $30,000 and in 1983 it grossed $95,000, the 100th anniversary of having picnics at Fancy Farm. During his stay at Fancy Farm some of these men spoke at the picnic-1975 Governor Wallace of Alabama, Representative Jim Wright of Texas, Senator John Sherman Cooper, Governors, John Y. Brown, Wendell Ford, Martha Layne Collins.

In 1983, Father became pastor of St. Sebastian and St. Charles in McLean Company He worked for six years, during which he acquired much property for the two churches there.

In 1989, he was sent to Sacred Heart Church, Russellville, KY. Did much of the work there to renovate the church, Parish Center, the rectory and Day Care Center.

In 1992 he was sent to Cloverport and Irvington.

Sister Jane Mariam is now teaching at the public school in Marion County. She teaches biology to the ninth and 10th graders. She has been there for 20 years and hopes to be there many more years. She is now 68 years old.

Sister Jane Irvin is now in Louisville. She takes care of seven retired priests.

Sister Jane Mariam; Sister Jane Irvin

Sister Jane Mariam will celebrate her 50th year of being an Ursuline Nun, Sister Jane Irvin will celebrate her 45th year of being an Ursuline Nun and Fr. Walter Hancock will celebrate his 45th year of ordination at Russellville, KY on May 24, 1992.

Their parents were married 65 years before they were called forth from this life. At their death they had 33 grandchildren, 55 great-grandchildren and four great-great-grandchildren.

HARDESTY, GERALD AND DOROTHY, Gerald A. was born May 7, 1929 and Dorothy was born April 7, 1933. Gerald is the son of Samuel A. "Fonce" Hardesty and Della Agnes Boarman Hardesty. She is the daughter of Herbert J. Hamilton and Mary W. Long Hamilton. They were married Nov. 15, 1952 at St. Lawrence Church, St. Lawrence, KY and recently celebrated their 40th Wedding Anniversary. They have six children: Brenda Kay Shively born March 23, 1954 in Nashville, TN; Linda Carol Appleby born April 15, 1955, Glen Burnie, MD; Richard Wayne Hardesty born Nov. 4, 1956, Evansville, KY; Randall Lee Hardesty born Feb. 4, 1958, Madisonville, KY; Debra Ann Karr born Sept. 7, 1959, Irmo, SC; and Ronald Gerald Hardesty born Nov. 9, 1965 in Owensboro, KY. They also have 10 grandchildren.

Gerald and Dorothy Hardesty

They currently live in Owensboro, KY, Daviess County and are members of Blessed Mother Parish since 1955. They are past members of St. Paul, Owensboro from 1952-1955. Gerald is former Cub Master of Troop 234; and former member of St. Vincent De Paul and Holy Name Society. Presently a Eucharistic Minister and a McAuley Minister, financial secretary and past Grand Knight of Owensboro Council #817 of the Knights of Columbus.

He served two years in the Army with the 101st Abn. Div. at Camp Breckinridge, KY during the Korean Conflict.

HARGIS, F.B., son of Viola Toone and Fred Hargis, and Anna L. Konsler, daughter of Waco Mattingly and Maurice Konsler both of Henderson County, KY were married Jan. 16, 1943, at Holy Name Church Rectory. It was World War II and he was drafted into the Army. He served in the U.S. Army in Italy, N. Africa and the U.S. Upon discharge from the Army they lived in Louisville, KY briefly before returning to Henderson. He operated a garage and then a home improvement business until his retirement. Ann was a homemaker and mother to six sons: Gene, Fred, Wayne, Tom, Bob and Cliff and two daughters Judy and Kathy. She went to work as a teacher aide in Henderson County Schools in 1970. She is coordinator for Parish Bereavement Dinners and does altar care. They will celebrate their 50th Wedding Anniversary at Holy Name on Jan. 16, 1993.

All of their children and several grandchildren were baptized at Holy Name. Their children and some of their grandchildren attended Holy Name School. Several of the boys served as altar boys. Daughter, Judy Edwards, is secretary at Holy Name School and great-grandson, Brandon Bassett, is a student at Holy Name. Some of the children were married at Holy Name Church. A granddaughter, Michelle Edwards Bassett, was married at Holy Name in July 1992. On Christmas Eve, 1991, this family gathered at Holy Name Church for a family portrait.

Hargis Family: Center-F. B and Ann; Cliff, Luke, Slade, Fred, Shelia A., Sara, Bob, Joe, Gene, Diane, Tiffany, Jennifer, Gena, Jacob, Paul, Leah, Adam, Sherri, Wayne, Christie, Tom, Karen, Kasey and Hillary Hargis; Dick, Judy, David, Elaine, Ryan, John, Angie and John K. Edwards; Kathy, Thad and Caleb Niehaus; Terry and Michelle Green, Brandon Bassett; Marsha, Scott, Kayla and Lindsey Crowder. (Newest members: Zeb Crowder and Alex Edwards).

HARL, ESTELL ANTHONY AND ROSE BERRY, Estell A. Harl's ancestors came from Ireland and settled in Virginia. They later moved to Marion County, KY. From there they came to Daviess County and settled in the St. Raphael area. They had heard that Daviess County had good farm land. Estell's grandfather, Thomas Harl belonged to St. Raphael Parish and was a personal friend of Fr. Paul Joseph Volk. Thomas Harl did some of the wood work on St. Raphael and St. Alphonsus Churches. Thomas Harl married Eliza Blandford on Nov.

Rose Harl and Family-Mary Margaret, Evonne and Mike

15, 1850. They had 10 children: Francis H., Thomas G., Sarah, James B., John W., Ella, Emma, Edward, Charles A. and Paul. One was Estell A. Harl who married Rose Berry, daughter of Hoarce and Eva Coffman Berry, on July 31, 1943. They had three children: Mary Margaret who married Daniel Decker on Feb. 25, 1977, Michael A. Harl who married Mary Ann Miller on Feb. 22, 1972, and Evonne M. Harl. Michael and his wife have five children: Kristena, Chad, Kevin, Matthew and Carrie. The Michael Harl family are members of St. Pius Tenth Church in Owensboro.

Estell died Jan. 21, 1981 and is buried in St. Alphonsus Cemetery. The Estell Harl family have been members of St. Alphonsus Parish for 40 years. One of Rose's fondest memories is Evonne's father carrying her down a gangplank to a truck so she wouldn't get mud on her shoes on her First Communion Day-1964.

HARPER, JIM AND JULIA

were married at St. Thomas More Church in 1962. Julia had already graduated from Murray State University. Shortly after their marriage they moved to Knoxville, TN where Jim graduated from the University of Tennessee. Julia taught school while Jim was finishing college. They have two grown children, Jim and Margaret Anne. Both children graduated from the St. Mary School System. Julia presently teaches kindergarten at St. Mary Elementary. She has also taught at St. John. Jim is a chemical engineer and is employed by B.F. Goodrich Chemical Company. Julia and Jim have been very active in their church lives and have served on various lay committees. Jim's parents are Elan Harper and the late Agnes Harper. Julia's parents are the late Julia and Fagin Whittington.

HARRISON-SPINKS-RAINER.

Lucy B. Cannon Harrison was born Aug. 5, 1987, died December 1971, was married to Professor B.F. Harrison in 1912 in Paducah, KY but attended St. Mary's in La Center. They only had Mass in La Center one day a month usually during the week. Professor Harrison was not Catholic, but their three children were raised in the church. Professor Harrison died in 1946.

The oldest daughter of Professor and Lucy B. Harrison was Nellie Harrison who married Faulkner Rollins of Wickliffe, KY and they moved to El Paso, TX, where he died and now Nellie resides in Ballard County. Nellie was born in 1913.

Ella Mae Harrison married Roy E. Spinks in 1939. Roy died in 1971. They had three children. Ella was born in 1916.

B.F. Harrison II left Ballard County and served in the war and moved to El Paso, TX, where he retired and died in 1989; born in 1922.

Ella Mae and Roy's children were raised in the church, and attended St. Mary's until they left Ballard County to work.

Roy Allen, served in the Vietnam War and returned to live here to help out when his dad broke his neck and was unable to work. He works for Jackson Purchase ECC; born in 1941.

Benjamin W. Spinks, born in 1944, now drives a semi and stays on the road the better part of the week.

Janie Spinks Rainer, born in 1946, resides in Ballard County and attends St. Mary's. She is married to Al Rainer, who is employed at Martin Marietta and also serves in the Army Reserves. They had two children, Roy, who served as an altar boy was born in 1966, while his dad was serving in the Vietnam crises. Roy is now serving in the Air Force and is stationed in Alaska, and has one child himself. Their daughter, Chyanne was born in 1971 and is a medical assistant and resides in Ballard County.

Ella Mae Spinks is one of the oldest members of St. Mary's as her mother was one of the original Cannon families to attend along with Curtis, Goughs and Ballards. When they attended St. Mary's the ladies from Paducah would come down and teach them their lessons. Later when Ella's children were in class, the nuns from Paducah would come down with the parish priest and have Sunday School. They were not even allowed to ride in the front seat with him, and they wore the long habits. They used the old Baltimore Catechism.

Everyone worked together each year at an annual barbeque picnic to raise money to build the new St. Mary's. All the men worked to build the church. Very little outside labor was used, even down to building the altars. The old church had a coal stove for heat, that had to be started before Mass.

We were small but proud, and being from a mostly protestant community, our children were always the outcasts and the brunt of a lot of teasing, especially on Friday, as our schools did not serve fish and we had to bring our lunches.

HATCHER, MATTHEW K.

who graduated from St. Mary in 1992 and Timothy R. Hatcher, who graduated from St. Mary in 1988, were the fourth generation in their family to graduate from St. Mary School. Their father, Kenneth R. Hatcher, was a 1962 graduate. He is married to the former Charlotte Workman and are members of St. Francis De Sales Church. Their grandmother, Dorothy Riley Hatcher, was in the 1935 Class, and great-grandmother, Nellie Yopp Riley, graduated from 1907.

HAYCRAFT, JACK C. AND MARY ANN STORM

were married July 1, 1961 at St. Paul's Catholic Church in Owensboro.

Jack was born and raised in Breckinridge County and was a member of St. Mary of the Woods Catholic Church in McQuady, KY.

Mary Ann was born and raised in Daviess County and was a member of Sts. Joseph and Paul Church. She taught the fourth and sixth grades at Our Lady of Lourdes School for two years. After the birth of her first child, she decided to stay at home and be a full-time mother.

The Haycrafts are the parents of 12 children, seven daughters and five sons. All the children have attended the Catholic schools beginning with Sts. Joseph and Paul School. Then after it closed, they attended the Cathedral School for the next four years. For the next nine years the children were enrolled at Mary Carrico Memorial School in Knottsville, KY. Presently the younger Haycraft children are attending the Catholic Consolidated School System.

During these years the entire family was involved in many ways with the school and church. Many hours were spent remodeling the rectory at Sts. Joe and Paul as well as work done on the school.

When St. Paul Church was burned, the family was found working, getting it back in order so services could be held there again.

Jack and Mary Ann both have been active on the school boards, lectoring, Eucharistic Ministers and serving on the Parish Councils.

When Sts. Joe and Paul school merged with St. Stephen, the summer was spent sanding desks and painting class rooms.

HAYDEN, BERNARD L.

was born Sept. 30, 1945 and Catherine S. Thompson born April 9, 1944 were married May 20, 1967. They have two children, Beverly Suzanne Hayden born Dec. 3, 1969 and John Patrick Hayden born Aug. 6, 1972. Bernard served in the Army from 1970-1977; completed his education through medical school at University of Kentucky. Catherine completed education through college. Beverly is in first year law school at George Washington Law School in Washington,

Bernard L. Hayden Family

D.C. John is a sophomore at St. Joseph College in Rennsselaer, IN. Bernard is now an obstetrician-gynecologist. They have been living in Paducah, KY, McCracken County since 1968. They are members of St. Thomas More Parish.

Cathy serves on Pastoral Council; both are Eucharistic Ministers. Bernard is a member of the McCracken County Medical Society. Cathy is a member of the McCracken County Medical Auxiliary.

Bernard's father is Charles Aloysious Hayden, deceased, member of Immaculate Parish in Owensboro. His mother is Virginia Medley Hayden, member of Immaculate Parish in Owensboro. Al Hayden was a retired fire chief of Owensboro.

Cathy's father is Jerome Hugh Thompson, deceased. Her mother is Mary Ellen Thompson, member of St. Thomas More Parish. Mrs. Thompson and family are owners of the Superior Care Nursing Home in Paducah.

HAYDEN, CHARLES WM.

was born and raised in Daviess County at Southerland, KY. He is the son of Charles R. Hayden and Mary Verna Hayden; Grandson of Charles Wm. Hayden and Malissa Hayden. His father and grandfather were farmers. Charles is married to Virgie Lynes; his first wife, May Leona Thompson, is now deceased. They are members of St. Anthony's Parish in Brownsville, KY.

Charles Wm. Hayden

Their children are: Charles Larry Hayden born June 22, 1944, married to Carol Fenwick; William Michael Hayden born Feb. 9, 1946, married to Sue Fogle; Delores DeVilley born Nov. 2, 1947, married to James K. DeVilley; and Donna Kager born Feb. 22, 1959, married to Michael W. Kager.

Charles and wife, Virgie, now live in Utica, KY.

HAYDEN, DELBERT J. AND MARY ELLEN

and family have been members of Holy Spirit Parish in Bowling Green, KY, since 1972. Kentuckians at birth, most of their lives have been spent in some part of Kentucky with the exception of two years when they enjoyed the warmth and friendship of Florida.

Back Row (L to R): Del, Ellen and John; Front Row (L to R): Beth and Jennifer.

Del grew up outside Owensboro in the farming community of Rome, KY with his parents, James U. and Mary Edna Hayden and nine sisters and brothers. Ellen's roots are in Louisville where her parents J. Sam and Margaret G. Quick reside. She was the fourth of six children.

Western Kentucky University has played a big part in their lives since bringing them to Bowling Green in 1969. Del is a professor of counseling and family studies at WKU. Ellen has taught for many years in child development and family living at the university.

Their two daughters are married and live away from Bowling Green. Jennifer, a middle school teacher, and her husband Drew DeLozier, live near Louisville in Crestwood, KY. Beth, a speech therapist, and her husband, Steve Bowlds, live in St. Louis. Their son, John, will be a freshman in college in the fall of 1992.

They have many fond memories of their years as members of Holy Spirit due to the outstanding priests and many fine people in the parish. Many families come to the parish and eventually move on which brings a certain sadness; however, new people come to fill the void. Ellen and a former parishioner, Mary Wawrukiewicz, were the first lay women allowed to lector at Holy Spirit back in 1973. She has served on the Parish Council. Del and Ellen were trainers for Renew and have been involved in many activities at Holy Spirit as well as with the diocese. For the past two years John has served as guitarist for one of the parish's choirs.

HAYDEN, DONALD EARL was born, Aug. 15, 1931, in Owensboro, KY, baptized in St. Stephen Church. His parents were Joseph Ferdinand Hayden born June 11, 1904 and Mary Borgia Higdon Hayden, born Nov. 4, 1905, both of Daviess County. Donald is the fourth of 10 children. He married Mary Teresa Powers on July 13, 1957. Mary Teresa born Feb. 7, 1931, was the 10th child of 12 children of Joseph Hubert Powers born Dec. 20, 1889 and Teresa Margaret McCarthy, born Nov. 19, 1889, who were married at St. Alphonsus Church on Nov. 19, 1912. Hubert and Margaret Powers farmed in the Curdsville area. Mary Teresa was born on Feb. 7, 1931 in Curdsville, KY and baptized at St. Elizabeth Church, by Fr. James Higdon. She has the following brothers and sisters: Joseph Powers born Aug. 25, 1913 died Oct. 29, 1988, Mary Agnes Powers born Dec. 29, 1915, Patricia Powers Garvin born March 27, 1918, Rev. Aloysius Powers, born Jan. 4, 1921, Robert Powers born Feb. 13, 1926, Elizabeth Powers Lattus, born July 8, 1924, Rev. Bernard Powers born Feb. 13, 1926, Martha Powers Taylor, born Sept. 23, 1927, Celine Powers Kahalley born June 22, 1929, Rev. Richard Powers born Oct. 6, 1932, and Maddalena Powers Leach born March 27, 1934. Don and Teresa Hayden have seven children: Patrick K. Hayden born July 7, 1958 married to Megan Hebert and they have a son, Matthew Ryan born Dec. 23, 1987. They are members of Sacred Heart Church in Russellville, KY. Joseph T. Hayden born April 13, 1960 married to Joan Wagner. They are members of the Immaculate Church, Owensboro, KY. M. Monica Hayden born July 24, 1961 lives in Covington, KY, Paul A. Hayden born April 5, 1963 married Constance Kertz and they have one son Nicholas Andrew born Oct. 8, 1992. Paul and Connie are members of St. Timothy Church, St. Louis, MO, Martin W. Hayden born Dec. 24, 1964, lives in Cincinnati, OH. Teresa A. Hayden born April 16, 1967 and David M. Hayden born July 24, 1969 are members of the Immaculate Church in Owensboro.

Donald Earl Hayden's brothers and sisters are: Elizabeth Ann Wheeler born Dec. 8, 1926, Francis Joseph Hayden born July 25, 1928, Herbert Anthony born April 23, 1930, Richard Otto born Feb. 3, 1935, Mary Rita Wassomer born Nov. 21, 1938, Lawrence Allen born Feb. 25, 1941, Denis Leo born March 19, 1944, Teresa Carolyn Gilles born Feb. 19, 1947, Sharon Rose Payne born Sept. 17, 1948. Donald is a CPA and a partner in the office of Hayden and Company Accounting Firm.

HAYDEN FAMILY, EDWARD FITZGERALD. Edward, born Jan. 28, 1923, married to Zita Mae (Cecil) Hayden, born April 27, 1923, seven children and their spouses, 23 grandchildren and one granddaughter-in-law.

Edward is the son of the late Francis Fitzgerald Hayden and Mary Angela (Payne) Hayden. Zita Mae is the daughter of the late James Norbert Cecil and Mary Lee Ura (McPherson) Cecil. All were natives of Daviess County, KY.

Ed and Zita attended rural school in their early years, and later, St. Francis Academy in Owensboro. They were high school sweethearts and graduated together in 1941. Ed attended St. Bernard College in Cullman, AL, while Zita attended Nazareth College. After college, they both worked in Evansville, IN in defense work during the World War II period. Even though they had lost contact during their college years, they resumed their courtship during their working years. They were married Sept. 23, 1944 at St. Paul Church in Owensboro by Fr. Charles Patrick Bowling.

In the first year of their marriage, they resided in Evansville, where Ed worked at Republic Aircraft and Zita worked at Servel Inc. Ed was tool and die designer (which profession he followed his entire working career). Zita was an IBM printer programmer (a computer programmer in today's language in the tabulating and payroll department).

Edward Fitzgerald Hayden and Zita Mae (Cecil) Hayden

In 1945 they moved back to Owensboro where all seven children were born and baptized at St. Paul Church. Ed continued to commute to work in Evansville (except for a short stint in Owensboro as an engineer during the construction phase of Green River Steel.) In 1956 the family moved to Bowling Green, KY, where he took a position at Holly Carburetor Company as chief tool designer.

With the move, the family became members of St. Joseph Catholic Church (the only Catholic church at the time) where Fr. C.P. Bowling was the pastor. The children attended St. Joseph Grade and High School (until it closed).

Five of the seven children attended Brescia College in Owensboro, due to the influence of their great aunt, Sr. Mary Cecelia Payne OSU, on the teaching staff there. The oldest son, Edward Jr. (Jerry) graduated from there, and gives credit to Brescia for his fine education and successful career in his computer business in Dallas, TX, where he resides with his family.

All the other children and their families live out of Kentucky, except the two youngest. They all have useful and successful careers and are active in community and church work.

When the Holy Spirit Parish was formed, the Haydens became members, due to the location. Ed and Zita have been active in parish work at both St. Joseph and Holy Spirit and were instrumental in the formation of some of these organizations: The Christian Family Movement, Sacred Heart League, The Catholic Women's Organization, the reorganization of the St. Vincent De Paul Society and it's Thrift Store.

Ed was the first SVDP president and Zita was the manager of the SVDP Store. As president, Ed served three terms on the local Holy Spirit, St. Joseph SVDP Conference and two consecutive terms as president of the SVDP Diocesan Central Council. His dad, "Fitz" was dedicated to the work of St. Vincent De Paul and was the first manager of the original store in Owensboro and passed along his zeal and example.

Zita's dedication to works of charity was learned early from the great example set by her parents. Both Ed and Zita are Eucharistic Ministers and have taught CCD.

The Hayden family is grateful to all relatives, priests, nuns, teachers and others who influenced their lives and have been a source of help and inspiration along the way.

HAYDEN, SISTER ETHELREDA was born Sept. 12, 1915 in Graves County, KY to Felix (Feb. 3, 1894-July 10, 1962) and Ethel (Buckman) Hayden (Aug. 6, 1893-March 26, 1985). She had the following brothers and sisters: Mary Catherine (deceased), Frances Virginia Hayden, William Felix, Charles Louis, Frances Eula Hayden Goode and Mary Elizabeth Hayden Willett.

Sister Ethelreda served in the following missions and locations from March 1936 until 1988: Brown's Valley, KY; Lebanon, St. Charles, St. Mary Home, Owensboro; New Haven, KY; Blanco, NM; St. Columba, Louisville; Lebanon, St. Charles; Paul, NB; Hillsboro, MO; Leitchfield, KY; St. Lawrence, Philpot, KY; Sorgho, KY; St. Benedict, Wax, KY; Beuchel, KY; San Fiedel, NM; Clementsville, KY; St. Theresa, Glennonville, MO; Mayfield, KY; Sacred Heart, Poplar Bluff, MO and Mount Saint Joseph. She served as cook and taught grades one through five.

HAYDEN, GEORGE NICHOLAS was the father of Helen Catherine Hayden Seabaugh of Jackson, MO, who was born June 29, 1932 in Perry County near Perryville, MO, one of eight children. Her father George Sr. was born 1896 at Silver Lake, MO and served in the U.S. Army in World War I and was gassed, Oct. 30, 1918, in Toul Sector receiving a medical discharge April 12, 1919. He attended college at Missouri University at Columbia, MO from 1921-24. Later he married (1926) Mary A. Schindler (1902-1984) at St. Mary Seminary at Perryville, MO and was a dairyman, farmer and in 1934 was elected to the office of Perry County Judge. He died 1940. His father was Wm. Ed Hayden (1869-1901) born near Biehle, MO, who married Regina Baudendistel; they have three children. He helped run the Mercantile Store at Silver Lake, MO. His father was George Anslem Hayden (1849-1896) born near Biehle, MO; who married Mary Elizabeth Brewer; they had 14 children. He was at one time a farmer, school teacher, and operated the store at Silver Lake, MO, where he died with TB as did his son Wm. Ed. later on at Perryville.

George Nicholas Hayden Sr. and Mary A. (Schindler) Hayden

His father was Charles Hayden (c 1812-1877) born in Nelson County, KY; married Matilda Mattingly (Faherty) in Perry County, MO. He farmed near Biehle and Brewer, MO. In 1874-76 he served in Missouri House of Representatives at Jefferson City, MO. He fathered 11 children (three marriages). His father was Wm. Hayden who is believed to have been born in St. Mary's County, MD, migrated to Kentucky and married Susan Stewart in Nelson County, KY on May 12, 1798 by Fr. S.T. Badin. They had eight children (records are missing but they could have been attending a smaller church out in the county, but the St. Joseph Parish at Bardstown, KY would have been the mother church) all born in Nelson County. They all moved to Perry County, MO in about 1826. There is a record book at St. Joseph Parish, Apple Creek, MO that is dated 1832-1839 that states the names of the members and they have William Hayden, Charles, William Jr., Joseph, Melvina Jacobaugle, Nelly (slave); later on his wife Susan and son James are listed as being baptized Nov. 22, 1838. The church was started in 1826; it is believed that they were charter members. He died in 1833 and she died in 1841, in Perry County. They believe that William's parents were George and Mary Hayden who lived and died in Maryland, having had five children, William being the oldest.

HAYDEN, GERALD AND MARY ROSE

have lived in Owensboro all their lives. William Gerald Hayden and Mary Rose Clark were married on Feb. 7, 1948 in St. Martin Church, Rome, KY by Rev. William Borntraeger. Mary Rose was organist at St. Martin's at the time.

They have eight children: Carol Marie Hayden Payne, Mary Joan Hayden, William Gerald (Jerry) Hayden, Patricia Rose Hayden Ward, Robert Clark Hayden, George Vincent Hayden, Rebecca Anne Hayden Sowders and John Paul (Jack) Hayden.

Six of their children still reside in the Owensboro Diocese. Patty Ward and her husband Denny and their three children live in Richmond, VA. Becky and her husband John live in Louisville, KY. Gerald and Mary Rose were members of St. Stephen Cathedral for a year and one-half after their marriage, then Sts. Joseph and Paul Parish until St. Pius the Tenth was built in 1957. Gerald owned and operated Hayden's Gulf Service at Fourth and Wing Ave. until he retired in 1987. Gerald's long hours at work left him little time for parish work. He also served early Mass at St. Pius when the appointed server "overslept." Gerald now serves as usher at the 7:00 a.m. Mass at St. Pius.

Mary Rose was the organist at St. Pius until she retired after 23 years. She now plays for funerals at St. Pius. She also served on the first school board and the first Parish Council.

Gerald and Mary Rose are very proud of their children: Carol, an RN; Joan, Hayden Electric Company; Jerry, Texas Gas; Patty, comptroller at James River Coal Company; Bob, I&M Power Plant; George, Kentucky Department of Reclamation: Becky, Paralegal in Louisville; Jack, UPS.

They now have 18 grandchildren and three step-grandchildren.

HAYDEN, HENRY AND ANNA.

William Henry was born Sept. 22, 1886 in Fancy Farm, KY, son of Samuel Willett Hayden and Margaret (Ryan). He married Anna Lucia (Elliott) Jan. 16, 1912, daughter of William Henry Elliott and Elizabeth Eugenia (Skinner). Anna was born April 12, 1892. They were baptized, confirmed, married and lived in St. Jerome Parish, Fancy Farm. He was a farmer, loving nature and the land. She was a music teacher, also the church organist for 13 of her young adult life. They were always interested and involved in parish activities. His philosophy of life was "Be kind and love one another." She was a devotee of the rosary and believed "that if you prayed together, you stayed together." Their house was filled with music, song and laughter.

Henry and Anna were blessed with five children: Mary Catherine, William Bernard, Margaret Mary, Samuel Joseph (married Ella Dean Elliott) and Helen Marie (Sr. William Ann, SCN). Six grandchildren, Kent Elliott, William Keith, Michael Louis, Lisa Ann, Patrick Del and Ellen Kaye; two great-grandchildren Phillip Joseph Thomas and Karson Elliott Hayden.

Henry and Anna celebrated their 50th Wedding Anniversary in 1962. Henry passed away in 1965 and Anna died in 1975.

HAYDEN, HENRY AND BERNADETTE,

when they moved to Ohio County, KY, after Henry finished law school at the University of Kentucky. They were the only Haydens in the county (in stark contrast to Daviess County). Both were originally from Daviess County. Henry was raised in Owensboro and lived in the St. Stephen's Cathedral Parish. Bernadette lived in the Rome community and was a member of St. Martin Parish. They were married on Nov. 26, 1964 at St. Martin in Rome by Monsignor Gilbert Henninger.

Henry's parents were Arthur F. Hayden Sr. and Georgia Roach Hayden of Owensboro, KY. Bernadette is the daughter of Mary Emma Reisz of St. Martin Parish, Rome and Robert S. Reisz of Owensboro.

Henry and Bernadette have four children: Kathy Hayden Young of Batesville, AR is married to Dennis Young and has two children; Deanna Marie Hayden of Nashville, TN, is employed by Arthur Anderson and Company; Henry E. Hayden II and Anne Elizabeth Hayden are still at home. Henry II is a senior and Anne is a freshman at Ohio County High School. The Hayden family has lived in Hartford, KY, since 1972, where Henry has his law practice.

Henry attended Owensboro Catholic High School, Brescia College University of Kentucky Law School. Bernadette graduated from Mount St. Joseph Academy and attended Brescia College.

They have attended the Holy Redeemer Catholic Church in Beaver Dam since they have lived in Ohio County. They have both been active in Parish affairs, having served in many capacities on the Pastoral Council and teaching various CCD classes. Bernadette is the president of the Pastoral Council and Henry is a past president.

HAYDEN, HENRY WALTER JR.

(March 9, 1896-June 19, 1973) and Mayola Mulligan Hayden (July 5, 1897-April 30, 1985), were born, raised, married and reared their 16 children (three died in infancy) on farms near Owensboro.

They were devoted, loyal and active members of St. Paul's Church until the formation of St. Pius X nearer their home. It quickly became their beloved parish-both were buried at St. Pius.

Walter and Mayola cherished and nurtured their Catholic Faith above all else. They often remarked that the three most important things in life were faith, family and pursuit of learning. Their lives reflected these deep-rooted convictions as they sacrificed greatly to foster, enrich and attain all three firm beliefs in their family life.

The highlight of their lives was a visit to the Holy Land made shortly after their 50th Wedding Anniversary, accompanied by their two priest sons and nun daughter. "It was the greatest thrill and blessing to see and walk on the holy soil where Jesus trod" both remarked on their return with eyes filled with emotion.

An insight into their lives may be taken from a letter Mayola wrote to be read after her death. To our children: "Do not grieve for us now that you have laid our bodies to rest in the earth from which we came. But please pray that our souls may go home to the Father in Heaven as we have finished the work we were created to do. We have fulfilled our vocation in life. Our years together have been full and over-flowing with graces and blessings beyond our understanding and deserving.

You, our children, are our riches and treasures. Each child was received with joy and gratitude and a gift from God."

HAYDEN, J. OTTO AND MARY JOE

and family became members of St. Joseph's Parish in Mayfield in 1950. They were married March 12, 1929 at St. Charles Parish in Carlisle County. Before moving to Mayfield, Otto and Mary Joe had been farmers. They gave up their farm life in Carlisle County when their sons grew up and left home.

Otto and Mary Joe had 10 children, with eight living, 34 grandchildren, 36 great-grandchildren and two great-great grandchildren. Their children are: Joseph L. Hayden of Cullman, AL; Simon S. Hayden of Ledbetter, KY; Margie E. Skrit of Drain, OR; William R. Hayden of San

Picture taken October 1987 for Henry and Bernadette's 25th anniversary-Front Row: Kathy holding Joseph, Henry, Bernadette and Deanna-Back Row: Denny, Henry, II and Anne.

William Henry and Anna Lucia (Elliott) Hayden

Henry Walter Hayden Jr. Family-Picture taken June 12, 1949 after Father Lucian's first Mass. Back Row: (left to right) David, Mary Nell, Henry Walter III (Hank), Fr. Lucian, John Paschal, Raymond, Helen (Sr. Marie Michael) and Fr. Michael-Front Row: (left to right) Dennis, Rose Marie, Mrs. Hayden, Paula, Mr. Hayden, Anne and Rachael (three children, Richard, Theresa and Gemma died as infants).

Diego, CA; Ellen F. Haggard of Murray, KY; Judy C. Lonne of Sunland, CA; Mary C. Stokes of Winchester, KY and Debra Ann Pickard of Mayfield, KY.

The J. Otto and Mary Joe Hayden Family

There are not too many jobs in plumbing, carpentry or electrical work that Otto cannot do. For 16 years he worked selling and servicing milking machines and other farm and garden equipment. He was maintenance supervisor for Holiday Inn for nine years, and a furniture salesman for four years prior to retiring.

Otto is a Fourth Degree in the Knights of Columbus serving as a trustee. He has been an active member for 18 years. Mary Joe, like her mother, has always been happy to be in the kitchen cooking a big meal for whoever, and however many friends or family happen to drop by for a visit. She remembers some weekends when it was like Grand Central Station with the children, grandchildren and friends coming and going from the house.

Mary Joe and Otto both enjoy their Tuesday afternoons; she plays cards with some ladies of their parish, while Otto plays pool with his friends.

HAYDEN, FATHER J. PASCHAL was born July 7, 1889 near Owensboro to H. Walter Hayden and Lilly Clarke Hayden. He was educated at old Columbia College, Owensboro, St. Mary College, St. Mary, KY and St. Meinrad, IN. He taught in the public schools of Daviess County for two years and at St. Mary College. He was ordained to the priesthood by the Rt. Rev. Joseph Chartrand, bishop of Indianapolis, at St. Meinrad Abbey on June 10, 1919, and celebrated his first Solemn Mass at St. Paul Church, Owensboro, June 15, 1919.

Father Hayden was the pastor of Church of the Holy Cross, Holy Cross, KY from 1919 to 1935. From 1935 to 1938 he served as pastor of St. Agnes Church, Uniontown. His health failing, he was stationed at Paducah as chaplain at St. Mary Convent from March 1938 until January 1939, when he became seriously ill. Upon his recovery he went to Mount St. Joseph.

A year before his ordination, while yet a student at St. Meinrad Seminary, he called the first organization of the Catholic Students Mission Crusade in 1918, a missionary society of young Catholics, after previous attempts to organize the society had failed.

Fr. Hayden was a pioneer in the rural cooperative movement. In this movement he received national recognition by being called as one of the speakers in the first National Rural Life Congress. He was also a pioneer in motor school busses, transporting the pupils to the school in a motor school bus. During his years at Holy Cross he built and maintained a community library and gymnasium. He was active in all civic and community affairs wherever he resided.

Fr. Hayden died in the rectory of Holy Name Church, Henderson, KY on Jan. 5, 1941.

HAYDEN, JOSEPH F. went to Cincinnati, OH to get a job. He got one at Formica Insulation Company. It was there that he met Gertrude. They just barely spoke to one another for awhile when they started going out with others from their work and then finally started dating. They were married at St. Augustine Church on Jan. 30, 1943.

They have nine living children, one son who is deceased, and 11 grandchildren. Gert is a convert having joined the church in North Bend, OH after the birth of their fourth child, George.

They moved back to Fancy Farm in 1956 where they had six more children, Timothy Roger who died at 10 days is buried in St. Jerome Cemetery.

Their children are: Joseph F. and wife Carolyn of Dyersburg, TN; Beverly and Jerry Dunn and daughter, Angela Logan, of Memphis; Robert Logan III in the U.S. Navy at Chicago; Sharon Marie who lives at home; George and Emma Hayden (who is also a convert) and two sons Timothy and Matthew of Mayfield; Ramona and David Petty, daughter Joy and son-in-law Steve Skaggs and children, Micky West, Missy and husband Gary Babb; Jacquelyn and Robert Langham all of Mayfield; Michelle, Donald and children, Wendy and Bradley Morgan; Victoria Theresa Wilson and children, Brandi Nocole and Jason Scott, all of Dyersburg, TN.

Standing L-R: Beverly Logan, Jackie Langham, George Hayden, Valerie Skaggs, Joseph Hayden Jr., Ramona Petty, Michelle Morgan. Sitting on couch L-R: Victoria Hayden (now Wilson), Joseph Hayden Sr., Gertrude (Kolb) Hayden and Sharon M. Hayden. Taken Jan. 30, 1983 on 40th Wedding Anniversary.

Joseph is a member of the Knights of Columbus at Fancy Farm, Monsignor Russell Council No. 1418; his wife belongs to the Fancy Farm Sr. Homemakers and sings in the church choir. She was one of the first Eucharistic Ministers at Fancy Farm. They belong to Square Dance Clubs, one at Paducah and one in Murray. They go to several of the rest homes around Paducah, Murray, Clinton, Kevil, Calvert City and Mayfield.

HAYDEN, SISTER JOSEPH MARK, was born May 13, 1909 in Fancy Farm, KY to J.J. Hayden (May 11, 1879-June 9, 1927) and Allie B. Courtney (April 25, 1881-May 17, 1920), both born in Fancy Farm. Her brothers and sisters were: Augusta Marie Hayden, Joseph Clayton, William Albert, Letha Virginia Carrico. She received her Habit, March 19, 1927, and took vows March 19, 1929 and March 19, 1932.

Her missions included: Curdsville, KY-Rome, KY; Cloverport, KY; Knottsville, KY; Hardinsburg, KY; St. Alphonsus, St. Joseph, KY; St. Columba, Louisville; St. Joseph, Owensboro; New Haven, KY; Shively, KY; St. Lawrence, KY; Earlington, KY; Stanley, KY; Mayfield, KY; Stanley, KY; Bardwell, KY; Cloverport, KY; Holy Cross, KY; Calhoun, KY; Paducah, KY, Rosary; St. Paul, Louisville, KY; St. Francis, KY; St. Columba, Louisville; Buechel, KY; Jeffersontown, KY; St. Ignatius, Louisville; Trinity High, Whitesville, KY; Clementsville, KY; St. Columba, Louisville; Central City, KY; Mount St. Joseph; St. Joseph, San Fidel, NM; St. Boniface Retirement Center; Motherhouse, November 1979, after brain tumor surgery;

HAYDEN, LARRY COLLINS was born and raised in Daviess County, KY. He married Rita Carol Merimee, daughter of William Alton Merimee, Aug. 10, 1907, farmer, and Mary Ethelreda O'Bryan Merimee, Nov. 4, 1916, homemaker. Her paternal grandparents are William Hagan Merimee, farmer, and Myzella Coomes Merimee. Her maternal grandparents are Benedict O'Bryan, Nov. 15, 1875, and Rasumond Vowels, Feb. 17, 1877. They are members of St. Mary of the Woods Parish. Rita is a Prep Class teacher. Their children include: Tracy Lynn born March 4, 1973, married with two children, Codi and Blake Shocklee; Jennifer Ann born Nov. 21, 1973, a college student; Brian Joseph born Feb. 11, 1976 and died Feb. 25, 1991 of leukemia; Bradley Collins born Sept. 22, 1982 a fifth grade student at St. Mary's. Served in many locations in Kentucky from 1928-1986, teaching grades four through eight.

HAYDEN, FATHER LUCIAN PAUL, was born Jan. 7, 1924 and baptized at birth by his father on the feast St. Lucian, so his parents named him "Lucian" and "Paul" after the pastor of their parish church. He was the third child of 16 born to Henry Walter Hayden Jr. and Mayola Mulligan Hayden. The other children are: John Paschal, Henry Walter III, Fr. Michael, Richard (died in infancy), Mary Nell, Theresa (died in infancy), Raymond, Helen (Sr. Marie Michael), David, Anne, Rose Marie, Rachael, Gemma (died in infancy), Dennis and Paula (who with her husband and infant were killed in a car accident at age 29 on Thanksgiving Day).

Lucian was taught by the Sisters of Charity at St. Francis Academy in Owensboro from grades one through 10, and received his seminary education under The Fathers of St. Sulpice at St. Charles College and St. Mary's Seminary in Baltimore, MD. During World War II seminaries went the year-round to school, so 10 scholastic years were completed in nine years.

Father Hayden was ordained by Bishop Francis Cotton at St. Stephen Cathedral on June 7, 1949. His first assignment was for nine years as an assistant at the Cathedral with one year at the Catholic University for Canon Law. He worked part-time for the next 12 years with the diocesan tribunal. He served as pastor: 1958-1966 St. Joseph, Central City with St. Charles, Livermore (Mission); 1966-1973 St. William's, Knottsville with St. Lawrence (Mission) The Knottsville Rest Home now Bishop Soenneker Home was established during this time. His father died in 1973; 1973-1982 St. Joseph's Bowling Green (Fr. C.P. Bowling, who had sent Father to the seminary, had been pastor in Bowling Green for 25 years. After retirement he often returned to visit and serve the people he dearly loved. He died on Feb. 11, 1980 on the Feast of Our Lady of Lourdes whose song "Immaculate Mary" he loved to sing); 1982-1989 St. Thomas More Church, Paducah (His mother died April 29, 1985 at Lourdes Hospital there); 1989-1992 St. Jerome, Fancy Farm; 1992-Sacred Heart Church, Russellville.

Father Lucian Hayden and fellow classmates met with Pope John Paul II in April 1990.

Father Hayden's brother, Father Michael Hayden, was ordained a Trappist Priest in 1954. After a number of years he was advised because of ill health due to certain allergies to move and work wherever it was best for him at the time. Fr. Michael therefore spent some of that time helping his brother Lucian in several parishes.

In the seminary Fr. Hayden did street preaching with the Catholic Evidence Guild. At Central City he had a daily radio talk program. Beginning at Central City, Father also found writing letters to the editor of the local papers a further providential opportunity to extend pastoral ministry to the public. His favorite lay organizations: The Legion of Mary and the St. Vincent De Paul Society. His most admired non-denominational group is AA (Alcoholics Anonymous).

If he had a motto, it would be, "The salvation of souls is the Supreme Law" or Mary's advice, "Do whatever Jesus tells you." (His own mother used to say to him, "You know what you have to do."); or St. Paul's question "Lord, what would you have me to do?"

HAYDEN, PAULINE

was born and raised in Daviess County, KY. She has been a member of St. Anthony Parish, Brown's Valley, since birth and baptism. She was the oldest daughter of Paul and Anna Wethington, also members of St. Anthony's Parish.

Pauline Hayden

After high school, Pauline married Charles S. Hayden Jr. a farmer, also a member of the parish. Together they raised 13 children. While Charles farmed, attended community meetings or conducted community meeting, Pauline nurtured the family through household chores, guiding whenever or whatever needed. Each one of Pauline's children can recall the huge breakfasts she prepared including pans of 60 biscuits.

Pauline is pleased with her children's career choices. Two sons followed their dad's farming career, while the others have high tech and diversified professional careers.

Pauline has 31 grandchildren and 17 great-grandchildren.

Over the years Pauline has devoted many hours to church work including the music ministry. She is and has been the church's organist for 37 years. She attends daily Mass.

HAYDEN, P.J. AND SARAH KEISER

were both born in Owensboro, KY. They were married at Sts. Joseph and Paul Parish in Owensboro in November 1966. P.J is the principal of St. Angela Merici School in Owensboro, and Sarah is self-employed in her home. She is a senior sales director for Mary Kay Cosmetics. P.J.'s parents are Charles Simeon Hayden Jr., now deceased. Sarah's parents are Mary Katheryn and Matthew Keiser, now also deceased. Mary Katheryn remarried Leo Fulkerson and they live in Owensboro. P.J. and Sarah belong to Immaculate Parish and they are Eucharistic Ministers and ushers.

P.J. and Sarah's children are: P.J. Jr. (25), Natalie (22) and Lauren (13). P.J. Jr. graduated from Owensboro Catholic High School and presently farms. He married Carol Duhart of Owensboro. They have one child, Nicholas Andrew (5), but are now divorced and Carol and Nicholas live in Bowling Green, KY where Carol attends Western Kentucky University. Natalie is a graduate of Owensboro Catholic High School and the University of Kentucky. She majored in advertising and communications and now has a job as the leasing consultant for the Aloisters, an apartment complex in Lexington, KY, where she lives. Lauren attends Owensboro Catholic Middle School where she is a cheerleader and is a member of the Immaculate Youth Group.

HAYDEN, PHILLIP BRENNAN SR.,

was born March 29, 1934 in Owensboro, KY, the sixth of nine children of Francis Fitzgerald and Mary Angela (Payne) Hayden. He was baptized at St. Paul Church, attended Blessed Mother Grade School, St. Mary High School and was graduated from St. Mary, Kentucky; college with a BA in philosophy in 1956. He studied Law at Creighton University, Omaha, NE and received his JD degree from the University of San Francisco in 1962.

He was married to Sara Nell (Schultzman) Hayden in 1960 at St. Thomas More in Paducah, KY. Sara Nell was born Dec. 14, 1940, the third of seven children born to Herbert Schultzman and Fredrica (Puryear) Schultzman, in Paducah, KY, and was baptized at St. Francis De Sales Church. She attended St Francis De Sales Grade School, Nazareth High School in Bardstown, KY, Brescia College in Owensboro, KY and the San Francisco College for Women; she received a BA degree in French from Brescia College.

Phil and Sara Nell have four children: Lynnelle (1962-1983); Dr. Francis Fitzgerald Hayden, M.D., graduated from Brescia College and the University of Kentucky College of Medicine and is practicing medicine in New York City; Philip Brennan Hayden Jr. graduated from the University of Louisville Speed School of Computer Engineering and is living and working in the D.C. area with his wife, Terri Davis Hayden; Jason Edward Hayden was graduated from Brescia College with a degree in graphic design and is living in Owensboro; he is director of Design and Communications at the Owensboro Museum of Fine Art.

Phil has practices law in Owensboro, KY, since 1962. In addition, he has served as trial judge, Daviess County Attorney, juvenile judge, and helped form the Owensboro-Metropolitan Planning Commission (OMPC). Both Phil and Sara Nell were active in the Christian Family Movement (CFM) and Renew; Phil is an original member of the Owensboro Diocese Pastoral Council. He is the author of the book *Law Guide for Teens and Parents*. As a representative of the Daviess County Bar Association he has conducted seminars for the last several years entitled "Law Day for Senior Citizens." At present he is practicing law at his office located in Owensboro, KY.

HAYDEN, WALTER AND MAYOLA,

This picture shows a 29 year old mother holding a sick baby. Many sleepless nights she spent caring for little Richard. Several nights later, on July 17, 1927, little Richard died. From then onward, each night at prayers the family said: "Little Richard help us to be good so that we come to Heaven with you." By 1937, Walter and Mayola Hayden were blessed with a family of 12 children, 10 on earth, two in Heaven. In following years, God blessed them with four more children, two of whom God took home to Heaven. A family history hinges on words recorded in the Bible in chapter nine of the Book of Wisdom: "Things of earth, scarcely do we guess; but things of Heaven, who can search them out? Thy purpose none may know, unless thou dost grant thy gift of wisdom. And thus were the paths of those on earth made straight by wisdom."

Living on a farm near Owensboro, KY, Walter and

Mayola Hayden prayed each night for wisdom, that they might have "a love for what is right and just." And thus they were given an appreciation for the gift of the Messiah. Each of their 16 children received the Messiah's gift of baptism. The Messiah's mother, the Virgin Mary, gave them a gift, the Rosary. They made good use of this gift. The Rosary helped them to go over in their minds each night the life of heroic love lived by Jesus, the Messiah. His life inspired them to live a life of love, a life of heroic love.

Over the years Walter and Mayola Hayden continued to pray each night for Wisdom, knowing all good things come in the company of Wisdom. And among these many, many good things, they placed great confidence in a promise made by Jesus to Saint Margaret Mary, in which Jesus assures us that his Divine Heart will be a safe refuge at the hour of death for all who would go to Holy Mass and receive the Holy Eucharist on the First Friday in nine consecutive months. Walter and Mayola lovingly fulfilled this request of Jesus many times. And, in turn, Jesus lovingly fulfilled his promise, seeing to it that Walter and Mayola did not die without receiving the sacraments. Each died a holy death. Engraved on their tombstones are the words reflecting the unwavering purpose of their life on earth, "Our constant prayer; Heaven for all our children."

HAYDEN, WILLIAM AND ELIZABETH (MATTINGLY).

Thomas Hayden was born c. 1780 in St. Mary's County, MD. Thomas married Elizabeth "Polly" Willett on Jan. 18, 1802 in Washington County, KY. Polly was the aunt of Samuel Willett, the first Catholic settler in Graves County.

Thomas and "Polly" had 13 children: Samuel, WILLIAM, James, George, John Joseph, Ann (Yaeger), Elizabeth (Pierceall), Thomas, Henry, Wilford, Philip, Mary (Ryan) and Bennett. "Polly" was buried at St. Rose, Springfield on Oct. 6, 1831.

Thomas, with most of his children, some of whom were married with families, migrated from Washington County to Hickman and Graves Counties around 1833.

William Hayden married Elizabeth Mattingly of Washington County on Oct. 13, 1827. Elizabeth Ann (1842-1913) was the eighth of their 10 children, and she married James Wilson in 1860 (see James Wilson biography). Emma Elizabeth Wilson was the second of their eight children. Emma (1864-1951) was married three times, all at St. Jerome. In 1884, she married Alexander Francis, son of Henry Jefferson and Susan (Willett) Carrico. They had four children: Ora Beatrice (1884-1905) married James M. Cash; Samuel Frederick (1886-1971) married Rosamond Shaffer; Mertie May (1888-1967) married Lawrence Elliott; and Joseph Leonard (1890-1949) married Lettie May Ledford.

L to R: Eugene E. Willett, James Alton Willett, Teresa (Toon) Willett, Delbert Leo Willett; taken Christmas 1942.

In 1895, Emma married second Thomas Jefferson (1846-1908), son of Jack and Florida Anne (Carrico) Willett. They had five children: Charles Ralph (born/died 1898); Mary Mabel (1900-1902); Anna Rubel, Sister Anna, SCN (1902-1969); James Alton (1904-1970) married Teresa Toon (see Athanasius Toon biography); and Thomas Claude (1908-1992) married Etol Melton.

In 1913, Emma married third James Buchanan "Buck" French (1849-1935). Emma died Nov. 16, 1951 in St. Louis, MO. She was buried in St. Jerome Cemetery.

James Alton and Teresa have two sons: Delbert Leo (born Aug. 11, 1925) and Eugene Emmanuel (born July 31, 1927) (see Jack Willett biography).

James Alton died April 3, 1970 in Belleville, IL, and was buried in Mount Carmel Cemetery, Belleville. Teresa died Dec. 13, 1993, and was buried with James Alton in Mount Carmel Cemetery.

HAYES, JAMES BERNARD (BERNIE),

was born in Scottsburg, IN Feb. 5, 1957 to Thomas M. and Patricia Kern Hayes (now of Cloverport), the third of 11 children.

Pamela Jean (Pam) Heuser was born in Louisville on Oct. 24, 1956, to George W. and Shirley Seefeldt Heuser (now of New Albany, IN), the fifth of seven children.

Bernie and Pam were married at St. Mary of the Knobs Catholic Church in Floyd Knobs, IN on Sept. 17, 1976. Pam worked as a nurse until July 1977, when Bernie graduated from United Electronics Institute in Louisville and took a job with Inland Steel Company, East Chicago, IN. They lived in Chesterton for the next four years. Pam became interested in social work and began pursuing education in this area at Valparaiso University.

In April 1981 they returned to Southern Indiana, when Bernie took a job with a chemical company in Louisville.

Their first son, Aaron Ray was stillborn on March 26, 1982 in Lousville. He is buried in St. Mary of the Knobs Cemetery.

Their second son, Adam Bernard, was born on March 24, 1983 in Louisville.

In September 1983, Bernie began work at Big Rivers Electric's D.B. Wilson Plant in Ohio County, KY.

In December of 1987, Bernie, Pam and Adam added four children to their family through adoption. These children are: Tonya Kimberly (Kim), born Jan. 16, 1977; Terrill James (T.J.), born June 22, 1978; Daniel George, born Feb. 3, 1982; and Kevin Thomas born Jan. 4, 1983. All five children continue to be a joy and a challenge.

Today, Bernie is in computer maintenance at Big Rivers. He is involved with the Boy Scouts Troop 173 of Ohio County and is a novice actor with the Courthouse Players Theatre Group in Hartford.

Pam is nearing her bachelor's degree in social work, is on the Board of Directors of the newly formed Adoptive Parent Association of Kentucky, and teaches prospective adoptive and foster parents.

HAYES, MARY ELLEN

is one of the oldest members in St. John the Evangelist Parish in Edmondson County. She has always lived in Sunfish, also her parents. She and her husband, Ebbon, were married at St. Joseph, Leitchfield by Rev. Louis Beruatto who baptized nine of their 12 children. Fr. Clement Borchers, a Glenmary priest, the first resident pastor at Sunfish, baptized the youngest child.

Ebbon died 16 years ago. He was a farmer as most of the men were then. Mary Ellen was a homemaker raising their family, four of whom have died. She is very proud of her 43 grandchildren, 47 great-grandchildren and five great-great-grandchildren.

Back Row: Johnnie, Dorothy, Junior, Otis, Louis, Betty, Wash and Linda; Front Row: Mary Ellen and Susie Hayes.

Mary Ellen had no modern conveniences. She tells of taking the laundry to the creek, heating the water and hanging the clothes on the bushes. In spite of this hard work and large family, she found time to help her neighbors. Following the Lord's command, "Love your neighbor," was practiced in many ways and made life enjoyable and pleasant along all the hardships and difficulties. Five of their children were born without the assistance of a doctor. She remembers, later, giving the doctor $5 to assist in the birth of one child.

Mary Ellen had one older sister and was the fourth child between four brothers which caused her to be a real "tomboy." She tells of some of their childhood recreations such as riding calves and catching frogs, at least a 100, and putting them in their neighbor's wagon.

During the time the Sisters of St. Francis from Wisconsin taught at St. John School, Mary Ellen operated the school cafeteria alone for eight years. The students thought she was the best school cook ever. Now at age 92, she makes beautiful quilts and has a garden.

HAYES, THOMAS M. AND PATRICIA C.

Thomas Melvin Hayes was born in Indianapolis, IN, Sept. 6, 1929. After about two months, his parents, Millard and Ruth Hayes, moved back to Sunfish, Edmondson County, KY. They lived with his grandfather, Pius Hayes. He died at Sunfish, St. John the Evangelist Parish in August 1936. After grade school, he attended St. Meinrad Minor Seminary, St. Meinrad, IN. In 1948, his parents moved the whole family, 11 children at the time, to Henryville, IN. He left the seminary in the spring of 1948. Then he started working for the New Washington State Bank, Henryville Branch, Henryville, IN. In March, 1951, he was inducted into the U.S. Army for two years.

After his release from the Army, he married Patricia Kern, at St. Ferdinand Church, Ferdinand, IN. He continued working for New Washington State Bank, until June 1976. At that time, they moved, with seven of the 10 children, to Cloverport, KY, becoming members of St. Rose of Lima Parish, Cloverport. He took a job with the Breckinridge Bank of Cloverport, soon becoming Vice-President. Martin, the oldest of the seven, who came with them, started college that fall, at St. Thomas Seminary in Minnesota, studying for the priesthood. Hilary, David, Mary and Emily graduated from St. Romuald High School, Hardinsburg, KY. Then, June 2, 1984, Martin was ordained a priest by Bishop John McRaith. Margaret and Stanley have since graduated from St. Romuald High School, and are now attending Bellarmine College. Since being ordained, Fr. Martin is now serving as pastor of three parishes: at Fulton, Hickman and Clinton in extreme Western Kentucky. Their third child, Bernie, has since moved with his wife Pam and son Adam, to Beaver Dam, KY, becoming members of Holy Redeemer Parish. At the present time, Bernie, Fr. Martin and David are members of the Owensboro Diocese. Margaret and Stanley are students at Bellarmine College.

HAYNES, MARY RUTH MONTGOMERY

was born on Dec. 8, 1903. She is the daughter of Benjamin D. and Emma Lillian Higdon Montgomery. Baptized at St. Paul Church, she attended Mass there and received the other sacraments including the Sacrament of Matrimony to her husband Newman Ignatius Haynes. After the wedding the couple moved to the St. William Parish and have remained there. Newman S. Haynes was born Sept. 28, 1904 to William E. and Soma Ann Roby Haynes of Knottsville. He was baptized at St. William and attended local schools in the area and later St. Joseph College in Bardstown. Newman and Mary Ruth have nine children, Agnes (deceased), James, Paul, Bernard, Helen, Regina, Edward, Robert and Francis.

Through the years the couple has remained dedicated to the church, participating in its functions, and ready to greet with a smile and a helping hand.

Newman passed away Dec. 17, 1986. Mary Ruth still lives at their home on Roby Road and still attends Mass at St. William. Though she doesn't get around as good as she used to, her stories of Newman and her, have and always will inspire the lives of their children, grandchildren and great-grandchildren.

HAZEL, LILLIAN FRANCES

(Sr. Francesca Hazel, O.S.U.) was born on July 28, 1903 in Owensboro. Her parents were Francis Hazel and Laura Clark Hazel, she had one sister, Pauline, and one brother, Charles. After her mother's early death, the children were sent to live with an aunt in Oklahoma. Lillian came to Mount St. Joseph Academy for school and after graduating entered the novitiate there to become an Ursuline Sister. She received the name, Sister Francesca, in 1926 and made vows in 1931. Early study and training directed her into the field of music and from then on music was an important part of her life. She earned a bachelor degree at Webster College in St. Louis and a masters degree from DePaul University in Chicago. She taught music at various levels in schools in Missouri, Nebraska and Kentucky leading many to a love of music both for church services and for their personal lives.

After nearly 30 years of music education, Sister Francesca was led into another field of concentration. Her work with young girls and women, her research and contacts with other professionals, opened another need and she developed a class in Christian Femininity with the encouragement and financial assistance of a medical doctor and psychiatrist, Dr. Philip Law. This class was built upon the principal motivation and inspiration of St. Angela Merici, the Ursuline foundress—to restore vitality to the Christian family through educating young women. It was Sister Francesca's desire to help women to develop a better image of their own identity and importance as women. The first class was offered at Mount St. Joseph Academy and then taken to Brescia College as a pilot course. Then it received full status as a course under the title The Contemporary Woman and became a 3-hour credit offering in Humanities, Theology and/or Sociology. With continual updating for the needs of this age, it still proves to be a source of spiritual enrichment and growth for both women and men.

Sister Francesca died on March 22, 1987 after a brief bout of acute pancreatitis.

HAZZARD, MARY E.,

was born March 2, 1941 in Evansville, IN to Lucille Theobald Hazzard and John Waven Hazzard of St. Paul Parish in Princeton, KY. Early memories include the summer religious education classes brought to Princeton from Earlington, the establishment of the Catholic School when she was in the second grade, and the summer parish and school picnics. Dad and a couple of other men built the swing set which was moved when the location of the school changed and still stands. Many people still remember the picnics held on their farm about two and one-half miles from town when Sister Carmencita would drive the jeep and wagon for the kids to drive. All enjoyed the food and fun.

Tracing the family history in the diocese, Lucille's parents were Henry Theobald and Carrie Courcier Theobald and their parents were John Theobald born in Ingbert, Germany and Mary Wurth born in McCracken County and Theodore Courcier and Lucy A. Morgan married at Hawesville, KY Jan. 29, 1867. The Theobald and Courcier families were members of St. Francis DeSales Parish in Paducah, KY and are buried in Mount Carmel Cemetery.

John Hazzard entered the Catholic Church receiving the Eucharist on Holy Thursday 1962 at St. Paul, Princeton. Mary was at the time attending Nazareth College in Louisville, KY working on the baccalaureate degree in nursing which was received in 1963. Mary attended New York University receiving her masters and Phd in nursing.

Mary and her daughter Mary Lucille moved to Bowling Green in 1979 when she became head of the Department of Nursing at Western Kentucky University. They are members of Holy Spirit and she has served on the St. Joseph School Board, Holy Spirit Parish Council, as Eucharistic Minister, lector, and RCIA catechist. Mary has been active with TEC and Cursillo.

HEAD, JOSEPH VIRGIL, son of Richard Emmett Head and Ada Matilda Payne and Mary Jacqueline Hagan, daughter of Ollie James Hagan and Catherine Lee Durvall, were married Jan. 19, 1957 at St. Mary of the Woods Church, Whitesville, KY.

Mr. Head is a farmer and also employed by Green River Steel Company, Owensboro. Mrs. Head is a homemaker and a teacher's assistant at Cathedral Pre-School, Owensboro. They are the parents of four sons and three daughters. The sons are: Robert Alan Head, Richard Joseph Head, Randal Virgil Head and Patrick Gerard Head. The daughters are: Lisa Faye Graham, Gina Gayle Sloon and Barbara Elaine Head.

Virgil, Jackie and Elaine live in Whitesville, KY. They are members of St. Mary Parish.

HEAVRIN, BENJAMIN, the son of William and Ann Heaverin, was born in Delaware in 1760. He had two brothers, William and Charles, who remained in Delaware, two brothers, Thomas and James, who moved to Eastern Kentucky and another brother, Robert who moved to Shelby and then Washington County, KY with Benjamin. All of the early Heavrins were farmers.

Robert Heavrin then moved to the Flint Island Community in Meade County, which was served by Fr. Elisha Durbin on his monthly circuit. Robert and wife Ann Kerrick are buried there at St. Theresa Church. They had many descendants, many of whom live in the Louisville area.

Benjamin Heavrin lived on a farm on Hardin Creek in Washington County. He and wife Ann attended St. Charles Church. They had three sons and four daughters. Benjamin's daughters Ann and Sally were two of the first six members of the Sisters of Loretto, founded by Fr. Charles Nerinckx in 1812 at St. Charles. Benjamin's son James, married Melissa Nation. They and their descendants lived mostly in the Shelby and Anderson County area. Benjamin's son, William, married Henrietta Riggs. In 1824, they moved to Union County, where they bought a 137 acre farm on Cypress Creek and raised three sons and four daughters. They attended Sacred Heart Church at St. Vincent, which was the headquarters of Fr. Elisha Durbin. Henrietta is buried there. William is buried near his farm at St. Ambrose Church, which was founded by Fr. Durbin in 1829.

William's youngest son, George, married Catherine Miller. They bought a farm in Grayson County. Their descendants had their name changed to Heaverin and many of them also live in the Louisville area. William's son, Joseph M., married Susan Norris. Most of their early descendants continued to farm in Union County. Their son, Samuel Rowan, married Jeanetta Oberhausen. They had 10 children, 41 grandchildren and 117 great-grandchildren.

HEEP, MARIETTA PIKE BLAKE, life-long member of St. Agnes Church, Uniontown, KY, daughter of Ignatuis Hite Pike and Elizabeth Burch Fenwick. She was born Jan. 21, 1911, baptized Jan. 23, 1911 at St. Agnes Church. First Communion June 5, 1917 at St. Agnes; confirmed June 29, 1917. Graduated from St. Agnes Grade School 1924 and St. Agnes High School in 1929. Married Richard Lengard Blake at St. Agnes April 23, 1934. They had one son Joseph Thomas Blake born April 7, 1935. Richard passed away in 1976. They were married 41 years.

Marietta Pike Blake-Heep

In December 1980 Marietta married James Franklin Heep, a convert. He died of a heart attack Oct. 6, 1991. Marietta is a retired teacher. The Pike family are members of the St. Agnes Church at Uniontown, KY since 1893, four generations.

HENNINGER, MONSIGNOR JOHN GILBERT, was born Dec. 18, 1907 in Stanley, KY to John Henry Henninger and Bertha Alvaria Miller. Baptized privately Dec. 18, 1907 at St. Peter Church in Stanley; First Communion June 15, 1916 at St. Peter; Confirmation Oct. 8, 1916; Priesthood May 22, 1937 in Louisville, KY. He attended grade school at St. Peter; high school at St. Meinrad, Meinrad, IN; junior college at St. Meinrad.

Msgr. John Gilbert Henninger

From September 1931 to June 1937, he studied Philosophy and Theology at St. Meinrad. He did his postgraduate work at Ottawa, Canada.

During his ministry, his residential appointments include work at the following: St. Peter, St. Rose, St. Benedict, St. Francis de Sales, St. Paul, St. Joseph, St. Francis, Ursuline Sisters, St. Anthony and St. Joseph.

His non-residential appointments include service: with the Chancery Office, March 19, 1938; as Vice-Chancellor, Feb. 9, 1939; as Chancellor, Sept. 20, 1939; as Concilium Administrations, March 18, 1941; as Notary for the First Synod, July 1, 1941; as Vicar General, Aug. 13, 1943; as Defensor Vinculi, July 16, 1946 and as director of Catholic Cemetery, Owensboro, KY.

Msgr. John Gilbert Henninger passed away on March 5, 1990. He is buried at Resurrection Cemetery.

HERIGES, ANNA MARIE BUCKMAN, married Anthony Earl Heriges at St. Ann Catholic Church on Aug. 14, 1976. Pastor Fr. Thomas Clark officiated. "Marie" raised in St. Ann Parish, completed grades one through eight at parish school. Attended Union County public school systems grade nine through 12. Graduated National Honors Society, but refused recognition.

Married "Tony" who was born in Hopkins County. He has lived most of his life in Union County. He is an active member of Morganfield First Baptist Church. The late "Buddy" Earl Davis Heriges and Junita Luvon Woosley Heriges are his parents, also of Morganfield, KY. Tony is a 1991 graduate of Union County High School and a member of United Mine Workers of America where he has been employed by Island Creek Coal Company for the past 20 years.

Marie and Tony lived in rural Waverly, KY (Hitesville) since married. Has rented a home on Buckman's family farm.

Laurel Elizabeth Ann "Lea" was born March 22, 1988 at Welborn Baptist Hospital.

Tony and Marie have owned five acres of wooded property in Forrest Hills Subdivision, Morganfield since 1980. In 1990 a new home was completed and in February a new residence was established on what is now addressed as Heriges Lane.

By the grace of God may we always have a loving, growing family and a warm home to dwell in.

HERRMANN, W. JOHN, was born Aug. 28, 1944 and graduated from Hesser College in 1988. He was a sergeant in the U.S. Army from 1961-64. Married Paula Mary Horvath Herrmann who was born March 24, 1947. They have one son Andrew Werner Herrman, born Sept. 19, 1969, a 1992 graduate of West Kentucky University. He is currently doing missionary work for Glenmary Home and missionaries with Chocktaw people of Tennessee. Their daughter Katherine Ann Herrmann was born Sept. 4, 1974, a 1992 graduate of Franklin Simpson High School and a student at West Kentucky University.

W. John Herrmann Family

They moved from New York City to New Hampshire and then to Franklin where they currently live. They purchased a 60 acre farm to raise Tennessee Walking horses. They are now members of St. Mary of the Woods Parish, of Franklin, Simpson Arts Council, Tennessee Walking Horse Association, Native American Indian Association and Cottonwood Singers.

HESEN, BENEDICT E., was born Nov. 14, 1931 at St. Mary Elizabeth Hospital in Louisville, KY to Herman O. Hesen and Pauline E. Finotti Hesen. He married Mary Martha Hemmerle who was born April 4, 1931, daughter of Anthony L. Hemmerle and Catherine Hazel Adams Hemmerle. They were married in Holy Spirit Catholic Church in Louisville, KY over 37 years ago. Benedict attended Catholic grade school, high school and college in Louisville. Ben and Mary have four sons, Ben Jr., Paul G., Anthony L. and Peter A., also four grandchildren. They have been members of St. William Parish in Marion, KY since 1986. Now living in Salem, Livingston County, KY. They are past members of Sacred Heart Parish in Jeffersonville, IN. Serves on Parish Council, and chairman of Building Committee. Trustee of Kentucky Hospital Association, past president of Twin Lakes Distr.

One day Sister Frances saw Ben and his maintenance crew from Livingston County Hospital marking off St. William Church "unmarked" lot. Ben said if anyone asked who did it tell them the "Angels" did it. Sister Frances said at last she had seen some Angels.

HIGDON, MONSIGNOR ANTHONY GEORGE, was born in Daviess County on Aug. 19, 1911. He is the son of Estil Edward Higdon (Feb. 5, 1883-June 13, 1964) and Henrietta Higdon Johnson (June 3, 1887-Aug. 13, 1978). His brothers and sisters were: Joseph Charles Higdon born July 15, 1913 married to Mary Ellen Fulkerson; Mildred born August 1915 and died three weeks later; Henrietta (Sr. Rose Henry) born January 1917; Olivia born June 1919, married L.M. Cassidy; James Estil Higdon born Aug. 16, 1921, married Eloise Ambs, died Oct. 27, 1988; Frances George Higdon (Bro. Maron) born August 1923, died 1984; and Victor Higdon born Dec. 15, 1927, married Marietha Dupont.

Father Anthony Higdon

He received First Communion at 7 years of age and confirmed 9 years of age. Attended St. Meinrad Minor Seminary for five years and the Major Seminary for six years. Ordained June 19, 1938. Served as associate priest at Holy Name in Henderson for one year; Associate at St Paul in Owensboro for two years; pastor at St. Anthony Brown's Valley, Vicar at St. Stephen Cathedral for 20 years; pastor at St. John Church, McCracken County; Pastor at St. Pius Tenth Church, Calvert City, KY; and Carmel Home in Owensboro, KY. First Priest ordained for the Diocese of Owensboro, the only one that year. Street preached for three summers at towns in Hancock and McClean Counties. Built church at Patesville, KY; built Catholic School at Hawesville, KY. Invested as a Monsignor 1973. Held the position of dean for about 30 years. He held other residential and non-residential appointments. Celebrated 50th anniversary of ordination June 1988 at St. Pius Tenth, Calvert City, KY.

Monsignor Higdon died at the age of 81 on Wednesday, Aug. 19, 1992 at the Carmel Home, where he was chaplain from March 1989 until a few months before his death.

HIGDON, CECELIA ULLAINEE, (Sister Georgetta) was born June 22, 1907. She was the daughter of Lawrence Henson Higdon, a dairyman and farmer born May 26, 1879 died July 7, 1987 and Mary Rose Coomes Higdon born Sept. 11, 1885 and died Dec. 4, 1977. They were both born in Daviess County, KY. Her brothers and sisters: Mary Esteleena who died at the age of 5; Francis Xavier (married Jimmie Logston who is now deceased); Lawrence Henson Jr. who is deceased (married Edna Shelton); May Rose married Norman Greenberg; Theresa Ursula married Paul Reitzel who is deceased; Mary Aloysius married William Eger; Thomas Andrew married Norma Faye; George Neihaus, died at 22 months; and Francis Marie who married Louis O'Bryan.

Cecelia attended St. Lawrence School and was interested in farm life. Entered convent Sept. 8, 1928 and missions include Curdsville, Stanley, Jeffersontown, Fairfield, Flaherty, New Haven, Blessed Mother, St. Denis, St. Margaret Mary, Farmington, NM, Hardinsburg, St. Joe and Paul, Paducah, Mayfield and Precious Blood. Her duties include music teacher and choir organist. She has travelled to Kodiak, AL; Virginia Beach; Denver, CO and Chicago to see Pope Paul IV.

HIGDON, DAYMOND LEE AND MARY ELLEN SANDERS, met for the first time on Jan. 9, 1971 through a friend. They were married on June 30, 1972 at St. Anthony Parish in Peonia by Fr. Joseph Miller.

Daymond was born Aug. 28, 1949 into a Catholic family of four brothers and seven sisters. He was baptized on Sept. 25, 1949 by Fr. Victor Boarman at St. Anthony Church. He attended St. Anthony School. His parents were Joseph A. Higdon and Elsie Marie Johnston Higdon who were married on Oct. 17, 1928 at St. Benedict in Wax. They became members of St. Anthony when they moved to Peonia and lived out their life there. Joseph G. Higdon died on Nov. 12, 1990, Elsie died on Nov. 26, 1978. They are buried in St. Anthony Cemetery.

Daymond and Mary Ellen Higdon

Mary Ellen was born into a Baptist family on Dec. 14, 1949. She had eight brothers and five sisters. Her parents are the late Edgar Sanders and Anna West Sanders of Leitchfield. She joined St. Anthony Parish Feb. 7, 1943. She was baptized by Fr. William Borntrager. They are members of St. Anthony Church in Peonia. Daymond works for the Walter T. Kelly Company. Mary Ellen is a housewife. They own their own farm where they raise beef cattle, pig, tobacco, etc. Daymond was born on this farm and has always lived there. They are active in several ministries in their church and feel this has helped them form a deeper faith and stronger commitment to follow God's way of life. They feel blessed to belong to the church family of St. Anthony, Peonia, KY.

HIGDON, JOSEPH CHARLES AND MILDRED LOIS CECIL, were born and raised in Daviess County, KY. After their marriage on Oct. 16, 1954, they moved to Owensboro, KY where they made their home and have lived since. They lived most of those years in Precious Blood Parish and are now members of Immaculate Parish. Joseph has served in Parish Ministry. Millie serves in parish and hospital ministry.

J.C. and Millie both come from large families of 10 and nine brothers and sisters respectively. They both grew up on farms, and often reflect back on the hard work and responsibility given throughout their young years, knowing full well, it would be beneficial in their up-bringing and prepare them for the challenges of the future. Now, as they look back, they know it was worth the trouble, whereas it provided good training to raise their own family. J.C. and Millie quickly concur, that their greatest challenge and ministry had been the rearing of their daughter and five sons. They both agree that their children often motivated them to persevere when times where hard and trying.

Their children have always been and will always be their pride and joy, the apple of their eyes. However, with all the good times, there must have been times of sorrow, such as experienced by J.C. and Millie, after the death of their daughter-in-law of one year and her pre-born son, as well as their 1 month old granddaughter. They realize that some sorrow and heartache is inevitable in raising a family, but, the joy they feel when they count their blessings far and away outweighs the sorrow which is displayed as they often gather as a family to celebrate their oneness!

Millie feels that so many prayers have been answered and she firmly believes that the Prayer of St. Francis said around the dinner table through the years was one of the greatest helps. Their six children, Greg, Alan, Patty, Perry, Billy and Ricky, all have good jobs, are all married in the church to very loving and caring spouses (four of whom converted into the Catholic Church). How grateful they are to be blessed with a long awaited adopted grandson, which blesses them with 11 grandchildren to love, and another on the way.

Joseph Charles Higdon Family

J.C. retired from Green River Steel after 31 years of service. Both J.C. and Millie can recall the difficult times in raising a family while at the same time dealing with a swing-shift schedule, but both look back and see some advantages. J.C had no problems putting his sons to work in order to help keep them on the straight and narrow, and being the perfectionist that he was, he made sure the work was done right.

Millie recalls fighting for survival at times, but feels blessed that J.C.'s good job gave her the opportunity to stay at home with the children. Millie's various ministries in church and volunteer work was a big help whereas her interaction with other adults enabled her to experience her commonness in addition to answering her personal call to serve the Lord.

As they say, anything worthwhile is worth the fight, and after all is said and done we have won the fight. We have been blessed with 38 years of marriage, six wonderful and successful children and their spouses, and 11 beautiful grandchildren. As we mature in our lives, it does both our hearts good to see that our own seeds have been sown, nurtured, grown and are maturing in their own lives. God and His creations have done nothing but bless us in our paths through life, and, for this we are forever thankful and in His debt.

HIGDON, the family of Buddie and Lenora Higdon have lived in Grayson County at Peonia most of their lives. Buddie and Lenora were married Oct. 26, 1924 at St. Anthony Church, Peonia. He was 24 and she was 18. They lacked 22 days being married 66 years. They had nine children. Charles Albert died as an infant. They have eight living children Helen, Russel, Mildred, Chester, Mary Catherine, Floyd, Anna Rose and Bernadette. All their children were baptized, made their First Communion and were confirmed at St. Anthony Church. All were married at St. Anthony except Chester. He was married at St. Helen Church in Louisville. Buddie and Lenora have 30 grandchildren and 42 great-grandchildren.

Higdon Family: Buddie, Lenora, Helen, Russell, Mildred, Chester, Mary Catherine, Floyd, Anna Rose and Bernadette (1989).

Buddie farmed all his life. When Buddie and Lenora were raising their family the only transportation they had was a roadwagon or on horseback. Buddie took his family to church in a roadwagon. Buddie was born May 17, 1900, the son of Charles and Mary Francis Higdon. He died Oct. 4, 1990. Lenora was born March 21, 1906, the daughter of Albert and Molly Miles Lush. Lenora was a housewife. She helped with the farming and raised her family. She made most of her children's clothes. Lenora is a member of St. Anthony Parish of Peonia.

HIGDON, MARGARET ELLOISE AMBS,
was born near Brown's Valley on Aug. 8, 1924 to Henry Francis and Alice B. Cheshire-Ambs and baptized at St. Anthony Church. She met her husband James Estil Higdon through Reverend Anthony G. Higdon (James' brother) who was pastor at the time at St. Anthony and her brother George Ambs who was in the service with James. It was love at first sight and although Jimmy and George were off fighting a war (World War II), Jimmy and Elloise wrote back and forth. After the war was over Jimmy and Elloise were married at St. Anthony and together they had 11 children, Eddie, Connie, Bernard, Jane, Mark, Ruth Ann, Phillip, Rita, Kevin, Angela and Benny. They resided in the Philpot area, belonging to the St. Pius Parish up until Jimmy's health began to fail. They, then moved to Lourdes Parish in Owensboro. After a long struggle with illness Jimmy died Oct. 27, 1989. Elloise still lives in the Lourdes area and is still an active member there.

So many good things can be told and remembered of them, their smiles and laughter, the big Sunday dinners, and a great feeling of love and shared happiness that will always be there.

HIGDON, THOMAS SR. AND JOYCE,
were married on April 23, 1965 in San Antonio, TX, while Thomas was in the Air Force and stationed there at Lackland Air Force Base. His military time ending the same year, they settled in Baytown, TX where three children were born: Thomas Jr. on Oct. 30, 1965, and twins Deborah and Denise on Oct. 15, 1966. After several moves in construction work, the family settled in Whitesville, KY where their fourth child was born Nov. 13, 1971.

The Higdons are members of the St. Mary of the Woods Parish of Whitesville where they have been active members. The children attended St. Mary of the Woods Grade School and Trinity High School. Tom Jr., is employed at Housner Hardcrome of Owensboro; Deborah married Marty Rhodes, also of Whitesville and has three children and is a nursing student at Kentucky Wesleyan College; Denise graduated from Western Kentucky University and is an interior designer with McCulloch and Company of Louisville, KY; and Christine is a student at KWC.

Thomas Sr. is from a long line of Daviess Countians. His parents trace their families to the earliest settlers of Daviess County and St. Lawrence, coming from Bardstown, KY. Norbert was a dozer operator and enjoyed pointing out to the grandchildren many roads and ponds he had built. He truly lives on in his work to help physically build Daviess County as well as through his 36 grandchildren and 10 great-grandchildren.

HIGGINS, MONSIGNOR JOHN MARTIN,
was born on Oct. 19, 1889, in Grayson Springs, KY. He was the oldest of 11 children (nine boys and two girls) born to Thomas Henry Higgins and Mary Catherine Tully Higgins. One of his earliest memories is of his mother cooking and baking in the country kitchen of their small modest home in Grayson County. He remembers his mother as the prettiest person he ever saw. He also remembers his father's horses on the farm, perhaps because one of his jobs was to help take care of them.

He attended Grayson Springs Public Schools until he was 16 years old, going to school about three months each year. Attendance at school was sporadic because of the distance from school, and the need to work on the farm. At age 17, he left his parents' home to go to St. Charles College in Catonsville, MD, and St. Mary Seminary in Baltimore. He was ordained a deacon by Cardinal Gibbons, and used to accompany him on daily walks through the streets of Baltimore, where he learned much about the church from this elderly cardinal.

Monsignor John Martin Higgins

He was ordained to the priesthood on June 19, 1918, by Bishop O'Donahue in St. Mary Magdalene Church in Louisville. He served as assistant pastor at St. Stephen Cathedral in Owensboro, and at Holy Cross in Louisville. His first pastorate was at St. Peter, Stanley where he built the present church. Those were sad and trying times, the years of the Depression in the 20s. On Nov. 15, 1928, he went to Sacred Heart Parish in Waverly, where he built the present church, and most of the buildings of old St. Vincent Academy. There is now a school there, Higgins Learning Center, named for him and dedicated to helping students who need special attention. He was pastor at Sacred Heart for 45 years, and chaplain at St. Vincent Academy where he also taught math, religion, English and Latin. He worked closely with the Sisters of Charity of Nazareth, whom he loved dearly.

Father Higgins was known as a person who radiated happiness and good cheer. On the occasion of the celebration of his Golden Jubilee, Bishop Soenneker said to him, "God gave him the gift of happiness." Indeed, he spread this happiness to each and every person he met along life's journey. After World War II, when Camp Breckinridge was established in Union County, he became auxiliary chaplain there. His rectory was always open to priests and chaplains, as well as to his parishioners and to the whole community. He was "everybody's priest". He was very ecumenical in his ministry, working with and for the Protestant ministers of Union County. He was very pastoral, ministering to people's needs without letting rules hinder him. He once said he always tried to do what in his heart he felt and believed was the right thing to do. He was given the title Monsignor in August 1948. While at Sacred Heart, there were two major events that were very sad for him. In March 1950 a fire destroyed the church. He built a new church that was dedicated in the fall of 1951. In June 1967 St. Vincent Academy was closed. Because he spent so much time at the academy as teacher and chaplain, it was like a part of his life was taken from him. He retired from active priesthood on Feb. 15, 1973. It was with much sadness and pain that he left his beloved Sacred Heart Parish. However, at the age of 83, he felt the need to slow down, to let go of the heartaches and headaches that go with administering and pastoring a parish.

After spending a year in Louisville with his sister Mary, and two years in New York with his sister Margaret, he returned to the diocese in 1976 and lived at Carmel Home in Owensboro. He never ceased to help God's people, and was always available to help in any way that he could. Many priests, sisters and lay people came to him for counseling during these years. He was the glue that held the diocese together through many difficult times.

Father Higgins had time for everything, time for everyone. He loved to celebrate and laugh and sing. In 1983, at age 94, he had the lead part in a Christmas play at Carmel Home playing "Grandpa Alexander." He never ceased to bring joy and happiness to others. In the early morning hours of Jan. 23, 1985, he left us quietly and peacefully. For those of us who were privileged to know and love him, there is a void in our lives that nothing or no one will ever be able to fill. However, his presence is still very much with us. It is being felt now as his life story is being written. His love and laughter live on in us and in this diocese.

HILL, MONSIGNOR RAYMOND GEORGE,
was born Feb. 21, 1907 in Louisville, KY, the son of Michael F. and Elizabeth Mulcahy Hill. Baptized Feb. 24, 1907 at St. John, Louisville by Fr. L.D. Bax. Attended grade school at St. James, Louisville; high school at St. Xavier and St. Meinrad; junior college at St. Meinrad. St. Meinrad and the Sulpician Seminary in Washington, D.C. prepared him for the priesthood. Bishop John A. Floersh ordained him to the priesthood in the Assumption Cathedral on May, 21 1932. He served in the parishes of St. Joseph, Bowling Green, St. John, Paducah, St. Agnes in Uniontown. In 1953 he was appointed Superintendent of Schools and served in this capacity for 15 years. Since 1964 he was chaplain of Mercy Hospital. He was involved in rehabilitating church interior and exterior at Uniontown, added office for Diocesan School Office at Uniontown.

Monsignor Raymond G. Hill

He also served as chaplain for the Carmel Home, the Owensboro Serra Club and Our Lady of Mercy Hospital. Hill was superintendent from 1953 to 1978 in the diocese, which consisted of 32 Western Kentucky counties.

Monsignor Hill died May 28, 1981, at our Lady of Mercy Hospital at the age of 74. He was survived by one sister, Elizabeth Hill of Louisville.

HINES, MARY LUCY (MOLOHON),
the youngest of five daughters of Loyola and Mamie Molohon, born in Curdsville, KY. Baptized by Fr. James Higdon at St. Elizabeth Church.

The Molohons owned a small farm near Curdsville, tobacco being the main crop. The daughters, not always willingly, helped with the planting and harvesting. There was such a low stretch of road between the Molohon home and the church which almost every year, the flood waters covered. This, however, was not an excuse to miss Sunday Mass, school, choir or play practice. Mr. Molohon would carry the daughters across when the water was shallow. As the waters became deeper, a wagon or boat was used for transportation.

Mary Lucy is a graduate of Mount St. Joseph Academy and attended Brescia College. She became a radio-

logical technologist and worked at the Owensboro Daviess County Hospital and Mayfair Square for Drs. Dixon, Wight, and Baumgarten.

In 1964, she joined the Extension Lay Volunteers (a lay missionary service) and was sent to Guthrie, OK. She, and 12 other volunteers from various states, staffed a small hospital at that location.

In 1971 she returned to Kentucky. Here she met W. Thomas Hines. Tom and Mary Lucy were married Jan. 6, 1973 at Immaculate Conception Church in Durham, NC.

The Hines' have lived in Friendly Village, south of Rome, KY for 18 years. Mary Lucy is a sales associate at Bacons Department Store. Tom is a supervisor at Alcan Aluminum in Sebree, KY. Mary Lucy is a member of Our Lady of Lourdes Parish in Owensboro, KY.

HINTON, JOHN F. (JEFF) AND VIRGINIA (JENNY) FLOOD,

joined St. Mary of the Woods, McQuady as a family after their marriage in 1948. Jeff had been a member of the parish from his birth in 1925. Jenny had been a member of St. Romuald, Hardinsburg where she was born and reared by her parents, Pete and Rachel Alexander Flood. Jeff's parents Willis and Gertrude Horrell Hinton were members of St. Mary's and reared their family there. Jeff, as his father before him, was a farmer all his life and the farm is still in the family. Jeff and Jenny were blessed with 11 children, seven boys and four girls viz; Don, Tony, Gary, Charlie, Becky, Marvin, Linda, Faye, Gerard, Mike and Debbie. They were all baptized at St. Mary Church and most of them were married there. From these children there are 13 wonderful grandchildren. The two older sons served in the military. Their children are now living in different areas of the state and country.

The Jeff Hinton Family

Jenny worked in the home and took care of the children until 1987 when she took the position of Breckinridge County Archivist. Jeff died on May 25, 1987 and is buried in St. Mary of the Woods Cemetery. Jeff served in the Marine Corp in World War II. He was a member of the Holy Name Society for many years and helped with the annual picnic each year. Both he and Jenny have served on the parish pastoral council. Jenny is a member of the choir, has been a member of the Christian Mothers since her marriage and taught CCD in the parish for 17 years. She is also serving on the cemetery committee and at present is helping to plat the map for future use of the parish which is greatly needed.

HINTON, RICHARD MARVIN AND MARY MAXINE (MATTINGLY),

were married Jan. 23, 1946, St. Anthony Catholic Church, Axtel, KY, Rev. Henry J. Friedel officiating. Richard Marvin's parents were Frank and Theresa (Crenshaw) Hinton. Mary Maxine's parents were Con and Mary (Storms) Mattingly. All the above were members of St. Anthony Parish. To Richard Marvin and Mary Maxine four children were born: Mary A., now Mrs. Roger Pierce, St. Joseph Parish, Leitchfield, KY; Francis Marie, now Mrs. Dennis Akers, St. Ambrose Parish, Cecilia, KY; Marian Anita, now Mrs. Adrian Durbin, St. Martin's Parish, Flaherty, KY and Theresa Ann who passed away at the age of 6 years old on July 21, 1954. Richard Marvin passed away Jan. 22, 1992. St. Anthony's continues to be Mary Maxine's home parish with Rev. Bruce Fogle, pastor.

HOBBS, JEROME AND ANGELINE (KING).

Jerome married first Margaret Jane Courtney in Hickman County in 1835. They were listed in the 1840 Hickman County Census as having three daughters: Catherine Ellen "Kitty" (Cissell), Mary Elizabeth (Estes) and Angeline (Denistin).

Jerome married second Mary Wooley in Hickman County in 1841. They had nine children: Martina, George Washington, Matilda Ann (O'Neal), Joseph Thomas, Philip Miles, Leatitia Jane, Jerome, John William, Lydia Joan (Redford). (Note: The above 12 children are listed, with birth dates in the Baptismal Registers at Sacred Heart, Waverly, Union County and at St. Jerome, Fancy Farm. And there is a baptism date of May 13, 1836 for Margaret Courtney, and of Oct. 23, 1842 for Mary Wooley).

Jerome married third Angeline King. They had six children: Benjamin Dudley, James Valentine, Richard, Oscar, Sarah (Hayden) and Ernest.

Benjamin Dudley (1866-1851), married first Mary Ellen Wilson (see James Wilson biography). They had six children: Olar (Burgess), James Everett, Romuald, Ruth (Burgess), Wm. Dewey (died age 3) and Alma (Echsner). "Dud" married second Catherine (Cissell) Burch in 1913 (no children).

James Everett (1894-1981) married Iva Gertrude Toon (see Athanasius Toon biography). They had 12 children: James Curtis (1915-1973) married Violet Carrico; James (stillborn); Mary Ella (1918-) married Joseph S. Carrico; Lyndal Bernard (1921-) married Patricia Liston; Joseph Earl (1923-1988) married Juanita Gore; Thomas Edward (1926-1978) married Mildred Lucille (1928-) married first Charles "Toby" Kilcoyne, married second Warren Robinette; Wm. Dewey (1930-) married Mary Ruth Murphy; Margaret and James (twins-premature-died shortly after birth); Robert Leon (1933-) married Verna Jean Wilson; and Thomas Howard (1936-) married Patricia Pitts.

Everett and Ivie (Toon) Hobbs Family

Lower L-R: Tom, Everett, Ivie (Toon), Bob; Upper L-R: Lucille, W.D., Edward, Earl, Mary Ella, Billy, Curtis

Mary Ella (1918-) married Joseph Samuel (1916-1981) son of Samuel Pius and Anna Ellis (Thompson) Carrico (see Francis Marion Carrico Biography), at St. Jerome, Fancy Farm on Nov. 10, 1942. They have nine children: James Samuel (1943), William Glenn (1946), Janet Elizabeth (1948), Larry Joseph (1949), John Edwin (1951), Philip Anthony (1952), Sharon Ann (1955), Kenneth Charles (1956) and Mark Eugene (1959).

Joseph S. Carrico died July 18, 1981 at Jefferson Barracks Hospital, St. Louis, MO, and was buried in Lake View Memorial Gardens, Belleville, IL. Mary Ella lives in Cahokia, IL. *Submitted by Mrs. Mary E. (Hobbs) Carrico.*

HOBBS, WILLIAM DONALD,

family began Jan. 23, 1961 with his marriage at Holy Name of Jesus Church to Maxine Elizabeth Linton, daughter of Ivo McAvoy Linton and Marie Elizabeth Deicken. He is the son of William Henry Hobbs and Ella Joan Pike. Don was born Aug. 15, 1941 in Paragould, AR. Attended St. Mary's School and moved to St. Vincent Academy 1957. Don, boasted that he was the only male boarder to graduate from the all girls boarding school in 1959. Maxine attended Holy School, graduating in 1958. Both attended Henderson Community College. Don is a lab technician at Eaton Corp.

Don and Maxine Hobbs

Don and Maxine have two sons, Charles Edward born Feb. 11, 1962, married Shelia Berry Russelburg Oct. 14, 1988. He has two step-children, Kelly Russelburg (1976) and Chad Edward Russelburg (Jan. 7, 1987). They reside in Uniontown, TN. William Christopher was born July 27, 1965, now a student at Murray State University.

Two daughters Elizabeth Ann born Aug. 2, 1963, married to Robert Christopher Raleigh, born April 28, 1960. They have two children, Jeremy Stewart born Jan. 7, 1985 and Lauren Nicole born July 22, 1988. They reside in Calletain, TN. Catherine Lynnett born Dec. 10, 1967, died Dec. 11, 1968.

HODGKINS, JAMES (JIM) I. AND ROSE (FISCHER).

Jim was born near Whitesville, KY the son of Philip John Hodgkins, born March 18, 1911 in Daviess County, KY and Ada Ann Payne born March 28, 1909 in Knottsville, KY. His grandparents were James D. Hodgkins (Jan. 17, 1864) and Ruey A. Ballman (Aug. 30, 1873); Marshall T. Payne (Jan. 9, 1861) and Mary Jane Raley (Sept. 16, 1885). His great-grandfather, Henry Ballman, emigrated from Ruhr, Germany.

Rose was born in Rome, KY to Robert John Fischer (born Aug. 24, 1899) and Helena Audrey Fischer (Dec. 30, 1910), both born in Daviess County, KY. Granddaughter of George Andrew Fischer (Feb. 4, 1871) and Margaret Wink (March 20, 1875); Joseph Henry Payne (April 6, 1864) and Mary Loran Stallings (Dec. 22, 1873).

James Hodgkins' Family-Jim, Rose, Amy, Julie, Jimmy, Stefani and Christopher.

Jim and Rose met while attending Brescia College. They now live in Owensboro, KY and are members of Blessed Mother Parish. Jim is employed as warehouse foreman at Owensboro Municipal Utilities and Rose teaches first grade at St. Angela Merici School. They have five children: Amy (20) a junior at Western Kentucky University majoring in music education; Julie (17) a senior at Owensboro Catholic High School; Jimmy (15) a sophomore at Owensboro Catholic High School; Stefani (12) a 7th grader at Owensboro Catholic Middle School; and Christopher (4) attends pre-school at St. Stephen's.

Jim is regional treasurer for St. Vincent De Paul, Eucharistic Minister, sings in choir and is on the picnic committee. Enjoys golfing and woodcrafting. Rose is charistic Minister, Children's Liturgy teacher, Vacation Bible School teacher.

HOLTSHOUSER, FANNIE ELLER,
was born June 13, 1885 in Kentucky. She was the daughter of John Francis "Jack" Holtshouser and Zerelda Bassett. Fannie married John Robert Skaggs Dec. 21, 1900 in Troy, Doniphan County, KS. She has 10 children and one stillborn male child: Forrest, Opal, Blanche, Carl, Connie Skaggs-Lenihan, Willard, Elmer and William.

Connie married Edward L. Lenihan on Aug. 12, 1928 in Ottawa, LaSalle County, IL. Their children were: Edward L. Jr. (1929-?) an electrical engineer for Boeing in Wichita, KS; Shelia (1944-) who married Robert Dennis Larson on Feb. 4, 1967 at the Trinity Lutheran Church in Genoa, DeKalb County, IL. Shelia and Robert have a daughter Michelle; Linda (1946-) who married Randall Charles Sellers March 26, 1972 at the "Church by the Side of the Road" in Rockton, Winnebago County, IL.

HOLTSHOUSER, GEORGE WASHINGTON,
was born July 25, 1798 in Nelson County, KY. George was the eldest child of John Holtshouser and Elizabeth Heavenhill.

George married Sarah (Sally) Langley May 16, 1821 in Nelson County, KY by J. Ferguson. Sally was the daughter of Thomas Langley. George farmed on Pottership Hill near Bardstown, KY just off Hwy. 150. The original homestead is still there and that is where George, Sally and two of their children are buried.

This author is not too convinced that George took on his mother's Catholic beliefs with much zeal. For one thing only a baptismal record for one of his children can be found and that was just a few months before her marriage in a Catholic church. George and Sally's boys are noted in local history for having a wild streak up their spine. It is probably the same as teenagers today taking a "joy ride" in dad's new car just to see how fast it would go. The Holtshouser boys would ride their horses as fast as they could up and down the streets of Bardstown shooting their guns in the air and scaring the wits out of people. Their son, John J. Crittendon, killed his brother, Daniel, very deliberately one day. Their other son, Robert, got into a squabble with a family friend, John Hardin, while at George's estate auction over the bidding of a horse. John outbid Robert on the horse and Robert reached for a gun, only to be shot several times.

Their children were: Sarah who was born March 18, 1825 in Nelson County, KY. Sarah was the second wife of William A. Roberts. Their children were George A. (1854), Mary W. Roberts Rapier (1855-1880), William A. Roberts (1857-1875), James J. Roberts (1865), Felix Christopher Roberts (1865) and Dixie J. Roberts (1862-1879). Sarah died Dec. 19, 1877 and was buried with her husband in the Holy Cross Cemetery.

Helena M. was born Feb. 28, 1829 in Nelson County and was baptized May 11, 1856 by Rev. Wuyts. Helena married John Thont Ballard on Dec. 9, 1856 in Nelson County, KY. Helena and J.T. had eight known children: Francis Murph (1860), James W. (1861-1883), George (1861), Mary Elizabeth (1858-1977), Ada Jane (1863-1932) married John Albert Medley, Albert Sidney (1864-1954) married Sarah Louie Riggs, Ida Louise (1867-1957) married Richard Medley, and Lena Frances Ballard (1869) married Charles Roberts. Helena died Aug. 11, 1880 in Marion County, KY and is buried in the Holy Cross Cemetery.

Daniel Webster was born Jan. 29, 1834 in Nelson County, KY. Daniel was shot one day by his younger brother John J. He was reading a newspaper one day at home when John J. entered the house, and without any words exchanged between the two, fired several shots. The newspaper is at the courthouse in Bardstown and you can see the bullets holes. Daniel died March 22, 1873 and is buried on the family farm on Pottership Hill near Bardstown.

John J. Crittenden was born in 1842 in Nelson County, KY. John married Eliza Ellen Boone Feb. 2, 1869 at the St. Joseph Cathedral in Bardstown. He was a Civil War veteran with Company B, Ninth Regt. Inf. Little else is known about John. In later years he unfortunately became a fugitive and wandered from family to family for shelter. John and Eliza had four children: Clarence (1869); Roxianna "Roxey" (1872-1931) married Stephen Jack Thompson. They had one son Jack Jr. who raised champion horses for a while in Kentucky; Mark Haber (1874) married a girl named Camille and later transferred to the Jefferson County, KY area. Mark and Camille had one son Muir (1906).

Ada Jane was born Oct. 14, 1838 in Nelson County. She later married a man named Showalter but nothing else is known about her.

Robert Peal Russell was born Aug. 14, 1848 in Nelson County. Robert married Susan Mary Boone on May 11, 1875. Robert and Susan had only been married one year at the time of his death at his father's estate auction. They had one son Custer Clarence (1876-1920). Custer never married and resided with his cousin, Clarence, in Louisville. Susan remarried a Thompson and had two other children, John and Fannie. Robert died Oct. 1, 1877 and is buried at the Holtshouser family farm on Pottership Hill with his parents.

Lizzie was born in 1839. Little else is known of her except that distant family believes that she married a Ball.

Henry Clay was born June 26, 1836. Henry married Jemima Ann Knott of Nelson County. Henry and Jemima belonged to the St. Thomas Catholic Church in Bardstown, KY and they farmed locally. They are mentioned in an adjoining section.

Missouri was born Jan. 28, 1827 in Nelson County. She married William C. Price in Nelson County on Nov. 26, 1849. Their children were: Jennie R. (1850-1889), Joseph (1852-1918), George N. (1852-1874), Charles, and Thomas Price (1857-1875). Missouri died Oct. 10, 1906 and is buried at the St. Joseph Catholic Church Cemetery at Bardstown.

Louisa Mary Holtshouser was born Dec. 1, 1831. She married James Coy and had two children, Amanda and Coy. She died before the 1870 Nelson County Census.

HOLTSHOUSER, HENRY CLAY,
was born June 26, 1836 in Nelson County, KY. He was the eighth child of George Washington Holtshouser and Sarah Langley. Henry grew up on Pottership Hill playing with his siblings and Heavenhill cousins. Henry married Jemima Ann Knott also of Nelson County on Nov. 25, 1862. Her family is also associated with a long line of Kentucky Catholic families. Their children are as follows: Sally Ann (1864-).

John Crittendon (1863-1927) who married Mary Jo Ritchie (1863-1903). They moved to Missouri in 1892. Their children are: Monica Ethel (1891-) who married Ernest Faulk; Bertha (1893-) who married John Spears; Edward (1894-1912). Stephen Ritchie (1897-) married May Jewell Wilcox and had a child Harold; Arn-Alberta (1895-) married Everett Fobey and had a son named Harold; Richard Eugene (1898-) married Gladys Young; Jessie (1900-) married Earl Vanskiski and had two daughters, Hazel Dean (1921) and Earlene (1925).

Theresa Ada (1867-1868).

John Webster (1868-).

Fabian (1871-).

Lee W. Holtshouser (1877-).

Henry and Jemima are buried in the St. Thomas Cemetery next to the old St. Thomas Catholic Church, which is a historical marker. Henry's headstone can no longer be found. Jemima's is surprisingly readable considering it is a weathered sandstone marker. Her headstone can be found just to the left at the beginning of the cemetery.

HOLTSHOUSER, HERBERT WENDELL,
was born in 1914 in Owensboro, Daviess County, KY. He is the son of William Alphonsus Holtshouser Sr. and Mabel Agnes Lashbrook. Herbert met and married Florence Christensen from Daviess County. Florence was a Seventh Day Adventist. They had six children, three boys and three girls: Barbara Ann, Wayne, Ruth, J.D., Richard and Jean. Herbert and Florence later relocated to Salt Lake City, UT.

HOLTSHOUSER, HOWARD DELOS,
was born Oct. 25, 1928 in Detroit, MI. His parents, like many, migrated away from their pioneer Kentucky roots in search of better economic prospects. Howard married Patricia Ruth Mary Korn Aug. 11, 1956 in Richmond, VA. To this union there were four children born.

Scott Howard Gerard Patrick Holtshouser was born Nov. 7, 1958 in Grosse Pointe, MI. Scott practices as an engineer. He married Erin Lafferty on Oct. 9, 1982 in Mount Clemens, MI and they have two children being raised in the Catholic faith—Kristina Marie was born July 2, 1985 in Michigan and Kendra Ann born Aug. 10, 1989, also in Michigan.

Stuart Robert was born May 16, 1963 in Detroit, MI. He works there as a sales representative. He married Lisa Jannette on Dec. 20, 1985 in Detroit, MI. They have no children yet.

Stephanie Helen married Richard Surzyn Aug. 9, 1986 in Harsens Island, MI. Richard is also Catholic and was baptized Nov. 20, 1960 in Detroit. They have one daughter, Kathryn Patricia born Nov. 18, 1990. Kathryn was baptized Feb. 3, 1991 in Mount Clemens, MI.

Steven John Joseph was born May 29, 1957 in Grosse Pointe, MI. He is employed there as an engineer. He married Regina Loretta Moses, April 25, 1987 in Mount Clemons, MI. They have no children yet. *Submitted by Diana Steele.*

HOLTSHOUSER, JAMES KENNETH,
was born Nov. 27, 1909 in Owensboro, KY. He was the son of William Alphonsus Sr. and Mabel Agnes Lashbrook. James met and married Mary Lillian Sapp, June 11, 1929 in Stanley, KY.

James and Mary had five children in Daviess County. They later relocated to Ft. Lauderdale, FL and are buried in the Queen of Heaven Cemetery there. Mabel died Jan. 4, 1971 (born Dec. 20, 1909) and James on Sept. 3, 1977.

Patricia Helen Holtshouser was born Aug. 16, 1932. She married Robert Truman. They have three children Micheal, David and Gina.

Barbara Jane was born Oct. 25, 1938 and she married Bill Dean. The author does not know if they have children.

Gerri Sue was born Dec. 4, 1940 and married Joseph Nugent.

Mary Josephine was born March 25, 1930 and married Art Layton.

Wilma Agnes was born Dec. 23, 1935 and married John "Jack" Thomas Considine, March 25, 1955 in Ferguson, MO. They are the parents to five children: John William, Richard Alan, Valerie Anne, Robin Mary and James Kenneth who was named for his grandfather. Jack owned and operated his own small business. They now live in Cameron Park, CA. John William was born Oct. 22, 1956 in St. Louis, MO. He married Michelle McBride July 14, 1979 in Reno, NV. Michelle was born Aug. 10, 1957. They have one daughter, Jenelle Marie, who was born Jan. 10, 1981 in Reno. Richard Alan was born Oct. 8, 1957 in St. Louis. Valerie Anne was born Jan. 11, 1959 in St. Louis. She married Dwight Joseph Rogers Dec. 15, 1979 in San Diego, CA. They adopted two beautiful children from Korea: Casey John born April 6, 1983 and Carly Anne born Jan. 7, 1985. Robin Mary was born Jan. 6, 1960 and married Lowell Henry Bronson in November 1977 in San Diego, CA. They have two daughters Shannon Marie born May 16, 1978 and Kelley Anne York born April 22, 1984. Also James Kenneth was born Oct. 4, 1962 in Pompano Beach, FL.

HOLTSHOUSER, JOHN,
was born Jan. 13, 1774 in Rowan County, NC. He was the son of Andrew and Anna Marie Wyandt Holshouser. Andrew was the son of Casper Holtzhausen, a German immigrant, who came to America in 1731.

John migrated to Nelson County, KY between 1792 and 1797. He met and married Elizabeth Heavenhill in 1797. Elizabeth was the daughter of Oliver Heavenhill and Elizabeth Miller. Heavenhill Distilleries is still in operation near Pottership Hill where Elizabeth grew up.

John and Elizabeth had many children whose Catholic descendants are numerous. The most famous, as far as published local history, has to be the children of George Washington Holtshouser. George's boys were known to have been a little on the wild side and would ride up and down the streets of Bardstown, KY on horseback shooting their guns in the air scaring the wits out of women and children.

John died 7 Nov. 1868 and is buried in the Saint Thomas Cemetery in Nelson County. Elizabeth died 10 years later and is also buried there.

Over the years the Holtshouser name has under gone many variations. Most people forget that "public" education, as far as reading and writing goes, is still fairly recent. The name has been found as Holtzhauser, Holthouser, Holshouser, and Holtzhousen. If it even sounds similar chances are that they're related in some way to John or his ancestors.

HOLTSHOUSER, JOSEPH WILLIAM, was born April 13, 1883 in Owensboro. He was the second child of Henry Charles and Fladgie Bellew-Holtshouser. Joseph married Bertha Ann Freels who was also born in Kentucky. Joseph and Bertha had five children: John Delle, Vivian, Fladgie and Lucy. Lucy died as a child and this author does not know where she is buried.

John Delle Holtshouser was born Sept. 6, 1901 in Spottsville in Henderson County, KY. He married Jennie Davis Nov. 23, 1926 in Cadillac, MI. John and Jennie had two boys Howard Delos and Floyd. Floyd died as an infant and is buried in Detroit.

Howard Delos was born Oct. 25, 1928 in Detroit, MI. He married on Aug. 11, 1956 in Richmond, VA, Patricia Ruth Mary Korn. They had four children: Scott Howard, Stuart Robert, Stephanie Helen and Steven John. Their descendants are covered in another section. Howard died April 25, 1984 in Detroit and is buried in the Cadillac Memorial Park Gardens.

Vivian Holtshouser was born Dec. 17, 1906 in Kentucky. She married Elton Eaves and little else in known to this author.

Fladgie Holtshouser was born Dec. 27, 1906. She married George Francis Greenwell who was born around 1904 in Kentucky. Fladgie and George moved around some and ended up in Orange, CA. One of their daughters was born in Indiana. They were blessed with four daughters: Lois Jean, Frances Arlene, Beverly and JoAnne. George died in 1989 and is buried in Orange, CA. Fladgie has failing health but her daughters are wonderfully attentive to her needs.

Lois Jean Greenwell was born Aug. 8, 1926 in Evansville, IN. She married Thomas Ralph Woodruff who was born in 1922 in Anniston, AL. They reside in Tustin, CA and have two children: Kathleen Carol who was born Aug. 18, 1946 in Davenport, IA and married Roger Neil Hand; blessed with a daughter Stacy Marisa born Nov. 2, 1970 in Palm Springs, CA and Thomas Alan was born June 9, 1951 in Anniston, AL.

Frances Arlene married Marlene LeRoy Priebe and they have two children: Eric LeRoy born in May 1980 and Jennifer Rose born Feb. 8, 1982.

Beverly J. married William Elton Barber. They have three children: Linda Louise, Loretta Lee (married a Barnhart) and William Elton II.

Linda Louise married Peter Eberhardt and they have two boys Peter Jr. and Bryan.

William Elton II married a Diane and they have three children: Melinda Ann, Joshua and Ryan.

JoAnne married Robert E. Allan and they have three children: Robert Daniel, Gary Eugene and Karen Marie.

Robert first married Julia Pance and they have a son named Aaron. Then he remarried a Lori and had two more children: Benjamin and Emily Rose.

Kathryn Holtshouser was born Feb. 24, 1912 in Evansville, IN. She married Jack Asaro and they currently reside in San Marino, CA. Kathryn and Jack have four wonderful daughters: Jacquolyn and Marolyn who are twins, Gloria Ann and Cathleen Diane.

Jacquolyn was born Feb. 14, 1933 in Los Angeles, CA. She married Dwight Sawyer and they have no children.

Marolyn married John Peterson and it is not known to the author if they have any children.

Gloria Ann was born Oct. 14, 1941 in Los Angeles. She married Leonard Cormier III.

Cathleen Diane was born July 22, 1943 also in Los Angeles. She married William Blackburn.

HOLTSHOUSER, JOSIE LEE, was born May 27, 1877 in Nelson County, KY. She was the daughter of William Russell and Martha Mudd-Holtshouser. She married Charles Thomas Head (1873-1921) on Feb. 10, 1903 in Nelson County. Josie and Charles were busy parents to 10 children:

William Francis Head (1903).

Mary Elizabeth was born Sept. 14, 1905 in Balltown, KY. She married Benjamin O'Bannion and had no children.

Russell Head (1906-1906) died at the tender age of 1 month.

Rosie Jane was born April 6, 1907 in Balltown. She married Harry L. Russell but had no children.

Bernard Leo (1909-1909) was born and died in Balltown, KY.

Thomas Richard Head was born Sept. 19, 1911 in Balltown, KY. Thomas married Mattie Brown (1911-1976) and had one son Tommy Lee who was born in 1930. Tommy died at age 6.

John Raymond was born Sept. 21, 1913 in Balltown. He married Elsie Lucille Goetzman who was born June 30, 1916. They had three children: Joyce Marie, born Dec. 8, 1947 and who married Charles L. Tabler. They have a son named Scott Toemayne.

Janis Lee, born Feb. 24, 1949 and she married Jimmie Donald Spann. Her children are Steven R., born Jan. 2, 1970 and Jennifer Lynn, born March 21, 1973.

Judith Raye, born Dec. 26, 1953 married Bruce Phillip Lynch. They have two children: Stephanie Marie, born July 7, 1974 and Bruce Phillip Jr., born Sept. 21, 1977.

Margaret Ellen (1915-1921) died as a child.

Nancy Ann Queen was born Aug. 6, 1917 in Balltown, KY. She married Elmer N. Hunter. Nancy died July 8, 1966 and is buried in the St. Michael Cemetery. Their children are: Lawrence, born July 11, 1946 and married Sherry Baker, they have a son named Benjamin, born March 3, 1978; Sharon, born Oct. 9, 1947 and married William Moss, with three children Nancy Lynn (Nov. 13, 1970), Brian Ernest (Aug. 9, 1973) and Erin Neil (Dec. 19, 1975); Rebecca (Oct. 3, 1956).

William Russell was born March 15, 1921 in Balltown, KY. He married Juanita Hazenbuhler (June 17, 1925) and had three children: William Charles who married Barbara Jane Mattie; Juanita Ann (July 8, 1944) who married Theodus Tumerlaine; and Richard Michael Head, born Dec. 19, 1964.

HOLTSHOUSER, MARGARET, was born Jan. 23, 1800 in Nelson County, KY. She was the second child of John Holtshouser and Elizabeth Heavenhill. Margaret grew up on Pottership Hill off of Hwy. 150 near Bardstown on the family farm. On Dec. 20, 1820 she was married to Nathaniel Langley in Nelson County by the Rev. Joseph Ferguson. Nathanial received a land grant near Danville in Vermillion County, IL for services during the War of 1812. Margaret and Nathaniel had four children: Elizabeth, Thomas, John, Charles and Casper James.

Elizabeth Langley (1823-1897) married Ernest Hayworth and little else in known. They are buried in Vermillion County.

Thomas John Langley (1828-1868) married Jane Hand in 1848 in Vermillion County, IL. Thomas and Jane were the parents to eight children: Sarah (1848-1849), Elizabeth Ann (1850-1850), Joseph (1852-1929), Margaret Langley-Jackson (1854-1898, she married James A. Jackson), Hellen Langley-McMillin-Young (1856-1928, she married Joseph Givins McMillin and then George Young), Clarissa Langley (1858-), Mary (?-1864) and Issabelle Jane "Jennie" Langley (1857-1913, who married Mack Tuttle).

Charles Langley (1831-1862) no issue. He died in Vermillion County, IL.

Casper James Langley (1835-1916) married Isabelle Anderson. Their children were Nora, Maggie, Hortense, Laura Belle and James Roscoe.

HOLTSHOUSER, MARY CARMEL, was born May 19, 1879 in Owensboro, KY. She was the eldest child of Henry Charles and Flagie Bellew-Holtshouser. Mary grew up in Owensboro surrounded by the Catholic cousins and family who had such an enormous impact on the spread of Catholicism to Western Kentucky. Mary Carmel married Charles Eugene Roberts who was from Union County, KY and they had two children: Mary Benita and Henry Ewell. Mary died Nov. 12, 1965 in St. Louis, MO and is buried in the Calvary Cemetery. Charles died Sept. 4, 1933 and is buried in Morganfield, KY at the St. Ann Catholic Cemetery.

Mary Benita Roberts was born Aug. 1, 1911 in Daviess County, KY. Benita was raised a strong Catholic and instilled this gracious gift to her children. Benita married Edward Bendon and they had three children who have blessed them with many grandchildren. They later relocated to St. Louis, MO. Edward died April 12, 1922 and is buried in Salem, MO where he and Benita retired a number of years ago. Benita remains there and is very active.

Charles Joseph Bendon was born Dec. 6, 1930 in St. Louis, MO. Charles married Imelda Ann Cowie and they had six children: Stephen Joseph, Charlene Marie (who married a Johnson), Pamela Jean (who married a McWilliams), JoAnn, Christopher Russell and Mary Teresa Bendon. Charlene has a child named Gabrielle who was born about 1983.

James Edward Bendon was born Jan. 29, 1935 in St. Louis, MO. He married Colleen Virginia Lay on Sept. 17, 1955. They have five children: Michelle Marie (married a Budzinski), Jeanine Carol (married a Mattconi), Suzanna Derinda (married a Wellerbrink), Dennie Edward and Timothy Jean Bendon.

Jane Frances Bendon was born Aug. 21, 1936 in St. Louis, MO. She was baptized in September of the same year at her families' Catholic church. Jane married Roland D. Fanning on May 25, 1957 in St. Louis, MO. Roland works for Lever Brothers, and Jane is a cook for the Walnut Grove School System. They have four children: Mark Joseph, Karen Marie, David Lee and John Edward.

Mark Joseph was born March 1, 1958 in St. Louis, MO and practices as an engineer. He married Denise Willen and they have three children: Mary Joseph Jr. (Sept. 28, 1983), Gregory F. (March 12, 1986) and Cory M. (March 11, 1989).

Karen Marie was born Aug. 24, 1959 and is a contract coordinator in the St. Louis area. She married Jerry Robertson June 16, 1984 in St. Louis.

David Lee was born Dec. 19, 1961 and is the plant manager for Image Printing. He married Donna Paule on March 31, 1984 and they have one son Christopher Fanning, born May 21, 1985.

John Edward was born Jan. 5, 1967 and works as an independent plumber. He married Denise Miller Sept. 29, 1990 in St. Louis.

HOLTSHOUSER, THOMAS THORNTON, was born June 21, 1855 in Nelson County, KY. He was the son of William Russell Holtshouser and Ann Lucretia Ballard and the grandson of John Holtzhouser and Elizabeth Heavenill.

Thomas was a devout Catholic. He met and married Anna Laura Clark, the daughter of Francis Marion Clark and Caroline Burch, in 1882 at the Saint Alphonsus Church in Saint Joseph, KY.

They had three children, William Alphonsus, Mary Olivia and Herbert. Mary Olivia became a nun. William married Mabel Agnes Lashbrook and they reared their family in Owensboro. Williams descendants are many and continue to carry on their Catholic faith.

Thomas, Ann, William and Mabel are buried in a family plot at Saint Andrew Cemetery in Owensboro.

HOLTSHOUSER, VALENTINE, was born in 1805 in Nelson County, KY. He was the fourth child of John Holtzhouser and Elizabeth Heavenhill. Valentine married Letitia Mahoney on April 18, 1836. Valentine died in

1897 and Letitia Mahoney in 1875. They attended St. Catherine Catholic Church in Nelson County, KY. Both are buried in Nelson County. Their children were:

Henry Casper (1837-1917). Casper is the name of Henry's third great-grandfather.

John Francis "Jack" (1838-1933) married first Zerelda Bassett and later a Matilda. John died in LaRue County, KY. His children were: Henry Valentine (1861) whose Baptismal sponsor was Louisa Hagan and the baptism occurred at the St. Catherine Catholic Church. The parish baptismal record spells the surname as Holtzhouser; John William (1863-); George William (1868-); Sarah Margaret (1868-); Mary Althea (1870-) who was also baptized at St. Catherine and her sponsor was Helen Wimsatt; Robert Chambige (unknown); Martha Ann (unknown); Lettitia (1877-); Richard E. (1880-); Fannie Eller (1885-1955) she married John Robert Skaggs and her descendents will be covered in another section; and Joseph Cleveland (1886-).

Mary Elizabeth (1842-1919) married Francis Uriah "Frank" Downs. She is buried in Nelson County although her children were born in Marion County, KY. Mary Elizabeth and Frank had eight children: Henry (1867-?), Mary L., Virginia (1873-?) who married Frank McGlothan, Ann L. (1875-?), John F. (1877-?), George B. (1879-?), Lizzie J. (1880-). Frank had a daughter from a first marriage named Josephine (born 1860).

Ruth Rebecca (1844-?) married Joseph S. Edwards.

William Harrison (1845-1865) served in the Civil War. He enlisted in June 1862 in Company K Sixth Regiment Cavalry. After his death his father collected a pension.

James William (1845-1911). His baptismal sponsor was Mary Louisa Clark at the Holy Cross Church in Nelson County. He was baptized on Feb. 27, 1845 by the Rev. Daniel Kelly.

George E. (1848-1932) was born in Nelson County. He married first Mary Barnes and then Ann Cissell. He had no children by either wife.

Susan Margaret (1849-?) was born in Nelson County, KY. She was baptized April 5, 1850 at the Holy Cross Catholic Church by Rev. A. Aud. Susan's baptismal sponsor was Nancy Hodgkins. She married Jack Ralph Nally Feb. 9, 1874 in Nelson County.

Charles Valentine (1854-1942) married Joyce Ann Saltsman on Nov. 12, 1883 in Larne, KY.

Mary Catherine (1855-) married Robert Nally, little else is known.

HOLTSHOUSER, WILLIAM ALPHONSUS II,

was born Nov. 30, 1905 in Owensboro, KY. He was the son of William Alphonsus Sr. and Mabel Agnes Lashbrook. William fell in love with Emma Catherine Mitchell. Emma was the daughter of John Edward and Mary Louise Mouser-Mitchell.

The Mitchell family has an interesting place in local Catholic history. Many were originally Baptist until the Civil War era. At that time there was a bloody fight in the Louisville area and it took the Bishop to encourage the people to put down their weapons for humanity. Several Mitchell families were so impressed with the bishop that they converted to Catholicism.

Emma and William reared their children in the Catholic faith. Emma could be found most anytime of day saying a Hail Mary or a rosary. They married Nov. 26, 1928 in Owensboro and immediately relocated to the St. Louis area. William had gotten a job as an aircraft builder for the now McDonnell Douglas Company and had moved there prior to their wedding.

Their first child was born in March of 1930. Emma had feared that since she did not become pregnant immediately after their wedding that she may be not able to bear children for William. In reality it was only one year and a half. She loved this child so much that she wanted to give it the family names of William and Spalding from her mother's and husband's long Catholic line. William and Emma Catherine were blessed with six wonderful children in all: William Spalding, Jean Ann, Elizabeth Louise, William Alphonsus III, James Edward and Joseph Lynn.

William Spalding was born March 27, 1930 in Owensboro, KY. He married Elaine Agnes Wellinghoff and they had three children: Steven Edward who was born in 1958; Robert Lewis who was born in 1961; and Becky Ann who was born in 1966. William Spalding is currently retired from McDonnell Douglas and resides in St. Louis close to his grandchildren.

Steven Edward married Ann Louise Bockelmann in St. Louis, MO. They are the parents of two lovely boys Michael Joseph (1987) and Matthew William (1989). Steven is an attorney with a practice in St. Louis.

Robert Lewis "Bobby" married Penny Kennedy and they have a son Andrew Thomas (1989). Robert was in the military and now resides in St. Louis with his family.

Becky Ann married Michael James Dunning. They have no children as of yet. In their spare time they have taken up genealogy and have done some interesting work on Michael's Dunning line.

Jean Ann was born June 19, 1932 in Daviess County, KY. She married Gilbert "Mick" Lewis Ambrow. Jean Ann and Mick have three children: Kevin Michael born 1959, Jackie Taylor born 1961 and Karen Lynn born 1957. They reside in a St. Louis suburb near their children.

Kevin Michael married Sharon Lee Deans. They have three wonderful children: Kevin Michael Jr. was born in 1985; John Lewis was born in 1987; and Diana Christine was born in 1990.

Jackie Taylor married Clemente Suraino. They resided for a while in Mexico and later relocated to Columbia, MO. They do not have any children yet.

Elizabeth Louise was born Jan. 19, 1934 in Daviess County, KY. The name Elizabeth Louise is a long traditional name among the Catholic "Spaldings" in Kentucky. Elizabeth married Jack Taylor Steele in 1954 in St. Louis. To this union five boys were born. Elizabeth is currently a medical transcriptionist who also does home day care. Jack is a family physician in St. Louis.

Mark Taylor was born April 17, 1956 in Coronado, CA. He was born there because his father Jack was completing a military assignment. Mark completed medical school and residency is now the chairman for the Emergency Medicine Program at Truman Medical Center in Kansas City, MO. Mark married Ginni Lynn Martino, a wonderful, petite Italian Catholic whose family also has a long Catholic history line, on April 23, 1988. Ginni is an obstetric nurse at a Kansas City hospital. They have had an exciting year! Alexander Taylor is a baby that they adopted who was born on Nov. 16, 1991. No more had the family gotten over that excitement when they found out that Ginni was expecting triplets! On June 20, 1992 Elizabeth Gabriele "Libby," Mallory Rae and Luke Gerard entered the world. Their good "Father" most certainly saw fit to bless this wonderful couple.

David Michael Steele was born Nov. 25, 1957 in St. Louis. He completed medical school and is residing in Madison, WI and completing a surgical residency. At this time he desires to further subspecialize in transplants. Michael married Mary Katherine Gowell, a dietician, and they have been blessed with three children: Michaela Marie was born June 24, 1989; Ann Elizabeth was born Nov. 9, 1990; and James Taylor was born March 8, 1992. All three children were baptized at St. Mary and Joseph Catholic Church in St. Louis on Sept. 5, 1992.

Jeffrey Scott Steele was born Feb. 28, 1960 in St. Louis. After completing medical school he entered the Navy for residency and subspecialized in cardiac anesthesia. While in medical school he met and married Diana Marie Craig, an ICU nurse, on Jan. 8, 1983 at Our Lady of Good Counsel Catholic Church in Kansas City by Fr. John Giacopelli. They relocated to the Washington, D.C. area in 1984 where their two children were born. Brian Christopher arrived Nov. 5, 1985. Brian made a long trek back to Kansas City when only a few weeks old to be baptized by Fr. John Giacopelli since he had married Brian's parents. Adam Joseph arrived May 1, 1990 and was baptized at St. Mary Catholic Church in Rockville, MD. In 1991, they relocated to Cape Girardeau, MO, where Jeff is employed at St. Francis Medical Center. Diana has put her career on hold until the baby enters school but remains busy with genealogy and community affairs. She has published for some local history books and is currently secretary for the Cape County Genealogical Society. She contributed the Holtshouser, some Spalding and allied family sections. Diana and Jeff discovered after relocating to Cape Girardeau that many Kentucky Catholic Spaldings are in their area. How exciting it has been for them to discover their cousins and share family history! Jeff and Diana are very active in their church, St. Vincent De Paul.

Brian and Adam Steele

John Thomas Steele was born March 15, 1962 in St. Louis, MO. John Thomas is a long name passed down among the Catholic Spaldings. John completed medical school and residency and is now employed for a hospital in Detroit, MI.

James Douglas Steele and Maggi Szylowski have a daughter Christine who was born July 30, 1991. Christine was baptized at the North American Martyrs Church in St. Louis. James is a CPA with Arthur Anderson, and Maggi is a pharmacist at De Paul Medical Center. *Submitted by Diana Steele.*

HOLTSHOUSER, WILLIAM APLHONSUS III,

was born Sept. 27, 1935 in Owensboro, KY. He was the second son of William Alphonsus I and Emma Catherine Mitchell. Imagine Emma Catherine's happiness at being blessed with a second son. The first to carry on her beloved family names of William and Spalding. Then another to carry on her spouses family names!

William "Bill" married Diana Bond Aug. 22, 1959 in Rockford, IL. They now reside in Manchester, NH and four children were blessed to their union: William Alphonsus IV, Stuart Macolm, Kent Mitchell and Susan Catherine who was named for her grandmother.

William Alphonsus Holtshouser IV was born Dec. 31, 1960 in St. Louis. He met and married JoMarie Sucato July 2, 1989. JoMarie is a wonderful Italian Catholic girl from an eastern shore family. William and she are expecting their first child in the fall of 1992. William is employed for IBM in New York.

Stuart Malcolm arrived June 13, 1963 in St. Louis. He met and married Kathleen Teresa Jacobson May 28, 1989 in Massachusetts. They are both employed near his parents home of Manchester.

Susan Catherine was born July 24, 1964 in St. Louis. She attended college in New Hampshire and relocated to the Washington, D.C. area. She plays hand bells in a church choir and sings at weddings. She has a splendid voice. In her spare time she also takes on musical roles with the area playhouses. Susan works for Allstate Insurance. *Submitted by Diana Steele.*

HOLTSHOUSER, WILLIAM ALPHONSUS SR.,

was born July 8, 1883 in Kentucky. He was the son of Thomas Thornton and Anna Laura Clark-Holtshouser. William's parents were married in the St. Alphonsus Catholic Church in Daviess County. The Alphonsus name has been carried out for four generations in this Kentucky Catholic family. William married Mabel Agnes Lashbrook (the daughter of John Samuel and Sophie Atherton-Lashbrook) July 26, 1904 in Kentucky. Mabel was born in Greencastle, IN, Aug. 5, 1883.

William and Mabel were blessed with three children: William Alphonsus II, James Kenneth, and Herbert Wendell. William reared his children in the Catholic faith and supported them financially by picking tobacco and being a factory laborer. William and Mabel raised their children in Owensboro.

Mabel died Dec. 18, 1958 and William followed her Sept. 14, 1970. They are both interred at the Mater Dolorosa Catholic Cemetery in Owensboro, KY although neither has a headstone marker. They are in the family plot with William's parents who do have markers. The author of these sections is currently taking donations from descendants to purchase two small markers for them.

William Alphonsus Holtshouser II was born Nov. 30, 1905 in Owensboro, KY. He married Emma Catherine Mitchell Nov. 26, 1928 in Owensboro. Their many descendants will be covered under his section.

James Kenneth Holtshouser was born Nov. 27, 1909 in Owensboro. He married Mary Lillian Sapp June 11, 1929 in Stanley, KY. James is buried in the Queen of Heaven Cemetery in Ft. Lauderdale, FL. His children are in his section.

Herbert Wendell Holtshouser was born about 1914 in Owensboro. Herbert married Florence Christensen, a Seventh Day Adventist. They resided in Owensboro for a while, but later relocated to Salt Lake City. They have six children: Barbara Ann, Wayne, Ruth, J.D., Richard and Jean.

HOLTSHOUSER, WILLIAM MARION, was born Sept. 5, 1845 in Marion County, KY. William was the second child of William Russell and Ann Lucretia Ballard-Holtshouser. He was baptized on Dec. 9, 1845 at the Holy Cross Catholic Church. William married May 4, 1867 Mary Bethania Greenwell (the daughter of Samuel and Julia Ann Ball-Greenwell, 1849-1886) and fathered seven children: William, John, Susanna, Mary, Cora, Frances and Ada Jane.

William farmed locally there his entire life and attended Saint Catherine Catholic Church. He and Mary are buried at Saint Francis, KY.

William Hilary was born April 16, 1868 in New Haven, KY. He was baptized June 2, 1868 at Saint Catherine Catholic Church by Father DeMeulder where his sponsor was Julia Greenwell.

John was born Feb. 22, 1870 and was baptized April 10, 1870 at Saint Catherines Catholic Church by Father DeMeulder. Little else is known except that his sponsors were John Tennelley and Julia Greenwell.

Susanna Margaret was born Oct. 13, 1872 in New Haven, KY. She was baptized Nov. 25, 1872 at the Saint Catherine Catholic Church in New Haven. She later married George Thomas Mattingly on Sept. 26, 1893 at the Saint Vincent De Paul Catholic Church. Susanna died April 4, 1953 and is buried in the Saint Francis Cemetery.

Mary Alice was born May 11, 1876 and baptized June 25, 1876 at Saint Vincent De Paul Catholic Church. Mary Alice first married Robert Theodore Nevitt and later Edward G. Mattingly.

Cora Frances was born March 23, 1878 in Nelson County. Her baptismal date is noted as March 31, 1878 at the Saint Vincent De Paul Catholic Church in New Hope. She married Washington Watson.

Frances Sidney was born April 18, 1882 in Nelson County, KY. He was baptized May 20, 1882 at Saint Vincent De Paul Catholic Church.

Ada Jane was born in Nelson County also. Little else is known except that she married a McDaniel.

HOLTSHOUSER, WILLIAM RUSSELL, was the sixth child of John HoltShouser and Elizabeth Heavenhill. William was born March 2, 1822 in Nelson County. He first married Ann Lucretia Ballard (the daughter of John Ballard and Elizabeth Nally 1822-1876) on June 25, 1842 in Nelson County by the Rev. Robert Byrne. William and Ann had nine children.

After Ann's death, William Russell remarried Martha Mudd (the daughter of John Thomas Mudd and Ann Ellen Nancy Queen 1839-1919) on Aug. 1, 1876 in Nelson County, KY.

A few sources also add a child named John as the 10th child of Ann and William although at present a record cannot be located to indicate this.

William and Ann's children: Ann Minerva has a birth date of April 16, 1843. She was born in Nelson County. There is a reported wedding date for her of Dec. 14, 1862 but unknown spouse at present.

William "Marion" Holtshouser was born Sept. 5, 1845 in Marion County, KY. He was baptized Dec. 9, 1845 at the Holy Cross Catholic Church. He married Mary Berthania Greenwell and their descendants are covered under his name.

Mary Lucretia was born Aug. 31, 1849. She was baptized Jan. 22, 1850 at the Holy Cross Catholic Church and her sponsor was R.C. Reid. After Lucretia's death Mr. Reid married two more times.

Henry Charles was born in August of 1852. Henry married Flagie Bellew on May 28, 1878 at the St. Stephen Cathedral in Owensboro, KY. They had two children: Mary Carmel and Joseph William.

Mary Carmel was born May 19, 1879 in Daviess County, KY. She married Charles Eugene Roberts. Charles died Sept. 4, 1933 in Morganfield, KY and is buried in the St. Ann Catholic Cemetery there. Mary Carmel died Nov. 12, 1965 in St. Louis, MO and is buried in the Calvary Cemetery. Their children will be discussed in another section.

Joseph William was born April 13, 1883 in Owensboro, KY. He married Bertha Ann Freels. Their children were raised in Los Angeles, CA and they are buried in the Forest Lane Cemetery. Their children will be covered in their section.

Thomas Thornton was born June 21, 1855. Thomas died as a fairly young father on Nov. 21, 1890. His baptismal sponsor was Mary Jane Brewer. He married Anna Laura Clark (the daughter of Francis Marion Clark and Caroline Burch (1860-1906) Feb. 20, 1882 in St. Joseph, KY at the St. Alphonsus Catholic Church. The St. Alphonsus Church must have had some very personal importance to this couple as they named one of their children William Alphonsus. The name William Alphonsus has been carried out to date for four consecutive generations of this Catholic family. Thomas was buried in the Mater Dolorosa Cemetery in the St. Andrew section. Their children were: William Alphonsus (1883-1970), Mary Olivia (1886-) who married Jessie Lee Gillespie) and Herbert Holtshouser (1889-).

After his death Anna remarried Frank W. Hazel (1859-? died in Louisville) a bookstore salesman. They had three children: Charles D. (1897-? who married Mary O'Brian), Mary Pauline (1895-?) and Lillian Hazel (1903-?). Lillian entered the convent at Mount St. Joseph, Maple Mount, KY. After Anna's death the children were placed among family members and he was noted to be residing with his brother Ralph in Louisville for the 1920 census.

Mary Helen was born April 18, 1858 in Balltown, KY. She married Charles Gregory Raphael Ferriell on May 7, 1884. Mary and Charles were the parents of five children: Nellie (1887-1970), Joseph (1889-1953), John W. (1891-), Mary Stella (1886-1970) and Herbert Ferriell (1895-1950). Mary, her spouse and children are all buried in the St. Francis of Assisi Catholic Cemetery. Charles was the son of John Cary Cerriell and Eliza A. Greenwell. John W. married Mary Frances Smith and they had a daughter Sarah. Herbert married Mary Lyons with unknown issue.

Francis was born June 11, 1860 and there is a baptismal date for him of Aug. 15, 1860.

Sidney has a date of birth from the 1860 census as 1859 although there are no other records. He must have died as a child and is probably in the St. Francis of Assisi Cemetery in the family plot.

Ann Elizabeth (1847-1941) was baptized on Nov. 11, 1847 at the Holy Cross Catholic Church. Her sponsor was Elizabeth Ballard. Ann married Pius Proctor Ballard on May 7, 1867 in Marion County, KY with the Rev. Francis Wuyts officiating. Ann and Pius had five children: Mary Louisa was born July 25, 1868 in Marion County. Her baptism was recorded on Aug. 23, 1868 at the Holy Mary Catholic Church by Rev. Wuyts. She never married and died June 14, 1885. Mary is buried at St. Francis, KY. Fannie was born in May of 1870. She married Dee Simons and had two children, Walter and Mary. Fannie died in Louisville, KY. Nicholas G. (1874-1960) married Josephine Barren. They had two children Ken and Leonard. Nicholas was buried in the Holy Cross Cemetery. William Bernard (1876-1931) never married. He died and was buried in Knoxville, TN. George Leo (1878?) married Regina Greenwell. They had a daughter named Bernadine Ballard. Regina died Oct. 30, 1952. Bernadine married Kenneth Johnson and she later died Aug. 24, 1960.

After the death of Ann Lucretia, William Russell remarried Martha Mudd. Their two children were: Josie Lee (1877-1977) was born in Nelson County on May 27, 1877. She married in Nelson County on Feb. 10, 1903 Charles Thomas Head. Her descendants are covered in a separate section. Charles (1873-1921) was buried in the St. Thomas Cemetery in Nelson County. Josie lived a month short of her 100th birthday. Our Blessed Father most certainly gave her a productive life! Josie was buried in the Calvary Cemetery in Louisville, KY.

William Russell Holtshouser Jr. (1881-1941) was born on May 25, 1881 in Balltown, Nelson County. William enlisted in the Army and was involved in the Philippine insurrection and World War I.

William Russell, Ann Lucretia and Martha are all buried in the St. Thomas Catholic Church Cemetery in Nelson County, KY.

HOOD, JOSEPH DOUGLAS, was born Dec. 24, 1939 in Philpot, Daviess County, KY, son of Newell J. Hood and Mary B. Hardesty. He married Dorothy Cecil who was born Feb. 20, 1940 in Owensboro on June 24, 1961. They have five children: Tracy Marie (1965), Kathryn Lynn (1966), David M. (1968), Mary Ann (1973), Paul Joseph (1976). Paul is the only child now at home. J.D. Hood is an accountant for Wetterau in Greenville, and Dorothy is a housewife and student at nursing college. They are members of St. Joseph Church in Central City, past members of St. Mary of the Woods in Whitesville. Past president of St. Joseph Parish Council and past president of St. Joseph School Board and choir. Also served as president for Greenville Kiwanis.

HOOD, NEWELL JUSTIN AND MARY BERNICE HARDESTY, were married at St. Paul Rectory on Jan. 13, 1934 by Rev. James F. Norman. They were very proud parents of 11 children-five sons and six daughters, all of whom live productive lives. Justin and Bernice were also blessed with 37 grandchildren and 28 great-grandchildren.

Newell Justin and Mary Bernice Hood

Justin supported his family by dairy farming. He was very proud of the fact that all of his children were educated in Catholic schools. They were members of St. Mary of the Woods Parish in Whitesville. Justin expired on Jan. 9, 1992 and was buried on their 58th Wedding Anniversary.

HOSKINS, ROBERT MARTIN SR., was born in Owensboro, KY and baptized at St. Joseph Church by Fr. Braun. His father, Bernard Raymond Hoskins, was from Owensboro and married Mary Martina Flanagan. Bernard and Martina Hoskins had three other children. Robert graduated from Owensboro Catholic High School in 1954 and attended Brescia College for two years receiving an associate degree and a BS in pharmacy from Duquesne University in 1959. Marylou Stine Hoskins married Robert Martin Hoskins Sr. on July 27, 1963. Marylou's parents are the late Carlton Lee Stine and Martha Regina Graham Stine of Monongahela, PA. Marylou graduated from Duquesne University Pharmacy School.

Robert Martin Hoskins Sr. family

Robert and Marylou Hoskins have four children. The oldest, Robert Martin Jr., graduated from OCHS in 1982. He graduated from United States Naval Academy in 1987. He is currently serving aboard the USS *Abraham Lincoln.*

Maryann Hoskins graduated from Apollo High School in 1984. She graduated from Tulane University in 1988. She received her law degree from Tulane in 1991. Maryann is currently practicing insurance defense litigation in New Orleans, LA.

Marylou Hoskins Jr. graduated from OCHS in 1986. She attended Samford Pharmacy School in Birmingham, where she is a candidate for a bachelor of science degree in pharmacy in 1993.

Carlton Lee Hoskins graduated from OCHS in 1989. He is a third year student at the United States Air Force Academy in Colorado Springs, CO. He is a candidate for a Bachelor of Science degree in May 1994.

Robert and Marylou Hoskins own Lincoln Pharmacy located in Owensboro, KY. They are parishioners of Our Lady of Lourdes Church, where their youngest three children were baptized.

HOSTETTER, FATHER LARRY,

was born in Nuernberg, West Germany. He is the son of Paul and Ann Cummings of Hopkinsville, KY. He and his family have lived in many places during his father's career with the military including: Arizona, Oklahoma, Germany and finally Kentucky.

Fr. Larry and his family moved to Kentucky in 1975 after his father was stationed at Ft. Campbell. He started the ninth grade at Hopkinsville High School and graduated in 1979. From there he went to Western Kentucky University. He stayed for two years; but during that time he felt the stirrings of a call to the priesthood. Being involved with the Newman Center, he consulted Fr. Bill Allard who encouraged him to pursue this vocation.

Fr. Larry Hostetter

During his junior year in college, Fr. Larry went to St. Pius X Seminary where he received his bachelors degree. From there he went to the Pontifical College Josephinum until he was ordained in 1987.

His first assignment was Our Lady of Lourdes in Owensboro. During these first two years he also taught at Brescia College in the Ministry Formation Program. His next assignment was at Blessed Mother Church in Owensboro which lasted only one year. He was then assigned to teach at Owensboro Catholic High School. During his third year at OCHS in 1992, Fr. Larry was also given the privilege of serving as pastor of St. Augustine Church in Reed.

HOWARD, ARNOLD AND ETHEL (NEE SHIVELY),

grew up in Daviess County. They were married Feb. 1, 1921 in St. Mary of the Woods Catholic Church with Monsignor Hugh O'Sullivan officiating. Ten children were born to them: Mary Josephine (Mrs. Naseeb L. Shory), Mildred Genevieve, James Leon, Eileen Marie (Sr. Eileen, OSU), Ita Isabelle, Robert Carl, Charles Elbert, Daniel Eugene, Michael Lee and Brice Dean. Ethel, age 91, still lives in the home place. Arnold died Aug. 3, 1969.

Church and school activities played an important role in this young family's life. Often, after Sunday Mass, kinfolk would gather at someone's home where a feast was shared in by all. Later, adults would play cards, while the children enjoyed various games with their cousins.

Arnold and Ethel Howard (nee Shively)

Farm life was hard in those days, but happy. Summers brought relief from school work, but meant hard field work and gathering and canning of garden produce. In Autumn, hungry children arriving home from school might find ginger bread, prepared by Mother, and fresh milk to eat and drink. Winter work days included: slaughtering and curing meats, feeding and milking cows, getting coal for a stove and other chores, but winter evenings were cozy. At a warm fireplace, stories were told of the day's happenings; at the kitchen table, after dishes were cleared away, school work was prepared by the light of a kerosene lamp, while Mother worked on a patch work quilt and Dad often popped corn. The coming of spring saw the children shedding their long stockings and long pants and walking barefoot! The entire family planted the garden and little feet ran after Dad as he plowed the soil for sowing the crops. Bird songs rode the wind and occasionally, a young rabbit would run from its grassy shelter. In any season, life in this household was never dull!

HOWARD, BRICE DEAN,

was born Aug. 18, 1946, the youngest of 10 children of Arnold Howard and Ethel Shively, was baptized at St Mary of the Woods Church, Whitesville, KY.

Marilyn Dorothy Reteneller, born Sept. 21, 1948, the third of four children and only daughter of Charles Reteneller and Aurelia Englert, was baptized at St. Martin of Tours Church, Louisville, KY.

Brice D. Howard Family

Brice and Marilyn were married April 20, 1974 at St. Martin of Tours in Louisville, KY.

They have four children, three boys and a girl. Lorin Matthew was born Nov. 30, 1975 and Kevin Nicholas born Dec. 6, 1976, were baptized at St. Stephen Cathedral, Owensboro. Jonett Marie, born Jan. 31, 1981, was baptized at St. Joseph and Paul in Owensboro. Iaian Patrick born Sept. 17, 1983, was baptized at Blessed Mother in Owensboro.

Brice served in the U.S. Army. He served one year in Vietnam. Today he is very active in many veteran organizations.

Marilyn taught religion at Owensboro Catholic High School from 1972-74, and is currently studying to be an elementary teacher.

The children are very involved in many school activities. The older three play in their school's band. The youngest expresses an interest in playing percussion when he becomes old enough.

The family now belongs to St. Joseph and Paul Church, Owensboro where they take a very active role in many ministries.

HOWARD, CELESTINE EDWIN,

was born in Whitesville, KY, and baptized by Fr. Hugh O'Sullivan. He is the son of Ivo L. Howard who was a rural mail carrier and farmer. His mother Mary Maudwina Higdon was born and raised in the St. Lawrence, KY area.

Margaret Louise Boarman was born in Philpot, KY, her father, Francis Lawrence Boarman, and mother, Mary Regina Hamilton, were farmers and lived in the Philpot area.

Celestine and Louise were married on Nov. 23, 1943 in St. Mary of the Woods Church in Whitesville by the brother of the bride Fr. Victor C. Boarman.

Celestine and Margaret Louise Howard

They are parents of eight children, five daughters and three sons all born near Whitesville. All eight attended and completed grade and high school at St. Mary's. They have 23 grandchildren and one great-grandchild. Celestine and Louise will celebrate their 50th Wedding Anniversary on Nov. 23, 1993.

HOWARD, CHARLES KEVIN,

was born Feb. 25, 1910 near Whitesville, Daviess County, KY. His father was Joseph Patrick Howard and his mother was Anna Stella Mattingly. They were farmers and members of the St. Mary Catholic Church in Whitesville. Kevin was member of the Boys Society, the Holy Name Society and the Temperance Society.

Kevin married Mary Myrtle Coomes of St. Lawrence, Daviess County, KY. She was born on May 8, 1911 and was the daughter of Joseph I. Coomes and Clara O'Bryan of St. Lawrence, KY. They were members of the St. Lawrence Catholic Church Parish and were farmers. The Rev. F.X. Laemmele officiated at Kevin and Myrtle's wedding on Feb. 10, 1931.

Kevin and his wife had six children with five born near Whitesville and the sixth in Owensboro. They were both farmers until 1942. He began working as an aviation parts clerk, in wholesale grocery services, then in auto assembly. In 1956 he began employment with American Tobacco Company in Owensboro and retired from there in 1975.

Myrtle worked at St. Joseph School cafeteria as a cook for two years. Later she worked as a furniture upholsterer seamstress. She retired from Whitehall Furni-

The Charles Kevin and Mary Myrtle Howard Family

ture Inc. in 1976. She believed in the rosary and found strength and peace in praying the beads. She died on May 21, 1985.

Kevin is a member of the Immaculate Parish of Owensboro and resides at his home alone. He still attends Mass regularly at the age of 82. He has six living children, 17 grandchildren, and 14 great-grandchildren. The children of Charles Kevin and Mary Myrtle Howard are: Mary Kevin Hermann, Charles Gilbert Howard, Joseph Carl Howard, Wilma Marie Dobric, Doris Jean Schwartz and Joyce Ann Lane.

HOWARD, DANIEL AND SUE,

and their family are life-long members of St. Mary of the Woods Parish in Whitesville. They have six grown children and 17 grandchildren. Dan is a son of Arnold and Ethel Shively Howard. Ethel, at age 91 still lives on the family farm at Whitesville. Arnold died in 1969. Sue is the daughter of O.J. and Catherine Duvall Hagan, both deceased.

After the completion of high school, Dan went to work in several diverse areas. First as a factory worker; after being laid off he went to work with a local oil drilling company. In 1959 he went to work at the Glenn Funeral Home, working there for seven years as a funeral director. In 1966 he worked at G.E. in Owensboro, until 1970 when he began work at Alcoa, where he is still employed.

Sue is a homemaker as well as being on the Altar Society, telephone committee and a lector.

The Daniel and Sue Howard Family

Dan and Sue have been on the RCIA team for the past few years as well as being members of several different prayer groups, both in their parish and other parishes.

They have been blessed by being able to participate in many different enrichment programs over the years. Some of these include: Marriage Encounter, Parish Renewal, Cursillo and Life in the Spirit Seminars. When Renew was offered in the diocese they were participants as well as team leaders. All of these have helped to bring the faith alive for them.

Being part of the Catholic faith community is something they thank God for daily.

HOWARD, DAVID AND MARY ANN,

were married on April 12, 1947 at St. Lawrence Church. They have 15 children: Donna, Melvin, Norman, Nick, Pat, John, Cathy, Joe, Roberta, Bernadette, Jane, Susan, George, Christine and Scott. All have graduated from Catholic schools. Twelve attended Brescia College; nine graduated from Brescia. Five have graduate degrees; three are teachers. All are still living.

David, a Navy veteran of World War II and a Kentucky Colonel, was picnic chairman for seven years at St. Mary's. He served the St. Vincent De Paul Society for 35 years, and was secretary and treasurer of the Owensboro Diocesan Central Council of SVDP. Mary Ann has donated many quilts to the parish and served the parish Ladies Altar Society. David was a member of the short-lived Diocesan School Board under Monsignor Hill in 1969. He also served as a fund raiser for Mercy Hospital in 1946.

David and Mary Ann have had three children serving in Diocesan Ministry positions at a parish and at the Catholic Pastoral Center. They had 10 children in parochial school at one time. Mel, the oldest son, is the founding editor of the *Western Kentucky Catholic*. Norman, third child, was one of the first four graduates from the Brescia Ministry Formation Program. Nick, fourth oldest, is the Assistant Grand Knight of the Owensboro Council 817 of the KCs.

Scott, Cathy, Janie, Susie, Chris, Nick, John, Joe, Norman, George, Melvin, Roberta, Bernadette, David, Mary Ann, Donna and Pat.

David and Mary Ann have 27 grandchildren: Julie, Mel's daughter, was a youth delegate to the 1991 Diocesan Synod.

David and Mary Ann have been a tithing family from the first week of their marriage. Strong believers in stewardship, they have always made sure their children contributed to the support of the church and found some way to serve in church ministry as children and as adults.

HOWARD, FRED AND ALICE,

family have lived in Whitesville all their lives. They were married June 26, 1965. Baptized Charles Frederick, he is the son of the late John Gerald and Hannak Mary Hamilton Howard. His wife, nee Alice Marie Aud, is the daughter of the late John Wellington (Weck) and Maud Dowell Leibfried Aud.

They have two children, David Allen Howard and Rachel Marie Howard. Both are graduates of St. Mary of the Woods Grade School and Trinity High School. Rachel graduated from Western Kentucky University. David served two years in the U.S. Army and completed the mechanics course at Daviess County Vocational School.

Fred, Alice, Howard, David and Rachel

Fred and Alice graduated from St. Mary of the Woods High School. They are active life-long members of St. Mary of the Woods Parish. Fred served three years in the U.S. Marine Corps and worked for over 30 years at H.R. Grace. Alice received a B.A. from Brescia and an M.A. from Western Kentucky University and has been a teacher in the diocese of Owensboro for over 25 years.

HOWARD, JAMES WALLACE AND MARJORIE,

were married at St. Anthony's June 21, 1958. Wallace is the son of the later Patrick M. and Xaveria Coomes Howard of St. Mary's in Whitesville.

Marjorie is the daughter of the late John Chissom and Elizabeth Howard Chissom of St. Anthony's, Browns Valley.

Wallace is a draftsman at Southwire, Hawesville. Marjorie is a sales associate at Bacon's, Owensboro. Both are life-long residents of Daviess County, KY. They have two daughters. Cheri Denice born April 7, 1960 is a graduate of Indiana School of Optometry and is practicing in Bloomington, IN. She is married to James F. Bohrer, a son of Max and Anna Roth Bohrer of New Albany, IN. Jeanna Marie born Nov. 10, 1963 is a graduate of Brescia and is a sales representative for Livingston Laboratories. She lives in Owensboro and is a member of St. Anthony's.

HOWARD, JOHN PHILLIP,

was the son of David Albert Howard and Frances Jane Christian. He was born June 30, 1878 near Whitesville, KY. He married Ola Stout May 7, 1907 and they reared four children-Alma, Pascal, Stanley and Anna Tom. John Philip helped build the old Catholic school, the barn where Monsignor Hugh O'Sullivan housed his horse "Old Laytail."

John Phillip was the son of David Albert Howard who married Frances Jane Christian in 1847 and they had nine children. Albert Howard was the son of Aloysius. Aloysius was married twice. He first married Mary Margaret Thompson and they had eight children-five boys and three girls. After her death, he married Martha Ann Shanks and this marriage produced three boys and seven girls. Aloysius moved to Marion County, KY from Virginia in time to have sons in both the Union Army as well as the Confederate Army. Personal feelings were so deep that the family never got back together after the war.

Stanley is the son of John Phillip and Ola. He was baptized by Monsignor Hugh O' Sullivan and was married Aug. 24, 1937 to Lorene Phillips of Whitesville by Monsignor O'Sullivan. This union produced three children-Mendel, Sheril and Lovella. Stanley worked his way through the University of Kentucky during the Depression and worked 30 years for the University of Kentucky and the Federal Extension Service before retiring. He has lived on a farm in Todd County since 1953. Stanley worked closely with Bishop Soenneker in establishing a Catholic Church in Elkton which is now known as St. Susan's and his two sons and their families attend church there. His son, Sheril, was selected to serve on St. Susan's first Pastoral Council. Stanley is presently serving on Pastoral Council. The present pastor is Father John Brown.

HOWARD, MEL AND BEV, were married at St. Joseph Church in Leitchfield on May 15, 1971 with Rev. William Field officiating. Both graduated from Brescia College in 1971, and both earned masters degrees to be teachers. Bev teaches students with learning problems in the Owensboro Catholic High School Learning Center, and was its founding teacher. Mel taught in high school for 14 years, and in 1985 became the founding editor of *The Western Kentucky Catholic,* Owensboro Diocesan newspaper. He is the member of the bishop's staff as director of communications.

Mel and Bev graduated from Catholic schools. She graduated from Grayson County Catholic High School in 1967 and from Brescia College in 1971. Mel graduated from St. Thomas Seminary in 1969 as a college sophomore and then attended Brescia College, graduating in 1971.

Mel and Bev have four children, all in Catholic schools in Whitesville. Julie graduates from Trinity High School in 1993. Ben is a sophomore at Trinity in 1992. Paul and Luke attend St. Mary Elementary.

Ben, Julie, Paul, Mel, Luke and Bev

Mel and Bev live on his grandfather's farm in Whitesville, and invite members of the J.L. and Mary Elve Howard family back to the homeplace for reunions. Keeping the continuity of the family history alive into the present and the future is important for the 130 plus descendants of J.L. and Mary Elve. Family ties are strong in the Howards.

Bev, Julie, Ben and Paul are members of the St. Mary's Youth Group, and are lectors at Mass. Luke also reads at Mass. Mel has been a parish musician on and off since 1969.

Mel is the second oldest of David and Mary Ann Howard's 15 children in Whitesville, and Bev is the second oldest of Daymon and Audrey Clemons' 11 children from Leitchfield, KY.

HOWARD, MYRON, was born in 1904 at Ralph, KY in Ohio County the oldest of two children to Ira and Laura Moseley Howard. He was baptized at Bell's Run Baptist Church. He attended Ohio County grade and high schools and attended Western Kentucky University for three and one-half years studying agriculture and education from 1926 to 1931 working his way through college. Myron taught school in Ohio County for 30 years and farmed all his life. He married Ethel Clark in 1929 and had one son, Billy. After she died, Myron married Juanita Sharp and had one son, Ira. After she died, Myron married his present wife, Georgia, a widow whose two former husbands, Arthur York and Wesley Teague, died. Georgia has four children, Annita, Carl, Martin and Joe.

Georgia is a Minister of Praise at St. Mary of the Woods Parish in Whitesville. Though not a Catholic, Myron comes to Mass with Georgia and shares with her activities of the parish. Both are 88 years old and retired, still living on their farm in Ohio County.

Georgia's parents were George William and Provie Narcissus Boarman of Whitesville. She is the seventh of nine children of the Boarman family. Baptized at St. Mary of the Woods, she was confirmed and received First Communion at St. Mary's. She attended Taylorfield School in Ohio County up to the eighth grade. Georgia has been a homemaker through her adult life.

Myron and Georgia are still active in their garden and though they rent out most of their farm, they continue to manage the land. Their work running the family farm, visiting their neighbors and continuing to be hospitable to people who come to their home make up much of their day. They share what they have with those who ask.

HOWARD, STEWART AND JOYCE, Stewart was born in Whitesville, the oldest son of Romanus and Della Mae Howard, the second child in the family of 13 children all living except one, Mitchell, who died in a car accident in 1968.

Joyce was born in Center Line, MI, the daughter of Viola and Harles Payne, originally from St. Lawrence and Knotsville area. They moved to Michigan to find work during the depression years. When Harles was killed by a car in 1944, Viola brought her family back to her home town to raise.

Stewart graduated from St. Mary School, Whitesville (1957). Joyce graduated from St. William School, Knotsville. She met her future husband through friends. They married Aug. 8, 1959 at St. Lawrence the church where her mom and dad said their vows many years ago. This made their wedding day special for her. Stewart said having Dr. Day was special because he was one of the first babies Dr. Day delivered when he came to Whitesville.

Stewart and Joyce Howard

Stewart and Joyce have five children: Bobby Howard who lives in Knotsville with his wife Donna Hayden and three children, Dusty, Lacey and Shawn; Denise who is their special child lived at home until she reached 30 and moved into independent living program in Owensboro; David who lives in Owensboro has two children, Brittany and Matt; Tina lives in Chicago with her husband Jody Carmack; Kimberly is a senior at Catholic High where all the Stewart children graduated except Denise, and she from Daviess County.

Stewart is an electrician at Willamette, IN and Joyce is an antique dealer. They are members of St. Pius X Church.

HOWARD, VIRGINA RUTH WHELAN, was born at St. Joseph, KY, May 23, 1919, and baptized at St. Alphonsus Church by her uncle, Fr. James Louis Whelan, pastor. Her parents were Florence Eugenia Neel and Joseph Leslie Whelan. She is the sixth child in a family of eight: Francis (who died at the age of 1 year), James Francis, Robert Vincent (both deceased), Mary deChantal, William Thomas, Charles Aloysius and James Louis.

Ruth attended St. Alphonsus Parochial School and graduated from Mount St. Joseph Academy in 1936 and attended Mt St. Joseph Junior College. While in college she attended the installation ceremonies of Bishop Francis R. Cotton, the first bishop of the newly created Owensboro Diocese. St. Stephen Cathedral was crowded and because Ruth was small, the usher sat her in the middle aisle. Because of her aisle seat, she was the only one in her group who saw any of the ceremonies.

Ruth was married to Thomas R. Howard on March 28, 1940 at St. Alphonsus Church by Fr. Robert A. Whelan, her first cousin. The couple lived for awhile in Evansville, IN, Henderson, KY, Cincinnati, OH and finally settled in Dayton, OH where their only son Thomas Howard Jr. was born Dec. 20, 1940.

Family of Ruth Whelan Howard, left to right: Thomas Howard, husband; granddaughter Christine; Ruth (Whelan) Howard; grandson, Thomas Joseph; Agnes (Geiger) Howard, daughter-in-law; and Thomas Howard Jr., son.

Thomas Jr. attended Chaminade High School and graduated from Dayton University. He married Mary Agnes Geiger. They have two children, Thomas Joseph and Christine Marie, both of whom are now graduated from college and are living in Dayton, OH and Toledo, OH.

When Ruth and Thomas Howard retired in Dayton, OH, they lived for awhile in Hawaii, but eventually moved back to Kentucky and are now living in Draffenville. Ruth is a member of St. Pius Tenth Church at Calvert City.

HOWE, HERMAN ABRAHAM, second of 12 children, born Feb. 27, 1930, of Joseph Herman and Bertha Mae McPherson Howe wed Mary Florence Morris, twin, ninth of 16 children, born May 11, 1927, of Joseph Benedict and Emma Dale Johnson Morris, at St. Mary of the Woods Church, Whitesville, KY, by Fr. Martin Nahstoll on Nov. 11, 1950.

With Mary working at General Electric and Herman at Servel and Glenmore Distillery, they rented a small house near Herbert, KY, where their first child of 13 was born. Together they built their first home on 11185 KY 764. While Herman attended vocational school as a electrician and later retired as an electrician from North American; they purchased 45 acres adjacent to their home, raising tobacco and pigs for slaughter on Thanksgiving Day, as was traditional for the Morris'.

Herman and Mary Howe

Throughout their faith-filled years, Mary chose to dedicate her life as a full-time wife and mother having all children baptized at St. Mary of the Woods. They faced the loss of a son, age 8 through open heart surgery, and a daughter three years later, died from third degree burns. The remaining 11 children all graduates of Trinity High with eight marrying and bringing 27 grandchildren.

Herman and Mary celebrated their 42nd Wedding Anniversary Nov. 11, 1992. They still live at their home in Whitesville and attend Mass at St. Mary of the Woods.

HUGHES, JAMES CHARLES AND BARBARA DUKE, were married Jan. 10, 1953 in Memphis, TN by Bishop Kearney. Charles was born in Philadelphia, PA, raised in Graves County, KY. He is the son of William E. and Dorothy Morris Hughes. Barbara was born in Graves County, raised there and still lives there. They are members of St. Joseph Parish in Mayfield, KY.

James Charles and Barbara Duke Hughes

Charles and Barbara's children are: Charles Michael born Jan. 7, 1954; Thomas William born July 26, 1955; Stephen Mark born Aug. 14, 1956; Kathy Marie born Sept. 20, 1958; and Barbara Rene born Dec. 1, 1967. They have 10 grandchildren.

HUGHES, PETER E., was born on Feb. 13, 1950 in Johnstown, PA. He was the fourth son of James and Margaret (nee Michinock) Hughes. His father James was born in Glasgow, Scotland, and his mother Margaret was born in Berlin, PA. His maternal grandparents came to the United States from Croatia, Yugoslavia. At the age of 2, his family moved to Cleveland, OH where he attended both parochial and public schools. He graduated from high school in 1968, attended Cleveland State University for a few years, and moved to New York City. It was from New York, that he applied for admission to the seminary of St. Mary's in St. Mary, KY. After a year at St. Mary's, he applied to Bishop Henry Soenneker for permission to study for the Diocese of Owensboro. A year later he was accepted as a seminarian of the Diocese. With the closing of St. Mary's, he was assigned to the seminary of St. Pius X in Erlanger, where he completed his senior year. His next assignment was to the Pontifical College Josephinum, in Worthington, OH. While at the Josephinum, he was a student member of the board of trustees. He was ordained in 1980 to the Diaconate by the Apostolic Delegate, Archbishop Jean Jadot; and a year later he was ordained to the priesthood by Bishop Soenneker. His first pastoral assignment was to Our Lady of Lourdes, and after four years he was next assigned to St. Rose of Lima, in Cloverport, and also to the faculty of St. Romuald High School. It was also during this time that Bishop McRaith asked him to take on the pastorate of St. Mary of the Woods Parish in McQuady. In all he spent five years in Breckinridge County. In June of 1990, he was transferred to St. Paul Parish in Princeton, and assigned as the Chaplain of the Catholic Correctional Complex, in Fredonia. It was during his work with the inmates at the state penitentiary that his convictions of being against the death penalty became stronger, and in 1991 became a member of the Diocesan Commission for the Right to Life. In June of 1992, Fr. Pete became pastor of St. Leo Parish in Murray, KY.

Peter E. Hughes

Fr. Pete's call to priesthood came early in life, and was encouraged by his family, and after years of preparation and prayer, they celebrated with joy his first Mass at the Church of the Immaculate in Owensboro. His first Mass was also a celebration of his roots, his great-aunt read one of the readings in Croation, and his uncle from Scotland played his bagpipes. Throughout his priesthood, Fr. Pete's love has been the church, and the people that he serves; he refers to himself as a "people-oriented" person. For relaxation he reads, and when time permits, loves to cook Chinese food, or do cross stitch.

HUNT, JESSE AND ANNETTE, Annette was the fifth child of Tillie and Hervie Toon. She was born on Nov. 29, 1931. Her first year she attended Sharon School, close to the Toon home. She was too small to walk the three and one-half miles to St. Charles. When she was old enough to attend second grade she went to St. Charles School. She attended Cunningham High School.

Jesse Hunt was the sixth child of Wash and Eulalia Hunt. He was born on Aug. 23, 1929. He attended Cunningham Elementary and high school. He managed the basketball team in 1947. That same year Annette began high school, but he did not notice her, she was only a green freshman. In 1948, they began dating. On Feb. 22, 1949 they were married at St. Charles Church. They have two children, Phyllis and Ricky. They also have four grandchildren. Kimberly and Matthew Hunt; and Leanne and Eric Ricciardi.

Jesse and Annette Hunt

Annette joined the Cunningham Homemaker's Club in 1949. In 1956 the club got so large they decided to start a young mother's club. It was called the Thrifty Club and Annette continues to be a member today. She has been a homemaker for 43 years.

Jesse and Annette are both members of St. Charles Church. Both have volunteered in work at the church, school and 4-H, as well as in the Cunningham community. Jesse and Annette are dairy farmers.

Annette began milking cows when she was 9 years old and helped her dad. She married at 17 and is still milking cows today. She says she has been milking for 50 years! Jesse likes to fish and has participated in all types of hunting.

HUNT, RICHARD WILLIAM (RICKY), was born on July 9, 1957 in Cairo, IL. He is the son of Jesse and Annette Hunt. He attended Cunningham Elementary and graduated from Carlisle County High School in 1975. He was a member of 4-H, FBLA, and BETA. He attended vocational school and became a certified welder. He likes to fish and is involved in all types of hunting. He was very involved in showing horses from 1964-75. He was a member of the Kentucky Horse Association. He has worked at Marine Ways, NCI, Shawnee Steam Plant (TVA) and now works at Walker Boat Yard in Paducah, KY.

Edrie Ann Clifton Hunt was born on Feb. 24, 1957 in Florence, AL. She travelled throughout the USA and in Germany during her childhood as her father was in the Army. She is the daughter of Floyd Matthew Clifton and Nell Summerville Clifton. Edrie Ann attended Symsonia High School in Graves County for the last of the senior year and graduated from there in May 1975. She then attended Murray State University in Murray, KY earning her bachelor's degree in social work in May 1981.

While attending MSU, Edrie met Ricky. They dated from July 1, 1976 until their engagement on Oct. 25, 1976. Ricky and Edrie were married on May 27, 1977 at St. Charles Church in Carlisle County, KY. The couple settled in Cunningham, KY. Edrie joined the church in 1987.

Ricky, Edrie Ann, Matthew and Kimberly Hunt

The couple has two children, Kimberly and Matthew. Kimberly was born on Aug. 10, 1980 in Paducah and Matthew was born Dec. 12, 1983 also in Paducah.

Edrie is employed as a social worker for the Department for Social Services in Mayfield, KY, specializing in child protection and juvenile services.

HUNTER, LUCIAN O. SR., was born March 4, 1883 in McDaniels, KY, son of J. Clint Hunter, who was a logger and later owned a lumber mill in Leitchfield, KY. Lucian O. Hunter was a salesman for Federal Chemical Company for 30 years, chairman of Grayson County Democratic party for 25 years.

Lucian O. Hunter Sr. was married on Oct. 7, 1908 to Virginia Monica Meredith, born July 26, 1887 at Peonia, KY. Virginia was the daughter of John Steven Meredith and Mary Elizabeth McClure. John Steven Meredith was a land owner and a tiller of the soil. Mary Elizabeth McClure was a school teacher. Virginia Monica Hunter died May 6, 1975.

Reverend Louis Beruatto, pastor of St. Joseph Parish from 1908 until 1956 married Lucian and Virginia Hunter, baptized all of their children, administered all their First Holy Communion, and married all of the children except Lucian Orestes Hunter, Jr. and Vida Lee who were married by Monsignor Joseph Orlet in Belleville, IL at St Mary Catholic Church on July 24, 1957. He also baptized all of the grandchildren and all were confirmed during Fr. Beruatto's tenure.

The children of Lucian O. Hunter Sr. and Virginia are: Charles Edward Hunter born March 17, 1909; Kathren McAtee Hunter born May 25, 1911; Nell Cannon Hunter born Dec. 20, 1913, now deceased; Lucian Orestes Hunter Jr. born July 15, 1916; Margaret Hill Hunter born Jan. 20, 1918, now deceased; Mary Elizabeth Hunter born Jan. 28, 1920, now deceased; John Allen Hunter and Jain Ellen Hunter (twins) born April 29, 1923; and James Crady Hunter born April 20, 1926.

1st row, from left - John Hunter Wycoff, Kenner Hay, Mrs. Lucian O. Hunter, Jakie Hay, Mr. Lucian O. Hunter, sitting in Mr. Hunter's lap-Lucian Hunter Hay, Meredith Hay Mucci. 2nd row, from left - Charles Walter Hay, Timmy (deceased), Mary Elizabeth Hunter Hay (deceased), James Crady Hunter, Mgr. Albert Thompson (deceased), Jane Ellen Hunter Hain, Jakie S. Hay (deceased), Vida Lee Hunter, Katheryn Hunter Wycoff, Joseph Addison Wycoff (deceased), Charles Edward Hunter. 3rd row, from left, John Allen Hunter and Lucian O. Hunter Jr. (These are the two men directly in back of Charles W. Hay.)

All four sons were altar boys under Fr. Beruatto. He was a very strict disciplinarian, if they made an error in their response from their Latin cards, after Mass, he would pull their hair and give them a slap or two on the face and march them back to the altar and continue practicing until they had it perfect. To this day, it is believed that the pulling of Lucian Orestes' hair was the chief cause of balding. Another incident that he will never forget, which occurred at St. John Evangelist Church at Sunfish, KY which was a mission of St. Joseph. During a mission at St. John's, Father had taken him along as an altar boy. One evening he put on his cassock and surplice and started over to the church and a dear old lady knelt down in front of him and said, "Father, please hear my confession, I have been a bad woman." This scared the dickins out of him and he ran back to the parish, again to be reprimanded by Fr. Beruatto.

During his engagement to Vida Lee of Butler County, a member of the Church of Christ, Monsignor Beruatto wrote him a letter advising him not to marry this girl and if he did, he would be committing spiritual suicide. They have been happily married for 35 years and the letter written by Fr. Beruatto is a collectors item of his.

The Hunter family had great respect for Monsignor Lewis Beruatto's strong convictions and the influence that he had in molding the character of each of them.

HURST, MILDRED JUANITA (OLIVER), was born March 31, 1925 in Hopkins County, KY, to Baptist minister James M. Oliver and Mildred Henley, one of 15 children. She married Gordon Hurst Nov. 17, 1943 in Indianapolis, IN. Blessed with two children, Paul and Colleen. Converted to Catholicism March 29, 1959 at St. Mary Cathedral. Confirmed by Bishop John J. Carberry May 1959. In 1970 she moved to Clearwater, FL and St. Cecilia Parish with Fr. Thomas Larken was pastor. In 1974, she moved back to West Layfayette, IN and St. Thomas Aquanis; 1976 to Madisonville, KY and Christ the King where Fr. Jerry Glahn was founder and pastor. She assisted Fr. Jerry Glahn in six parish renewals of Christ the King. Served as lector, Eucharistic Minister and had prayer group in her home from 1979-82. Phone ministry at home from 1979-90. Made Cursillo number 20 in 1979 St. Stephen Cathedral Owensboro, KY. Tended the dying on request of family and/or Fr. Glahn.

Juanita Hurst

She states that she felt the Holy Spirit was her guide from childhood. Learned to read the Bible at an early age but did not like how it was taught in the churches that she attended. She taught Sunday School so that her children would not be misled. Then at age 32 went in search of the origin of the Bible. She found her answers in the Catholic teaching. At age 33, chose to become a member of the Body. Juanita had dreamed for years of returning to Madisonville-to build a house on the hill above the highway leading north. In 1976, they moved to Madisonville to find that God had already built her home on that hill, Christ the King Parish. And, had a loving new family to welcome her. She is now disabled and finds peace in knowing that God's love unites all his children.

HUSKISSON, TENSLEY AND BARBARA, live in Lewisport, KY. Tensley (Huck) is the son of the late Aubrey and Martha Huskisson of Owensboro. Barbara is the daughter of Vincent H. and Anna Sue Payne of Lewisport, KY. Barbara and Huck were married on Nov. 4, 1967 at St William Church in Knottsville.

Huck is retired from the U.S. Army after having served 20 years. In his travels, he has been in France, Germany, Korea and various other places. He entered the Army when he was only 17 years of age; therefore, he was able to retire at the age of 38. During his military career, he was able to pursue his goal of attaining the rank of sergeant major. He and Barbara then returned to Daviess County where they built a house at the current address. Huck then pursued another career by becoming a sales person for one of the major heating and air-conditioning companies.

Barbara graduated from Brescia College in 1965 and obtained a teaching position at Owensboro Catholic High where she taught for four and one-half years. Due to military transfer, she then taught in Tennessee, Mississippi, Texas, Chicago and West Virginia before settling back home. Barbara's biggest challenge was teaching in an all-black school in Mississippi to poor rural children, and for seven years this was true mission work as these students were deprived beyond belief. Currently she teaches at Trinity High School in Whitesville, KY, going on her 10th year there.

Huskisson Family 1985: Bottom Row: Barbara and Huck; Top Row: Lori Ann and Kenneth.

Barbara and Huck have two children, Kenneth Lee and Lori Ann. Lori, is also a Brescia graduate and is teaching in a Catholic school in Memphis; Kenneth is working at a local medical supply store.

INGRAM, ROBERT AND JO ANN, entered the church by joining the parish of St. Thomas More, Easter Eve, April 14, 1990. They have lived in Paducah, KY all their lives. They had previously belonged to the Methodist church.

They own and operate Ingram Sheet Metal. Jo Ann is also a registered nurse.

They have three grown children and three grandchildren. Their son, William Randall Ingram, his wife Gaye and their two children, Billi Nicole and Robert Christopher, have also come into the church.

Another grandson, Justin Anthony Ingram, was baptized Easter morning, April 15, 1990.

Robert, Jo Ann and Justin Ingram

They are active members and extremely happy in the church. Robert is a member of the Knights of Columbus and serves as usher. Jo Ann is a member of the Legion of Mary, Eucharistic Minister and lecturer. Justin is a member of the children's choir. All three grandchildren attend St. Mary Elementary School.

They feel that God has blessed them abundantly. The love and friendship that they have found, as well as the opportunity to serve in various ways, is no small part of that blessing. It has changed and enriched their lives in so many ways.

During Holy Week, just before her confirmation, Jo Ann expressed her feelings in this way. "I was baptized at age 12. I am now 52. I feel like one of the Israelites, who having wandered in the wilderness for 40 years, is now about to enter the Promise Land."

ISBILL, BARRY AND CYNTHIA (CYNDI), and family now live in Whitesville and belong to St. Mary of the Woods Parish. They have three children, Christopher, Shana and Isaac.

Before their marriage on Nov. 18, 1983, Barry was a member of St. William's Parish in Knottsville. He made T.E.C. #37 while in high school. Barry is a son of Mary and Walter "Buck" Isbill Jr. of Knottsville. Barry is presently unemployed since the closing of Barmet Aluminum Corp. in June 1991, where he was a production supervisor. He is now busy in the community. He is co-chairman of the parish picnics and also an active member of the Knights of Columbus since 1988. He has been on the Whitesville Volunteer Fire Department since 1985. He is also an assistant coach of Christopher and Shana's Tee-ball team.

The Isbill Family—First Row: (L to R): Shana, Isaac and Christopher. Back Row: (L to R): Barry and Cynthia.

Cyndi grew up in Whitesville and has always been a member of St. Mary's. She made T.E.C. number 35 while in high school. Cyndi is a daughter of Sue and Daniel Howard Sr. of Whitesville. She is now a full-time mother and homemaker.

Christopher attends St. Mary Elementary School and Shana will begin first grade there during the 92-93 school year. They enjoy going to the Children's Litergy at the Sunday Masses. Until Isaac starts school in a few years, he is content to stay home with his mother.

JARBOE, JAMES AND MARY ALICE (POTTS), were married Nov. 3, 1942 at St. Romuald in Hardinsburg. They have six children: Don, Judy who married Logan Tivitt, Joe, Paul, Betty Carroll who married Rufus Tivitt, Jeanne who married Dave Lee.

James and Mary Jarboe

The Jarboe's worked hard and sacrificed much to send all of their children to Catholic schools. They especially worked hard at the church picnic's in the 1950s, frying chicken, making pies, serving food and telling stories entertaining friends and cousins. Mr Jarboe is retired from the State Highway Department, Mrs. Jarboe is retired from doing excellent needle work at Eleanor Beard Studio and American Needlecraft. In 1986 Mrs. Jarboe designed and stitched many blocks on the anniversary quilt that hangs in the back of the church today.

The Jarboe's have 12 grandchildren, seven of whom attend St. Romuald Grade School at present. The faith goes on.

JARBOE, RICHARD ROBERT AND MARY JANE (PATE), were married sometime in the late 1850s. They had five children, William, John, Frank, Alonzo and Racheal who married Will Beauchamp. They are all buried at St. Romuald in Hardinsburg.

Mr. Jarboe was a farmer and also ran a poor house. This was in the days before Social Security and welfare checks. Many of the paupers are buried at the Poor House Farm on Jarboe Road. Mr. Jarboe died at the age of 35 after having an accident. He was buried at St. Romuald in June 1872.

JARBOE, MONSIGNOR WILLIAM BYRNE, was born March 13, 1901 in Lebanon, KY to James Walter and Helen Louise Elder Byrne. He was baptized March 24, 1901 at St. Augustine Church by J.A. Hogarty; First Communion March 12, 1912 and confirmation June 18, 1912.

Monsignor Jarboe-first pastor at Blessed Mother

A graduate of St. Augustine Grade and High School in Lebanon and St. Meinrad College and Seminary, St. Meinrad, IN. He was ordained a priest in 1928 and was named a monsignor in 1939 by Pope Pius XII. He served as assistant pastor and pastor of several parishes in Kentucky, including St. William Catholic Church, Knottsville and St. Paul Catholic Church in Owensboro. He served as pastor of Blessed Mother Catholic Church, Owensboro, for 17 years. The last parishes he served were St. John and Rosary Chapel in Paducah and St. Rose in Cloverport. He retired in 1974. Monsignor Jarboe died Sept. 14, 1984 at the Carmel Home. He was 83 years old.

JARBOE, WILLIAM AND ELIZA (HENDRICK), were married in 1890 at St. Romuald in Hardinsburg. They had nine children, eight sons and one daughter: Carl Sr., Lon, Bill, Bob, Paul, Herbert who was killed in coal mine in 1940, Bernard a World War II veteran, Helen and James who still belong to St. Romuald Parish. The Jarboe's were farmers but their second love was baseball. They had their own team which was almost unbeatable in the 1930s. They were zealous members of the congregation. When their present church was constructed in 1900, Mr. Jarboe along with his brother, Frank, donated one of the stained glass windows in memory of their father Robert. The Eighth Station of the Cross was donated by them also, and the Ninth Station was donated by William's brother Lon and his wife Maggie.

In 1986 when St. Romuald was readying the church for their 175th anniversary, many of the descendants helped strip the woodwork around the windows that was donated in his name. What a glorious feeling having the faith passed on by such hardworking and loving persons.

The William and Eliza Hendrick Jarboe Family

JENNINGS, BOBBY DALE, was born in Henderson County on March 28, 1932. Son of Ivan Wise Jennings and Jewell Mozell Powell. The family moved to Sturgis, KY in Union County in 1934. He served in the United States Air Force from 1951 to 1955. He met his wife Irene while in the Air Force in Munich, Germany. Irene was born in Munich-Allach, Germany on Nov. 23, 1930. She is the daughter of Jacob Neuner and Kreszenz Lichtenwald. Her father died on Feb. 19, 1944. Bobby and Irene married in Morganfield, KY at St. Ann's Church on Aug. 11, 1956. Bobby Dale was converted to the Catholic faith and baptized in 1968 at St. Ann. They have two children: Jacob Erich, born Dec. 31, 1962 and Anastasia Simone, born Dec. 16, 1965. Jacob graduated from Brescia College and is a sportswriter for *The Messenger-Inquirer*. Anastasia married Mark K. Wilkerson on May 26, 1990. They have a daughter, Christina Rachelle Wilkerson, born Oct. 22, 1991. Mark works for PBS in Henderson, KY, and is presently attending RCIA. Anastasia is a beautician. Bobby lectors at St. Agnes, Uniontown. Irene and Bobby are also Eucharistic Ministers and choir members at St. Agnes. They are active in Cursillo. Irene's mother, "Kreszenz" lived with Bobby and Irene for 11 years. She often travelled back to Germany to see her son, Erich. Irene's mother died June 25, 1969 and is buried at St. Agnes Cemetery in Morganfield, KY.

JENNINGS, JAMES AND JULE, and family have lived in Paducah, KY most of their lives. Jule moved, with her parents, to Paducah at the age of 4 from St. Stephen Parish in Owensboro, KY.

James was born in Paducah. His parents were Nick Jennings of Union County, KY (a convert to the Catholic faith) and Anne Foster of Livingston County, KY. He had one sister, Martha and one brother, William (Red).

Jule's parents were Eugene H. Cocke Sr, born in Peewee Valley, KY and Clara Ben Hagen of Owensboro, KY. She had four brothers, Gene, Bob, John and Tom.

James and Jule Jennings family

James (better known as "Soup") retired from the Modine Mfg. Company after 30 years as personnel manager. He served as president of the West Kentucky Personnel Club for two terms and was on the Chamber of Commerce's first Labor Management Team. He served in WWII for five years and participated in the "Battle of the Bulge." He was awarded the Bronze Star.

Soup is a life member of the Knights of Columbus, was on the first advisory board of Lourdes Hospital as well as the first Advisory Board of the new St. Mary High School and is a Charter Member of the Rolling Hills Country Club. Jule has belonged to the Daughters of Isabella for many years as well as the Altar Society, first at St. Francis de Sales and later at St. Thomas More. She was active in the USO during World War II and was active in the Red Cross Swimming Program for a number of years. She has been an active member of the Lourdes Hospital Auxiliary for over 20 years.

James and Jule had two children, a daughter, Judith Anne and a son, James Richard, (he was killed in an accident at age 26). The Jennings celebrated their 50th Wedding Anniversary.

JENNINGS, JULIA, was born in Livermore, KY in 1948, the ninth of 10 children of Thomas Hugh and Jennie Mae Barr Rhodes, who were members of St. Charles Church. They were active members of the parish, and were often praised for their children's behavior in church. The children became choir members, each joining when he could behave nicely by himself. During their formative years, the children attended St. Joseph School in Central City, which has since been demolished.

In 1962 the family bought a home in Livia, KY, and the family joined the congregation of St. Anthony at Brown's Valley. The two youngest children attended that grade school, razed in 1967. Julia remembers the church picnics that were held in the grove of trees just north of the church grounds, and the Grotto depicting Our Lady of Lourdes, that was southwest of the church. Both Hugh and Jennie Mae attended this church until their deaths; his in 1973, hers in 1986.

Julia moved to Owensboro to 1967, where she attended Mass at St. Stephen Cathedral. In 1973, she met Larry Wayne Jennings, and in 1974 they moved into the St. Pius X Parish where they were married, and their children, Summer Leigh and Cody Morgan were baptized.

The Larry Jennings Family

In 1987 the family moved to Pettit and again became members of St. Anthony Church, where they continue to feel at home. Julia and Summer are lectors, and Cody is an altar boy. They belong to The Army of Mary and are active in the parish social life and services.

Julia credits her continued growth in faith to her parents' example and to supportive brothers and sisters. She remembers the family rosary as a daily part of growing up, and continues to foster devotions to Jesus and Mary as a vital part of daily life.

JOHNSON, CLARA ALICE, is the fourth of 11 children born Feb. 22, 1948, to Ruth and Justin Johnson in Daviess County, KY. She was a member of St. Lawrence Catholic Church, Philpot, and went to St Lawrence School until it burned in the fall of 1959. She finished grade school and high school at St. William, Knottsville, KY.

The Ursuline Sisters taught her all 12 years of grade and high school and they, along with the deep faith life of her parents and family, had a strong influence on her becoming a religious.

In August 1966, she entered the convent at Mount St. Joseph. Aug. 14, 1967, became a Novice and took a new name, Sister Joseph Clara Johnson. On Aug. 15, 1969, she professed temporary vows of poverty, chasity, obedience and instruction. July 21, 1974, she made perpetual vows, giving herself to the mission of God, the church and the MSJ community.

Sister Clara Johnson, OSU

During the Novitiate and Juniorate, she studied religious life, the vows, the Scriptures, prayer and community life, etc. while also taking classes through Brescia College, Owensboro, for a bachelor's degree in elementary education in May 1971 and a master's degree in library science from Spalding University, Louisville, in May 1979.

Sister Clara Johnson has taught school, been librarian and pastoral minister at St. Bartholomew, Louisville; St. Francis, Loretto; St. Romuald, Hardinsburg; St. Charles Albuquerque, NM; MSJ Academy; St. Mary Elementary, Paducah, KY and St. Ann, Morganfield.

She has just celebrated a year of jubilee (25th) with her community, her family and the parish of St. Ann, Morganfield. She gives thanks to God for being so good to her and for blessing her with such a great, wholesome family, a wonderful community and all the students, parents and parishioners who have shared their faith's journey with her.

JOHNSON, FRANCES CECILIA, second daughter of Loula Ramage Johnson and Ernest Duval Johnson, was born on Troy Avenue in Hickman, KY in her grandmother's (Mary Ann Ramage) renting house, next to the public school on Sept. 27, 1908. Her baptism took place at Sacred Heart Church on Oct. 12, 1908.

Frances attended the Hickman schools through the ninth grade, then attended Nazareth Academy in Nazareth, KY graduating from high school there in June 1926.

Frances Cecilia Johnson

During her work years, Frances was employed at Hickman Bank and Trust Company, *Hickman Courier* and the city of Hickman, KY in the capacity of city clerk from 1936 to May 1974. During most of these years, she would also serve as clerk in her precinct on election days.

At the present time, Frances resides in Hickman, KY.

JOHNSON, GEORGE ALBIN, born in Hancock County on Jan. 30, 1893, was named after his father George Albinus "Al" Johnson. He followed in his father's footsteps, bought and farmed an adjoining farm. His mother, Rose Matilda Shoemaker was originally from Union County, KY. His wife, Emma Josephine Hagman born Aug. 19, 1894 at Skillman, was the daughter of a prominent and successful Hancock County farmer and sawmill owner. Her parents were Victor Hagman and Theresa Ballman. Albin and Emma were married in 1930 in the church of St. Catherine, St. Albany, NY. Emma was living with and working for her sister Cecilia Hagman Rives.

After their marriage, this couple moved back to Hancock County and became involved members of St. Lawrence Parish. Albin served as one of two trustees for several years. Their three children, Victor Albin, Eugene Joseph, Mary Eula were all baptized at St. Lawrence. Mary Eula entered the Sisters of Charity of Nazareth in 1951.

Emma was widowed in 1956. She lived to be 97, attending liturgy every Sunday and other special occasions until she died in 1991. The first Sunday after her burial a white bow was placed on the pew she occupied for 56 years by a parishioner. Emma had a great love for the missions and she sponsored a number of children and seminarians of India through the Catholic Near East Association.

George Albin and Emma Hagman Johnson, wedding day 1930.

Her grandchildren and great-grandchildren were left a legacy of a gentle, dedicated and faithful woman devoted to family, friends, neighbors and the church.

Interesting story: Bishop Cotton mandated that all Catholic children should attend a Catholic school. Their son, Victor got up at 4:30 a.m., rode a horse four miles and housed it with Raymond Jarboe, then walked two miles to attend St. Lawrence School. He did this for two years as a seventh and eighth grader. Their other two children walked a least a mile for one year to catch the bus to attend St. William School, until the bus route changed.

During times of flooded or impassable roads, it was not unusual for the family to drive 30 miles to reach church only six miles away to attend Sunday Mass. At times it meant driving until the car got stuck and the family would walk the remainder of the journey to church.

JOHNSON, RAPHAEL LAWRENCE, was born near Knottsville on Jan. 2, 1927 and was baptized at St. Lawrence Church. He attended St. Lawrence and St. William Schools. He was one of 10 children of Raphael Johnson and Julia Wathen Johnson. He served in the U.S. Army. He is a retired Chrysler employee, carpenter and farmer. He was maintenance man at the Knottsville Personal Care Home for 10 years.

Dortha Lanham was born in Daviess County on June 3, 1933 and was baptized at St. William Church. She is one of nine children of John Lanham and Pearl Mae Kanoble. Dortha attended St. William School and graduated in 1951 with 12 years perfect attendance. She worked at General Electric for five years, was a nurse aide at Knottsville Personal Care Home for eight years and presently works in the Dietary Department at the Carmel Home.

Lawrence and Dortha were married on Sept. 22, 1951 at St. William Church. They had 10 children: Jeanetta born June 27, 1952 married Philip Ballard; William L. born Oct 10, 1954 married Katherine Jodell Morris; Susan born Jan. 23, 1956 married Ronald Bickett; Kenneth born Feb. 18, 1957 married Amanda Boarman; Patrick born Oct. 28, 1958 born Tamara Stock; Karen born Oct 1, 1960 married David Allen; Cynthia born May 25, 1962 married Barry Mills; Bruce born Nov. 22, 1963 married Julia Mills; Randall born Oct 4, 1964, deceased July 31, 1965; and Joseph born Aug. 29, 1967 married Coral Howard. They have 32 grandchildren and one great-grandchild. They live in Knottsville and are members of St. William Church.

JOHNSON, SUSANNAH RUTH, was born in Hancock County, KY, six miles from St. Lawrence Church in Daviess County, KY. Her father, George Albinus Johnson, married Rose Matilda Shoemaker in Union County, KY on Feb. 4, 1885 at Sacred Heart Church. They built a home on part of the land Grandfather Johnson bought when he came to Kentucky in 1834 from Lenordtown, MD. John Lewis, her grandfather married Elizabeth Dorothy Payne at St. Lawrence. She is the youngest of the 12 children of George Albinus and Rose Johnson.

Mary, the oldest child, married Will O'Bryan. Next was Henrietta who married Estil Higdon. Joe, the oldest son, married Regina Coomes. Harry married Ada Fichtor. Albin married Emma Hagman. Eulalia never married; she became a nurse. William married Lylia Carroll. Susannah Ruth died at the age of 1. Lillian also never married. She lived on the farm. Dorothy married Harold Hagman. Thomas married Ruth Payne. Susannah Ruth is single and has lived on the farm all her 86 years. St. Lawrence has been her parish all her life. Father Lucian Clements baptized her and she made her First Communion under his leadership. Father George Neihaus was her pastor from 1914 to 1931. He had a great devotion to poor souls. He was the last resident pastor of St. Lawrence. After 1931 all other pastors were resdents of St. William's Parish in Knottsville, KY.

She belongs to Poor Souls Society, League of Sacred Heart, Sodality of Blessed Virgin Mary and the Legion of Mary. She hopes to be buried in St. Lawrence Cemetery in the family lot.

JOHNSON, THOMAS E. AND ELIZABETH ANN ISBILL, were married Oct. 2, 1965 at St. William Church in Knottsville. Thomas was born and raised in Knottsville. Elizabeth and Thomas Johnson were both in CCD for three years while daughter was attending. Elizabeth worked outside the home until her third child was born. She returned to work after a few years.

The Johnsons are the parents of three children, one daughter and two sons. All the children have attended the Catholic schools beginning with St. Pius X and have graduated from Owensboro Catholic High School. Thomas Johnson has served on the Parish Council and still remaining. He is head cook for the church picnic each year. Elizabeth and her daughter also work at St. Pius X Picnic every year. Thomas, Elizabeth and daughter were in the church choir for 10 years.

Thomas and Elizabeth believe that Catholic education gives the students a good moral environment. Catholic students pray together, share with each other, and treat each other as a family. Catholics are taught religion which is very important for their spiritual well being for their entire life. Students in Catholic schools have the best teachers. Students are taught to be respectable, loving and understanding. Students are encouraged to learn all they can and to further their education

Elizabeth graduated from St. William High School in Knottsville in 1963. She began working for General Electric right out of high school and remained there for 10 years. She now works for Glenmore Distilleries. She has been with that company for 21 years. Thomas graduated from St. William High School in Knottsville in 1963. He enlisted in the Navy for two years. When he got out of the Navy, he worked at Coca-Cola Bottling Company for one year. He bought a service station for two years, then went to work for Big Rivers for 11 years. Their children all graduated from Owensboro Catholic High School. Their oldest son David is in dental school. Their middle child, Duane, worked at Square D Company for one year. Their last child, Donya, is in college.

JOHNSON, VICTOR A., son of Albin Johnson and Emma Hagman Johnson, was born on the site of his present farm in Hancock County near the eastern Daviess County line. Except for the four years he attended high school at St. Bernard, Cullman, AL and the two years serving in the U.S. Navy, Victor has lived at the same location, a part of the original farm belonging to his grandparents G. Albin and Rose Matilda Shoemaker Johnson.

He married Lois Brasher in 1955 at St. Lawrence Catholic Church. They have eight children: Noel, Philip (killed at age 18), Albin, Chris, Rita, Ann and Anthony (Tony) twins and Nancy. Two of the sons, Albin and Tony still reside nearby and are active members of St. Lawrence Parish.

Lois Brasher grew up in St. Peter Parish, Stanley and St. Anthony, Brown's Valley before moving to St. Lawrence with her family at age 16. Her parents were Hershel E. Brasher and Rita Jane Sapp from the Bonharbor section of Daviess County.

Both have been active in parish, school and civic activities and committees including parish picnics, parish council, finance, school board (Mary Carrico and Trinity), farm bureau and soil conservation and Lois has been principle organist at St. Lawrence 1968.

JOHNSON, VIRGIL LOUIS, was born in Daviess County, KY on Dec. 4, 1914. His father, Timothy Sylvestor, was a farmer and his mother Hilda Jane Millay was a homemaker. They lived in Daviess County. Anna Mural Millay was born in Daviess County, KY on Sept. 5, 1919. Her father Joseph Benjamin Millay was a farmer also. Her mother Anna Louise Payne was a homemaker. Virgil and Anna Mural were married in a double ceremony with his brother, Paul and Annastasia on April 12, 1939 at St. Lawrence Catholic Church in Knottsville, KY. They moved to Iowa for two years before coming back to Daviess County, KY. He farmed and was a custodian of St. Lawrence Church and cemetery.

They raised eight sons and six daughters in Daviess County. After retiring from farming he continued as custodian of St. Lawrence Church and the cemetery. He retired as a custodian after 27 years in 1978.

Virgil Louis and Anna Mural Johnson

Anna Mural and Virgil were married 46 years. Anna Mural died on Jan. 9, 1985 with cancer. Virgil lived at their home at St. Lawrence until he passed away on Jan. 22, 1992. They left 14 living children, 43 grandchildren and four step-grandchildren and three great-grandchildren (they were also preceded in death by a grandson and a great-grandson).

JOHNSON FAMILY, In 1834, four Johnson brothers came to Kentucky from Leonardtown, MD. William Peter, the eldest, Joseph Leonard, John Louis and Michael Henry. They lived at Lewisport, KY. Michael donated the land for St. Columba Catholic Church at Lewisport in 1850 and they are both buried in the cemetery about two miles east of Lewisport along with their wives and some other members of their families. The other two from which many of their descendants are still living came up to the Daviess-Hancock County Line and settled. Joseph Leonard Johnson was born Feb. 22, 1819; He married Martha Ann Payne, Jan. 12, 1847. Joseph Leonard died March 16, 1901; Martha Ann died September 1896; they had the following children: Michael B. Nov. 13, 1850; who married Rose Eva Coomes on Nov. 11, 1874, daughter of William Peter Coomes and Margaret A. Mattingly, they had one son, Francis. Mary Ann, born on Oct. 13, 1852; died on July 29, 1853; Helen born on Aug. 24, 1853, died Sept. 14, 1859. Martha L. born on June 21, 1854, married Ignatius Coomes on Nov. 19, 1878. Their daughter, Agnes G. Coomes married Frank Higdon. Elizabeth Ellen born on Aug. 25, 1857. Joseph Lewis born on Oct. 22, 1864, died Feb. 24, 1923, was married to Mary Elizabeth Haynes, March 1, 1886. Catherine Rose born on Nov. 24, 1862, married Robert Ignatius Knott, on Nov. 25, 1884. Robert Ignatius born on Sept. 9, 1860. Margaret Virginia (Mag) was born on March 22, 1868, she died on July 3, 1944 and was married to Joseph Nemrod Martin.

Agnes Coomes as was mentioned above married Frank Higdon and from that union their chldren were: Audry Miles, Carmel Hoskins, Norbert Higdon, Bernardine Wright, Frances Higdon, Mildred O'Bryan and Justin Higdon. Agnes Coomes went to Gatewood School and then to Mount St. Joseph. All the children of Francis Higdon went to St. Lawrence Grade School. Most of the children were employed in the agricultural industry and in homemaking, raising tobacco, wheat, pigs, turkeys and etc.

Bernadine Wright's children are: Francine, Sarah, Bernard, Michael, Frieda, Lawrence, Elmo. Mildred O'Bryan's children are: Larry, Wilma Knott, Bevery Aud, Carl, David, Ronnie, Paula Wells and Gerald. Carmel Hoskins had Joseph, Charles, Edward, Mark and Justin.

Audry Miles' chldren were Edith Jackson, Dennnis Miles, Martha Johnson, Morris and Antoinette Wolker. Adury Miles played the organ at St. Lawrence for many years.

John Lewis Johnson brother of Joseph Leonard was born April 17, 1817. He married Elizabeth Dorothy Payne Nov. 21, 1843. He died of pneumonia Jan. 6, 1890 Elizabeth Dorothy (a sister of Martha Ann) died Oct. 22, 1898. She was born May 7, 1821.

They had the following children.

Joseph Edwin born June 28, 1846, died may 25, 1916, Waverly, KY. John Lewis, born March 8, 1848, died July 2, 1918 married Serophine Speak Oct. 22, 1872.

James William born Aug. 30, 1849, died in infancy.

Benjamin Michael born Feb. 9, 1851 died July 10, 1851.

George Albin born March 1, 1853 died June 6, 1933; married Matilda Rose Shoemaker, Feb. 4, 1885.

Francis Titus born Jan 4, 1855 died April 18, 1920.

Thomas Rosenwald born Feb. 7, 1856, died March 5, 1877. in Seminary at Bardstown, KY.

Richard Cyrillus born July 9, 1858 died July 28, 1903.

Henry Peter born Feb. 22, 1860 died Dec. 28, 1922. He married Mary Marulline Hazel, Feb. 7, 1882.

JOHNSTON, EWELL (THOMAS), was born on Sept. 30, 1907, son of Theodore and Annie Clemons Johnston. On Oct. 3, 1926, he married Mary Vera Bradley, who was born on Aug. 7, 1911, daughter of J.T. and Millie Bradley. They lived their early years together in Dog Creek, KY (Hart County). Approximately 15 years after their marriage, they bought a farm of their own and moved across the Nolin River to Grayson County. Ewell and Vera spent their lives farming. They both had eighth grade educations.

Ewell had seven sisters: Lissie Higdon, Elsie Higdon, Leona Miller, Bertie Pierce, Wanda Pierce, Edith Clemons and Pearl Stinson; he had four brothers: Hubert, Earl, Robert and Quintin Johnston.

Vera had two brothers, Alvey and George.

The couple had 14 children: Bernita (Sims), Juanita (Higdon), Odaline (Clemons), Royce, Wildred, Lorena, Freeman, Armond, Georgetta (Smith), Denise (Sims), Judy (Clemons), Wayland, Dwight and Maryla (White).

In the early 1960s, before all their own children had left home, Vera's mother, Millie, came to live with the family. She stayed there until she died in 1976.

In 1977, their son Armond was killed in an automobile accident, and eventually all three of Armond's teenage sons, Mickey, Steven and Jimmy, came to live with their grandparents. With the care of extended family in both generational directions, the couple had very few retirement years.

Ewell and Vera Johnston

Vera and Ewell belonged to St. Benedict Parish, Wax, all their lives. In her last years, Vera served on the Bereavement Committee of the parish.

Vera died in 1984 of lung cancer. Ewell died in 1989 of heart failure. Besides the 14 children, at Ewell's death, the couple had 69 grandchildren, 46 great-grandchildren and one great-great-granddaughter.

JOHNSTON, ROSALINE, born Aug. 29, 1907, is the last member of 10 children born to Benjamin Thomas and Mary Francis Pierce Johnston and has been a lifetime member of the diocese. She experienced the loss of her brother, Claude and two sisters, May Dell and Lois Johnston within three years.

The origin of the Johnston family can be historically traced to Spotsylvania County, VA to William Johnston I, who was a member of the House of Burgesses for Spotsylvania, 1736-1740. He was married to Ann Chew, whose father was also a Burgess. Rosaline's ancestors are thought to have come to the United States from Scotland.

Rosaline Johnston

B.T. Johnston's grandparents, Absolan and Elizabeth Thomas Johnston were among a group of two early Catholic settlers who settled on the banks of the Nolin River in the early 1800s. They settled in what was later known as Wax, Grayson County; Dog Creek, Hart County. These two settlements were separated by the Nolin River and spiritually cared for from one location. Rosaline's reat-grandfather, Absalon, donated land for the first St. Benedict Church which was located on the north bank of Vax, Grayson area. Although Dog Creek, Hart County is officially located in the Louisville Diocese the residents presently attend church in Grayson County.

Her family was born and grew up on a farm bordering the Hart County Bank of the Nolin River. Due to almost impassable roads, there were many hardships practicing Catholicity in the early days. She recalls her parents having the honor of hosting the Right Rev. Denis O'Donoghue and a visiting priest from Louisville, as overnight guests, previous to confirmation in the parish. Their home was a second home for Rev. Paul Joseph Volk, who was pastor, 1918-19. The Most Rev. Henry J. Soenneker, second bishop of Owensboro, dined with the Johnston when he substituted for pastors at St. Benedict.

The Johnstons were always active in church ministry and have contributed, financially, to St. Benedict Church. Her brother, the late Claude Johnston left a generous trust fund for the general upkeep of the church and cemetery. Rosaline made a generous contribution for the renovation of what is now the Catholic Pastoral Center in Owensboro.

During her lifetime, Rosaline has witnessed change and progress in Catholicity in Western Kentucky. She is thankful for the generosity and untiring zeal of many pastors and bishops. As the Johnston family slowly give themselves back to God, they will always have descendents to carry on the Catholic Apostolic Ministry.

JONES, REV. MARK ANTHONY, was born Feb. 17, 1959 in Owensboro, one of five children of William Thomas Jones, deceased and Wanda Marie McBride Jones. He has three brothers, William Joseph, John Thomas and Jeffrey Scott and one sister, Mary Joanna Jones. He has several nieces and nephews: Michael Brian Jones, Christopher Joseph Jones, Nicholas Clayton Jones (deceased), Adam Charles Jones, Holly Elizabeth Jones and Amanda Renea Jones.

Fr. Jones attended St Anthony School, Our Lady of Lourdes Elementary, Southern Junior High School and Owensboro Catholic High School.

Rev. Anthony Jones

He attended Western Kentucky University, The Pontifical College Josephinum (BA, 1984) and the Athenaeum of Ohio (M. Div., 1989).

Fr. Jones was ordained to the priesthood on May 27, 1989 by Bishop John McRaith.

He served a year as an intern at St. Jerome in Fancy Farm (1986-1987). Her served as associate pastor at Holy Spirit in Bowling Green (1989-1991); St. Francis De Sales, Paducah, 1991-1992; he was campus minister at St. Mary High School and St. Mary Middle School; he is presently associate pastor at St. Stephen Cathedral in Owensboro.

Fr. Tony Jones has been involved with Teens Encounter Christ (TEC) and the Cursillo Movements. He has served as spiritual advisor for retreats at both Owensboro Catholic High School and at St. Mary High School in Paducah.

JONES, RICHARD JOSEPH, was a 10 year old Baptist boy growing up on a farm in McLean County in 1966. Unknown to him, his future wife, Birgit Atherton, had, a year before, received her First Holy Communion at the St. Paulus Church in Trier, West Germany and was now on her way to the U.S. with her parents.

Rick and Birgit grew into their teens without meeting until one July day in 1973 their friendship began. At first they dated and occasionally attended church together. As their love grew, so did Rick's curiosity about the Catholic faith.

Rick Jones and Birgit Atherton were married on Nov. 29, 1975, by Fr. Richard Powers. The next year, Rick finished the instructions that he had begun with Fr. Powers and became a member of St. Charles Parish in Livermore, KY.

During the first years of marriage, Rick farmed and worked as a millwright while Birgit attended Brescia College majoring in art.

Their first child, a son, Rowan Neil, was born in 1978 and in 1979 Birgit received her bachelor of arts degree from Brescia. In 1981 a daughter, Erika Marie, arrived. Rowan attended Our Lady of Lourdes School kindergarten-second grade and then the family moved from their farm in Livia to another farm in McLean County so that Rick would be closer to the land that he now farmed with his father. With the relocation, came a change to public school for Rowan and Erika.

Rick and Birgit Jones with Rowan, Erika and Mark

In 1988 a third child, Richard Mark, was born. By this time, Rick had been farming full-time for two years and the family was home for good in McLean County.

In 1990, Rick and Birgit answered a call to better educate their children in the church. They joined the parish of The Immaculate and Rowan and Erika began attending Owensboro Catholic Middle School and Catherine Spalding even though they lived in McLean County. It requires three daily trips to the county line to catch the bus, but the good of a Catholic education far outweighs a little extra effort.

Rick, who is still farming, is a member of the Immaculate Men's Club, Knights of Columbus, and is a lector at Immaculate. Birgit is a homemaker, farm secretary and is kept busy transporting children to their various activities. Rowan attends OCMS, plays on the Aces basketball team, is an altar server and a member of the Immaculate Youth Group. Erika attends Catherine Spalding School and helps her mother with little brother Mark.

It is a happy coincidence that the Jones' once again find themselves with Fr. Richard Powers as their pastor, now at Immaculate.

JONES, TONY AND KATRINA RICKE. Katrina was born in Erie, PA on Aug. 30, 1960. Tony Jones was born in Gary, IN on Dec. 15, 1964. They married on Nov. 30, 1991 at Wesleyan College and became Mr. and Mrs. Tony Jones. Katrina works as a receptionist at Wendell Foster Center and Tony works at Big Rivers. Katrina's parents are Mr. and Mrs. Ed Ricke of Immaculate Parish. Ed works at Owensboro Regional Airport as an air traffic controller. Katrina has two children, Katie Drury, 13, who attends Owensboro Catholic Middle and Bradley Drury, 11, who attends Daviess County Middle School. The family belongs to Immaculate Parish. Katie is active in the youth group that meets every Sunday.

JORDON, WALTER AND ANN, and family moved to Hopkins County, KY in 1963, from a tour of duty on Okinawa. They joined Immaculate Conception Church, Earlington.

Walter, son of James Asberry and Ada Shoemaker Jordon, was born and attended school in Louin, MS. He entered the U.S. Air Force in 1941, serving in Cuba, Hawaii, Guam, England, Germany and Okinawa. Walter received many awards during his years in the service. He retired as senior master sergeant in 1966 and opened Economy Rentals in Madisonville, KY.

Ann, daughter of Elva D. and Anna Mark Allen, was born and attended school in Henderson. She graduated from University of Kentucky, Lexington, KY and Michael Reese Hospital Dietetic Internship, Chicago, IL.

Walter and Ann were married May 12, 1947 by Fr. Robert Gipperich at Holy Name Catholic Church, Henderson. The family lived in Louisville, KY; Memphis, TN; Broadstairs, England; Greenville, MS; and Okinawa during Walter's 24 years in the Air Force.

The Jordon children consist of six sons and a daughter. All their sons received the Ad Altari Dei, the Catholic Scouting Award and the Eagle Scout. Their daughter received the Girl Scout Curved Bar. Walter and Ann were involved in scouting for 40 years. They were recognized as "Council Scouting Family of the Year" in 1979, and received the Bronze Pelican, Silver Beaver and District Award of Merit in Scouting.

The Walter T. Jordon Family

Six of the children, Walter Allen, Margaret Ann, John David, James Richard, Robert Anthony and Joseph Andrew are married. Walter lives in Richmond, VA, and Margaret in Somerset, KY. The other four and Paul Wayne live in Florida. The Jordons are blessed with wonderful children, in-laws and 11 grandchildren.

Both Walter and Ann served the Parish Council and PTAs for years and continue to participate in church and community activities.

JOSEPH, LESLIE E. AND MARY L., Leslie E. is the fifth of eight children born to fundamentalist Protestant parents, Elihue and Oma Combs Joseph in Powell County in Eastern Kentucky. He married Mary Louise Emge, the sixth of seven children born to second generation American-German Catholics, Raymond and Josephine Renner Emge, from Haubstadt, IN. Les received four sacraments of the Catholic Church in one week-in September, 1960-baptism, confirmation, Holy Communion and matrimony. But let's back up.

The Leslie E. Joseph Family

Les was a Korean War veteran; a G.I. Bill educated, newly graduated accountant from University of Kentucky working in St. Louis, MO when he met Mary Lou who was a St. Louis University graduate student (after receiving a bachelor's degree in theology from St Mary's College, Notre Dame, IN). When he asked and she said no, she wouldn't marry him because she "didn't want the total responsibility for the religious formation of a family," he gave her shock of her life, "I didn't say I wouldn't be Catholic!"

Les and Mary Lou married in September 1960 and have seven children. Jeanne Marie and Jill were born in St. Louis; Sidney, Raymond and Jennifer were born in Nashville, TN; and George and Christopher in Paducah, where the family finally "came home to Kentucky". This was in 1969 when Les entered into a CPA partnership in Paducah.

The family has been members of St. Thomas More Parish ever since. Except for Christopher who is a Down syndrome special child, all the Joseph children attended St. Thomas More Elementary and St. Mary High School. (Mary Lou taught religion at St. Mary High School for eight years during which time she taught all of her own children). Subsequently, Jeanne Marie graduated from Murray State University in computer management. She married Jeffrey Nash and they have one child, Lesley. Jill graduated from Western Kentucky University in accounting. She married Randolph Thompson and they have four children: Amanda, Kathryn, Jessica and George. Sidney graduated from Auburn University in accounting. Raymond attended Western Kentucky University and Technical-Vocational School. He is a draftsman, and recently married West Paducahan, Cindy Worley. Jennifer and George are both graduates of Southern Illinois University-Jennifer in elementary education and George in business management.

The Joseph nest emptied completely in July 1992 when special Christopher went to live at Anderson Woods Residential, Inc., in the beautiful hills of Southern Indiana, under the twin spires of St. Meinrad Archabbey, Monastery. His "new mom" is a Benedictine Sister from Monastery Immaculate Conception in nearby Ferdinand. Mary Lou says her life has come full circle. That monastery is her high school Alma Mater and there's nowhere on earth she'd rather have Chris live out his special life.

JOYNER, LESLIE A., was born Jan. 9, 1956. Received an associate degree from Madisonville Community College, graduate of American Medical Record Association Independent Study Program in Medical Record Technology 1984; Passed accreditation examination for Accredited Record Technicians in 1985; employed by Dawson Springs Health Care Center as director of medical records since 1977; promoted to Indiana Regional Medical Record Coordinator in 1991 (part-time) with National Health Corp. Currently living in Dawson Springs and a member of Resurrection Church, past member of Christ the King in Madisonville, KY.

Leslie A. Joyner

Former member and secretary of Parish Council; member and former secretary of Altar Society, member of Western Deanery Council, Schedule Minsters (lectors, gift bearers,) for parish.

KAMINSKI, CHESTER ANTHONY, born in Rockford, IL to Chester Peter Kaminski and Sarah Loretta Molitor. Deanna Berniece Lanham and Chet were married in St. Paul Church in Owensboro in 1960. She is the daughter of Tony Lanham and the former Inez Alvey. Two of their sons, Dennis and Joseph were born in Rockford, IL. Steven and Christopher were born at Mercy Hospital in Owensboro. November 1992, saw the fulfillment of one of the blessings of the Nuptial Mass, "and may you see your children's children" for the Kaminskis, when Frances Claire Strange Kaminski was born to son Chris and Jennifer Strange.

Chester served as Eucharistic Minister, lector and commentator when a member of St. Stephen Cathedral Parish and as a member of the Parish Council. The Kaminskis chaired the committee for the Chrismon Tree during the 70s. At Blessed Mother Parish, Chester continues to serve as minster of Communion. Deanne has been on the Parish Advisory Board and the Parish Council. The family was responsible for making and hanging many of the large altar banners used during the Liturgical seasons of the 80s.

Chester and Deanna Kaminski

Board of directors for the Optimists and the Kiwanis civic clubs and involved in the Literacy Program. He was awarded the distinction of Kentucky's Outstanding Volunteer Literacy Tutor by First Lady Martha Wilkerson and the Owensboro Board of Education Golden Apple in 1991. He currently serves on the Literacy Council.

Deanne is a member of Extension Homemakers, serving her club in various leadership roles. She was elected to a term as county treasurer for this 600 member organization, and served a term as county president. She is a medical technologist. Chester and sons, Joe and Chris own and operate Kaminski Electric and Service Company.

KAMMER, MR. AND MRS. EDWARD N. Kammer and the former Lillian Knadler were married May 29, 1941, in Louisville. They have one son, Stuart Kammer of Madison, AL. They also have two grandchildren.

Mr. and Mrs. Edward N. Kammer (news photo)

KARL, FR. KEVIN, the son of Leo F. Karl and Elizabeth (Betty) Weis Karl was born in 1954 in Bowling Green, KY. He was the third of their four children, two older sisters, Sharon and Debbie and a younger brother, Greg. Baptized at St. Joseph Parish in Bowling Green, he went to school in that parish, educated by the Sisters of Charity of Nazareth. In 1973, he entered the seminary of St. Pius X, in Erlanger, KY, and later finished his priesthood preparation at St. Meinrad Seminary in Southern Indiana. He was ordained for the Diocese of Owensboro on Jan. 12, 1980. His first assignment was at St Ann Parish in Morganfield, and Sacred Heart in Union County. From there, in 1983 he returned to St. Meinrad as associate director of Spiritual Formation in their College Seminary. During these years he returned to school in the summers to get a degree in the diocese in 1987 as the director of vocations and as associate at the Cathedral Parish.

Fr. Kevin Karl

In 1989 Fr. Kevin was named pastor of St. Mary Magdalene Parish in Sorgho, a year later, in 1990, he became pastor of Sts. Joseph and Paul Parish in Owensboro, where he presently serves. Fr. Kevin is a member of the Diocese Marriage Tribunal and is active as a Spiritual Director for many people.

KARL, LEO F., was born in New Washington, (Crawford County), OH, the son of Henry J. and Julia (Mahl) Karl in 1922. Betty, (Elizabeth D. Weis) was also born in New Washington, OH, in 1925, the daughter of Walter F. and Inez Milliron Weis. The Weis family came to Kentucky in 1936 and settled in Bowling Green, as members of St. Joseph Parish. Among other employments, the Weis's owned a boarding house for students at Western Kentucky State Teachers College. Leo was stationed at Western for pre-flight training during World War II. The Weis family still took the Ohio hometown paper which told where all their local soldiers were stationed. The Weis's invited Leo to supper and reaquaintence began. Sometime later the couple began a war romance dating mostly through the mail. After the war Leo and Betty married at St. Joseph Church in 1945. The couple remained in Bowling Green, raising four children: Sharon who later married Gene Cohron; Debbie, who married Dale Goins; Kevin who became a priest for the diocese in 1980; and Greg who married Teresa Young.

Leo F. and Elizabeth "Betty" Karl

Through the years Leo co-owned a service station, worked for the post office and later managed and co-owned Weis Funeral Supply. After many years as a housewife, Betty later joined Leo at their office as his secretary and bookkeeper working everyday together. They were active members of their parish at St. Joseph where all their children went to school. They were founding members of Holy Spirit Parish. Their oldest daughter, Sharon died in 1982. Leo died in 1984. Betty still lives in Bowling Green, active in Holy Spirit Parish and still working in the business. The couple has seven grandchildren.

KAUFMAN, RAYMOND JOSEPH, son of Wilfred O. and Rose Lattus Kaufman was born Aug. 13, 1928, in Paducah, KY. Anne Mary Burke born June 28, 1925 in Cedar Hill, TN, the daughter of Thomas H. Burke and Ora Crawford Burke. Thomas H. was born Feb. 2, 1885 and died Aug. 19, 1958. Ora was born July 30, 1897 and died Aug. 16, 1982. Grandparents, Michael Burke, born in Ireland in 1828 and Honora Warner Burke, born of Ireland immigrant Nov. 11, 1828. Charles Crawford and Ella Porter. Charles died in 1922 and Ella in 1953.

Raymond and Mary were married Nov. 23, 1957, at Our Lady of Lourdes, in Springfield, TN. Four children were born to this union: David Joseph, born Jan. 10, 1959; Mary Agnes, born Nov. 28, 1961; Carolyn Marie, born Dec. 9, 1962; and Richard Stephen, born April 7, 1965. Raymond Joseph died Jan. 29, 1981. Mary Agnes was married to James Richard Williams, July 6, 1979. The son of Logan and Maxine Williams of Hickman, KY. To this this union was born Jill Marie, July 7, 1982 and James Richard born Jan. 28, 1986. Carolyn Marie married Barry Lynn Harrison, of Hickman, KY on Sept. 3, 1988.

KEENY, JUNE, was born on May 27, 1941 and baptized at St. Raphel Church by Fr. Glenn. He was the pastor of St. Elizabeth Church and since St. Raphel's was a mission church he presided over both of them. Her parents, James and Mary Joe Ballard Knight were married at St. Elizabeth Church. They belong to St. Stephen Cathedral, since moving to Owensboro, KY in 1959. Her grandparents, Joe and Ellen Hayden Ballard Sr. lived on the Wayne Bridge Road and belonged to St. Raphel Church. They are laid to rest in the church's cemetery. Great-grandparents, John Brown and Deliha Powers Ballard lived in West Louisville, KY and went to St. Alphonsus Church.

Douglas and June Keeny

June grew up in Rome, KY area. She attended St. Martin School and Church. She made her First Communion in 1947 by Fr. Joseph Borntraeger and was confirmed by the Most Rev. Francis R. Cotton in 1955. Graduated in 1957 and went to Owensboro Catholic High. She married out of her church in 1981 by Judge Bennett, but in 1986 Fr. J. Edward Bradley remarried her husband, Douglas Lloyd Keeny, and her in the church and she is proud to say that she belongs.

KEITH, CAPTAIN JOSEPH J., and daughter Lura T. Keith and pet fox terrier dog, Tiny, arrived in Russellville, KY, Nov. 11, 1950 after visiting relatives in California, Abilene, TX and Dallas, TX.

They joined the Sacred Heart Catholic Church. The Russellville people were so friendly that they decided then to make Russellville their home.

Before settling here, they lived in Baguio City, the summer capital of the Philippine Islands.

The Americans came early in 1900. The Spanish explorers came in 1572 and governed for 200 years.

The township of Baguio became a chartered city on Sept. 1, 1909. It is one of the largest cities in the world, having an area of 49 square kilometers of loveliness.

Most romantic and exhilarating of all cities in the Orient, Baguio nestles with an alluring charm on a lovely pine-clad forest plateau at about 5,000 feet above sea elevation in the rugged Cordillera Mountains, 250 kilometers north of Manila. Also, this is the only place in the world where Benguet lilies are grown, found in places seldom tread by man. Baguio was the first place in the Philippines to be struck by the Japanese. Camp John Hay (a military vacation outpost) was bombed by 15 Japanese bombers on the morning of Dec. 8, 1941.

Captain Joseph J. Keith and daughter Lura T. Keith

It was on Dec. 27, 1941 that Chief Keith was informed that the Japanese were on the outskirts of the town. Taking three Japanese civilians from the prison camp who spoke English, Keith got in his car to meet the Japanese. When Keith saw the Japanese in the road, he stopped the car and stepped out while lifting his arms in a gesture of surrender. Keith told who he was and asked the Japanese to not bother civilians, as there were no soldiers. The Japanese thanked him politely and entered Baguio without a single shot being fired. Chief Keith surrendered Baguio to the Japanese.

At the time there were about 500 Americans in Baguio, they interned themselves in the American Brent School. The Army post had been evacuated and only two of Chief Keith's 125 policemen retreated to the mountains, together with the people, fled to the mountains. The Japanese interned most of the Americans at the empty Army post. About 35 old and sick Americans were not interned.

The Japanese occupied Baguio for three years and four months, Dec. 27, 1941, withdrawing April 27, 1945. Two American tanks of the 129th Infantry of the 33rd Division liberated Baguio.

Captain Joseph J. Keith (Chief Keith to many) was chief of police of Baguio from 1910 to 1942, retired in 1946. Chief Keith was a towering six foot two inch Texan (resembling Mr. Dillon of "Gunsmoke") who spent his youth cattle punching on the Crowfoot Ranch in New Mexico. When the general call went out for volunteers to aid Uncle Sam in the Spanish American War in 1899, he kissed his mother goodbye and joined the 34th Infantry U.S. Volunteers. He fought three engagements in the Spanish American War, one of which was a two day skirmish with Aguinaldo's insurrectos.

Upon receiving his Army discharge, Keith joined the Metropolitan Police Force in Manila for 10 years. He was then made assistant to the Secret Service Director. Due to his ability and height he was appointed as chief of police in Baguio in 1910, when the little city was a stopping place for Army pack mules with husky American "mule skinners" and miners to drown their nostalgia in "wine bars and six saloons." Life was really rough for the cops. In accordance to the promise from the United States, the Philippines were granted independence and were inaugurated on July 4, 1946.

Captain Keith was a member of the Knights of Columbus. Lura with her brother, James, were schooled with the good Belgian Sisters (Agustinian order) at their Holy Family Girls College in Baguio. Lura was a member of the Children of Mary Sodality. The Belgian Fathers built the beautiful Baguio Cathedral on a hill overlooking the city of Baguio. One could always hear the beautiful huge cathedral bells, imported from Belgium. These bells were donated by the company president of one of the largest gold mines. The beauty of the stained glass windows surround the inside of the church.

Before the war, Baguio had a population of about 50,000 about 500 Americans and the city was governed by the Americans and the American flag flew high.

Baguio's mountains are rich with gold, copper, manganese, chrome and other metals. Many varieties of vegetables are grown and flowers can be seen in every yard.

Strawberries are grown six months of the year. Several kinds of sweet potatoes, bananas and coffee are grown. The average temperature is 64.4 degrees. Baguio is often called the Shangrila of the Orient.

Captain Keith passed away in 1953. Lura's brother, James, passed away in 1977. Lura took up nursing in 1953 and later became an industrial nurse at the famous Rockwell International Industry in Russellville, KY. She retired in 1982 and is now enjoying gardening, organ music, painting as well as volunteer work at Logan Memorial Hospital in Russellville.

KELLER, LUCIAN DENIS (BUDDIE), son of George Charles and Mayme Goetz Keller was born Sept. 25, 1920 at residence on Keller Road, Owensboro, KY. Baptized at St. Martin Church, Rome, KY. Attended school at St. Martin, St. Francis Academy in Owensboro and graduated from Daviess County High in 1939. Married Mary Regina (Jean) Cecil, daughter of Oliver Cecil and Loretta Murphy Cecil, in December 1941 at St. Joseph Catholic Church in Owensboro, KY.

Children include (sons): Gary Denis, David Richard, Lucian Denis Jr. (deceased), Mark Edward, Brian Francis and daughters Carol Jean Rhodes, Patricia Rose, Mary Ann Alvey, Diana Marie Warren and 21 grandchildren.

Spent three years in military service during World War II with Army Air Force, tour of duty in European Theatre of Operations, flying over enemy occupied territory.

Now living on their farm on Keller Road, Daviess County, Owensboro, KY in the Rome community.

They attend St. Martin Catholic Church, member of the Men's Club. Both Jean and Buddie are Eucharistic Ministers at Mass, hospital and parish shut-ins and sick.

They have received many, many blessings, have a great family and enjoy the beauties of God's creation.

KELLER, ROSE REGINA SCHRECKER, was an amazing woman whose faith in God meant everything to her. She wanted to serve the Lord with her whole life. She entered St. Mary of the Woods Convent, Indiana to become a nun. But God had different plans for Rose. She became sick with appendicitis and was sent home. Then she met George Keller and they became engaged. They were married on May 16, 1911 at St. Martin Church. They lived in a house near Panther Creek where their eight children were born between 1912 and 1924. Paul, Willie, Mary, George Jr., Pauline, Anne, Joseph and Herman were all born at home. In 1924, George and Rose moved to a farm on Keller Road in Rome, KY.

Rose's prayer life and spiritual discipline formation she received while at St. Mary of the Woods Convent prepared her for life. Her faith sustained her through raising her family of eight children alone after the death of her husband, George in 1933 during the Depression and the death of her son, George Jr. at the young age of 21 years.

She had a strong devotion to daily Mass and Communion. The priest at St. Martin Church, Rome, KY, even gave her a key to the church because she came so early before Mass to pray. She had a strong devotion to Mary and the rosary and she died on the Feast of Our Lady of the Rosary, Oct. 7, 1981.

George and Rose Keller

She wanted to help others so much that she did volunteer work when she was 70 years old. She was a Gray Lady volunteer at the hospital. She volunteered at the Wendell Foster Center for spastic children in Owensboro. She supported the missions financially. She was friend to the Passionist Sisters of Owensboro and helped them in many ways.

The world truly was a better place because Rose Keller lived.

KELLY, WANDA, in 1955 Wanda Kelly and her three children, along with her parents, Mr. and Mrs. Warren Prewitt, moved from Louisville, KY, to Butler County to the small town of Woodbury, which is nestled along the Green River, and was once the port for the river steamers which plied the river from Cumberland to Henderson. Mr. Prewitt had decided to retire in the country where he had visited so often and had enjoyed fishing for so many years.

Wanda was raised in Louisville, and converted to the Catholic faith before her marriage in July of 1951 at St. Patrick Church. She was later confirmed at the Cathedral of the Assumption in Louisville. Her three children, Bobbie, Danny and Paula, have been brought up in the Catholic faith. At the present time, her two grandchildren, Lindsay Graham and Misty Givens, are being reared in the Church.

After several years, Mrs. Prewitt accepted the faith, received baptism at the Holy Trinity Church in Morgantown from Father Joseph O'Donnell, and was confirmed by Bishop Henry Soenneker. She was a proud lady, and found great comfort in the Church in her declining years until her death inn 1970.

In the first years of its existence, Holy Trinity Parish had very few members and could be accommodated in a small white frame, two room dwelling which served as the church. From that small beginning in the 1950s the church in Butler County has grown to many members.

A beautiful church, designed by Father Patrick O'Donnell, and a church hall which includes a rectory, were built in 1965, under the direction of Father Carl Boehler, and with the workmanship of Glenmary Brothers Robert Hoffman, Peter McQuade (now deceased) and Gregory Woods, as well as the assistance of several parishioners. In years to come, growth in faith and love continue to be the goal of the parish.

KEMP, TARRY QUINLAN, was born on July 10, 1947 to Lawrence Bernard Kemp, a small business owner, and Dorothy Jane Kemp, a housewife, in Iowa. They attended Nativity Church. When he went to nursing school he met Linda Marie Barry who was born on April 19, 1947 in Streator, IL. She was the eighth child of John Thomas Barry, a switchman on the railroads and Catherine Paulin (Meyer) Barry, a housewife. They attended Immaculate Church. Linda and Tarry fell in love and got married in Immaculate Conception Church on June 22, 1968. The ceremony was performed by Father Howard Meyer, Linda's uncle.

Now Tarry, a hospital administrator and an RN, and Linda, an RN instructor, have four kids. The two girls, Amiee Catherine Kemp (15) and Tara Linn Kemp (13), live at home in Owensboro, KY and the family attends Our Lady of Lourdes Church. The oldest daughter helps at church by being in the choir and the youngest is in the choir at her school, Owensboro Catholic Middle School. The oldest son, Timothy Quinlan Kemp (23), goes to college in Subugue, IA. The youngest son, James Christopher Kemp (22), is married and lives in Athens, GA.

In the year of 1988 both Dorothy Kemp and John Barry passed away. Linda and Tarry are now 45 and have four kids, one daughter-in-law and a grandson on the way.

KETTLER, STEPHEN MARK, was born and raised in Paducah, KY, the son of Fred M. Kettler (born Sept. 9, 1918 in Paducah, KY) and Elizabeth Irene Hobbs Kettler (born May 27, 1917). His grandparents were Tobias F. Kettler, Eva Mae Hawkins Kettler, Henry E. Hobbs and Mary Elsie Phipps Hobbs. He is a member of St. Thomas More Parish in Paducah, and a principal/teacher.

He has two sons, Stephen Mark Kettler II, born April 18, 1973, a sophomore at Murray State University and Keven Michael Kettler, born June 17, 1979, an eighth grader at St. Mary Middle School.

KETZER SISTER MARY BARBARA, was born July 4, 1915 to Frank and Tillie Schillinger Ketzer. Frank was born in Bavaria, Germany and Tillie in Toledo, OH. Mary was baptized by Rev. J.B. Kiebel in St. Rose Church, Perryburg, OH. This priest was also to give her, her first teaching position in that same parish school which she attended. Her brother, Rudy, was born June 26, 1917. He died Jan. 26, 1984 of an inoperable malignant brain tumor. His wife, Evelyn, lives in Santa Rosa, CA with their daughter, Judy. Three sons: Bob, also lives in Santa Rosa; Tom in North Carolina; and John in Ohio.

After obtaining a BS degree from Creighton University and an MA from Rosary College, her teaching experiences took her to St. Alphonsus School, Nebraska City, Flaherty and then in 1956 to Brescia College Library where she was reference librarian for 33 years. In 1989, she celebrated her 50th Jubilee and also retired from happily driving the Sisters to their appointments, crocheting, tending Switchboard and playing Skip-Bo.

Sr. Mary Barbara Ketzer

One of the greatest joys of her life was taking care of her parents for the last years of their lives. They came from Florida where they had lived for 11 years and were at the then Knottsville Personal Care Home for almost 10 years. The Ketzer Family will always be grateful to the Diocese of Owensboro for the Bishop Soenneker Home. Her dad was allowed to pursue his gardening and help beautify the place. Forty trees and many shrubs are a memorial to his ability. Bishop Soenneker would bring out the trees and say, "Frank, plant and water these and don't let them die." Frank and Tillie celebrated their 60th Wedding Anniversary in November 1974 with Bishop Soenneker and Father Henry Willett concelebrating. All the Ketzer family were present. Her father died in 1975 and mother in 1980. They are buried in St. William Cemetery at their request.

KING, CLARA EVELYN ROBERTS, the youngest of eight children of William Emilous Roberts and Della Utley Roberts who were married by Father Tierney at Holy Name Church in Henderson. Clara was preceded in birth by Regina, Harold, Marvin, Roberta, Spalding, Nina Rene and Claude Homer Roberts. Clara's father was born in Union County but farmed in Henderson County.

The Roberts children attended the local elementary schools. The three older girls graduated from Mount St. Joseph Academy. The older boys graduated from high school at Jasper, IN. Claude Homer and Clara graduated from Niagara High School. The Roberts' girls attended Western Kentucky Teachers' College. Clara earned college hours from Mount St. Joseph Junior College. To their mother's delight all of the girls taught school until they were married.

Clara married Cecil W. King on Nov. 19, 1942. During World War II, Cecil was stationed at Ft. Crockett, TX and in Germany. After the war, he returned to the States, his wife and his former job with Pure Oil Company.

On Dec. 24, 1946, Cecilia Claire was born, Carole on Feb. 17, 1948, Claudia Celeste on Nov. 23, 1949. Cathryn Harriet on Feb. 13, 1952. The King children attended Holy Name School.

Cecilia attended Brescia and Henderson Community College and Secretarial College. She is married to Larry D. Abbot, they have one son, Paul and reside in Henderson.

Carol graduated from St. Louis University, spent 10 months as a nurse on Hope Ship in Maceio, Brazil. Attended Storrs University in Connecticut and received a master's degree in nursing. She married Michael J. Stevenson and have two sons; Michael King and Eric Christian Stevenson. They reside in Ranchos Palos Verdes, CA.

Claudia attended Henderson Community College and University of Kentucky. She married Larry A. Green and have two children, Lindsey Celeste and Stuart Allen. They reside in Henderson.

Cathryn graduated from University of Kentucky. She married Randall Manion, They have four children: Marcy, Maicie, Mark and Marley. They are members of St. Bartholomew Church in Louisville.

Cecil suffered a fatal heart attack on August 2, 1985. Clara attends Mass at Holy Name and enjoys her children and grandchildren.

KIPPER, FRANCIS NICHOLAS, born Nov. 28, 1907 and Nell Agnes Drury, born Aug. 9, 1911, were married on Aug. 14, 1929.

They had 12 children, 11 are now living-one dead: Mary LaVerne (Kipper) Thomas born May 28, 1930; Francis Charlene (Kipper) Watson born March 8, 1932; Martha Ann (Kipper) Lampton born Jan. 23, 1934; John Nicholas Kipper born Aug. 11, 1936; Marvin Simon Kipper born Jan. 18, 1938; Wayne Edward Kipper born April 20, 1941 (died at age 2); Judy Nicole (Kipper) Nelson born March 17, 1943; Joseph Wayne Kipper born June 10, 1944; James Richard Kipper born Jan. 10, 1946; Michael Ray Kipper born July 2, 1947; Harilyn Jane (Kipper) Harris born Aug. 17, 1948; Thomas Carroll Kipper born Oct. 21, 1950.

Nell (Drury) Kipper was the daughter of Clint (Pete) Drury and Anna (Storms) Drury. She was born and raised in Grayson County around the St. Paul and Big Clifty area. As a young woman she moved to Louisville where she met Frank (Bud) Kipper. They were married three months later. They lived in Louisville until March 1948, when they moved back to Grayson County.

Frank and Nell Kipper wedding picture

Bud and Nell Kipper lived in the small community of St. Paul where they raised their children. All of their children but the oldest girls attended St. Paul School. They were married for 43 years, when Bud died of cancer in May 1974. Nell now lives in Big Clifty, KY.

Three of their children belong to St. Paul Parish, several grandchildren and great-grandchildren live at St. Paul, and attend St Paul School. Three of their children belong to St. Joseph. The rest of their children live in Bardstown and Louisville.

KIPPER, JOHN N. (JACK) AND DEANNA CATHRAN DARST,

were married at St. Paul Church, Nov. 4, 1961 by Rev. Pike Powell. Deanna was born and always lived in St. Paul Parish. Jack was born in Louisville, but has lived in St. Paul Parish for most of his life. They are both active in church and school work. Jack is a member of the Parish Council. Jack and Deanna have both been on the St. Paul School Board in years past.

Jack is a builder and a farmer. His work is mostly in Louisville. He drives back and forth every day. Jack works around the church and school, helping with others in the parish with building and remodeling as it is needed.

Deanna is secretary of St. Paul School. She is on the picnic committee. In January of 1986 she helped to start a bingo at the parish hall for school tuition and other parish expenses.

Jack, Deanna and Nick Kipper

A son, Nick, was born Oct. 24, 1962. Nick loves St. Paul and the country around it. He has said, "When the Lord comes to earth, He will set His feet in St. Paul's." Nick is an agriculture teacher at Central Hardin High School in Hardin County, KY. He is a very committed and dedicated teacher and is admired by his students. A parent of one of his students remarked that she hoped her son would follow in Mr. Kipper's footsteps.

Jack is the son of Frank and Nell (Drury) Kipper. Deanna is the daughter of Joseph E. and Ruby (Tackaberry) Darst.

KIRCHHOFF, CHARLES,

immigrated to America in 1882 from Anrochte, Westfalen, Germany, at the age of 23. He came to avoid an enforced apprenticeship (cobbler). He was welcomed in Paducah by his brother Frank who was already established in the bakery business.

Charles and Wilhelmina Korte Kirchhoff with children, Theresa and Mary

In Paducah in Frank's bakery he met Wilhelmina Korte, a young woman from Strohen Province of Hanover, Germany. Wilhemina had been preceded by brothers, a sister, Mary, and uncles who had settled near Round Knob in Southern Illinois; they were acquiring farm lands. Charles and Wilhelmina were married in the rectory of St. Francis de Sales on May 13, 1886. Charles became a very successful grocery owner, establishing financial footing in a little cobbler shop. He retired at the age of 48. Charles and Wilhelmina had three children: Charles Jr. died in infancy; Mary and Theresa. Both Mary and Theresa attended St. Mary's Academy, Paducah. Theresa went on to become a legal secretary; she was the first touch typist in Paducah. Mary remained at home because of her father's failing health.

KIRCHHOFF, THERESA

married August (Gus) Legeay II whose grandfather, August (Joe) Legeay immigrated from LaJutiere in Western France in 1858 and settled on Old Cairo Road in McCracken County, KY, where a colony of French truck farmers was developing. The land was well-suited to garden and farm activities. Here August met and married Annie Daily, of Irish descent, who at age 16 came as a governess to children of the Menard family, also immigrants from France. Both were Catholics and they were married at St. Francis de Sales Church in Paducah. Of this union six children were born: Augustine (Singery), Camille (Roof), Helen (Seitz), August II, Paul and Alfred. Educational background of the six children is rather sketchy, except it is known that August (Gus) attended a one-room school. Distance prevented regular church attendance and the faith was not strong. However, four of the children married Catholics while two married non-Catholics. Children of all six were raised in the church. August died at the age of 65 and Annie lived to be 84.

Theresa Kirchhoff and August (Gus) Legeay II met when card playing was the foremost from of entertainment of the day. They were married in St. Francis De Sales Church on Nov. 8, 1910. It is of interest that the organist for the wedding was fired from her business position because Fr. Henry A. Connolly preached too long on the value of the Catholic marriage. (She was reinstated.) Of this union seven children were born, three survived to adulthood: Ann, Gus and Suzanne. Two died at birth, Mary Helen at 12, and Theresa Catherine at one year.

The early years of Gus and Theresa were happy and prosperous. Gus's livelihood came from operating a market garden on 45 acres. All of the produce was sold from Stall 48, Market House. Today it is the Market House Museum. Roots for the market gardener and his family are imbedded deep in the good earth. From early spring with the appearance of the asparagus shoots and radishes, through strawberries, sweet corn, watermelons, squash, to root cellars, bleached celery, turnip greens cut out of the cold and snowy fields, the cycle was repeated yearly with soul stirring anticipation and God's beauty and handiwork below and above the soil.

The Great Depression of 1929 hit and the bottom fell out of the market. Gus died at the age of 48 in 1931, leaving Theresa with three children: Ann (16), Gus (8) and Suzanne (5). Theirs was a real story of what the "crash" could do, and surviving through Love of God and one another. Foreclosure took the home and land, Aunt Mary (Theresa's sister) provided a home, and Theresa eventually moved into the work-day-world. She was soon polling a Catholic vote where needed and became deputy county clerk, remaining for 20 years. Shortly after retiring at age 72, she suffered a stroke and died at the age of 87.

KISTER, FRANCIS LEOPOLD,

was born in France in 1833. The family moved to Sinsheim, Grand Duchy of Baden (Germany) around 1837. Francis and his brother John came to America in 1851. In Louisville they met the Fritz family, emigrating from Effingham, Baden. In 1853, the rest of the Kister family came, settling in Nelson County where the father, who was an architect and master builder, was commissioned to construct the Trappist Monastery at Gethsemane. The Annals of the Abbey relate: Frank Kister put the church under roof by Winter 1855, but after finishing the north wing in 1856 he returned to Germany. (His wife had died in 1855). In 1857, John married Cecelia Fritz and Francis (Frank) married Frances Fritz-both at the Monastery.

In 1859 at the request of Fr. Joseph DeVries, Frank moved to Bowling Green to build the church there. So Francis Kister and Frances Fritz, who had lived five miles apart in Baden, but only met and married after coming to America, put their roots down in Bowling Green. They raised 12 children at 717 Barry St., within the shadow of St. Joseph Church-which he designed and built through the three stages of its development, from the first small brick church in 1860; through the enlargement of 1871-72 and through the magnificent Gothic completion of 1889. Frank Kister Jr. (1862-1931) at age 22, became his father's chief carpenter in 1884 for the final enlargement and completion of the church.

Eleven of the 12 children of Frank and Frances Fritz Kister with their spouses and children gather for Christmas morning breakfast at the family home at 717 Barry Street in 1897.

Frank Kister Sr. died in 1920 and Frances in 1928-both funerals from their Barry St. home to their beloved St. Joseph's.

Felix Francis Spugnardi, son of Wilhelmina Kister Spugnardi; Henry E. Keiffer III, grandson of Rosa Frances Kister Keiffer; Kathryn T. Garrison, granddaughter of Frank L. Kister Jr. and Lorene H. Batson, granddaughter of Mary Kister Bittner are descendents living in Bowling Green today.

1897 photograph of Frank L. Kister Sr. Family

KNIGHT, FRANCIS, was born Dec. 2, 1914 in Breckinridge County, KY, to William Knight and Mary Helen Ballman Knight, who were farmers. Catherine Lenora Shellman was born Jan. 21, 1918 in Breckinridge County, KY to Lewis A. Shellman and Rachel Oelze Shellman. They also farmed. Francis and Nora married April 7, 1942 at St. Romuald in Hardinsburg, KY. They owned a nearly 300 acre farm on the western tip of Breckinridge County, where the first seven of their 13 children were born. The remaining children were born at the local hospital. Their children include: Mary Helen, Rita, Marie, George, Ruby, Frank, Bill, Sue, Beth, Wayne, Alice, Don and Bobby. They also have 25 grandchildren and eight great-grandchildren. Francis passed away Oct. 5, 1988. Nora sold the farm and now lives in Cloverport where she attends St. Rose.

KNIGHT, ROBERT JOSEPH, was born Aug. 18, 1964 in Breckinridge County, KY, the youngest of 13 children born to Francis and Catherine Lenora Stellman Knight. Lori Lynn Stephens was born July 3, 1965 in Louisville, KY to Bobby Stephens and Barbara Probus Stephens.

They were married on March 16, 1984 at St. Rose of Lima in Cloverport by Fr. Maury D. Riney. They live in Cloverport and have one son, Robert Francis Knight who was born Nov. 27, 1988.

KNOTT, MICHAEL RAY AND KAREN ANITA ROGERS, are members of St. Mary Parish in Whitesville, KY. Michael was born Dec. 3, 1956, the son of Al Knott and Doris Hagan Knott. Karen was born Dec. 7, 1958, to Irvin Porter Rogers and Anna Lois Logsden Rogers. They are the parents of Nathan Michael, born April 17, 1983 and twins, Natalie Anna and Nicholas Ray, born Sept. 5, 1986. Michael is an electrician and Karen an instrument technician.

KOGER, MIKE AND DONNA HAYDEN, were born and raised in Daviess County, KY. Mike is the son of Charles and Maybelle Koger. Donna is the daughter of Charles William and Leona Hayden. They are members of St. Anthony Parish in Brown's Valley, KY. Mike and Donna are the parents of Holly Koger, a senior at Apollo High School and Jason Koger an eighth grader at Burns Middle School. Mike is a self-employed mechanical contractor.

KORTZ, EDWARD J. JR. AND PATRICIA R., and family are members of St. Thomas More Parish in Paducah. They were married on Oct. 11, 1952 at St. Francis De Sales Church.

Before retiring Ed was an accountant and Patricia was a staff registered nurse at Lourdes Hospital.

Ed and Patricia are proud of their four children. Julia is a registered nurse and is married to a pediatrician, William Weber. They live in Louisville, KY and have three children. Elizabeth is a registered nurse and works at the McCracken County Health Center. Both Julia and Elizabeth are graduates of Spalding College in Louisville. John, a graduate of Murray State University, is married to the former Valerie Singery and they have two children. John is a salesman for Welders Supply Inc. and Valerie is employed by Peoples First National Bank and Trust Company, both of Paducah. Ellen received her degree in special education from Brescia College in Owensboro, KY and recently was awarded a master's degree by Western Kentucky University. She is married to Michael Wolford and they have three children. Ellen is employed as a special education teacher at Apollo High School in Owensboro, and Michael is the Maintenance Department supervisor at Glenmore Distilleries, also in Owensboro.

Ed has been a member of the Mount Carmel Cemetery Board of Directors for over 15 years and has been chairman for the last several years.

Patricia's father, the late William J. Rance and her mother, Elizabeth, originally from Freeport, IL, moved to Paducah in 1943. Ed's late parents, Ed and Olga Kortz, were lifelong residents of Paducah. His father was a letter carrier for the U.S. Post Office and his mother was a leader of the Altar Society and Daughters of Isabella.

KRAMER, JOHN DAVID AND AMY JOAN, reside in St. Peter Parish in Waverly, KY. John David was born Nov. 14, 1968 in Union County, KY. His parents are the late George David and Virginia Ann Adamson Kramer. He has two sisters, Carrie Kramer Floyd and Kelly Ann Kramer. He attended Morganfield Elementary Grade School and graduated from Union County High School in 1987. He graduated from Madisonville Vocational High School with a degree in tool and die making. He is employed as a machinist at Thompson Tool Inc. in Henderson, KY.

Amy Joan was born June 11, 1966 and baptized at St. Ambrose Church by Rev. William Hagman. Her parents are Billy Don and Joyce Carroll Greenwell. She has four brothers and three sisters. She attended St. Ann's Grade School and graduated from Union County High School in 1984. She has worked as a beautician at Mane Tamer's and Linda's Beauty Shop but is opening her own shop, Bold Elegance, in Morganfield, KY.

They were married July 5, 1991 at St. Peter Church with Rev. E.E. Willett officiating.

KRAMPE, ANTIONETTE, was born Aug. 31, 1896 in St. Joseph, KY, while her father Joseph Anthony Krampe, was overseer at Mount St. Joseph 1883-1897. As overseer he insisted that he would only hire those who attended services on Sunday in the Catholic Church or a church of their choice. All the Cheshire family entered the church and were baptized Catholic, Anne Belle Cheshire (Sister Inez) among them. Mary Jane Thompson joined the family; she had been mistreated in her home, and Mr. Krampe took her to live with his large family at Brown's Valley when he found the meager salary he received at the Mount insufficient to sustain them. It is his donation of land at Brown's Valley that the church there rests on; the early picnic grounds are also his donation to the church. This same spirit of generosity must have been a natural gift from her father that caused Mary Aloysius, when she became Sister Antionette in the Order, to offer herself for the many needed duties that she accepted during her 66 years of active service in Kentucky, Missouri and New Mexico.

In 1918, when the flu epidemic was at its peak, and nurses were not available, she with Sister Agatha and Sister Patrice volunteered to nurse the soldiers at Camp Taylor. Not one of the three took the flu. When tuberculosis patients at the Mount were without much care, and no one seemed to know what to do for them, Sister Antionette had the balcony on the third floor of St. Angela's screened, and there they received the attention and care that was given to tuberculosis patients at that time. When later they were moved to the whitehouse, Sister Antionette went with them. She ate and slept there so as to be near should they have need of her.

During her two terms at the Mount 1923-1928, and 1961 until she was no longer able to take on major responsibilities there she worked in the milk house, the bake room, at the guest house where she made all visitors welcome and made the Sisters in the summer months feel equally welcome from their missions. She was one who kept the house for Bishop Cotton in Owensboro 1951-1957.

Weeks before her death, she began to fail, and she was confined to the infirmary at the Motherhouse. On the morning of Wednesday Aug. 27, 1980, she was not able to receive Holy Communion and seemed to be dying. At 3:30 p.m. she quietly passed away. Her funeral took place August 30. Father Anthony Zeigler and Monsignor Bernard Powers concelebrated the Mass. Bruce Fogle, seminarian and nephew of Sister's, was reader.

KRIMPLE, LEO ANTHONY, oldest son of George and Mary Ann Poat Krimple, was born July 14, 1899 at St. John's, KY. Leo's grandfather, Andrew Krimple, was the only Krimple born in Germany who came to the U.S. His maternal grandmother was Mary Catherine Haesely Poat, niece of Rev. Charles Haesely, builder of St. Jerome Parish, Fancy Farm, KY, who came from Switzerland.

Leo married Anna Christine Hovekamp on June 11, 1923. Anna's parents were Benjamin and Margaret Mary Sanders Hovekamp from established McCracken County families.

Leo and Anna were the parents of James Anthony Krimple, born Nov. 26, 1924 and died Aug. 12, 1991; and of Barbara Helen (Sister Mary Loretto, SCN) born April 30, 1928.

Front Row: (Left to Right) James Anthony, Anna Christine, Mary Loretto, SCN. Standing: Leo Anthony Krimple.

Leo Krimple was a master machinist at Southern Textile Machinery Company, Paducah, a master gardener until age prevented it and a good neighbor. He and Anna were loyal members of St. Francis de Sales Church, Paducah, active in Holy Name and Altar Societies, in picnics and bazaars for the church and for St. Mary's Academy which both children attended. Anna, born on April 19, 1900, died Oct. 14, 1968. Leo survived her until Jan. 14, 1989.

Sister Mary Loretto, SCN, has been an elementary teacher in Kentucky and Tennessee. For 11 years, she taught refugees, relocated in Paducah, and helped them to obtain employment. Sister also cared for her father and brother after the death of her mother. Presently, Sister ministers in Community Service at Nazareth Home, Newburg Road, Louisville, KY.

KURZ, PAUL N. JR. AND PALLIE, have been members of St. Leo Parish since 1970. Both were born and reared in Daviess County and were members of St. Stephen Parish. St. Stephen's will always seem like "home" to them since they were baptized, received the Sacraments of penance, Holy Eucharist, confirmation and were married in the Cathedral.

Paul is the son of Paul N. (Smokey) and Mary Lee Bauer Kurz. He attended Brescia College and is a graduate of the University of Dayton, Dayton, OH. Pallie, the daughter of Hayden C. and Kathleen Head Thompson is an R.N. having graduated from St. Mary's School of Nursing, Evansville, IN. Their children, (two sons and three daughters) were all born in Ohio where they resided until 1969 when they returned home to Kentucky. They were members of St. Thomas More Parish in Paducah for 18 months before moving to Murray in August 1970. One son and one daughter and four of their six grandchildren still reside in the area.

Paul and Pallie Kurz Family, November 3, 1990, (Left to Right) Back row: Jennifer, Paul, Pallie, Mary Ann Bell, Jeffrey Bell, Chris Kurz, Rita Kurz, Holly Kurz, Emily Kurz, Mike Kurz. Front row: Stephanie Kurz, Jacob Bell, Brian Kurz, Paul C. Kurz.

They immediately became actively involved in building parish community. Father Martin Mattingly was pastor at that time and he asked Paul to serve as a trustee. He has been a member of the finance committee since 1975 and as chairman, he also is a PPC member.

He was director of the CCD program in the parish for 10 years and is a Eucharistic Minister and lector at the present time. He is a charter member of the Fr. Russell Council of the Knights of Columbus. He was elected Grand Knight in 1978. The following year, he was elected treasurer, an office he has held since that time.

Pallie is chairperson of the liturgal committee, serves on the PPC and is a member of the Ladies Guild. She, too, is a Eucharistic Minister and lector.

LAMB, GARY NEAL AND JANIE MILDRED O'NAN,

were both born in McCracken County, KY. Gary was born Oct. 5, 1946 to Earl E. Lamb and Maurine (Jackson) Lamb; Janie was born July 10, 1949 the daughter of Jesse Paul O'Nan and Ethel (McElroy) O'Nan. They were married Sept. 15, 1965. Gary and Janie are members of St. Thomas More Church. He is employed as an engineer for Paducah and Louisville Railroad and Janie is an LPN at Lourdes Hospital.

They have two living children and one which is deceased: Gary Neal Jr., born May 2, 1968 who was killed in a four wheeler accident Aug. 11, 1981; Syrena Danette Gamble (Lamb) born March 25, 1966, married to Rodney Gamble with children Megan Lynn, Trevor Neal and one due December 1992; and Christina Antionette Lamb born Nov. 26, 1976, a student at St. Mary Middle School.

LAMBERT,

the four Lambert sisters and their brother officially joined St. Francis De Sales Church in Paducah, KY, on Dec. 12, 1959, but had been associated with St. Mary's Academy for many years previously.

Front (L to R): Barbaranelle and Gladys-Back (L to R): Laura Jane and Henrietta; Stanley Boy Lambert

Barbaranelle, Gladys Clinton, Henrietta Marie, Laura Jane and Stanley Boyd (Bo), children of the late Wesley and Janie Lambert, are all graduates of St. Mary's Academy in Paducah. Barbaranelle has been registrar at St. Mary High School for the last 27 years, preceded by working in the office of St. Mary's Academy for two years. Gladys taught kindergarten and primary grades for 27 years at both the academy and St. Francis Elementary School. She is presently secretary at St. Francis De Sales Church, where she has served for the last 10 years. Henrietta taught both in the Academy and St. Francis Elementary School for 17 years in the primary grades and served as secretary/bookkeeper for St. Francis De Sales Church for 21 years, until her death on Jan. 4, 1991. She also drove the school bus for several years. Laura has taught middle school and junior high school grades at both the Academy and St Francis Elementary School. When the elementary schools in Paducah consolidated, Laura went to St. Mary High School, where she began her 35th year of teaching in August 1992. She received the 1988 Distinguished La Sallian Educator Award from the Christian Brothers Community. Bo entered the teaching profession, but is now a free lance writer.

The sisters are Associates of the Sisters of Charity of Nazareth and members of the Daughters of Isabella. They have been involved in a variety of volunteer service to the Catholic community in Paducah.

LAMPTON, JOHN W. JR.,

and his wife, Bonnie S. (Portman) Lampton are members of St. Paul Parish in Grayson County, KY. Although they reside near Leitchfield, KY, also in Grayson County, they were both born and raised in Jefferson County, KY.

John, a carpenter and factory worker, is the son of John W. and Martha Lampton. Bonnie is the daughter of George R. and Anna F. Portman. John and Bonnie have two children. The oldest, Timothy Michael, was born Feb. 3, 1980 and is presently in seventh grade at St. Paul School. The newest addition to the Lampton household is Katie Elizabeth, who was born on Sept. 14, 1992.

LANCASTER, SR. ANNALITA,

is the daughter of Joshua A. and Anna McCracken Lancaster; the granddaughter of Joshua and Amelia Bolin Lancaster and Josephine Spalding McCracken. She was born and raised in Meade County, KY, in the parish community of St. Martin, Flaherty. She has resided in the Owensboro Diocese since 1943 as a member of the Ursuline Community at Maple Mount, engaged in the teaching mission of the Community within the United States and South and Central America. Educated in Meade County Public Schools, Flaherty, through high school; graduate of Bellarmine College and Spalding University, Louisville; post graduate studies at Catholic University, Washington, D.C. Currently serving as pastoral associate, St. Jude, Clinton.

LANCASTER, PAUL MARTIN AND MARY THERESA ROE,

were married in their home church St. Martin's, Flaherty, KY on May 24, 1980. Paul was born in Hardin County and raised in Meade County. He is the son of Robert Paul Lancaster and Mary Ann Whelan Lancaster. Mary Theresa was born in Breckinridge County and raised in Meade County, the daughter of Robert Louis Roe Sr. and Gwendolyn Lamar Langley Roe. They are currently living in Irvington; Breckinridge County. Members of Holy Guardian Angels Parish in Irvington. Paul is a self-employed farmer and Theresa is a nursing student and CCD teacher.

They are the parents of Emily Nicole Lancaster born March 1, 1982; Joshua Martin Lancaster born April 25, 1983; and Kyle Robert Lancaster born Nov. 23, 1987.

LANGLEY, THOMAS JOHN,

was the second child of Margaret Holtshouser and Nathaniel Langley originally of Nelson County, KY, and who migrated to Vermillion County, IL. Thomas was born in Vermillion County Feb. 22, 1828. On April 23, 1848 Thomas married Jane Hand who was the daughter of Elisha and Sally Hand. Thomas and Jane reared their family in Vermillion County. Thomas died young at age 40 and was buried in the Gordon Cemetery. When the city of Danville, IL decided to dam a creek to make Lake Vermillion, more than half of the old burial sites in Gordon Cemetery went under water. Thomas Johns headstone was lost. Jane died in 1898 and was buried in the Niccum Cemetery.

Sarah (1849-1849).

Elizabeth Ann (1850-1850).

Joseph Langley (1952-1929).

Margaret (1854-1898) married James A. Jackson, it is not known if they had any children.

Hellen (1856-1928) married Joseph Givens McMillian and later married George Young. Hellen was buried in the United States Church of Christ Cemetery in Henning, IL. Joseph was buried in 1887 in the Gordon Cemetery. Helen and Joseph's children were: Mary Cyndisa (1875-1946). Mary married Asa E. Crawford and was buried in Potomac, IL. Mary and Asa's children were: Paul (1896-1979, buried Lebanon, IN), Edgar (1901-1915, buried Potomac, IL), Joseph (1899-1899), unnamed male baby (1906-1906, buried Potomac, IL), Lewis Curtis (1910-1952 buried Savona, Italy) and Mary Marguerite born Dec. 13, 1913 in Indiana. Mary Marguerite married Milton Frederick Droege March 11, 1934 in West Lafayette, IN. Mary was a music teacher for a number of years. She and her husband ran a hardware store. Delia May (unknown) Reason Hazel (unknown) buried in the Gordon Cemetery. Gaffer G. McMillian (1882-1974). Gaffer was buried in Henning, IL Cemetery. Logan G. (1884-1943),. Martha Onita (1886-),. Clarissa (1858-),. Mary (unknown-1864),. Isabelle Jane "Belle" (1857-1913) married Mack Tuttle.

LANGSTON, W.T. TOMMY AND EVELYN LANGSTON,

family began when they were married by Rev. John Hallihan in the St. Francis De Sales Rectory on Feb. 20, 1938. Tommy was a Paducah City fireman for 22 years. Evelyn became a convert and was baptized by Fr. Thomas Libbs in 1943.

Their marriage was blessed with two sons and one daughter, Fr. Micheas Langston OSB, Robert L. Langston and Judith Giovannucci. During World War II Tommy served three years in the U.S. Coast Guard as a port security specialist. After the war they bought a home near St. Thomas More Church. Evelyn decorated the St. Thomas More altars for many years with beautiful flowers from her garden.

(L to R): Judy, Fr. Micheas, Evelyn, Tommy and Robert.

Tommy left the fire department in 1959 to join the Air Products Company as safety director. He was a first aid instructor for 38 years and was one of the first EMTs in Western Kentucky. He has been a member of Knights of Columbus for over 50 years, is a past Grand Knight of Holy Rosary Council Number 1055 and past navigator of Fr. Fallon Assembly, Fourth Degree K of C. He petitioned the local priests for permission to lead the rosary in 1978, 15 minutes before the Masses during October and May, and the next year the council started making rosaries to give people who had none. This practice still continues.

Tommy and Evelyn celebrated their 50th Anniversary on Feb. 20, 1988. The Mass was celebrated by their son Fr. Michaes Langston OSB, now an Army chaplain of 25 years. Their Mass and reception was attended by over 200 family and friends. They now have five grandchildren and one great-grandson. Both are very active in charity work of the church, St. Vincent De Paul, and Knights of Columbus.

LANHAM, ANTHONY (TONY) VERNON,

was born near Knottsville, KY. He is the son of John V. (Diddle) and Wanda Meserve Lanham. He attended school at Mary Carrico in Knottsville for eight years and four years at Whitesville Trinity High. He graduated in 1974. His grandparents are Joseph and Rose (Morris) Lanham and Emmitt and Cecil (Harley) Meserve.

Tony married Sandra Kay Goetz in 1980 at St. Lawrence Catholic Church. She attended school at St. Joseph and Paul for eight years and four years at Owensboro Catholic High she graduated in 1975. She worked at Ragu Foods Inc. for eight and half years. She is the daughter of John A. Goetz (deceased) and Martine (Alvey) Goetz of Owensboro.

Her grandparents are Nick and Bertha (Geisler) Goetz and Manford and Juliet (Osborne) Alvey.

They have now been married for 12 years and live in Knottsville and have three beautiful children; Tonea Kay, age 10; Brandon Vernon, age 7 and Jordan Michael, age 4. The children attend Mary Carrico School in Knottsville.

Tony has worked in coal mining in 17 years. Anne is now the owner of Lanham Mining Company Inc. Sandy is a housewife and has been since she quit working at Ragu in 1983. They also raise livestock (cattle) and do some farming on the side.

LANHAM, JOSEPH ANTHONY "TONY," was born in 1917 in Knottsville, KY and married Inez Louise Alvey in 1938. Inez was born in Evansville, IN while her father worked for the railroads. Tony's grandfather John Thomas Lanham married Elizabeth Ellen Hanley in 1821, in Washington County, KY and moved to the St. Lawrence Church community near Knottsville in Daviess County in 1850. Their son, Thomas Henry, married Mary Ellen Higdon. Inez's family long influenced by the strong Catholic faith of Henry Alvey, born 1821 in Washington County. He married his second wife, Isabella Thompson, at St. Joseph's Academy, Maple Mount in 1870. Their youngest son Charles Volk was named in part for Father Volk, the priest accredited for praying the "miracle of the bricks" for Mount St. Joseph Academy. Charlie married Mary Delora Hayden in 1900.

Tony and Inez Lanham

Almost life-long members of St. Paul's, Tony and Inez were married there on a very rainy day. The water was so deep that the car had to be driven up to the front door. In later years they established Lanham Electric and located just across from those same front doors. Except for a short period of time in the early years of their marriage they lived one and one-half blocks from St. Paul's until Thanksgiving Day in 1986 when their home burned while they were at Mass. Forced to relocate, they moved across town and tried a new parish. Celebrating their 50th Wedding Anniversary at St. Paul's, they now drive across town to their home parish. Their children Deanna, Michael, David, Tonya, Randy and Marian attended Sts. Joseph and Paul School, Owensboro Catholic High School and Brescia College, serving the church as choir girls and altar boys. The Lanhams have 13 grandchildren and two great-grandchildren.

LANHAM, JOSEPH LAWRENCE, was born Oct. 25, 1927, the youngest son of Lawrence Lanham and Hattie Hagan. They made their home south of Whitesville, and because of their location Joe attended school in Ohio County until his eighth grade which he spent at St. Mary of the Woods in Whitesville. He is a life-long member of St. Mary of the Woods Parish and is a Minister of Praise. He is also active in the Knights of Columbus, having served in various offices during his 17 years of membership. He has been member of the local Lions Club since 1974, also having served in some of the offices in that organization. Each year during October a large group of relatives and friends visit with Joe to celebrate his birthday; they bring many home cooked dishes and all have a generally good time. He has lived alone since his mother died in 1973 but has many friends in his faith family whom he can call on when needed.

LANOWSKI, JIM AND SUSAN RUDYINSKI, met at Creighton University where they both attended, and on Nov. 29, 1970 they were married. Jim was born Feb. 24, 1945 and Susan was born June 6, 1947. She lived in Nebraska. After their marriage they moved to Seymour, IN where Jim worked for his father at his store (Big Blue Store). A few years later, Jim and Susan had their first child, Lindsey Allison born June 1, 1977. Two years later, they had a son, James Andrew, born April 17, 1979. In 1983, the family moved to Owensboro, KY, and began another Big Blue Store. They then became part of Blessed Mother Parish, and are to this day.

Lindsey, now 15, is counting off the days until she gets her drivers license. She attends Owensboro Catholic High School and plays the piano as she has for nine years. Her brother, Andrew is now 13 and attends Owensboro Catholic Middle School. Andrew plays soccer and is very good. Jim and Susan love golfing, play together often, or with the rest of the family.

LATTUS, DONALD HUGH AND DEBORAH GAIL HUTCHINS, were married on March 13, 1976 at St. Edward Church in Fulton, KY. Don is the son of Hugh Leonard Lattus and Doris Burchman Lattus of Hickman, KY. Deborah is the daughter of Lewis Roscoe Hutchins and the late Hazel Campbell Hutchins of Fulton, Ky. Don and Deborah live in Hickman where Don farms, and Deborah is employed with the Fulton County School System.

They have two children, Jason Donald and Carrie Genet'. Jason is a sophomore at Fulton County and plays baseball, football and basketball. Carrie is in the eighth grade and enjoys playing basketball for the Fulton County Junior High Pilots.

The Don and Deborah Lattus family are members of Sacred Heart Church in Hickman, KY.

LATTUS, HUGH LEONARD AND DORIS JEWELL BURCHAM, were married on Feb. 13, 1946 at the Immaculate Conception Church in Union City, TN.

Hugh is the son of the late Jacob A. Lattus and Elizabeth Hogg Lattus of the community of Brownsville. Doris is the daughter of the late Robert Elbert Burcham Sr. and Fannie May McDaniel of Woodland Mills, TN.

Hugh and Doris have spent their entire married life in the Hickman area. They have two children, Barbara Jane who is married to Maurice Risner and lives in Louisville, KY and Donald Hugh who married Deborah Hutchins from Fulton, KY and lives in Hickman, KY. Don and Deborah have two children, Jason Donald and Carrie Genet'.

Hugh and Doris Lattus are members of Sacred Heart Church in Hickman, KY.

LATTUS, JOHN HUBERT, was born Nov. 29, 1897 in Hickman, KY, the youngest son and fifth child of Joseph Benjamin Lattus, a Polish immigrant, and Margaret Priska Stahr, daughter of Jacob Stahr and Augustina Scheible. He was baptized, made his First Communion and was confirmed at Sacred Heart Church.

On Nov. 16, 1921, he married Elizabeth Pauline Neel from Fancy Farm, KY at St. Jerome Church. She was born April 29, 1903, the eldest of 10 children of John Fielding Neel and Sarah Elizabeth Willett. John and Pauline had seven children, Mary Anita (Aug. 28, 1922), Rose Colesta (Feb. 1, 1925), Elizabeth Ann (July 10, 1928-Dec. 26, 1988), Frederick Joseph (Dec. 16, 1929), Herman Joseph (April 24, 1932), John Louis and William Lawrence (Sept. 8, 1937). The family were members of Sacred Heart Church and the children attended Catholic school.

Mary Anita married Joseph Crostic Youree and they have one son, Gregory Andrew. Rose Colesta married Robert Lafayette Harrison Jr. (1920-1969) and they have four children, Elizabeth Ann (born and died Nov. 11, 1946), Robert Joseph, Myriam Anita and James Frederick. Elizabeth Ann is Sister Elizabeth Ann, a Sister of Charity of Nazareth, KY. Frederick Joseph married Elizabeth Marie Poiners and they have two children, Benjamin Richard and Janet Marie. Herman Joseph, single. John Louis married Frances Ann Neumann and they have two children, Michael Dean and Sara Pauline. William Lawrence is single.

John Lattus served as usher, was a member of the Holy Name Society and a member of the Knights of Columbus, and served in other capacities when needed. Pauline belonged to the Altar Society, was manager of the school cafeteria at Sacred Heart for many years.

John Hubert Lattus died Jan. 27, 1971 and Pauline Neel Lattus died April 30, 1978. At the present time Joe and Anita Youree live in the family home and are members of Sacred Heart Church.

LATTUS, JOSEPH BENJAMIN, a Polish immigrant, born 1851, died 1900, moved to Hickman, KY from South Bend, IN and married Margaret Prisha Stahr, born Feb. 12, 1867. They lived on a farm west of Hickman and to this union six children were born Jacob Andrew, Joseph Benjamin, Catherine Augusta, Charles Anthony, John Hubert and Rosa Isabella.

After Joseph Benjamin's death, Margaret Stahr Lattus married her widowed brother-in-law Henry Maregold who had five children, Henry Herman, Philip Ernest, William Andrew, Mary Anna and George Bernard. They had one son, Raymond Victor. She helped rear a total of 12 children. All were members of Sacred Heart Church and very active in the Church. Henry Maregold died Dec. 13, 1935 and Margaret "Maggie" died Jan. 28, 1951.

LAUZON, FATHER PETER EDWARD, was born on July 8, 1953, in Owensboro, KY, the fourth of five children born to Joseph and Martha Baumgarten Lauzon. Since both parents and doctors knew a boy would be named "Pete," his birth was not announced to his parents with the traditional, "It's a boy," but rather with "Pete's here!"

Pete attended Immaculate Grade School and Owensboro Catholic High School, graduating in 1971. He then entered the seminary at St. Pius X in Erlanger, KY, graduating in 1975 with a BA in philosophy. He continued his education at Mount St. Mary's Seminary in Emmitsburg, MD, earning an MA in theology. He was ordained to the Dioconate on May 27, 1978, and to the priesthood on a snowy Jan. 6, 1979, at St. Stephen Cathedral by Bishop Henry Soenneker.

Fr. Peter Edward Lauzon

After ordination he served as associate pastor in Holy Spirit Parish, Bowling Green; St. Pius Tenth Parish, Owensboro; and Holy Name Parish, Henderson. In June, 1983 he was named pastor of St. Romuald Parish, Hardinsburg, serving there until assigned to study Canon Law in 1985 at Catholic University in Washington, D.C. He earned his Licentiate in Canon Law in May 1987, returning to the diocese to work in the Marriage Tribunal and serve as associate pastor at Immaculate and later at St. Pius Tenth, Owensboro. He was named pastor of St. Anthony Parish, Brown's Valley in June 1990, living at St. Martin's, Rome, while a new rectory was being built at Brown's Valley. He has worked with Engaged Encounter since 1980, and presently continues as pastor of St. Anthony Parish and working at the Catholic Pastoral Center as Adjutant Judicial Vicar.

Joseph L. Lanham

He loves priesthood and is a gifted homilist. He is also devoted to his family, and enjoys his time off by fishing, golfing, reading or spoiling his faithful dog, Barkley.

LaVOICE, ROSE AND HARRY, moved from Louisville to Paducah in May of 1974 because the FAA transferred Harry to Barkley Field. That summer they joined St. Francis De Sales Parish. In the earlier years Rose served as a Brownie and Girl Scout leader, CCD teacher, chairperson of the parish's Liturgy Committee, while Harry also taught CCD, and was a Webelo and Boy Scout Leader. Later, both became involved with TEC, and both the Catholic and Ecumenical Cursillo. Both Rose and Harry have served on the parish's CCD Board, and Rose was a member of the Diocesan Liturgical Committee for six years.

Harry, Rose and Julie LaVoice

When the Catholic Churches in Paducah merged their CCD programs, Rose became the associate director, and is currently serving the Catholic community in this capacity. Both Harry and Rose sing in the choir, where, in addition, Harry plays the guitar and banjo. Also, Rose serves as a lector, minister of the Eucharist and chairperson of the St. Francis De Sales Food Pantry.

The LaVoices are the parents of four children: Jeffrey Lewis, age 26, in the Air Force and stationed with his wife, Donna, at Elmendorf AFB in Anchorage, AK. They were the parents of Lucas, who died in 1987. Lisa Rose, age 22, also lives in Anchorage, working as a computer operator and attending the University of Alaska part-time. In Wurzburg, Germany with the USA is Michael Patrick, also 22, and Lisa's twin. Along with his wife Donna, and children Krista and Logan Michael, Michael is still celebrating being back from seven months in Saudi Arabia, Iraq and Kuwait. Julie Katherine, age 14, and the family's caboose is in the eighth grade and serves at St. Francis De Sales as a crossbearer, Minister of Hospitality, and a member of the choir.

LEACHMAN, MALINDA, was born on Sept. 13, 1905 in Center Point, IN, the only child of George Meek and Minerva Dennis Leachman. She was baptized in the United Brethren Church in the summer of 1912. Her paternal grandfather was John Meek Leachman, M.D. who practiced medicine and did both minor and major surgery in homes before the advent of modern antiseptics, antibiotics and anesthetics. Her maternal grandparents Cyrus Harry and Lucy Ann Tanner Leachman, whose lineage dates back to the pioneer settlers of McLean County, KY. Malinda was 10 when her father died. In 1915 her mother, Minerva, was diagnosed as having a terminal illness with only a few months to live. Knowing the exceptional quality of the Catholic Church's educational system, she officially set up a long range plan so that immediately after her mothers' death, Malinda would be enrolled at Mount St. Joseph Boarding School. Malinda graduated in June 1924. After passing the State Board Teachers examination she started teaching. Her career covered 44 years in the public schools of McLean and Daviess County, KY. On June 26, 1928 Malinda married Robert Lee Coakley, the Rev. Felix Sanders of the United Methodist Church officiated. They had two children; Connie Jan Coakley Clary and Robert Michael Coakley. Connie is a teacher in Las Vegas, NV and Robert Michael has been an employee of the CSX Railroad for the past 23 years. Malinda has seven grandchildren and eight great-grandchildren.

Malinda Leachman

Malinda received her undergraduate degree from Brescia College in 1958 and did graduate work at Western Kentucky University. Malinda and Robert Coakley celebrated their Golden Wedding Anniversary at Stephen Cathedral on July 6, 1978. Rev. Joseph Rhodes, the late Monsignor Anthony G. Higdon and the late Rev. John Bartolomucci, TOR, participated. Robert Coakley died five months later.

In referring to Catholicism, Chesterson once said, "When they (Protestants) cease to shout it down, they listen to it with pleasure."

Starting soon after her enrollment at Mount St. Joseph Academy in 1917 Malinda's thinking and loyalty was gradually becoming pro-Catholic. She was listening to it "with pleasure." Many years later, during a course in Ethics at Brescia College she faced the issue squarely, that she must do something with her life NOW. In spite of her Catholic mentality she was still active in the Methodist Church which the Coakley family attended regularly. In 1957 at the age of 52, Malinda was received into the Catholic Church. Her daughter, Connie, followed shortly and so did son, Michael. The Robert Coakley family who was originally 100 percent Protestant became 100 percent Roman Catholic when Robert was received into the church on June 2, 1974 at the age of 76.

To paraphrase: The Church is a House with many gates and no two people enter at the same angle. Malinda knows that at any particular time, if she is harassed, embarrassed, dumb, scared, or sinful that she is infinitely precious to Almighty God and that His hands are outstretched to her as tenderly as to any queen. Malinda is sometimes approached by Protestants and Catholics with the question, "Why did you embrace Catholicism?" What better answer can she give than simply; "Because I love it and I believe in it."

"O gift of gifts
O grace of Faith
My God how can it be
That Thou who has discerning love
Should give this gift to me?"

LEGEAY, ANN, GUS AND SUZANNE, were born to Gus and Theresa Kirchoff Legeay (see story p. 82) at home on the Cairo Road, McCracken County, KY. All three were baptized, made their First Communion and were confirmed at St. Francis De Sales Church. They attended St. Mary's Academy for 12 years. Transportation during the early years (five miles) was by horse and buggy. A glass enclosed buggy was pulled by Dyersburg who knew his way to the livery stable near old St. Mary's where she stayed and ate oats and hay while his "wards" were learning arts and letters two blocks away. Carpooling in the late 20s replaced the primitive mode of transportation.

Ann entered the Sisters of Charity of Nazareth at the age of 38, leaving a position with the Social Security Administration. Her years in community have been in teaching and counseling high school in Massachusetts and Paducah; Director of Students at Nazareth College, Louisville (now Spalding University), Administrator of St. Peter Home for Children, Memphis, and in recent years parish minister in Whitesville and Hickman, KY. She is presently engaged as co-director with Sister Theresa Ann in activities program for retired Sisters at Maple Mount.

(L to R): August Legeay III (Gus) Sr. Ann Legeay, SCN and Sr. Theresa Ann Legeay, OSN.

Gus served in the Navy after completing a degree in chemical engineering at Notre Dame as a recipient of the Matthew J. Carney Scholarship. He married Marion Riley, daughter of M.T. Riley and Nellie Yopp, Paducah, while stationed at Cornell University. Upon release from the Navy, he resumed his education at Notre Dame and secured employment with Union Carbide in Paducah and Martin Marietta in Oak Ridge. He spent 20 years in Gaseous Diffusion in Paducah and 12 years as production manager in Oak Ridge, TN. They have three sons: Michael, Gus III and Stephen, six grandchildren. Gus and Marion attend St. Mary Church, Oak Ridge where he is active in ministry.

Suzanne (Sr. Theresa Ann, OSU) attended Mount St. Joseph Junior College after graduating from St. Mary's Academy. One year later she entered the Ursuline Order. Sister Theresa Ann has had many years of teaching and principalship in elementary schools. She taught in Jeffersontown, KY, Affton, MO, principal St. Thomas More in Paducah, Curdsville, KY, Glennonville, MO, Precious Blood and Cathedral, Owensboro. She was elected to and served on the administrative Council of the MSJ Ursulines for four years. Today, she and Sister Ann are working with the retired Sisters at the Mount in the spiritual, physical, psychological and social areas of later life.

LENNON, KEVIN J., family in Logan County dates back to the 1850s when many Irish families came west with the railroad construction. Kevin's family has owned and farmed the land one mile south of Russellville along Highway 79 for nearly 100 years. His mother's family, the Strobels, originated in Germany and settled in Tell City, IN.

Kevin's wife, Laura, came to Russellville from Paducah. Her father's family, the Carrico's, are from the richly Catholic area of Fancy Farm in Western Kentucky. Her mother, a Ledbetter, moved north from Red Bay, AL.

Mr. and Mrs. Kevin Lennon

Kevin and Laura farm 130 acres along Highway 79 South, raising cattle, sheep and tobacco. Kevin is also employed by Miles Farm Supply in Allensville, KY, where he is the assistant manager of a retail chemical and fertilizer store. Laura has been teaching piano in her own private studio for four years in addition to her farming duties.

Both are graduates of Western Kentucky University, holding B.S. degrees in agriculture.

Kevin serves the Sacred Heart Parish as a member of the Parish Council, as well as lector, usher and Eucharistic Minister.

Laura has been the organist and music co-ordinator for Sacred Heart for nearly seven years.

LEWIS, DAVID RAPHAEL, was born June 12, 1959, married Marilyn Gail Ford March 24, 1982. Educated Owensboro Catholic High School, and worked as supervisor at Owensboro Grain Company. Marilyn was born March 21, 1962 and educated Apollo High School and Henderson Community College with a associate degree in nursing. She is now a housewife. They have two sons and two daughters, Jason David, born Oct. 2, 1982, Brenton Ford, born Oct. 26, 1984, Kaitlyn Nicole born May 22, 1990 and Aubrey Danielle Lewis, born Sept. 28, 1993. They have lived in Utica, KY, Daviess County since April of 1989. Members of St. Anthony Parish. David currently serves on the Parish Council and member of the St. Anthony Men's Club.

David R. Lewis Family

David is the son of Joseph Leopold Lewis and Francis Lee Hockgeiger Lewis. Their children in order of birth: Michael Joseph, David Raphael, Patrick Andrew, Mary Carolyn, Diane Elizabeth and Stephen Lee.

Marilyn is the daughter of Elmer Earl Ford and Mary Bell Nation Ford. Their children in order of birth: Gerald Ray, Joyce Nell, Keith Nation and Marilyn Gail.

LILLY, TOM AND LaNELL, family joined Blessed Mother Parish in Owensboro in June 1988. They have three children, Sarah Elizabeth, born Jan. 27, 1982; Tressie Virginia, born July 5, 1984; and Charles Thomas (Chas), born May 3, 1989. Sarah and Tressie both attend St. Angela Merici Grade School.

The Tom and LaNell Lilly Family

Tom and LaNell were both born and raised in Morganfield, KY in Union County. Tom graduated from Union County High School in 1977, LaNell in 1979. Tom graduated from the University of Southern Indiana with a degree in communications, LaNell holds an associate degree. LaNell is the daughter of Stewart and Ruth (Mills) Lovell, and was born on July 26, 1961. She is a convert, and received her First Holy Communion on their wedding day, June 23, 1979. Tom is the son of Robert Y. and Martha (Clements) Lilly, and was born on June 26, 1959.

LaNell and Tom became active in the TEC (Teens Encounter Christ) Retreat Program after observing the 25th TEC retreat held in Owensboro's St. Stephen's basement in October 1980. They have served with that organization in various capacities. Tom co-chaired the 1983 National Convention, and served as the Western Kentucky board chair in 1984. In addition, the Lilly's have been involved with two different degrees CCD, RCIA, The Knights of Columbus, Children's Bible School and various prayer groups. They attended the 44th and 45th Cursillo in Princeton, KY, and LaNell currently serves as a Eucharistic Minister for the shut-ins at Hillcrest Nursing Home in Owensboro, is involved with school activities at St. Angela Merici Grade School, and is a member of the Parish Council at Blessed Mother.

The family moved to Owensboro when Tom joined the staff of Owensboro Catholic High School as its first development director in January of 1988. In June of 1991, he became the director of stewardship for the diocese.

LINDOW, DAVID FREDERICK, was born Feb. 14, 1954 in Washington, D.C. He went to Lourdes and then went on to Daviess County. He served in the Air Force for seven years and now works at Allstate, where he has been for 10 years. His parents were Bob Lindow and Jean Wake. They belonged to Lourdes Church.

Catherine Marie Barna was born June 6, 1955, in Owensboro, KY. She went to St. Stephen Cathedral and then went on to Catholic High. She worked as a waitress in Briarpatch for 12 years, and now is a substitute waitress for Briarpatch. Her parents were Wally Barna and Margaret Spalding. She belonged to St. Stephen Church.

David and Cathy have four children. Their oldest child is Courtney Renee' Lindow. She was born Dec. 1, 1978, and attends Owensboro Catholic Middle School where she is a cheerleader. Dave and Cathy's youngest child, Natalie Brooke Lindow was born Feb. 3, 1982. She attends St. Angela Merici School, and is also cheerleader.

LINDSEY, ROY, was born Sept. 7, 1928 to Elizabeth and Siman Lindsey. Mable Hardy was born Sept. 13, 1928 to Sara and Joseph Hardy. They met in high school and were married Oct. 8, 1949. They had three children, Steve, Kim and Lesely.

Steve met Diane Hodges at Daviess County High School and were married on April 14, 1973. They attend St. Joseph and Paul Church and have two children, Maranda who was born April 25, 1974 and Ashley born Aug. 8, 1979.

LING, JAMES LEO, was born near Glenville, KY on Dec. 13, 1915. He worked at MSJ Academy from 1938-1940. His father Joseph Lewis Ling, a farmer, his mother, Flora Gertrude Hagan Ling, a homemaker. James had five brothers and five sisters.

Cecilia LaFern Ward Ling was born at Stanley, KY on June 22, 1924. Her father, Romie S. Ward, a farmer and Hosier Cardinal employee in Evansville, IN. LaFern's mother, Pearle A. Boarman, was a homemaker. She has six brothers and one sister.

The James Ling Family

James and LaFern were married April 13, 1948 at St. Augustine Church in Reed, KY. Moved to Detroit, MI for two years and had two children. They then came back to Kentucky, lived in St. Mary Magdalene Church, Sorgho, from 1951-1958. They had 10 children, one who died Dec. 7, 1975, 20 grandchildren and four great-grandchildren. They live in Philpot, KY, and are members of St. Mary of the Woods in Whitesville, KY. Parish activities include Eucharistic Minister, Knights of Columbus.

LING, RONALD EUGENE, was born in Philpot, KY. His father, James Ling was a farmer and worked at Sherval, Evansville, IN. His mother, LaFern Ward Ling, was a homemaker.

Jana Rowland Ling was born in Owensboro, KY. Her father, William DeChamp Rowland, is a union electrician, her mother, Charlotte Lowe Rowland, is a homemaker.

Ronnie and Jana Ling were married Oct. 16, 1982 at St. Mary of the Woods in Whitesville, KY. They have two sons and reside in Philpot, KY. They are members of St. Mary of the Woods Church and Ronnie is a member of the Knight of Columbus.

LITTLE, ED AND ANN McBRIDE, were married at St. Francis De Sales Church in Paducah, KY by Fr. Albert Thompson on Sept. 14, 1940. After spending four years in Biloxi, MS in the Air Force, they returned to Paducah.

Their son, Tom was born on Jan. 18, 1948. While in Paducah, they became members of St. Thomas More Church where both Ed and Ann were active in the parish and the school for several years. Ed was Scout Master for the Parish troop while Ann was Den Mother. Ann was also active in the Altar Society and the Legion of Mary, and a volunteer lunchroom worker. Ed spent years as baseball manager in all age groups with many Catholic youths.

Another son, John, was born Jan. 7, 1960. In 1962, the Little family moved to Madisonville, KY after Ed was transferred by his company (Kentucky Utilities). They became members of Immaculate Conception Church in Earlington, KY, where all were active in various church activities. Ann became lunchroom manager at Immaculate Conception School, and served for six years. She has been a member of the Altar Society for 50 years and served as president for three terms.

Tom graduated from Centre College in Danville, KY; he is married and lives in Lexington, KY. They have three children.

John graduated from the University of Kentucky (1982) and decided to enter the seminary. After spending five years in the Pontifical College Josephinum at Columbus, OH, he was ordained a priest on May 30, 1987.

Ed passed away on June 12, 1987. Ann spends her time doing volunteer work for Immaculate Conception Church. John is currently University Pastor of the Newman Center at Western Kentucky in Bowling Green, KY. Tom is currently vice-president of the Mentor Computer Company in Lexington, KY and is a lieutenant colonel in the National Guard.

LONG, JAMES L. AND REGINA HEAVRIN, were married Dec. 28, 1927 in the old Sacred Heart Rectory at St. Vincent's. Fr. Kiel officiated at the marriage. At that time the ceremony could not be held in the church, because James Long was not a Catholic. He belonged to the Presbyterian Church until his death in 1964. Despite this, he was instrumental in the decision to build a Catholic Church in Sturgis. Regina was the daughter of Joseph Benjamin Heavrin and Isabella Marie Thompson, both life long residents of Union County. Regina attended St. Vincent Academy before her marriage.

Mr. Long was affiliated with a coal company in Sturgis and an investor in real estate. He had options on some lots where the church stands and wanted to donate one lot to the church. Bishop Cotton, however, refused to accept only one lot for the church. Regina used her influence to persuade her husband to offer the entire front of the block to the bishop who accepted his generous gift. This area now has the church of St. Francis Borgia, a rectory, an educational building and a parish hall on it. The bishop was very foresighted in wanting room for growth.

James and Regina Long had two sons, James L. Jr. and Robert Joseph. The wedding of James L. and Nancy McDonnell was the first Nuptial Mass celebrated at St. Francis Borgia. Robert died at the age of 41. Regina is still very active in the community and faithful in her attendance at Mass. She has 10 grandchildren and 13 great-grandchildren. She is amazed at the changes which have occurred in Sturgis since the construction of St. Francis Borgia and is very proud to have been a part of the Catholic community in Sturgis.

LONG, MARIE HART, daughter of Edward and Adelaide Long, born Jan. 26, 1929. Educated in parochial elementary, junior high school and high school, attended New York University BBA program. Employed as Legal Secretary for Lord and Taylors; Civil Service Commission New York City and State and U.S. Federal Civil Service Commission; Executive Assistant to Personnel Directors, Gambel Bros., Kentucky; Manager of St. Francis de Sales Dept. of Agriculture School Lunchroom Program prior to and during start of cost accounting procedures.

On Dec. 6, 1947 she married Thomas Long at the Church of Incarnation Rectory.

T.L. Long and Marie Long

She has served as an Altar Society Member, Parish Choir and member of the Parish Council when the first Eucharistic Ministers were started at Midnight Mass, Dec. 25, 1970. She has been a member of the Legion of Mary since 1979. She served as State Treasurer for the daughters of Isabella from 1987-1991. She was a St. Francis de Sales Circle #258 Regent from 1988-1933. She has been a Boy/Girl Scout Leader; participated in PTAs; Parish Choir; St. Mary High School Band Officer and CCD Instructor.

She is a Navy wife of 18 years and Navy mother of seven and one-half years.

LONG, MITCHELL C. AND MABEL JOSEPHINE GRATZER, were married in 1946 by Rev. Charles P. Bowling of St. Paul Church in Owensboro. A native of Rosine, Ohio County, KY, he is the son of Benjamin F. Long and Anna Mae Young, and is a distant relative of Harry S. Truman and Kit Carson. During World War II he was at the Battle of the Bulge and was a prisoner of war. For over 30 years he was an employee of E.S. Peters Construction Company of Owensboro.

Jerry (on left) and Mitchell Long, sons of Mitchell C. Long and Mabel J. Gratzer. Taken in 1964 on the steps of St. Michael Catholic Church, in Cannelton, IN, which several generations of their mother's family had been members.

Mabel Long, a native of Owensboro, her parents Ernest P. Gratzer and Mable Catherine Paulin, and her grandparents, Benedict Gratzer and Josephine McCallister, had been members of St. Paul Church. From 1951 to 1959 Mrs. Long's family were members of the Blessed Mother Parish; of Our Lady of Lourdes, 1959-1965, and subsequently of Blessed Mother. For over 30 years she has been a member of the Legion of Mary and since 1985 has been a volunteer at the Owensboro Daviess County Hospital.

Mr. and Mrs. Long have two sons, Mitchell C. and Jerry. They attended grade school at Blessed Mother and Our Lady of Lourdes, and are graduates of Owensboro Catholic High School and Brescia College.

Mitchell Long Jr. attended St. Maur Priory at South Union, KY for two years. For several years he operated his own business, F.M.Hi-Fidelity, in Owensboro, and is now general manager of Faith Tool and Die Company. In 1968, he married Linda Jean Rivette, a daughter of Albert P. Rivette and Mary Margaret Yeand. Their children are: Christy Michelle, Heather Rene, Brian Mitchell and Katherine Jean. They attend Our Lady of Lourdes Church.

Jerry Long, a Magnum Cum Laude graduate of Brescia College, works in the Kentucky Room at the Owensboro Daviess County Public Library, also for McDowell Publications of Pleasant Ridge, KY and as a professional genealogist. He is vice-president of the West Central Kentucky Family Research Association, is a lifetime member of the Kentucky Historical Society and of several other historical and genealogical organizations. He has published several articles and books on History and Genealogy. He attends church at St. Pius.

LONG, REV. RICHARD EDWARD, eldest child of Marie and Thomas Long, was born April 11, 1956 at New York City. He was baptized at the Church of Incarnation. He received his first communion at St. Francis Solano, CA. He received his Confirmation at St. Thomas More, Paducah, KY.

Rev. Richard Edward Long

Rev. Long has served as an altar boy, youth high school representative, first male center in Paducah. He was educated in parochial elementary and high school. Attended the University of Kentucky and Paducah Community College. He attended Murray State University where he graduated May 1978 with a BBA in Political Science and marketing; B.S.; MBA - 1981 from the University of Kentucky. He holds a Master of Divinity from the Seminary of Immaculate Conception.

Ordained Deacon April 1990. Ordained to Priesthood June 2, 1990 for the Diocese of Brooklyn, NY. Served his pastoral year at St. Theresa June 8, 1990, assigned as Associate Pastor, St. Theresa of Lisieux. He studied at the Foreign Language Institute, Douglaston, KY.

LONG, THOMAS EDWARD, second son of Marie and Thomas, born March 2, 1958 in New York City. Baptized at the Church of Incarnation. Received communion and confirmation at St. Francis de Sales Church. Attended Parochial kindergarten, elementary and high school, Paducah, KY. Attended the University of Kentucky, Paducah Community College and Murray State University.

He served in the United States Navy for seven and one-half years at Orlando, FL. USN Training School, Security Station, Sicily; USS *Forrestal*, USS *Saratoga*, USS *Eisenhower*, USS *FDR*, USS *Nimitz*. He attended Naval Station Training School, Mississippi and Millington Naval Station, Millington, TN.

Thomas Edward Long

He served as an altar boy and in both the school and church choir, Paducah TEC #1, Eucharist Minister at St. Francis de Sales and Lourdes Hospital. He is presently employed at Lourdes Hospital.

LUCKETT, CLEMENT, born Sept. 15, 1872 and Lillian Josephine Caldwell born May 26, 1876 were married Jan. 21, 1896 in Marion County, KY. Soon thereafter they moved to Union County and became members of St. Ann Parish. Born to that marriage were five daughters, Catherine, Mary, Corrine, Lucille and Florence, and six sons, Harold, Preston, Ernest, Joseph, Leo and William. All children, except William, grew into adulthood in the parish. Harold became a priest, later a monsignor and was pastor of St. George Church in Louisville at the time of his death on July 24, 1936. Lillian passed away Sept. 12, 1917.

Joseph Luckett married Blanche Boswell in 1940 and they have one daughter, Mary Jo, who with her husband, Eddie Steward, are members of St. Ann Parish.

Joseph's paternal grandparents are Charles Preston Luckett and Catherine Spalding Luckett who lived in Marion County. "Joe" is a direct descendant of Samuel Luckett who came to America from Kent County, England in 1678. Samuel married Elizabeth Hussey, Charles County, MD. Son, Thomas Hussey Luckett, born of this marriage was a Revolutionary War First Lieutenant of Port Tobacco, Charles County, MD.

Through the genealogical line of his grandmother, Catherine Spalding Luckett, "Joe" is a direct descendant of Ignatius Spalding and his wife, Ann Pottinger who moved to Union County in 1821 where he donated land in Morganfield for St. Ann Church.

Through his maternal genealogical line, Joe is a direct descendant of John Caldwell, born in Lifford Parish, Ireland, and came to America in 1727. Joe's great-great-grandfather, John C. Caldwell (Sept. 22, 1758 to Nov. 9, 1804) was the second elected Lt. Governor of Kentucky and died in office in 1804. He was a major general in the Indian Wars. Caldwell County, KY was named for him. His burial in the State Lot in the Frankfort Cemetery was authorized by Act of the Kentucky Legislature.

LUCKETT, JOHN MILLS, the John Mills Luckett family had their ancestral roots in St. Mary County, MD. From there, they moved to Marion County, KY and finally migrated to Union County, in Western Kentucky in the early 1800s. The late John Mills Luckett II was the fifth of seven children. He and Mary Ethelreda (Hancock) parented eight sons and three daughters, the youngest of whom died 13 hours after birth. At the same time the mother also went to God (1931). This brought a minor breakup in the family. John "Jack" was the fire chief in Morganfield and wishing to raise his sons, ranging in ages 2 to 17, requested permission of the city officials to make adjustments suitable for bringing boys to live at the Fire Department. Permission granted, the unusual manner of raising a family started and lasted for 16 years. Life-style in this public building was quite unique.

The two daughters were given a home with an aunt and uncle in the country and attended school at St. Vincent

John Mills Luckett Family
1929 (Fifty-Years) 1979

John Mills Luckett Family 1929 and fifty years later in 1979. Left to right: Charles, Terry, Jerry, Bettye, Lloyd, Jack, Thomas, Rose Marie (Sister Martha Rita), Robert and Marion.

Academy as day pupils. After graduation, the older of the two girls chose to give her life to God to be of service of others. Along with seven other members of her class, she entered the community of the Sisters of Charity of Nazareth, KY in 1935. The younger daughter married and settled in California. The distance being so great, visiting home was a rare event for her, but she managed to keep in touch with all of the family by mail and by telephone.

All feel their mother is in Heaven and has been guiding "her flock" from on high. Their father died in 1963. They are a close knit family and collectively have produced 102 off-spring. May God, His Mother and the Luckett parents be praised and thanked!

LUCKETT, JOSEPH CYRIL, was born in Marion County and baptized by Father Durbin at Calvary May 28, 1920. Father Durbin had a son named Cyril, hence the name (he also became a priest).

He married Roberta Sanderson upon returning from the Pacific, April 27, 1946. Roberta was Baptist when they were married, hence the mixed marriage in Lexington by Father Garland O'Neal. She was baptized Catholic some three months later by the same saintly priest.

First two children, Joseph Currie and Peter Michael were born in college at Ohio State University while father became a veterinarian.

Father Harold Luckett (25th Year of Priesthood)

The family became members of Sacred Heart Parish upon moving to Russellville in June 1950 to establish a veterinary practice. They were made welcome by the Glenmary Home Missioners. Both priests and sisters who were here at that time. They had established a Catholic school there and gratefully all Luckett children received their primary school education from them, including Jim, born in 1951 and Marcia in 1954. The Glenmary Nuns were not educated as teachers but through their supreme effort and the Grace of God they did a superb job. Nearly every year a Sacred Heart graduate would receive the highest honors upon graduation from Russellville High.

Dr. Luckett established the Logan County Animal Clinic which still thrives with five veterinarians and some 10 or 11 lay assistants.

He retired in March 1986 and is now enjoying being actively engaged in parish activities and running a small cattle ranch. They live on the same block as the church.

LUSH, EDWIN, son of Leo and Ida Johnston Lush was born May 22, 1922. He has lived in Eastern Grayson County all his life. Edwin received his early education in the one-room Blue Springs Public School. For a time he was faithful in getting to school before his peers and building fires for a nickel a day.

He received the sacraments of Baptism, Penance, Eucharist and Confirmation in a frame church built at St. Benedict. In his lifetime, Edwin remembers worshiping in four parish churches. The first was taken by age, second by water, to give way for construction of the Nolin River Dam, third, erected by government financing, by fire. The fourth, and present church, is now serving the people of God.

Edwin Lush

Following the example of a wholesome Catholic family, he has served the Lord faithfully, by attending the Sunday Mass and lending a helping hand when needed. During World War II, Edwin was the only one of the four Lush boys remaining on the farm. He worked hard to help his parents support the family while his brothers, Arnold, Clevie and Joyce Lush served their country in the Army and Navy.

Edwin's physical abilities and lifestyles were slowed down at an early age. Due to health purposes, his right leg was amputated at St. Joseph Infirmary, in Louisville, KY on July 4, 1947. His handicap left him somewhat dependent on others. He lives on the Lush homestead with his sister, Carrie Alvey.

Edwin's cheerful disposition, a smile for everyone, patient suffering and endurance for many years, in climbing the many steps leading up to the churches are a valuable contribution for giving Christian witness to all who knew him.

LUSH, LURA MAE, (SISTER WALTER LOUISE), daughter of Leo and Ida Johnston Lush, was born Dec. 7, 1914. Their ancestors are thought to have come to the U.S. from England and Scotland. Her parents were born and reared in the Dog Creek, Hart County area. After marriage they moved across the Nolin River to Wax, Grayson, in early 1900s.

Lura, the seventh child of a large family received the sacraments in the first frame church at St. Benedict, Wax. Her memories of these sacraments are vague; however, she clearly remembers sitting on Fr. John Dudine's lap for first Reconciliation. Other than the slight tap on the cheek, Confirmation also left memories of the Most Rev. John A. Floerish putting his arm around her.

Her early education in a one-room school at Blue Springs, provided a foundation which later enabled her to complete high school at Mount St. Joseph Academy, pursue a BS at Brescia College, Owensboro, and MA at Eastern Kentucky University, Richmond.

Sister Walter Louise Lush

Her hard-working parent's fidelity to Sunday Mass and family prayer were factors which prepared her for a vocation to the religious life. She entered Mount St. Joseph Novitiate, Maple Mount, KY, Sept. 8, 1935; received the habit of the Ursuline Order, Aug. 14, 1936. She chose the name of Sr. Walter Louise, and made first Vows, Aug. 15, 1938. This marked the first occasion for the Most Rev. Francis R. Cotton to celebrate the Mass of Religious Profession at the Mount, and receive vows from eight young Sisters. She celebrated a Golden Jubilee in Religion, August 1986.

Sister's ministry has been principally in rural schools in Nebraska and Kentucky. She served as Activity Program Director at her Motherhouse for four years. After semi-retiring in 1986, Sister had been active in Parish Ministry, serving five years at St. Romuald Parish, Hardinsburg. In July 1991, the Most Rev. John J. McRaith established a Catholic presence in Caneyville, KY, Western Grayson County. When offered the position, Sister accepted the challenge to minister to the people, and work with other churches of the community to spread the Good News. Her superior, Sister Mary Matthias Ward gave her support. A dedication Mass and blessing were held, Aug. 19, 1991, at the new Holy Spirit Convent, with Bishop McRaith officiating, assisted by the pastor, Rev. Greg Trawick and visiting clergy.

Since the time of Bishop John A. Floerish, to the present, the growth of Catholicity in Western Kentucky has been astounding. To preserve the heritage, Sister feels her need to pray harder for many more zealous priests and religious to maintain and further the Ministry of Apostolic work in God's Kingdom.

LUSH, RODNEY AND TERESA, live in Clarkson, Grayson County, KY and are members of St. Paul Parish in Leitchfield. Rodney is the son of Bernard Lush and Gladys

Rodney and Teresa Lush

Tincher Lush. Teresa is the daughter of Tony Darst and Rebecca Clark Darst. They were married Sept. 11, 1987 at St. Paul Church by Rev. Thomas Clark, uncle of Teresa. Eucharistic Minister was Rodney's dad, Bernard. Their attendants were Lisa Darst (Teresa's sister) and Joey White.

Teresa attends Western Kentucky University to earn a degree in elementary education. Rodney is Grand Knight of the Knights of Columbus Council, following in the footsteps of his father. They help with many activities of the parish.

MAITZ, THE TONY AND LEE MAITZ FAMILY,
moved to Bowling Green, KY in 1981 when the Corvette Plant relocated from St. Louis, MO where they had lived for 23 years. With two of their five children, they joined Holy Spirit Parish; Lee becoming active in the Legion of Mary and CWO (Catholic Women's Organization) and Tony as an usher.

Tony and Lee were born and raised in Austria. They left as a result of the war for Argentina where they spent three months looking for a Catholic Church and a priest who spoke German so they could be married and celebrate the sacraments. After 10 years in Argentina they came to the U.S.—St. Louis for a family reunion and stayed. When in Buenos Aires they belonged to Santa Teresita Parish and the children went to school there. It was hard learning the language, but the Latin Mass made them feel at home! Learning prayers in Spanish was a fond memory! In St. Louis they belonged to Holy Cross Parish and St. Casmier Parish and had many German friends and family members. Tony belonged to a German Club Choir and Lee was very active in the Mother of Purpetual Help Group and school activities with the children. One of her fondest memories is helping her son make a rosary which he gave her on Mother's Day and she still uses.

Tony and Lee Maitz family.

Moving to Kentucky was not easy but Barbara and Ken (who worked at the Corvette plant) made the Maitz's feel very welcome. Lee can still see them waving to them across the pews.

Being separated from her husband due to job move, two teenagers, with a house to sell and a full time job at Red Lobster she devoted her spare time between crying and praying a novena. Things fell into place. They moved on September 8, the Blessed Mother's birthday, her being the Patron Saint of the Vincentian Priests. Sold their house on November 27, the "Feast of the Miraculous Medal" to Sisters of Charity for Vietnamese Refugees. Father Ed celebrated with them, him being a Vincentian Priest.

MANION, THE CHARLES J. AND ZENA OVERFIELD FAMILY,
moved to Owensboro in 1938. They were married Nov. 25, 1913 in Henderson County. She was a convert and he was an Irish Catholic (his mother coming from Ireland at 15). Charles repaired watches and was an optometrist in Henderson and later Owensboro. He belonged to Holy Name Society and Knights of Columbus. Zena worked at Sherman Williams and managed Foy Johnston Paint Stores before retiring in 1963. She was an artist and painted tabernacle veils for most churches in Owensboro and repainted statues. She was active in the D of I and was the first president of the Altar Society in Henderson.

Charles J. and Zena Overfield Manion family.

They had four children, Charles Jr., Harold, Richard and Mary Alice. Charles Jr., Harold and Mary Alice graduated from Holy Name School in Henderson. Richard went to St. Joseph Church after the family moved to Owensboro. Charles Jr. married Virginia Montgomery Sept. 28, 1940 at St. Paul Church. They had five children: C.J. III, Pat, Kay, Judy and Bob. Harold married Lela Rowland in Evansville and had three children: Tony, Nancy and Tommy, all live in Eureka, MO. Mary Alice married Kenneth Bopp Oct. 18, 1947 at St. Stephen's Cathedral. Richard married Theresa Vollman in 1942 at St. Joseph Church and have five children: Richard Jr., Marty, Joyce, Tony and Mike who all live in Louisville. Charles, Zena and their three sons are deceased. Mary Alice works in the Foster-Grandparent Program, volunteers at Mercy Hospital and sings in the choir at St. Stephen's when possible. Charles Jr. has two children in Owensboro, Judy Thornberry who is a Realtor and Bob Manion who is in insurance.

MANN, HENRY THOMAS AND MARY ELIZABETH POWELL
became husband and wife on March 27, 1937. Henry, better known as "Buby," met Mary when he was in his early 20s. His baptism had been delayed, but he was received into the church at Christmastime 1931 at the age of 24.

Henry Thomas and Mary Elizabeth Powell Mann.

Those depression days were not easy. Henry worked on the farm, raised a little crop and was at one time police chief at Uniontown.

Seven children were born of this marriage: Ted, Joe, Dick, Frankie, Martha, Millie and Jimmy, all of whom are still living.

Buby's parents were George Allen and Lucy Davis Mann. His relatives came from Allen County. Mary, daughter of Edward Fenwick and Martha Elizabeth Pike Powell, was born on Dec. 18, 1906. Buby, on Aug. 7, 1907. After 34 years of marriage, on Aug. 17, 1971, Buby was called to his eternal reward. Although Mary suffers from diabetes and has a prosthesis, she, at 85, does quite well and is able to attend Sunday Mass. In times past she made it a point to attend daily Mass at St. Agnes Church. She lives by herself in her mobile home in Uniontown. Her children visit her regularly and see that she has the things she needs. There are 20 grandchildren and 16 great-grandchildren. Most of Mary's life has been spent in St. Agnes Parish. The only survivor of the Class of 1927 from what was then St. Rose High School, needless to say, she is not interested in a class reunion!

MANNING, MILDRED VOWELLS,
In 1892 James I. Mills and his wife Alice Hardesty Mills and their 12 children came from Marion County, KY to Union County, KY. James was a farmer. He was told about the fertile land in Union County. He rented a farm near Uniontown, KY. He, his wife and his 12 children came by boat from Louisville, KY to Uniontown. The day they came was Ash Wednesday. All on the boat were amazed at the big family. They were served meat in all their meals, not realizing it was Ash Wednesday. When they did later they hurried to confession.

Mildred Manning

They were met at the ferry in Uniontown, by Jack Luckett, grandfather of Tommy Luckett and Edd Marie Padgett. Mr. Luckett came with two wagons to take the Mills family to his home. The Lucketts had nine children. The Mills family stayed at the Lucketts' for a few weeks until the house on the farm they rented was vacated.

Mary Ann Mills told of her sleeping on the dining room table on a feather bed at the Lucketts' home.

Mary and Peter Vowels who was born in Uniontown, were married at St. Agnes Church in 1906. They had six children. Twin girls, Mary Catherine and Mary Louise, only lived two months. Other children were Douglas, Samuel, Joseph Elbert (Hick) and Mildred. Shortly after Mary and Peter were married they moved to Waverly, KY where they farmed and lived until 1967 when they went to live at the Little Sisters of the Poor in Evansville, IN. They both died there. Peter was 87 and Mary was 101 when they died.

Mildred went to St. Peter School in Waverly along with her brothers.

In 1933 Mildred married Paul Manning, who was from Breckinridge County, KY. They had five children, Jerry, Pat, Sam, John and Charlotte. Paul died in 1969 in Carmi, IL. Mildred now lives in Morganfield, KY. She worked at the Dairy Maid for 15 years. She is a member of St. Ann Church where she is a week-day lector, Eucharistic Minister and on the R.C.I.A. team and a gift bearer.

MANNING, THOMAS JOSEPH,
was born in Rhodelia, KY near Brandenburg, and was baptized by Fr. John Sullivan. His father, Paul Thomas, was a school teacher and grocer at Rhodelia and Louisville. His wife was Eula Margaret Nevitt Manning. She was from near Rhodelia, KY. Her father was Gabe Newitt, a farmer near Rhodelia, KY. His father was Thomas Henry Manning who came from Owensboro, KY. They belonged to St. Theresa Parish in Rhodelia, KY.

Thomas is now living with his wife at Cave Hollow Bay in Edmonson County and belongs to St. John Catholic Church in Sunfish, KY. His wife is the former Verena Oser from Jasper, IN. She is a gardener and cook. He is presently retired and has lived at Cave Hollow Bay on Lake Nolin for the past 10 years. Their children were all born in Louisville, KY. He belonged to the Knights of Columbus, the American Legion, Veterans of Foreign Wars, etc. His wife's parents were Avis Oser and Francis Oser. Avis lived to be 101 years old. They are both deceased. They were great people. Thank God for all.

Their children are Thomas Jr., Pat, Phillip, Marty, Theresa, Bridget, Mary, Buddie Leon, Elaine and Tony.

They decided to join St. John Parish because the people were so friendly and nice to them and it was only

13 miles away. They liked the atmosphere very much. They worked at the church, painted the parish house and were general managers for nine of the 10 years. They have cleaned and done general repairs around the place. They are now retired and stay at home most of the time. They attend Mass on Sundays and Wednesdays at St. John.

MARREN, J. THOMAS, born and raised in St. Louis, MO, married Helen L. Vertin, born and raised in St. Joseph, MO, on May 4, 1946. They resided in St. Louis with their three sons, Thomas Joseph, John Patrick and Francis Jerome and were members of the North American Martyr Parish until January of 1964. While a member of the North American Martyr Parish, Tom was extremely active in the Vincent De Paul Society and the Boy Scouts, where all three of their sons obtained their Eagle Scout Award.

J. Thomas and Helen V. Marren

The family transferred by Emerson Electric Company from St. Louis to Russellville, KY, where Tom assumed the position of production superintendent. The family became members of the Sacred Heart Parish in Russellville. Tom and Helen's three sons graduated from Brescia College, Owensboro, KY and now live out of state, as do their two grandchildren, Tim and Susan. Tom was very active in the Sacred Heart Parish, serving on numerous committees until his death on Oct. 21, 1983. He was buried in St. Mary Cemetery in St. Louis, MO. Helen continues to be an active member, serving on several church committees of the Sacred Heart Parish in Russellville, KY.

MARRETT, JAMES FRANCIS AND EMMA LOU, were married at St. Stephen Cathedral on April 26, 1980; Rev. Richard Meredith officiated at the ceremony.

Jim is the son of Louise Mulligan and the late Francis A. Marrett. He was baptized and confirmed at the cathedral.

James Francis and Emma Lou Marrett

Emma Lou, who is the daughter of the late Alice Mae Sharp and Zedock William Embry, was raised in Louisville, KY as a Protestant. Her first encounter with the Catholic faith community was through Jim. Because his faith was so strong and his beliefs so binding, she felt compelled to explore his Catholic religion. She began instructions with Fr. Meredith, and what a blessing that was. Fr. Meredith is a brilliant Biblical scholar and a truly inspired man of God. The instructions progressed to the desired conclusion when Emma Lou was confirmed at the cathedral on Nov. 24, 1980.

The Marretts have five children, Larry, Jamey, Robin, John Mark and Cindy and four grandchildren.

Jim has been a letter carrier with the U.S. Postal Service for 27 years. Emma Lou retired from the Owensboro-Daviess County Hospital in 1989, where she was supervisor of the Neuro-Surgical Unit.

The Marretts believe their life together is far richer because of their shared Catholic faith.

MARRETT, LOUISE MULLIGAN, was born in the small community of West Louisville, KY, on Aug. 12, 1910, the youngest of eight children of Henrietta O'Daniel and Joseph H. Mulligan. The family attended Mass at St. Alphonsus Church in St. Joseph where Louise was baptized on Aug. 15, 1910 by Rev. Richard Maloney.

Francis and Louise Marrett

Her favorite activities while growing up on the family farm were riding the horses and dancing to the music of her Edison victrola. She still loves to reminisce about her favorite horse and the many hours she enjoyed while riding around western Daviess County.

Almost her entire lifetime has been spent in Owensboro and Daviess County. She left home only during her high school years to attend St. Catherine Academy in Springfield, KY.

Louise was married to Francis A. "Nick" Marrett at St. Alphonsus on Nov. 23, 1932; Rev. Joseph Diemert officiated at the ceremony. The Marretts moved to Owensboro following their marriage and subsequently built their home in the parish served by St. Stephen Cathedral.

Nick was born in the West Louisville area on Nov. 19, 1910, the only child of Mary Blandford and Hardin Marrett.

Nick and Louise had four children, James, Robert, Joan and Rebecca and 18 grandchildren. Three of the Marrett children still reside in the Owensboro Diocese.

The Marretts had been married 58 years when Nick died on June 10, 1991.

Louise has been a member of the Cathedral for more than 57 years. She has been active in the Altar Society and has worked at the Cathedral Soup Kitchen. She also volunteered at the St. Vincent De Paul Society Store and at Mercy Hospital.

Her life has been devoted to her children. She raised them in a loving Catholic home and instilled in them the values of their Catholic faith.

MARTIN, THE CARROLL AND GERTRUDE FAMILY, The family of Jesse Martin moved from Marion County, KY to Union County around 1895 and settled in the Grove Center, St. Ambrose Community.

Jesse, the oldest in the Martin family, married Shellie Kibby, the oldest in the Thomas Kibby family.

The couple had only one child, a son. And when he was born on April 21, 1915, the selection of a name began. Jesse wanted the name of Joseph, his father's name. Shellie wanted her father's name, Thomas. And the owner of the farm where the Martins resided, Carroll Wallace, stated that his name must be used.

So the son of Jesse and Shellie Martin was christened Joseph Thomas Carroll Martin. Throughout his life he has been known as Carroll Martin.

Carroll attended a one-room school—Old Bethel—through the eighth grade and then attended the old Grove Center High School, one of four county high schools in Union County.

Family of Carroll and Gertrude Martin—Mark's wedding June 1984. Bottom row, left to right: R.J., Anna, Maria, Mark, Barbara and Tom. Top row, left to right: Gertrude and Carroll.

Carroll graduated from Grove Center High School and labored with his father as a small, tenant/sharecropper. Carroll also worked on nearby farms.

Jesse Martin died in 1936 and Carroll continued the farming operation, supporting his mother.

In 1940, Carroll married Anna Gertrude French, one of 11 children. The couple were united in Holy Matrimony on May 14, 1940 at St. Ambrose, the second oldest Catholic Church in Union County.

Carroll and Gertrude have remained in the St. Ambrose Community all their married lives and their union produced five children—three boys and two girls.

Carroll entered public work, first as manager of Kroger's in Morganfield. He later worked in the shipping and receiving department at MoVac, a vacuum metalizing firm.

Carroll was elected to two terms as Union County's Property Valuation Administrator and served in that capacity for eight years. He retired as a certified water plant treatment operator for the city of Morganfield.

Carroll served 27 months in the U.S. Navy.

He is a third degree member of the Durbin Council 1004 Knights of Columbus, based in Morganfield and is a fourth degree member of the St. Vincent Assembly, based in Henderson.

Carroll has been active in St. Ambrose as a parish council member, Eucharistic Minister and as a lector.

Gertrude was kept busy raising the couple's five children and being a dedicated housewife. She has found time to be an Altar Society member at St. Ambrose and is also a member of the choir and of the Ladies Guild.

The couple celebrated their 50th Wedding Anniversary on May 14, 1990 at St. Ambrose.

MATTHEWS, ALVA M. AND GRACE COMPTON, married July 9, 1919, at St. Anthony Church, Axtel, Breckinridge County, KY. Alva (1892-1968) and Grace (1898-1977) were lifelong farmers, except for the 10 years that the family, with the four oldest sons lived in Detroit, MI.

After coming back to Kentucky, three more children were born. (A baby girl, Patricia, died.) All were members of St. Anthony Parish until 1946 when the parents moved to Hardinsburg, KY in St. Romuald Parish.

Alva and Grace Matthews family (1963). Standing, (L to R): Thomas, Claud, Francis, Gerald, Joseph. Seated, (L to R): Grace, Mary Rita (Sister Mary Angela), Alva.

Of the six Matthews children, Joseph of Rockford, IL married Audrey Krueger and they had seven children. Gerald of Janesville, WI married Lavina Symonds and they had five children. Francis of Hardinsburg, KY married Margaret Whitfill. They had 10 children. Claud of Hardinsburg, KY married Martha Ann OReilly. They had 11 children. Mary Rita joined the Ursuline Order of Mount St. Joseph, Maple Mount, KY and is known as Sister Mary Angela. Thomas of Salem, OH, married Joen Trolinger. Tom and Joen have four children. Joseph died in 1976.

MATTHEWS, JERRY, born Feb. 28, 1953, married Lavida Ann Hinton, born Feb. 4, 1959 on April 15, 1978.

Jerry was raised in Breckinridge County and moved to the Owensboro area to be with his grandparents in his early teen years. Jerry entered the Catholic faith April 1991 at Our Lady of Lourdes Church. A joyous occasion for all! Jerry is presently a supervisor with Western Ky. Gas Company.

Lavida has been a member of Lourdes Parish since its birth. Immediately after high school, she started her training in banking with a local finance company. She currently manages TranSouth Financial Services.

Jerry and Lavida have two children: a son, Jerred Lee, born Feb. 18, 1981 and a daughter Marissa Faith-Lynn born Aug. 21, 1987, both are enrolled at Catherine Spalding Elementary.

Jerry's first love is his children and the time spent with them. Jerred shares his father's second love for hunting and the outdoors. Jerry is an avid hunter and displays many trophies.

"All my memories of growing up are memories of love because I grew up in a large family" said Lavida. "My brothers were the special kind of brothers who always looked out for the *little sister*. Family is very important."

"I am also very thankful for the opportunity to visit Medjugorje in '88" added Lavida. "It was truly an enlightening experience: a reaffirmation of all that we believe in."

Jerry is the son of James and Nadine Blair of Cloverport, KY. Lavida is the daughter of Raymond Hinton and Wilma Hagan, both from Whitesville, KY and James R. Baird of Utica, KY.

MATTINGLY FAMILY, "Big George" Austin Mattingly, (born Oct. 30, 1802, Washington [Marion], KY, died Oct. 31, 1883), the son of Basil (born 1772, Maryland) and Monica (Miles) Mattingly, was married Jan. 19, 1828, Washington County, KY, to Ann Nancy Johnson, (born Dec. 15, 1807, died Oct. 27, 1867), daughter of Henry and Catherine (Flannagan) Johnson. Their known children: Augustine, Amanda Catherine (born 1820, died 1912, was married Oct. 23, 1848 to Thomas Monarch, by W.S. Coomes, C.P.), Austin (I), Benjamin, John R./H., Harriett, Ellen, Milton, Eliza J., Mary A./Margaret, Austin (II), Nancy and Patrick. In 1821 George attended the very first session of St. Mary's College, Marion County, KY. Upon moving to Daviess County, George was to become one of the earliest residents of Boston Precinct. He settled there in 1832. His holdings included a 176 acre farm in Boston Precinct No. 5. George and Nancy were apparently members of St. Lawrence Catholic Church. They were respected Christian citizens, landholders and slave owners. They are buried in St. Lawrence Catholic Cemetery, Daviess County, KY.

George Mattingly's immigrant ancestor, Thomas Mattingly I, came to America in 1663/1664 settling in St. Mary County, MD. The Kentucky Mattinglys descended from this man. The Maryland ancestral home of the Mattinglys was known as "Mattingly's Hope," remaining in the Mattingly family for over 300 years. George Mattingly's grandfather, Leonard Mattingly, is said to have emigrated from Maryland to Kentucky sometime around 1780.

MATTINGLY, CHARLES CELESTINE JR. AND MILDRED KANNAPEL, Paternal grandparents: John and Mattie Jolly Miller and James Robert and Rose Sheeran Mattingly. Paternal parents: Charles C. and Mildred Miller Mattingly. Maternal grandparents: John and Mary Sheeran Roach and William and Mary Sohn Kannapel. Maternal parents: Ethel J. and Nora Roach Kannapel.

Charles C. was born in Breckinridge County, Hardinsburg, KY on Sept. 7, 1928. He died on July 12, 1985 in Hardinsburg, KY. Mildred was also born in Hardinsburg on June 17, 1931. She still resides there.

They are members of St. Mary of the Wood, McQuady, KY. Charles C. served in the Army during the Korean War, farmed and worked at Olin Chemical. Mildred owns H & R Block Tax Service in Hardinsburg, KY. They have four children.

Rosanne Mattingly Cunningham, born Sept. 14, 1960, lives in Bowling Green, KY. She works at Bowling Green Medical Center as Neuro-Diagnostic Technician and has three children: Beth, Christina and Cody.

Charles C. Mattingly III was born on Feb. 24, 1962 and lives at Greensburg, KY. He is an attorney.

Harry Jerome Mattingly was born on Feb. 5, 1968 and attends pharmacy school at Samford University, Birmingham, AL.

Michael Mattingly was born Sept. 10, 1970 and attends Brescia College, Owensboro, KY.

All four graduated from St. Romuald High School, Hardinsburg, KY.

MATTINGLY, JOSEPH EARL AND MARY R. HAMILTON, Joseph is the son of Claude I. Mattingly and Loney Hartly Mattingly. Mary's parents are Charles Justin and Mary A. Bowlds Hamilton. They were farmers and members of St. Anthony Parish in Daviess County.

Joseph and Mary were born in Daviess County and now live in Owensboro, KY. They are members of St. Pius X Parish. Their children include:

Mary Jane, married to Leon Brasher of Bowling Green, KY attend Holy Spirit Parish. Rita Faye, married to Tom O'Bryan of Whitesville, KY attend St. Mary. Mary Earline, married to Danny Brasher, attend Blessed Mother Parish. Joseph E. Mattingly Jr., married to Janice Fitzerald. Charles Justin, married to Ina Conder, of Whitesville attend St. Mary. Judy, married to Mike Pate, of Lewisport, KY attend St. Columba Parish. Patricia, married to Darrel Clark, of Daviess County attend St. Pius X Parish. Eddie L. Mattingly, married to Tammy Jackson, of Maceo, KY attend St. Pius X Parish. Ricky Martin, married to Sharon Howard, of Maceo, KY attend St. Pius X Parish. Tommy B., married to Lisa Millay, of Lewisport, KY attend St. Columba Parish. Kenny Joseph Mattingly, married to Becky Craig attend St. William Parish. A daughter, Margret Ann Mattingly, died in 1955 at the age of 6 months.

MATTINGLY, JOSEPH WENDELL, was born at Curdsville, KY, Daviess County, on July 17, 1907. He was baptized at St. Elizabeth Church there. He is the son of Henry Elbert Mattingly, a teamster, and Mary Fonda Vowels, a seamstress.

Muriel Calhoun was born at Curdsville, KY on Sept. 26, 1906. She was baptized at St. Alphonsus Church, St. Joseph, KY. She is the daughter of James Paul Calhoun and Irene Clements, farmers.

They were married on June 27, 1927, at Sacred Heart Church, Whiting, IN. Wendell retired from the steel mills in East Chicago, IN, and Muriel retired as secretary from St. Mary School, Griffith, IN. They moved back to Kentucky in 1969.

Joseph and Muriel Mattingly

They had 12 children, nine still living; 48 grandchildren and 70 great-grandchildren. They liked to travel and play cards. They celebrated their 50th Wedding Anniversary in 1977, and took a trip to Hawaii.

Wendell passed away on Feb. 16, 1990. Muriel lives in Curdsville and attends St. Elizabeth Church there.

MATTINGLY, FATHER MARTIN, was born on April 24, 1925 at Curdsville in western Daviess County, the son of Ignatius Mattingly and Mabel Green. He was baptized on the day of his birth by Father James Higdon, pastor of St. Elizabeth Church in Curdsville. (Martin's father said, "You can't tell when babies might die; I want to be sure he is baptized.") The Mattingly family lived on a farm two miles from Curdsville until 1932, when they moved to Owensboro.

Fr. Martin Mattingly

He attended grade school at St. Joseph School and St. Frances Academy. After his sophomore year in high school at St. Frances, he entered the seminary at St. Mary College near Lebanon, KY. He finished high school and two years of college at St. Mary's and was transferred to St. Mary Seminary in Baltimore, MD, where he finished his preparation for the priesthood. He was ordained by Bishop Francis R. Cotton on May 30, 1950.

He was stationed temporarily at St. Mary of the Woods at Whitesville, then at Hickman, KY, where he served primarily mission parishes at Fulton and Murray. In 1952 he transferred to Hawesville with missions at Lewisport, Patesville and Pellville. He became pastor of St. Anthony Parish at Brown's Valley in 1955. He then pastored churches at Murray, Hopkinsville, Paducah and Earlington. He taught philosophy and theology at Brescia College 1952-1961 while serving the parishes in the Hawesville circuit and of St. Anthony in Brown's Valley. After his transfer as pastor to St. Leo Parish in Murray, he was Catholic chaplain at Murray State University 1961-1981. He qualified as faculty member of Bellarmine College in Louisville and taught an extension course in theology to nursing students in Paducah.

He is now pastor of Immaculate Conception Parish in Earlington and of Resurrection Parish in Dawson Springs. He recently celebrated his 67th birthday and the 42nd anniversary of his ordination.

MATTINGLY, SISTER MARTIN GERTRUDE, was born on Nov. 21, 1907 at Knottsville, KY to Martin and Gertrude Bowlds Mattingly. She was baptized on Dec. 14, 1907 as Stella Mae and had her Confirmation on Oct. 25, 1915. She entered the convent on Sept. 7, 1927 and took her vows on March 19, 1930 and March 19, 1933. Her brothers and sisters include: Mary Edwina Loyd, Sister Merici, OSU, Mary Theresa McBride, Anna Geraldine Staples, Mary Margaret Payne, Joseph Edward, Thomas Leo, Martin Spalding, Vincent Eugene, Merici Benita Millay.

Her missions include: St. Charles, Bardwell, KY, Hardinsburg, KY, Earlington, KY, St. Columba, Louisville, Flaherty, KY, Raywick, KY, Wax, KY, St. James, Louisville, Jeffersontown, KY, St. Bartholomew, Louisville, St. Martin, Rome, KY, St. Margaret Mary, Louisville, St. Leonard, Louisville, Motherhouse, St. Bernard, Louisville, Immaculate, Owensboro, Cathedral, Owensboro, Mary Carrico, Knottsville, KY, and Motherhouse.

MATTINGLY, SISTER PAUL JOSEPH,

was born on Oct. 17, 1896 and died on Oct. 22, 1977. She was the daughter of William J. and Roxanna Vowells-Mattingly of St. Joseph, KY. She was baptized as Pauline on Nov. 26, 1896 and entered the convent on March 19, 1915. She received her habit on Aug. 10, 1915 taking her final vows on Aug. 5, 1923.

Brothers and sisters include: Dan, Billy, Jude (Brother Martin, OP), Georgia Cecil, Joe, Angela Thompson (half-sister), Mayme Wethington (half-sister).

Pauline attended school at the Mount from 1903 to 1915. She was probably a day student since she lived at St. Joseph, KY. On Nov. 10, 1905, Archbishop George Montgomery of San Francisco, a relative of Sisters Columba and Bernard, visited Mount St. Joseph. As he was introduced to the students he spied Pauline, and he asked "Where does this little red head live?" She replied, "Across the hitching lot."

Pauline received the name of Sister Paul Joseph at investment. Her missions took her to Blanco, NM; to Jefferson, Marion, Nelson, Breckenridge, Union, Daviess Counties in Kentucky. She taught at Mary Carrico School, Knottsville, for seven years. Here she taught in the grade school, but most of her work was done in high school as librarian and teacher of English.

Inclined to be scrupulous in her own observance of poverty, she would mend her stockings with something lasting, such as umbrella material. She was not exactly particular about her personal appearance, but she was particular about seeing that the poor were clothed and fed. She was motherly in the care of the nieces and nephews left upon the death of their mother, Angela Thompson. She was outgoing, and tried to help people in any way she could. It was while she was at Blanco that the school took on a lunch program.

When she retired to the Mount in 1972 she took upon herself the organization of the St. Ursula Library, and she enjoyed this kind of retirement so much that she could be found working with the books late at night. When not busy with books she enjoyed making bright colored flowers (posies) of fabrics and wire in the craft room.

She died at Mercy Hospital, Owensboro, at 1:45 in the afternoon, Oct. 22, 1977, after several days of illness, although she had not been well since 1972 when she retired from teaching. Her death had been expected for several days. Her nieces, Sister Mary Eva Thompson and Sister George Ann Cecil, were with her when death came. They had been quite attentive to her in her illness, as she had been toward them when they were children and in their early days in the convent.

Funeral Mass which was said at 2:00 p.m., October 24, was concelebrated by 10 priests: Father Jerry King, OP (Superior at Dover, MA) celebrant, Monsignor George Hancock from the chancery office, Monsignor Bernard Powers, Father Jude Weisenbach (of Brescia College), Father Henry Willett, Father Phillip Riney, Father Carroll Wheatley, Father Anthony Ziegler, Monsignor Edward Russell, Father D.P. Thibault (St. Louis Bertrand, Louisville). Father Ziegler gave the homily in which he compared Sister's life to that of the seasons. Survivors included three brothers, Martin, St. Stephen Priory, Dover, MA; Dan, Lafayette, LA; and, Joe, Curdsville, and a sister, Georgia Cecil of Owensboro.

MATTINGLY, SISTER THERESE MARTIN,

the second child of Hugh Bernard Mattingly and Lila Lyon Mattingly was born on March 2, 1907, at Loretto, KY. She was given the name of Mary Alice. She had one older sister, Edith who was married to Victor O'Daniel and died April 18, 1954. A younger sister, Pauline, married Joseph E. Dugan, and died April 18, 1964. Two younger brothers, Hugh Bernard, who died Oct. 29, 1913 and Henry Lyon, who married Evelyn Pontrich and lives at Lanesville, IN. She attended St. Charles Elementary and High School in Lebanon which was taught by the Mount Saint Joseph Ursulines. On Sept. 7, 1926, Mary Alice entered the Mount Saint Joseph Novitiate and received the name of Sister Therese Martin.

Her teaching career took her to: St. Columba School, Louisville, St. Ann Howardstown, St. Bernard School, Clementsville, St. Andrew School, Harrodsburg, Holy Name of Mary School, Calvary, St. Denis School, Louisville, KY, St. Charles School, Lebanon, St. Paul School, Leitchfield, Grants, NM, St. Augustine School, Lebanon, St. Bartholomew, Louisville, and Benton, KY, being present to the people with whom she comes in contact.

Sister Therese Martin Mattingly

Sister Therese Martin loved all of her teaching experience with the exception of the one year at Clementsville when she had 36 students, 29 of whom had the last name of Wethington. The people told her that she had to learn who the fathers and grandfathers were before she could really remember the students.

MAYFIELD, JOSEPH,

was born on Sept. 22, 1963, the eldest child of J. Anthony and Barbara R. Haynes Mayfield. A native of Daviess County, he was baptized at St. Paul's in Owensboro and attended Mass at St. William's in Knottsville. Angela, his wife was born Dec. 16, 1962. She is the youngest daughter of James E. and Margaret E. Ambs Higdon of Philpot. She was baptized at St. Pius and attended Mass there. On Oct. 23, 1982, Joseph and Angela were married at St. Pius. Her uncle, Monsignor Anthony G. Higdon officiated.

As of this date the young couple have three beautiful children, Sarah, Laura and Maria. The family resides near Knottsville and are members of the St. William Parish.

During the 17th century their ancestors came to America from England and France and later in the late 19th century, Germany. With them they brought the Catholic faith, passing it on to each generation.

Joseph and Angela Mayfield with their children, Sarah, Laura and Maria.

During the 19th and early 20th century their families settled in the areas of St. Lawrence, St. William's, St. Mary's and also in the area of St. Anthony's in Brown's Valley. This brief history is dedicated to all those in their family who have died and gone, but left them so very much: the loving memories, the special friendships and more, but most of all for showing the way to our Heavenly Father through the church.

MAYFIELD, KENNETH L AND DEBORAH (CECIL) FAMILY,

Kenneth, a paper worker, is the son of Mr. and Mrs. Jerome Mayfield. Deborah is the daughter of Mr. and Mrs. Claude O. Cecil. They were born and raised and continue to live in Daviess County, where they are members of St. Mary's, Whitesville.

Kenneth and Deborah have three children. Brad, born Sept. 29, 1976, is a freshman at Trinity High School. Travis, born March 26, 1980, is in the seventh grade at St. Mary's. Aaron, born May 30, 1982, is in the fourth grade at St. Mary's.

McBRAYER, WILLIAM ANTHONY,

was born in Pellville, KY. His father, Shelby Walton, was a farmer and pipefitter and his mother, Beatrice Elizabeth Bickett, a housewife. Rebecca Ann Goetz was born in Owensboro, KY. Her father, John August Goetz, was a farmer. Her mother was Virginia Martine Alvey, the daughter of Manford Aloysius Alvey.

William and Rebecca Ann McBrayer

They were married Nov. 27, 1969 on Thanksgiving Day at St. Paul Catholic Church in Owensboro and moved to Pellville, KY where they farm and Bill works at National Southwire Aluminum.

McBRIDE, GORDON AND ALMA,

have called Western Kentucky home throughout their lives and have been members of Sacred Heart Parish in Union County for the 40 years of their marriage.

Alma was born to Leonard Wurth and Mary Pauline Poat in the St. John's community outside of Paducah. The Wurth family moved to Morganfield in 1942 when Fr. Barrett asked Leonard to be the caretaker for St. Ann's. Gordon grew up in Union County, the youngest son of Will McBride and Agnes Pritchett.

Center: Gordon and Alma McBride. Bottom: left, Vicki Higginson; right, Staci McBride. Top, left to right: Tom McBride, David McBride, Gary McBride and Larry McBride.

Alma and Gordon were married on June 10, 1952 at St. Ann's by Fr. Spaulding. They have six children and seven grandchildren. Their oldest son, Gary, married Diana Johnson of Las Vegas and they now live in Niceville, FL, with their three children, Joe, Mike and Heather. David married Debbie Clark of Owensboro where they reside with their two daughters, Katie and Laura. Vicki married Brad Higginson of Henderson where they live with their two sons, Chase and Logan. Larry was ordained a priest for the Owensboro Diocese in 1987 and is currently the pastor of St. Pius X Parish in Owensboro. Tom married Kari Boyd of Marion and they live in Reidland. Staci graduated from Brescia College and works as an accountant in Owensboro.

Alma and Gordon drawing from their deep roots in Catholicism are very active in their church. Their involvement in the parish has ranged from teaching religious education to working on the parish picnic. They have also been involved in the TEC program. Their active involvement in the church has been passed on to their children. Gary is active in Cursillo. David and Debbie are involved in Engaged Encounter. Vicki and Brad have worked on Cursillo weekends. Tom, Kari and Staci have been involved in the TEC program and Staci participated in the Ministry Formation program while at Brescia.

They are a family with a rich Catholic heritage who continue to celebrate that heritage with an active faith participation.

McCARTY, GARY LEON, was born to Dora Ann and Joe McCarty on September 18. He is a graduate from Catholic High. He has been employed at Colonial Bakery for 18 years. He attends Precious Blood Catholic Church.

Mary Sharon Thomas was born to Barbara Ann and Robert Eugene Thomas on September 10. She is a graduate from Mount Saint Joseph Academy. She is employed at Owensboro Daviess County Hospital for 11 years. She attends Precious Blood Church.

Gary and Sharon have three children. Jennifer Leigh McCarty who is 13 and is in eighth grade at OCMS. She also attends Precious Blood. Scott Alan McCarty who is 9 and is in the third grade at Bishop Soenneker Elementary. He also attends Precious Blood. Heather Nicole McCarty is Gary and Sharon's youngest. She is 3 years old. She attends Precious Blood with her family.

Gary and Sharon have been married for 16 years.

McCARTY, JAMES MICHAEL AND THERESA ROSE HAGMAN, were united in marriage in the old Immaculate Conception Church at Hawesville, KY. Their marriage was one of the last in the old stone church. They began their married life on a dairy farm near Curdsville in western Daviess County. There they were members of St. Elizabeth Church and where their first six children were baptized. In 1959 they moved to Hawesville and at that time they were able to worship in the new Church of the Immaculate Conception. After two years, they were back in Daviess County and in 1963 they bought a farm in the Utica-Livia area of southern Daviess County and became members of St. Anthony Parish at Brown's Valley. They liked the area because of the elementary school at St. Anthony's. After a couple of years, they received word that their school would be closed. They were very disappointed as now their children,

Mike and Theresa McCarty Family—40th Wedding Anniversary.

13 in number by now, would have to be bused to the Catholic schools in Owensboro. Because they wanted their children to have a Catholic school education, Mike began work at ALCOA in Newburg, IN in addition to his farming operation.

All 13 children are graduates of Owensboro Catholic High School and all continued their education after graduation. They are all successful in their chosen work. They have also given their parents 28 grandchildren.

Mike served on the first Parish Council at St. Anthony's. He is presently serving a term on the Pastoral Council. He is also a member of St. Anthony's Men's Club. After her children were almost grown, Theresa took the job as parish bookkeeper. She also is a member of the Finance Committee. Both Mike and Theresa are lectors and Eucharistic Ministers at St. Anthony's.

McCARTY, JOHN MICHAEL FAMILY, began on Oct. 25, 1952, when John, the second of 13 children, was born to James Michael McCarty and Theresa Rose Hagman. One year later, his future wife, Carolyn Ann Drury, was the first of five children born to Archie Joseph Drury Jr. and Frances Theresa Reisz.

John attended St. Elizabeth, Immaculate Conception, St. Joseph and Paul, St. Anthony and Our Lady of Lourdes parochial grade schools and Owensboro Catholic High School. Carolyn attended The Immaculate Grade School as well as Mount St. Joseph Academy and Owensboro Catholic High School. Carolyn and John first met while students at Owensboro Catholic High School.

Upon their graduation from high school in 1971, John and Carolyn attended the University of Kentucky in Lexington. They graduated from U.K. in 1975, John with a bachelor of science in agriculture and Carolyn with a bachelor of arts in education. They were married in Owensboro at the Immaculate on July 26, 1975.

After John and Carolyn taught one year in Marion County, John was accepted into the University of Louisville School of Law. On May 13, 1979, John graduated from law school and he began practicing law in Owensboro. Carolyn taught first grade at Our Lady of Lourdes School until May 22, 1980 when Zachary Stuart was born. In 1981 John opened his own law practice in Hawesville. On Feb. 6, 1983, Benjamin Simon, was born. Later that year, the family moved to Hawesville where they live today. On Feb. 15, 1986 Christopher Martin was born. On Jan. 18, 1990 Emily Coleen was born.

Zachary and Ben attend Immaculate Conception Grade School. Christopher is in kindergarten at Hawesville Elementary. Carolyn has retired from teaching and is a full time mother and homemaker. John is the Commonwealth Attorney for the 38th Judicial District.

McCARTY, SISTER PAULETTA, O.S.U., is the daughter of Ignatius Paul McCarty (1885-1958) and Nettie Rose Mahoney (1896-1973). Her father was a farmer who was born in Daviess County, KY. Her mother, born in Nelson County, KY, was a housewife.

Sister Pauletta was born Helen Marie McCarty on July 17, 1921 in Daviess County. She is a member of St. Elizabeth Church, Curdsville. The third of eight children, she attended St. Elizabeth School, Mercy Academy in Louisville and Mt. St. Joseph Academy in Maple Mount, KY. She graduated from Mt. St. Joseph in 1939 and entered the Novitiate at Mt. St. Joseph Ursuline Convent in January 1941.

Retired to M.S.J. in 1992 after 49 years of ministry in teaching and/or pastoral care in Kentucky, Missouri and Nebraska.

McCASLIN, JILL ANNETTE, was born on Dec. 20, 1979 in the Owensboro-Daviess County Hospital. The proud parents were Mike and Marilyn McCaslin. She has an older sister, Julie. The proud grandparents were Russell and Flora McCaslin of Hawesville, and Paul and Anastasia Johnson of St. Lawrence.

During the Great Depression, Paul Johnson worked for 50 cents a day, six days a week. It was difficult finding a job then. He paid 7 cents for a gallon of gasoline. He and his family grew their own wheat for flour, and they raised hogs and cows as a source of meat and milk. They also raised chickens as a source of food. It was a treat to go to Owensboro at least once a year. There was no such thing as buses back then. He walked three miles to get to school and church every day.

These may not seem like much now, but back then they were very proud of their accomplishments!

Jill McCaslin is now 12 years old and she is attending Immaculate Conception School.

McILVOY, DANIEL B., is married to Polly and they have daughters, Mary Anne Zaya, Carol Kersting and Linda Penn. They also have six grandchildren.

Old St. Patricks at Danville, KY, dedicated 1810.

The McIlvoys have lived in Bowling Green, KY, Warren County since 1945 and are members of St. Joseph and Holy Spirit.

Daniel McIlvoy House, 1806.

Daniel is a physician—pediatrician. His family is from Ireland.

McKENDREE, ARVIL LEWIS, was born in Marshall County, the son of Haze and Lucille (Green) McKendree. Arvil has three brothers and five sisters. Ruth Ann McKendree was born in McCracken County, the daughter of Richard Anthony and Helen Marie (Luigs) Durbin. Ruth has seven brothers and two sisters. Ruth was a member of the last graduating class from St. John High School.

Arvil and Ruth were married April 20, 1974 at St. John Church in McCracken County. They lived in Paducah for 14 years and attended St. Thomas More Church. They moved to the St. John Community in 1988 and are members of St. John Church. They have two daughters, Jennifer Helen and Jessica Ann. Jennifer is a freshman at St. Mary High School. Her hobbies include dance, sports and music. Jessica is a fourth grader at St. John Elementary. Her hobbies include dance, acrobatics and being a Girl Scout.

Arvil was baptized a Catholic during the Rite of Christian Initiation of Adults on April 2, 1988, at St. Thomas More Church. He is a wholesale salesman for Kentucky Wine and Spirits Company. He is a member of the Lone Oak Lions Club and the St. John's Knights of Columbus organization. Ruth is employed by Alco Health Services in Paducah, working in the sales department.

McNEILL, CATHERINE AUGUSTA LATTUS, was the third child born to Joseph Benjamin Lattus and Margaret Priska Stahr Lattus (Jan. 12, 1892). She was baptized April 17, 1892, made her First Communion Aug. 17, 1902 and was confirmed Nov. 3, 1902 at Sacred Heart Church, Hickman, KY.

On Feb. 3, 1913, she married Roy McNeill, son of Tom McNeill and Molly Reed McNeill. They lived on a farm east of Hickman until Roy's death on Sept. 17, 1921. After his death she went into grocery business on Dec. 8, 1922 and remained at the same location for 53 years helping her church, family and friends.

Catherine Augusta Lattus McNeill "Katie McNeill".

After retiring in 1975, Mrs. McNeill lived at her home until she fell and went to live with her niece and her husband, Joe and Anita Youree, until her death.

Aunt Katie, as she was known, belonged to the Sacred Heart Altar Society, had food sales for the church at her store and was very active in all church activities. She paid tuition for many children at Sacred Heart School for many years. She was a daily communicant and attended Mass and church services any time there were any.

On Dec. 26, 1988, she and her niece, Sister Elizabeth Ann Lattus, visiting for the holidays, were killed in an automobile accident after attending Mass in Union City, TN. After a double funeral "Aunt Katie" was laid to rest in the Hickman City Cemetery at age 96, two weeks short of her 97th birthday. Sister Elizabeth Ann was buried in the S.C.N. Cemetery, Nazareth, KY.

"Aunt Katie" was one of her church's greatest benefactors both during her lifetime and after death, leaving a large sum of money to the church in her will. She lived for her God, her family and her friends.

McNULTY SR., THE MARTIN A. FAMILY, began when Anita Reisz born Sept. 13, 1916 to Rosa Fischer and Daniel Reisz, married Martin on June 5, 1937, at Stephen Cathedral.

Anita's baptism, First Communion and confirmation took place at St. Martin Church, Rome, KY. In 1961 with her four sisters, one brother, many friends and family, all joined in Mass, celebrating Rosa and Daniel's 50th Wedding Anniversary on November 28th, at St. Augustine Church, Reed, KY. A memorable reception followed at their home.

Martin, born April 1, 1915 to Mae Coleman and John McNulty I, had four sisters and one brother. His baptism, First Communion and confirmation took place at St. Stephen Cathedral where his family were members all their lives.

Martin and Anita were blessed with 16 children, 38 grandchildren and 13 great-grandchildren to date. Listed are their 16 children's name and year of birth.

Marty, 1938; Rosemary, 1940; Dan, 1942; John, 1943; Pat, 1945; Ruth, 1947; Mike, 1948; Helen, 1949; Martha, 1950; Rachel, 1951; Bill, 1953; Jimmy, 1954-1966; Maggie, 1955; Mary Ann, 1956; David, 1958; Jeanne, 1960-1962.

The McNultys belonged to St. Stephen Parish, with the exception of several years, until their 16th and last child was baptized there. In the fall of 1960, with the expansion of the diocese, they became members of Precious Blood Parish. June 5, 1962, was Martin and Anita's 25th Wedding Anniversary celebrated with a Mass at Precious Blood Church and a beautiful reception at the school hall.

Time marched on and with 16 children things can get complicated, but Martin and Anita's ideals modeled that

April 1, 1990, Daddy's 75th Birthday celebration. Front row from left to right: Martha, Mary Ann, Martin (Daddy), Anita (Mother), Rosemary, Margie, Helen. Back row, left to right: Dan, Pat, Rachel, Marty, Ruth, Bill, John, Mike, David.

of the Holy Family and it became clear their religion and family came first.

Of the 14 surviving McNulty children all have been Brescia College students, 11 are college graduates from various colleges, three with a master's degree. There's been a McNulty child or grandchild attending Owensboro Catholic High School since 1952, the second year after it was built.

A McNulty has served as an usher when all three bishops were installed in the Diocese of Owensboro at St. Stephen Cathedral. In 1938, Martin McNulty Sr. for Bishop Francis R. Cotton; 1961, John McNulty III for Bishop Henry J. Soenneker; 1982, John McNulty IV for Bishop John J. McRaith.

During the mid 1960s six McNulty sisters participated in the Precious Blood Church adult choir.

June 5, 1987 Mr. and Mrs. Martin A. McNulty Sr. celebrated their 50th Wedding Anniversary, honored with a Mass at St. Stephen Cathedral followed with a grand reception celebration at their home.

As far back as any of the McNulty children can recall, daily prayer was and is a way of life. The McNulty Motto is: "The Family That Prays Together Stays Together." Twice a year, without exception, once in the summer and at Christmas time the McNultys travel for miles to be together to carry on their family heritage and traditions. They meet at what has been the McNulty Home Place for close to 130 years, located in the beautiful Bon Harbor Hills, outside Owensboro, KY. The celebration of the Holy Mass and recital of The Family Prayer are always the heart of all McNulty Reunions and functions.

When Martin McNulty passed on Feb. 14, 1991, he had his beloved wife and most of his children gathered around him in prayer. "As you live, so shall you die."

Anita McNulty is still a member of Precious Blood Church and is frequently visited by her many friends and family she has so deeply touched in her own special way over the years.

McRAITH, BISHOP JOHN JEREMIAH, was born on Dec. 6, 1934, in Hutchinson, MN. He received his grade school education in a one room country school and graduated from Saint John Prep School in Collegeville, MN in 1952. Bishop McRaith is a graduate of Loras College in Dubuque, IA and received his seminary training at Saint Bernard Seminary in the same city. Bishop McRaith was ordained to the priesthood on Feb. 21, 1960, for the Diocese of New Ulm, MN.

Bishop McRaith was the executive director of the Catholic Rural Life Conference from 1971-1978. In 1978 Bishop McRaith was appointed as vicar general/chancellor of the Diocese of New Ulm. Bishop McRaith was ordained bishop of Owensboro on Dec. 15, 1982.

McRAITH, MARIE HANLEY, was born on Jan. 2, 1900 in Meeker County, MN. Marie Hanley married Arthur L. McRaith on Aug. 17, 1926 in Litchfield, MN. Marie and Arthur had five children: James A., born Sept. 4, 1927, John Jeremiah, born Dec. 6, 1934, Jane, born Nov. 9, 1936, Mary Win, born Jan. 1, 1939 and Margaret Mary born June 15, 1944. Jane married Charles Moening and they have four children: Bernadette, Brian, Sarah and Shannon. Margaret Mary married Eugene Madder and they have three children: Molly, Meghan and Matthew. James A. married Mary E. McCormick and they have four children: Mary Beth, Timothy, Barry and Daniel. John J. was ordained a priest for the Diocese of New Ulm, in Minnesota, on Feb. 21, 1960. He was appointed bishop of the Diocese of Owensboro Oct. 23, 1982, and his Episcopal Ordination and installation as the third bishop of the Diocese of Owensboro took place on Dec. 15, 1982. Arthur L. McRaith died in Minneapolis on Dec. 25, 1983.

Marie McRaith

In December, 1991 Marie Hanley McRaith moved from Minneapolis, MN to Owensboro, KY. She is presently residing at the Carmel Home on Old Hartford Road where she enjoys the visits of her son, Bishop John J. McRaith, her many friends and the other residents of Carmel Home.

McWILLIAMS, THE ROY AND CAROLYN FAMILY, became members of Holy Name of Jesus Parish in 1968 after moving from Evansville, IN to Henderson, KY. Roy and Carolyn are originally from Evansville, where they were married in St. Theresa Church on Aug. 29, 1959. Roy, a pharmaceutical sales representative, joined Mullen and Haynes Company in Owensboro in the spring of 1968. Carolyn has been content working at home, caring for her husband and four children.

In 1971, as president of the Holy Name Men's Club, Roy was instrumental in reviving the parish fall festival. Roy and Carolyn have worked together in the Cursillo Movement, the Charismatic Prayer Group and on the RENEW parish team. They presently are members of the Holy Name Rosary Prayer Group and are serving in ministry as Eucharistic Ministers.

Roy's hobbies include woodworking, bird watching and rose gardening. Carolyn enjoys decorating, reading biographies and lives of the saints and listening to music. They also enjoy traveling together. One of the highlights of their travels was visiting the Holy Land and Rome in 1985.

Roy and Carolyn McWilliams

Their four children, Sherri, Randy, Mindy and John are now grown and all live within 30 miles of Henderson. Roy and Carolyn have been blessed with six grandchildren; all are healthy and happy. Thanks be to God.

MEDLEY, SISTER CHARLES CATHERINE, was born on Aug. 16, 1914, at Holy Cross, KY to Wesley Medley (July 5, 1886-Aug. 31, 1970) of Holy Cross and Catherine Blandford (June 29, 1894-Dec. 24, 1933) also of Holy Cross. She was baptized as Marguerite. She entered the convent on Sept. 7, 1932 and took her vows on March 18, 1933, March 19, 1935 and March 19, 1938. Her brothers and sisters include: Madeline Medley (deceased), Anna Belle Medley-Cambron, Jane Marie Medley (Sr. Miriam OSU), Charles A., Joseph Bertrand, Joseph Adrian, Francis Gerald (deceased) and Mary Kathleen Medley-Daugherty.

Sister Charles Catherine's missions include: St. Paul, Louisville, Brown's Valley, KY, St. Mary's, Nebraska City, NE, Fairfield, KY, Brown's Valley, KY, Howardstown, KY, San Fidel, NM, Farmington, NM, St. Francis, Raywick, KY, St. Andrew, Harrodsburg, KY, St. Theresa, Grants, NM, St. Denis, Louisville, San Fidel, NM, Grants, NM, St. Bernard, Louisville, St. Bartholomew, Buechel, KY, St. Augustine, Lebanon, KY, St. Denis, Louisville, St. Francis, Loretto, KY, and Mount Saint Joseph.

MEDLEY, GEORGE W. AND ANNA CAROLINE, Names of children and births are from Joshua Lancaster Bible record. Joshua Lancaster married two daughters of George Medley and Caroline Montgomery. Marriage from Meade County Marriage bonds. Death Records from St. Martin's Cemetery, Flaherty, KY and St. Rose near Springfield, Washington County, KY. George Medley and Caroline moved to Meade County from Washington County c. 1834-35. Caroline Montgomery Medley's mother was Sarah Ozborne, daughter of Thomas Ozborne and Priscilla Miles.

Hardin and Daviess Counties families. John B. Higdon, born ca. 1804-5, died Dec. 13, 1848. Buried at St. Patrick Cemetery, Stithon, KY (Fort Knox), son of Ignatius and Lucy Higdon. He married Levina Carrico (born 1813-14). They were married on Oct. 25, 1831 at St. Rose, Springfield, Washington County, KY.

Their children:

Matilda C. Higdon, born 1834, married a Mr. Fry.

Benedict or Benjamin Joseph Higdon, baptized Dec. 27, 1835, St. Rose, married Sarah Ann Simpson.

Mary E. Higdon, baptized Dec. 2, 1837, St. Rose, married John M. Miles.

Thomas Polin Higdon, baptized April 21, 1839, died ca. 1840 (St. Rose).

Thomas Polin Higdon, born March 25, 1842, baptized May 15, 1842, St. Patrick's, married Mary Elizabeth Wayne.

Pius Ignatius Christopher Higdon, born July 3, 1844, baptized Sept. 15, 1844, St. Patrick's, married first Catherine Shircliff, married second Mary Ellen Hill.

John Lloyd Higdon, born Sept. 6, 1846, baptized Nov. 15, 1846, St. Patrick's, married Elizabeth Appollonia Miles.

Maternal ancestors descend from Catholics who settled in Maryland and migrated to Kentucky. Some of the family names are Higdon, Hamilton, Carrico, Medley, Edelen, Montgomery, Ozborne, Maddox, Spalding, Wayne, Cissell, Rhodes, Cambron, Wathen and Hagan.

MEDLEY, MARY ELIZABETH, was born Sept. 6, 1843, in Meade County, KY. Confirmation in 1859 at St. Martin, Flaherty, KY, Meade County. Married Joseph Marion Hamilton (bond) on Oct. 8, 1861 in Marion County, KY (married) Aug. 10, 1861. Their children are William Buford Hamilton, Leonard Joseph Hamilton, born July 12, 1867, Flaherty, KY, St. Martin's Records, George Marion Hamilton, born March 23, 1864, Flaherty, KY, St. Martin's Records, Anna May Hamilton, Sarah Regina Hamilton, born 1875 and Thomas Parker Hamilton.

George W. Medley born July 15, 1808, Washington County, KY, died Nov. 27, 1870 Meade County, KY, buried St. Martin Cemetery, Flaherty, Meade County, KY (son of Thomas Medley and Alice Edelen) married Nov. 11, 1832 Washington County, KY, Anna Caroline Montgomery, daughter of James S. Montgomery and Sarah Ozborne. Anna Caroline Montgomery born Dec. 13, 1817 in Washington County, KY, died Dec. 6, 1870 in Meade County, KY, buried St. Martin's Cemetery. Their children:

Richard T. Medley, born Aug. 12, 1833, in Washington County, KY, baptized Oct. 14, 1833, at St. Rose Church, Washington County, KY, sponsor Mrs. James Montgomery.

Sarah Jane Medley, born April 23, 1835, married Joshua Hamilton (from Bible of Joshua Lancaster).

James W. Medley, born Nov. 6, 1836, died Oct. 18, 1912 (tombstone at St. Martins, Flaherty, KY; Helda G. Medley Jan. 8, 1840-Jan. 22, 1910).

Robert T. Medley, born Aug. 12, 1838 (Cemetery Records of St. Martin-Robert S. Medley Jan. 7, 1838-Jan. 30, 1885; Sarah C. Medley March 6, 1843-March 25, 1867).

Sarah C. Medley, born Nov. 30, 1841, died June 27, 1862, buried St. Martin, Meade County, KY, married February 1856 Joshua Lancaster, Meade County, KY. (Joshua Lancaster Oct. 17, 1836-Oct. 30, 1926-tombstone).

Mary E. Medley, born Sept. 6, 1843, died March 27, 1917, married Joseph Hamilton (bond Oct. 8, 1861).

Theresa E. Medley, born Dec. 10, 1844, died Aug. 20, 1883, buried St. Martin Catholic Cemetery, Flaherty, KY, married William Edelen. (William Edelen Aug. 9, 1842-Sept. 4, 1899 tombstone St. Martins).

Joseph E. Medley, born Nov. 14, 1846.

George Anne Medley, born Dec. 8, 1847, died Dec. 12, 1882, second wife of Joshua Lancaster, buried at St. Martins.

Mahala Ann Medley, born Jan. 20, 1850, Meade County, KY, died March 26, 1916, buried at St. Rose, Washington County, KY, married Oct. 19, 1869 in home of George Medley, Meade County, KY, by C.I. Coomes, R.C.P., to Benedict E. Cambron (born Sept. 19, 1841 Marion County, KY, died April 20, 1921 Washington County, KY, buried at St. Rose).

Rose C. Medley, born Dec. 15, 1853.

John Francis Medley, born Aug. 14, 1854, died Nov. 5, 1867, buried St. Martins, Meade County, KY.

William Henry Medley, born April 21, 1856.

Luella Estine Medley, born Aug. 17, 1858.

MEREDITH, BRUCE AND CATHY, live near Grayson Springs, Clarkson, KY. They are members of St. Paul Parish, Leitchfield, KY. They were married Jan. 15, 1982, by Rev. Charles DeNardi in St. Paul Church with Neil and Lynda Crawford as attendants.

Bruce and Cathy Meredith Family

Bruce is the son of Clarence Meredith and Temple Logsdon Meredith. Cathy is the daughter of Tony Darst and Rebecca Clark Darst. They have two children; Brad, age 4 and Casey Marie, age 2.

Cathy and Bruce are active members of the parish.

MEREDITH, REV. CHARLES RICHARD, was born Oct. 1, 1952, the third child of Percy and Margie Meredith, members of St. Joseph Church, Leitchfield. Richard grew up in Leitchfield, attending St. Joseph Elementary School (1958-1966) and Leitchfield High School, graduating in 1970. He attended St. Pius X Seminary College, Erlanger, KY (1970-1974), graduating with a B.A. in philosophy in 1974. That same year Richard began graduate theological studies at the Josephinum School of Theology, Columbus, OH. On June 11, 1977, Bishop Henry J. Soenneker ordained him to the order of deacon at St. Joseph Church, Leitchfield. That summer he served at the Immaculate Parish in Owensboro, with Monsignor Bernard Powers, the pastor, and with Rev. Ed Bradley, the associate pastor. June 3, 1978, Bishop Soenneker ordained Richard to the order of presbyter at St. Stephen Cathedral, Owensboro.

From June 1978 to June 1980 Richard was assistant to Rev. Joseph V. Rhodes, rector of St. Stephen Cathedral. From June 1980 to May 1983 he taught in and chaired the religion department of Owensboro Catholic High School. During that assignment he was also Catholic chaplain at Wendell Foster Center, Owensboro, (June 1980-June 1983) and chaplain with Monsignor John Higgins at the Carmel Home, Owensboro, (June 1980-June 1982).

Rev. Charles Richard Meredith

By May 1983 Richard completed the thesis and received the M.A. in theology from the Josephinum. Bishop John J. McRaith then directed him to begin studies in pursuit of the Ph.D. in systematic theology at The Catholic University of America, Washington, DC. These studies required residency in Washington through the end of 1988. Candidacy for the Ph.D. was awarded in March 1988 with the dissertation topic being: "Themes of Thomistic Eschatology in the Ecumenical Theology of Yves Congar." Due to the terminal illness of his father, Richard returned to the diocese that December to finish the dissertation work and to prepare for a new assignment at Brescia College.

In August 1989 he began helping coordinate the Ministry Formation Program at Brescia College with Sr. Mary Margaret Cooper, SCN, while residing at St. Stephen Cathedral with Rev. Ed Bradley, pastor and Rev. Darrell

Venters, associate pastor. His assignment included full time teaching as an assistant professor in Ministry Formation and Religious Studies. Between the summers of 1991 and 1992, however, Richard interrupted this assignment to complete his dissertation, taking up residence at St. Meinrad School of Theology, St. Meinrad, IN. A complete draft of all six chapters was ready late in 1992. [The projected date of defense is now the spring 1993.] In June 1992, Richard resumed his duties at Brescia College and residence at St. Stephen Cathedral, again with Rev. Ed Bradley and Rev. Tony Jones, associate pastor.

THE MEREDITH FAMILY, Eleazer Meredith (July 12, 1832-Nov. 21, 1905) and Harriet Porter McClure (Aug. 20, 1832-April 28, 1875) settled on a farm on the banks of Bear Creek, south of Leitchfield, sometime early in the second half of the 19th century. At least nine children were born to the couple: Sarah Catherine (May 12, 1855-March 16, 1877), Nannie Jane (Jan. 1, 1857-May 31, 1884) and her twin William Elisha (died before 1870), George (ca. 1859-Sept. 13, 1927), Jack (Dec. 17, 1860-Aug. 30, 1891), James (Sept. 25, 1862-Oct. 30, 1889), Thomas (June 1865-), Richard Owen Frederick (Jan. 12, 1868-Aug. 7, 1924) and Henry "Harry" (November 1870-June 10, 1962). There is record of Catherine's baptism by Fr. Michael F. Melody (March 3, 1877). Harriet was also baptized by Fr. Melody (April 27, 1875), the day before she died. It is said that Eleazer was baptized at the same time as Harriet, but there is no record. Nannie Jane, James, Thomas, Richard and Harry were later baptized together by Fr. H. Bronsgust, S.J. (Oct. 2, 1877). Instructions in the Catholic faith may have been limited to Sunday catechism. It appears that not many of the children continued in the practice of the faith.

After Harriet's death, Eleazer (also called Eli and "El") married her niece, the widow Sarah McClure Goldsberry (March 7, 1858-Dec. 9, 1931). To "El" and "Aunt Sallie" (as the older children called Sarah) were born Juanita Marie (June 15, 1894-Jan. 20, 1961), Eli Vernon (April 12, 1895-Aug. 1, 1968) and Monica (May 8, 1899-June 1, 1901). The family relocated to Leitchfield during this time, settling at 112 West Walnut Street. "El," Harriet, "Sallie" and a number of the older children are buried at St. Augustine Cemetery, Grayson Springs.

Wedding of Michael and Lori, June 11, 1988, St. Edward Church, Fulton, KY. Left to right, back to front. Back row: John Meredith, Bill Johnston, Bill Meredith, Richard Meredith, Patrick Meredith. Middle row: Dawn Johnston, Betty Johnston, Lori Haddad Meredith, Michael Meredith, Margie Meredith, Debbie Meredith. Taller children: Meredith Johnston, Bill Meredith, Matthew Meredith. Smaller children: Patrick Meredith, Christopher Meredith.

Richard Owen Meredith married Frances Elizabeth Higdon (Feb. 28, 1879-Dec. 5, 1969), daughter of Alexius Higdon (March 5, 1855-1890) and Martha Heaverin (1854-1895) at St. Joseph Church on April 16, 1900, Fr. Martin O'Connor officiating. The Higdon family was Catholic in long standing. The Richard and Frances Meredith family has maintained membership at St. Joseph Church ever since. The couple first made their home at the Meredith farm on Bear Creek where the following children were born: George Henry (Jan. 15, 1901-April 7, 1940), Owen Frederick (June 17, 1902-April 26, 1959), Herman Porter (Aug. 8, 1904-Oct. 2, 1975), Richard Schley (Aug. 5-6, 1907-Oct. 31, 1976) and William Percy (April 4, 1912-Feb. 18, 1989). Fr. Martin O'Connor baptized George (May 11, 1901) and Owen (Sept. 7, 1902). Fr. Rudolph Ruff baptized Porter (Sept. 13, 1904). Fr. Joseph Minch baptized Richard (Oct. 15, 1907). Fr. Louis Beruatto baptized Percy (June 12, 1912). Frances is said by the children to have often ridden side-saddle to church carrying some of the children. Around 1914 the family purchased a farm northeast of Leitchfield, on what is now highway 1214, from Alfred Lee. After settling there Marie Frances was born (Aug. 8, 1916) and was baptized (Sept. 16, 1916) by Fr. Beruatto. Marie worked in town and on the farm, staying with and caring for her mother until Frances died. Marie still lives on the home place.

Porter married Mary Agnes Hughes (July 8, 1906-Dec. 4, 1991), daughter of David Lemuel Hughes (1870-1952) and Mary Ellen Hughes (1873-1943), at St. Joseph Church Jan. 25, 1936, Fr. Louis Beruatto officiating. The couple eventually moved into Mary Agnes' childhood home on West Walnut Street, which served as their home until 1991. A great tragedy for them, each of their three daughters died shortly after birth: Mary Frances (1936), Martha Ellen (1938) and Catherine Marie (1941). A great joy for them, Porter and Mary Agnes were loving godparents to many of their nieces and nephews. Porter, Leitchfield postmaster for 30 years and a pharmacist, also served many years as a trustee of the parish. Mary Agnes was for many years the church organist. The couple was devoted to daily Mass and service to the church until illness and age eventually intervened.

Percy married Marjorie May Simpson (Oct. 16, 1928), daughter of Charles Bethel Simpson (July 7, 1890-March 29, 1966) and Callie Marie Nash (Aug. 18, 1895-June 12, 1980), at St. Joseph Church April 17, 1949, Fr. Louis Beruatto officiating. The couple built and moved into their new home on Grayson Springs Road, on land adjacent to the Meredith farm, in 1954. This continues as the family home and gathering place. Percy was employed before and after World War II with the state highway department, serving 45 years; in the latter years as resident engineer until retirement (July 31, 1974). Margie began employment with Grayson County Hospital in 1974. Since 1979 she has worked as a critical care technician in CCU. The following children were born to the couple: Elizabeth Marie (Feb. 12, 1950), William Percy II (May 26, 1951), Charles Richard (Oct. 1, 1952), John Robert (Dec. 1, 1954), George Patrick (Jan. 3, 1959) and Michael Andrew (Jan. 7, 1964). Fr. Beruatto baptized Betty (March 19, 1950), Bill (July 1, 1951), Dick (Nov. 2, 1952) and John (Feb. 27, 1955). Fr. Albert Thompson baptized Patrick (Feb. 1, 1959) and Fr. Raymond Berthiaume baptized Michael (Feb. 2, 1964). Margie was baptized by Fr. Charles M. Hughes of Glenmary (May 4, 1957) and the next day received her First Communion, as her daughter, Betty, also made her First Communion. The older children attended St. Joseph School until it closed and otherwise continued in the religious education programs and activities of the parish. Betty married David Lee Johnston at St. Joseph Church on Dec. 27, 1969. To them were born: Charles William (Jan. 22, 1972), Elizabeth Dawn (Sept. 1, 1974) and Meredith Leigh (March 31, 1978). Bill married Joyce R. Hutton at Marykirk, Scotland (Dec. 7, 1973). To them were born: William Percy III (March 2, 1977) and Christopher Robert (Jan. 31, 1980). Richard was ordained to the priesthood for the Diocese of Owensboro June 3, 1978. John was ordained to the priesthood for the Diocese of Owensboro Jan. 12, 1980. Patrick married Deborah June Tomes at St. Joseph Church on Jan. 7, 1977. To them were born: Matthew Whitney (July 28, 1978) and Patrick Andrew (Jan. 14, 1985). Michael married Loretta Nell Haddad at St. Edward Church, Fulton, KY, on June 11, 1988. To them have been born: Michael Andrew II (Oct. 10, 1989) and Joshua Simon (Jan. 16, 1992).

MEREDITH, REV. JOHN R., was born Dec. 1, 1954, the fourth child of Percy and Margie Meredith, members of St. Joseph Church, Leitchfield. John grew up in Leitchfield, attending St. Joseph Elementary School (1960-1968) and Leitchfield High School, graduating in 1972. After one year of study at Western Kentucky University, Bowling Green, John entered St. Pius X Seminary, Erlanger, KY, from which he graduated in 1976 with a B.A. in philosophy. He then pursued theological studies at Mount St. Mary's Seminary, Emmitsburg, MD, from which he received the M.A. in theology in 1984. Ordained deacon, May 12, 1979, John served for one summer at Holy Spirit Church, Bowling Green, with Fr. Joe Mills, pastor. January 12, 1980, John was ordained to the order of presbyter. His first assignment began that spring as associate pastor of St. Francis De Sales, Paducah, serving with the pastor, Fr. Paul P. Powell. In the summer of that same year, however, along with other clergy changes, John was reassigned to serve as associate pastor of St. Mary of the Woods, Whitesville, with the pastor, Fr. Phil Riney. Throughout the spring and summer of 1981, at the bishop's direction, John undertook and completed 12 hours of course work in education at Brescia College. He moved to Owensboro during the summer term, taking up residence with his brothe,r Fr. Richard Meredith, and with Fr. Jerry Riney. In August 1981 John returned to Whitesville, having been assigned to serve as instructor and chaplain at Trinity High School. He continued in this assignment through the spring of 1983.

Rev. John R. Meredith

From June 1983 to June 1985, John served as associate pastor at Immaculate Parish, Owensboro, first with Monsignor Bernard Powers and then with Fr. Bill Allard as pastor. In June 1985 John was named pastor of St. Edward Church, Fulton and Sacred Heart Church, Hickman. In June 1988 John was named to his current pastorate of Christ the King Church, Madisonville. He also currently serves as dean of the Central Deanery, as a member of the Priests' Council and as diocesan liaison to the charismatic renewal.

MERIDETH, WILLIAM JENNINGS BRYAN, was born in 1900 in Edmonson County, KY. He was the son of Thomas McClellan Merideth and Susie Napper Merideth (non-Catholics). They had four other children.

Mary Cleophas Bradley, born in 1903 in Hart County, was from a Catholic family of seven children born to William Thomas "Booker" Bradley (parents: Nick and Sarah Lush Bradley) and Mary Tom "Molly" Croghan Bradley (parents: Martin and Arabella Wood Croghan).

The Bradley family attended Mass at St. Benedict Church in Wax. Cleo played the organ and sang at Mass; and she decorated the church with flowers, often gathered on her way to Mass.

On June 21, 1920 at St. Benedict, Bryan (who had become a Catholic) and Mary Cleo were married. They became the parents of 10 children: Howard, Bernice, Eugene, Ella, Rudolph, Isaac, Clarence, Ralph, Rosemary and Patricia. In the mid 1920s they lived for a short time in Louisville, then returned to Edmonson County. Bryan ran a store, farmed or did what work was necessary to support the growing family.

In 1943 the family moved to Hardin County and became members of St. Ignatius Parish. Bryan was a farmer and received the Master Conservationist Award in 1955. Cleo took care of her family, home, garden and grew flowers to decorate the church. She was a member of the Altar Society.

In 1974 Bryan and Cleo and some other family members became parishioners of St. Paul Church, Leitchfield, in Grayson County. Bryan died in 1974, and Mary Cleo died in 1989; both are buried in St. Paul Cemetery.

Bryan and Cleo were very happy to have a large family. Their descendents now include nine living children, 67 grandchildren, 108 great-grandchildren and three great-great-grandchildren. Many of them are very active in their various parishes.

MERRITT, KAVIN LYNN AND EDRA JEAN BURCH,
are the children of Jewell and Rose Merritt and George and Cathy Burch. Employment includes Transmix Concrete, Burch Machine Shop and Faith Tool and Die. The Merritts are from Philpot while the Burches are from Whitesville. Some of the Merritts are members of South Hamptons Baptist while others belong to St. Mary's.

Merritts include: Mona Jones, Donna Kuder, Paula Moore, Annie Hunnicut. Burches are Gary and Jeanie Merritt.

MESSENGER,
The Minor and Anna Messenger family have lived in Grayson County all their lives. They were married on June 12, 1965. Father Warren performed the ceremony at Saint Anthony Church, Peonia. After they were married they moved to Leitchfield and became members of Saint Joseph Parish.

Minor and Anna have five children; Michael, Sheila, Monica, Karen and Jorge. Sheila is married to Kevin Brown. They have one son Neil and are expecting their second child. Monica is married to Kenny Horn. They have two children; Ashley and Kendrea. The Messenger children were all baptized, made their First Communion and were confirmed at Saint Joseph Church. Minor and Anna are very proud of their children and grandchildren.

Anna grew up in the Saint Anthony Parish, Peonia. She is the daughter of Buddie and Lenora Higdon. Anna was baptized by Father Dienes. Father Boarman was pastor of the parish when she made her First Communion and was confirmed. She attended Peonia School for eight years and graduated from Saint Paul High School in 1963.

Messenger Family—Minor, Anna, Mike, Sheila, Monica, Karen and Jorge.

Minor is the son of Ruby Messenger and the late Woody Messenger. He attended Leitchfield High School. After school he joined the Air Force for four years. Minor was a non-Catholic when they married. [He is now taking RCIA classes to become a Catholic.] He is looking forward to becoming a Catholic and participating in the parish functions.

Both Minor and Anna are proud to be a part of Saint Joseph Parish.

MESSICK, REV. SEVERIN, O.S.B.,
(baptized Mark Stephen) was born in Indianapolis, IN on July 12, 1954. He is the son of Henry Max and Anna Louise (McGuire) Messick. He attended Immaculate Heart of Mary Grade School and Chatard High School in Indianapolis. At a very early age he felt a call to serve Christ as a priest. After graduating from high school in 1973, he entered the seminary at St. Meinrad, IN. After graduating from the College at St. Meinrad, he entered the Novitiate of St. Meinrad Archabbey. On Aug. 6, 1978, he professed vows as a Benedictine monk receiving the name Br. Severin.

Rev. Severin Messick, OSB

After four years of theology, he was ordained a priest for St. Meinrad Archabbey on May 2, 1982. From 1983 to 1985, Fr. Severin was associate-pastor of St. Mary of the Woods Church, Whitesville, KY, where he also taught religion at Trinity High School. From 1985 to 1986, he served as associate-pastor at St. Ann Church in Morganfield, KY. From 1986-1992, he served as associate-pastor of St. Mary's, in Huntingburg, IN in the Evansville Diocese. He returned to the Owensboro Diocese to become pastor of St. Ann's in Morganfield, KY on June 16, 1992. Morganfield is in Union County, KY.

MILES, MARK GORDON,
was born in 1948, the son of Al and Ruth Miles. In elementary school he went to St. Joe and Paul. Later in high school he attended Catholic High. He lettered in football and was co-captain of the team. He went to Brescia College and majored in chemistry. After college he served in the Navy. When he left the Navy he used his degree to get a job at NSA.

Becky Jean Stowers, daughter of Richard Stowers and Lydia Stowers, was born in 1948. In grade school she went to St. Mary Magdalene. In high school she attended Catholic High. After high school she jot a job at the GRAD Office.

Mark and Becky were introduced by friends while Mark was on shore leave. After Mark served his term in the Navy he and Becky went out for some time and eventually got married. In 1974 they had a son William Nicolos Miles. Today he is going to ITT Technical Institute. In 1979 they had another son Richard Louis Miles. Now he is going to school at Owensboro Catholic Middle School.

Mark quit his job at NSA for certain reasons and started his own business Miles Custom Woodworking. A short time later Becky started helping with the office work and quit her job at the GRAD Office.

MILLAY,
The Carl and Brenda Millay family have lived in the Stanley area except for the first three months of their marriage. They were married Dec. 28, 1968, by Fr. Martin Nahstoll at St. Peter of Alcantara Church. During those first three months, they resided in Owensboro where a man was robbed and murdered for $7.00 down the street from their home. Brenda said they were moving back to Stanley because people don't get murdered there. And so they did the following day.

Since then, Carl has worked at a number of factories—Whirlpool, Millay's Plastering, Ohio Valley Forgy, Smith Machines and is now in maintenance at National Southwire. Brenda received her license as a hairdresser, worked at Joli for 22 years and now has her own business, Kuntry Kutter. Together Carl and Brenda have found a caboose, had it moved to their back yard and are making it a Gift Shoppe.

Carl and Brenda are proud to have three beautiful children who help with all that goes on with the business and home. Don, age 23, works for Ohio Valley Marine and is a certified diver. Lisa, age 21, works at Wax Works Warehouse and is an artist. Ronnie, age 18, a senior at Catholic High, has registered to attend vocational school, training in industrial electricity and is also applying to the National Evangelization Team.

Carl has served on the Parish Council, is head of maintenance, and is a member of the Men's Club at St. Peter's. Carl and Brenda both head committees at Catholic High for Project Graduation. Brenda is now serving on the Parish Council and is a member of the Ladies Auxiliary at St. Peter's.

Next year Carl and Brenda will celebrate their 25th Wedding Anniversary and plan a second honeymoon traveling through the New England states.

MILLER, BRUCE DAVID AND TERESA ELAINE GOFF,
were married on Dec. 1, 1984. Bruce, born April 5, 1963, is a self employed farmer. Elaine, born Oct. 29, 1964, is a homemaker. They reside in Magnet, IN, Perry County, since 1984 where they are members of St. Augustine Catholic Church in Leopold, IN. They are former members of St. Martin, Rome, KY and St. Mary Magdalene, Sorgho, KY. Elaine attended St. Mary Magdalene (grade one), St. Martin (grades two-eight) and Owensboro Catholic (grades nine-12). She is the daughter of Leander and Janet Goff, members of St. Martin Parish, Rome, KY.

Their children are Kayla Elaine Miller born Sept. 15, 1989 and William Garrett Miller born July 20, 1992.

MILLER, JAMES AND DOROTHY,
were married in November 1949, St. Paul Church, by Father Charles DeNardi. James was in the service, at that time, at Fort Knox, KY, Dorothy was a housewife. In 1952 the Army sent James to Alaska, Dorothy went along, it was a great two years, a good place to live. In 1954 they came back to Fort Knox. They moved to Louisville, KY to live. In 1956 they adopted their first son, James Larry and in 1962 they adopted their second son, Richard Lee. They adopted them from a Catholic Home in Louisville, KY. Those two days were the most important days of their life. Then in 1963, James retired from the Army, they stayed in Louisville, James went to work there. Then in 1973 they moved to a little farm in the St. Paul neighborhood, where they raised their boys. They had good neighbors and their family around them. James farmed and did carpenter work. The boys went to school at St. Paul. They are both grown now, have homes near James and Dorothy.

They have two sweet grandchildren, who go to St. Paul School. Dorothy, her boys and now her grandchildren all went to St. Paul School which is a great school and they have a good parish.

MILLER, LAURA ANN (HOLLIE) HAMLET AND RICHARD MATHIAS JR.,
were married on Oct. 26, 1991 at St. Romuald Parish, in Hardinsburg, Breckinridge County, KY by Fr. Brad Whistle. To this union Laura brought her children Julie Michele Hamlet and Michael Glenn Williams.

Mathias and Laura Miller Jr.; Julie Hamlet and Michael Williams.

Laura was baptized at the request of her parents Sue Ann (Potts) Hollie and Larry D. Hollie Dec. 8, 1968 at St. Joseph Catholic Church in Vinton, LA.

Julie and Michael enjoy spending time in the county with their grandparents Sue Ann (Potts) Hollie Hale and Harold Hale.

MILLINER, THOS. DALE AND BETTY SUE,
were married on May 25, 1968 at St. Paul by Rev. Richard Danhauer. Dale was born on April 1, 1949 and Sue was born on May 24, 1950. Their children include Edward Thomas Milliner born Feb. 14, 1969, Ronald Craig Milliner

born Oct. 11, 1970 and Stacie Denise Milliner born Dec. 31, 1971.

Dale and Sue have lived in Leitchfield, KY, Grayson County, since 1961 where they are members of St. Paul. He is a former member of Holy Guardian Angels, Louisville and Sue is a former member of St. Anthony, Peonia.

The Thomas Dale and Betty Sue Milliner Family.

Dale and Sue have been Eucharistic Ministers since it started. They were the first chosen to set an example. They have both been involved in the CCD program and have helped with all the youth activities. They are lectors at church along with their three children who enjoyed doing their share. The boys were servers at Mass until they graduated (and still do on occasion). Stacie has helped with CCD and Bible School. All are always ready to become involved wherever they are needed.

Dale descends from Gilbert and Ersie Milliner, Willie and Ann Mary Casey and Tom and Margaret Milliner. Sue descends from John Benny and Minnie Sims, B.W. and Cora Kidwel and Samuel Thos. and Gladys Sims.

MILLS FAMILY, Arnold Sylvester Mills, son of William Lawrence Mills and Rachel Florence Ward, was born in Ohio County and baptized at St. Mary of the Woods Church, Whitesville, KY, in 1923. Rose Mary Monaghan, daughter of John Monaghan and Mary Louise (Minnie) Coffey, was baptized in 1924 at St. Joseph Church in Central City, KY, the city of her birth. Arnold and Rose married at St. Joseph on Sept. 18, 1943 and, like many other Kentuckians during World War II, they moved to northern Indiana. In 1952 they returned to Kentucky and joined St. Augustine Parish in Reed, KY. Arnold worked 32 years at Whirlpool in Evansville; in July 1964 he also became caretaker at St. Augustine and currently serves as business administrator for the parish.

Arnold S. and Rose Mary Mills

They have nine living children: Connie, Carol (married Richard Bruce Raley), Jean (married Robert G. Carrico), Jan (married James O. Gish), James Monaghan (married Rebecca Elder), David (married Anne Gregory), Donnie (married Hideyo Neshige), Patricia (married Tom Reynolds) and Erin. Arnold and Rose, much influenced by their teachers in parochial schools, made many sacrifices to send their children to Catholic Schools in the diocese: St. Augustine, St. Peter Alcantara in Stanley, Mount St. Joseph, Holy Name in Henderson, Owensboro Catholic High School and Brescia College. Encouraged by their parents and teachers, the Mills children have earned four master's degrees, five bachelor's degrees, two associate's degrees and countless additional hours in college and technical training. Sixteen grandchildren share the same love for learning and seem destined to outdo their parents.

Arnold and Rose represent two important Catholic groups in Kentucky. Most of his ancestors were English and Irish Catholics who settled in Maryland, moved to the Kentucky "Holy Land" of Nelson, Washington and Marion Counties, and continued their trek to Daviess County. Most of her ancestors were Irish Catholics who emigrated to the United States after the Civil War. Throughout their years together Arnold has delighted Rose about her one renegade English grandmother. Both cherish their legacy of Catholic faith.

MILLS, CHARLES OWEN, was born at Whitesville, KY and baptized by Father Hugh O'Sullivan. His father, Joseph Ireneous Mills, was a farmer, and his mother, May Catherine Howard was a housewife. They were lifelong members of Saint Mary of the Woods Parish at Whitesville.

Joyce Edge was born at Knottsville, KY. Her father, Patrick Joseph Edge, was a farmer, her mother, Anna Leah Payne, was a housewife.

They were married on Sept. 14, 1957 at St. William in Knottsville, KY. They lived a short while at Whitesville. After serving two years in the United States Army, moved to Knottsville, KY. He worked at Commonwealth Aluminum Co. in Lewisport for 24 years before retiring. Charles also farms.

They have six children, 10 grandchildren. They are active in church and community affairs. Charles has cooked for the annual church barbecues for 30 years. They love to travel and enjoy country living with their family. Charles and Joyce celebrated their 35th Wedding Anniversary in 1992. They live on Short Station Rd. near Knottsville, KY and attend Mass at St. Williams at Knottsville.

MILLS, DONALD W. AND RHONDA, are members of Resurrection Church, Dawson Springs, KY. They have four children; Casey Jo, Clark Jacob, Chase Alvey, Chelsea Don. Donnie works for Kentucky Utilities in Dawson Springs as district superintendent. Rhonda is a homemaker. They are involved actively in school and summer athletic programs as well as CCD and other youth attended church activities.

MILLS, HELEN LINGANG, was born Helen Claire Lingang, daughter of Joseph Lingang and Josephine Danhauer Lingang, on Dec. 19, 1896, in Owensboro. She had one sister, Viola, and one brother, Sylvester. Baptized at St. Paul in Owensboro, she was educated at St. Frances Academy, and was active in musicals and plays at school and in the local community. When she became engaged in 1921 to Leo Kendrick Mills, a young pharmacist working at Mills Drug Store, they went to see their pastor, Fr. Edward Fitzgerald, at St. Paul, and requested that a Mass be offered once a week for the intentions of the newly-engaged couple and for their coming marriage. Over the years, she has seen to it that a Mass was offered each week for the family. Once their son was ordained, he assumed the responsibility of offering that Mass each week. That practice continues to this day.

Helen Lingang Mills

L. K. and Helen had seven children: Randall, Kay Rhodes, Sr. Ann Miriam (Passionist Monastery), Fr. Joe Jack, Mollie Bissmeyer and Bill. There are 15 grandchildren and 16 great-grandchildren.

Over the years, Helen has enjoyed all the children and all those who make up the extended families, along with the in-laws. For years she has kept up with all the birthdays and family celebrations. Her birthday party is a gala gathering of all the children who sit around and listen as she carefully reads each of the cards and opens her gifts. Her sense of humor has added a special flavor to all the family gatherings.

She was very active in her parish, serving as president of the Altar Society. She and L. K. were daily communicants for many years. In May of 1992, she gave up her home where she had lived alone since L. K. died on July 7, 1961, and moved to Carmel Home. She now enjoys the opportunity of going to daily Mass, attending the holy hours and the bingo parties. A special delight of hers is to be with many of her friends she has known and loved over the years. She is a member of the Immaculate Parish but presently she calls Carmel Home her home.

MILLS, FATHER JOSEPH M., was born on Sept 6, 1927, in Owensboro and baptized at St. Paul Church, on Sept. 1, 1927. The fourth of seven children born to Leo Kendrick (+1961) and Helen Lingang Mills, his siblings are: Randall, Kay Rhodes, Sr. Ann Miriam (Passionist) Jack, Mollie Bissmeyer and Bill. He attended St. Frances Academy, the Minor Seminary at St. Meinrad, Catholic University of America, and was ordained by Bishop Cotton on May 26, 1953, at the Cathedral.

His first assignment was assistant at Cathedral then at St. Agnes, Uniontown (1953-1959). He studied canon law in Rome, Italy (1959-1961). Then Bishop Soenneker asked him to teach theology at Brescia College (1961-1973). He was made pastor of Holy Spirit, Bowling Green (1973-1982). Precious Blood was his pastorate for a brief five months before Bishop McRaith appointed him judicial vicar (1983) and pastor of St. Anthony, Brown's Valley, where he was pastor until June 1985. Cathedral once again became his residence until he was appointed pastor of St Martin, Rome (1989).

Fr. Joseph M. Mills

He has been a member of the priests' council (1981-), was appointed Director for the Propagation of the Faith (1991) and vicar general (1992). His priestly ministry has seen him working with the Cursillo, the Charismatics, Marriage Encounter, RENEW, Serra Club Jesus Caritas Fraternity for Priests, Task Force on Aids boards at St. Meinrad and Brescia College. He also belongs to an Ecumenical Group Re-union.

His greatest thrill is celebrating the Eucharist each day. He enjoys preaching and administering the sacrament of reconciliation. Working at the Catholic Pastoral Center is a privilege and a responsibility, as he sees it.

His favorite scripture verse is John 15:15. His prayer life focuses principally on friendship with the Lord Jesus especially in the Eucharist. For years, his religious "practices" include a daily dialogue (journal) with the Lord. He has loved being a priest, and can't imagine a more fulfilling way to spend one's life.

"I could never begin to thank the Lord for all his gifts," he concluded.

MITCHELL FAMILY, CLEMENT LEE, Near the year 1900 Clement Lee Mitchell and his wife, Lucy Vanover Mitchell, moved from McLean County into St. Peter Parish about one and one-half miles west of Stanley. They were not Catholics at this time. They had two sons, Joseph Estill and Clement Lee. Clement Lee died at the age of 2 years. Estill joined the Catholic church at the age of 14 and attended school at St. Peter.

In 1920 the Mitchells moved one mile east of Stanley on the Oakford Road adjacent to the former site of St. Peter Church and rectory.

Joseph Estill and Mary Gertrude Russell were married at St. Peter in 1926 by Rev. James Whelan. They had one child also named Clement Lee. Joseph Estill died in 1940. His father, Clement Lee, who had joined the Catholic Church near 1935 died in 1942. Both were buried from St. Peter by Father Martin Nahstoll.

Clement Lee Mitchell and Anita Keller were married at St. Peter in 1947. Both attended school from grades one through 10 at St. Peter. The school had not been built at this time. Fathers C.P. Bowling and Martin Nahstoll were pastors during this time.

Clement and Anita had nine children, Vicki, Marty, Jill, Sally, Eddie, Jane, Billy, Johnny and Cathy, all of whom received their elementary education at St. Peters.

One of their children, Eddie, died in 1985 and was buried from St. Peters by Father Pike Powell.

Vicki, Jill, Sally and Jane were all married at St. Peters.

Three of their children still reside in the parish. Vicki with her husband, Jackie Stogsdill and their three daughters; Marty with his wife, Becky and their one daughter and two sons; and Cathy who plans to be married in August of 1992 by Father Powell.

MITCHELL, JESSE WILLARD (PETE), JR., was born in Princeton, KY in August 1939. He is the son of Jesse W. Mitchell and Mary Catherine (McKinney), both of Princeton.

Mary Ann Pardon was born in Owensboro, KY in June 1942. She is the daughter of Frank H. Pardon and Mary Rose Karn of Daviess County. Her mother, Mary Rose Karn is the daughter of C. Robert Karn and Rose Aud. Frank H. Pardon worked as an optometrist in Owensboro for 30 years.

Pete and Mary Ann were united in marriage July 27, 1961 at Our Lady of Lourdes, Owensboro, with Father Boarman officiating. They have eight children: Jesse Willard Mitchell III, Brian Karn Mitchell, Clifford Stewart Warren Mitchell, Mary Kelly Sikes, Mary Katherine Caruthers, Christina Leigh Claypool, Mary Ann Mitchell and Nancy Rose Mitchell. They also have nine grandchildren.

Pete and Mary live in Paducah, KY and attend St. Pius X Church in Calvert City, KY where Pete is active in the Knights of Columbus. He enjoys cooking bar-b-que with his fellow Knights, all proceeds going to charity. Pete is also an active member of the Elks and Lions Clubs.

(See photo on page 362.)

MITCHELL FAMILY, JOHN T., John T., born March 2, 1854-died March 10, 1918 and Mollie Mitchell, born Feb. 1, 1847-died March 28, 1922 were parents of Lawrence B. Mitchell, born Sept. 6, 1889-died June 17, 1959. Lawrence married Mary C. O'Daniel of Marion County, born May 19, 1886-died June 14, 1972. Her parents were Henry E. O'Daniel of Marion County, born May 2, 1855-died April 6, 1941 and Mary E. Mulligan of Daviess County, born Jan. 15, 1862-died Dec. 15, 1931 in Marion County. Lawrence owned and operated Mitchell Cleaners until retirement. Mary C. was a school teacher. They had seven children.

John Mitchell had five children; Norma, Larry, Pat, Steve and Bill. All graduated from Catholic High. John has eight grandchildren. He owned and operated Mitchell Cleaners upon his father's retirement. He and his wife drowned together in 1988.

Mary Regina (Ramsey) a R.N. has one son, Greg and two grandchildren.

Elizabeth Theresa (Gilman) died on May 7, 1990. She had one son, Warren who died on July 16, 1974.

Mary Lawrence Mitchell, secretary L & N, died Sept. 5, 1976.

Margaret Ozetta Mitchell, R.N., retired, member of Cathedral Parish.

Hattye Rose (Boyle), housewife, married David Boyle and has six children; Anne Weaver, Denise, Mollie, Mary Babbitt, David and Margaret Dugan. She also has eight grandchildren. Resides in Louisville.

Anna Jane Ward, housewife, married Marvin Ward. They have three children; John, Libby and Mike and three grandchildren. They reside in Fort Wayne, IN.

All seven children of Lawrence and Mary were baptized and made First Communion at St. Stephens. Mary C. taught Monsignor Jarboe as a lad in Marion County. Lawrence was an active member in the YMI and K.C.-Catholic organizations.

MITCHELL FAMILY, ROBERT J. AND ANNA R., became members of St. Augustine Parish by birth, being born in 1918 and 1919. They were in the parish in 1944 and became parents to six children who were also baptized at St. Augustine's.

Front, left to right: Dee Anna, Anna R., Robert F. Next: Laura Bea, Mary Martin, Jay A. Back: Ralph E., Robert J.

Their children are Robert F. of Henderson, Dee Anna Booker of Reed, Ralph E. of Reed, Mary M. Cooper of Henderson, Jay Aloysius of Henderson and Laura Bea of Owensboro.

Over the years Robert has helped with the annual picnic and other fund raisers. Anna has been active in the Altar Society and other activities in the parish.

MITCHELL, WILLIAM CLYDE AND ROSEMARI, Clyde was born in Millersburg, KY (Bourbon County) in 1926 and was raised in that area. He served in the Army during World War II. Rosemari was born in Romeo, MI in 1932. Her father was a forest ranger and was transferred around a lot to different forests in the mid-West.

William C. and Rosemari Mitchell.

They were married in St. Helen Catholic Church in Louisville, KY at Eastertime in 1979. It wasn't the first marriage for either of them, and between them they have 11 children, 24 grandchildren and one great-grandchild.

Clyde retired from Gordon Foods where he was superintendent of Maintenance. Rosemari worked for a while at Churchill Downs.

After raising the children, a grandchild for a few years and an invalid mother for several years, they were able to retire to High Plains Road this spring. They are looking forward to getting better acquainted with the people of Irvington and Holy Guardian Angels Parish.

MOMAN, CLARA MARGARET CECIL, was born July 6, 1910 in Graves County, KY, the youngest of six children. (See Roland Cecil story). At the age of 19, she married Frederick Owen Collins. (See John Wickliffe story). Clara Roberta was born Sept. 19, 1930 and Ada Agnes was born Aug. 28, 1931. In less than two years (from marriage on Nov. 28, 1929 to Fred's death on Oct. 24, 1931), Margaret was a widow with two babies to raise by herself. Most of her younger life, she lived with her parents, until their death in early 1940.

On Dec. 26, 1949, Margaret married Herman Richard Moman, a childhood "sweetheart." He had been previously married, also. Herman had lost his first wife when his family was young, also. He had four girls living, and had lost his first child, a boy—James Richard, when he was still a baby. Sarah Belle and Cornelia Ann, "Neelie," were about the age of Margaret's two girls. Carolyn Jane and Betty June were younger.

Herman Roland Moman was born Dec. 10, 1952 and Margaret Anne was born Nov. 8, 1955. Then on Nov. 22, 1963, Herman passed away. Once again Margaret was faced with the job of raising two young children alone. She very often said that she thought that her vocation in life must be "being a widow."

When still a small child, Margaret's family moved back to Union County, where she spent most of her adult life, at St. Ann's Parish in Morganfield.

All of Margaret's children grown, with families of their own. She has 15 grandchildren and 18 great-grandchildren.

MONARCH, JAMES, (born 1790, St. Marys County, MD), son of Francis and Mrs. Elizabeth (Mattingly) Melton Monarch, moved to Kentucky with his mother and other siblings shortly after the death of his father in 1801. James Monarch and Ruth Russell, (born 1792), daughter of Charles and Jane (Mattingly) Russell, were married Jan. 27, 1812, Washington (Marion) County by Father Charles Nerinsky. Their children: Thomas, John, David A., James and Nancy. James Monarch owned a 235 acre farm in Knottsville, Precinct 4. James died (1854) and Ruth (1874), and both are buried St. Lawrence Catholic Cemetery, Daviess County, KY.

Mary Lee (Simmons) Townsend, Paul Monarch Townsend, Florence (Simmons) Drury.

Thomas Monarch, (born 1817, Kentucky), son of James and Ruth (Russell) Monarch, was married Oct. 23, 1848, Daviess County by Father W.F. Coomes to Amanda Catherine Mattingly, (born 1830, Kentucky), daughter of "Big" George and Ann Nancy (Johnson) Mattingly. Their children were all born Daviess County, KY: Georgeanna (born Aug. 29, 1849, married Alfred Hays), Mary Rosetta, (born Jan. 14, 1852, married H. Burton) both baptized by W.L. Coomes; an unnamed infant daughter, (born and died 1854); Alice M. (born Feb. 2, 1858, died March 8, 1861); Ellen Generose (born March 8, 1861, married Milicious G. Howard) baptized by M.M. Coghlan; Henrietta/Harriet Lee (born Sept. 5, 1862/1863, baptized Oct. 25, 1863, St. Lawrence Catholic Church by Father M.M. Coghlan, died 1894, buried Mater Dolorosa Cemetery, Owensboro, Daviess County, married John C.

Simmons). Thomas and Amanda had a 100 acre farm in Boston Precinct No. 5. Both Thomas (died 1864) and Amanda (died 1912) Monarch were members of St. Lawrence Catholic Church, near Knottsville, Daviess County, KY and are buried in St. Lawrence Catholic Cemetery.

There are many Monarchs remaining in Kentucky and Daviess County today carrying on the work begun by these early stalwart Christian settlers.

MONARCH-SIMMONS FAMILY, Henrietta/Harriet (Hettie) Lee Monarch, (born Sept. 5, 1862 (marker) or 1863, St. Lawrence Baptismal Records, Daviess County, KY), daughter of Thomas and Amanda (Mattingly) Monarch, was born Daviess County, KY. She was baptized in St. Lawrence Catholic Church, Knottsville, KY, Oct. 25, 1863 by Father M.M. Coghlan and sponsored by Caroline M. Williams. She married John Calvin Simmons, (born 1853, Kentucky, died 1920, Lindale, Smith County, TX). Their children: Florence (1881); Mary Lee, (born 1883, Whitesville, Daviess County, KY, died 1929, Houston, TX, buried Glendale Cemetery, Lufkin, Angelina County, TX, married George Eli Townsend, children: Paul Monarch, Zoe Mary, Jesse Calvin, Jane Elizabeth, George W. and Rebecca Marie); Thomas Jesse (1886), baptized by John Sheridan; Rosa Agnes (1887), baptized by T.J. Jenkins, married Keith Mewburn, children: Lettie, Jessie, William and Claude); Joseph (1889, died as a baby and buried St. Mary of the Woods Catholic Cemetery near Whitesville).

Henrietta died Sept. 7, 1894 and is buried in Mater Dolorosa Catholic Cemetery, Owensboro, Daviess County, KY, (away from all of her family). After the death of his wife, John C. Simmons took the younger three children, Mary Lee, Thomas Jesse and Rosa Agnes to Texas. Florence remained in Daviess County living with her grandmother, Amanda (Mattingly) Monarch. Florence was married to Hilary G. Drury in 1907 at Knottsville by L.H. Spalding. They had at least one son, William Francis Drury. They are both buried in St. Lawrence Catholic Cemetery.

Very little is known about John Calvin Simmons or any of his family.

MONARCH FAMILY, The Monarch Family was believed to be of French Catholic descent and came to Kentucky from St. Marys County, MD. After the American Revolution, many of these Maryland Catholic families began migrating to central Kentucky (Nelson, Washington and Marion counties). Later on, many of these same families or their descendants migrated on to Daviess County, KY. Some of these early Monarchs were to become champions in the whiskey distilling business, noted throughout Kentucky and America. Kentucky is of course now world famous for its (past and present) whiskey distilleries.

Francis Monarch, the progenitor of the Kentucky Monarchs, (born Maryland, died Feb. 25, 1801, St. Marys County, MD) and was married to Mrs. Elizabeth (Mattingly) Melton. Before his apparent untimely death, he had begun making plans to move to Kentucky. His death bed wish was that his wife carry out these plans and so in April 1801, she and the children left Maryland crossing the mountains to Wheeling then taking a flat boat down the Ohio River disembarking at Bear Grass Creek (present day Louisville). Elizabeth, an undoubtedly strong, steadfast and faithful woman, settled her family, (including these sons, James, Edward and newborn son, Thomas) in Washington County, KY in an area later to become Marion County near Lebanon in the St. Charles Catholic Church community. Elizabeth died there in 1835. She was a Mattingly and it is said that some of the Maryland Mattingly families joined the league of 60 families that migrated to Nelson County, KY after the Revolutionary War. The above mentioned sons each with their families later migrated into Daviess County, KY making their mark in their new chosen home land as good farmers, good businessmen and good Christian citizens.

MONTGOMERY, RIGHT REV. GEORGE, D.D., Bishop Montgomery, when he became bishop of Monterey and Los Angeles, was physically in the prime of life. Born in Kentucky, Dec. 30, 1847, he was in his 49th year. He had been ordained to the priesthood in Baltimore, Dec. 20, 1879. When he came to Los Angeles as coadjutor, he virtually took over the administration of the diocese because of Bishop Mora's precarious health. Earnest and energetic, with a particularly kindly personality, Bishop Montgomery from the very beginning of his residence here became a power in the life of Southern California, not only in his position as a churchman, but in his ready willingness to assume the burdens and responsibilities of a civic leader. His popularity was great with all classes of our citizenry, as may be seen from an editorial tribute in the *Los Angeles Times* at the time of his death in 1907.

It was fortunate for Catholic interests here that his merit as a public figure was so generally recognized, because he came to Los Angeles at a time when the county was passing through the throes of a resurgent epidemic of anti-Catholic bigotry. The so-called American Protective Association, popularly known as the A.P.A. was engaged in a campaign to exclude Catholics from public office and from remunerative mercantile employment. A covert, and sometimes overt, boycott of Catholic businessmen was part of the program of intolerance. Unfortunately, Los Angeles was to a very large extent affected by this un-American movement. In 1894, the A.P.A. element made a considerable showing in the city elections. Absurd charges and fantastic stories of Catholic disloyalty to American ideals were made from many platforms and from some pulpits. In the face of this campaign of proscription Bishop Montgomery acted promptly and decisively. A branch of the Catholic Truth Society of San Francisco was organized a series of popular lectures on Catholic doctrine was given by able speakers, among them the late Father Peter C. Yorke, who had carried on a successful newspaper controversy in San Francisco with a whole bevy of opponents. Sermons appropriate to the demands of the time were preached every Sunday night in St. Vibiana's Cathedral. The Catholic schools of the city took a notable part in the Fourth of July parade in 1895 in defiance of cowardly threats made, so to speak, in the dark. In fine, the Catholics of the city and diocese were well organized to meet the onslaughts of the A.P.A., and in the end the whole movement ignominiously collapsed, particularly after its motives were repudiated in 1896 by the leaders of both our great parties. Bishop Montgomery had rendered a signal service, not only to his own people, but to the principles of good American citizenship itself. One of the results of the campaign against bigotry was the establishment of the Tidings, as already mentioned; and later in 1899, the founding of the Newman Club of Los Angeles (which, after 41 years, still holds its regular monthly meetings) helped further to strengthen Catholic social and intellectual life in Los Angeles. The Club had from the beginning the bishop's hearty approval.

It may therefore be fairly said that, in the long run, the A.P.A. outbreak reacted beneficially on the Church in Southern California. This was, indeed, the judgment of the daily press when good Bishop Montgomery regretfully left Los Angeles a few years later.

Appointed Archbishop. In September 1902, word was received of the appointment of Bishop Montgomery as coadjutor, with the right of succession, to Archbishop Riordan of San Francisco. He became titular Archbishop of Osimo. The archbishop was recipient of many testimonials of esteem from his fellow-citizens, and a large public gathering paid him merited honors on the eve of his departure. He left Los Angeles for his new post on the evening of Feb. 3, 1903. Very Rev. Patrick Harnett was appointed administrator of the diocese.

Civic Tribute. The following fine tribute was paid to the Archbishop by a non-Catholic editorial writer in the *Los Angeles Herald* (then a morning paper). It forms a fitting conclusion to this brief survey of his episcopal career in the diocese:

"Bishop Montgomery has been the central figure of at least two memorable and significant banquets given in this city within the last few years. At the first banquet there met around the board ministers of practically every religious denomination to listen to and discuss an address by Bishop Montgomery on 'Religious Tolerance.' On the second occasion, last Wednesday night (Jan. 29, 1903), the bishop was greeted in sympathy and warm affection, not only by his hosts, the Newman Club, but by men of many creeds and various professions, who esteemed it a high privilege to be able to pay tribute by their presence to so liberal a thinker and ardent worker as the guest of honor had proven himself to be.

"Bishop Montgomery's place in Los Angeles and in the hearts of all sorts and conditions of men may not be filled; but, nevertheless, we welcome the fact that he has been preferred to a still more important post, where his devotion to humanity and his sound liberal judgment may wield a still wider influence. The agnostic may have received—we say it with all reverence—as great a blessing from the life and example of George Montgomery as the most devout churchman, nor will the Protestant yield to the Catholic in the warmth of his admiration for the noble character of this remarkable man.

Whatever his future dignity, wherever he may be summoned by his church, Los Angeles will not forget her friend nor the lesson that Bishop Montgomery had ably demonstrated to this community, 'the greatest thing in the world,' and Christ's single law—'Love One Another'."

Most Rev. George Montgomery was born Dec. 30, 1847 at St. Lawrence, KY. He was baptized and made First Communion, confirmation at St. Lawrence. He was ordained a priest on Dec. 20, 1879 in Baltimore, MD. Consecrated bishop April 8, 1894 in Monterey and Los Angeles, CA.

Appointed coadjutor archbishop of San Francisco, CA Sept. 17, 1903. Returned to St. William's, Knottsville, KY May 28, 1898 to ordain his first cousin, Rev. Lucien E. Clements to the priesthood in St. William Church.

Visited Daviess County, November 1905 as archbishop of San Francisco. Visited Mount St. Joseph Nov. 10, 1905, visited his three first cousins, Sisters Bernard, Columba and Mary Paul, all of Montgomery family.

MONTGOMERY, JAMES LUCIAN, was born on Sept. 6, 1913 near St. Lawrence, KY. He was the son of Ira Ignatius Montgomery, born Oct. 24, 1879 and Mary Daisy Lambert, born Oct. 5, 1882. Ira and Daisy were married on Feb. 11, 1907. Ira was the son of William Kendrick Montgomery, born Sept. 21, 1842. William Kendrick was one of 12 children of Thomas Montgomery and Clotilda Wathen, who were married on Jan. 23, 1815. Kendrick's eldest brother Pius, born Jan. 20, 1816, was the father of George Thomas Montgomery, who became the coadjutor archbishop of San Francisco. William Kendrick married Laura A. Higdon, born Nov. 25, 1849. Two of his daughters, Sister Bernard and Sister Columba, were Ursuline nuns at Mount St. Joseph, KY.

Lucian and Ruth Montgomery, 50th Wedding Anniversary.

James Lucian was baptized at St. Lawrence Church by Fr. Lucien E. Clements, his namesake, who had been ordained by Archbishop George Thomas Montgomery, his first cousin. He married Helen Ruth Roby, born Oct. 3, 1916, on Feb. 8, 1941 at St. William Church. She was the eldest daughter of Marcus J. Roby, a farmer, born June 8, 1890 and Mary M. Mattingly, born July 12, 1894. The latter were married on Nov. 17, 1915 at St. William Church by Fr. F.J. Timoney, who also baptized Helen Ruth.

Helen Ruth's grandparents were John Alexander Roby, born Oct. 25, 1858 and Amanda Bell Wagoner

Roby, born Nov. 14, 1866. They were married on Feb. 5, 1886. John Alexander was the son of James Lawrence Roby, born May 1, 1833 and Sarah Elizabeth Evans, born May 21, 1841.

Both Lucian and Ruth witnessed the burning of their respective schools which they attended. Ruth was in the second grade when St. William Grade School burned on Friday morning, April 23, 1926. The school, auditorium, library and the Sisters' living quarters were all destroyed in the fire. St. Lawrence School, a two room frame building, burned on Tuesday evening, Oct. 18, 1960. Lucian saw the black smoke and heard the church bell ringing from his farm, but by the time he arrived, the school was completely burned.

Lucian and Ruth have farmed ever since their marriage. They live on Monarch Road, south of Knottsville, and have been members of St. William Parish for the past 49 years. They have seven children, 20 grandchildren, one deceased and eight great-grandchildren. They celebrated their 50th Wedding Anniversary on Feb. 8, 1991.

MONTGOMERY, JOHN RAYMOND, was born Aug. 17, 1948 near Knottsville, KY. He is the fourth child of James Lucian and Helen Ruth Montgomery of St. William Parish in Knottsville. His brothers and sisters are James L. Jr., born March 17, 1942; Mary Margaret, born Dec. 13, 1943; Joseph Francis, born Aug. 23, 1945; William Eugene, born Sept. 6, 1951; Robert Anselm, born June 25, 1953; and Martha Ann, born June 15, 1957. Ray attended St. William Grade School and Mary Carrico Memorial High School, with two years of high school at St. Thomas Seminary in Louisville. He graduated Brescia College in 1971 with a B.S. degree in history and mathematics. He attended Western Kentucky University, where he obtained a master's degree in education. He has taught math and history in the parochial schools of the Owensboro Diocese for 17 years.

He married Peggy Jorene Smith from Burkesville in Cumberland County, KY on Dec. 19, 1970. She is the daughter of Hill A. Smith and Christine L. Shepherd, both of Cumberland County. She is the second of three children: Donald A., born June 30, 1947; Peggy, born Sept. 8, 1948; and James E., born May 23, 1950. She attended Owensboro Jr. College of Business, where she earned her secretarial degree in 1971.

Ray and Peggy Montgomery

Ray and Peggy have three children, Christina Elizabeth, born Dec. 30, 1973; Timothy Ray, born Feb. 6, 1977; and Thomas Alexander, born March 3, 1980. Tina graduated from Catholic High in Owensboro in 1992; Tim is now a sophomore at Catholic High and Tommy attends Owensboro Catholic Middle School.

The Montgomerys are members of St. Pius X Church in Owensboro and presently reside on Jach Hinton Rd. in Philpot.

MOORE, JOHN JOSEPH, lived in the St. Vincent area while growing up. He is the son of Charles Lonnie Moore and Helen Allen. He went to Sacred Heart Church and attended school at St. Vincent. He married Judy Elnora Willett, daughter of Martha Helen O'Nan and Herman Willett (died January 1991).

They have three children; Chastity Dawn, Angela Diane and John Joseph II. When Johnny and Judy were married at Waverly in 1971, there was a deep snow on the ground. Judy was stuck in the snow until the grader came by. Johnny lived outside of Waverly at that time. He rode his horse as far as Peak Bros. while wearing his tuxedo. They had a beautiful wedding. Everyone remembered that wedding!

Judy and Johnny have always been Catholics. Both of their fathers were always Catholics. Both of them had a mother who joined the church after their marriage.

Johnny is the grandson of Beulah Nelson and Harvey Allen. Judy is the granddaughter of Jessie Coney and John E. Willett. Jessie was the inspiration for Judy's faith life. She tried to pattern her life after her grandmother.

Johnny belongs to the K.C.'s of Waverly. Johnny and Judy have one grandson, John Dillion Miller. Their son J.J. is an altar boy. He was trained by Father E.E. Willett. J.J. attends St. Ann School.

Johnny and Judy like to go on pilgrimages to the shrines of Mary. They have been to Birmingham, AL and to Conyers, GA. They attended a Marian Congress in Chicago, IL. There they met Fr. Ken Roberts and Joseph Terelya.

They both like music. Johnny plays the guitar at church at St. Peter's on the first Friday of every month. Judy leads the singing at that time.

Judy attended St. Peter School.

MORRIS, CAROL, Erin Morris's parents are Philip and Carol Morris. Philip's parents are Albert and Alta Morris. Albert was born to Raymond and Dorothy Morris on Feb. 20, 1933 in Bartholomew County, IN. He is a retired farmer and truck driver. Alta (Dillman) Morris was born to Charles and Gertrude Dillman on Oct. 20, 1932 in Jennings County, IN. She is a secretary at Bartholomew County Hospital in Columbus, IN. Albert and Alta were married Aug. 31, 1952 at First Baptist Church in Columbus. They have two kids, Philip and Brian, and four grandkids.

Carol (McCarthy) Morris's parents are William and Lucille McCarthy. William was born in Chicago, IL on March 19, 1918 to William and Helen McCarthy. He was a wholesale lumber dealer. Lucille (Kraimer) McCarthy was born May 8, 1928 in Kennan, WI to Frank and Anna Kraimer. She is a retired bookkeeper at the Indiana Veteran's Home. William and Lucille were married Sept. 29, 1949 at St. Anne Church in Kenman, WI. They have four kids, Patrick, Barbara, Carol and Michele, and nine grandkids. She is a member at St. Lawerence Church in Lafayette, IN.

Philip Morris was born on June 24, 1953 in Columbus, IN. He is a senior engineer at Texas Gas. Carol Morris was born Jan. 13, 1954. She is a homemaker. Philip and Carol were married at St. Lawrence Church in Lafayette, IN on May 31, 1975. In 1979 they moved to Owensboro, KY and became members of Immaculate Parish.

Erin Morris was born Sept. 24, 1979 in Owensboro. She is 13 years old and attends OCMS. Kevin Morris was born June 13, 1988 in Owensboro. He is 4 years old and goes to Faith Lutheran Pre-School.

MORRIS, FRANCES AGNITA, born in Daviess County near Knottsville, KY. Baptized in St. William Church. Parents were Joseph B. Morris and Emma Della (Johnson). Had nine brothers and six sisters.

Frances Agnita Morris

Entered the Ursuline Order at Mount St. Joseph in February 1943. August 14, 1943 received the habit and the name Sister Joseph Emma. August 1945 made vows. Served in Fairfield, Louisville and Mount St. Joseph, KY; Wilhelmena, MO and Blanco and Waterflow, NM. Presently she lives at the Mount doing various jobs. Her hobbies are sewing and crocheting. She will celebrate her Golden Jubilee in Religion in 1993.

MORRIS, FRANCIS DENNIS, was born in Whitesville, KY. His father, William Otis Morris, was a farmer, and his mother Mary Dessie Hawkins was a housewife also from Whitesville. Dorothy Mae Edge, daughter of Patrick Joseph Edge and Anna Leah Payne, grew up on a small farm in Knottsville, KY. Francis, who goes by the nickname of "Red," and Dorothy were married April 11, 1964 at St. William Parish in Knottsville. They moved into a home on Highway 144 where they still live.

Francis Dennis Morris and Dorothy Morris

Their five children, three boys and two girls, Dennis, Timothy, Brian, Angela and Theresa, were born in Owensboro, and grew up at their small farm in Knottsville area. Red has worked at W.R. Grace for 26 years, and Dorothy worked at the General Electric Plant for 10 years. The family has been working together to raise tobacco for many years.

They have been involved at St. William Church since their marriage, and have been very active with bingo, the Catholic Grade School, parish picnics and many other church activities. They celebrated their 29th Wedding Anniversary in 1992. They still live in their home on Hwy. 144 with their two youngest and continue to attend Mass at St. William in Knottsville.

MORRIS, JOSEPH BENEDICT AND EMMA DELLE JOHNSON, were married at St. Lawrence Church in Knottsville on April 29, 1919. Rev. George Niehaus witnessed the marriage.

Joe was born Feb. 8, 1895. His parents were John William Morris and Lilly Isabelle Long. Joe grew up working in the coal mines near Knottsville and served a short term in the U.S. Army.

Emma Delle was born on Jan. 11, 1895. Her parents were John Lewis Johnson and Saraphine Speaks.

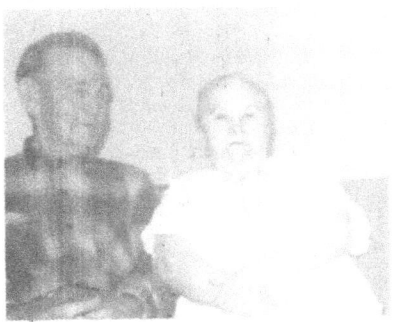

Joseph B. and Emma D. Morris

Joe and Emma Delle married at the age of 24. They lived in several places in the Knottsville area before moving to Whitesville in 1942. Their primary occupation was farming.

Joe and Emma Delle had 16 children. Three of whom died as babies: James Louis, Lilly Mae and Michael.

The oldest child Mary Augustine married James Samuel Harley. They had 14 children.

Joseph Marvin married Mildred Harley. They had 10 children.

Frances Agnita entered the Ursuline Sisters of Mount St. Joseph.

William Bernard married Barbara Sue Lanham. They had seven children.

Francis Leo married Stella Harley. They had three children.

John Aloysius (Tom) married Carole Howard. They had seven children.

Joseph Lawrence married Wilma Dean Carmen. They had four children.

Mary Florence married Herman A. Howe. They had 13 children.

Patrick married Shirley Fuqua (deceased). They had five children. He later married Brenda Carmen Hawkins.

John William married Pauline Howard. They had 10 children.

Emma Louise married Raymond Elwood Whistle. They had four children.

Catherine Marie married Sherman Chandler. They had four children.

Barbara Ann married Carroll Shively. They had six children.

Emma Delle died April 8, 1970. Less than a year after her death, Joe went to the Knottsville Personal Care Home. He married Ada Head on Sept. 30, 1972 and they lived at the Knottsville Personal Care Home. Joe died on Oct. 6, 1980.

MUDD, SR. GIA THERESE, OSU, was born in Louisville, KY on June 4, 1960 and baptized at St. Edward Church in Jeffersontown, KY. Her father, Francis Eugene Mudd Jr., is a retired electrical engineer and her mother, Cecil Ann (Kelly) Chinn, is a former bookstore manager.

In the 1950s and early 1960s, Sr. Gia's siblings attended St. Edward Elementary School. A majority of the school's teachers were Ursuline sisters from Mount St. Joseph's Convent in Maple Mount, KY and the Mudd family formed close ties to the small community of Ursulines that had come from Daviess County to teach in the Jefferson County city of Jeffersontown.

Sr. Gia Therese Mudd

Though Sr. Gia's family moved from the area and she did not attend St. Edward's, her mother's continued relationship with one of the Mount St. Joseph's teachers, Sr. Mary Ann Krampe, prompted Gia to consider the Mount St. Joseph's community and the Ursuline order as the place to fulfill her vocation. Eventually, she elected to become and was accepted as a novitiate at the Maple Mount Convent.

In the mid-1980s she attended Brescia College and then transferred to the University of Louisville to complete her studies toward a bachelor's of science in nursing. On May 14, 1988, she graduated from the University of Louisville with highest honors.

After graduation, she returned to Mount St. Joseph to work in the convent infirmary as a nurse and later would become director of personnel. On July 22, 1989, she made her perpetual profession in a ceremony celebrated by Bishop John J. McRaith.

In the summer of 1991, Sr. Gia went to South America as a missionary and is currently working in the Archdiocese of Valparaiso, Chile.

Sr. Gia is a descendant of the Mudd, Hoskins, Stallings and Shepherd families of Daviess County, KY.

MUDD-RINEY, Joseph B. Mudd, son of Clyde F. and Catherine Hill Mudd married Mary Louise Riney, daughter of Thomas Len and Irmine Mulligan Riney on April 11, 1953 at St. Stephen Cathedral in Owensboro. They had seven children; Jeffrey Thomas, born Jan. 13, 1954, died Sept. 5, 1977; Judith Lynn, born Jan. 20, 1955; Donna Marie, born July 18, 1956; Susan Kay, born Aug. 9, 1957; Gregory Joseph, born June 10, 1958; and twins, Phillip Riney and Patrick Hill, born Aug. 8, 1959.

Judith Lynn married Robert Rutledge June 25, 1976, they have three children; Christopher Allen, Matthew Roy and Meggan Riney Rutledge. Donna Marie married Charles (Chuck) Cecil on Sept. 2, 1984, they have three children: Kathleen Louise, Joseph Charles and Patrick Aaron. Susan Kay, married James Coy on April 9, 1988, Gregory Joseph married Diane Elder in May 1978. They have three children: Chad Robert, Jeffrey Chase and Chelsey Renee. Phillip Riney Mudd lives in Lexington, KY and Patrick Hill Mudd died on June 8, 1989.

MULLIGAN, ERLE A., Daddy was a full fledged Catholic for each of his 94 years. He was respectful and tolerant of other Christian's beliefs, and practiced being neighborly with one and all. He was christened at St. Raphael's, the product of parentage having roots from Pottingers Crossing, thence to St. Alphonsus for a life of farming in the same community as Mount St. Joseph. He was a parishioner of St. Mary Magdelene, Sorgho, KY, in retirement until his departure from this life while under the care of the Carmalite Nuns in the Owensboro Carmel Home for a brief period.

His personal service to the community was never challenged in seniority for serving on the school board. He gave tirelessly of time in his efforts to gain approval for the amendment of rules for school buses to permit transport of parochial students. This successful change did not occur over night. It began through the election of a superintendent who was empathic to the cause and a willingness to work in concert with the other board members. Today the results of his efforts are realized each day of the school year, when the yellow and black lettered buses routinely pick-up and drop off students at our Catholic elementary and high schools.

The Erle A. Mulligan Family

Condensing Daddy's family within a short article is not without challenge. His brother, Lum, was the master mechanic during the early days of the automobile. His oldest sister, Ermine, married Leon Riney, the parents of Father Phil. Another sister, Louise, married into the Merritt family, and Laurita married Bernard Clark at St. Alphonsus. His marriage to Corine Riney was to be blessed with three sons: Billy, Harrold and John M. who were to perpetuate the family name along the pathway of history. Their eight daughters: Suzetta, Marion, Geraldine, Frances, Mildred, Ruth Ann and twins - Martha Jean and Mary Jane, all were to receive their schooling from the Ursulines at Mount St. Joseph in preparation for a Christian life. Their heritages through matrimony will probably frustrate genealogists in extending the Mulligan/Riney family clan to include: Ebelhar, Mattingly, Simmons, Boswell-O'Bryan, Timbrook, Kauffeld and Alexander.

Daddy may best be remembered for his empathy toward his fellow man, to always see that his family practiced the rules of the church, and his admonition to never judge. His favorite and frequent quote was, "One never can be sure, when I get inside those pearly gates, I just may look upward while climbing the ladder and recognize Brother Probust standing on the rung above me." Grandchildren and their children and the children in the first three grades in school at Angela Merici, Sorgho, were to be his comforting thoughts throughout his days during his twilight years.

MULLIGAN, JAMES FRANCIS JR. FAMILY, James Francis Mulligan Jr. and Laura Ann Taylor were married on July 2, 1947 in the rectory of Saint Joseph Church, Central City, KY. Father Victor Boarman officiated.

Four children were born from this union - James Francis Mulligan III, Anne Conway Mulligan, Michael Thomas Mulligan and Mary Catherine Mulligan.

Laura Ann and daughter Ann Conway

James Francis Mulligan Jr. attended Notre Dame University and graduated Magna Cum Laude. James served four years in the Navy during World War II. Laura Ann attended Virginia Inteemant College in Bristol, VA.

Two of the four children are living. Anne Conway lives at home. Michael Thomas is married to the former Kathy Huddleston. They have three children, Christy, Thomas and Lillie-Ann. They reside in Earlington, KY and attend Immaculate Conception Church. James Francis Mulligan III died in 1963. Mary Catherine Mulligan died in 1981.

Laura Ann and daughter Anne Conway are members of Saint Joseph Church, Central City, KY. Father Francis Mastravito is the pastor. Presently they are active in small groups participation, R.C.I.A. and church music and choir. Laura Ann is presently serving on the Rural Deanery Council of Western Kentucky and represents that council on the Diocesan Pastoral Council.

MULLIGAN, JOHN SIMEON, member St. Mary Magdalene Parish, Sorgho, KY married Mary Christine Edge, member of St. Mary of the Woods, Whitesville, KY on June 20, 1956.

Children: Yvonne Marie Mulligan (married David Hileman in Lexington, KY), John Simeon Mulligan Jr. (married to Cynthia Annett Beemer), Vernon Dale Mulligan, Hugh Milton Mulligan, Timothy Joseph Mulligan, Mary Katherine Mulligan (married Jeffrey Lynn Hayden); and Thomas Carl Mulligan.

Grandchildren: Jeffrey Lynn Hayden Jr., Kimberly Annett Mulligan and John Andrew Mulligan.

MURPHY, BERNARD LOUIS, was born Oct. 10, 1924. On Nov. 22, 1951 he married Lillian Theresa Hayden, born June 24, 1928. He worked as an union electrician and Lillian was a full-time mom of 11 children, five boys and six girls. They have lived in Owensboro, KY since 1960 and are members of St. Martin Parish, Rome, KY.

Children: Thomas Aquinas Murphy, born Sept. 19, 1952, named after Bernard Louis Murphy's brother, Father Thomas Aquinas Murphy Sept. 8, 1915 to Jan. 13, 1978. He married Terri Lynn Boling on April 25, 1975 and they have four children: Lynn Nichole, Kellie Elizabeth, Carrie Ann and Thomas David.

Barbara Anita Murphy, born Jan. 22, 1953.

Monica Jane Murphy Gilstrap, born Sept. 17, 1955, married Feb. 27, 1976 to Gerald Donald Gilstrap. Children; Jamie Lynn and Miranda Kay.

Sandra Leona Murphy Thompson, born Nov. 4, 1956 married March 4, 1977 to Christopher Matthew Thompson. Children; Jesse Louis, Lisa Anne, Diane Michelle and Michael Joseph.

Esther Lisa Murphy Clouse, born Jan. 21, 1958 married June 26, 1976 to Paul Martin Clouse. Children; Melissa Kay, Valerie Jean and Martin Anthony.

Bruce Louis Murphy, born Jan. 9, 1960.

Deborah Louise Murphy, born May 4, 1961.

Marvin Terry Murphy, born Jan. 22, 1963.

Larry Robertus Murphy, born Aug. 2, 1968.

Donna Sue Murphy, born Aug. 22, 1971.

Kevin Lee Murphy, born May 25, 1973.

MURPHY, SISTER EDWARDINE, (Feb. 13, 1914-Nov. 2, 1984) was the daughter of James Patrick and Mary Ellen McGowan-Murphy. She was born in Central City, KY, and baptized as Mary Callista on March 8, 1918. Entered Mount Saint Joseph Ursulines: Sept. 7, 1932. Received habit: March 18, 1933, No. 409, Final Vows: March 19, 1938.

Mary Callista was born into a family of nine brothers and sisters whose parents both had an Irish background. She was one of these nine: James Patrick, Arthur Thomas, Kathleen Virginia, Margaret Lenora, Elizabeth Ellen, Joseph Patrick, Charles Alfred, Jack Dugan and Mary Callista.

Mary Callista, who after she received the habit, became known as Sister Edwardine, taught in Jefferson, Marion, Meade and McCracken counties of Kentucky, and at Wilhelmina, MO and Waterflow, NM. No doubt the most significant of her missions was the opening and operating of Rosary School in Paducah. In her own words she says of it: "I had the privilege to live in 'Jim Crow' era. We lived in the ghetto and we were able to win many over to the Catholic faith with the grace of God. With the help of Father Rhodes we opened our school with 13 non-Catholics. We had a Baptist choir and a Catholic service. This was the first and only all-black school the Ursulines conducted. Father Edward Russell was dean of the area. He played a great part in helping us to organize. I spent eight of my happiest years at Rosary from 1947-1955."

Sister Edwardine was a very bright person and a good teacher. She did not stick to the book; she did projects with her classes that kept them interested. She was dissatisfied with the texts in geography and history, and threatened to write her own. She made these subjects "come to life" for her own class. Sister George Marie Wathen called Sister Edwardine a true follower of St. Angela in that she favored the poor and would do anything to help those who had very little. Not only did she go out to the children at Rosary, but when she was at St. James, a more affluent parish, she helped in any way she could the poor children that Father Paul Russell would bring into the school.

Throughout life, joy and a sense of humor were perhaps the most predominant qualities that Sister Edwardine portrayed. At Rosary when Bishop Cotton visited the school and she was embarrassed by her failure to have instructed the children on the proper way to greet a bishop; nevertheless, she kissed his ring. When the Bishop left they asked her if he were her "boy friend." When she asked why they said such a thing, they replied that she kissed his hand. In order to avoid scandal, and while he was still in the area at St. Francis, she called him and asked him to return and explain to the students this mark of respect for the hierarchy. He returned, and graciously removed Sister Edwardine's fears with his explanation of protocol on this point.

Any number of funny stories could be told of her eight years at Rosary. This one she must have laughed at many a time: She was to watch to see that the church was locked at night. Father Rhodes had been away on retreat, and when he returned late at night he tried the church door since he had given his key to his house to Sister Edwardine. When she saw someone trying the church door, she called the police. They came at once and picked up the "intruder" to take him to jail. He asked to pass by the convent building where he called the Sisters to throw him his house key.

Colonel Bradley, who owned a horse farm in Lexington, was a friend of her family whom they called "Uncle Ed." He was quite generous with Sister Edwardine, and from time to time he sent her all or part of his winnings. With these she supplied Mount St. Joseph with one of the chapel windows and with the statue of the Little Flower on All Saints Avenue.

Sister Edwardine had Parkinson's disease for years before she died, and she finally had to retire to the Mount, and here she patiently suffered her inability to do for herself. She remained happy and full of fun to the end. Her ability as a poet came to light for many of us when we read for her her own Way of the Cross. At her Wake service her poem "Maples and Aspens" was read; the final stanza:

the end comes with winter rains

which mat and soak and finally wash away

the aspens and the maples found going not so hard in all this glory -

but then aspens and maples believe in spring.

Sister Edwardine died at 8:00 p.m. on Nov. 2, 1984. On November 5 Father Anthony Ziegler offered the funeral Mass.

MURPHY, GARY AND BETTY, reside in Owensboro, KY, where they have lived for 13 years. They were married at St. Pius Tenth June 19, 1976. They have three children: Jennifer, Michael and Kannetha. Gary attended St. Pius Tenth Elementary and went on to Owensboro Catholic High where he graduated in 1973. Betty went to St. Mary of the Woods Elementary and went to attend Daviess County Jr. High, and graduated at Owensboro Catholic High in 1976. Jennifer attends Catholic High, Michael attends Catholic Middle and Kannetha is still at home.

Gary and Betty have been members of Precious Blood Parish for 13 years and are active in the community. Gary is the treasurer for the Booster Club and before that he was the Athletic Director of Booster Club. He coaches the women's softball and helps at bingo. Betty is the concession stand chairman of Athletic, helps at bingo, ushers at Mass and cleans the church. Gary works at Commonwealth Aluminum where he is a crane operator. Betty is a sales clerk at a local department store.

Gary is the son of Martin Murphy and Veda (Ellis) Murphy. Martin and Veda were married Oct. 10, 1942. They have five sons and four daughters. Martin worked at G.E. July 8, 1935 where he worked for 43 years before he retired in December 1978. Veda worked for G.E. in 1935, went to beauty school and then became a housewife.

Betty is the daughter of Marvin Morris and Millie (Harley) Morris. Marvin and Mildred recently celebrated their 50th Wedding Anniversary, they were married Nov. 15, 1941. Marvin and Millie have 10 children, five boys and five girls. Marvin worked for National Southwire Aluminum Jan. 1, 1973 until he retired. Mildred worked for Green River Tobacco Company for 15 years and then became a housewife.

Both the Murphys and the Morrises live in Owensboro, KY.

MURPHY, JAMES ROBERT AND MARY TERESA RUMMAGE, were born in Daviess County in late 1800 and were married Feb. 10, 1910. James was born on Feb. 8, 1887 and Mary was born on Feb. 8, 1890. They had 11 children: John Robert married Irene Ballard; Daniel Edward married Lucille Bickett; Mary Anita died at the age of eight; Thomas Aquinas was ordained to the priesthood May 4, 1943; Lawrence Robertus married Mary Margaret Hayden; Benedict Martin married Mary Rita Wedding and was killed on D Day in 1944; Hubert Rock, chiropractor, married Mary Frances Gatton; Joseph Christopher married Imogene Riney; Bernard Louis married Lillian Hayden; Theresa Marie was professed as a Sister of Charity of Nazareth on July 19, 1949; Murray married Della Jean Mattingly. Four of the boys served in World War II.

Last complete family picture of James Robert Murphy and Mary Teresa Rumage (except for Mary Anita who died in 1922). Date: 1942. First row: Mary Teresa, Murray, J.R. Second row: Bernard, Dan, Martin, Hubert, Theresa Marie (Sister Theresa Murphy SCN). Third row: John R., Robertus, Christopher, Aquinas Murphy (Father Thomas Aquinas).

Robert (J.R.) and Teresa lived on a farm about a mile from St. Joseph, KY for many years. They worked hard to make ends meet during Depression. Here they taught their children prayers and real values of the Catholic faith which is being passed down to 50 grandchildren and about 80 great and great-great-grandchildren. Thus, this faith will continue for many years to come. Much credit goes to the influence of St. Alphonsus Parish, but the real credit goes to Robert and Teresa. They prayed morning and evening prayers. If neighbors came during that time, they had a choice of joining or waiting outside. Most of the boys remained successful farmers, even to this writing in 1992.

The above picture was made by a favorite maple tree in the front yard of the homeplace. This was the last time the family was together before Martin was killed in France. Hubert was leaving and Dan was coming home on furlough, when by chance, they met at St. Alphonsus Church. They returned home for a few minutes, during which time this last complete family snapshot was taken.

MURPHY, JOSEPH CHRISTOPHER, was born March 7, 1922 and married Frances Imogene Riney Feb. 15, 1947. Imogene was born Sept. 15, 1926 and died Aug. 12, 1971. They had 14 children: Robert Stephen born Dec. 5, 1947, married Janice Hardin Sept. 10, 1966; Thomas Martin born July 12, 1949, married Charlotte Bartram July 10, 1971; Joseph Christopher Jr. born Aug. 15, 1950, married Jeanie Payne Oct. 27, 1973; Barbara Jean born Nov. 4, 1951, died Feb. 3, 1952; Patrick Sylvester born Dec. 31, 1952, married Sheila Broadley Nov. 21, 1980; Bernadette Marie born March 1, 1954, married Michael Barnard Aug. 24, 1979; Joan Cecilia born March 3, 1956, married Andrew Keith Dant Aug. 3, 1974; Imelda Louise born July 8, 1957, married Rick Millay April 30, 1982; Frances Ursula born March 3, 1959, died Feb. 13, 1982; Aloysius Gerard (Wally) born Feb. 22, 1961, married Kim Donahue Aug. 19, 1983; Harold Dominic born May 25, 1963, married Patricia Knott March 2, 1985; Linda Deloris born Aug. 3, 1964; Michael Anthony born Sept. 24, 1966, married Tonya Kamuf June 6, 1987; Phillip Edward born Jan. 21, 1968, married Tammy Drury July 6, 1990.

The Joseph Christopher Murphy Family

Christopher and Imogene went through many hardships, the loss of one of their children, Barbara Jean, loosing their home to a fire in 1966 and a stable with the winter feed for their farm animals in 1969. Christopher and his children lost their beloved wife and mother in 1971, leaving Christopher alone to raise and provide for the remaining 11 children still at home and then in 1982, Christopher lost another child, Frances.

Through all of these hardships, the family never lost their faith in God. In fact, their Catholic upbringing is what pulled them through.

To this day in 1992, the family still remains strong in their faith. Most of the family still remain in and around the farm home in Elba, with others located in Daviess County. There are 22 grandchildren and five great-grandchildren, so the Catholic faith for the Murphy family will continue for a long time.

MURPHY, SISTER MARY HUGH (NANCY), was born on Sept. 16, 1941 at Curdsville, KY to Hugh Murphy, Feb. 9, 1912-June 27, 1955 and Helen Hamilton, born Aug. 5, 1915, both of West Louisville, KY. She was baptized as Nancy Elizabeth on Oct. 5, 1941 and had her confirmation on Oct. 13, 1948. She entered the convent on Sept. 7, 1960 and received her Habit on Aug. 14, 1961 taking her vows on Aug. 15, 1963 and Aug. 15, 1968. Her brothers and sisters include: Tom, Monica Sue Murphy-Blandford, Sally Ann Murphy-Buford, Mary Rose Murphy-Riney, Jim, Peggy Murphy-McCarthy, Betty Kathleen Murphy-Rogers and Billy.

Missions: St. Margaret Mary, Louisville; St. Edward, Jeffersontown, KY; New Haven, KY; Calvary, KY; St. Thomas More, Paducah, KY; St. Ignatius; St. Angela, Florissant, MO; Mere Marie, Owensboro, Brescia; Motherhouse.

MURPHY FAMILY, WILLIAM BERNARD, After serving 47 months on the USS *Nashville*, William Bernard, eldest son of J. Thomas and Mary Augusta Bickwermert of Newman, KY, became engaged to Mary Helen Kerrick, daughter of James Miles Kerrick and Mary Lillian Hayden of Owensboro, KY.

On Nov. 28, 1945, they were married at St. Paul Catholic Church of Owensboro, KY by the Rev. Charles Patrick Bowling. God has sent to them many blessings and a few sorrows. The Murphy's have been very active in church work, especially during picnic times. They lived on a farm in the Newman Community raising 11 children. They moved to Knottsville, KY in 1966, where their children attended both grade and high schools.

Bernard was employed at the Green River Steel Mill and is a charter member of the Lion's Club in Knottsville. He joined the Knights of Columbus Council No. 817 in Owensboro and both he and Mary Helen work with the Knight's Fish Fry Suppers every Friday night until Good Friday. Mary Helen was a member of the Altar Society in Reed and is now active in the Ladies Guild, as well as having served on two school boards.

Their family consists of 11 children and 31 grandchildren. The children and their spouses are: Miles F. (Patricia Thompson), Daniel T. (Agnes M. Boteler), Dennis B. (Janet Jones), Dorothy M. (Bill Hall-convert), Alan G. (Linda Shields-convert), Gwendolyn A. (Martin E. Howard), Sheila M. (Earl V. Harrington), Pamela J. (Randall Wayne Howard), Bonnie Lee (Gerald P. Castlen), Donald R. (Cristine Ann Bonetti) and Linus C. (Suzanne M. Mattingly).

Their 31st grandchild arrived in February 1992. Mary Helen was needed by the family when the newest grandchild arrived and she felt like she had turned back the pages of time.

Most of their life Mary Helen has been blessed with a camera and has all of their family's memories recorded on film. She has also found time to quilt each grandbaby a special baby quilt. However, not to be outdone, the children put together for Bernard and Mary Helen a quilt with the hands of each family member on a block and it is quite unique. One grandson, Ben Murphy, asked them "How can you sleep under all those hands?" Mary Helen told him, "Oh Ben, I've washed all those hands!"

After Bernard had open heart surgery in 1985 and Mary Helen had sleep apnea in 1985, they are looking forward to many more years of good health and continued happiness.

MYRICK, GILBERT L. AND CONNIE, moved to Kentucky in 1977. They moved to Ballard County, Monkey's Eyebrow in 1980 where they are members of St. Mary of the Fields in LaCenter, KY. They are previous members of St. Ann in Ridgecrest, CA. Their children are: Daniel Myrick, Sabra Parker, Jeffrey Myrick and Christiane Myrick.

Gil serves as usher, Eucharistic Minister, Parish Council two terms. Connie's activities include, Parish Council one term, CCD teacher seven years, lector. Gil helped repair and maintained the parish church and grounds, Cursillo. They are past assistant Boy Scout leader and Webelo Leader, Girl Scout leader, Den Mother in Boy Scouts.

They have two children going to Brescia College. It was Sister Elaine Byrne who took her daughter and her friend to the school to visit the first time. Many of their parish members are in a rural area. Everyone enjoys the fellowship after Mass and visiting while their children are in CCD. In all the churches they have belonged to never have they felt more welcome than at St. Mary's. Gil is a convert. Connie was born Catholic and thanks God she is.

MYRICK, JAMES MARTIN, was born in Paducah, KY on Sept. 12, 1931. His father, Ira Alton, worked for Home Ice Co. and his mother, Jessie Mae Sexton, worked at Star Laundry and later ran Myrick Nursing Home. His parents were born in Hampton, KY in Livingston County and came to Paducah, KY in 1928. Betty Jo Ward Myrick was born at Riverside Hospital June 16, 1931 in Paducah, KY. Her parents were James William Ward and Martha Cleo Hudson. They came from Obion County in Tennessee. They moved to Ledbetter, KY, Livingston County in 1970 and are members of St. Francis De Sales. They are previous members of St. Thomas More and serve as Eucharistic Ministers.

Children: Howard James, Feb. 14, 1951; Linda Faye, Brenda Kaye, Sept. 9, 1951; Kenneth Raymond Dec. 23, 1952; Joseph Martin Sept. 12, 1956; Robert Anthony July 16, 1958. Grandchildren: Yancey Wayne, James Norman Lane, Tara Jo Venters, Rodney Lynn Myrick, Anthony Childers, Phyllis Jessica Myrick, Kristen D'Shane and Whitney Erin Myrick.

James retired from IC Railroad after 32 years of service in 1982. Betty will retire at Lourdes Hospice after working for 20 years. James and Betty love to travel and plan on more travel in the future.

NAAS, RAYMOND F. AND MURIEL W., came to Paducah, KY and St. Thomas More Parish in 1951. The family at that time included four children: Frederick (Fritz) Arthur, Joanne Marie, Helen Jeanne and Judy Kathryn. Since arriving in Paducah, another two members were born into the family: Anthony Raymond and Christopher Alan. The family came here from St. Mary Church in Eldorado, IL. Ray and Muriel have been active members of St. Thomas More since that time, and the family has expanded.

Family reunion, June 1992. Jeanne, Tony, Joanne, Judy, Ray, Muriel and Fritz.

Fritz married Ruth Ann Hamilton of St. Frances De Sales. They reside in Elizabethtown, KY and have four sons: Keith, Mark, Alan and Matthew.

Joanne married John L. Shoulta of St. John's. They reside in Shelbyville, KY and have 10 children: Carol, Stephen, Edward, Theresa, Ellen, Jerry, Jeff, Lisa, Brian and Eric.

Jeanne married Robert E. Yates (deceased) and they had four daughters: Sandra, Loretta, Cheryl and Christina. Jeanne recently returned to live in Paducah and is active in St. Francis De Sales Parish.

Judy married Larry Trabucco from Symsonia. They live in Paducah, are active at Rosary Chapel, and have two children, Derek and Angela.

Tony and his wife Sharon live in Lexington, KY.

Chris and his wife Mary reside in LaCenter, KY.

As of this writing, November 1992, there are 15 great-grandchildren. Ray and Muriel celebrated their 50th Wedding Anniversary with all their children and many of the grandchildren and great-grandchildren present at St. Thomas More on Nov. 3, 1984.

NAHSTOLL, MARTIN EDWARD, was born on Dec. 22, 1901 in Jeffersonville, IN to George Nahstoll and Christina Kleespies. He was baptized on Dec. 29, 1901 at St. Anthony Church, Jeffersonville, IN by Rev. Leonard Reich O.M.C. At the age of 7 he had his First Communion, St. Anthony Church, Rev. Louis Hammer, O.M.C. His confirmation was May 30, 1911, St. Anthony Church, Rt. Rev. Jos. Chartrand. He was ordained to priesthood: May 29, 1928, St. Meinrad, Mt. Rev. Jos. Chartrand.

Father Martin Edward Nahstoll

Father Martin attended St. Anthony School; Jr. and High school at Jeffersonville Public; Junior College at St. Mary College, Kentucky; Philosophy and Theology, St. Meinrad, IN.

He was appointed assistant at St. Mary Church, Indianapolis; Instructor, Gibault Home for Boys, Terre Haute; assistant, St. Martin Church, Louisville; Incardinated in Louisville Diocese July 2, 1935; pastor, St. Martin Church, Rome, St. Peter Alcantara Church, Stanley, St. Mary of the Woods, Whitesville.

He died June 20, 1978.

NEAL, THOMAS AND LUCY HANCOCK, Thomas Edward Neal was born May 4, 1935, in Owensboro. His parents were Lucile Arnold (died 1975) of Owensboro and Judge Sidney B. Neal (died 1983) of Paris, KY. His maternal grandparents, Anna Brokramp and Nick T. Arnold, a jeweler, moved from Crawfordsville, IN, to Owensboro in 1901; they were members of St. Paul Church, then later of St. Stephen Cathedral. Tom's B.S. and L.L.B. are from the University of Kentucky. He is a partner in the law firm of Connor, Neal and Stevenson.

On Feb. 11, 1961, Tom married Lucy Frances Hancock, who was born Jan. 5, 1937, in Waverly. Her parents were Virginia Price (died 1942) of Providence and John Gip Hancock (died 1952) of Corydon. Her paternal grandparents, Lucy Gip Clements and James Thomas Hancock, a Henderson County farmer, were members of Sacred Heart Parish. The Sisters of Charity of Nazareth lived with Lucy's ancestors while St. Vincent Academy was being built in 1820. Lucy is a graduate of Nazareth Academy, Bardstown, KY, has a B.A. from Maryville College of the Sacred Heart, St. Louis, and a M.A. from the University of Kentucky, and is a former Brescia College faculty member.

Thomas and Lucy Neal

Lucy and Tom's daughters were born in Owensboro, Lucy Gip on Dec. 18, 1964, and Lee Ann on April 15, 1969. All are members of St. Stephen Cathedral.

Tom's church activities include vice chairman Passionist Monastery Advisory Board (1991-); Diocesan Synod Committee 1990-91; Parish Council 1978-81, (president 1981); Knights of Columbus third degree, Advocate (1985-); president Brescia Boosters (1969-71).

Lucy's church activities include Glenmary Western Kentucky Committee (1991-); Eucharistic Minister to the sick (1984-89); president Catholic Woman's Club (1984-85); Army of Mary, 1983- (secretary-treasurer 1983-87); president La Fiat Guild of Brescia College (1972-73); Altar Society (1961-).

NELSON, RALPH AND ERNESTINE, of St. Joseph Church, Mayfield, KY were the parents of eight children, four boys and four girls. Mary Ruth, the oldest, remembers the great religious devotions her parents had. Her dad, a convert before he married, taught them the power of prayer.

First row (l to r): Mary Ruth Elder, Bart and Donald. Back row (l to r): Ed and Helen.

They prayed the rosary every day. He would pass out the rosaries that hung on a nail on the kitchen wall beside her daddy's chair, after the evening meal.

Each person took their turn giving out a decade of the rosary until every one had given out a prayer, even the youngest.

Mary Ruth married the second son of Ross and Christine Hayden Elder on Dec. 28, 1957. She and Donald have three children.

Helen married Andy Elliott on March 19, 1976. He is the son of Tommy and Juanita Elliott of Fancy Farm. They have three daughters, Amy, Mary and Callie.

Ed married Carol Elliott on June 19, 1983, daughter of Judy and Rudy Elliott, a native of Fancy Farm. They have three sons, Jacob, Cody and Nathaniel.

Their youngest son, Bart, married Tracy Russelburg on March 10, 1990, the daughter of Earl and Onida Russelburg of Hickory, KY. Bart is in the Air Force, they are stationed in Germany.

NEWBY, STEVE ALLEN AND CATHERINE MARIE HOWARD, were married on July 7, 1979. Steve, born July 13, 1957, holds an emergency medical technician certificate in Kentucky since 1991. He is the general manager of St. Vincent De Paul Store in Owensboro. He also works part-time for ARROW Ambulance (EMT) in Owensboro. Cathy, born April 28, 1956, is the daughter of David L. and Mary Ann Howard. She earned her master's degree in elementary education and is a teacher at St. Mary of the Woods in Whitesville, KY. They are members of St. Mary of the Woods Parish and have lived in Whitesville, KY, Daviess County since 1982. Former parishes include Sts. Joseph and Paul Church and Blessed Mother Church in Owensboro, KY. Their parish activities include parish picnic worker, Bible School in summer (teacher).

Steve and Cathy have four children: Rachel Leah Newby, born Jan. 6, 1981; Sarah Marie Newby, born July 21, 1983; Stephanie Aleena Newby, born Aug. 27, 1985; and Bridget Jo Newby, born Aug. 11, 1989-died July 17, 1990.

Steve's activities include Whitesville Volunteer Fire Department, Knights of Columbus while Cathy is a representative of faculty for Diocese of Owensboro Catholic Educators (DOCE).

They were the second couple to be married in the newly built St. Mary Church (1978-1979 model).

Cathy's parents are David L., a retired purchasing agent for Green River Steel Corp. and Mary Ann Howard, a homemaker. Her paternal grandparents are John Louis Howard and Mary Elve Payne Howard. Her maternal grandparents are Joseph Augustine Carrico and Mary John Fowler Carrico.

NEWTON, SISTER AGNES LEO, was born on June 2, 1911 at Manton, KY to Joseph L. Newton (Aug. 10, 1972-Aug. 17, 1947), Marion County, KY and Alice Hughes (Dec. 13, 1978-Aug. 18, 1917), Meade County, KY. She was baptized on Sept. 2, 1911 as Marcella and received her confirmation on Sept. 26, 1920. She entered the convent on Sept. 7, 1926 and received her Habit on March 19, 1927 taking her vows on March 19, 1929, March 19, 1932 (renewed one year-too young) and March 19, 1933. Her brothers and sisters include: Rose Parilee married Melvis Riggs, (second marriage) James A. Hagan, Mary Agatha married William Wimsatt, Mary Golda married Bowman Wimsatt, Frances Ethel, Mary Ada, Joseph Eugene married Lela Downs, and Mary Ruth.

Missions: Rome, KY; St. Lawrence, KY; Central City, KY; Mayfield, KYr; Sorgho, KY; St. James, Louisville; Brown's Valley, KY; Affton, MO; Hillsboro, MO; Buechel, KY; St. Raphael, KY; St. Rose, Cloverport, KY; St. Paul, Leitchfield, KY; Holy Cross, Loretto, KY; St. Catherine, New Haven, KY; Curdsville, KY.

NICHOLSON, MRS. REX W. (MARY B.), was born in Paducah, KY to Charles Hasby Mitchell and Ruby Hart on July 13, 1916. They lived at 925 Broadway for the first 21 years and moved to 30th Broadway (after the 1937 flood) for a few years; lived in the Idd apartments one year. Her father died in 1939 at 49 years of age. They moved to a small community called Camelia on the Blandville Rd. until she married.

Graduated from St. Mary Academy in 1935. Worked at Penneys a few years until Rex W. Nicholson and she met and married May 28, 1940 in the rectory of St. Francis De Sales Church by Rev. Albert Thompson.

Mary and Rex Nicholson

Rex and Mary moved to Reidland Rd. in a house he and his father, Charles E. Nicholson, built before they married. They have spent 52 years of married life in the same house and hope to complete their life there.

They have been blessed with three lovely daughters.

Joanne, born April 1, 1941, married Dale Litzsinger on Aug. 14, 1965. They have one daughter, Sara, born March 28, 1977 and live in Spring, TX.

Beverly Kaye, born July 29, 1942, married Jim Martin on Aug. 7, 1964. They have three children, Philip Martin, born Aug. 21, 1972; David Martin, born Nov. 22, 1973; and Kathy Martin, born Aug. 15, 1978. They live in Sulphur, LA.

Mary Elizabeth, born April 30, 1947 married Richard Zapalo on Jan. 6, 1973. They have one daughter, Kimberly, born Aug. 23, 1977 and live in La Porte, IN.

Mary has been a member of St. Francis De Sales Church all her life, Rex is a member of the Reidland Methodist Church.

Rex was a city letter carrier for the post office and fire chief of Reidland Volunteer Fire Dept. for 16 years and a charter member of the Reidland Lions Club and a past president.

Mary was president of P.T.A. at St. Mary Academy one year while their children were in school. She trained for first aid and home nursing and taught first aid courses. Rex served as the operator for their volunteer fire department several years; and did volunteer work at Lourdes Hospital and was a charter member of the Reidland Lioness Club and a past president.

They celebrated their Golden Anniversary on May 20, 1990.

Mary had two brothers, Charles Howyer Mitchell and William Joseph Mitchell deceased.

Twenty-three ladies, of them all classmates and mothers, were in school together and they did P.T.A. work together. They have a birthday club and that friendship continues on.

NOAH, STEVEN LEE AND MELINDA ANN BARBER, were married on June 20, 1981. Steve was born on Aug. 28, 1959 and Melinda was born on Aug. 28, 1962. They have two children; Christopher Grant, born Aug. 24, 1985 in North Carolina and Megan Marie born May 3, 1987 in North Carolina. Steven was in service, Air Force, from February 1981-July 1992. He is an A & P mechanic, receiving training in Air Force where he received an honorable discharge. Melinda is a legal secretary graduating from Madisonville Health Occupations as a medical secretary in June 1980.

They have lived in Earlington, Hopkins County, KY since 1992 and are members of Christ the King Parish. Steve and Melinda are former members of Our Lady of the Snows, Alaska; St. Michael, North Carolina; Resurrection, Dawson Springs, KY; and Immaculate Conception, Earlington. She participates in choir, military council for Catholic Women, hospitality, church picnic and fund raisers.

NORMAN, REV. JAMES F., was born Aug. 2, 1875 at Manchester England. He was ordained May 7, 1907 at

Cathedral in Louisville by Bishop John B. Morris. After ordination he was called to Little Rock, AR to assist Bishop Morris as his secretary, being given a leave of absence from the Louisville Diocese. He remained there 18 months, during which time he also served as vicar of the Cathedral in Little Rock, and chaplain at St. Vincent's.

Rev. James F. Norman

Upon his return to the Louisville diocese Father Norman was assigned to Taylorsville in 1909, where he remained one year. He was then named assistant at St. Cecelia Church, Louisville. In 1911 he was named pastor of St. Romuald Church, Hardinsburg where he remained for about 15 years. He was then transferred to Waverly, KY, where he served as pastor until he was named pastor of St. Paul, Owensboro.

He died on Nov. 2, 1938 with burial in Providence, RI.

NORRIS, LEE ANN and Richard Val Norris, Richard was born on Sept. 29, 1960 in Owensboro, KY. He went to Sutton Elementary School and Owensboro High School. His father was Richard Norris, born on Dec. 28, 1935 in Owensboro, KY. His mother was Carol Kantlehnar, born on Dec. 3, 1937 in Louisville, KY. Lee Ann Ebelhar was born on July 12, 1960 in Owensboro, KY. She went to Immaculate Elementary School and Owensboro Catholic High School. Her father was Dennis Ebelhar, born on Sept. 5, 1933. Her mother was Martine Payne, born on Nov. 11, 1934. Val and Lee Ann married at Immaculate Church on Dec. 16, 1978. They are both 32 years old. Val works at Big Rivers Electric Corporation. Lee Ann is a housewife and a Tupperware saleswoman.

Valerie Ann Norris was born on June 22, 1979. She is 13, in eighth grade at Owensboro Catholic Middle School. Natalie Nicole Norris was born on Dec. 28, 1981. She is 10, in fifth grade at Catherine Spalding School. Chad Dennis Norris was born on Dec. 4, 1984. He is 7, in second grade at Catherine Spalding. Logan Richard Norris was born on Aug. 22, 1986. He is 6, in kindergarten at Catherine Spalding. Valerie and Natalie both enjoy cheerleading and gymnastics, and are cheerleaders for their school. Chad and Logan both enjoy baseball. They play pee wee ball, for the Yankees, at Immaculate Parish.

Their family is a member of Immaculate Parish. Lee Ann is secretary of P.T.O. at Owensboro Catholic Middle School. She is also a cheerleading coach at O.C.M.S. and Catherine Spalding School.

NUNN-ROGERS, St. Francis De Sales Church history, the first marriage of record was the nuptials of Phillip Nunn and Regina Eich, Oct. 24, 1848 by Rev. Cor Opperman.

Phillip Henry Nunn April 28, 1818-Aug. 10, 1887, born Kolitzhein, Germany. Regina C. Eich, Nov. 11, 1828-Feb. 13, 1901 born Grunetal, Bavaria. Children:
Andrew Louis, born Nov. 3, 1850.
Ella May, May 30, 1852-May 6, 1928, married Edwin Farley on Oct. 3, 1871.
Mary Barbara, Oct. 22, 1853-Nov. 11, 1928, married John Rogers Feb. 12, 1878.
Rosa, June 27, 1855-July 18, 1910, married J.E. Robertson Oct. 5, 1880.
Henry Phillip, April 23, 1857-Feb. 3, 1937, bachelor.
Anna Regina, April 9, 1859, married A.R. Elder Dec. 29, 1881.
Eudora Kathrine, June 20, 1861-Feb. 22, 1936, married John H. Friant May 19, 1886.

Peter Rogers married Ellen Gillespy, both of Reading, MA, on Oct. 12, 1851, Father James Conway of St. Marys Church, Salem, MA. Peter Rogers, Aug. 24, 1826-May 31, 1883 born County Fermangh, Ireland. Ellen Gillespy, March 17, 1826-Nov. 18, 1899 born County Donegal, Ireland. Children:
Mary Ann, July 29, 1852-April 26, 1913, married John Bolger August 1871.
John, Dec. 11, 1853-July 10, 1937, married Mary B. Nunn Feb. 12, 1878.
James, June 23, 1856-Dec. 1, 1934, bachelor.
Peter, Aug. 24, 1859-Oct. 23, 1903, married Augusta Rupertus.
(See John Rogers Family.)

OBERST, ANDREW AND MARY JOSEPHINE TENNES, were married at St. Joseph Church, Owensboro, KY, on Sept. 12, 1976 with Rev. Westermann officiating. Andrew was born in Mandel, Germany, on Dec. 5, 1853. His parents were Johann Oberst and Katherina Mackworth. At age 14 he went to England where he learned the baker's trade. He left England and arrived in New York at age 17 with 15 cents in his pocket. Andrew came to Owensboro to join his sister, Christina, and operated a bakery and confectionery at St. Ann Street across from the court house. Later he became manager of the brickyard of the Paul Tennes estate, and of the rental property of his wife. He died Feb. 2, 1922.

The Andrew Oberst Family Picture. Front row: Louis, Mr. Oberst, Mrs. Oberst, Eugene. Middle row: Frank, Joseph, Mary, Andrew, Josephine, John, Herman. Back row: Father Bonaventure, Albert.

Mrs. Oberst was born on Aug. 6, 1857 in Dubois County between Huntingburg and Jasper, IN. Her parents were Paul Tennes and Josepha Kieffer who were of German parentage. Paul Tennes was born in Bavaria and his first wife is believed to have come from Alsace Lorraine. Mrs. Oberst died on her birthday Aug. 6, 1939. They had nine sons and two daughters: Andrew, Josephine, Paul Joseph, Albert, John, Herman, Joseph, Mary, Frank, Louis, Eugene. Paul Joseph became Father Bonaventure of the Congregation of the Passion.

All the children were brought up in the Catholic faith, went to St. Joseph School, and later some became members of St. Stephen Church. Many of the Oberst family are buried at Mater Dolorosa Cemetery in Owensboro, KY.

The stained-glass window of St. Boniface at St. Joseph Church, now the property of the Museum of Fine Arts, was given in memory of the above Paul Tennes, Fred Arnold Sr. (Paul Tennes' son-in-law) and Amelian Breidenbach.

OBERST, CHARLOTTE LEONA, daughter of Andrew Albert and Charlotte Marie Blau Oberst. Granddaughter of Andreas Oberst Mandel by-the-Rhine, Germany and George Blau of Alsac-Lorraine, France. Andy and Lottie were married in 1909 and raised seven children. All were baptized at St. Joseph German Catholic Church except Lottie, who was instructed, baptized, confirmed and married at St. Paul Church by Reverend Edward Fitzgerald. Their family became members of St. Stephen Church in 1925. Charlotte is the sixth of seven children, all born in Owensboro.

George Paul (deceased 1983), owner of Medical Book Publishing Company, St. Louis, MO, married in 1940.

Cyril, (deceased 1985), proprietor of a grocery, Owensboro, KY, married in 1939.

Bernardine (deceased 1991), co-owner of McFarland's Photography, Owensboro, married in 1953.

Robert Sr. (deceased 1974), superintendent of National Life/Accident Insurance, Evansville, IN, married in 1939.

Anna Catherine (deceased 1977), self-employed stenographer, secretary.

Margaret who died in infancy in 1917.

Charlotte L., the remaining living member of Andy/Lottie family, is a self-employed registered nurse, physical therapist and skin care consultant.

Education includes St. Frances Academy Owensboro; Nazareth School of Nursing, Louisville; dermo-neuro musculo therapy, University of Minnesota; physical therapy, University of Kansas School of Medicine; advanced rehabilitation, New York University, NY. Returned to Owensboro at the tragic death of mother in 1957 and opened the first Physical Therapy Department, as the first licensed physical therapist, serving Owensboro 27 years as director at Owensboro Daviess County Hospital. Practiced nursing and physical therapy in Owensboro; St. Louis; Washington, D.C.; Minneapolis; Farmington, Michigan; New Jersey; and New York City.

Honors: Listed in *Who's Who Women of the World* and first edition of *Who's Who in Rehabilitation*. Member: Chamber of Commerce, Society of Lady Kentucky Colonels, St. Stephen Cathedral Altar Society and a life member of American Physical Therapy Association, Beta Sigma Phi International Sorority and Optimist International. *Submitted by Charlotte L. Oberst.*

OBERST, JOHN LUKE SR. AND EMMA ISABELLE CRISP, were married at St. Paul Catholic Church, Owensboro, KY, on April 25, 1911 with Reverend Edward Fitzgerald officiating. John, born in Owensboro, was a member of St. Joseph Church. After marriage the family were members of St. Stephen Church. He was one of 11 children of Andrew Oberst and Mary Josephine Tennes Oberst. John was head of the Money Order Division of the post office on Fifth and Frederica Streets until his death on Aug. 22, 1942. Emma was born in Whitesville, KY, one of eight children of John Alexander Crisp and Mary Elizabeth Cecil Crisp. Her mother died when she was an infant and she was raised by her uncle, George Richard Cecil and Flora Ann Clark Cecil. Before moving to Owensboro, she played the organ for services at St. Mary of the Woods Catholic Church. In Owensboro she was executive secretary and office manager at the Owensboro Wagon Factory on East Third and Leitchfield Road before her marriage. She died Feb. 25, 1977.

They had five children:

Richard Cecil Oberst Sr. who married Marcelia Hoover King. They have two sons. He retired from Owensboro Municipal Utilities.

Mary Josephine Oberst, retired army nurse, was prisoner of war of the Japanese in the Philippines during World War II and assistant director of St. Mary's Hospital School of Nursing in Evansville, IN.

Dorothy Lucille (Sister Dorothea) joined the Sisters of Charity of Nazareth, KY, taught in elementary and secondary schools, taught mathematics four summers at Catherine Spalding University in Louisville, KY. Sister taught basic mathematics, algebra I and II and geometry at Owensboro Catholic High School for 17 years.

John Luke Jr. married Gladys Kasey and had three children. He retired from Texas Gas Transmission. He died Aug. 21, 1981.

Lawrence Allen operated Industrial Marking Company after retirement from Owensboro Municipal Utilities. He married Marvadean Mason and had two children. He died Aug. 4, 1982.

OBERST, ROBERT ANDREW, was born Sept. 18, 1918 in Owensboro, KY. His father Andrew Albert Oberst was the eldest of 11 children born of German immigrants and was employed by the Owensboro Foundry. His mother was Charlotte Marie (Blau) the daughter of a railroad engineer. Estelle Marie Hagan (March 19, 1920) was born in Owensboro, KY. Her father, Joseph Birch Hagan was a draftsman, and her mother is Stella Mae Hamilton, who is a resident at the Carmel Home and was born the daughter of a farmer. Robert and Estelle were married on Feb. 12, 1940, and spent the majority of their married years in Owensboro, where Robert worked for the National Life and Accident Insurance Company.

They had eight children who were raised mainly in Owensboro, KY and later in Evansville, IN. Sandra Marie (Feb. 28, 1941) married Darrell Eugene Flatter and they have one daughter, four sons and two grandsons. Robert Andrew, Jr. (Nov. 23, 1942) married Barbara Joan (Adler) and they have three sons, one granddaughter and two grandsons. Patricia Faye (Nov. 6, 1945) married Douglas Roger Cole and they have one son. Charlotte Anne (Aug. 25, 1948) married John Thomas Hood and they have one son and one daughter. Margaret Josephine (May 9, 1950) married Raymond Louis Flittner and they have one daughter and two sons. Thomas Wayne (Dec. 30, 1952) has a son by a previous marriage. Sarah Elaine (Feb. 3, 1955) married James Michael McCoy and they have one daughter and three sons. Cynthia Louise (June 10, 1959) married William Clayton Jackson and has one son and one daughter.

Robert A. Sr. passed away on Oct. 23, 1974. Estelle still lives in Owensboro and attends Mass at Precious Blood Church.

O'BRIEN, ED AND CLARA,
were married at Sacred Heart Church in 1945. They have three daughters, eight grandchildren, and four great-grandchildren.

Ed has always lived in Sacred Heart Parish, but Clara became a convert to the Catholic faith in 1943 while in Ursuline College in Louisville, KY.

Ed and Clara O'Brien

James and Rose O'Brien, Ed's grandparents, were among the first 15 or so families who came to Logan County, KY, in the late 1850s with the coming of Louisville and Nashville Railroad. They were from Waterford County, Ireland.

Ed is almost a legend at Sacred Heart Parish. Former pastors have described him as pouring himself out for the church. Ed has been on every council and committee that the church has to offer at some time. He is a lector, Communion Minister, usher and active in Knights of Columbus. He has been a daily Mass server since the school closed in 1986. His total years of serving Mass have been 69.

From 1975 to 1986, Clara did special tutoring at Sacred Heart School, volunteering to teach refugees who came to Sacred Heart through Owensboro Refugee Services. In 1982, Clara taught a Laotian refugee family for about three years. She taught English conversation and American customs. Clara earned the President Reagan Volunteer Citation in 1983 for reaching out to those people less fortunate.

The O'Brien's supported their church and family mostly by farming and by Ed working as city clerk, and Clara teaching in public schools.

Ed and Clara are chairpersons for Pro-life activities and Clara works with Right to Life and Opportunities for Life.

The O'Brien daughters report they are grateful for having grown up in a Christian home. All attended Catholic schools from grade one into Catholic High School and College.

O'BRIEN, SISTER MARY ROSALINE S.C.N.,
grew up in Sacred Heart Parish, the daughter of Edward and Mary Phillips O'Brien, and sister to Ed O'Brien. Sister received her high school education from the Blessed Sacrament Sisters, Nashville, TN and her college degree from Sisters of Charity's Spalding College.

Sister Mary Rosaline O'Brien

Sister was a faithful and kind nun and school administrator for 57 years. Sister Mary Rosaline is Sacred Heart Church's only professed religious, thus far.

O'BRIEN, TIMOTHY (THADY),
was born Aug. 21, 1958 to William and Terry O'Brien, Galway, Ireland. His family was very involved in the Catholic church and faith. His dad, an agricultural adviser, just retired.

Thady married his wife, Elizabeth, in Craughwell, Ireland April 1983. Elizabeth's parents also from Ireland are Aidan and Angela O'Toole and are also very devout Catholics. Both families come from generations of Irish Catholics. Her father, Aidan, runs his own confectionery business in Ireland. Elizabeth was born in New York after her parents came to the states in the 60s. They, parents and three children, returned to Ireland in 1965 and another three family members were born. Thady also comes from a good size family of three brothers and one sister, all Irish.

Thady and Elizabeth O'Brien Family.

Timothy and Elizabeth's first son, Morgan, was born in Ireland in 1984 before they immigrated to the states in 1985. Beginning in Chicago, Thady got his first job in his agricultural degree field in Illinois—promoted to Texas. His two daughters, Genevieve and Maria, were born in 1987 and 1989 in Texas. He then accepted an assistant manager's position in Turner Dairies, Fulton, KY, where they now reside.

Elizabeth became involved in AMS Montessori training from Illinois, and uses it from a home base with her young family. Thady and Elizabeth were involved in many church ministries since coming to the states. Now nine years married, they thank God for His life's miracles through their healings of children's illnesses, for the unity and prayers from their families, and deceased grandparents, Warners, O'Briens, O'Tooles and Courtneys, and for the gift of marriage and children, with its many blessings and even trials, which only helped to strengthen them more.

O'BRYAN, ELIZABETH THERESA OBERST,
was born in Atlanta, GA and moved to Owensboro at the age of 7. Her mother, Anna Winkler Oberst was born in New York and her father, Herman Simon Oberst was born in Owensboro. The Obersts were members of St. Joseph Parish in Owensboro. Elizabeth married Marion Albin O'Bryan, a member of St. Paul Church in Owensboro. Elizabeth and Albin gave birth to four children: Rose Marie (Sister Rose Marita, a Mount St. Joseph Ursuline Sister), Marion Albin Jr., H. Joseph and David E.

Elizabeth O'Bryan

Sister Rose Marita was baptized by a great uncle, Rev. Bonaventure Oberst, C.P. at the Cathedral. Marion Albin was baptized at the Cathedral by Rev. William M. McAtee. H. Joseph (Joe) was baptized at the Cathedral by Rev. Charles Saffer and David E. was baptized at Blessed Mother by Rev. William B. Jarboe.

The Marion Albin O'Bryan family were members of Blessed Mother Parish from the very beginning of Blessed Mother's early days. Marion Albin Sr. died on Nov. 15, 1978 and was buried from Blessed Mother Parish. Elizabeth Theresa Oberst O'Bryan is a member of Blessed Mother Parish. She has five grandchildren.

O'BRYAN, ELMO AND MARGIE,
were married in 1933 at St. Joseph Church in Owensboro, KY. Elmo is the son of Richard and Nancy of Henry County. He was born in 1909 in Daviess County. Margie Dishman is the daughter of Lawrence and Lura Dishman. She was born in 1909 in Daviess County. They have five sons.

Robert Eugene O'Bryan married Charolet Rudy.
Jame Donald O'Bryan married Nancy Newbauer.
William Joseph O'Bryan married Adell Bell.
Charles Edward O'Bryan married Theresa Castlen.
John Thomas O'Bryan married Terry Bonvillain.

Elmo and Margie have 22 grandchildren and 20 great-grandchildren.

O'BRYAN, HARRIETTE (HALLIE) VIRGINIA,
was born in Owensboro, KY Sept. 22, 1915. Baptized by Fr. Edward F. Fitzgerald and made her First Communion at St. Paul Church. She graduated from St. Francis Academy and attended business school. Her father, William Meigs O'Bryan was born at Crab Orchard, KY and was employed at Central Bank and Trust. He was, at one time, mayor of Owensboro. Her mother, Marybelle (Mable) Murphy was born at West Louisville, KY. Her family were members of St. Paul and her mother was active in the choir.

Miller Graham and Hallie were married at St. Paul's rectory by Fr. James F. Norman on June 18, 1936. They had two sons and six daughters. All the children, with the exception of one, graduated from Owensboro Catholic High. Her oldest son, Captain John Meigs Graham, was killed in Vietnam Jan. 16, 1971.

Now that all the children are grown, she lives at Roosevelt House and attends Immaculate Parish.

O'BRYAN, H. JOSEPH (JOE),
was born in Owensboro, KY, the second son of Marion Albin and Elizabeth Oberst O'Bryan. Joe married Margaret Mary (Maggie) Sims on June 2, 1972 at Blessed Mother Church. Maggie is the daughter of C.C. Sims and Mary Leona Ballard of Marion County, KY.

O'Bryan Family (l to r): Jill, Maggie, Jennifer, Joe and Michael.

Both Joe and Maggie continue to be very active in Catholic education. Joe ministered at Owensboro Catholic High for 16 years as religion teacher and as principal there for six years. In July 1991 Joe became superintendent of schools for the Owensboro Diocese. Maggie ministered as teacher in the intermediate grades at Immaculate School in Owensboro from 1972-1988. She is currently teaching at St. Angela Merici School in the third grade. Between them at this time, Maggie and Joe share almost 45 years of Catholic school involvement.

Maggie and Joe have three children: Jennifer Michele, Michael Joseph and Jill Marie. The family are members of Blessed Mother Parish.

O'BRYAN, MARY CECILIA, was born in Owensboro, KY on Nov. 11, 1910. She was baptized by Father Edward Fitzgerald, made her First Communion, was confirmed, and was a member of the choir at St. Paul Church. She attended and graduated from St. Francis Academy. After graduation she worked at Central Bank and Trust and then later at The First Owensboro Bank and Trust Company. Her father was William Meigs O'Bryan, an employee of Central Bank and Trust Company, and at one time, mayor of Owensboro. Her mother, Marybelle (Mable) Murphy, was a member of St. Paul and lead singer in the choir.

John Abell Medley was born in Owensboro, KY on Sept. 2, 1910. He was baptized by Father Edward Fitzgerald, made his First Communion, and was confirmed at St. Paul Church. He attended St. Francis Academy through the eighth grade and graduated from Owensboro High School. He then attended the University of Dayton where he was a band member, played football, and graduated in 1933. His father, Thomas Aquinas Medley was a distiller, and his mother was Florence Ellen Wathen from Lebanon, KY.

John Medley and Cecilia O'Bryan were married at St. Paul Church by Father James F. Norman on Oct. 25, 1935. Like his father, John also became a distiller. When Owensboro became a diocese they were moved to St. Stephen Parish, and then again to Blessed Mother Parish. When the Immaculate Parish originated, they became charter members of that parish and John was very active in its establishment. John and Cecilia had five boys and four girls of which they all attended Catholic grade schools, Owensboro Catholic High and Catholic colleges. There are 26 grandchildren and 11 great-grandchildren. John passed away in April, 1981, and Cecilia is still living at their home in Owensboro and attends the Immaculate Church.

O'BRYAN FAMILY, The O'Bryan's of Western Kentucky Diocese of Owensboro, began their family Catholic heritage from the Irish Catholics, St. Mary's County, MD, beginning from Peter and Jane (Gardner) O'Bryan. Thence to Lewis and Mary Ann (Blandford) O'Bryan who parented both Paul's great-grandfather the fifth of their 12 children and their 10th child who established their history via their second child James Pius O'Bryan. Records of these beginnings were recorded from 1800 to 1837, when Pius came to St. Lawrence with his widowed mother. He married Frances R. Hoskins and after eight children of this marriage, then married Nancy (Snyder) Lawson, a widow with two children. This marriage was to be blessed by six additional children. To narrow their story a bit they focus on the third child of this second marriage - Joseph Martin O'Bryan. In 1904 Martin married Regina Ivo (Mattingly) and their children swelled to 10. Mary Ursula the first, served her stewardship as a Mount St. Joseph Ursuline, the third Aloysius was to be ordained to the priesthood serving until his retirement in the Louisville Diocese. Father Henry, their fifth having his stewardship via Catholic High as teacher and principal thence to the diocese superintendent of Catholic schools needs no further introduction to the history pages.

The O'Bryan Family

Genealogies always become ultra complex - even when the population traveled via dirt country roads, but return to Lewis and Mary's fifth child - Paul's great-grandfather, Thomas Fielding O'Bryan. Thomas married Hannah (Whaelan) and their 10th child Urban P. was married to Paul's grandmother Sarah Ann (Thompson) the mother of the four boys in the above picture, the older boys, Mike, Jim and Irv, are sons of a first marriage to Urban (deceased from clearing land and pneumonia at the age of 31) and the baby son, Roscoe, is held by (uncle) Thomas J. O'Bryan. Grandma's second marriage to yet another O'Bryan. This is one family of Catholic O'Bryan's coming from the environs of Nelson and Marion counties surrounding Bardstown. Space precludes Paul's mentioning three other O'Bryan related families - also they did not have a Father Aloysius O'Bryan (retired) to do all the genealogical research.

These folks did much to aid in filling the churches now comprising the 16 in Daviess County, especially Sts. Alphonsus and Raphael. Paul's immediate forefathers were all baptized by Father Vonthurstenburgh. Grandpa cleared the land and helped to finance all of what they call the permanent buildings. Daddy, masterminded the planning for and building of the roads for the travel of the school buses which today transport their children to Catholic High. Their picnics with mutton, burgoo and chicken would have never been annual financial successes to operate the schools had not the good and faithful Catholics pulled together to enable their schools to function. And last, but definitely not the least, to be acclaimed in the successes they have experienced is the services of their good Sisters from Nazareth and the Mount St. Joseph who toiled for less than poverty returns while surviving in furnishings that were for many years rural communities of the frontier. Catholics did not originate in this diocese from a bountiful table.

O'BRYAN, WM. WALLACE, was born near West Louisville, KY, the son of Ben O'Bryan and Rausemond Vowels. He was a member of St. Alphonsus Parish. On March 29, 1932, he married Sophia Kaelin, daughter of John Kaelin and Rose Birchler of St. Martin Parish. Wallace, a farmer and Sophia, an R.N. had three daughters, Jacquelyn Greenwell (deceased), Mary Jane Blandford and Beverly Ann Smith. They have six grandchildren and two great-grandchildren.

Wallace and Sophia were active members of St. Alphonsus Parish until 1990 when they moved to the Carmel Home, where they attend daily Mass and services. They celebrated their 60th Wedding Anniversary in March, 1992.

Wallace and Sophia O'Bryan

O'DONNELL, FATHER JOSEPH, was born in Chicago on Feb. 22, 1922. After attending Resurrection Grade School he entered the high school seminary of Chicago and continued his seminary studies in the Diocesan Chicago Seminary in Mundelein, IL. In 1946 he joined the Glenmary Home Missioners and finished his last two years of study at Mount St. Mary Seminary in Cincinnati, OH. He was ordained on May 16, 1948. His first permanent assignment as a Glenmary priest was in Sunfish, KY from 1949 to 1952. After special study at Catholic University he then taught in the Glenmary Home Missioner Seminary from 1953 to 1965. In October 1965 he was appointed the pastor of Holy Redeemer Church in Beaver Dam and was there until July 1976. At that time he began to serve as the liaison in Southern Baptist—Roman Catholic relations for the Bishops' Committee on Ecumenical and Inter-Religious Affairs. He lived in Atlanta, GA doing this work from 1976-81.

Father Joseph O'Donnell

In November 1981 he returned to Beaver Dam as the pastor of three parishes: Holy Redeemer in Beaver Dam, Holy Trinity in Morgantown and St. John in Fordsville. He continues now as the pastor of those three churches.

At present Father O'Donnell is the director of the Office of Ecumenism for the Diocese of Owensboro. On a part-time basis he does ecumenical work with the various state and diocesan ecumenical programs.

He has always enjoyed his experience as a priest in Western Kentucky.

OELZE, CLETUS STEPHEN, was born near Hardinsburg in 1913. He was baptized at St. Romuald by Father James Norman. His father, Sherman Oelze, was a farmer, his mother, Annie, died when he was 4 years old. His father later remarried Mary Roach and they had three children.

Cletus married Regina Wethington. Her father and mother, Paul and Minnie Wethington, also lived near Hardinsburg. He was a mail carrier and a farmer. They had 10 children. Regina was born in 1916 and baptized by Father Norman.

Both families were always faithful members of St. Romuald. All the children of both families were baptized and married at St. Romuald.

Cletus and Regina married Sept. 29, 1936. They were blessed with 13 wonderful children. They were all baptized and attended both grade and high school and graduated at St. Romuald. Eight children married at St. Romuald.

Cletus and Regina Oelze Family. Back row: Mary, Minnie, John, David, Joe, Sherman and Paul. Middle row: Peggy, Shirley, Jamesetta, Lettie, Danny. Front row: Mom and Dad, Cletus, Regina and Dorothy.

Cletus was a farmer and mail carrier. Three of their sons served the armed service. Cletus and Regina celebrated their 50th Wedding Anniversary in 1986. Cletus passed away Feb. 10, 1991. Two children preceded him in death. They still have 11 living children, 48 grandchildren, and 19 great-grandchildren. Their big family was always their pride and joy. Neighbors visited neighbors, had music parties and played games. Someone played a piano, some a violin, guitar and banjo, everyone sang. When the party was over they ate cake, popcorn balls and pickles. Some kids think cake and pickles sound silly but they sure were good. They didn't have much money but they sure had a lot of love and fun, love for their family and love for God. For many years they have been sending clothes, toys and household items to mission countries.

OSBORNE, DAVID, was born on Nov. 26, 1952. His father, Tony Osborne owned a gas station. When David grew up he worked with his father at his gas station. David would pump gas and wash windows. David's mother, Mary Osborne, was a housewife who took care of six kids. When David got older he worked with his brothers, Tommy and Mike Osborne, as a brick layer. David then met Vickie Hardesty who was born on Sept. 30, 1952. Vickie's father, Ott Hardesty, was a bomber in World War II. Vickie's mother, Edna Hardesty, worked at Goodlow School. Then Edna became a housewife. Edna raised the family while Ott worked at a furniture store.

Vickie and David then got married on May 26, 1973. Vickie and David had three children. Amanda born on Dec. 21, 1978, now attends Owensboro Catholic High School. Amber born on Sept. 25, 1979, now attends Owensboro Catholic Middle School. Andrew, born on May 4, 1985, now attends Audubon Elementary. Vickie now works at Cravens Elementary. David is a Kentucky State Police. Vickie and David are Communion ministers at Precious Blood Church. David is also president of the St. Vincent De Paul Society. They attend church every Sunday.

PARKER, BEN AND SARAH, Prior to World War II in 1941, Ben and Sarah Parker with their three children, Agnes, Ben Jr. and John moved to Russellville from Pensacola, FL. Two more children, Sarah, Chris and George, were added later.

The Parkers came to run the family business, Parker Hardware and Furniture Store. Ben Parker left behind nine years of coaching an outstanding football team at Pensacola High School.

Sarah Conroy Parker met Ben at a wedding reception in her hometown of Clarksville, TN. At the time, Ben was completing his law degree while quarterbacking and playing linebacker for Vanderbilt University, Nashville, TN. He was voted to the "All Southern" squad on several occasions. Parker graduated from law school in 1931.

On Aug. 13, 1942, Ben Parker was received into the Catholic Church and was baptized at Sacred Heart Church by Father John Hallahan.

In 1942 the Glenmary priests of Cincinnati assumed care of Sacred Hearth Church at the request of Most Reverend Francis Cotton, bishop of Owensboro. The Glenmarians were a missionary order. They began work to establish a parochial school. By 1947, almost enough money had been donated to purchase a large dwelling house for students and four Glenmary nuns. However, funds were insufficient, and Ben Parker's family came to the rescue donating $2500 to complete the property purchase. In addition, the Parker's completely furnished the convent for free.

Benjamin F. Parker, about 1941; Sarah Conroy Parker, about 1941.

Although the school closed in 1986, the Parker family's generosity will be remembered by the 175 graduates—at least two of whom attended Harvard University.

In 1944 Russellville School Superintendent, Moss Walton, was short a football coach and three of his best players were fighting in the war. Parker volunteered to coach and told Moss he didn't want "nothing, nothing at all" for his time. Ben Parker practiced his Christian ethics on the ball field as well as in his business dealings.

Parker's former employees say he cared about them and their families. He always knew when someone needed toys or furniture. His former bookkeeper, Richard Young, said Parker gave without wanting praise or favors.

Coach Parker took over the team from seventh grade and what was left of the high school players. Parker was a strategist who believed his greatest asset was "imagination," teaching the young men to outsmart opponents rather than overpower them every time.

One of Parker's former players, Harold "Tubby" Hinton, said. "Ben Parker gave Russellville Panthers a new life. He not only taught us football fundamentals but also how to play the larger game of life; to be honest, work hard, to be disciplined, never give up and when we're right to hold onto our convictions."

Former Panther, Bobby Murphy, tells how Coach Parker watched the practice sessions from the bleaches sending word to the field by messenger about plays.

Parker and Coach Harold Hunter, together, molded quite a team that started the "glory years" with an undefeated team in 1950 under Coach Jimmy Haynes, whom Parker had brought to Russellville. Haynes had played three years for Parker in Pensacola.

Sarah was the perfect business partner going to the furniture markets with Ben and dressing the store windows. Her art talent was given generously in decorating Sacred Heart Church for weddings and holidays.

The Parker family moved to Louisville in 1950 so that the children could attend Catholic high schools. There, Parker taught at St. X High School until 1972.

Ben and Sarah Parker are now deceased. Their five children are outstanding business and professional people. According to son, John, at "last count" there were 16 grandchildren and 12 great grandchildren.

What a remarkable Christian family and what a legacy.

Information gathered from Jim Turner, sportscaster, Steve Meredith, sportswriter, former Panthers and business associates.

PATE, SISTER JOSEPHINE, parents were Austin and Mary Oelze Pate. She was born in Hardinsburg, KY. Baptized Ruby Rose April 10, 1892. Entered Mount St. Joseph Novitiate July 25, 1911 and received habit Nov. 21, 1912. Final vows, Dec. 30, 1920.

Missions: St. Alphonsus; St. Francis, Chicago, KY; St. Bernard, Nebraska City, NB; New Haven; MSJ Academy; St. Charles, Lebanon; Brescia College.

Of Sister Josephine, Sister Jane Frances said: "She knew how to run a school; she was a good principal, and she knew how to place her teachers and get the most out of them." Everyone who knew Sister Josephine would agree with this summing up of her as one in charge. Sister Mary Anselm said: "She impressed me as having a kind of overpowering personality, and seemed to get people and affairs going her way with a minimum of effort.

1947-1962 her teaching and manual labors contributed much to Brescia's success in its trying and formative years. She was mathematics and engineering drawing instructor. She was also in charge of keeping the campus beautiful; she likewise was purchasing agent for Brescia's needs and in charge of the cleaning staff. Under her supervision, the first brick building was erected in 1950-1951. In 1955 it was she who directed the enlargement of the administration building to which was added a new $200,000 front to Brescia College. She knew the best business firms in the city and patronized them. They in turn knew and respected her business ability. Her wit and wisdom talked many folks out of the right thing at the right price. By her conversational ability and tact she could turn "foe into friend."

Sister Josephine died Friday, July 21, 1967 at 1:00 p.m. after 49 years of hard work. She was buried July 24 at 10:00 with Mass said by Monsignor Thompson.

PATTERSON, LINDA BIVIN, though not born in Sacred Heart Parish, Russellville, returned in 1969 to the home of her ancestors along with sons, Gregory and Christian and daughter, Shelby. Having had the privilege of a Catholic education taught by Ursulines and Benedictines, Linda was happy for her children to attend Sacred Heart School. In the 1950s she had gone to Sacred Heart School when the Glenmary Sisters were teaching. From 1969 until 1986, she took an active role in her children's education and in support of the school by directing school plays, chaperoning outings, teaching P.R.E.P. classes, serving as an officer of both school board or P.T.A. She is currently active in the women's church group and as a lector.

Linda Bivin Patterson Family, 1990; Linda and granddaughter, Elizabeth, on her lap, Christian, Gregory and his wife, Tina and Shelby.

Maternal great-grandparents, Adam and Lena Bauer Stein, came to Logan County in the late 1800s working on the Louisville and Nashville Railroad. Adam was born in Alsace -Lorraine, France and worked as a stone mason. His artistry is still evident on headstones in the Maple Grove Cemetery. Lena Bauer was born in Berne, Switzerland.

Linda's mother, Josephine (deceased) was the daughter of Joe and Rose McCann Stein (deceased). Rose was born in Warrenton, MO. She had two older brothers, Elder and Norman. Josephine married Arlo Bivin from Todd County; and they moved to Dayton, OH.

A cousin to Linda's family and member of Sacred Heart Parish is Agnes Donovan Barrett. Agnes' mother, Annie, was a sister to Joe Stein. Annie died at 29 leaving two young daughters, Virginia (deceased) and Agnes.

Several of Elder (deceased) and Anna Lee Stein's children (they had 10) live in Christian County. Norman and Maxine Prather Stein (deceased) had one child, Lucretia Farquahar, who lives in Douglasville, GA.

PAYNE, SISTER ANGELINA, was born Jan. 31, 1904 at Knottsville, KY. She is the daughter of Sydney I. Payne (Feb. 16, 1874-Jan. 12, 1964, Knottsville, KY) and Agnes J. Millay (Dec. 19, 1878-Oct. 29, 1956, Knottsville, KY). She has 10 siblings: James Paulinus, Edward Ivo, Mary Roberto (deceased), Mary Frances Payne-Stimmle, Agnes Edna Mae Payne-Millay, Mary Vetta Payne (deceased), Mary Ethel Payne-Coomes (deceased), Joseph Bernard, Augustine Fabisn and Gerald Willima (deceased).

Sister Angelina taught various grades 1-6 at the following locations: St. Charles; Stanley, KY; Jefferson town, KY; St. Columba, Louisville; Farmington, NM; Blanco, NM; St. Paul, Louisville; Holy Cross, Kentucky; St. Francis, Kentucky; Wax, KY; Blanco, NM; Calvary, KY; Glennonsville, MO; Plattsmouth, NE; Peonia, KY; Flaherty, KY; Immaculate Conception, Hawesville, KY; Fredericksburg, KY; Holy Cross, KY; San Fidel, NM; Curdsville, KY; St. Francis, Loretto, KY.

She is presently retired at the motherhouse.

PAYNE, BEN AND MARY, met in their First Communion Class, the first ever in the new St. Mary of the Woods Church at McQuady, KY, in 1911.

Ben was the son of Henry Louis Payne and Josephine Midkiff and was born in Hancock County, Oct. 17, 1900. He was baptized in the Old St. Thomas Church which was built on land donated by his grandfather, Charles Payne. He was a descendant of the Maryland Catholic pioneers who came to Daviess County via Nelson County and settled near St. Lawrence. Henry brought his family to Breckinridge County in 1910.

Mary's parents were Dennie Sherron and Mary Frances Ryan. She was born near Tarfork, KY, Sept. 16, 1900. The Sherrons were just one generation away from Ireland having come to Cloverport during the potato famine. Mary was a 1921 graduate of Maple Mount and attended Western State Teachers College, returning to teach at the one room schools for a number of years.

Ben and Mary were married Oct. 26, 1927 by Father John F. Knue at St. Mary of the Woods. They settled into farming and a growing family just in time to face the hardest of economic times, the Great Depression. The family of four girls and three boys took a great deal of pride in what they could accomplish working together.

Ben and Mary Payne

The family will always remember a Christmas in the 30s. The roads of that time were dirt roads which quickly turned to mudholes in wintertime. The Model A Ford couldn't make it so Ben hitched a team of mules to the farm wagon filled with hay and enough quilts to cover five children. The trusty mules slogged through six miles of mud to Christmas Mass.

Ben died March 2, 1990. Mary still lives on the family farm and faithfully attends St. Mary of the Woods.

PAYNE, REV. GARY LEO, was born on April 5, 1959. He was the second of six children born to Herman Junius Payne and Edith Catherine Clark Payne who were at that time living at Browns Valley, KY. Soon after, the Payne family moved to Whitesville which became their permanent residence. Gary's sister and brothers are: Wayne, Diana, John, Mark and Glenn.

Rev. Gary Leo Payne

Gary was baptized by Rev. Martin Mattingly on April 15, 1959 at St. Anthony Church, Brown's Valley. Gary attended St. Mary of the Woods Catholic Elementary and Trinity High School at Whitesville. He attended Kentucky Wesleyan College in Owensboro in 1977 where he studied theater. In January 1979 Gary entered St. Pius X Seminary in Erlanger, Kentucky graduating with a BA in philosophy. In 1981 he entered the School of Theology at Mount Saint Mary in Emmitsburg, MD. In 1982 he transferred to St. Meinrad School of Theology where he completed his master's of divinity in 1985. On June 23, 1984 he was ordained as a deacon in his home parish of St. Mary of the Woods. On May 11, 1985, he was ordained a priest by Bishop John J. McRaith in Owensboro. His first assignment was to Holy Name Parish in Henderson as an associate pastor. After two years he was assigned to Holy Spirit in Bowling Green as an associate pastor. In 1987 he became pastor of three parishes in Grayson County, St. Anthony, Penoia, St. Benedict, Wax and St. Augustine, Grayson Springs. This is his current ministry as well as being a member of the Diocesan Pastoral Council and the Diocesan Liturgy Committee.

PAYNE, GEORGE AND ROSEMARY FAMILY, have been members of Saint Peter Parish in Waverly for most of their married life. St. Peter Church is located on land that was originally owned by the Payne ancestors. George lived with his parents, Walter and Elizabeth Higginson Payne until he married Rosemary Stockton at Saint Ann Church in Morganfield on Aug. 3, 1954 officiated by Father Joseph Spalding. In 1960 they moved back to the Payne's family farm in Waverly. They had six children. Two baptized at Saint Ann and the others at Saint Peter.

George was a farmer and carpenter. They were both active in parish work. George served on the church board, ushered, worked at the annual picnics, and was always available to do odd jobs around the church rectory. He was a Grand Knight and financial secretary for the Waverly Knights of Columbus. He died of cancer at the age of 55 on Oct. 2, 1987.

Rosemary is the church organist, the co-ordinator for the Parish Grade School CCD Program, teaches CCD, is a member of the Altar Society and serves on the Liturgy Committee.

Social worker, nursing, carpentry, farming and oil field worker are the professions the children are engaged in. Four still live in this diocese. Diane (married to Paul Henshaw) has three children, is a hospice nurse and attends Saint Ambrose Church. George Jr. is married to the former Cynthia Henshaw. They have two sons and are active in Saint Peter Parish. Cindy was received into the church in 1989. Rosemary (married to Joe Park) has four children and attend Saint John Parish in the Evansville Diocese. Cecilia works as a travel nurse, so has the opportunity to be a part of many parishes. Joe, Steve and his son still live on the family farm with their mother.

PAYNE, GILBERT T. AND MARY CECILIA (PAYNE), Gilbert is a steelworker and Mary is a office manager for M & I Newspaper. Paternal-Alec Payne and Lenora Tierney; maternal-Francis A. and Mary Elizabeth Cook, father, mechanic (auto) and mother, RN. Paternal farmer and mother housewife.

They were born and raised in Daviess County and presently live in Utica, KY-Daviess County.

They are members of St. Anthony Brown's Valley.

Their children are Jeannette, Nov. 24, 1955; Ronald, Feb. 25, 1957; Terry, May 27, 1960; Roxanna, Jan. 27, 1962; Carla, May 26, 1964 and Melanie, Aug. 25, 1970.

PAYNE, HENRY BERRY, was born June 24, 1924. He was baptized and confirmed at St. Stephen Cathedral.

He graduated from St. Francis Academy in 1942 and enrolled in Naval ROTC at Notre Dame. He graduated as an ensign in 1945, and went to sea, on a baby flat too after World War II was over.

Father Maloney built the present St. Stephen Cathedral. In the early 30s, on his 25th anniversary as a priest, there was a program to raise money to send him to Rome. There was a "bride and groom" wedding procession. Henry as the groom (portraying Fr. Maloney) and was dressed in a velvet morning coat. Mary Rita McAtee was the bride (the church) in a wedding dress.

Boy in the black velvet suit is Henry Berry Payne at Father Mahoney's 25th anniversary of the priesthood.

Later, Henry was an altar boy under Fr. Boehmicke.

He (Henry) was in on the celebration in 1937 when Bishop Cotton became the first bishop in Owensboro. He suggested Henry study law or medicine, but Henry became an engineer.

Henry's grandfather Henry Scott Berry, was the weatherman for Daviess County for 37 years. He and his brother-in-law (Samuel Ridley) Ewing were the two incorporators of the Catholic Diocese of Owensboro. Mr. Berry was famous for making the burgoo for the annual church picnic.

PAYNE, HENRY D., (1878-1941), son of Thomas Henry and Elizabeth Russell Payne was born in Owensboro. His education was at the Monks School in Marion County, KY and the Spencerian Business School in Louisville, KY. As a teenager, Henry D. Payne was employed by the E.W. Smith Furniture Co. Later he and a partner, James S. Leach bought the business and operated it until Mr. Payne's retirement in 1934. His father, Thomas H., was born in Meade County, a member of St. Tresea Parish, baptized by Fr. Eliza Durbin. He and his brothers moved to Owensboro and engaged in the whiskey industry.

Elizabeth C. O'Flynn Payne (1875-1967, the wife of Henry D. Payne, was born in Owensboro. She and her husband were members of St. Paul Parish; both are buried in the old Catholic Cemetery on West Ninth Street. Her parents were Richard and Thersa O'Flynn. Mrs. Payne was educated at the Mount St. Joseph Academy, Maple Mount, KY.

Richard O'Flynn was engaged in the tobacco industry, having operated a Stemmery for years. Mrs. Payne's grandfather, William Coomes Jr. was an early Daviess County resident and a member of St. Lawrence Church. His Ohio River farm home was used as a chapel by visiting priests from St. Vincent in Union County prior to St. Stephen Church in Owensboro.

Children of Henry D. and Elizabeth C. Payne were all born in Owensboro. Angela (Mrs. F.F. Hayden); Thomas E. (wife: Elizabeth Berry); Agnes (Sr. Agnes Miriam SCN), Nazareth, KY; Dorothy (Sr. Mary Cecilia OSU) Maple Mount, KY; Mary Louise, Helen (Mrs. Paul E. Gilles), Chattanooga, TN; Heny D. Jr. (Hank), Mount Carmel, IL.

PAYNE, HERMAN AND EDITH, have lived in Daviess County all of their lives. They were married June 25, 1955 by Rev. Walter Hancock at Saint Mary of the Wood Church, Whitesville.

Herman is the son of the late Lawrence and Anna (Wathen) Payne. They were originally from Knottsville, but moved into Owensboro where they were members of Blessed Mother Parish.

Edith is the daughter of the late Kyran and Delpha (Ryssellburghe) Clark. They were life long members of Saint Mary, Whitesville.

Herman and Edith have six children, five sons and a daughter and eight grandchildren.

Joseph Wayne, after graduating from Trinity High School, went to Navy for two years.

Wayne married Joan Hagan June 23, 1983. They have five children, two sons, three daughters, Ryan (deceased), Katie, Curtis, Marci and Andrea.

Gary Leo went to college at KY Weselyn two years and transferred to Saint Pius X Seminary in Erlanger, KY. He went to Mount Saint Mary, MD for one a half years of theology and transferred to Saint Meinrad in Indiana to finish his schooling.

Gary was ordained priest May 11, 1985. His first assignment was associate at Holy Name in Henderson.

Then Holy Spirit in Bowling Green as associate for two years. Since June 1989 he has been pastor at Saint Anthony Peonia Saint Augustine Grayson Springs and Saint Benedict at Wax.

Gary has officiated four of our children's weddings and has baptized all the grandchildren.

Diana married Richard Beaven Nov. 29, 1991. They are making their home in Corydon, KY.

John married Imelda Hagan June 14, 1986. They have two sons, Johnny and Jason. God has blessed them with another on the way.

Mark married Paula Bean Sept. 17, 1988. They have a son, Zachary, and live in Henderson.

Glenn married Deanna Johnson June 23, 1990. She is a registered nurse for Mercy Hospital.

Herman is usher and Edith is Eucharistic Minister at Saint Mary, Whitesville.

PAYNE, HERMAN VINCENT (BUTCH) AND JOYCE CECILIA, was born July 3, 1955. Married Joyce Cecilia Payne, born Jan. 14, 1956. They were married Oct. 4, 1975. Their children are: Isaac Lee Payne, born Jan. 23, 1978; Luke Andrew Payne, born Jan. 11, 1980; Chelsea Elizabeth Payne, born April 30, 1982, daughter; Emily Ann Payne, born Oct. 24, 1983, daughter; Jesse Thomas Payne, born Jan. 14, 1985, son.

They have resided in Whitesville, KY, Daviess County. They are members of St. Mary of the Woods, Whitesville, KY. They have been members of Blessed Mother, Owensboro from Oct. 4, 1975 to Oct. 30, 1981.

Butch was a lecturer, on the grade school board and chairman of the picnic for three years. Joy teaches children's liturgy. Butch was on the Synod Delegate Committee for St. Mary Parish. Butch and Joy were on the Stewardship Committee and shared their testimony at St. Mary and Immaculate Parishes.

Herman Vincent (Butch) Payne Family

Joy is a Girl Scout leader and Cub Scout leader. Butch's parents and grandparents were members of St. William, Knottsville. Joy's parents were members of St. Mary. Butch was a member of St. William until married and Joy a member of St. Mary.

Butch and Joy entered diocese Oct. 4, 1975. Member of Blessed Mother Parish. They joined St. Mary of the Wood Oct. 30, 1981. Moved from Blessed Mother. Butch is an electrician. Joy is a full time homemaker.

They belonged to Blessed Mother for six years when they first got married. Then they moved to Whitesville and joined St. Mary of the Woods. Butch started working at Toyota in September 1992. In December 1992 they are moving to Lexington, KY and they are joining Mary Queen of the Holy Rosary Catholic Church.

PAYNE, IGNATIUS CHESTER SR., was born near Knottsville, KY on Jan. 31, 1904. His father, Ignatius Raphael, was a farmer, and his mother, Margaret Millay, was of the Knottsville community. Agnes Gerald Kennedy was born at St. Lawrence, KY on Nov. 13, 1904, and was baptized by Father Lucian Clements. Her father, Andrew Kennedy, came to Kentucky from County Wexford, Ireland in 1846. He was a teacher and also farmed near St. Lawrence and Whitesville, KY. Her mother was Theresa Ann Payne of St. Lawrence.

Mr. and Mrs. Payne

Chester and Agnes were married April 12, 1926 at St. William Church, Knottsville. The Rev. Joseph McAleer officiated. In the early years of their marriage, they lived near Knottsville where he was a farmer and six of their children were born. In the mid 1930s she taught Cathecism in her home to children of non-practicing Catholics, under the direction of the pastor, Rev. William B. Jarboe. In December 1940, they moved to Owensboro, KY where they were members of St. Paul Parish. Two of their children were born in Owensboro. He was a machinist at the Wright Machine Co.

They later moved back to the country, where he enjoyed gardening for several years. They were members of St. Pius X Parish, and were active in church activities in the beginning years of the parish.

In 1971, they moved to Owensboro, KY, where they still live.

They have eight children: Ruth Anna Cureton, Margaret Cleophas Foster, Rose Mary Bender, Mary Audeline Meffert, Theresa Marie Pedley, Dolores Rita Hartz, Ignatius Chester Payne Jr. and Joseph Anthony Payne, 28 grandchildren and 27 great-grandchildren.

They celebrated their 66th Wedding Anniversary on April 12, 1992, and are members of St. Stephen Parish, the Army of Mary, the Ministry of Praise and the Legion of Mary.

PAYNE, JAMES P., son of Sidney I. Payne and Jane (Anne) Millay Edith Marie, daughter of Thomas Tierney and Anne Bickett.

J. Pauline and Marie have lived in Knottsville all of their 68 years of married life. Farming and carpentry helped them in the rearing of their 12 children. They have been an inspiration to the 69 grandchildren and 90 great grandchildren. Many are active in the church ministry.

Both have been active in the Legion of Mary, Altar Society, Miraculous Medal, the Sacred Heart and the St. Benedict leagues. Their lives center around St. William Church and the many priests and nuns who have influenced them.

They have known sorrows, including the loss of four children. Their faith has been renewed with many miraculous events they have experienced, especially the miraculous cure of a granddaughter from leukemia.

The J.P. Payne Family

They keep active and feel blessed that they were able to travel to Italy in their 70s.

Music is a highlight of family gatherings as Marie plays the piano. Everyone enjoys a joke or a story of Daniel Boone from Pauline. The highlights of grandchildren's visits was to search for granddaddy's "hamburger tree" in the woods.

Pauline at 90 and Marie at 87 still enjoy their farm home. They tell of their love of Christ and their thanks to all who have journeyed with them through life.

Their children are: Lillian Weafer, Owensboro; Cyril, deceased; Thomas, deceased; Patrick, Louisville; Vincent, Knottsville; James Sidney, deceased; Edna Marie, deceased; Joseph Daniel, Indiana; Mary Ann Adams, Owensboro; Regina Toon, Toledo; Paul, Owensboro.

PAYNE FAMILY, from Maryland via Virginia to Kentucky, John, Cornelius, Edward Payne. John Payne 1769-1846 was born in St. Mary's County, MD. John married Dorothy Drury (1794) in St. Mary's County, MD where all their children: William, John Lewis, Ignatius,

Herman Payne Family

Cornelius and Denis H. were born. Cornelius (1803-1835) married in 1832 in Washington County, KY to Mary Payne daughter of Basil Payne and Sarah Mattingly, moving to Daviess County where John, Cornelius died and buried at St. Lawrence Catholic Church.

Cornelius's children: John Thomas born 1827, Edward Norris born 1831, Charles Hillary, born 1833, Cornelius Jr., born 1835 were all born in Daviess County, KY; all were baptized at St. Lawrence Catholic Church. Edward Norris moved to Breckinridge County where he married in 1853 to Sarah Arnold (1854-1867) at Flint Island Catholic Church. After the death of Sarah, Edward married (1870) to Lydia Ann Hardesty (born Dec. 3, 1843, died April 27, 1929) at Flint Island Catholic. Edward, Sarah and Lydia are all buried at St. Theresa Catholic Church.

Edward and Lydia Hardesty Payne

John Thomas (born Nov. 26, 1872, died Feb. 26, 1958) married at St. Theresa Catholic Church to Hallie Lillian Payne (born Jan. 12, 1876, died March 23, 1947) daughter of James M. Payne and Mary Rhodes. John Thomas and Hallie were the parents of 13 children. John Thomas and Hallie attended Mass every Sunday regardless of the weather, traveling by horse and wagon to St. Theresa. The horses had worked hard all week in the fields planting crops. John Thomas would hitch the team of horses at the foot of the hill to St. Theresa as the horses needed the rest. John Thomas's son, Thad Payne (born Nov. 13, 1915) married (1938) Lillie Mae Wright and was the father of six children: Margaret, Dorothy, Grace, Mildred, Mary Linda and Marilyn. Thad's family attended Holy Guardian Angel Church, Irvington where Lillie Mae and Margaret are still members.

PAYNE, JOSEPH ANTHONY AND ROSE MARIAM FAMILY, joined St. Pius Parish in February 1973. They were married May 29, 1971 at St. Mary of the Woods Church at Whitesville, KY. They have two children, Chris and Sheila. Chris is a sophomore at Owensboro Catholic High School and Sheila is in seventh grade at Owensboro Catholic Middle School.

The Joseph Payne Family

Joseph Anthony's parents, Chester and Agnes Payne, grew up in St. William Parish at Knottsville, KY and are now members of St. Stephen Parish in Owensboro. Rose Mariam's parents, C.G. (Coke) and Annie Hamilton, grew up in St. Mary of the Woods Parish in Whitesville, KY and are still living there.

Joseph Anthony was baptized at St. William Parish in Knottsville, and confirmed at St. Paul Parish in Owensboro. He graduated from Owensboro Catholic High School, served four years in U.S. Air Force. He has worked at Big Rivers Electric for 23 years. Rose Mariam was baptized and confirmed at St. Mary of the Woods Parish in Whitesville, KY. She graduated from St. Mary of the Woods School and from Owensboro Business College. She worked as a dental assistant for 10 years.

Both Joseph and Rose enjoy participating at parish picnics and various other fund raisers. Chris and Sheila enjoy youth group activities.

PAYNE, JOSEPH P., was born near Whitesville, KY Dec. 25, 1925 the son of Wm. Guy Payne and Mary Bertha Boarman. He attended 12 years of grade school and high school at St. Mary's, was drafted into the service and was wounded in World War II. He married Rose Angela Howard, daughter of Ivo L. Howard and Maudwina Higdon on April 19, 1947 by the Rev. Wm. B. Jarboe at St. Mary's Church. Rose and Joe attended both grade and high school together. They made their home on 19 acres (and still live) just west of Whitesville where they part-time farmed and raised cattle. Joe worked for Texas Gas 36 years before retiring in 1987. They have five children: Marilyn R. Beyke, Theresa Marie Payne, Jane Ann Gayhart, Kenneth P. Payne and Mark A. Payne and five grandchildren.

Mr. and Mrs. Joseph P. Payne

All five of their children earned their college degrees with two of the daughters and the youngest son entering the teaching profession and the oldest son is an engineer.

PAYNE, JOSEPH WAYNE, born in 1957 was baptized at St. Anthony's by Father Martin Mattingly. He attended St. Mary of the Woods Grade School and was a 1975 graduate of Trinity High School. He served in the U.S. Navy. He is now employed with I&M Power.

His father is Herman J. Payne. His grandparents were Lawrence A. and Anna Wathen Payne. His great-grandparents were Thomas and Sue Montgomery Payne. His mother is Edith C. Clark Payne daughter of Kyram and Delpha Rysselburghe Clark. Kyram's parents were Leo and Mary Church Clark. Leo's parents were Wilfred and Matilda Clark.

Joan Marie Hagan was born in 1961. She attended St. Mary of the Wood Grade School and was a 1979 graduate of Trinity High School in Whitesville.

Her father is Audrey L. Hagan, the son of William Kernie and Mary Etta Ward Hagan. Her great grandparents were Joseph and Nancy Sharp Hagan.

Her mother is Martha R. Howard Hagan, the daughter of Clarence Patrick Hagan Howard and Carmel Greenwell Howard Edge. Their parents were Joseph Patrick and Julia Clark Howard; Eugene and Mary John Hardesty Greenwell. Joseph W. and Joan Hagan Payne were married on Sept. 24, 1983, St. Mary of the Wood Church in Whitesville by Rev. Steve Dunn.

Their children are Ryan Junius born and died on Jan. 4, 1985. Catherine Marie born July 2, 1986; Curtis Wayne, Sept. 4, 1987, Marci Jo, June 13, 1989; Andrea Ryan, May 21, 1990.

All their children were baptized by Father Gary L. Payne, Joseph's brother. The Payne family live in Whitesville and are members of St. Mary of the Wood Church.

PAYNE, KENNETH E., and his wife, Beverly and their two children, Robbie-13, and Laura-7 reside in Irvington. Robbie and Laura attend St. Romuald Interparochial School in Hardinsburg.

Kenny is a native of Breckinridge County and grew up in St. Mary of the Woods Parish where he attended the Parish School through the sixth grade. In the seventh grade, he transferred to St. Romuald School and graduated from high school there in 1962.

Beverly is a native of Russell County where she grew up Baptist and graduated from Russell County High School.

After their high school years, their lives took them in various directions before they eventually met while both were living in Louisville. Growing dissatisfied after several years of city living, Kenny returned to Breckinridge County at their present address, with Beverly joining him upon their marriage.

Though Beverly was Baptist, she began attending Holy Guardian Angels Church. After several years, she began attending adult education classes taught by Father Tony Stevenson and joined the Catholic Church, making her First Communion at Easter '92 and was confirmed the next month in May.

PAYNE, LARRY S., was born near Knottsville, KY and attended St. William Church and School. His father, Sylvester Payne was a farmer. His mother, Cora Skinner, was a homemaker. They had eight living children and attend St. William Church at Knottsville.

Ann Genetta Johnson was born near Knottsville, KY and attended St. Lawrence Church and School. She graduated from Mary Carrico Memorial School at Knottsville. Her father, Paul E. Johnson was a farmer. Her mother, Anastasia Coomes was a homemaker. They had nine children and belong to St. Lawrence Church.

After graduation from high school, Larry spent three years in the Navy. He graduated from the University of Evansville with a bachelor of liberal studies degree. He has been employed at Alcan Aluminum for the last 19 and half years. They married on June 29, 1968 at St. Lawrence Church. They have seven children and live at Utica, KY.

Larry S. and Ann Genetta Payne

They are members of St. Anthony Church at Browns Valley, KY where Larry is a Eucharistic Minister and lector. Gennie is presently serving on the Pastoral Council.

PAYNE, MARK ALAN, was born on Oct. 29, 1964 in Owensboro, KY. He is the son of Herman J. Payne and Edith Clark Payne of Whitesville, KY. He was baptized Nov. 8, 1964 by Fr. Benedict Huff. As a member of St. Mary of the Woods Catholic Church, he attended St. Mary Elementary School and graduated Trinity High School in 1982. Mark has one son Zachary Devan B. Payne born Aug. 12, 1990 in Henderson, KY. He was baptized Sept. 30, 1990 by his uncle, Fr. Gary Payne.

They have resided in Owensboro, Daviess County, since Aug. 1, 1992. Member of Precious Blood, Owensboro, KY. Past membership Holy Name of Jesus in Henderson, KY 1988-1992.

Late Kyran and Delphia Clark, St. Mary of the Woods and the late Lawrence and Anna Payne, Blessed Mother.

Mark is material handler at Aeroquip in Henderson.

PAYNE, OWEN ALOYSIUS, was born near Knottsville, the son of Martin Payne and Agnes Sophie Bowlds.

Anna Virginia Roberts was born near Maceo, the daughter of Lawrence Roberts Sr. and Agnes Maud Hartley. They were married on Aug. 18, 1931 at St. William Church in Knottsville. Their attendants were Manuel Roberts brother of Anna Virginia, Sis to many of her friends, and Clara Johnson who later became Sr. Anna Francis OSU. They moved to Detroit after their first child Greta was born to look for work in the auto plants. Two of Owen's sisters and their families had already moved there.

Owen and Virginia Payne

After Greta died in a tragic accident at the age of 20 months, Owen and Virginia moved back to Knottsville. Owen started farming and they had nine more children. Owen eventually went to work at Green River Steel where he retired from in 1973. After retiring they moved to Owensboro. Owen died May 20, 1980. Their oldest daughter Jean Ann had an aneurism on April 16, 1986 and laid in a vegetative state for two and a half years before dying Nov. 22, 1988. Owen and Virginia have 36 grandchildren and 28 great grandchildren. Virginia still resides in Owensboro and attends Blessed Mother Catholic Church.

PAYNE, PAUL A. was born in Daviess County Hospital in 1955 to Roy I. Payne and Margaret W. Payne. They were Catholics and attended Saint Joseph and Paul Church. They moved to Knottsville when he was almost 9.

Karen Turner was born in a house in Ensor in 1958 to Elizabeth Turner and Jocient A. Turner. They moved once when she was 14 to Knottsville and attended Saint William Church. Karen and Paul met in Karen's mother's restaurant and married on Aug. 16, 1975.

The next year on Karen's birthday, Sarah Payne was born. Three years later in September Adam Payne was born. Just before Adam was born they moved to Knottsville. Two more children, one in 1987 named Clinton, another in 1989 named Ryan were born. Sarah attends OCHS. Adam attends OCMS. Clint attends a public kindergarten and Ryan a public daycare. Karen works as a paramedic in Indiana and Daviess County. Paul has been teaching at OCHS for 13 years. They serve in other parish activities and Adam as an altar boy.

PAYNE, RAYMOND ALVA AND EVELYN TALLEY, were born at Reynolds Station in Ohio County. Raymond, son of Albert and Lula Payne Payne, was a driller and oil field worker. Evelyn is the daughter of Oliver, a farmer of Derby, IN, and Mary Zuma Moseley Talley, a teacher in Ohio County. Raymond and Evelyn were married by Fr. Hugh O'Sullivan in the rectory of St. Mary of the Woods, Whitesville on Feb. 11, 1930.

Mr. and Mrs. Payne were blessed with five children. Virginia, the eldest, married Aubrey Lewis Mayfield, a successful farmer. Ginny and Aurb have seven children; the couple are lifelong members of St. Mary's, Whitesville.

Edna Lucille Payne, like her grandmother Talley, is a teacher in the Ohio County School System and has traveled widely.

Harold Payne, an oilfield worker, married Connie Payne and is the father of six children. They are St. Mary's parishioners also.

Herman G. Payne, a graduate of Trinity High School, was a Marine who lost his life in Quang Tri, Vietnam. He had been named for his uncle, Herman Talley, soldier in World War II who became a prisoner of war in the Philippines. He was among American POWs being transported to another prison camp by the Japanese when American soldiers mistakenly torpedoed the ship, thinking it carried only Japanese. Thus Mrs. Evelyn Payne is the keeper of her brother Herman's Purple Heart and of her son Herman's Purple Heart.

Raymond A. and Evelyn Talley Payne seated, with youngest children Carmel Rose and Herman G. Payne standing. (Picture from 1954 St. Mary of the Woods, Whitesville, parish directory.)

Carmel Rose, youngest daughter, married Darrel Crabtree, an electrician. Carmel, mother of three, is a homemaker and self-employed upholsterer.

Raymond and Evelyn moved to St. Pius X Parish in 1972 where they were active members until Raymond passed away Jan. 19, 1990. They have 16 grandchildren and 23 great-grandchildren. Evelyn and Lucille reside in Owensboro.

PAYNE, THAD AND LILLIE MAE WRIGHT, Lillie Mae Wright, the oldest daughter of Edgar (1883-1962) and Clarissa Durbin (1892-1930) Wright. Lillie Mae and her two sisters, Georgia Lee and Loretta lost their mother at a young age. The children of Clarissa continued in their Catholic faith even though their father was not a Catholic. They would walk to church as well as school in all types of weather.

Lillie Mae's grandparents, Thomas J. (1855-1922) and Malissa Logsdon (1858-1920) Durbin were from a long line of Catholics. Lillie Mae's great-grandparents, Phillip Edward (born 1819) and Margaret McCaffery (1822-1881) were Catholics as was William Joseph Logsdon (died 1891) and Elizabeth Theresa (1810-1880) Durbin ancestors were Kentucky pioneer Catholics.

Lillie Mae Wright married (1938) to Thad Payne who was from a very long Catholic family line. The Payne family came to Kentucky in ca 1796 from St. Mary's County, MD. Thad and Lillie Mae started out as farmers and continued to farm, and Thad went to public work in the early 1950s. Thad and Lillie Mae became the parents of six daughters: Margaret, Dorothy, Grace, Mildred, Mary Linda and Marilyn Deloris. The Payne family came to be members of Holy Guardian Angel Church at Irvington, KY in the early 1950. Lillie Mae and Thad had 10 grandchildren and seven great-grandchildren and three step-grandchildren.

PAYNE FAMILY, VINCENT H., have lived in and around Knottsville most of their lives. Vincent H. Payne, youngest of three of Hillary Payne and Mary Florence Higdon of St. Lawrence was born Dec. 25, 1914. Anna Sue Isbill, daughter of Joseph Earnest Isbill and Mary Bernadette Payne was born on Oct. 13, 1915. Anna and Vince were married on Feb. 12, 1935 at St. William Church by Father Jarboe, and for over 50 years have lived and worked in the same area in which they still live, Lewisport, Kentucky. They have belonged to St. William Parish in Knottsville all their lives.

Vince had a dual occupation as a mechanical technician and as a part-time farmer. Anna has been a homemaker and aided Vince in his part-time farming. Anna suffered many trials and tribulations having had four children being still-born; however, she and Vince were blessed with three living children-Ernie, born Jan. 17, 1937; Barbara, born Nov. 18, 1942; Gary, born Nov. 8, 1952.

Vincent and Anna Payne 50th Wedding Anniversary February 1985. From left to right, Gary, Ernie, Vince, Anna Sue and Barbara Ann.

Through many sacrifices, all their children were able to receive a 12 year Catholic education with Barbara and Gary obtaining further degrees from Brescia College and Ernie owning and operating a successful garage business. All three of their children have found stable careers, and all live nearby in Daviess County. Vince and Ann have seven grandchildren and seven great-grandchildren.

Vince and Ann have always helped in their parish by working regularly at the annual picnics and supporting the church faithfully.

PAYNE, WM. HENRY, was born Jan. 11, 1987, Roseville, KY, died May 20, 1957. Mother, Mary Ollie Mattingly, died June 28, 1993, Balltown, KY, died Nov. 26, 1981. Father baptized by Fr. Henry, St. Thomas Church near Roseville, KY. Mother baptized at Old St. Mary's near McQuady, KY, pastor unknown. Parents education included third to fifth elementary grades. They farmed all their lives in Hancock (Fr. before marriage) and in Breckinridge Counties. They lived about five miles east of McQuady.

Member of St. Mary of the Woods, McQuady, KY. Past member of Father-Modern Woodmen of America, Holy Name Society, Mother-Altar Society and Christian Mothers Society.

"Pup Creek" John Payne, Daviess County, is the origin of family in Diocese of St. Lawrence in Daviess County. His grandfather was a farmer.

Descendents to present. Fr. (Chas. L. Payne), Henry Lawrence Payne (Fr.). Mother - parents were Francis Marion Mattingly and Jennie Ruppert. Her grandparents were Benedict Mattingly and Sara Eliz. Monarch and John Phillip Ruppert and Annie Bowers.

My father's (Wm. H. Payne) mother was Josephine Midkiff, daughter of Wm. Curtis Midkiff and "Matilda" Garth.

St. Mary of the Woods was the newer St. Mary and was located at McQuady, as it was a little settlement, while "old" St. Mary was out in the deep woods. Fr. John F. Knue, a huge, handsome six foot six inch man was the founder and pastor. He was beloved by both Catholics and Protestants and broke down the prejudices against Catholics. He is buried at St. Mary Cemetery in McQuady. His heart never left his parish there.

PEAK, SISTER JEAN MADELINE, came to the Diocese of Owensboro Sept. 8, 1933, when she entered the Novitiate of the Ursuline Sisters at Mount St. Joseph, Maple Mount, KY.

Sister was born and reared in Holy Cross, KY, Marion County. She was the only child of John and Nettie Medley Peak. When she was 2 months old her father died leaving her and her mother to make their home with maternal grandparents, Albert and Ada Jane Medley.

When she was 9 she became the step-daughter of Thomas Blanford. After a few years there were in the Blanford family my child, your child and our children. What a happy and devoted family!

Sister Jean Madeline Peak

Her elementary education was in the public schools of Marion County, taught by the Sisters of Loretto and lay teachers.

Some years were spent in a one-room school with Anna Mary McKenna and Irene Osborne as teachers. She attended high school at Mount St. Joseph and received college degrees at Brescia College and Eastern Kentucky University.

Sister received the Ursuline habit March 18, 1934, made her profession of final vows March 19, 1939, celebrated her Silver Jubilee at St. Benedict, Wax, Kentucky, 1959 and her Golden Anniversary at St. Bartholomew, Louisville, 1984.

During her years of teaching she served in the Archdioces of Louisville, Missouri and Owensboro Diocese, 25 years as principal. She enjoys recalling the years when she taught four grades, served as principal and local superior of the convent. Nothing was thought of teaching 62, 64 or 70 pupils in one classroom.

In June 1985, after 18 years at St. Bartholomew School, 15 as its principal, Sister's retirement ended 48 years in the schools. In July of that year she went to St. Joseph Parish, Leitchfield, KY, where she began her new ministry of serving shut-ins, visiting the rest homes and hospitals.

During her first five years in St. Joseph Parish, Sister worked with one of her former grade school students, Rev. Jerry Calhoun. She continues as pastoral minister at St. Joseph under the leadership of Rev. Gregory Trawick, pastor.

PEERMAN, ANGELA BLAIR, was born in 1953 in Daviess County, KY to Mr. and Mrs. J.P. Blair. She attended St. Augustine Grade School for four years, St. Peter Grade School for the next four years and graduated from Mount St. Joseph Academy High School in 1972. Upon graduation, Angela moved to Evansville, IN to attend ITT College.

Mr. and Mrs. Dennis Peerman Family

Angela married Dennis Wayne Peerman in 1974 at her home parish, St. Augustine, Reed, KY with Fr. Carl Asplund officiating. Dennis graduated from Reitz High School in Evansville. They have two sons, Scott and David; one daughter, Miranda. The family returned to St. Augustine in 1980, where Angela is now active in the Altar Society, CCD, Youth Group and is a Eucharistic Minister. The children are active youth group members. Scott and David are altar boys and Miranda is a lector and cantor. All are active in helping with the church picnic.

Dennis worked at Adkins Molded Rubber in Evansville for 15 years. Angela has worked at Kentucky Distillery in Stanley, KY for eight years. The boys attended Apollo High School and Miranda attends North Junior High School in Henderson, KY.

PEKAREK FAMILY, ED AND ELINOR, entered the Diocese of Western Kentucky at a time memorable to members of St. Paul Church. In 1971 the church and rectory properties in downtown Princeton were sold to the General Services Administration to make possible expansion of the adjoining post office. The weekend of the last Mass celebrated in that church building in January 1972 coincided with the Pekarek's move to Princeton.

Ed and Elinor Pekarek

Ed and Elinor have their roots in Cleveland, OH. They both are graduates of Case-Western Reserve University. They met in 1939 while Elinor was a sophomore at Flora Stone Mather College and Ed was a metallurgical engineer beginning his 32 year career with TRW Inc. They were married on Jan. 17, 1942 in St. Clement Church in Lakewood, a western suburb of Cleveland. They have four children, two boys and two girls and four grandchildren. Their younger daughter, Beth, now a psychiatrist practicing in North Carolina, is the only one of their children to grow up in Kentucky. The Pekarek's have concluded that their decisions to move to Western Kentucky in 1972 and retire here in 1982 were the most important and favorable ones in their married life of more than 50 years. Their move from Ohio came about when Ed changed jobs and accepted a position with Federal Mogul Corp., now Special Metals Corp., to work in a newly built vacuum melting facility.

The Pekareks continue to be active in St. Paul Church. They both organized the campaign to raise funds for a new church and are members of the St. Vincent DePaul Society. Ed has been president for 12 years. Elinor taught CCD and was director of religious education for five years when St. Paul Parish School operated with all lay teachers.

PERRY, MICHAEL WILLIAM SR. AND CONNIE WISEMAN, Michael William Perry Sr. was born Aug. 30, 1949 the second son of Joseph Henry Perry Sr. and Evelyn Sullivan Perry in Potsdam, NY. Early years of life was spent in Parish, NY, and after high school graduation from Altman-Parish-Williamstown High School, he attended Manilus Military Academy, a preparatory school, prior to Murray State University. Michael received a B.S. in 1973 from Murray State and taught chemistry and biology at Nelson County Sr. High School in Bardstown, KY. Then he received his doctor of dental medicine from the University of Louisville School of Dentistry in 1980. He moved to Paducah to practice dentistry and has been a member of St. Thomas More since moving to Paducah.

Connie Wiseman Perry, born Aug. 14, 1948, is the third of four children and only daughter of Tillen Wayne Wiseman Jr. and Emma Louise Gravely Wiseman. Connie's early life was spent in St. Louis, MO where she graduated from Mehlville High School, Class of 1966. She received her B.S. at Murray State University in 1971 in English and business. Connie received her master's in guidance and counseling from Murray State University in 1975 prior to teaching at My Old Kentucky Home Jr. High School in Bardstown, KY. She taught at Spencerian Business College in Louisville from 1976-1980.

Michael and Connie have been blessed with five children: Corrine Monique 1978-1984, Michael William Jr., Tillen Joseph, Seth Gregory and Adam Quenten. All four sons attend St. Mary Elementary School.

PHILLIPS, GILBERT A. AND SHIRLEY HUNDLEY, were born in Allen County, KY. Raised in Simpson County, KY. Living in Daviess County. They are members of St. Elizabeth Parish in Curdsville. Parents are Herschel and Mae Phillips, Allen County, KY.

Gilbert is plant and personnel director, Mount St. Joseph and Shirley is medications tech. at Mount St. Joseph. He is state director of Ancient Order of Hibernians.

PIERCE, ROGER AND MARY PIERCE, were married Oct. 30, 1971, at St. Joseph Church by Father Robert Wilson, who has passed away.

Roger is originally from Leitchfield, and is the second oldest of eight children, born to Leonard and Wanda Pierce.

Mary is from Breckinridge County, belonging formerly to St. Anthony Church, Axtel. Her parents are Marvin (deceased) and Maxine Hinton, and she is the oldest of three daughters.

They met at Paper Novelty Manufacturing Company, 1968 where they both operated machines that produce Christmas decorations.

In 1972 after Paper Novelty closed their company, Roger was employed by Houchens Market in Leitchfield, and Mary began working at Huron Copysette, until their first child, Angie, was born in September of 1977. Two other sons named Keith and Kevin were born Nov. 11, 1979 and June 6, 1984.

Roger remained at Houchens until Dec. 22, 1985, when he was injured at work. A case of drink bottles fell on his right ankle, cracking the ankle bone. The bone healed, but as a result of this injury, he has reflex sympathetic dystrophy. The nerves in the right heel of his foot are extremely sensitive to the slightest touch. He now walks with crutches.

The Roger Pierce Family - Roger, Mary, Angie, Keith and Kevin.

After 26 sympathetic blocks to his spine and four surgeries, nothing has taken away this severe pain. The doctors don't know anything more to do to help him.

Through it all, when you ask Roger how he's doing, he'll always smile and say, "I'm doing okay."

Their family went through a period of discouragement, through all the surgeries, but with the help of their pastor, Rev. Greg Trawick, and by attending daily Mass, their faith has give them the strength to see Our Lord's hand pulling them closer together. They know that He will take care of them.

PIERCEALLS, came to Kentucky from Maryland in 1795. Patriarch of the family was Richard Pierceall, a Revolutionary War veteran and farmer, who was born at St. Mary's County, MD in 1744. Joining their fellow Maryland Catholics in the trek westward, the Piercealls settled in Washington County near the Rolling Fork River, where Richard and his wife (her name is unknown) raised nine children. The year of Richard's death isn't recorded,

Benedict Joseph Pierceall and family, Fancy Farm, Kentucky 1890. Back row l to r: Martin Andrew Pierceall (face partly missing from tear in photo), infant Sarah Bernardine Pierceall (held by mother Rena Toon Pierceall), William Clement Pierceall (holding daughter) Elizabeth Catherine), Benedict Joseph Pierceall Jr., John J. Pierceall, Bell Cissell Pierceall, Allen Gregory Curtsinger, Isabelle Pierceall Curtsinger (holding daughter Teresa Laurentia), Marietta Ellen Pierceall (holding accordion), Enos Curtsinger (standing behind wedding portrait of Benedict Joseph Jr. and Amelia Willett's 1870's wedding), Elizabeth Almina Willett (face partly cropped). Front row, l to r: Mary Geraldine Pierceall, Anna Leona Pierceall, Johanna Elizabeth Curtsinger, Susan Robinson Pierceall (holding infant son, Joseph Ernest Pierceall, whose known birthdate of Nov. 29, 1889, dates the photo to early 1890), Benedict Joseph Pierceall (holding unidentified pictures with grandson William Roy Pierceall leaning on his shoulder), Mary Elizabeth Austin Pierceall (with granddaughter Mary Agnes Curtsinger at her knee), Clara Alberta (Bertie) (Curtsinger, May Mary Pierceall, Lucy Augustine Pierceall, Clapp and Wilson.

though he is counted in the 1840 Census, age 96. He was buried at Calvary Cemetery by Holy Name of Mary Church near Lebanon.

Richard's elder sons, Clement (1784-1863) and Joseph (1788-1850), moved to Missouri by way of Union County, KY, where nine of Joseph's children were baptized by Fr. Elisha J. Durbin. The families of their sisters, Mary Fowler and Susanna Buckman, were in residence there as well.

Richard's third son was John Benedict Pierceall (1798-1855), a blacksmith and farmer who first came to Graves County in 1835. Eight of his children were also baptized by Fr. Durbin, who also recorded the death of his sister Susanna Buckman in 1833, possibly during a cholera epidemic. Widowed by the death of first wife Matilda Wimsatt in 1830, John remarried to Teresa Mills and his 18 children by both wives sets a family record. John died on Wolf Island near Columbus.

John B.'s son, Benedict Joseph Pierceall (1823-1912), was a brickmason who remained in Graves County after his father moved on. He married Mary Elizabeth Austin at St. Jerome's in 1846 and worked a farm near Mayfield Creek. Today, the descendants of Benedict Joseph and Mary E. Austin Pierceall include the allied families of Burd, Carrico, Curtsinger, Hayden, Hobbs, Thomas, Thompson, Toon and Willett, many of whom live in the area still and are well represented in the local histories and church records of St. Jerome, St. Denis and St. Joseph parishes.

PIERCEFIELD, JOHN THOMAS (J.T.),

was born in Grant County, KY, Sept. 3, 1929 to Eva and Daniel Piercefield. His father was founder of Piercefield Panel Homes in Erlanger, KY where his mother Eva and two brothers, Harry and Roy live. On Feb. 10, 1949, John was baptized into the Catholic faith by the Reverend Father Paul Brinker in Saint James Church, Ludlow, KY. His wife, Mary Cecilia, was born and raised in Latonia, KY. Mary Cecilia was born on May 8, 1930 to Anna Mary (Robke) Reinecke and Herman C. Reinecke, she had three brothers: Herman, Edward and Robert Reinecke all of Latonia. She was baptized in Holy Cross Church, Latonia, KY and attended Holy Cross School there. Her maternal grandfather, John Robke helped organize in the building of Holy Cross Church back in the 1890s.

The Piercefields have four children, John Jr., Daniel, Mary Patricia and Jim. Also eight grandchildren. They moved to Western Kentucky almost 20 years ago. They attend Mass at St. Henry Church, Aurora, KY. John and Mary Cecilia think the area they live in is one of the most beautiful in Kentucky. Their granddaughter, Kirby Lawrence Lane, was the first baby to be baptized in St. Henry Church where Rev. Monsignor George Hancock is the pastor.

PIKE, SISTER MARY GERTRUDE,

was born in Waverly, KY. She was baptized Frances Rosalia March 25, 1895 by Father William Hogarty, St. Vincent, KY. Entered the Ursuline Convent Aug. 5, 1910. Took final vows, Aug. 9, 1919. Her parents were Samuel and Lucina Ann Maher Pike. Her brothers and sisters are: Annie, William Paul, Ella, Joseph Valentine, Jesse Oswald, Ignatius, Denis, Elizabeth.

Served in following missions: In Kentucky: Raywick, Hardinsburg, Curdsville, Sorgho, Brown's Valley, Holy Cross, St. Raphael, Knottsville, Owensboro, New Haven, Lebanon; St. James, St. Ignatius, Mother of Good Counsel, in Louisville; in Nebraska: Wynot, Snyder, Nebraska City, Bow Valley, Plattsmouth, Paul, St. Benedict; in New Mexico; Blanco, Waterflow; in Missouri: Glennonville.

Frances Rosalia's mother died when she was 2 years old. She went to live with Uncle Joe and Aunt Mary (Hite) Pike near Uniontown, KY, until her father remarried, at which time she returned home to live with her brothers and sisters.

She had her first years of formal education in the public school in the Uniontown area called Hite School with George Pike as her teacher. Later she attended public schools in Waverly, KY. When she was 16 her father died, and at this time she and her sister Ella went to Mount St. Joseph to school. Here she was taught by Sister Amadeus and Sister Aquina.

On Aug. 5, 1910, Frances entered the community and received the name Sister Mary Gertrude. On Tuesday, November 13, 1990 she died. Funeral Mass was concelebrated by Father Pike Powell, a relative of Sister's; Father James Hite, also a relative, and Father Bernard Powers.

John and Mary Cecilia Piercefield

PIKE, THE PIKE SISTERS,

These five sisters known as "The Pike Sisters" are the daughters of the late Ignatius Hite Pike and Elizabeth Fenwick Pike.

They grew up on "Maple Ridge Farm" located three miles east of Uniontown, KY.

They attended St. Agnes School in Uniontown and became elementary education teachers after receiving their degrees from Brescia College and Spalding College.

Bottom row - left to right: Lucy Pike Willett, Elizabeth Pike; Top row - left to right Nancy Pike French, Patrice Pike and Marietta Blake Heep.

All of these teachers have taken an active part in all religious and civic activities including the teaching of CCD, Bible School, members of the church choir, the Altar Society, the Lioness Club, P.T.A., K.E.A., N.E.A. and are Kentucky Colonels.

As elementary school teachers they contributed a total of 151 years to the education of youth in Western Kentucky.

They attribute their many successes to their religious home training by their parents and to the Catholic education received from the Sisters of Charity of Nazareth and the Ursuline Sisters of Mount St. Joseph, Maple Mount.

PISKULA, LOUIS F.,

On Jan. 14, 1940, eight days after he was born Fr. Louis F. Piskula was welcomed into the family of God through the sacrament of baptism at Blessed Sacrament Church in Milwaukee, WI. He intensified his relationship with Jesus through First Holy Communion on May 29, 1949 and sealed his membership in the Church Oct. 19, 1954 by receiving the sacrament of confirmation at St. Joseph Church in Big Bend, WI. The youngest of four boys born to Ben Piskula and Sylvia Long (nee: Hirsch) he grew up in the rural community of Muskego, WI. Not having the benefit of Catholic schools he depended upon his family and the School Sisters of Notre Dame for his religious training.

Fr. Louis F. Piskula

He worked in a factory, ran a service station, was a night watchman, drove school and charter bus as well as semi trucks before entering college seminary at Mount St. Paul College in Waukesha. He finished his bachelor of arts degree at Domincan College in Racine, WI. It was at college that he met and studied with a number of our diocesan priests. At the invitation of Fr. Benjamin C. Powers (died 1978) he visited and joined the Owensboro Diocese in 1969. Receiving his master of divinity from St.

Meinrad School of Theology, he was ordained to the priesthood by the Most Rev. Henry J. Soenneker, D.D. May 10, 1975.

His assignments include assistant pastor at St. Stephen Cathedral until June 1977; then Blessed Mother in Owensboro until August 1982; appointed pastor at St. Leo and Newman Chaplain at Murray State University until 1985; pastor at St. John, outside of Paducah until June 1989 when he assumed duties as pastor of St. Mary of the Woods,Whitesville, Kentucky. During his priesthood he also served as director for handicap ministry, chaplain for: Serra, Knights of Columbus, Daughters of Isabella, secretary of St. Joseph Clerical Aid Society, member of Diocesan Pastoral Council and continuing education for priest committee.

PLUMMER, CHARLES AND DEBORAH,

joined Sacred Heart Parish in 1986, Russellville, KY. Formerly from Michigan City, IN resided there 12 years and attended Queen of all Saints Church.

Charles and Deborah were born and raised in central Pennsylvania, whose families were always quite active in their home parish. It was wonderful to grow up around relatives and closeness of friends, says Deborah.

Charles, Deborah, Melissa, Matthew and Nicholas Plummer.

Russellville is a wonderful little town to raise a family. We have been very much involved with our new parish. Our daughter Melissa is an organist for Sacred Heart Church. Melissa is 16 and active with school, community service and church. Our sons Matthew, 15 and Nicholas, 12 serve as alter boys and also active with school sports and their personal interests. Deborah is an Opportunities For Life volunteer for Logan County, treasurer for Catholic Womens Club and choir member for Sacred Heart. Charles is Eucharist Minister and member of Knights of Columbus at Sacred Heart.

At the time of our arrival to Russellville, Father Robert Drury was pastor, since then we have had the pleasure of visiting Father Drury while in Owensboro, attending Palm Sunday Mass at Precious Blood Church.

POAT-HAESELEY FAMILY,

church, census and taxation records verify the emigration to America from Germany of the early Poat families to the St. John community in the late 1830s. The Poat surname has many variations in spelling on these records, including Poath, Poarth, Poth, Pote, Poot and Poart. Even though they were German speaking people, it is not certain where in Germany (or possibly Alsas Loraine) these immigrants originated.

The Graves County tax list of 1841 lists Anthony Poat with 80 acres of farm land in the Boaz precinct at Mayfield Creek. The 1950 census of Graves County registered Anthony "Anton" Poat, age 27, born in Germany, as farming 300 acres and support five dependants: Madeline (Welker), his wife, age 43, born in Germany; Barbara, age 11; Madeline, age 4; John, age 2; and Margaret Conn, age 74, born in Germany and presumed to be the mother of his wife, Madeline. The three children are listed as being born in Kentucky and were baptized at St. John in 1838, 1845 and 1848.

The 1850 Graves County Census also lists Matthew Poat, age 23, born in Germany on Oct. 21, 1828, as farming 300 acres with his wife Christina (Englert), age 18, born in Germany on Nov. 30, 1832. They were married by Father McNicholas on Feb. 15, 1848. They had 10 children: Anthony, Martin, John, Edmond, Phillip, Cecilia, William Henry, Philomena, Mary Elizabeth and Aloysius.

Anthony, born April 10, 1850, married Barbara Elizabeth Schneider and they had two children, William E. and Mary Barbara. After Barbara Elizabeth died at age 20, Anthony married Mary Catherine Haeseley, born Jan. 19, 1847. She was the niece of Father Peter Haeseley, who performed the wedding between Anthony and Catherine in September 1874. She also had a brother Charles who became a priest and was pastor at St. Jerome, Fancy Farm at one time.

Peter Joseph Haeseley was born July 1, 1830 at Gipf near Frick, Switzerland. Having the baker's trade he came to America in May 1856. The following year he was employed as a baker at St. Thomas Seminary in Nelson County, where he expressed a desire to study for the priesthood and was accepted as a student at the seminary. He was transferred to the Provincial Seminary of Mount St. Mary, Cincinnati, in 1865, to complete his theology. He was ordained by Bishop J.L. Luers of Fort Wayne in the Cathedral of the Assumption, Louisville on Dec. 22, 1867.

Father Haeseley's first assignment was a pastor of St. John the Evangelist Parish in McCracken County, where he built a frame church to replace the log church built by Father Elisha Durbin. His next appointment was to St. Joseph Parish (a German Parish) in Owensboro in February 1878. In May of that year, the original church was struck by lightning and burned. Father Haeseley, with the support of the German community and donations from German people in Indiana and Illinois, a new brick church was constructed. This 86 by 43 foot church was completed in 1880. But before it was totally completed at a cost of approximately $10,000, it was blessed on March 7, 1880 by Father Haeseley and used for the worship services of the German immigrants. (Because the people had decided to build the church at Fourth and Clay Streets instead of Seventh and Frederica where Bishop McCloskey wanted, he did not come and officially dedicate the church until 1883.)

When Father Haeseley was first ordained and was appointed pastor of St. John the Evangelist, he didn't have a housekeeper. So he wrote to his sister, Mary Anne, and asked her to send her daughter, Catherine, to keep house for him. The request was granted but the parents decided to send along Catherine's little brother, age 12, to protect her. Catherine was 21 at the time.

Six years later Mary Catherine became the wife of Anthony Poat and her little brother, Charles, was ordained a priest on September 1, 1878 by Bishop McCloskey at Nazareth. For a while he was pastor of St. John's and then pastor at St. Jerome, Fancy Farm. There he built the church and school.

The young Father Haesley's uncle, Peter Haesley performed the marriage of Anthony and Mary Catherine (Haeseley) Poat, and he himself performed the marriage ceremony of Ida Philomena Poat who was married to Phillip Clark Willett, my parents and grandparents respectively. The Fathers Haeseley were great-great uncle and great uncle respectively to me and my brothers and sisters.

Anthony and Catherine had eight children: Mary Ann (Mrs. George Krimple), Rosa (Mrs. Henry Younker), Cecilia, who died at age 18, John (Mae Grief), Ida Philomena (Mrs. Phillip Clark Willett - see "Willett Family" below), Mary (Mrs. Charles Schmitt) and Dorothea Catherine "Dora" (Mrs. Riley Durbin).

Carl Matthew married Rosie Younker on Jan. 11, 1905. They operated a farm within sight of St. John Church. They had five children: Mary Lenora (Mrs. Melvin Cissell), Joseph Oscar (Frances Paulette Reason), Mary Kathleen (Mrs. Raymond Wurth, whose grandson is studying for the priesthood); John Melvin (Elsie Marie Gibson) and Anthony Leroy (Marie Juanita Moore).

John married Mae Grief on February 5, 1907. They had five children who survived to adulthood: Mary Pauline (Mrs. Leonard Wurth), Clifford, Aubrey, Sylvester and Marguerite.

Details about the girls of the family are given with their husband's family history. Most of this history is taken from the Poat family as recorded in the *Sesquicentennial History Book of St. John Community*.

POGUE, WILLIAM THURMAN,

was born in Daviess County on September 15, 1942. William farmed for most of his younger years then went to the restaurant business. Now he presently works for Clarks Detective Agency and is owner at Pogue's Bar-B-Que.

His parents, Ellis Glen Pogue and Ednell Lowell Moore, were both from Muhlenberg County Church. Ellis was born January 10, 1920 and Ednell was born June 15, 1921. Patricia Zielinski (Pogue) was born in Chicago, IL on Jan. 31, 1946 and worked for W.R. Grace Inc.

Her parents Stanley Zielinski and Loretta Komola (Zielinski) are both members of the Holy Trinity Church. William and Patricia were married on August 27, 1963 and then moved from Illinois to Kentucky.

William T. Jr. was born on Feb. 15, 1979 and presently attends Owensboro Catholic Middle School and a member of the Blessed Mother Parish. April Lynn was born April 10, 1984 and presently attends St. Angela Merici and also attends Blessed Mother Parish.

William also spent three years in the Army. On Jan. 13, 1989 Patricia Pogue passed away.

POLASHOCK, MICHAEL STEPHEN AND BETTY LOUISE (MCGOWAN),

Michael came to Paducah, KY from Linden, New Jersey in 1959. He worked as a chemical engineer supervisor at a chemical plant in Calvert City. Michael had also served in the U.S. Army serving as an officer in the Chemical Corps. Shortly after arriving in Paducah, he met Betty McGowan who is a Kentucky native from her mother's side since the early 1800s. Her father was from Jackson, TN and came to Paducah in the 1920s. He was employed by Illinois Central Railroad. Her parents are Anthony Bernard (A.B.) and Louise (Glidwell) McGowan. Betty was a school teacher when she met Michael, and continued teaching for a while after they married in July 1960. They married at St. Francis De Sales Church where Betty and her parents and brothers and had been life long members. Both of Betty's brothers, Bernard and James, graduated from Notre Dame University and later became doctors. All attended St. Mary Academy receiving their education from the Sisters of Charity of Nazareth. Betty graduated from Spalding University in Louisville and did graduate work at Murray State University.

After marriage, Michael and Betty moved into the St. Thomas More Parish. Michael's parents were from New Jersey and his grandparents from Pennsylvania. When he settled in Kentucky, he liked it so much that he never wanted to leave. His education was by the Dominican sisters and Benedictine priests and brothers, Newark College of Engineering and a master's in business from Murray State University. He now works for the University of Kentucky through the Paducah Community College as business and industry liaison.

Michael and Betty have been actively involved in all phases of parish and school activities in the course of their marriage and rearing their three children and continued their participation after the children left. All attended the St. Thomas More and St. Mary School System for 12 years each. All children are living in Nashville, TN now. Margaret is married to Jeffrey Flowers and Gregory is married to Lois Fawns Polashock.

Marian graduated from Western and is assistant manager at a Kroger store. Margaret graduated from Middle Tennessee State University and is a properly manager with Trammell Crowe, Gregory graduated from the University of Kentucky and manages several restaurants.

RENEW has been the most inspirational event since Vatican II for both. "It opened us up and our lives changed and we feel the St. Thomas More Parish changed too. Cursillio has also made a difference for the better. We are also blessed with wonderful priests in Paducah.

POOSER-HAGMAN FAMILY,

Krisandra Leigh Pooser was born on May 27, 1978 at Perry County Memorial Hospital in Indiana, to Dorothy Mae Hagman and Frank Simmons Pooser. Dorothy M. Hagman was born on July 17, 1940 in her parents home, in Hawesville, KY, there, she grew up on a farm, attended Immaculate Conception School in Hawesville, graduated, then moved to Florida, from which there, she met her husband Frank S. Pooser, then married while Frank was still in the Air Force on February 17. Dorothy M. Hagman is the daughter of Harold Victor Hagman (born Oct. 17, 1898, died October 1987) of Hawesville, KY and Dorothy Rose Johnson of the St. Lawrence area.

Frank S. Pooser is the son of Bertha Ruth Christensen (born Oct. 24, 1915) and Frank Giles Pooser both from Charleston, SC.

Krisandra Pooser will be graduating from Immaculate Conception School in Hawesville, KY, and will be attending Hancock County High School.

POPE, KENTON JOSEPH,

was born in Lakewood (Long Beach), CA and was later baptized at a Baptist Church at the age of 14. He was confirmed and made his first Holy Communion on Easter of 1989 at St. Francis De Sales Church in Paducah.

His father is Joseph Pope Jr. of Festus, MO, his mother, Mildred Roddy of Barlow, KY. He also has a stepfather, Jack Roddy, of Barlow and a stepmother, Donna Pope of Festus, MO.

Kenton Joseph Pope and Kaela Judith Sherise Pope

His maternal grandfather was Josh Kenton Lovelace of Barlow. He owned the M and H Grocery until he retired. His maternal grandmother was Lucille Lovelace Evens of Barlow. She was a registered nurse.

His paternal grandparents, Joseph and Imogene Pope, lived in Festus, MO, where his grandmother still lives. His grandfather worked at Pittsburg Plate Glass Company.

He has one daughter, Kaela Judith Sherise Pope, who was born in Paducah, KY on Oct. 9, 1990. Kaela and Kenton are parishioners at St. Francis De Sales in Paducah and he attends Mass often at St. Mary Church in La Center.

POPE, LORIE KAY HAMILTON,

was born in Paducah, KY and was baptized in Kevil Methodist Church as a baby. Her father, Joseph Lee Hamilton and her mother, Sharon Kay Griffin Hamilton, are both mail carriers at the Kevil Post Office.

She converted into the church at Easter in 1989 and is a member of St. Francis De Sales Parish in Paducah, KY.

Lorie has two daughters, Kaela Judith Sherise Pope, born Oct. 9, 1990 and Karie Adriene Lee Pope, born Nov. 18, 1992 died June 19, 1993.

Ever since she first started going to St. Francis De Sales Parish, she has always felt at home. This Parish has been a great support and inspiration to her, especially with the past year of her life. She and her husband separated shortly after she became pregnant with their second child. When Karie was born she had a very serious heart defect and had to have open-heart surgery immediately. She stayed in the hospital three weeks and was able to come home. Unfortunately, she started having more complications being hospitalized again and having four more open-heart surgeries, being placed on a heart-lung bypass machine (ECMO) twice for five days each time and having more than 20 operations total. She spent six of her seven months on this earth in an intensive care unit 230 miles away from home. Without the grace of God and everyone praying for her, she would not have made it as long as she did. Having to go through all of this has really strengthened Lorie's relationship and faith in God. She now has an angel up in heaven.

Kaela and Karie Pope January 1993

Lorie and Kaela Pope

POTTS, JAMES FLOOD AND MARY LILLIAN (BROWN),

joined St. Romuald Parish, Hardinsburg as a family after their marriage on Nov. 20, 1934. James's parents, John Harvey and Agnes Bridget (Flood) Potts, and Mary Lillian's parents, Oscar Alysious and Eva Elizabeth (Mattingly) Brown, were all members of St. Romuald Parish. James and Mary Lillian had seven children; two sons are buried at St. Romuald and another in Louisville, four living children survive. Doris Jean (Potts) Critchelow and Mary Agnes (Potts) Brown are members of St. Anthony Parish, Axtel and James Leo Potts and Sue Ann (Potts) Hollie Hale are members of St. Romuald Parish.

James F. and Mary Lillian Potts

James farmed in the New Bethel community until the onset of heart trouble when the family moved to Hardinsburg in 1962. James was always active as a parish member. James joined the Holy Name Society, was an usher, cleaned church grounds and cemetery and helped with yearly picnic. James died Sept. 3, 1973 and is buried at St. Romuald Cemetery. Mary Lillian sang in the choir, always been a member of the Altar Society and helps with yearly picnic. Mary Lillian is well known for her spotless house and preparing delicious meals for her family, friends and parish priest.

POTTS, JOHN HARVEY AND AGNES BRIDGET (FLOOD),

were married Nov. 20, 1907, at St. Romuald. Harvey's parents were Joseph Smith Potts and Sarah Elizabeth (Wheatley). Agnes' parents were James Joseph and Elizabeth (Carroll) Flood. Harvey and Agnes had four children, William Francis, James Flood, Elizabeth Carroll (now Weatherholt), Mary Alice (now Jarboe).

Harvey was an active member of the parish, as well as a friend to the pastor. Fr. Martin Rosengarten was bird hunting with Harvey, when he ran from the back field of the Hinton farm to get medical help when Harvey had his first heart spell. Harvey died June 28, 1949 at age 63.

John Harvey Potts and Agnes Bridget (Flood) Potts

Agnes, a widow, lived in her two story white house in Hardinsburg for 38 years until her death in December 1987 at age 98 a half. Agnes would sit on her front porch in her swing and greet each passerby. Agnes remembered going out in the middle of the night to help deliver a baby, nursing a sick child or helping pray with the dying. She also remembered her own mother dying young, then her father being killed in a dynamite explosion leaving younger orphan siblings. Agnes was example for all times - a dedicated wife and mother, taking on the challenges of everyday life. She took on the responsibilities of making a living, took pride in her voting privilege and cherished her Irish Catholic roots. Agnes prayed her rosary often, and walked to church daily until her health began to fail at age 94. Agnes' dying words to her maker were "O'God, take me home, take me home."

POWELL, CLARENCE IGNATIUS AND MARY VIRGINIA WOLFE,

married on Feb. 26, 1946. Clarence, the son of Edward Fenwick and Martha Elizabeth Pike Powell, was born June 16, 1914, the middle son of five, he had three sisters, two of whom are still living. All the boys are still living.

Mary Virginia was the oldest of 12 children, born Oct. 6, 1918, to Willie and Florence Willett Wolfe.

Mr. and Mrs. Clarence I. Powell

Like so many during those years, money was scarce and job opportunities were few. Clarence saved enough money to buy himself a mare which bore one horse colt and four mules. Along with a little he was saved while in the Army for four years, this was his "start" after the war.

Having lost two or three children at birth, they have six living children: Elizabeth Ann, Irene, Viola, Clarence Jr., Elsie and Cecilia. There are 15 grandchildren.

Clarence and Virginia farmed for a number of years and for about 10 years before Clarence retired, they bought a home in Waverly and he worked for the state. Virginia was always a full-time homemaker. Her collection of dolls and other "treasures" makes Clarence pray that he will go to heaven first, so he won't have to dispose of it all! Virginia is still looking for garage sales to find more dolls. Clarence spends his time piddling in his garage, working in his garden and chatting with the neighbors.

Until moving to town they were members of Sacred Heart Parish, but are now in St. Peter Parish, Waverly. Although they suffer from the usual ailments, God has blessed them with reasonably good health and both seem to enjoy their retirement and the time they can give to their children and grandchildren.

POWELL, EDWARD FENWICK AND MARTHA ELIZABETH PIKE,

On Feb. 6, 1906, were joined in marriage at St. Agnes Church, Uniontown, KY. Of that union nine children were born. Mary married Henry T. Mann on March 27, 1937. Joe died at about the age of 6. Leo, whose first wife Beatrice O'Donnell died in childbirth, has been married to Mary Manning since Feb. 14, 1953. Christina, who never married, died June 3, 1988 at 75. Clarence's wife is the former Virginia Wolfe whom he married on Feb. 26, 1946. George and Alice wed on the same day—Feb. 6, 1939 to Catherine Mann and Carl Richard Utley. Richard Leonard married Linnie V. Davis on Dec. 30, 1950. Paul Pike was ordained to the priesthood on April 5, 1948. Five still live in Henderson and Union County. Leo moved to St. Petersburg, FL after retiring. Fr. Powell is pastor of St. Peter, Stanley. Alice's and Mary's husbands died in 1961 and 1971.

E.F. and Martha Powell Family

After spending a couple of years in Henderson County, Mr. and Mrs. Powell lived the rest of their lives on a 61-acre farm three miles north of Uniontown. Mr. Powell died on March 27, 1948, having been received into the Catholic Church on his deathbed. Mrs. Powell died on Feb. 22, 1988. Two or three grandchildren died in infancy; three of George's died in a drowning accident in 1961; the remaining 42 grandchildren live within a few miles of their birthplace.

In the 42 years together, the Powells did not accumulate much of this world's goods. Six of the children graduated from St. Agnes High School. While they were afflicted by the health problems experienced by any large family, the Lord blessed all with the ability to work and earn an honest living for their families. The Catholic Faith has remained strong among all of Ed and Martha's sons and daughters: divorce was never considered by any of them; their average age at this time of the seven living, is 76 years. God has been good to the Powell family!

POWELL, GEORGE LOUIS AND MARY CATHERINE MANN,

were married on Feb. 6, 1939. It was a double wedding, with his sister Alice and Carl R. Utley. It was also the 33rd anniversary of George's parents' wedding.

Catherine's parents were George Allen and Lucy Davis Mann. George worked on the farm before and after marriage and later in a plastic factory in Henderson.

Tragedy struck their growing family on Palm Sunday, 1960 when three of their children, Betty K., Charlie Bill and Kenneth, were drowned when the car they were riding in went into a creek near Henderson. Two of their cousins were also drowned. Faith and neighbors carried them through this event and God blessed them with four more children, making 12 presently living: Norman, David, Carolyn, Linda, Ronald, Paul, Mike, Robert, Glenn, Jane, Philip and Bonnie.

George Louis and Mary Catherine Mann Powell

Needless to say, Catherine never worked outside the home, but worked hard to make life comfortable for all on the modest income that was theirs. George was forced to retire at age 59 because of emphysema.

For a number of years they have lived in Henderson and have been members of Holy Name Parish since 1952. The pastor and Eucharistic ministers faithfully bring them Communion on Sundays and first Fridays. George missed being a leap year baby by one day, being born on Feb. 28, 1916. Catherine was born on March 20, 1918.

POWELL, LEO FRANKLIN AND MARY MANNING,

have been married since 1953 on St. Valentine's Feast Day. Leo, the son of Edward Fenwick and Martha Elizabeth Pike Powell, was born Feb. 4, 1911. He prides himself on being two days older than Ronald Reagan!

After graduating from St. Agnes High School in 1930, he had various jobs during those Depression years. He was acquainted with the WPA shovel! In 1940 he enlisted in the February 1942, since World War II had begun.

Somewhere along the way he had taken a course in diesel engineering and in 1947 went to Chicago to make his "fortune."

Leo F. Powell and B_____ O'Donnel Powell

Because of his stature, he was known as "Shorty," but was quite a mean catcher on the local rural ball team appropriately known as the "Agricolas."

In Chicago he took a liking to the Irish and married Beatrice O'Donnel whose parents were from Ireland. Unfortunately, a year later she died in childbirth along with their newborn son.

In 1953 Leo married Mary Manning who was direct from the "Old Sod," from County Galway. Leo worked for the City Transit Authority for 25 years as a repairman. Mary had a civil service job and worked as a food specialist in one of the hospitals of Chicago. They both retired in 1972. While they had no children of their own, they played a big part in rearing Mary's sister's four children. Mary's sister was killed in a St. Patrick's Day dance when the dance floor collapsed. The accident made international news.

Leo F. Powell and Mary Manning Powell

After retirement both Mary and Leo were active in the Legion of Mary in Holy Family Parish in St. Petersburg, FL. While he temporarily lived there, Leo especially felt St. Agnes, Uniontown, was still his home. Leo F. Powell died on Nov. 24, 1992, and was buried the day after Thanksgiving.

POWELL, MILDRED CHRISTINA,

daughter of Edward Fenwick and Martha Elizabeth Pike Powell, was a life-long member of St. Agnes Parish, Uniontown, KY. The fourth child and second of two girls, she never married.

When World War II came along, with three of her brothers in the service, Christina found herself helping run the farm with her Daddy, who was in failing health. These were not easy years for "Cricket," as she was called, but Divine Providence has a hand in everything. Her father needed much attention in his waning years and she was there to provide it. After his death in 1948, Christina lived on with her mother on the farm. Despite the chores, they found time to attend daily Mass quite regularly.

Mildred Christina Powell

Even after the death of her mother in 1968, Christina continued on the farm, tending a few calves and pigs. In 1976 she sold the farm and moved to Fifth Street in Uniontown. When her brothers were helping her find a home, one of them remarked: "Don't take the first thing you see; this might be your last move." She responded: "This will be my first move!" Sixty-four years in the same home! For a number of years after moving to town, she helped out in the Catholic School cafeteria.

Since she had 45 nieces and nephews, she lacked no experience in dealing with children. When a new one came along, you know who took care of its siblings until the mother was able. As long as she lived, they remembered what "Aunt Tee" did for them.

About four years before she died, Christina was afflicated with Alzheimer's disease and was in a nursing home for two and a half years. On June 3, 1988 God called her home. Her simple tombstone in St. Agnes Cemetery which read: "Born 12/12/32; died 6/3/88" does not tell the whole story.

Although she has been dead these four years, she was so much a part of the life of St. Agnes Parish that this writer believes she deserves a place in this diocesan history book.

POWELL, THE REV. PAUL PIKE, first saw the light of day in a small frame house near Uniontown, KY on Feb. 1, 1923. The last of eight living children, he was born to Edward Fenwick Powell and Martha Elizabeth Pike.

For 12 years he attended St. Agnes School. In those Depression years food was simple but plentiful; the same could not be said for clothes or money to buy books, tablets and pencils. His father hauled coal from the local mines with wagon and team for four or five weeks each year to fill the five parish buildings with fuel. This helped pay tuition.

September 1941 found Pike packing his few belongings to enroll in St. Mary College in Marion County. Pike received his AB degree on his birthday in 1945. A few days later he was at St. Meinrad, IN for his theological training.

Rev. Paul Pike Powell

His father's faithfulness in helping Mrs. Powell raise all the children properly in the Catholic faith reaped its reward: Mr. Powell was baptized on Holy Thursday and died on Easter Sunday, just eight days before Father Powell's ordination on April 5, 1948. Sadness and joy met in a special way that week!

A brother, Joseph, died long before Pike was born. The other siblings, Mary, Leo, Clarence, George, Alice and Leonard are married and still living. Christina, who never married, died in 1988 at the age of 75.

Father Powell served as assistant at St. Stephen Cathedral and St. Jerome, Fancy Farm. While at the cathedral he was in charge of Blessed Sacrament Chapel for four years. He has been pastor at St. Paul in Grayson County; Sacred Heart, Russellville; St. Pius X, Owensboro; St. Francis De Sales, Paducah. He has been at St. Peter of Alcantara, Stanley since Dec. 6, 1982. He was also pastor of St. Augustine, Reed, from June 1987 to June 1992.

Maybe his ministry is reflected in this little story. When he first went to one of his parishes, the editor of the grade school paper came over to interview Father Powell. Not sure the young editor would know the difference between a pastor and an assistant, Father Powell said: "I have helped out in three parishes and have run two others." When the paper published the article, it read: "Father Powell has helped out in three parishes and has ruined two others." Father Powell leaves it to the parishioners and history to determine whether that was a typographical error or accurate reporting on the part of the young editor!

POWELL, RICHARD LEONARD, was born on Sept. 7, 1920 and graduated from St. Agnes High School on June 1, 1941. Immediately he joined the CCC and volunteered to go "anywhere in the USA." He ended up in Henderson and later in Paducah. Out of the CCC by December because of the war, he was in uniform by the fall of 1942. After seeing combat in France and Germany and being involved in the Battle of the Bulge, he came home with only two injuries. He got a broken tooth in a little pugilistic encounter with a fellow-American and hurt his shoulder doing stunts on a motorcycle "captured" from the Germans. He is still waiting for his Purple Heart!

After the war Leonard farmed for a while, met and married Linnie who had migrated from Eastern Kentucky. In October of 1951 their home burned. It was off to Louisville to make his fortune with the railroad. In short order he lost an eye, then his job and they were back in Union County. They bought a home and small acreage near Robinsonville, where they have lived ever since. For some 28 years he worked for Southern Stages in Morganfield, and was forced to retire in 1983 because of a heart attack.

Richard and Linnie Powell

One of the highlights of Leonard's life was when Linnie joined the church in 1954. The only thing bigger than the day were the mosquitos flying around little St. Francis Church in Henderson County during the baptism! Fr. Edelen had given Linnie instructions; Fr. Powell had the privilege of baptizing her; Same Pike and Christina Powell were the sponsors. (Later St. Francis Church was closed and they have become members of St. Agnes.

They have eight children: Dennis, Eddie Joe, Paul Jean, Mary Lou, Billy, Beverly, Carl and Mark. Linnie and Leonard seem to enjoy their retirement years. Linnie is quite a seamstress and Leonard looks after his pets: horses, goats, rabbits, dogs and cats. But he never gets so attached to his goats that they avoid ending up on the barbeque grill!

POWELL, WILLIAM A. (BILL) AND JOANNE I. (JOEY), married Dec. 26, 1959 at Our Lady Queen of Apostles Parish in Detroit, MI. Bill is the swimming coach at Western Kentucky University. He is the only swimming coach that Western has had: he started the program in 1969. Joey is the principal of St. Joseph School and also teaches in the Art Dept. at WKU.

They have resided in Bowling Green (Warren) since 1969. They are members of St. Joseph and Newman Center (WKU). They have past memberships at St. Joseph Parish in St. Joseph, MI.

Bill is the faculty advisor for the Newman Club and a lector. Joey is a Eucharistic Minister. She has taught in various Catechetical programs in years past, been a lector and served on the Parish Council.

The William and Joanne Powell Family—Back row: Dan, Bill, Mary Beth; Front row: Katie, Joey and Anne.

Involved in Warren County Tomorrow Commission, Landmark Association, Capital Arts Center Arts Alliance and Fountain Square Players.

Bill, Joey and their four children are members of Newman Center WKU. They joined in 1969 after moving from Michigan. They are both educators.

Mary Beth married Edo van der Zee May 26, 1990. They were married at St. Joseph Parish in Bowling Green. She is an attorney. He is a pilot. They live in Jacksonville, FL. Anne Powell is a computer systems analyst in Indianapolis, IN working on an MBA. Dan Powell owns and runs video stores in Bowling Green and surrounding towns. Katie married Barry Hannah Jr. Sept. 3, 1988. She is working on a doctorate in English at Southern Mississippi University. He is the lead guitarist in a band called Beanland. Through the years the Powell family spent many weekends on the road usually because of swim meets involving teams that Bill coached or that the children swam for. This gave them the opportunity of taking part in Mass in a great many different churches across the country. This provided a wonderful basis for the children, especially, to know the universality and unity that comes from being a part of the Catholic Church. It also taught the lesson that no matter what obstacles are in the way, we participate in Sunday Mass wherever our travels take us.

POWERS, REV. ALOYSIUS F., Past state K.C. chaplain, was born Jan. 4, 1921 in Daviess County, KY. He received his primary education in the local parish school of St. Elizabeth, Cursdville. He entered St. Meinard Seminary, St. Meinard, IN, to begin his training for the priesthood in 1935. He was ordained to the priesthood in April 5, 1948 for the diocese of Owensboro.

Rev. Aloysius F. Powers

Father Powers is one of 12 children; two of his four brothers are priests of the Owensboro Diocese. His father and three of his four brothers are third and fourth degree members of the Knights of Columbus.

Father Powers joined the Knights in the spring of 1969 at Sorgho Council No. 6101. He has been chaplain for Council 6101, Sorgho, 1055 at Paducah and 1004 at Morganfield. He served as state chaplain from 1978 to 1990. Presently he is chaplain of 1055 in Paducah and Faithful Friar of the Father Fallon Assembly in Paducah. He is now pastor of St. Pius Tenth Church, Calvert City, KY.

POWERS, MONSIGNOR BERNARD ALPHONSUS, is a priest in the diocese of Owensboro and has served in Western Kentucky since his ordination in 1952. His Catholic faith is the heritage of his maternal great-grandparents, John Michael McCarthy, born in Cork County, Ireland and Elizabeth Bowlds, born in St. Lawrence, KY, the first Catholic parish in Daviess County. His paternal great grandparents, Sylvester Powers and Mollie Johnson, were of the Catholic settlement in Nelson County, KY. His maternal grandparents were John Michael and Mary Aurora Byrne McCarthy; the paternal grandparents were Robert Abell and Susan Helen Clements Powers. He was born of Joseph Hubert and Teresa Margaret McCarthy Powers in Curdsville, seventh of 12 children: four brothers, Joseph, Father Aloysius, Robert, Father Richard and his seven sisters, Mary Agnes, Patricia Garvin, Elizabeth Lattus, Martha Taylor, Celine Kahalley, Teresa Hayden and Maddalena Leach.

As a young priest, Monsignor Powers was assigned to Owensboro Catholic High as teacher and dean of students. Here he served for 12 years and then was transferred to St. Joseph, Leitchfield as pastor and also as teacher as Grayson County Catholic High. The time in Grayson County was short and Monsignor was called to Mount St. Joseph as chaplain for the Ursuline Sisters and teacher in the academy at Mount St. Joseph where his mother had attended school in 1904. The presence at Mount St. Joseph gave the opportunity to become involved in retreat work. The nine years at the Mount was opportunity for spiritual growth as well as challenges in teaching. July of 1976 brought another call and this was to Immaculate Parish in Owensboro. The diversity of priestly ministry found joy in celebrations, called for compassion in the presence of sufferings, and challenged one in the presence of a growing faith community.

Monsignor Powers serves as pastor of St. Alphonsus and also as associate director of the Mount St. Joseph Center where he conducts days of prayer, retreats and programs of spiritual enrichment. He has an appreciation of the beauties of nature and a love for the Sacred Scriptures. A hobby is that of writing. Several of his reflections have been published in national magazines. He has found a real joy in the priesthood and through his ministry has touched and enriched the lives of many people.

POWERS, JAMIE MICHAELLE, born May 1, 1978 the fifth child born to Judith G. and William F. Powers Jr. William F is the son of Nellie D. Powers and the late William F. Powers Sr. Nellie Powers is the daughter of Joe and Effie Gray.

William F. Powers Sr. is the son of Albert and Francis Powers. William F. Powers Sr. was a solider in World War II. Judith G. Powers is the daughter of James H. and Helena G. Estes. James H. died Jan. 2, 1978 and Helena G. died May 20, 1989.

William F. Powers Jr. is currently working at Commonwealth Aluminum and has been working there for 26 years. Jamie Powers is currently attending Immaculate Conception in Hawesville. Jamie is in eighth grade, she is preparing to attend Hancock County High School.

PRICE, ROBERT P., born in Pittsburg, PA, raised in Rochester, NY and Weston, CT and has lived in Marion, KY, Crittenden County since 1992. He has three brothers, no sisters. Member of St. William Parish, Marion, KY.

Robert P. Price

Member of Knights of Columbus, church lector. Graduate of the University of Notre Dame and of the University of Southern California. Teaches high school CCD. Lector at church. Engaged to be married to Colleen F. Harris of Genoa, NE in July 1993. She will be an elementary school teacher after their marriage. They plan to make an engagement encounter in Owensboro in the spring. They will be married in the Catholic church in Kansas.

PRUNTY, MARSHALL EDWARD, was born in Heidelberg, Germany. He was adopted from a Catholic orphanage by James and Peggy Mullins Prunty. He came to the United States after his father completed his stint in the Army. Melinda Ann Gibbons was born in Ashland, KY to Leon and Mary Jane Gibbons. She was baptized at First United Methodist Church and accepted Christ as her personal Savior in 1971. They met at the University of Kentucky. They were married Dec. 28, 1978, by Melinda's brother after obtaining a dispensation.

They established their home in Muhlenberg County in 1984 when Eddie set up his medical practice in Greenville. Melinda is a physical therapist by profession. She has been employed primarily by Muhlenberg Community Hospital's Home Health Service.

They, along with their three daughters, Kaci (12/80), Lindsay (10/82) and Hillary (6/87) make their parish home at St. Joseph in Central City. Melinda joined the Catholic Church at Easter in 1988. Both she and Eddie have been very active teaching Senior High Religious Education and sponsoring the Senior High Youth Group for many years. They have taken several mission trips and have also participated in several diocesan events such as CLI, Quest, Youth Rally and Youth Congress.

Eddie has served on the parish council. He is also active in Rotary, Greenville Chamber of Commerce, Muhlenberg County Children's Fund Inc. and Concerned Christians/Citizens for a Better Future. Melinda has served on the Education Committee as well as YMTN and YMAC.

PUCKETT, WALTER LEE, was born March 20, 1925 in Hart County, KY. His parents were Lawrence Clifton and Pearl Etola James Puckett. He had three sisters and four brothers. They were of the Methodist faith. Walter married Martha Elizabeth Puckett on Dec. 30, 1948. Martha was born Dec. 2, 1931, daughter of Lawrence Calvert and Kathryn Marie Wilkerson Puckett. They were also Methodist. Martha's father died May 30, 1932. Her mother remarried and had two more children.

After their marriage, Walter and Martha moved to Indianapolis where they were employed by AT&T. They have one son and two daughters and eight grandchildren. Walter retired in September 1981. Martha retired in August 1982. They moved back to Hart County in August of 1982.

Both Walter and Martha attended the Methodist Church after retiring. They joined the Catholic Church in April 1984, and were baptized on Holy Saturday.

Martha is a member of the Parish Council. Both Walter and Martha are Eucharistic Ministers and Dismissal Catechists at St. Benedict.

They now live on Cub Run Highway, Cub Run, KY.

PURDY, ANNA ROSETTA, (Sister Jean Catherine, OSU) was born Dec. 6, 1908 on a farm about two miles from Saint Elizabeth Church and school. She was baptized, made first confession, Holy Communion and was confirmed in Saint Elizabeth Church, Curdsville, KY.

She attended Saint Elizabeth School in grade one through 11. She had a happy home life and enjoyed her school days.

She grew up with four brothers, one had gone to heaven about six months before she was born. Her three sisters entered the convent when she was too young to remember them. But several years later she followed them and entered the novitiate at Mount Saint Joseph Sept. 7, 1926, leaving her dear mother alone. Her father had died June 23, 1923.

Novitiate days were happy but busy ones. There was no lay help in those days, and the young Sisters, postulants and novices really worked.

After she made final profession March 19, 1932, she started teaching and continued for almost 50 years. During those years she taught all eight grades (not at the same time).

In June 1979 she retired from teaching and came to the Mount.

Now all her sisters and brothers have followed our parents into eternity. Only she is still living.

RACHELS, THURMAN E., married Wilma M. Hartz from the Newburg, IN area. Thurman served in

The Rachels' Family, November 1984 (L to R): JoAnn, Larry, Thurman and Wilma

World War II from 1941-1945. He is a retired coal miner and she is housewife. They are members of Holy Redeemer Catholic Church. Past members of St. Joseph in Central City, KY. They have lived in Beaver Dam since 1964. Wilma has helped with the rummage sales that Holy Redeemer had several years ago.

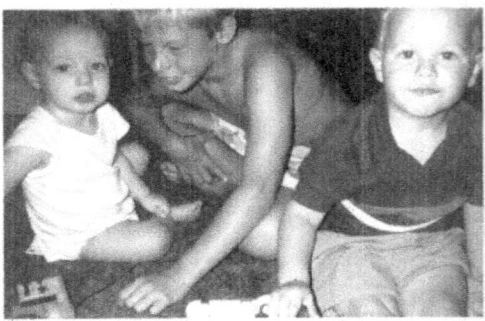

June 1992 (L to R): Derek, Matthew and Tyler

Their son, Larry E. Rachels (32), runs a loader at Medussa Aggregates in Hartford and has three children; Matthew E. Rachels who is 9 1/2 years old; Eric Tyler Rachels who is 3 1/2; and Derek Thurman Rachels who is 1 1/2.

RALEIGH/BOHN/HAGAN FAMILY HISTORY, My name is Mary Louise Raleigh. I am a widow. I was married to Klee Raleigh for 36 years before his death in 1986. I work at Holy Name Church and have for the past 25 years.

Our oldest son, Steve, married Pamela Kenney and they are the parents of five children. Becky is the oldest daughter and she is married to John R. Ricketts and they are the parents of three children. Richard is next in line and he is married to Debbie O'Nan and they have six children. Mary Jane is our fourth child and she is married to Daniel Hawkins, and they have two children. Susan is our fifth child and she is married to Gary Vetter and they have three daughters. David, our sixth child, is married to Dolores Rafferty and they have three children. Christopher is married to Beth Hobbs and they have two children. Bill is our youngest and is single and lives at home. Four of our in-laws have converted to the Catholic faith and the other three were already Catholic.

My maiden name was Bohn and I was oldest of five children, two sisters, Betty, who married Karl Christ and Sister Laurita Bohn who is Sister of Charity of Nazareth. My two brothers are John, who is married to Marie Fenwick and Bob who is married to Catherine Nally. My father, Gregory Bohn, was the middle child of five children and his parents were George and Louise Herbert. They were both immigrants from Germany but married at Holy Name after coming here.

My mother was Amy Hagan and she was the daughter of Thomas J. Hagan and Louise Logsden. They came to Henderson County by way of Union County but were born in Marion County, KY. My grandmother Hagan had three sisters who were Dominican Nuns and one was Mother General at St. Catherine's, Springfield, KY. My grandfather Hagan's mother was a Spalding and I can remember being told she was a sister of Bishop Spalding.

My Catholic roots are very deep and go way back in history. My prayer is that my grandchildren and their offspring will continue the faith.

RALEY/BYRNE/HENDERSON/STOKES, As I began writing this short history of my family the thing that I was most aware of was all the ones who had to be omitted because of time and space. "Thank You," to each one of them for all the hardships they endured to carry on the faith.

The passage of our Raley ancestors from St. Mary's County, MD to Kentucky began shortly after the close of the Revolutionary War. Basil and John Raley (brothers) took possession of land on the Rolling Fork River, Washington County, KY during 1787.

Basil Raley (son of Basil who moved from Maryland) and Elizabeth Spalding married in Springfield, KY, January 1811. They purchased a farm near Thompson's Station (Flournoy), about two miles west of Waverly. They had 10 children. Their first born, Hilary LaFayette (my great-grandfather) was born Sept. 19, 1857.

Hilary LaFayette married Mary Elizabeth Bell at Sacred Heart Church, St. Vincent. From this union came six children one of which was Mary Margaret (my grandmother), born April 26, 1891. Mary Margaret (Mayme) Raley married David Vantrece Byrne at Holy Name Church, Henderson. They had five children: David Clarence (deceased), married Peggy Baird, Henderson, KY (divorced); Edith Cavanaugh (divorced), Baltimore, MD, with one daughter, Shelia; and Gladys Lewis, Smith Mills, KY.

Elizabeth Martina, married: (Daniel Shacklett Henderson, Holy Name Church, Henderson. Three daughters; Annette, Josephine and Patricia (twins).

Dorothy Gertrude married Douglas Staples, Henderson, KY with one daughter, Nancy Gail. Douglas died in 1941. Dorothy married Robert Garfield Hayes, Henderson, KY. They had two children: Judith Yvonne and Paul Vincent.

Irvin Johnson married Ruth Pfingston (divorced), no children.

Charles Thomas married Pauline Mills, Henderson, KY. They had nine children: Michael, Paulette, Sondra, Tonya, Theresa, Tina, Jeanette, David and Tim (not in birth order).

Annette Henderson married Forrest Edward Stokes. They have four daughters: Rebekah Jean, Edythe Jayne, Regina Susan and Nancy Elaine. Rebekah J. married Thomas Warren Rideout. They have three daughters: Erin and Amie (twins) and Kristen. Edythe J. married Terry Ray Thompson. They had a son Joshua Ryan and a daughter, Jessica Renay. They divorced. Edythe married Owen Ray Mays. Regina S. married Harold Lee Butler (no children). Nancy E. married Phillip Breeding in Dubois County, IN. They had one daughter, Chasity Dawn. Divorced, Nancy married Dale Fulkerson, Henderson.

RANCE, WILLIAM J. AND ELIZABETH W.,
In the fall of 1943, they moved to Paducah and the Diocese of Owensboro when he was transferred by his employer, the Illinois Central Railroad. He was named general foreman at the Paducah shop.

Bill and Elizabeth grew up in Freeport, IL and attended St. Mary Church where they were married in 1926. In 1941 the family moved to Vicksburg, MS and spent two years before coming to Paducah. Bill retired in 1969 having spent 51 years in railroading.

Two of their daughters, Patricia Ann and Barbara Jane were born in Freeport and attended schools there and in Vicksburg before entering St. Mary Academy in Paducah.

Later, in Paducah, another daughter, Elizabeth Sue, was welcomed to the family.

All three of the daughters became registered nurses. The family was active in the St. Francis De Sales Parish and in the St. Mary's organizations.

Patricia is married to Ed Kortz, has four children and eight grandchildren. Barbara is married to J. Keith Beauvais, has four children and eight grandchildren. Sue is married to Paul Derouen and has two children. Patricia and Sue live in Paducah and are members of St. Thomas More Parish and Barbara lives in Rockford, IL.

Bill passed away in 1990. Elizabeth, now 90 years of age, resides at the Ritz Apartments and attends St. Thomas More Church.

RAY, EDITH ELIZABETH, was born Aug. 7, 1910. She is the daughter of Joseph Lawrence (Lon) Ray (June 4, 1874-Feb. 1, 1982), a farmer from Meade County, KY, and Mary Elizabeth Mills (May 30, 1883-Sept. 5, 1957) a housewife also from Meade County. They were married Dec. 30, 1902. Edith received her education at St. Theresa Academy, Mount St. Joseph, St. Joseph College and Creighton University. She entered the convent Jan. 21, 1929. Her name as a Sister became Sister Elizabeth Ann, OSU. She taught in Kentucky for 21 years; Missouri for one year; and New Mexico for 32 years. Retired from teaching in June 1985, and since then she has served as assistant Archivist at Mount St. Joseph, Maple Mount, KY.

Lawrence and Mary's other children were: Sallie Mary (Dec. 1, 1904) married Francis Heavin; Ann Mildred (March 14, 1906) married James C. Miller; Joseph Jefferson (April 24, 1907) married Theolinda O'Bryan; Catherine Addillon (Nov. 6, 1908) married Joseph Jennings Whelan; William Louis (April 29, 1912) married Rita Staples; James Thomas (Nov. 7, 1913) married Mary Flaherty; Lawrence Allen (April 3, 1915) married Mary (Payne) Troutman; Charles Albert (Dec. 10, 1916) married Anita Flaherty; Rhoda Aloysius (March 14, 1919) married Martha (Willett) MacAllister; Inez Irene (July 16, 1922) married Hardin Whelan; and Benjamin Baskett (Jan. 9, 1925) married Helen Henshaw.

RAY, GERALD, the son of Gerald Ray and Hallie Yates, was married Lucille Whelan, daughter of Gus Whelan and Minnie Mattingly at St. Martin Church, Flaherty, Meade County, KY, in 1948.

Their marriage was blessed with 13 children: Thomas, Gerald, James, Steven, Elaine, Jeanette, Phyllis, Kenneth, Mary, Michael, Anita, Joseph and Cheryl. All have settled in Kentucky except Joseph and Cheryl who live in Albuquerque, and Anita, who lives in Germany. Among them, they have given Lucille and Gerald 18 grandchildren, one of whom died in 1989.

The Gerald Ray Family

Gerald was employed for 36 years by Texas Gas, and the family moved many times during the early years of marriage, living the longest period in Mitchell, IN. They moved to Madisonville in 1965, joined Immaculate Conception Parish, Earlington, and enrolled their children in the parish school, until Christ the King Church in Madisonville was completed.

Gerald helped to clear the trees, erect the three crosses and lay the form for the the outdoor altar atop the hill behind the church. Their youngest child, Cheryl, was the first baby to be baptized in the new church, and hers was the first name entered on the Baptismal Register.

Gerald retired in 1985, but he and his wife are still faithful members of Christ the King Parish. Lucille was a member of Altar Society for many years, and today loves to quilt and crochet rosaries, which she distributes to anyone who promises to use them.

Among the Rays' earliest memories is a visit from Gerald's uncle, Fr. Anthony Ray, a Holy Ghost Father from Michigan who entertained them for hours with stories of his missionary work among the Seminole Indians in Everglades, FL. Times were hard, and he showed them his trousers mended with twine. His shoe laces too were twine. Fr. Anthony is now deceased.

REED, LESTER RAY, was born June 13, 1924 in Manchester, OH. He married Martha Wilhelminia Kirk who was born Jan. 14, 1924 in Owensboro, KY on Aug. 1, 1946. Lester served in the U.S. Air Force in World War II in Germany. They live in Owensboro, KY and are members of Immaculate Parish, past members of Blessed Mother Parish. Martha is hospitality minister at Immaculate. Lester retired from Whirlpool after 36 years. Martha retired from General Electric after 34 years.

The Lester and Martha Reed Family

They have eight children: Edward Ray Reed (May 29, 1947) served in U.S. Air Force in Vietnam; Mary Linda Reed (July 25, 1949); Catherine Belle Reed (May 23, 1951); Daniel Lee Reed (March 7, 1954) served in Germany with the U.S. Army; Stephen Kirk Reed (July 22, 1955); John Lester Reed (July 9, 1958); Timothy Allen Reed (Jan. 12, 1965); Lori Kaye Reed (March 21, 1969). They also have 24 living, one deceased grandchildren, seven great-grandchildren. All eight of the children attended Immaculate School at one time or another.

REYNOLDS, CHARLES H. AND PATTY NUSZ, were married by Fr. Joe Spalding on Jan. 28, 1947 at St. Joseph Church in Bowling Green. Patty attended St. Joseph School and then attended and graduated from Nazareth Academy. Several of her aunts were Sisters of Charity of Nazareth. Charles converted to Catholicism during World War II while serving in the Pacific Theatre. After they married, Charles finished law school and practiced law for over 20 years. He later served as Court of Appeals Judge for 14 years and in 1990 was elected to the Supreme Court of Kentucky. Bishop McRaith led the invocation at his investiture at the state capital in Frankfort. Patty has stayed very busy the past 45 years helping to rear their 11 children.

Justice and Mrs. Charles H. Reynolds Family

When Holy Spirit Parish was formed in the late 1960s, Charles and Patty became active there. Charles served as a parish trustee and Patty served on the Parish Council. Most of their children belong to St. Joseph Parish and are involved with parish and school function there. All 11 children attended and finished at St. Joseph School. Their children include: Mike (attorney); Kevin (finance officer); Dan (farmer/businessman); Father Pat (a priest of the Owensboro Diocese since 1980); Mary Anne (mom/housewife); Kenny (construction supervisor); Laura (teacher); Margaret (pharmacist); Tom (salesman); and Brian and Trish (college students). When Trish, the youngest, finished at St. Joseph School in 1984, Charles and Patty where given an award for attending PTA meetings at St. Joe for 31 consecutive years! At present count there at 15 grandchildren, most of whom are now attending St. Joseph School also.

REYNOLDS, C. MICHAEL, 44, was born in Bowling Green, KY, graduated from St. Joseph High School, Bowling Green. Graduated from Western Kentucky University (BA), University of the Americas and University of Louisville School of Law. He married

Mary Dale Reynolds, 39, who was born in Jackson, TN, graduated from Louisville Westport High School, Louisville, KY and from Western Kentucky University (BA). They were married Aug. 2, 1980 in St. Joseph Catholic Church, Bowling Green. All four of their children were born in Bowling Green, KY: Emily Lynn (11); David Michael (8); Christopher Lee (4); Gregory Hilliard (8 months). They currently live in Bowling Green and are members of St. Joseph Parish. Mr. Reynolds is past president of the St. Joseph Parish Council; past chairman of the school board and chairman of the Finance Council of St. Joseph; member of Chamber of Commerce, Elks Lodge, Bowling Green Rotary Club and Phi Alpha Delta. Mrs. Reynolds is past president of the Altar Society and a member of Alpha Delta Pi.

RHODES, GORDON PATRICK, was born on a farm near McDaniels, Breckinridge County, KY on Nov. 28, 1892. He was baptized by Fr. Hugh O'Sullivan, pastor of St. Anthony Church, Axtel, KY. He was a life-long member of St. Anthony's, as was his father and grandfather before him. He was the son of James and Alice Mattingly Rhodes. His grandfather, Francis was the son of Elias Rhodes, who came to Breckinridge County, KY. before St. Anthony Church was established in 1812. There are two stories about Elias Rhodes that tell of his journey and arrival in Breckinridge County. One says that Elias was born in 1781 in Loudan County, VA, and was brought to Kentucky when about 10 years old by Richard Mattingly. They came down the Ohio River on a flatboat from Pittsburgh, PA and settled in Washington County, KY, where he remained until 1801 when he came to the southern part of Breckinridge County. The other story says that Elias came from Maryland in 1795 with Barton Mattingly-also from Maryland. Elias was married to Margaret Mattingly eldest daughter of Richard Mattingly on June 1, 1807. The ceremony was performed by Father Badin and took place in the open air in the presence of a great crowd of invited guests.

Gordon Rhodes married Elizabeth Critchelow-also a member of St. Anthony Church July 10, 1917. The ceremony was performed by Father Odendahl. They were the parents of 10 children. Three children are still members of St. Anthony Parish. Also several grandchildren and great-grandchildren. Gordon died Feb. 21, 1970. His wife Elizabeth died May 5, 1934.

RHODES, JOSEPH (TONY), was born in Reed, KY. His father Arthur (Doodle) Rhodes was a farmer all of his life. His mother Elsie (Head) Rhodes was a homemaker. Mary Helen Higdon was born in Knottsville, KY. Her father, Gus Higdon, was a barber in Owensboro, KY. Her mother, Jamie (Aud) Higdon, was a homemaker. Tony and Mary Helen were married on April 15, 1961, at St. William Church in Knottsville and lived in Thurston, KY until 1962. They have four children: Lisa, Chris, Serena (deceased), Carisa, and are expecting their first grandchild in November 1992. Tony works at Whirlpool, is a songleader at church and likes to sing at local square dances. Mary is a homemaker, has served on the Parish Council, grade school and high school boards, and was a representative at the Diocesan Synod in Owensboro. Both are active in the parish. They have been members of St. William and St. Lawrence Church all of their lives. Tony and Mary are happy with the small parish communities and the closeness and caring of the parish members.

RHODES, MARTIN EUGENE, was the fifth of 10 children of Thomas H. Rhodes and Jennie Mae Barr. Born near Whitesville, KY and raised at Livermore where he attended St. Charles Church in Livermore and St. Joseph School in Central City, where he graduated in 1957.

Theresa Marie Kuegel was the fifth of 13 children of George Henry Kuegel and Mary Pauline Newman. Born in Owensboro, moved to Stanley where she attended St. Peter's Church and her first seven grades of school. She attended St. Joseph in Owensboro in the eighth grade. Went to St. Francis Academy for three years then graduated the first senior class from Owensboro Catholic High School. They were married on Feb. 10, 1984 at Immaculate Church in Owensboro and now reside in Livia, KY. They are members of St Anthony Church at Brown's Valley. They are both members of the Army of Mary, and Martin is the parish representative on the rural Deanery Council.

Martin and Theresa Rhodes

RHODES, NANCY CAROLYN BOONE, was born on April 1, 1939 in Owensboro, daughter of Raymond O. Boone, accountant and Mary Robert Hayden. She was baptized at St. Joseph Church. She attended St. Joseph School for eight years, graduated from Owensboro Catholic High School, and was a student at Brescia College when she married.

Nancy was married for 18 years to Donald Bartlett Rhodes, born Oct. 16, 1936 in Detroit, MI. He was the son of Rollie E. Rhodes, Whitesville, a local insurance agent and Opal Pierce of Daviess County.

Nancy and Don were married by Fr. Thomas Clark at St. Stephen's Rectory on Dec 28, 1959. They resided in Bowling Green, KY, while Don attended the Business University. After returning to Owensboro, they moved into Immaculate Parish where their five sons and one daughter attended elementary school. Don was a graduate of Brescia College and practiced accounting in Owensboro. He was a member of Immaculate Men's Club and Immaculate Boy Scout master. Nancy was a Girl Scout leader and a member of the Immaculate Parish choir. Two sons and their daughter were married at Immaculate Church.

Don died on April 12, 1978, and Nancy is currently employed in the business division of Brescia College. She still resides in Owensboro and attends Immaculate Church.

RICCIARDI, PHYLLIS ANN HUNT, is the daughter of Jesse and Annette Hunt. She was born on April 9, 1953 in Cairo, IL. She was delivered by Dr. Brackin. She attended Cunningham Elementary then Carlisle County High. She graduated in May 1971. She was a cheerleader. She also participated in 4-H, FBLA and Beta Club. She did a lot of charity work for school, church and the Carlisle County community. She graduated from Murray State University with a bachelor's degree in nursing.

Danny and Phyllis Ricciardi, Leanne and Eric

She married Daniel Ricciardi on Sept. 17, 1977. They were members of St. Thomas More Church in Paducah, KY. They now live in Cincinnati, OH and belong to a parish there. Danny works for Midland Enterprises as manager of barge maintenance and repair. Phyllis works for Kreindler Medical and Associates. She is director of nursing, Clinical Research Coordinator and Occupational Health Coordinator. The Ricciardi's have two children: Leanne, born Feb. 12, 1985 and Eric, born March 27, 1990.

RILEY, CECIL ANTHONY, was born near Mayfield, KY on Oct. 22, 1903. He was baptized at St. Denis Church in Ballard County. His parents were Bartholomew Harrison Riley and Vera Emaline Roberts. Cecil Anthony has three brothers and three sisters: Ruth, William Gentry, Charles Shelborn, Mary Estelle, Flossie Ann and Claude Joseph.

Cecil Anthony (Jake) married Mary Lucille Sanderson. Lucille was born on March 27, 1910 near Mayfield, KY. Her parents were Charles Edward Sanderson and Nola Cornelia Sanderson. Lucille was next to the youngest of their six children (Lela, Vallie Mae, Charles Diseral, Pauline, Mary Lucille and Samuel).

The Cecil Anthony and Mary Lucille Riley Family

Jake was a livestock dealer, a farmer and an acetylene welder. He and Lucille lived on Jimtown Road near Mayfield for the early part of their married life. Jake worked on the natural gas pipeline for about five years. During this time he and his family lived in several different places in Illinois, Wisconsin and Michigan. Lucille was not a Catholic when she and Jake were married, but she was baptized a Catholic at St. Joseph Church in Mayfield on Dec. 24, 1934.

In 1942 Jake and Lucille bought a farm on Backusburg Road east of Mayfield. They moved there with their 10 children: Cecil Howard, Margie Marie, Wilma Juanita, Joseph Bud, Mary Opal, James Samuel, Teresa Ann, John Marvin, Ruth Jane and Roy Patrick. Jake and Lucille celebrated their 50th Wedding Anniversary in 1974, and Jake died in 1975. Lucille still lives on Backusburg Road. She has 34 grandchildren, 58 great-grandchildren and two great-great grandchildren. Four of Jake and Lucille's sons (C. Howard, Joseph B., James S. and John M.) and one daughter (Margie Brittain) live near Mayfield. Wilma Kline lives in Warren, MI; Mary O. (Nivita) Yothment and Ruth Dickins in Tucson, AZ; Sr. Teresa Riley in Owensboro, KY; and Roy P. Riley in Lawrenceburg, IN.

RINEY, C. PHILIP, was born Nov. 5, 1924, near St. Joseph, the sixth of 11 children of T. "Len" Riney and Irmine (see T. Len Riney history) Mulligan Riney. The family moved to Owensboro in January of 1929. He attended St. Joseph Grade School and St. Frances Academy.

Father Phil Riney

Phil felt the call to priesthood since childhood. He enrolled at St. Mary College (St. Mary, KY) September 1941, completing four years of high school and four years of college. The diocese sent him to St. Mary University (Baltimore, MD) for theology training. Bishop F.R. Cotton called Phil for ordination to the priesthood April 5, 1948 at the young age of 23 years and six months, requiring a dispensation from Rome. He was not allowed to hear confessions for six months.

Father Phil was associate at St. Paul Church (Owensboro) for one year. He was assigned to St. Ann (Morganfield) August 1949, and spent six wonderful years as associate to Fr. Joe Spalding. In addition to other duties, Fr. Phil taught at St. Vincent Academy and initiated an athletic program to attract boys to the previously all-girls' school. A new parish started and a church building was erected in Sturgis, KY during this time.

In June 1955, Fr. Phil was appointed pastor of Rosary Chapel (Paducah) and St. Mary (LaCenter). St. Mary dedicated it's new church Nov. 5, 1956. Bishop Cotton blessed the new Rosary Church Feb. 11, 1959.

Bishop Soenneker transferred Fr. Phil to pastor four small parishes in Hancock County, June, 1962. He worked with volunteers, remodeling the school that served the whole county, was substitute bus driver and did everything necessary to build up the body of Christ and improve the physical buildings. He led the parishes in a decision to close the small high school and to put all their resources and energies into a quality grade school.

Father Phil's transfer back to Paducah, July 19, 1969, to old St. Francis De Sales (downtown) was like coming home. Renewal of Vatican II, renovation of the church for the new liturgy, ecumenical services and social justice efforts with other churches of Paducah, involvement in civic affairs, etc. made the years extremely busy, but fruitful. St Francis and Grace Episcopal were in the process of forming a covenant relationship when Father suddenly was moved to St. Mary Church (Whitesville).

At Whitesville, these generous people paid off an old grade school debt, planned and and built a new church (dedicated Oct. 7, 1978), operated a free first grade through high school and paid off all debts by 1981.

Bishop John McRaith appointed Father Phil Riney pastor of Holy Name Parish (Henderson) on June 7, 1983. Holy Name had a beautiful, cathedral-type church and an excellent grade school. Many Catholic Schools were losing students and some were closing, but in 1986 Holy Name added a new wing for middle school students. They also built a new Parish Center attached to the church that provided much needed office space and education rooms. In the middle of this construction, the bishop moved Fr. Phil to Blessed Mother Church (Owensboro), June 13, 1989.

Owensboro Daviess County Parish Schools consolidated July 1, 1989, consuming most of this parish's time, energy and money. Blessed Mother Pastoral Council called the people to stewardship April, 1991. The parish is living what it preaches, giving tithe to the poor. It is most exciting and rewarding to see the vision of Vatican II come to fruition.

Father Phil said: "I will be a priest 44 years April 5, 1992. I have many friends throughout Western Kentucky and being back in my home town is the last lap of my journey, God willing."

RINEY, F.G. AND WINNIE, The F.G. and Winnie Riney family have lived at West Louisville in the western part of Daviess County all of their lives, coming from adjoining parishes of St. Alphonsus and St. Raphael's.

Their family ancestry came from England, Ireland and Scotland to Maryland and then to Nelson and Marion Counties in Kentucky.

Francis Guerdon Riney Jr. (F.G.) and Winifred Marie Cecil were married at St. Alphonsus Church, St. Joseph, KY on Dec. 28, 1939. Rev. James Higdon officiated. Fr. Higdon had much influence on their lives. He was once pastor of the mission church of St. Raphael's and F.G. was an altar boy for him until he was 16 years old. Back then the roads were dirt and Father couldn't travel by car from Curdville. F. G. would meet him at West Louisville and take him two miles in horse and buggy to and from church every Saturday afternoon for confessions and again on Sunday morning. Later Fr. Higdon became pastor at St. Alphonsus, married them and baptized five of their 14 children.

Dec. 28, 1991 at the occasion of Laurie and Greg Payne's wedding day and F.G. and Winnie's 51st anniversary. First Row (L to R): Doug Riney, Ann Roby, F.G., Winnie, Winnie Lynn, Cohron, Linda O'Nan. Second Row: Cathy McClish, Martha Kamuf, Sister Judieth Nell, Becky Jean Reisz. Third Row: Kay Beth Riney, Mary Carol Riney, Keith Riney, Laurie Payne, Pam Higdon and Frank Riney.

F.G. farmed the land of his father and Winnie was the homemaker. Times were hard but all the children learned how to work and take responsibility. All 14 children attended St. Alphonsus Grade School. The girls attended Mount St. Joseph Academy just as their mother did and the boys graduated from various high schools. The children then put themselves through Brescia College.

The Rineys are very proud of their children, all of whom have found useful careers. Of the 14, two are elementary school teachers, one music teacher, a medical technologist, a librarian, pharmacist, two accountants, three secretaries, an electrician, a homemaker and a farmer. They are also very proud of their 29 grandchildren and one great-grandchildren.

The Rineys celebrated their 50th Wedding Anniversary in December of 1989 with their family and many friends in the same church where they were married.

RINEY, JOSEPH C. AND SUE THOMAS, Joseph was born on April 5, 1924 on the Riney farm near West Louisville, KY, the third son of William G. and Mary Josephine Merrimee Riney, who died during during childbirth in August 1925.

The Riney family moved to Mount St. Joseph, Maple Mount, KY in December 1933 where William Gerald Riney was farm manager for 28 years. Joe attended St. Alphonsus Grade School, three years at St. Joseph High School in Owensboro, graduation in 1942 from Vine Grove High School in Hardin County. Joe then returned to work at Maple Mount Farm. He was one of the two boys who attended Mount St. Joseph Junior College.

The Joseph C. and Sue Thomas Riney Family

On Sept. 27, 1944 Joe married Sue Thomas, the third daughter of Joseph R. and Edna Tong Thomas. Sue was born on Aug. 3, 1924, attended St. Raphael's Elementary School and graduated from Mount St. Joseph Academy in 1942 and attended Owensboro Business College. Joe was drafted into the Army on Nov. 11, 1944. Attained the rank of regimental sergeant major in the First Calvary Division, served two years in the Philippine Islands and Japan. Joe returned to the Maple Mount Farm where he was manager for 29 years.

Joe and Sue have eight children: Mary Jo Kirby, T. Edward, Wm. Jerry, Janet Murphy, Robert E., Jane Gaffey, Maria Thompson, Ann Carver and 15 grandchildren. Mary Jo, Janet, Jane and Maria graduated from Mount St. Joseph Academy. Ann and Ed graduated from Owensboro Catholic High School. Jerry graduated from St. Mary's Seminary in Marion County, KY. Bob graduated from Daviess County High School.

Mary Jo and Ed graduated from Brescia College with degrees in business and accounting respectively. Janet is pursing a business degree. Jerry graduated from St. Mary's College, received his masters degree in theology from North American College in Rome, Italy, and was ordained Aug. 9, 1975 at St. Stephen Cathedral. Maria received a BS degree in nursing from Western Kentucky University. Ann graduated with a degree in mechanical engineering from the University of Kentucky. Bob is a licensed airline transport pilot. Jane attended Western Kentucky University and is property manager for Balcor in Denver, CO.

Joe retired as Maple Mount farm manager in 1990. He and Sue moved to Owensboro and are members of Immaculate Parish. Joe is a member of the Men's Club, Fr. Connor K.C. Council, has served on numerous boards, including Owensboro Catholic High School, First Diocesan School Board, St. Alphonsus trustee, Daviess County Democratic Committee and is presently chairman of the West Daviess County Water Board.

RINEY, J. GARY, was born Nov. 20, 1936 in West Louisville, KY, one of 10 children to James Louis and Kathryn Wimsalt. His father was county commissioner from 1969-1980, his mother was a housewife. He was a lifetime member of St. Alphonsus Parish. Graduate of St. Alphonsus and attended Brescia College.

J. Gary, Mary Helen and Susan Kathryn Riney

J. Gary married Mary Helen Knight who was born Jan. 2, 1943, the daughter and oldest child of 13 of Francis Knight and Lenora Shellman Knight of Cloverport, KY. She graduated from St. Romuald's High School, attended Brescia College and Western Kentucky University. They were married May 30, 1964. Currently living in West Louisville, Daviess County, KY. Members of St. Alphonsus in St. Joseph, KY. J. Gary works is employed as manager of Old Hickory Barbecue in Owensboro, KY. Mary Helen is an elementary school teacher. She taught at Immaculate School in Owensboro and West Louisville School. They have one daughter, Susan Kathryn Riney, born Aug. 2, 1973. She is a graduate of Owensboro Catholic High, now attending Bellarmine College in Louisville, KY.

RINEY, LEN, The Rineys of Kentucky were in a group of colonists sponsored by Lord Baltimore who settled in Charles County, MD in 1632. In 1793 some of them migrated to Washington County, KY and from there William Ray, moved to Daviess County in 1863.

In 1915 Len, grandson of William Ray, married Irmine Mulligan at St. Alphonsus Church, St. Joseph, KY. During the next 20 years, they were blessed with 11

Front row, left to right: M. Virginia, Thomas L., David, Irmine, M. Lou; Back row, left to right: C. Philip, James E., Trudy, Richard D., Joe Leon, Ruth Helen, Jeanne and Patricia. The Len Riney Family.

children: Joe Leon of Owensboro, Richard D. of Louisville, Sister Mary Leon, OSU, Sister Ann Clare SCN, James E. of Louisville, Mary Gertrude of Clarksville, IN, Rev. C. Philip of Owensboro, Patricia Cheshire of Memphis, David of LaJolla, CA; Mary Lou Mudd of Owensboro, M. Virginia Dorsten of Dayton, OH.

To support his family, Len farmed near West Louisville until 1930 when he moved to Owensboro, and served as deputy tax commissioner or as tax commissioner until 1946. His untimely death in 1946, left his widow with four children in school. Her great faith and resourcefulness manifested itself; her children recall with great admiration her business acumen and her unshakeable faith in God.

For more than 40 years, Irmine was a daily participant at the early morning Mass at St. Stephen Church. She survived her husband 39 years, going to her reward at the age of 91, survived by 10 children, 52 grandchildren and 72 great-grandchildren.

Three of the children entered the service of the church: Ruth, Jeanne and Phil. Sister Mary Leon and Father Phil between them have contributed 70 years of service to the Owensboro Diocese (Sister also taught in the Louisville and Lincoln Dioceses). Currently Sister Mary Leon is assigned to Madisonville as pastoral minister, Sister Ann Clare is part-time Sister Visiter at Sts. Mary and Elizabeth Hospital in Louisville, Father Phil is pastor of Blessed Mother Parish in Owensboro (elsewhere in this book, you will find his history of service).

RINEY, OZETTA, was born Oct. 4, 1907, in Beech Grove, McLean County, 10th child of Sidney and Victoria Blandford Hayden. Ancestors came from Maryland to Washington County, KY, later to Daviess County, KY, settling in St. Raphael's, St. Alphonsus area in the early 1800s.

Mary Ozetta Hayden, daughter of Joseph Sidney Hayden and Theresa Victoria Blandford born Oct. 4, 1907 married Richard Lamar Riney on Aug. 23, 1930, son of W.G. Riney and Susan Ann Thompson born Oct. 19, 1901 and died Sept 25, 1979. This picture was made Sept. 23, 1930.

The farm and woods across from "The Mount" was owned by Ozetta's grandparents, Aquilla Pius and Louise Medley Blandford, who provided the first five Ursulines, who arrived earlier than expected, with their first meal of buttermilk and watermelon and temporary lodging. At that time Fr. Paul Volk, founder and builder of Mount St. Joseph, was pastor at St. Alphonsus. Ozetta fondly remembers when Father Volk returned from serving in the missions in Central America. During this stay he organized the Temperance Society and offered Mass in the Mission Church of St. Benedict's of Beech Grove. In August 1916, she received her First Communion from his holy hands. This was very special to her as a child, since Father was credited with several miracles and was considered a saint by his parishioners.

August 23, 1930, she married Lamar Riney, son of W.G. and Susan Thompson Riney, at St. Joseph Church in Owensboro. They had four children: Richard Lamar Jr. married Benita Mudd Aug. 23, 1955; Sidney Jean married Clarence Ebelhar May 24, 1952; Mary Joan married Tom Schartung Sept. 20, 1958; and Madge Marie married Joe Fleming July 7, 1962. They have 16 grandchildren and 18 great-grandchildren.

Aquilla Pius Blandford born Oct. 23, 1836 died Dec. 14, 1923. Louise Catherine-his wife born Nov. 4, 1846 died Dec. 10, 1923. This was the original homeplace across the road from Mount St. Joseph Academy-now belonging to the Mount. Grandparents of Ozetta Hayden Riney.

They moved to West Louisville in 1943, back to Owensboro in 1960. Lamar was district engineer for Kentucky Highway Department and worked in the diocese on many church properties. He was active in Precious Blood, St. Vincent De Paul Society, Men's Club and Building Committee.

Lamar's funeral was at Precious Blood, Sept. 28, 1979 with burial in St. Alphonsus Cemetery.

Ozetta was a teacher and later a librarian in the Daviess County School System for 22 years. She received her BS degree from Brescia College in 1962. After retirement she volunteered to work as librarian to get Precious Blood School accredited. She also catalogued the church library for Fr. Maurice Tiell. Ozetta presently resides in the homeplace on Bittel Road, Owensboro.

RINEY, RICHARD LAMAR "LARRY" JR., has lived in Daviess County all his life. He is the son of Lamar and Ozetta Riney and is one of four children. His mother is a retired school teacher. He is a retired professional engineer who was employed by the Kentucky Department of Transportation for more than 31 years. His father, Lamar Sr. (deceased) was also employed by the state and was district engineer at Madisonville upon retirement.

Benita Riney is the daughter of Robert and Helen Mudd who were lifetime farmers. She was born in Lebanon, KY and is one of 13 children.

Larry and Benita attended Brescia College in Owensboro. After serving in the Air Force during the Korean War, Larry returned to Brescia. They were married at St. Charles Church, her home parish, at Lebanon, KY in 1955. They are the parents of four children. They have a son and a grandson, named for Larry's dad, who are expected to carry on the Riney family name. Richard III, and his family live in Denver. Their daughters are Mary, Janet and Karen who are all married and live in Los Angeles, Owensboro and Atlanta respectively. They have four grandchildren.

The Richard L. Riney Jr. Family

The Rineys have been members of St. Mary Magdalene Parish for 34 years where all their children attended school before going to Owensboro Catholic High School.

Benita enjoys singing in the church choir and is a member of Christian Mothers. She has been a teacher for 31 and one-half years. She taught for five years at Mount St. Joseph Ursuline Academy and has taught 26 and one-half years in the Owensboro Public Schools. Larry serves as a Eucharistic Minister, takes Communion to the sick, is a member of the Men's Club and the Knights of Columbus. He attends and serves at daily Mass. One other very rewarding experience is his volunteer work in Kentucky prisons with the Kentucky Prison Ministries, a group of lay ministers. His hobbies are woodworking and gardening.

RINEY, TIM AND JUDY, were married at St. Mary's of the Woods in Whitesville, on May 3, 1980 with Rev. Phil Riney officiating. Tim graduated from Brescia College in 1977 and earned his bachelor of arts (BA) degree. Tim and Judy went to Catholic schools all their lives.

Tim attended Immaculate Grade School (one-eight) and Owensboro Catholic High School for four years. Judy attended Precious Blood (one-eight) and also Owensboro Catholic High School for four years. They have three children who also attend Catholic schools. Jeremy who will graduate in 1993 from Owensboro Catholic. John and Melissa who attended Bishop Sonneker.

Tim plans to build in the future in Whitesville on his 20 acre farm. The family spends a lot of spare time in the peaceful county of Whitesville.

Jeremy is an usher at Precious Blood Church and John is an altar boy. Tim also helps with St. Vincent De Paul outside his busy schedule. Judy is a good mother who stays around the house and cleans and enjoys playing softball in the summer and fall. The Riney's go back several centuries and hope to carry on in the future. Overall the Riney's are a good down to earth family.

RINEY, WILLIAM GERALD, was born Aug. 2, 1896, at Stanley, KY, and was baptized at St. Peter's Church, Stanley. He was the oldest son of William Morton (W.G.) Riney and Susan Ann Thompson. His ancestors came from Maryland to Washington County, KY, and hen they moved to Daviess County. Gerald lived in the West Louisville-St. Joseph area for 61 years of his life. During this time, he was a member of St. Alphonsus Church. He was also an active member of the Holy Name Society.

Gerald married Mary Merimee in June 1919 at St. Alphonsus Church. There were three sons by this marriage-Gerald, Marnell and Joe. Mary died August 1925. He married Katherine Fitzpatrick five years later. She was a native of Monroe County, MS. There were two daughters of this marriage, Mary Catherine and Patricia Ann. Katherine died August 1977, at the age of 84.

William Gerald Riney

Gerald served in the Medical Corps in World War I and was a life-long member of the American Legion. Most of his early years were spent farming. He truly loved the land and found great satisfaction in a productive harvest. In 1933, he was appointed supervisor and manager of the farm at Mount St. Joseph, Maple Mount, KY. He served in this capacity for 28 years. He instilled pride, cooperation and mutual respect among his employees. All of which resulted in efficiency. He was frequently consulted on many issues and served various other needs of the Sisters.

In 1961, Gerald retired. His youngest son, Joe, succeeded him as supervisor and manager. For 29 years, he continued many of the traditions established by his father and in the same exemplary manner.

Gerald and Katherine moved to the former home of his parents in West Louisville. They were active members of St. Raphael Church. In December 1972, they moved to Owensboro where they were members of Immaculate Church.

His five children, 22 grandchildren and 29 great-grandchildren were a source of great pleasure and utmost pride. Two outstanding highlights of his life were the ordination of his grandsons, Fr. Jerry Riney and Fr. Maury Riney, both whom are serving the Diocese of Owensboro. Love of and loyalty to his country were among his strongest convictions. Therefore, he was proud to have had three sons serve in the Army and Navy during World War II.

Gerald was a man greatly admired, loved and respected by all who knew him. He was a gentle, kind, considerate and caring person-one who inspired confidence and trust. He had many friends and touched many lives. He had strong convictions regarding his family and faith. To have known him was to have loved him! He lived a long and productive life. He died at the age of 95, April 26, 1992.

ROACH, JACK AND NELLIE, along with their 3 year old daughter, Mary Elizabeth, moved to Cloverport in 1923. They moved from a farm near Stephensport with the meager supply of furniture in a wagon pulled by a team of mules.

From that day, St. Rose Parish became an integral part of their family life. Nellie and Mary Elizabeth attended daily Mass. It was from her mother that Mary E. first learned about the Catholic faith. Nellie's answer to her questions gave her the fundamentals of faith which have remained with her.

As the years went by the family became more and more a part of St. Rose. Holy Name Altar Society and Sodality were most meaningful in their lives. Confession and Communion were vital on those special weekends.

Mary Elizabeth's elementary education was at St. Rose School where the Ursuline Nuns continued her religious education. Bible History and catechism were stressed. Visits to the Blessed Sacraments were encouraged, as well as devotion to the Blessed Mother.

Jack worked at Murray Tile Company and sold milk and vegetables from his garden to supplement his income. He was able to raise a bountiful garden until his 90th birthday. Nellie was the homemaker and ever present loving mother and wife. She raised chickens, canned vegetables and did intricate needle work for Eleanor Beard Studio.

Mary Elizabeth completed high school at Frederick Fraize, received her bachelor's degree from Spalding University and a master's degree from the University of Louisville. She married Wilfred Kidder and lived in Louisiana until his death. She then returned to Kentucky and continued teaching. She retired in 1976 after 35 years of teaching.

Nellie died in 1975 at the age of 82. Jack joined her in death in 1981 at the age of 91. Mary Elizabeth continues to live in the Cloverport home.

ROBERTS, GENE AND ANNA MARIE, have lived at Rome, KY in St. Martin Parish for 15 years. They were married April 17, 1971 at St. Mary of the Woods Church in Whitesville, KY. They lived a short while in Owensboro and at Masonville, KY before moving to Rome. Gene, the son of Lola Mae Roberts and the late Thelbert Roberts, is the fifth of six children. He grew up in the St. Martin Parish Community, attended St. Martin School, Owensboro Catholic High and Brescia College. He has worked for the telephone company for 27 years. Anna Marie, the daughter of G.C. (Coke) and Anna Virginia Russelburg Hamilton of Whitesville, attended school at St. Mary of the Woods High School (currently Trinity High). She worked at General Electric and is now employed as secretary at St. Martin Church.

Gene, Anna Marie and Bridgette Roberts

Gene and Anna Marie have one daughter, Bridgette. She graduated from Owensboro Catholic High School in 1992 and is planning to attend Western Kentucky University next year. She was active in D.A.R.E. and Thespians in high school. Bridgette is active in the Youth Group at St. Martin, where she is a member of the Core Team. She is employed part-time at A&W Hot Dogs and More in Towne Square Mall in Owensboro. Gene is a member of St. Martin Men's Club, past president of the Holy Name Society and has chaired the parish picnic for three years. He is active in the Knights of Columbus and is currently the State Warden elect. Anna Marie is a member of the Altar Society, serves as a lector and is currently involved in the youth group at St. Martin Parish, where she is a member of the Core Team. She has worked for many youth interests over the past years. The Roberts' believe strongly in an active participation in family, church and community.

ROBERTS, HARRY DEAN AND PATRICIA LAURICELLA, were married on Aug. 5, 1972 at St. Mary of the Woods Church in Whitesville; Fr. Charles Fischer officiated at their wedding. Pat's homeplace is in Dayton, OH, the oldest child of Louis and June Lauricella; Harry is from Lewisport, KY, the oldest child of Harry Dean and Betty Jean Roberts. Pat is a member of St. Columba Church, Lewisport. The Roberts live near Lewisport with their sons, Sean and Craig.

Pat earned a BA in sociology from Brescia and a MSSW in social work from the Kent School of Social Work, University of Louisville. She works as a independent living coordinator for the Green River District of the Kentucky Department of Social Services. Harry has a BA in history from Kentucky Wesleyan College and a MA in counselor education from Western Kentucky University; he teaches social studies at Hancock County Middle School.

Pat and Harry Roberts Family

Sean is a graduate of Immaculate Conception School, Hawesville. Pat has been a lector, a member of the picnic committee, a catechist, a choir member, data collection committee member. She participated in her parish's RE-NEW groups which she feels got her more involved in parish life.

Pat came to the Diocese of Owensboro from Dayton in 1968 as a Brescia student to attend a Catholic college which she felt was important for her course to study in social work. She knew no one here, but has since "adopted" the David and Mary Ann Howard family of Whitesville, as they have her. Having a family and community connection to church has become more important for Pat as her immediate family grows and as she continues to find her place in God's plan.

ROBERTS, LAWRENCE AND ROSE ANN, family have lived in Knottsville in eastern Daviess County since 1947. Before relocating to Knottsville, the Roberts family lived in Lewisport, KY, and were active members of St. Columbus Catholic Church.

Lawrence was the son of the late Lawrence and Maud Roberts, having five brothers and two sisters. Lawrence met Rose Ann Johnson of St. Lawrence, KY. Rose Ann had seven sisters and three brothers. They were married at St. William Catholic Church in Knottsville on May 24, 1938, with late Monsignor William B. Jarboe officiating the wedding.

Lawrence and Rose Ann had 10 children, which nine are still living in the Owensboro Diocese. They had one child, Judith Catherine, to die on Nov. 16, 1946, just before moving on their farm in Daviess County. They have always been very proud of all their children. There has always been some hard times during the Depression years, but Lawrence and Rose Ann always found the means to see that all their children received a Catholic education. They have 24 grandchildren and 11 great-grandchildren. They celebrated their 50th Wedding Anniversary on May 24, 1988, in the same church they were married.

Lawrence was a farmer and worked at the steel mill in Owensboro, KY until his retirement. After retirement Lawrence and Rose Ann travelled overseas to visit the Holy Land and travelled each year out west and the southern states.

In 1984, Lawrence became very ill and could not travel any longer. Rose Ann, a housewife and mother, stayed home raising their family and nursing her husband until his death on May 22, 1990. She has continued to live on their farm in Daviess County and is an active member of St. William Catholic Church in Knottsville, KY.

ROBERTS, MARK, was born April 17, 1953 at Mercy Hospital. Mark's father, Wallace, was born in Owensboro and his wife, Frances, was born in Russellville.

Cathy's father, Alphonso, was born in Owensboro and his wife, Mildred, was born in Hardinsburg, KY.

Cathy was born Feb. 9, 1953 at Mercy Hospital. Mark and Cathy were married at St. Joe and Paul Church on July 13, 1974. She is now working at Drs. Blackstone and Schmitt and is assistant office manager. Mark works at Indiana Hardwoods and is a national lumber inspector. He is a member of the choir at Blessed Mother Church.

Renee Roberts was born at Owensboro Daviess County Hospital on Aug. 27, 1975. Renee was baptized Sept. 14, 1975. She helps with children's Liturgy at Blessed Mother.

Matthew Roberts was born at Community Methodist in Henderson April 5, 1983 and baptized April 17, 1983.

Joshua Roberts was born at Community Methodist in Henderson on July 2, 1979 and baptized July 14, 1979.

ROBERTS, M.C. AND BARB, were both raised on farms in Daviess County. M.C. had one brother, one sister and two step-sisters; Barb has 14 brothers and sisters. They were married in St. Mary of the Woods Church on Oct. 29, 1960. They lived outside Chicago until the spring of 1962, then moved back to Daviess County. In 1966, they moved to Louisville, KY for a while then returned to Daviess County and lived there until four years ago. They have seven children: Dwayne, Kelly Coomes, Chad, Chris, Bruce, Jodie and Donna Roberts. All the children received their First Communions, were confirmed and went to school at Mary's Elementary and Trinity High School. M.C. and Barb have always been very proud of their children and what they have done with the gifts God gave them...and their 10 grandchildren.

The M.C. and Barb Roberts Family

M.C. has been a carpenter, school bus driver, electrician, factory worker, truck driver, farmer and a mechanic. Barb has worked in the school system since 1974, 11 of those years as a secretary at Trinity High School, and two years as secretary to the superintendent of Catholic Schools. They both have served on the boards of St. Mary's Elementary School and Trinity High School.

At one time four of their sons were in the military service but only Bruce was there to participate in the Persian Gulf War. They are thankful for the help of family and friends during hard times. M.C. had heart surgery in October 1966, and they were given money and toys for the children at Christmas time. He lost one of his eyes in September 1970, and again friends and family pitched in and harvested their crops. Their generosity and friendship is appreciated tremendously.

M.C. and Barb moved to Ohio County in December of 1988 and Fr. Joe O'Donnell and the people of Holy Redeemer made them feel very welcome.

ROBINSON, LARRY J. AND MARIANNA WILLETT, were married Aug. 1, 1964 and moved to Ohio County upon returning from their honeymoon. Larry had accepted a position with the accounting firm with which he is presently a partner, Clemons, Guthrie and Robinson, CPAs. Larry was one of seven children of William A. Robinson and Thelma (Tillie) Carrico. They were members of St. Alphonsus Church. Marianna was one of four children of Harvey Willett and Mary Ben Carrico and grew up in St. Peter of Alcantra and St. Joseph and Paul Parishes. When Larry and Marianna moved to Ohio County in 1964, there were few Catholics in the area. They maintain that, largely through the efforts of the Glenmary Missionary Society, they have seen the parish grow immensely. They add that their association with the Glenmary priests, sisters, brothers and candidates has been a source of joy as well as a faith-enriching experience for their family.

Larry and Marianna now have three grown children: Martina Todd Robinson, age 27, a registered nurse residing in Louisville, KY; Matthew Tray Robinson, age 25, works in hotel management in Louisville, KY; Allison Leigh Robinson, age 22, continues to work toward a master's degree in clinical speech pathology at Western Kentucky University. After their three children were grown, Marianna obtained an advanced degree and resumed her teaching career where she is presently on the faculty at Ohio County Middle School.

ROBY, CHARLES LAWRENCE, was born at Knottsville, KY, and baptized at St. William's Church by Father Jarboe. His parents Hobert and Bernadette Speaks Roby owned and operated a grocery store in Knottsville. Charles used to drive Father Hallahan to various places like St. Lawrence for Mass or to town. He spent 11 years in ac-tive reserve. His unit was activated during the Berlin Crisis.

Olivia Ann Riney Roby was born at West Louisville, KY, and baptized at St. Alphonsus Church at St. Joseph, KY by Fr. James Higdon. Ann is the oldest of 14 children born to F.G. and Winifred Cecil Riney.

Charles and Ann were married at St. Alphonsus on Aug. 20, 1966. They made their home at Knottsville and are members of St. William Church.

Both Charles and Ann are teachers in the Daviess County School System; both have taught for over 30 years. Charles is in 34th year and Ann in her 31st. Charles received a BS degree from Brescia College, a master's degree and Rank I from Western Kentucky University. He is a biology teacher at Daviess County High School. Ann is a reading teacher at Audubon Elementary School. She received an AB degree from Brescia College, a master's degree and Rank I from Western also.

Both Charles and Ann are members of N.E.A. (National Education Assoc.), D.C.E.A. (Daviess County Education Assoc.) and K.E.A. (Kentucky Education Assoc). They have taught CCD at St. William's for a number of years. Charles served on the first school board for Trinity High School. He has served as a lector. He makes rosaries and has sent many to Guatemala with Father Allard. Ann is a member of Women's Guild at St. William's and International Reading Association.

Their son, Steven Lawrence Roby, was born on Sept. 21, 1980 in Owensboro, KY. He was baptized at St. William's Church by Fr. Henry Willett. Steven is currently in the sixth grade. He enjoys music and takes both piano and organ lessons.

ROCHA, JOSEPH, was born Nov. 25, 1939 in Havana, Cuba. He had 14 years schooling with Christian Brothers-LaSalle School. Came to the U.S. in 1960, and served in the U.S. Army.

Daisy Winstead was born Oct. 22, 1942 in Paducah. Converted to Catholicism in 1964 with Rev. Robert Wilson giving her instructions.

Joseph and Daisy were married Sept. 3, 1966 at St. Francis De Sales in Paducah, KY. Joseph is currently transportation manager at PB&S Chemical Co. in Henderson, KY. Daisy is a teacher at Webster County High School. They are members of Christ the King Parish in Madisonville, KY. They are past members of St. Francis De Sales; St. Thomas More Church; Queen of Apostles, Pennsville, NJ; St. Michael's Sebree; Holy Name, Henderson, KY; and Our Lady of Victory, Tallmadge, OH. Joseph is the president of Evansville Traffic Club; Daisy plays the organ and has taught CCD. They currently live in Slaughters, KY.

They have one son, Alex, who was born Feb. 5, 1970. He is currently employed for PB&S Chemical and resides in Henderson. He was server at Mass for several years.

ROGERS, JOHN, On Feb. 12, 1878 the rites of matrimony between John Rogers and Mary Barbara Nunn were performed by Fr. J.C. Freehan at St. Francis De Sales Church, Paducah, KY.

Their children, all born in Paducah, are: Wilford E. (Feb. 7, 1879, died Dec. 25, 1926) married Ella Robinson (June 26, 1899); Phillip W. (Oct. 8, 1881, died Sept. 11, 1946) married Edith Lowe (Dec. 1, 1904); John R. (Sept. 25, 1885, died Sept. 23, 1936) married Daisy Wallace (Jan. 13, 1925); Wallace (Nov. 20, 1890, died Nov. 18, 1892); and Mary Ellen (Feb. 16, 1892, died July 9, 1971) married George H. Shelton (Oct. 12, 1916).

The John Rogers Family-First Row (L to R): John R., Mary Barbara, Mary Ellen, John and Ella R. Rogers. Back Row (L to R): Phillip Rogers, Mrs. Hessian (housekeeper), Wallace Rogers (picture) and Wilford E. Rogers.

On Oct. 12, 1916 the rites of matrimony between George H. Shelton and Mary Ellen Rogers by Fr. B.H. Dorshel of St. Cyril's Church, Chicago. IL. Their children are: John R. born Feb. 16, 1918, married Sara K. Fergerson June 14, 1941 and lives in Paducah; Mary Barbara born Jan. 29, 1920, married Frank Bacon Sept. 12, 1949 and lives in Detroit, MI; Margaret Ellen born Aug. 31, 1924, married Stanley Saunier May 15, 1948 and lives in Lexington, KY; Betty Ann born Feb. 25, 1927 in Nazareth, joined Sisters of Charity Sept. 28, 1945; and George H. born Oct. 18, 1933, married Carol Hurley Dec. 28, 1957, and they live in Chicago, IL.

John Rogers Shelton and Sara Kathryn Shelton were married June 14 by Fr. A. J. Thompson at St. Francis. Their children, born in Memphis, are: Edgar F. born Sept. 1, 1942, married Charlene Metters on Oct. 2, 1965; Sally G. born Oct. 28, 1947, married Barry L. Crowe Sept. 10, 1976.

Second marriage, Fr. Bob Willett married John R. Shelton and Mildred B. Shannon Nov. 9, 1990 at St. Francis Church. John, Edgar and Sally attend St. Francis Church.

ROGERS SR. MARY VICTOR, OSU, was born in Nelson County, KY, now living in Daviess County. She is a member of Mount St. Joseph Community. She serves as curator of museum and organist.

ROHRER, JOE PHILIP, son of Philip and Nora Rohrer, was born in Russellville, KY on Oct. 18, 1925. He was a member of the Third Div., 15th Infantry during World War II. He was wounded in Northern France in November of 1944, but was sent back to the front line soon after. Winter was very severe and he suffered from frost bite. In 1945, he was sent to Troyes, France, where he met his future wife, Lucette, a governess. The family lived across the street from Joe's depot. Each evening all would go out for a walk, noticing this one G.I. sitting alone on a window ledge. One of the children wanted to ask this G.I. for a stick of gum, but the G.I limped across the street pulling gum out of his pocket, to the children's delight. The mother could speak English and invited him in. That was July 17, 1945. Soon afterwards Joe was sent to Germany. There he looked into the Catholic faith, was instructed and baptized by their chaplain, Fr. Tompkins, a priest from Louisville, KY. On July 30, 1946 Joe married Lucette Simone Aubry, daughter of Lucien and Celile Aubry in her hometown church of Gye-Sur-Seine. He returned to the U.S. in August, she in October. They became members of Sacred Heart Church and still are today. Joe worked for T.V.A. for 22 years. In 1979 he became disabled.

July 30, 1946

May 8, 1992 (L to R): Marie, Mary Agnes, Elizabeth, Frances, Michael, Michelle, Philip, Monica with Lucette and Joe.

One day Lucette was called by Sacred Heart School to help. The cook was ill. It was the first day of 13 wonderful years as manager and cook. She taught CCD to high schoolers for seven years.

They have eight children. All proudly attended Sacred Heart School receiving the best in education and religion. Today, all are the parent's pride.

They have 15 grandchildren so far.

ROLLINS, ANNA THARP, is the daughter of May McCauley and Thomas Tharp. May died in January 1925, leaving Tom to raise their five children. Her funeral Mass was celebrated by Rev. Cotton who became the first bishop of the Diocese of Owensboro.

May died when Anna was 5 years old. Their father explaining to his children that their mother's death was a blessing considering her pain and suffering. He said they should remember she was in Heaven watching and praying for them. They always felt that she saw everything they did, good or bad. By being taught that death was God's will, they did not grieve their losses as most did but prayed to accept it. They never questioned "why" when there was illness, accidents or death. He taught them to offer pain and suffering for their sins.

Tom Tharp was baptized a Methodist as a boy, but friends and neighbors told his children he taught them the way he knew their mother would have wanted them to be taught.

As the children grew older they realized he was a Catholic at heart. He took them by train to Cairo, IL every week for Mass. He became Catholic in 1939 shortly before his death.

Anna married Homer (Bubba) Rollins on Jan. 23, 1938. She and Bubba lived at Barlow with her father and her son, Tom Parker by a previous marriage. Both of Anna's marriages were by justice of peace, but in 1940 her marriage to Bubba was blessed by Rev. Hugh Taylor.

Anna and Bubba had five daughter: JoAnn, Kay, Gayle, Gloria Jean and Kathy Sue who was still-born.

JoAnn married James Donald Roberts and had four children. JoAnn and Don were killed in an auto accident in July 1966, leaving their four sons to be raised by Anna and Bubba. Kay married John E. Bussey and had two children. John Earl was killed in an auto accident in 1963. Kay later married Rex Alexander and had three children. Gayle married Roy E. Waltmon and had three children. Gloria Jean married David Henderson and had two children. Tom Parker married Mae Howard and had one son. Tom died in June 1988.

Homer (Bubba) Rollins and Anna Rollins with Gayle Rollins Waltman and Gloria Rollins Henderson. The grandchildren of Homer and Anna are seated on the front row left to right: Donnie, Bill, Michael and Terry Roberts (sons of JoAnn Rollins and Donnie Roberts).

All five of Bubba and Anna's children were baptized, made their First Communion and confirmed at St. Mary's Church.

Bubba and Anna served on the financial board while canvassing for money pledges to build the new church. Bubba donated his work while building the new church as all the men did. When he was unable to work at the church because of farm work he would hire a man to work in his place at church and pay him.

Their son Tom and their four grandsons (Roberts) were altar boys and lectors. Their son-in-law, David Henderson, organized the first active guitar group for Sunday Liturgy. Bubba died Oct. 22, 1982.

RUARK, JAMES D. SR., was born July 7, 1915 in Uniontown, KY. Camilla Mason was born Nov. 3, 1915 in Morganfield, KY. They were married Sept. 11, 1941. Now living in Morganfield. J.D. is a graduated of the University of Kentucky and an attorney. Camilla graduate from Rosemont College in Philadelphia, PA, receiving a BA degree. J.D is a member of Morganfield Methodist Church; Camilla a member of St. Ann Catholic Church.

They have four children: James Dorris Ruark Jr., born Sept. 12, 1942-died March 2, 1956; Gordon Mason Ruark, born Sept. 11, 1943; Aaron Waller Ruark, born Jan. 5, 1947; and Allen Chapman Ruark born Nov. 20, 1950, married Deborah Jean Moore April 16, 1977.

RUDY, JOE, was a farmer from 1946, when he was born, until when he married Bev Bellew. They were married in 1970 at St. Stephen Cathedral. Bev was born in 1946 also. They both belong to Immaculate Parish and are Hospitality members there. After being married for six years they had two kids, Lee and Hadley.

Hadley is 20 and works at Wax Works, she attends community college. Lee is 14, he goes to OCMS. Joe now 47, works at Big Rivers. Bev, 46, works at Phil Clark Insurance. The family resides in Owensboro, KY.

RUSHING, KENNETH G. AND DORIS BARKAU, returned to their hometown in 1983 after an absence of 27 years to become an active part in St. William's Catholic Church in Marion, KY.

Both Ken and Doris were born and raised in Crittenden County, both are graduates of University of Maryland, and both are converts to the Catholic faith.

Ken spent 25 years on active duty with the U.S. Air Force and an additional six years working for the federal government as a civilian before returning to Crittenden County. The Rushings have resided in seven states and three foreign countries, raised three children (Nick of Tybee Island, GA, Gina of Fairfax, VA and Bill of Meridan, MS), and have each retired from one career and set forth on another. Ken is currently claims manager for Atlas Van Lines World Headquarters in Evansville, IN. Doris, a former medical social worker, is now a licensed insurance agent with the Ford Agency in Marion.

Are they happy to be a part of the Diocese of Owensboro? You bet! "In 1983, we came from a parish with three priests to a priest with three parishes," says Doris, "but it is an uplifting experience to be members of this warm Christian community."

Doris serves on the Parish Pastoral Council and as lector at St. William, and Ken serves as usher.

RUSSELL, JOSEPH EDWARD, son of Leslie McGill and Pauline Carrico Russell and Celeste Mae, the daughter of William Irie and Ida Stahr Willett, were married on May 15, 1954, at St. Jerome Church, Fancy Farm, KY. They have been active members of St. Thomas More Parish in Paducah all their married life. Joe has been a Eucharistic Minister and lector. Having been introduced to the retreats at the White House Jesuit Retreat Center in St. Louis by his father, Joe has returned annually for the past 33 years.

Celeste, a charter member of St. Thomas More choir, is a homemaker and mother of four children. Besides her interest in ceramics, she works at the computer at home when Joe's work calls for it.

Joe and Celeste chose St. Thomas More and St. Mary High School for their children's education until they reached college age. Pictures and memories record hours spent at games, plays, dances, outings on Russett Farm where horseback riding and cookouts, sunrise services and three wheeler mudding taking them through seasons and years. All four attended Paducah Community College for at least one year. Louis Edward obtained BS and MS degrees in animal science from University of Illinois. After completing two years at Paducah Community College Robert Joseph was drafted by the St. Louis Cardinals and pitched for four years in their organization. After an injury he finished his education at University of Kentucky earning a BS degree in mechanical engineering. Stephan Christopher, after earning a BS in computer science at U.K and accepting a job with AT&T in Richmond, VA, earned a MS in computer integrated manufacturing (CIM) from Brigham Young University. Ann Celeste, after a year at Brescia College in Owensboro, earned a BS in communications sciences and disorders. She is currently pursuing a master's degree in speech and language pathology at St. Louis University.

All are married except Ann. Joe and Celeste are the proud grandparents of two boys and four girls.

SANDERSON, BEV, and her family have been members of St. Francis De Sales Church in Paducah for about eight years. Bev, the oldest of 12 children, grew up in Joliet, IL. She is a nursing school graduate and for many years worked in the Critical Care unit of several hospitals before retiring home to raise her family.

During the past year, Bev has been studying to get reinstated into nursing. Soon, she will begin her practical experience hours and then will commence work as a registered nurse in one of the local hospitals.

Bev and her family are very active in their parish and community. She has taught CCD classes for four years, been a minster of the Eucharistic both at weekend Masses and takes Communion to the sick and shut-ins. Currently, she is also serving as an RCIA sponsor. In addition, Bev serves as a Brownie as well as a Webelo Scout Leader.

The Bev Sanderson Family

Amy Sanderson, age 17, is a junior at Marshall County High School where she runs track. In the parish, she is a CCD aid and a crossbearer. Both Mel and Nathon, age 13 and 11 respectively, serve as altar boys and CCD aids. At North Marshall, Mel, is a member of the band; while at Sharp Elementary, Nathon plays football and is a member of the Academic team. Both boys are in Boy Scouts. Katie, age 9, will soon be a junior Girl Scout. All four children attend weekly religious ed classes with the Paducah CCD program.

SAUER, MAX FIELDING, one of 13 children of William Henry and Aline O'Nan Sauer, has lived all his life, except for two years in U.S. Army in Henderson County, KY. Marian came to Henderson with her parents, Robert Simen and Frances Whittinghill Hayden, from Owensboro where her father sold life insurance. She has two brothers and four sisters. After graduating from Brescia College, Max and Marian were married in 1956 at Holy Name. They have been blessed with 11 living children and two angels in Heaven.

The Max and Marian Sauer Family

John Hayden, employed at Accuride, is married to Wanda Wood and they have three children, Daysha, Zebulan and Ariel.

Linda Susan, a teacher, lives in Zionworth with her son, Max Logan. In 1988 she donated one of her kidneys to her dad, who suffered renal failure due to kidney disease.

Timothy Max and his wife, Jackie, have a 3 year old son, Timmy. Timothy works at Thompson Bet and she is a respiratory therapist.

Donna Maxine, after teaching several years, is now attending Catholic University in Washington, D.C. studying law.

Robin Jeanne lives in Cincinnati, OH and is an insurance underwriter.

Amy Francis lives in Evansville, IN with her 3 year old son, Nicholas and is a housekeeper at a nursing home.

Barbara Carol attended Art and Design School in Chicago, IL, and is employed there by a publishing company.

Dennis Patrick helps with the family farm and also does carpentry work.

William Brian is in his last year at Western and is studying business management.

Connie Elizabeth is attending the University of Kentucky at Lexington.

Brad Eric is helping on the farm and going to community college.

Marian is a Eucharist minister and serves on the Pastoral Council.

SCHADLER, EUGENE FRANCIS SR., was born in Louisville, KY and baptized at St. Aloysius Church. He is the son of Alphonsus Schadler and Bernadine Kamuf Schadler. In July 1940, they moved to Curdsville, KY and became members of St. Elizabeth Parish. Gene graduated from St. Alphonsus High School. He is presently a part-time farmer and employed at Glenmore Distillery.

Mary Kareen Head was born in Sorgho, KY, the daughter of George Head and Rose Cecilia Beyke Head. She was baptized at St. Mary Magdalen Church, Sorgho. Kareen graduated from Owensboro Catholic High.

They married on Aug. 7, 1965 at St. Mary Magdalene Church, and took residence at 6335, where they are now living. They are members of St. Stephen Cathedral.

Gene and Kareen have six children. Rosanna Schadler is a graduate of Owensboro Catholic High and Brescia College, with degrees in sociology and ministry formation. She is coordinator of Youth Ministry for Holy Spirit and St. Joseph Parishes in Bowling Green, KY.

The Eugene Francis Schadler Sr. Family

Marianna Schadler Romero is a graduate of Owensboro Catholic High and Brescia College, with degrees in sociology and ministry formation. She is Pastoral Minister of Rosary Chapel in Paducah, KY.

Eugene Schadler Jr. is a graduate of Owensboro Catholic High, Thomas More College and the University of Louisville with a master's degree in social work. He is a therapist with Bluegrass East Comprehensive Care Center in Lexington, KY.

George Schadler is a graduate of Owensboro Catholic High and ITT Technical Institute with an associate degree in electronic engineering. He is employed at Big Rivers.

Elisa Schadler is a graduate of Owensboro Catholic High. She is a junior at Brescia College studying psychology and ministry formation.

Cynthia Schadler is a graduate of Owensboro Catholic High. She is a freshman at Kentucky Wesleyan College studying accounting.

SCHAIBLEY, JOHN AND LINNIE, were born in LaSalle County, IL, currently living in the Smithland, KY area, which is Livingston County. John is the son of Oscar and Alana Schaibley, who were factory workers. John and Linnie are members of St. Williams Parish in Marion, KY, St. Peter and Paul Church in Leonore, IL.

John and Linnie Schaibley

They have six children: Jon born Feb. 2, 1960; Mark born Jan. 2, 1961; Denise born Feb. 7, 1962; Janet born Jan. 11, 1965; Michael born April 26, 1968; and Melissa born Oct. 3, 1970.

They serve as lectors, on the parish pastoral council, usher, and work at the church.

SCHEIDEGGER, EUGENE M. AND ANNA JANE CLARK, were married at St. Joe and Paul Church on Sept. 27, 1958. They spent six years together before they had Timothy G. Scheidegger on Jan. 20, 1964. Then six years later, they adopted Sara Jane Scheidegger on April 30, 1970. Then four years later they had Philip Martin Scheidegger on April 7, 1974.

Eugene M. Scheidegger had a job at A&P Store for 28 years. They then closed down and now he has a job at Commonwealth Aluminum. Anna Jane Scheidegger worked at G.E. for a long time, then retired and went to babysitting. Tim Scheidegger graduated in 1982 from Owensboro Catholic High. Then went to the Navy. In 1988 Sara Scheidegger graduated from Owensboro Catholic High, and is a senior at Murray State University. Now Philip Scheidegger is in school at Owensboro Catholic High and will graduate in 1993. Eugene was part of the first class to graduate from Owensboro Catholic High. Anna Jane graduated from St. Francis Academy. They lived on Lewis Lane, then in 1973 they moved over on Christie Place and have been there ever since.

The Scheidegger family has belonged to Immaculate Parish for 28 years. Eugene and Anna have been involved in Cub Scouts as troop leaders. The Scheidegger family has been around for 34 years and with God's help it will be around for a long time to come, because good Catholic families are the best to live and grow up in.

SCHELL, ROBERT, was born March 4, 1939 in Daviess County, KY. He is the fourth of six children of Simon and Lucy Schell. He grew up in Pettit, KY and went to St. Anthony Catholic Church in Brown's Valley. He attended school at St. Anthony's and Owensboro Catholic High where he graduated in 1958. He attended Nashville Auto Diesel College in Nashville, TN and graduated in 1962. He worked at Short Brothers then W.R. Grace.

Judith was born Sept. 8, 1946 in Evansville, IN at Deaconess Hospital. She is the oldest of six children of Charles and Mary Jane Williams. She lived in Boonville, IN, Newburg, IN and Evansville, IN, before moving to Owensboro in the seventh grade. She attended Central Presbyterian Church in Owensboro. The schools she attended in Evansville were Columbia School and Washington School. Then Foust Jr. High, Eastern Jr. High and Owensboro High School where she graduated in 1964. She was a Candy Striper at Mercy Hospital the last three years of high school. They met when he was a patient and she a nurse's aid at Mercy.

They were married July 16, 1966 at St. Anthony's in Brown's Valley. The Rev. William Borntraeger officiated at the wedding. In August 1966 she graduated from Owensboro School for Practical Nurses.

They belonged to St. Joseph and Paul and Precious Blood before they moved to Our Lady of Lourdes Parish in 1977. While they were at Precious Blood Parish, she joined the Catholic Church in 1976.

The Schell Family (L to R): Front: Mary E., Robert L., Joseph A., Judith K., Stephen M., Patrick C. Second Row: Cisa K., Pamela M., Debra J. Back Row: John C., Robert E., Ronald David and Timothy A.

They have 11 living children, the 12th, Thomas Mark, was stillborn in 1987 when Judith was six and one-half months pregnant. The 13th miscarried in 1988 when she was three months pregnant.

Robert is a Fourth Degree Knights of Columbus member, Our Lady of Lourdes Men's Club, cooking team for the festival on the river and parish picnic. He is a member of the Moose and an officer of the Fraternal Order of Eagles.

Judith is a member of K.S.A.P.N. and N.F.L.P.N., Our Lady of Lourdes Altar Society, Daughters of Isabella and Fraternal Orders of Eagles Auxiliary.

They are both very active in Owensboro Right to Life and have attended the march in Washington, D.C. for the last four years.

They celebrated their 25th Wedding Anniversary July 20, 1991 at St. Anthony's with over 100 people attending.

SCHEPERS, ELMER LEO, was born Nov. 1, 1934 in Jasper, IN, the son of Raymond B. Schepers and Theresia (Seger) Schepers. He served in the U.S. Army from 1954 to 1956 in Korea; attended Brescia College, and employed as manager Employee Relations.

Mary Marcella Howard was born May 14, 1933, the daughter of John Louis Howard and Mary Elve (Payne) Howard. She attended Brescia College and employed as a teacher and housewife.

Elmer and Marcella were married Jan. 3, 1956. They are members of St. Mary of the Woods Church and have seven children.

Dr. Theresa Mary Schepers Alloy, graduate of Western Kentucky University and University of Louisville. She is employed as a research scientist.

Mary Lou Schepers Anderson, graduate of Western Kentucky University and University of Kentucky School of Pharmacy. Employed as a pharmacist.

Marilyn Suzanne Schepers Teitloff, graduate of Western Kentucky University School of Nursing and employed as a registered nurse.

Annette Marie Schepers Hamlin, graduate of Western Kentucky University School of Business. She is employed as a C.P.A.

Jeanne Marie Schepers Lancaster, graduate of Western Kentucky University School of Business, employed in banking.

Joseph Gerard Schepers, married to Christine Danhauer. A graduate of University of Kentucky School of Engineering. Employed as a civil engineer.

Eric Jude Schepers, a graduate of Bellarmine College School of Biology. Employed in Research in Entomology at University of Kentucky.

SCHERM, SISTER EUGENIA, was born Aug. 25, 1888 in Owensboro, KY, the daughter of Michael and Mary Grausz Scherm. She was baptized Mary Pauline Sept. 8, 1888.

Mary's early school days, along with her brothers, Paul, Lee and William and sisters, Rose, Lucy and Catherine were spent in her home under of the supervision of several governesses. After completing the eighth grade, she was sent to Mount St. Joseph Academy to continue her education. She came to the academy in September of 1904, and graduated in June of 1908. In the fall of 1907, while Mary was a junior, her father took her and her sister Rose on a tour of the eastern part of the United States, including the Jamestown Exposition. In the summer of 1908, Mary and her father decided again to go travelling, this time to see Europe. Margaret Miller, a classmate, made the trip with them. Their first stop was England, then Belgium, Germany, and from Germany to Italy and Western Austria. Mr. Scherm knew his daughter's love for history, and this travel was the greatest way of preparation for her later teaching in high school and college.

Mary entered the Ursuline novitiate at Mount St. Joseph on July 4, 1909 and made her vows Dec. 30, 1912, a member of the first class to make vows after the community was granted its independence of 1912. Because of her knowledge of German she was instrumental in helping with the separation of Mount St. Joseph from the Louisville Ursulines. Her class was the last class to make the vow of instruction of youth, until the year 1940.

She did not cease to travel after entering the convent. In 1915 Mother Aloysius asked Bishop O'Donohue for Sister and Sister Vincentia to go to the west coast and the Canal Zone. Once on this occasion they missed boarding a ship that they found out later had been totally destroyed in a hurricane; the second ship they boarded was also caught in a terrible hurricane. During the storm they made a promise to Our Lady of Prompt Succor, if she would avert the danger and bring all safely into port, they would erect a shrine in her honor and would spread devotion to her. Upon reaching home safely, the project was endorsed by Mother Aloysius, and they were given permission to use the funds left over from their trip for that purpose. The shrine was erected in 1927 at Mount St. Joseph.

Her 55 years of teaching include 34 at the Mount, nine in western states and 12 at Brescia College. In 1963 Sister Eugenia returned to the Mount where her time was devoted chiefly to collecting and preserving data for the Archives. During the last two years of her active life she wrote the biographical story of Mother Aloysius Willett which she offered as a loving tribute to her former teacher and Mother Superior. On Nov. 12, 1972 Sister slipped and fell on the dining room floor after supper, breaking her hip, from which accident she never recovered. Deafness and poor vision made her suffering greater. On June 30, 1973, she peacefully died with the nurses and Sisters watching at her bedside. Mass was said by Monsignor Powers as celebrant with Monsignors. Russell and Peter Braum from St. Joseph and St. Paul. Fathers Aloysius O'Bryan and Michael Volkmer, C.P.S. were in the chapel. Monsignor Powers' homily was taken from the title of her book *Born to Lead* to which he compared her life as born to follow in love and humility and obedience.

SCHMUKE, MRS. J.E., at 3 o'clock Tuesday morning, Aug. 26, 1902, Mrs. Joseph E. Schmuke passed calmly into the bright beyond. Sorrowing hearts surrounded the death bed, grieved and stricken as they watched their loved one peacefully responding to the call of death's angel who was hovering near to guide her pure spirit over the borderland into realms prepared for such as she.

It seems but yesterday that these columns contained glowing accounts of the marriage of one of the rarest young ladies Cape Girardeau has ever produced. And now, today, our theme is changed—the bridal robes are converted into a shroud: the wedding bells have ceased their peals of gladness and solemnly they toll the weird funeral knell: the deep organ that resounded scarce a year ago to the glad hosannas of a bright wedding morn, today gives out in requiem aeternum in cadence solemn, sweet and low.

Philomene Dempsey was born Feb. 13, 1874. On Nov. 6, 1901 she was married to Joseph E. Schmuke of Jackson, a marriage that gave every evidence of being an ideal one in all respects. Three weeks ago an infant daughter was born and their cup of happiness apparently full. But dread disease overtook the young mother and all that the best medical science and tenderest care could perform, availed nothing. Death had marked her for his own and with the beautiful Christian resignation that through life has always characterized her, she awaited the summons from on high and was ready to fill the vacant place prepared for her on heaven's fair distant shores. Born and raised in Cape Girardeau, Philomene was a favorite with all who knew her. Beloved by young and old for the rare and beautiful traits of character her daily life unfolded, her death has brought many heartaches and has left a void that can never be filled. It is hard to be reconciled to her being called away in her bright young life when all was so alluring and full of promise: but "God's ways are not our ways," and we must seek to be resigned to His will for "He doeth all things well."

Universal sympathy is felt for the young husband who is left with the tiny, motherless babe and whose devoted wife was taken from him on the anniversary of his brother Will's death, which occurred in St. Louis just a year ago today. A fond, devoted mother has been forced to give up her only daughter-human consolation can never assuage the intense grief that rends her heart today and forever. Three brothers always caring and thoughtful of their only sister are left to mourn her untimely end. God alone can comfort the aching hearts of the bereaved ones in this hour of deep affection.

SCHWARTZ, ARTHUR LEE, was born on July 21, 1940 in Daviess County, KY near Owensboro. His father was James Everett Schwartz, a mechanic and farmer. His mother was Lona Belle Schwartz a housewife, mother of eight and a Catholic convert. His father gave him the nickname "Sonny" a few weeks after birth. Doris Jean Howard was born on March 3, 1941 in Owensboro. She was the daughter of Charles Kevin and Mary Myrtle Howard, members of Sts. Joseph and Paul Parish.

They were married on Dec. 26, 1959 in St. Paul's Church. Their pre-marriage instructions were taught by Rev. Gerald J. Glahn but Rev. Bernard A. Powers officiated the wedding Mass. Because two couples were marrying that morning the two priests flipped a coin to decide who would perform the first Mass.

The Arthur Lee Schwartz Family

He attended Catholic schools at St. Joseph, St. Stephen and Owensboro Catholic High School, graduating in 1958. He attended classes at Kentucky Vo-Tech trade school, Owensboro Police Academy, EKU Law Enforcement Academy, U of L National Crime Prevention Institute, KY State Police Academy and Kentucky Department of Criminal Justice Annual training. His public employment began in 1958 as an offset printing press operator.

In 1962, he joined the Owensboro Police Department and worked as a street cop and also a second job as a printer. He was promoted through the ranks to Lt. Col., assistant chief and on July 1, 1992 he was appointed Col. chief of police with 30 years of service. He was an altar boy, active in St. Peter Parish picnics, in the mid-teens he assisted Rev. Maurice Tiell escort boys on tours to the seminary in St. Meinrad, IN.

She attended Catholic schools at St. Joseph and Owensboro Catholic High and graduated in 1959. She prays the holy rosary on a regular basis. She was a housewife, mother of four, a Cub Scout den mother in Immaculate Parish. She was an employee of Our Lady of Mercy Hospital several years as admitting clerk in the Emergency Room. She was an Owensboro police woman and served as a school crossing guard for 16 years.

He has been involved in several civic and community organizations: Optimist Club Member, Boy Scout post advisor, chairman GRCC Champions Against Drugs, coordinator Just Say No and D.A.R.E. rallies, Council on Homeless member, GRR Crime Commission, Dimas Charities Advisory Council member, ex. dir. of Mayors Crime Prevention Commission, chairman of Board Owensboro Area Spouse Abuse Shelter.

He is a member of: International Association of Chiefs of Police, Kentucky Association of Chiefs of Police, Kentucky Peace Officers Association, Kentucky Law Enforcement Council, Fraternal Order of Police as past president of treasurer.

On their 25th Wedding Anniversary (1984) a Mass was scheduled for celebration at St. Paul's Church and they were going to attend. Upon their arrival a notice was posted, the church had burned Christmas evening. They were disappointed and saddened. They prayed to Jesus and asked that the church be saved.

Their four children were born in Owensboro: Karen Lee Christian, Stephen Dale Schwartz, Keith Allen Schwartz and David Arthur Schwartz. They are the grandparents of five grandchildren. They attend Mass regularly at St. Stephen Cathedral Parish.

SCWARTZ, JAMES EVERETT, was born on June 11, 1920 near Stanley, Daviess County, KY. His father Arthur Conrad Schwartz was a farmer, and his mother, Annie Elizabeth Shively, was the daughter of Henry Shively and Susan Beaven who were also farmers. These families were members of St. Peter Catholic Parish in Stanley.

James married Lona Belle Clark of Owensboro, Daviess County, KY on June 17, 1939 at St. Peter Church officiated by Rev. Martin Nahstoll. He was a member of the Holy Name Society and the parish picnic cooking team. He was confirmed by Bishop Francis R. Cotton and he received an eighth grade certificate from St. Peter School.

Lona Belle was born on July 31, 1917, the daughter of Lee Alender and Clara Young Clark of Owensboro, KY. Lee was a carpenter and built homes. They were members of the First Christian Church.

James and his wife had eight children, five were born near Owensboro and three were born near Stanley. His work began in the oilfields until 1942, and he then worked as a welder in the Evansville shipyard. In 1944 he started work as an auto mechanic, also trucks, tractors and other farming machinery. He spent years farming on the side and when he left farming he worked for the city of Owensboro maintenance garage and retired from there.

Lona Belle had a daughter very ill and was going to require surgery. She was a regular church attender and she prayed to God for the safety of her child. In her prayers she promised God that if the child was saved, she would convert to the Catholic faith. With the guidance and teaching provided by the Rev. Aloysius F. Powers she joined the Catholic Church in 1947. She loved the holy rosary and remained a devout Catholic through out her life until succumbed by death from cancer on May 18, 1974.

James resides alone in Owensboro, is a member and regular attender of Mass at Sts. Joseph and Paul Parish.

He has eight living children, 20 grandchildren and eight great-grandchildren.

The children of James Everett Schwartz and Lona Belle Schwartz are: Arthur Lee "Sonny" Schwartz, Joyce Marie Williams, Anna Jane Mansfield, Patricia Ann Lambert, Clara Mae Doom, James Wetzel Schwartz, Terri Sue Powers and Cynthia Gale Johnson.

SCOTT, JAMES ORVILLE,

son of Harry Franklin Scott and Reba Oda Scott, married Oct. 9, 1965 at St. Francis De Sales, Mary Madeline Walker, daughter of Ernest Allen Walker of Toronto, Canada and Margaret Monica Conway of Greenwich Village, NY.

The Scott Family—Back Row: Mary and James Front Row: Steve and Philip.

James and Mary were born in Paducah, KY and baptized at St. Francis De Sales, as were their sons. They first met at St. Mary Academy. James was in the second grade, Mary in the first. Both classes were combined in the same classroom. Their academic years were spent in St. Mary's and St. Thomas More.

James entered the Army after high school, Mary attended Charity Hospital School of Nursing. The Catholic Youth Club brought them together.

James has worked for Bell Telephone for 27 years. Mary retired as an LPN to raise their sons. She also worked as a bookkeeper for the Boy Scout Office, is the recipient of the Silver Beaver Award, and is a doll artisan.

James and Mary were active in Boy Scout Pack and Troop 7 where Philip Gregory and Stephen Allen earned the Pavuli Dei, Ad Altari Dei and Eagle Scout. Besides scouting, the family was active in square dancing, Paducah's Swim Team, Boy's Choir, Tilghman Band Boosters, Steve was a band member and American Legion Bugler. Both boys were school photographers for Tilghman High School where they graduated. As summer employment, they were lifeguards at Noble Park Pool and taught Red Cross swimming lessons.

Philip was listed for two years in *Who's Who Among High School Students*. Steve was a member for three years in Academic All American Scholar Program. They both received scholarships to Murray State University where Philip graduated in 1991, he is presently employed as assistant manager at Sherwin Williams and helps with a youth group. Steve still attends M.S.U. At M.S.U., they were in the Newman Club, Alpha Kappa Psi Fraternity and worked at Harry Lee Waterfield Library. Steve was in marching and jazz bands as a trumpeter. He also plays with St. Francis Choir. Steve had perfect attendance for 12 years in CCD. Other organizations: Usher, Knight of Columbus, D of I, Altar Society, Paducah Piecemakers Quilt Club and Heartland Lace Guild.

SCOTT, WILLIAM ADDISON AND CATHERINE LEONORA (SPALDING),

were cradle Catholics born in Union County while it was still part of the Louisville Diocese. Add (1891-1955) was the son of Gordon General Winfield Scott (1853-1932) and Susan Mary (Hardesty) Scott (1855-1935). Add attended the public schools and Lockyear Business College, Evansville, IN. He worked as bookkeeper for the IC Railroad, as an insurance agent and agriculture agent, but the major part of his life work was on a farm near Sacred Heart Church and St. Vincent Academy.

William Addison and Catherine Leonora (Spalding) Scott

Leora (1891-1957) was the daughter of T. Ross (1861-1949?) and M. Laura (Wight) Spalding (1863-1955) cradle Catholics of Union County. In 1911 Leora graduated from Mount St. Joseph Academy, Maple Mount, KY. She and Add Scott were married April 2, 1913. They had nine children: Addison, Ralph, Helen, Elizabeth, Ben, Jane, Rosemary, Rita and Jimmy. All of the children went as day scholars to St. Vincent Academy and seven graduated from high school there. Addison and Ralph had to transfer to public schools for high school since SVA did not have males in the high school until later. Add and Leora spent their lives caring for their children, nursing their parents and feeding and caring for those they found in need.

SEGEBARTH, RONALD J.,

was born in Shreveport, LA, while his father, Ralph, was serving in the military. His mother was Virginia A. Throop Segebarth. He took instructions in the Catholic faith from the late Fr. Jerry Glahn in 1967. He married Marsha L. Craft, daughter of William and Margaret Craft. Fr. Jerry married the couple in Immaculate Conception Church in Earlington, KY in August 1968. He continued to be a good friend of the couple and hunted and fished with Ron.

After their marriage the couple lived in Speedway, IN for two years then moved to Omaha, NE where Ron attended dental school at Creighton University, graduating in 1974. During this time Marsha completed her bachelors degree in medical technology and began a master's degree.

Segebarth Family

In 1971, James Andrew "Andy" Segebarth was born. He was followed by Christopher "Scott" in 1973, Paul Bradley "Brad" in 1975, Cynthia "Suzanne" in 1979, Mary Katherine "Katie" in 1982 and Jennifer "Meagan" in 1984.

The family moved to Madisonville and became members of Christ the King Parish in May 1974. The boys attended Christ the King School for several years before transferring to Hanson Elementary School. The girls attend CCD classes at Christ the King.

Ron and Marsha serve on the Diocesan Family Life Committee, have served on the Christ the King School Board, have been members of the Christ the King Parish Council, and Marsha has served as a CCD teacher and is active in her local Right to Life group. She also serves as a lector and in the RCIA Program. Ron currently serves on the Diocesan Pastoral Council.

Ron has a dental practice in Madisonville, KY and Marsha is a part-time instructor at Madisonville Community College, having completed her master's degree before Brad's birth.

Andy and Scott are currently attending the University of Kentucky, both majoring in business.

SEILER, THEODORE JOSEPH,

married Margie Carol (Nenninger) Aug. 22, 1970. He is an auto worker at General Motors and she is a housewife. They have two children, Michael Joseph, who attends WKU, and Tammy Jo, a senior at Butler County High School. They reside in Morgantown, KY and are members of Holy Trinity Parish. Past members of Our Lady Parish in Festus, MO, St. John's in Leopold, MO and St. Joseph in Advance, MO. Margie taught religious education for three years. Teddy is a member of Knights of Columbus 5898 St. Johns, Leopold, MO.

SENG, GEORGE,

was born in Simpson County, KY on April 20, 1898. His parents were Peter and Mary Alice (Aaron) Seng; his only sibling, Sarah, died at the age of 16 in 1908. George's home for his entire life was Simpson County. During the years of his childhood and early adulthood, St. Mary was a mission of Sacred Heart Church in Russellville, and George, his parents, and his mother's family were some of the dwindling number of Catholics in the area. He was proud of being Catholic in an era when anti-Catholicism was strong, and was very public about being a member of St. Mary. Due to his outgoing and optimistic personality, George was involved over the years in a number of businesses that made him well-known and well-liked in the city of Franklin and the surrounding county. He was fond of saying that he never met a person he could not talk to and find some area of agreement, even if the discussion began on an anti-Catholic note.

George Seng

George never married, but he had a good friend, Edith Crafton, who took care of him for many years. Though he was virtually house-bound from the early 1980s, he still enjoyed visitors and their reports of the goings-on around town and church. He lived to see his parish grow from six families in 1946 to over 100 families at the present. George died peacefully in his sleep on Oct. 22, 1992 at the age of 94. When he died, he had a unique distinction: he was the last practicing Catholic who had been in Simpson County before World War II. George was part of the parish for 94 of its 124 years!

SHAVER, JACOB L. AND MARY JO, moved to Sturgis shortly after their marriage in 1959. Jacob, usually known as "Pat" is a dentist, and Mary Jo is a nurse-educator who teaches at Union County High School.

While there are a number of Shavers in Western Kentucky, notably Muhlenberg County, Pat is one of the few who have converted to Catholicism. His baptism after his conversion was by Fr. Allard, who was serving St. Francis Borgia as pastor at that time. Mary Jo Shaver, nee Hildesheim, was born in Louisville and attended Holy Trinity School, Presentation Academy and St. Anthony School of Nursing in the city before her marriage.

The Shavers have been active in the growth of St. Francis Borgia Parish. Both have served on the Parish Pastoral Council and each have chaired that body. When the CCD Program was first introduced into the parish, each taught for number of years. At present Mary Jo is a Minister of Music for the church. They enjoy participating in the Catholic community in Sturgis.

Jacob L. and Mary Jo Shaver

Pat and Mary Jo have raised three children. Mary Shannon is married to Bill Cleavenger and presently resides in Morganfield with her three children, Eddie, Jake and Chris. Steve Shaver is married to the former Lindy Bruce from Mayfield. Samantha attends the University of Louisville School of Dentistry.

SHAVER, MICHAEL DEAN AND KATHY LORETTA ROBERTS, were married on June 12, 1992. Mike is the son of Harrold and Judy Shaver of Owensboro. Mike has an 8 year old daughter, Amy Lee Shaver. Mike graduated from Daviess County High and is employed at Owensboro Municipal Utilities as an equipment operator.

Kathy is the daughter of Rose Ann Roberts and the late Lawrence Roberts Jr. She is the youngest of nine children. Kathy graduated from Daviess County High and is employed at Carmel Home as social service director.

Mike and Kathy are members of St. Joseph and Paul Catholic Church. Mike is involved in church soft ball and enjoys fishing and hunting. Kathy enjoys craft activities. Mike and Kathy are living on Old Mill Lane.

SHEERAN, Elias and Margaret Rhodes, Ignatius and Sarah Coomes and the Fowler family migrated to Kentucky with the first Catholic settlers. A few years later Margaret Sheeran, a widow, came from Ireland with her sons and daughters. These were men and women of strong faith who proclaimed the Good News by their daily lives. Among their descendants have been many priestly and religious vocations, dedicated single persons and married couples who have passed the faith on through the generations. Among these latter were Denis Sheeran and Elizabeth Coomes who were married in St. Romuald Church on Nov. 5, 1902. As they could not afford a honeymoon, Denis took his bride home that same day. The house was poor, but Elizabeth began at once to make it a beautiful home. They were always poor in material things, but rich in virtue. They worked hard and made many sacrifices for their children.

The children attended the one-room school in Kirk where one teacher taught all eight grades. Each week Fr. Knue came to the school and, with permission, took the Catholic children to a nearby Catholic home where he taught Catechism and Bible History. When the five month school ended Elizabeth taught her children and some of the neighbor's children in her home for about three months. After finishing the eighth grade some of the children went to St. Romuald's High School.

Edna Sheeran is the only member of the family who still lives in St. Romuald Parish. She and Cecilia Wheatley have lived together for many years. Cecilia is a descendant of Elias and Margaret Rhodes and Leonard Wheatley who was also among the pioneers who settled in Kentucky. Edna and Cecilia continue the good works of their concern for their neighbors and their countless acts of charity.

SHELTON, JAMES EDMOND AND SHERYL LYNN, Sheryl Lynn McWilliams, daughter of Roy and Carolyn McWilliams was born in Evansville, IN. She was baptized at Holy Spirit Parish in Evansville. In 1968, the McWilliams family, including children Sherri, Randy and Mindy, moved to Henderson. In 1975 Sherri graduated from Holy Name Grade School. After graduating from Henderson County High School in 1979, she enrolled in the nursing program at Henderson Community College. She met her husband, Jim Shelton (a Henderson native) and they were married on Nov. 2, 1979 at the First United Methodist Church in Henderson. When Joshua Roy was born, Sherri withdrew from college to become a full-time wife and mother. Sherri and Jim have three other children, Brandon James, Dane Joseph and Scarlett Bethany. While participating in the parish's fall festival, Jim met many friends and decided to attend RCIA classes in 1987. Sherri became involved with the Welcoming Committee and the Prayer Line at Holy Name and Jim became an usher. After receiving an annulment of his first marriage, Jim and Sherri were remarried at Holy Name in June of 1989, Jim also received the sacraments of Holy Communion, reconciliation and confirmation on that same day with Fr. Phil Riney presiding.

The Sheltons-Jim, Sherri, Josh, Brandon, Dane and Scarlett.

Josh, Brandon and Dane are currently attending Holy Name School. Sherri is now completing her associate degree in nursing; Jim is presently employed with Gibbs Die Cast and Aluminum as a trim manager.

In the spring of this year, Jim and Sherri attended the Cursillo weekend in Princeton, KY.

Currently, the Shelton family are members of the Holy Name Rosary Prayer Group and have plans to become more involved in serving Holy Name Parish.

SHOEMAKER, CHARLES MICHAEL (MIKE), was born June 10, 1958 in Owensboro, KY. He was baptized at St. Stephen Cathedral. His parents are Charles and Mary Ruth Shoemaker. He has three brothers and four sisters. He received his early education at St. Stephen Cathedral Grade School, and graduated from Owensboro Catholic High School. He liked Catholic schools because of their religious beliefs. After graduation, he worked several years for Green River Steel in Owensboro. He works as a self employed builder now. He enjoys his home and loves to work in his yard.

He is a member of St. Stephen Cathedral. For his hobbies, he enjoys reading the Bible and American history. He also enjoys walking. He is a member of several Bible study groups.

Mike recalls helping his dad, brothers and sisters cleaning estate homes for sale to help pay their tuition to attend Catholic schools. While attending Owensboro Catholic High, he worked part-time as a gas station attendant and enjoyed meeting and talking to many different people.

Charles Michael Shoemaker

He appreciates his Catholic education from Owensboro Catholic High and the teacher and principals who helped him. He continues his education by attending Adult Learning classes.

SHOEMAKER, DAVID AND DIANE JOHNSON, were married at Holy Name Catholic Church on June 4, 1976 by Fr. E.E. Willett.

David is the son of Ray and Evelyn Shoemaker of Henderson. David has been a member of Holy Name Church all of his life. He attended Holy Name School until the high school was closed his junior year. Then he attended Henderson County High School his senior year.

Diane was raised a Baptist, but had a strong Catholic influence. Most of her best friends and neighbors were Catholic and attended Holy Name. Diane attended Holy Name Church with David for many years and became a Catholic member in 1985 after going through the RCIA Program.

Diane and David have two girls, Amanda and Sara. Amanda is 12 years old, and Sara is 9 years old. Both girls attend Holy Name School.

Both David and Diane are active in different activities at Holy Name Church and Holy Name School. David has been active in the Knight of Columbus since 1972. He was Grand Knight from 1990-1992. He has been active with the Fall Festival and Summer Social. Diane helps with bereavement dinners, fall festivals and different religious receptions. She does most of her volunteering at the school for many different projects. Both David and Diane made a Cursillo in 1988.

SHOEMAKER, MARY ROSE, was born near St. Joseph in western Daviess County on Feb. 27, 1922. She was the daughter of Andrew and Margaret Lee Shoemaker. She thinks family, prayer, attending Mass and Catholic schools influenced her careers in life. She participated in Mission projects in high school. They gave her ideas of missionary work which developed in her education at St. Louis University. She volunteered to read to the aged priests at the university and they related their missionary work to her.

She volunteered in many Catholic missionary projects in varied parts of the country with missionaries. She taught, worked, tutored foreign students and the poor there.

Mary Rose Shoemaker

She worked in careers of Naval records, medical records librarian, teaching and anthropology research. She graduated from Mount St. Joseph and Brescia College. She received a master's degree in anthropology and did post graduate work at St. Louis University. She was awarded grants from the Universities of St. Louis, Washington, D.C., Pace in New York, Chicago and Freedoms Foundation of Valley Forge, PA. She received a National Freedom Award in 1974 and in 1981 from Freedoms Foundation. She is a recipient of many state and local awards. She received Golden Poetry awards from World Poetry Press in California where her poems are published. She is a member of "Who's Who in Poetry" there. She is a member of Catholic and professional organizations.

Since her retirement, she is a Eucharistic minister to sick at Mercy Hospital and in her parish at St. Stephen's Cathedral. She works at funeral meals, bulletin folding and minister of hospitality there. She appreciates the continued religious education provided by the diocese hospital and parish for her volunteer work. She has enjoyed and thanks God and many people who influenced her life.

SHOEMAKER, RAY AND EVELYN SCHWEIZER,

were married on Oct. 18, 1947, at Holy Trinity Catholic Church, Evansville, IN. Ray worked as an insurance investigator for Retail Credit Company and was transferred to Illinois where they lived until October 1952, when Henderson became home.

They brought with them their four children, Donna, Teresa, JoAnn and Danny and were subsequently blessed with eight other children David, Eddie, Annette, Patrick, Mary Evelyn, Rita, Kelley and Jimmy.

Eight children were baptized, 11 confirmed, and eight married at Holy Name Church. They all graduated from Holy Name Grade School and four graduated from Holy Name High School.

JoAnn's husband, Jack Jacobs, became a member of Holy Name through the RCIA program, as did David's wife, Diane, and Eddie's wife, Betty.

In the early years at Holy Name, Ray was president of the PTA and Grand Knight of the Knight of Columbus. He also served as Eucharistic minister, usher and church council member, and volunteer at St. Vincent De Paul. Evelyn became active in PTA, Altar Society and the Knights of Columbus Ladies Auxiliary where she has served as president, and a volunteer for St. Vincent De Paul. Both Ray and Evelyn made Cursillo in 1970.

In 1953, the family bought a home on Bishop Lane at Graham Hill where they lived until 1988. Ray was insurance agent for Knights of Columbus from 1976 until his retirement in 1988. Ray and Evelyn now reside in Henderson, where their children and 21 grandchildren can come visit often. Needless to say, it is also convenient to Holy Name Church and school where the family is still deeply involved.

SHUMAKER, JAMES L. M.D.,

was born Nov. 3, 1934. He graduated from St. Mary Academy, Paducah, KY in 1952; University of Notre Dame in 1956; Indiana University Medical School in 1960. Served in the U.S. Army from 1961-1967. Residency in pediatrics 1967-1969. Moved back home to Paducah in 1969 to open a practice of pediatrics.

Camilla Mason Campbell Daniels Shumaker was born Dec. 31, 1945 in Morganfield, KY. Graduated from St. Ann Grade School in 1959; St. Vincent Academy in 1963; Fontbonne Catholic Girls College 1963-1965; and graduated from the University of Kentucky in 1967. Married James Ron Daniels from Valparaiso, IN on May 18, 1968. Daughter Vicki Lynn Daniels was born May 29, 1970, graduated from University of Kentucky in 1992. Son James Christopher Daniels was born Jan. 28, 1972, now attending Georgetown College. Married James L. Shumaker Jan. 3, 1979. Children: James Link Shumaker Jr. born Jan. 3, 1979, attending St. Mary Middle School; Paul Daniel Shumaker born Jan. 28, 1982, attending St. Mary Elementary School; and John Jerimiah Shumaker born March 6, 1985, now attending St. Mary Elementary School.

They are currently living in Paducah, KY, McCracken County since 1969 for Camilla, and since birth for James, except for education and service. They are members of St. Thomas More Parish and past members of St. Francis De Sales (James) and St. Ann's in Morganfield (Camilla). Members of Parish Council, parenting step program, RENEW, Genesis II, Life in the Spirit seminar, Eucharist minister, altar boys, lector and Bereavement Committee.

The James L. Shumaker Family

Camilla is the daughter of Benson Walker Campbell Jr. and Margaret Clements Mason Campbell; step-mother LaVonne Campbell. Granddaughter of Allen Gordon Mason (deceased), not Catholic and Margaret Clements Mason (deceased), member St. Ann's, Morganfield, KY. Also Benson Walker Campbell Marietta, OK, non-Catholic; Belle Bunting Campbell (deceased), non-Catholic, Beulah Campbell (deceased) step-grandmother.

Camilla works as a homemaker and bookkeeper at her husband's office.

Jim and Camilla shared one of the same Sister of Charity teachers during their high school years. They appreciate their pastor, Fr. Jerry Riney and all the priests in Paducah.

SIMON, ANNA LAURA,

in religion Sister Mary Thomas of the Handmaids of the Lamb of God, was born May 2, 1936 near Curdsville, in Daviess County. She is the daughter of Thomas Louis and Gertrude Coomes Simon. The fourth of 16 children of which 10 were reared to adulthood.

Sister remembers walking with two of her sisters from their home at West Louisville to St. Alphonsus on Saturday mornings for classes. The weather was hot and the way a bit long, yet the only real obstacle was a big red bull that would always come running to the fence making it seem dangerously impossible to continue the route. In August 1954 the three were allowed sacraments.

Sister Mary Thomas

Gratitude will always be to Rev. Joseph McAleer who gently instructed them and to Rev. Henry Willett who planted an active love for the church in their hearts.

September 1955, Sister was confirmed by Bishop Cotton in his private chapel. With his blessing Sister left for France to join community and thus fulfilled an inner yearning of service to God and others.

September 1958, she took vows and returned to Owensboro. September 1965, she was graced with final vows. February 1970 brought sorrowful news to the family and parish. James Martin Simon, age 19, gave his life during the Vietnam War.

In January 1976, the father died. The mother followed him in death in 1986.

The nine remaining children are: Francis Ivo Simon, Helen Marie Boarman, Thomas Robert Simon, Sister Mary Thomas, Connie Mae Hood, Mary Emma Howard, William Edward Simon, Margaret Rose Cannon and Judy Katherine Warner.

William is single and has the home place. Others are married and living in the Owensboro Diocese except Francis who, after the Korean War, married and remained in Northern California.

For the last 10 years Sister has found contentment caring for Marie Ziegler, the mother of Fr. Anthony Ziegler in the Diocese of Owensboro.

SIMS,

The Mary Teresa (Tong) and Joseph Robert (J.R.) Sims family began in Rome, KY when the two neighbors married at St. Martin's Church on Nov. 23, 1935, witnessed by the Rev. Carlos Poole. Mary's parents were Columbus O. and Mary Teresa (Mullican) Tong. Jimmy was the son of Joseph Henry and Jesse (Beavin) Sims. Mary was a schoolteacher and Jimmy a tenant farmer and they moved from Rome to Calhoun, back to St. Joseph, KY and later bought their first farm on Reid Road in Eastern Daviess County (now the site of the Greenbrier Subdivision). Mary stopped teaching when they married and the family grew to 11 children, two of whom died as infants. Surviving children are: Gertrude Marie Frey, Timothy Joseph, Alan Douglas, Stephen Matthew, Rita Suzanne, Philip Rex, Thomas Mark, Mary Teresa McGraw and Delores Kay Turnage.

Early in the 1960s, another farm was purchased and in 1962 the family farm was sold and they moved a short distance to Thruston while Jimmy farmed the 200 acre farm in southern Indiana and later sold this to become a farm implement salesman. He died suddenly in 1969. Meanwhile, the youngest child had begun Catholic elementary school at St. Pius X in Owensboro and Mary began teaching there and taught for 23 more years. All the children had a Catholic education throughout elementary and high school, and all were married, except Suzanne who entered the Mount St. Joseph Ursuline Community in 1966 when she finished high school. Mary also worked simultaneously at a nursing home in Owensboro for 17 years on weekends as an aide and moved to Owensboro in 1981 where she retired from teaching but continued part-time at the nursing home until 1989. She now resides at the Carmel Home in Owensboro. There are 26 grandchildren, who live in Kentucky, Florida, Indiana and New Jersey and 10 great-grandchildren.

Jimmy was proud of a family who would "fill up the pew" on Sunday's, but also on First Fridays. He was active in St. Vincent De Paul and Holy Name ocieties all his adult life and loved cooking burgoo for the parish picnics. Mary went back to college in the 1960 to gain more credits to teach and to update herself in the "new math." She also had a huge garden each summer which she preserved and canned as well as doing a lot of sewing for each child. While teaching she took a summer job at the former Camera Shop in Owensboro for a few years.

Prayer was always a daily family activity in their family and the rosary a family prayer, especially during May and October. Baptisms, First Communions, Confirmations, weddings and religious profession have always been big family events for celebration.

Each year the family gathers for reunion the weekend after the Fourth of July for a barbecue, volleyball, cards and lots of other fun.

SIMS, SAMUEL THOMAS AND GLADYS KIDWELL, were united in marriage in January 1927 at St. Benedict Church at Wax. Gladys was not a Catholic at the time but later joined the church. They had 15 children together, 10 boys and five girls throughout their 27 years of marriage. Tommie died of a heart attack in 1954 leaving Gladys with nine children under of the age of 15. She did the best she could to send them to school and church but without a car it was hard. A neighbor (her brother-in-law) had a large farm truck that he drove to church on Sunday's and he would pick up anyone along the way who wanted to go to St. Anthony's at Peonia.

Six years later Gladys married Jurial Hill. They bought a farm and moved into the St. Paul Parish. With seven children still at home it was rough. They didn't have any children together but they shared lots of grandchildren and great-grandchildren. Jurial died of cancer after 23 years of marriage leaving Gladys alone. She has lost three of her sons in the past 10 years. She still has a garden and pieces quilts and cooks a lot for her family. She attends St. Paul's Church on Sunday mornings with several of her children and their families. Gladys is now 81 years of age and has 60 grandchildren and 61 great-grandchildren. In April of 1993 she is expecting her first great-great-grandchild. Hope she has many more.

SLOBIG, FATHER CHARLES B., of Louisville, KY, received a master's in education. He is a member of Carmelite Order. Received first degree in February 1936; fourth degree in November 1985. He is presently chaplain of Blessed Mother. Retired in 1985.

SMITH, DOUG AND MARY, belong to the St. Paul Parish near Leitchfield, KY. They have two young children, Jared and Wesley.

The Smith Family

Mary has been a member of St. Paul Parish all her life. Doug is originally from Peonia, KY and was a member of St. Anthony Church in Peonia. They were married on May 17, 1986 at St. Paul's Church with Rev. Tony Stevenson performing the ceremony.

Doug is an engineer for the Kentucky State Department of Transportation and an active member of the Knights of Columbus. Mary works in the home caring for their children and babysitting.

Presently, they are building a new home which they plan to be living in soon.

SMITH, EUGENE, was born at Grayson Springs, Grayson County, KY on Aug. 29, 1939, the youngest of 12 children of George Allen Smith and Bertha Belle Clemons Smith. Eugene was baptized by Rev. Benedict F. Huff on Sept. 9, 1939 at St. Augustine Church on Bear Creek at Grayson Springs.

George and Bertha owned the farm on the south and west side of the St. Augustine Church property and lived in a large two story house adjoining the cemetery where Eugene and the younger children were born. George was a carpenter, blacksmith, miller, part-time farmer and a bridge construction foreman by trade. In 1930 when George and Bertha bought the farm they traded with Rev. Edward Russell, the pastor at St. Anthony's in charge of the St. Augustine mission, to tear down a large rectory at St. Augustine which was no longer needed and to build a small three room house on the site. In return for this, George was to get all the excess material. From this he built the two story house, into which the family, consisting of eight children moved upon completion. George was born March 20, 1891 across Nolin River from the St. Benedict Church in Hart County, KY. He was not born of the Catholic faith. His parents were Theodore "Thee" H.M. Smith and Sarah Ellen Wood. Smith moved to and spent the rest of their lives in Grayson County near the site of the old St. Benedict Church on Nolin River at Wax, KY. Most all the families in the area were Catholic. George courted and married Bertha Belle Clemons from a devout Catholic family. She was the daughter of Andrew Jackson Clemons and Margaret Thomas Clemons, Clemons, first cousins, and both descendants of Thomas W. Clemons and Letticia Duell who were married Oct. 12, 1836 in St. Joseph Cathedral by Rev. M. J. Spaulding.

George and Bertha were married and George was baptized into the Catholic faith on April 9, 1910 by Rev. Anthony Helling at St. Elizabeth Church in Clarkson, KY. The churches of St. Anthony, St. Augustine and St. Benedict were missions of St. Elizabeth at the time as Father Helling had left the St. Augustine rectory two years earlier and the new St. Anthony Church was not completed.

Probably through the influence of George and Bertha and others in the community, George's parents and his five living sisters were all converted as Catholics before their death. Both his and Bertha's parents are all buried at St. Benedict Cemetery at Wax.

George died Sept. 19, 1980 and was preceded in death by Bertha Jan. 26, 1968. Both are buried just over the line from their home of 50 years in St. Augustine Cemetery.

Eugene grew up on Bear Creek at Grayson Springs, attended Peonia Grade School, a public school taught by the Ursuline Nuns, entered St. Paul High School and graduated in the class of 1957. In September of 1957 he went to work for the Kentucky Highway Department on the construction engineering crew at Leitchfield, KY. A.B. "Happy" Chandler was governor at the time and the state was preparing to enter into the construction era of the interstate highway system. Eugene was one of about 300 high school graduates who were hired and trained over the years for this purpose. He attended several mandatory and voluntary training sessions over the next several years, became both a registered professional engineer and a licensed land surveyor and moved up through the ranks to the position of district maintenance engineer at highway district Number Four office in Elizabethtown, KY. He retired from this position at the age of 48 with 30 years service on Sept. 1, 1987. Eugene is presently a part-time farmer, property developer, and practices his engineering and land surveying profession on a part-time basis.

Eugene was married on Oct. 25, 1958 by Rev. Victor C. Boarman to Georgetta Johnston, one of a family of 14 children of Ewell Thomas Johnston and Mary Vera Bradley Johnston at the old St. Benedict Church on Nolin River at Wax, KY. The Johnston family was also of the Catholic faith. Ewell (born Sept. 30, 1907-died April 8, 1989), Vera B. (born Aug. 7, 1911-died July 20, 1984), along with both their parents Theadore "Dode" Johnston and Annie Elizabeth Clemons Johnston and John Thomas "Dick" Bradley and Millie Easter Wilson Bradley are buried at St. Benedict Cemetery.

Georgetta was born Nov. 6, 1939 at Dog Creek just across the river from Wax in Hart County, KY and was baptized by Rev. Benedict F. Huff on Dec. 8, 1939 at St. Benedict. The family soon moved across the river to Grayson County and the children attended St. Benedict Catholic Grade School. Georgetta attended St. Paul High School for two years.

After marriage Eugene and Georgette lived in a small house built by his father just across the cemetery from St. Augustine Church. In 1961 they purchased a farm on the Huffman Road in the Meredith Community about two miles from St. Anthony Church in Peonia. Since that time they have been members of the St. Anthony Parish. They are the parents of five children: Douglas Eugene (born Oct. 13, 1959) married Mary Darst, Philip Ray (born Feb. 9, 1961) married Tracie Lusby, Annete Marie (born Jan. 19, 1962) unmarried, Thomas Allen born (Jan. 26, 1963) unmarried and Joseph Gil (born Dec. 17, 1964), unmarried. Eugene and Georgetta are the proud grandparents of four boys, Jared Douglas born Oct. 22, 1988; Wesley Adam born Aug. 3, 1990 (Douglas and Mary); Alexander Phillip born Sept. 26, 1988; and Matthew Thomas who was born Jan. 14, 1992 (Phillip and Tracie).

In 1972 Eugene and Georgetta owned and operated a local store business which later became known as "Smitty City." The business catered somewhat to the local trade, but mostly served the tourist trade to nearby Nolin Lake and Mammoth Cave. The store is now owned by Bill and Alberta Sims.

Eugene and Georgetta are both active in the operation of St. Anthony Parish. He serves on the Parish Council, is the leader of the finance committee, an usher and is Deputy Grand Knight of the Father Carroll White Council of the Knights of Columbus. He has just completed a two year term as the St. Anthony's representative to the Eastern Deanery Council and was St. Anthony's delegate to the recent Diocese of Owensboro Synod. Georgetta serves as a Eucharistic minister, is on the Social Concerns Committee and is the director of the Funeral Bereavement Meal Committee. Both served on the renovation committee in the 1991 renovation of St. Anthony Church.

Joseph Gill, still living at home, works for the parishes of St. Anthony, St. Augustine and St. Benedict as the grounds keeper.

SMITH, SR. FRANCIS XAVIER, was born Aug. 1, 1893 in Owensboro, KY, the only daughter of Cornelius and Frances Long Smith, and a sister to six boys. Baptized Martha Serena Aug. 25, 1893. She came to Mount St. Joseph to enter when she was 17. She was invested with the habit on Aug. 30, 1910, together with 12 other young ladies. She probably knew the farm hands here well since she lived at Brown's Valley, and she would ask them for donations for treats for herself and her classmates. Peanut butter and crackers were a real treat at that time, and it was probably treats like this that she may have gotten, but Sister Stanislaus said she was embarrassed just the same about her asking for these things. Almost her entire life in religion was spent in the parochial school of Marion and Washington Counties, at Raywick and Howardstown, where she was recognized as a zealous and efficient teacher.

She was deeply concerned with the study for the priesthood of her brother Leo. She was afraid that he would be drafted into the war, and this thought prompted her to write the following letter to Our Blessed Mother, which is in her personal file:

Dearest Mother, promising you to have 10 Masses offered in your honor, under the title of Our Lady of Victory, for the suffering souls of priests-souls that are dearest to the heart of Your Divine Son, if you will help to obtain exemption from the draft law and his perseverance in his studies. I will persuade relatives to have these Masses offered as my Vow of Poverty will prevent me from saying that "I" will have it done. I pray always to remain your grateful child. (Signed Sister Francis Xavier). Obtain for me perfect resignation to the Will of your Son in all trials and crosses. If Malcolm is to die on the battlefield, accept his life as a great prayer for Leo's exemption.

Leo became a priest and served for long years in the parishes of the Diocese of Louisville; Ursuline Sisters taught for him at Calvary up until his death on Dec. 30, 1972. At Leo's ordination and First Mass Malcolm was present in 1922. *The Record* of that year spoke of Malcolm as a "wounded hero of the Great War."

Sister Francis Xavier died on Sunday morning, Sept. 7, 1924 at St. Anthony's Hospital were she had undergone a major operation on that previous Tuesday. Her remains were conveyed to the Mount where the funeral services were held on the feast of Our Lady's Nativity. Besides her parents and her brother, Fr. Smith, she is survived by her brothers, Malcolm, Charles, Monroe, Beckham, Jean and Aloysius.

SMITH, GEORGE ALLEN, the only son of Theodore Harman Monthavale Smith and Sarah Ellen Wood, was born March 20, 1891 near Wax, Grayson County, KY. On April 9, 1910, he was baptized and married Bertha Belle Clemons at St. Elizabeth Church, Clarkson, KY with Rev. Anthony Helling officiating. Bertha Belle Clemons, the daughter of a local merchant, Andrew Jackson Clemons and Margaret Thomas Clemons, members of St. Benedict Church, Wax, KY, was born March 15, 1895 at Pearman, KY.

They lived in various communities within the St. Benedict Parish. Mr. Smith farmed, did carpentry work, operated a general store and was postmaster of Snap, KY. When fire destroyed their home and business at Snap, the family moved frequently and, for a brief period, they lived at Peonia in St. Anthony Parish.

Prior to September 1926, the Smith family settled at Grayson Springs. On April 1, 1930, they purchased 68 acres on Bear Creek bordering the St. Augustine Church property. Here Mr. Smith built a house with material salvaged from the old St. Augustine Rectory he had razed.

At Grayson Springs, the Smiths became active members of St. Augustine Parish. The parish church had great importance for them and their Catholic faith was their way of life. They established a family of strong Catholic principals and devout religious practices. Their faith supported them when their infant son died in 1934 and again in 1943 when a son was killed in Northern Africa. Their prayers went with four sons as they served their country during World War II.

George Allen Smith and wife, Bertha Belle Clemons with child, Mary Ruth Smith (1912).

They had 12 children: Mary Ruby (Higdon), Clifford Anthony, Delbert Augustine (deceased), William Cletus (deceased), Carlos Leo, Edsel James (deceased), George Allen, Anna Catherine (Kelty), Rosemary (Dawood), Joseph Ray (deceased), Elizabeth Joyce (Hopper) and Ambrose Eugene Smith.

Mrs. Smith died Jan. 29, 1968 and Mr. Smith died Sept. 16, 1980. They are buried in St. Augustine Cemetery.

SMITH, JOHN PAUL, was born at Sorgho, KY, the son of the late Bernard Smith and Lillian McCann. He was a member of St. Mary Magdalene Parish. On Feb. 27, 1965, he married Beverly O'Bryan, daughter of Wallace O'Bryan and Sophia Kaelin (presently residents of Carmel Home) from St. Alphonsus Parish. They lived in Our Lady of Lourdes Parish where their sons, John Paul II and Brad Williams were born before moving to St. Alphonsus Parish where Michael was born. Their oldest son was married in April 1992, and their second son joined the community of The Sons of Mary in Rome as a seminarian in September 1992. He is serving his postulant and later plans to study at the Angelicum.

The John P. and Beverly Smith Family

Paul and Beverly are active in the Army of Mary and the Family of the Sons and Daughters of Mary. They also transport the Pilgram Virgin Statue from home to home to anyone desiring to have a visit from the Blessed Mother.

Paul is a lector and has served as a Eucharistic minister. Beverly is an officer in the Altar Society-Christian Mothers and was bookkeeper for several years in the parish school.

SMITH, ROBERT W. JR., was born in Breckinridge County, the son of Robert W. Smith Sr. and Gladys Marie Spink. Robert W. Jr. and his three brothers and four sisters were born on a farm adjoining the Mount Merina Church, the early Catholic Church at Irvington. The Smiths lived on the Kasey farm in the early years then bought the joining farm where they continued to live from birth until they married and moved away from home. Most of them lived close to their roots. They belonged to Holy Guardian Angel Church from birth to adulthood. Robert W. Jr.'s grandparents on his mother's side came from a long line of Catholics.

Robert W. Jr. married Margaret Mary Thompson and they became the parents of three daughters, Vickie Elaine, Rhonda Ann and Sharon Faye Smith. Their mother died at the age of 26. Several years later Robert W. Jr. married Margaret Payne and the family joined Holy Guardian Angel Church that Robert had grown up as a member of. Robert Jr. had five grandchildren, Jonathon Rory Todd, Jessica Todd, Brandi and Tara Margaret Dore and Lauren Paige Hall. Rhonda Dore Smith and her two daughters, Brandi and Tara Margaret were members of Holy Guardian Angel Church at Irvington, KY. The daughters of Rhonda made their First Communion at the church where their grandfather had been baptized, First Communion and was married at their second marriage.

SNYDER, JOSEPH BRENT AND RUTH ANN ATHERTON, were married in Pleasant Hope General Baptist Church Calhoun, KY on Nov. 6, 1976. Ruth joined the Catholic Church on June 10, 1979. Joe and Ruth were remarried by Rev. Henry O'Bryan at this time in St. Anthony's Parish at Browns Valley, KY.

Joe graduated from St. Martin Elementary, and then went on to graduate from OCHS in 1972. Ruth attended McLean County High School in Calhoun, KY. Joe and Ruth have two sons. Brandon is a freshman at OCHS and Tommy is in the seventh grade at OCMS. Brandon and Tommy have been altar boys since 1987. They have served weddings, funerals and regular Masses. Brandon is active in their youth group at Our Lady of Lourdes and has been playing football since he was in the fourth grade. Tommy played football and was active in Cub Scouts.

Joe is the oldest son born to Joseph Bertraum Snyder and Judith Rachel Raferty Snyder. Joe has one younger brother and sister. He was born and raised in West Louisville, KY, St. Joseph area.

Ruth is the youngest of four daughters born to Ray Haswell Atherton and Mildred Rae Atherton. Ruth was born in Kansas City, MO, where her father was stationed in the U. S. Air Force. Her family moved to Daviess County, KY in the late 60s.

Joe helped coach the first Catherine Spalding football team where Brandon and Tommy both played that season. As a team they were undefeated in regular season and the championship games. The team put their trophies in the new school.

SNYDER, MARY BELLE CHILES, was born June 17, 1906 at Maxon Mill, McCracken County, KY, daughter of Garland and Gertrude Fenwick Chiles. Her grandparents Thomas and Amanda Fenwick were among the 11 Catholic families in the county.

They helped build St. Thomas More Catholic Church in the Summer of 1903 on the Paducah and Cairo gravel road two miles west of Maxon Mill.

The property for the church was given by her uncle J.C. Reeves on Jan. 10, 1893 to Rt. Rev. William George McCloskey Roman Catholic Bishop of Louisville, KY. The church was blessed by Rev. McCloskey in November 1903.

Fr. A. O'Sullivan drove two horses and buggy on gravel and dirt roads 19 miles on the first Tuesday of each month and spent the night with her grandparents, Thomas and Amanda Fenwick, drove to church, said Mass, returned for breakfast, then back to Paducah.

Her grandparents retired. Fr. Francis Cotton (later became Bishop Cotton) came to her parents home for the night, ate breakfast and returned home.

Paulist Fr. Clinton Allord conducted a mission at St. Thomas in 1915. Her father joined the church.

A tornado swept through the county about midnight March 28, 1924, taking the church from the foundation. The building was badly twisted and damaged. Attempts were made to replace and repair it. Yet the damage was so great the structure was unsafe. Her mother purchased the material March 15, 1930 that could be salvaged and built a house in West Paducah, KY.

J. Raymond and Mary Belle Snyder

She married Aug. 31, 1926 to J. Raymond Snyder, had a daughter, Glorya Juyne Snyder Wemple. All members of St. Thomas are dead except her brother, Bush Chiles, Billy Fenwick, Elizabeth and Emery McKinney, Frances O'Nan, Richard and Vickie Grief, Ann Criswell, J. Raymond and Mary Belle Snyder, who attend St. Francis De Sales.

SNYDER, SONDRA ANN, was born Sept. 16, 1951. She grew up in a family of four sisters and parents with the name of Charles Francis Bickwermert and Lettie Pearl Bickwermert. Joseph Brent Snyder was born on March 8, 1954. They were married on Oct. 2, 1992.

Sondra has two children, Tracy Lynn McLean and Charles Michael McLean. Tracy was born on Oct. 30, 1971. She goes to Eastern Kentucky University, she is a full-time student and works at Pizza Hut. Michael was born on Oct. 14, 1977 and goes to OCMS. He serves for St. Stephen's Cathedral. Joseph also has two children, Joseph Brandon Snyder and Thomas Richard Snyder. Brandon was born June 13, 1977 and goes to OCMS and Tommy was born Oct. 15, 1979 and attends OCMS. They all became one big family on Oct. 2, 1992 and belong to St Stephen's Cathedral.

SOENNEKER, HENRY JOSEPH, was born in Melrose, MN, on May 27, 1907 to Henry and Mary Soenneker, immigrants from Neuenkirchen, Germany. He attended the Pontifical College Josephinum from 1921 until his ordination in 1934. From his earliest days as a priest, people remembered him as a patient listener in time of trouble, an ardent advocate of devotions to Mary and a zealous teacher in the schools. His kindness and gentleness as a confessor, his well-prepared sermons, his interest in every person especially those in need or in sorrow, endeared this tall simple priest to all his parishioners. Father Soenneker filled many positions during his priestly career.

He was chaplain, spiritual director, vocation director, presiding judge of the Diocesan Court all of this while at the same time serving as pastor. Henry J. Soenneker was consecrated bishop on April 26, 1961 and installed as the second bishop of the Diocese of Owensboro on May 9, 1961 at the St. Stephen Cathedral. He served the Diocese as Bishop from 1961-1982, when he reached the mandatory retirement age. He remained in Owensboro until his death from a heart attack on Sept. 24, 1987. His memory will last with us forever.

SPAIN, SR. JAMESINA, was born April 21, 1911 in Nelson County, at New Haven, KY. Her paternal grandparents were James R. Spain I, born June 9, 1832 and Elizabeth Thornberry, born Oct. 10, 1832. He was a farmer and blacksmith who served in the Civil War. They were lifelong members of St. Catherine Church, New Haven, KY. Her maternal grandparents attended Holy Cross Church, Holy Cross, KY. No other information is known about them.

Jamesina Spain

Her father, James R. Spain II, was born Oct. 15, 1874. Her sisters were Gertrude, Ethel, Edith, and Geraldine. She was baptized Margaret Elizabeth. Her mother died May 5, 1912 when she was 13 months old. She was cared for by her father and her two older sisters until she was six years old at which time her father remarried.

Her elementary school education was in Nelson County Public Schools. Secondary education was at St. Catherine High School, New Haven and St. Charles High School in Marion County. Upon graduation from St. Catherine in June 1930, she entered Mount St. Joseph Novitiate.

Sr. Jamesina began teaching in 1933. She taught 18 years in the public schools of Meade and Marion Counties and more than 20 years in numerous parochial schools in the Archdiocese Louisville and the Diocese of Owensboro.

As a second career she served as DRE and Pastoral Minister in the Archdiocese of Louisville and the Diocese of Springfield/Cape Girardeau, MO.

In 1986 she came to Mount St. Joseph where she used her gifts in the Ursuline Community Archives at Maple Mount.

SPALDING, The Spalding's of Cape Girardeau, MO. About 1844 a group of Kentucky Catholics from the Washington County area set out for Cape Girardeau, MO. They were a highly enthusiastic group of Mattinglys, Wathens, Spaldings and other allied families. Cape was originally settled by a strong group of Catholics from the 1700s. The Vincentians had a monastery, college and small Catholic church nestled along the shoreline of the worlds only fresh water, and it was on the mighty Mississippi. An earlier group of Catholic pioneers settled in Perryville just north of Cape County so there would at least be cousins close by.

Edmund Franklin Spalding was among one of these pioneers. Edmund was the son of Edward Spalding and Elizabeth Spalding Wathen Spalding. Edward was the son of Bennet and Eleanor Fenwick Spalding. Elizabeth was the daughter of Benedict and Alethaire Abell Spalding. Edmund was baptized at Holy Name of Mary Church at Calvary, KY, a year later on Dec. 18, 1818.

Edmund met and married Martha Ann Walker on Feb. 6, 1844 in Washington County, KY. She was the daughter of William Walker and Catherine Wathen. Immediately after their marriage they set out for Missouri. Their first child was born in Cape Girardeau in December that year. In June of 1846 their next three children were born in Lebanon, Marion County, KY. We can at least be assured that in the early years they must have been back and fourth several times.

Edmund was a farmer in the Cape area. In fact, one of the original Spalding farms operated west of the city near the present interstate of I-55. When St. Francis Medical Center needed to expand they purchased part of the property and built their present facility. The old farm house and barns still remain nestled in between Route K and the front porch of the medical center. Times were tough for Edmund and family. One granddaughter told the author years later that she could remember the family not having enough money to donate to the church, so Edmund would allow the nuns to pick out one of his best hogs every year and some other assorted garden crops to help feed them. Edmund and Martha had nine children that the author can prove. There is always the possibility of some dying enroute or in Kentucky with the spacing between them.

Edmund died Nov. 7, 1899 in Cape Girardeau. He is buried in a family plot at the Old Lorimer Cemetery in downtown Cape. The Old Lorimer Cemetery sits high on the side of a hill that overlooks the mighty Mississippi. The entire family has no headstones on their plots for probable economic reasons. It is also possible that there were earlier markers but that they have been destroyed. Unfortunately, Old Lorimer Cemetery, like many others, has been vandalized with the resulting loss of some of the city's oldest markers. Fortunately, the county residents saw a need to fence the property to cut down on this and funds were collected to place a large iron fence around the property.

Martha died Jan. 2, 1902 in Cape Girardeau and is buried in the St. Mary Catholic Cemetery.

William Edward Spalding was born Dec. 17, 1844 in Cape Girardeau. He met and married Sophia M. Scherer who was born in Switzerland. She was the daughter of John J. Schearer and Judith Schoenhalzer. Notice how the fathers surname changes with Americanization. They were married in Cape April 17, 1865 by Fr. Guedrey C. M. They had six known children and possibly a seventh. Their children will be discussed in this section.

Catherine "Kate" Elizabeth Spalding was born June 28, 1846 in Lebanon, Marion County, KY. It is unclear if both her parents went back to Kentucky at this time or if perhaps just her mother Martha with brother William. Kate married Joseph M. Schmuke at St. Vincent's on March 30, 1864 by Rev. J.F. McGerry C.M. Their children are discussed in her section.

Martha Jane Spalding was born May 29, 1849 in Lebanon, KY. She never married. Martha died April 14, 1888 and is believed to be in the family plot at the Old Lorimer Cemetery. It was the only one in the area that had a Catholic section and about three-fourths of the interred people there have no markers.

John Thomas Spalding was born Sept. 9, 1850 in Lebanon, KY. John Thomas is an old traditional name among the Spaldings. Nothing else is know of him.

Annie Mary Spalding was born Nov. 21, 1853 in Cape Girardeau, MO. Annie never married. She lived for years directly across the street from the St. Mary Catholic Church in downtown Cape. There are a few old homes still standing, but it is mostly commercial property now. Annie died Oct. 7, 1937 and is buried in the St. Mary Cemetery.

Benjamin Ignatius Spalding was born March 17, 1856 in Cape Girardeau. He died as a baby and is buried in the St. Mary Cemetery although he has no marker.

Richard Oscar Spalding was born Oct. 8, 1857 in Cape Girardeau. His descendants are covered in his section. His first wife, Virginia E. Randol died in childbirth and is buried in the Old Lorimer Cemetery. Richard and his second wife Mary Lenora Baehre (pronounced Bear) are buried in the St. Mary's Catholic Cemetery in Cape.

Martha Alice Spalding was born Oct. 20, 1861 in Cape Girardeau. She never married. She died Sept. 21, 1886 in Cape. Local death records state that she is buried in the nonexistent old cemetery on the grounds of the seminary. It is this authors belief that she is buried in the Old Lorimer Cemetery with the other family members.

Virginia E. Spalding was named for her brother Richard's first wife who died in childbirth. She was either a stillborn or died shortly after birth, as the death register gives the same date for birth and death Jan. 18, 1868. She is buried in the Old Lorimer Cemetery with no marker.

SPALDING, CATHERINE "KATE" ELIZABETH, was born in Lebanon, Nelson County, KY on June 28, 1846. She was the second child of Edmund Franklin Spalding and Martha Ann Walker. Catherine married Joseph M. Schmuke (pronounced smoke-ee). Joseph and two other brothers migrated together from Switzerland. One of his brothers got off of the boat and declared citizenship in Mississippi. Joseph declared his at Cape Girardeau. Another brother declared in Washington, MO. Kate and Joseph married March 30, 1864 at St. Vincent's Catholic Church in Cape Girardeau with the Rev. J.F. McGerry officiating. Their children were born in Cape Girardeau although later they relocated to Jackson, the county seat. Joseph died Jan. 23, 1887. Kate died Sept. 14, 1941. They are both buried in the Old Jackson City Cemetery. One of their granddaughters Mary Hunter Schmuke lives across the street from the cemetery to this day. They were the parents to six children.

Anna Schmuke was born April 22, 1867. She married William Schaefer. Anna and William had six children, although they are evasive to the author. Both are buried in the Old Jackson City Cemetery close to her parents.

John F. Schmuke was born March 26, 1868. He died Oct. 14, 1891. John never married and is also buried in the Old Jackson City Cemetery.

Joseph Edmund Schmuke was born in 1871. His first wife was Philomina Dempsey. They married Nov. 6, 1901 at St. Vincent's Catholic Church in Cape Girardeau. Philomina died immediately after childbirth (Aug. 26, 1902) and was laid to rest in the Old Lorimer Cemetery in the Spalding family plot. The infant, Catherine A. died Oct. 17, 1902 and was laid next to her mother. Joseph later married Mary Hunter. Joseph and Mary were blessed with six wonderful daughters from their union. Joseph died Feb. 3, 1947 and Mary Feb. 13, 1970. Both are in the Russell Heights Cemetery in Jackson, MO. Their children are: Catherine Schmuke Statler, Mary Hunter Schmuke, Martha Schmuke Penzel, Agnes Schmuke O'Loughlin, Betty Schmuke Seabaugh, JoAnn Schmuke Hill and Laura Schmuke Lewis.

Albert was born in 1874. Little else is known other than his wife's name was Hattie and he died in Wichita, KS.

William P. Schmuke was born Oct. 30, 1877. He died Aug. 26, 1901 and is buried in the Old Jackson City Cemetery.

Bernard Schmuke was born and died on the same day in Cape Girardeau (1872). He is buried in the family plot in Old Lorimer Cemetery.

SPALDING, JOHN LUCIAS, was born July 8, 1867 in Scott County, MO. He was baptized at the St. Denis Catholic Church in Benton. He married Ida Josephine Proffitt Aug. 26, 1890 in New Hamburg, MO at the St. Laurence Catholic Church. For years John ran the county's poor farm. He died April 30, 1943 and is buried in the St. Denis Cemetery with Ida who died Nov. 30, 1938.

331

Charles "Doc" Spalding was born in Benton, MO. Lillian was also born in Benton.

Joseph Lucius Spalding was born Nov. 18, 1901 in Benton. He married Mary JoAnna Enderle who was also a Catholic from the Kelso area of Scott County. Mary was born Nov. 22, 1903. They were married Feb. 24, 1925 in Illmo, Scott County, by Fr. Gronner. Joseph died Feb. 21, 1952 and is buried at the St. Denis Cemetery in Benton. Their children are: Martha Ann Spalding, born Sept. 24, 1926 in Benton. She was baptized at the St. Denis Catholic Church. She first married John E. Ulmer on April 21, 1945. Later on May 21, 1949 she married Daniel Monroe Dempster. Daniel died in September 1991 and is buried in the St. Denis Cemetery in Benton. John Edwin "Pete" Ulmer was born Oct. 23, 1946. He has a daughter Courtney Nicole Oct. 3, 1983. Daniel Russell Dempster was born Aug. 6, 1951 and baptized at St. Denis in Benton. He married Diane Johnson in November of 1971 and they have three children: Stacey Len, Marla Danielle and Cody Diane. Geraldine Lynn Dempster was born Aug. 25, 1958. She first married Larry McClain Feb. 10, 1984 and later Mark Cheathum. She has a daughter Erin Elizabeth Dempster born Feb. 22, 1980 at Cape Girardeau. Erin was baptized at St. Denis Church. Teri Ann Dempster was born Oct. 21, 1960. She first married Fred Lee Welter on Feb. 10, 1984 and to this union Andrew Dempster Welter was born July 6, 1984 in Cape Girardeau. Later she married James Buchenmeyer in 1990. James and Terri have a son Jacob Albert from this union which was born March 18, 1991 at Poplur Bluff, MO.

Joseph "Amos" John Spalding was born July 9, 1930 in Kelso, MO. He married Lois Rebecca Dirnberger Sept. 26, 1953 at the St. Laurence Catholic Church in New Hamburg by Fr. Herbert Mellies. Amos owns a trucking company and his son works there with him. Lois is a social worker with the Cape Girardeau Department of Social Services. Joseph Wayne was born in Cape Girardeau on July 29, 1954. He was baptized at St. Denis Catholic Church. He married Michelle Mary Melton Aug. 16, 1986 at St. Denis in Benton, MO. They have two sons, Joseph Melton, (1987) and Justin Thomas (1990). John Darryl was born June 13, 1961. He also works with the family trucking company. He married Lisa A. Duke Nov. 27, 1981 at St. Denis. They have two daughters who were also baptized at St. Denis: Emily Elizabeth (1983) and Katie JoHanna (1987). Rebecca Mary was born March 7, 1956. She married Oct. 6, 1979 Charles Albert Schwartz. Rebecca was baptized, married, and her three children baptized at St. Denis in Benton: Suzanna Rebecca (1980), Stephen Joseph (1983) and Gregory Charles (1986). Melissa Rose was born July 29, 1959. She too was baptized and married at St. Denis. Melissa and Jeffrey D. Lee are the parents of two boys were both born in Springfield and baptized there at Immaculate Conception: Jared David (1987) and Jeffery Jordon (1991). Melissa and Jeffery operate a funeral home.

Ida Louise was born Feb. 5, 1933 in Benton and baptized at the St. Denis Catholic Church where she was also married. James E. Roper worked for the highway department in Sikeston, MO until his death in 1978. They adopted a beautiful boy James Lee Roper who was born July 22, 1968. James Lee married July 22, 1989 Beverly Cochran. He was baptized at the St. Xavier Catholic Church there. They have one son, Christopher Wayne who was born in Rockford, IL in 1990.

Mary Alice was born Feb. 15, 1936 in Benton and was baptized at the St. Denis Catholic Church. Mary Alice married Melvin O. "Bud" Schweer June 23, 1962 also at St. Denis. Bud was a native of Oak Ridge in Cape Girardeau County. Mary is the deputy assessor for Scott County. Melvin Oscar Schweer married Laura Kay Pobst on Aug. 21, 1963. They have two children who were born in Cape Girardeau: Grant Alexander (1987) and Lexie Elizabeth (1988). Mary Anna was born Nov. 25, 1964. She too was baptized at the St. Denis Catholic Church.

Blanche Marie "Sally" was born Feb. 10, 1939. She was married July 15, 1961 at St. Denis to Alfred Charles Asmus. Alfred was baptized at Guardian Angel Catholic Church in Oran, MO. Sally is a bookkeeper at a bank. Their children are: Mark Allen born June 9, 1962. He married at the Guardian Angel Church on Oct. 11, 1980 Carolyn Ruhl.

Carolyn is a native of Sikeston. Mark is a school teacher and Carolyn is an interior designer. They have a son David Charles who was born Sept. 30, 1985. Teal Ann was born March 10, 1964. Teal was baptized and later married at Guardian Angel. She is a teacher also. Teal and her husband Kent A. Mangels who is a native of Cape Girardeau married April 8, 1989. They have a daughter Kirstie Lynn, born Aug. 28, 1990. John Gerard arrived March 9, 1968. He married Tami Moore. Their son Christopher Bryant was born June 19, 1989. Tina Marie was born March 15, 1969. She too was baptized and married at Guardian Angel. Her spouse is Jeffrey Scherer. Tara Lynn was born June 9, 1975. She was baptized at Guardian Angel.

Blanche Spalding died as a teenager from a ruptured appendix. She is buried in the St. Denis Cemetery. Her sandstone marker is severely weathered and is illegible for dates.

Ada Belle is the last child and she remains elusive to the author.

SPALDING, REV. JOSEPH LANCASTER, was born Sept. 17, 1901 in Lebanon, KY, the son of John Martin and Ann Lancaster. Baptized Sept. 22, 1901 at St. Augustine's in Lebanon, by Rev. J.A. Hogarty. Confirmed June 8, 1912. Attended grade school at St. Augustine; St. Augustine High School; University of Kentucky; St. Charles in Catonsville, OH; St. Gregory in Mount Washington, OH; Mount St. Mary, Norwood, OH. Ordained June 14, 1930 in Cathedral of Assumption, Louisville, KY by the Most Rev. John A. Floersh. Served as assistant pastor of Cathedral, Louisville, KY from July 1930 until September 1930; St. George, Louisville from September 1930 until 1933. He was a member of "Priest Mass League" of the Diocese of Owensboro. Also member of the Louisville Sodalitium.

Rev. Joseph L. Spalding

Rev. Spalding died Feb. 8, 1965. He is buried at St. Ann Cemetery in Morganfield, KY.

SPALDING, SR. PRAXEDES, was born Nov. 15, 1912 in Calvary, KY, the daughter of Mark (Sept. 22, 1886-May 30, 1950) and Lula Spalding (Dec. 2, 1889-May 2, 1970). Entered Sept. 7, 1932 and received Habit March 18, 1933. Made vows March 19, 1935 and March 19, 1938 in Nebraska City, NE. She served in various missions from 1935 until her retirement in January 1986, teaching grades one through eight.

She has three sisters Ann Margaret, who married Joseph Bruce Thomas; Harriet Elizabeth, who married Joseph H. Mattingly; and Anna Rebecca, who married James Sherman Raley.

SPALDING, RICHARD OSCAR, was born Oct. 8, 1857 in Cape Girardeau, MO. He was the son of Edmund Franklin and Martha Ann Walker Spalding the Washington County, KY Catholic immigrants. Richard was baptized at the St. Mary's Cathedral in Cape. Richard was raised with a full and rich Catholic heritage.

Richard married Virginia E. Randol Nov. 3, 1886 at the St. Vincent Catholic Church by Rev. P.M. Hale C.M. Unfortunately Virginia died in childbirth on the Dec. 6, 1888. She and the baby are buried in the Old Lorimer Cemetery in Cape.

Richard was devastated by this loss. Ten years later he married Mary Lenora Baehre (pronounced Bear) on June 7, 1896 at St. Vincent's by Rev. P. Cuddy C.M. Mary was born in May of 1876 and the daughter of Henry and Mary Vaehre. Richard was blessed with nine children to this union. He and Mary are buried in the St. Mary's Catholic Cemetery in Cape.

Mary Inez was born on June 11, 1900. She married Walton Brown. Little else is know about her. Her children include: unknown infant was not named, but its burial is recorded in the same plot as its grandparents Richard and Mary Spalding at St. Mary's; Robert Brown; Walton Brown Jr.; Doris Brown; Jerry Brown; and Larry Brown.

Baby boy Spalding. Born and died Feb. 18, 1918. There is no headstone for him. He is buried at the feet of his parents grave.

Unknown male child, who was also stillborn on Jan. 5, 1917. His birth was noted in the records of the old St. Francis Medical Center. There is no record of a place of burial but the author assumes him to be at St. Mary's with the parents.

Virginia Spalding died at age 2.

Edmund Spalding was the first male child to live for Richard. He was named for his grandfather. Unfortunately he lived only about a year and one-half from January 1898 to Aug. 14, 1899.

Richard Henry Spalding arrived March 5, 1902. What a joyous event this must have been for them!! Richard is a very traditional name among the Spaldings of Kentucky. Richard married Dec. 10, 1924 at the St. Mary Cathedral Dora Marie Christina Hager. They were blessed with six children. Richard died May 9, 1981 and Dora June 29, 1978. They are both buried in the New Lorimer Cemetery in Cape. Their children are: Robert Alyn was born July 3, 1937. He has been a trucker for most of his life. He met and married Juanita Irene Lee Jan. 8, 1973. Juanita is employed with Kens Cape Cleaners. She is very active in genealogy and her church. Virginia R. Spalding was born Sept. 30, 1923. She was tragically killed in a car accident while serving active duty with the Marine Corp Oct. 1, 1945. She is buried next to her parents. Melvin Eugene Spalding was born Nov. 11, 1927 and died March 26, 1989. Elizabeth Louise Spalding was born Jan. 23, 1930. She married Albert Burgger and they live in Jackson, MO. Marilyn Vondell Spalding was born Jan. 23, 1925, married Ronald Rutherford. They reside in Colorado Springs, CO. Richard Kenneth Spalding was born Nov. 13, 1925. His wife is unknown to the author, but he survives two children: Kenneth W. Spalding (1950-1984) and Richard S. Spalding (1952-1972).

Edward Franklin Spalding was born Oct. 1, 1904. He died Feb. 25, 1974. His wife Erna survives him. They were married May 1, 1926 in Cape Girardeau. Their only child Carolyn Ruth lived only a few weeks from Feb. 18, 1939 to March 2, 1939. She is buried in her parents plot at the Fairmont Cemetery next to the St.Vincent De Paul Catholic Church.

Anna Marie Cecilia Spalding was born May 25, 1907 in Cape Girardeau. She married Nov. 26, 1927 Clarence Martin Siemers. Clarence died six weeks before the birth of his second child (1904-1933). They were they parents of two sons: Clarence Albert (1929-1951) and Kenneth (1933-1970), who was killed on a construction job in New Madrid, MO when he fell off a scaffolding.

Albert Oscar Spalding was born Aug. 31, 1911.

SPALDING, ROBERT LOUIS, son of Thomas and Mabel (Wilson) Spalding (see James Wilson biography) married Patricia (Drew), daughter of Jack and Agnes (Dorsch) Drew in Chicago, IL in 1960. Three of five children were born there. Bob longed to return to Fancy Farm, which they did in 1970. Bob enjoys farming and has continued in his vocation as a building contractor.

Bob and Pat find fulfillment in helping others through volunteer work in church, school, and other community affairs (Matthew 25:40). Bob has served as president of the Fancy Farm Volunteer Fire Department for 18 years, and remains active therein. He has been either chairman or co-chairman of the famous Fancy Farm Picnic for 18 years. In 1978, he was elected to the Graves County Board of Education and was soon chosen chairman. He believed strongly in better education for every student in the county and after several years of dedicated work, voter approval was achieved and in August of 1985, the Graves County High School became a reality.

Front row (L-R): Grandfather-Tom Spalding, Lynn Prather, Heather and Brittany. Second row: Belinda Spalding, Diane Spalding, Pat Spalding. Third row: David Spalding, Bob Spalding Jr., Bob Spalding Sr. Top row: Phillip Prather, Kathy Spalding.

Pat works very closely with Bob in all he undertakes, believing that a family that works together is happy. For several years, she wrote a column called "The Fancy Farm Scene" for the *Mayfield Messenger*. Presently, she is editor of the *St. Jerome Journal*, a church sponsored community paper.

Bob and Pat's oldest child, Lynn (Phillip) Prather, is a registered nurse and the mother of two daughters, Brittany and Heather. Bob Jr., a carpenter and wife, Belinda (Franklin) are the parents of a son, Robert. Diane teaches sixth grade; Kathy is a parts manager in an automotive store; and David is a high school student. Already, each child has shown a tendency to follow in their parents footsteps by showing a concern for and a willingness to help others.

SPALDING, ROSS AND LAURA (WIGHT),

cradle Catholics, were members of the Diocese of Owensboro (then Louisville) from birth; were descendants of Catholic families who came to Kentucky in 1791 or soon after. Mr. Spalding was the great grandson of Benedict Spalding Jr. who led a large group of Catholic families from Maryland to a part of Nelson County which later became Washington County, KY. Ross (1864-1949) Spalding was the son of Robert and Catherine Ann (Martin) Spalding.

Ross and Laura (Wight) Spalding

Ross was a farmer and a self educated man. In 1884 he married Laura Wight Spalding (1863-1955), daughter of Thomas and Susan (Pike) (Wight), whose Catholic families came to Kentucky from Maryland. Laura attended St. Vincent Academy for a time. She had musical talent and laughed when she said that when she had laryngitis she lost her voice so she was taken out of school. Laura always said, "I had 10 children, five in heaven to pray for me and five here on earth to take care of me?" She was devoted to the Blessed Mother and named all her daughters Mary ___ except Leora. At Leora's funeral sermon, Father Vincent Spalding could not remember her full name so he called her Mary Lenora. Grandmama got her way in the end!

SPALDING, WILLIAM EDWARD,

is the eldest child of Edmund Spalding and Martha Walker. He was born Dec. 17, 1844 in Cape Girardeau, MO. Close to the time that William was born there was a huge influx of German Catholic immigrants into Cape Girardeau County. This accounts for his wife's family in the area. Some of these new German Catholics moved westward one county and settled in Scott County. There are to this day many small but fiercely devoted German Catholic communities such as Kelso and New Hamburg.

William married Sophia M. Scherer April 17, 1865 in Cape Girardeau by the Father F. Guedrey C.M. There were six known children to this union and possibly others that escaped the authors knowledge since census years.

Sophia died Oct. 25, 1895 in New Hamburg, Scott County, MO. She is buried in the Saint Laurence Catholic Cemetery there. In the plot with her are Carina Spalding (died March 18, 1893) and Eudela Spalding (died Nov. 20, 1895). It is unclear if these are children from a possible first marriage of their son John or if indeed they are the children of William and Sophia. The stones are elaborately done and written in German.

William died Jan. 5, 1915 in Benton, Scott County, MO. He was buried in the Benton City Cemetery. His marker there is badly worn and towards the back of the cemetery.

John Lucias Spalding was born July 8, 1867 in Scott County. He was baptized at the Saint Denis Church in Benton. He met and married Ida Josephine Proffit on Aug. 26, 1890. Their descendants are numerous and are listed under his section.

William E. Spalding was born in 1866 in Cape Giradeau. There is little personal info available on him. He married Ivy Jane Sadler-Ryon and they married Nov. 28, 1942 in Benton, MO. This was Ivy's second marriage. Ivy died in 1976 and is buried near her family in the Saint Denis Catholic Cemetery at Benton. William is buried in the cemetery at Commerce, MO.

The remaining four children have disappeared from the author. They appear on the 1880 Cape County Census but no other records are available. Kate was born in 1870. Rosine was born in 1874. Sophia was born in 1876. Annie B. was born in 1879.

SPINK, GLADYS MARIE,

daughter of Cecilia Emma Vessels (1884-1950) and James Samuel Spink (1883-) was from a long line of Catholics. Robert Thomas Vessels (1850) and Mary Etta O'Bryan, grandparents of Gladys were Catholics. Great-grandparents of Gladys, Thomas (1812) and Sarah (1814) Vessels were Catholics. Henry O'Bryan and Cecilia Osborne were also life-long Catholics.

Gladys Spinks married Robert W. Smith Sr., son of Frank Smith (1871-1934) and Mary "Emma" Carter (1879-1967). The Smith's were Baptist, but Gladys raised their eight children in the Catholic faith: Robert W. Jr., Richard, Edward, Kay, Phyllis, James, Mary Helen and Gail. The Smith family children were all born on a farm joining the land where Mount Merino Catholic Church was located. Mount Merino was the early Catholic church at Irvington. All the children of Gladys were baptized at Holy Guardian Angel Church and received all the other sacraments there. Gladys and Robert have 22 grandchildren and 22 great-grandchildren.

Gladys, Robert W. Jr. and Gail have continued as members of Holy Guardian Angel Church, Irvington. Rhonda Smith Dore, Kimberly, Nicholas, Bobby and Allison Decker, grandchildren of Gladys and Robert attend Holy Guardian Angel Church. Great-grandchildren, Brandi and Tara Dore, Robert and Russell Lyons belong to Holy Guardian Angel Church.

STAHR, JACOB,

(originally Stoehr) was the first of the Stahrs to come to Fulton County. He was born in Irslingen, Wurtenberg (July 20, 1825), the son of Johann Stöehr and Katherina Von Zimmern. He married Augustina Scheible, daughter of Mattaus and Agatha Seeburger Scheible of Gobblingen, Wurtemberg. Their first child, Valentine, was born Feb. 14, 1852 in Wurtemberg.

The Stöehrs came to this country in the wave of German immigration of the early 1850s. Many German Catholics came during this period escaping persecution they suffered after the German Revolution of 1848.

Shortly after Valentine's birth, Jacob and Augustina immigrated to this country settling first in Ohio and Indiana and then came to Hickman, KY around 1868-1870. In addition to Valentine, there were nine more children. John Hubert born Dec. 22, 1855, Joseph born 1857, Stephen born 1859, Katherine Agatha, born 1861, William Areton born 1863, Mary Cecelia born 1865, Margaret Priska born 1867 and Gertrude Barbra born 1870.

All were members of the Catholic Church in Hickman and were the corner stones of the church as it is today.

STEELE, DAVID,

and family have been members of the diocese for 17 years. In that 17 years they have been members of St. Pius Tenth, Immaculate, and now are members of St. Stephens. David and Cindy both attended public schools but were raised as Catholics. David attended Blessed Mother Parish, and Cindy attended Immaculate Parish. David's parents are Beverly and Charlie Steele. He has three brothers and three sisters. Cindy's parents are Don and Margie Whitney, she has three sisters also. David and Cindy have two children, Scott and Whitney. Scott is a 17 years old senior at Owensboro Catholic High, and Whitney is eight years old, and a third grader at St. Angela Merici.

Scott was baptized in the Immaculate Parish in 1975, received his First Communion at St. Pius Tenth, and made his confirmation at St. Stephen Cathedral. Whitney was baptized at St. Pius and made her First Communion last year at St. Stephen. David works for his father Charlie Steele at a rock quarry. Cindy works as a clerk at Lloyd and Pat's Jewelry store. The family attends Mass regularly and donates some of their time to church activities.

STEELE, JEFFREY SCOTT,

was born Feb. 28, 1960 in Saint Louis, MO. Jeff was born to Elizabeth Louise Holtshouser and Jack Taylor Steele M.D. Elizabeth was the daughter of William Alphonsus Holtshouser Jr. and Emma Catherine Mitchell.

Jeff met and married Diana Marie Craig while completing medical school in Kansas City, MO. He served seven years in the Navy in the Washington, D.C. area and during Desert Storm. They have been truly blessed with two boys, Brian Christopher and Adam Joseph. They relocated to Cape Girardeau, MO where Jeff joined a group practice and enjoys golf and his boat. Diana has put her nursing career on hold until the youngest enters school but has taken up genealogy and volunteer work. They are very active in their parish serving the flood victims, shut ins, teaching SRE Classes and Cub Scouts.

STEELE, VINCENT JOSEPH,

was born Nov. 5, 1897 to parents John Kennedy Steele and Annie Goodwin (Barrow) Steele. He married his wife, Pauline (Hagan) at St. Peter's Catholic Church, Stanley, KY on May 19, 1925. They were united by Rev. J.M. Higgins, Celebrant; Rev. E.S. Fitzgerald, deacon; Rev. Guido Mensa, sub deacon and Rev. J.J. Rives, Master of Ceremonies. Pauline was the daughter of Sylvester Hagan and Laura (Smith) Hagan.

Vincent Steele

Vincent Joseph and Pauline had eight children. Vincent J. Steele Jr.; Mary Anne Steel, deceased; Charles

Carroll Steele; Robert Hagan Steele; Pauline Steele, deceased; Ruth H. Steele; John Kennedy Steele and Sarah Steele (Mrs. James L. Edge). They have 24 grandchildren and 21 great grandchildren.

Vincent was a member of St. Paul's Catholic Church and former Grand Knight of the Knights of Columbus. He was a friend of Fr. Robert Connor and helped establish Blessed Sacrament Church in Owensboro. He also was the 33rd person to receive lifetime membership in the University of Notre Dame Honor Committee.

At the age of 12 he began working for his Uncle Marshall Barrow in the coal business. Later he owned his own coal company and wholesale beer distributorship. Mr. Steele also built and operated WVJS, whose call letters are the initials of Mr. Steele. WVJS went on the air for the first time Thanksgiving Day, Nov. 27, 1947. He also owned and operated Kentucky's first full time stereo station, WSTO FM (formerly WVJS-FM). He constructed Owensboro Cablevision in 1974. It was one of the most modern and sophisticated systems in the nation, with approximately 200 miles plant, serving 20,000 homes. He passed away April 15, 1975 in Ft. Lauderdale, FL.

The Steel family, through the Steele Foundation, continue their support of the Catholic Church. The Foundation is responsible for building and dedicating the Infant of Prague Infirmary (in memory of Vincent J. Steele, at the Carmel Home) and recently purchased 150 acres near Whitesville for the relocation of St. Joseph Monastery for the cloistered Passionist Nuns.

STENGER, GARY PROCTOR AND BRENDA LOVELL,
although Gary was born in Alabama and Jarrod was born in Missouri, all five were raised in Union County and have lived just outside Morganfield in Union County most of their lives.

Gary is a graduate of UK and Brenda received her master's from Western Kentucky University. Gary is a grain farmer-livestock producer and Brenda is a teacher.

They are members of St. Ann Parrish.

Members of Gary's family include Thomas Jarrod Stenger, born Feb. 24, 1969, Tammie Lynn Stenger, born July 25, 1971 and Carrie Proctor Stenger, born July 10, 1977.

THE STEWART FAMILY,
the Norman and Jo Ann Stewart family moved to Marion County, Crittenden County in 1968, from Union County. The family consists of Wompie, Juliane, Debbie and Trevor who live with them here while Jimmy and Billy Joe live out of state. Juliane is still at home but is attending Madisonville Community College studying to be a respiratory therapist.

Norman, Jo Ann and Juliane belong to St. William Parish. Jo Ann and Juliane joined the parish in 1991, after going through the RCIA program. Wompie, his wife Christine and their two children, Jessica and Jordan are in the present RCIA preparing to join the Catholic Church, St. William, this Holy Saturday. Norman and Jo Ann have seven other grandchildren, of who they are very proud.

Norman and Jo Ann are the chief "barbequers" for St. William's Church. Norman sleeps under the tree while Jo Ann takes care of the barbequeing. Anyhow they are both good at it and love to do it for their "pot lucks" at St. Williams.

Norm and Jo Ann

Jo Ann is employed in the Food Service Department at Crittenden County Elementary School and has been for several years. She enjoys her work with the children and has made many friends there, among the teachers and students.

Norman's hobby is deer hunting and soon his daughter, Juliane wants to join him. Jo Ann stays home to cook because when they return from hunting they are hungry.

The Stewart family are very active members of St. William Parish. Right now they "putting fire" under the building committee, for a new parish hall to be a reality, not just talk.

STIFF, PERRY,
Perry Carlton was raised by Rita Mae and Lowell Richard Stiff I in Owensboro, then moved to Texas and back to Owensboro. Deborah Kay was raised by her parents, Joseph Albert and Patricia Ann O'Bryan in Owensboro, KY. Perry and Deborah met at Catholic High and dated several years before marrying on Sept. 23, 1977 at St. Joseph and Paul. Deborah Kay works at home and is a homemaker. Perry Carlton is a mechanic at Titan Feb.

Perry and Deborah have six kids; Beth Anne, Daniel Perry, Serena Marie, Patrick Bryan, Rose Marita and Briana Kathleen. Beth attends school at Owensboro Catholic Middle School. While Daniel, Serena and Patrick attend school at Catherine Spalding, the family attends church at Our Lady of Lourdes. Perry does some coaching for pee wee baseball, while Deborah is a lector, teacher at children's liturgy, singer and also cleans the church.

STONE, MARTHA JULIETTE HAYDEN MAGEE,
one of the pioneer Catholic families in Kentucky were the Haydens. One branch now located in Owensboro, Paducah and Fancy Farm came from St. Mary's County, MD to Washington County, KY. This line goes William Ben, John, Pius, Emanuel and William Gross who had two daughters, Mary Kathleen Henderson, deceased, the mother of eight children and Juliette Magee Stone, the mother of three, Michael Dennis Magee, Frankfort; Ava Siener, Paducah; and William Gross Magee, Cairo, IL. Mrs. Stone's mother, Stella Rickman Hayden, is still alive at 94 and is a resident of Life Care Center in Cairo.

Mrs. Stella Hayden and daughter, Juliette Magee Stone

Mrs. Stone, a past member of St. Frances De Sales and St. Mary's at La Center, is now a member of St. Joseph's in Central City where she lives with her second husband Larry Stone, who is the father of four sons. Her first husband, Alfred J. Magee, of Nyack, NY, died in 1967. They started in the newspaper business after he was discharged from service in 1945 after nearly five years in the Army. Her second husband is also a veteran of World War and is also a newspaper man connected with the *Times-Argus* in Central City.

The Magee family owned four newspapers in Western Kentucky which Mrs. Magee operated after the death of her husband. All three of her children were in the newspaper business. She retired last year after 47 years in the newspaper business and sold the businesses. She was publisher of the *Advance-Yeoman,* Wickliffe, the *Livingston Ledger,* Smithland, the *Hickman County Gazette,* Clinton and the *West Kentucky News,* Paducah.

Mrs. Stone is also an author and in addition to her newspaper work has written eight histories and is continuing a writing career. She has two grandchildren, Jacob

Magee Siener and Sarah Elizabeth Magee. She likes reading, writing, arithmetic, card playing and crossword puzzles.

STREHL, KATTIE MAE,
wife of John Strehl, was born Nov. 22, 1905 in Owensboro, KY. She was raised in Owensboro, KY. Katie Mae is a retired nurse. She is a member of Blessed Mother Church.

STREHLE, LAWRENCE AND MARY FRANCES (MILLS),
became regular members of St. Ann's Church, Morganfield, KY in October 1952.

Lawrence was born in Hoboken, NJ, received the sacraments of baptism, penance, Holy Eucharist and confirmation at Our Lady of Grace Church, Hoboken, NJ.

Mary Frances was born in Union County, was baptized and was married to Lawrence at St. Ann's in Morganfield. She received all other sacraments at St. Agnes, Uniontown, KY, also attended and graduated from St. Agnes School.

Lawrence served three years in the Army during World War II. He and Mary Frances met while he was stationed at Camp Breckinridge and she was attending nursing school at St. Mary's Hospital Evansville, IN.

Lawrence and Mary Frances Strehle

After his return from the war they were married May 4, 1946. They have six living children, Lawrence, Elaine, Mary Ann, Kenny, Joan, Bruce. David died at age 7 months.

They lived in Hoboken, NJ for six years before returning to Morganfield, KY. All of their children attended St. Ann's Grade School and received all of the sacraments at St. Ann's.

They are now retired and both are active in volunteer services to the local nursing home and to St. Anthony Hospice. They belong to Our Lady's rosary makers and in their spare time make mission rosaries.

STUART, SR. HELEN ANN,
baptized as Mary Rita June 25, 1922. She was born May 25, 1922 in Daviess County, KY. Entered Feb. 1, 1949. Received habit Aug. 14, 1949. First vows, Aug. 15, 1951, and final vows Aug. 15, 1954.

Her father was Joseph Stuart born June 9, 1897 in Daviess County and died Aug. 14, 1964. Her mother Minnie Ballard was born Oct. 1, 1893 in Daviess County and died March 18, 1957.

Her brothers and sisters include Joseph Marvin, William Gerald, Helen Marie Stuart-Warren, Theresa Martina Stuart-Greenwell.

Served in missions: St. James, Louisville, Mayfield, Jeffersontown, Precious Blood, St. Joseph, St. Alphonsus, St. Leonard, St. Francis, Motherhouse, Brescia, St. Romuald, Mount Saint Joseph from 1951 until 1990 teaching grades 1-2.

STUART/LEWIS/COOMES,
Sarah Stuart was born Oct. 19, 1757 (tombstone) in Maryland, probably St. Marys County. She was married during the late 1770s, probably to a William Lewis, and had a number of children by him, including one Thomas W. Lewis, born about 1778. But William Lewis died and Sarah Stuart Lewis then married an Ignatius Coomes (Coombes). She died May 5, 1850 (tombstone) and is buried next to her second husband, Ignatius, in the southwest corner of the cemetery

of St. Romuald Catholic Church in Hardinsburg, Breckinridge County, KY.

Ignatius Coomes (Coombes) was born Oct. 28, 1767 (tombstone) in Maryland (St. Marys County ?) and died March 25, 1851 in Hardinsburg, KY, and is buried next to his wife at St. Romualds'. An excellent book, *The Jesuit Missions of St. Mary's County, MD*, by Edwin Warfield Beitzell, 1976, contained numerous Coomes family references, but not this branch.

Ignatius Coomes and wife Sarah had several children, among them: Linus Coomes born 1792, who became a priest; Walter S. born 1794, who also became a priest; and Francis Xavier born 1796. Ignatius and family joined many Catholics from Maryland in migrating to the new land of Kentucky, supposedly stopping in Loudon County, VA and probably is Surry County, NC, before ending up in the Axtel neighborhood near Tuels Creek in Breckinridge County, KY. They seem to have followed a famous migration trail down the valley of Virginia and then into Kentucky. A good reference is *Marylanders to Kentucky 1775-1825*, by Harry C. Penden Jr. 1991. Ignatius and family apparently became affiliated with St. Romualds Catholic Church in Hardinsburg, KY, since they were buried there.

Thomas W. Lewis, born ca 1778 (VA or MD), and keeping his birth name, apparently migrated to Kentucky with his mother and step-father, Ignatius. Thomas had 15 children by two wives, among them a Simon P. Lewis, born ca 1810, supposedly in Virginia. Simon seems to have married Oct. 28, 1832 in Jefferson County, KY, to Maria P. Brown (born ca 1816). They had a daughter, Mary Jane Lewis who was born July 10, 1842 and married July 7, 1859 in Hawesville, Hancock County, KY to a George Kernard Green. George was born Nov. 16, 1836, maybe in Indiana and he served during the Civil War in the Kentucky Cavalry, CSA.

Wedding of Mary Jane Lewis to George Kernard Greene, 1859. (Photo submitted by Ken Craft).

Mary Jane and George had a daughter, Daisy Boyd Greene, born Nov. 17, 1871 in Hardinsburg, KY, who married a John Wesley Piland (born June 27, 1871). From Louisville, she moved to Dexter and Poplar Bluff, MO and Arkansas before ending up in Willow Springs, MO. Their daughter, Eunice Alma Piland, born April 19, 1894 in Louisville, married Oct. 20, 1919 to Joseph Henry Noennig.

TACKETT, BOB L. AND BARBARANELLE HAAS,
were married on Oct. 15, 1960. Bob was born on Jan. 18, 1936 and moved to Paducah, McCracken County, KY in 1959. Barbaranelle was born on May 23, 1937 and has lived in Paducah since birth. They are members of St. John the Evangelist and participate as Eucharist Ministers, on Parish Finance Board and past church trustee.

Their children include: Colleen Ann Tackett Tincher, married to Bruce. They have two children, Kyle and Meagan. Cynthia Rose Tackett Sandefer, married to Erik. They have two children, Adam and Kathryn. Carol Maria Tackett Kupper, married to Ron. They have one daughter, Lauren.

When Bob joined the Catholic faith in April of 1960 he chose as his Baptismal sponsors the same sponsors as his bride-to-be (Barbaranelle), which were Syl and Elizabeth Roof.

TALIAFERRO, ERNEST E. JR.,
was born Aug. 1, 1948 in Owensboro. He was married to Shirley Osborne, born April 24, 1949 in Indianapolis, on May 23, 1970 at St. Paul's Church in Owensboro.

Shirley, born of Charles and Marilyn Osborne, the owners of Daveco Drive-Thru, was a teacher at Blessed Mother School when she married Ernie. They had two children while she taught before expecting her third and getting out of teaching. Her husband Ernie, born of Theresa Taliaferro, then working for General Electric, substituted teaching before teaching two years at St. Stephen's Cathedral School and then getting on for a job at Texas Gas.

They have six children, Matt, 17; Kara, 16; Ryan, 14; Allison, 11; Jordan, 5; and Katlyn, 2. All were born in Owensboro and members of Immaculate Parish. Matt, Kara, Ryan and Allison attended Immaculate Grade School before it closed because of consolidation. Now, Matt is a senior and Kara is a junior at Owensboro Catholic High School. Ryan is in eighth grade at Owensboro Catholic Middle School and Allison is in sixth grade at Catherine Spalding Elementary School. Jordan attends Cathedral Pre-School and Katlyn is not in school yet.

Ernest, a graduate of Immaculate Grade School, Owensboro Catholic High School, Brescia College and Murray State University, and Matt are Eucharistic ministers at Immaculate Parish while Ryan is an altar server.

TENNES, PAUL,
was born in Bavaria, Dec. 13, 1830 and died Aug. 23, 1877. He is buried in Mater Dolorosa Cemetery in Owensboro, KY. He married Josepha Kieffer on Nov. 24, 1855 in Jasper, IN. Josepha's family is believed to have come from Alsace Lorraine. Paul and Josepha had five children: Mary Josephine born Aug. 6, 1857; Caroline born Sept. 9, 1861; Anna Marie born Dec. 6, 1864; John Joseph born Dec. 27, 1867; and Albert J. born Dec. 12, 1869.

Their baptismal records are at St. Joseph Church at Jasper, IN.

In Paul Tennes' plot at Mater Dolorosa Cemetery there is a marker that reads John P. next to a marker that says Anna Marie and a marker that says "Father."

Mary Josephine, John Joseph and Albert were living when Paul Tennes remarried after the death of his first wife, Josepha.

Paul Tennes had several brothers: Mike, Adam, John and perhaps, Joe.

Paul Tennes and Christina Oberst married Feb. 18, 1873. Christina was born in Prussia Aug. 23, 1843 and died March 19, 1910. They had two daughters: Catherine Sophie, known as Katie and Frances Josephine born July 17, 1876. In the summer of 1945, Katie received the "Pro Ecclesia et Pro Deum" Award for 60 years of service as organist at St. Joseph Church in Owensboro, KY. Frances married Fred W. Arnold. They had two children, Paul and Frederick. Paul had one daughter and Fred had eight children among whom are Reverend Edward Arnold and Sister Catherine Arnold, Sister of Charity of Nazareth, KY.

THOMAS, DOUGLAS JOSEPH AND ELIZABETH HAZEL HAYDEN,
have been married 41 years. They are presently retired and all children are married. They have lived in Fancy Farm, Graves County, KY since May 1991. They are members of St. Jerome where they participate in choir and serve as lector and usher. They are former members of St. Charles, Carlisle County.

The Douglas Thomas Family

Their children include: Janice Boyd, Kay Wilson, Gail Elliott, Jeanie Stamper, Deborah Underwood, Richard Thomas, Cindy Redden, Sandy Goatley, Lori Wilson, Leah Hayden and Deah Hayden.

People always ask why they moved to Fancy Farm and they tell them "where else could we go to find three daughters Eucharistic ministers, one daughter a lector, two grandsons altar boys, Mother and Dad choir members, all at one Mass." They have 11 children, 22 grandchildren and are expecting their first great-granddaughter. Nine of their children attend St. Jerome Church.

THOMAS, JOSEPH LEONARD (KINKY),
was born Dec. 5, 1921 and died Jan. 12, 1979. He married Helen Dean Greenwell Thomas, born June 2, 1927, at St. Agnes Catholic Church, Uniontown, KY on Feb. 12, 1947.

They have nine children, Mariam Theresa (Dec. 17, 1947) married John William Richard of Arlington, VA on Aug. 23, 1969. They have three daughters, Carolyn Dean born June 30, 1972, Jennifer Mariam born May 29, 1975 and Mary Susan born Nov. 2, 1981. They live in Pittsburgh, PA.

Thomas Family

Deborah Louise Thomas (July 17, 1949) married Dr. William Courtney Tapp on June 19, 1971. They have three daughters, Holly Ann born Oct. 6, 1974, Audrey Jean born Sept. 3, 1977 and Laura Marie born Oct. 14, 1978 in Morganfield, KY.

Joseph Donald Thomas (Aug. 29, 1951) married Cheryl Jean French on June 10, 1972 and they have a daughter, Mechelle Leigh born May 25, 1975 and a son Donald Wayne born June 8, 1977. They live on the Thomas Family Farm.

William Raymond Thomas (Nov. 26, 1952) named after his great-grandfather married Linda Faye Girten on Aug. 31, 1974. They have three sons, Cory Andrew born Dec. 6, 1976, William Kevin born Feb. 9, 1980 and Wade Anthony born Aug. 16, 1983. They also live on the Thomas Farm near Morganfield, KY.

Jacqueline Ann Thomas (Oct. 12, 1955) married Alan Singleton on April 24, 1982. They have two sons, Lee Thomas born Nov. 30, 1984 and Michael Newman born Jan. 16, 1987. They reside in Floyd's Knobs, IN.

Darrell Leonard Thomas (Dec. 21, 1959) married Donna Gale Thomas on Feb. 21, 1986. They have one son Matt Logan born Feb. 1, 1990.

Regina Ellen Thomas (Jan. 8, 1962) married Don Cunliffe Pearson on March 19, 1988. They have one son Thomas Cunliffe Pearson born Nov. 26, 1989. They live in Bells, TN.

Ida Jill Thomas (Dec. 3, 1963) married Gary Alan Utley on Aug. 24, 1984. One son Alex Leonard born Sept. 13, 1989 and a daughter Morgan Renee born Aug. 21, 1991. They live in Uniontown, KY.

Phillip Wade Thomas (Sept. 21, 1966) is engaged to Andrea Lee Simms.

Joseph Leonard Thomas was killed on Jan. 12, 1979 when his tractor overturned on icy roads. He was a Fourth Degree Knight. His wife, Helen Dean, still lives on the Thomas family farm which has been in the family for four generations.

THOMAS AND HOBBS FAMILIES,
The Hobbs and Thomas family ties cross many times. Jerome C. and

Annie Bettie (Hayden) Hobbs parents of Kelvie Hobbs and William Fred and Mary Emma (Thompson) Thomas parents of Mary Thomas were married by Fr. Haeseley at St. Jerome's Church on the same day 1903. The Hobbs family traveled by wagon train to New Mexico to farm new lands. After a year of crop failure young Kelvie and his family returned to Fancy Farm. There he began his first year of school in the new school building completed in 1909. Both families had nine children of which the oldest Hobbs son Wm. Kelvie, and the third Thomas child, Mary A. united in marriage.

William Kelvie Hobbs married Mary Anthonia Thomas Feb. 5, 1927 in Chicago, IL at St. Bernard Church. The marriage was witnessed by Fr. Ryne. They had migrated as young working singles from their home in Fancy Farm, Graves County, KY. The couple lived in Chicago for five years, birthing their first daughter Emma Dolores, before the Depression necessitated their return to their native Kentucky. They farmed 62 acres for 40 years and raised their six children, five daughters and one son. They communicated principles of church, community and education and the children strive to live them out. Dolores (Toon), Dianna Carol (Hayden) married home town boys and live in the Fancy Farm community. Shelley (Kresse) and Mary Ann (Purcell) returned home with "northern" boys and raised their families. The son, Donald and remaining daughter June settled out of state and return often to visit family and friends. Twenty-three grandchildren and 24 great-grandchildren come from the Wm. Kelvie and Mary (Thomas) Hobbs family.

THOMAS, MYLES AND RUTH ANN, live in the St. Paul Parish located near Leitchfield, KY. They have two young children, Joshua and Amanda.

Ruth Ann has belonged to the St. Paul Parish all her life. She works at Citizens Bank and Trust Co. of Grayson County in Leitchfield. Ruth Ann attended Brescia College in Owensboro, KY and this is where she met Myles. About a year after her graduation, Myles and Ruth Ann began dating. They were married on Sept. 27, 1986 at St. Paul Church with Rev. Anthony Stevenson performing the ceremony.

The Thomas Family

Myles grew up in Owensboro, KY and belonged to St. Stephens Parish. He plays the guitar monthly for Sunday Mass at St. Paul Church and occasionally for special occasions. Myles is a computer programmer for Field Packing Company in Owensboro and commutes to work daily.

Approximately two years ago, they bought their home which is adjacent to Ruth Ann's parents' farm (Michael and Hettie Darst). Here they enjoy the small quiet community where they can relax, walk and spend time with their children.

THOMAS, OWEN, was born 1731 in Wales. Married Polly Harden, daughter of Major John Harden and Catherine Marr. They came to Frederick County, VA. Their children were Enas, Henry, Hezekiah, John, Catherine, Polly, Harden, Lewis.

Second Generation. Enas who was born in Virginia, moved with his parents to Fayette County, PA and had a son named Henry.

Various Thomas families came to Washington County, KY in 1776 where they were given land grants for their military service in the Revolutionary War. Enas and his son Henry began the tradition of farming in Kentucky.

Third Generation. Henry moved from Washington County to Harden County and in 1798 married Nancy Vanscite. They had a son named John who lived only one year. Henry died shortly thereafter.

Nancy then married Elias Drury and had a son named John who married Rebecca Durbin.

Fourth Generation. John and Rebecca had a son Elias, who married Mary Elizabeth Hagan. For nine years Elias and Elizabeth continued farming and raising their children, Jane, Martha Ellen, Mary Elizabeth, Virginia, Walter Raymond, John, Hilary Sylvester and Henry Thomas who was the grandfather of Ray Thomas of Holy Name parish. Walter came to Union County and bought several 100 acres of land. His brothers followed him except Henry. He stayed in Harden County.

Fifth Generation. Henry Thomas married Sarah Jane French and had a son named Gregory Thomas. (Ray Thomas' father). When Gregory was 20, he moved from Harden County to Union County.

Sixth Generation. Gregory Thomas married Emma Martin Barker Hite. They had six children. Ray, Carl, Lorena, Lucille, Noel and Edith. Ray Thomas married Nolan Vancleave both born in 1912. Ray died in 1988.

Carl Thomas married Tilitha Beaven. Both are deceased.

Lorena (Sister Jean Louise, SCN) only one living.

Lucille Thomas married Charlie Thomas. Both deceased.

Noel Thomas married Thelma. Noel is deceased.

Edith Thomas married Chuck Sweitzer. Edith is deceased.

Ray Thomas who married Nolan Vancleave had six children. They belong to Holy Name Parish in Henderson, KY as do several of their children.

Tony Thomas married an English girl Joan Hill. Five children.

Ramona Thomas married Dan Lauterwasser. Four children.

Joe E. Thomas married Mary Ann Gastenveld. Three children.

Andy Thomas married Brenda Blanford. Three children.

Gladelle Thomas married John Hardenbergh. Two children.

Yvonne Thomas married Thomas Drury. Two children.

THOMAS, RUDY K. AND JOANN M., live in Cromwell, KY. They moved there in the spring of 1992 and have been members of Holy Redeemer Catholic Church since 1964. They are former members of St. Joseph in Central City, KY. Rudy served in the Vietnam War for 12-1/2 months during 1969 and 1970. He is a truck driver for Eddy Ashby in Beaver Dam, KY. Joann is a teller at Beaver Dam Deposit Bank. Her maiden name was Rachels.

Rudy and Joann Thomas

Joann used to be a youth group leader and an Eucharistic minister. She is still very active with the social life of the church, parish council meetings and reads some for the church and also sings some for the Christmas choir and occasionally on Sundays. She has made a lot of beautiful friendships through the church. Her church life is of great importance to her.

THOMPSON, AL AND MOLLY FAMILY, entered the diocese and joined Blessed Mother Parish in Owensboro in June 1988. They have three young children: Megan, Kathleen and Melinda.

Before relocating here they lived in Evanston, IL, where they were active in Northwestern University's Catholic Newman Center. They moved to Owensboro after graduation when Al took a management position with Owensboro Electric Supply Company, now Midwest Electric Supply Company. It meant a change for Molly, reared in an Irish-Catholic family in the Los Angeles area, but a homecoming for Al, who grew up in Precious Blood Parish in Owensboro.

Al and Molly Thompson Family with (l to r): Melinda, Kate and Megan.

Al's mother, nee Cloa Johnson, grew up in Blessed Mother Parish; his father, A.M. (Mike) Thompson was raised on a farm in Precious Blood Parish; and most of Al's extended family still reside within the diocese.

Al has chaired Blessed Mother's annual picnic, is a member of the parish Pastoral Council, and recently joined Serra Club. Molly chaired the External Data Committee for the diocesan Synod held in October 1991 and participated as a parish delegate for that event. At Blessed Mother she is a lector, takes part in a women's prayer group, and helped start a Parents and Young Children's Group.

Al and Molly made Cursillo weekends in Princeton, KY, in the spring of 1992. Their experiences helped them refocus their priorities as Christians, both within their family and in their community. The Thompsons enjoy participating in their parish and the larger diocesan church.

THOMPSON, ANNA Z. Fancy Farm, KY is a small town located about 30 miles north of Paducah, 10 miles east of Mayfield and about 17 south to Fulton, and west, 30 miles to Wickliffe, KY.

The town she has known since birth, April 17, 1909.

Her parents Wm. Stanislous and Nancy Catherine Hayden.

She had four sisters and two brothers but now only two sisters and one brother.

She was married to Norris Thompson Oct. 19, 1937 lived in Chicago, IL until June 1945.

They went to California to make their home in 1945 since her parents and rest of family lived there.

In 1948 their first child Robert J. Thompson was born April 2, 1948.

Then on Aug. 14, 1950 they had twins, Thomas Michael and Mary Ann.

They lived in California until the fall of 1979. Norris had retired and wanted to come back to Kentucky so they did.

But during the next few years Norris' health became bad.

The place he loved so much wasn't to be. In the spring of 1984 his health got worse.

On Feb. 15, 1984 he passed away, their plans were not to be.

But the good Lord knows best and she will continue to make the best of everything.

At least Norris' dream came true and he did what was best for both of them.

THOMPSON, CHRISTOPHER MATTHEW AND SANDRA L. MURPHY,

were married on March 4, 1977. Chris, born Sept. 21, 1954, is a maintenance mechanic. Sandra, born Nov. 4, 1954, is a secretary and full-time mother. They have four children: Jesse Louis Thompson born Nov. 22, 1980, Lisa Anne Thompson born Aug. 4, 1983, Diane Michelle Thompson born Aug. 17, 1985 and Michael Joseph Thompson born Dec. 31, 1989. The Thompsons have lived in Philpot since March 17, 1990 and attend St. Mary of the Woods. They are former members of Our Lady of Lourdes. Sandra is active in Girl Scouts with Lisa and Diane and Jesse in Boy Scouts. Diane sings in the children's choir.

Chris is the son of William Joseph (Bill) Thompson and Rose Mary Dockermeyer Thompson. Bill was a draftsman for Texas Gas and Rosemary was a full-time mother. They had two daughters and four sons: Lynda Thompson Edwards; Bernard (Benney) Thompson; Christopher Thompson, Tommy Thompson, Francis (Franky) Thompson and Darlene Thompson May. They are members of St. Alphonus Church in St. Joseph, KY.

Sandra is the daughter of Bernard Louis Murphy and Lillian Theresa Hayden Murphy. Bernard's occupation - construction electrician; Lillian - full-time mother of 11 children: five boys and six girls. They are Thomas A. Murphy, Barbara Anita Murphy, Monica Jane Murphy Gilstrap, Sandra Leona Murphy Thompson, Esther Lisa Murphy Clouse, Bruce Louis Murphy, Deborah Louise Murphy, Marvin Terry Murphy, Larry Robertus, Donna Sue Murphy and Kevin Lee Murphy. Members at St. Martins Church Rome, KY, Owensboro, KY.

THOMPSON, JAMES CUMMINGS SR.,

(1902-1990) was born in Marion County, KY. His parents were Edgar Thomas Thompson (1873-1955) and Agnes Winifred Cummings (1877-1935), both Catholic and natives of Kentucky. When James was very young his parents moved to East St. Louis, IL where his father was employed with the railroads. Nevertheless, Edgar and "Min" sent James and his two sisters, Winifred Rita (Johnson) 1904-1990 and Bernadette Alphonsa (Williams), back to Louisville to be educated in the Catholic school system, there. James graduated in 1921 from St. Francis Xavier High School. In addition, he and his two sisters spent most of their summers and vacations visiting their Thompson-Cummings relatives in Louisville and in Marion and Bullitt counties.

In 1925 James graduated from St. Louis University's School of Commerce and began his long career as a Certified Public Accountant. In 1935 he founded the firm of James C. Thompson and Co. of which he was president until his death in 1990. He was one of the few C.P.A.s to be permitted to practice before the federal tax courts and he authored several articles dealing with corporate tax law. For a time he was an officer of the Missouri Society of Certified Public Accountants. Throughout his long career he devoted his expertise to several Catholic charitable organizations, guiding them through the complex and changing tax laws governing their not-for-profit status. In 1984 in recognition of his support of Catholic higher education he was named an Honorary Dean of St. Louis University's DuBourg Society.

In 1931 James married Alice Igoe Thompson of a prominent Catholic family in St. Louis. They had four children, James Cummings Thompson Jr., Mary Elizabeth Thompson (Walrond), Alice Anne Thompson, Ph.D. and Virginia Thompson (Reynolds). They also have eight grandchildren.

James is a direct descendant of the Thompson and Mattingly families whose members migrated from Maryland to Washington County, KY in the 1780s. His great-great-grandparents, John Thompson and Susannah Mattingly were one of the first Catholic couples married by Bishop Charles Nerinx. His (James) grandfather, John Bermard Thompson 1841-1910 had four sisters who were among the earliest members of the Loretto order and his great aunts, Mary and Nancy Rhodes were the society's first two superiors. His paternal grandfather, on his mother's side, was James Broderick Cummings, (1833-1903) an architect and college professor from the Commought region of Ireland. He fled to the U.S.A. in the 1840s and designed churches for Baptists and Catholic congregations in New York, Cleveland and Kentucky. In 1863 he married Mary Alphonsa Mooney of Bardstown Jct., daughter of John Francis Mooney (1802-1872) and Hannah Letitia Spraggins (1823-1894). Providing their children with a Christian home environment and education were the premier goals of the Thompson-Cummings families of Kentucky and continues today among the descendants of James Cummings Thompson, Sr.

THOMPSON, JAMES HERMAN AND MARY KATHLEEN RUSSELBURG,

were married on Jan. 3, 1987 at Immaculate Church, Owensboro, KY by Fr. Danny Goff. James, now retired, is the son of Ralph Thompson and Eva Church. Mary, employed by Behr's (Towne Sq. Mall) in Owensboro, is the daughter of Bill Russelburg and Rose C. Edge.

James and Mary Thompson

James and Mary live in Daviess County, Philpot, KY and attend St. Mary's, Whitesville, KY. Mary is a former member of St. Thomas, Roseville, KY and Immaculate parish, Owensboro, KY. James is a lifetime member of St. Mary's parish. Both attended St. Mary's grade school and Mary graduated from St. Mary's High School in 1952.

James Herman has two sons and two granddaughters. Mary Kathleen has three living sons and seven grandchildren.

THOMPSON FAMILY, JOSEPH BERNARD JR. AND IMOGENE,

live in Sorgho where they have been members of St. Mary Magdalene for 40 years. They were married at St. Mary's in Whitesville on Feb. 9, 1952 by Father Martin Nahstoll. They have five children and two grandchildren. Their son, Glenn and wife, Julia (Mullican) with children live in St. Martin Parish. The four daughters live outside the Owensboro Diocese.

Bernard Jr. (Hank) has lived in the Sorgho area all his life and is a retired farmer. His parents are Bernard and Anabel (Wimsatt) Thompson. He is fourth of 12 children and was one of the young men in the parish who helped build the present church and school. Hank is a member of the Men's Club and was on the team that won the Championship Title for St. Mary Magdalene, in 1979, at the First International Barbecue Festival. He also is an active member of Knights of Columbus Council 6101.

Imogene was born in Whitesville. Her parents are Patrick M. and Xaveria (Coomes) Howard. She is the oldest of seven children and played the organ for St. Mary's all four years of high school. She attended Nazareth College before taking X-Ray training in Little Rock, AR. After living there four years, Imogene came to Mercy Hospital in January 1951 to become their first full-time X-Ray technician. She worked about three years before becoming a full time homemaker. She presently is a member of Christian Mothers and The Army of Mary.

Bernard and Imogene have been devoted to their parish community. Along with the annual picnics, they were the first lay people involved with counting Sunday Collections. After 26 years, Imogene retired in 1991 as church organist. Their stewardship also included the Stone Church Sign in front of church and missalette racks on the pews inside.

THOMPSON, LORA (MARISE) CLEMONS AND (THOMAS) LAMAR,

were married on Nov. 12, 1983 at St. Benedict's Church, Wax, KY.

Lora and Lamar Thompson

Lora, the seventh child of Odaline and Carmel, was born on Feb. 25, 1964; Lamar was born on Aug. 9, 1963, and is the only child of Doris Jean Croghan and Randy Thompson of Cub Run, KY. Lora attended Peonia and Clarkson Grade Schools, Grayson County Middle School

Seated: James Cummings Thompson Sr. and wife Alice Veronica Igoe Thompson Standing L-R: Alice Anne Thompson, Ph.D., James C. Thompson Jr., Mary Elizabeth Thompson (Walrond), Virginia Thompson (Reynolds).

The Joseph Bernard, Jr. and Imogene Thompson family.

and St. Paul School; she graduated from Grayson County High in 1982. Lamar attended Blue Lick, Prestonia, St. Rita's Grade Schools in Louisville and Cub Run Grade School; he graduated from Hart County High School in 1981. The couple met at St. Benedict's Religious Education classes.

Lora has taken classes at Western Kentucky University and is currently working towards certification in the CPCU (Chartered Property Casualty Underwriters) Program. She is presently employed at Van Meter Insurance in Bowling Green. Lamar works in sales at R & J Industrial Supply Company.

The couple belong to Holy Spirit Parish in Bowling Green. In their spare time, they like to work on their new home and yard, and they enjoy traveling.

THOMPSON, SISTER MARGARET MARY S.C.N., professed 50 years on July 19, 1990. This concerns her relation to His Excellency Most Reverend Francis Ridgely Cotton, first bishop of Owensboro, KY.

Her great-grandfather, Joshua Morris Cotton, was a half-brother to James Wright Cotton, grandfather of Bishop Cotton.

The Cottons of Virginia and Kentucky were Baptists to her grandfather who became a Catholic late in life as did Charles Robertson Cotton, father of the bishop.

In 1983 she visited the niece, Virginia Jones Cota, and her husband, Al Cota, and their family in Santa Maria, CA. Her mother was Louise Cotton Jones.

The older sister, Mildred, married first, Henry Lobley and had two children, Cameron and Mary Catherine. Second marriage was to Jay Culliton. They all lived in Seattle, WA.

THOMPSON, SISTER MARY EVA, (April 21, 1917-April 30, 1992) was the daughter of Ambrose Vincent and Ellen Angela Mattingly Thompson, born in St. Joseph, KY. She was baptized Mary Lillian on May 6, 1917 by Rev. James L. Whelan, St. Alphonsus Church. Invested: Aug. 14, 1937 No. 450. Final Profession of Vows: Aug. 15, 1942.

Mary Lillian was welcomed into the family by Cecelia, Catherine and Bill. Later she would welcome James, Paul and Frank. In 1924 her mother died. Cecilia, Catherine and Lillian came to Maple Mount. Bill, James, Paul and Frank went to St. Thomas Home, Louisville, KY. After a year Mr. Thompson took the girls to Stanley where Cecelia contracted infantile paralysis and died. Catherine and Lillian returned to the Mount. Lillian's formal education began at St. Anthony School, Brown's Valley, KY. Sister Madeline Buckman was her teacher. She continued grade school at the Mount; then entered high school where Sisters Agnita, Joseph Marie, Eugenia, Mary Jean and Aquina were her teachers. In 1933 she graduated from high school. Lily lived the next year in Louisville with her sister Kate and attended Nazareth College. After the year Lily returned to the Mount and continued college at Mount St. Joseph Junior College.

Christ called and Lily responded by entering the novitiate Sept. 7, 1936. The following Aug. 14, 1937, with seven other young ladies, Miss Mary Lillian Thompson received the Ursuline habit and became Sister Mary Eva, O.S.U. Novice days were too short for Sister Mary Eva - so much to learn, so much to do. Characteristics that she had acquired - determination, hard work, independence, uniqueness, a sense of being with God, love of Jesus in the Blessed Sacrament, the Mass and devotion to Our Lady began to foreshadow her life as she began teaching religion, English and Latin at the Academy.

Sister Mary Eva's first mission away from home was at Flaherty, KY as teacher of religion, English, Latin and commercial subjects. Next she went to St. Bernard Academy, Nebraska City as religion, English, Latin and journalism teacher. Then Brescia College in Owensboro had many needs, and for the next 10 years Sister Mary Eva served. Brescia College needed a librarian and claimed Sister for the rest of her life. During these years Sister Mary Eva furthered her education by attending summer schools and work shops in San Antonio, TX; Creighton, NE; Chicago, IL; and Austin, TX.

The community remembers Sister Mary Eva as a true Ursuline Sister - womanly, loving, compassionate, enjoying her duties, even being jury and judge of little-boy squabbles and peacemaking afterwards - teacher, librarian, writer, musician, artist, liturgist, sacristan, a prayerful religious. She loved her family, and kept in touch with them in their joys and sorrows. They remember her in her last years of suffering, fighting cancer, determined to keep on until the last. She came to Lourdes Infirmary April 8, 1992. They remember how considerate she was of nurses, Sisters and aides who kept watch with her. From then until her death Thursday, April 30, 1992, her sister, Kate and Sister,s were present to her. While the community were receiving Holy Communion in the Chapel, Sister Mary Eva began her fullness of life.

The funeral liturgy was at 10:00 a.m. in St. Alphonsus Church.

THOMPSON, WM. J., son of the late Wm. Gobel Thompson, a farmer and the late Myra V. Payne, was married to Rose Mary Dockemeyer, daughter of the late Bernard J. Dockemeyer, farmer, and Lillian Beaven on Jan. 20, 1951 at St. Alphonsus Church.

They have lived in St. Alphonsus Parish, except for two of their married years.

They have two daughters and four sons.

Lynda married Danny Edwards on Dec. 4, 1971. Bernard (Benny) married Paulette Beaudry on Oct. 4, 1975. Chris married Sandra Murphy on March 4, 1977. Tommy married Donna Simmons on Dec. 21, 1984. Darlene married Keith May on March 23, 1985. Franky is not married. A fifth son, David, died at 6 weeks of age.

Lynda has two girls, Karen and Christie. Benny has a boy and girl, Patrick and Amanda. Chris has two boys and two girls, Jesse, Lisa, Diana and Michael. Tommy has two stepchildren and twin daughters, stepchildren are Beth and Robbie, twin daughters are Kyndal and Kerrie. Darlene has three children, Krystal, Erica and Nathan.

Bill was a minister of Communion. He was born in Louisville, KY in 1929 and moved to New Mexico as a small child. Then in 1943 he moved back to Kentucky. He retired from Texas Gas in February 1990 after 35 years. Rose Mary was born in St. Raphael Parish and moved to St. Martin then to St. Alphonsus. They both love to travel, cooking out and seeing their children and grandchildren.

THRASHER-HAMILTON, Cecil Thrasher Jr., son of Cecil and Margaret Marsch Thrasher, born Sept. 7, 1921 in Lewisport, KY was baptized at St. Columba Catholic Church in Lewisport.

Cecil married Mary Ann Hamilton June 25, 1955 in Holy Name Catholic Church in Henderson, KY. Mary Ann was born May 18, 1932 and baptized at Holy Name Catholic Church. She is the daughter of Samuel Richard Hamilton Jr. and Mary Kathryn Carroll.

Cecil and Mary Ann had three children, John Cecil, Mary Anne and Margaret Jane. John Cecil was born Oct. 27, 1960 and married Laura Frances Brackett on Nov. 20, 1987 at the Newman Center in Lexington, KY. They now reside in Columbus, OH. Mary Anne was born July 3, 1965 and married Bradford Thomas Boyd on Aug. 2, 1985 in Holy Name Catholic Church. They have two daughters, Caroline Elizabeth and Abigail Thrasher Boyd. They reside in Henderson. Margaret Jane was born May 26, 1972 and is a student at Purdue University in West Lafayette, IN.

Mary Ann is a housewife and a volunteer at Holy Name Church and in the community.

Cecil is a veteran of World War II. He served in the Eighth Army Air Force in Polebrook, England. He was an armorer gunner flying waist position on 29 missions. He was in the 351st Bombardment Group, 511th Bomb Squadron.

Cecil has been active in Holy Name Church since moving to Henderson in 1950 as City Art Supervisor. He later taught at Henderson City High School and Henderson Community College. He has been in the insurance business for 35 years. He is past president of Henderson Rotary Club, Paul Harris Fellow, and is presently treasurer of Kentucky Rotary Youth International Exchange.

THRELKELD, THOMAS GILHOOLEY AND ANNA LISLE HARRISON, were both born in Marion County. After Tom finished medical school at University of Louisville they moved to Russellville, KY in 1954. They are members of Sacred Heart in Russellville. Thomas was born on May 9, 1924 in Lebanon, KY to John C. Threlkeld and Marguriete Gilhooley. Anna was born on Nov. 3, 1926 in Lebanon, KY to Anna Mae Duncan and George Harrison.

Thomas and Anna Threlkeld

They have five children, Mike born Nov. 3, 1950 is married to Janice Guron; Tommy born July 11, 1952 is married to Carolyn Savage; Mary Cret born July 19, 1953 is married to Danny Johnson; Ann Duncan born June 14, 1954 is married to Roger Gower; and Meg born July 11, 1958 is married to Gary Hancock. They also have nine grandchildren, Ryan Gower, Clay Johnson, Julie Threlkeld, Robert Threlkeld, Tyler Johnson, Lynn Anne Gower, Michael Threlkeld, Morgan Hancock and Mary Duncan Hancock.

THWEATT, IRENE C., was born June 22, 1913 in Portageville, MO to Andrew and Myrtle Carter. She received the three sacraments of Baptism, Holy Communion and Confirmation at St. Eustachius Catholic Church in Portageville.

She moved to St. Louis, MO where she wed Francis P. Cronin in 1931. She has one daughter, Mary Catherine Cronin Blackwell who was born Sept. 3, 1932. She attended St. Theresa's and Sacred Heart Parishes while in St. Louis.

Irene Thweatt and Mary C. Thweatt

On Feb. 12, 1942 she wed Landon L. Thweatt. They moved from St. Louis to Symsonia, KY in 1946. At this time she became a member of St. Francis De Sales Parish in Paducah, KY. She had been a member of St. Francis De Sales Parish until she moved her membership to Rosary Chapel in 1981. She has two grandchildren, Victoria L. Auchenbach of St. Louis, MO and Brian D. Blackwell of Fort Worth, TX. She has two great-grandchildren, Lauren Michelle Auchenbach of St. Louis, MO and Sean M. Auchenbach of Atlanta, GA.

Her Catholic faith was exemplified to her by her parents who raised nine children on modest means in the bootheel of Missouri. They all learned to share, respect and love each other, along with their fellow man.

TIELL, FATHER MAURICE JEROME, was born to Albert and Evangeline (Hoepf) Tiell on April 3, 1923 at New Riegel, OH. He grew up on a 73 acre farm a mile and a half southeast of Berwick, OH. He received his First Holy Communion at St. Nicholas Church at Frenchtown, OH April 24, 1932 and was confirmed there four days later. After completing the ninth grade at an area public school at McCutchenville, OH, he entered The Pontifical College Josephinum at Worthington, OH to begin his studies for the priesthood. When Bishop Francis R. Cotton visited the Pontifical College Josephinum to ask for volunteers for the Diocese of Owensboro, Maurice volunteered because he was interested in home mission ministry.

Father Maurice Jerome Tiell

On June 3, 1950 Father Tiell was ordained for the Diocese of Owensboro at the Pontifical College Josephinum by the Most Reverend Amleto Cicognani, Apostolic Delegate to the United States. Father Tiell was assigned to Sts. Joseph and Paul Parish in Owensboro as assistant to Monsignor Peter Braun on June 23, 1950 until he was sent to St. Stephen Cathedral as assistant to Monsignor Anthony G. Higdon on July 6, 1950. Fr. Tiell was named pastor of St. William at Knottsville with the Mission to St. Lawrence Parish on Aug. 26, 1959. Bishop Henry J. Soenneker appointed him pastor of Precious Blood Parish in Owensboro on Aug. 2, 1966, pastor of Sts. Joseph and Paul Parish in Owensboro on July 20, 1976, and then pastor of St. Francis De Sales Parish in Paducah on Dec. 9, 1982 with missions to Rosary Chapel and St. Mary, LaCenter, KY. Bishop John J. McRaith decided to make him pastor of Webster County on June 7, 1983 to serve St. Michael Parish (residing in a mobile home in Sebree, KY) and Holy Cross Parish of Providence, KY. On Aug. 19, 1986 Fr. Tiell spent three months on a sabbatical with 50 priests from around the world at the University of Notre Dame. Then on June 10, 1987 Fr. Tiell was given the "Dream Appointment" to establish a parish in Lyon County with headquarters in Eddyville, KY (the last county in the diocese without a parish church.) On July 8, 1988 Bishop McRaith asked him to become the pastor at St. William Parish of Marion, KY and minister to the people of Crittenden and a good part of Livingston Counties.

Fr. Tiell has been active in ecumenical affairs wherever he has been assigned and has served as assistant spiritual director of the Inter-Father Cursillo Movement in Kentucky and in Ministerial Associations.

He likes to remember the restoration of St. Lawrence Church, the building of Mary Carrico School, starting the Knottsville Credit Union, the restoration of St. Paul Church in Owensboro, and lastly the building of the St. Mark Church-Hall and Rectory in Eddyville, KY.

With the encouragement of Bishop Soenneker when he served on the First Liturgy Commission of the Diocese, he wrote *Be Reconciled to God,* a catechism for the new rite of penance. He has composed three volumes of poems entitled "Over My Shoulder" and is presently working on a fourth volume. Fr. Tiell will tell you that he is glad to be a priest of the Diocese of Owensboro, KY.

TIPTON, NELVIS RAY (BUDDY) JR., was born on December 12 in Owensboro, KY. His parents are Nelvis Ray Tipton and Jean Lyle. He married Sharron Alexander and had two children, Keysha Lynn Tipton and Zachery Ray Tipton. Then they were divorced. Buddy remarried Rhonda Ann Blandford. Her parents are William D. Blandford and Joyce Mattingly. She was born on October 18 in Owensboro, KY.

Buddy and Rhonda had two children. The first was Nicole Anne Tipton, who was born on Feb. 27, 1979. She is 13 years old and goes to O.C.M.S. The other child, named Kimberly Ann Tipton, was born on Feb. 17, 1983. Both children were born in Owensboro, KY. Kim is 9 years old and attends school at Sutton Elementary where she is in the fourth grade.

Buddy is a member at Yellow Creek Baptist Church. Rhonda and the children were members of St. Pius but now they have moved to Hill Ave. so they switched parishes. Now they are members of Blessed Mother Parish.

TIVITT, LOGAN AND JUDY JARBOE, were married Jan. 30, 1965. Mrs. Tivitt has served on the Parish Council, also been an officer in the Altar Society and PTO, chairman of the church picnic and coordinator of the 175th Anniversary of St. Romuald Parish. She is also a member of the chair and a Eucharistic Minister. She works as a postal clerk and is a homemaker and mother of five children.

Logan and Judy Tivitt and family

Mr. Tivitt is an asst. manager of Galante Studio, where he has worked for 27 years. Although Mr. Tivitt is not a Catholic he generously supports St. Romuald Church and school. All of the couple's children attended St. Romuald School: Taylor, Tony, Julie, Jamie and Josh. Taylor after getting six years electronics training in the Navy is employed as an electronics technician for K.E.W.S. of Kentucky. Julie is a senior at Spalding University in Louisville. Tony a Desert Storm veteran is employed as a machinist at Falls of Rough, KY. Jamie and Josh are in grade school at St. Romuald.

TOLENTINO, OSCAR VILLAMOR AND ROSA BELLA FAMILY, came to Paducah in 1988 and joined St. Thomas More Parish. They have one daughter, Kristin Mariel.

They got married in the Philippines on Jan. 18, 1973 and came to America in September, 1974. They lived in Cleveland, OH for two and one-half years before relocating to San Jose, CA where they lived for 11 years. They were active in the Diocesan Council of Filipino Catholics and Santa Teresa Parish where Rosa Bella served as organist. They moved to Paducah when Oscar took the position of plant engineer for Lafarge Corp. (then Missouri Portland Cement) in Joppa, IL.

Having attended Catholic schools from elementary through college, they made it their priority to enroll Kristin in one. She is presently attending St. Mary Middle School.

Rosa Bella started playing the organ in church since 1956. She will never forget the time when she learned to play the harmonium and got it in one day. She had a fever that night from fatigue caused by pedaling for one day. In college, she was the chapel organist for the Far Eastern University Student Catholic Action.

Currently, Rosa Bella is an organist at St. Thomas More.

TOON, ATHANASIUS AND THEODOSIA (MAXEY). Athanasius Hagen "Dock" (1843-1915) was the sixth of the 10 children of Hillary and Cinthia (Tharp) Toon. "Dock's" paternal grandparents were Stanislaus and Jenny (Blandford) Toon. Hillary and Cinthia were in the 1830s pioneer settlers of "the Fancy Farm Community" in Graves County. (Note: St. Hilary and St. Athanasius were outstanding theologians in the fourth century, and both have

been designated as **Doctors of the Church.** They were very close friends. The writer of this sketch believes that the above explains why Hillary named his son Athanasius, and why Athanasius was nicknamed "Dock". This may have been a suggestion of Father Alfred Hagan, who baptized Athanasius on May 7, 1843, at St. Jerome, Fancy Farm, KY.) "Dock" died on July 7, 1915, in Carlisle County.

Seated: Theo (Maxey) Toon (1916). Standing: Teresa (Toon) Willett. Bottom right: A.H. "Dock" Toon.

Theodosia Ernest (1857-1948) was the sixth of seven children of Wade W. and Mary (McGary) Maxey. Wade and Mary were from Chesterfield County, VA. They are listed in the 1840 Graves County Census. Theo's paternal grandparents were John and Nancy (Langsdon) Maxey. (John fought at Yorktown in the Revolutionary War.) Theo's maternal grandparents were Thomas Duke and Polly (Rudd) McGary of Chesterfield County, VA.

The Hillary Toon farm in Graves County was next to that of the Wade Maxey farm. The Toons were Catholics, and the Maxeys were Baptists. Theo was baptized at St. Jerome on Oct. 31, 1891, at the age of 34.

"Dock" and Theo had eight children: William Peter (1882-1936) married first Ida Burgess, married second Marvis Stonner; Charles Milford (1885-1963) married Mamie Gore; William Claud (1887-1949) married Catherine Roberts; Robert Bernard (1890-1915) married Lillian Hobbs; Iva Gertrude (1893-1962) married James Everett Hobbs (see Jerome Hobbs biography); Clarence Harden (1896-1966) married first Ruby Pearl Burgess, married second Catherine (Wooley) Hayden; James Aubrey (1900-1925) married Eulah Mae Brower (Aubrey was killed in an automobile accident near Arlington); and Teresa (1903-1993) married James Alton Willett (see Jack Willett and William Hayden biographies).

Theo and "Dock" had 45 grandchildren, with 37 reaching adulthood. It was always a treat going to and staying at grandma's. Theo died on Oct. 6, 1948. Theo and "Dock," with four of their children (Robert, Aubrey, Iva and Clarence), were buried in St. Jerome Cemetery.

TOON, EARL, was born near Fancy Farm, KY. A veteran of World War II. His father Elvis Toon was a farmer. His mother Idella Hobbs was a homemaker. Rubel Cissell was also born near Fancy Farm, daughter of James Noel Cissell. He was a farmer also. Her mother Josephine Carrico was a homemaker. Both were baptized at St. Jerome.

Earl and Frances Toon—50th Wedding Anniversary

They married on Sept. 28, 1940 at St. Jerome Church, Fancy Farm, KY and moved to a farm. They are the

Front row: Sonny, Pat, Georgia, Annette, Will Ed, Tootsie. 2nd row: James, Papa, Mama, Mary Joe. Back row: Father Russell, Tommy Cash.

parents of 10 living children, one deceased, 30 grandchildren and four great-grandchildren.

Earl and Rubel Toon celebrated their 50th Wedding Anniversary in 1990. They reside near Fancy Farm and enjoy retirement and attend church at St. Jerome.

TOON, JOSEPH AND MARY BLANFORD.

Joseph "Hervie" Toon Sr. was born on June 6, 1896 and died on Jan. 16, 1969. He married Mary "Tillie" Blanford in January 1917. Hervie was the son of Chris and Lucinda Toon. Tillie was the daughter of George and Nettie Blanford. She was born on July 27, 1900 and died April 20, 1987. They were farmers and members of the St. Charles Church in Carlisle County, KY. They lived one-half mile from Kirbyton close to where St. Charles Church is located. In 1962 they moved to Fancy Farm and are buried there. They had eight children.

James, born on Feb. 13, 1920. He lived in Chicago and married Helen Baker. They have five children. James died on Jan. 16, 1990.

Mary Joe, born on Aug. 3, 1922 and lives in Graves County. She married Jack Cash and they have four children.

Agnes "Tootsie," born on April 20, 1925. She married W.L. Cash. They have three children.

Hervie Jr. "Sonny," lived in Carlisle County. Born March 28, 1928. He died on Dec. 30, 1982. He married Betty Hayden and they had 12 children.

Annette, born Nov. 29, 1931, lives in Carlisle County. Married Jesse Hunt. They have two children.

William Edward, born May 9, 1934 and lives in Rolla, MO. Married Maybelle Hobbs and had two children. Second marriage to Rose Delcour.

Mary Pat, born May 28, 1937, lives in Graves County. Married to Robert Elliott. They have five children.

Georgia Mae, born on Nov. 14, 1941, lives in Paducah. Married to Dan Sullivan. They have two children.

TOON, STANISLAUS AND JENNY (BLANDFORD).

Stanislaus Toon married Jenny, daughter of William and Joannah (Pidgeon) Blandford, on Jan. 19, 1801 in Washington County. They had nine children. They were members of St. Rose Priory Parish (Dominicans), Springfield, KY.

Although Stanislaus and Jenny never lived in western Kentucky, they were and are a considerable part of what became the Owensboro Diocese through their children and descendants, mainly in St. Jerome Parish, Fancy Farm. Five of their children migrated to Graves and Hickman Counties in the 1830s, and one, Matilda Goatley, migrated to Graves County after her husband's death. Another child, Elizabeth, migrated with her husband and family to Daviess County before 1840.

The six children of Stanislaus and Jenny Toon, who migrated to St. Jerome parish were: Theresa (born 1806), who married Alfred Hobbs, 10 children; William (1808), who married Perdelia Carrico, 11 children; Hillery (1810), who married first, Cinthia Catherine Tharp, 10 children (see Athanasius Toon biography and accompanying picture of John Hilary Toon Family); Hillery, who married second, Mrs. Jane (Tharp) Gibson, three children; Sarah (1811), who married first, Ambrose Hobbs, one child; Sarah, who married second, Thomas F. Curtsinger, three children; Matilda (1812) who married William Goatley, 12 children; and Stanish Lloyd (1817), who married Jane Ryan, 10 children.

Another child of Stanislaus and Jenny, Elizabeth (1814), who married Joseph B. Mitchell, was living in Owensboro before 1840. One of their five children, Martha Ann (1842), married Freeman B. Eaton. Their seven children were baptized at St. Stephen, Owensboro. One of these, Anna (1873), married John W. Stout. Their four children were baptized at St. Stephen's. One of these, Mildred (1898), married Charles E. Field. Mildred and Charles were generous supporters of Mercy Hospital and Brescia College in Owensboro.

Rose (1858), another daughter of Elizabeth (Toon) Mitchell, married Vitus Higdon at St. Stephen's in 1877. Rose and Vitus moved to Fancy Farm in 1880s. They had six children.

TOON, WILLIAM CHRISTOPHER AND LUCINDA.

William Christopher Toon was born on April 20, 1856 and died March 13, 1939. He married Lucinda Frances Elliott in 1884. She was born on March 3, 1866 and died Aug. 29, 1919.

They had 14 children, Phillip, Bonnie, Louisa, Roy, Ira, Elizabeth, Hervie, Larney, Daisey, Randell, Laura, Minnie, Agnes and Mary Magdalene. They were farmers and members of St. Charles Church in Carlisle County, KY.

TOON, WILLIAM R. AND JEAN.

William, known as Sammy, and Jean Wynn were married at St. Francis De Sales, Paducah, KY on Nov. 11, 1950. He was born Aug. 3, 1927. His parents were William Randle and Flora Poat Toon. He was the third of four children, was baptized, made First Communion, confirmed and served as an altar boy at St. Francis DeSales. Father Albert Thompson said he was the most perfect altar boy that he ever had to serve Mass for him. He graduated from St. Mary's Academy in 1945. Served in the Navy during World War II and the Korean Conflict. Jean was born April 6, 1932. Her parents were William B. and Anna Simmons Wynn of Obion, TN. She was the youngest of nine children. After the death of her father they moved to Paducah. She graduated from Tilghman High School in 1950. Two years after marriage she joined the church.

Having served as a supervisor in the Mechanical Department, Sammy retired after 41 years with the railroad in 1989.

Jean retired from Citizens Bank after 29 years of service. At the time of her retirement she was assistant vice-president and manager of Ky. Oaks Mall Branch.

John Hilary and Teresa Neomia Willett Toon family. Back, l to r: Joseph, Harrison, James, Lee, Felix, Robert. Front: Catherine Marie, Edna Lorena, Anna Daisy, Cornelius R., Alvey.

William Christopher and Lucinda Toon with Daisey (baby) sitting, Randel sitting and Laura standing.

William R. and Jean Toon

They have two children, William Michael and Cynthia Kay. Both graduated from St. Mary's High School and the University of Kentucky and reside in Lexington, KY. They also have two grandchildren, Cassandra Ann and Stephen Michael.

Jean and Sammy reside in Kuttawa, KY and attend St. Mark Catholic Church in Eddyville, KY. They are active in their church.

TOWERY FAMILY. The James and Susan Hayden Towery family have lived in the St. Joseph, Beech Grove, KY area all their lives. Both of them received their sacraments at St. Alphonsus Church, St. Joseph, KY. They were married there on June 10, 1972, by Fr. Walter Hancock.

James, Susan, Alex and Eric Towery.

Jim is a self-employed farmer and Susan is a school teacher.

They have two teenaged sons, Alex and Eric.

Their parents are the late Joseph G. and Mary Louis Stallings Towery and Joseph Henry and Verna Ball Hayden.

TRAWICK FAMILY. Louise was born in Vitebsk, Russia during the height of the Stalin oppression. Her mother and maternal grandmother were born in Riga, Latvia. They were of Polish heritage. Her father was Russian and Polish. All were raised Roman Catholic.

The family's anti-Communism came to the attention of the authorities. The family had to abandon their home and fled to Southern Russia. When German troops entered Russia, they were caught back and forth under fire. The family witnessed many atrocities of World War II. During the retreat of the Germans from Russia, the family was herded like cattle into crowded trucks and then trains and sent to labor camps in Austria.

Surviving the war, the family came to the United States in September of 1949 under the sponsorship of two families in Natchitoches, LA.

Louise was 17 at the time and spoke Russian, Polish, German but no English. With a strong faith, determination and a dictionary as a constant guide, she overcame the language barrier.

André was born on a small farm in a remote rural area, Little Woods, LA, on the outskirts of New Orleans, LA. That rural area doesn't exist today; it is now a New Orleans suburb.

Louise and André met at L.S.U. They were active in the Newman Club where the then Father Wm. Borders (later archbishop of Baltimore) deeply touched their lives.

The Trawick Family

After L.S.U. André attended Loyola Law School. Louise and André married while he was still in law school. Their five children were born in New Orleans. Louise and André have always been active in their church parish. They were speakers for 12 years in the New Orleans Pre-Cana programs. The family moved to Dallas in 1972. Four of the five children graduated from Bishop Dunne High School. That school and St. Elizabeth's Parish was the nucleus of the Trawick life in Dallas.

In 1980 the Trawicks moved to Henderson, KY, when André received an appointment as a Federal Administrative Law Judge. That year Louise and André celebrated their 25th wedding anniversary (occasion of picture). The oldest son, Andy, is married, has two children and lives in Salt Lake City, UT. Their second son, Greg, was ordained a priest in the Diocese of Owensboro on May 11, 1985. The other three children, Armand, Corinne and Steve, presently reside in Kentucky.

TRAWICK, FATHER GREGORY GORDI-JENKO, was born Nov. 6, 1957 to André and Louise Trawick in New Orleans, LA. He was the second of the Trawick's five children. He was named after his mother's grandfather. Greg attended Catholic Schools. While in New Orleans he was enrolled in Our Lady of Lourdes and St. Andrew Elementary Schools. He attended one year of high school at Jesuit. His father's large French family and "Life in New Orleans," including Mardis Gras, made his early years most memorable.

Father Gregory Gordijenko Trawick

The family moved to Dallas in 1972 and he completed his high school at Bishop Dunne. He attended St. Mary's University in San Antonio, TX where he received his B.A. While in high school and college he was active in various organizations.

Following his graduation he moved with his family to Henderson, KY. He worked for one and one-half years at a savings and loan in Evansville before entering the seminary. He received his master's of Divinity from St. Meinrad Seminary in 1985. He was ordained a deacon on May 26, 1984 and spent some time at St. Jerome's in Fancy Farm with Fr. Jerry Riney. He was ordained to the priesthood on May 11, 1985 with Daniel Goff, Gary Payne and Terry Devine. His first assignment was at Holy Spirit. He served with Fr. Thomas Clark from 1985-1987. In June of 1987 he was transferred to Blessed Mother in Owensboro where he served with Fr. Charles Fischer until June of 1989. He was then named pastor of St. Joseph, Leitchfield and St. John the Evangelist, Sunfish. One of his first projects was to bring to fruition a parish center at St. Joseph's. As a priest he has been a part of Ecumenical Organizations, various community boards, and was elected Dean of the Eastern Deanery.

TRUCINSKI, LEO STANLEY (LEON STANISLAS TRYCINSKI), was born in Nancy, France, one of six children. The family had moved from Ciechanow, Poland to escape the oppression in their homeland. The family sailed from Cherbourg, France aboard the R.M.S. *Aquitania* of the Cunard steamship line. From Ellis Island they settled in New Philadelphia, OH and became members of Sacred Heart Church. Leo served in U.S. Army in Europe during World War II.

He met and married Martha Marie Hulsey while both were in service. She in the 113th W.A.C. Hospital Co. They were married in the Chapel of Nichols General Hospital, Louisville, KY by Fr. Aloys Selhorst.

Leo and Martha came to Madisonville in 1951 and were members of Immaculate Conception Church in Earlington until Christ The King Church in Madisonville was built.

They have one son, John and two grandsons.

TURNER, KENNETH WAYNE AND BENITA FAYE, were married on Feb. 28, 1981 at St. Mary of the Woods. Kenneth, born Nov. 23, 1959, is the son of Robert Earl Turner and Anna Louise Edge. Benita, born Oct. 4, 1960, is the daughter of Joseph Cecil Payne and Frances Marie Higdon. They have lived in Knottsville, KY, Daviess County since 1981 and are members of St. Williams. Benita is formerly from St. Mary's at Whitesville. They both participate in their parish picnic and both are 1978 graduates of Trinity High School.

Kenneth and Benita Turner

Kenneth and Benita have five children, Jesse Wayne Turner, born Oct. 1, 1983; Hannah Marie Turner, born Jan. 14, 1985; Andrew Thomas Turner, born June 4, 1986, died Dec. 19, 1986; Audrey Faye Turner, born March 7, 1988; and Kelsey Jo Turner, born May 30, 1989.

Kenny is a volunteer fireman and emergency medical technician. He is employed as a control room operator at Dart Polymers.

TURNER, MICHAEL EZRA AND KATHY CLARK, Michael was born on Aug. 26, 1952 and is employed as cemetery maintenance construction worker. Kathy was born on Sept. 30, 1954. They reside in Daviess County and are members of St. Mary of the Woods Parish.

The Michael Turner Family—Kathy, Daniel, Joshua, Abram, Julie and Maghan.

They have five children, Daniel Ezra Turner, ninth grade, born April 11, 1977; Joshua Michael Turner, seventh grade, born May 2, 1979; Abram Jeremiah Turner, fourth grade, born Oct. 3, 1982; Julie Marie Turner, third grade, born July 7, 1984; and Maghan Kathleen Turner, born Dec. 6, 1988.

TURNER, RICHARD ALLEN AND PEGGY MARIE WILLETT, settled in Morganfield, KY. Peggy had attended Catholic schools during grade school. There was no Catholic high school in Union County at that time. Ricky was a Baptist when they were married. He joined the Catholic church in 1984. Father Al Powers gave him instructions. Ricky is active in many things. He joined the Knights of Columbus in Morganfield. He is the Pro-Life chairman. Peggy and Ricky went on a Pro-life march in Washington D.C. one year. They have been to a pro-life seminar in Louisville. They pass out literature for the pro-life people.

Ricky is a volunteer fireman for the city of Morganfield.

Ricky and Peggy have three children. Joshua John Williams was the first born. He was named for both grandfathers. Shawnna Marie is the only girl. Marshall Derek is the youngest one. Josh and Shawnna attend St. Ann's School. Derek is in kindergarten.

Peggy and Ricky went on a pilgrimage to Medjugorje, Yugoslavia. It was a trip of a lifetime. When they returned home, they gave talks about their trip and answered questions. They received many blessings while on their trip. Peggy went on another pilgrimage with a tour group. Her mother went with her that time. They went to Fatima, Portugal and to Medjugorje, Yugoslavia.

Ricky and Peggy have gone to Birmingham, AL where the Blessed Virgin Mary has appeared to one of the visionaries from Medjugorje, Maria.

Peggy does volunteer work at St. Ann's School. She does whatever is needed from work in the lunchroom to field trips. She also visits nursing homes.

TURNER, ROBERT EARL AND ANNA LOUISE EDGE, were married on July 7, 1951. Robert, the son of Focient Adolphus Turner and Mary Ilean Heady, served in the Korean War for two years and is a carpenter. Anna, daughter of Patrick Joseph Edge and Anna Leah Payne, is a housewife and foster mother. They are the parents of nine children, Robert Eugene Turner born July 22, 1954, Janice Marie Turner born June 30, 1956 (deceased), Joseph Patrick Turner born April 6, 1958, Kenneth Wayne Turner born Nov. 23, 1959, James Anthony Turner born July 19, 1962 (deceased), James Edward Turner born Dec. 30, 1963, Margaret Ann Turner born July 13, 1965, Martin Earl Turner born July 10, 1968, and Stephen Darrell Turner born Nov. 8, 1972.

The family has lived in Knottsville, KY, Daviess County since 1952 and are members of St. William. They were members of St. Mary's, Whitesville, for one year. They have been very active in their parish picnics, bingos, Alter Society and Conference of Christian Mothers (when there was one).

Involved in Knottsville Fire Dept. since 1973. They have been foster parents for 16 years.

Robert attended both St. William grade and high school. Anna attended St. William School for 12 years. All their children attended Mary Carrico and Trinity High. The two deceased children died at birth.

UHING, SISTER MARY BERNICE, was born on Oct. 23, 1916 at Bow Valley, NE to Herman Uhing and Anna Promes, both of Hartington, NE. She was baptized, Alma, on Oct. 26, 1916 and had her confirmation in May 1925. She entered the convent on Sept. 8, 1935 and received her Habit on Aug. 14, 1936. Sister Mary took her vows on Aug. 15, 1938 and Aug. 15, 1941. She was recommended by Rev. A. Birnbach at St. Peter and Paul Parish, Bow Valley, NE. She has four brothers and sisters, Julia Uhing-Leise, Edmund, Cyril, and Hubert.

Her missions include: Waterflow, NM, Mt. St. Joseph, Waverly, KY, Earlington, KY, Radcliff, KY, Fredericktown, KY, St. Edward, Jeffersontown, KY, St. Christopher, Radcliff, KY, Brescia, Hawesville, KY St. James, Louisville, KY, Plattsmouth, NE, St. James, Louisville, St. Theresa, Grants, NM, Motherhouse, Christ the King School, Madisonville, and Motherhouse.

UNDERWOOD, HERSCHEL AND POLLY, Polly grew up in Cedar Hill, TN, where the absence of priests made it difficult to receive the sacraments. One day Father Brown from Nashville lined up Polly, her brothers, sisters and mother in their living room and baptized them all. Mass at St. Michael's was first celebrated every fourth Sunday, then every second and fourth Sunday, and eventually every Sunday. One evening when Polly was at Church, a storm came up, and she and about 14 others had to stay overnight in the church because the creek had flooded and they couldn't get home.

Herschel and Polly Underwood

During the war, Polly worked as a riveter on B-24s in a factory outside Detroit.

Herschel grew up in Arkansas and after serving over four years in the Army Air Force, he was employed by the New York Central Railroad in Michigan. Herschel was not a Catholic when he and Polly met, and it was a couple of years after they were married on Oct. 24, 1948, that he was received into the church. They had eight children, (five boys and three girls), seven of whom are still living and doing well.

After retiring, Herschel and Polly moved to Western Kentucky in 1984 and joined St. Henry Church in Aurora, where they are both very active. Both have served on the Parish Council, the cemetery committee, and the grounds committee. Herschel is an usher and Polly is an Eucharistic minister and lector. She also tries to keep flowers around the altar. Some of the flowers are from their garden at home and some are wild flowers found in the fields.

The Underwoods are thankful for the guidance of their pastor, Monsignor George Hancock, and appreciate the opportunity to attend Mass five days a week. They are truly enjoying their retirement.

URSULINE SISTERS AT MARION, KY. In July of 1985 Sister Ethel Sims and Sister Frances Miriam Spalding, Mount St. Joseph Ursulines, arrived in Marion, KY to be the first resident sisters to minister to the people in St. William Parish and to others in Crittenden and Livingston Counties. At first they were very apprehensive as to this assignment since this area was truly the "Bible Belt," with only this one Catholic Church among the other 67 churches, most being Baptist. However, at the very beginning and during the seven years of their residence there, they have felt only acceptance and love, not just from the Catholics but from all other religious denominations.

In the absence of a resident priest, they as pastoral ministers, help to care for the spiritual needs of these people. They are involved in the RCIA programs, CCD teachers, caring for the shut-ins, nursing homes, hospitals, participating in the literacy programs, minister to the needy and anything else the Lord sends their way. Each day is a different challenge.

Sister Rose Theresa Johnson and Sister Francis Miriam Spalding

The first three years they ministered not only to St. William Church, but to St. Francis in Sturgis and St. Ambrose in Henshaw, doing the same kind of work. Father Hank Cecil, in residence at Sturgis, was the pastor for all three parishes. When he was transferred to Mayfield, their extended places of ministry changed from St. Francis and St. Ambrose to St. Mark in Eddyville, with Father Maurice Tiel as pastor in residence at Eddyville.

The family of two Ursuline Sisters has not grown in number of sisters these seven years, but a change in Sisters has. After two years Sister Ethel Sims was replaced by Sister Jamesetta Knott. Then two years later, she was replaced by Sister Rose Theresa Johnson, who has been at St. William for three years. Sister Francis Miriam has given seven years in ministry with these great people. She and Sister Rose Theresa are both looking forward to being in the midst of these people at Marion, Salem and Eddyville and walking with them as they journey with our God, for years to come.

UTLEY, CARL RICHARD AND MARTHA ALICE POWELL, were one couple of a double wedding that took place on Feb. 6, 1929. Carl, born June 30, 1916, the son of John Robert and Susan Gertrude Utley, farmed early in life and worked in a foundry at Morganfield later on. Alice's parents were Edward Fenwick and Martha Elizabeth Pike Powell. She was the youngest of three daughters and was born on Sept. 12, 1918. There were three older and two younger brothers. All but Christina still live.

Carl and Alice were members of St. Ann's Parish most of their married life. They have 10 children: Peggy, Jerry, Joe, Jack, Sue, Tommy, Rose, Richard, Helen and Powell. One son, Joseph Michael, died at birth.

Carl was stricken early with cancer and died Aug. 14, 1961, leaving Alice with nine children at home, the youngest only 21 months old. But faith and friends saw them through; she held the family together, and worked for a number of years at the public library in Morganfield to supplement her Social Security.

Carl Richard and Martha Alice Powell Utley

A few months ago her oldest daughter, Peggy and her husband Walter Murphy, who recently retired from the post office in Massachusetts, moved back to Morganfield. This makes all her children just a few miles distance from her. So, she is never alone or lonesome, because of the coming and going of children and grandchildren. Large families are rewarding!

Alice lives in Morganfield by herself and attends Mass almost daily at St. Ann's.

VAUGHAN, THOMAS ARTELLE (TOMMY),
was born in Centralia, IL on May 1, 1927, the only son of Rupert Artelle Vaughan and Fay Henley. After moving to Paducah and graduating from St. Mary's Academy in 1944 he married his classmate Ann Cloys on May 29, 1947 and worked for the Illinois Central Railroad. Ann Cloys, born in Paducah on Feb. 27, 1927, is the daughter of Otho Cloys and Marguerite O'Donnell.

The Thomas A. Vaughan family.

Tommy and Ann lived in Paducah throughout their marriage and had six children. The oldest child, John Richard, was ordained a priest in 1974. After serving in several parishes in Western Kentucky he was vicar general of the diocese for seven years and currently is on the faculty of his alma mater, the North American College in Vatican City. The other five children currently live in Paducah and are members of St. Thomas More, St. John's and St. Francis De Sales parishes. All six of the Vaughan children attended Catholic schools in Paducah and so have all their children.

Lynn Ann married Dan Brown and they have three children. William Joseph married Nancy Purcell and they too have three children. Mary Lee also has three children and now is married to Keith Galloway. Carol Fay married Kenny Shoulta and they are the parents of four sons and a daughter. The youngest, James David, is married to Tana McManus. David has one son by a previous marriage and he and Tana have one child.

After Tommy's death in 1965 Ann began working for a dentist in Lone Oak. She remained in the same office until her retirement in 1992. She has been a member of the adult choir at St. Thomas More for over 25 years and has sung in the diocesan choir. In retirement she volunteers for a variety of parish activities.

VEATCH FAMILY, BENJAMIN, Benjamin Veatch
was born Sept. 16, 1828 in Woodford County, KY. He was the son of James Powers Veatch and Matilda Ann Lewis. The date he moved to Union County is unknown, but there is a record of Martha Ann and Isabella, his two oldest children, being baptized at Sacred Heart. These were from a previous marriage, and there is a possibility that he moved here as a widower, but no records have been located.

Eliza Magdalene Bartley Veatch with her son, George.

He met and married Eliza Magdelene Bartley, who was born in Union County, KY on Feb. 17, 1839. The marriage took place at Sacred Heart Church, on Jan. 16, 1866. Benjamin Veatch died Oct. 9, 1908 and Eliza Magdalene died on Dec. 12, 1929. Eliza was the daughter of Hezekiah K. Bartley and Eleanor Madden.

Ben and Eliza raised six children and lost two at an early age. The children are: Henry E., who married Florence Hause and started a furniture store in Morganfield; Mary Magdalene married John Wickliffe Collins (story under Collins); Ellen Ruth married George Simpson Collins and remained in St. Ann Parish raising seven of nine children; James William died young; George Martin married Rose Etta Lee and after raising their family in Union County moved to California; Matilda died young; Lydia Priscilla married Harry B. Carrico and settled in Owensboro, KY; Benjamin Jerome married Hazel Pearl Wilson and raised their family in Cannon City, CO. No record has been found of Martha Ann and Isabella.

Benjamin and Eliza and the children that remained in Union County are all buried in St. Ann's Cemetery.

Tradition has it that Ben was a big red haired man, noted for raising good thoroughbred horses. It was said that he turned his horses loose, to prevent Union soldiers from capturing them.

VENTERS, FATHER DARRELL, was born in
Fairfield, IL. He is the fifth of six children born to Mrs. Lucille Venters and the late Mr. Lester Venters. He attended Fairfield Community High School, and received a bachelor of science in agri-business from Murray State University, Murray, KY. He was baptized in the First United Methodist Church and was received into full Communion to the Catholic Church in August 1982 at St. Francis De Sales, Paducah, KY.

Father Darrell Venters

He entered St. Meinrad Seminary in 1984 and received his masters of divinity in 1989. He was ordained a deacon, November 1988, and a priest May 1989 for the Diocese of Owensboro by the Most Reverend John J. McRaith. He was associate pastor at St. Stephen Cathedral, Owensboro for two years and St. Thomas More, Paducah for one year. He is currently pastor of Precious Blood, Owensboro.

VICTOR, STEVEN E., son of Harold and Irene
Victor, was born May 11, 1949 in Brookston, IN. Harold worked farming popcorn and Irene was a housewife. Peggy Cummings, daughter of Joseph and Betty Cummings was born July 13, 1943 in Grand Rapids, MN. Joseph worked in business while Betty worked as a teacher. Steven and Peggy met while at a hospital meeting. They were married on Feb. 15, 1974. Steven works for the Eli Lilly Company. Peggy is a former medical records technician and is now attending college for a degree in journalism.

Steven and Peggy had two children, Jessica and Nathan Victor. Jessica attends Apollo High School while Nathan attends Owensboro Catholic Middle School. Nathan is an altar server for Immaculate Parish. Jessica baby sits for the people at Zion Baptist Church. Nathan mows yards. Jessica is now 17 and Nathan is 14.

VINSON, CHESTER FAMILY, Chester, son of
Thomas and Rebecca Vinson served in the armed forces during World War II. He returned to West Virginia and worked two years in the coal mines in Mingo County before coming back to Paducah and marrying Pearl, daughter of Riley and Dora Durbin, on Oct. 21, 1947 at St. John.

Chester Vinson Family

They were the parents of six children, Dorothy Jeane, Deanna Rose, Donna Sue, David Chester, Daniel Lee and Donald Gerard, all attended St. John and were all graduates of St. Mary High.

Dorothy married Gary Shaffer on June 21 at St. John and they have three children: Ginny Michelle, Gary Lynn and Jeffrey Vinson. Deanna Rose married Jim Bealmear from Hopkinsville on Sept. 3, 1971. They have one daughter Melissa Ann and belong to St. Stephens in Cadiz. Donna Sue resides in Columbus, OH and works as a nurse. She is in St. Leo's Parish. David Chester married Lori Labazon on April 20, 1985 in the cathedral in Columbus and they have two children, David Chester and Kristen Marie. They live in Pittsburg, PA and are members of St. Catherine of Sienna Catholic Church. Danny Lee married Patti Robinson at St. John on Feb. 10, 1977. They have two daughters, Danielle Nicole and Sarah Ruth. They belong to St. John Parish. Donald Gerard married Paula Sue Humpert at the Blessed Sacrament Church in Fort Milchell on Nov. 19, 1988.

Chester worked for the Illinois Central Railroad for 29 years. He died Feb. 25, 1977 and was buried in St. John's Cemetery.

WAGNER, PHILLIP MATHEW, was born to
Harriet Josephine and Fred George Wagner, born Oct. 24 and 25, 1888, who were farmers. He was born and raised in Rock County, WI and now lives in Marshall County on Kentucky Lake at Jonathan Creek area. He is a member of St. Frances De Sales parish.

His children include: Phillip, born Aug. 19, 1955; Mark David, born July 12, 1957; Thomas Alan, born June 25, 1958; Craig Martin, born May 13, 1960; Debra Ann, born Jan. 10, 1962; and Kimberly Renee, born June 8, 1963. All college grads with honors.

He is a member of the Lions Club, Parish Council, Berea Team, Administrative Group and Building Committee.

WALDRIDGE, CHARLES AND ANNELLA MARIE WILLETT,
On Aug. 12, 1967, a new life began for Annella Marie Willett. She was joined in holy matrimony to Charles Fredrick Waldridge, a widower with five children ranging in age from 11 to 16. Charles' wife had died quite suddenly 15 months earlier and at age 37 he felt God was giving him a second chance for happiness. Annella, at age 32, had found the good husband she was looking for when she joined a square dance club to which Charles belonged. Charles and Annella were married at St. John the Evangelist Church by Monsignor William B. Jarboe.

Annella was born on Jan. 27, 1935, the third of 10 children born to Arthur Anthony Willett and Margaret Frances Wurth. Charles was born on Feb. 24, 1930, the youngest of 10 born to Louis Marvin Waldridge and Alcestra McKinney. His 2 year old brother dubbed him "Baby Charles," a name that followed him throughout his life.

On March 11, 1950, Charles was married to Bobbye June Hutchins. God blessed their marriage with three sons and two daughters; Charles Jr., William, Sharon, Jack and

Karen. Charles and the children were members of Cumberland Presbyterian Church. When he and Annella married, Charles began going to the Catholic church with her. They drove the 10 miles from Paducah to St. John's to attend an early Mass. Then Charles would go to the Presbyterian Church with his children. Occasionally the three younger children would go to the Catholic Church with them.

Charles, Annella and Janice Waldridge.

On July 20, 1968, Charles and Annella were blessed with daughter, Janice Marie so Annella looked for a "home parish" closer to home. She decided on Rosary Chapel, a small "homey" parish in Paducah. In 1973 when the organist at Rosary left, Annella called on her experience as organist at St. John's during her school years and volunteered as organist at Rosary Chapel, a "job" she continued for more than 12 years. Charles began going to choir practice every Tuesday night with Annella and eventually went to the rectory to do "odd jobs" for the pastor, Fr. Emillian. One night after choir practice when Annella was preparing for bed she noticed a catechism laying on the dresser in the bedroom. When questioned about it, Charles admitted the "odd jobs", in part at least, had been taking instructions in the faith. During the Easter Vigil Services on March 30, 1975, Charles was baptized in the Catholic faith, received First Holy Communion and was confirmed. What a glorious day for Annella and Janice! His daughters, Sharon and Karen later followed his example and joined the church also.

From the first, Charles embraced his new religion with enthusiasm. He became very active in the parish serving as lector, usher, Eucharist Minister and two terms on the Parish Council. He became a one-man welcoming committee. Annella arrived at church 30 minutes early to get the music ready and Charles spent the time at the church door greeting everyone, but especially the elderly ladies who attended there because of the easy access to the church (there were no steps) and assisting them in any way possible. One lady in particular who used a walker Charles always watched for. He'd help her out of the car and up the center aisle to her place in the front pew so to make it convenient for Father to give her Communion. Little Janice walked beside her Daddy carrying the lady's purse. Mrs. Dorian called Janice her little Guardian Angel.

If for some reason they were a little late getting to church and the ladies were already in their places, Charles made the rounds to the pews greeting and chatting with them. One of the nuns who was pastoral assistant at Rosary used to kid Charles and say he missed his calling - he should have been a priest. He would answer, "If I ever get rid of Annella I may do that."

In 1979 Charles and Annella built a new home in the St. John community but they continued to attend Rosary Chapel. Charles had to retire in 1985 after by-pass heart surgery, so they moved their membership to St. John's because it was closer. However, Charles's heart was still at Rosary and many a Sunday morning he attended Mass there - sometimes alone if Annella was engaged as organist at St. John's. The people were always glad to see him, he was liked and admired by all. In his quiet, simple way Charles touched the lives of so many people. He died from the heart disease on Aug. 4, 1987 - just eight days before his and Annella's 20th Wedding Anniversary. Annella still lives at their home in the St. John community and continues to take her turn as organist at the week-end Masses.

A year after her father's death, Janice married Brian Fredrick Kopischke and they also are building a new home in the St. John's community.

WALTER, ELIZABETH LINHUBER, was born on Jan. 30, 1917 to Anna and Mathias Linhuber of Austria, Europe. She was born and raised in Austria and now lives in Benton, KY, Marshall County. She belongs to St. Pius Tenth Church in Calvert City.

Elizabeth Walter

Elizabeth has one daughter Eva Walter Quint who lives in Michigan.

WALZ, HENRY, eldest son of Lawrence and Frances Crile Walz married Martha Clara Ballmann Feb. 29, 1885 at Immaculate Conception, Hawesville. They were both born in Kentucky. Ambitious, dedicated and God fearing servants they became the parents of Frances, Henry and Charles (twins), William and Joseph (twins), Otto, Frank, Rosa, Lawrence, John, Victor and Lena Walz. Eleven children reached adulthood. At present Rosa, 98 years of age and Lena age 91 years are members of Immaculate Conception.

Henry was a carpenter, truck farmer and dairyman while Martha was his strong companion and homemaker. Deep embedded faith they passed on to their children. One of their gifts to the church was the sixth station of the Cross which can be seen in their present church.

Martha died in 1936 and Henry in 1942 after 51 years of marriage. They rest peacefully in the Walz family cemetery now Calvary Cemetery the land given by them to the church.

Lena, Rosa and Frances, the three daughters have given over 60 years of selfless service as sacristans to Immaculate Conception which has been the center of their life's work.

WALZ, LAWRENCE AND FRANCES CRILE, Immaculate Conception Church Hawesville, KY was the strengthening strand to their faith brought from Germany. Lawrence and Frances, both born in Baden, Baden Bavaria met and married in Hawesville on July 13, 1860 before the first church was built. In 1858 the lot, on which the church was built, was bought through Father Bede O'Conner of St. Michael's Cannelton, IN at the request of Bishop Spalding of Louisville.

With pioneer determination the first hand hewn stone edifice was finished in 1871 through the labors, prayers and sacrifices of the small group of Catholics in the area. Each family contributed as their means permitted. Lawrence and Frances gave two pews and a stained glass window to the little church nestled next to the L&N and St. L Railroad on the banks of the Ohio River. The stained glass window can be seen in present church.

Lawrence was a cabinet maker and Frances the homemaker. To this union was born Henry, John, Lawrence and Rosa. Henry remained in Hawesville. John died in Hawesville and Lawrence Jr. moved to Missouri. Little Rose died of serious burns at an early age.

Lawrence Sr. died in 1896 and is buried in Calvary Cemetery formerly the Walz family cemetery later donated to the church. Frances died in 1905 and is buried in Jasper, IN at her request.

WALZ, OTTO GEORGE, sixth child of Henry and Martha Ballmann Walz married Ida May Brown at St. Rose Cloverport, KY on June 15, 1920. They were both born in Kentucky. St. Rose was their parish until 1947 when Immaculate Conception became their parish at the request of their pastor.

Martha Walz Gammon

Otto was a farmer but worked at numerous trades which didn't prevent his giving wholly his time and energy to both Immaculate Conception Church and the schools. Much of his time was given in repair service at the schools. He was one of the builders of their present church in 1958. May also gave service in the school cafeteria.

May's death came in 1973 and Otto's in 1980 after 52 years of marriage they remained unrelenting God fearing servants. As family Regina, Dorothy Jackson, Sister Joan of Arc Walz, George Edward and Martha Gammon respected their dedication, sacrifices and strong faith passed on to them.

In 1967, Martha Walz Gammon, widowed with a young son, came to Immaculate Conception which became her strengthening strand to her faith. Now retired from sales and nursing, much of her time is given in christian service, as lector, catechist and member of the Altar Society, associate member Legion of Mary, etc.

Over 132 years a Walz has been an active member at Immaculate Conception. Presently Miss Rosa and Miss Lena Walz, Miss Regina Walz, the George Gammon family and Martha are members.

May Immaculate Conception always remain a beacon as they give their thanks for the privilege to serve.

WANINGER, GREGORY, was born in Tell City, IN. Moved to Owensboro, KY when he was 10 years old. He went to Immaculate School, then he went to O.C.H.S. He went to college for two years at Kentucky Wesleyan. He works at Kenway as a salesman. Kennetha Waninger was born in Owensboro, KY. She went to Precious Blood and went to O.C.H.S. Now she works as a teacher's aide at Bishop Cotton School. They were married at St. Stephen. They go to Immaculate Church and are ushers.

They have three children. The oldest is Nicholas Waninger, 14, goes to O.C.M.S. and is a server and is in the youth group. Nathan Waninger, 12, goes to school at Catherine Spalding and is a server. Natalie Waninger, 7, goes to Catherine Spalding.

WARD, JOSEPH DONALD AND AMELIA PAULA (GREENWELL), were married on Oct. 5, 1968. Joseph was born on Nov. 23, 1946 and Amelia was born on Feb. 27, 1947. They have lived in Whitesville, Daviess County since August 1969 and are members of St. Mary of the Woods. Mr. Ward is a former member of St. Joe and Paul in Owensboro and Mrs. Ward is a former member of St. Mary Magdalene. Mr. Ward has coached girls basketball and softball for the grade school since 1982 while Mrs. Ward has been school volunteer and school board member since 1982.

Their children are Tabatha Marie Ward, July 1, 1969; Tracy Ann Ward, May 9, 1971; Tina Louise Ward, April 29, 1973; and Terra Suzanne Ward, April 28, 1980.

WARREN, JOHN "CHRIS," was born on Sept. 25, 1953 to Benjamin Hubert Warren and his wife, Lois Eileen Warren. On Dec. 27, 1973 at Lourdes Church, he married Vickie Ann Shreclner. She was born to Russel

Antony Hayden and Margery Ann Shreclner on Oct. 16, 1953. Chris works at Commonwealth Aluminum and Vickie is a teacher at Foust Elementary School. They go to Saint Stephen Cathedral to celebrate Mass. They are both 39 years old.

Stephen "Scott" Warren who is 13 is the oldest child in the Warren family. Alex "Nick" who is 10 is the middle child. The youngest children are Erin Lee, Ryan Benjamin and James Russel Warren. They are 5 year old triplets. Scott and Nick are both servers and Scott is in St. Stephen's youth group. Scott goes to O.C.M.S. while Nick, Erin, Ryan and James go to Saint Angela Merici.

WARREN FAMILY, ROBERT AND JANETTE,

The children of the Robert and Janette Warren family have a rich heritage in the Western Kentucky Diocese sprouting from both sides of their family tree. Bob and Janette's home is built on the farm owned by his great-grandfather, John O. Warren, who along with Bob's father and grandfather, is buried in St. Alphonsus Cemetery. Janette's great-grandfather, Aquilla Blandford, is mentioned as one of the first Catholic settlers in Kentucky, and on the site of his log home now stands facilities of Mount St. Joseph Educational Center. The heritage has continued down the generations and today finds the Warrens serving in a diversity of ways. Bob has been a church councilman and a school board chairman. All of the Warren children attended St. Alphonsus grade school. Both Bob and Janette have been C.C.D. teachers.

Bob and Janette Warren

But their special gift to the diocese would probably be in the area of music. Bob has served as music leader at St. Alphonsus for over 20 years. He plays the organ also, and two of his daughters have been church organists. He and Janette have taken part in Diocean Choral Events. Bob also plays the piano weekly for one of the area nursing homes. Bob has worked for 36 years for Bell South.

Bob and Janette's pride and joy is their strong family. Each of their nine children are active in their respective churches and have succeeded in their chosen professions. Nothing pleases Bob more than looking down their long dining room table and seeing his children and their spouses, along with his six grandchildren, gathered to celebrate a holiday or special family event. They are an affectionate and supportive clan, despite their geographic spread over five states. Bob and Janette have ensured that the rich heritage of faith and service to God they received from their ancestors has been passed along to the next generation.

WATHEN, SISTER GEORGE MARIE,

was born on April 15, 1909 in Calvary, KY to George Wathen (Aug. 12, 1882-March 18, 1965) and Myrtle Raley (June 18, 1884-April 26, 1931) both of Marion County, KY. She was baptized, Mary Catherine, on April 25, 1909. Sister George Marie entered the convent on Sept. 7, 1927 and received her Habit on March 19, 1928. She took her vows on March 19, 1930 and March 19, 1933. Her brothers and sisters include: Harry, Josephine Wathen, Paul, Isabel, Anna, Louise, Mary Rose, Cecilia George (half-brother).

Sister George Marie's missions include: St. James, Louisville; St. Joseph, Central City, KY; Rosary, Paducah; St. Margaret Mary, Lyndon, KY; St. Benedict, Wax, KY; St. Leonard, Louisville; Seven Holy Founders, Affton, MO; St. Margaret Mary, Lyndon, KY; St. Ignatius, Louisville; St. Angela Merici, Florissant, MO; St. James, Louisville; Mt. St. Joseph; and Motherhouse.

WATHEN, SISTER MARGARET ANN,

was born on Nov. 5, 1909 in Calvary, KY to Linus Wathen (March 14, 1886-Feb. 2, 1968) and Bertha Gribbons (1888-Jan. 14, 1919) both of Marion County, KY. She was baptized, Elizabeth Beatrice, on Nov. 14, 1909. Sister Margaret Ann entered the convent on Sept. 8, 1930 and received her Habit on March 19, 1931. She took her vows on March 20, 1933 and March 20, 1937. Her brothers and sisters are Charles, James C., Joseph (half-brother), Margaret Ann (half-sister), Hubert (half-brother), Robert (half-brother), Adrian (half-brother) and Mary Jo (half-sister).

Sister Margaret Ann's missions include: Howardstown, KY; Bow Valley, NE; St. Charles, Lebanon, KY; St. Mary Home, Owensboro; Flaherty, KY; St. Charles, Lebanon, KY; Waverly, KY; St. Francis, KY; Buechel, KY; St. Joseph, Owensboro; Central City, KY; Princeton, KY; Hillsboro, MO; St. Joseph, Leitchfield, KY; Holy Cross, KY; Sacred Heart, Farmington, NM; Jeffersontown, KY; Immaculate, Owensboro.

WATHEN, SISTER MARIE BOXCO,

was born on July 24, 1924 in Finley, KY to George Wathen and Annie Myrtle Raley. She was baptized, Margaret Cecilia, on Aug. 2, 1924 and received her confirmation on May 18, 1931. She entered the convent on Sept. 7, 1942 and received her Habit on Aug. 14, 1943. Sister Marie took her vows on Aug. 15, 1945 and Aug. 15, 1948. Her brothers and sisters are: William Harry (deceased), Susan Josephine (deceased), Sister George Marie OSU, Joseph Paul, Mary Isabelle Wathen-Abell, Anna Myrtle Wathen-Thomas, Mary Louise Wathen-Buckman-Payton, Mary Rose Wathen-Bryant and George Robert.

Sister Marie's missions include: New Haven, KY; Affton, MO; St. Bartholomew, Buechel, KY; Our Lady of Good Counsel; Immaculate, Owensboro; Affton, MO; Brescia College, Owensboro.

WATHEN, MICHAEL FRANKLIN,

was born near Rome, KY and baptized at St. Martin by Father Saffer. His father, John Martin was a farmer and his mother, Mattie Sue O'Bryan was a housewife.

Martha Louise Chappell was born and baptized at St. Joseph, KY, her father, Charles William Chappell was a laborer. Her mother was Mary Rose Fenwick, the daughter of a farmer.

They married Nov. 24, 1990 at Our Lady of Lourdes Church in Owensboro. The priest was Father Delma Clemons. They live in Owensboro.

Martha has three children and four grandchildren.

WATSON, EARL AND FRANCES,

Frances Anita Watson, daughter of Charles Rowan Ballard and Anna Maud Ballard (both deceased) married Earl Edwin Watson Feb. 2, 1946 at St. Raphel Church in Chicago, IL. They moved to Western Kentucky in December 1946.

Frances has always been a member of St. Mary's Church of LaCenter, and Earl joined the church in 1972. They have three sons.

Rodney Watson, now married to Joanie Carrico of Mayfield. They have two children, Allison, a sixth grader at LaCenter Elementary, and Adam, a third grader at LaCenter Elementary.

Glen Watson, married Sally Boulton. They have three children, Jennifer, a student at Paducah Community College, Brian, an 11th grade student at Ballard Memorial H.S., and Amanda, a seventh grade student at Ballard Middle School.

Mark Watson married Loraine Giles. They have two children, Joshua, a second grade student at LaCenter Elementary, and Holley, a pre-school student at Barlow, KY.

Earl and Frances have been married for 47 years. Earl is now retired and they currently reside in the LaCenter community.

WATSON, EDWARD STANISLAUS JR. AND MILDRED GLENN SMITH,

were born in Logan County, KY. They became high school sweethearts and were married, while Stan was in the service in World War II. They and their daughter have lived most of their lives in and around Sacred Heart Parish in Russellville, KY. Glenn taught catechism lessons to all four daughters as they were growing up and became a convert to the Catholic faith in 1984.

Stan's great-grandfather, Joseph Watson, served his apprenticeship in England during the Industrial Revolution and sailed across the ocean and up the Cumberland River with the machinery to build a grist mill on the Red River at the community of Dot, KY.

In the 1830s, the Joseph Watson family, along with three other Catholic families, formed a group known as the Byrne Catholic Colony, located just across the state line in Tennessee. These families were responsible for constructing St. Michael Catholic Church in 1842—the oldest Catholic church still in use in Tennessee. The Watson family attended St. Michael's in Robertson County, TN until Sacred Heart Church was built in Russellville, KY.

Stan's father, Ed Watson, married Victoria Orndorff, whose father owned and operated Orndorff Flour Mill on the Red River at Schley, KY. They had two sons. Victoria later became a convert to the Catholic faith.

Stan, now retired, worked for the Civil Service at Fort Campbell, KY and Glenn is a homemaker. They arranged for their daughter to attend Sacred Heart Parochial School, where they were taught by the Glenmary Nuns.

Stan and Glenn have five grandchildren and have made their home in Schley, KY on the banks of the Red River since 1954.

WATSON, RODNEY AND JOANIE,

Rodney Lee Watson was born to Earl Watson and Frances (Ballard) Watson near LaCenter, KY, and is a lifetime member of St. Mary of the Fields. His father owned the town's feed mill until his retirement, and his mother was a homemaker. Rodney attended school at LaCenter Elementary, Ballard Memorial H.S. and received a bachelor of science degree in business administration from Murray State University. He has been employed for the past 20 years at Ballard Rural Telephone Cooperative as a Central Office Repairman.

Joanie (Carrico) Watson is the daughter of Frank Carrico (deceased) and Lucille (Garland) Carrico of Mayfield, KY. Her father was the manager of Barton's Men's Wear in Mayfield, and her mother was the bookkeeper there. She attended St. Joseph Catholic School in Mayfield, and was a parishioner there until she moved to LaCenter. She graduated from Murray State University with a bachelor of science degree in social work, and moved to LaCenter to take a position with the Ky. Department of Human Resources. She worked as an employment interviewer for five years.

They married at St. Mary Church in LaCenter on April 30, 1977, and have two children, Allison and Adam, both students at LaCenter Elementary.

The Rodney Watson family attends St. Mary's Church in LaCenter where Rodney serves on the cemetery board, finance council, and is an usher and Eucharistic Minister.

Joanie serves on the finance council, is volunteer bookkeeper, and serves as a reporter to the *Western Kentucky Catholic*.

WEAFER, RICHARD E. AND LILLIAN PAYNE,

were married at St. Williams Church, Knottsville, KY, in 1946. They had nine children and were members of St. Stephen's parish most of their married lives.

Their children (and spouses) are as follows: Lucy and Gerald Goetz; James and Dixie Higdon Weafer; Stephen and Sarah Taylor Weafer; Dennis and Pam McCarthy Weafer; Janice and Michael Flamion; Barbara and Joseph Cecil; Richard Jr. and Dee Boling Weafer; Michael and Sharon Murphy Weafer; Lillian (Reenee) and Vincent Fogle. The children attended Catholic elementary schools, graduated from Owensboro Catholic High School, and attended Brescia College. Four received degrees from Brescia and one from the University of Kentucky. All family members currently reside in the

Owensboro area, except Stephen, who lives in Lexington, KY. There are 26 grandchildren and the family is still growing!

Richard E. and Lillian Weafer Family

Lillian, born and raised in Knottsville, KY, was the oldest of 12 children. Her parents are James P. and Marie Tierney Payne. Richard was born in Brookline, MA. His home was in Dorchester, MA and Vermont. He attended North Eastern University in Boston, then was in the army during World War II. While stationed at Camp Breckenridge, KY, he met Lillian. After their marriage, they resided in Boston, then returned to Kentucky. He completed his studies at Brescia College and became a Certified Public Accountant in 1958.

At the time of Richard's death in 1989, he was Vice President of Business Affairs at Brescia College. Richard was very active in his church and community. In 1970, he was blessed as an Eucharistic Minister, among the first in the area. Lillian is Eucharistic Minister for the sick at Daviess County Hospital, a choir member at St. Stephen Cathedral, and does volunteer work in the community.

WEDDING, MARTIN JOHN AND SARAH ANN BOARMAN, were married in 1881 at St. Mary of the Woods Church, Whitesville, KY. In the early 1890s Martin and Sally, with their four living children, moved from Union County to Fancy Farm in Graves County. After a few years as tenants, they bought a large tract of land in Carlisle County where they built a home, but they remained members of St. Jerome Parish in Fancy Farm. They had 11 children: Alonzo Vincent (1886-1954) married first Dora Rhodes (1887-1915), married second Victoria Stahr (1888-1982) daughter of Wm. Anthony and Clara Josephine Davis Stahr; Joseph (died in infancy); Maude married Paul Johnson; Hattie (1890-1985) married Fred Crawford; Bertha (1892-1985) married Roy (1891-1966) son of Christopher and Lula (Elliott) Toon; Celestine married Lola Riley; Milburn (1895-1971) single; Sadie Genevieve (1899-) married Solon Anthony (1898-1979) son of Wiley and Catherine (Roberts) Higgins; Nell (1904-) married Bernard son of Herman and Kate Stahr Mangold; Ellie (1904-1906) a twin; and Agnes (1906-1974) married Nolan (1905-1975) son of Wm. Aaron and Elizabeth Skinner Robb. Sadie Higgins lives in Fancy Farm and Nell Mangold in Cordova, TN.

Martin J. and Sarah (Boarman) Wedding

Alonzo V. and Dora Rhodes Wedding had four children: Herbert Haeseley (1912-1988), married Lillian Siebenaler; Martha (1914-) single, residing at Nazareth Village, Nazareth, KY; Margaret Rhodes and John Justin died in infancy. Alonzo V. and Victoria Stahr Wedding had four children; Wm. Martin (1919-1966), married Maggie Bethel Clements; Vincent de Paul (1921-) married Geraldine Herring, residing in Meade County, KY; Mary Hildegarde, now Mary Wedding, SCN, residing at Nazareth, KY and Mary Winifred born and died 1931.

Sister Mary Wedding taught at St. Agnes School in Uniontown from 1951-1959; at St. Vincent Academy in Union County from 1961-1965, and at Owensboro Catholic High School from 1971-1973.

Many other Wedding descendants reside in the Diocese of Owensboro.

WEIDENBENNER, SISTER MARY CELINE, was born June 4, 1944 to Isaac Weidenbenner, a farmer and Frances Stenger Weidenbenner, housewife. She was raised in Southeast Missouri (Dunklin County), Glennonville, MO and presently lives in McCracken County, KY. She is a member of St. Francis De Sales Parish. She is a teacher.

Sister Mary Celine attended St. Theresa's Grade School in Glennonville and one year freshman at Campbell High in Campbell, MO. Attended 10-12 years of school at M.S.J. Academy in St. Joseph, KY. Entered the Ursuline Convent in September of 1962 and has had teaching jobs in Stanley, KY, Holy Cross, KY, Calvary, KY, St. Joseph, KY, St. Alphonsus, KY, Mayfield, KY, and now St. Mary Middle School in Paducah, KY.

WEISE, TONY AND THOMASINE, have been members of St. Martin Parish in Rome since 1965. He grew up in the parish as a child, but left it to join the service and later married and lived in St. Sebastian in McClean County. Their two daughters, Debra and Donna attended St. Martin School until the eighth grade. His parents were members since their children were of school age. He had two aunts who were Ursuline nuns at Mt. St. Joseph, Sr. Mary Francis and Sister Mary Fidelis. They told their two brothers one of whom was Tony's father that there was work to be had there. They left their home in Breckenridge County and came to work there for two years. They hauled coal and worked in the boiler room stoking the furnace. Many a young boy in the neighborhood came to watch and admire the exceptional strength and perseverance of these two men. They earned themselves quite a reputation for hard work. Walter later met and married Virgie Hodgskins and his brother married her sister. They had five children, 24 grandchildren and 25 great-grandchildren, several of whom attend St. Martin Church, most of the others are in the diocese.

They belong to the Army of Mary, the choir and she is presently helping to put together a cookbook for St. Martin Parish Altar Society.

WEITLAUF-FELLER, Michael Anthony Weitlauf was born May 27, 1964 at Paducah, KY the son of Thomas Edward and Rose Marie Schmitt Weitlauf. Baptized May 31, 1964 at St. Francis De Sales Church Paducah, KY by Father Robert Wilson. Received First Holy Communion Nov. 14, 1971. Confirmed Feb. 10, 1974 by Bishop Henry J. Soenneker. Attended St. Mary High School, Paducah Community College and Murray State University where he received a B.S. degree in construction engineering technology in December 1986. Married Ann Arleen Feller at St. Pius X Church in Calvert City, KY Oct. 6, 1988. They have one child Emilie Elisabeth born Jan. 23, 1992. They are members of St. Lawrence Catholic Church in Lawrenceburg, KY. He is a member of the church choir.

Ann Arleen Feller born May 26, 1964 in Chicago, IL daughter of Max Henry and Sara Alice Gleason Feller was baptized at Our Lady of the Wayside Church in Arlington Heights, IL. Received First Holy Communion May 1971 at St. Pius X Church at Calvert City, KY. Confirmed February 1974 by Bishop Henry J. Soenneker. Attended Marshall County High School. Graduated from Murray State University in 1988 with a B.S. degree in nursing.

WEITLAUF-GERTEISEN, Rita Ann Weitlauf Gerteisen born March 8, 1961 at Paducah, KY daughter of Thomas Edward and Rose Marie Schmitt Weitlauf was baptized March 12, 1961 at St. Francis De Sales Church in Paducah, KY by Father Charles De Nardi. Received First Holy Communion Dec. 22, 1968. Confirmed March 14, 1972 by Bishop Henry J. Soenneker. Attended St. Mary High School and Brescia College in Owensboro, KY where she received her B.S. degree in communication sciences and disorders in 1983. She obtained a master's degree in audiology from Lamar University in Beaumont, TX on Dec. 22, 1984. Married Michael Lindy Gerteisen at St. Francis De Sales Church in Paducah, KY on July 27, 1985. Children: Kristen Rose born April 25, 1988 and Hannah Elizabeth born June 25, 1991.

They are members of St. Stephen Cathedral in Owensboro. She is a lector, a member of American and Kentucky Speech and Hearing Association and past president of Western Kentucky Speech and Hearing Association and a past president of Brescia College Alumni Association.

Michael Lindy Gerteisen born Aug. 5, 1959 at Owensboro, KY son of Lindy and Betty Rowans Gerteisen was baptized, received First Holy Communion and confirmed on July 4, 1985 by Father Tony Bickett at St. Stephen's Cathedral. Attended Owensboro Senior High School and Owensboro Vocational-Technical School.

WEITLAUF-GLASS, David Thomas Weitlauf born April 7, 1951 at Paducah, KY, son of Thomas Edward and Rose Marie Schmitt Weitlauf was baptized April 15, 1951 at St. Francis De Sales Church, Paducah, KY by Father Albert J. Thompson. Received First Holy Communion on May 11, 1958. Confirmed April 3, 1960 by Bishop Francis R. Cotton. Attended St. Mary High School, Paducah Community College and University of Kentucky received a B.S. degree in physical therapy in 1974. Married Belinda Sue Glass at Rosary Chapel in Paducah on Aug. 19, 1978. Children are Jea Scott born July 24, 1970 and Sarah Renee born Jan. 12, 1979.

The Thomas and Rose Weitlauf Family.

They are members of St. Joseph Catholic Church, Mayfield, KY. He has served as lector, a member of the school board and financial board. He is a member of the YMCA Board and the Kiwanis Club.

Belinda Sue Glass born Aug. 9, 1950 at Princeton, KY is the daughter of Alvin Jefferson and Wilma Sue Cummins Glass. She was baptized on Aug. 4, 1978 at Rosary Chapel by Father Harold Diller. Made her First Holy Communion and confirmed on her wedding day Aug. 19, 1978 by Father Harold Diller. Attended Caldwell County High School, Murray State University and became a Certified Ward Secretary for the Paducah School of Nursing. She is a lector at St. Joseph's, a member of the school board and YMCA Board, Girl Scout Leader and a member of the Junior Welfare League.

WEITLAUF-KINGSLEY, Joseph Raymond Weitlauf was born Dec. 26, 1959 at Paducah, KY, the son of Thomas Edward and Rose Marie Schmitt Weitlauf. Baptized Jan. 3, 1960 at St. Francis De Sales Church, Paducah, KY by Father William O. Fields. Received First Holy Communion Oct. 30, 1966. Confirmed March 4, 1970 by Bishop Henry J. Soenneker. Attended St. Mary High School, received an associate degree from Brescia

College. Graduated from Murray State University in 1982 with a B.S. degree in computer engineering technology. Married Paula Jo Kingsley at St. Francis De Sales Church in Paducah, KY Sept. 21, 1985. They are members of St. Francis De Sales Church where he is an usher-greeter.

Paula Jo Kingsley was born Dec. 12, 1958 at Paducah, KY the daughter of Allen Eugene and Ann Elizabeth Belford Kingsley. Baptized Dec. 25, 1967. Received her First Holy Communion June 23, 1985. Confirmed June 23, 1985 by Father Patrick Bittel. Attended Pope County High School, Golconda, IL, Southeastern Illinois College, received a B.S. degree in radio-television productions at Bradley University in Peoria, IL in 1981. She is a lector and a member of the Worship Committee. Has membership in the Zonta Club.

WEITLAUF, MARY VIRGINIA, was born June 23, 1952 at Paducah, KY, the daughter of Thomas Edward and Rose Marie Schmitt Weitlauf. Baptized on June 29, 1952 at St. Francis De Sales Church, Paducah, KY by Father Albert J. Thompson. Received First Holy Communion May 10, 1959. Confirmed April 3, 1960 by Bishop Francis R. Cotton. Attended St. Mary High School, Paducah Community College and Murray State University, received a B.S. degree in mathematics in 1973 and a master's degree in education. Received her Rank One in school administration from Western Kentucky University at Bowling Green, KY. She is a student at Fred Astaire Dance Studio in Louisville, KY.

A member of St. John the Apostle Catholic Church in Brandenburg, KY where she lives and teaches at Meade County High School. She is a past-president of Brandenburg Woman's Civic Club and a three term president of the Nite Owls Homemakers Club.

WEITLAUF-SCHMITT, Thomas Edward Weitlauf born March 20, 1921 in Paducah, KY son of John Henry Weitlauf (Sept. 15, 1893-Oct. 20, 1951) and Lucille Virginia Jones Weitlauf (May 8, 1899-April 23, 1984), grandson of George William Weitlauf (1852-June 5, 1922) and Catherine Melber Weitlauf (Oct. 12,1861-Jan. 29, 1937) and Thomas Walter Jones (Dec. 5, 1868-Jan. 2, 1908) and Mary Ann Joyce Jones (1867-1902). Baptized by Father John D. Fallon on May 3, 1921 at St. Thomas Church, Maxon Mills, KY. Confirmed by Bishop Alphonse J. Smith on May 13, 1928 at Sacred Heart Church, Memphis, TN. Married Rose Marie Schmitt on Sept. 14, 1948 at St. Francis De Sales Church, Paducah, KY. They are the parents of six children: David Thomas, Mary Virginia, Charles Henry, Joseph Raymond, Rita Ann and Michael Anthony. He is a fourth degree member of the Knights of Columbus, has been a Knight for 46 years. They are both active members of the Legion of Mary and the Army of Mary, Lourdes Auxiliary and collection volunteer for St. Francis De Sales. He is an usher-greeter.

Rose Marie Schmitt Weitlauf born Oct. 21, 1925 Paducah, KY is the daughter of Charles James Schmitt (Jan. 21, 1888-Feb. 11, 1963) and Mary Teresa Poat Schmitt (May 23, 1887-June 29, 1977) and the granddaughter of Charles Schmitt (May 13, 1849-July 12, 1913) and Mary Philomena Seitz Schmitt (May 25, 1847-July 25, 1932) and Anthony Poat (April 10, 1850-Nov. 19, 1936) and Mary Catherine Haseley Poat (Jan. 19, 1847-March 17, 1916). Baptized by Father Paul Barrett on Oct. 25, 1925 at St. John's Church, Paducah, KY. Received First Holy Communion June 5, 1933. Confirmed by Bishop John A. Floersh at St. John the Evangelist Church, on May 26, 1936. Attended St. John School for 10 years and graduated from St. Mary Academy in Paducah with a scholarship to Nazareth College and the distinction and honor of not missing a day of school in the complete 12 years.

She is a 48 year member of the Daughters of Isabella. Served two terms as Regent of the local Circle #258 and one year as Kentucky State Regent. She is a member of the church cleaning group.

WEITLAUF-STELTENPOHL, Charles Henry Weitlauf was born Feb. 18, 1955 at Paducah, KY, the son of Thomas Edward and Rose Marie Schmitt Weitlauf. He was baptized on Feb. 27, 1955 at St. Francis De Sales Church, Paducah, KY, by Father Albert J. Thompson. Received First Holy Communion Oct. 28, 1962. Confirmed May 2, 1965 by Bishop Henry J. Soenneker. Attended St. Mary High School, Murray State University and Indiana University and Perdue University at Indianapolis where he received a B.S. degree in occupational therapy in 1977.

Married Sharon Lee Steltenpohl at Corpus Christi Church in Newport, KY on July 29, 1978.

Children are John Thomas, born Aug. 22, 1985 and Phillip Charles born March 22, 1987.

They are members of The Church of the Nativity in Indianapolis. He has served on the Parish Council and is an Usher-Greeter.

Sharon Lee Steltenpohl was born May 30, 1955 at Fort Thomas, KY, the daughter of Jerome George and Donna Louise Whitehead Steltenpohl. Baptized June 26, 1955 at St. Bernard Catholic Church in Dayton, KY. Received First Holy Communion April 21, 1963. Confirmed March 9, 1964. Attended Bishop Brossart High School, Alexanderia, KY, William Booth Hospital School of License Practical Nurse. Received B.S. degree in nursing from Indiana University and Perdue University in Indianapolis, IN in 1983.

She has served as usher-greeter at church and is a member of the Ladies Club. She is a teacher for Bible School.

WELDON, WALTER NEIL, was born in 1925 in the Cottonpatch community of Crittenden County. His father, Walter A. Weldon, was a farmer, his mother, Reeta Heath Rankin, a housewife. Walter had one brother and two sisters.

Margaret Ann Dyer was born in 1931 in Marion, KY. Her father, Richard Leon Dyer, was a well-known mechanic. Her mother, Mary Louise Raley was a housewife and later a nurse. Margaret had two brothers.

Walter and Margaret were married in 1950. They lived in Marion and Crittenden County all their lives. They both attended school in Crittenden County and Marion. Walter served in the Army during World War II, stationed in New Guinea, the Philippines and Okinawa. After his discharge, he worked for a contractor and for the state highway dept. (Engineers). He retired in 1986. He is working for Crittenden County on roads and bridges and is serving as 911 DES coordinator at present time.

With the arrival of her family, Margaret became and has remained a mother and homemaker. She was one of the original members of St. William Catholic Church, having services in James F. Mills home before a church was built. She was active in the church, playing the organ, cleaning, teaching CCD classes and belonging to the Altar Society.

Walter and Margaret have always been devoted to their family, often making sacrifices to make ends meet. Walter often had to drive great distances to work. They have lived in the Forest Grove Community for 30 years, in a house with a big yard, which is a necessity when the family congregates for weekend barbeques and fish frys.

The Weldons have six children. Virginia Lee 1950, Walter Thomas 1951, Michael Neil, 1959, Patricia Ann 1966, Margaret Louise (1967-1967) and Nancy Heath 1970. Walter and Margaret have six grandchildren.

WELLS, EDWARD DOUGLAS, was born in Fordsville, KY son of Marvin and Mabel (Hendricks) Wells. Grew up with two brothers and two sisters. He married Mary Joan Edge, daughter of Louis and Nora (Van Rysselburghe) Edge of St. Mary's parish in Whitesville, KY. Joan is the eldest of 14 children growing up with eight brothers and five sisters (one brother and two sisters now deceased). Ed took instructions and became a convert to the Catholic Faith from the late Father Herman J. Miller of Sacred Heart Parish where, on Sept. 15, 1955, Ed was baptized.

Ed and Joan were married in Whiting, IN. Four of their sons were born in Indiana and baptized at Sacred Heart, one son died there in 1960. Ed worked in a steel mill while living in Indiana. In 1962 they moved to Whitesville and are now members of St. Mary's. Ed went to work at a steel mill and they had three more children, one daughter and two sons.

Edward and Joan Wells Family.

Ed has been an usher and Joan a member of the Altar Society for several years, both active in the parish picnics. Four of their sons have been in the military, three of whom are still active in the military, as is their son-in-law, two of their sons, live in Whitesville, one lives in Florida and two in Pennsylvania. Their daughter lives in Tennessee. Ed and Joan have 10 grandchildren.

Ed is now semi-retired and Joan is a nursing assistant and works with the elderly. They live on Oklahoma Laffoon Road in Whitesville.

WESTERFIELD, ALLIE DAVID JR., was born in Owensboro, KY and was converted to Catholicism in December of 1943.

His father, Allie David Sr., was a carpenter and his mother, Aura Bell Maglinger, was a homemaker. They were from Owensboro, KY.

Allie David and Mary Mildred Westerfield Jr.

Mary Mildred Myers was born and baptized in Ravenna, KY. Her father was Clay Harper Myers and her mother was Mary Bell Owen.

A.D. and Mildred were married on June 26, 1942 by Father C. P. Boling at St. Paul Catholic Church in Owensboro, KY. Their eight children were born in Owensboro, KY. They have 17 grandchildren and four great-grandchildren.

A.D. is a retiree of General Electric and his hobby is wood working. Mildred is retired from Owensboro Senior High School where she was a lunchroom matron.

A.D. and Mildred celebrated their Golden Wedding Anniversary in June of 1992. They reaffirmed their wedding vows at Mass celebrated by Fr. Darrell Venters at Precious Blood Parish.

The Westerfield's reside in Owensboro, KY and are active members of Precious Blood Parish.

WESTERFIELD, JAMES EDGAR AND AGNES MARIE EDGE, Agnes born Oct. 1, 1915 to George T. and Melinda Ann Edge was one of 12 children. She married James on Oct. 24, 1942. He was wounded in World War II and received the Purple Heart and Good Conduct Medal. James died Sept. 14, 1978.

They had two children, one of which died when a baby. The other child, Mary Jo, married John Snyder.

Agnes presently lives in Whitesville, KY, Daviess County and attends St. Mary of the Woods. She retired from G E in Owensboro.

WESTERFIELD, KENNETH AND MARTHA FAMILY, have belonged to St. Mary's of the Woods

Parish in Whitesville all their lives. They were married Sept. 22, 1956. Reverend Martin Nahstoll officiated at their wedding.

Kenneth worked in Evansville, IN, at International Harvester before their marriage. He was drafted into the armed forces during the Korean War for two years, 18 months of which was served overseas. He is a cattle farmer and drilling contractor who began his business in July 1955.

Martha worked at General Electric Company before their marriage. After marrying Kenneth, she worked in the home raising their children and helped Kenneth with bookkeeping in his business.

Kenneth and Martha Westerfield Family

The Westerfields have three children and three grandchildren of which they are very proud. Daughter Geralyn, is married to Edward Early and has three children. Son Mark, is serving his country in the United States Marine Corp. Daughter Lori, attends college, studying to be a nurse.

Kenneth and Martha are active in their parish. Kenneth served on St. Mary's Grade School Board for six years. He was on the first grade school board, which started on Sept. 2, 1971. He also served on the Trinity High School Board for three years. He served on the Parish Council, Finance Committee and Picnic Committee. He belongs to the Knights of Columbus organization and has been a lector in St. Mary's Parish for 20 years.

Martha scheduled and helped with the altar servers for eight years. She has belonged to St. Mary's Altar Society for 35 years, and is an active member. She also belongs to St. Mary's Quilters. Nora and Louis Edge welcome the quilters into their home once a week to quilt for St. Mary's Parish Picnics. A lot of piece making goes on there.

WESTPHELING FAMILY, Paul and Johanna Westpheling came to Fulton in the spring of 1947 from Washington DC. At age 31 and a college graduate, he had nine years experience (advertising staff/manager on five previous newspapers) plus four years domestic and foreign duty in the Army in World War II. He resigned his job with the *Washington Post* to make this change. Johanna, his wife, also resigned her staff position with the Veterans Administration. During the war years she had been on the staff of the Office of War Administration (OWI) in Washington, with previous experience including 10 years with a daily paper in her home town. Both elected to seek their fortunes with their own newspaper in Kentucky.

Paul is a native of St. Joseph, MO, the oldest of seven children, a communicant in the Cathedral Parish of that city, a graduate of Christian Brothers High School and the University of Missouri. Johanna, a native of Clarksdale, MS, a member of the Immaculate Conception Parish of that city and a graduate of schools in New Orleans, was one of 13 children of Mr. and Mrs. John Serio of her city.

Their first child, Robert Paul Westpheling III, was born in Fulton that fall. A second, a daughter Mary Johanna, was born in 1960. Both attended St. Edward's Catholic School in Fulton and subsequent diocesan schools in neighboring Union City (TN) and Hickman, (KY). Paul graduated from Murray State University at Murray, KY and began a career in radio broadcasting. After having been associated with all three major networks, he is now a staff member of the Voice of America (VOA) in Washington, DC. He and his wife Kathy make their home in Vienna, VA. They have no children.

Mary Johanna attended the Academy of the Sacred Heart in St. Charles, MO and graduated from the University of Tennessee at Martin (TN) with a degree in accounting. After a career in that field, she opened her own office in Fulton as a CPA and is now administrator of the Parkway Regional Hospital in Fulton. She has three sons, Todd, a graduate of Rhodes College in Memphis; Rob, a senior at the McCallie School in Chattanooga (TN); and Paul, a sophomore at home.

In their active careers in Kentucky, both Paul and Johanna have been honored as influential citizens both in their community and in their chosen endeavors.

Paul has served as president of the Kentucky Press Association, president of the Fulton Rotary Club, chairman of the Hickman-Fulton Riverport Authority, a member of the Kentucky Economic Development Commission, a member of the Boy Scout Council of the area, and a member of the building committee that enlarged St. Edward's Church to its present size. He is a retired veteran and a long-time professional musician (pianist) and former orchestra leader.

Johanna's long list of accomplishments included being active in state political circles, state president of the 1982 Kentucky Bicentennial, a long-time member of the State Democratic Central Committee, a delegate to five Democratic national conventions, a five-time president of the International Banana Festival and state and national offices of the Business and Professional Women's Clubs.

Some years ago Paul and Johanna sold their interests in the radio station and newspapers in Fulton and purchased the *Hickman Courier*, a weekly newspaper at Hickman, KY, which Paul continues as publisher.

Johanna passed away in March, 1986. Paul has since remarried and he and his wife continue to make their home in Fulton on West State line.

WETHINGTON, PAUL VOLK AND ANNA MURPHY, Paul, born April 28, 1880 at West Louisville, KY; died Sept. 16, 1948. Anna, born June 4, 1885 at Brown's Valley, KY; died June 27, 1962. Paul and Anna, married Nov. 26, 1907 at St. Anthony Church, Brown's Valley. Paul was a farmer, Anna was a seamstress. Paul and Anna were staunch members of St. Anthony Parish. Being of strong Catholic faith, they fully supported the church, the school and the pastor.

Paul and Anna, parents of 14 children: Bernard, Bert, Mary Pauline Hayden, William, Anna Louise Grant, Herman, Mary Elizabeth Martin, Margaret Anderson, Helen Blandford, Angela, Sister of Charity of Nazareth, KY, Rita Husted, Father Paul Volk Jr., Joseph and James.

All 14 children were born at Brown's Valley and baptized at St. Anthony Church. The 14 children represent many areas of the United States and embrace a variety of professions.

Paul and Anna were grandparents to 66 children and great-grandparents to 105 children.

The name, Paul Volk, a prominent name in this family, is taken from Rev. Paul Volk, founder of Mount Saint Joseph, Maple Mount, KY.

WETHINGTON, SISTER ROBERTUS, (May 28, 1886-June 19, 1963) was born to Alec and Martha Thompson Wethington in St. Joseph, KY. She was baptized, Mary, June 6, 1886 and entered the convent on May 9, 1909. Received Habit July 14, 1909. Final vows Dec. 30, 1912. Brothers and sisters: Paul, Leo, Joe, Gonzaga, Hortense (Sr. Augustine), Gertrude (Sister Richard) and Christine Wethington-Aud. Missions: Hardinsburg, New Haven, St. Charles, Supervisor of Schools, Fredericktown, MSJ Academy, Fairfield, Motherhouse.

Sister Robertus was truly "a fighter for the rights of the underdog." One of the Sisters characterized her in those words; she herself, in an article titled "A Sister Speaks," gives evidence of the truth of this title that she earned by hard work and by calls for her dismissal from a school where she was principal. The composition "Three Worshippers at the Crib" is a touching tribute to her years of work for social justice for the black people. She introduced a course in the study of the psychology of racial prejudice, probably the first in Kentucky.

Sister Robertus was an intelligent woman and a prophet before her time, who at Catholic University was involved in a movement she aroused concerning the denial of educational advantages to the black people. She knew her materials and could relate to church, community, politics, - all phases of life, what oppression of the Blacks would bring to pass here and elsewhere in the course of time. Here at the Academy in her teaching, no matter what the class, the national sins and world sins against the Blacks were the subject of her militant treatment on discrimination against them. She lived to be 77 and wore herself out proclaiming what she believed.

One of her former students from New Haven says she feared and revered Sister Robertus. She says: She discovered I had a mind and she taught me to use it. She taught me to outline and to organize my materials. She was not a leader, but a pusher. Her philosophy was that if you pushed people far enough they would succeed in whatever they wanted to do, and she declared she pushed harder those she loved the most.

Sister died June 19, 1963 of brain cancer.

WHELAN, SISTER DOROTHY ANN, Sister Dorothy Ann Whelan's roots are from Maryland. She was baptized at St. Ann's, Howardstown, KY. She came from a family of nine; three sisters and five brothers. She entered the Ursuline Order of Mount Saint Joseph in 1930. Sister made her First Vows in 1933 and Final Vows in 1936. She started teaching in 1933 with 65 pupils in the first four grades, plus being organist at Little Saint Joseph in Marion County. She also taught at Raywick, St. Charles, St. Francis, Loretto and Calvary in Marion County, Clementsville in Casey County, Peonia in Grayson County, Mayfield in Graves County, St. Bernard's and St. Paul's in Jefferson County, Immaculate in Daviess County, St. Benedict's and Plattsmouth in Nebraska. She taught school for 49 years, thirty-four of those years in the public school system staffed mostly by Sisters. Sixteen of those years she was principal and teacher. Before Vatican II, she taught the Latin for the Requiem Mass to grade school children. This training was accomplished between the first day of school and All Souls Day on November 2.

Sister Dorothy Ann Whelan

She celebrated her Silver Jubilee while teaching at St. Paul's in Louisville, her Golden Jubilee at Loretto, KY, and her 60th Jubilee at St. Joseph's, Leitchfield.

After retiring from the classroom, she taught music for six years. She was a Pastoral Ministry worker at St. Joseph's, Leitchfield, KY. Thank God for the blessings of good health for all these years.

WHELAN, SISTER MARY deCHANTAL, was born at St. Joseph, KY, Nov. 10, 1914. Since both her mother and father's parents were dead, her parents, Florence Eugenia Neel and Joseph Leslie Whelan, moved from Paducah, KY in 1909 to St. Joseph, KY in order to be near Father James Louis Whelan, her father's oldest brother, who was pastor of St. Alphonsus Church and later chaplain of Mount St. Joseph Convent and Academy.

DeChantal is the fourth child in a family of eight: Francis Jr, who died at the age of 1 year, James Francis, Robert Vincent, (both deceased), Mary deChantal, William Thomas, Virginia Ruth, Charles Aloysius and James Louis.

DeChantal was baptized by her uncle, Father James Louis Whelan, at St. Alphonsus Church, attended the Parish Parochial School, and graduated from Mount St.

Joseph Academy in 1933. In September 1933, she entered Mount St. Joseph Ursuline Convent, took the habit of the order in 1934, and made first vows on March 19, 1936.

Sister deChantel

She received her B.A. and M.A. degrees from St. Louis University, MO. She taught grade school and high school in St. Louis, MO, Louisville, New Haven, Holy Cross, Loretto, KY. She was assigned to Brescia College in 1958 and taught journalism and English there until 1967 when she attended graduate school at Indiana University. She earned her doctorate in English in 1970 after which she returned to Brescia and taught English until she began working in the grants office in 1988, where she is working at the present.

She lives at the Brescia College Convent, Owensboro, KY.

WHELAN, SISTER MARY EMILY, was born Howardstown, KY, Aug. 16, 1918. Parents were Nicholas L. Whelan, 1876-1955, Howardstown, KY, farmer. Addie (Boone) Whelan, 1877-1957, Howardstown, KY, housewife. Her sisters and brothers are Sister Dorothy Ann Whelan (Dorothy Cecilia) April 14, 1912; Mary Pauline Rogers (1902-1989); James Virgil Whelan (1904-1960); Joseph Edward Whalen (1906-1968); Agnes Lucille Cecil (1908-1985); Charles Henry Whalen (1910-1963); William Martin Whalen (1913-1971); and Robert Anthony Whalen (1916-1944). Attended St. Ann School, Howardstown, KY; Mount St. Joseph Jr. College, Maple Mount, KY; Nazareth College, now Spalding University, Louisville, KY; Catholic University of America, Washington, DC; Columbia University, New York City, NY; Fisk University, Nashville, TN.

Sister Mary Emily Whelan

Entered Mount St. Joseph Novitiate, Feb. 2, 1939. First profession Aug. 14, 1939, final profession, Aug. 15, 1941.

Ministered: St. Charles School, St. Mary, KY; St. Columba School, Louisville, Ky; St. Bernard Academy (now Lourdes High School), Nebraska City, NB; Brescia College, Owensboro, KY; librarian 1959-1989. 1989 retired from the library and working as a receptionist in the counseling center.

She has traveled through the Midwestern States, the New England States; Canada.

WHISTLE, RAYMOND ELWOOD AND EMMA LOUISE MORRIS, were married in Whitesville at St. Mary of the Woods Rectory on Dec. 27, 1952. Rev. Martin Nahstoll witnessed the marriage.

Elwood was born on May 6, 1933. He served two years in the U.S. Army and worked for Whirlpool in Evansville for 38 years where he retired in June of 1990. Elwood is a member of Karns Grove Baptist Church near Philpot.

Elwood's parents were Turner "Doc" Whistle and Helen Canary Whistle. Turner worked and retired from Fleischmann Distillery and was a farmer. He died in October of 1988. Helen was a housewife and helped on the farm. She died in November of 1990.

Emma Morris Whistle was born on April 29, 1933. She is a housewife and helps on the farm. Emma has been a life-long member of St. Mary of the Woods Church in Whitesville.

Emma's parents were Joseph B. Morris and Emma Delle Johnson. Joe was a farmer and Emma Delle a housewife. Joe died in October of 1980 and Emma Delle died in April of 1970. They were members of St. Mary of the Woods Church in Whitesville.

Raymond and Emma Whistle

Elwood and Emma have four children.

The oldest son Robert Leon was born on May 6, 1954 in Whitesville and married Patricia Dickens. They have three boys: Troy, Brandon and Nicholas. They also had twins, Keith and Kevin, who died shortly after birth.

The second son, James Bradley was born on June 18, 1955 at Fort Hood, TX. He was ordained a priest for the Diocese of Owensboro in January, 1981.

Brenda Louise, the third child, was born at home in Philpot on Feb. 24, 1957. She is married to Donald Edge. They have seven children: Terri, Jamie, Dustin, Jeffery, Todd, Corey and Casey.

Curtis Ray, the fourth child, was born in Owensboro, on Nov. 16, 1959. Curtis is married to Donna Hamilton and they have two children, Kristi and Chad.

Elwood and Emma plan to do a little traveling if Elwood will ever retire from farming. Emma works with quilt tops and other crafts when she is not working on the farm. Elwood piddles around at the garage. They live in Philpot, KY.

WHITE, CHARLES HUBERT AND JOHN LILLIAN HULTZ, were married at St. Anthony's Church at Peonia, KY by the Reverand Victor Boarman on Sept. 26, 1953. Charles' parents were Leona Grant and Charles Harvey "Bunk" White. Lillian's parents were Laura Ellen Hazelwood and John Hultz. Her father, who was a blacksmith, died three weeks before Lillian was born. Hence the reason her mother named her John Lillian.

Lillian joined the church and made her First Communion on her wedding day. They have been members of St. Augustine Parish at Grayson Springs ever since. They are proud of the church community there.

Charles and Lillian have seven living children.

Joyce Anne, the oldest is married to Edward Johnson. They have one son, Kyle and live in Lexington, KY.

Mary Jane weighed only three pounds and lived only two days. She died within an hour after having been baptized.

Veronica Sue has one son, Scott and a daughter Bethany Gibson. She is divorced.

John Christopher, the oldest son, is married to Wendy Hawkins. Wendy is a convert. Both are CCD teachers and are very active in St. Augustine's Church. They have two sons, Christopher and Johnathon.

Charles Harvey is a builder of beautiful homes in Leitchfield. He is married to Kelli Claypool.

Laura Jean is married to Greg Hughes of Lexington. Greg is a convert. They have two children, Amanda and Adam.

Kerry Kim is a recent graduate of University of Kentucky. His wife is Victoria Rae Mercer. Their daughter is Kayla Kim. Kerry was known as their "Miracle Baby" since the doctors said there was little chance he would be born alive and not much chance that Lillian would live. Thanks be to God. Kerry was delivered naturally and both baby and mother did great!

The Charles White Family

Michael Gerard is a very "special" son. Michael has Down's syndrome. Three hours after his birth, the doctor said he would never walk, talk, smile, would not know his parents and that he would never know what love was. He strongly suggested Michael be given up for science to study. They told him "No" and have tried to treat him as they did the others. Michael is retarded but "Thank God" he can walk, talk, laugh, run and play and do most things other kids do. Michael has been blessed with an abundance of love that he receives from almost everyone he meets and love he gives to everyone!

A very wonderful priest, Rev. Ray Goetz, took the time to teach Michael to serve at Mass and to make his First Communion. Michael loves to serve!

One unusual and rare note on the White family.

The white satin wedding dress that Lillian wore when she married was the same dress that all three of her daughters wore when they married.

WHITE, EMMETT O. FAMILY, Ruby Lee Barnes, born June 3, 1916, was the second child of Cletus Barnes and Mary Lile who married in 1913. Cletus and Mary Barns reared eight children, all baptized at St. Joseph Church in Leitchfield, KY. Mary was a convert. Ruby Lee Barnes married Emmett O. White on March 15, 1937.

Emmett was the seventh child of Washington White and Rua Wilson. He married Ruby Barnes in Louisville, Kentucky at St. Leo Church. Emmett converted to Catholicism shortly after his marriage. With the exception of 10 years, they have lived in Grayson County all their lives and Ruby Barnes White has been life-long member of St. Joseph Parish.

The Emmett O. White Family

Emmett and Ruby had 10 children: Joseph E. White born March 9, 1938, James Cletus White born Oct. 3,

1939, deceased Oct. 4, 1940, Kenneth E. White born June 28, 1941, Janice M. White born April 9, 1943, Lloyd R. White born May 13, 1947, deceased Sept. 14, 1989, Martina White born Aug. 28, 1948, Catherine L. White born Feb. 25, 1951, John A. White born Aug. 24, 1952, Phyllis J. White born March 14, 1953, Rita K. White born Dec. 25, 1957. These children have all married and there are 28 grandchildren and four great-grandchildren. Three of the families are presently members of St. Joseph Parish.

The Catholic tradition at St. Joseph's has long been a part of the Barnes' family. Grandfather, Harrison Barnes, who was born in 1870, told of an Italian priest, Father Louis Beruatto, coming to St. Joseph and his trouble with the English language. Many tales of going to church on horseback or in wagons are recalled by the Barnes/White family at St. Joseph Parish, Leitchfield, KY.

WHITE, GLEN FREDERICK AND VIDA LEE MEREDITH,

were born in Peonia, KY, but did not meet until 1959 when Fr. Walter Hancock, who was pastor at the time, started a teen club in what he called the crystal green room, which was the church basement. Fred went to school at St. Anthony and St. Paul. Vida went to St. Benedict. They were married Feb. 24, 1962 at St. Anthony by Fr. Walter Hancock. They lived in Chicago the first three years of marriage. Moved back to Peonia, they've been there since. Fred is employed with American Bread Co. Vida is a homemaker. They have two sons, William F. is married to Diane Pilot of Kalamazoo, MI. James G. is married to Tammy Clark of St. Paul, KY. William and Diane have two daughters, Meredith and Callie. Fred and Vida's parents, grandparents and great-grandparents were all life long members of St. Anthony and Augustine parishes. Fred is a member of the Knights of Columbus, Fr. Carroll White Council. Fr. Carroll a cousin to Fred, died in a car accident in December 1969.

Fred and Vida White

Fred and Vida are involved in several ministries in the church. They helped with the 50th anniversary renovation of St. Anthony Church. It was very humbling for them to read the history that was compiled for the rededication ceremony and see the names of parents and grandparents who helped to build the church and realize the responsibility of passing on the faith.

WHITE, SISTER REBECCA,

was born Sept. 20, 1957 at Campbell, MO. She was baptized Rebecca Regina. She was baptized Sept. 20, 1957. Entered Aug. 27, 1978. Received habit June 30, 1979. Her father is Ben White and mother Geneva Hagan. They were both born in Blytheville, AR. Her father was born July 27, 1925 and her mother March 13, 1925.

She had brothers and sisters: Benjamin Edward, Thomas Larry, Dolores Anna White-Welman, Loretta Marie White-Handy, Francis Randal and Mary Kathleen White-New.

She became an RN before entering Mount St. Joseph Ursuline Community. As an Ursuline she ministered in the Motherhouse Infirmary and later continued her studies to earn a BS in nursing. Further study was directed toward a Masters degree in Women's Studies.

WHITEHOUSE, MARK AND MARGARET,

married Aug. 11, 1984 at St. Anthony's Parish in Browns Valley, KY, then began their married life together at Bowling Green, KY and there attended and were active members at the Western Kentucky University Newman Center. Their first child, Erika was born and baptized there, then they all relocated to Owensboro in June 1986 after Mark graduated from Western Kentucky University and began working at North American Phillips. They currently have three children: Erika, Jason and Collin. Jason and Collin were both baptized at Immaculate Church where they are current members.

The Mark and Margaret Whitehouse Family

Mark was raised in Philpot and attended Sts. Joe and Paul Parish. He is a son of Gordon and Mary Rose Whitehouse. After 12 years of Catholic education he joined the Navy for four years, then returned to Western to receive an electrical engineering degree. He currently works at Indiana-Michigan Power Company in Rockport, IN. He serves as a hospitality minister at Immaculate.

Margaret was raised in Utica, belonged to St. Anthony's Parish in Browns Valley. She also attended 12 years of Catholic education before going on to nurses training. She completed her nursing from Western Kentucky University and currently works at Owensboro Daviess County Hospital. She is one of 13 children of Mike and Theresa Rose McCarty. She has been involved in the RCIA program and the "I am special" preschool program.

WHITFILL, J. MICHAEL FAMILY,

was born Feb. 19, 1945. He married Joyce L. Whitfill, born April 18, 1944, Sept. 28, 1968. Michael attended St. Paul Elementary and Grayson County Catholic High School. Joyce attended Custer Elementary School and Irvington High School. They had a son, Joseph M. Whitfill. He was born Sept. 18, 1970. He is single and attended St. Paul Elementary School, Grayson County High School, and attended Western Kentucky University. He graduated from high school in 1988.

Mike was employed with GE for 27 years. Served in the military from Oct. 28, 1963 to Oct. 28, 1965. Joyce employed with Tell City Chair Company for 17 years. Joseph has been employed with Wal Mart for two years.

The J. Michael Whitfill Family

They have lived in the Saint Paul community, Leitchfield, KY since 1973. They were member of Saint Paul Parish, Grayson County from 1968 to 1973.

He is chairperson of parish council 15 plus years. Past Saint Paul School Board president eight of 10 years. Member Knights of Columbus, Eucharistic Minister, lector, deanery council (Eastern), everything else where needed (all purpose).

Mike helps with East Grayson County Fire Department Festival (fry chickens), senior citizens dinner in December.

He is son of Cletus and Clara Whitfill, St. Paul Parish. Members from birth, 1913 and 1910. They moved from Maryland in the 1800s. Cletus was a farmer. Some descendants include: J.S. and Elizabeth Whitfill, grandparents, three children; Cletus and Clara Whitfill, parents, 11 children.

Joyce Whitfill was born Joyce Pile in Custer, KY. Her family was Methodist and members of Eastern Star and MYF. She was baptized to Catholicism in 1968. Since St. Paul Church had burned down in 1966, they married in Clarkson, St. Elizabeth by Fr. Richard Danhauer.

WHITLER, JAMES MARCUS JR. AND MILA SULPA,

came to reside permanently in Hardinsburg in April 20, 1986. Marcus was born in Glen Dean, grew up in Cloverport and joined the Armed Forces in 1940. He finished business administration and went overseas to work in Saudi Arabia and in Alyeska Pipeline, AK. He went back to Saudi Arabia and worked as senior contract administrator with Bechtel Co. He met his wife Milly (nickname) through his Filipino secretary. In Nov. 12, 1978 they got married at the Ellinwood Cathedral, Manila, Philippines.

Marcus and Milly Whitler

Milly comes from a Catholic family of nine. She graduated BS agriculture, majored in plant pathology and worked with the governor in Daet, Camarines Norte. She was working as research assistant in Forest Research Institute, Laguna, when they met in June 1978. She joined her husband in Jubail, Saudia Arabia in September 1979. During their seven years stay in Saudia Arabia, they traveled in different countries. Milly traveled around the world seven times and visited religious places like Lourdes, France; Vatican City, Rome; Ephesus, Turkey and Egypt. In Jubail Milly used to attend Catholic Mass in secret since it is prohibited to hold any Christian ceremony in public.

Marcus retired from Bechtel in Jan. 26, 1986. He was a Methodist but went with Milly to Catholic church. He liked the solemnity of the Mass especially the Eucharist. In March 26, 1989 he joined the St. Romuald Church. He served as lector and usher while she is a Eucharistic minister and both helped the RCIA team.

He had three children from first marriage, Dr. James Wesley, Evelyn and Helen, and eight grandchildren; Jason, Kelly, Joshua, Becky, Chris, Lukey, Marcus and Michelle. They have four dogs, Shaggy Boy, weights 135 lbs; Tippy, Jackie and PeeWee, all were blessed on St. Francis Assisi's Feast by Fr. John Little.

WILBORN, KATHLEEN SYNDER AND MALCOM,

were married at Blessed Mother Church by Father Fisher. Malcolm graduated from Owensboro Business College in 1971, while Kathleen graduated from American Institute of Banking in 1988. Malcolm has worked as manager for three years with Tribbles Maytag; prior to working there Malcom worked in banking where he met Kathleen who also worked at Citizens State Bank located in Owensboro.

Kathleen attended and graduated from Owensboro Catholic High School in 1974. During this time she was a member of the pep club and president for two consecutive years of the Junior Spastic Guild. This was formed to help promote income for the local Wendel Foster Center here in Owensboro, which was formally named Spastic Home.

Malcolm graduated from Daviess County High School in 1969, where he participated in football, band, choir and the Junior Achievement Program for three years.

Ann Celene was born on March 22, 1974 at Saint Anthony Hospital in Louisville, KY. The birth was the brightest moment of Kathleen's life. She was completely healthy which was a wonderful miracle in itself since the doctors didn't expect such good results. They transported Ann Celene home to Owensboro right after four major tornados touched down in Louisville and Brandenburg.

She first was baptized at Blessed Mother Church by Father Clemons performing the ceremony then later her First Communion. Besides her regular school studies Ann took gymnastics, organ lessons, roller skating and then clarinet; this started while in middle school under the direction of Richard Skaggs who also taught her father. She continued with band at Owensboro Catholic High under the direction of Jay Morgan. During band she was introduced to flag corp which she is a member of for the past five years and has served as Flag Corp Captain.

WILKERSON, MARY LOUISE, Sister Theresa Marie, OSU, attended St. Francis Academy for four years and was transferred with her brother to St. Joseph's where she graduated in 1939. Her greatest pleasure in high school was playing in the orchestra and band and taking part in the many plays and musicals put on by the Sisters. Her school days were happy ones with many wonderful Ursuline teachers and great classmates. At age 16 she went to work at Newberry's Five and Ten at 8 cents an hour. Working on Saturdays only netted $1.49. She was glad to get that. At the age of 20 she entered Mount St. Joseph Ursuline Community because she wanted to teach very badly and give herself to God at the same time. Her dreams were realized in the 38 years of teaching in Kentucky, Nebraska and Missouri. She never regretted this choice because she never taught one student she did not like. In 1980 when Mount St. Joseph Academy, where she taught for seven years seemed to be about to close she accepted the job of settling refugees. During the past 12 years sister has settled many many refugees all over the diocese. The flow is not so many now, but more and more migrants and aliens needing help in immigrations are entering the diocese. Her life has been work filled and full. Many happy summers were spent at Omaha where she received her BA in history and at St. Louis University where she received an MA in history. Sister accepted many grants in the summer to many universities. One of her teachers was Emmanuel Teller, inventor of the atom bomb. These opportunities were always a time of growth and enlightment. God has been good, very good to her in calling her to a wonderful community of Sisters who are loving, supportive kind and understanding. She give thanks to God each day for calling her to this great community and this way of life.

Her parents were Wallace Wilkerson, born in Daviess County 1897. Was a telegraph operator and printer. Her mother, Earmina Hay was born in Daviess County of Caroline Hurley and John Hay. Was a milliner.

Mary Louise Wilkerson was born May 16, 1920 in Daviess County.

Her brothers and sisters include: James Wallace Wilkerson Jr. Sept. 19, 1922, worked for Lever Brothers in Gary, IN until his death in 1987. He was married to Phyllis Caise, and they had three children.

Thomas Carl Wilkerson, born Feb. 28, 1926. He has been in the plastering and accoustics business all his life. He was married to Lois Hamilton who died in 1976. Now married to Hallie Miles. They have nine children.

Robert Louis Wilkerson, born Oct. 20, 1930 has worked in the grocery business and affiliates all his life. Is married to Kathryn Gordon. They have three children.

Gerald Martin Wilkerson, June 19, 1933 was a shoe salesman and died of throat cancer 1990. He wrote the history of Sts. Joseph and Paul Church.

John Owen Wilkerson, March 27, 1927, married to Norma Goetz, has worked for Alcoa for 27 years. They have four children, the eldest, David is deceased.

WILLETT, AMBROSE AND MARY DENISE (SCHEER), married in St. John Catholic Church on Nov. 21, 1946.

Ambrose came from a family of 11 children. His father died before the last baby was born leaving his mother with 10 children to raise.

Mary Denise came from a family of nine children.

Ambrose and Mary Denise had six children, three boys and three girls: William Clark, James Edward, Ruth Ann, Hilda Marie, Betty Louise and Harold Louis.

William Clark was in the Vietnam War. He was enlisted in the Army on Feb. 27, 1970. He was in combat duty in Vietnam, Saigon, L.Z. Oasis and Chu Loi.

James Edward was enlisted in the Army on Oct. 2, 1969. He was in the infantry. He was discharged on Aug. 2, 1971. William Clark married Laura Mae Carper on May 2, 1970. They have two children, Philip Dewain and Andrew Joy. Philip Dewain married Peggy Ann Kirby on Dec. 4, 1991 and they are expecting their first baby in November. Andrew Joy is now in service at Fort Jackson, SC.

James Edward married Wendy Lou Reis on Sept. 10, 1971. They have four children: James Edward Jr., Jesse Alan, Joseph Gerald and Sarah Suzanne. James and Wendy have one grandchild, Gage Willett.

Ruth Ann married Earl Kaufman. Hilda Marie married Kenneth Eugene Brewer. They have two children Leigh Ann and Kristina Lynn. Betty Louise married Ricky Allen McManus. They have two children, Jennifer Lynn and Rachael Michale.

Harold Louis married Sally Joe Beckman on Feb. 22, 1992. William Clark, James Edward, Ruth Ann, Hilda Marie, Betty Louise and Harold Louis married in St. John's Church. All the children live in Paducah except James Edward. He and his family live in New Richmond, WI.

WILLETT, ARTHUR ANTHONY AND MARGARET FRANCES, were married at St. John the Evangelist Church in McCracken County on Nov. 26, 1929 by Rev. Paul Barrett.

Arthur was born on Oct. 10, 1906, the eldest of 11 born to Philip Clark Willett and Ida Philomena Poat. Margaret was born on March 9, 1911, the sixth of seven born to Joseph Henry Wurth and Rosena Thecla Matilda Englert.

Arthur Anthony Willett Family

Arthur and Margaret are the parents of three sons and seven daughters. The eldest son, Paul, died with cancer at the early age of 27, leaving a pregnant wife and four small children. They have 35 grandchildren, five step-grandchildren, 25 great-grandchildren and 15 step-great-grandchildren.

In the early years of their marriage Arthur and Margaret moved to the Poat homeplace within a half mile of St. John Church where they still reside. In the days of stoker coal furnaces, Arthur kept the coal hopper filled so the church was always warm and cozy - a job his father had for many years. In 1941, to help support his growing family, Arthur took a janitorial job at St. Francis De Sales Parish in Paducah. The 10 mile trip was made by Greyhound Bus. When a school bus was purchased for St. Mary's Academy, the Catholic school in Paducah operated by the Sisters of Charity of Nazareth, the duty of school bus driver was added to his list of cleaning church and rectory, cutting grass, washing pastor's car on Saturday afternoon and general "Jack-of-all-trades." When St. Francis Parish no longer needed his services, Arthur worked for the McCracken County School a number of years, and finally ended up as janitor at St. John Elementary until Parkinson's Disease forced his retirement in 1986.

Margaret was kept busy being a wife and mother but found time to do the church laundry at St. John's for several years and cooked many a meal for the pastor or a visiting priest when the housekeeper was unavailable. As the children got older and time permitted she found it relaxing piecing and quilting quilts. For 18 years Margaret has donated a hand-made quilt to be raffled at the St. John's Picnic, and many years also gave a quilt for the Country Store.

Arthur and Margaret were always active in the church and taught their children the values of faith and morals. The boys were all acolytes and five of the girls took their turns as organists. An amusing story that still brings laughter is when an electrical storm knocked out the electricity on a Sunday afternoon during Benediction, Arthur was called on to manually pump the pipe organ. Not being able to see around the huge pipes to know what was going on, he continued to pump and pump until the old organ, filled with air, had to let off steam and so began to play all by itself. You can imagine the giggles from the school children choir before Sister would send someone to the back to tell Arthur to slow it down a bit.

After retirement Arthur and Margaret attended daily Mass at St. John. Even when Arthur was forced to give up driving, the faithfulness of a few friends and neighbors enabled them to attend daily. Now that Arthur is in a wheelchair most of the time it is still a rare occasion that they do not attend a week-end Mass, and they are still active members of the St. Vincent De Paul Society. For many years they were members of the Right-to-Life Movement. Just recently Arthur became a charter member of the new council of Knight's of Columbus formed at St. John's in memory of Monsignor Anthony G. Higdon, a former pastor.

Arthur and Margaret celebrated their 60th Wedding Anniversary in 1989.

WILLETT, BERTRAM, born Jan. 25, 1912, one of seven sons and four daughters of the Clark and Ida (Poat) Willett family. On Nov. 21, 1939, He married Lydia Myrtle Dunaway, daughter of Robert and Ellen Dunaway. They had one daughter and four sons. Martha Ellen was born on April 28, 1941. She married Richard Gipson, and they have one son and two daughters. Dewain, born Jan. 5, 1965, married Sara Burrows. Ella Marie born May 4, 1967, married Christopher Garland and Darla, born May 26, 1969, married Keith Martin.

Their sons are Roscoe, born Feb. 21, 1944, and married to Jeanie Callendar. They have two sons, Clint, born Aug. 8, 1972 and Brent, born March 2, 1978.

Marvin, born March 24, 1946, married Clara Marie Murphy. They have two sons, Jeffery, born Sept. 1, 1971 and Chad, born Jan. 4, 1979. Henry, born April 8, 1948, married Phyllis Riepe. They have two sons, Michael, born Dec. 18, 1976 and David, born Feb. 29, 1980.

Aubrey, born May 6, 1950, married Monselle Wiley. They have two daughters and one son. Sondra, born Dec. 17, 1975, Justin, born June 28, 1978 and Kelly, born Feb. 14, 1983.

He is very proud of each and every one of them, and they have very close family ties. Four of the families live within sight of their home, and the other family lives within just a few minutes drive of their home.

His first wife, Lydia, their mother and grandmother, died April 29, 1973. They all missed her very much and they were very sad and lonely, but with the help of God, they all lived through it. About two years later, in 1975, he met Lois McElwain Metcalf. They married April 30, 1977.

Lois's husband, John A. Metcalf, had been called home by God eight years prior to that time. They had two sons. John, born Dec. 11, 1944, married Susan Wolschena. They have two sons and one daughter. Andrew Allen, born Nov. 3, 1975, Jessica Lynn, born May 18, 1977, and Christopher John, born Feb. 26, 1979.

The Bertram Willett Family

James, born Dec. 19, 1946, married Melinda Collis. They have two sons, Reid, born April 5, 1978, and Cameron, born April 16, 1981. Both John and James are medical doctors.

He was born and raised on a farm, and has farmed most of his life, and at age 80 he still enjoys farming. he hired one of his grandsons (Dewain) to help. He has worked for him all his life and they both enjoy it. They plant and harvest about 1600 acres each year.

There have been many changes in farming during his life. Now, with no-till and other conservation practices, they can feed the world and preserve the land for the future generations. He did the first no-tilling in their community about 22 years ago, and has served on the McCracken County Soil Conservation Board of Supervisors for 20 years, serving as chairman of the board for the past 18 years. He is proud to be a part of soil conservation, since it is very important to save the soil.

As he was born and raised near St. John's Catholic Church, their daddy and the boys did lots of church work. They fired the coal burner stoves to heat the church and took care of the kerosene lamps to light it. They helped a lot with mowing the cemetery, etc. He is very proud to still be able to do certain activities at church, such as Eucharistic Minister at church and take Communion and visit the sick and shut-ins. He also takes his turn as lector at Mass.

Lois is a registered nurse. She worked 25 years at the McCracken County Health Dept. for many years as head nurse, before she semi-retired. Since then, she works for her son, Dr. James Metcalf in Paducah. She enjoys it very much and he is proud to have his mother helping.

WILLETT FAMILY OF THE ST. JOHN COMMUNITY. The Willett family originated in Wales. In the early 17th Century several of them migrated to the New World and settled mostly in Prince George County, MD. But apparently some of them settled in New York, previously known as New Amsterdam. Captain Thomas Willett became the first mayor of New York in 1665. The first pewterer known in Maryland was also a Willett. Toward the end of the 18th Century a group of the Willetts migrated to Kentucky through the Cumberland Gap. Some of these settled in Washington County and later moved to Fancy Farm.

Another branch of the family settled in Nelson County, around Bardstown and Pottinger's Creek. Among these were George Willett who was born in Maryland in 1757. He married Elizabeth Sanders, who bore him 11 children. He died near Bardstown on March 25, 1814. One of his sons, Samuel born Sept. 8, 1896, married Mary Dant who had 17 children. The fifth of these children was named McMurray (the mother's maiden name). McMurray married Mary Florence Greenwell on July 6, 1880 at Sacred Heart Church in Union County. This couple, my grandparents, were blessed with 10 children, the oldest being Philip Clark, born Feb. 8, 1882. He and six of his brothers and sisters were born in Union County and were baptized at Sacred Heart Church.

In 1898 McMurray and Mary Florence moved the family to Maxon Mill (now known as West Paducah).

Three years later the family moved again to Adrian, a small community with a post office, which later became known as St. John's. Here the other three children were born. Joseph Lucian was born Jan. 7, 1902 and died the same day. The other children were born to McMurray and Florence were Mary Edna (July 22, 1884); Joseph Leonard (Oct. 11, 1886); Joseph Gordon (Dec. 16, 1888); Bernard Uriel (Nov. 30, 1892); Mary Rita (Jan. 30, 1896); Mary Mahala (Sept. 9, 1898); Joseph McMurray (Oct. 15, 1903); and Joseph Celestine (May 19, 1907).

McMurray was not a Catholic but he helped his wife rear the children as Catholic. Finally on June 29, 1907, he was baptized and received into the Church. The next day he and his son, Uriel, made their First Communion together.

The three oldest children married and settled at St. John. The rest of the family moved to Jonesboro, AR in 1912. Mary Mahala joined the Olivetan Benedictine Sisters in Jonesboro on July 2, 1919 and took the name Sister Mary Regina. After many years in the classroom, she retired to the Mother House where she died May 21, 1990.

Joseph C., the youngest son, is the only child still living. He lives in Jonesboro, and is a very young 85 years of age.

Those who remained at St. John were John Leonard, who married Blanche Englert, daughter of Joseph and Mary (Clark) on Jan. 26, 1909. Mary Edna married Martin Andrew Englert, son of John and Magdalene (Krimple) on Jan. 20, 1904. Phillip Clark had received his Catholic education at Sacred Heart School for boys at St. Vincent, KY. On Nov. 21, 1905, he married Ida Philomena Poat, daughter of Anthony and Catherine (Haeseley) Poat, at St. John with Father Charles Haeseley, uncle of the bride, performing the ceremony. Their home is now Walker's Antiques.

Clark Willett Family

Clark and Ida were blessed with 11 children, seven boys and four girls. They are Arthur (Oct. 10, 1906); Mary Cecilia (May 27, 1908); Anna Elizabeth (Feb. 5, 1910); Bertram Paul (Jan. 25, 1912); Martin Joseph (March 27, 1914); Henry Louis (Aug. 19, 1916); Raymond Phillip (April 20, 1919); Margaret Regina (April 29, 1921); Joseph Ambrose (June 5, 1922); Angela Rita Mae (Dec. 25, 1924); Joseph Leonard (Dec. 2, 1928). Regina died on May 27, 1921. Mary Cecilia died June 30, 1985. The rest of the children are still living. Phillip Clark died on Oct. 27, 1928, about five weeks before the youngest son, Joseph, was born. Ida died on Oct. 20, 1949.

The two surviving daughters, (Anna) Sister Annella, O.S.B. and (Rita) Sister Brenda, O.S.B, joined the Olivetan Benedictines in Jonesboro, AR, on Aug. 15, 1932 and Aug. 15, 1962 respectively. Sr. Annella will be celebrating her Diamond Jubilee on July 11, 1992, the Feast of St. Benedict.

Henry, the middle child, was ordained to the priesthood on Feb. 24, 1945, in Owensboro by the Most Rev. Francis R. Cotton, D.D., the first bishop of Owensboro. During the past 47 years, it has been his privilege and blessing to serve the diocese in many areas of the diocese. He went into active retirement in June of 1990, but has been more active than retired during the past two years.

Arthur married Margaret Wurth, daughter of Joseph and Rosina (Englert) on Nov. 26, 1929. They were blessed with 10 children - three sons and seven daughters, all of whom are happily married. Bertram married Lydia Dunaway, daughter of Robert Henley and Mary Ellen (Snyder), on Nov. 21, 1939. They were blessed with one daughter, Martha Ellen (Gipson) and four sons, Roscoe, Marvin, Henry and Aubrey. Lydia died on April 29, 1973. On April 30, 1977 Bertram married Lois McIlwain Metcalf.

Martin married Armella Mary Ruden on Sept. 14, 1943 in Remsen, IA. They were blessed with three sons - Clarence, Phillip, Allen and one daughter, Jo Ann.

While Raymond was in military service in France in World War II, he married a French lady, Lucienne Romand, on Aug. 13, 1945, at St. Remi Cathedral in Riems, France. They have two sons, Gabriel and Daniel and two daughters, Jacqueline and Lillian.

Ambrose was in the Marine Corps in World War II. After his honorable discharge on Aug. 21, 1946, he soon took up another kind of service as the husband of Mary Denise Scheer, daughter of William and Odelia (Roof), on Nov. 21, 1946. They were blessed with six children - William Clark, James Edward, Ruth Ann, Hilda Marie, Betty Louise and Harold Louis. All of the children are happily married.

Joseph Leonard was united in marriage to Thelma Ona Johnson on Nov. 24, 1949 at St. John. They were blessed with six wonderful children - Ida Mae, Patricia Joe, Barbara Jean, Charles Lynn, Brenda Kay and Nancy Roberta. About five years after their marriage, they moved to Madisonville, where three of their six children were born.

Although their family is spread all over the country, they have a wonderful relationship. Each summer when the Sisters are home for vacation, they have a large family gathering of 75 to 100 members of the immediate family. If they had them all together, the number would probably reach 150. They thank God for his many blessings on them all.

One great blessing in disguise was the fact that they (their mother and seven small children) went through the Depression, with no father as a bread winner. Their mom did a magnificent job and they all had to work and sacrifice together in order to make ends meet. They had a small and very poor farm of 40 acres. The land produced very meager crops. They had to rent most of their crop land. When he went to the seminary in 1932, that meant one less "farm hand" and one extra financial burden. He remembers one time after he went back to school in September, Mom wrote to him telling him that they had only 36 cents in the treasury. But with a lot of prayers and hard work they made it. Remembering those times helps us to appreciate and love each other more. So thanks be to God for His blessings in disguise.

WILLETT, SISTER DOROTHY MARIE was born Sept. 8, 1921 at Waverly, KY. She was baptized Ursula, November 1921. Entered Sept. 7, 1940. Received habit Aug. 14, 1941. First vows Aug. 14, 1943. Second vows Aug. 14, 1946. Her parents were Edward and Jane Purdue Willett. Her father was born in Waverly, KY Aug. 29, 1889 and died Jan. 21, 1958. Her mother was born Dec. 15, 1897.

Her brothers and sisters are as follows: Thomas Edward (dec.), Dorothy Jane Willett-Massey, Rose Marie

Willett (Sr. Rosita OSU), Mary Kathleen Willett-Dunkel, Joseph Vernon, Theresa Bernadett Willett-Trapp, Doris Hiltrude Willett-Trapp.

She served in the following missions from 1943 through 1989 with grades one through six and in Food Service as liaison with lay directors, assistant local superior and in personal and pastoral care: St. Paul, Vine Grove, Earlington, Curdsville, St. Raphael, SS Joseph and Paul, St. Thomas More, Buechel, KY, Precious Blood, Motherhouse, Blessed Mother, Nebraska City, NB, Mount St. Joseph.

WILLETT, FATHER ERNEST EZRA,

The Rev. Ernest Ezra Willett, 73, of Waverly died Wednesday, Dec. 9, 1992, at Deaconess Hospital in Evansville. He was born at Fancy Farm, the son of James Elmer and Ann Elizabeth Melbourne Willett. He was the pastor of St. Peter Church and Sacred Heart Church, both in Waverly. He attended elementary and high school at St. Jerome in Fancy Farm, attended St. Mary College from 1937-1941 and St. Meinrad Seminary from 1942-1945. He was ordained a priest by Bishop Francis R. Cotton on Feb. 24, 1945, at St. Stephen Cathedral in Owensboro. His first assignment was at St. Stephen from June 1945 to June 1948. He was assistant pastor of St. Francis De Sales in Paducah from 1948-1950, pastor of St. Joseph in Central City from 1950-1957, pastor of Sts. Peter and Paul in Hopkinsville from 1957-65, pastor of St. Thomas More in Paducah from 1965-1969, pastor of Holy Name in Henderson from 1969-1983 and was pastor of the churches in Waverly since 1983. He served on various committees of the Diocese of Owensboro, was on the original Diocesan Education Committee and was appointed to a second term on the Diocesan Committee for Administration, a position he held at the time of his death.

Survivors include a brother, Thomas Willett of Long Beach, CA; two sisters, Rita Saalwaechter of Cincinnati and Sister Rita Ann Willett of Nazareth Home, Louisville; and several nieces and nephews.

Two funeral Masses were celebrated for Fr. Willett in Waverly on December 11 and in Fancy Farm on December 12. Burial was in St. Jerome Cemetery in Fancy Farm.

WILLETT, FRANCIS PATRICK KENDRICK,

born in Graves County on July 28, 1837 was the fifth child of Samuel Willett and Elizabeth Hobbs. Francis married on Nov. 27, 1860 at St. Jerome's, to Sarah Ellen Austin the daughter of Benedict Austin and Margaret Yates. Francis and Sarah had nine children. Eugene married first Ellen Bowlds, second, Ophelia Linz. Charles, William B. married Mary Fenwick. Oscar Willett born Oct. 22, 1867. Nancy C. born 1870 died by 1880. Margaret born 1872 died by 1880. Mary married Mr. Cash. Elizabeth born 1877 married Benjamin Burch. Maud married John Crowdus. Francis and Sarah's Catholic faith brought them through many tragedies. Francis' sister died in infancy and both of Sarah's parents died before her 14th birthday. Later three of their children died. Francis owned a farm and was a postmaster of Fancy Farm during the Civil War and a sewing machine agent. After Francis died on March 4, 1917, Sarah lived with her daughter and son-in-law B. Burch. Sarah died on June 7, 1923.

Francis P.K. Willett and his wife, Sarah Ellen Austin

Oscar Willett, the son of Francis and Sarah married Mary Bowlds. After Mary's death Oscar married Hattie Buckman the daughter of William Buckman and Ann Shanks at St. Jerome's on Feb. 7, 1898. Oscar farmed and owned Willett Tobacco Enterprise with his brother Benedict. Mystery shrouds his death on Aug. 2, 1898. His obituary states he had a cramp and mistakenly took carbolic acid which he thought was medicine. His son Oscar Jr. and others in town heard that it was suicide. Oscar's death was a tragic loss, as he never lived to see his son. Hattie worked to support her son, as a dressmaker. Hattie was a devoted Catholic and passed this down to her son Oscar, who attended St. Meinrad's Seminary but decided that God called him to married life.

WILLETT, HARBERT PATRICK "HARVEY" AND MARY BEN CARRICO,

were married July 11, 1939, at Sts. Joseph and Paul Church in Owensboro, KY with Father C.P. Bowling officiating. Harvey, a native of Stanley, KY was employed at Fleishmann's Distillery for 25 years; Mary Ben, born in Union County, KY, retired from General Electric after 35 years. The couple were members of St. Peter of Alcantara Church (Stanley), Sts. Joseph and Paul (Owensboro) and in 1964, moved into St. Stephen's Cathedral Parish. Mary Ben was active in Daughters of Isabella, Altar Society, and the Ursuline Club. Following retirement, she was a regular volunteer at St. Stephen's Church. Her retirement years included traveling extensively in the U.S. and Europe. The four children born to Harvey and Mary Ben included three daughters and one son: Dorothy P. Halbleib, Marianna Robinson, Benjamin Willett and Mildred Faye Wilkerson. The couple enjoyed their seven grandchildren during retirement years. Because of her declining health, Mary Ben became a resident of a nursing home in Hartford, KY following Harvey's death in 1989.

WILLETT, HAROLD,

On Aug. 25, 1941, Harold Willett, son of Roy Willett and Verena Elliott Willett, and Ann Toon, daughter of Ernest Toon and Mary Weitlauf Toon, were married in St. Jerome Church in Fancy Farm, where both were baptized and are still active members. While busy raising a family of nine children on a farm in Carlisle County, they remained very involved in the life of St. Jerome Parish where their children received the sacraments of baptism, confirmation, Eucharist, penance and marriage. Anna Belle's (the oldest daughter) funeral Mass was celebrated there in December 1949, as well as Bob's (oldest son) ordination to the priesthood in February 1968. Other sad gatherings at St. Jerome for this family include the funeral Masses for two grandsons killed in car accidents: Jason Towery (4 years old) in August 1982, and Neil Hayden (15 years old) in January 1987. Joyful events include Harold and Ann's Golden Wedding Anniversary in August 1991, and Glenn (Wilson) and Barbara Sue's Silver Wedding Anniversary in September 1991.

Their parish and community involvement over the years include active membership in the St. Vincent De Paul Society, the Altar Society, the Knights of Columbus, the Credit Union, the Water/Sewage System Board, the VFW, American Legion, Carlisle County Soil Conservation, Parish Finance Committee, Parish Maintenance Committee, Cemetery Committee, Picnic Committee and Ministers of Care.

Besides Anna Belle who died at the age of 5, their children and their spouses are: Bob, Tom (Judy Cole), Barbara Sue (Glenn Wilson), Becca (Sam Higdon), Joyce (Hardy Hayden), Sam, Donnie (Patty Ellegood), Nancy (Dale Towery). They also have 19 grandchildren.

WILLETT, REVEREND HENRY L.,

The day was Saturday, August 19 in the year 1916, when Phillip Clark and Ida Philomena Poat Willett were gifted with their sixth child, Henry Louis. This was only the half-way point for this fruitful marriage which produced a total of 11 children. Henry Louis was the middle child - three boys and two girls older and three boys and two girls still to come.

They were a poor but happy family living on a poor 40 acre farm some 10 miles south of Paducah, on Highway 45. The children were blessed with very religious parents who unquestionably put God first in their lives. They were a living example of what being Christian is all about. Due to the good example and prayers and encouragement of Clark and Ida, he had a strong inclination toward the priesthood from a very early age.

He attended the St. John Catholic School, taught by the Sisters of Mercy. They exerted a very strong influence on him. Sister Mary Callista especially encouraged him to pray and think about becoming a priest.

When he completed his grade school, he told his pastor, Father Paul Barrett that he though he would like to be a priest. He relayed this information to the bishop, John A. Floersch, D.D. of Louisville. He graciously accepted his application and sent him to St. Mary's College where he spent six years of preparatory studies. After that he studied at the Basselin Foundation in Washington, D.C. After three years, Bishop Francis R. Cotton, the First Bishop of Owensboro, sent him to St. Mary Seminary at Roland Park in Baltimore. After completing his theological studies, he was ordained a priest on Feb. 24, 1945, which happened to be the seventh anniversary of Bishop Cotton's Consecration. This was a day of joyful celebration for St. John the Evangelist Parish, since he was the only priest ordained from St. John's in more than a century of history.

After ordination he worked in several places before receiving his first real appointment. He was in Fancy Farm and the mission parishes there. He spent about six weeks in Hopkinsville and Princeton and then came back to the Cathedral, where he had been during Holy Week. And in July he was sent to Morganfield as assistant to Father Paul Barrett. After four years in Morganfield, he was named administrator of St. Augustine at Reed with St. Mary Magdalene, Sorgho as a mission. He went there on his birthday in 1949 and on his birthday in 1950, he was duly sworn in as pastor of St. Elizabeth, Curdsville, with St. Raphael as a mission.

Reverend Henry L. Willett

On Aug. 19, of 1961, their new Bishop, Henry J. Soenneker, D.D., assigned him to Immaculate Conception in Earlington, with St. Paul, Princeton, as a mission. He had the privilege of establishing a new parish in Madisonville, under the title of Christ the King. They had procured land for the new church and were in the process of getting architectural plans for the building, when Bishop Soenneker, transferred him to Bowling Green, where they established the new Holy Spirit Parish. Ground was broken on Aug. 10, the second anniversary of his assignment as pastor. On Thanksgiving Day 1970, they celebrated a private Mass of Thanksgiving in our new church which was solemnly blessed by the bishop on December 6 of that year. He was happy to serve as pastor there for three more years and then was given the parishes of St. William and St. Lawrence on July 26, 1973 at Knottsville. After some nine years there, he was assigned to Sts. Joseph and Paul Parish in Owensboro. He took up the pastorate there on Dec. 9, 1982, just six days before our third and present Bishop John J. McRaith, D.D., came to Owensboro as our chief shepherd. He enjoyed eight fruitful years there. These exciting years with a very serious church fire, the demolition of the old St. Joseph school and church, two total renovations of St. Paul Church, and the construction of a much needed parish hall.

In June of 1990 he resigned as pastor and has enjoyed working full time ever since. He had the privilege of building a church or school or some other important building in almost every parish he served. These were all good experiences. But not as nice to just "be busy" without the worry and anxiety that goes with the pastoral administration. After 48 years of priesthood, he can only say "Thank you Lord, for this tremendous gift."

WILLETT, JAMES LAFAYETTE, was born July 30, 1922. He was the oldest son of Robert Benjamin Willett and Sarah Altheir Mills Willett. He had one sister, Anna Mae Bullock of Holy Name Parish, Henderson, KY and two brothers, Thomas Gregory Willett and Basil Andrew Willett of St. Peter Parish, Waverly, KY.

James attended St. Peter High School in Waverly, KY and the University of Evansville.

He was a veteran of World War II, a supervisor at Spencer Chemical Company in Henderson, KY and was self employed on his farm where he lived his entire life.

James married Lucy Pike Willett of St. Agnes Parish, Uniontown, KY on Feb. 2, 1963.

Lucy received her degrees from Brescia College, Spalding College and Indiana University.

They were members of St. Peter Church, Waverly, KY and participated in many civic and religious activities including teachers of C.C.D. and Bible School, members of the church choir, the Altar Society, the Parish Church Board, Kentucky and National Education Association, Parent Teachers Organization and were Kentucky Colonels.

James and Lucy Willett

Lucy taught 49 years in the elementary schools of Western Kentucky and is still substitute teaching in various schools as her love for the youth has not failed.

While Lucy taught in Crittenden County there was no Catholic Church therefore she rode a bus home on weekends in order to attend Mass.

This couple had no children of their own but as Lucy states, "We feel that we have a claim on the hundreds of children that we helped to educate."

James passed away on Feb. 13, 1989.

WILLETT, JOHN ELBERT, born Jan. 31, 1886, died March 14, 1972. John Elbert was the second child of a large family of six boys and five girls. Their parents were Claude Richard and Ollie Jane Nally Willett. Johnny's family included his twin brothers. Johnny was baptized at St. Vincent. Two of his brothers were in service in the military. Claude chose the military as a career. He was stationed in France. Steve was in Germany and in the Panama Canal.

Johnny's grandfather, Richard D. Willett, was a soldier in the Civil War. He was in Co. G, first Kentucky Confederate Cavalry. Richard D.'s father Richard came to Union County in 1822 from Nelson County.

Johnny had just started his instructions in religion at age 15 when his Father died suddenly. As the oldest boy he had to go to work to help support his family.

The Willett's came from Virginia and Maryland to Kentucky. They settled in Nelson County. George Willett Jr. was the first family member to convert from a protestant to a Catholic during the early 1800's.

Their faith was always important to the family. Johnny's brother Owen had a daughter who became a Nun. She is called Sister Gemma and she lives in Dearborn Heights, MI.

Johnny married Jessie Coney in 1912 at Sacred Heart Church. Jessie was born Feb. 12, 1888 to Margaret Ellen Graham and Patrick Coney. Patrick and his brother John came here from Ireland with their parents and lived in Louisville for a short time. Their father worked on the railroad and died soon after arriving there. The boys came to Union County where they were adopted but they kept their own name. The priest at the wedding was Fr. Cunningham.

Johnny was a farmer and lived with Jessie at Hitesville, KY in Union County. They had four sons and five daughters. Jessie was a happy, cheerful person and enjoyed being a wife and mother. She visited her neighbors, went to church and said her prayers. She had gone to school at St. Vincent Academy. It was a boarding school for girls and a day school for girls and boys. Jessie had lived there for awhile. The nuns taught her about the Catholic faith. All of the children were baptized as soon as possible. The family went to church in a buggy.

Johnny and Jessie came from a closeknit family. They kept in touch with each member of the family. Johnny's brothers and sisters are: Agnes, Johnny, Anne Virginia (Virgie), Owen, Henry Benjamin, Stephen and his twin Cleveland, Margaret Mary (Mag), Claude (Chick), sister Clyde, Mary Lucy.

Johnny and Jessie taught their children to live their Catholic faith in their lives. They said the rosary as a family together. They had a huge cross on their wall. They had an altar in their home every May and a permanent one when the children were gone from home.

Jessie was very good with horses. One day she hitched her favorite horse to the buggy, told Johnny that she was going to Waverly to buy some groceries. She left the younger children in the care of the older ones. It was very cold that day. When she finished her shopping and came outside to the buggy it was sleeting. Soon the road was covered with ice. She was an expert with horses and was well trained so she had no problem until she started up a steep hill. The horse kept sliding on the ice. Jessie got out of the buggy, took off her sturdy shoes. She used the high heels to chop a hole in the ice for the horse so he could step in the cleared spot. The horse wanted to get home as much as Jessie did. He soon caught on to what she wanted and step by step they reached the top of the hill and went on their way.

Two of their sons served in the Armed Forces. Herman was in Germany in World War II. Johnny was in Korea. They were not seriously injured. Mother Jessie and Father Johnny followed them with their prayers and their rosaries.

These are the children of the family: William (Dynamite), Mary Leo Buckman, Claude, Viola Duncan, Herman, Elizabeth (Bessie), Barnaby, Susie Duncan, Theresa Nelson, John Lucian.

Johnny liked working outside. He raised a garden when he was elderly. He liked to walk around Waverly and visit his friends. They moved away from the farm. He couldn't see very well by this time. He took his dog with him every time he left home. The dog would sit by the road until it was safe to cross, then the two of them went on their way. Johnny was called Papa by all of his children and most of his grandchildren.

He was unable to attend church and climb the steps so he sat outside under the shade tree during all the funerals and prayed for his friends and listened to the church bell toll one for each year of life. He worked for Fr. Higgins during his last years. He took care of the cemetery. He died quietly in his sleep with no previous illness.

John and Jessie Elizabeth Willett

Jessie liked music and flowers. She could play the organ and the accordion. She always burned blessed candles during a time of crisis such as a storm. She put palm on the trees and buildings and her home. She put palm crosses on everything. She sprinkled Holy water throughout the house every night and also on each person present. When she had skin cancer on her face she used holy water from Lourdes, France and prayed every day. The cancer went away just before the scheduled operation.

Jessie and Johnny had 71 grandchildren. Each of them was baptized by a Catholic priest. Many of their descendants are involved in the Catholic church as Eucharist Ministers, cantors, organists, in the choir, CCD teachers, lectors. There are many altar boys. Some of the family work with the St. Vincent De Paul Society and some with the bereavement dinners hospice, Knights of Columbus, as helpers at the local Catholic School, and workers at the funding picnics and hospitality committee.

Some of the family members have visited Marian Shrines here in this country and in Europe.

Jessie and some of her friends walked to church every day after she moved to Waverly. She said "When I get to heaven, I am going to ask Jesus if I can spend my time making sure my children and grandchildren remain in the church and return to it if they stray."

WILLETT, JOHN LUCIAN, was born into a large Catholic family in 1930. His family had practiced their faith for several generations. He served in the U.S. Army for three years. He was in Korea for one year. He was in communications as a pole lineman.

Johnny married Betty Jean Nelson. Betty did not belong to any church. She joined Sacred Heart Catholic Church in 1954. They lived just behind the church and Betty borrowed books from Father Higgins. The first time Father Higgins saw her at the mailbox, he told her to return to high school. He thought she was a student!

John and Betty had four children: Barbara, Michael, Timmy, Peggy. In 1963 they moved to Waverly where they joined St. Peter Church.

When Betty first joined the Catholic church there were many questions and much confusion. Johnny's mother, sisters and other family members were patient and answered all of the questions. Why did they keep weeds in the house and burn them and display them (palm)? Why did they stop suddenly before going into the pew (genuflect)? Why did they wash their fingers when going into church? Why did they make strange movements with their hands (Sign of Cross)? Why did the priest turn his back to us? What strange language did he speak? Why did he change the colors he wore? Why did the church year start in December?

All of their children attended Catholic school. They were all baptized, confirmed and married in the church. Barbara played the part of the child Jesus while attending St. Vincent in second grade with the high school students. She was chosen because she had long golden hair.

Johnny liked to be outside. He worked on a farm. Betty sewed most of their clothes including the uniforms for school. A nun at St. Vincent asked Betty to make a new habit for her, but Betty was scared of Nuns.

Johnny raised a big garden and Betty canned the vegetables and later froze some of them. When Peggy, the youngest child, was 3, Betty went outside the home to work as a seamstress. She made raincoats, and later men's caps.

John and Betty Willett

Johnny helped with whatever work was needed at the church. He helped setup the outdoor manger at Christmas, helped with new sidewalks and other repairs with Father Reisz. He helped set up the stands for the annual barbeque and also worked at the picnic.

Betty was a member of the Legion of Mary. She is a member of the Altar Society and is a Lector. She has taught CCD for many years, helps prepare the young people for confirmation. She is a volunteer for St. Vincent De Paul Society and helps with the reading at St. Ann School for the second grade. She has volunteered to help with the Literacy Council.

Betty wrote a book on the Willett family. There were around 800 or 900 books published and distributed to family members. The book is also in many libraries such as Bardstown, Morganfield, Henderson, Evansville, Chicago and the Library of Congress.

Johnny and Betty have 11 grandsons and three granddaughters.

Betty and her daughter, Peggy, went on a pilgrimage to Fatima, Portugal and Medjugorje, Yugoslavia. It was an unforgettable experience.

WILLETT, JOHN WILLIAM "JACK,"

(1821-1909) son of John and Matilda (Summers) Willett was born after his father's death. He had an older brother, Samuel (see Samuel Willett biography) and six sisters. According to Fr. Charles Haeseley's article in 1911, Jack at age 8 joined his brother in Graves County around 1830.

In 1845 at St. Jerome, Jack first married Florida Anne "Rhody" (1823-1869) daughter of Cornelius and Theresa (O'Bryan) Carrico, nine children. Jack second married Elizabeth Gale Burgess prior to 1880, four children; Jack third married Angeline Mary Potter on Jan. 8, 1889 at St. Jerome, one child.

Fr. Haeseley wrote in 1911: "In 1888 'Uncle Jack' Willett left his beautiful country near Fancy Farm and moved to Mayfield, the county seat, where he resided, the friend of everyone, till his death on Oct. 5, 1909." He was buried in St. Jerome Cemetery.

Thomas Jefferson (1846-1908), the oldest child of Jack and Rhody Willett, and their only son to reach adulthood, first married Frances Ann Pierceall (1856-1893), four children; married second, Emma Elizabeth Wilson (1864-1951) on July 15, 1895 at St. Jerome (see James Wilson Biography), five children.

James Alton (1904-1970) son of Thomas Jefferson and Emma, married Teresa Toon (1903-1993) on Sept. 28, 1924, at St. Joseph, East St. Louis, IL (see William Hayden and Athanasius Toon Biographies). They have two sons: Delbert Leo (born Aug. 1, 1925) and Eugene Emmanuel (born July 31, 1927).

Delbert Leo professed his first religious vows in the Society of Mary (Marianists) at Galesville, WI on Aug. 15, 1944. He is known in religion as Brother Leo Willett, S.M. He has spent his years as a Marianist, mainly in high school teaching and administration.

Eugene married Dorothy Mae (born July 19, 1926) daughter of Emery and Mildred (Shepherd) Webb, four children: Michael Eugene (1951) married Nancy Sturgeon; Teresa Diane (1954) married Dennis C. Nizinski; Donna Marie (1955); and Marsha Ann (1961) married Mark Williamson. Eugene and Dorothy have two grandchildren: Dennis E. Nizinski (1973) and Robert E. Williamson (1987). Eugene is retired from Benjamin Moore Paint Co., St. Louis, and he and Dorothy live in Trenton, IL.

WILLETT, JOSEPH HAROLD,

born and raised in Graves County near Fancy Farm, KY. Baptized, First Communion, confirmed and married at St. Jerome Church.

His father Roy Bernard was a farmer and his mother Anna Verena Elliott was a housewife.

Harold attended grade school at St. Jerome.

Anna Rose Toon, born in Graves County. Her father Ernest Toon was born in Graves County and was a tenant farmer. Her mother Mary Ann Weitlauf was born in McCracken County, was raised in Graves County by her grandmother after her mother died.

Ann attended four different one room grade schools and high school at St. Jerome.

James Alton and Teresa (Toon) Willett Family

In 1939 Harold went to Cincinnati and worked at St. Francis and Good Samaritan Hospital and Wrights Aeronautical Co.

In 1940 Ann went to Norwood, OH. Worked at St. Mary's Seminary and later at Good Samaritan Hospital, Cincinnati.

Harold and Ann Willett

On Aug. 25, 1941 Harold and Ann were married at St. Jerome and lived in Cincinnati until Harold was called to serve in the U.S. Navy in June 1944.

The oldest son Joseph Robert was born in Cincinnati, the remaining eight: Anna Belle, Wm. Thomas, Barbara Sue (Wilson), Rebecca (Higdon), Joyce (Hayden), Samuel, Donald and Nancy (Towery) were born in Graves and Carlise County.

The second child Anna Belle died at age 5.

Seventeen living grandchildren; two grandsons killed in auto accidents. The oldest son Robert, is the first and only ordained priest from Carlisle County, where he lived for 30 years.

Harold and Ann celebrated their 50th Wedding Anniversary Aug. 24, 1991.

Harold is a member of the Knights of Columbus and Parish Cemetery Committee.

Ann is a Eucharistic Minister of Care and Altar Society member.

They have always attended St. Jerome Church except the five years in Cincinnati.

WILLETT, MAURICE CHARLES,

and Helen Eckman Willett have been lifelong members of the Owensboro Diocese and members of St. Agnes Catholic Church in Uniontown, KY since their marriage on Nov. 28, 1953.

They are the parents of three children: Kerry Michael, Gregory Scott and Sara Kaye.

Kerry is married to Leslie Baird and they have three girls: Kara Michelle, Katie Marie and Krista Jo. Scott is married to Kristi Kinnamon and they have a daughter, Morgan Nicole. Sara is married to Lindol Adkisson from Henderson County. They have two children: Lindol Tyler and Kelsey Ellen.

Maurice is a retired farmer and Helen retired as office manager for the U.S. Department of Agriculture, ASCS.

Their children attended St. Agnes Grade School through grade eight, then attended public schools where they graduated from Union County High School. Kerry started farming after high school and is presently employed by Union County Livestock, Inc. He is part-owner of another business. Scott graduated from the University of Kentucky and is employed by the Kentucky Department of Agriculture in Frankfort, KY. Sara attended Western Kentucky University and received an associate degree from Locklear College in legal secretarial.

Maurice serves as lector at St. Agnes and is currently serving as District Deputy for the Knights of Columbus. He has served as chairman of the Parish Council and for several years co-chaired the St. Agnes Knight of Columbus annual barbeque. He is a former two-term member of the Union County Board of Education and has served on two redistricting committees for the county.

Helen also serves as lector at St. Agnes and is a member of the Deanery Council. She served as a delegate from St. Agnes to the Diocesan Synod, is a volunteer in the Community Methodist Hospital Auxiliary and is a member of the Citizens Advisory Board for Solid Waste in Union County.

WILLETT, OSCAR CHESNEY,

the only child of Oscar and Hattie (Buckman) was born in Fancy Farm, KY on Dec. 16, 1898 two months after his father's death. On Feb. 7, 1919 Chesney married Mary Leona Cash born May 9, 1899 daughter of William Taylor Cash and Mary Irene Willett. Chesney and "Lena" were devout Catholics and went to school and church at St. Jerome's until Chesney had to go to Akron in 1927 to work at Goodyear Rubber factory in order to support his family. They learned many things at St. Jerome besides reading, writing and arithmetic, like the value of hard work, the family, and the wisdom in following church teaching. Five of their eight children, "Hattie Mae," Dean, a World War II pilot shot down over "Normandy," Margaret, Ralph and Sylvia were born in Mayfield and the other three John F., Kenneth and Richard were born in Akron, OH.

Stephen and Kathy Redle with Daniel (baby) and Michael

John F., born April 19, 1933 married on May 5, 1955 to Mary Eleanor Gabelman (born Jan. 16, 1933 daughter of Jacob Gabelman and Mary Ellen McQuillan). John a retired tax accountant from Goodyear and Eleanor an oncology nurse had four children, namely, James a Gulf War veteran and nurse anesthetist; Robert a vice president/rubber broker married Kim Villemain (their daughter Sara born Jan. 4, 1984), second wife Jo Ann Comernisky had Shannon C. in May 1993; Kathleen Marie a former art teacher; and Julie a pediatric nurse married Sean Francis, had Shannon M. on April 2, 1993.

Kathleen Willett born Oct. 11, 1961 in Akron, OH married on July 30, 1988 to Stephen Redle born Nov. 4, 1960 (son of David Redle and Elizabeth Cunningham). They have three children Michael born Oct. 4, 1989, Daniel Aug. 26, 1991 and Julie born Jan. 17, 1993. The Redles attend St. Martha's in Akron where Kathy lectors and Steve taught PSR. Steve is a psychology assistant with the mentally retarded and is working on a PhD in Psychology. They reside in Akron, OH.

WILLETT, SAMUEL AND ELIZABETH (HOBBS)

Samuel (1808-1892) son of John and Matilda (Summers) Willett, who was born the year the Diocese of Bardstown had been created, married Elizabeth daughter of Jesse and Mary (Elder) Hobbs in Washington County on Sept. 22, 1828, probably at St. Rose, Springfield. Samuel's uncle was Fr. William Thomas Willett (1790-1824), Dominican, who was the first native Kentuckian to be ordained a Catholic priest.

Samuel and Elizabeth were "the founders" in 1829 of "the Catholic Settlement" in far Western Kentucky, the counties of Graves and Hickman. In the 1830s, several of their relatives and friends from St. Rose Priory Parish, Washington, County, migrated to "the Catholic Settlement." St. Jerome, the first Catholic Church in the Jackson Purchase, was built in 1836, under the leadership of Fr. Elisha J. Durbin, the patriarch of the Catholic Church in Western Kentucky (Owensboro Diocese). Fr. Charles Haeseley, the pastor of St. Jerome from 1888-1920, wrote in 1911: "These two brothers (Samuel and "Jack" Willett) were the pioneers of St. Jerome's congregation, and remained identified with it as its foremost and most active members...(Samuel) won the love of all who knew him by his clean, noble and Christian life and conduct .... Though broken down in health and enfeebled by old age, in 1890 and 1891 he strenuously urged the building of a new and larger church to supply the needs of the growing congregation...."

Samuel and Elizabeth had 12 children: John William (born 1829-died before 1892) married Mary Elvina Carrico; Susan Mary (1831-1917) married Henry Jefferson Carrico; Samuel Thomas (1833-1893) married Cecilia Ann Roberts; Elizabeth Appolonia (1835-1912) married first James Philip Hayden, married second Thomas F. Curtsinger; Francis P. Kendrick (1837-1917) married Sarah Ellen Austin; Josephine Matilda (1840-1926) married Ignatius Carrico; Elisha Joseph (1842-1911) married Theresa Ann Pierceall; Eliza Jane (1844-1922) married Francis Marion Carrico; Nancy Ann Elder (1846-1926) married Samuel Abell Thomas; James Alexander Philip (1848-1926) married Augusta Ann Elliott; Charles Constantine (1850-1909) married Anna Isabelle "Belle" Cash; Frances Eugenia (1852-1853). Samuel and Elizabeth had 89 grandchildren.

Samuel married second Elizabeth M. (1830-1910) daughter of John S. and Juliann (Adams) Roberts at St. Jerome on April 3, 1878. Samuel died June 10, 1892; his first wife died May 4, 1877; his second wife died Jan. 30, 1910; all three are buried in St. Jerome Cemetery.

(For information on the ancestors and descendants of Samuel and Jack, see *The Willett Family of Maryland, Colonial Pewterers, Kentucky Pioneers*, 1983, by Sr. M. Louise Donnelly, Box 97, Ennis, TX).

WILLETT, SISTER ANNELLA

Diamond Jubilee Celebration for Sister Annella and Sister Geraldine (July 11, 1992). Rt. Rev. Abbot Jerome, Rev. Priests, Deacon Stepka, brothers, sisters, relatives and all other friends. (and we don't have anyone present who does not fit into one or more of those categories):

We are assembled here today, not only to eat and be merry, but to honor two of our sisters, of our relatives and/or friends, who have given God and community, 120 years of service in His name: Sister Annella Willett and Sister Geraldine Homer.

"And they each served God over 300 years, and God looked on them and saw that their service was good." or so the account might read if we used Biblical language, where the term "40 years" could denote any number of successful years in a field, or location.

Our Jubilarians have both served God in a number of fields of work and at various locations, and are today being honored as witness to their life and their work.

Sister Annella Willett was born to Clark and Ida Willett on Feb. 5, 1910, in Paducah, KY. She has seven brothers: Arthur, Bertram, Martin, Henry, (now Father Henry), Raymond, Ambrose and Joe: and three sisters: Cecilia, who died June 30, 1986 and Regina, who died as an infant, and Rita Mae (Sister Brenda) who is a religious here at Holy Angels. We are so glad to have Bertam and his wife Lois, Father Henry, Raymond and Luciene, Ambrose and Mary, Joe and Juanita and Sister Brenda with us today. We regret that Arthur and Martin could not attend. Several of Sister's nieces, nephews and grandnieces and nephews are present with her, today also.

Sister Annella left home to enter the convent in 1930, and made her first religious profession of vows in 1932. She began her service of God, her sisters, and brothers, in the culinary department of Holy Angels Convent, spent time working in St. Bernard's Hospital diet kitchen and at St. John's Seminary, where her cooking art kept body and soul of many recipients together. I'm sure she can count a great number of priests among those she served.

One year Sister spent as moderator of the boarding students in the now closed Holy Angels Academy. (I'm sure, having experienced boarding school life, there myself, she not only kept bodies and souls together during that year, but also, clothing, books and entire persons).

Sister worked as executive housekeeper in St. Bernard's Hospital for some time, as housekeeper and cook for the Sisters at Sacred Heart School in Muenster, TX, and at St. Andrew's School in Little Rock for nine years. (I can attest to at least one of those years at St. Andrew's, having been stationed there with Sister, as a very young person on my first ministry mission. I must say, her loving attention, her sense of humor, her bows and her smiling face, helped this green religious to face many predicaments).

Many parishes in the diocese benefited from the fruit of Sister's work as she baked the altar breads for a number of years, at the same time working in various areas of the convent. From 1962 to 1967, Sister Annella worked at and managed St. John's Place in Hot Springs. In fact, she was there when it closed to give place for the building of Benedictine Manor. Subsequently, she worked at the hospital in Eureka Springs for a short time before going to Washington, D.C. for studies where she earned her certificate in Hotel-Motel Training at Lewis Training School.

For some 22 years Sister worked with the diocesan poverty program, becoming executive director of the Helping Hand in 1970. Sister enjoyed this work very much, and found that she not only provided food and clothing to the needy, but also had daily opportunities for consoling and cheering the helpless and poor. (For a good write-up, and more information on her work see the *Arkansas Catholic* for Jan. 19, 1992. And the *Arkansas Catholic* is not giving me a commission for that plug).

Sister retired from "outside the convent" ministry this spring 1992. She was given a fond farewell party, attended by many of her volunteer workers and friends whose appreciation was shown through the years, and is evidenced by the plaques on the "Sister Annella" Wall outside the Chapel, and by many encouraging words and signs. Thus ends Sister's 300 years of service to this time. Sister Annella now has time for her needlework, reading and music which she enjoys so much. But Sister, let us remind you of what Father Blaise Truck said during one of our retreat conferences:

"We never really retire from ministry (It has to keep growing) (give plant) Because we still have the Sisters to minister to, with a smile, a helping hand, an open heart, or just our presence" all of which you do so well, Sister Annella. (Here is a reminder of the tools you will be needing) (give box). God bless you, Sister, and give you many more useful years in which to serve God and your Sisters.

WILLETT, W. IRIE,

grandson of Samuel and Elizabeth Hobbs Willett (1829 founder of the Catholic settlement known as Fancy Farm) was a son of Constantine and Anna Belle Cash Willett. Irie's first wife, Alberta Hobbs, died leaving one son, Harold. Irie (1887-1976) married Ida Mary Stahr (1891-1988). They had nine children. Harold (married

William Irie and Ida Stahr Willett Family. Clockwise from upper left hand corner: Joseph Harold, William Edward, Mary Elizabeth, Rachel, SCN, Joseph Emmanuel, Mary Lenora, William Irie, Celeste, Clara, SCN and Charles Conrad.

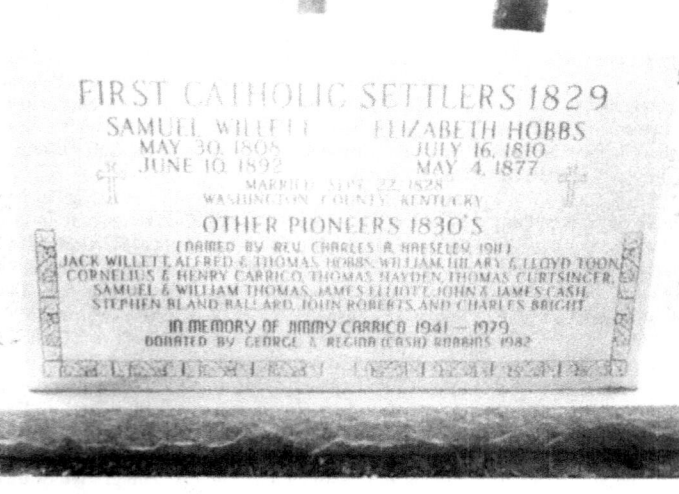

Monument to Pioneer Catholic settlers

Mary Eula Mills), successful farmer in Graves County; Clara Isabel (William Maria, SCN), teacher/principal in elementary schools, later in ministry to the elderly in Nazareth Village, KY; Conrad (married Helene Schueler) World War II, farmer in Carlisle County; Edward (married Phyllis Owens, married second Geri Agee), retired U.S. Marine Captain in World War II and Korean Wars, later stock market broker; Elizabeth (married Arthur Federle), homemaker/mother in Cincinnati and Sacramento; Rachel (Jerome, SCN), teacher/principal in elementary and secondary schools, instructor in college; first secretary to Bishop John J. McRaith; Jos. Emmanuel (married Dorothy Thomas), Ph.D, founder and president of Comprehensive Care of Northern Kentucky for 25 years; Lenora (married Wilbur Turney), homemaker/mother, currently assistant to the vice-chairman of the Joint Chiefs of Staff, Pentagon; Celeste (married Joseph E. Russell), homemaker/mother, charter member of St. Thomas More Choir; Irie Jr. (married Mary Smith) U.S. Air Force and Lawn Care Service. Irie and Ida were lifelong members of St. Jerome Parish, attending/supporting its school. (The value of Catholic education prompted Ida's parents, Wm. Anthony and Clara Josephine Davis Stahr, to sell their farm in Hickman and move to Graves County ca 1902.)

Ida taught in one-room schools. Both Irie and Ida were involved in parish events: K of C, Altar Society, treasurer for picnic. They lived through almost a century of changes with a rare resilience. Their home was open for Block Rosary, RENEW groups, frequent visitors, with many a card game or heated political debate. In the family name, Ida donated a stained-glass window depicting the Sacred Heart, symbolizing the faith and trust they had always placed in God, a heritage they left to their children and generations to come.

WILLIAMS, SISTER AGNES CATHERINE, baptismal name - Mary Agnes. She was born Jan. 29, 1905 in Owensboro, KY. Entered Jan. 21, 1925. Received habit Aug. 15, 1925. Vows, Aug. 15, 1927 and Aug. 15, 1930. She served St. Stephen Parish. Her father was Asa Williams, born Oct. 25, 1865 in Posey County, IN. He died Dec. 17, 1950. Her mother, Catherine Stengell, was born Oct. 8, 1865 in Fulda, IN. She died Sept. 15, 1966.

Her family: (See Sister Charles Asa Williams), John L. George I., Eva (Sr. Joseph Marie OSU), Wilbur A., Jessie (Sister Charles Asa OSU), James S., served in the following missions/locations from 1926 until 1988 teaching primary-third grade. St. Alphonsus, St. Joseph, KY; St. Columba, Louisville; St. Alphonsus, St. Joseph, KY; Calvary, KY; Raywick, KY, Sts. Joseph and Paul, Owensboro; Holy Founders, Affton, MO; Mount Saint Joseph.

WILLIAMS, JAMES RICHARD, was born Sept. 10, 1957 in Hickman, KY. The youngest son of Earnest Logan and Betty Maxine Williams. Logan and Maxine were married Sept. 5, 1948 in Corinth, MS. To this union were born two other children, Debra Renee and Michael Logan.

Jim was married to Mary Agnes Kaufman, on July 6, 1979 in Hickman, KY. Agnes was born Nov. 28, 1961 in Obion County, TN. Agnes is the daughter of Raymond J. and Mary Burke Kaufman. They have three other children, David, Carolyn and Richard.

The James Richard Williams Family

Born to Agnes and Jim, a daughter, Jill Marie, on July 7, 1982; a son James Richard II, Jan. 28, 1986. Jim's paternal grandparents were Charles Hubbard and Mary Ellen Young Williams. Hubbard Williams was born March 9, 1893, in Fulton County, KY. Mary Ellen was born Dec. 18, 1895 in Fulton County, KY. To this union were born seven children. Charles, Cecil, Monk, Logan, Pat, Jerry and Jim.

Jim's maternal grandparents were James Richard and Etoile Ermine Nunley Thompson. To this union were born three girls, Mary, Maxine and Sue.

Agnes' paternal grandparents were W.O. Kaufman and Rose Lattus Kaufman.

Her maternal grandparents were Thomas H. Burks and Ora Crawford Burke of Cedar Hill, TN.

WILLIAMS, W. ASA, was born in Posey County, IN Oct. 25, 1861. He died Dec. 17, 1950. Came to Owensboro in the 1880s. Married Aug. 5, 1888 at St. Joseph Church. He was an electrical engineer. He married Catherine (Kate) Stengell, born in Fulda, IN Oct. 8, 1865, and died Sept. 15, 1966.

Children born to this union:

John L. born June 27, 1889, died July 2, 1962; George I., born May 4, 1893 died Oct. 17, 1967; Eva born Sept. 27, 1895, died April 21, 1989. Joseph lived only a week; Wilbur A. born Aug. 22, 1899 died June 10, 1983; Jessie M. born June 7, 1902; M. Agnes, born Jan. 29, 1905; James S. born Aug. 28, 1907 died Dec. 21, 1981.

All children attended St. Frances Academy; only James graduated there.

All three girls entered Ursuline Convent, Maple Mount, KY. Eva, Sr. Joseph Marie; Jessie, Sr. Charles Asa; Agnes, Sr. Agnes Catherine.

Children baptized at St. Paul, Owensboro but also attended St. Stephen-St. Joseph.

WILLIAMSON, AUDREY RAY AND MARTHA JEAN, Martha Jean was born to Mildred and Myrtle Hagan Dec. 23, 1928 and was baptized at St. Paul's Church two weeks later. Her father worked for Owensboro Grain Company for 42 years. Her mother was manager of the gift shop located in Daviess County Hospital. She was the oldest of five children. She attended St. Frances Academy for four years and transferred to St. Joseph School.

Married to Audrey Ray Williamson April 28, 1947, at St. Joseph Church. They have three sons. Their oldest son Michael Ray, was born in Owensboro, KY and baptized at St. Joseph Church. He attended St. Stephen School for his first five years. They moved to Logan County, KY in 1959 at which time he started to Sacred Heart School. He graduated from Sacred Heart School as an honor student. He belonged to the Squires for several years. He later graduated from Russellville High School as an honor student also. He enlisted in the U.S. Marine Corps during the Vietnam conflict. After returning home he was employed by the TVA in Hixon, TN. He married Paula Farmer and has a step-daughter.

Their second son Stephen Lynn, was also born in Owensboro and was baptized in St. Stephen Church. He also attended Sacred Heart School and was an honor student. His favorite past time appeared to be breaking the school window while learning to play baseball. Mr. Gleason, God Bless him, would repair it for them. He also loved to visit and work at St. Mark's during harvest time. He also graduated from Russellville High School and was awarded the DeGraffenreid Award. He is married to Regina Moore and they have two children, Sarah Lynn, age 7 and John Moore, age 12. He is a project manager at Wright Industries in Nashville, TN.

Martha Jean Williamson and Audrey Ray Williamson

Their third son Patrick Neal, was born in Logan County. Baptized at Sacred Heart and attended Sacred Heart School. He graduated from Russellville High School and married Mary Ann Shifflett. They have two sons, Matthew Neal, age 9 and Kyle Ray, age 4. Patrick is a sergeant in the U.S. Air Force stationed at Lakenheath Air Force Base, England. He spent six months in Saudia Arabia during the Mid East Conflict in 1991. They have been in England three years and are scheduled to return to the United States in December 1993.

Audrey and Martha worked for the Louisville Stores in Owensboro and then transferred to Russellville store where it was called the Peoples Store.

They worked for the company a total of 33 years. Audrey had to medically retire in 1980. He has suffered with emphysema for 12 years.

Martha was active in the Sacred Heart Parrish in several different programs. She was president of the PTA for two terms, School Board Member off and on for 11 years, sung in the church choir for several years, president of Women's Club for two terms, helped start bingo in the parish, started the Memorial Fund, belonged to the Legion of Mary for three years, also served as Eucharist Minister. She is now serving as substitute Eucharist Minister and makes sure the altar and church is decorated at all times.

Martha has worked for 48 years and is now semi-retired. She works three days each week at Bert's Auto Parts. Her favorite time of the year is the Christmas season.

WILLS, BESSIE MAE, was born July 25, 1912, Paducah, KY. Her parents were William Randol and Flora Poat Toon from St. John's. Her grandparents were Stephen and Emma Toon and Phillip and Louisa Poat. She was baptized at St. John's. She is the oldest of four children. She made her first Holy Communion and was confirmed at St. Francis De Sales in Paducah. She attended St. Mary's Academy and graduated in 1930. In 1937 she was married to Paul H. Wills at St. Francis De Sales. Her husband was not a Catholic but later joined the church. In 1939 they moved to Macon, GA, where she attends St. Joseph Church.

Bessie Mae Wills

During the war she worked at Warner Robins, Warner Robins, GA, as an assistant supervisor over the tool cribs. They issued tools to the employees repairing the air planes before going over seas. Later she went to work for the Georgia Loan and Trust Company, a mortgage company, as secretary to the president. She worked there for 30 years until her retirement. At the time of her retirement she was secretary of the company and on the board of directors. After retiring, as her husband deceased and she had no children, she moved back to Paducah to care for her mother and aunt, both now deceased. After an illness she moved to Kuttawa to live with her brother and sister-in-law, Sammy and Jean Toon. She attends St. Mark Catholic Church, Eddyville, KY.

WILSON, JAMES EWING, AND MARTINA (PIERCEALL). James Ewing (1912-1987) son of Robert Leo and Anna Belle (Hobbs) Wilson married Lucille Martina (1914-) daughter of Thomas Guy and Mary Artie (Cissell) Pierceall on Feb. 1, 1932 at St. Charles Church in Carlisle County.

Ewing and Martina had 12 children: James Rudolph (Jan. 9, 1933-April 13, 1967) married Dorothy Hayden (Oct. 12, 1935) Sept. 23, 1952; Vivian Ann (Oct. 29, 1934)

J. Ewing and Martina (Pierceall) Wilson Family

married Edward Goatley (March 1, 1922) Dec. 31, 1955; Wanda Jean (Sept. 27, 1936) married Joseph Mathys (Jan. 29, 1935) Nov. 3, 1962; Robert Leo (R.L.) (Jan. 27, 1938) married Carolyn Koeck (Nov. 12, 1938) Nov. 19, 1960; Annette (Sept. 19, 1941) married Paul Hammrich (Nov. 11, 1939) Feb. 24, 1968; Thomas Terry (Aug. 6, 1943) married Hettie Brannon (April 9, 1944) Oct. 19, 1963; Darlene (June 20, 1946) married Thomas Greuel (Jan. 12, 1942) Oct. 19, 1963; Mary Artie (June 25, 1947) married Claude Brannon (Jan. 8, 1947) Feb. 12, 1966; Eva Nell (Oct. 2, 1949) married Ronald Alderdice (Aug. 26, 1946) Aug. 8, 1970; Betty Lou (Nov. 29, 1951) married James O'Guinn (Feb. 16, 1951) Oct. 2, 1971; Catherine Marie (April 30, 1954) married Steven Grey (March 18, 1955) June 30, 1973; and James Ewing, Jr. (Sept. 10, 1955) married Cindy Cook (Oct. 16, 1957) March 1, 1975. Ten were married at St. Jerome, Fancy Farm, Rudy at St. Charles, Carlisle County, and R.L. at St. Ann in South Dakota. At this writing, Ewing and Martina have 39 grandchildren, 32 great-grandchildren and five great-great-grandchildren.

Ewing quit school at a young age to farm. His hobby was fishing and hunting. He retired from farming 1974. He sold his farm to his third son, Terry. Ewing and Martina celebrated their 50th Wedding Anniversary 1982. Ewing died Jan. 26, 1987 and is buried in St. Jerome Cemetery, Fancy Farm. Martina lives in their home in Fancy Farm, Graves County.

WILSON, JAMES AND ELIZABETH ANN (HAYDEN). Joseph Wilson married Nancy, daughter of Richard and Mary (Murphy) McKay Sr. in Nelson County, KY on May 1, 1821. They migrated to Hickman County in the 1830s.

On Jan. 31, 1860 at St. Jerome, Fancy Farm, James son of Joseph and Nancy married Elizabeth Ann Hayden. James and Ann had eight children: Josephine (died young), Emma Elizabeth (see William Hayden biography), Sarah Josephine, Mary Ellen (see Jerome Hobbs biography), Robert Leo, Thomas Ewing (died young), and family tradition has it that there were twins boys, who died young of poisoning after eating the skimmings from molasses.

James Wilson was baptized on Nov. 6, 1891 at St. Jerome. He died about 1904, and he was buried on his farm. Elizabeth Ann died on July 12, 1913, of apoplexy, and she was buried in St. Jerome Cemetery.

Sarah Josephine (1866-1893) married Thomas Henry Carrico. They had four children: Mary Augusta, James Roy, Alvin and Sarah Lillian.

Robert Leo (1881-1955) married Anna Belle (1882-1977), daughter of Joseph Thomas Hobbs (see Jerome Hobbs biography) and Mary Redford on Oct. 22, 1900 at St. Jerome. Leo and Annie had 10 children: Leslie (1902-1973) married Beatrice Cissell (see Joseph Benjamin Cissell and Leslie Wilson biographies); Vodra (1904-1953) married Mary Ethelene Willett; Mable (1907-1962) married Thomas Louis Spalding (see Robert L. Spalding Biography); Marie (1909-) married Bernard Leo Harmeling; William Dewey (born-died 1911); Ewing (1912-1987) married Martine Pierceall (see Ewing Wilson biography); Everett (1914-) married Anna Rita Courtney (see Leo Byrl Courtney biography) Gladys (1917-), Sister Ann Leo, SCN: Lera (1919-), Sister Judith Ann, SCN; and Paul (1923-) married Grace Snyder.

Leo told the following story to Leslie: "One Sunday I decided it would be more fun to remain in the wagon with my father than attending Mass with my mother. My mother gave me such a yank from the wagon that day, that the importance of attending Mass on Sunday never left me."

WILSON, JOSEPH LESLIE AND BEATRICE (CISSELL). Joseph Leslie Wilson (1902-1973) son of Robert Leo Wilson and Annie Belle Hobbs married Beatrice Cissell (1901-1985) daughter of Joseph Benjamin Cissell and Hettie Jane Hayden on Nov. 9, 1921 at St. Charles Church in Carlisle County.

Leslie and Beatrice had 11 children: Pauline (Jan. 5, 1922 died at birth); Joseph Leo (Oct. 28, 1924) married Magy Masterson (Sept. 28, 1927) Nov. 25, 1948; Thomas Cloyd (Aug. 29, 1926) married Dorothy Marie O'Neill (Dec. 31, 1928) Jan. 7, 1947; Dorothy Mae (June 1, 1928) joined Sisters of Charity of Nazareth Sept. 24, 1947; James Harold (April 16, 1930) married Elizabeth Hayden (Oct. 6, 1934) Feb. 5, 1952; Patricia Ruth (Dec. 7, 1931) married Billy Joe Collins (June 30, 1929) March 1, 1957; Charles Albert July 13, 1934 married Linda Bennett (Feb. 24, 1942) March 30, 1959; Frances Shirley (March 29, 1936) married Donald Leo Westerman (Dec. 13, 1935) Feb. 6, 1960; Rose Nell (Oct. 17, 1937) married Robert Collyer Douthit (Dec. 29, 1942) May 30, 1966; James Jerome (June 16, 1939) married Agnes Kay Goatley (April 23, 1940 - Aug. 17, 1989) Feb. 7, 1959; Philip Anthony (Jan. 11, 1942) married Joyce Marie Mills (June 1942) Feb. 9, 1963.

Leslie and Beatrice were a proud farm family and pleased that all six sons chose farming as their way of life. They were active members of St. Jerome Parish and wanted their children to attend St. Jerome School. Living three miles away and not being able to take off from work to transport them, they bought a horse and buggy so they could do it themselves (until bus service was available).

The year Dorothy Mae was born it rained every day of May and June. The bridge between their home and St. Jerome had been washed away. Since it was expected that a baby be baptized within two weeks of birth, Leslie arranged with Alice (Beatrice's sister) and Herman Curtsinger to meet him on the other side of the creek with their buggy to take them to church. Leslie frequently told the story of how he "swam the creek" to get his daughter baptized. *Submitted by Mrs. Dorothy (O'Neill) Wilson.*

WILSON, JOSEPH LEO, oldest son of Leslie and Beatrice and grandson of Leo and Anna Bell Wilson and Joe Ben and Hettie Jane Cissell all of Carlisle County, KY. A member of St. Jerome Church, a farmer, married Magy Masterson, Nov. 25, 1948, Sacred Heart Church, Louisville, KY.

Front: Magy and Joseph. Left: Denis, Wayne, Ronald, Karen, Elaine, Lanny and Ricky.

Purchased first farm spring 1948. He and his family milked cows and grew tobacco. Joseph Wayne was born Oct. 14, 1949, married Diane Ballard. Lanny Francis born Sept. 13, 1950, married Linnea Bostrum, Chicago, IL. Denis Michael born Dec. 13, 1951, married Denis Toon. Karen Ann born Dec. 18, 1952, married Walter Shup, Mayfield, KY. Richard Dale born Oct. 27, 1954, married Margaret Sandefur, Beaver Dam, KY. Ronald Leo born Oct. 29,

Robert Leo and Anna Belle (Hobbs) Wilson married October 1900. Children: Leslie, Vodra, Everett, Ewing, Mabel, Sr. Ann Leo, Sr. Judith Ann, Paul, Marie. (Golden Wedding Anniversary)

Leslie and Beatrice Wilson Family (August 1953)—Back row: Cloyd, Rose Nell, Joe, Dorothy Mae, Harold, Shirley, Charlie, Ruth; Front row, left to right: James, Leslie, Beatrice, Philip.

1956, married Cinda Reddick. Elaine Marie, born Feb. 7, 1961, married Jimmy Lynn Hogancamp, Bardwell, KY.

All the children have at least four years college. Two self-employed farmers, two doctors of medicine, one CPA accountant (who owns his own business) one school teacher and a nurse. All settled in Western Kentucky except a son in Hinsdale, IL.

They have 23 grandchildren. Two already graduated from high school.

Joe was a Marine in World War II, has been active in the church and is still a Eucharistic Minister and a fourth degree member of the Knights of Columbus. Was a Farm Bureau director and tobacco director for many years. Was on the Fancy Farm Water Board and was one of the ones to start the Credit Union under Father Russell. He's presently on Farmers Home Administration Board and Extension Service through University of Kentucky.

Magy has been active in the church. A cantor for many years. Is secretary-treasurer of Altar Society. President of Garden Club of Mayfield and president of Senior Citizens at Fancy Farm and a member of Homemakers.

WILSON, STEVE ALAN, was born Jan. 1, 1958 in Warren County, KY and Mary Jane Goodin Wilson, born Feb. 18, 1958 in Marion County, KY, were married on Aug. 22, 1981 in Lebanon, KY at St. Augustine Catholic Church. Steve graduated from Western Kentucky University in 1979 and went on to receive his law degree from Chase College of law in 1982. He is currently Commonwealth's Attorney in Warren County. Jane graduated from WKU in 1980. She spent three years working as a television news anchor/reporter before joining Merrill Lynch as a stock broker in 1983.

Steve is currently in the Jaycees, the Rotary Club, B.G. Bar Association and on several boards of local charities. Jane is currently an advisor to Alpha Omicron Pi Social Sorority at WKU, member of B.G. Bar Auxiliary, as well as above church and school activities.

Steve is from Bowling Green, First Church of Nazarene.

Jane Ashlee and Anne Taylor are members of Holy Spirit. Jane, St. Augustine Parish in Lebanon, KY. Jane lector, pre-school Sunday School teacher, co-ordinator of parish nursery, served on church building fund-raising committee, member of St. Joseph School Board.

Steve and Jane have two children, Jane Ashlee, born Oct. 29, 1986 and Anne Taylor, born May 27, 1989. Both girls were baptized at Holy Spirit Church. Ashlee is now in kindergarten at St. Joe. Shortly after Ann Taylor's birth, Jane retired from Merrill Lynch to become a fulltime mother and housewife.

WIMSATT, CARMEL AND ROBERT, (deceased), married on Jan. 16, 1940 at Saint Mary, Whitesville, by Father (Monsignor) William B. Jarboe.

Robert was a successful farmer and livestock producer. He retired about one and half years before his death, July 21, 1980. He was a member of the Holy Name Society, worked for church picnic's and other related church functions.

The Wimsatt Family May 3, 1990. Seated Fred, Ann, Carmel, Juanita, Tom; Standing Judy, Frances, Hugh, Doris, Elaine.

Carmel, a housewife and mother of 10, earned college credits before marrying. She attended Brescia College after the children were in school and taught at St. Mary's Grade School, Whitesville, Lourdes in Owensboro, then again at Whitesville, Trinity. She has been a member of the Altar Society for 52 years, is a Eucharistic Minister, does volunteer work at the Pastoral Archives, Catholic Schools Office and where needed. Carmel also quilts with the club at Whitesville.

Living in a family of 10, emotions are perpetual - a wellspring of laughter and strength, tears and joy, knowledge and understanding. The Wimsatt home was a place to linger and inevitably to leave. Carmel and Robert were proud of their children, and passed on to them the desire to find their potential. Juanita: supervisor in unemployment, tax division, State Department. Tom: territory manager for Supersweet Company. Ann: credit supervisor with GMAC, Nashville. Doris: principal at Catherine Spalding School. Joe was killed in a traffic accident, Jan. 4, 1980, employed as supervisor at Willamette Corporation, Hawesville. Elaine holds vice-president capacity of CGNA Insurance Corporation. Frances works as seamstress and crafter. Hugh, full time farmer and livestock producer. Fred: Recovery second helper with Willamette Corporation. Judy: sales administrator with Kuhlmar Corporation in Versailles, KY.

The Wimsatts have 25 grandchildren pictured in "Grandma's Hall of Fame."

WIMSATT, THOMAS EUGENE, husband and father, July 14, 1942. Attended St. Mary's Grade School and high school, Whitesville; Western Kentucky University, B.S. in 1966. U.S. Army Air Defense June 6, 1968. Married Patricia Simon Wimsatt, July 3, 1950. Attended St. Joe Grade School. Graduate of Bristow High School and Western Kentucky University with MA.

The Tom Wimsatt Family

Sarah Emily Wimsatt, daughter Nov. 28, 1978 attends CCD at St. Joe and Warren East Middle School. Michael Thomas Wimsatt, son July 1, 1980, altar boy at St. Joseph. Attended Warren East Middle School. Jennifer Elizabeth, daughter Feb. 19, 1986 CCD at St. Joseph and Oakland Elementary School.

They have lived in Oakland Warren, 1979. He is a member of St. Joseph. Past members of Holy Spirit, St. Mary's Whitesville.

Parish activities include Deantry Council, Parish Council, teaches CCD. Civic/fraternal activities include Warren East Optimist Club, president-elect, Knights of Columbus.

Joined the parish in 1980. Tom is territory manager; Patty, teacher, Oakland Elementary. Tom's father, Robert Noel Wimsatt; grandfather Charles Wimsatt. Tom's mother, Mary Carmel Hardesty Wimsatt. Grandfather Ben Hardesty.

WINK, MARY LOUISE, was born near Pettit, KY and baptized by Father Walter Hancock. Her father Charles Aloysius Wink is a retired farmer and egg man. He was born at Sutherland, KY. Her mother Melba Marsh Wink is a housewife. She was born in Monticello, KY, they were married Oct. 5, 1940 at St. Anthony's Church, Brown's Valley, KY.

Paternal grandparents, Joseph Simon Wink born in Fulda, IN. Julianna Mehling Wink born in Ferdinand, IN They were farmers in Daviess County, KY.

Paternal great-grandparents. Michael Wink born near Pittsburg, PA. Mary Katherine Hildebrand born in Bavaria, Germany.

Great-great-grandparents, Valentine Wink born in Prussia, Germany and Appolonia Stroebel born in Braden, Germany.

Her maternal grandparents William Thomas Marsh born in Monticello, KY was an oil driller. Lina Ethel Carter Marsh born in Monticello, KY. Her maternal great-grandmother, Josephine Craft Carter, was part Cherokee Indian whose Indian name was Corn Blossom.

Mary is fourth child of seven. Children: Charles Patrick, John William, a veterinarian in Russellville, AR; Joseph Martin, a farmer in Utica; Anita Marie Mathews, who lives in Fort Collins, CO; Rebecca Ann Mills who works for hospice; and David Gerard who is a farmer in Utica.

Mary's hobbies are needlework and cooking. She works as an LPN. She has 16 nieces and nephews and a great-niece and a great-nephew.

Her Aunt Lois sent her a T shirt with this written on it, "Every child should have an Aunt Mary."

Mary lives on Hill Bridge Rd. and attends Mass at St. Anthony at Brown's Valley.

WINK-GOETZ, Valentine Wink, married Barbara Goetz, Feb. 22, 1887 in St. Boniface Catholic Church, Fulda, IN. Valentine had worked in Owensboro for a number of years as a farm hand for Mike Scherm.

Valentine bought a 83 acre woodland farm across the road from the Scherm farm. This he cleared and after their marriage moved to Daviess County.

In 1904 a new home was built and is still on the farm land.

They were life-long members of St. Joseph Church. Children baptized there and attend St. Joseph School.

In this church were beautiful stained glass windows which came from Munich, Germany.

Michael and Valentine donated one window, also Nick and Frank Wink shared another one.

In 1911 Valentine and two brothers gave a beautiful station at Mount St. Joseph for the chapel. (It is heart breaking knowing these magnificent stations have been removed from the chapel). These items demanded great sacrifices for these families. We of this generation reap the fruits from the sacrifices.

They thank them for the strong faith and love they had for the German Catholic Church.

They taught us how to work, to share and appreciate Gods creation.

They worked as a family on all projects on the farm.

An outstanding memory she has of their parish, is when they would attend evening services, this was not too often, as they drove the three mile with horse and surry.

Martine recalls how excited they were about seeing the hundreds of lights lit in the dome of their Church for night services. Thank God every day for having been a member of St. Joseph Parish they were indeed a one family parish. The youngest of eight children.

WOLFE, JAMES AND HELEN BLANFORD, is the son of William J. Wolfe and Florence Buckman Wolfe. Helen Blanford was the daughter of Herman Blanford and Laura Girten Blanford of La Salle, IL, formerly of Union County, KY. James Wolfe and Helen Blanford were married Oct. 26, 1942 at Sacred Heart Church at St. Vincent by Monsignor John M. Higgins. They celebrated their Golden Wedding Anniversary in October 1992. James has

James and Helen Wolfe

been a farmer, construction worker, and has retired from the Bureau of Highways of Kentucky, and is spending his retirement from the Bureau of Highways of Kentucky, and is spending his retirement years farming.

James and Helen had six children, two girls and four boys. The two daughters are Jeannie Wolfe Girten and Barbara Wolfe Jenkins. The four sons are: Arnold Wolfe, Gary Wolfe, Billy Wolfe who died in 1968 and Kenny Wolfe. They have 11 grandchildren and 11 great-grandchildren. James belongs to the K. of C. of Waverly.

WOLFE, WILLIAM PAUL AND DOROTHY SHEFFER, were born and raised in Union County, KY. Both are from large families.

His parents are William J. and Florence Buckman Wolfe. They had 12 children. Her parents are Robert St. Clair and Mary T. Abell Sheffer. They had 10 children.

William Paul and Dorothy had eight children. They also have 27 grandchildren and seven great grandchildren. Their children went to St. Peters School and St. Vincent Academy School.

They were married on Aug. 11, 1941 at St. Ann Catholic Church at Morganfield, KY. They have been members of St. Peter's Catholic Church at Waverly, KY for 46 years. They are active in the parish and so are the children.

The William Paul Wolfe Family

He is an honorary life member of the Knights of Columbus and pro life chair member since 1973. They work diligently for Pro Life and make the annual trip to Washington for the March for Life on January 22.

She has been a member of the Altar Society for 46 years. She was past president of the Society. She helps her husband with Pro Life and is always willing to help anyone sick or in need.

They celebrated their 50th Wedding Anniversary on Aug. 11, 1992 with a large crowd of friends and relatives.

There has been many changes in their life time. They used to go to church in a wagon or horseback and fast from midnight for Holy Communion. Since Vatican II and improved roads and auto they don't have to sacrifice like they did then. Since they retired they go to Mass almost daily.

WOOLDRIDGE, JOSEPH WARD SR., was born July 11, 1900 in Big Clifty, KY. He is one of the younger children of 12. The family moved to Mayfield, KY when Joseph Ward was 9 years old and he has lived there all of his life except for a few years when he lived with a daughter in Louisville and in a nursing home there. He is back in Western Kentucky in a nursing home. He has five children: Julia Wooldridge, Joan Delcher, Helen Maravich, Martha Mathis and Joseph Ward Jr. He has 12 grandchildren and several great-grandchildren. He married Mary Veatrice Hobbs from Mayfield originally from Fancy Farm. She passed away in 1969.

Ward was a member of St. Joseph Church in Mayfield and the children attended school there with the Ursuline Sisters from Mount Saint Joseph near Owensboro.

Ward has been a farmer most of his life. After retirement he did painting and carpentry work.

He is from a family that dates back to 1678 from England. The family came through Virginia and at the time of the Revolutionary War, a grandfather (fourth generation back) was given a land grant on Cumberland Lake, where they lived for several years. Jamestown, KY near Cumberland Lake, was named for one son for having donated land for the town to be built.

Joseph Ward Wooldridge Sr.

The Wooldridge family has been Catholic since about 1849 when the grandfather was converted to Catholicism. Mary Malinda Skees was a staunch Catholic and left a deep rooted faith to the generations that followed.

Joseph Ward and Mary Veatrice were strong in their faith. There was the daily family rosary. Holy water and blessed palm was essential items in the home. Every night the house was sprinkled with holy water and blessed palm was burned during a storm.

WRIGHT, FRED AND BERNADINE, Fred was born April 15, 1913. Bernadine Oct. 27, 1914. Married Feb. 4, 1936 at St. Lawrence. Their children are Wm. Bernard (Nov. 26, 1936) Frieda Marie (Jan. 23, 1939), Lawrence Edward (June 9, 1941), Elmo Ignatius (April 5, 1943), Martha Agnes (Feb. 21, 1945) died Nov. 6, 1945. Michael Eugene (Aug. 23, 1946), Francis Gertrude (Jan. 18, 1948), Sarah Ann (Oct. 29, 1949). They have 29 grandchildren and 17 great-grandchildren.

They have resided in St. Lawrence, Daviess County since 1942. They are members of St. Lawrence Parish. Past members of St. Mary's, Whitesville, KY. They work at picnics and cemetery committee.

All of their children are members of St. Lawrence except Lawrence who is a member of St. Mary's, Whitesville, KY and Elmo who is a member of St. Martin, Rome, KY.

WURTH, The forefather of the Wurths is Englebert Wurth. He was born in 1806. Englebert married Rosena. They had seven children.

Stephen one of their children married Catherine Englert. They had six children.

Denis the youngest of the six married Edith Durbin on Oct. 4, 1939. She is the daughter of Riley and Dora Poat Durbin. They have six children. Roscoe, Margie, Dottie, Bobby, Jerry and Denis Jr.

Roscoe married Joyce Carrico they have two children, Renee and Dwayne. Renee married James Bayette. They have a daughter Crystal.

Dwayne married Mary Merger. They have a son Derick.

Denis Wurth Family

Margie married Bill Wurth. They have two children, Gregg and Gina.

Gregg married Rachel Jones. Gina is engaged to Eric Holeman. A spring wedding is being planned.

Dottie married Milton Grief they have one son Chad.

Bobby married Vickie Gilbert. Bobby has a son Robbie.

Jerry married Barbara Burns.

Denis married Diann Neihoff. They have three children, Sherry, Stephanie, Stephen. Roscoe, Jerry and Denis reside in McCracken County. Bobby in Lovelaceville. Margie in Princeton, KY. Dottie in Brentwood, TN. Denis and Edith and all their children were born and raised in the St. John's Community.

WURTH, HILARY AND HELEN. This family has always been a part of the diocese. Hilary N. Wurth, son of Robert H. Wurth and Mary E. Weitlauf Wurth of Melber, and Mary Helen Saffer, daughter of George N. Saffer and Clara Mary Whitman Saffer of Paducah, were married Jan. 20, 1942. The wedding was performed in the church of St. Francis De Sales, Paducah, by Rev. Charles A. Saffer, brother of the bride.

Hilary and Helen Wurth

They started their family in the parish of St. John the Evangelist, Paducah, and are still dedicated members. Their children, Rita A. Wurth, Vivian W. Stout, Charles V. Wurth, Barbara W. Parker and Robert L. Wurth, have all settled in the Paducah area. They have six grandchildren. Hilary, a retired farmer, and Helen, wife and mother, live on the family farm in Melber, in the house where he was born.

In January 1992, Hilary and Helen celebrated their 50th Wedding Anniversary with an open house hosted by their children and their spouses and grandchildren.

YATES, J.K. (JACK) AND COLLETTA BOWLING, (deceased). William K. and Margaret Austin Yates and William and Sarah Hardesty Bowling are the parents of J.K. Yates and Colletta Bowling Yates. They are farmers.

Jack Yates was born and raised in Union County. Colletta was born and raised in Daviess County. They are also farmers. Members of St. Peter Parish in Waverly, KY.

Adrian was born Oct. 8, 1904. Married Jessie Pierce, Nov. 25, 1931 and died March 8, 1976. Bernadine born April 5, 1906, married Raymond LaRoe, Jan. 23, 1954; died Nov. 2, 1988. Lillian born June 10, 1910. Entered MSJ Convent Jan. 20, 1930 as Sr. Margaret Louise, made vows Aug. 15, 1932.

Clarence born Sept. 16, 1916, married Heloise O'Bryan April 21, 1947. Presently living in Sacramento, CA. Their children: Philip, Margaret, Louise and Ginny.

James Walter (Jack), born Dec. 2, 1918, married to Helen Allen May 18, 1946. Presently living in Evansville, IN. Two children, Kenneth and Janice. (Served in the Navy in World War II. Ship bombed Dec. 7, 1941).

Earl, born Jan. 3, 1921. Married Ivo Gish Sept. 8, 1946, died April 30, 1978. Served in World War II.

YEISER, JOYCE BITTEL, Goebel Bruce Yeiser was born on May 17, 1947. He grew up in Daviess County in a farming community called Thurston and attended Daviess County Schools. He then graduated from Murray State University in Murray. His parents are Pauline Smith, 81 and Goebel Yeiser who died in 1986 at the age of 86. He and his family were Baptist. Joyce Elaine Bittel was born on Oct. 4, 1947. She grew up on a farm near the airport. She

attended Sorgho Elementary School, went to Catholic High School and then graduated from Brescia College.

Her parents are Anthony Bittel and Mary Beiz. Her whole family was Catholic. Joyce and Bruce met when they were showing horses and then married at St. Stephens Cathedral on May 22, 1971. Bruce now farms and works for the city of Owensboro. Joyce works at the State Building in employment services.

Wesley Bryant Yeiser was born on July 19, 1978 and was baptized at St. Piux X Church. He is now 14 years old and goes to school at Owensboro Catholic Middle School. He works on the farm during the summer with his dad for a summer job. Wes is getting ready to celebrate the sacrament of confirmation and attends the school's youth group.

YOUNGBLOOD-WEBB, DOROTHY ROSE (BOURGOIS),

born in Cairo, IL July 22, 1922 to Louis George Bourgois Sr. and Margaret Geneva Courtney Bourgois. She is a descendant of Solomon Courtney, son of the pioneer settlers of this area and August Bourgois, who came to Cairo, IL from Paris, France in the 1840s. Her grandparents were George Allen and Mary Imelda Toon Courtney of Fancy Farm, KY and George and Annie Bourgois of Cairo, IL. She was baptized at St. Joseph Catholic Church in Cairo and attended grade school there. In the fall of 1936 She moved to St. Louis, MO with her mother and brother. She attended Rosata-Kain High School there. Dorothy's mother died in October 1939 and is buried at Fancy Farm. On April 3, 1941 she was married to Paul Edward Youngblood in Cairo, IL. Shortly afterwards they moved to Henderson, KY where her husband worked at an Evansville, IN war plant. They moved to Paducah in May of 1944, where he went to work for the Illinois Central Railroad. In 1951 he was transferred to Jackson, TN where they made their home until his death in August 1976. They had two children, Michael Stephen Youngblood and Michelle Ann McLauren.

In 1982 Dorothy was remarried to Macon Webb of Jackson. They continued living in Jackson until she retired as head of the area Meals on Wheels program in 1989. At that time they moved back to Paducah, where she is a member of St. John the Evengelist Church.

YOUREE, JOSEPH CROSTIC,

was born May 22, 1921, the sixth child of seven children of Hoyte Youree and Mary Inez Crostic Youree.

After attending Hickman Schools and serving in the Army in World War II he returned to Hickman and became engaged to Mary Anita Lattus (Aug. 28, 1922). On Jan. 26, 1947, he was baptized in Sacred Heart Church and they were married Jan. 29, 1947. Anita attended Sacred Heart Catholic School and Hickman High School. She was organist at church for 10 years.

In 1949 they moved to Detroit, MI, then moved to Southern California and returned to Hickman with their 3 year old son, Gregory Andrew Youree (Feb. 4, 1966) in 1969. As members of Sacred Heart Church, Greg attended CCD classes and was a server and lector. Joe served on the church council finance committee and is a member of the Knights of Columbus. Anita belonged to the Altar Society serving as president one year, served on the church council and is a lector.

Joe and Anita are still in Hickman and have a business in Union City, TN. Greg attended Fulton County Schools, spent one year at U.T. Knoxville then transferred to U.T. Martin.

On June 17, 1989, he married Stephanie Speed and they have a daughter, Corey Ann born July 28, 1991 and are living in Dyersburg, TN. Greg is with the Dyersburg Police Department and Stephanie teaches in elementary school.

ZAMBRANO, NATALIE BOONE AND ALAN CHARLES,

Natalie was born in Owensboro on May 21, 1940, daughter of Raymond O. Boone and Mary Robert Hayden. She was baptized at St. Joseph Church and attended the parish school there for eight years. Graduated from Owensboro Catholic and attended Sacred Heart College in Cullman, AL.

Alan was born Dec. 23, 1940 in Manhattan, NY the son of Jose Aurelio Zambrano, a diplomat from Quito, Ecuador and Gloria Anaya of Manhattan.

Natalie and Alan married on June 3, 1961 at St. Stephen Cathedral in the presence of Father Bernard Boone, her uncle of the Louisville Diocese.

They have four sons and two daughters, all of whom attended St. Stephen Elementary School and graduated from Owensboro Catholic High School. During that time Natalie was a Girl Scout Leader and Alan served on the School Board and was also a lector and Eucharistic Minister.

Two of their children were married at St. Stephen and two of their four grandchildren were baptized there.

Alan and Natalie are still parishioners at St. Stephen as are three of their children.

ZIEGLER, FATHER ANTHONY,

Tony was the oldest of two children born to Anthony and Marie Ziegler. He was born in New Orleans, Dec. 31, 1933, and baptized two weeks later at Holy Spirit Church, Hammond, LA. A few months after his birth, his parents moved back to Western Kentucky and settled at Hopkinsville. His sister, Mary Carolyn, was born there in 1937. Anthony made his First Communion and was confirmed at Sts. Peter and Paul Parish. His religious instructions were weekly sessions with the Pastor, Fr. Joe Spaulding, and with the Ursuline Sisters of Mount St. Joseph who came for two weeks in the summer, for there was no Catholic School at that time. He attended Virginia St. Public School. He began serving Mass as soon as he was tall enough to light the candles — about 8 or 9 years old.

In February 1944, the family moved to Owensboro. Tony attended Blessed Mother School at the K of C Hall at Seventh and Frederica, where grades one-five were held. He then went to St. Frances Academy for grades sixth through nine. He has always been most grateful to the Sisters of Charity of Nazareth who taught him through these years. At the end of his freshman year he made the decision to study for the priesthood and in the fall of 1948 he went to St. Charles Seminary in Catonsville, MD.

He spent the remainder of his high school and college years in Baltimore with the Sulpicians, at St. Charles and then at St. Mary's on Paca St. In 1955 he was sent by Bishop Cotton to St. Maur's School of Theology at South Union, KY.

Fr. Anthony Ziegler

Tony was ordained by Bishop Cotton on May 1, 1959. His first assignment was to be assistant to Monsignor Raymond Hill at St. Agnes, Uniontown. There he assisted Monsignor in the office of the superintendent of Schools, and taught religion in the high school (60 students), and was "coach" of the basketball team. On the weekends he assisted Fr. E.E. Willett at Hopkinsville. In 1962 the office of Superintendent of Schools was moved to Owensboro. Tony was moved to Owensboro where he was assistant at the Cathedral, taught full-time at Owensboro Catholic High School, and was athletic director there. In 1964, he was made the head of the Religion Department, and turned over the athletic department to Mr. Harold Mischel. He stayed at the high school until 1973. While there he served as pastor at St. Sebastian Church at Calhoun 1968 - 1971, where he continued the tradition of driving the school bus into Owensboro. This discontinued in 1970.

In 1973, Tony moved to Brescia College, and was chair of and taught in the Religious Studies Department. He remained teaching there until 1982. During that time (1976-1982) he also served as chaplain at Mount St. Joseph Motherhouse.

In August 1982 he was appointed as pastor to Our Lady of Lourdes Church in Owensboro by Bishop Soenneker. In October, John McRaith was appointed as bishop of Owensboro and asked Tony to function as director for Continuing Education for the priests of the diocese, a role he had unofficially assumed through Brescia College. Bishop McRaith later asked him also to open and set up an Office of Worship. In 1985, Tony took on these jobs full-time as part of the staff of the Catholic Pastoral Center.

ZIEGLER, MARIE M.,

currently living in Owensboro was born near Flaherty in Meade County, KY, Dec. 20, 1894 and was baptized at St. Martin Church there. She was the daughter of Alex and Minnie (Schwabenton) Montgomery, the parents of nine children. During high school Marie boarded at Bethlehem Academy and graduated there in 1913. After graduation she taught for several years in a one-room school in Meade County and later worked as a secretary in Louisville, KY, where she met her husband, Anthony Ziegler. He was born Jan. 17, 1896 in Lawrenceburg, IN. Growing up in Meade County included memories of farm life, her father shipping livestock to market by railroad to Louisville and going to "Soon" church on Sundays. "Soon" church meant the early activities at the parish church which included confessions and Communion so that the parishioners could eat a sack breakfast while waiting for the Mass which did not begin until much later. If there was only one priest, there could be only one Mass.

Marie M. Ziegler

When Marie and Anthony Ziegler married, June 17, 1927, Mr. Ziegler worked for the Illinois Central Railroad. Shortly after their marriage he was transferred to Vicksburg, MS and then a few years later to Hammond, LA. Their first child, Anthony Jr., was born on the last day of 1933 in New Orleans, LA.

A few months after the birth of their first child, the couple moved back to Western Kentucky. Their second child, Mary Carolyn, was born in Hopkinsville, KY, in January 1937, and was baptized at Sts. Peter and Paul Church by Father Joseph Spaulding, his first baptism as pastor. Mary Carolyn was later baptized a "second" time at the Ziegler home because Fr. Spaulding was afraid that the water he used the first time was not "holy."

Marie and her husband were members of Sts. Peter and Paul Parish in Hopkinsville when the Diocese of Owensboro was established in 1937. The Ziegler family made the trip to Owensboro to be present for the installation of Bishop Cotton, the first bishop. In February 1944, the Ziegler family moved from Hopkinsville to Owensboro and became members of St. Stephen Parish.

The couple became involved in the life of the parish, belonging to the parish groups such as the Altar Society, the Sacred Heart League. Marie often made house to house calls to distribute the monthly Sacred Heart leaflets to parish members. Son, Anthony Jr., was ordained priest of the Owensboro Diocese on May 1, 1959. Daughter, Mary Carolyn, was married to John Herbert Kurz on May

11, 1963 at St. Stephen Church. After Mr. Ziegler's retirement in 1962, he assisted Father Anthony Higdon with the Monday morning counting of the Sunday collection money, and later kept the financial books for the parish. Marie and Anthony were seen at daily Mass frequently. The husband died in September 1975 and was buried from St. Stephen Parish.

With the devoted assistance of Sister Mary Thomas, A.D., and her son Fr. Anthony Ziegler and daughter Mary Carolyn Kurz, Marie continues at the ripe age of 97 to live at the home on Freeman Avenue they moved into in 1944.

ZOELLER, FR. ANDREW C., became seriously ill at the Altar (before the First Gospel) on Friday morning, February 26, just four days after receiving the title of Monsignor at the Banquet which closed the First Synod of the Diocese of Owensboro.

Before this, Father Zoeller's health was apparently normal; he conducted the weekly Holy Hour Services as usual, the previous evening. From the Chapel Father Zoeller went to his room and to his bed from which he was never to arise.

Fr. Andrew C. Zoeller

It is customary at a person's death to review some of the qualities of his life. His life is the life of Christ, so that St. Paul could say, "I live, now not I, but Christ liveth in me."

When Father Zoeller came to Mount Saint Joseph as Chaplain, Sept. 27, 1935, he left behind him a record of more than 40 years of faithful, fruitful Priesthood in the Diocese of Louisville. At Raywick, Marion County, the field of his longest and most arduous labors, and at St. Denis, Jefferson County, where he organized a parish, opened a Parochial School, and erected a beautiful imposing Church, the Ursulines of Mount Saint Joseph were privileged to labor with Father Zoeller, approximately 15 years; hence, he came not as a stranger to THE MOUNT, but to a spot long-beloved by him, and to friends by whom he was known and appreciated.

Father Andrew Christian Zoeller was born at St. Matthews, Jefferson County, KY, April 1, 1871. He often referred to his Christian home of nine children, the very atmosphere of which was respectful obedience to authority. His studies for the Priesthood were begun at St. Francis, Cincinnati, continued at St. Meinrad, Indiana, and completed at St. Mary's Seminary, Baltimore; in his large class for ordination, was the late Father James L. Whelan, whom Father Zoeller succeeded as Chaplain at Mount Saint Joseph; his ordination by the late Bishop William George McCloskey took place in the Cathedral of the Assumption, Louisville, Dec. 27, 1894; a younger brother, Rev. August Zoeller, died in 1916.

At Left: Sons and Daughters, Jesse W. Mitchell, II. Front (L to R): Tina Mitchell, Nancy Mitchell, Kathy Caruthers. Middle: Brian Mitchell, Annie Mitchell, Kelly Sikes, Back: Cliff Mitchell and Pete Mitchell.

Roman Catholic Diocese of Owensboro Index

A

Abbot 276
Abel 174
Abell 11, 18, 19, 35, 38, 118, 121,124, 126, 127, 147, 162, 169, 209, 213, 216, 236, 331, 345, 360
Able 147
Abney 220
Ackerman 147
Adair 208
Adams 79, 92, 161, 169, 248, 257, 307, 356
Adamson 278
Adkisson 355
Adler 303
Admas 148
Agee 357
Ahern 61
Akers 239, 260
Alderdice 358
Aldridge 214
Alexander 117, 203, 239, 298, 323, 339
Allan 262
Allard 94, 110, 132, 135, 166, 177, 243, 292, 327
Allen 196, 208, 224, 271, 273, 297, 360
Allman 67, 68, 73, 84, 93, 228
Allord 330
Alloway 135
Alvey 72, 95, 115, 123, 127, 196, 197, 211, 221, 231, 274, 275, 279, 280, 284, 288
Alveys 11
Amberg 170
Ambo 223
Ambrow 263
Ambs 258, 259, 288
Anderson 196, 228, 229, 236, 325, 348
Andrews 201
Anthony 197
Appleby 250
Aquinas 299
Arbogast 184
Archabbey 87
Arcilesi 94, 147, 156, 174, 197
Armbruster 34, 134
Armes 239
Arms 172
Armstrong 57, 105
Arnold 301, 302, 308, 335
Artysiewicz 107
Asaro 262
Ashby 336
Askin 215
Askins 153
Asmus 332
Asplund 162, 310
Atherton 263, 273, 330
Atkinson 242
Aubrey 16
Aubry 322
Auchenbach 202, 338
Aud 11, 35, 36, 147, 155, 174, 192, 197, 198, 263, 266, 272, 295
Auer 29, 190
Aull 55, 70, 93
Austin 224, 311, 353, 356, 360
Auxilium 182

B

Babb 254
Babbitt 295
Bachi 149
Bachmann 25
Bacon 198, 322
Baden 140
Badin 10, 12, 13, 14, 15, 18, 19, 22, 118, 124, 169, 253, 318
Baehre 331, 332
Bair 78
Baird 148, 287, 317, 355
Baker 94, 108, 113, 133, 156, 158, 165, 198, 199, 262, 340
Ball 198, 203, 239, 261, 341
Ballard 62, 137, 156, 198, 203, 229, 244, 245, 246, 261, 262, 264, 271, 275, 299, 303, 334, 345, 359
Ballards 251
Ballman 260, 271, 278
Ballmann 344
Balster 154
Bambury 127
Bambury 115, 116, 124, 137, 143, 159
Barber 262, 301
Barkau 323
Barker 336
Barkley 93
Barna 282
Barnard 299
Barnes 263, 349
Barnett 110, 202, 212
Barnhart 262
Barr 63, 224, 237, 243, 270, 318
Barren 264
Barret 122
Barrett 23, 24, 33, 34, 35, 36, 37, 43, 44, 49, 115, 120, 121, 123, 124, 137, 139, 155, 200, 224, 230, 305, 347, 351, 353
Barriere 13, 18
Barron 198
Barrow 199, 333, 334
Barry 115, 276
Bartholome 57
Bartlett 318
Bartley 199, 222, 343
Bartolomucci 34, 281
Barton 92, 184, 199
Bartram 299
Basehart 79
Basham 208, 215
Baskett 317
Bassett 250, 261, 263
Batman 156
Batson 199, 200, 277
Baudendistel 252
Bauer 44, 154, 278, 305
Bauman 172
Baumgarten 54, 63, 64, 184, 260, 280
Baush 247
Bax 22, 23
Bayer 200
Bayette 360
Bealmear 343
Bean 307
Bear 331, 332
Beatty 200
Beauchamp 270
Beaudry 338
Beauvais 317
Beaven 200, 307, 325, 336, 338
Beavin 153, 154, 232, 328
Beck 241
Becker 47, 76
Beckett 96, 107, 179
Beckman 351
Bedwell 52
Beemer 298
Beitzell 335
Beiz 361
Belcher 224
Belford 69
Bell 205, 213, 224, 225, 278, 303, 317
Bellchase 127
Bellew 262, 264, 323
Bender 307
Bendon 262
Benedict 116
Benham 239
Bennett 95, 182, 229, 275, 358
Benny 294
Bernadette 36, 56
Bernardin 69
Berry 68, 92, 209, 224, 248, 251, 306
Berthianume 143
Berthiaume 292
Bertrand 291
Beruatto 31, 34, 35, 43, 44, 49, 129, 140, 143, 231, 243, 256, 268, 269, 292, 350
Bethel 200
Beyhurst 115, 137
Beyke 200, 308, 324
Bickett 62, 93, 94, 105, 123, 156, 174, 200, 201, 202, 206, 209, 212, 240, 271, 288, 299, 307, 346
Bickwermert 201, 216, 300, 330
Bielefield 214
Biggs 60, 70
Bihn 169
Binghams 122
Birchler 220, 304
Bird 41, 202
Birkhead 246
Birnbach 342
Bishop 71, 140, 143, 157, 179, 182, 243
Bissert 240
Bissmeyer 294
Bittel 94, 144, 161, 201, 347, 361
Bittner 94, 199, 277
Bivin 305
Bivins 62, 206
Black 93, 201, 202
Blackburn 262
Blackwell 202, 338
Blahn 161
Blair 202, 203, 287, 310
Blake 257
Bland 203
Blandford 69, 197, 218, 247, 248, 250, 286, 291, 300, 304, 320, 339, 340, 345, 348
Blanford 144, 203, 309, 336, 340, 360
Blau 303
Blincoe 205, 210, 246
Blount 172
Blue 200
Boarman 33, 34, 52, 67, 95, 111, 126, 127, 130, 150, 192, 203, 204, 206, 207, 211, 213, 214, 215, 216, 219, 221, 240, 248, 250, 258, 265, 267, 271, 282, 293, 295, 298, 308, 328, 329, 349
Bobbett 200
Bockelmann 263
Boddie 200
Boehler 105, 107, 276
Boehman 248
Boehmann 204
Boehmicke 43, 44, 49, 50, 95, 96, 108, 112, 113, 151, 161, 164, 167, 242, 306
Boemiche 58, 67
Boemicke 53, 56, 61, 67
Boggess 204
Bohanon 161
Bohn 316
Bohrer 266
Boland 63, 107
Bolands 140
Boles 12
Bolger 302
Bolin 279
Boling 299, 345, 347
Bolling 207
Bomensatt 34, 63, 67, 95, 132
Bompart 244
Bonaventure 302
Bond 263
Bondurant 236
Bone 73
Bonetti 300
Bonvillain 303
Booker 295
Boone 76, 77, 80, 89, 92, 127, 184, 192, 205, 231, 261, 318, 349, 361
Booth 184, 236
Bopp 285
Borchers 107, 140, 256
Borgia 94
Borntraeger 126
Borntraeger 34, 43, 44, 49, 108, 133,159, 163, 170, 206, 253, 275, 324
Borntrager 143, 258
Bosecker 229
Bostick 200
Bostrum 359
Boswell 205, 283, 298
Boteler 55, 183, 214, 300
Bouchet 37, 169
Boulton 345
Bourgois 205, 206, 361
Bourke 29, 35, 36, 115, 116, 137
Bowen 123
Bowhmicke 160
Bowlds 95, 198, 206, 218, 252, 287, 309, 353
Bowles 11, 72, 73, 84, 92, 184, 206
Bowling 34, 35, 36, 43, 45, 49, 51, 59, 66, 91, 141, 160, 162, 176, 188, 206, 221, 244, 246, 252, 254, 283, 295, 300, 353, 360
Boyd 289, 335, 338
Boyle 110, 170, 295
Brackett 338
Brackin 318
Braddock 135
Bradley 67, 70, 76, 92, 93, 115, 134, 171, 182, 200, 207, 221, 242, 247, 272, 275, 291, 292, 299, 329
Brady 171
Bramlette 103
Brandle 207
Brandon 207, 208
Brannon 358
Brashear 227
Brasher 272, 287
Braum 325
Braun 34, 43, 44, 49, 134, 146, 160, 208, 221, 264, 339
Brazil 196
Breeding 317
Brenkus 154
Brewer 11, 213, 252, 264, 351
Brey 29, 30, 31, 35, 37, 103, 163, 222
Bright 137, 243
Brinker 311
Brittain 318
Broadley 299
Broffey 215, 239
Brokramp 301
Bronk 243
Bronsgust 292
Bronson 261
Brooks 222
Brothers 248
Brower 339
Brown 94, 172, 191, 208, 209, 224, 229, 233, 239, 240, 248, 249, 250, 262, 266, 275, 293, 313, 332, 335, 342, 343, 344
Browning 70, 79, 84, 92, 93, 96, 110, 208

Bruce 327
Brumfield 78
Brumlow 209
Bryan 209, 211, 247
Bryant 345
Buchenmeyer 332
Buchman 79
Buckman 79, 92, 209, 240, 241, 244, 246, 252, 257, 311, 338, 345, 353, 354, 355, 360
Buechlin 87
Buehrle 92
Buerhle 79
Buford 300
Bugg 213, 218
Bullock 156, 354
Bumpus 125
Bunch 114
Burch 33, 137, 205, 210, 219, 234, 236, 262, 264, 293, 353
Burcham 280
Burchman 280
Burchs 239
Burd 210, 311
Burden 220, 227, 230
Burgdorf 95
Burgess 115, 196, 234, 260, 272, 339, 355
Burgger 332
Burich 196
Burk 215
Burke 60, 92, 96, 275, 357
Burkes 116
Burkhead 159
Burks 357
Burns 192, 200, 360
Burris 219
Burrows 241, 351
Burshears 225
Burtle 143
Burton 295
Busam 91, 92, 196, 209, 211
Buser 92
Bush 200
Bussey 323
Butler 124, 317
Byerly 208
Byrd 95, 211
Byrne 55, 94, 156, 205, 212, 230, 233, 264, 270, 300, 315, 316, 317

C

Cain 201, 241
Caise 351
Caldwell 283
Calhoun 62, 67, 68, 73, 84, 92, 93, 106, 140, 143, 159, 165, 182, 184, 192, 201, 212, 213, 220, 287, 310
Calhouns 95
Callahan 115, 162
Callendar 351
Calvert 11
Cambon 147
Cambron 123, 213, 235, 291
Cameron 176, 192
Campbell 214, 280, 328
Cannon 143, 156, 251, 328
Canty 68
Carberry 269
Carey 245
Cargile 123
Carmack 267
Carman 144, 239
Carmanns 159
Carmen 298
Carmens 127
Carney 239, 281
Carol 103
Caroline 107
Carper 351
Carr 65, 206
Carrico 34, 38, 43, 44, 49, 55, 65, 110, 115, 129, 132, 137, 173, 186, 192, 210, 213, 214, 215, 218, 220, 225, 234, 241, 254, 255, 260, 272, 281, 291, 294, 301, 311, 322, 323, 339, 340, 343, 345, 353, 355, 356, 358, 360
Carrigan 188
Carroll 13, 14, 18, 104, 115, 140, 163, 184, 199, 200, 215, 236, 239, 244, 245, 249, 271, 313, 329, 338
Carson 283
Carter 163, 222, 333, 338, 359
Caruso 241
Caruthers 295
Carver 319
Carwile 239
Casey 96, 159, 294
Cash 55, 94, 110, 137, 139, 149, 156, 203, 210, 215, 216, 224, 232, 234, 242, 255, 340, 353, 355, 356
Caslen 184
Cassidy 124, 258
Castlen 62, 63, 73, 184, 216, 300, 303
Castrale 36
Caswell 184
Cates 215
Catlett 115
Caudill 184

Cavanaugh 317
Cecil 60, 64, 67, 69, 73, 75, 89, 93, 122, 124, 135, 144, 175, 216, 217, 222, 224, 230, 252, 258, 264, 275, 288, 295, 298, 302, 319, 342, 345, 349
Cereny 203
Cerhan 217
Cerriell 264
Chabrat 15, 18, 20, 24
Chambige 21, 127
Chandler 298, 329
Chaplain 61
Chapman 246
Chappell 345
Charlesine 36
Charlet 130
Charters 107
Chartrand 38, 39, 41, 254, 300
Cheathum 332
Cherry 232
Cheshire 259, 320
Chessin 67
Chew 272
Childers 300
Chiles 330
Chinn 298
Chiodo 144
Chissom 266
Chittenden 200
Christ 316
Christensen 261, 264, 313
Christian 235, 266, 325
Christie 324
Christopher 128, 208
Church 156
Ciagnio 68
Ciccolella 198
Cicognani 339
Cimprich 149
Cinnamon 156
Cinnamond 218, 246
Cissell 11, 19, 35, 127, 169, 217, 218, 248, 260, 263, 291, 312, 339, 357, 358
Clan 123
Clapp 196
Clark 11, 19, 61, 62, 66, 67, 73, 74, 93, 94, 106, 110, 111, 113, 119, 122, 123, 127, 159, 161, 176, 188, 196, 199, 200, 203, 206, 218, 219, 224, 226, 227, 228, 231, 236, 238, 241, 248, 249, 253, 256, 262, 263, 264, 267, 285, 287, 291, 298, 302, 306, 307, 308, 318, 325, 326, 341, 350, 352
Clarke 245, 254
Clarkson 186, 213
Clary 243, 281
Claussner 191
Clay 15
Claypool 349
Clayton 134
Cleavenger 327
Clements 34, 35, 37, 43, 44, 49, 52, 95, 108, 113, 115, 121, 122, 127, 13
9, 144, 147, 161, 174, 190, 220, 244, 249, 271, 282, 287, 296, 301, 307, 315, 328, 346
Clemons 62, 67, 73, 75, 78, 82, 93, 111, 113, 161, 196, 220, 221, 232, 238, 247, 248, 267, 272, 329, 330, 337, 345, 351
Cleveland 230
Clifton 268
Clouse 299, 337
Cloys 343
Cochran 332
Cocke 222, 270
Coenen 27, 28, 31, 35, 108
Coffey 294
Coffman 251
Coghlan 147, 155, 295, 296
Cohron 274
Colburn 184
Colby 70, 86
Cole 222, 223, 303, 353
Coleman 290
Collens 95
Collignon 241
Collins 62, 95, 122, 191, 199, 217, 222, 223, 250, 295, 343, 358
Collis 352
Combs 273
Comernisky 356
Concepta 154
Conder 192, 222, 287
Cone 144
Coney 297, 354
Conklin 143
Conley 93, 207
Conlon 117
Conn 223, 312
Connelly 29
Conner 171, 223
Connolly 32, 35, 37, 124, 163, 277
Connor 34, 52, 58, 248, 334
Conroy 144
Considine 261

Conway 298, 302, 326
Cook 306, 358
Coombes 334, 335
Coomes 19, 20, 21, 22, 30, 35, 36, 61, 62, 76, 92, 118, 127, 129, 147, 155, 171, 184, 197, 200, 212, 222, 223, 229, 230, 254, 258, 265, 266, 271, 272, 287, 291, 295, 306, 308, 327, 328, 334, 337
Cooper 79, 80, 92, 93, 248, 250, 295
Corbett 62
Corley 63
Cormier 262
Corrigan 188
Cossey 223
Cota 338
Cotton 16, 31, 33, 34, 38, 41, 44, 47, 48, 49, 50, 51, 52, 53, 54, 55, 56, 63, 77, 78, 87, 92, 109, 110, 112, 114, 116, 119, 122, 126, 129, 130, 131, 135, 143, 144, 146, 148, 150, 156, 160, 166, 167, 171, 173, 178, 181, 182, 183, 186, 189, 196, 197, 199, 223, 236, 242, 249, 254, 267, 271, 275, 278, 284, 287, 290, 299, 305, 306, 319, 323, 326, 328, 330, 338, 339, 346, 347, 352, 353, 361, 362
Courcier 256
Courtney 205, 218, 224, 254, 260, 303, 358, 361
Covington 157, 172
Cowie 262
Cox 197, 229
Coy 261, 298
Crabtree 93, 224, 309
Craft 264, 335, 359
Crafton 327
Craggs 157
Craig 333
Crane 171
Craney 103, 122, 123
Cravens 115
Crawford 224, 275, 279, 291, 346, 357
Crawley 118
Creary 124
Cremer 197
Crenshaw 260
Crews 10, 12, 15, 16, 153
Crisp 224, 302
Criswell 330
Critchelow 78, 224, 313, 318
Critchlow 239
Crittenden 261
Crittendon 261
Croghan 26, 292, 337
Croghn 162
Cronin 27, 118, 160, 163, 174, 202, 338
Crostic 361
Crouse 223
Crow 198
Crowder 250
Crowdus 353
Crowe 201, 212, 224, 322
Crowley 124
Crune 198
Cuddy 332
Culliton 338
Cummings 225, 337, 343
Cummins 346
Cunningham 118, 215, 249, 287, 354, 356
Cureton 307
Curlin 198
Curran 126
Curry 199, 247
Curtin 164
Curtis 156, 251
Curtsinger 137, 144, 204, 218, 241, 311, 340, 356, 358
Cusick 115

D

Daily 277
Dalton 32, 172, 215
Daly 120
D'angelo 226
Danhauer 61, 93, 132, 133, 135, 143, 148, 159, 170, 173, 184, 223, 227, 293, 294, 325, 350
Daniel 192, 223
Daniels 328
Dant 14, 212, 242, 299, 352
Darnall 199
Darnell 245
Darst 218, 219, 224, 226, 227, 277, 285, 291, 329, 336
Dauby 228
Daugherty 192, 291
Davenport 184, 227
David 12, 13, 15, 16, 19, 20, 120, 186, 231
Davidson 65

Davis 25, 26, 37, 68, 114, 115, 200, 227, 248, 262, 314, 346
Dawood 330
Day 161, 227, 267
Dayberry 122, 200, 209, 240
De Mareo 55
De Nardi 346
De Sai 241
De Vries 22
Dean 261
Deanery 79
Deans 263
DeChristopher 34, 126, 134
deChristopher 128
Decker 251, 333
DeGaulle 111
Degauquier 20, 21, 35, 38, 140, 143
Degauzuier 124
DeGrandis 72
Deicken 260
Delcher 360
Delcour 340
Delehunt 192
Delphin 49
DeMeulder 264
Dempsey 325, 331
Dempster 332
DeNardi 43, 44, 49, 95, 132, 133, 137, 159, 219, 225, 226, 227, 293
Denistin 260
Dennis 188
Deparcq 20, 36
Dequaquier 127
DeRohan 169
deRohan 18
Derouen 317
DeSmet 140
DeVilley 251
Devine 93, 94, 111, 132, 149, 227, 243, 341
Devins 112
DeVries 23, 27, 28, 35, 116, 141, 152, 277
deVries 22
DeWeese 228
Deweese 186
DeWitt 248
Dickens 349
Dickins 318
Diddle 279
Diemert 286
Dienes 34, 43, 44, 49, 50, 110, 126, 143, 144, 148, 171, 207, 221, 293
Diermert 121
Dierolf 228
Dietrich 228
Diller 34, 114, 346
Dillman 297
Dillon 115, 120, 124
Dirnberger 332
Dishman 303
Dixon 241, 244, 260
Dobric 266
Dockemeyer 338
Dockermeyer 337
Doepker 210
Doggett 233
Doland 215
Donahue 122, 228, 238, 299
Donnelly 204, 356
Donoghue 239
Donohoe 103, 124, 229
Donovan 25, 74
Doom 326
Doran 228
Dore 229, 330, 333
Dorian 344
Dorn 105, 107, 138
Dorsch 332
Dorshel 322
Dorsten 320
Dorth 230
Dosh 186
Dossett 215, 229
Dotson 218
Doughty 229
Douling 239
Douthit 358
Dowden 245
Dowdy 229
Dowell 78, 94
Downes 188
Downey 170
Downing 248
Downs 161, 248, 263, 301
Dozier 62
Drace 227
Drane 239
Dreckmann 116
Dreville 116, 121
Drew 332
Driscoll 213
Driskill 210
Droege 279
Drur 229
Drury 29, 30, 35, 37, 41, 79, 94, 112, 117, 121, 134, 156, 174, 188, 191, 198, 212, 213, 229, 276, 289, 295, 296, 299, 307, 312, 336
D'Shane 300
Ducette 244
Dudine 126, 140, 284
Duell 329

Duerr 10, 12
Duff 245
Duffy 95
Dufresne 230
Dugan 288, 295
Duggan 148
Duggins 77
Duhart 255
Duke 332
DuMaine 32, 33, 137, 210
Dunaway 241, 351, 352
Dunbar 230
Duncan 230, 338, 354
Dunkel 353
DunLaney 64
Dunn 17, 23, 35, 37, 60, 61, 67, 95, 115, 126, 156, 164, 165, 170, 221, 254, 308
Dunnigan 183
Dunning 263
Dupont 258
Durbin 10, 17, 19, 20, 21, 22, 23, 25, 26, 27, 31, 32, 34, 49, 62, 66, 108, 110, 116, 118, 119, 120, 122, 123, 124, 127, 132, 136, 137, 139, 140, 147, 152, 155, 161, 164, 174, 190, 210, 229, 231, 232, 246, 257, 260, 284, 289, 306, 311, 312, 336, 343, 356, 360
Durbins 170
Durry 163
Durvall 257
Dutsehke 239
Duvall 232, 266
Dworzan 205
Dyer 217, 222, 232, 233, 347

E

Early 348
Eastwood 229
Eaton 340
Eaves 262
Ebelhar 79, 233, 298, 302, 320
Eberhardt 262
Echmans 54
Eckman 355
Eckmans 93
Edelen 34, 43, 44, 49, 66, 120, 122, 143, 155, 223, 233, 244, 291, 315
Edge 198, 202, 203, 214, 233, 234, 294, 297, 298, 308, 334, 337, 341, 342, 347, 349
Edwards 142, 250, 263, 337, 338
Effinger 115
Egan 43, 44, 49, 116, 117, 155, 171, 174, 223
Egart 40, 127, 143, 159, 215
Eger 258
Eggermont 25, 121, 147, 155, 170
Eich 302
Elder 137, 188, 213, 222, 234, 270, 294, 298, 301, 302, 356
Ellegood 132, 353
Elliott 34, 55, 137, 207, 210, 215, 218, 225, 234, 241, 253, 255, 301, 335, 340, 346, 353, 355, 356
Ellis 232, 299
Embry 220, 286
Emge 273
Emilian 344
Enderle 332
Engelman 156
Englert 110, 176, 265, 312, 351, 352, 360
Ernest 198
Erwin 144, 234
Eskridge 239
Espy 235
Estep 235
Esterkamp 179
Estes 260, 316
Eubank 79
Evely 61
Evans 235, 297
Evens 313
Ewing 65
Ezell 235

F

Fagan 108
Faherty 252
Fahrenbach 127
Fahrendorf 238, 239
Fallon 32, 347
Fanelli 44
Fanning 238
Farenback 159
Farley 73, 235, 302
Farmer 357
Farquahar 306
Farrell 69
Farris 200
Faulk 261
Faunt 162
Fawns 312
Feaster 238
Federico 239
Federle 357
Feehan 26, 37, 115, 137, 164
Fegan 25
Feirstein 244
Feix 235
Feldpausch 203
Felhoelter 215
Feller 76, 346
Felton 139
Felts 218
Fenelly 124, 169
Fenton 148, 154
Fentress 235
Fenwick 11, 12, 14, 18, 236, 249, 251, 257, 285, 311, 313, 314, 316, 330, 331, 342, 345, 353
Fergerson 322
Ferguson 262
Ferrell 196
Ferreri 67
Ferriell 236, 264
Fichtor 271
Field 115, 132, 140, 148, 155, 160, 236, 267, 340
Fields 126, 143, 346
Finegan 160
Finley 235
Finn 152
Finotti 257
Fischer 93, 95, 120, 133, 155, 159, 163, 170, 192, 202, 215, 236, 237, 238, 239, 241, 243, 260, 290, 321, 341
Fisher 60, 63, 206, 350
Fitter 239
Fitzerald 287
Fitzgerald 82, 35, 125, 160, 192, 294, 302, 303, 304, 333
Fitzgibbon 122, 239
Fitzmorris 176
Fitzpatrick 321
Flaget 12, 13, 15, 17, 18, 19, 20, 21, 22, 118, 139, 141, 169, 231
Flaherty 79, 184, 237, 317
Flamion 345
Flanagan 239, 264
Flannagan 287
Flatter 303
Fleischman 69
Fleischmann 70, 237, 238, 239
Fleming 223, 320
Flittner 303
Floerish 178, 284
Floersch 32, 48, 353
Floersh 16, 32, 38, 39, 103, 130, 146, 164, 259, 332, 347
Flood 203, 215, 236, 239, 260, 313
Floresh 36, 48, 57, 139
Floyd 244, 278
Fobey 261
Fogle 93, 94, 124, 132, 149, 154, 162, 167, 198, 202, 232, 247, 251, 260, 278, 345
Ford 27, 28, 74, 115, 124, 127, 137, 138, 144, 155, 159, 240, 250, 282
Forester 241
Forgey 215
Forrestal 115
Fortier 185
Foster 270, 307
Fouriner 169
Fournier 13, 124
Fowler 31, 132, 210, 217, 232, 233, 240, 301, 311, 327
Fox 247
Foy 210
Francis 55, 240
Francken 31
Frank 198
Frankberger 66
Franklin 200, 333
Frantz 95, 120
Franzen 198
Freehan 322
Freels 262, 264
Freking 94, 107
French 207, 209, 222, 229, 236, 240, 241, 256, 286, 311, 335, 336
Frey 241, 247, 328
Friant 302
Friedal 302
Friedel 44, 260
Friedman 182
Friel 153
Frink 209
Frisz 96, 148
Fritz 67, 277, 300
Froede 103
Froehlich 242
Froelich 242
Froning 79, 81, 93, 241
Fry 291
Frye 96
Fuerst 216
Fulkerson 61, 65, 79, 198, 212, 248, 255, 317
Fuller 192

Fuqua 224, 234, 298

G

Gabe 124, 127, 159, 169, 235
Gabelman 356
Gaddis 201
Gaffey 319
Gallagher 121, 134, 176, 210
Gallo 60, 69, 85, 86, 93
Galloway 230, 248, 249, 343
Gamble 279
Gambon 28, 146, 171, 174
Gambron 294
Gammon 344
Gardiner 11, 21, 186
Gardner 93, 304
Garey 236
Garland 234, 241, 345, 351
Garnett 215
Garrett 224, 241, 243
Garrison 207, 277
Garth 309
Garvin 112, 252, 315
Gasser 110
Gastenveld 336
Gatton 110, 299
Gavin 130
Gaw 109
Gayhart 308
Geary 230
Gehres 68, 175
Geiger 267
Geisler 279
General 25
Gerneral 45
Gerst 109
Gerteisen 346
Gerten 60
Gentry 249
Gibbons 259, 316
Gibbony 131
Gibbs 172
Gibson 93, 137, 184, 192, 200, 205, 210, 218, 222, 223, 234, 236, 240, 245, 246, 247, 249, 257, 263, 266, 278, 280, 282, 287, 291, 301, 303, 307, 308, 316, 333, 336, 339, 350, 357
Gilbert 58, 360
Giles 345
Gilhooley 338
Gilkey 248
Gill 139
Gillenbeck 134
Gilles 214, 252, 306
Gillespie 264
Gillespy 302
Gillim 216
Gillock 184
Gilman 295
Gilstrap 241, 299, 337
Giovannucci 279
Gipperich 34, 43, 44, 49, 66, 235, 244, 273
Gipson 241, 351, 352
Girten 200, 335, 360
Gish 228, 244, 361
Givens 276
Glahn 34, 62, 66, 67, 72, 84, 94, 113, 115, 121, 148, 149, 158, 165, 167, 170, 197, 203, 242, 269, 325, 326
Glaser 115
Glass 346
Gleason 148, 346, 357
Glenn 34, 43, 44, 49, 134, 173, 207, 291, 300, 303, 308, 313, 321, 338, 351
Glennon 36, 206
Glidwell 312
Glisson 218
Goatley 210, 335, 340, 358
Goeff 80
Goetz 76, 94, 110, 119, 126, 137, 156, 177, 214, 225, 275, 279, 288, 345, 349, 351, 359
Goetzman 262
Goff 93, 95, 151, 243, 293, 337, 341
Goins 229, 274
Gold 69
Goldsberry 292
Goldsburry 143
Goldwasser 227
Goode 252
Goodin 315
Goodwin 248
Gootee 166
Gordon 213, 234, 351
Gore 260, 339
Gorline 232
Gorman 184, 185
Gorny 105, 107, 138, 179
Gough 156, 238
Goughs 251
Gowell 263
Gower 338
Grace 227
Graham 257, 264, 276, 303, 354
Grant 68, 70, 76, 93, 112, 162, 196, 243, 348, 349
Gratzer 243, 244, 283
Grausz 325
Gravely 310

Graves 235
Gray 170, 188, 233, 316
Greathouse 208
Greayer 198
Green 188, 238, 239, 250, 276, 289, 335
Greenberg 258
Greene 335
Greenfield 249
Greenwell 11, 33, 34, 43, 44, 49, 79, 119, 128, 151, 184, 202, 205, 208, 215, 236, 244, 249, 262, 264, 278, 304, 308, 334, 335, 344, 352
Greenwood 224
Gregory 294
Gresham 149
Greuel 358
Grey 358
Gribbons 345
Grief 139, 245, 312, 330, 360
Griffin 215, 313
Griffith 133, 165, 174
Griggs 232
Grimmelsman 56, 178
Groghan 162
Gronner 332
Gross 334
Guedrey 331, 333
Guerin 115
Guillerman 245
Guillory 224
Gupton 218
Guron 338

H

Haas 34, 92, 245, 335
Haddad 245, 292
Haddon 225
Haeseby 164
Haeseley 24, 26, 28, 32, 35, 115, 132, 137, 139, 224, 312, 336, 352, 355, 356
Haesely 278
Haesley 234
Hagan 21, 62, 68, 72, 89, 93, 95, 137, 184, 192, 200, 205, 210, 218, 222, 223, 234, 236, 240, 245, 246, 247, 249, 257, 263, 266, 278, 280, 282, 287, 291, 301, 303, 307, 308, 316, 333, 336, 339, 350, 357
Hageman 105
Hagen 270
Hager 208, 332
Hagman 95, 115, 122, 128, 132, 135, 138, 151, 155, 156, 162, 166, 188, 247, 271, 272, 278, 287, 312
Haight 197
Hain 268
Haire 221
Haislip 67
Halbleib 353
Hale 239, 240, 247, 248, 293, 332
Haley 257
Hall 148, 198, 248, 300, 330
Hallahan 34, 43, 44, 49, 116, 163, 206, 207, 305
Hallihan 279
Hallows 211
Hamilton 188, 192, 215, 222, 246, 248, 249, 265, 266, 287, 291, 300, 303, 308, 313, 321, 338, 351
Hamlet 293
Hamlin 325
Hammer 300
Hammerlin 238
Hammrich 358
Hancock 58, 59, 66, 67, 72, 76, 77, 80, 92, 93, 94, 103, 105, 117, 121, 126, 129, 132, 137, 138, 143, 155, 163, 170, 207, 208, 225, 233, 249, 250, 283, 288, 301, 307, 311, 338, 341, 342, 350, 359
Hand 246, 279
Handley 188
Handy 350
Haney 225
Hanley 75, 280, 290
Hannah 315
Hanning 236
Hansen 72, 87
Hanson 211, 223
Haragan 219
Harden 336
Hardenbergh 336
Hardesty 192, 228, 239, 246, 250, 264, 285, 305, 308, 326, 359, 360
Hardin 261, 299
Hardy 282
Hargett 241
Hargis 250
Harl 250
Harley 298, 299
Harmeling 358
Harms 235
Harnett 296
Harold 61
Harper 208, 239, 251

Harrington 61, 300
Harris 159, 198, 220, 276, 316
Harrison 156, 251, 275, 280, 338
Hart 204, 301
Hartley 208, 309
Hartly 287
Hartwick 115
Hartz 227, 307, 316
Harvey 228
Haseley 347
Hatcher 93
Havelburg 122, 127, 159, 161
Hawkins 276, 297, 298, 316, 349
Hay 268, 351
Haycraft 251
Hayden 11, 20, 34, 43, 45, 49, 50, 51, 52, 59, 60, 62, 65, 67, 69, 70, 73, 76, 79, 85, 87, 91, 92, 93, 94, 95, 104, 117, 120, 132, 137, 142, 156, 168, 173, 174, 182, 184, 192, 197, 205, 207, 208, 215, 216, 218, 219, 220, 225, 233, 234, 236, 240, 251, 252, 253, 254, 255, 260, 267, 275, 278, 280, 298, 299, 300, 301, 306, 311, 315, 318, 320, 324, 334, 335, 336, 337, 339, 340, 341, 345, 348, 353, 355, 356, 358, 361
Hayes 25, 32, 34, 35, 37, 43, 44, 49, 51, 75, 93, 94, 115, 141, 149, 164, 184, 199, 200, 211, 231, 243, 256, 317
Haynes 214, 256, 272, 288, 305
Hays 295
Hayse 78
Hayworth 262
Hazel 174, 256, 264, 272
Hazelwood 219, 349
Hazenbuhler 262
Hazzard 256
Head 61, 110, 198, 203, 214, 237, 257, 262, 264, 278, 298, 324
Heady 342
Heally 118
Healy 116, 157
Heavenhill 261, 262, 264
Heavenill 262
Heaverin 257, 292
Heavin 317
Heavrins 122
Hebert 252
Heep 257, 311
Hehir 69
Heichelbeck 60
Heim 209
Helfrich 211
Helling 30, 31, 34, 35, 38, 43, 44, 49, 52, 126, 133, 147, 159, 218, 226, 329, 330
Hellner 115
Helm 234
Hemmerle 257
Henckens 26
Henderson 72, 222, 236, 317, 323, 334
Hendricks 347
Hengstebeck 179
Henkel 148
Henley 269, 343, 352
Henn 95
Hennessy 163
Hennesy 103
Henniger 57, 67
Henning 147, 172, 188, 198, 203, 215, 239
Henninger 34, 35, 38, 43, 44, 49, 59, 61, 150, 162, 242, 253, 257
Henry 59, 124, 163, 258
Henshaw 306, 317
Henshaws 122
Henson 258
Herbert 172, 316
Herberth 31, 35, 150, 170
Heriges 209, 257
Hermann 266
Hernas 60
Herring 346
Herrmann 257
Hertel 93
Hesen 257
Hessian 322
Hester 249
Heuser 225, 256
Hevern 12
Hick 285
Hicks 216
Higdon 34, 35, 38, 43, 45, 49, 52, 53, 65, 79, 92, 93, 95, 96, 109, 121, 124, 126, 127, 133, 134, 143, 149, 151, 156, 162, 166, 170, 171, 184, 188, 196, 198, 200, 212, 216, 217, 220, 221, 246, 252, 256, 258, 259, 265, 271, 272, 280, 281, 287, 288, 291, 292, 293, 296, 308, 309,

365

318, 319, 330, 339, 340, 341, 345, 351, 353, 355, 362
Higgins 28, 32, 34, 35, 38, 43, 45, 49, 66, 118, 119, 124, 127, 162, 163, 164, 168, 201, 225, 235, 236, 240, 259, 291, 333, 346, 354, 360
Higginson 288, 289, 306
Higgs 96, 183
Hildebrand 210, 359
Hildesheim 327
Hileman 298
Hill 34, 35, 39, 43, 44, 49, 54, 58, 61, 110, 120, 121, 127, 162, 164, 184, 192, 196, 203, 221, 232, 240, 249, 259, 291, 298, 329, 331, 336, 361
Hinchey 208
Hines 62, 259, 260
Hinton 124, 154, 215, 248, 260, 287, 305, 310
Hirsch 311
Hisgen 164
Hite 63, 93, 122, 134, 135, 174, 217, 229, 249, 311, 336
Hixon 79, 92, 114
Hobbs 20, 55, 137, 224, 229, 234, 260, 276, 311, 316, 335, 336, 339, 340, 353, 356, 357, 358, 360
Hockgeiger 282
Hodde 96
Hodges 282
Hodgkins 260, 263
Hodskins 230
Hoepf 103, 124, 338
Hoffman 95, 107, 182, 276
Hoflinger 207
Hogan 229
Hogancamp 359
Hogarty 32, 115, 118, 270, 311, 332
Hogg 280
Holder 223, 241
Holeman 113, 223
Holieran 103
Holinde 103
Holmes 211
Holshouser 261, 262
Holthouser 262
Holtzhausen 261, 262, 263, 264, 279, 333
Holtzhauser 261
Holtzhauser 262
Holtzhouser 262
Holtzhouser 263
Honnold 219
Hood 65, 217, 264, 303, 328
Hooivelad 128, 151
Hoover 235, 302
Hopper 330
Horatio 137
Horn 293
Horrell 143, 260
Horseman 233, 234
Horvath 257
Hoskins 264, 272, 298, 304
Hostetter 79, 92, 93, 94, 111, 128, 265
Hovekamp 278
Howard 11, 60, 63, 67, 68, 69, 72, 73, 74, 76, 79, 85, 92, 93, 132, 134, 172, 192, 198, 199, 218, 219, 223, 224, 233, 237, 246, 265, 266, 267, 269, 271, 287, 294, 295, 298, 300, 301, 308, 321, 323, 325, 328, 337
Howe 227, 267, 298
Howell 247
Hoying 169
Huckebys 122
Huddleston 184, 298
Hudson 300
Huff 34, 35, 39, 43, 44, 49, 126, 132, 133, 155, 163, 173, 220, 237, 308, 329
Hughes 82, 87, 94, 96, 143, 148, 154, 161, 163, 213, 267, 268, 292, 301
Hulsey 341
Hultz 349
Hummel 211
Humpert 343
Hundley 310
Hunnicut 293
Hunt 268, 318, 340
Hunter 34, 62, 66, 114, 123, 262, 268, 305, 331
Hurley 322, 351
Hurm 192, 214
Hurst 269
Huskisson 269
Hussey 283
Husted 348
Huston 93
Hutchens 103
Hutchins 20, 230, 280, 343
Hutton 292
Hygins 124
Hyland 144

I

Ingram 269

Intravia 69
Iott 113
Irons 184
Isbill 269, 309
Itschner 64, 75
Ivie 215

J

Jackson 107, 110, 223, 229, 262, 272, 279, 287, 344
Jacobaugle 253
Jacobs 205, 328
Jacobson 263
Jadot 268
James 198, 316
Jansen 29, 35, 37, 115
Janson 29
Jarboe 11, 34, 43, 44, 45, 49, 115, 127, 132, 155, 160, 163, 174, 201, 203, 206, 213, 214, 229, 233, 235, 239, 240, 270, 271, 295, 303, 307, 308, 309, 313, 321, 322, 343, 359
Jean 167
Jefferson 255
Jelinski 179
Jenkins 11, 25, 108, 118, 124, 147, 164, 174, 296, 360
Jenne 124, 134, 151
Jennings 249, 270
Jerkins 208
John 55
John XXIII 56
Johner 73
Johnson 79, 92, 93, 94, 115, 123, 131, 134, 135, 184, 188, 192, 198, 200, 201, 205, 213, 214, 225, 228, 230, 244, 247, 249, 258, 262, 264, 267, 270, 271, 272, 287, 289, 295, 297, 301, 308, 309, 313, 315, 321, 326, 332, 336, 337, 338, 342, 346, 349, 352
Johnsons 116
Johnston 129, 196, 207, 220, 221, 258, 272, 273, 284, 292, 329
Jolly 239
Jones 93, 106, 110, 226, 228, 238, 239, 273, 292, 293, 300, 338, 347, 360
Jonson 239
Jordon 273
Joseph 93, 94, 273
Joyce 110, 124, 127, 143, 159
Joyner 274

K

Kaelin 67, 70, 72, 84, 243, 304, 330
Kager 251
Kahalley 252, 315
Kaiser 154
Kaminski 274
Kamuf 92, 227, 299, 319, 324
Kanaly 184, 185
Kanapple 239
Kannapel 287
Kanobie 271
Kantlehnar 302
Kapelsohn 93
Kapusha 203
Karl 70, 72, 84, 92, 93, 119, 146, 151, 274
Karn 295
Karr 250
Kasey 302, 330
Kauffeld 298
Kaufman 66, 115, 232, 275, 351, 357
Kazel 74
Kean 228
Kearney 164, 267
Keeling 210, 229
Keenan 63
Keene 205
Keeny 275
Keiffer 277
Keightley 198
Keil 118
Keiser 360
Keith 275
Kellehur 133
Kellenaers 26, 28, 29, 31, 35, 120, 122, 123
Keller 80, 189, 197, 218, 275, 276, 295
Kelley 107, 161
Kelly 16, 87, 127, 215, 217, 263, 298
Kelty 330
Kemp 276
Kempf 55
Kendrick 294, 356
Kennedy 57, 95, 107, 154, 182, 184, 241, 263, 307
Kenney 316
Kenny 80
Kenrick 37
Keough 62
Kern 211, 256

Kerrick 216, 257, 300
Kersting 289
Kertz 252
Kettler 276
Ketzer 276
Kibby 286
Kidder 215, 239
Kidwel 294
Kieffer 302, 335
Kiebel 276
Kiel 282
Kilcoyne 260
Kimble 196
King 26, 37, 57, 75, 103, 115, 144, 155, 203, 206, 260, 276, 288, 302
Kingsley 347
Kinkel 95
Kinnaird 84, 88
Kinnamon 355
Kinney 144
Kipper 276, 277
Kipply 62
Kirby 210, 319, 351
Kirchhoff 277
Kirchoff 281
Kirk 317
Kister 277
Kletzel 148
Kleuk 216
Klien 237
Kline 318
Knadler 274
Knight 248, 275, 278, 319
Knoerr 115
Knott 11, 174, 198, 223, 261, 272, 278, 299, 342
Knue 30, 124, 153, 154, 306, 309, 327
Koblenz 241
Koch 154
Koeck 358
Koenig 96, 179, 208
Koger 278
Komola 312
Konsler 215, 244, 250
Koonce 75
Kopischke 344
Korn 261, 262
Korte 117, 132, 277
Kortz 317
Kraimer 297
Kramer 69, 70, 213, 244, 278
Krampe 216, 239, 248, 278, 298
Kreidt 115
Kresse 336
Krimple 278, 312, 352
Krueger 287
Kuder 293
Kuegel 318
Kuhn 30, 38, 126, 127, 129
Kunkel 120
Kupper 335
Kurz 73, 92, 247, 278, 362

L

La Beau 238
Labazon 343
Laemmle 265
Laemmle 174
Lafferty 261
Lamb 201, 279
Lambert 296, 326
Lampton 276, 279
Lancaster 67, 73, 84, 93, 162, 208, 279, 291, 325, 332
Lanceste 149
Landall 154
Landoll 32
Lane 148, 203, 206, 266, 300, 311
Langan 112
Lange 184, 185
Langham 254
Langley 261, 262, 279
Langsdon 339
Langston 245, 279
Lanham 155, 192, 201, 217, 218, 247, 271, 274, 279, 280, 298
Lanowski 280
Larimore 184, 185
Larken 269
LaRoe 360
Larson 261
Lashbrook 237, 261, 262, 263
Lashley 207
Laslie 239
Lattus 115, 252, 280, 289, 315, 357, 361
Lauer 60
Laur 192
Lauter 93
Lauterwasser 336
Lauzon 34, 73, 84, 92, 93, 106, 110, 125, 247, 280
Lavely 236
Lavialle 16, 24
LaVoice 281
Law 256
Lawler 277
Lawrence 60, 67, 192
Lawson 208, 304

Lay 262
Layton 261
Leach 252, 306, 315
Leachman 170, 281
Lear 209
Leary 360
LeBeau 238
Leber 141
Lebre 144
Lechner 66, 175
Ledford 255
Lee 235, 239, 248, 269, 332, 343
Lees 11
Leet 216
Legeay 67, 115, 156, 208, 277, 281
Leibfried 266
Leiedecker 238
Leigh 198
Leneave 132
Lenihan 144, 261
Lennon 117, 281
Lennarts 44
Lennons 116
Leonard 144
Lewis 20, 65, 135, 235, 239, 271, 282, 317, 331, 334, 335, 343
Libbs 115, 279
Libs 34, 52, 148, 165, 170
Lichtenwald 270
Lickteig 225
Liedecker 239
Likens 202
Lilly 72, 81, 182, 282
Linder 189
Linderman 132
Lindles 122
Lindow 282
Lindsey 230, 282
Ling 282
Lingang 294
Linhuber 344
Linton 161, 260
Linz 353
Liston 260
Little 92, 96, 154, 163, 177, 237, 350
Litzsinger 301
Livoti 183
Lobley 338
Loftus 161
Logan 68
Logdson 247
Logsdon 17, 19, 140, 192, 231, 244, 291, 309
Logston 258
Lombardi 199
Loney 212
Long 131, 135, 236, 240, 241, 244, 282, 283, 297, 311, 329
Lonne 254
Lorenes 216
Lott 206
Lovelace 313
Lovell 282
Lowe 282, 322
Lowery 75, 114
Loyd 287
Lucas 226
Lucid 153
Luckett 92, 94, 123, 130, 132, 144, 283, 284, 285
Luers 24
Luigs 232, 289
Luke 188
Luley 128
Lusby 329
Lush 31, 126, 196, 259, 284, 292
Luther 60, 61, 91, 92, 94, 133, 135, 148, 166
Luttrell 230
Lynch 30, 31, 79, 92, 262
Lynes 251
Lynn 172
Lyon 93
Lyons 10, 14, 15, 17, 19, 20, 21, 22, 23, 24, 26, 27, 28, 29, 30, 31, 32, 33, 36, 37, 38, 39, 40, 41, 42, 116, 117, 248, 264, 333
Lyvers 203

M

MacAllister 317
MacDougall 61
Mackey 233
Mackin 216
Mackworth 302
Madden 199, 343
Madder 290
Maddox 291
Magee 334
Maglinger 347
Maher 311
Mahl 274
Mahoney 262, 289
Maier 201
Maitz 285
Makin 189
Malone 75
Maloney 35, 39, 64, 87, 128, 162, 171, 176, 204, 286, 306
Mandel 302
Mangels 332
Mangold 115, 346

Manion 276, 285
Mann 285, 314
Manning 119, 239, 285, 314
Mansfield 326
Maravich 360
Maregold 280
Mark 92, 192
Markey 235
Maron 223, 258
Marr 336
Marren 286
Marrett 286
Marsch 131
Marsh 131
Marshall 61, 142, 213, 232
Martin 36, 184, 242, 248, 272, 286, 301, 333, 348, 351
Martino 263
Martter 184
Marvel 214
Mason 134, 242, 323, 328
Massarella 107
Massey 353
Masterson 358
Mastravito 298
Mastrovito 142, 144, 165, 240
Mathews 359
Mathias 293
Mathis 360
Mathys 358
Matthews 211, 286
Mattie 262
Mattingly 11, 18, 45, 55, 68, 92, 93, 94, 108, 113, 124, 127, 128, 143, 148, 153, 154, 155, 156, 165, 183, 198, 200, 215, 216, 219, 222, 223, 230, 234, 235, 243, 248, 250, 252, 255, 260, 264, 265, 272, 287, 288, 295, 296, 298, 299, 300, 304, 306, 308, 309, 313, 317, 318, 332, 337, 338, 339
Mattox 246
Mauzey 143
Maxey 339
May 61, 142, 337, 338
Mayes 218, 245
Mayfield 237, 288, 309
Mays 203, 218, 317
McAleer 34, 35, 43, 45, 49, 121, 174, 197, 214, 307, 328
McAtee 34, 52, 61, 117, 128, 132, 134, 151, 166, 171, 268, 303, 306
McAuley 24, 178
McAuliffe 107
McBrayer 288
McBride 84, 93, 148, 156, 167, 188, 261, 273, 287, 288
McCabe 67, 96, 154, 234
McCaffery 309
McCallister 244, 283
McCann 305, 330
McCarthy 121, 134, 252, 297, 300, 315, 345
McCarty 60, 63, 95, 125, 156, 170, 228, 289, 350
McCary 115
McCaslin 289
McCauley 56, 323
McClain 332
McClish 319
McCloskey 16, 17, 23, 24, 25, 26, 27, 28, 29, 30, 31, 32, 33, 37, 38, 39, 40, 42, 115, 123, 137, 146, 156, 160, 163, 170, 193, 312, 330, 362
McClosky 108, 138, 143, 162
McClure 268, 292
McConnell 26, 27, 31, 35, 171
McCormick 290
McCoy 303
McCracken 279
McCrory 37
McDaniel 238, 264, 280
McDermott 115
McDonald 115
McDonnell 283
McDonough 16
McElroy 279
McElwain 352
McFarland 184
McGarry 245
McGary 339
McGee 128, 206, 222
McGehee 202
McGerry 331
McGill 36, 171, 186, 210, 323
McGlothan 263
McGovern 161
McGowan 299, 312
McGraw 328
McGrew 226
McGruder 79, 92
McGuire 128, 162, 201, 293
McIlvoy 289
McIlwain 352
McIntosh 93, 132, 184
McKaey 196
McKay 316
McKearney 162
McKendree 232, 289
McKenna 310
McKenzie 210

McKeown 65
McKinley 221, 234, 241
McKinney 161, 245, 295, 330, 343
McLaughlin 170
McLauren 361
McLean 330
McMahan 223
McMahon 41
McMannis 200
McManus 343, 351
McMichael 198
McMillian 279
McMillin 262
McMurray 352
McNally 245
McNamara 161
McNEIL 39
McNeil 29, 30, 32, 35, 130, 144
McNeill 290
McNicholas 124, 169, 312
McNichols 137
McNulty 67, 290
McNutt 66
McParland 108
McPherson 121, 218, 252, 267
McQuade 107, 276
McQuaid 40
McQuillan 356
McRaith 47, 66, 67, 68, 69, 70, 71, 72, 73, 74, 75, 76, 77, 78, 80, 81, 82, 84, 85, 86, 87, 88, 89, 90, 91, 92, 93, 108, 111, 115, 121, 126, 131, 132, 133, 135, 143, 146, 148, 149, 160, 169, 171, 181, 183, 185, 189, 197, 211, 212, 221, 230, 231, 242, 243, 256, 268, 273, 284, 290, 291, 294, 298, 306, 317, 319, 339, 343, 354, 357, 361
McShane 115
McSweeney 127
McTiques 116
McWilliams 262, 291, 327
Meador 239
Meadors 207
Meadows 75
Meagher 24, 25, 35
Meany 138
Medley 11, 142, 220, 251, 261, 291, 304, 309, 320
Meffert 307
Mehlbauer 110
Meiring 103, 124
Meister 73
Melbourne 353
Mellies 332
Melody 27, 35, 127, 143, 164, 174, 292
Melone 245
Melton 255, 296, 332
Menard 187, 277
Menke 32, 162
Mensa 35, 39, 115, 121, 128, 168, 333
Mercer 220, 349
Mercy 167
Meredith 79, 84, 92, 93, 94, 110, 115, 143, 156, 232, 268, 286, 291, 292, 305
Merger 360
Merici 54, 90, 175
Meridith 93
Merimee 227, 254, 321
Merjavy 208
Merritt 210, 293, 298
Mertins 25, 116, 152
Merton 12
Meserve 279
Meshew 55
Messenger 293
Messick 73, 94, 123, 156, 293
Metcalf 221, 352
Metters 322
Mewburn 296
Meyer 130, 276
Meyerhofer 148
Meyering 29, 35, 40, 103, 125, 130
Micale 200
Michinock 268
Midkiff 306, 309
Migacz 149
Mikulcik 148
Miles 23, 237, 238, 239, 259, 272, 287, 291, 293, 351
Millard 144
Millay 234, 237, 238, 239, 272, 287, 293, 299, 306, 307
Miller 61, 95, 108, 120, 121, 126, 142, 197, 241, 243, 244, 247, 251, 257, 258, 261, 262, 272, 287, 293, 297, 317, 347
Milligan 247
Milliner 159, 219, 226, 227, 293, 294
Milliron 274
Mills 92
Mills 11, 19, 34, 43, 44, 49, 55, 59, 61, 67, 72, 77, 84, 86, 88, 89, 92, 93, 94, 106, 112, 123, 128, 132, 138, 150, 156, 163, 166, 184, 211, 215, 219, 223,

233, 240, 244, 248, 271, 282, 285, 292, 294, 311, 317, 347, 354, 357, 358, 359
Minch 103, 115, 124, 130, 143, 292
Minnis 216
Mischel 65, 110, 361
Mistkowski 238
Mitchell 162, 228, 263, 264, 295, 301, 333, 340
Moening 290
Molitor 274
Mollhorne 127
Molloy 96
Molohon 176, 259
Moman 158, 217, 295
Monaghan 142, 147, 294
Monarch 30, 65, 162, 287, 295, 296, 309
Monica 209
Monnin 154
Montgomery 21, 29, 30, 37, 110, 192, 229, 256, 285, 288, 291, 296, 297, 308, 361
Montini 58
Moodey 205
Mooney 337
Moore 11, 48, 170, 184, 185, 188, 223, 239, 293, 297, 312, 323, 332, 357
Moorman 239
Morgan 211, 254, 256, 351
Morphew 246
Morris 11, 39, 40, 82, 93, 110, 245, 267, 271, 279, 297, 299, 302, 349
Morrow 191
Mort 134
Moseley 172, 309
Moser 161
Moses 261
Moss 161, 262
Mott 67
Mouser 263
Mucci 268
Mudd 62, 127, 143, 188, 223, 224, 262, 264, 298, 320
Mueller 40, 160
Mulcahy 259
Mulchrone 107
Mullen 239
Muller 199
Mullican 328, 337
Mulligan 79, 92, 242, 253, 254, 286, 295, 298, 319
Mullins 316
Murnian 68
Murphy 34, 40, 63, 66, 69, 72, 103, 111, 115, 120, 122, 124, 125, 134, 144, 148, 184, 202, 203, 212, 216, 229, 260, 275, 298, 299, 300, 303, 304, 305, 319, 337, 338, 342, 345, 348, 351, 358
Muscovalley 196
Muyssen 128, 143
Myers 347
Myrick 300

N

Naas 95
Nagele 140, 170, 172
Nahstall 66
Nahstoll 34, 43, 44, 49, 155, 162, 170, 171, 202, 217, 233, 267, 293, 295, 300, 326, 337, 348, 349
Nall 210
Nally 79, 263, 264, 316, 354
Narcissus 267
Nash 107, 274, 292
Nation 257, 282
Nazaria 192
Neagle 117
Neal 301
Neale 204
Neel 267, 280, 348
Neely 233
Neesen 134
Neeson 163, 243
Neff 239
Neihaus 40, 271
Neihoff 360
Nelson 276, 297, 354
Nenninger 326
Nerinckx 10, 12, 13, 14, 15, 18, 19, 49, 118, 124, 126, 127, 140, 147, 155, 159, 169, 209, 240, 257
Nerincx 159
Nerinsky 295
Nerinx 104, 337
Neshige 294
Netherton 207
Neudecker 209
Neumann 280
Neuner 270
Nevitt 264, 285
New 350
Newbauer 303
Newby 301
Newcom 197
Newcomb 205
Newman 122, 318
Newton 11, 236, 248, 301
Nicholson 301
Nieborowski 25

Niedergeses 87
Niehaus 29, 35, 103, 147, 163, 250, 297
Niesen 162
Nisz 317
Nizinski 355
Noah 301
Noennig 335
Nolan 139
Norman 34, 35, 40, 43, 44, 49, 51, 160, 242, 264, 302, 304
Norris 246, 257, 302
Norsworthy 209
Novak 61
Novicke 148
Nugent 198, 261
Nunley 357
Nunn 184, 185, 302, 322
Nussbaun 249

O

O' Sullivan 266
O'Bannion 262
Oberhausen 257
Oberhulsman 137
Oberlinkels 121, 124, 134
Oberst 224, 246, 302, 303
O'Brian 264
O'Brien 303
O'Brien 94, 95, 107, 117
O'Briens 116
O'Bryan 52, 61, 65, 66, 67, 68, 69, 70, 85, 93, 94, 95, 115, 138, 151, 155, 166, 170, 172, 182, 205, 214, 216, 223, 225, 238, 239, 254, 258, 265, 271, 272, 287, 298, 303, 304, 317, 325, 330, 333, 334, 345, 355, 360
O'Calligan 22
O'Callaghan 35
O'Callaghan 22
O'Callagran 170
O'Callahan 171
O'Connell 25, 187
O'Connells 116
O'Conner 143, 344
O'Connor 28, 108, 109, 115, 117, 149, 292
O'Cornor 103
O'Daniel 286, 288, 295
Odendahl 122, 124
Odendall 162
Odengahl 128
O'Dohaghue 41
O'Donaghue 16, 30, 31, 32, 38, 40, 41, 142, 163
O'Donahue 206, 259
O'Donnel 140
O'Donnell 67, 73, 76, 81, 92, 93, 94, 105, 107, 117, 138, 172, 179, 248, 276, 304, 317, 343
O'Donoghue 169, 219, 244, 273
O'Donohue 132, 325
O'Driscoll 115
O'Dwyer 40
Oechsli 225
Oelze 78, 304
O'Flynn 306
O'Guinn 358
O'Hara 113
O'Keefe 185
O'Keefe 184
Oldham 164
O'Learys 122
Olejnicak 67
Oliver 200, 269
O'Loughlin 331
O'Nan 279, 297, 319, 324, 330
O'Neal 260, 284
O'Neil 163, 239
O'Neill 201, 358
Opperman 302
Orange 161
OReilly 287
O'Reilly 67
O'Riley 143
Orlet 268
Orndorff 345
O'Rourke 11
Ortize 62
Osborn 77
Osborne 94, 112, 184, 208, 242, 246, 279, 305, 310, 333, 335
Oser 285
O'Sullivan 35
O'Sullivan 28, 30, 34, 40, 43, 45, 49, 51, 115, 121, 124, 127, 143, 144, 155, 156, 161, 186, 192, 200, 204, 233, 234, 265, 266, 294, 309, 318, 330
O'Toole 303
Outland 200
Overfield 285
Overstreet 236
Owdziej 201
Owen 347, 354
Owens 143, 357
Ozanam 65, 192
Ozar 68
Ozborne 291

P

Padgett 208, 285
Pance 262

Panzera 148
Papciak 79, 92
Pardon 295
Paris 222
Park 306
Parker 149, 300, 305, 360
Parrette 31, 132
Parrott 215
Pate 203, 287, 305
Patry 128
Patten 211
Patterson 305
Paul Paul VI 62
Paul VI 33
Paule 262
Paulin 244, 283
Paydon 235
Payne 11, 31, 33, 35, 41, 73, 78, 79, 92, 93, 94, 95, 106, 110, 114, 126, 138, 150, 154, 163, 198, 200, 201, 204, 212, 216, 219, 220, 227, 229, 234, 237, 238, 243, 244, 248, 249, 250, 252, 253, 255, 257, 260, 267, 269, 271, 272, 287, 294, 297, 299, 301, 302, 306, 307, 308, 309, 317, 319, 325, 330, 338, 341, 342, 346
Payton 345
Peak 220, 309
Peake 236
Pearl 133, 159, 219
Pearson 335
Pease 218
Pedley 307
Peebles 137
Peerman 310
Pekarek 310
Penn 289
Pennaman 79
Penzel 331
Perdue 236
Perkins 215
Perlman 198
Perry 60, 310
Peterson 66, 112, 262
Petitt 167
Pettit 34, 52, 55, 108, 110, 112, 113, 115, 144, 148
Petty 184, 254
Pfingston 317
Philip 320
Phillips 116, 248, 303, 310
Philpot 44
Phipps 218, 276
Pickard 254
Pidgeon 340
Pieper 198
Pierce 105, 221, 243, 260, 272, 310, 318, 360
Pierceall 137, 210, 224, 240, 255, 310, 311, 355, 356, 357, 358
Piercefield 311
Piersall 218
Pierson 122, 135
Pieters 120
Pike 27, 29, 31, 35, 103, 113, 116, 124, 128, 134, 162, 164, 170, 188, 216, 219, 240, 249, 257, 260, 288, 311, 313, 314, 315, 333, 342
Piland 335
Pilger 122, 135
Pilot 350
Pinkston 234
Pio Laghi 76, 87
Pirtle 119
Piskula 75, 79, 95, 148, 156, 184, 247, 311
Pitt 32, 49, 53, 182
Pitts 260
Placzek 107, 172
Plummer 312
Poart 312
Poarth 312
Poat 232, 278, 288, 312, 340, 347, 351, 352, 353, 357, 358
Poath 312
Pobst 332
Pogue 312
Poiners 280
Pokagon 14
Pollard 184, 185
Pontrich 288
Poole 156, 198, 328
Pooser 312
Poot 312
Pope 248, 313
Pope Gregory XVI 21, 178
Pope John Paul 68
Pope John Paul II 63, 66, 75, 80, 84, 91, 245, 254
Pope John XXII 58
Pope John XXIII 57, 58, 171
Pope Leo IX 29
Pope Paul IV 258
Pope Paul VI 58, 63
Pope Pius IX 26
Pope Pius X 30
Pope Pius XI 33, 48, 49, 171
Pope Pius XII 50, 119,

270
Popham 215
Porter 246, 275
Portman 279
Pote 312
Poth 312
Potter 355
Pottinger 248, 283
Pottkoetter 154
Potts 215, 239, 240, 293, 313
Powell 20, 92, 95, 103, 117, 127, 128, 129, 132, 133, 148, 149, 159, 162, 167, 169, 184, 185, 221, 270, 277, 285, 292, 295, 311, 313, 314, 315, 342
Power 22, 23, 115, 124
Powers 22, 62, 64, 65, 66, 67, 70, 78, 92, 93, 94, 96, 106, 109, 110, 112, 119, 121, 123, 128, 140, 143, 144, 146, 148, 151, 154, 158, 162, 173, 208, 223, 227, 237, 238, 252, 275, 278, 288, 291, 292, 311, 315, 316, 325, 326, 342, 343
Prather 333
Preske 117
Prewitt 276
Price 216, 261, 301, 316
Priebe 262
Priester 149
Prince 172
Pritchett 288
Proctor 249, 334
Proffit 333
Proffitt 331
Promes 342
Puckett 316
Purcell 30, 224, 336, 343
Purdue 353
Purdy 316
Puryear 255

Q

Queen 264
Quick 251
Quigg 130
Quigley 188, 248
Quint 344
Quirk 170

R

Rachels 316
Raferty 330
Rafferty 316
Raffo 124
Rahm 35, 37, 41, 122, 123, 126, 213
Rahrig 189
Raibley 204
Rainer 251
Raleigh 260, 316
Raley 11, 41, 207, 233, 260, 294, 316, 317, 332, 345, 347
Ramage 198, 271
Ramon 197
Ramsey 295
Rance 278, 317
Randol 331, 332
Randolph 113, 241
Rankin 347
Rapier 204, 244, 261
Rathman 217
Ratley 244
Rauch 31
Ray 232, 317
Raymer 208
Rearidon 170
Redden 335
Reddick 359
Redford 260, 358
Reding 172
Redle 356
Reed 94, 95, 122, 135, 290, 317
Reeves 330
Regan 176
Regis 36
Reich 300
Reid 264
Reil 196
Reinecke 311
Reis 351
Reising 93
Reisy 154
Reitmier 22
Reitz 208
Reitzel 258
Remedios 117
Renfrow 207
Renner 154, 273
Resser 245
Reteneller 265
Revlett 230
Reynerson 229
Reynolds 67, 72, 84, 92, 95, 123, 169, 230, 240, 294, 317, 318, 337
Rhoades 199
Rhodes 12, 52, 55, 59, 61, 67, 73, 92, 95, 114, 156,

171, 213, 240, 259, 270, 275, 281, 291, 294, 299, 308, 318, 337, 346
Rhody 113
Ricciardi 268, 318
Richard 335
Richardson 142, 206
Richardsville 161
Ricke 273
Ricketts 316
Rickman 334
Rideout 317
Ridley 306
Riedl 199
Riepe 351
Riggs 199, 218, 248, 257, 261, 301
Riley 28, 55, 93, 134, 137, 150, 170, 211, 215, 251, 281, 318, 346
Riney 61, 63, 65, 67, 73, 76, 92, 93, 94, 110, 114, 131, 132, 133, 135, 137, 149, 154, 155, 156, 158, 159, 163, 173, 208, 212, 217, 223, 225, 227, 233, 278, 288, 292, 298, 299, 300, 318, 319, 320, 321, 322, 327, 328, 341
Riordan 296
Risner 280
Ritch 209
Ritter 188
Rives 109, 128, 163, 271, 333
Rivette 283
Roach 215, 253, 287, 304, 321
Robb 346
Robbins 109, 203
Roberts 32, 103, 131, 137, 192, 204, 206, 209, 219, 222, 227, 229, 230, 235, 242, 245, 249, 261, 262, 264, 276, 297, 309, 318, 321, 322, 323, 327, 339, 346, 356
Robertson 262, 302
Robeson 202, 203
Robinette 221, 260
Robinson 76, 82, 200, 248, 322, 343, 353
Robke 311
Roby 127, 192, 203, 238, 239, 296, 319, 322
Rocha 322
Roche 183
Rock 26, 131, 147, 160
Roddy 313
Rode 212
Rodgers 55, 124
Rodman 188, 241
Roe 279
Roetteis 139
Rogers 143, 169, 261, 278, 300, 302, 322, 349
Rogge 249
Rohling 183
Rohrer 322
Rohter 121
Rollins 232, 251, 323
Rolph 246
Romand 352
Romero 74, 94, 324
Roof 63, 73, 95, 110, 113, 139, 161, 163, 245, 277, 335, 352
Roper 332
Rose 25, 78, 235
Rosengarten 44, 103, 313
Rospert 115
Ross 55, 176, 210, 241
Rowans 346
Rowland 282, 285
Ruark 323
Ruck 94
Ruckdaschel 223
Rudd 160, 339
Ruden 352
Rudy 303, 323
Rudyinski 280
Ruff 120, 124, 142, 143, 292
Ruhl 332
Ruihe 244
Rule 55
Rumage 201, 299
Rupertus 302
Ruppert 153, 309
Rushing 323
Russelburg 200, 260, 301, 337
Russelburghe 200
Russell 34, 35, 41, 43, 44, 49, 66, 73, 126, 137, 148, 203, 224, 225, 241, 262, 288, 295, 299, 306, 323, 325, 329, 357, 359
Rutherford 170, 332
Rutledge 298
Ryan 24, 59, 116, 117, 124, 152, 153, 210, 253, 255, 306, 340
Ryans 116
Ryne 336
Ryon 333
Rysselberghe 233, 307, 308, 347

S

Saalwaechter 353
Sadler 333

Saffer 27, 34, 43, 44, 49, 52, 59, 66, 123, 144, 148, 150, 173, 224, 226, 227, 241, 243, 303, 345, 360
Saia 68
Salmon 140, 169
Saltsman 263
Sandefer 245, 335
Sandefur 249, 359
Sanders 157, 198, 215, 232, 258, 278, 281, 352
Sanderson 284, 318, 323
Sansbury 19
Sapp 261, 264, 272
Sauer 55, 62, 244, 324
Saunier 322
Savage 338
Sawyer 262
Schaacht 146
Schacht 23, 24, 25, 35, 121, 150, 171, 188
Schact 23
Schadler 69, 93, 106, 114, 218, 264
Schaefer 331
Schaeffer 127
Schaibley 324
Schartung 320
Scheer 351, 352
Scheible 280, 333
Scheidegger 324
Schell 324
Schenk 172
Schepers 325
Scherer 331, 333
Scherm 325, 359
Schiebert 176
Schill 189
Schillinger 276
Schindler 252
Schmitt 134, 143, 170, 312, 346, 347
Schmitz 55
Schmuke 325, 331
Schneider 312
Schoenborn 92, 107, 179
Schoenhafer 25
Schoenhalzer 331
Schonofer 22
Schrecker 218, 275
Schueler 357
Schuhmann 79, 183
Schuler 96, 179
Schultzman 255
Schumakers 93
Schuwey 131
Schwab 172
Schwabenton 361
Schwartz 266, 325, 326, 332
Schweer 332
Scott 182, 220, 223, 235, 326
Schumann 215
Seabaugh 252, 331
Seaford 215
Sebree 172
Seeburger 333
Seefeldt 256
Segebarth 79, 92, 93, 326
Seger 325
Seiler 326
Seitz 55, 153, 183, 277, 347
Selhorst 341
Sellers 215, 261
Seng 326
Serio 348
Serra 184
Seton 63
Settles 93
Severs 239
Sexton 300
Shackelford 72
Shade 79
Shaffer 255, 343
Shain 217
Shakelford 76
Shank 206
Shanklin 172
Shanks 266, 353
Shannon 322
Sharkey 148
Sharp 267, 286, 308
Shaver 327
Shaw 198
Sheehan 199
Sheeran 153, 210, 287, 327
Sheffer 209, 360
Shehan 218
Shehees 116
Shellman 278, 319
Shelton 200, 220, 258, 322, 327
Sheperd 132
Shepherd 297, 298, 355
Shercliffe 11
Sheridan 155, 163, 174, 296
Sherran 215
Sherron 115, 153, 154, 306
Sherry 96
Shields 300
Shifflett 357
Shipley 228
Shipp 110
Shircliff 291
Shively 224, 250, 265, 266, 298, 325

Shock 248
Shocklee 254
Shoemaker 123, 271, 272, 273, 327, 328
Shonis 70, 95, 96, 105, 138
Shory 265
Shoulta 245, 300, 343
Showalter 261
Shreclner 344
Shumaker 328
Shup 359
Siebenaler 189, 346
Siemers 332
Siener 334
Sikes 295
Silva 79
Simmons 131, 184, 185, 199, 216, 223, 295, 296, 298, 338, 340
Simms 335
Simon 55, 107, 117, 172, 179, 187, 203, 223, 246, 328, 359
Simons 264
Simpson 93, 143, 184, 185, 291, 292
Sims 79, 127, 149, 207, 221, 241, 272, 294, 303, 328, 329, 342
Singery 277
Singleton 335
Sinnott 249
Sipes 50
Skaggs 254, 261, 263, 351
Skees 161, 360
Skinner 253, 308, 346
Skrit 253
Slack 184, 236
Slaybough 229
Slobig 329
Sloon 257
Slusher 211
Smith 34, 43, 44, 49, 51, 52, 54, 122, 123, 127, 162, 163, 191, 206, 214, 222, 224, 228, 229, 231, 232, 239, 244, 248, 249, 264, 272, 297, 304, 329, 330, 333, 347, 357, 361
Snow 63, 133, 159
Snowden 109
Snyder 183, 207, 223, 304, 330, 352, 358
Soenecker 188
Soennecker 61, 171
Soenneker 34, 38, 47, 57, 58, 59, 61, 62, 63, 64, 65, 66, 76, 77, 78, 87, 90, 92, 95, 103, 105, 106, 107, 112, 113, 115, 117, 119, 132, 138, 143, 149, 151, 154, 158, 159, 161, 163, 166, 169, 170, 172, 177, 181, 182, 183, 184, 189, 191, 192, 212, 214, 233, 242, 254, 266, 268, 273, 276, 280, 290, 291, 294, 312, 319, 331, 339, 346, 347, 353, 361
Sohn 287
Soldo 225
Soubirous 181
Sourd 107
Southard 199
Sowders 253
Spain 331
Spalding 10, 11, 12, 15, 16, 17, 18, 21, 22, 23, 24, 25, 26, 28, 30, 34, 35, 36, 37, 41, 43, 44, 49, 93, 94, 103, 109, 115, 118, 119, 123, 131, 135, 141, 153, 155, 161, 164, 166, 174, 182, 186, 187, 188, 193, 216, 223, 249, 263, 273, 279, 282, 283, 291, 296, 306, 316, 317, 319, 326, 331, 332, 333, 342, 344, 358
Spann 262
Spaulding 171, 209, 289, 329, 361
Speak 198, 272
Speaks 95, 144, 297
Spears 261
Speed 361
Spiess 30, 128
Spink 186, 210, 229, 330, 333
Spinks 251
Spoelker 116

Spraggins 337
Springer 248
Spugnardi 277
Spurlock 60, 95, 182
Stafford 241
Stahr 55, 62, 115, 280, 289, 323, 333, 346, 357
Stallings 260, 298, 341
Stammerman 44
Stammermen 148
Stamper 335
Staples 182, 287, 317
Starkey 220
Statler 331
Steel 54
Steele 110, 115, 234, 261, 263, 333
Stein 305
Steltenpohl 347
Stengell 357
Stenger 70, 71, 85, 334, 346
Stennett 246
Stephens 92, 213, 278
Sterber 193
Sterckx 28
Sterett 62, 63
Stevens 79
Stevenson 94, 103, 124, 133, 143, 159, 161, 227, 276, 308, 329, 336
Steward 283
Stewart 199, 200, 253, 334
Stiff 334
Stimmle 306
Stine 264
Stinson 207, 272
Stock 154
Stockton 306
Stoehr 193
Stogsdill 295
Stokes 254, 316, 317
Stone 109, 334
Stonner 339
Storm 93, 124, 251
Storms 103, 260, 276
Stout 266, 340, 360
Stowers 293
Straney 170
Strange 274
Stratton 170
Strehl 111, 212, 334
Stribling 93
Strobel 246
Stroker 205
Stuart 12, 334
Stuemueller 61
Sturgeon 239, 355
Sublett 192
Sucato 263
Sullivan 67, 69, 134, 159, 184, 210, 285, 310, 340
Sulpa 350
Summers 355, 356
Summerville 268
Suraino 263
Surzyn 261
Sutton 228
Swanberg 93
Sweeney 87, 144, 161
Sweitzer 336
Swenson 196
Swink 235
Sylvester 141
Symonds 287
Synder 350
Szylowski 263

T

Tabler 262
Tabor 233
Tachenberry 62
Tackaberry 219, 226, 277
Tackett 245, 335
Taliaferro 335
Talley 309
Tamborn 196
Tanner 281
Tapp 335
Tarltons 11
Tarrant 115
Taylor 133, 137, 176, 183, 238, 248, 252, 298, 315, 323, 345, 359
Teague 267
Teill 66
Teitloff 325
Telegdy 117, 122, 135
Templeton 218
Tennelley 264

Tennes 302, 335
Terelya 297
Tharp 323, 339, 340
Tharpe 156
Thayer 13, 169
Theobald 256
Theriault 206
Thibault 288
Thiry 209
Thomas 34, 43, 45, 49, 61, 112, 118, 120, 122, 123, 137, 155, 203, 213, 215, 226, 230, 236, 241, 245, 253, 272, 276, 289, 311, 319, 328, 329, 330, 332, 335, 336, 345, 356, 357
Tompkins 109, 120
Thompson 11, 33, 34, 35, 41, 43, 44, 45, 49, 79, 92, 93, 114, 121, 123, 127, 132, 137, 143, 148, 162, 171, 177, 184, 202, 205, 207, 225, 228, 229, 234, 237, 241, 242, 246, 247, 251, 260, 261, 266, 268, 274, 278, 280, 282, 288, 292, 299, 300, 301, 304, 305, 311, 317, 319, 320, 330, 336, 337, 338, 340, 346, 347, 348, 357
Thornberry 285, 331
Thrasher 76, 249, 338
Threlkeid 338
Thweatt 202, 338
Tibbs 218
Tidwell 79, 92
Tiel 342
Tiell 94, 112, 135, 146, 149, 158, 174, 320, 325, 338
Tierney 27, 35, 104, 276, 306, 307, 346
Tillman 148
Timbrook 298
Timoney 174, 296
Tincher 245, 285, 335
Tipmore 241
Tipton 339
Tisch 64, 184
Tivitt 269
Todd 31, 62, 330
Toffler 61
Toler 198
Tomes 231, 292
Tompkins 34, 43, 44, 49, 131, 322
Tong 62, 328
Toon 137, 203, 205, 222, 224, 234, 241, 255, 260, 268, 307, 311, 339, 340, 346, 353, 355, 357, 359, 361
Toone 250
Topper 184
Toth 218
Touhey 144
Towery 341, 353, 355
Towerys 170
Townsend 296
Trabucco 300
Trapp 353
Trawick 92, 94, 95, 106, 140, 143, 243, 284, 310, 341
Trent 198
Tripp 345
Trolinger 287
Tromly 237, 238
Troutman 317
Truijello 62
Truman 261, 283
Trunk 170
Tucker 34, 65, 188, 199
Tuley 151
Tully 38, 259
Tumerlaine 262
Turk 93
Turnage 328
Turner 216, 219, 305, 309, 341, 342
Turney 357
Tuttle 262, 279
Tweddell 249

U

Uhing 342
Ulmer 332
Ulrich 93
Underwood 335, 342
Utley 276, 314, 335, 342

V

Vaehre 332

Valenza 107
Van de Vyver 31
Van den Branden 38
Van den Branden de Rethe 41
van der Zee 315
Vance 113, 161, 164, 211
Vancleave 336
VanConey 248
VandeMergel 27
Vandemergel 23, 24
Vandermerel 159
Vandermergal 126, 127
Vandermergel 143, 159
Vandiver 222
VanFroostenberghe 120
Vanover 235, 295
Vanscite 336
Vanskiski 261
Vantroostenberghe 168
Vantroostenberghe 26, 35, 42
Varble 192
Vaughan 76, 77, 78, 80, 84, 87, 89, 92, 95, 343
Vaughn 70, 72, 76, 163
Veatch 199, 217, 222, 343
Venters 93, 112, 292, 300, 343, 347
Vertin 286
Vessels 333
Vetter 316
Vetterl 211
Victor 343
Villemain 356
Vinson 343
Vize 31
Volk 24, 25, 26, 31, 35, 121, 126, 146, 170, 193, 216, 236, 250, 273, 280, 320, 348
Volkmer 325
Vollman 285
Von Zimmern 333
Vonthurstenburgh 304
Vosko 173
Vowells 288
Vowels 254, 285, 287, 304
Voyles 239
Voytek 149

W

Wachter 240
Wade 179
Wadell 221
Wagner 252, 343
Wagoner 296
Wajiuckecwicz 203
Wake 282
Waldeck 95
Waldridge 343
Waldrons 116
Waldruff 132
Walker 161, 184, 214, 217, 326, 331, 332, 333
Wallace 239, 250, 322
Walrond 337
Walsh 61, 115, 122, 123, 176
Walter 344
Waltman 323
Waltmon 323
Walton 288, 305
Waltrudis 55
Walz 344
Waninger 344
Ward 34, 52, 65, 84, 96, 108, 121, 122, 128, 151, 155, 163, 201, 253, 282, 284, 294, 295, 300, 308, 344
Warden 224
Warner 328
Warners 303
Warren 79, 80, 126, 155, 192, 198, 212, 229, 275, 293, 334, 344, 345
Washington 214
Wassomer 252
Wasterman 103
Wathen 20, 35, 103, 123, 133, 142, 147, 155, 168, 169, 170, 171, 174, 188, 197, 219, 271, 291, 296, 299, 304, 307, 331, 345
Watson 79, 245, 264, 276, 345
Watts 209
Wawrukiewicz 252
Wayne 153, 291, 300
Weafer 217, 307, 345
Weatherholt 313
Weaver 196, 220, 237, 238, 239, 295
Webb 20, 22, 26, 29, 127, 139, 184, 197, 355, 361
Weber 198
Webster 139, 261
Wedding 110, 240, 299, 346
Weedman 39
Wehmhoefer 183
Wehr 243
Weidenbenner 156, 346
Weigand 134
Weimer 245
Weise 130, 274
Weise 154, 230, 346
Weisenbach 288
Weiss 115, 144, 206
Weitlauf 346, 347, 355, 360
Welch 161
Weldon 347
Welge 245
Welker 312
Wellenhoff 263
Wellington 266
Wells 186, 235, 248, 272, 347
Welman 350
Welsh 29, 164
Welter 332
Wemple 330
Werner 115, 215
Wersing 114
Wessel 57
West 258
Westerfield 233, 347
Westerman 358
Westermann 302
Westpheling 348
Wethington 73, 213, 255, 288, 304, 348
Whaelan 304
Whalen 103, 134, 169
Wheatley 11, 62, 63, 95, 124, 155, 199, 239, 248, 288, 313
Wheeler 252
Whelan 33, 34, 35, 43, 45, 49, 120, 121, 140, 162, 174, 208, 229, 247, 267, 279, 295, 317, 338, 348, 349
Whistle 67, 94, 106, 123, 126, 169, 298, 349
Whitaker 117, 245
White 11, 34, 66, 127, 143, 155, 192, 207, 221, 233, 235, 239, 247, 272, 285, 349, 350
Whitehead 347
Whitehouse 350
Whitfield 200
Whitfill 227, 287, 350
Whiting 95, 191
Whitler 350
Whitman 360
Whitney 333
Whittaker 248
Whitten 93, 226
Whittinghill 324
Whittington 251
Whittler 78
Wibbles 154
Wickliffe 295
Wieder 93, 106, 111, 184, 214
Wigger 238
Wiggins 201
Wight 116, 260, 326, 333
Wightman 216
Wilborn 350
Wilcox 261
Wiley 351
Wilfrid 188
Wilhelm 62
Wilhite 211
Wilkerson 62, 67, 75, 83, 93, 143, 270, 316, 351, 353
Wilkinson 148
Williams 224
Willen 262
Willet 227
Willett 10, 18, 20, 31, 32, 34, 55, 60, 61, 62, 63, 67, 92, 94, 95, 106, 108, 112, 119, 121, 122, 123, 128, 129, 132, 134, 137, 144, 146, 156, 163, 164, 165, 173, 174, 201, 208, 209, 210, 213, 215, 225, 232, 241, 242, 252, 255, 256, 276, 278, 280, 288, 297, 311, 312, 313, 317, 322,

239, 295
Webb 20, 22, 26, 29, 127, 139, 184, 197, 355, 361
Weber 198
Webster 139, 261
Wedding 110, 240, 299, 346
Weedman 39
Wehmhoefer 183
Wehr 243
Weidenbenner 156, 346
Weigand 134
Weimer 245
Weise 130, 274
Weise 154, 230, 346
Weisenbach 288
Weiss 115, 144, 206
Weitlauf 346, 347, 355, 360
Welch 161
Weldon 347
Welge 245
Welker 312
Wellenhoff 263
Wellington 266
Wells 186, 235, 248, 272, 347
Welman 350
Welsh 29, 164
Welter 332
Wemple 330
Werner 115, 215
Wersing 114
Wessel 57
West 258
Westerfield 233, 347
Westerman 358
Westermann 302
Westpheling 348
Wethington 73, 213, 255, 288, 304, 348
Whaelan 304
Whalen 103, 134, 169
Wheatley 11, 62, 63, 95, 124, 155, 199, 239, 248, 288, 313
Wheeler 252
Whelan 33, 34, 35, 43, 45, 49, 120, 121, 140, 162, 174, 208, 229, 247, 267, 279, 295, 317, 338, 348, 349
Whistle 67, 94, 106, 123, 126, 169, 298, 349
Whitaker 117, 245
White 11, 34, 66, 127, 143, 155, 192, 207, 221, 233, 235, 239, 247, 272, 285, 349, 350
Whitehead 347
Whitehouse 350
Whitfield 200
Whitfill 227, 287, 350
Whiting 95, 191
Whitler 350
Whitman 360
Whitney 333
Whittaker 248
Whitten 93, 226
Whittinghill 324
Whittington 251
Whittler 78
Wibbles 154
Wickliffe 295
Wieder 93, 106, 111, 184, 214
Wigger 238
Wiggins 201
Wight 116, 260, 326, 333
Wightman 216
Wilborn 350
Wilcox 261
Wiley 351
Wilfrid 188
Wilhelm 62
Wilhite 211
Wilkerson 62, 67, 75, 83, 93, 143, 270, 316, 351, 353
Wilkinson 148
Williams 224
Willen 262
Willet 227
Willett 10, 18, 20, 31, 32, 34, 55, 60, 61, 62, 63, 67, 92, 94, 95, 106, 108, 112, 119, 121, 122, 123, 128, 129, 132, 134, 137, 144, 146, 156, 163, 164, 165, 173, 174, 201, 208, 209, 210, 213, 215, 225, 232, 241, 242, 252, 255, 256, 276, 278, 280, 288, 297, 311, 312, 313, 317, 322, 323, 325, 327, 328, 339, 342, 343, 351, 352, 353, 354, 355, 356, 358, 361
William 267
Williams 87, 192, 237, 249, 275, 293, 324, 326, 337, 342, 357
Williamson 355, 357
Willoughby 93, 106
Wills 357
Wilson 34, 43, 44, 49, 61, 66, 114, 126, 128, 129, 132, 134, 151, 167, 184, 202, 212, 215, 218, 221, 224, 235, 239, 242, 254, 255, 260, 310, 311, 322, 329, 332, 335, 343, 346, 349, 353, 355, 357, 358
Wimsatt 319
Wimsatt 11, 230, 246, 248, 263, 301, 311, 337, 359
Wink 201, 216, 225, 248, 260, 359
Winkler 214, 303
Winstead 247, 322
Wirt 235
Wise 79, 113, 176
Wiseman 188, 310
Wisor 94
Witting 115
Wolf 116, 132, 134, 179
Wolfe 313, 314, 360
Wolford 63, 95
Wolfram 185
Wolker 272
Wolschena 352
Womack 63
Wood 33, 94, 224, 292, 324, 329, 330
Woodcock 249
Woodruff 235, 262
Woods 31, 107, 172, 216, 276
Woodward 55, 62, 93, 94, 187
Wooldridge 204, 360
Wooley 260, 339
Woosley 257
Workman 251
Worland 223
Worley 274
Worth 73
Wright 30, 134, 151, 222, 250, 272, 308, 309, 360
Wring 235
Wrinkles 249
Wuest 107, 157, 172
Wurth 55, 62, 256, 288, 312, 343, 351, 352, 360
Wurtz 139, 190, 232
Wuyts 261, 264
Wyandt 261
Wyatt 68, 215\
Wycoff 268
Wynn 340

Y

Yaeger 255
Yanz 92, 245
Yates 11, 143, 300, 317, 353, 360
Yeand 283
Yeiser 361
Yopp 245, 251, 281
York 28, 115, 144, 267
Yorke 296
Yothment 318
Young 66, 115, 201, 223, 236, 244, 253, 261, 262, 274, 279, 305, 326, 357
Youngblood 205, 361
Younker 312
Youree 280, 290, 361
Yunker 34, 66, 107, 138

Z

Zachman 115
Zambrano 361
Zapalo 301
Zarnowiecki 196
Zaya 289
Zeigler 62, 67, 72, 73, 278
Zeitler 107
Ziegler 84, 93, 95, 111, 248, 288, 299, 328, 361
Zielinski 312
Zimmerman 225
Zoeller 34, 43, 45, 49, 103, 127, 133, 159, 362
Zumberge 124
Zumberger 103
Zwinger 22

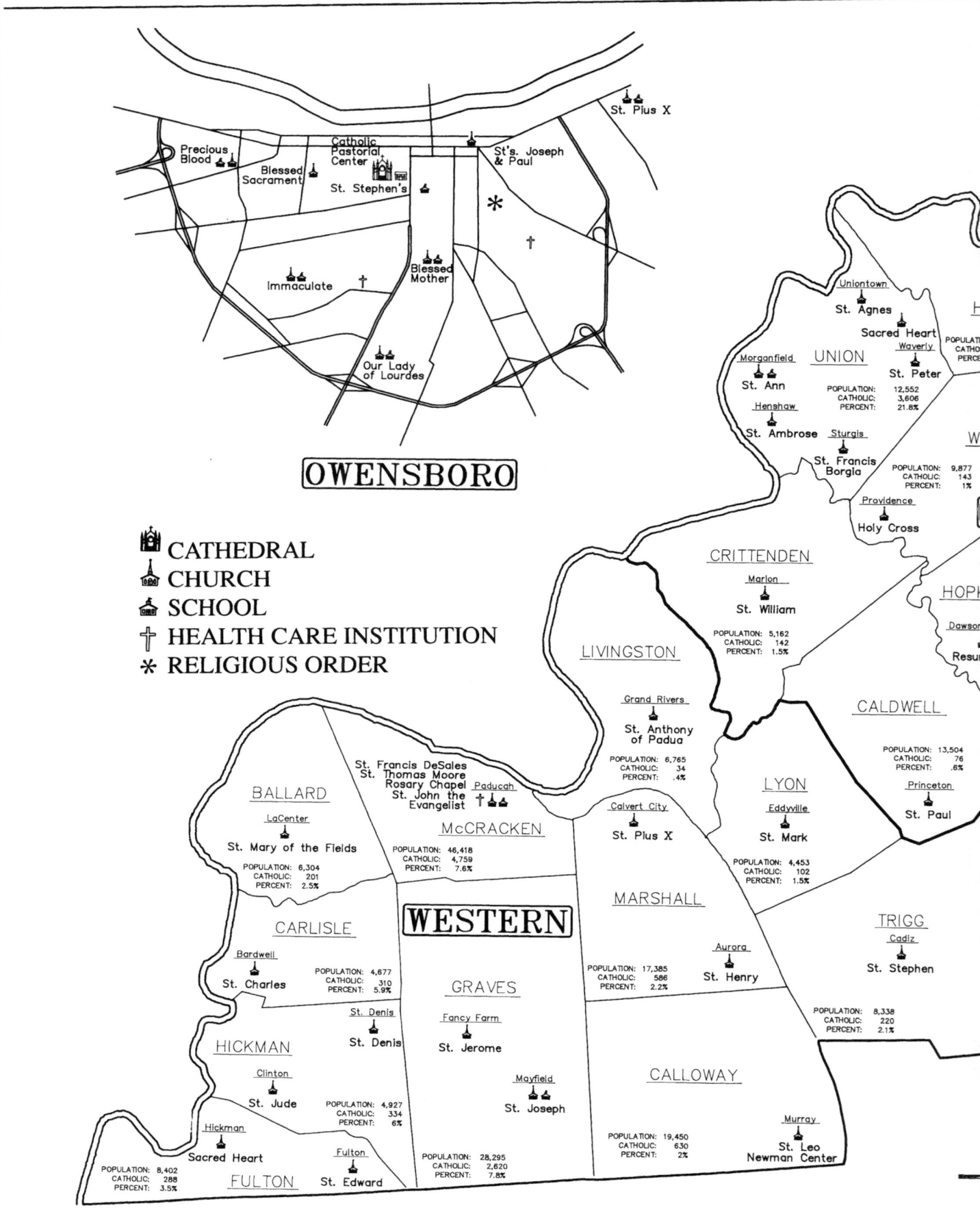

MAP SUBMITTED BY STEPHEN J. WALL

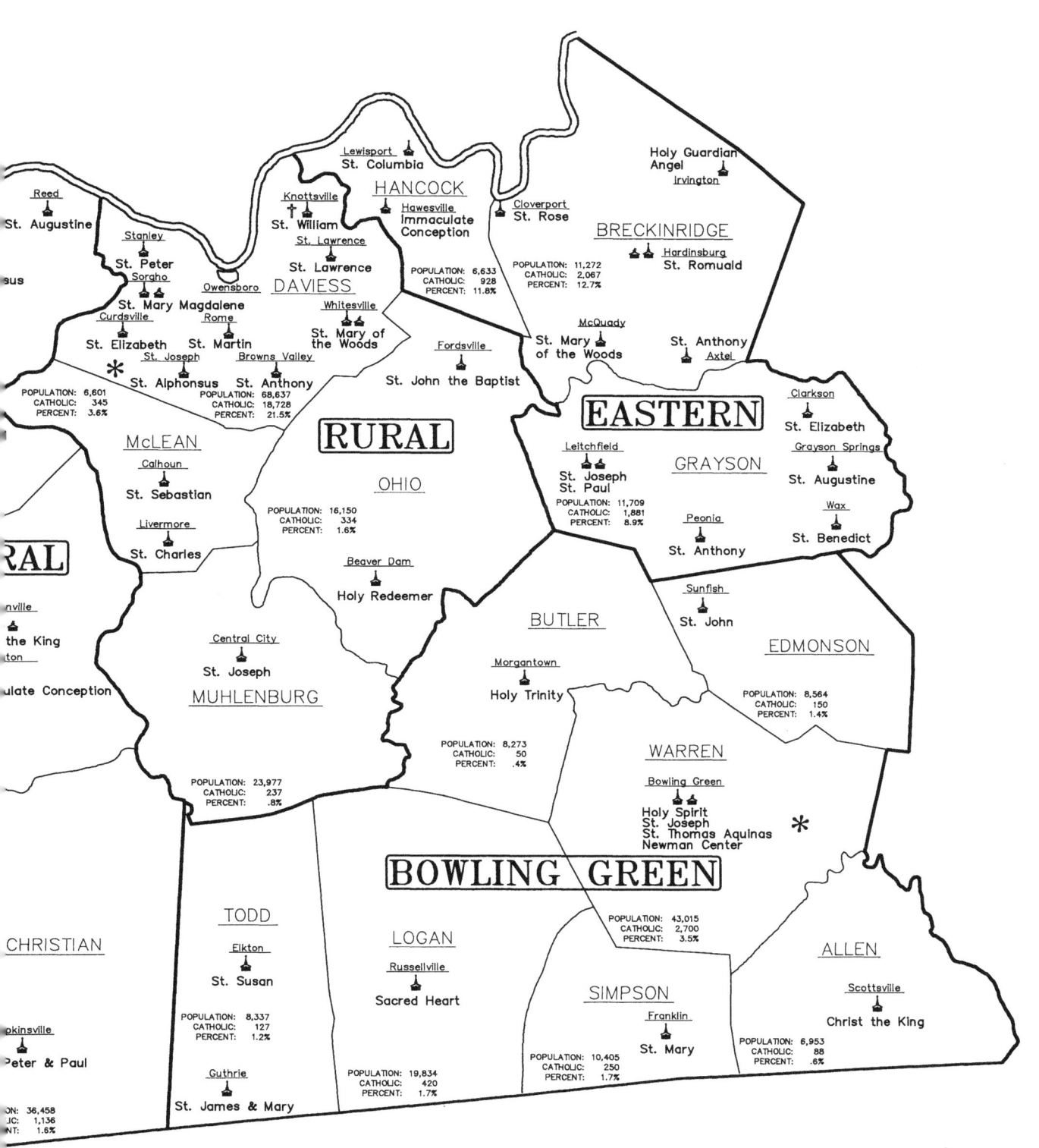

DIOCESE OF OWENSBORO, KENTUCKY

ESTABLISHED 1937

As of January, 1993   Figures based on 1990 census

www.ingramcontent.com/pod-product-compliance
Lightning Source LLC
Chambersburg PA
CBHW060229240426

43671CB00016B/2896